W9-AAD-077

THE COMPLETE
★★★★★ BOOK OF ★★★★★
U.S. PRESIDENTS

THE COMPLETE
★★★★★ BOOK OF ★★★★★
U.S. PRESIDENTS

WILLIAM A. DEGREGORIO

SIXTH EDITION

"The President is at liberty, both in law and conscience, to be
as big a man as he can. His capacity will set the limit."

—Woodrow Wilson

Published by Barricade Books Inc.
185 Bridge Plaza North
Suite 308-A
Fort Lee, NJ 07024

www.barricadebooks.com

Library of Congress Cataloging-in-Publication Data
DeGregorio, William A., 1946
        The Complete Book of U.S. Presidents /William A. DeGregorio—6th ed.
               p. cm.
        Includes bibliographic references and index.
        ISBN 13 978-1-56980-286-1
        ISBN 10 1-56980-286-6
        1. Presidents—United States. I. Title.
E176.1D43
973'.099-dc20

Second Printing Sixth Edition

To Alfred W. DeGregorio,
Mallie Sasso DeGregorio,
and Roslyn P. DeGregorio,
for their love, encouragement,
and support
from October 23, 1946

CONTENTS

PREFACE

My interest in the presidents is long-standing. I got hooked at age eight when, sick with the mumps, I was given a toy revolving disc, which, when turned, revealed facts about each president through windows in the disc. Afterward, I began reading juvenile biographies of the presidents and at length progressed to the adult versions. In 1969 I started to amass a personal library of presidential biographies and related materials, which has since swelled to hundreds of volumes. By the late 1970s I had written dozens of freelance articles on a variety of presidential activities.

In 1980 I decided to compile and write a reference work on all the presidents, in one large and easy-to use volume, that would combine basic information for the student, the researcher, and the amateur historian—and intriguing, little-known facts for the browser and trivia buff. Under consistent headings and subheadings, this book provides quick access to facts about the lives of the presidents as well as many other related illuminating and surprising bits of historical information.

In the George Bush chapter, for example, under "Education," one learns not only which schools he attended but also of his encounter with Babe Ruth while the future president was playing first base for Yale. Elsewhere, reading of the personal tragedy shared by former First Lady Barbara Bush and former President Clinton: each lost a parent in a freak one-car accident.

In the Clinton chapter, find out how Clinton earned the dubious honor of becoming the youngest ex-governor in U.S. history, what First Lady Hillary Clinton said as a graduating college student that was important enough to make the pages of *Time* and *Life* magazines, and follow the numerous scandals that plagued the Clinton presidency.

The George W. Bush chapter includes details of the outrageous presidential election of the year 2000, the most controversial and bitterly contested election since the 1876 presidential race between Rutherford B. Hayes and Samuel J. Tilden.

A reader seeking the date of birth of Franklin D. Roosevelt can reach for any almanac or encyclopedia. But here you will learn not only that FDR entered the world on the evening of January 30, 1882, but also how the attending physician's misjudgment nearly killed FDR. Similarly, many sources provide the religion of each president. In *The Complete Book of U.S. Presidents*, one learns that Theodore Roosevelt not only belonged to the Dutch Reformed church, but also that he so strongly believed in the absolute separation of church and state, that as president, he attempted, unsuccessfully, to remove "In God We Trust" from all U.S. coins. The First Ladies merit a brief mention in most collective presidential works. *The Complete Book of U.S. Presidents* furnishes not only profiles of the presidents' wives but also sketches of early romantic interests and mistresses of the presidents.

This book consists of 43 chapters, one for each president (Grover Cleveland, the 22nd and 24th president, is treated in two chapters). Each chapter is divided into headings, where applicable, in the following order:

Name	Career before the Presidency, jobs,
Physical Description	offices held
Personality	Party Nomination for President
Ancestors	Opponent(s)
Father	Campaign and the Issues
Mother	Election as President
Siblings	popular vote, electoral vote,
Collateral Relatives	states carried
Children	Inaugural Address
Subsequent Descendants	Vice President(s)
Birth	Administration Cabinet
Childhood	significant programs and events
Education	Supreme Court Appointment(s)
Religion	Ranking in 1962 Historians Poll
Recreation	Retirement
Early Romance	Death
Marriage(s)	President Praised
Extramarital Affair(s)	President Criticized
Post marital Affair(s)	Quotes of President
Military Service	Books about President

Beginning with the Clinton chapter, I have eliminated footnotes, choosing instead to give the source for quotes and controversial information within the body of the text.

I am indebted, first of all, to the legion of biographers, living and dead, who from the disorder of the original source material brought forth reliable, readily digestible, yet detailed accounts of the presidents' lives. Without them no reference work such as this could be written in one author's lifetime. *Burke's Presidential Families* (Burke's Peerage, 1981) was especially valuable as a starting point in research the sections pertaining to the presidents' relatives. The ranking of the presidents in each chapter was based on the 1962 poll of 75 historians conducted by Arthur M. Schlesinger, Sr., who ranked 31 presidents as follows: 5 great presidents, 6 near great, 12 average, 6 below average, and 2 failures. Helpful, too, were numerous other books dealing with specialized aspects of the presidents' lives.

I am grateful to the late S. Arthur Dembner of New York City, whose early guidance helped forge the book into a reference tool more useful that it otherwise would have been. This work also benefited significantly from the scrutiny of my editors, the historians Dennis Ryan and Joanna Ryan, as well as Anna Dembner. I wish to thank Mrs. Betty Tilson, staff assistant to Mrs. Lyndon B. Johnson, and Anna M. Parks, associate director for development at the Carter Presidential Center in Atlanta, for providing me with research materials, and the children of presidents who replied to my requests for information, namely John Coolidge of Farmington, Connecticut, the late Franklin D. Roosevelt, Jr., and John S. D. Eisenhower of Valley Forge, Pennsylvania.

I owe much to the staff of the Stark County District Library for their assistance in securing research materials both at the main facility in Canton, Ohio, and through the interlibrary loan service. I am also grateful to the staffs of the New York Public Library and the Akron-Summit County Public Library for the use of their facilities.

Special thanks go to Roslyn P. DeGregorio for her patient assistance in proof-reading the manuscript.

And finally, I extend thanks to an anonymous breadman, who decades ago left at our doorstep that toy revolving disc. It stirred within me an enduring interest in the presidents that resulted in this book.

GEORGE WASHINGTON

1ST PRESIDENT

NAME: George Washington. He was probably named after George Eskridge, a lawyer in whose charge Washington's mother had been left when she was orphaned.

PHYSICAL DESCRIPTION: Washington was a large, powerful man—about 6 feet 2 inches tall, 175 pounds in his prime, up to more than 200 pounds in later years. Erect in bearing, muscular, broad shouldered, he had large hands and feet (size 13 shoes), a long face with high cheekbones, a large straight nose, determined chin, blue-gray eyes beneath heavy brows and dark brown hair, which on formal occasions he powdered and tied in a queue. His fair complexion bore the marks of smallpox he contracted as a young man. He lost his teeth, probably to gum disease, and wore dentures. According to Dr. Reidar Sognnaes, former dean of the University of California at Los Angeles School of Dentistry, who has made a detailed study of Washington's bridgework, he was fitted with numerous sets of dentures, fashioned variously from lead, ivory, and the teeth of humans, cows, and other animals, but not from wood, as was popularly believed. Moreover, he was not completely toothless. Upon his inauguration as president, Washington had one of his own teeth left to work alongside the dentures. He began wearing reading glasses during the Revolution. He dressed fashionably.

PERSONALITY: A man of quiet strength, he took few friends into complete confidence. His critics mistook his dignified reserve for pomposity. Life for Washington was a serious mission, a job to be tackled soberly, unremittingly. He had little time for humor. Although basically good-natured, he wrestled with his temper and sometimes lost. He was a poor speaker and could become utterly inarticulate without a prepared text. He preferred to express himself on paper. Still, when he did speak, he was candid, direct, and looked people squarely in the eye. Biographer Douglas Southall Freeman conceded that Washington's "ambition for wealth made him acquisitive and sometimes contentious." Even after Washington had established himself, Freeman pointed out, "he would

1

insist upon the exact payment of every farthing due him" and was determined "to get everything that he honestly could."[1] Yet neither his ambition to succeed nor his acquisitive nature ever threatened his basic integrity.

ANCESTORS: Through his paternal grandmother, Mildred Warner Washington, he descended from King Edward III (1312–1377) of England. His great-great-grandfather the Reverend Lawrence Washington (c. 1602–1653) served as rector of All Saints, Purleigh Parish, Essex, England, but was fired when certain Puritan members accused him of being a "common frequenter of Ale-houses, not only himself sitting daily tippling there, but also encouraging others in that beastly vice."[2] His great-grandfather John Washington sailed to America about 1656, intending to remain just long enough to take on a load of tobacco. But shortly after pushing off on the return trip, his ketch sank. Thus John remained in Virginia, where he met and married Anne Pope, the president's great-grandmother.

FATHER: Augustine Washington (1694?–1743), planter. Known to friends as Gus, he spent much of his time acquiring and overseeing some 10,000 acres of land in the Potomac region, running an iron foundry, and tending to business affairs in England. It was upon returning from one of these business trips in 1730 that he discovered that his wife, Jane Butler Washington, had died in his absence. On March 6, 1731, he married Mary Ball, who gave birth to George Washington 11 months later. Augustine Washington died when George was 11 years old. Because business had kept Mr. Washington away from home so much, George remembered him only vaguely as a tall, fair, kind man.

MOTHER: Mary Ball Washington (c. 1709–1789). Fatherless at 3 and orphaned at 12, she was placed, in accordance with the terms of her mother's will, under the guardianship of George Eskridge, a lawyer. Washington's relationship with his mother was forever strained. Although she was by no means poor, she regularly asked for and received money and goods from George. Still she complained, often to outsiders, that she was destitute and neglected by her children, much to George's embarrassment. In 1755, while her son was away serving his king in the French and Indian War, stoically suffering the hardships of camp life, she wrote to him asking for more butter and a new house servant. Animosity between mother and son persisted until her death from cancer in the first year of his presidency.

SIBLINGS: By his father's first marriage, George Washington had two half brothers to live to maturity—Lawrence Washington, surrogate father to George after the death of their father, and Augustine "Austin" Washington. He also had three brothers and one sister to live to maturity—Mrs. Betty Lewis; Samuel Washington; John Augustine "Jack" Washington, father of Supreme Court Justice Bushrod Washington; and Charles Washington, founder of Charles Town, West Virginia.

COLLATERAL RELATIVES: Washington was a half first cousin twice removed of President James Madison, a second cousin seven times removed of Queen Elizabeth II (1926–) of the United Kingdom, a third cousin twice removed of Confederate General Robert E. Lee, and an eighth cousin six times removed of Winston Churchill.

CHILDREN: Washington had no natural children; thus, no direct descendant of Washington survives. He adopted his wife's two children from a previous marriage, John Parke Custis and Martha Parke Custis. John's granddaughter Mary Custis married Robert E. Lee.

BIRTH: Washington was born at the family estate on the south bank of the Potomac River near the mouth of Pope's Creek, Westmoreland County, Virginia, at 10 A.M. on February 22, 1732 (Old Style February 11, the date Washington always celebrated as his birthday; in 1752 England and the colonies adopted the New Style, or Gregorian, calendar to replace the Old Style, or Julian, calendar). He was christened on April 5, 1732.

CHILDHOOD: Little is known of Washington's childhood. The legendary cherry tree incident and his inability to tell lies, of course, sprang wholly from the imagination of Parson Weems. Clearly the single greatest influence on young George was his half brother Lawrence, 14 years his senior. Having lost his father when he was 11, George looked upon Lawrence as a surrogate father and undoubtedly sought to emulate him. Lawrence thought a career at sea might suit his little brother and arranged for his appointment as midshipman in the British navy. George loved the idea. Together they tried to convince George's mother of the virtues of such service, but Mary Washington was adamantly opposed. George, then 14, could have run away to sea, as did many boys of his day, but he reluctantly respected his mother's wishes and turned down the appointment. At 16 George moved in with Lawrence at his estate, which he called Mount Vernon, after Admiral Edward Vernon, commander of British forces in the West Indies while Captain Lawrence Washington served with the American Regiment there. At Mount Vernon George honed his surveying skills and looked forward to his twenty-first birthday, when he was to receive his inheritance from his father's estate—the Ferry Farm, near Fredericksburg, where the family had lived from 1738 and where his mother remained until her death; half of a 4,000-acre tract; three lots in Fredericksburg; 10 slaves; and a portion of his father's personal property.

EDUCATION: Perhaps because she did not want to part with her eldest son for an extended period, perhaps because she did not want to spend the money, the widow Washington refused to send George to school in England, as her late husband had done for his older boys, but instead exposed him to the irregular education common in colonial Virginia. Just who instructed George is unknown, but by age 11 he had picked up basic reading, writing, and mathematical skills. Math was his best subject. Unlike many of the Founding Fathers, Washington never found time to learn French, then the language of diplomacy, and did not attend university. He applied his mathematical mind to surveying, an occupation much in demand in colonial Virginia, where men's fortunes were reckoned in acres of tobacco rather than pounds of gold.

RELIGION: Episcopalian. However, religion played only a minor role in his life. He fashioned a moral code based on his own sense of right and wrong and adhered to it rigidly. He referred rarely to God or Jesus in his writings but rather to Providence, a rather amorphous supernatural substance that controlled men's lives. He strongly believed in fate, a force so powerful, he maintained, as "not to be resisted by the strongest efforts of human nature."[3]

RECREATION: Washington learned billiards when young, played cards, and especially enjoyed the ritual of the fox hunt. In later years, he often spent evenings reading newspapers aloud to his wife. He walked daily for exercise.

EARLY ROMANCE: Washington was somewhat stiff and awkward with girls, probably often tongue-tied. In his mid-teens he vented his frustration in such moonish doggerel as, "Ah! woe's me, that I should love and conceal,/ Long have

I wish'd, but never dare reveal,/ Even though severely Loves Pains I feel."[4] Before he married Martha, Washington's love life was full of disappointment.

Betsy Fauntleroy. The daughter of a justice and burgess from Richmond County, Virginia, she was but 16 when she attracted Washington, then 20. He pressed his suit repeatedly, but, repulsed at every turn, he finally gave up.

Mary Philipse. During a trip to Boston to straighten out a military matter in 1756, Washington stopped off in New York and there met Mary Philipse, 26, daughter of Frederick Philipse, a wealthy landowner. Whether he was taken with her charms or her 51,000 acres is unknown, but he remained in the city a week and is said to have proposed. She later married Roger Morris, and together they were staunch Tories during the American Revolution.

Sally Fairfax. From the time he met Sarah Cary "Sally" Fairfax as the 18-year-old bride of his friend and neighbor George William Fairfax, Washington was infatuated with her easy charm, graceful bearing, good humor, rare beauty, and intelligence. Although the relationship almost certainly never got beyond flirtation, the two had strong feelings for each other and corresponded often. In one letter written to her in 1758, at a time when he was engaged to Martha, he blurted his love, albeit cryptically lest the note fall into the wrong hands. He confessed he was in love with a woman well known to her and then continued, "You have drawn me, dear Madam, or rather I have drawn myself, into an honest confession of a simple Fact. Misconstrue not my meaning; doubt it not, nor expose it. The world has no business to know the object of my Love, declared in this manner to you, when I want to conceal it."[5] As heartbroken as Washington appears to have been over the hopelessness of the relationship, the anguish might have been greater had he pressed the affair, for the Fairfaxes would not come to share Washington's passion for an independent America. In 1773, the year American resentment over British taxes erupted in the Boston Tea Party, Sally and George Fairfax left Virginia for England, where they settled permanently, loyal subjects to the end.

MARRIAGE: Washington, 26, married Martha Dandridge Custis, 27, a widow with two children, on January 6, 1759, at her estate, known as the White House, on the Pamunkey River northwest of Williamsburg. Born in New Kent County, Virginia, on June 21, 1731, the daughter of John Dandridge, a planter, and Frances Jones Dandridge, Martha was a rather small, pleasant-looking woman, practical, with good common sense if not a great intellect. At 18 she married Daniel Parke Custis, a prominent planter of more than 17,000 acres. By him she had four children, two of whom survived childhood. Her husband died intestate in 1757, leaving Martha reputedly the wealthiest marriageable woman in Virginia. It seems likely that Washington had known Martha and her husband for some time. In March 1758 he visited her at White House twice; the second time he came away with either an engagement of marriage or at least her promise to think about his proposal. Their wedding was a grand affair. The groom appeared in a suit of blue and silver with red trimming and gold knee buckles. After the Reverend Peter Mossum pronounced them man and wife, the couple honeymooned at White House for several weeks before setting up housekeeping at Washington's Mount Vernon. Their marriage appears to have been a solid one, untroubled by infidelity or clash of temperament. During the American Revolution she endured considerable hardship to visit her husband at field headquarters. As the First Lady, Mrs. Washington hosted many affairs of state at New York and Philadelphia (the capital was moved to Washington in

1800 under the Adams administration). After Washington's death in 1799, she grew morose and died on May 22, 1802.

MILITARY SERVICE: Washington served in the Virginia militia (1752–1754, 1755–1758), rising from major to colonel, and as commander in chief of the Continental army (1775–1783), with the rank of general. See "Career before the Presidency."

CAREER BEFORE THE PRESIDENCY: In 1749 Washington accepted his first appointment, that of surveyor of Culpepper County, Virginia, having gained much experience in that trade the previous year during an expedition across the Blue Ridge Mountains on behalf of Lord Fairfax. Two years later he accompanied his half brother Lawrence to Barbados. Lawrence, dying of tuberculosis, had hoped to find a cure in the mild climate. Instead, George came down with a near-fatal dose of smallpox. With the deaths of Lawrence and Lawrence's daughter in 1752, George inherited Mount Vernon, an estate that prospered under his management and one that throughout his life served as welcome refuge from the pressures of public life.

French and Indian War, 1754–1763. In 1752 Washington received his first military appointment as a major in the Virginia militia. On a mission for Governor Robert Dinwiddie during October 1753–January 1754, he delivered an ultimatum to the French at Fort Le Boeuf, demanding their withdrawal from territory claimed by Britain. The French refused. The French and the Ohio Company, a group of Virginians anxious to acquire western lands, were competing for control of the site of present-day Pittsburgh. The French drove the Ohio Company from the area and at the confluence of the Allegheny and Monongahela rivers constructed Fort Duquesne. Promoted to lieutenant colonel in March 1754, Washington oversaw construction of Fort Necessity in what is now Fayette County, Pennsylvania. However, he was forced to surrender that outpost to superior French and Indian forces in July 1754, a humiliating defeat that temporarily gave France control of the entire region. Later that year, Washington, disgusted with officers beneath his rank who claimed superiority because they were British regulars, resigned his commission. He returned to service, however, in 1755 as an aide-de-camp to General Edward Braddock. In the disastrous engagement at which Braddock was mortally wounded in July 1755, Washington managed to herd what was left of the force to orderly retreat, as twice his horse was shot out from under him. The next month he was promoted to colonel and regimental commander. He resigned from the militia in December 1758 following his election to the Virginia House of Burgesses.

Member of House of Burgesses, 1759–1774. In July 1758 Colonel Washington was elected one of Frederick County's two representatives in the House of Burgesses. He joined those protesting Britain's colonial policy and in 1769 emerged a leader of the Association, created at an informal session of the House of Burgesses, after it had been dissolved by the royal governor, to consider the most effective means of boycotting British imports. Washington favored cutting trade sharply but opposed a suspension of all commerce with Britain. He also did not approve of the Boston Tea Party of December 1773. But soon thereafter he came to realize that reconciliation with the mother country was no longer possible. Meanwhile, in 1770, Washington undertook a nine-week expedition to the Ohio country where, as compensation for his service in the French and Indian War, he was to inspect and claim more than 20,000 acres of land for himself and tens of thousands more for the men who had served under him. He had taken the lead in pressing the Virginia veterans' claim. "I might add, without much arrogance," he later wrote, "that if it had not been for my unremitted attention to every favorable circumstance, not a single acre of land would ever have been obtained."[6]

Delegate to Continental Congress, 1774–1775. A member of the Virginia delegation to the First and Second Continental Congresses, Washington served on various military preparedness committees and was chairman of the committee to consider ways to raise arms and ammunition for the impending Revolution. He voted for measures designed to reconcile differences with Britain peacefully but realized that such efforts now were futile. John Adams of Massachusetts, in a speech so effusive in its praise that Washington rushed in embarrassment from the chamber, urged that Washington be named commander in chief of the newly authorized Continental army. In June 1775, delegates unanimously approved the choice of Washington, both for his military experience and, more pragmatically, to enlist a prominent Virginian to lead a struggle that heretofore had been spearheaded largely by northern revolutionaries.

Commander in chief of Continental Army during Revolution, 1775–1783. With a poorly trained, undisciplined force comprised of short-term militia, General Washington took to the field against crack British regulars and Hessian mercenaries. In March 1776 he thrilled New Englanders by flushing the redcoats from Boston, but his loss of New York City and other setbacks later that year dispelled any hope of a quick American victory. Sagging American morale got a boost when Washington slipped across the Delaware River to New Jersey and defeated superior enemy forces at Trenton (December 1776) and Princeton (January 1777). But humiliating defeats at Brandywine (September 1777) and Germantown (October 1777) and the subsequent loss of Philadelphia undermined Washington's prestige in Congress. Richard Henry Lee, Benjamin Rush, and others conspired to remove Washington and replace him with General Horatio Gates, who had defeated General John Burgoyne at the Battle of Saratoga (October 1777). Washington's congressional supporters rallied to quash the so-called Conway Cabal. Prospects for victory seemed bleak as Washington settled his men into winter quarters at Valley Forge, Pennsylvania, in December 1777.

"To see men without clothes to cover their nakedness," Washington wrote in tribute to the men who suffered with him at Valley Forge, "without blankets to lay on, without shoes, by which their marches might be traced by the blood from their feet, and almost as often without provisions as with; marching through frost and snow, and at Christmas taking up their winter quarters within a day's march of the enemy, without a house or hut to cover them till they could be built, and submitting to it without a murmur, is a mark of patience and obedience which in my opinion can scarce be paralleled."[7] Of course, some did grumble— and loudly. "No pay! no clothes! no provisions! no rum!"[8] some chanted. But remarkably there was no mass desertion, no mutiny. Patriotism, to be sure, sustained many, but no more so than did confidence in Washington's ability to see them through safely. With the snow-clogged roads impassable to supply wagons, the men stayed alive on such fare as pepper pot soup, a thin tripe broth flavored with a handful of peppercorns. Many died there that winter. Those that survived drew fresh hope with the greening of spring and the news, announced to them by General Washington in May 1778, that France had recognized the independence of America. Also encouraging was the arrival of Baron Friedrich von Steuben, who, at Washington's direction, drilled the debilitated Valley Forge survivors into crack troops. Washington's men broke camp in June 1778, a revitalized army that, with aid from France, took the war to the British and in October 1781 boxed in General Charles Cornwallis at Yorktown, thus forcing the surrender of British forces.

General Washington imposed strict, but not punitive, surrender terms: All weapons and military supplies must be given up; all booty must be returned, but the enemy soldiers could keep their personal effects and the officers could retain their sidearms. British doctors were allowed to tend to their own sick and wounded. Cornwallis accepted, but instead of personally leading his troops to the mutually agreed-upon point of surrender on October 19, 1781, he sent his deputy Brigadier Charles O'Hara. As he made his way along the road flanked by American and French forces, O'Hara came face to face with Washington and the Comte de Rochambeau, the latter decked out in lavish military regalia. O'Hara mistook Rochambeau for the senior commander, but the French officer quickly pointed to Washington, and O'Hara, probably somewhat embarrassed, turned to the American. Unwilling to deal with a man of lesser rank, Washington directed O'Hara to submit the sword of capitulation to his aide General Benjamin Lincoln. In his victory dispatch to Congress, Washington wrote with obvious pride, "Sir, I have the Honor to inform Congress, that a Reduction of the British Army under the Command of Lord Cornwallis, is most happily effected. The unremitting Ardor which actuated every Officer and Soldier in the combined Army in this Occasion, has principally led to this Important Event, at an earlier period than my most sanguine Hope had induced me to expect."[9] In November 1783, two months after the formal peace treaty was signed, Washington resigned his commission and returned home to the neglected fields of Mount Vernon.

President of Constitutional Convention, 1787. Washington, a Virginia delegate, was unanimously elected president of the convention. He was among those favoring a strong federal government. After the convention he promoted ratification of the Constitution in Virginia. According to the notes of Abraham Baldwin, a Georgia delegate, which were discovered only recently and made public in 1987, Washington said privately that he did not expect the Constitution to last more than 20 years.

ELECTION AS PRESIDENT, FIRST TERM, 1789: Washington, a Federalist, was the obvious choice for the first president of the United States. A proven leader whose popularity transcended the conflict between Federalists and those opposed to a strong central government, the man most responsible for winning independence, a modest country squire with a winsome aversion to the limelight, he so dominated the political landscape that not 1 of the 69 electors voted against him. Thus, he carried all 10 states—Connecticut, Delaware, Georgia, Maryland, Massachusetts, New Hampshire, New Jersey, Pennsylvania, South Carolina, Virginia. (Neither North Carolina nor Rhode Island had ratified the Constitution yet. New York was unable to decide in time which electors to send.) Washington was the only president elected by a unanimous electoral vote. John Adams of Massachusetts, having received the second-largest number of votes, 34, was elected vice president.

ELECTION AS PRESIDENT, SECOND TERM, 1792: Despite the growing strength of Democratic-Republicans, Washington continued to enjoy virtually universal support. Again he won the vote of every elector, 132, and thus carried all 15 states—Connecticut, Delaware, Georgia, Kentucky, Maryland, Massachusetts, New Hampshire, New Jersey, New York, North Carolina, Pennsylvania, Rhode Island, South Carolina, Vermont, and Virginia. John Adams of Massachusetts received the second-highest number of votes, 77, and thus again became vice president.

INAUGURAL ADDRESS (FIRST): New York City, April 30, 1789. ". . . When I was first honored with a call into the service of my country, then on the eve of an arduous struggle for its liberties, the light in which I contemplated my duty required that I should renounce every pecuniary compensation. From this resolution I have in no instance departed; and being still under the impressions which produced it, I must decline as inapplicable to myself any share in the personal emoluments which may be indispensably included in a permanent provision for the executive department, and must accordingly pray that the pecuniary estimates for the station in which I am placed may during my continuance in it be limited to such actual expenditures as the public good may be thought to require. . . ."

INAUGURAL ADDRESS (SECOND): Philadelphia, March 4, 1793. (This was the shortest inaugural address, just 135 words.) "Fellow Citizens: I am again called upon by the voice of my country to execute the functions of its Chief Magistrate. When the occasion proper for it shall arrive, I shall endeavor to express the high sense I entertain of this distinguished honor, and of the confidence which has been reposed in me by the people of united America.

"Previous to the execution of any official act of the President the Constitution requires an oath of office. This oath I am now about to take, and in your presence: That if it shall be found during my administration of the Government I have in any instance violated willingly or knowingly the injunctions thereof, I may (besides incurring constitutional punishment) be subject to the upbraidings of all who are now witnesses of the present solemn ceremony."

VICE PRESIDENT: John Adams (1735–1826), of Massachusetts, served 1789–1797. See "John Adams, 2d President."

CABINET:

Secretary of State. (1) Thomas Jefferson (1743–1826), of Virginia, served 1790–1793. See "Thomas Jefferson, 3d President," "Career before the Presidency." (2) Edmund Jennings Randolph (1753–1813), of Virginia, served 1794–1795. Author of the Randolph (or Virginia) plan, favoring the large states, at the Constitutional Convention of 1787. Transferred from attorney general, he remained aloof of the struggle between Jefferson and Alexander Hamilton. Denounced by supporters of both, he was largely ineffective and was forced to resign amid unfounded charges that he had misused his office for private gain. (3) Timothy Pickering (1745–1829), of Massachusetts, served 1795–1800. Transferred from war secretary, he was a staunch Hamiltonian and stayed on in the Adams administration.

Secretary of the Treasury. (1) Alexander Hamilton (c. 1755–1804), of New York, served 1789–1795. President Washington's closest advisor, he was a great admirer of British institutions and a master of power politics. He saw his role in the government as that of prime minister. His influence went beyond economics to include foreign affairs, legal matters, and long-range social planning. He advocated and helped create a strong central government at the expense of states' rights. He put the infant nation on sound financial footing by levying taxes to retire the national debt and promoted the creation of a national bank. He also advocated tariffs to insulate fledgling American manufacturing from foreign competition. Hamilton's vision of America's future encompassed the evolution from a largely agrarian society to an industrial giant, a national transportation program to facilitate commerce and blur regional differences, a strong permanent national defense, and a sound, conservative monetary system. Even after resigning his post, he kept his hands on the controls of power. Washington continued to consult him. Hamilton's successor, Oliver Wolcott, and others in the cabinet took his advice. He even helped draft Washington's Farewell address. The foremost conservative leader of his day, he was anathema to Thomas Jefferson and his supporters. (2) Oliver Wolcott (1760–1833), of Connecticut, served 1795–1800. A lawyer and Hamilton supporter, he stayed on in the Adams administration.

Secretary of War. (1) Henry Knox (1750–1806), of Massachusetts, served 1789–1794. Chief of artillery and close adviser to General Washington during the Revolution and war secretary under the Articles of Confederation, he was a natural choice for this post. He pressed for a strong navy. Fort Knox was named after him. (2) Timothy Pickering (1745–1829), of Massachusetts, served January–December, 1795. A lawyer and veteran of the Revolution, he strengthened the navy. He resigned to serve as secretary of state. (3) James McHenry (1753–1816), of Maryland, served 1796–1800. He had served as a surgeon during the Revolution and was a prisoner of war. He stayed on in the Adams administration. Fort McHenry at Baltimore was named after him.

Attorney General. (1) Edmund Jennings Randolph (1753–1813), of Virginia, served 1789–1794. He helped draft President Washington's proclamation of neutrality. Washington disregarded his opinion that a national bank was unconstitutional. He resigned to become secretary of state. (2) William Bradford (1755–1795), of Pennsylvania, served 1794–1795. He was a state supreme court justice at the time of his appointment. (3) Charles Lee (1758–1815), of Virginia, served 1795–1801. He was a brother of Henry "Light-Horse Harry" Lee. He urged, unsuccessfully, that the United States abandon its policy of neutrality and declare war on France. He stayed on in the Adams administration.

ADMINISTRATION: April 30, 1789–March 3, 1797.

Precedents. "Many things which appear of little importance in themselves and at the beginning," President Washington observed, "may have great and durable consequences from their having been established at the commencement of a new general government."[10] With this in mind, then, he proceeded cautiously, pragmatically, acting only when it seemed necessary to flesh out the bare-bones framework of government described so sparingly in the Constitution: (1) In relying on department heads for advice, much as he had used his war council during the Revolution, he set the pattern for future presidents to consult regularly with their cabinet. (2) Because Congress did not challenge his appointments, largely out of respect for him personally rather than out of principle, the custom evolved that the chief executive generally has the right to choose his own cabinet. Congress, even when controlled by the opposition party, usually routinely confirms such presidential appointments. (3) How long should a president serve? The Constitution did not then say. Washington nearly set the precedent of a single term, for he had originally decided to retire in 1793, but remained for a second term when it became clear that the nonpartisan government he had so carefully fostered was about to fragment. Thus he set the two-term standard that lasted until 1940. (4) When John Jay resigned as chief justice, Washington went outside the bench for a successor rather than to elevate one of the sitting justices to the top position, as many had expected him to do. In disregarding seniority as a necessary qualification to lead the Supreme Court, Washington established the precedent that has enabled his successors to draw from a much more diverse and younger talent pool than that of a handful of aging incumbent jurists.

Indian Affairs. In 1791 President Washington dispatched forces under General Arthur St. Clair to subdue the Indians who had been resisting white settlement of the Northwest Territory. St. Clair failed, having been routed by Miami Chief Little Turtle on the Wabash River. Washington then turned to Revolutionary War veteran "Mad" Anthony Wayne, who before launching the expedition spent many months training regular troops in Indian warfare. He marched boldly into the region, constructed a chain of forts, and on August 20, 1794, crushed the Indians under Little Turtle in the Battle of Fallen Timbers near present-day Toledo, Ohio. Under the terms of the Treaty of Greenville (1795), the defeated tribes ceded disputed portions of the Northwest Territory to the United States and moved west. Through diplomacy, President Washington tried with limited success to make peace with the Creeks and other tribes in the South. In 1792 the president entertained the tribal leaders of the Six Nations confederation, including Seneca Chief Red Jacket, whom Washington presented with a silver medal, a token that the Indian treasured the rest of his life. Red Jacket, who had led his warriors against Washington's army during the Revolution, rallied to the American cause during the War of 1812.

Proclamation of Neutrality, 1793. In the war between France, on one side, and Britain, Austria, Prussia, Sardinia, and the Netherlands, on the other, President Washington in 1793 declared the United States to be "friendly and impartial toward the belligerent powers." Although he avoided using the word *neutrality*, his intention was clear. Critics denounced the proclamation as reneging on the U.S. commitment to its first ally, France. However, it kept the nation out of a war it was ill-prepared to fight. The French minister to the United States, Edmond Genet, pointedly ignoring Washington's policy, fomented pro-French sentiment among Americans and arranged for American privateers to harass British ships—activities that prompted President Washington to demand his recall.

Whiskey Rebellion, 1794. To help pay off the national debt and put the nation on a sound economic basis, President Washington approved an excise tax on liquor. Pennsylvania farmers, who regularly converted their corn crop to alcohol to avoid the prohibitive cost of transporting grain long distances to market, refused to pay it. On Hamilton's advice, Washington ordered 15,000 militia to the area and personally inspected troops in the field. This show of strength crushed this first real challenge to federal authority.

Jay's Treaty, 1795. Washington was roundly criticized by Jeffersonians for this treaty with Great Britain. To forestall further conflict with the former mother country and impel Britain to withdraw its forces from outposts in the Northwest Territory, as it had promised under the terms of the Treaty of Paris concluding the American Revolution, Washington relinquished the U.S. right to neutrality on the seas. Any American ship suspected of carrying contraband to the shores of Britain's enemies was subject to search and seizure by the British navy. And Britain regarded as contraband virtually any useful product, including foodstuffs. Moreover, Jay's Treaty failed to resolve one of the key disputes standing in the way of rapprochement with Britain—impressment. Britain's policy of "once an Englishman, always an Englishman" meant that even after renouncing allegiance to the crown and becoming a duly naturalized U.S. citizen, a British immigrant was not safe from the king's reach. If while searching an American ship for contraband, the British spotted one of their own among the crew, they routinely dragged him off and pressed him into the Royal Navy. But for all this, and despite the added strain on relations with France in the wake of Jay's Treaty, the pact did postpone the inevitable conflict with Britain until 1812, when America was better prepared militarily. After the Senate ratified the treaty, the House asked the president to release all pertinent papers relating to its negotiation. Washington refused on the constitutional ground that only the upper chamber had approval rights over treaties. He thereby set the precedent for future presidents to resist such congressional petitions.

Pinckney's Treaty, 1795. Under its terms, Washington normalized relations with Spain by establishing the boundary between the United States and Spanish Florida at the thirty-first parallel. Even more importantly for the future of American commerce, the pact granted U.S. vessels free access to the entire length of the Mississippi River and to the port of New Orleans for the purpose of export.

In other acts of lasting importance, President Washington signed into law bills creating or providing for:

1789 Oaths of allegiance to be sworn by federal and state officials
     First tariffs to protect domestic manufacturers
     Department of State and War and the Treasury
     Office of postmaster general
     Supreme Court, circuit and federal district courts, and position of attorney general (Judiciary Act). Washington, of course, appointed all the first judges to these courts.
1790 First federal census
     Patent and copyright protection
     Removal of the capital to Philadelphia in December 1790 and to Washington 10 years later
1791 Bank of the United States
1792 Presidential succession, which placed the president pro tempore of the Senate and the Speaker of the House next behind the vice president in line of succession to the presidency
     U.S. Mint of Philadelphia
1795 Naturalization law, which lengthened residency requirement from two to five years

Farewell Address, 1796. President Washington announced his retirement in his celebrated Farewell Address, a pronouncement that was printed in the Philadelphia *American Daily Advertiser* on September 17, 1796, but never was delivered orally. In it he warned against the evils of political parties and entangling alliances abroad. Throughout his term he had tried to prevent the rise of partisanship, but he had succeeded only in postponing such division by serving a second term. The Federalists under Hamilton and Adams and the Democratic-Republicans under Jefferson joined battle soon after he announced his retirement. Washington's warning to remain aloof from European struggles was better heeded. "The great rule of conduct for us in regard to foreign nations," he advised, "is, in extending our commercial relations to have with them as little *political* connection as possible. So far as we have already formed engagements let them be fulfilled with perfect good faith. Here let us stop."[11] Isolationism remained the dominant feature in American foreign policy for the next 100 years.

States Admitted to the Union. Vermont (1791), Kentucky (1792), Tennessee (1796).

Constitutional Amendments Ratified. Bill of Rights (first 10 amendments, 1791): (1) Freedom of religion, of speech, of the press, to assemble and petition for redress of grievances. (2) Right to bear arms. (3) Restrictions on quartering soldiers in private homes. (4) Freedom from unreasonable search and seizure. (5)Ban on double jeopardy and self-incrimination; guarantees due process of law. (6) Right to speedy and public trial. (7) Right to trial by jury. (8) Ban on excessive bail or fines or cruel and unusual punishment. (9) Natural rights unspecified in the Constitution to remain unabridged. (10) Individual states or the people retain all powers not specifically delegated to the federal government or denied to states by the Constitution. Eleventh Amendment (1795): A citizen from one state cannot sue another state.

SUPREME COURT APPOINTMENTS: (1) John Jay (1745–1829), of New York, served as chief justice 1789–1795. As the first chief justice, he established court procedure. While on the bench he negotiated Jay's Treaty (see "Administration"). He resigned to serve as governor of New York. (2) John Rutledge (1739–1800), of South Carolina, served as associate justice 1789–1791. His appointment as chief justice in 1795 was rejected by the Senate. (3) William Cushing (1732–1810), of Massachusetts, served as associate justice 1789–1810. He was the only Supreme Court justice to persist in wearing the formal wig popular among British jurists. (4) James Wilson (1742–1798), of Pennsylvania, served as associate justice 1789–1798. A Scottish immigrant, he was a signer of the Declaration of Independence. Speaking for the Court in *Chisholm* v. *Georgia* (1793), he ruled that a citizen of one state was entitled to sue another state, a decision so unpopular that it prompted passage of the Eleventh Amendment (1795), specifically nullifying it. (5) John Blair (1732–1800), of Virginia, served as associate justice 1789–1796. A friend of Washington—they had served together as Virginia delegates to the Constitutional Convention—he brought to the bench many years of experience on Virginia state courts. (6) James Iredell (1751–1799), of North Carolina, served as associate justice 1790–1799. An English immigrant, he was at 38 the youngest member of the original Supreme Court. His lone dissent in *Chisholm* v. *Georgia* (1793) formed the basis of the Eleventh Amendment (1795). (7) Thomas Johnson (1732–1819), of Maryland, served as associate justice 1791–1793. A friend of Washington since the Revolution, he served as the first governor of Maryland and chief judge of the state's General Court. He resigned from the Supreme Court for health reasons. (8) William Paterson (1745–1806), of New Jersey, served as associate justice 1793–1806. He helped draft the Judiciary Act of 1789 creating the federal court system. In *Van Horne's Lessee* v. *Dorrance* (1795) he established the Court's authority to strike down as unconstitutional a duly enacted state law, a precedent that anticipated judicial review of federal laws. (9) Samuel Chase (1741–1811), of Maryland, served as associate justice 1796–1811. Irascible and acid tongued, his gratuitous attacks on President Jefferson in 1803 led the House to impeach him, but the Senate fell four votes short of the two-thirds necessary for conviction. He was the only Supreme Court justice to be impeached. Speaking for a unanimous Court in *Ware* v. *Hilton* (1796), he established the supremacy of national treaties over state laws. (10) Oliver Ellsworth (1745–1807), of Connecticut, served as chief justice 1796–1800. He was the principal architect of the Judiciary Act of 1789, creating the federal court system. In *United States* v. *La Vengeance* (1796), he spoke for the majority in extending federal authority to all inland rivers and lakes.

RANKING IN 1962 HISTORIANS POLL: Washington ranked second of 31 presidents and second of 5 "great" presidents. He ranked above Franklin Roosevelt and below Lincoln.

RETIREMENT: March 4, 1797–December 14, 1799. Washington, 65, returned to Mount Vernon to oversee much-needed repairs. He played host, often reluctantly, to an endless parade of visitors, many longtime friends, others perfect strangers there just to ogle the former president and his family. Briefed on affairs of state by War Secretary McHenry and others, he maintained a keen interest in the course of the country. With tensions between the United States and France threatening to erupt into war in the wake of the XYZ Affair (see "John Adams, 2d President," "Administration"), Washington was commissioned lieutenant general and commander in chief of American forces on July 4, 1798, the only former president to hold such a post. He accepted the commission on the condition that he would take to the field only in case of invasion and that he had approval rights over the composition of the general staff. He promised the cause "all the blood that remains in my veins." Fortunately the undeclared "Quasi-War" that followed was limited to naval encounters and Washington's services were not required. In his last year Washington faced a liquidity crisis: Money owed him from the sale or rental of real estate was past due at a time when his taxes and entertainment bills were climbing. As a result, at age 67 he was compelled for the first time in his life to borrow money from a bank.

DEATH: December 14, 1799, after 10 P.M., Mount Vernon, Virginia. On the morning of December 12, Washington set out on horseback around the plantation. With temperatures hovering around freezing, it began to snow; this turned to sleet, then rain, and back to snow by the time Washington returned indoors five hours later. Still in his cold, wet clothes, he tended to some correspondence and ate dinner. Next morning he awoke with a sore throat, and later in the day his voice grew hoarse. About 2 A.M. on December 14 he awoke suddenly with severe chills and was having trouble breathing and speaking. Three doctors attended him—his personal physician and longtime friend Dr. James Craik and consultants Drs. Gustavus Richard Brown and Elisha Cullen Dick. They diagnosed his condition as inflammatory quinsy. The patient was bled on four separate occasions, a standard practice of the period. Washington tried to swallow a concoction of molasses, vinegar, and butter to soothe his raw throat but could not get it down. He was able to take a little calomel and tartar emetic and to inhale vinegar vapor, but his pulse remained weak throughout the day. The physicians raised blisters on his throat and lower limbs as a counter-irritant and applied a poultice, but neither was effective. Finally, Washington told his doctors to give up and about 10 P.M. spoke weakly to Tobias Lear, his aide, "I am just going. Have me decently buried and do not let my body be put into a vault in less than two days after I am dead. Do you understand me?" "Yes, sir," replied Lear. " 'Tis well,"[12] said Washington. These were his last words. Soon thereafter he died while taking his own pulse. After a lock of his hair was removed, his body was placed in a mahogany coffin bearing the Latin inscriptions *Surge Ad Judicium* and *Gloria Deo*. The funeral services, conducted by the Reverend Thomas Davis on December 18, were far from the simple ceremony Washington had requested. A procession of mourners filed between two long rows of soldiers, a band played appropriate music, guns boomed in tribute from a ship anchored in the Potomac, and the Masonic order to which Washington belonged sent a large contingent. His remains were deposited in the family tomb at Mount Vernon. In his last will and testament, a 42-page document executed in his own hand in July 1799, Washington provided his widow with the use and benefit of the estate, valued at more than $500,000, during her lifetime. He freed his personal servant William with a $30 annuity and ordered the rest of the slaves freed upon Martha's death. He left his stock in the Bank of Alexandria to a school for poor and orphaned children and ordered his stock in the Potomac Company to be applied toward the construction of a national university. He forgave the debts of his brother Samuel's family and that of his brother-in-law Bartholomew Dandridge. He also ensured that his aide Tobias Lear would live rent free for the rest of his life. To nephew Bushrod Washington he left Mount Vernon, his personal papers, and his library. His grandchildren Mrs. Nellie Lewis and George Washington Parke Custis received large, choice tracts. In sundry other bequests, the gold-headed cane Benjamin Franklin had given him went to his brother Charles, his writing desk and chair to Doctor Craik, steel pistols taken from the British during the Revolution to Lafayette, and a sword to each of five nephews on the assurance that they will never "unsheath them for the purpose of shedding blood except it be for self-defence, or in defence of their country and its rights, and in the latter case to keep them unsheathed, and prefer falling with them in their hands, to the relinquishment thereof."

WASHINGTON PRAISED: "A gentleman whose skill and experience as an officer, whose independent fortune, great talents and excellent universal character would command the approbation of all America and unite the cordial exertions of all the Colonies better than any other person in the union."[13]—John Adams, in proposing Washington as commander in chief of the Continental army, 1775.

"You would, at this side of the sea [in Europe], enjoy the great reputation you have acquired, pure and free from those little shades that the jealousy and envy of a man's countrymen and contemporaries are ever endeavouring to cast over living merit. Here you would know, and enjoy, what posterity will say of Washington. For a thousand leagues have nearly the same effect with a thousand years. The feeble voice of those grovelling passions cannot extend so far either in time or distance. At present I enjoy that pleasure for you, as I frequently hear the old generals of this martial country [France] (who study the maps of America and mark upon them all your operations) speak with sincere approbation and great applause of your conduct; and join in giving you the character of one of the greatest captains of the age."[14]—Benjamin Franklin, 1780.

"More than any other individual, and as much as to one individual was possible, has he contributed to found this, our wide spreading empire, and to give to the Western World independence and freedom."[15]—John Marshall.

"To the memory of the Man, first in war, first in peace, and first in the hearts of his countrymen."[16]—Henry "Light-Horse Harry" Lee, 1799.

WASHINGTON CRITICIZED: "If ever a nation was debauched by a man, the American nation has been debauched by Washington. If ever a nation was deceived by a man, the American nation has been deceived by Washington. Let his conduct, then, be an example to future ages; let it serve to be a warning that no man may be an idol."[17]—Philadelphia *Aurora,* 1796.

"An Anglican monarchical, and aristocratical party has sprung up, whose avowed object is to draw over us the substance, as they have already done the forms, of the British government. . . . It would give you a fever were I to name to you the apostates who have gone over to these heresies, men who were Samsons in the field and Solomons in the council, but who have had their heads shorn by the harlot England."[18]—Thomas Jefferson, in the wake of Washington's support of Jay's Treaty, 1796.

"You commenced your Presidential career by encouraging and swallowing the grossest adulation, and you travelled America from one end to the other, to put yourself in the way of receiving it. You have as many addresses in your chest as James the II. . . . The character which Mr. Washington has attempted to act in this world, is a sort of non-describable, camelion-colored thing, called prudence. It is, in many cases, a substitute for principle, and is so nearly allied to hypocrisy, that it easily slides into it. . . . And as to you, sir, treacherous to private friendship (for so you have been to me, and that in the day of danger) and a hypocrite in public life, the world will be puzzled to decide whether you are an apostate or an imposter, whether you have abandoned good principles, or whether you ever had any?"[19]—Thomas Paine, in an open letter to Washington, 1796.

WASHINGTON QUOTES: "It is easy to make acquaintances but very difficult to shake them off, however irksome and unprofitable they are found after we have once committed ourselves to them. . . . Be courteous to all but intimate with few, and let those few be well tried before you give them your confidence; true friendship is a plant of slow growth."[20]

"As the sword was the last resort for the preservation of our liberties, so it ought to be the first to be laid aside when those liberties are firmly established."[21]—1776

"Precedents are dangerous things; let the reins of government then be braced and held with a steady hand, and every violation of the Constitution be reprehended: if defective let it be amended, but not suffered to be trampled upon whilst it has an existence."[22]—1786

"[Political parties] serve to organize faction, to give it an artificial and extraordinary force to put, in the place of the delegated will of the Nation, the will of a party; often a small but artful and enterprizing minority of the community; and according to the alternate triumphs of different parties, to make the public administration the mirror of the ill-concerted and incongruous projects of faction, rather than the organ of consistent and wholesome plans digested by common counsels, and modified by mutual interests. However combinations or associations of the above description may now and then answer popular ends, they are likely in the course of time and things, to become potent engines, by which cunning, ambitious, and unprincipled men will be enabled to subvert the Power of the People and to usurp for themselves the reins of Government; destroying afterwards the very engines which have lifted them to unjust dominion."[23]—1796 (Farewell Address).

BOOKS ABOUT WASHINGTON: Cunliffe, Marcus. *George Washington: Man and Monument.* Boston: Little, Brown, 1958.

James T. Flexner. *George Washington: A Biography.* 4 vols. Boston: Little, Brown, 1965–1972.

Freeman, Douglas Southall. *George Washington: A Biography.* 7 vols. New York: Scribner's sons, 1948–1957; abridged to 1 vol. by Richard Harwell, New York: Scribner's Sons, 1968.

Wright, Esmond. *Washington and the American Revolution.* London: English Universities Press, 1957.

NOTES

1 Douglas Southall Freeman, *George Washington: A Biography*, New York: Scribner's Sons, 1948–1957, vol. II, p. 389.

2 Ibid., vol. I, p. 529.

3 Ibid., vol. II, p. 387.

4 Ibid., vol. I, p. 260.

5 Ibid., vol. II, p. 337.

6 James T. Flexner, *George Washington: A Biography*, Boston: Little, Brown, vol. I, p. 301.

7 Freeman, *Washington, An Abridgement by Richard Harwell of the seven-volume George Washington*, New York: Scribner's Sons, 1968, p. 385.

8 Ibid., p. 374.

9 Ibid., p. 492.

10 Alfred Steinberg, *The First Ten: The Founding Presidents and their Administrations*, Garden City, N.Y.: Doubleday, 1967, p. 15.

11 Henry Steele Commager, ed., *Documents of American History*, New York: Crofts, 1945, Doc. no. 100, p. 174.

12 Freeman, *Abridgement*, p. 752.

13 Anne Husted Burleigh, *John Adams*, New Rochelle, N.Y.: Arlington House, 1969, p. 135.

14 Carl Van Doren, *Benjamin Franklin*, New York: Viking, 1938, pp. 610–611.

15 Robert Haven Schauffler, ed., *Washington Birthday*, New York: Moffat, Yard, 1910, p. 142.

16 John Marshall, *Life of George Washington*, Philadelphia, 1805, vol. V, p. 767.

17 Coley Taylor and Samuel Middlebrook, *The Eagle Screams*, New York: Macaulay, 1936, p. 63.

18 Merrill D. Peterson, *Thomas Jefferson and the New Nation*, New York: Oxford University Press, 1970, p. 571.

19 M. Lincoln Schuster, ed., *A Treasury of the World's Great Letters*, New York: Simon & Schuster, 1940, pp. 180–184.

20 Freeman, *Abridgement*, p. 516.

21 Ibid., p. 325.

22 Ibid., p. 534

23 Schauffler, p. 292.

JOHN ADAMS

2D PRESIDENT

NAME: John Adams. He was named after his father.

PHYSICAL DESCRIPTION: Adams was short, about 5 feet 6 inches, stocky in his youth, and portly in middle age. He had quick blue eyes and fine brown hair. Ironically, Adams, the longest-living president, was beset by a train of maladies throughout his 90 years. "My constitution is a glass bubble,"[1] he once said. He caught cold at the slightest draft; Boston's air gave him acute chest pains; headaches, heartburn, and general weakness slowed him down. His eyes were weak from his youth. In Amsterdam in 1781 he contracted a severe fever and lapsed into a five-day coma before shaking off this "Dutch complaint," which lingered three months. By the time he became president, his hands shook with palsy, and most of his teeth had fallen to pyorrhea. He refused to wear the ill-fitting dentures of the period and thus from this time talked with a lisp.

PERSONALITY: "There are few people in this world with whom I can converse," Adams once admitted. "I can treat all with decency and civility, and converse with them, when it is necessary, on points of business. But I am never happy in their company."[2] This confession sums up the paradox of Adams's personality; he genuinely loved and had deep compassion for humanity but never learned to deal with individual human beings. To his immediate family, he was a warm, generously loving man; to outsiders, he appeared cold, aloof, conceited. As a youth he was driven by ambition. He was determined to be a man of substance and, if circumstances afforded the opportunity, a great man. Throughout his life he wrestled with his passions. From his mother he inherited his pugnacity, drive, ready temper, and broad mood swings. He frequently fell to black despair, fits of depression that were triggered usually by the onset of some illness, public criticism, or lack of recognition of his achievements. Some historians believe that he may have been manic-depressive. Somewhat paranoid, too, he was quick to see in his unpopularity a plot by others to discredit him and steal credit for themselves. A proper Puritan, he was shocked by the open sexuality of eighteenth-century France. At a dinner party in Bordeaux in 1778, a Madame de Texel, addressing Adams with innocent frankness, wondered aloud how Adam and Eve ever learned how to have sex, for no one else was around to explain the facts of life to them. Adams was thoroughly embarrassed, having never before heard a woman discuss such matters. He blushed but quickly regained his composure to explain with mock seriousness. "There was a physical quality in us resembling the power of electricity or of the magnet, by which when a pair approached within a striking distance they flew together like the needle to the pole or like two objects in electric experiments."[3]

ANCESTORS: Through his paternal grandmother, Hannah Bass (1667–1705), Adams was a great-great-grandson of Pilgrims John and Priscilla Alden. The first Adams ancestor to arrive in the colonies was his great-great-grandfather Henry Adams, a farmer and maltster, who left Somersetshire, England, with his wife, Edith Squire Adams, and some nine children to settle in Braintree, Massachusetts, by 1640. John Adams's great-uncle Dr. Zabdiel Boylston introduced the practice of inoculation in America. During the smallpox epidemic in Boston in 1721, Doctor Boylston, encouraged by Cotton Mather, vaccinated some 240 persons, including his own children; only a handful subsequently died from the disease.

FATHER: John Adams (1691–1761), farmer and leather craftsman. A pillar of the community, he served Braintree Township variously as a lieutenant in the militia, selectman, constable, tax collector, and deacon of the church. In warm weather he diligently toiled his fields, and during the winter he handcrafted shoes, harnesses, and other leather goods. "The honestest man I ever knew,"[4] his most famous son said of him. It was his example that fueled young John's ambition. He died in the flu epidemic of 1761.

MOTHER: Susanna Boylston Adams (1709–1797). She married John Adams in 1734. She is among the least well known of the famous Adams family, for her name appears infrequently in the large body of Adams writings. However, her son's diary reveals that she had a fiery temper. Part of her husband's job as selectman was to see that the town's indigent were cared for, and he fell into the habit of bringing stray needy children home with him. "I won't have all the town's poor brought here, stark naked, for me to clothe for nothing," she scolded Adams one day in 1758 when he introduced yet two more penniless girls to the household. "I won't be a slave to other folk's folk for nothing. . . . You want to put your girls over me, to make me a slave to your wenches."[5] Five years after the death of her husband, she married a Lt. John Hall, who apparently did not get along with her grown children. Like George Washington's mother, she died in the first year of her son's presidency.

SIBLINGS: Adams had two younger brothers—Peter Boylston Adams, farmer, militia captain of Braintree, and Elihu Adams, who while a company commander in the militia during the American Revolution, died from "a contagious distemper."

COLLATERAL RELATIVES: John Adams was a second cousin to Samuel Adams, patriot and signer of the Declaration of Independence, and a third cousin to his own wife, Abigail Smith Adams.

CHILDREN: Adams had four children to live to maturity.

    Abigail "Nabby" Adams (1765–1813). Having broken off her engagement to Royall Tyler, a high-spirited, somewhat irresponsible youth, she in 1784 married William Stephens Smith, a veteran officer of the Revolution and secretary to her father in London. While Adams was president, Smith was surveyor of the port of New York and, from 1813 to 1815, served as a U.S. congressman from New York. She died of cancer, having endured three years of severe pain.

John Quincy Adams (1767–1848), sixth president.

Charles Adams (1770–1800), lawyer. A bright, engaging young man, an outstanding personality in this reserved family, he died an alcoholic at age 30.

Thomas Boylston Adams (1772–1832), lawyer. From his first case, a sensational trial at which he defended the owners of a local brothel, he built a modest practice in Philadelphia and served abroad as secretary to his older brother John Quincy, but he, too, drank excessively and died in debt.

SUBSEQUENT DESCENDANTS: For the noteworthy descendants of John Adams, see the chapter "John Quincy Adams," sections "Children" and "Subsequent Descendants."

BIRTH: Adams was born on October 30, 1735 (New Style) at the family homestead in Braintree (now Quincy), Massachusetts.

CHILDHOOD: In his autobiography, John Adams chose to deny posterity the details of his childhood in Braintree but revealed a portrait of a carefree youth conspiring to get out of schoolwork to enjoy the pleasures of outdoors. He made toy boats and sailed them on local ponds and brooks. He flew kites, drove hoops, shot marbles, played quoits (a ring-toss game), wrestled, swam in summer, and ice-skated in winter. But his favorite pastime was hunting. Every spare moment he spent tramping through the woods after deer, partridge, grouse, squirrel, and any other animal available and fit for a New England table. He even began to tote his gun along to school so that he could take to the field at dismissal without having to go home first. All this sport was fine training for a young colonist, but Mr. Adams began to worry that his intellectually gifted son was frittering away his education for a sackful of game. Having tried, repeatedly and unsuccessfully, to interest him in books, Mr. Adams in exasperation put the question point-blank to his 10-year-old son: "What would you do, child?" "Be a farmer," the lad shot back. "I will show you what it is to be a farmer," Mr. Adams said. "You shall go with me to Penney ferry tomorrow morning and help me get thatch." Early next morning father and son set out for a full day's work along the creek. That night young John returned home dog tired, caked in mud, his enthusiasm for farming no doubt dimmed. "Well, John, are you satisfied with being a farmer?" Mr. Adams asked, confident that he had driven home his lesson. "I like it very well, Sir,"[6] the boy answered. The Adams men were stubborn.

EDUCATION: Having been taught to read by his father while still a tot, young Adams had a leg up on the other pupils at Mrs. Belcher's one-room schoolhouse. After digesting *The New England Primer*, he progressed to Joseph Cleverly's Latin school. Adams hated Cleverly as much as he did the dreary assignments he undertook there. He clearly had an aptitude for math and resented Cleverly for not letting him progress at a faster clip. Disgusted, he worked through the math problems on his own at home. Except for math, he had little use for school and especially disliked Latin. But Mr. Adams had his heart set on his son attending Harvard and becoming a minister, so John agreed to take his lessons more seriously if his father would just get him out of Cleverly's school and into the more challenging classes of Joseph Marsh. During his year of study under Marsh, John at last began earnestly to explore the world of knowledge. In 1751 Adams entered Harvard College. Class standing in those days depended not on scholastic achievement, but rather on the social position of one's family. Of respectable, yet humble, stock, Adams thus ranked slightly below average, fifteenth of 24 students in the class of 1755. There he studied Latin, Greek, logic, rhetoric, philosophy, metaphysics, physics, geography, mathematics, geometry, and theology. He most enjoyed math and philosophy. Adams joined a reading club at which members took turns reading aloud some new publication, poetry, or drama. The recitation demanded a certain theatrical flair, and the enthusiastic applause Adams received for his hearty renditions apparently started him thinking about a career as a trial lawyer. His four years at Harvard turned him around intellectually. "I soon perceived a growing curiosity, a love of Books and a fondness for study," he wrote of his college days in his autobiography, "which dissipated all my inclination for sports, and even for the society of the ladies." He graduated with a bachelor of arts degree in 1755. He studied law under James Putnam of Worcester and was admitted to the Massachusetts bar in November 1758.

RELIGION: Unitarian branch of Congregationalism. "My religion is founded on the love of God and my neighbor," Adams reflected as he approached death, "on the hope of pardon for my offenses; upon contrition; upon the duty as well as necessity of supporting with patience the inevitable evils of life; in the duty of doing no wrong, but all the good I can."[7] Adams believed that although Christ was a great and good man whose example of piety, love, and universal brotherhood was the ideal that all people and nations should emulate, he was, after all, still a human being, not the Son of God, not the Word made flesh. If he were God, reasoned Adams, why would he allow his own creatures to nail him to a cross. Adams also rejected the idea of a Blessed Trinity. To say that one is three and three is one was, to Adams, sheer mystical gimmickery. He abhorred rigid Calvinism. That only a few are selected for salvation and that every man's fate is predetermined at birth conflicted with his belief in a fair and just God. On the other side of the religious spectrum, Adams found Deism equally unacceptable. Although he respected the beliefs of Jefferson and others who held that God created the universe and then withdrew from mundane affairs, Adams deeply believed in continuous divine intervention, that God does indeed note the fall of a sparrow and guide the affairs of men. Similarly, Adams was confident of life after death. Adams had little use for the trappings of organized religion. One need only follow the good conscience God gave him and follow the precepts set forth in the Bible in order to be a solid Christian, Adams believed.

RECREATION: For exercise and stimulation Adams walked outdoors daily, often as much as five miles at a stretch. "It sets my blood in motion much more than riding,"[8] he said. He began smoking at age eight and, except for sporadic periods of abstinence, continued using tobacco henceforth. He also enjoyed fishing and an occasional hand of whist. But his most absorbing hobby was his private library. A voracious reader whose eyes raced across the page at times too quickly for him properly to digest its contents, he built a fine library whose volumes he spoon-fed to his children and grandchildren. Not content simply to read a book, Adams critiqued the text, festooning the pages with incisive marginalia. Among his regrets in old age was that he did not have enough time left to learn Chinese and the Semitic tongues in order to read their ancient texts. Although he had little opportunity to utilize his math background during his career, he kept his mind nimble by taking son John Quincy through Euclid's algebra and trigonometry. An inveterate diarist, Adams recorded fine word sketches of people, places, and events. He also collected souvenirs from his many travels. At Stratford-upon-Avon, he shamelessly carved out a sliver of wood from a chair in Shakespeare's birthplace.

EARLY ROMANCE: Although overweight, Adams exuded a certain rustic masculinity and intellectual vigor that made him very popular with girls. "I was of an amorous disposition," he wrote in his autobiography, "and very early from ten or eleven years of age, was very fond of the society of females. I had my favorites among the young women and spent many of my evenings in their company and this disposition although controlled for seven years after my entrance into college returned and engaged me too much till I was married." However, having been warned by his father that illicit sex almost automatically brought with it venereal disease, Adams remained celibate until marriage. "No virgin or matron ever had cause to blush at the sight of me, or to regret her acquaintance with me," he boasted from the perspective of old age. "No father, brother, son or friend ever had cause of grief or resentment for any intercourse between me and any daughter, sister, mother, or any other relation of the female sex. My children may be assured that no illegitimate brother or sister exists or ever existed." Although he declined to enumerate his "youthful flames," he assured the readers of his autobiography that "they were all modest and virtuous girls and always maintained this character through life."[9]

Hannah Quincy. One girl known to have lured Adams to the brink of engagement was Hannah Quincy, daughter of Colonel Josiah Quincy and sister of the Josiah Quincy who later joined Adams in defending British soldiers accused of the Boston Massacre. A year younger than Adams, Hannah was a witty, unusually well-read, attractive brunette who kept several suitors dangling simultaneously. At 23, Adams, still a struggling lawyer, was deter-mined to avoid marriage until his finances improved, but Hannah kept drawing him closer and closer to a commitment. So many Sunday evenings did Adams spend at her home that his father warned him that people were beginning to talk as if they were already engaged. Adams dismissed such rumors as so much "tittle tattle" but was increasingly entranced by the charms of his "Orlinda," his pet name for Hannah. One spring afternoon he found himself alone with her in her drawing room. Amid the soft, relaxed conversation, the dim light, and the release of spring, Adams for an instant forgot his career and the cost of matrimony. Just as he was about to propose, the door swung open and in walked two of their friends. Adams returned home shaken over this close call, vowing to redouble his efforts to resist similar temptations in the future. As for Hannah, she tired of waiting and in 1760 married Dr. Bela Lincoln of Hingham. After his death, she wed Ebenezer Storer, who also left her widowed. Adams never forgot her. In 1820, more than six decades after their courtship, Hannah called on the ex-president, himself now a widower. "What! Madam," the 84-year-old Adams exclaimed, beaming, "shall we not go walk in Cupid's Grove together?" "Ah, sir," Hannah replied, "it would not be the first time that we have walked there."[10] Hannah died in 1826, the same year as Adams.

MARRIAGE: John Adams, 28, married Abigail Smith, 19, on October 25, 1764, at the home of the bride's parents in Weymouth, Massachusetts. Born in Weymouth on November 23, 1744 (New Style), the second of three daughters of the Reverend William Smith and Elizabeth Quincy Smith and a granddaughter of longtime Massachusetts legislator Colonel John Quincy, Abigail Smith was a sickly child, too sick to send to school. With absolutely no formal education, then, she became one of the most erudite women ever to serve as First Lady and is today regarded as an early heroine of the women's liberation movement. Although Adams had known the Smith family since he was a boy, he paid no attention to the delicate child nine years his junior. But in 1762, when he tagged along to Weymouth with friend Richard Cranch, who was engaged to the oldest Smith girl, Mary, he was quickly attracted to the petite, shy seventeen-year-old brunette who was forever bent over some book. He was surprised to learn that she knew so much about poetry, philosophy, and politics, especially because her parents had discouraged her reading as inappropriate training for a wife. Although Abigail's father approved of the match, Mrs. Smith was appalled that a Quincy would throw her life away on a country lawyer whose manners still reeked of the farm, but eventually she gave in. The bride wore a square-necked gown of white challis. The groom appeared in a dark blue coat, contrasting light breeches and white stockings, a gold-embroidered satin waistcoat his mother had made for the occasion, and buckle shoes. The bride's father performed the nuptials. After the reception, the bridal couple mounted a single horse and rode off to their new home, the small cottage and farm that John had inherited from his father in Braintree. The American Revolution and Adams's role in it meant many long separations, but John and Abigail maintained an intimacy in regular correspondence. Abigail, a keen observer of current events, kept Adams posted on developments at home. During the momentous year of 1776, as America scrapped the royal statutes, she urged her husband to include women in the new order: "Remember the ladies and be more generous and favorable to them than your ancestors! Do not put such unlimited power into the hands of the husbands. Remember all men would be tyrants if they could. If particular care and attention is not paid to the ladies, we are determined to foment a rebellion, and will not hold ourselves bound by any laws in which we have no voice or representation."[11] All this made little impression on Adams, who saw no reason "to repeal our masculine systems," which, he insisted, "are little more than theory"[12] anyway. With the removal of the capital to Washington in 1800, Abigail Adams became the first First Lady to preside over the White House, or President's House, as it was then known. She found the unfinished mansion in Washington "habitable" and the location "beautiful" but complained that, despite the thick woods nearby, she could find no one willing to chop and haul firewood for the First Family. Mrs. Adams's health, never robust, suffered in Washington. In 1801 she returned home to Massachusetts, where she remained the rest of her life. In later years she renewed correspondence with Thomas Jefferson, whose political opposition to her husband had hurt her deeply. She died of typhoid fever on October 28, 1818.

MILITARY SERVICE: None.

CAREER BEFORE THE PRESIDENCY: From his admittance to the Massachusetts bar in 1758, Adams steadily built his law practice in Boston and held such local offices as surveyor of highways and selectman for Braintree. In his first notable case in 1768–1769, he succeeded in having charges dropped against John Hancock for allegedly having smuggled wine into the port of Boston without paying the required duty. But his most celebrated defense, a courageous one that nearly cost him his career, was that of the British soldiers charged with perpetrating the Boston Massacre.

Boston Massacre, 1770. On March 5, 1770, an angry mob of Bostonians taunted a group of eight armed British soldiers under the command of Captain

Thomas Preston. Some threw snowballs and debris, others wagged heavy sticks under the troops' noses, still others tried to snatch their rifles from them. "Why don't you fire?" the crowd taunted. Suddenly one of the redcoats did just that; the others then fired in rapid succession. Three Americans lay dead, including the burly black Crispus Attucks, and eight were wounded. The British muskets had barely cooled before all of Boston was buzzing about the wanton slaughter of "hundreds" of innocent peaceable citizens. Paul Revere hastily turned out an engraving that depicted Captain Preston ordering his men to fire on a defenseless throng, a work of art that among the virulently Anglophobic citizens of Boston was regarded as visual proof of British atrocity. To calm the people, the royal government arrested the soldiers and promised a fair trial. But no colonial lawyer would touch the case for the defense—no one but John Adams and Josiah Quincy. Even though he supported the colonial effort that was inexorably advancing toward open rebellion and even though he knew it would make him extremely unpopular with his fellow citizens, Adams accepted the case because he believed these British soldiers to be innocent and in danger of being railroaded to the gallows just to satisfy a mob thirst for vengeance and because he felt it important to establish the supremacy of justice over political expedience. Preston, as commanding officer, was tried first. Adams convinced the jury that the men had fired on their own without orders from Preston. With Preston's acquittal, Adams began preparing for the defense of the other eight, who were tried as a group. During jury selection, Adams wisely challenged prospective jurors from Boston itself, so that the final panel consisted solely of rural residents, less likely to be swayed by the anti-British hysteria rampant in the city. Before four justices of the Superior Court of Judicature, the prosecution (Robert Treat Paine and Samuel Quincy) produced witnesses who testified that the soldiers fired gratuitously into a peaceable assembly of citizens. Adams for the defense painted a very different picture. He conjured up for the jury "a motley rabble of saucy boys, Negroes, and mulattoes, Irish teagues and outlandish jack tars . . . shouting and hazzaing and threatening life . . . whistling, screaming and rending an Indian yell . . . throwing every species of rubbish they could pick up in the street." He asked each of the jurors to put himself in the shoes of the soldier who was clubbed off his feet and struck about the chest. "You expect he should behave like a stoic philosopher, lost in apathy?" Adams asked sarcastically. "You must suppose him divested of all human passions, if you don't think him at least provoked, thrown off his guard."[13] The jury acquitted six of the defendants and found the other two guilty only of manslaughter. The two were branded on the thumbs and released. Adams was exhausted. As expected, he was villified by townsmen for championing a British cause. Some even charged that he took the case just for the fee, which came to less than twenty guineas for both trials. Eventually, his lonely stand against trial by passion and his insistence that it is more important to protect the innocent than to punish the guilty was vindicated.

Member of Massachusetts legislature, 1770–1774. Elected as the Boston representative to the General Court (lower house), Adams served as legal adviser to the legislature. In 1773 he was elected by his colleagues in the Court to serve on the Governor's Council (upper house), but his election was vetoed by the royal governor. Adams applauded the Boston Tea Party as a fitting protest against British colonial policy.

Member of Continental Congress, 1774–1777. In 1774 Adams was elected a Massachusetts delegate to the Continental Congress, where he sought to broaden the base of the incipient rebellion to include the southern colonies. To that end he nominated George Washington to be commander in chief of the Continental army. Among his committee assignments were the secret Committee on Foreign Correspondence, charged with obtaining foreign aid, and the panel assigned the task of drafting the Declaration of Independence; the latter duty was left to Thomas Jefferson. He also served as president of the War and Ordnance Board. Besides Jefferson, he is the only president to have signed the Declaration of Independence.

Diplomat Abroad, 1778–1788. Appointed to replace Silas Deane as a member of the commission to France that included Benjamin Franklin and Arthur Lee, he arrived in Paris in 1778. He accomplished little there, for his blunt nature irritated the French and his Puritan disdain for Franklin's sexual adventures as well as his jealousy of Franklin's popularity in France caused friction within the delegation. He returned to the United States in 1779. As a delegate to the Massachusetts Constitutional Convention of 1779–1780, he drafted the state constitution. In 1780 he was sent as minister to the Netherlands, where during the next two years he obtained from the Dutch diplomatic recognition of American independence and the first of several substantial loans. As the Dutch, whom Adams likened to "a school of sharks" when it came to money matters, were not known for bankrolling lost causes, the success of Adams's mission was an important psychological boost to the Americans. Adams returned to Paris in October 1782, flush with his diplomatic coup at The Hague, to help conclude a peace treaty with Britain. Upon his arrival, however, he was appalled to learn that Congress had instructed the American negotiators to be guided by the French foreign ministry in hammering out peace terms—this despite France's willingness to accept the Appalachian Mountains as the western boundary of the United States, leaving the Ohio country and the rest of the sparsely populated region between the mountains and the Mississippi River under British control. Adams, Franklin, and John Jay, who had since joined the team, baldly ignored their instructions and concluded the Treaty of Paris (1783) without French approval and with the western boundary of the United States fixed at the Mississippi. In 1785 Adams was appointed the first American minister to Great Britain. However, the wounds were still too fresh for genuine rapprochement with the former mother country, and Adams, having accomplished little, requested his own recall, effective February 1788.

Vice President, 1789–1797. "My country has in its wisdom contrived for me the most insignificant office that ever the invention of man contrived or his imagination conceived."[14] So John Adams summed up his duties as the nation's first vice president. His term, in addition to being boring, injured Adams's reputation, for it was as vice president that he acquired the image of a monarchist. Presiding over the Senate in its early days, he became bogged down in the minutiae of form, protocol, and precedent. How should visitors to the chamber be received? Should senators listen to a presidential address while seated or standing? How should the chief executive be addressed? To the latter, Adams proposed His Highness, the President of the United States and Protector of their Liberties. The motion was hooted down. To many, all this concern over pomp smacked of the same British royalty that the young nation had just thrown off. Legislators began referring to Adams derisively as His

Rotundity, the Duke of Braintree, His Superfluous Excellency, and Bonny Johnny Adams. His critics further charged that he was grooming himself to succeed Washington. Adams disclaimed any such ambition. "I am not of Caesar's mind," he noted. "The second place in Rome is high enough for me."[15]

FEDERALIST PRESIDENTIAL NOMINATION, 1796: Neither Adams nor his opponent was formally nominated. As vice president and with the endorsement of retiring President Washington, Adams became the de facto candidate of the Federalists. Thomas Pinckney (1750–1828) of South Carolina was the Federalist candidate for vice president.

OPPONENT: Thomas Jefferson (1743–1826) of Virginia, Democratic-Republican. Having resigned from Washington's cabinet, Jefferson was free to challenge the Federalist candidate once Washington retired. He enjoyed the universal, broad-based support of the faction opposed to Federalism—the party that survives today as the Democratic party. See "Thomas Jefferson, 3d President." Aaron Burr (1756–1836) of New York was the Democratic-Republican candidate for vice-president.

CAMPAIGN AND THE ISSUES, 1796: The Jeffersonians, so long frustrated with having to mount their opposition to Federalism without appearing to offend the venerable Washington, charged into this, the nation's first real presidential campaign, eager to bloody Adams. Pamphleteers for both sides worked overtime smearing the opposition: Adams was characterized as a despot who longed for American monarchy and distrusted the people. Jefferson, the Federalists charged, was a demagogue, preying on people's fears to further his own political fortunes. Stripped of their excess, the two characterizations pointed up the real issues separating the candidates. Adams distrusted the masses. He favored life terms for the Senate as a check on the popularly elected House. Government, he believed, is best left to the pros, the politicians, the bureaucrats. He vowed to reinforce Washington's strong central government. Jefferson, on the other hand, advocated a dissipation of power from the federal government to the states. He rode the wave of popular fears of insidious royalism, but he genuinely shared those fears and was not merely preying on them to win an election. In foreign affairs, Adams condemned the French Revolution as mobocracy; Jefferson, while wincing at its excesses, applauded the effort to overthrow the French royal family. Jefferson still saw Britain as America's principal enemy; Adams considered France the greater threat. French minister to the United States Pierre Adet campaigned openly for Jefferson. President Washington made it clear that he preferred Adams as his successor. The endorsement was crucial for Adams in this close election, for many still revered the general's opinion. The federal bureaucracy, every important member of which owed his job to Washington, also lined up behind Adams. Alexander Hamilton, although a Federalist, privately opposed Adams, because he was too independent, too unpredictable to control. He therefore hatched a scheme to deny the presidency to both Adams and Jefferson and deliver it to the Federalist vice presidential candidate, Thomas Pinckney. This maneuver was possible because at that time each elector cast two votes without distinguishing which was for president and which for vice president. Whoever received the most votes became president; the man with the next highest total became vice president. By inducing southern electors to vote for Pinckney and anyone else except Adams, and trusting that loyal Federalists in New England would vote for Adams and Pinckney, Hamilton hoped to make Pinckney president. However, the plan backfired when New Englanders learned of it and deliberately reduced Pinckney's total in the region. Although the effect of Hamilton's plot was to narrow Adams's margin of victory, it also dragged Pinckney down to third place behind Jefferson. Ironically, then, Hamilton indirectly helped his old enemy win the vice presidency, a springboard Jefferson used to good advantage four years later.

ELECTION AS PRESIDENT, 1796:

Electoral Vote: Adams, 71; Jefferson, 68.

States Carried: Adams won the majority of electors in nine states— Connecticut, Delaware, Maryland, Massachusetts, New Hampshire, New Jersey, New York, Rhode Island, and Vermont. Jefferson won the majority of electors in seven states—Georgia, Kentucky, North Carolina, Pennsylvania, South Carolina, Tennessee, and Virginia.

INAUGURAL ADDRESS: Philadelphia, March 4, 1797. ". . . to a benevolent human mind there can be no spectacle presented by any nation more pleasing, more noble, majestic, or august, than an assembly like that which has so often been seen in this and the other Chamber of Congress, of a Government in which the Executive authority, as well as that of all the branches of the Legislature, are exercised by citizens selected at regular periods by their neighbors to make and execute laws for the general good. Can anything essential, anything more than mere ornament and decoration, be added to this by robes and diamonds? Can authority be more amiable and respectable when it descends from accidents or institutions established in remote antiquity than when it springs fresh from the hearts and judgments of an honest and enlightened people? For it is the people only that are represented. It is their power and majesty that is reflected, and only for their good, in every legitimate government, under whatever form it may appear. The existence of such a government as ours for any length of time is a full proof of a general dissemination of knowledge and virtue throughout the whole body of the people. And what object or consideration more pleasing than this can be presented to the human mind? If national pride is ever justifiable or excusable it is when it springs, not from power or riches, grandeur or glory, but from conviction of national innocence, information, and benevolence. . . ."

VICE PRESIDENT: Thomas Jefferson (1743–1826), of Virginia, served 1797–1801. See "Thomas Jefferson, 3d President."

CABINET:

Secretary of State. (1) Timothy Pickering (1745–1829), of Massachusetts, served 1795–1800. A holdover from the Washington administration, he was asked to resign after Adams learned that he had been conspiring with Hamilton against administration policy. When he refused to resign, Adams dismissed him; Pickering is the only secretary of state to be fired directly. (2) John Marshall (1755–1835), of Virginia, served 1800–1801. Having declined Adams's invitation to serve as war secretary, he reluctantly accepted this post. He argued against war with Franch and asserted the U.S. position on neutral rights at sea. He resigned near the end of Adams's term to become chief justice.

Secretary of the Treasury. (1) Oliver Wolcott (1760–1833), of Connecticut, served 1795–1800. A holdover from the Washington administration and a Hamiltonian, he criticized Adams behind his back for departing from what he considered to be orthodox Federalism. (2) Samuel Dexter (1761–1816), of Massachusetts, served January–May 1801. Transferred from war secretary, he stayed on briefly in the Jefferson administration.

Secretary of War. (1) James McHenry (1753–1816), of Maryland, served 1796–1800. A holdover from the Washington administration, he, too, schemed with Hamilton to thwart Adams's policies and was forced to resign. (2) Samuel Dexter (1761–1816), of Massachusetts, served 1800–1801. He resigned to become Treasury secretary.

Attorney General. Charles Lee (1758–1815), of Virginia, served 1795–1801. A holdover from the Washington administration, he remained loyal to Adams against the intrigue of Hamiltonians. He alone in the cabinet argued for outright war against France.

Secretary of the Navy. Benjamin Stoddert (1751–1813), of Maryland, served 1798–1801. The first to serve in this cabinet post, he made the U.S. Marine Corps a permanent branch of the Navy, expanded the fleet amid hostilities with France, and established shipyards at Norfolk, Virginia, Portsmouth, New Hampshire, and Brooklyn, New York.

ADMINISTRATION: March 4, 1797–March 4, 1801.

Relations with France, the XYZ Affair. Without regard for the political consequences, President Adams ignored the popular clamor for war with France and with patience forged a lasting peace with that country. By the time Adams took office, relations with France had deteriorated badly under President Washington's pro-British foreign policy. With French privateers regularly harassing American merchant ships, it seemed that the two nations were headed for war. In 1797 Adams dispatched a three-man mission, Charles Cotesworth Pinckney, John Marshall, and Elbridge Gerry, to Paris to try to resolve the differences, but French Foreign Minister Talleyrand refused to receive them directly. Instead, he sent three men, Bellamy, Hauteval, and Hottinguer, to demand of the Americans a $250,000 bribe before he would even consider normalizing relations. The Americans refused. When Adams learned of this diplomatic extortion, he was enraged and prepared immediately for war. Republicans, including Vice President Jefferson, thought Adams was exaggerating the incident as an excuse to declare war. They asked to see the diplomatic dispatches. Adams refused on grounds of executive privilege, only reinforcing the Republican belief that Adams had trumped up the whole episode. Finally, at the urging of Hamilton and other Federalists who hoped to silence the opposition once and for all, Adams released the documents after substituting the letters X, Y, and Z for the real names of the French agents. The incident that thus became known as the XYZ Affair turned the nation against France. Republicans kept a low profile, as citizens who once flew French flags now cursed the nation that had tried to blackmail America. "Millions for defence, but not a cent for tribute" was the slogan of the day. Although Adams had effectively destroyed the pro-French opposition in Congress, he now faced the danger of being swept into a conflict that the United States was ill-prepared to fight. Amid an intensifying clamor for war, Adams remained determined to seek a peaceful solution. For two years U.S. frigates and armed privateers engaged French vessels at sea in what came to be called the Quasi-War, but Adams refused to press for an outright declaration of war. In 1799, against all political advice, he sent another peace mission—Patrick Henry, Minister to the Netherlands William Vans Murray, and Chief Justice Oliver Ellsworth—to Paris, having received private assurances from Talleyrand that they would be treated respectfully. This time it worked. Under the terms of the Convention of 1800, France accepted U.S. neutrality rights at sea and discharged the U.S.

from its obligations under the alliance formed during the American Revolution. In return, the United States granted France most-favored-nation status as a trading partner.

Logan Act, 1799. In a sincere effort to normalize relations with France following the XYZ Affair, Dr. George Logan of Pennsylvania, on his own initiative without authorization from the U.S. government, entered into negotiations with French officials in Paris. In 1799 Congress reacted by passing the Logan Act, which specifically outlawed such private diplomacy. The statute remains in effect.

Alien and Sedition Acts, 1798. Amid the anti-Republican sentiment rampant in the wake of the XYZ Affair, President Adams in 1798 signed into law four bills designed to crush the opposition: (1) The Naturalization Act made it more difficult for immigrants (most were Jeffersonians) to become citizens. (2) To rid the nation of the more vociferous pro-Republican immigrants, the Alien Act permitted the president to deport any alien considered dangerous. (3) The Alien Enemies Act, directed at French immigrants, authorized the president to round up and imprison enemy aliens during wartime. (4) In a severe blow to freedom of the press, the Sedition Act threatened with fine and imprisonment anyone who "shall write, print, utter or publish . . . scandalous and malicious writing or writings against the government of the United States, or either House of the Congress . . . or the President . . . with intent to defame . . . or to bring them . . . into contempt or disrepute; or to excite against them . . . the hatred of the good people of the United States."[16] The Naturalization Act was repealed in 1802. The other three acts, enacted with a two-year expiration date, were allowed to lapse in 1800.

Fries Rebellion, 1799. In July 1798 President Adams approved legislation levying federal taxes on property. The next spring John Fries led a group of his fellow Pennsylvanians in armed resistance against tax assessors and collectors. He was arrested, convicted of treason, and sentenced to be hanged, but in May 1800 President Adams, after considerable deliberation, pardoned him and others who took part in the rebellion.

Midnight Appointments. Bitter about his defeat by Jefferson in 1800, President Adams spent the final hours of his administration appointing a slew of Federalists to the judgeships and lesser court offices created by the hastily passed Judiciary Act of 1801. These so-called midnight appointments were designed to deny the incoming administration the opportunity to leave its mark on the courts and to guarantee a strong Federalist check on Republican executive action. Having done this, Adams chose to end his term with one last slap at his opponent. On March 4, 1801, he rose before dawn and slipped out of town to avoid the inaugural of his successor. President Jefferson removed many of these appointees.

SUPREME COURT APPOINTMENTS: (1) Bushrod Washington (1762–1829), of Virginia, served as associate justice 1798–1829. A staunch Federalist like his uncle George Washington, he aligned himself with Chief Justice John Marshall. (2) Alfred Moore (1755–1810), of North Carolina, served as associate justice 1799–1804. A Revolutionary War veteran, he was a state superior court judge at the time of his appointment. (3) John Marshall (1755–1835), of Virginia, served as chief justice 1801–1835. He is generally considered to be the greatest chief justice of the United States. Through forceful written opinions and a determination to set in concrete the legal underpinnings of a strong central government, he saved the Court from lapsing into a vestigial third branch of government, transforming it into a vital element in the troika of checks and balances. He strengthened the Court's influence by doing away with the usual practice of having each justice draft a separate opinion and instead assigned a single jurist to write for the majority. This system allowed the Court to speak with one voice even when its members disagreed. A prodigious worker, he assigned himself about 50 percent of the opinions, including the most important ones. He personally drafted two of the most important decisions ever handed down: In *Marbury* v. *Madison* (1803), he established the precedent of judicial review, the right of the Court to declare acts of Congress unconstitutional. In *McCulloch* v. *Maryland* (1819), he upheld the constitutionality of the Bank of the United States under the implied powers granted to Congress by the Constitution. Although its immediate effect was to promote the conservative economic system envisioned by Alexander Hamilton, it also formed the constitutional basis of the liberal social welfare legislation of the twentieth century. By virtue of his lifetime appointment, Marshall was the last prominent Federalist to remain in power.

RANKING IN 1962 HISTORIANS POLL: Adams ranked tenth of 31 presidents, the fifth of six "near great" presidents; ranked above Cleveland, below Truman.

RETIREMENT: March 4, 1801–July 4, 1826. Repudiated at the polls (see "Thomas Jefferson, 3d President," for the election of 1800), Adams returned to his homestead at Quincy (formerly Braintree), Massachusetts, expecting to enjoy a few years of peaceful retirement before passing. Instead, he embarked on an intellectual adventure that lasted more than a quarter century. His mind remained alert, his curiosity insatiable, to the end. He read new books and reread the classics. When cataracts clouded his vision, he enlisted his grandchildren and other relatives to read aloud to him. He undertook a voluminous correspondence with old friends from the Revolution. In 1805 he renewed ties with Benjamin Rush, whose anti-Federalist politics had strained their relationship. At Rush's intercession, then, Adams and Jefferson buried their differences in a flurry of letters that rekindled the warm friendship they had enjoyed during the Revolution. In 1820 he interrupted his retirement briefly; as a presidential elector, he cast one of Massachusetts's 15 electoral votes for the reelection of President Monroe. That same year he also served as an elected delegate to the Massachusetts state constitutional convention. Finally, at 89, he enjoyed a thrill denied to every other former chief executive—to see his son John Quincy Adams elected president.

DEATH: July 4, 1826, about 6 P.M., Quincy, Massachusetts. Adams's health had been failing for several months. He was invited to attend the grand celebration marking the nation's fiftieth birthday in Boston, but he had grown too weak to venture outdoors. In his last days he was confined to his upstairs bedroom. On the morning of July 4, he lapsed into a coma. Shortly after noon he rallied just long enough to utter these last words: "Thomas Jefferson still . . ." (The last word was indistinct but was thought to be "survives.")[17] He awoke again a bit later but was unable to speak and early that evening died peacefully from heart failure and pneumonia. He was at 90 years and 247 days the longest-living president. In one of the most remarkable coincidences in American history, Jefferson also died that day, a few hours before Adams. Thus the only two signers of the Declaration of Independence to become president died simultaneously—on the fiftieth anniversary of the adoption of that great document.

Adams was buried beside his wife beneath the Congregational church in Quincy. Inscribed on the white marble stone inside the church is a lengthy epitaph, composed by his son John Quincy Adams, which reads in part: "This house will bear witness to his piety; / This town, his birth-place, to his munificence; / History to his patriotism; / Posterity to the depth and compass of his mind."[18] In his last will and testament, executed in 1819, Adams left the family house in Quincy, some 100 surrounding acres, and his papers, books, and other personal belongings to his son John Quincy Adams, on the condition that he pay $12,000 to the estate and a sum equal to one-half the value of the books to John Adams's other surviving son, Thomas Boylston Adams. He also left eight acres of land to the town of Quincy for the construction of a new church and school. The residue of his estate, about $42,000, was to be divided equally among his two sons, eleven grandchildren, and one niece.

ADAMS PRAISED: "The man to whom the country is most indebted for the great measure of independency is Mr. John Adams of Boston. I call him the Atlas of American independence. He it was who sustained the debate, and by the force of his reasoning demonstrated not only the justice but the expediency of the measure."[19]—Richard Stockton of New Jersey, signer of Declaration of Independence, 1776.

"Adams has a heart formed for friendship and susceptible of its fondest feelings. He is humane, generous and open; warm in his friendly attachments, though perhaps rather implacable to those whom he thinks his enemies."[20]—Jonathan Sewall, American Tory refugee living in London while Adams was minister to Britain.

"Mr. A [dams] . . . has always appeared to me to add an ardent love for the public good, and his further knowledge of the world seems to have corrected those jealousies which he is represented to have once been influenced by."[21]—Alexander Hamilton, 1788

"You stand nearly alone in the history of our public men in never having had your integrity called in question or even suspected. Friends and enemies agree in believing you to be an honest man."[22]—Benjamin Rush

"I never felt a diminution of confidence in his integrity, and retained a solid affection for him."[23]—Thomas Jefferson

ADAMS CRITICIZED: "You will never make a soldier. You can only talk about it. You have the head for strategy—but not the heart for fighting. . . . I have searched your heart. Tired with one year's service as Representative, dancing from Boston to Braintree and from Braintree to Boston. Moping about the streets of this town as hipped as Father Flynt at ninety. You don't care for anything but to get money enough to carry you smoothly through this world!"[24]—James Otis of Massachusetts

"He means well for his country, is always an honest man, often a wise one, but sometimes, and in some things, absolutely out of his senses."[25]—Benjamin Franklin, 1783

"Mr. Adams and his Federalists wish to sap the Republic by fraud, destroy it by force, and elect an English monarchy in its place."[26]—Thomas Jefferson

"However dangerous the election of Mr. Jefferson may prove to the community, I do not perceive that any portion of the mischief would be avoided by the election of Mr. Adams. We know the temper of his mind to be revolutionary, violent, and vindictive. . . . His passions and selfishness would continually gain strength; his pride and interest would concur in rendering his administration favorable to the views of democrats and Jacobins."[27]—Oliver Wolcott, Treasury secretary under Adams

"Whether he is spiteful, playful, witty, kind, cold, drunk, sober, angry, easy, stiff, jealous, cautious, confident, close, open, it is always in the wrong place or to the wrong person."[28]—James McHenry, war secretary under Adams

ADAMS QUOTES: "Let me have my farm, family and goose quill, and all the honors and offices this world has to bestow may go to those who deserve them better and desire them more. I court them not."[29]

"By my physical constitution, I am but an ordinary man. The times alone have destined me to fame—and even these have not been able to give me much."[30]

"The people, when they have been unchecked, have been as unjust, tyrannical, brutal, barbarous, and cruel, as any king or senate possessed of uncontrollable power. The majority has eternally, and without one exception, usurped over the rights of the minority."[31]

"Modesty is a virtue that can never thrive in public. . . . A man must be his own trumpeter . . . he must get his picture drawn, his statue made, and must hire all the artists in his turn, to set about works to spread his name, make the mob stare and gape, and perpetuate his fame."[32]

"The loss of paradise, by eating a forbidden apple, has been many thousand years a lesson to mankind; but not much regarded. Moral reflections, wise maxims, religious terrors have little effect upon nations when they contradict a present passion, prejudice, imagination, enthusiasm or caprice."[33]

"The history of our Revolution will be one continued lie from one end to the other. The essence of the whole will be that Dr. Franklin's electrical rod smote the earth and out sprang General Washington. That Franklin electrified him with his rod—and thenceforward these two conducted all the policies, negotiations, legislatures, and war."[34]

BOOKS BY ADAMS: *A Defense of the Constitutions of Government of the United States of America* (3 vols., 1787–1788) and *Discourses on Davila* (1805), in *Diary and Autobiography of John Adams*, ed. L. H. Butterfield. 4 vols. Cambridge, Mass.: Harvard University Press, 1961.

BOOKS ABOUT ADAMS: Bowen, Catherine Drinker. *John Adams and the American Revolution.* Boston: Little, Brown, 1950.

Burleigh, Ann Husted. *John Adams.* New Rochelle, N.Y.: Arlington House, 1969.

Chinard, Gilbert. *Honest John Adams.* Boston: Little, Brown, 1933.

Smith, Page. *John Adams.* 2 vols. New York: Doubleday, 1962.

Shaw, Peter. *The Character of John Adams.* Chapel Hill, N.C.: University of North Carolina Press, 1976.

NOTES

1 Page Smith, *John Adams*, New York: Doubleday, 1962, p. 1102.

2 Ibid., p. 263.

3 L. H. Butterfield, ed., *Diary and Autobiography of John Adams*, Cambridge, Mass.: Belknap Press, 1961, vol. IV, p. 36.

4 Smith, p. 8.

5 Butterfield, vol. I, p. 65.

6 Ibid., vol III, p. 257.

7 Charles Francis Adams, ed., *The Works of John Adams, Second President of the United States*, Boston, 1850–1856, vol. X, p. 170.

8 Butterfield, vol. II, pp. 42–43.

9 Ibid., vol. III, pp. 260–261.

10 Smith, p. 1128.

11 Janet Whitney, *Abigail Adams*, Boston: Little, Brown, 1948, p. 129.

12 Ibid., p. 130.

13 Smith, pp. 124–125.

14 Alfred Steinberg, *The First Ten: The Founding Presidents and their Administrations*, New York: Doubleday, 1967, p. 59.

15 Adams, vol. VIII, p. 494.

16 Howard F. Bremer, ed., *John Adams 1735–1826, Chronology—Documents—Bibliographical Aids*, Dobbs Ferry, N.Y.: 1967, pp. 55–56.

17 Smith, p. 1136; Marie B. Hecht, *John Quincy Adams*, New York: Macmillan, 1972, pp. 436–437.

18 Adams, vol. I., p. 643.

19 Smith, pp. 268–269.

20 Catherine Drinker Bowen, *John Adams and the American Revolution*, Boston: Little, Brown, 1950., p. 633.

21 Smith, p. 740.

22 Anne Husted Burleigh, *John Adams*, New Rochelle, N.Y.: Arlington House, 1969, p. 390.

23 Merrill D. Peterson, *Thomas Jefferson and the New Nation*, New York: Oxford University Press, 1970, p. 560.

24 Bowen, p. 420.

25 Butterfield, vol. I, p. lxiii.

26 P. L. Ford, ed., *The Writings of Thomas Jefferson*, New York: Putnam, 1892–1899, vol. VIII, p. 67.

27 Smith, p. 1039.

28 Steinberg, p. 71.

29 Smith, p. 262.

30 Butterfield, vol. II, p. 362.

31 Adams, vol. VI, p. 10.

32 Smith, pp. 380–381.

33 Ibid., p. 721.

34 Steinberg, p. 75.

THOMAS JEFFERSON

☆ ☆ ☆ ☆ ☆ ☆ ☆ ☆ ☆

3D PRESIDENT

NAME: Thomas Jefferson. He was named after his paternal grandfather, Thomas Jefferson II (c. 1677–1731), a prominent landowner, militia captain, and justice of Chesterfield County, Va.

PHYSICAL DESCRIPTION: Tall (6 feet 2½ inches) and thin, Jefferson had small hazel eyes, an angular nose, thin lips, sound straight teeth, a pointed chin, a long neck, and reddish hair that turned sandy as it grayed. In his youth he was heavily freckled and rather gawky. His hands and feet were large. He walked in a loping gait and maintained poor posture. "He sits in a lounging manner on one hip, commonly," observed Senator William Maclay, "and with one of his shoulders elevated much above the other."[1] He paid little attention to fashion but dressed in whatever was most comfortable, often mixing styles from different periods. When Anthony Merry, British minister to the United States, called on President Jefferson, he was appalled to find the chief executive "not merely in undress, but actually standing in slippers down at the heels, and both pantaloons, coat and under-clothes indicative of utter slovenliness and indifference to appearances, and in a state of negligence actually studied."[2] His health generally was good, except for severe headaches that struck usually after a personal loss and sometimes lingered for weeks. In later years he suffered from rheumatism. From 1786 his right hand was crippled (see "Postmarital Affairs, Maria Cosway").

PERSONALITY: "Mr. Jefferson displays a mild, easy and obliging temper," commented the duc de La Rochefoucald-Liancourt, "though he is somewhat cold and reserved. His conversation is the most agreeable kind."[3] Jefferson was open and approachable, yet he maintained an impregnable core of inner feeling that has frustrated his biographers. He had an insatiable curiosity about all aspects of life. His fondness for structure and order can be seen in the meticulous records he maintained on plant life and weather conditions at Monticello. Despite his many years in politics, he never acquired two attributes usually considered essential to success in that profession: a thick skin and a gift for oratory. He was acutely sensitive to public criticism and, although captivating in small groups, delivered notoriously unmoving speeches before large crowds. He tended to mumble softly out of earshot of much of his audience.

ANCESTORS: Through his maternal grandfather, Isham Randolph, Jefferson descended from King David I (1084–1153) of Scotland. The immigrant ancestor of the Jefferson (possible original spelling *Jeaffreson*) line is unknown. The president, who could trace his paternal ancestry only to his grandfather, recounted in his later years the family tradition that the Jeffersons had emigrated to the New World from the Mount Snowden area of northern Wales.

FATHER: Colonel Peter Jefferson (1708–1757), planter, surveyor, public official. In 1739 he married Jane Randolph. Industrious, inquiring, tall, and more muscular than his famous son, Peter Jefferson was a prominent landowner, acquiring clear title to some 5,000–7,000 acres in sparsely populated Goochland (later Albemarle) County in western Virginia. He held many local offices, including magistrate, sheriff, justice of the peace, and Chancery Court judge. From 1745 he was a leader of the county militia, first as lieutenant colonel and later as general commander. He also represented his county in the House of Burgesses during 1754–1755. As assistant county surveyor under Joshua Fry, he helped fix the boundary between Virginia and North Carolina in 1749. Shortly thereafter Fry and Jefferson were commissioned to undertake a comprehensive survey of Virginia. Their map, completed in 1751, was long regarded as the definitive guide to the colony. Peter Jefferson died of unknown cause at 49, when Thomas was 14 years old.

MOTHER: Jane Randolph Jefferson (1720–1776). Born in London, she came to America with her family as a child. Very little is known of her, for Jefferson rarely mentioned his mother in his writings. She was said to have been mild tempered. According to biographer Merrill Peterson, she represented a "zero quantity" in her son's life. She died from a stroke a few months before Jefferson wrote the Declaration of Independence.

SIBLINGS: The third of eight children to live to maturity, Jefferson had six sisters and one brother—Jane Jefferson, who died unmarried at 25; Mrs. Mary Bolling, whose husband, John, served in the Virginia House of Burgesses; Elizabeth Jefferson, mentally retarded; Mrs. Martha Carr, whose husband, Dabney, helped launch the underground Committee of Correspondence in Virginia on the eve of the Revolution; Mrs. Lucy Lewis; Mrs. Anna Scott Marks; and Randolph Jefferson. Anna and Randolph were twins.

COLLATERAL RELATIVE: Jefferson was a second cousin, once removed of Chief Justice John Marshall.

CHILDREN: Jefferson had two daughters to live to maturity.

Martha "Patsy" Jefferson (1772–1836). Tall and slim, with angular features and red hair, she closely resembled her father, to whom she was devoted. From age 12 to 17, she lived in Paris while her father served as U.S. minister to France. Jefferson enrolled her at Abbaye Royale de Panthémont, an exclusive convent school, after receiving assurances that Protestant students were exempt from religious instruction. Nevertheless, Patsy not only expressed a desire to convert to Catholicism but also informed her father that she was thinking about becoming a nun. Jefferson promptly withdrew her from school. She returned to Virginia in 1789 and the next year married her second cousin, Thomas Mann Randolph (governor of Virginia 1819–1822). She served for a time as official hostess at the White House while her father was president. A destitute widow after the death of her husband in 1828, she accepted cash gifts totaling $20,000 from the states of South Carolina and Louisiana.

Mary "Polly" Jefferson (1778–1804). Smaller, prettier, and more delicate than her older sister, Polly was said to have resembled her mother. In the care of slave Sally Hemings, she at nine sailed to England, where Abigail Adams, wife of U.S. Minister John Adams, looked after her before she joined her father in Paris. Polly attended the same convent school as her sister and was withdrawn with her. With her father and sister, she returned to Virginia in 1789 and lived for a time in Philadelphia while Jefferson was secretary of state. In 1797 she married John Wayles Eppes. She died at 25 after giving birth to her second child. It was her death that prompted Abigail Adams to extend written condolences to President Jefferson, thus ending the long silence between the two families that had been brought on by political differences.

SUBSEQUENT DESCENDANTS:

Thomas Jefferson Randolph (1792–1875). The president's grandson, he served in the Virginia state legislature and presided over the 1872 Democratic National Convention.

George Wythe Randolph (1818–1867). The president's grandson, he served as the first secretary of war of the Confederacy.

Thomas Jefferson Coolidge (1831–1920). The president's great-grandson, he served as U.S. minister to France 1892–1896.

Archibald Cary Coolidge (1866–1928). The president's great-great-grandson, he was professor of history at Harvard University and author of *The United States as a World Power* (1908).

Jefferson Randolph Anderson (1861–1950). The president's great^3-grandson, he served in the Georgia House 1905–1906 and 1909–1912 and Georgia Senate 1913–1914.

George Wayne Anderson (1863–1922). The president's great^3-grandson, he served as Richmond city attorney in 1921.

BIRTH: Jefferson was born on April 13, (April 2 Old Style), 1743, at Shadwell plantation, Goochland (now Albemarle) county, Virginia. His birthplace was destroyed by fire in 1770.

CHILDHOOD: Jefferson's earliest recollection was of when he was about age three riding with a slave on horseback, a pillow beneath him to absorb the shocks of the 50-mile trip from Shadwell to Tuckahoe, where his father was taking the family in order to discharge his duties as executor of the will of his late friend William Randolph. Randolph had ordered that on his death, Peter Jefferson was to manage his Tuckahoe plantation and raise his orphaned children. One of these children was Thomas Mann Randolph, two years older than Thomas Jefferson. The two, who no doubt played together, became in-laws when Randolph's son married Jefferson's daughter. After about six years at Tuckahoe, the Jeffersons returned to Shadwell. Little is known of Thomas's childhood there, except that he was bookish, enjoyed tramping through the woods and observing nature, and prowled the eastern slopes of the Southwest Mountains in search of deer, turkey, and other wild game.

EDUCATION: From about age 9 to 14, Jefferson studied under the Reverend William Douglas at Saint James parish in Northam. Because it was some distance from Shadwell, he boarded with the clergyman during the school term, returning home for three or four months each year. Under Douglas, whom he disliked, he learned Greek, Latin, and French. From age 14 to 16 he attended the Reverend James Maury's school at Fredericksville, which was close enough to Shadwell to permit Jefferson to spend weekends home. Maury, who also taught James Madison and James Monroe, encouraged Jefferson's linguistic ability and instilled in him an appreciation for the classics in their original languages. He also studied dance for six months under a Mr. Inglis. In 1760 Jefferson enrolled at the College of William and Mary at Williamsburg. During his two years there, his studies included science, mathematics, rhetoric, philosophy, and literature under Dr. William Small, who, Jefferson later said, "probably fixed the destinies of my life."[4] A serious student, Jefferson reportedly studied 15 hours a day. Small introduced Jefferson to George Wythe, later to become the first American law professor, and Francis Fauquier, colonial governor of Virginia. Wythe, Fauquier, and Jefferson often dined together. The intellectual excitement at these dinners thrilled young Jefferson, who claimed that there he "heard more good sense, more rational and philosophical conversation than in all my life besides."[5] While at college, he belonged to the Flat Hat Club, a social fraternity. During 1762–1767, Jefferson studied law under George Wythe (who also taught John Marshall and Henry Clay). A five-year law apprenticeship was long by the standards of the day, but Jefferson used his time well. He plowed through the tedious tomes of Cooke's *Institutes of the Lawes of England* and other books to emerge an unusually well read lawyer upon his admission to the Virginia bar in April 1767.

RELIGION: Deism. Jefferson grew up an Anglican but from early adulthood professed faith in a Creator uninvolved in the affairs of this world. He relied on reason, not revelation, to fashion a moral code that adhered to Christian precepts, but he had little use for the church itself. "I am a real Christian," he wrote in retirement, "that is to say, a disciple of the doctrines of Jesus."[6] He felt that these doctrines, though "the most perfect and sublime that has ever been taught by man,"[7] had since been "adulterated and sophisticated"[8] by the clergy. He belonged to no church but did attend services from time to time and contributed to the support of various denominations. He advocated reading the Bible with the same critical eye that one would cast on any other book. Above all, Jefferson considered religion a wholly personal matter and favored absolute separation of church and state. He drafted the Virginia Statute of Religious Liberty (1786), which asserted "that no man shall be compelled to frequent or support any religious worship . . . but that all men shall be free to profess, and by argument to maintain, their opinion in matters of religion."[9] Translated and reprinted abroad, the document gained for Jefferson an international reputation as a champion of religious freedom, but American churchmen, who thrived under state-supported religion and compulsory attendance, denounced him as an atheist. To Jefferson the issue was not whether God does or does not exist, but rather that all views on the subject ought to be tolerated. "It does me no injury," he asserted, "for my neighbor to say that there are twenty gods, or no god. It neither picks my pocket nor breaks my leg."[10]

RECREATION: A true Renaissance man, Jefferson found diversion in a wide range of interests. Architecture, botany, animal husbandry, meteorology, mechanical engineering, books—all competed with politics for his attention. He designed his grand home at Monticello and meticulously landscaped the grounds. He built into the house such unique features as a two-faced clock visible indoors and outdoors, beds that were retractable into a wall, an indoor indicator connected to the weather vane to permit him to determine wind direction without venturing outdoors, and a dumbwaiter used to haul goods from the cellar to his dining room table. In 1987 Monticello archaeologists discovered a stone-lined air shaft that had been installed by Jefferson to ventilate his outhouse. Labor-saving devices always intrigued him. One of his favorites was the polygraph, a contraption of flexible rods connecting two pens that reproduced precisely the hand movements of a writer and thus provided perfect copies of much of Jefferson's correspondence. He invented the swivel chair and designed an adjustable table that tilted for easy sketching, remained flat for writing, or could be raised to enable him to work standing up. His invention of a plow moldboard that turned the soil more efficiently than those then in use won him a gold medal from a French agricultural society. He encouraged Italian grape growers to settle in Virginia and from them learned how to raise, in addition to wine grapes, such exotic foods as garlic, oranges, and wild endive. From Spain Jefferson imported America's first Merino sheep, prized for their superior wool, but the stock did not do well in the New World. He carefully recorded daily high and low temperatures and made note of precipitation levels and dates of seasonal changes. For exercise and to clear his head, Jefferson enjoyed horseback riding alone for one or two hours a day. When president he used this daily regimen to get out and meet the people, often without their knowing who he was. Jefferson did not smoke. He drank only wine with dinner. A connoisseur of fine wines, he preferred the light French varieties to the heavier wines of Italy, although Montepulciano pleased him. His wine bill during his eight years as president exceeded $10,000. He enjoyed music and was himself a good fiddle player. He collected books all his adult life. After his first library was destroyed in the fire at Shadwell, he immediately began to amass a new one, which eventually totaled some 6,500 volumes.

EARLY ROMANCE:

Rebecca Burwell. Jefferson's first known love, Rebecca Burwell, was an orphan of a prosperous Virginia family who was said to be both beautiful and pious. She was 16, Jefferson 19, when they began seeing each other. Jefferson, then a law student with ambitions to tour Europe, wanted her to wait for him to return from abroad (he did not make the trip after all). He tried to propose in October 1763 while they danced in the Apollo Room of the Raleigh Tavern in Williamsburg but was so nervous that he could not get the words out straight. All he could muster, he later lamented to a friend, was "a few broken sentences, uttered in great disorder, and interrupted with pauses of uncommon length."[11] By the next spring Jefferson grieved to learn that his "Belinda," as he called her, had agreed to marry Jacquelin Ambler. In time she had two daughters, one of whom, Mary, married a young veteran of the Revolution named John Marshall, later chief justice of the United States.

Betsey Walker. The wife of Jefferson's friend and neighbor John Walker, Betsey Moore Walker was the subject of a scandal that broke out in the press while Jefferson was president. All that is known for certain about the affair is what Jefferson admitted: "When young and single I offered love to a handsome lady. I acknowledge its incorrectness."[12] John Walker, who had so trusted Jefferson that he had named him executor in his will and had asked him to look after his wife and daughter while he was away, became a laughingstock in the press. Mortified, he published in 1805 his version of events: Jefferson had tried repeatedly and unsuccessfully to seduce Walker's wife over an 11-year period, a siege Jefferson continued even after he married. Once, Walker claimed,

Jefferson burst into her room while she was dressing. Another time he tried to grab her outside her chamber. But, Walker insisted, Betsey resisted every time. Walker also stated that his wife had kept all this from him until after Jefferson left for France in 1784. His honor now publicly at stake, Walker challenged the president to a duel. However, Jefferson arranged to meet with him privately at the home of James Madison and quietly talked him out of settling the matter with pistols. Historians generally discount Walker's charge that Jefferson continued recklessly to chase his wife, because it seemed so out of character for Jefferson. Biographer Dumas Malone dismissed Walker's story as grossly exaggerated.

MARRIAGE: Thomas Jefferson, 28, married Martha Wayles Skelton, 23, a widow, on January 1, 1772, at The Forest, the estate of the bride's father in Charles City County, Virginia. Born in Charles City County on October 30, 1748, the daughter of John Wayles, a prominent lawyer and landowner, and Martha Eppes Wayles, Martha Wayles at 18 married Bathurst Skelton. Upon Skelton's death in 1768, she moved back to her father's house with her infant son, who died a few years later. She probably met Jefferson in Williamsburg about 1770. Following their wedding, the Jeffersons honeymooned about two weeks at The Forest before setting out in a two-horse carriage for Monticello. They made the 100-mile trip in one of the worst snowstorms ever to hit Virginia. Some miles from their destination, their carriage bogged down in 2–3 feet of snow; they had to complete the journey on horseback. Arriving at Monticello late at night after the slaves had banked the fires and retired for the night, the couple settled in the freezing one-room brick building that was to be their home until completion of the famous main house at Monticello. No portrait of Martha survives, but she was said to have been pretty, with hazel eyes, auburn hair, and a trim figure. She played the harpsichord, often accompanied by Jefferson on the violin, and sang well. According to legend, two of her other male suitors gave up when one day they heard Jefferson and her singing and playing music happily together. Throughout their 10-year marriage, they appear to have been wholly devoted to each other. Seven pregnancies sapped her strength; she died on September 6, 1782, four months after giving birth to her last child, a daughter who died two years later. According to slaves who attended her in her final days, Jefferson promised his wife that he would never remarry. He never did. Jefferson was inconsolable in his loss. It is said that he collapsed just before she died. After the funeral, he refused to leave his room for three weeks. Then he spent endless hours riding horseback alone around Monticello. Not until mid-October did he begin to resume a normal life.

POSTMARITAL AFFAIRS:

Maria Cosway. During August–October 1786, while serving as minister to France, Jefferson spent much of his time in the company of Mrs. Maria Hadfield Cosway, a beautiful artist with great blond curls who shared his love of music. He was 43, she 27. Her husband, Richard Cosway, was an accomplished miniaturist. Just how involved the relationship became is uncertain. From Jefferson's subsequent letters to her, however, it is clear that he loved her deeply. On September 18, 1786, while they were out strolling, Jefferson momentarily forgot his age as he tried to leap a fence. Unfortunately he tripped and dislocated or broke his right wrist. In excruciating pain, he saw a doctor, who set the joint improperly. His right hand thereafter remained crippled, though eventually it mended well enough for him to write. A week after the Cosways left Paris, Jefferson, using his left hand, wrote her a long letter in which he confessed to being "solitary and sad" without her. He then related a conversation that he said he had overhead between his head and his heart. His head, rational, unmoved by passion, warns his heart to stop placing "your affections, without reserve, on objects you must so soon loose, and whose loss when it comes must cost you such severe pangs."[13] They were together again in Paris for a few months in 1787, but after that, only letters passed between them.

Sally Hemings. Author Fawn Brodie, in her book *Thomas Jefferson: An Intimate History* (1974), made the most convincing case for the long-held suspicion that Jefferson fathered several illegitimate children by his slave Sally Hemings. In presenting the evidence, admittedly circumstantial, Brodie asserted that Jefferson did not debauch Sally, as other masters commonly did with their slave girls but rather engaged in a mutually fulfilling love affair that lasted 38 years. Sally Hemings was the offspring of the slave Elizabeth Hemings and a white master, John Wayles, Jefferson's father-in-law. Thus Sally was a half sister of Jefferson's wife. It was Sally who accompanied Jefferson's younger daughter abroad in 1787. Her son Madison Hemings claimed publicly that Sally was Jefferson's concubine. But other Jefferson biographers remain unconvinced. Merrill Peterson doubted that Jefferson would stoop to such exploitation of his slaves; he believes that the paternity of Hemings's children probably could be charged to Jefferson's nephew Peter Carr. In a letter written to her husband in 1858 but not made public until 1974, Ellen Randolph Coolidge, the president's granddaughter, reported hearing that the father of Hemings's children was either Peter Carr or his brother Samuel. The latter she described as "the most notorious good-natured Turk that ever was master of a black seraglio kept at other men's expense."[15]

MILITARY SERVICE: None

CAREER BEFORE THE PRESIDENCY: Upon his admission to the bar in 1767, Jefferson practiced law on the circuit, covering most of the counties in Virginia.

Member of House of Burgesses, 1769–1774. One of two members representing Albemarle County in the House of Burgesses in the last years of that body, Jefferson aligned himself with those opposed to British domination of the colonies. In "Summary View of the Rights of British America" (1774), he eloquently made the case against Parliament's authority over America. He was active in the underground Committee of Correspondence in Virginia, a vital link with rebels in other colonies on the eve of the Revolution.

Declaration of Independence, 1776. As a member of the Continental Congress 1775–1776, Jefferson was appointed to the committee charged with drafting a declaration of independence. The other members of the committee— John Adams, Benjamin Franklin, Roger Sherman, and Robert R. Livingston— agreed that Jefferson was the logical choice to draft the document because he had a reputation for powerful prose, he was generally popular with other members, and he represented Virginia, the most influential of the southern colonies. During June 11–28, 1776, Jefferson composed the founding document of the Revolution unaided by reference book or pamphlet. His guiding purpose, he explained many years later, was "not to find new principles, or new arguments, never before thought of, not merely to say things which had never been said before; but to place before mankind the common sense of the subject, in terms so plain and firm as to command their assent, and to justify ourselves in the independent stand we are compelled to take . . . and to give that expression the proper tone and spirit called for by the occasion."[16] Congress debated and amended Jefferson's declaration. Most of the changes were minor. One significant alteration, however, was the deletion of Jefferson's stinging indictment of George III for trafficking in slaves. Representatives from Georgia and South Carolina found this passage particularly offensive. Indeed, the sudden revulsion against the slave trade by colonies that had and were continuing to profit from the system seemed hypocritical to many. Even as amended, the Declaration of Independence clearly bore Jefferson's mark. Its bold assertion of fundamental human rights, still relevant today, succinctly enunciates the American philosophy of government: "We hold these Truths to be self-evident, that all Men are created equal, that they are endowed by their Creator with certain unalienable rights, that among these are Life, Liberty, and the Pursuit of Happiness—That to secure these Rights, Governments are instituted among Men, deriving their just Powers from the Consent of the Governed, That whenever any Form of Government becomes destructive of these Ends, it is the Right of the People to alter or to abolish it, and to institute new Government, laying its Foundation on such Principles, and organizing its Powers in such Form, as to them shall seem most likely to effect their Safety and Happiness." Jefferson then proceeded to list the "long Train of Abuses and Usurpations" suffered at the hands of the king and finally declared, "That these United Colonies are, and of Right ought to be, Free and Independent States." Realizing that with this revolutionary document they were literally laying their necks on the line, the signers pledged "to each other our Lives, our Fortunes, and our sacred Honor." Jefferson joined six other Virginians, including Benjamin Harrison, himself progenitor of two presidents, in signing the Declaration.

Member of Virginia House of Delegates, 1776–1779. Delegate Jefferson worked to abolish entails and primogeniture and to promote religious freedom and education.

Governor of Virginia, 1779–1781. Jefferson's two years as governor of Virginia during the Revolution were largely unsuccessful. The office of governor at that time was in fact little more than an extension of the assembly. The executive had no veto power and was more or less bound by the consensus of the Council of State, eight men elected by the legislature to advise the governor. During Jefferson's administration, Britain brought the war to Virginia soil. Helpless to resist, the entire state government abandoned the capital at Richmond and took temporary refuge in Charlottesville. Shortly after his term as governor had expired but before a successor was named, Jefferson learned that a British unit was advancing on Monticello, where he had retired. He hastily arranged for the safe departure of his family and then fled himself just ahead of the enemy. Later he was roundly criticized for what was seen in some quarters as a cowardly escape. A special committee appointed to investigate his conduct, however, fully vindicated him. The legislature even adopted a resolution praising his "ability, rectitude, and integrity" and thanking him for his "impartial, upright, and attentive administration whilst in office."

Member of Continental Congress, 1783–1784. At Annapolis, then the temporary capital, Congressman Jefferson of Virginia helped establish the decimal system and worked to organize the government of what became the Northwest Territory.

Minister to France, 1785–1789. Minister Jefferson helped negotiate commercial treaties and was a keen observer of European events.

Secretary of State, 1790–1793. Appointed by President Washington, he was the first secretary of state. He organized the department, which at that time encompassed domestic affairs, excluding those under the purview of the Treasury and war secretaries, as well as diplomacy. He urged closer relations with France and was skeptical of British intentions. Although he enjoyed the complete confidence of the president, constant wrangling with Treasury Secretary Alexander Hamilton, especially over American policy toward Britain and France, blunted his effectiveness. Still, Jefferson managed to put the department on sound footing with an annual budget of less than $10,000. Among his handful of employees at State was Philip Freneau, a French translator who moonlighted as editor of the *National Gazette*, from whose pages he attacked Hamilton mercilessly. The appointment and Jefferson's refusal to fire or muzzle Freneau further undermined his position in the cabinet. Jefferson resigned when it became clear that Washington was adopting Hamilton's world view.

Vice President, 1797–1801. Having received the second highest number of votes (68) in the presidential contest against John Adams (71 votes) in 1796, Jefferson was elected vice president ("see John Adams, 2d President," for the election of 1796). Jefferson, who disliked the inactivity of the vice presidency, fulfilled his responsibility as presiding officer of the Senate with utmost fairness and courtesy. In his free time he compiled *A Manual of Parliamentary Practice*, which is today still in use in the Senate. Jefferson was the only vice president to later be elected to and serve two full terms as president.

REPUBLICAN PRESIDENTIAL NOMINATION, 1800: Republican congressmen in caucus chose Jefferson, the undisputed leader of the party, as their candidate for president. Aaron Burr of New York was the Republican nominee for vice president.

OPPONENT: President John Adams (1735–1826) of Massachusetts, Federalist. Without having been formally nominated, President Adams stood as the Federalist candidate for reelection, and Charles Cotesworth Pinckney of South Carolina the Federalist candidate for vice president.

CAMPAIGN AND THE ISSUES, 1800: The campaign waged by the partisan press of both camps was bitter and personal. Federalists were able to blunt the Republican campaign by prosecuting opposition editors under the Sedition Act. Operating under no such restraint, Federalist campaigners urged voters to choose "God—and a religious President" over "Jefferson . . . and no God." They warned that if Jefferson was elected, "Murder, robbery, rape, adultery and incest will be openly taught and practiced."[17] Foreign affairs played a lesser role than it did in the campaign of four years before, because the United States and France had backed away from war by this time, and the rise of Napoleon dampened Jefferson's enthusiasm for France. Rather, the campaign turned on domestic issues, specifically federal authority versus states' rights. Jefferson and James Madison had written the controversial Virginia and Kentucky Resolutions, 1798–1799, which declared the Alien and Sedition Acts unconstitutional. The principle of state nullification of federal laws did not prevail ultimately, but the resolutions became a rallying point for anti-Federalism and Republicans. Adams's defeat was virtually assured in the spring of 1800 when Republicans ousted the Federalists in the New York State legislature. New York went to Adams in 1796, because the Federalist-controlled legislature selected the presidential electors. Now, with Republicans in charge, Jeffersonian electors were sure to be chosen. The shift of New York's 12 electoral votes from Adams to Jefferson was enough to tip the election to the Republicans.

ELECTION AS PRESIDENT, FIRST TERM, 1800:
Electoral Vote. Jefferson, 73; Burr, 73; Adams, 65. Because Jefferson and Burr received the same number of votes, the election was thrown into the House of Representatives. Even though it had always been clear during the campaign that Jefferson was the presidential candidate and Burr the vice presidential candidate, the latter refused to concede, thus forcing the issue to a vote in the House. Jefferson and Burr won the majority of electoral votes in eight states—Georgia, Kentucky, New York, North Carolina, Pennsylvania, South Carolina, Tennessee, and Virginia. Adams and Pickney won the majority of electors in seven states—Connecticut, Delaware, Massachusetts, New Hampshire, New Jersey, Rhode Island, and Vermont. Maryland electors were evenly split.

The House, with each state casting one vote based on the majority of that state's delegation, took 36 ballots during February 11–17, 1801, to decide the contest in Jefferson's favor. Alexander Hamilton played a key role in bringing Federalist support to Jefferson, whom he considered the lesser of the two evils. In the final tally in the House, Jefferson carried 10 states—Georgia, Kentucky, Maryland, New Jersey, New York, North Carolina, Pennsylvania, Tennessee, Vermont, and Virginia. Burr carried four states —Connecticut, Massachusetts, New Hampshire, and Rhode Island. Delaware and South Carolina cast blank ballots. Jefferson was thus declared president, Burr vice president. The deadlock prompted passage of the Twelfth Amendment (1804).

REPUBLICAN NOMINATION FOR REELECTION AS PRESIDENT, 1804: In February 1804, congressional Republicans in caucus unanimously nominated Jefferson for reelection. George Clinton of New York was nominated for vice president.

OPPONENT: Charles Cotesworth Pinckney (1746–1825) of South Carolina, Federalist. Born in Charleston, South Carolina, Pinckney was educated in England, where he practiced law before returning to South Carolina in 1769. During the Revolution, he served as an officer with South Carolina forces and was captured by the British. As a delegate to the Constitutional Convention in 1787, he pressed for the requirement that treaties be submitted to the Senate for ratification. He supported ratification of the Constitution in South Carolina. With John Marshall and Elbridge Gerry, he served on the mission to France in 1797 that ended in the XYZ Affair (see "John Adams, 2d President," "Administration"). Pinckney, when told that the Americans must pay a bribe for the privilege of meeting French officials, responded, "No! No! Not a sixpence!" He was the Federalist candidate for vice president in 1796. He again ran for president in 1808 (see "James Madison, 4th President," "Opponent"). Rufus King of New York was the Federalist candidate for vice president.

CAMPAIGN AND THE ISSUES, 1804: President Jefferson handily checked a feeble challenge from the dying Federalist party. The Federalists went into the campaign discredited by radical elements of the party in Massachusetts, the so-called Essex Junto, which sought to escape the effects of Jeffersonian democracy by seceding from the Union. Junto leaders hoped to enlist neighboring states in forming a New England Confederacy. The movement failed. With the outcome never in doubt, the presidential campaign was lackluster. In addition to his traditional southern base of support, Jefferson made significant inroads in once solidly Federalist New England. Die-hard Federalists managed to mount a significant challenge to Jefferson only in Connecticut, Delaware, and Maryland.

ELECTION AS PRESIDENT, SECOND TERM, 1804:

    Electoral Vote. Jefferson, 162; Pinckney, 14.

    States carried. Jefferson won the majority of electoral votes in 15 states—Georgia, Kentucky, Maryland, Massachusetts, New Hampshire, New Jersey, New York, North Carolina, Ohio, Pennsylvania, Rhode Island, South Carolina, Tennessee, Vermont, and Virginia. Pinckney won the majority of electors in two states—Connecticut and Delaware.

INAUGURAL ADDRESS (FIRST): Washington, D.C., March 4, 1801. ". . . All, too, will bear in mind this sacred principle, that though the will of the majority is in all cases to prevail, that will to be rightful must be reasonable; that the minority possesses their equal rights, which equal law must protect, and to violate would be oppression. Let us, then, fellow-citizens, unite with one heart and one mind. Let us restore to social intercourse that harmony and affection without which liberty and even life itself are but dreary things. And let us reflect that, having banished from our land that religious intolerance under which mankind so long bled and suffered, we have yet gained little if we countenance a political intolerance as despotic, as wicked, and capable of as bitter and bloody persecutions. During the throes and convulsions of the ancient world, during the agonizing spasms of infuriated man, seeking through blood and slaughter his long-lost liberty, it was not wonderful that the agitation of the billows should reach even this distant and peaceful shore; that this should be more felt and feared by some and less by others, and should divide opinions as to measures of safety. But every difference of opinion is not a difference of principle. We have called by different names brethren of the same principle. We are all Republicans, we are all Federalists. If there be any among us who would wish to dissolve this Union or to change its republican form, let them stand undisturbed as monuments of the safety with which error of opinion may be tolerated where reason is left free to combat it. . . ."

INAUGURAL ADDRESS (SECOND): Washington, D.C., March 4, 1805. ". . . I know that the acquisition of Louisiana has been disapproved by some from a candid apprehension that the enlargement of our territory would endanger its union. But who can limit the extent to which the federative principle may operate effectively? The larger our association the less will it be shaken by local passions; and in any view is it not better that the opposite bank of the Mississippi should be settled by our own brethren and children than by strangers of another family? With which should we be most likely to live in harmony and friendly intercourse? . . ."

VICE PRESIDENT: Aaron Burr (1756–1836), of New York, served 1801–1805. Born in Newark, New Jersey, and orphaned in infancy, he was raised by an uncle. Graduating from the College of New Jersey (now Princeton) in 1772, he studied law briefly before serving with distinction as an officer in the Revolution. After the war he practiced law in New York and soon entered politics. Rising swiftly, he was elected by the state legislature to the U.S. Senate (1791–1797) but failed to win a second term. A Democratic-Republican, he was instrumental in wresting control of New York State government from the Federalists in 1800; his efforts were a key element in Jefferson's victory in the presidential contest that year. Burr lost favor with Jefferson when he refused to concede the presidential election to him without a fight in the House (see "Election as President, First Term,1800"). Disagreements over patronage and other matters further strained their relationship. Burr was replaced by George Clinton as the vice presidential candidate in 1804. That year he ran for governor of New York but was defeated, largely because of Alexander Hamilton's opposition. During the campaign, Hamilton had called Burr's character into question, insults that prompted Burr to challenge him to a duel. The two squared off on July 11, 1804, at Weehawken, New Jersey, where Burr fatally wounded Hamilton. Indicted for murder (the charges eventually were dropped), Burr fled New York and traveled throughout the West. He conspired with General James Wilkinson and others, allegedly to instigate war with Spain, to seize control of the lands acquired under the Louisiana Purchase, and to separate this area from the United States, with himself as leader of an independent nation. Burr was arrested in 1807 while attempting to lead a band of followers down the Mississippi. Tried for treason before Chief Justice John Marshall, he was found not guilty. Thoroughly discredited despite the acquittal, he spent several years in exile in Europe before resuming his law practice in New York in 1812. He died in New York.

George Clinton (1793–1812), of New York, served 1805–1812. Born in Little Britain, New York, he became a lawyer and served in the Continental Congress 1775–1776. He missed signing the Declaration of Independence, because that summer he was commanding New York militia in the field. He served as the first governor of New York (1777–1795, 1801–1804). An outspoken critic of the federal Constitution, he worked in vain to prevent its ratification. He was a supporter of Aaron Burr. Clinton ran for the Republican presidential nomination in 1808 but settled for another term as vice president under James Madison.

CABINET:

Secretary of State. James Madison (1751–1836), of Virginia, served 1801–1809 (see "James Madison, 4th President," "Career before the Presidency").

Secretary of the Treasury. (1) Samuel Dexter (1761–1816), of Massachusetts, served 1801. A holdover from the Adams administration, he agreed to stay on to help in the transition of power until Jefferson's appointee could assume his post. (2) Albert Gallatin (1761–1849), of Pennsylvania, served 1801–1814. A Swiss immigrant, he had been a Republican leader in the U.S. House and Senate, where he demonstrated a firm grasp of financial matters. As Treasury secretary, he reduced the national debt despite severe drains on federal coffers by the Louisiana Purchase and the war against the Barbary pirates. Jefferson looked to him for advice on both foreign and domestic issues. He stayed on in the Madison administration.

Secretary of War. Henry Dearborn (1751–1829), of Maine, served 1801–1809. A veteran officer of the Revolution, he as war secretary strengthened defenses in the west. During the War of 1812 he was appointed commander of the Army of the North but performed poorly and was relieved of command. He served as minister to Portugal under President Monroe.

Attorney General. (1) Levi Lincoln (1749–1820), of Massachusetts, served 1801–1804. A lawyer, he later served as governor of Massachusetts. (2) John Breckenridge (1760–1806), of Kentucky, served 1805–1806. Reluctant to take Breckenridge out of the Senate, where he had been a loyal supporter and especially helpful in smoothing the way for the Louisiana Purchase, Jefferson chose him after two others declined the appointment. Breckenridge died in office. (3) Caesar A. Rodney (1772–1824), of Delaware, served 1807–1811. He was actively involved in bringing Aaron Burr to trial for treason. Dissatisfied with Burr's acquittal on narrow constitutional grounds, he advocated broadening the definition of treason to include conspiracy. He stayed on in the Madison administration.

Secretary of the Navy. Robert Smith (1757–1842), of Maryland, served 1801–1809. An admiralty lawyer, he was Jefferson's fifth choice for the post.
ADMINISTRATION: March 4, 1801–March 3, 1809.

Revolution of 1800. Jefferson's defeat of Adams is sometimes referred to as the Revolution of 1800, because it marked the fall of Federalism and the rise of Republicanism. Jefferson set out at once to roll back what he regarded as the most offensive Federalist measures. The Alien and Sedition Acts (see "John Adams," "Administration") were allowed to lapse. The residency requirement for naturalization was reduced again to five years. The federal tax on liquor that had touched off the Whiskey Rebellion (see "George Washington," "Administration") was repealed. The Judiciary Act of 1802 effectively nullified the last-minute rigging of the federal court system by the previous administration (see "John Adams," "Administration, Midnight Appointments").

Tripolitan War, 1801–1805. The pirates of the Barbary states of Morocco, Algiers, Tripoli, and Tunis had long been preying on Mediterranean Sea traffic, looting and shanghaiing the seamen of those nations that refused to pay tribute. Most countries, including the United States, found it cheaper to buy protection than to go to war with the Barbary pirates. Jefferson had long opposed in principle paying such tribute but continued the practice briefly until May 1801, when Tripoli suddenly demanded more money. When the president refused, Tripoli declared war on the United States. American naval forces dispatched to the region at first accomplished little. In 1803 pirates seized the *Philadelphia*, along with its crew, and turned its guns against the rest of the American fleet. Then, in a bold thrust in 1804, Lieutenant Stephen Decatur sailed to the Tripoli coast and burned down the *Philadelphia*. Capitalizing on this victory, Jefferson sent virtually every available vessel to the region. As the war turned against the pirates, Tripoli in 1805 agreed to end demands for annual tribute. Meanwhile, the officers and crew of the *Philadelphia* continued to be held hostage in Tripoli. To secure their release Jefferson agreed to pay $60,000 in ransom. The United States continued to pay tribute to the other three Barbary states until 1815.

Louisiana Purchase, 1803. For $15 million, a paltry three cents an acre, the United States purchased from France the Louisiana Territory, a vast region between the Mississippi and the Rockies that comprised all or part of the present-day states of Louisiana, Arkansas, Missouri, Iowa, Minnesota, North and South Dakota, Nebraska, Kansas, Oklahoma, Texas, New Mexico, Colorado, Wyoming, and Montana. Jefferson had authorized his negotiators, Robert R. Livingston and James Monroe, to buy only New Orleans and West Florida. Napoleon, hard pressed for cash on the eve of war with Britain, surprised the Americans with an offer to sell all of Louisiana. Although Jefferson was unsure of the constitutionality of such a purchase, he hastily agreed lest Napoleon change his mind. The Senate eventually ratified the treaty by a vote of 26–5. The Louisiana Purchase, which doubled the size of the United States, was the most significant achievement of the Jefferson administration.

Lewis and Clark Expedition, 1804–1806. To explore the vast unknown expanse between the Missouri River and the Pacific had been Jefferson's goal even before the Louisiana Purchase. Now with that territory firmly in U.S. hands, the president was all the more eager to learn more about the West. He commissioned his private secretary Meriwether Lewis and William Clark to lead the expedition. In a two-and-one-half-year, 8,000-mile trek, the party ascended the Missouri River, crossed the Continental Divide, rode the Columbia River to the Pacific, and then more or less retraced their steps to St. Louis. Their published observations provided scholars of the day with much new information.

Abolition of the Slave Trade. In March 1807 President Jefferson signed into law the bill that banned the importation of slaves from January 1, 1808. Slaves continued to be smuggled into the country until the Civil War, but the numbers were greatly reduced.

Executive Privilege. President Jefferson was subpoenaed to testify at the Burr treason trial (1807; see "Vice President," Aaron Burr) and to bring with him certain papers bearing on the case. In declining to appear and releasing only such information as he chose, Jefferson established the precedent of executive privilege.

Embargo, 1807–1809. During the Napoleonic Wars, the United States found itself abused by both Britain and France, as each belligerent regularly seized or otherwise harassed American ships bound for the other's ports. In one of the most flagrant of such offenses, the British warship *Leopard* in June 1807 fired on the U.S. frigate *Chesapeake*, forcibly boarded her, and impressed four of its crew. To end these indignities, President Jefferson signed the Embargo Act in December 1807. Under its terms, no American ship was permitted to sail to foreign ports, and no foreign vessel was allowed to unload its cargo at American ports. Jefferson had hoped that Britain and France would be so severely injured by the loss of American trade that they would readily agree to respect the neutrality of U.S. shipping. Instead, the European powers bore up well under the embargo, while the American economy suffered serious dislocation. With U.S. ports closed, dockworkers, sailors, and others whose livelihood depended on sea trade, were suddenly unemployed. Merchants went broke. Farm surpluses languished in storage. Although it proved a boon to domestic manufacturers, who no longer had to compete with foreign products, the embargo became increasingly unpopular as it crippled the economy without accomplishing its original goal—to win U.S. neutral rights at sea. Shortly before he left office in 1809, Jefferson approved the Non-Intercourse Act (see "James Madison, 4th President," "Administration"), partially lifting the embargo. During its 14-month existence, the embargo cost the United States some $16 million in lost customs revenues alone.

State Admitted to the Union: Ohio (1803).

Constitutional Amendment Ratified. Twelfth Amendment (1804). Electors vote separately for president and vice president; enacted in response to Jefferson-Burr tie vote (see "Election as President, First Term, 1800").

SUPREME COURT APPOINTMENTS: (1) William Johnson (1771–1834), of South Carolina, served as associate justice 1804–1834. He alone of Jefferson's appointees succeeded in countering Chief Justice Marshall's domination of the Court. In doing so, he established the tradition of the "great dissenter." Though a southerner, he opposed nullification. (2) Brockholst Livingston (1757–1823), of New York, served as associate justice 1806–1823. He was unable to exert any significant influence on the Court dominated by Chief Justice Marshall. (3) Thomas Todd (1765–1826), of Kentucky, served as associate justice 1807–1826. He also fell under the domination of Chief Justice Marshall and left no lasting mark on the Court.

RANKING IN 1962 HISTORIANS POLL: Jefferson ranked fifth of 31 presidents, the lowest of 5 "great" presidents; ranked above Jackson, below Wilson.

RETIREMENT: March 4, 1809–July 4, 1826. Upon the inauguration of James Madison, Jefferson retired to Monticello, content with his performance as a public figure and eager to enjoy the blessings of retirement. Tragically, however, he departed Washington about $24,000 in debt. His only prospective income was the several thousand dollars a year generated from the sale of crops, flour, and nails produced on his estate. In 1815, after the British had burned the Capitol, destroying the Library of Congress, Jefferson sold his 6,500-volume collection to the United States for $23,950. Transported overland to Washington in 11 wagons, it formed the core of a new national library. Unfortunately, about two-thirds of the Jefferson collection was destroyed in a fire at the Library of Congress in 1851. Jefferson spent much of his time in retirement writing letters. It gave him great pleasure to renew through correspondence his friendship with John Adams. Jefferson's most important project in retirement was the founding of the University of Virginia at Charlottesville. He designed the buildings, directed their construction, drew up the course of study (pointedly omitting religious instruction), handpicked the faculty, and served as university rector. One innovation he introduced was the system of student electives—"to leave everyone free to attend whatever branches of instruction he wants, and to decline what he does not want,"[18] he said. The University of Virginia opened in 1825.

DEATH: July 4, 1826, 12:50 P.M., Monticello estate, Virginia. Already wracked by rheumatism, Jefferson developed an enlarged prostate and spent his last months in great pain. He took laudanum, the tincture of opium, to allow him to sleep. His condition was compounded by chronic diarrhea, which mortally sapped his strength. Because of his weakened condition, he declined an invitation to attend the Fourth of July festivities in Washington. According to the attending physician, Dr. Robley Dunglison, he lapsed into a "stupor, with intervals of wakefulness and consciousness" on July 2. Most of the next day he spent unconscious. About 7 P.M. he awoke to ask, "Is it the Fourth?" His doctor replied, "It soon will be." He fell back to sleep and died peacefully the next day, July 4, 1826. Coincidentally, John Adams also died later that day. Thus the only two signers of the Declaration of Independence to become president died simultaneously—on the fiftieth anniversary of the adoption of that great document. In accordance with his instructions, Jefferson was buried in a simple ceremony at the family cemetery on the Monticello grounds. The local Episcopalian rector conducted graveside services. Jefferson had designed his own tombstone and composed the modest inscription it was to bear: "Here was buried Thomas Jefferson, Author of the Declaration of Independence, of the Statute of Virginia for Religious Freedom, and the Father of the University of Virginia." He declined to mention his service as president. In his last will and testament, executed in March 1826, Jefferson left Monticello to his sole surviving daughter, Martha. Unfortunately, he died with debts totaling $107,274. To satisfy these claims Monticello was sold, its furnishings auctioned. Also in his will, Jefferson freed five of his slaves: Madison Hemings and Eston

Hemings, sons of Jefferson's alleged slave mistress Sally Hemings; John Hemings, a cabinetmaker and Sally's half brother; Joe Fossett, a blacksmith, and Burwell, Jefferson's personal servant, both half nephews of Sally.

JEFFERSON PRAISED: "He is an old friend with whom I have often had occasion to labor on many a knotty problem, and in whose abilities and steadiness I always found great cause to confide."[19]—John Adams, 1784

"No better minister could be sent to France. He is everything that is good, upright, enlightened and clever, and is respected and beloved by every one that knows him."[20]—Marquis de Lafayette

"His dress and manners are very plain; he is grave, or rather sedate, but without any tincture of pomp, ostentation, or pride, and occasionally can smile, and both hear and relate humorous stories as well as any other man of social feelings. . . . He is more deeply versed in human nature and human learning than almost the whole tribe of his opponents and revilers."[21]—Representative Samuel Latham Mitchill of New York, 1802

"So long as virtue, wisdom and patriotism continue to be revered in the world, so long will his character remain a distinguished monument of the triumph of liberty and the rights of man over despotism and aristocracy, around which the sons of freedom will rejoice to rally."[22]—Representative George W. Campbell of Tennessee, 1807

"He lives and will live in the memory and gratitude of the wise and good, as a luminary of Science, as a votary of liberty, as a model of patriotism, and as a benefactor of human kind."[23]—James Madison, 1826

JEFFERSON CRITICIZED: "How long it is since that gentleman's real character may have been *divined* . . . I am not sufficiently acquainted with the history of his political life to determine; but there is always a *'first time'* when characters studious of artful disguises are unveiled; when the visor of stoicism is plucked from the brow of the epicurean; when the plain garb of Quaker simplicity is stripped from the concealed voluptuary; when Caesar *coyly refusing* the proferred diadem, is seen to be Caesar rejecting the trappings but grasping the substance of imperial domination."[24]—Alexander Hamilton, 1792

"A ridiculous affectation of simplicity, stiling himself in the public papers and on invitation cards, plain Thomas, and similar frivolities, a pretended outcry against Monarchy and Aristocracy may have had a momentary effect with the few ignorant and unsuspecting, but have long ago excited the derision of the many, who know that under the assumed cloak of humility lurks the most ambitious spirit, the most overweening pride and hauteur, and that *externals* of pure Democracy afford but a flimsy veil to the *internal* evidences of aristocratic splendor, sensuality and Epicureanism."[25]—Representative William Loughton Smith of South Carolina, 1792

"The coward wretch at the head, while, like a Parisian revolutionary monster, pratting about humanity, could feel an infernal pleasure in the utter destruction of his opponents. We have too long witnessed his general turpitude—his cruel removals of faithful officers, and the substitution of corruption and baseness for integrity and worth."[26]—Senator Timothy Pickering of Massachusetts, 1804

JEFFERSON QUOTES: "Of all the cankers of human happiness, none corrodes it with so silent, yet so baneful a tooth, as indolence. . . . Idleness begets ennui, ennui the hypochondria, and that a diseased body."[27]—1787

"Nature intended me for the tranquil pursuits of science, by rendering them my supreme delight. But the enormities of the times in which I have lived have forced me to take a part in resisting them, and to commit myself on the boisterous ocean of political passions."[28]—1809

"Education . . . engrafts a new man on the native stock, and improves what in his nature was vicious and perverse into qualities of virtue and social worth. And it cannot be but that each generation succeeding to the knowledge acquired by all those who preceded it, adding to it their own acquisitions and discoveries, and handing the mass down for successive and constant accumulation, must advance the knowledge and well-being of mankind, not *infinitely*, as some have said, but *indefinitely*, and to a term which no one can fix or foresee."[29]—1818

BOOK BY JEFFERSON: *Notes on the State of Virginia* (1785).

BOOKS ABOUT JEFFERSON: Brodie, Fawn. *Thomas Jefferson: An Intimate History*. New York: W. W. Norton, 1974.

Malone, Dumas. *Jefferson and His Time*. 6 vols. Boston: Little, Brown, 1948–1981.

Peterson, Merrill D. *Thomas Jefferson and the New Nation*. New York: Oxford University Press, 1970.

Cunningham, Nobel E., Jr. *In Pursuit of Reason: The Life of Thomas Jefferson*. Baton Rouge: Louisiana State University, 1987.

NOTES

1 Merrill D. Peterson, *Thomas Jefferson and the New Nation*, New York: Oxford University Press, 1970, p. 399.
2 Ibid., p. 731.
3 Ibid., p. 520.
4 Ibid., p. 12.
5 Fawn Brodie, *Thomas Jefferson: An Intimate History*, New York: Norton, 1974, p. 60.
6 Peterson, P. 960.
7 Ibid., p. 957.
8 Dumas Malone, *Jefferson and His Time*, Boston: Little, Brown, 1948–1981, vol. I, p. 109.
9 Henry Steele Commager, ed., *Documents of American History*, New York: Crofts, 1945, Doc. no. 80, p. 126.
10 Malone, vol. I, p. 275.
11 Brodie, p. 65.
12 Ibid., p. 76.
13 Ibid., p. 483ff.
14 Ibid., p. 32.
15 *New York Times*, May 18, 1974, p. 31.
16 Malone, vol. I, pp. 220–221.
17 Peterson, pp. 637–638.
18 Ibid., p. 975.
19 Ibid., p. 298.
20 Ibid., p. 316.
21 Malone, vol. IV, p. 94.
22 Ibid., vol. V, p. 470.
23 Ralph Ketcham, *James Madison: A Biography*, New York: Macmillan, 1971, pp. 665–666.
24 Malone, vol. II, pp. 471–472.
25 Ibid., vol. II, p. 474.
26 Ibid., vol. IV, pp. 403–404.
27 Brodie, p. 51.
28 Malone, vol. V., p. 668.
29 Peterson, p. 972.

☆ ☆ ☆ ☆ ☆ ☆

JAMES MADISON

☆ ☆ ☆ ☆ ☆ ☆

4TH PRESIDENT

NAME: James Madison, Jr. He was named after his father.

PHYSICAL DESCRIPTION: Madison, the shortest and slightest president, stood about 5 feet 4 inches tall and weighed just 100 pounds. He had brown hair, blue eyes, and a rather tawny complexion. His nose was scarred from once having been frostbitten. He wore a size 7¼ hat. Until his last years he always appeared young for his age. From his youth, he was sickly, weak, and nervous, though he toughened his constitution somewhat in later years through rigorous exercise. He suffered from what his principal biographer, Irving Brant, has called "epileptoid hysteria," psychosomatic seizures similar to those of epilepsy that suspended the intellectual functions. Madison spoke in a thin, low voice. His speeches before deliberative bodies usually went unheard in the back benches. Even the recorder at the Virginia legislature complained that he could not always make out Madison's words clearly. Neat in appearance, Madison dressed carefully, usually in black.

PERSONALITY: Madison was shy and reserved with strangers and never learned the politically useful art of small talk. Because of this shyness, as well as his small stature and weak voice, he made a very bad first impression. Contributing to his poor image was his deliberative nature. He deferred decisions whenever possible until all sides had been considered thoroughly. For this, some regarded him as weak and indecisive. But others agreed with Treasury Secretary Albert Gallatin, who said, "Mr. Madison is . . . slow in taking his ground, but firm when the storm rises."[1]

ANCESTORS: "In both the paternal and maternal line of ancestry," Madison wrote of his forebears, "they were planters and among the respectable though not the most opulent class."[2] The immigrant ancestor of his paternal line was John Maddison (the second *d* eventually was dropped), a ship's carpenter from England who in 1653 was granted 600 acres of land in Virginia through the headright system, that is, in exchange for paying the passage of a specified number of immigrants, who commonly came to America as indentured servants. By 1664 Maddison had acquired nearly 2,000 acres in this way.

FATHER: James Madison, Sr. (1723–1801), planter. Fatherless at nine, he grew up on the estate in Orange County, Virginia, that he inherited on reaching manhood and that he passed on to his son and namesake. He acquired still more property and became the largest landowner and leading citizen of Orange County. During the Revolution he served as county lieutenant. He also from time to time held the posts of sheriff, justice of the peace, and vestryman. He married Nelly Conway in 1749. Madison exerted a profound influence on his son and is generally credited with instilling in him the virtues of morality, sobriety, and sense of purpose. He died less than a week before James, Jr., was appointed secretary of state.

MOTHER: Eleanor "Nelly" Rose Conway Madison (1731–1829). Born at Port Conway, Virginia, the daughter of a prominent planter and tobacco merchant, she remained very close to her most famous son. Although plagued by chronic malaria, she was otherwise a remarkably strong woman. She lived to be 98 years old and until the end remained lucid, able to read without glasses, and, one observer noted, less wrinkled than her son, the 77-year-old former president.

SIBLINGS: The oldest of seven children to live to maturity, Madison had three brothers and three sisters—Francis Madison, planter of Orange County, Virginia; Ambrose Madison, planter and captain in the Virginia militia, looked after the family interests in Orange County; Mrs. Nelly Hite; William Madison, veteran of the Revolution and lawyer, served in the Virginia legislature; Mrs. Sarah Macon; Mrs. Frances "Fanny" Rose, wife of a doctor. By his siblings Madison had more than 30 nieces and nephews to live to maturity.

COLLATERAL RELATIVES: Madison was a half first cousin twice removed of President George Washington and a second cousin of President Zachary Taylor.

CHILDREN: Madison had no children; thus, he has no direct descendants.

BIRTH: Madison was born at midnight on March 16, 1751, (March 5, 1750, Old Style) in the home of his maternal grandparents at Port Conway, King George County, Virginia. He was baptized on March 31, 1751, by the Reverend William Davis of Hanover Parish in King George County.

CHILDHOOD: Not long after his baptism in King George County, the infant Madison returned with his mother to Orange County and the small wooden home built by his grandfather. There, within view of the Blue Ridge Mountains, on the plantation that came to be called Montpelier, Madison grew up. Although little is known specifically about his childhood, clearly the most traumatic event of these early years, besides a smallpox epidemic, was the French and Indian War (1755–1762). News of Edward Braddock's defeat by French and Indian forces in 1755 sent shock waves through Virginia. The possibility of an Indian attack, though it never came, was much discussed at Montpelier. This early threat permanently prejudiced Madison against Native Americans. According to biographer Irving Brant, the boy "had seen the tomahawk and torch too vividly in his mind's eye to permit him to view the Indian as anything but a savage."[3] The major positive event of his childhood was the construction of the great house, to replace the small dwelling his grandfather had built, which, with subsequent additions, served as Madison's principal residence for the rest of his life. At its completion about 1760, young Madison helped move some of the lighter pieces of furniture from the old house to the new one.

EDUCATION: From age 11 to 16, Madison studied under Donald Robertson, an instructor at the Innes plantation in King and Queen County, Virginia. "All that I have been in life," Madison later wrote of this fine teacher, "I owe largely to that man."[4] From Robertson, Madison learned math, geography, and modern and ancient languages. He became especially proficient in Latin. At 16, he began a two-year course of study under the Reverend Thomas Martin, who tutored the lad at Montpelier in preparation for college. Unlike most college-bound Virginians of his day, Madison did not choose William and Mary, because, he explained, the lowland climate of Williamsburg might have strained his delicate health. Instead, in 1769 he enrolled as a sophomore at the College of New Jersey (now Princeton). Through diligence and long hours of study that at times robbed him of his sleep, he managed to graduate in two years. His studies there included Latin, Greek, science, geography, math, rhetoric, and philosophy. Great emphasis also was placed on speech and debate. Among his closest friends in college were Philip Freneau, whose anti-British verse later earned him the title "poet of the American Revolution," and William Bradford, later attorney general under President Washington. Although he engaged in his share of campus mischief, notably as a member of the American Whig Society, his generally studious nature prompted university president John Witherspoon to recall that he had never known young Madison "to do, or to say, an improper thing."[5] After graduation, Madison remained at Princeton to study Hebrew and philosophy under Witherspoon before returning to Montpelier in the spring of 1772. Madison studied law sporadically but never gained admission to the bar.

RELIGION: Episcopalian. Madison professed the basic tenets of his faith but was not zealous. He believed in a divine creater but doubted men's ability to know him.

RECREATION: Madison found stimulation in walking, observing nature, and horseback riding. An avid reader, he remained proficient in Latin and Greek all his life and poured over the ancient texts again and again. He also played chess.

EARLY ROMANCE: Madison was very shy with women. If he was seriously involved with anyone before he entered his 30s, the relationship has not yet been exposed.

    Kitty Floyd. (Details of Madison's courtship and engagement to Catherine "Kitty" Floyd did not become known until publication of the second volume of Irving Brant's biography in 1948. In his later years, Madison had inked out enciphered passages of letters relating to the affair. In time the ink faded, exposing the underlying numerical cipher sufficiently for Brant to decrypt it.) Madison met Kitty in 1780 when she was still a child of 13. Both were living at the boardinghouse of Mrs. Mary House in Philadelphia while Madison and Kitty's father, William Floyd of New York, served together in the Continental Congress. Madison began to take a romantic interest in Kitty when she reached 15, he then was 31. They saw much of each other from November 1782 and by the next April had agreed to marry after the close of Congress, probably sometime in the late fall of 1783. Madison was elated at the prospect of marriage, as his encrypted letters to Thomas Jefferson reveal. Without disclosing his wedding plans, he informed Virginia supporters that he would not be available to serve another term in Congress. Then suddenly, in July 1783, Kitty broke off the engagement. The reason is not known for certain. However, it seems likely that she simply loved someone else. William Clarkson, a medical student at the College of Philadelphia, had been calling on Kitty at about the time Madison first took an interest in her. In 1785, the year of Clarkson's graduation, he and Kitty were married. Madison never saw Kitty again. Dr. Clarkson quit medicine after nine years to become a Presbyterian minister and died in 1812. Kitty died in 1832.

MARRIAGE: James Madison, 43, married Dolley Payne Todd, 26, a widow with one son, on September 15, 1794, at Harewood, the estate of the bride's sister and brother-in-law, Lucy and George Steptoe Washington (nephew of President Washington), in what is now Jefferson County, West Virginia. Born on May 29, 1768, at the New Garden Quaker settlement in North Carolina, where her parents John Payne and Mary Coles Payne lived briefly, Dolley Payne spent her early years on the family plantation in Goochland County, Virginia. When she was still a young girl, her father, a devout Quaker convert, freed his slaves, sold the plantation, and moved his family north to Philadelphia, where he went bankrupt as a starch manufacturer. In 1790 Dolley married John Todd, a 26-year-old Quaker lawyer. He died in the yellow fever epidemic of 1793, leaving Dolley with one son, John Payne Todd. As a member of Congress, Madison had doubtless met the widow Todd at social functions in Philadelphia, then the nation's capital. But in May 1794 he took formal notice of her by asking their mutual friend Aaron Burr to arrange a meeting. The encounter apparently went smoothly, for a brisk courtship followed, and by August she had accepted his proposal of marriage. For marrying Madison, a non-Quaker, she was expelled from the Society of Friends. Four days after the wedding—a small, family-only affair performed by the Reverend Alexander Balmain, husband of one of the groom's cousins—the couple visited Madison's sister Nelly for two weeks. Unfortunately, Dolley suffered a recurring attack of malaria there. When her health was restored, the couple returned to Philadelphia. They did not take up residence at Montpelier until 1797. Dolley Madison was a vivacious, buxom beauty who charmed official Washington as no First Lady had before and few have since. During the Jefferson administration, she occasionally served as official hostess. As First Lady she instituted her popular Wednesday "drawing rooms." Typically clad in a feathered turban and otherwise lavishly dressed, she was the focus of every social event she attended. With architect Benjamin Latrobe she oversaw the remodeling of the White House. During the War of 1812, she courageously remained at the Executive Mansion as British troops advanced on the capital in August 1814 until she was able to arrange for the safe transport of certain national treasures. From the White House, she wrote her sister: "I am still here within sound of the cannon! Mr. Madison comes not; may God protect him! Two messengers covered with dust come to bid me fly; but I wait for him. . . . A wagon has been procured: I have filled it with the plate and most valuable portable articles belonging to the house. . . . I insist on waiting until the large picture of General Washington is secured, and it requires to be unscrewed from the wall."[6] With time running out, she had the full-length Washington portrait by Gilbert Stuart cut from its frame and spirited safely away. She then fled the capital to join her husband. After three days the Madisons returned to Washington to find the White House a burned-out shell. They took up residence at the Octagon House as the three-year process of reconstruction began. In 1817 she retired with the president to Montpelier. After his death in 1836 she moved back to Washington, where she spent the rest of her days, once again a popular figure on the capital's social circuit. She was by this time, however, virtually destitute. Her entertaining as well as demands from her spendthrift son, John Todd, proved a severe drain on her finances. To satisfy her creditors she sold Madison's papers to Congress and eventually was forced to sell Montpelier. Dolley Madison died on July 12, 1849, and was buried in Washington. In 1858 her remains were taken to Montpelier for reburial next to the president.

MILITARY SERVICE: American Revolution. In October 1775, Madison was commissioned a colonel in the Orange County militia. However, his frail health limited his activities to drill, target practice, and recruiting. He saw no action during his brief service.

CAREER BEFORE THE PRESIDENCY: Returning home from Princeton in 1772, Madison had not yet settled on a career. He decided to study law to broaden his knowledge, but he had no intention of practicing law. In 1774 he was elected to the county Committee of Safety, which his father chaired.

Delegate to the Virginia Convention, 1776. Madison served on the Privileges and Elections Committee and the committee assigned the task of drafting a declaration of rights and a plan of state government.

Member of Virginia House of Delegates, 1776–1777. According to the state constitution adopted at the convention of 1776, all delegates were to serve *ex officio* as the first members of the newly created House of Delegates until regular elections could be held. Thus Madison took his seat in October 1776. He was instrumental in securing passage of the religious freedom statute and generally supported the liberal initiatives of fellow-delegate Thomas Jefferson. In April 1777 Madison was defeated for reelection by one Charles Porter, largely because Madison refused to conform to the popular campaign custom of passing out free whiskey to voters.

Member of Council of State, 1778–1779. Madison disliked the Council of State, calling it "the grave of all useful talents,"[7] because it attempted to run the state by committee and stood in the way of strong, effective executive leadership. Under Virginia law, the governor required council approval for every substantive action. Serving under governors Patrick Henry and Thomas Jefferson, Councillor Madison helped direct the state's war effort during the Revolution.

Member of Continental Congress, 1780–1783. At 29 the youngest member of the Congress, he remained in the background at first, but by the end of his term he assumed a position of leadership. He supported the concept of a strong national government over that of a loose confederacy, pressed for more money and supplies for the Continental army, and favored the separation of the western lands from their parent states.

Member of Virginia House of Delegates, 1784–1786. He led the opposition to reestablish the Episcopal church in Virginia. Supporters, led by Patrick Henry, sought to levy a tax on all Virginians "for the support of the Christian religion or of some other Christian church, denomination or communion of Christians or of some form of Christian worship."[8] The measure was subsequently changed to support "teachers of the Christian religion," but Madison still objected to it. Against intense lobbying by the clergy, Madison managed to defeat the measure that threatened his cherished concept of separation of church and state. In the wake of this victory, Madison engineered passage of a bill that decriminalized heresy and abolished the religious test for public office. As chairman of the Commerce Committee, Madison pressed for the upgrading of Virginia seaports to enable them to compete with those of the North.

Delegate to Annapolis Convention, 1786. Called to consider disputes of interstate commerce, the convention resolved nothing. Madison joined other delegates in calling for a constitutional convention to be held in Philadelphia the next year.

Father of the U.S. Constitution. As a delegate to the Constitutional Convention in 1787, Madison earned the title Father of the Constitution for his role in drafting much of the document, arguing successfully for the creation of a strong central government, maintaining a comprehensive record of the proceedings, and marshaling public opinion in favor of its ratification. In addition to taking an active part in the debate, Madison daily kept copious notes of virtually everything that transpired in session. Because the convention was held behind closed doors and thus was not covered by the press or other outside observers, Madison's account constitutes the definitive record of the Constitutional Convention. After adoption of the Constitution came the formidable task of securing its ratification by the necessary nine states. In Virginia, Madison led proratification forces to a narrow (89–79) victory over Patrick Henry, leader of the opposition. With Alexander Hamilton and John Jay, Madison wrote *The Federalist Papers*, a collection of essays stressing the advantages of the proposed Constitution over the outmoded Articles of Confederation and allaying fears that a strong central government might pose a threat to individual freedoms. In "Federalist No. 51," writing under the pseudonym Publius, Madison put forth the best case for the system of separation of powers and the value of checks and balances: "The great security against a gradual concentration of the several powers in the same department, consists in giving to those who administer each department the necessary constitutional means and personal motives to resist encroachment of the others. . . . Ambition must be made to counteract ambition. . . . It may be a reflection on human nature, that such devices should be necessary to control the abuses of government. But what is government itself, but the greatest of all reflections on human nature? If men were angels, no government would be necessary." His efforts on behalf of the Constitution won him a powerful enemy in Patrick Henry, who saw to it that Madison was denied a seat in the newly created U.S. Senate.

U.S. Representative from Virginia, 1789–1797. Elected to the U.S. House over James Monroe in 1789, Madison introduced and steered to passage the Bill of Rights, the first 10 amendments to the Constitution, which were ratified in 1791 (see "George Washington, 1st President," "Administration: Constitutional Amendments Ratified"). He early became one of President Washington's leaders in the House. However, as partisan differences emerged between the federalism of Alexander Hamilton and the democratic principles of Thomas Jefferson, Washington increasingly supported Hamilton, and Madison lined up behind Jefferson. Although Madison and Washington remained on cordial terms personally, they had split politically by the beginning of the latter's second term in 1793. Madison opposed Jay's Treaty (see "George Washington, 1st President," "Administration").

Virginia Resolutions, 1798. Madison drafted the Virginia Resolutions, adopted by the state legislature in 1798, which declared the Alien and Sedition Acts to be unconstitutional (see "John Adams, 2d President," "Administration"). Jefferson wrote a similar resolution adopted in Kentucky at about the same time. Although the principle of state nullification of federal laws did not prevail ultimately, the Virginia and Kentucky Resolutions became a rallying point for antifederalism.

Member of Virginia House of Delegates, 1799–1800. Madison defended his Virginia Resolutions and campaigned for the election of Thomas Jefferson as president.

Secretary of State, 1801–1809. Appointed by President Jefferson, Secretary of State Madison supported the purchase of the Louisiana Territory from France, encouraged resistance to the tribute demanded by the Barbary pirates, and, more than any other cabinet member, pressed for the embargo against Britain and France in response to their harassment of American ships. He vehemently denounced the British practice of impressment. "That an officer from a foreign ship," he fumed, "should pronounce any person he pleased, on board an American ship on the high seas, not to be an American citizen, but a British subject, and carry his interested decision on the most important of all questions to a freeman into execution on the spot, is . . . anomalous in principle . . . grievous in practice, and . . . abominable in abuse."[9] (For more about the Louisiana Purchase, Barbary pirates, and Embargo Act, see "Thomas Jefferson, 3d President," "Administration.")

REPUBLICAN PRESIDENTIAL NOMINATION, 1808: For the first time, Republicans were divided over their choice for president. Thomas Jefferson, now retiring after two terms as president, so commanded the affections of the party that the nomination had been his for the asking. Jefferson openly favored Madison as his successor. The endorsement was a big boost toward the nomination, but Madison still faced opposition from two quarters—the old-line Republicans of the South, lead by John Randolph, who supported James Monroe of Virginia; and the supporters of George Clinton of New York. Monroe Republicans distrusted Madison for his strongly nationalist view of government. Clinton hoped to break Virginia's grip on the presidency to become the first New Yorker to hold that office. In January 1808, Republican congressmen in caucus chose Madison as their nominee on the first ballot. With the numbers clearly against them, most Monroe supporters boycotted the caucus, thus ensuring Madison an overwhelming victory: Madison, 83; Monroe, 3; Clinton, 3. Clinton was nominated for vice president.

OPPONENT: Charles Cotesworth Pinckney (1746–1825) of South Carolina, Federalist. He had run for president on the Federalist ticket against Thomas Jefferson in 1804. Without a formal caucus, Federalists again accepted Pinckney as their candidate for president and Rufus King of New York for vice president. After his defeat by Madison, Pinckney served as the first president of the Charleston Bible Society.

CAMPAIGN AND THE ISSUES, 1808: Madison was vulnerable on just one issue—the embargo. It had failed to persuade Britain and France to respect the neutral rights of American ships at sea while at the same time severely damaging the U.S. economy. Federalists roundly criticized Secretary of State Madison for advocating the embargo as a means of building up domestic manufactures at the expense of those whose livelihood depended on foreign trade. The unpopularity of the embargo revitalized the Federalist party, particularly in the Northeast, but the sentiment was insufficient to overcome the Republican majority that had become entrenched during the Jefferson administration. President Jefferson played a key role in wooing back Monroe's followers to support the party's nominee. Immediately after the nominating caucus, old-line Republicans denounced Madison as "unfit to fill the office of President in the present juncture of our affairs."[10] But in the end, the South and West went solidly for Madison. George Clinton, even though he accepted the Republican vice presidential nomination, criticized the caucus nominating process and allowed his supporters to campaign for him for president. A viable candidate only in his home state, he won 6 of New York's 19 electoral votes.

ELECTION AS PRESIDENT, FIRST TERM, 1808:
Electoral Vote: Madison, 122; Pinckney, 47; Clinton, 6.

States Carried. Madison won the majority of electoral votes in 12 states—Georgia, Kentucky, Maryland, New Jersey, New York, North Carolina, Ohio, Pennsylvania, South Carolina, Tennessee, Vermont, and Virginia. Pinckney won the majority of electoral votes in 5 states—Connecticut, Delaware, Massachusetts, New Hampshire, and Rhode Island.

REPUBLICAN NOMINATION FOR REELECTION AS PRESIDENT, 1812: In May 1812 Republican congressmen in caucus unanimously (82–0) nominated Madison for reelection. The New York delegation boycotted the caucus. John Langdon of New Hampshire was nominated for vice president, but at age 70 he declined. Elbridge Gerry of Massachusetts was then nominated for vice president.

OPPONENT: DeWitt Clinton (1769–1828) of New York, Federalist-backed Republican. Born in Little Britain, New York, he was a nephew of George Clinton, vice president under Madison. Graduating from Columbia College in 1789, he became a lawyer and, in 1798, was elected to the New York Assembly. In between terms in the state senate, 1798–1802, 1806–1811, he served in the U.S. Senate 1802–1803, where he introduced the Twelfth Amendment to the Constitution, establishing the modern procedure for the election of president and vice president. As mayor of New York City, 1803–1807, 1810–1811, 1813–1815, he promoted public education, the rights of immigrants, and other liberal reforms. In May 1812, Republican state legislators of New York nominated Clinton for president. Federalists, meeting in New York in September declined to select a presidential nominee, thus ensuring Clinton overwhelming Federalist support. Jared Ingersoll of Pennsylvania was nominated for vice president. Following his defeat by President Madison in the general election, Clinton turned his energies to the construction of the Erie Canal, connecting the Hudson River and Lake Erie. He was elected governor of New York in 1817 but was ousted in 1821 by the Tammany machine of Martin Van Buren. Returned to office in 1825, he remained governor until his death.

CAMPAIGN AND THE ISSUES, 1812: The War of 1812 dominated the campaign. Because the United States suffered early defeats in the West, Clinton supporters blasted the president for incompetence in directing the war effort, a war Federalists denounced as groundless. Madison campaigners defended the war as necessary to establish American neutral rights. Clinton sought to appeal to hawks and doves alike. "No canvas for the Presidency was ever less creditable than that of DeWitt Clinton in 1812," wrote historian Henry Adams, who accused the candidate of duplicity in "seeking war votes for the reason that he favored more vigorous prosecution of the war; asking support of peace Republicans because Madison had plunged the country into war without preparations; [while] bargaining for Federalist votes as the price of bringing about a peace."[11] The South and West again gave Madison a majority. Even some Federalists rallied around the president because of the war. Opposition to Madison was strongest in New England.

ELECTION AS PRESIDENT, SECOND TERM, 1812:
    Electoral Vote: Madison, 128; Clinton, 89.

    States Carried: Madison won the majority of electoral votes in 11 states—Georgia, Kentucky, Louisiana, Maryland, North Carolina, Ohio, Pennsylvania, South Carolina, Tennessee, Vermont, and Virginia. Clinton won the majority of electoral votes in 7 states—Connecticut, Delaware, Massachusetts, New Hampshire, New Jersey, New York, and Rhode Island.

INAUGURAL ADDRESS (FIRST): March 4, 1809. ". . . Indulging no passions which trespass on the rights or the repose of other nations, it has been the true glory of the United States to cultivate peace by observing justice, and to entitle themselves to the respect of the nations at war by fulfilling their neutral obligations with the most scrupulous impartiality. If there be candor in the world, the truth of these assertions will not be questioned; posterity at least will do justice to them. . . ."

INAUGURAL ADDRESS (SECOND): March 4, 1813. ". . . As the war [of 1812] was just in its origin and necessary and noble in its objects, we can reflect with a proud satisfaction that in carrying it on no principle of justice or honor, no usage of civilized nations, no precept of courtesy or humanity, have been infringed. The war has been waged on our part with scrupulous regard to all these obligations, and in a spirit of liberality which was never surpassed.

"How little has been the effect of this example on the conduct of the enemy! . . .

"They have not, it is true, taken into their own hands the hatchet and the knife, devoted to indiscriminate massacre, but they have let loose the savages armed with these cruel instruments; have allured them into their service, and carried them to battle by their sides, eager to glut their savage thirst with the blood of the vanquished and to finish the work of torture and death on maimed and defenseless captives. . . ."

VICE PRESIDENTS: George Clinton (1739–1812), of New York, served 1805–1812. He had served as vice president during President Jefferson's second term. Having opposed Madison even as they shared the Republican ticket in 1808, Vice President Clinton remained aloof of the administration. His most significant action was to cast a tie-breaking vote in the Senate against renewing the charter of the Bank of the United States in 1811. The Madison administration had supported renewal. Vice President Clinton died in office.

    Elbridge Gerry (1744–1814), of Massachusetts, served 1813–1814. Born in Marblehead, Massachusetts, he graduated from Harvard University in 1762 and served in the Continental Congress 1776–1785. He signed the Declaration of Independence. A Massachusetts delegate to the Constitutional Convention of 1787, he refused to sign the document as adopted. He served in the U.S. House 1789–1793. With John Marshall and Charles Cotesworth Pinckney, he represented the United States in what came to be called the XYZ Affair (see "John Adams, 2d President," "Administration"). As governor of Massachusetts, 1810–1812, he approved a redistricting plan that ensured Republican domination of the state. The shape of one new district resembled that of a salamander, prompting Benjamin Russell, editor of the Boston *Centinel*, to coin the term *gerrymander*, which has entered the political lexicon to signify redistricting for partisan advantage. Republicans chose Gerry for vice president in order to add

New England balance to the ticket, but, more significantly, because at age 68 he posed no threat to the presidential ambitions of James Monroe, whose support was important to Madison's fortunes. Vice President Gerry died in office.

CABINET:

Secretary of State. (1) Robert Smith (1757–1842), of Maryland, served 1809–1811. He had served as navy secretary under President Jefferson. Having reluctantly appointed Smith to appease opposition senators William Branch Giles and Samuel Smith (brother of Secretary Smith), Madison placed little confidence in him. The president berated his sloppy correspondence and upbraided him for criticizing administration policy behind his back. When Treasury Secretary Gallatin threatened to resign if Smith remained any longer, Madison dismissed Smith. (2) James Monroe (1758–1831), of Virginia, served 1811–1817 (see "James Monroe, 5th President," "Career before the Presidency").

Secretary of the Treasury. (1) Albert Gallatin (1761–1849), of Pennsylvania, served 1801–1814. A holdover from the Jefferson administration, he continued to call for a balanced budget even though it meant reducing military expenditures on the eve of the War of 1812. He helped negotiate the Treaty of Ghent ending the war. He later served as minister to France under Presidents Madison and John Quincy Adams. (2) George W. Campbell (1769–1848), of Tennessee, served February–October 1814. A native of Scotland, he was a former senator and "War Hawk." (3) Alexander Dallas (1759–1817), of Pennsylvania, served 1814–1816. Taking over a Treasury depleted by the war effort, he restored it to solvency with a program of increased taxes. He was a key figure in the creation of the Second Bank of the United States in 1816. (4) William H. Crawford (1772–1834), of Georgia, served 1816–1825. Transferred from war secretary, he stayed on in the Monroe administration.

Secretary of War. (1) William Eustis (1753–1825), of Massachusetts, served 1809–1812. Blamed for the early defeats of the war, he was dismissed and in 1814 was appointed minister to Holland. (2) John Armstrong (1758–1843), of New York, served 1813–1814. Blamed for the failure of the American expedition against Montreal and the British invasion of Washington during the war, he, too, was forced to resign. (3) James Monroe served 1814–1815, temporarily discharging duties of both State and War departments (see "James Monroe, 5th President," "Career before the Presidency"). (4) William H. Crawford served 1815–1816. He resigned to become Treasury secretary.

Attorney General. (1) Caesar A. Rodney (1772–1824), of Delaware, served 1807–1811. A holdover from the Jefferson administration, he was criticized for spending so much time on his private law practice in Wilmington. (2) William Pinkney (1764–1822), of Maryland, served 1811–1814. He was a popular figure in Washington renowned for his eloquent courtroom oratory. After resigning, he served in the War of 1812 and was wounded at Bladensburg. (3) Richard Rush (1780–1859), of Pennsylvania, served 1814–1817. He accompanied President Madison on his flight from Washington in advance of the British invasion. He edited the *Laws of the United States 1789–1815*. He stayed on in the Monroe administration.

Secretary of the Navy. (1) Paul Hamilton (1762–1816), of South Carolina, served 1809–1812. An alcoholic, he resigned when the disease began affecting his job. (2) William Jones (1760–1831), of Pennsylvania, served 1813–1814. Coming on duty in the middle of the war, he performed ably. Madison thought he was the best Navy secretary up to that time. (3) Benjamin Crowninshield (1772–1851), of Massachusetts, served 1815–1818. He stayed on in the Monroe administration.

ADMINISTRATION: March 4, 1809–March 3, 1817.

Non-Intercourse Act, 1809–1810. With the failure and repeal of the embargo (see "Thomas Jefferson, 3d President," "Administration"), President Madison sought to end British and French abuses of American shipping by enforcing the Non-Intercourse Act, passed in the final days of the Jefferson administration, which permitted U.S. trade with all nations except Britain and France. In addition the United States promised to exempt either nation from the act if it agreed to respect the neutrality of American ships. As it became clear that the policy was having no effect, Madison sought to achieve the same goal in a different way with Macon's Bill No. 2.

Macon's Bill No. 2, 1810. This law repealed the Non-Intercourse Act, with the offer that if either Britain or France agreed to respect the neutrality of American ships, the United States would suspend trade with the other nation. Napoleon agreed to this, and the United States reimposed non-intercourse with Britain.

War of 1812, 1812–1814. Causes: (1) British impressment of American seamen and seizure of goods in international waters. (2) Indian unrest, encouraged and exploited by Britain, in the West. (3) Rise of such "War Hawks" as Henry Clay and John C. Calhoun, who saw in war the opportunity to seize Canada.

Declaration of war: Unable peacefully to induce Britain to respect American neutral rights at sea, President Madison came to agree with the War Hawks that war was inevitable. Accordingly, on June 1, 1812, Madison asked Congress for a declaration of war. In his war message Madison condemned Britain for continuing impressment, in which "thousands of American citizens . . . have been torn from their country and from everything dear to them; have been dragged on board ships of war of a foreign nation and exposed, under the severities of their discipline, to be exiled to the most distant and deadly climes, to risk their lives in the battles of their oppressors, and to be the melancholy instruments of taking those of their own brethren." A badly divided Congress declared war on Great Britain on June 18, 1812. With the West and South voting for war and New England against it, the House approved the declaration 79–49; the Senate, 19–13.

The war: Even with the cream of the British army involved in Europe against Napoleon, the War of 1812 began disastrously for the Americans. Madison's first objective was to take Canada. He chose General William Hull, an obese aging veteran of the Revolution, to advance on Fort Malden at modern Windsor, Ontario. As Hull made his way cautiously across Canadian soil, he grew increasingly fearful of Indian attacks and withdrew to Detroit. There, subsequently surrounded by an inferior force of British and Indians, he surrendered Detroit without firing a shot. (Hull later was court-martialed and sentenced to death but was pardoned because of his service in the Revolution.) Madison handed command of the Northwest to William Henry Harrison, who got bogged down in the swamps of northwestern Ohio. A foray into Canada led by Henry Dearborn also failed. Surprisingly, the United States fared better in the naval war despite Britain's longtime supremacy at sea. The *Essex*, the *Constitution*, and other U.S. vessels won decisive engagements against British ships.

Stunned by these setbacks, the British threw a blockade against the American coast and successfully bottled up the U.S. fleet for the duration. Britain dominated Lake Erie until September 1813 when Captain Oliver Hazard Perry led his eight-vessel fleet from Put-in-Bay and in a three-hour battle took control of the strategic lake. "We have met the enemy and they are ours," wrote Perry in his famous dispatch. With Lake Erie secure and the British flushed from Detroit, William Henry Harrison pursued the enemy into Canada and in October 1813 scored a signal victory at the Battle of the Thames, at which the Indian leader Tecumseh was killed. To the southeast, however, the British penetrated the feeble American defenses in the Chesapeake Bay region to march into Washington and burn the White House, the Capitol, and other buildings in August 1814. The blitz forced President and Mrs. Madison to take refuge in Virginia. The next month British guns pounded Fort McHenry at Baltimore but failed to force its surrender—a glorious spectacle to observer Francis Scott Key, who celebrated the event in song, "The Star-Spangled Banner," which became the national anthem. By this time both sides were sufficiently war weary to talk peace.

Treaty of Ghent, 1814: In December 1814 the U.S. negotiating team—John Quincy Adams, James A. Bayard, Henry Clay, Albert Gallatin, and Jonathan Russell—concluded with British commissioners the Treaty of Ghent ending the War of 1812 *status quo ante bellum*, that is, with each side retaining territory held prior to the war. Impressment and other areas of conflict were left unsettled.

Battle of New Orleans 1815: Before news of the Treaty of Ghent reached North America, crack British veterans of the Napoleonic Wars, now since concluded, attempted to capture New Orleans. In a stunning defensive victory, frontier militia under General Andrew Jackson laid down a withering barrage of rifle fire that dropped more than 2,000 British troops. American casualties numbered just 21.

Results: The War of 1812, often called the Second War of Independence, marked the end of U.S. economic dependence on Britain. Domestic industry, having filled the vacuum created by a suspension of trade with Europe, emerged from the war a vital, expanding force in the economy. America had taken its first steps in the evolution from a largely agrarian nation into an industrial giant. Of the 286,730 Americans to serve in the war, 2,260 were killed, 4,505 wounded.

Hartford Convention, 1814–1815. New England Federalists opposed to the war convened in Hartford, Connecticut, in December 1814 to air grievances and consider solutions. Connecticut, Massachusetts, and Rhode Island sent delegates; New Hampshire and Vermont did not. Although radical Federalists urged secession, cooler heads prevailed. The convention proposed constitutional amendments designed to reduce the influence of the South, especially Virginia. The recommendations were buried in the euphoria of Jackson's victory at New Orleans and the end of the war.

Second Bank of the United States, 1816–1836. With Madison's support, Congress chartered the Second Bank of the United States in 1816. The bank remained in operation until President Jackson blocked renewal of its charter.

Internal Improvements. Although he supported federal subsidies for the development of interstate transportation, Madison, in his last act as president, surprised his own supporters in vetoing a bill authorizing federal funds for the construction of highways and canals. In his veto message, he asserted that such a program, though beneficial, exceeded Congress's constitutional authority to provide for the general welfare. He recommended a constitutional amendment.

States Admitted to the Union. Louisiana (1812), Indiana (1816).

SUPREME COURT APPOINTMENTS: (1) Joseph Story (1779–1845), of Massachusetts, served as associate justice 1811–1845. He was Madison's fourth choice for the appointment; John Quincy Adams was among those declining. A Republican, he was put on the Court to balance the Federalism of John Marshall. Instead, he joined Marshall in strengthening federal authority over states' rights. Story's sound legal scholarship complimented Marshall's statesmanship. In his first years on the Court he organized the tangle of maritime laws into a consistent, rational body of opinion. In *Martin* v. *Hunter's Lessee* (1816), Story delivered the majority opinion that established the Supreme Court's right to review the decisions of state courts. With Marshall's death and the appointment of Chief Justice Roger B. Taney in 1836, Story found himself increasingly in the role of dissenter. In addition to his duties on the bench, Story from 1829 also served as professor of law at Harvard University, where he helped establish Harvard Law School. He wrote numerous articles and books, notably the *Commentaries* (9 vols. 1832–1845) on the Constitution, equity, and other aspects of the law. (2) Gabriel Duval (1752–1844), of Maryland, served as associate justice 1812–1835. He worked in the shadow of Chief Justice Marshall, whose strong nationalist views he supported. He occasionally raised his voice in dissent, notably in *Mima Queen and Child* v. *Hepburn* (1812), in which he chastised the majority for denying freedom to two slaves manumitted by their master on his deathbed simply because the blacks' only proof of the dying wish was based on hearsay. "The right of freedom is more important than the right of property," Duvall argued. "And people of color, from their helpless condition under the uncontrolled authority of a master, are entitled to all reasonable protection."

RANKING IN 1962 HISTORIANS POLL: Madison ranked twelfth of 31 presidents, the best of 12 "average" presidents; ranked above John Quincy Adams, below Cleveland.

RETIREMENT: March 4, 1817–June 28, 1836. Upon the inauguration of James Monroe, Madison retired to Montpelier. Although he was among the largest landowners in Orange County, Virginia, a succession of poor tobacco and wheat harvests produced little income. Moreover, Madison felt obligated to cover the gambling debts of his ne'er-do-well stepson. Madison shared Jefferson's interest in the creation of the University of Virginia. He served on the board of regents and succeeded Jefferson as rector in 1826. In 1829 Madison represented Orange County at the Virginia Constitutional Convention in Richmond. He tried, unsuccessfully, to reconcile the competing interests of the large slaveholders of the east, who had long dominated state government, and the settlers in the burgeoning western frontier. At this same time, Madison was drawn into the debate over Nullification. Southerners supporting the right of states to declare federal laws unconstitutional and therefore null and void in their respective states cited as precedents Jefferson's and Madison's Virginia and Kentucky Resolutions of 1798. Madison publicly repudiated the Nullification movement, protesting that it had never been his intention to grant to the states the power to dissolve the Union. He denounced the doctrines of Nullification and Secession as "twin heresies." Madison had for many years believed that the perpetuation of slavery undermined the Union. He favored a gradual abolition and resettlement of freed blacks in Africa. To this end he in 1819 helped organize the American Colonization Society, which three years later founded Liberia in West Africa as a colony for former American slaves.

DEATH: June 28, 1836, after 6 A.M., Montpelier estate, Virginia. Crippled by rheumatism, confined to his room for the last six months of his life, Madison suffered bilious attacks and steadily weakened. Dr. Robley Dunglison attended him during the final month. Madison reportedly was offered stimulants to keep him alive until July 4, so that he could join three former presidents in dying on that historic date, but he refused. Sometime after 6 A.M. on June 28, 1836, he seemed to have trouble swallowing his breakfast. "What is the matter, Uncle James?" asked one of his nieces. "Nothing more than a change of *mind*, my dear," he replied. These were his last words. His head suddenly dropped. He died quietly from heart failure at 85. He was buried next day at the family plot at Montpelier. Episcopal services were conducted at graveside before numerous relatives, friends, and neighbors and some 100 slaves. His headstone bore simply his last name and the dates of his birth and death. Discovered among his papers was a brief message, intended for posthumous publication, entitled "Advice to My Countrymen." In it Madison pleaded "that the Union of the States be cherished and perpetuated." In his last will and testament, executed in April 1835, Madison ordered that his comprehensive journal on the Constitutional Convention be sold. From the proceeds (Congress eventually paid $30,000 for it), he directed the following bequests: $6,000 for the education of various relatives, $2,000 to the American Colonization Society, $1,500 to the University of Virginia, and $1,000 each to Princeton and a college at Uniontown Pennsylvania. He left his personal library to the University of Virginia, 240 acres of land to his brother-in-law, John C. Payne, and $9,000 to be divided among his nieces and nephews. The entire residue of his estate—including Montpelier, the slaves (none was to be sold against his will unless he committed some crime), his personal effects, and the balance of the proceeds from the sale of his notes on the Constitutional Convention—went to his widow.

MADISON PRAISED: "Madison was enviable in being among the few young men who were not inflated by early flattery and could content themselves with throwing out in social discourse jewels which the artifice of a barren mind would have treasured up for gaudy occasions."[12]—Edmund Randolph of Virginia, on Madison at 25

"No man had a higher reputation among his acquaintance for probity and a good honorable feeling, while he was allowed on all sides to be a gentleman in his manners as well as a man of public virtue."[13]—British diplomat Augustus J. Foster, 1807

"Never was a country left in a more flourishing situation than the United States at the end of your administration; and they are more united at home and respected abroad than at any period since the war of the independence."[14]—former Treasury secretary Albert Gallatin, 1817

"I can say conscientiously that I do not know in the world a man of purer integrity, more dispassionate, disinterested, and devoted to genuine Republicanism; nor could I in the whole scope of America and Europe point out an abler head."[15]—Thomas Jefferson, 1812

"He had as much to do as any man in framing the constitution, and as much to do as any man in administering it."[16]—Daniel Webster

"Mr. Madison . . . rendered more important services to his country than any other man, Washington only excepted."[17]—Senator Henry Clay, 1836

MADISON CRITICIZED: "Mr. Madison, a gloomy stiff creature, they say is clever in Congress, but out of it he had nothing engaging or even bearable in his manners—the most unsociable creature in existence."[18]—Martha Bland (wife of Theodorick Bland, Virginia delegate to Continental Congress), 1781

"I think him a good man and an able man, but he has rather too much theory, and wants that discretion which men of business commonly have. He is also very timid and seems evidently to want manly firmness and energy of character."[19]— Representative Fisher Ames of Massachusetts, 1789

"In my opinion 'the virtuous and amiable Madison' is (and perhaps I may eventually prove him to be) utterly devoid of political integrity."[20]—Senator Timothy Pickering of Massachusetts, 1810

"Our President tho a man of amiable manners and great talents, has not I fear those commanding talents, which are necessary to controul those about him. He permits division in his cabinet."[21]—Representative John C. Calhoun of South Carolina, 1812

"I firmly believe that Madison, who is but the puppet of Jefferson, is only qualified to ruin his country. I cannot believe that the Union will survive another four years of his administration—or if it should survive, I believe it must be at the expense of the best blood of the Northeastern states, to be shed by the New Englanders themselves."[22]—former navy secretary Benjamin Stoddert, 1812

MADISON QUOTES: "To the press alone, chequered as it is with abuses, the world is indebted for all the triumphs which have been gained by reason and humanity over error and oppression. . . . That to the same beneficent source the United States owe much of the lights which conducted them to the ranks of a free and independent nation, and which have improved their political system into a shape so auspicious to their happiness."[23]—c. 1800

"A popular Government without popular information, or the means of acquiring it, is but a prologue to a farce or a tragedy; or, perhaps both. Knowledge will forever govern ignorance; and a people who mean to be their own Governors, must arm themselves with the power which knowledge gives."[24]

BOOKS BY MADISON: *The Papers of James Madison* (3 vols., 1840), selected and edited largely by Madison himself; includes "Notes on the Federal Convention of 1787."

BOOKS ABOUT MADISON: Brant, Irving. *James Madison*, 6 vols. Indianapolis: Bobbs-Merrill, 1941–1961.

Ketcham, Ralph. *James Madison: A Biography*. New York: Macmillan, 1971.

Rutland, Robert A. *James Madison: The Founding Father*. New York: Macmillan, 1987.

NOTES

1 Ralph Ketcham, *James Madison: A Biography*, New York: Macmillan, 1971, p. 473.
2 Irving Brant, *James Madison*, Indianapolis: Bobbs-Merrill, 1941–1961, vol. I, p. 33.
3 Ibid., p. 48.
4 Ibid., p. 60.
5 Ketcham, p. 35.

6 Brant, vol. VI, p. 303.

7 Ibid., vol. I, p. 316.

8 Ibid., p. 343.

9 Ketcham, pp. 449–450.

10 Ibid., p. 467.

11 Henry Adams, *History of the United States during the Administration of Jefferson and Madison*, New York, 1889-1891, vol. VI, p. 410.

12 Brant, vol. I, p. 206.

13 Ibid., vol. IV, p. 46.

14 Ibid., vol. VI, p. 419.

15 Ibid., vol. I, p. 273.

16 Richard Kenin and Justin Wintle, eds., *Dictionary of Biographical Quotation*, New York: Knopf, 1978, p. 513.

17 Brant, vol. VI, pp. 521–522.

18 Ibid., vol. II, p. 33.

19 Ibid., vol. III, p. 262.

20 Ibid., vol. V, p. 141.

21 Ketcham, p. 532.

22 Brant, vol. VI, p. 97.

23 Ketcham, p. 401.

24 Asa Martin, *After the White House*, State College, Pa.: Penns Valley, 1951, p. 87.

☆ ☆ ☆ ☆ ☆ ☆ ☆

JAMES MONROE

☆ ☆ ☆ ☆ ☆ ☆ ☆

5TH PRESIDENT

NAME: James Monroe.

PHYSICAL DESCRIPTION: Slightly over 6 feet tall, Monroe was sturdily built with broad shoulders and a large frame. He had a high forehead, and from early adulthood deep bays indented his hairline. The dark wavy hair of his youth had grayed almost completely by the time he became president. His angular face was distinctive for its oversized nose, wide-set blue-gray eyes, and dimpled chin. He always appeared well groomed but did not keep up with fashion changes in clothes. His health generally was good.

PERSONALITY: Monroe's greatest asset was his disarming, warm personality. Although conceding that Monroe lacked brilliance and a nimble mind, biographer Harry Ammon pointed out that he "had a rare ability of putting men at ease by his courtesy, his lack on condescension, his frankness, and by what his contemporaries looked upon as his essential goodness and kindness of heart."[1] Monroe at least partially overcame an early shyness but remained markedly low-key and reserved, especially among strangers. Acutely sensitive to criticism, he at times took offense where none was intended. Rather than lash back at his critics, however, he usually bottled up his feelings. "Operating as he did with such an elevated sense of his own integrity," Ammon has written, "he could not easily adjust when old friends failed to approve his conduct."[2]

ANCESTORS: Through his paternal grandfather, Andrew Monroe, James Monroe descended from King Edward III (1312–1377) of England. According to family tradition, the paternal line descended from the Munro family of Fowlis, Scotland. The immigrant ancestor of the Monroe line is believed to have been the president's great-grandfather, Andrew Monroe, an officer under Charles I at the Battle of Preston (1648), who was taken prisoner and exiled to Virginia.

FATHER: Spence Monroe (?–1774) planter, carpenter. According to his most famous son, Spence Monroe was a "worthy and respectable citizen possessed of good landed and other property."[3] In addition to having been a moderately prosperous planter he also had learned the carpenter's trade. In 1752 he married Elizabeth Jones. In 1766 he joined George Washington and other Virginians in calling for a boycott of British goods to protest colonial policy. He died when James Monroe was about 16.

MOTHER: Elizabeth Jones Monroe (d. ante 1774). "A very amiable and respectable woman, possessing the best domestic qualities of a good wife, and a good parent,"[4] Monroe wrote of his mother. She was born of Welsh heritage apparently in King George County, Virginia, and was said to be better educated than most women of her day. Little else is known of her.

SIBLINGS: The second of five children to live to maturity, Monroe had one older sister and three younger brothers—Mrs. Elizabeth Buckner of Caroline County, Virginia; Spence Monroe, who reportedly died young; Andrew Monroe of Albemarle County, Virginia; Joseph Jones Monroe, clerk of the District Court of Northumberland County, Virginia, private secretary to President Monroe, settled in Missouri.

CHILDREN: Monroe had two daughters to live to maturity.

Eliza Monroe (1787–?). Educated at the exclusive French school of Madame Campan (former lady-in-waiting to Marie Antoinette) while her father was minister to France, Eliza appeared to many a haughty, pompous socialite quick to remind others of her good breeding and lofty station. In 1808 she married George Hay, a prominent Virginia attorney who had served as prosecutor in the trial of Aaron Burr. He later ran his father-in-law's campaign in Virginia and was appointed a federal judge by President John Quincy Adams. During the Monroe administration, Eliza often substituted as official White House hostess for the ailing First Lady. Eliza soon alienated much of Washington society for her refusal to call on wives of the diplomatic corps, as was the custom. She caused another social furor in closing her sister's wedding to all but family and friends. For all her apparent vanity, however, she demonstrated genuine compassion during the fever epidemic that swept Washington during Monroe's term. She spent many sleepless nights selflessly caring for victims. Following the deaths of her husband and father she moved to Paris, converted to Catholicism, and lived in a convent.

Maria Hester Monroe (1803–1850). Still a child when her father was elected president, Maria finished school in Philadelphia before moving into the White House in 1819. On March 9, 1820, she married her first cousin Samuel L. Gouverneur in the first wedding ever performed at the White House. Many in Washington criticized the Monroes for keeping the wedding private; just 42 members of the family and close friends were invited. Friction between Maria's husband and her outspoken sister strained family relations thereafter. The Gouverneurs settled in New York City. Former President Monroe, upon losing his wife in 1830, moved in with them. President John Quincy Adams appointed Samuel Gouverneur postmaster of New York City.

BIRTH: Monroe was born on April 28, 1758, in Westmoreland County, Virginia.

CHILDHOOD: Few details of Monroe's childhood are known. Upon the death of his father, Monroe, then about 16, fell under the guidance of his maternal uncle Joseph Jones, executor of his father's estate and a member of the Continental Congress. Under the system of primogeniture, Monroe inherited all his father's estate and assumed responsibility for the welfare of his younger brothers. He was a very athletic youth.

EDUCATION: From age 11 to 16, Monroe studied at Campbelltown Academy, an excellent school run by the Reverend Archibald Campbell of Washington Parish. There he progressed through Latin and math at a rate faster than that of most boys his age. Among his classmates was John Marshall, later chief justice of the United States. At 16, Monroe entered the College of William and Mary. However the atmosphere on the Williamsburg campus was not conducive to study in 1774. The prospect of revolution charged most of the students, including Monroe, with patriotic fervor. In June 1775, after the battles of Lexington and Concord had sounded the opening guns of the Revolution, Monroe joined 24 older men in raiding the arsenal at the Governor's Palace. The 200 muskets and 300 swords they stole helped arm the Williamsburg militia. Next spring Monroe dropped out of college to join the Continental army (see "Military Service"). He never returned to earn a degree. During 1780–1783, he studied law under Thomas Jefferson.

RELIGION: Episcopalian. His writings do not reveal the extent of his faith.

RECREATION: Monroe enjoyed horseback riding and hunting.

EARLY ROMANCE:

Nannie Brown? While serving as aide-de-camp to Lord Stirling, General William Alexander, in 1778, Major Monroe met a young lady who has never been positively identified but who is thought to have been Nannie Brown, a relative of Lord Stirling. In a letter to Theodosia Bartow Prevost, the pro-American wife of a British officer who later married Aaron Burr, Monroe complained of his overly possessive girlfriend. The couple quarreled over Monroe's desire to study in France. Whether this disagreement drove them apart or, as some believe, Monroe never was serious about her, is unknown, but it is generally believed that it was Monroe who ended the relationship. By the spring of 1779, they had stopped seeing each other.

MARRIAGE: Monroe, 27, married Elizabeth Kortright, 17, on February 16, 1786, in New York City. Born in New York on June 30, 1768, the daughter of Laurence Kortright, an officer in the British army and prominent merchant who lost much of his fortune during the Revolution, and Hannah Aspinwall Kortright, Elizabeth early acquired social grace and elegance. A statuesque beauty with raven hair and blue eyes, she first caught Monroe's attention in 1785 while he was in New York as a member of the Continental Congress. After a brief honeymoon on Long Island, the newlyweds returned to New York to live with her father until Congress adjourned. In Paris, as wife of the American minister during the Reign of Terror, she helped secure the release of Lafayette's wife from prison. Mrs. Monroe suffered from an unidentified chronic ailment that forced her to curtail her activities as First Lady. Her elder daughter, Eliza, often substituted for her as official hostess. The decisions not to pay courtesy calls on Washington hostesses and to have a private White House wedding for her younger daughter made the First Lady extremely unpopular. Although she regained a measure of respect and admiration during her husband's second term, she compared poorly with her predecessor, Dolley Madison, who had captivated Washington society, setting a standard by which future First Ladies long were measured. In 1826, a year after retiring with the former president to their Oak Hill estate in Loudoun County, Virginia, she suffered a violent seizure during which she collapsed into the fireplace and sustained severe burns. She died on September 23, 1830.

MILITARY SERVICE: American Revolution. Monroe served in the Continental army from March 1776 to December 1778, rising from lieutenant to major. In March 1776 Monroe dropped out of college to enlist in the Third Virginia Regiment under Colonel Hugh Mercer. After basic training at Williamsburg, Lieutenant James Monroe and the 700-man regiment marched north to join General George Washington at Manhattan in September 1776. That Christmas, Monroe was among those crossing the Delaware with Washington to take part in the Battle of Trenton. There Lieutenant Monroe helped lead a bold charge against the enemy in order to capture two 3-pound cannons that were about to be turned against them. In the raid he was severely wounded in the shoulder and had to be carried from battle. He would have bled to death if it were not for the immediate attention of one Doctor Riker, a local resident who had just joined the unit after it landed in New Jersey. For his heroism, Monroe was promoted to captain. In 1777 he took part in engagements at Brandywine and Germantown and was promoted to major. As aide-de-camp to Lord Stirling, he survived the brutal winter of 1777–1778 at Valley Forge. At the Battle of Monmouth in June 1778, he scouted for General Washington and, when Lieutenant Colonel Francis Barber was wounded, filled the breach as Lord Stirling's adjutant general. By December 1778 Monroe had grown restless as Stirling's deputy and resigned his commission to return to Virginia, where he tried unsuccessfully to raise sufficient volunteers to form a command of his own. In 1780 Governor Thomas Jefferson appointed him military commissioner of Virginia with the rank of lieutenant colonel. His exemplary service during the Revolution earned him the lasting gratitude of his commander in chief. "He has, in every instance, maintained the reputation of a brave, active, and sensible officer,"[5] General Washington wrote.

CAREER BEFORE THE PRESIDENCY:

Member of Virginia Assembly, 1782–1783. Monroe served on the eight-man Council of State.

Member of Continental Congress, 1783–1786. Elected to three successive one-year terms, Monroe championed the rights of the West. He favored granting western lands to veterans of the Revolution. He pressed for free navigation of the Mississippi River. His proposal that Congress be granted authority to regulate both foreign and interstate commerce later became part of the U.S. Constitution.

From 1786, when he was admitted to the Virginia bar, until 1790, Monroe practiced law at Fredericksburg, Virginia. He represented Spotsylvania at the Virginia Ratifying Convention (1788), where he voted against ratification of the U.S. Constitution. However, he was quickly reconciled to it and wholeheartedly, though temporarily, supported the new national government under President Washington. In a friendly campaign against James Madison for a seat in the first U.S. Congress, Monroe lost by 300 votes.

U.S. Senator, 1790–1794. He sided with the Anti-Federalists to become a chief lieutenant of Thomas Jefferson. He proposed (1791) and obtained (1794) a rule change opening the Senate sessions to the public for the first time. Senator Monroe at first supported President Washington's Proclamation of Neutrality but came to fear that once the right of the chief executive to proclaim neutrality had been established, a future president might cite this precedent as a basis for asserting his right to declare war, thus usurping congressional authority. Monroe also opposed creation of a standing army.

Minister to France, 1794–1796. Appointed by President Washington to succeed Gouverneur Morris, Monroe found it difficult to reconcile his fondness for France with the administration's policy of strict neutrality. At his official reception in Paris, Minister Monroe was so lavish in his praise of France that he drew an official reprimand from the U.S. secretary of state. Monroe interceded with French officials to secure the release of Thomas Paine, who had been imprisoned in Paris for opposing the execution of King Louis XVI. Believing Paine to be mortally ill, Monroe allowed him to stay at the American minister's residence. Paine recovered, however, and immediately attacked President Washington in blistering terms for allowing him to languish in prison so long. The episode further diminished Monroe in the president's esteem. Monroe opposed Jay's Treaty with Great Britain (see "George Washington, 1st President," "Administration"). However, as U.S. minister in Paris, he neither stated his objections publicly nor conveyed them to French officials. Still, the Federalist administration expected him actively to support the treaty, to defend it against French objections. This Monroe did not do. For his silence, President Washington recalled him.

Governor of Virginia, 1799–1802. Elected by the state legislature over Federalist James Breckenridge, Governor Monroe put down an incipient slave revolt, promoted education, and in 1800 campaigned for Thomas Jefferson for president.

Special Envoy, 1803. Monroe joined U.S. Minister Robert R. Livingston in Paris to negotiate the Louisiana Purchase (see "Thomas Jefferson, 3d President," "Administration").

Minister to Great Britain 1803–1807. Appointed by President Jefferson, Monroe found his reception in London increasingly chilly as British-American relations deteriorated. He attempted to induce Britain to abandon its policy of impressment. Failing that, Monroe and William Pinkney signed a commercial treaty with Britain, which, because it failed to resolve the impressment issue, was rejected by Jefferson. Meanwhile, Monroe traveled to Spain to attempt, unsuccessfully, to fix the Florida boundaries.

In 1808, following his return to the United States, Monroe was a candidate for the Republican presidential nomination, supported by John Randolph and other southerners in the party opposed to James Madison.

Governor of Virginia, January–March 1811. Governor Monroe used his influence to keep disaffected Republicans in the state from bolting the party.

Secretary of State, 1811–1817. Appointed by President Madison, Monroe set out to find a peaceful solution to the problems alienating the United States and Great Britain. He soon came to realize, however, that the two nations had drifted too far toward open hostility to avoid what was to become the War of 1812. Moreover, with Britain's continued harassment of American ships, Monroe concluded that war "could not do us more injury than the present state of things" and "would give activity to our infant manufactories, which would soon be able to shut the door on British industry."[6] When British troops landed on Maryland's western shore in August 1814, Monroe personally led a scouting party to the region. Realizing that the enemy was about to march on Washington, he ordered all State Department records and documents, including the Declaration of Independence, removed to a place of safety in Virginia. After the British sacked the capital and withdrew, President Madison appointed Monroe secretary of war and military commander of the Federal District.

Secretary of War, 1814–1815. Monroe held this post while retaining his duties at the State Department. Failing to convince congress of the need to establish a military draft, he nevertheless strengthened the regular army by offering greater land bounty to volunteers and other inducements to service. His tireless efforts in the twin cabinet posts earned him widespread acclaim as the tide of the war turned in America's favor. He emerged the heir apparent to retiring President Madison.

REPUBLICAN PRESIDENTIAL NOMINATION, 1816: Monroe was the favorite candidate of both former President Jefferson and retiring President Madison. However, he faced stiff competition from Secretary of War William H. Crawford of Georgia. Also, there was widespread sentiment, especially in New York, that it was time to end the Virginia dynasty. But Monroe's long service at home and abroad had made him a fitting candidate to succeed Madison. He was particularly popular among state party leaders around the country. Crawford never formally declared himself a candidate, because he believed that he had little chance against Monroe and feared that such a contest might deny him a place in the new cabinet. Still, Crawford's supporters posed a significant challenge. In March 1816, Republican congressmen in caucus chose Monroe over Crawford, 65–54. Governor Daniel D. Tompkins of New York was nominated for vice president.

OPPONENT: Rufus King (1755–1827), of New York, Federalist. Born at Scarboro in what is now Maine, King, a lawyer, served in the Continental Congress 1784–1787 and, as co-author of the Northwest Ordinance, led the successful drive to ban slavery in the Northwest Territory. A delegate to the Constitutional Convention, he joined those advocating a strong central government and later helped secure ratification of the Constitution in Massachusetts. Moving to New York in 1788, he was elected one of that state's first two U.S. senators, serving from 1789 to 1796. He became a leading Federalist and enthusiastic supporter of Alexander Hamilton's policies. Appointed minister to Britain by President Washington in 1796, he served in London until 1803. In 1804 and again in 1808, he ran unsuccessfully for vice president on the Federalist ticket with Charles Cotesworth Pinckney. Returned to the Senate in 1813, he was among the last Federalists to cling to power. Although the Federalist party did not officially nominate a candidate in 1816, it supported King. John E. Howard of Maryland was the principal Federalist candidate for vice president. After his defeat by Monroe, Senator King emerged a leading opponent of slavery. He proposed gradual abolition, with due compensation to slaveholders, and resettlement of blacks outside the United States. Appointed minister to Great Britain by President John Quincy Adams in 1825, he served only briefly before failing health forced his retirement. He died on Long Island in 1827.

CAMPAIGN AND THE ISSUES, 1816: Monroe's nomination was tantamount to election, for the Federalist party was moribund after the War of 1812. The party's opposition to the war had accelerated its decline. A few die-hard partisans rehashed Monroe's diplomatic failures abroad, but candidate King put up only token opposition. Monroe's supporters did little campaigning, preferring to sit on their commanding lead until the election.

ELECTION AS PRESIDENT, FIRST TERM, 1816:
Electoral Vote: Monroe, 183; King, 34.
States Carried: Monroe won the majority of electoral votes in 16 states—Georgia, Indiana, Kentucky, Louisiana, Maryland, New Hampshire, New

Jersey, New York, North Carolina, Ohio, Pennsylvania, Rhode Island, South Carolina, Tennessee, Vermont, and Virginia. King won the majority of electoral votes in three states—Connecticut, Delaware, and Massachusetts.

REPUBLICAN NOMINATION FOR REELECTION AS PRESIDENT, 1820: Monroe's renomination was such a foregone conclusion that few Republicans bothered to attend the nominating caucus in April 1820. Rather than to name the president with only a handful of votes, the caucus declined to make a formal nomination. Thus President Monroe and Vice President Daniel D. Tompkins became de facto candidates for reelection.

OPPONENT: None.

CAMPAIGN AND THE ISSUES, 1820: With the incumbent president standing unopposed for reelection, of course, there was no campaign. Not since George Washington had a president enjoyed such broad-based support. Even former President John Adams, a pillar of the Federalist party, came out of retirement to stand as a Monroe elector in Massachusetts. It was indeed an "Era of Good Feelings" (see "Administration"). Only 1 of the 231 electors voted against Monroe—Governor William Plumer of New Hampshire, who cast his ballot for Secretary of State John Quincy Adams. According to legend, Plumer voted against Monroe to preserve Washington's record as the only president unanimously chosen by the electoral college. However, Plumer genuinely disliked the president and, according to a biography of the governor written by his son, voted against Monroe in earnest.

ELECTION AS PRESIDENT, SECOND TERM, 1820:
    Electoral Vote: Monroe, 231; John Quincy Adams, 1.
    States Carried: Monroe carried the majority of electoral votes in all 24 states—Alabama, Connecticut, Delaware, Georgia, Illinois, Indiana, Kentucky, Louisiana, Maine, Maryland, Massachusetts, Mississippi, Missouri, New Hampshire, New Jersey, New York, North Carolina, Ohio, Pennsylvania, Rhode Island, South Carolina, Tennessee, Vermont, and Virginia.

INAUGURAL ADDRESS (FIRST): March 4, 1817. ". . . Possessing as we do all the raw materials, the fruit of our own soil and industry, we ought not to depend in the degree we have done on supplies from other countries. While we are thus dependent the sudden event of war, unsought and unexpected, can not fail to plunge us into the most serious difficulties. . . .

"If we look to the history of other nations, ancient or modern, we find no example of a growth so rapid, so gigantic, of a people so prosperous and happy. In contemplating what we have still to perform, the heart of every citizen must expand with joy when he reflects how near our Government has approached to perfection; that in respect to it we have no essential improvement to make; that the great object is to preserve it in the essential principles and features which characterize it, and that that is to be done by preserving the virtue and enlightening the minds of the people; and as a security against foreign dangers to adopt such arrangements as are indispensable to the support of our independence, our rights and liberties. . . ."

INAUGURAL ADDRESS (SECOND): March 5, 1821. ". . . In our whole system, national and State, we have shunned all the defects which unceasingly preyed on the vitals and destroyed the ancient Republics. In them there were distinct orders, a nobility and a people, or the people governed in one assembly. Thus in the one instance there was a perpetual conflict between the orders in society for the ascendency, in which the victory of either terminated in the overthrow of the government and the ruin of the state; in the other, in which the people governed in a body, and whose dominions seldom exceeded the dimensions of a county in one of our States, a tumultous and disorderly movement permitted only a transitory existence. In this great nation there is but one order, that of the people, whose power, by a peculiarly happy improvement of the representative principle, is transferred from them, without impairing in the slightest degree their sovereignty, to bodies of their own creation, and to persons elected by themselves, in the full extent necessary for all the purposes of free, enlightened, and efficient government. The whole system is elective, the complete sovereignty being in the people, and every officer in every department deriving his authority from and being responsible to them for his conduct. . . ."

VICE PRESIDENT: Daniel D. Tompkins (1774–1825, of New York, served 1817–1825. Born in present-day Scarsdale, New York, Tompkins, a lawyer, served briefly in the New York State legislature before being appointed to the state supreme court in 1804. As governor of New York 1807–1817, he promoted education and opposed banking interests. In addition to his gubernatorial duties during the War of 1812, he was responsible for the defense of the state. When the state legislature refused to appropriate the funds necessary to meet soaring military expenditures, Governor Tompkins borrowed the difference, offering as collateral his own property. After the war neither the state nor federal government came forward to repay the loans. Thus creditors promptly attached Tompkins's personal fortune. Ensuing litigation, which continued until 1824, when the U.S. Congress agreed to reimburse him for the war debts, took a heavy toll on Tompkins's health and performance. He fell to alcoholism and as vice president at times presided over the Senate while drunk. He died a few months after leaving office.

CABINET:

Secretary of State. John Quincy Adams (1767–1848), of Massachusetts, served 1817–1825. Among the greatest secretaries of state, he negotiated successfully with Britain to fix the U.S.-Canadian border, gained Florida from Spain, and helped inspire the Monroe Doctrine (see "John Quincy Adams, 6th President," "Career before the Presidency").

Secretary of the Treasury. William H. Crawford (1772–1834), of Georgia, served 1816–1825. A holdover from the Madison administration, he was the most blatantly political member of Monroe's cabinet as he jockeyed for position in anticipation of the 1824 presidential election. "A worm preying upon the vitals of the Administration,"[7] Secretary of State Adams called him. Relations between Crawford and the president became increasingly strained, erupting finally near the end of Monroe's second term in a violent exchange. Growing impatient over Monroe's delay in making certain political appointments he had recommended, Crawford in abusive terms criticized the president for being indecisive. Monroe, taken aback by his tone, chastised the secretary for such disrespect. Then, according to Navy Secretary Southard, who later recounted the event based probably on what Monroe had told him, Crawford raised his cane as if to strike the president and yelled, "You infernal scoundrel." In self-defense, Monroe grabbed the fireplace tongs and ordered Crawford to get out. At this point the secretary backed away, apologizing for his behavior. Monroe graciously accepted, and the two shook hands. Despite his uncontrollable temper, however, Crawford was an able, efficient Treasury secretary who did much to alleviate the economic hardships wrought by the panic of 1819. To the many persons who had purchased public land in good times under the conventional terms of 25 percent down and 25 percent in each of the next three years and now found themselves in hard times unable to keep up the payments, Crawford offered an alternative to foreclosure. Under the Crawford plan, as approved by Congress, such debtors could either take up to eight years to complete the payments or pay off on time at a discount or gain clear title for whatever portion of land had already been purchased and forfeit the remainder (see also "John Quincy Adams, 6th President," "Opponents").

Secretary of War. John C. Calhoun (1782–1850), of South Carolina, served 1817–1825. A superb administrator who insisted on efficiency, he was able to reduce the cost of maintaining enlisted men by 34 percent. However, following the panic of 1819, Congress began insisting on deeper cuts in the war budget. He resisted, unsuccessfully, a congressionally mandated reduction in army manpower. With the president's approval, Calhoun constructed military outposts throughout the frontier acquired under the Louisiana Purchase. (see also "John Quincy Adams, 6th President" "Vice President"; "Andrew Jackson, 7th President," "Vice President"; "John Tyler, 10th President," "Cabinet: Secretary of State").

Attorney General. (1) Richard Rush (1780–1859, of Pennsylvania, served 1814–1817. A holdover from the Madison administration, he served simultaneously as acting secretary of state pending John Quincy Adams's return from abroad. As acting secretary, he negotiated the Rush-Bagot Agreement (see "Administration"). He resigned to become minister to Great Britain. He later served as Treasury secretary under John Quincy Adams and minister to France under James K. Polk. (2) William Wirt (1772–1834), of Virginia, served 1817–1829. He organized department records and initiated the practice of publishing the opinions of the attorney general. Renowned for his eloquence, he argued before the Supreme Court in such landmark cases as *McCulloch* v. *Maryland* (1819) and *Dartmouth College* v. *Woodward* (1819). He supported President Monroe's opinion that the use of federal funds for internal improvements (see "Administration") was unconstitutional. He stayed on in the John Quincy Adams administration.

Secretary of the Navy. (1) Benjamin Crowninshield (1772–1851), of Massachusetts, served 1815–1818. A holdover from the Madison administration, he resigned after being reprimanded by Monroe for a logistics foulup during a presidential inspection tour. (2) Smith Thompson (1768–1843), of New York, served 1819–1823. He resigned to accept appointment to the U.S. Supreme Court. (3) Samuel L. Southard (1787–1842), of New Jersey, served 1823–1829. He constructed naval hospitals; he stayed on in the John Quincy Adams administration.

ADMINISTRATION: March 4, 1817–March 3, 1825.

Era of Good Feelings. The phrase that came to be associated with the Monroe administration first appeared in the Boston *Columbian Centinel* to describe the euphoria attending President Monroe's triumphant tour of New England, once a Federalist stronghold, in 1817. During this brief period in American history when a single party commanded the affections of virtually all segments of society, the absence of partisan struggle did indeed generate, on the surface at least, an "era of good feelings." Monroe, who as the last Revolutionary War officer to reside in the White House was enormously popular, personified this national unity. But behind the facade of good feeling ticked the twin time bombs of slavery and protectionism, issues that would soon restore partisanship and ultimately lead to civil war.

First Seminole War, 1817–1818. Seminole Indians and fugitive slaves operating together out of sanctuaries in Spanish Florida frequently raided settlements in Georgia, massacring residents. When it became clear that Spain would do nothing to check these incursions, President Monroe assigned General Andrew Jackson to deal with the problem. Jackson promptly invaded Spanish Florida, crushed the Seminoles, destroyed their villages, and overthrew the Spanish governor. He also captured and executed two British citizens, Alexander Arbuthnot and Robert Ambrister, who had incited the Seminoles to commit atrocities against Americans. Because he had taken such bold action without specific authorization from the president, Secretary of War Calhoun and others urged that Jackson be reprimanded. However, no action was taken. The episode, while straining relations with Britain briefly, convinced Spain that the United States was capable of seizing Florida at will. This belief was a powerful inducement for Spain to sell the territory and thus paved the way for the Adams-Onís Treaty.

Rush-Bagot Agreement, 1818. This disarmament agreement between the United States and Great Britain demilitarized the Great Lakes. Acting Secretary of State Richard Rush and British Minister Charles Bagot negotiated the pact at Washington in 1817; it was ratified the next year.

Convention of 1818. This agreement between the United States and Great Britain granted American fishermen the right to work certain eastern Canadian waters and fixed the present U.S.-Canadian border from Minnesota to the Rockies.

Adams-Onís Treaty, 1819. Under its terms, Spain ceded Florida to the United States, which agreed to assume damage claims amounting to about $5 million that American citizens had lodged against Spain. It also fixed the southwestern boundary between the United States and Spanish territory at the Sabine River, thus leaving all of modern Texas under Spanish control. Spain also relinquished its claims to Oregon. U.S. Secretary of State John Quincy Adams and Spanish Minister Luis de Onís concluded the agreement.

Panic of 1819. Shoddy banking practices, fervid land speculation in the West, and renewed competition from European imports following the War of 1812 all combined to thrust the United States into its first major economic depression. The Monroe administration offered some relief in relaxing mortgage terms on land purchased from the government (see "Cabinet," Secretary of Treasury Crawford). The depression lasted until 1821.

Missouri Compromise, 1820. This law maintained the precarious balance between slave and free states by admitting Missouri to the Union as a slave state and Maine as a free state. It also provided that within the rest of the territory obtained through the Louisiana Purchase (see "Thomas Jefferson, 3d President," "Administration"), the section north of latitude 36°30' was to be free, that south of the line slave. Representative Henry Clay of Kentucky was architect of the compromise. President Monroe considered vetoing the measure on the ground that Congress lacked constitutional authority to ban slavery in the territories. He even drafted a veto message to that effect. But in the end the president signed the bill amid fears that a veto might have precipitated civil war.

Internal Improvements. President Monroe encouraged improved transportation in the West but believed that in the absence of a constitutional amendment specifically authorizing such federal intervention, construction of roads and canals must be left to the states. The West grew impatient over what residents considered legal hairsplitting, pointing out that the federal government had seen fit to construct lighthouses and other coastal improvements to facilitate trade along the Eastern Seaboard. Henry Clay denounced the apparent double standard. In 1822 Congress passed a bill authorizing federal construction and maintenance of toll booths on the Cumberland Road; the proceeds were to finance the westward extension of the highway. Monroe exercised his only veto in killing the measure.

Monroe Doctrine, 1823. Responding to concerns that Spain might attempt to recapture her former colonies in Latin America and that Russia might extend its claims in Alaska to include the Oregon territory, President Monroe delivered a message to Congress warning the European powers against intervention in the Western Hemisphere. The message came to be called the Monroe Doctrine. Great Britain, whose commercial interests were better served by an independent Latin America, had invited the United States to issue a joint declaration. However, Secretary of State Adams convinced the president to issue a unilateral statement in order to avoid the appearance of "a cockboat in the wake of the British man-of-war." Still, it was universally understood that to enforce the Monroe Doctrine the United States would need to rely on British sea power. In asserting that "the American continents . . . are henceforth not to be considered as subjects for future colonization by any European powers," Monroe laid down what was to become the cornerstone of American foreign policy for the rest of the nineteenth century. As modified by the Roosevelt Corollary (see "Theodore Roosevelt, 26th President," "Administration") and the Good Neighbor Policy (see "Franklin Delano Roosevelt, 32nd President," "Administration"), the Monroe Doctrine continues to be an integral part of American foreign policy.

States Admitted to the Union: Mississippi (1817), Illinois (1818), Alabama (1819), Maine (1820), Missouri (1821).

SUPREME COURT APPOINTMENT: Smith Thompson (1768–1843), of New York, served as associate justice 1823–1843. Only reluctantly did Thompson give up his post as secretary of the navy to accept appointment to the Court, for he wanted to run for president in 1824. He joined those opposing the nationalism of Chief Justice John Marshall.

RANKING IN 1962 HISTORIANS POLL: Monroe ranked eighteenth of 31 presidents, seventh of the 12 "average" presidents; ranked above Hoover, below Van Buren.

RETIREMENT: March 4, 1825–July 4, 1831. Monroe remained three weeks at the White House following the inauguration of his successor, John Quincy Adams, because Mrs. Monroe was too ill to travel. The Monroes then retired to their recently built estate Oak Hill in Loudoun County, Virginia. The house had been designed by former president Thomas Jefferson. Monroe entered retirement some $75,000 in debt. He pressed the federal government for payment of tens of thousands of dollars due him for past service, but only after a protracted struggle did he get from Congress part of the total. In 1826 he was named to the board of regents of the University of Virginia. Three years later he represented the Loudoun-Fairfax region at the Virginia Constitutional Convention in Richmond and was elected president of that body. With the death of his wife in 1830, Monroe could no longer bear to remain at Oak Hill. He moved north to live with his daughter and son-in-law, the Gouverneurs, in New York City. He made his last public appearance in November 1830 at a Tammany Hall celebration of the overthrow of Charles X of France. In retirement Monroe began but never completed his memoirs as well as a book comparing the United States with ancient Greece and Rome.

DEATH: July 4, 1831, about 3:15 P.M., New York City. Monroe developed a nagging cough, perhaps a sign of tuberculosis, and steadily weakened during his final months. Retaining his faculties until the end, he died peacefully from heart failure, the third of the first five presidents to expire on the Fourth of July (John Adams and Jefferson had died exactly five years before). On July 7, following eulogies at New York City Hall and funeral services at St. Paul's Episcopal Church, thousands of mourners followed the hearse in procession up Broadway to the Marble Cemetery on Second Street, while church bells tolled and guns boomed from the Battery once for every year of the president's life. His body remained there in the Gouverneur family vault until 1858, when it was removed to Hollywood Cemetery in Richmond, Virginia. In his last will and testament, executed in May 1831, Monroe left $6,000 to his daughter Mrs. Maria Gouverneur to compensate for his having already given real estate to his other daughter, Mrs. Eliza Hay. The residue of his estate was to be divided evenly between the two daughters.

MONROE PRAISED: "Turn his soul wrong side outwards and there is not a speck on it."[8]—Thomas Jefferson, 1787

"The old notions of republican simplicity are fast wearing away, and the public taste becomes more and more gratified with public amusements and parades. Mr. Monroe, however, still retains his plain and gentle manners; and is in every respect a very estimable man."[9]—Justice Joseph Story

"Tho' not brilliant, few men were his equals in wisdom, firmness and devotion to the country. He had a wonderful intellectual patience; and could above all men, that I ever knew, when called on to decide an important point, hold the subject immovably fixed under his attention, until he had mastered it in all of its relations. It was mainly to this admirable quality that he owed his highly accurate judgment. I have known many much more rapid in reaching a conclusion, but few with a certainty so unerring."[10]—Vice President John C. Calhoun, 1831

"There behold him for a term of eight years, strengthening his country for defense by a system of combined fortifications, military and naval, sustaining her rights, her dignity and honor abroad; soothing her dissension, and conciliating her acerbities at home; controlling by a firm though peaceful policy the hostile spirit of the European Alliance against Republican South America extorting by the mild compulsion of reason, the shores of the Pacific from the stipulated acknowledgment of Spain; and leading back the imperial autocrat of the North, to his lawful boundaries, from his hastily asserted dominion over the Southern Ocean. Thus strengthening and consolidating the federative edifice of his country's Union, till he was entitled to say, like Augustus Caesar of his imperial city, that he had found her built of brick and left her constructed of marble."[11]—John Quincy Adams, 1831

MONROE CRITICIZED: "If Mr. Monroe should ever fill the Chair of Government he may (and it is presumed he would be well enough disposed) let the French Minister frame his Speeches. . . . There is abundant evidence of his being a mere tool in the hands of the French government."[12]—George Washington, c. 1797

"Virginia's misfortunes may be comprised in one short sentence; 'Monroe is elected Governor!'"[13]—*Richmond Federalist*, 1799

"[Monroe] is one of the most improper and incompetent that could be selected [for president]. Naturally dull and stupid; extremely illiterate; indecisive to a degree that would be incredible to one who did not know him; pusillanimous, and of course hypocritical; has no opinion on any subject and will always be under the government of the worst men. . . . As a lawyer, Monroe was far below mediocrity. He never rose to the honor of trying a cause of the value of a hundred pounds."[14]—Aaron Burr, 1815

"Mr. Monroe has just been re-elected with apparent unanimity, but he has not the slightest influence in Congress. His career was considered as closed. There was nothing further to be expected by him or from him."[15]—Henry Clay, 1821

"[Monroe was] one of those respectable mediocrities in high public station, with whom people are apt to sympathize in their troubles, especially when unnecessarily attacked and humiliated by persons of greatly superior ability."[16]—Journalist, political leader Carl Schurz

MONROE QUOTES: "The earth was given to mankind to support the greatest number of which it is capable, and no tribe or people have a right to withhold from the wants of others more than is necessary for their own support and comfort."[17]—1817

"Surely our government may get on and prosper without the existence of parties. I have always considered their existence as the curse of the country, of which we had sufficient proof, more especially in the late war. Besides, how keep them alive, and in action? The causes which exist in other countries do not here. We have no distinct orders."[18]—1822

"The condition of the aborigines [Indians] within our limits, and especially those who are within the limits of any of the states, merits particular attention. . . . To remove them from it, the territory on which they now reside, by force, even with a view to their own security and happiness would be revolting to humanity and utterly unjustifiable. Between the limits of our present States and Territories and the Rocky Mountains and Mexico there is a vast territory, to which they might be invited with inducements which might be successful."[19]

BOOK BY MONROE: *A View of the Conduct of the Executive in the Foreign Affairs of the United States* (1797).

BOOKS ABOUT MONROE: Ammon, Harry. *James Monroe: The Quest for National Identity*. New York: McGraw-Hill, 1971.

Cresson, W.P. *James Monroe*. Chapel Hill: University of North Carolina Press, 1946.

Styron, Arthur. *The Last of the Cocked Hats: James Monroe and the Virginia Dynasty*. Norman: University of Oklahoma Press, 1945.

NOTES:

1 Harry Ammon, *James Monroe: The Quest for National Identity*, New York: McGraw-Hill, 1971, p. 373.

2 Ibid., p. 268.

3 Ibid., p. 2.

4 Ibid.

5 Ibid., p. 28.

6 W. P. Cresson, *James Monroe*, Chapel Hill, N.C.: University of North Carolina Press, 1946, pp. 252–253.

7 Ibid., p. 454.

8 Julian P. Boyd, ed., *The Papers of Thomas Jefferson*, Princeton, N.J.: Princeton University Press, 1950– , vol. XI, p. 97.

9 Cresson, p. 370.

10 Ammon, p. 369.

11 Ibid., p. 573.

12 Ammon, p. 169.

13 Arthur Styron, *The Last of the Cocked Hats: James Monroe and the Virginia Dynasty*, Norman, Okla.: University of Oklahoma Press, 1945, p. 221.

14 Ibid., pp. 338–339.

15 Ammon, p. 472.

16 Richard Kenin and Justin Wintle, eds., *Dictionary of Biographical Quotation*, New York: Knopf, 1978, p. 544.

17 Ammon, p. 536.

18 Ibid., p. 508.

19 Cresson, p. 466.

JOHN QUINCY ADAMS

NAME: John Quincy Adams. He was named after his great-grandfather Colonel John Quincy, Speaker of the Massachusetts Assembly, member of the Governor's Council, and militia officer. John Quincy died soon after the birth of his namesake. His daughter, John Quincy Adams's maternal grandmother, suggested naming the infant in his memory.

PHYSICAL DESCRIPTION: Adams was 5 feet 7 inches tall and weighed about 175 pounds. He had penetrating black eyes. By the time he became president he was almost completely bald. He dressed plainly and without great care. He spoke in a high, shrill voice. His health generally was poor. He frequently complained of various aches and pains. Insomnia, indigestion, nervous anxiety, and eye discomfort chronically plagued him. Intermittently throughout his life he wrestled with bouts of mental depression, what he called "uncontrollable dejection of spirits" and "a sluggish carelessness of life." He admitted having at times "an imaginary wish that [life] were terminated."

PERSONALITY: Because he was both introspective and uncommonly candid in admitting his own shortcomings, Adams remains the best source for a description of his personality. "I am a man of reserved, cold, austere and forbidding manners," he confided to his diary, "my political adversaries say, a gloomy misanthropist, and my personal enemies, an unsocial savage. With a knowledge of the actual defect in my character, I have not the pliability to reform it."[1] In a letter to his wife he admitted, "I never was and never shall be what is commonly termed a popular man, being as little qualified by nature, education, or habit for the arts of a courtier as I am desirous of being courted by others. . . . I am certainly not intentionally repulsive in my manners and deportment, and in my public station I never made myself inaccessible to any human being. But I have no powers of fascination; none of the honey which the profligate proverb says is the true fly-catcher."[2] Ironically, a man famous for his cold demeanor was the most successful American diplomat of his time. In the ticklish art of negotiation, Adams assiduously checked his temper and performed the diplomatic amenities.

ANCESTORS: Through his maternal line, John Quincy Adams descended from King Edward III (1312–1377) of England. For his paternal ancestry, see "John Adams, 2d President" "Ancestors"; see also "Name".

FATHER: John Adams (1735–1826), second president. The only president whose son also became president, John Adams died while John Quincy Adams was in the White House.

MOTHER: Abigail Smith Adams (1744–1818). The only woman to be wife of one president and mother of another, she died while John Quincy Adams was secretary of state (see "John Adams," "Marriage").

SIBLINGS: The second of four children to live to maturity, Adams had one older sister and two younger brothers—Mrs. Abigail Smith of New York, whose husband was secretary to John Adams in London and later served in the U.S. House; Charles Adams, a lawyer, who died of alcoholism at 30; Thomas Boylston Adams, a lawyer, who served as secretary to John Quincy Adams abroad (see "John Adams," "Children").

COLLATERAL RELATIVES: John Quincy Adams was a second cousin once removed to Samuel Adams, patriot and signer of the Declaration of Independence, and a third cousin once removed to his own mother, Abigail Smith Adams.

CHILDREN: Adams had three sons to live to maturity.

George Washington Adams (1801–1829), lawyer. Born at Berlin in what is now Germany, he was brilliant, though unstable, and considered a likely candidate to carry on the Adams tradition of national public service. He graduated from Harvard, studied law in the Boston office of Daniel Webster, and in 1826 was elected to the Massachusetts legislature. Unfortunately, he developed a debilitating nervous condition and became careless in his habits. He neglected his law practice, ran up huge debts that his father had to pay off, and got a girl pregnant. He began hallucinating and became paranoid. Aboard a steamer en route to New York he accused other passengers of plotting against him. A short time later, he either jumped or accidentally fell overboard. His body washed up on City Island in Long Island Sound six weeks later.

John Adams II (1803–1834), presidential aide. Born on the Fourth of July at Quincy, Massachusetts, he attended Harvard but was expelled in his senior year for taking part in a student riot. He studied law under his father, who, upon becoming president in 1825, brought him to the White House as his private secretary. Fiercely loyal to his father, young Adams got into a scuffle with Russell Jarvis, an editorial writer for the antiadministration Washington *Daily Telegraph*, in 1828. In response to certain disparaging remarks young Adams had made about him, Jarvis physically assaulted him in the Capitol Rotunda, and Adams fought back. A House committee appointed to investigate the incident voted to censure, but not punish, Jarvis for his action. After President Adams's defeat by Andrew Jackson in 1828, John Adams II ran a Washington flour mill owned by his father. But his health soon failed, and he died suddenly in 1834. His loss, coming as it did just five years after the drowning of his older brother, was yet another source of anguish to the former president. "A more honest soul, or more tender heart never breathed on the face of the earth,"[3] John Quincy Adams wrote of him in his grief.

Charles Francis Adams (1807–1886), diplomat, public official, author. Born in Boston, he from age two to eight grew up in St. Petersburg while his father was minister to Russia. In 1815 he traveled by carriage with his mother from the Russian capital to Paris amid the tumult of the fall of Napoleon. Educated in England and at Harvard, he studied law briefly but soon decided upon a literary career. Eventually he edited the papers of his father and his grandfather, President John Adams, as well as the letters of his grandmother, Abigail Adams. In 1837 he published *Reflections upon the Present State of the Currency*. Having come to share his father's opposition to slavery, he spoke out for abolition as a member of the Massachusetts legislature 1840–1845 and in 1848 accepted the vice presidential nomination of the Free Soil party on the ticket with former president Martin Van Buren. He served one term 1859–1861, in the U.S. House. Appointed minister to Great Britain, 1861–1868, by President Lincoln, he was the third generation of Adamses to serve at the Court of St. James. It was largely through his efforts that Britain remained officially neutral during the Civil War despite widespread sentiment in that country in favor of recognizing the independence of the Confederacy. In 1871 President Grant appointed him to the international commission formed to settle damage claims arising out of Britain's aid to the South during the Civil War. Adams won for the United States a $15 million indemnity from Great Britain. In 1872 Adams was touted as the most likely candidate to challenge Grant's reelection. At the convention of Liberal Republicans in Cincinnati that year, he led on the first five ballots but ultimately lost the nomination to Horace Greeley.

SUBSEQUENT DESCENDANTS:

Charles Francis Adams, Jr. (1835–1915). A grandson of President John Quincy Adams and great-grandson of President John Adams, he was a railroad executive and historian. He exposed corruption in the railroad industry following the Civil War and served as chairman of the Massachusetts Board of Railroad Commissioners during 1872–1879. In 1884 he became president of the Union Pacific Railroad but was ousted six years later by Jay Gould. He returned to Quincy, Massachusetts, where he promoted educational reform. His writings include *Chapters of Erie* (1871), *Individuality in Politics* (1880), *Life of Charles Francis Adams*, his father (1900), and his autobiography (1916).

Henry Adams (1838–1918). A grandson of President John Quincy Adams and a great-grandson of President John Adams, he was a noted historian. During 1870–1876 he was professor of history at Harvard University and editor of the *North American Review*. His works include biographies of Albert Gallatin (1879) and John Randolph (1882), a nine-volume history of the United States during the administrations of Presidents Jefferson and Madison (1889–1891), and his celebrated autobiography *The Education of Henry Adams* (1906).

Brooks Adams (1848–1927). A grandson of President John Quincy Adams and great-grandson of President John Adams, he was a noted historian who warned of the evils of unchecked capitalism and predicted the ultimate decline of the United States. His works include *The Law of Civilization and Decay* (1895), *America's Economic Supremacy* (1900), and *The Theory of Social Revolutions* (1913). He correctly predicted that by 1950 the United States and Russia would be the two major powers in the world.

Charles Francis Adams III (1866–1954). A great-grandson of President John Quincy Adams and great-great-grandson of President John Adams, he served as secretary of the navy under President Hoover.

Abigail Adams Homans (1879–1974). A great-granddaughter of President John Quincy Adams and great-great-granddaughter of President John Adams, she was until her death at 94 the delightfully iconoclastic matriarch of the Adams family in Boston. Perhaps her most famous remark occured during a visit from Lady Bird Johnson. While conducting the First Lady through the restored homes of her presidential ancestors, Mrs. Homans, then 88, accidentally knocked over some antique glassware. The room fell uncomfortably silent for a moment until she quipped, "Hell, I hope it isn't historic."

BIRTH: Adams was born on July 11, 1767, in Braintree (now Quincy), Massachusetts.

CHILDHOOD: Literally a child of the American Revolution, Adams was a brilliant, precocious lad who grew up amid more excitement than perhaps any other president. At age eight, he and his mother witnessed the Battle of Bunker Hill from a vantage point atop Penn's Hill. With his father away much of the time working on behalf of the rebel cause, he, the oldest son, took seriously his responsibilities as the man in the family. It was a frightening time for a young boy amid the prospect of being, as he wrote, "butchered in cold blood, or taken and carried into Boston as hostages by any foraging or marauding detachment"[4] of British soldiers. From age 10 to 17, young Adams lived in Europe, except for a brief return home in 1779. Because he spoke French fluently, he in 1781 was chosen to serve as secretary to Francis Dana on his mission to Russia (French was the language of diplomacy at St. Petersburg). Dana had hoped to convince Catherine II to recognize American independence but failed even to win an official audience. Young Adams summed up his impressions of St. Petersburg in one sentence: "There is nobody here but slaves and princes."[5] While Dana remained in the Russian capital, 15-year-old John Quincy Adams joined his father at The Hague, having traveled five months, much of the time alone, by way of Helsinki, Stockholm, Göteborg, Copenhagen, Hamburg, Bremen, and Amsterdam. By the time he returned to America in 1785, John Quincy Adams was an urbane, mature young man with more first-hand knowledge of world affairs than many American politicians twice his age.

EDUCATION: With regular school suspended in Braintree during the Revolution, young John Quincy Adams learned the fundamentals at home under the tutelage of his parents and a pair of his father's law clerks, John Thaxter and Nathan Rice. By age 10 he already was reading Shakespeare. He received his first formal education at the Passy Academy outside Paris, where, together with the grandsons of Benjamin Franklin, he studied fencing, dance, music, and art in addition to the classics. With his father he worked through problems in algebra, geometry, trigonometry, and calculus. In Amsterdam, his father enrolled him in a Latin School, but he disliked it there and in 1781 transferred to Leyden University, where he continued his study of the classics. By the time he returned to America in 1785 Adams had mastered Latin, Greek, French, Dutch, and, to a lesser extent, Spanish. In order to qualify for advanced placement as a junior at Harvard, Adams studied for a time under his uncle the Reverend John Shaw in Haverhill, Massachusetts. At Harvard 1785–1787, Adams felt somewhat out of place after having spent most of his formative years abroad with few American friends. He took no part in campus mischief. He was a member of the Phi Beta Kappa Society and played flute in the band. He graduated second of 51 students in the class of 1787. At commencement exercises he delivered the senior English oration, entitled "The Importance and Necessity of Public Faith to the Well-Being of a Nation." Although Adams was highly critical of his teachers at Harvard, he never regretted attending college there. Upon his return from Europe he had a rather inflated idea of his own importance and place in society. He credited his experience at Harvard with reducing "my opinion of myself and of my future prospects to a nearer level with truth."[6] During 1787–1790 Adams studied law under Theophilus Parsons at Newburyport, Massachusetts. In his spare time he learned shorthand and read voraciously everything from ancient history to popular literature. He particularly enjoyed Thomas Jefferson's *Notes on Virginia* and called Fielding's *Tom Jones* "one of the best novels in the language." Adams was admitted to the bar in July 1790.

RELIGION: Unitarian branch of congregationalism. Adams formally joined no church until after he became president, at which time he took his first communion at the Unitarian Church in Quincy, Massachusetts. "I have at all times," he wrote late in life, "been a sincere believer in the existence of a Supreme Creator of the world, of an immortal principle within myself, responsible to that Creator for my conduct upon Earth, and of the divine mission of the Crucified Savior, proclaiming immortal life and preaching peace on earth, good will to men, the natural equality of all mankind, and the law, 'Thou shalt love thy neighbor as thyself.'"[7] Indeed, Adams was a devout Christian. He attended church regularly and often worshipped twice on Sunday. While president he frequently was seen at morning services in the Unitarian church and in the afternoon at the Presbyterian church. All his life, before retiring each night, he recited the familiar bedtime prayer, beginning, "Now I lay me down to sleep." In the morning, he invariably read several chapters of the Bible before starting his day. Adams believed that Christ was superhuman but remained unconvinced of his divinity. Adams also was skeptical about the virginity of Mary. And he was unable to accept as undisputed fact the various miracles referred to in the Bible.

RECREATION: Adams enjoyed shooting billiards (he installed the first billiard table in the White House), reading, keeping a diary, observing nature, domesticating wild plants, walking, horseback riding, swimming, the theater, and fine wines. He had a very discriminating palate. It is said that at a wine sampling following dinner one night, he correctly identified 11 of 14 Madeiras. He vented his feelings in a diary, which he kept assiduously from age 17. "There has perhaps not been another individual of the human race," he wrote of himself, "of whose daily existence from early childhood to fourscore years has been noted down with his own hand so minutely as mine."[8] Indeed, from age 29 to 49, he wrote something in his diary every single day. Adams kept fit with a daily regimen of exercise. As president he walked to the Capitol and back to the White House often before dawn. In warm weather he went skinny-dipping in the Potomac early in the morning. An expert swimmer, he at 58 swam the width of the river, about a mile, in one hour. Once he nearly drowned during a sudden squall. He resumed swimming the Potomac, though less frequently, when he returned to Washington as a congressman. He took his last nude dip in the river at age 79.

EARLY ROMANCE: Adams's first love was an actress. He was 14, she about the same age, when he first saw her perform as part of the company at the Bois de Boulogne outside Paris. He never worked up the courage to go backstage to meet her but suffered in stoic silence for two years. Even after his ardor had cooled, she appeared in his dreams for many years. "Of all the ungratified longings that I ever suffered," he admitted, "that of being acquainted with her, merely to tell her how much I adored her, was the most intense."[9]

Nancy Hazen. Adams met Nancy Hazen when both were boarding with the Reverend John Shaw in Haverhill in 1785. He was 18, she 17. Although she was not especially beautiful, Adams was attracted to her mature manner, good figure, and dazzling eyes. It seems to have been a casual romance that quickly flickered out.

Mary Frazier. Adams was more deeply in love with Mary Frazier than with any other woman prior to his marriage. They met in Newburyport while he was studying law under Theophilus Parsons in the late 1780s. He was 22, she 18. He was so taken with the blond, blue-eyed Miss Frazier that he confided to a friend that all his hopes of future happiness depended on her. But, alas, his mother convinced him that as a struggling young lawyer he was unable properly to support a wife. The young lovers agreed to go their separate ways. In 1802 Mary married Daniel Sargent, a friend of John Quincy. Two years later Adams learned that she had died.

MARRIAGE: Adams, 30, married Louisa Catherine Johnson, 22, on July 26, 1797, at All Hallows Barking parish in London, England. Born in London (she was the only foreign-born First Lady) on February 12, 1775, the daughter of Joshua Johnson, an American merchant, and Catherine Nuth Johnson, an Englishwoman, Louisa grew up in London and Nantes, France, where the family took refuge during the American Revolution. It was in Nantes that four-year-old Louisa first met her future husband, who at 12 was traveling through France with his father. When she had blossomed into a pretty, slender young lady with delicate features, reddish blond hair, and brown eyes, she again met Adams, this time in London, where her father had been appointed American consul. Adams at first showed interest in her older sister Nancy but soon settled on Louisa. His father, John Adams, then president of the United States overcame initial objections to his son marrying a foreigner and welcomed his daughter-in-law into the family. When her father was forced into bankruptcy, President John Adams appointed him U.S. director of stamps. Louisa Adams was sickly, plagued by migraine headaches and frequent fainting spells. She had several miscarriages. As First Lady she became reclusive and depressed. For a time she regretted ever having married into the Adams family, the men of which she found cold and insensitive to women. In fact, during her first year in the White House, she began, but never completed, an autobiography in which she recited a litany of abuse she had suffered as Mrs. Adams. The untimely deaths of her two oldest sons added to her burden. "Our union has not been without its trials," John Quincy Adams conceded on his fourteenth wedding anniversary. He acknowledged "many differences of sentiment, of tastes, and of opinions in regard to domestic economy, and to the education of children, between us." But, he added, "she always has been a faithful and affectionate wife, and a careful, tender, indulgent, and watchful mother to our children."[10] After her husband's death in 1848, Louisa Adams remained in Washington until her death on May 15, 1852. She was buried next to him in Quincy.

MILITARY SERVICE: None.

CAREER BEFORE THE PRESIDENCY: Following his admission to the bar in 1790, Adams opened a law office in Boston but attracted few clients.

Minister to the Netherlands, 1794–1797. At least partially to reward Adams for political articles he had written in support of the administration and because he was among the few Americans familiar with Holland and fluent in the Dutch language, President George Washington appointed him minister to the Netherlands in 1794. His primary mission was to see that payments on the debt arising from Dutch loans to America during the Revolutionary War proceeded properly. Adams also observed the course of the French Revolution and sent back insightful reports (formal ones to the secretary of state and informal observations to his father, then vice president).

Minister to Prussia, 1797–1801. President Washington had appointed Adams minister to Portugal, but before his arrival in Lisbon he received word that his father, now president, had changed the appointment to minister to Prussia. In Berlin, Adams concluded the Prussian-American treaty of 1799, a commercial pact, and continued to send back perceptive reports on European developments.

Massachusetts State Senator, 1802. Returning to the United States in 1801, he was elected the next year to represent Suffolk County in the state senate. He unsuccessfully promoted apportionment reform. In 1802 he was the Federalist candidate for the greater Boston seat in the U.S. House; he carried the city, but by a margin insufficient to offset losses in the outlying areas. He lost narrowly (1,899–1,840) to Dr. William Eustis.

U.S. Senator (Federalist-Massachusetts), 1803–1808. Elected to the U.S. Senate over Timothy Pickering, Adams was nominally a Federalist but came to support the Republican administration of President Thomas Jefferson. He was the only member of his party in either house to support the Louisiana Purchase; he also voted for the imposition of the embargo (see "Thomas Jefferson, 3d President," "Administration"). In perhaps his most significant achievement in the Senate, he won rejection of the King-Hawkesbury Convention of 1803. Its defeat ultimately preserved for the United States what is now the northern half of Washington State, the northern tip of Idaho, the northern third of Montana, the northern half of North Dakota, and the northwest corner of Minnesota. Senator Adams voted in the minority against the Twelfth Amendment to the Constitution, providing for the separate election of president and vice president. He unsuccessfully promoted a federal plan of internal improvements. Because of his support for the Jefferson administration, the Federalist-dominated Massachusetts legislature voted (248–213) to replace him with James Lloyd, Jr. Adams resigned his seat in June 1808.

Minister to Russia, 1809–1814. Appointed by President Madison to be the first U.S. minister to Russia, Adams maintained very cordial relations with Czar Alexander, whom he admired for his resistance to Napoleonic domination. He persuaded the czar to grant neutral American ships access to Russian ports and to use his influence to secure the release of American ships then under detention in Denmark. While in St. Petersburg, Adams was offered a seat on the U.S. Supreme Court but declined. During Napoleon's ill-fated invasion of Russia in 1812, Minister Adams sent back to Washington vivid accounts of this turning point in European history and rejoiced in Russia's ultimate triumph.

Chief Negotiator of Treaty of Ghent, 1814. President Madison appointed Adams to head the five-man American delegation to negotiate a peace agreement with Great Britain ending the War of 1812. Assisted by Treasury Secretary Albert Gallatin, Senator James A. Bayard of Delaware, House Speaker Henry Clay, and Minister to Sweden Jonathan Russell, Adams negotiated the Treaty of Ghent, settling none of the disputes that caused the war but restoring territory to the status quo prior to the outbreak of hostilities.

Minister to Great Britain, 1815–1817. Assisted by Albert Gallatin and Henry Clay, Minister Adams concluded with Great Britain the Commercial Convention of 1815. He also began discussions on the demilitarization of the Great Lakes and fishing rights.

Secretary of State, 1817–1825. Appointed by President James Monroe, Adams was among the most gifted and accomplished secretaries of state. With Britain he secured the Convention of 1818, establishing U.S. fishing rights off certain Canadian coasts and fixing the present U.S.-Canadian border from Minnesota to the Rockies. With Spain he concluded the Adams-Onís Treaty (1819), transferring Spanish Florida to the United States, fixing the southwestern boundary of the United States at the Sabine River, and removing Spanish claims to Oregon. He persuaded President Monroe to withhold diplomatic recognition of Latin American nations until they had stabilized sufficiently to maintain their newly won independence. During the formulation of the Monroe Doctrine (see "James Monroe, 5th President," "Administration"), Secretary Adams was the foremost proponent of a unilateral American declaration warning European nations not to interfere in the affairs of the Western Hemisphere. Against the advice of such prominent figures as former presidents Jefferson and Madison, who advocated accepting Britain's invitation to issue a joint declaration, Monroe came to agree with Secretary Adams's assertion that "it would be more candid, as well as more dignified, to avow our principles explicitly . . . than to come in as a cockboat in the wake of the British man-of-war."[11] Within the department, Adams organized the diplomatic correspondence files and improved accounting procedures. He refused to fill vacancies with patronage appointments and instead drew about him a capable staff.

PRESIDENTAL NOMINATION, 1824: At a time when the nominating caucus had fallen into disrepute but before the appearance of national political conventions, the presidential candidates came forward on the basis of regional endorsement. No party labels were used. In February 1824 Adams supporters held a mass rally at Boston's Faneuil Hall, and on June 10 the Massachusetts legislature formally nominated him for president. The rest of New England quickly lined up behind him. By this time the Kentucky legislature had already nominated native son Representative Henry Clay, and other western states had flocked to his banner. Similarly, in August 1822 the Tennessee legislature nominated Andrew Jackson of that state; rallies in several western cities confirmed his popularity. Only Treasury Secretary William H. Crawford of Georgia looked to the discredited congressional caucus system for support. On February 14, 1824, a rump caucus consisting of less than a third of those eligible to attend overwhelmingly endorsed Crawford for president. John C. Calhoun offered himself as a presidential candidate for a time but withdrew to run as vice president.

OPPONENTS:

Andrew Jackson (1767–1845), of Tennessee. His frontier roots and success on the battlefield made him the most popular figure in the race. Of the four candidates, he alone had substantial support outside his regional power base. He was elected as the seventh president in 1828.

William H. Crawford (1772–1834), of Georgia. Born in Amherst County, Virginia, and raised in South Carolina and Georgia, Crawford became a lawyer and in 1803 was elected to the Georgia legislature. From 1807 to 1813 he served in the U.S. Senate, the last year as president pro tem. In 1813 President

Madison appointed him minister to France and, two years later, named him to succeed James Monroe as secretary of war. In 1816 he was transferred to become secretary of the Treasury. That year Crawford emerged as Monroe's principal rival for the Republican presidential nomination. He remained at the Treasury in the Monroe administration, during which time he performed ably but alienated many, including the president. During the 1824 campaign, Crawford suffered a paralytic stroke from which he never completely recovered. Despite poor health, however, he continued to harbor presidential ambitions. He spent his last years in Georgia as a state circuit court judge.

Henry Clay (1777–1852), of Kentucky. Born in Hanover County, Virginia, Clay, a lawyer, was largely self-educated. He settled in Lexington, Kentucky, as a young man and soon entered politics. After serving in the state legislature 1803–1806 and 1807–1810 and filling unexpired terms in the U.S. Senate 1806–1807 and 1810–1811, he was elected to the U.S. House and promptly chosen Speaker. He served there 1811–1821 and 1823–1825. He later returned to the Senate 1831–1842 and 1849–1852. Clay was a leading War Hawk during the War of 1812 and helped negotiate the Treaty of Ghent, 1814, ending that conflict. He devised and championed the American System, a program of high tariffs and federally sponsored internal improvements. His persuasive oratory and tireless efforts to defuse a series of sectional crises that despite his leadership ultimately led to the Civil War earned him the nickname the Great Compromiser. He played key roles in passage of the Missouri Compromise (see "James Monroe, 5th President," "Administration"), the Compromise Tariff of 1833 (see "Andrew Jackson, 7th President," "Administration"), and the Compromise of 1850 (see "Millard Fillmore, 13th President," "Administration"). President John Quincy Adams appointed him secretary of state in 1825. Clay was the Whig presidential nominee in 1832 and in 1844 but lost to Andrew Jackson and James K. Polk, respectively.

CAMPAIGN AND THE ISSUES, 1824: The campaign turned on sectional rivalries and the strong personalities of the four candidates. Adams's apparent aloofness and formal manner compared unfavorably with Jackson's down-home style. All four candidates supported in varying degrees a protective tariff. A federal program of internal improvements also had wide appeal. Slavery had not yet become a divisive issue. Adams enjoyed the solid support of his home base of New England and the manufacturing interests. He also had a large following in New York; among those campaigning for him there was 27-year-old Thurlow Weed, later a political boss in the Whig and Republican parties. Jackson and Crawford drew from the South, Jackson and Clay divided the west.

ELECTION AS PRESIDENT, 1824:

Popular Vote. Jackson, 152,933 (42%); Adams, 115,696 (32%); Clay, 47,136 (13%); Crawford, 46,979 (13%).

Electoral Vote: Jackson, 99; Adams, 84; Crawford, 41; Clay, 37.

States Carried: Jackson won the majority of electoral votes in 11 states—Alabama, Illinois, Indiana, Louisiana, Maryland, Mississippi, New Jersey, North Carolina, Pennsylvania, South Carolina, Tennessee. Adams won the majority of electoral votes in seven states—Connecticut, Maine, Massachusetts, New Hampshire, New York, Rhode Island, Vermont. Crawford won the majority of electoral votes in three states—Delaware, Georgia, Virginia. Clay won the majority of electoral votes in three states—Kentucky, Missouri, Ohio.

John C. Calhoun of South Carolina was elected vice president, having received 182 electoral votes, to 79 scattered among five other candidates.

Because none of the four presidential candidates received a majority of the electoral vote, the election was thrown into the House of Representatives. In accordance with the Twelfth Amendment to the Constitution, the House was directed to choose the president from the top three electoral vote getters; thus Henry Clay was dropped from consideration. Clay thereupon supported Adams. On February 9, 1825, the House, with each state casting one vote based on the majority of its delegation, elected Adams president on the first ballot with the barest majority. Adams carried 13 states—the seven states he had won in November, the three states that had gone for Clay, plus Illinois, Maryland, and Louisiana (former Jackson states). Jackson held on to just seven states— Alabama, Indiana, Mississippi, New Jersey, Pennsylvania, South Carolina, Tennessee. Crawford carried four states—his original three plus North Carolina, a former Jackson state.

DEFEATED FOR REELECTION: See "Andrew Jackson, 7th President," for the presidential campaign of 1828.

INAUGURAL ADDRESS: March 4, 1825. ". . . Ten years of peace, at home and abroad, have assuaged the animosities of political contention and blended into harmony the most discordant elements of public opinion. There still remains one effort of magnanimity, one sacrifice of prejudice and passion, to be made by the individuals throughout the nation who have heretofore followed the standards of political party. It is that of discarding every remnant of rancor against each other, of embracing as countrymen and friends, and of yielding to talents and virtue alone that confidence which in times of contention for principle was bestowed only upon those who bore the badge of party communion. . . ."

VICE PRESIDENT: John C. Calhoun (1782–1850), of South Carolina, served 1825– 1832. Born in Abbeville, South Carolina, Calhoun, a lawyer, served in the South Carolina legislature 1808–1810 and the U.S. House 1811–1817. As chairman of the House Foreign Affairs Committee, he was a leading War Hawk during the War of 1812. He served as secretary of war 1817–1825 under President Monroe. As vice president under Adams, he early alienated the president by his behind-the-scenes attempts to place supporters in key posts. Calhoun was reelected in 1828 (see "Andrew Jackson," "Vice President").

CABINET:

Secretary of State. Henry Clay (1777–1852), of Kentucky, served 1825– 1829. Clay's support of Adams over fellow-westerner Jackson in the House presidential runoff election in 1824 and President Adams's prompt appointment of Clay as secretary of state smacked of a political deal to Andrew Jackson and his followers. Although both Clay and Adams denied any collusion, the persistent charge of a "corrupt bargain" dogged the administration. Clay answered the vituperative attacks of one of his severest critics, John Randolph of Roanoke, with a challenge to a duel. The two squared off with pistols, exchanged fire, but missed each other. Secretary Clay oversaw completion of routine commercial treaties with the Scandinavian countries and certain Latin American nations. On Indian affairs, Clay was a hopeless victim of the blind prejudice of his times. He saw native Americans as worthless, incorrigible, doomed savages. "I believe they are destined to extinction," he asserted at one cabinet meeting. "Although I would not use or countenance inhumanity towards them, I do not think them, as a race, worth preserving. . . . Their disappearance from the human family will be no great loss to the world."[12]

Secretary of the Treasury. Richard Rush (1790–1859), of Pennsylvania, served 1825–1829. He had served as attorney general under Presidents Madison and Monroe and as acting secretary of state had negotiated the Rush-Bagot Agreement (see "James Monroe, 5th President," "Administration"). He was minister to Great Britain when Adams offered him the Treasury post. A close friend of the president, he ran unsuccessfully for vice president on the ticket with Adams in 1828. He later served as minister to France under President Polk.

Secretary of War. (1) James Barbour (1775–1842), of Virginia, served 1825–1828. He was a longtime advocate of states' rights. He resigned to become minister to Great Britain. (2) Peter B. Porter (1773–1844), of New York, served 1828–1829. He was a veteran general of the War of 1812.

Attorney General. William Wirt (1772–1834), of Virginia, served 1817–1829. A holdover from the Monroe administration, he was a leading opponent of Adams's program of internal improvements. He ran for president as the nominee of the Anti-Masonic party in 1832.

Secretary of the Navy. Samuel Southard (1787–1842), of New Jersey, served 1823–1829. He was a holdover from the Monroe administration.

ADMINISTRATION: March 4, 1825–March 3, 1829.

Internal Improvements. Adams was the first president both to endorse wholeheartedly federally sponsored internal improvements and to harbor no constitutional qualms about their implementation. In his first annual message to Congress in December 1825, Adams reminded the nation that "the great object of the institution of civil government is the improvement of the condition of those who are parties to the social compact, and no government, in whatever form constituted, can accomplish the lawful ends of its institution but in proportion as it improves the condition of those over whom it is established."[13] He went on to propose the construction of a network of roads and canals, a national university, and an astronomical observatory, the latter to be manned by a full-time astronomer. The program was too ambitious for Congress, however. Adams obtained only the westward extension of the Cumberland Road into Ohio and the construction of the Chesapeake and Ohio Canal. At the canal's groundbreaking ceremony on the Fourth of July, 1828, President Adams proudly turned over the first shovelful of earth.

The Panama Congress, 1826. President Adams supported U.S. participation in the Panama Congress, convened by South American patriot Simón Bolívar to foster Pan-American cooperation. Southern congressmen, who feared that the meeting might be used as a forum to condemn slavery, combined with Adams's political opponents to delay confirmation of the U.S. delegates long enough to make it impossible for them to reach Panama in time to attend the congress.

Tariff of Abominations, 1828. President Adams proposed a high tariff on imported manufactured goods to protect domestic industry, then centered in New England. According to many historians, the supporters of Andrew Jackson, who opposed the tariff, sought to kill the measure by amending it to include a stiff tariff on the imported raw materials used to manufacture products in New England. Adams opponents hoped by this to create a tariff package so odious to North and South alike that it would be defeated. Instead, New

England legislators voted in favor of the bill despite its flaws, and the Tariff of 1828, or the Tariff of Abominations, as it was quickly dubbed, became law. Although its steep rates were soon rolled back, the tariff act was significant as it prompted Vice President Calhoun to draft the South Carolina Exposition condemning the tariff as "unconstitutional, oppressive, and unjust" and claiming the right of a state to nullify such federal laws.

SUPREME COURT APPOINTMENT: Robert Trimble (1776–1828), of Kentucky, served as associate justice 1826–1828. During his brief service, he supported the nationalism of Chief Justice John Marshall.

RANKING IN 1962 HISTORIANS POLL: Adams ranked thirteenth of 31 presidents; second of the 12 "average" presidents. He ranked above Hayes, below Madison.

RETIREMENT: March 4, 1829–February 23, 1848. Without attending the inaugural of his successor, Andrew Jackson, Adams took up temporary residence at Meridian Hill outside Washington before returning to his home town, Quincy, Massachusetts, in June 1829. The next year he was elected to the U.S. House as an Anti-Mason (he later became a Whig). He was the only former president to serve as a U.S. representative. During his 17 years in the House, Adams often found himself in the minority: he supported continuation of the Bank of the United States, opposed the annexation of Texas, and voted against the declaration of war with Mexico in 1846. But he scored a singular victory in his eight-year struggle against the gag rule. In 1836 the House had voted to table automatically without debate any petition critical of slavery. To circumvent this gag order and uphold the right of petition, Adams overcame the infirmities of old age to read into the record a myriad of antislavery petitions, which abolitionists around the country were sending him daily. In 1844 the House relented and repealed the gag rule. Meanwhile, in 1841, Adams argued successfully before the Supreme Court to win freedom for slave mutineers aboard the Spanish ship *Amistad*. He also led the fight to accept the bequest of James Smithson of England, who in his will directed that his fortune be turned over to the United States for the creation of an institution to disseminate knowledge. The $500,000 gift was used to establish the Smithsonian Institution. Having been thwarted in his attempt as president to build a national observatory, Adams eagerly accepted an invitation to speak at the laying of the cornerstone of the Cincinnati Observatory in 1843. At 76 he endured the rigors of western travel to lend his presence to what he considered an event of great national importance. It was during this his second career in Congress that the former president earned the nickname of Old Man Eloquent.

DEATH: February 23, 1848, 7:20 P.M., U.S. Capitol Building, Washington, D.C. On November 20, 1846, Adams suffered a mild stroke while strolling with a friend in Boston. After several weeks rest, he recovered sufficiently to resume his congressional duties in Washington. On February 21, 1848, just minutes after casting a very loud No! against a proposal to decorate certain generals serving in the Mexican War, Adams suffered a second stroke, this one massive, and slumped over his House desk into the arms of Representative David Fisher of Ohio. He was carried away on a sofa to the Speaker's room, his entire right side now paralyzed. Attending him were five doctors—William Newell, Thomas Edwards, George Fries, Samuel Peyton (all four members of the House), and Harvey Lindsley. Realizing the gravity of his condition, Adams said, "This is the end of earth" and then added either, "but I am composed," or "I am content."[14]

These were his last words. He slipped into a coma and died two days later. He was 80. For two days mourners filed by the open casket in a House committee room. On February 26, the House chaplain, the Reverend R. R. Gurley, conducted funeral services before a packed House chamber. Adams was buried at the family tomb in Quincy. Upon the death of his wife in 1852, the two were buried with his parents, John and Abigail Adams, beneath the Congregational church in Quincy. A memorial plaque, placed there by his son Charles Francis Adams, reads, in part, "For more than half a century, / Whenever his Country called for his Labors, / In either hemisphere or in any Capacity, / He never spared them in her Cause." In his last will and testament, executed in January 1847, Adams left his 8,500-volume library and personal papers, as well as his home and grounds at Quincy, to his sole surviving son, Charles Francis Adams, provided that for the house the son paid $20,000 to the estate. The bulk of the residue of his estate, which included various other properties in and around Boston and Washington, cash, and stock, he divided among four heirs—his wife, daughter-in-law Mary Hellen Adams (widow of his son John Adams II), granddaughter Mary Louisa Adams, and son Charles Francis Adams.

ADAMS PRAISED: ". . . Mr. Adams is the most valuable public character we have abroad. . . . There remains no doubt in my mind that he will prove himself to be the ablest, of all our diplomatic corps."[15]—George Washington, 1797

"The greatest ornament and the ablest member of the American Senate, who if he but persists in his dignified course must one day attain to the highest station in our republic."[16]—Boston *Independent Chronicle*, 1808

"I have found in him since I have been associated with him in the executive government as little to censure and condemn as I could have expected in any man."[17]—Henry Clay

"This Convention views with eager interest the important position relative to the cause of human freedom now held by the venerable John Quincy Adams, formerly President of the United States; and while admitting the moral heroism with which he had thrown himself into the breach, we will not cease our prayers to the Giver of all good gifts, that his hands may be strengthened for the great work to which he has given himself, and that his valuable life may be mercifully prolonged until he shall witness the abolition of slavery, not only in his own country, but throughout the world."[18]—World Antislavery Convention, London, 1843

"The slave has lost a champion who gained new ardor and new strength the longer he fought; America has lost a man who loved her with his heart; religion has lost a supporter; Freedom an unfailing friend, and mankind a noble vindicator of our inalienable rights."[19]—Theodore Parker, Massachusetts clergyman and reformer, 1848

ADAMS CRITICIZED: "Like a kite without a tail he will be violent and constant in his attempts to rise . . . and will pitch on one side and the other, as the popular currents may happen to strike, without soaring to his intended point."[20]—Stephen Higginson, Boston banker, c. 1817

"It is said he is a disgusting man to do business. Coarse, *Dirty* and clownish in his address and stiff and abstracted in his opinions, which are drawn from books exclusively."[21]—William Henry Harrison

"This is the first Administration that has openly run the principle of patronage against that of patriotism, that has unblushingly avowed, aye and executed its purpose, of buying us up with our own money."[22]—Senator John Randolph of Virginia, 1826

"He was educated as a monarchist, has always been hostile to popular government, and particularly to its great bulwark the right of suffrage, . . . he affected to become a Republican only to pervert and degrade the Democratic party; and to pave the way for such a change in the Constitution as would establish the United States an aristocratical and hereditary government."[23]— Representative Samuel D. Ingram of Pennsylvania, 1827

"You are perfectly insane and should apply for admission to the Lunatic Asylum. You have cost the Government more than half your state is worth. You are a curse to the Whig Party and to the nation."[24]—letter from one Isaac Milne of Ohio, 1842, objecting to Adam's efforts against the gag rule

ADAMS QUOTES: "Individual liberty is individual power, and as the power of a community is a mass compounded of individual powers, the nation which enjoys the most freedom must necessarily be in proportion to its numbers the most powerful nation. But our *distribution* of the powers of government is yet imperfect. . . . We have not succeeded in providing as well for the protection of property as of personal liberty. Our laws between debtor and creditor are inefficacious and secure justice to neither. Our banks are for the most part fradulent bankrupts. Our judiciary is not independent in fact, though it is in theory; and according to the prevailing doctrine our *national* government is constituted without the power of discharging the first *duty* of a nation, that of bettering its own condition by internal improvement."[25]—1822

"The art of making love, muffled up in furs, in the open air, with the thermometer at Zero, is a Yankee invention, which requires a Yankee poet to describe."[26]—1832

"Why does it follow that women are fitted for nothing but the cares of domestic life, for bearing children, and cooking the food of a family, devoting all their time to the domestic circle—to promoting the immediate personal comfort of their husbands, brothers, and sons? . . . The mere departure of woman from the duties of the domestic circle, far from being a reproach to her, is a virtue of the highest order, when it is done from purity of motive, by appropriate means, and the purpose good."[27]—1838

BOOKS BY ADAMS: *Dermot MacMorrogh or, The Conquest of Ireland: An Historical Tale of the Twelfth Century* (book of poetry, 1832); *The Lives of James Madison and James Monroe* (1850).

BOOKS ABOUT ADAMS: Bemis, Samuel Flagg. *John Quincy Adams and the Foundations of American Foreign Policy.* New York: Knopf, 1949.

Bemis, Samuel Flagg. *John Quincy Adams and the Union.* New York: Knopf, 1956.

Falkner, Leonard. *The President Who Wouldn't Retire: John Quincy Adams, Congressman from Massachusetts.* New York: Coward-McCann, 1967.

Hecht, Marie B. *John Quincy Adams: A Personal History of an Independent Man.* New York: Macmillan, 1972.

NOTES

1 Samuel Flagg Bemis, *John Quincy Adams and the Foundations of American Foreign Policy*, New York, Knopf, 1949, p. 253.
2 Adriene Koch and William Peden, eds., *Selected Writings of John and John Quincy Adams*, New York: Knopf, 1946, p. 320.
3 Samuel Flagg Bemis, *John Quincy Adams and the Union*, New York: Knopf, 1956, p. 199.
4 Marie B. Hecht, *John Quincy Adams: A Personal History of An Independent Man*, New York: Macmillan, 1972, p. 11.
5 Hecht, p. 34.
6 Ibid., p. 53.
7 Bemis, *JQA and Union*, p. 106n.
8 Ibid., p. 526n.
9 Bemis, *JQA and Foreign Policy*, p. 18.
10 Ibid., p. 82.
11 Graham Stuart, *The Department of State*, New York: Macmillan, 1949, p. 63.
12 Bemis, *JQA and Union*, p. 83.
13 Henry Steele Commager, ed., *Documents of American History*, New York: Crofts, 1945, Doc. no. 130, p. 242.
14 Hecht, p. 627.
15 Bemis, *JQA and Foreign Policy*, p. 89.
16 Ibid., p. 148.
17 Stuart, p. 70.
18 Bemis, *JQA and Union*, p. 470n.
19 Ibid., p. 545.
20 Bemis, *JQA and Foreign Policy*, p. 123.
21 Freeman Cleaves, *Old Tippecanoe, William Henry Harrison and His Time*, Port Washington, N.Y.: Kennikat Press, 1969, p. 241.
22 Hecht, p. 430.
23 Bemis, *JQA and Union*, p. 143.
24 Ibid., p. 438.
25 Koch and Peden, p. 342.
26 Bemis, *JQA and Foreign Policy*, p. 23.
27 Bemis, *JQA and Union*, p. 369.

☆ ☆ ☆ ☆ ☆ ☆ ☆ ☆
ANDREW JACKSON
☆ ☆ ☆ ☆ ☆ ☆ ☆ ☆

7TH PRESIDENT

NAME: Andrew Jackson. He was named after his father, who had died just before he was born.

PHYSICAL DESCRIPTION: Long and lean, Jackson stood 6 feet 1 inch tall and weighed about 140 pounds. His narrow, angular face was topped by a mass of unruly reddish-sandy hair that had completely grayed by the time he became president. His complexion generally was pale and somewhat pockmarked. He had penetrating, steely blue eyes. He began wearing false teeth at about age 60. For many years he carried in his body two bullets from separate encounters. One fired from the pistol of the brother of Thomas Hart Benton in 1813 greatly reduced the mobility of his left arm until the lead was removed nearly 20 years later. The other from Charles Dickinson (see "Career before the Presidency") in 1806 lodged dangerously near his heart, where it remained, causing him periodic discomfort for the rest of his life. Jackson outgrew a childhood habit of slobbering, which persisted into his teens. While president, he was chronically wracked by headaches, abdominal pains, and a hacking cough that often brought up blood. A gaunt figure who relied on a cane to steady his faltering gait, President Jackson was considered a likely candidate to become the first president to die in office. But he survived the fires of two contentious terms to enjoy several years of retirement. Despite his reputation as a backwoodsman, Jackson dressed fashionably while in Washington.

PERSONALITY: A charismatic figure, Jackson was combative, quick-tempered, and thin-skinned. To his friends he was generous, considerate, and above all loyal; to his enemies, mean-spirited and spiteful. "When Andrew Jackson hated," Robert V. Remini, a modern Jacksonian scholar, has written, "it often became grand passion. He could hate with a Biblical fury and would resort to petty and vindictive acts to nurture his hatred and keep it bright and strong and ferocious."[1] He at times exploded with anger, but it is believed that he never really lost his temper. Rather, he launched into tirades quite purposefully either to intimidate his opposition or to end debate on a matter that was dragging on too long. Martin Van Buren, his closest adviser, marveled at Jackson's ability to turn his anger on and off at will. One minute he could be shrieking at the cabinet in the high register his voice invariably had whenever he was agitated; the next moment, alone with Van Buren after the others had left, he was relaxed and in good humor. At social occasions Jackson surprised many with his grace, poise, and charm. Around women he shed his backwoods manner and earthy language to engage comfortably in social discourse. He delighted in disappointing those who, he said, "were prepared to see me with a tomahawk in one hand and a scalping knife in the other."[2]

ANCESTORS: Jackson was Scotch-Irish, his ancestors having emigrated from Scotland to northern Ireland sometime after 1690. His paternal grandfather, Hugh Jackson, was a weaver and merchant in Carrickfergus, a seaport on the northern shore of Belfast Lough 10 miles northeast of Belfast.

FATHER: Andrew Jackson (d. 1767). A farmer in County Antrim, Ireland, he married Elizabeth "Betty" Hutchinson and had two small children. In 1765 he sold his land and emigrated to America. The Jacksons probably landed in Pennsylvania and made their way overland to the Scotch-Irish community in the Waxhaw region straddling the border between North Carolina and South Carolina. There Jackson injured himself lifting a log and died in early March 1767, leaving his wife pregnant with the future president.

MOTHER: Elizabeth "Betty" Hutchinson Jackson (d. 1781). An indomitable woman from whom Jackson inherited his reddish hair and blue eyes, she attempted to raise her three fatherless boys amid the hardships of the American Revolution. After seeing Andrew through a near-fatal case of smallpox, she went to Charleston to help nurse captured American soldiers languishing on British prisoner-of-war ships. There she contracted cholera and died. Jackson, 14, never saw his mother again. But he never forgot the final words she spoke to him before departing for Charleston. She warned him not to lie, steal, or quarrel as long as his manhood was not in jeopardy. She also cautioned him not to look to the courts for relief against slander. "Settle them cases yourself,"[3] she advised.

SIBLINGS: Jackson had two older brothers, both born in northern Ireland and both of whom lost their lives in service during the American Revolution. Hugh Jackson died of heat exhaustion after taking part in the Battle of Stono Ferry in 1779. Robert Jackson, taken prisoner along with Andrew, contracted smallpox and died days after his release in 1781.

CHILDREN: Jackson had no natural children; thus, no direct descendant of Jackson survives. In 1809 the Jacksons legally adopted one of Mrs. Jackson's nephews, one of the twin boys recently born to Mr. and Mrs. Severn Donelson. They named him Andrew Jackson, Jr.

BIRTH: Jackson was born posthumously on March 15, 1767, in the Waxhaw region straddling the border between North Carolina and South Carolina. The exact site of his birth remains in dispute. After burying her husband, Mrs. Elizabeth Jackson, then nearly due to deliver Andrew, decided to move in with her sister Mrs. Jane Crawford in present-day Lancaster County, South Carolina, where many believe she gave birth. But some historians argue that enroute to the Crawfords, Mrs. Jackson stopped to visit another sister, Mrs. Margaret McCamie, in what is now Union County, North Carolina, where she suddenly went into labor and gave birth to the future president. As for Andrew Jackson, he accepted the first version and often referred to himself as a native of South

Carolina. Still, the dispute continues. In 1979 local officials in the two counties decided to settle the matter in a unique way: Each year high school football teams from Union County and Lancaster County square off in the Old Hickory Football Classic. The victorious county wins the right to claim the seventh president as a native son and to place a 17-inch stoneware bust of Jackson in its courthouse for one year.

CHILDHOOD: Fatherless at birth and orphaned at 14, Jackson grew up a spirited, combative youth, quick to punch anyone who dared cross him. He was especially sensitive to any kind of criticism. Boys foolish enough to make fun of Jackson's peculiar habit of slobbering were asking for a fight. He was a good fistfighter and fast runner, but he was too light to wrestle well. As a public reader of news for the many illiterate residents of the Waxhaw region, nine-year-old Andy read aloud the Declaration of Independence when newspapers carrying it reached the area in 1776. After the Revolution (see "Military Service"), Jackson was utterly alone, having lost his mother and both brothers in the war. He lived alternately with two uncles for a time and spent six months apprenticed to a saddler. Then at age 15 he inherited some £350 from his grandfather Hugh Jackson of Ireland. If invested in land, a business, or education, such a sum could have provided the orphan with a solid stake in life. Instead, Jackson squandered the entire inheritance gambling and carousing in Charleston. He returned home to the Waxhaw region chastened by his profligacy and determined to succeed.

EDUCATION: Because his mother had her heart set on her youngest son becoming a Presbyterian minister, young Andrew received a better education than his older brothers. From age 8 to 13 he learned the fundamentals and studied the classics under first Dr. William Humphries and then the Reverend James White Stephenson. But Jackson never was a particularly good student and certainly had no inclination to enter the clergy. He remained a poor speller all his life; his grammar was faulty. Returning to the Waxhaw region after squandering his inheritance (see "Childhood"), he resumed his studies briefly at the New Acquisition school of Robert McCulloch. Then he taught school himself one year but quickly tired of the tedium of preparing lessons and in 1784 left the Waxhaw region, permanently as it turned out, to become a lawyer. In Salisbury, North Carolina, he studied law for two years under Spruce McCay and spent another six months at the law office of John Stokes. He did what was expected of him but little more. In his spare time he gambled, drank, chased women, and took dancing lessons. In September 1787 Jackson was admitted to the North Carolina bar.

RELIGION: Presbyterian. Although not especially religious, Jackson was not the heathen many churchmen believed him to be. He frequently skipped Sunday services and from his youth peppered his speech with salty language, but he also enjoyed reading the Bible and considered himself a practicing Christian. He delayed formally joining a Presbyterian church until after he had retired to Tennessee, but only because he wanted to avoid charges that he was doing so for political effect.

RECREATION: Jackson's favorite pastime was breeding and racing horses. He also raised gamecocks and entered his birds in cockfights in Nashville. Jackson loved a good practical joke: While studying law in Salisbury, North Carolina, he was chosen to manage the Christmas ball, the town's most important annual social event. For laughs, Jackson sent formal invitations to two prostitutes, a mother-and-daughter team well known in Salisbury. Few besides Jackson thought it funny when the unwelcome pair appeared at the ball. Jackson read newspapers voraciously. His favorite novel was Oliver Goldsmith's *Vicar of Wakefield*. He maintained a large collection of pipes from all over the world but preferred the sweet taste of his crude corncob one.

EARLY ROMANCE: Mary Crawford. Little is known of Jackson's romance with his cousin Mary Crawford in the Waxhaw region when he was 17. He never saw her again after leaving the area in 1784, but he fondly remembered the interlude long afterward. From the White House a half century later, President Jackson sent Mary, now the widow of Dr. Samuel Dunlap, a silver snuff box for, he wrote, "the endearing recollection of the pleasure he enjoyed in his boyhood."[4]

As a young law student in Salisbury, Jackson was very popular with girls. One Nancy Jarret spoke for many of the single women in town when she described the lanky, fun-loving young man as "most captivating" and added, "There was something about him I cannot describe except to say that it was *a presence.*"[5]

MARRIAGE: Andrew Jackson "married" Rachel Donelson Robards in August 1791 at Natchez, Mississippi. They were both 24. The marriage was invalid, because Rachel's divorce from her first husband, Lewis Robards, had not yet become final. They remarried, this time legally, on January 17, 1794, at Nashville, Tennessee. Born in present-day Halifax County, Virginia, on June 15, 1767, the daughter of Colonel John Donelson, a surveyor and member of the House of Burgesses, and Rachel Stockley Donelson, Rachel Donelson moved with her family to Tennessee and later to Kentucky. Although a dowdy, forlorn figure in middle age, famous for smoking a corncob pipe, she was in her youth a comely, vivacious creature popular with men. At 17 she married Lewis Robards in Kentucky and lived with him there while her parents returned to Tennessee. Insanely jealous, Robards repeatedly accused Rachel of having affairs with other men. Despite her pleas of innocence, he ordered her to return to her family in Tennessee until he called for her. Soon after she had rejoined her mother, now a widow, near Nashville, Andrew Jackson arrived as a boarder at the Donelsons. Eventually Jackson and Rachel fell in love. Nevertheless, when Robards came to Nashville to reclaim his wife, Rachel dutifully returned with him to Kentucky. She soon learned, however, that he had done nothing to curb his rages of jealousy. Told of her unhappiness, Jackson raced to Kentucky and rescued her. In December 1790, at Robards's request, the state legislature passed an enabling act permitting him to sue for divorce. Mistaking this preliminary action for a final divorce decree, Jackson, who as a lawyer should have known better, "married" Rachel in 1791. Robards learned that his wife was living with Jackson and sued for divorce on grounds of adultery; the decree was issued in September 1793. Jackson was furious, Rachel mortified, to learn that they had never legally been married. Unfortunately, their remarriage in 1794 did not end the matter. The charge of adultery was to haunt the couple thereafter. Scurrilous attacks on Rachel's character poisoned the presidential campaign of 1828. Although Jackson tried to keep such reports from his wife, who had a history of heart trouble, Rachel heard enough to realize that her past was being raked up in the national press. At least in part as a result of her anguish, she grew ill and died suddenly on December 22, 1828. Jackson forever blamed his political opponents for her death. "In the presence of this dear saint," President-elect Jackson solemnly vowed at her burial, "I can and do forgive all my enemies. But those vile wretches who have slandered her must look to God for mercy."[6]

MILITARY SERVICE:

American Revolution. At 13 Jackson, along with his older brother Robert, joined the Continental army. He served as a mounted orderly or messenger under Colonel William Davis and was present at the Battle of Hanging Rock in August 1780. The following April the Jackson brothers were surprised by a British unit at the home of their cousin Thomas Crawford and taken prisoner. The British officer in charge ordered the boys to clean his boots. When they refused, the officer whacked them with his sword. Andrew's left hand was cut to the bone, and he sustained a gash on his head that left a prominent white scar, a permanent reminder of his hatred for the British. Without dressing their wounds, the redcoats led the lads on a 40-mile forced march, without food or water, to the prisoner-of-war camp at Camden, South Carolina. There they subsisted on a diet of stale bread until their release as part of a prisoner exchange in late April 1781. They had spent about two weeks in captivity. Jackson was the last veteran of the Revolution to become president and the only president to have been a prisoner of war.

Burr Conspiracy, 1805–1806. Having been narrowly elected major general of the Tennessee militia in 1802, Jackson was for a time an unwitting accomplice in Aaron Burr's ill-fated conspiracy in the West (see "Thomas Jefferson, 3d President," "Administration"). Assured by Burr that he was merely preparing to defend the United States against a Spanish invasion, Jackson provided him with a list of reliable officers and two riverboats. However, when Jackson learned of President Jefferson's proclamation warning the nation of the subversive nature of Burr's plan, he dissociated himself from the enterprise.

War of 1812. Appointed major general of U.S. Volunteers by Governor William Blount of Tennessee in 1812, Jackson led 2,070 raw Tennessee recruits to Natchez, Mississippi, only to be ordered by General James Wilkinson to demobilize his force. Rather than dismiss them there, Jackson marched the volunteers back to Tennessee under severe conditions. It was on this return trek that his men nicknamed him first Hickory, for his toughness, and later Old Hickory.

Following the Creek Indian uprising in which 250 whites were massacred at Fort Mims in what is now Alabama, Major General Jackson led 2,500 Tennessee volunteers against the Creeks in October 1813. At Talladega in November, he defeated a force of 1,000 Indians, killing 300 and putting the remainder to flight. Although wracked by dysentery and hampered by inadequate provisions and threats of desertion, Jackson subdued the Creeks under Chief Red Eagle, crushing them at Horseshoe Bend in March 1814 after patiently awaiting the safe evacuation of Indian women and children. Serving under Jackson in the battle was a 21-year-old ensign named Sam Houston.

Promoted to major general in the regular army in May 1814, Jackson invaded Florida in October and captured Pensacola the following month. He then marched to New Orleans, where he undertook the defense of that city against imminent British attack. In a controversial program designed to establish his complete authority over the city during the emergency, he imposed martial law, ordered the dissolution of the state legislature, executed deserters, suppressed free expression, and ignored a federal judge's writ of habeas corpus. (For this last act he was subsequently fined $1,000, but in 1844 the U.S. Congress refunded the money). On January 8, 1815, Jackson led his forces in a stunning defensive victory over crack British veterans who attempted to advance on New

Orleans under cover of early morning fog. At Jackson's order, the Americans laid down a withering barrage of rifle fire that dropped more than 2,000 British troops. American casualties numbered just 21. General Jackson was awestruck at the spectacle of British survivors rising up from the heaps of their fallen comrades to come forward and surrender—a scene he likened to the final Resurrection. The Battle of New Orleans, although it occured after the Treaty of Ghent (see "James Madison, 4th President," "Administration") had officially ended the war, was the most decisive American victory of the conflict. From it Jackson emerged a national hero.

First Seminole War, 1817–1818. Responding to raids on Georgia settlements by Seminole Indians and fugitive slaves operating out of sanctuaries in Spanish Florida, President James Monroe instructed General Jackson to check the incursions but to refrain from invading Spanish territory except in hot pursuit of the enemy. Jackson exceeded these instructions. In 1818 he invaded Florida, destroyed Seminole villages, captured Pensacola, and overthrew the Spanish governor. He also captured and executed two British citizens, Alexander Arbuthnot and Robert Ambrister for having incited the Seminoles. Because Jackson had taken such bold action without presidential authorization, Secretary of War John C. Calhoun and others privately urged that he be reprimanded. However, no action was taken. A congressional motion of censure failed. Jackson served as military governor of Florida for several months in 1821, during which time he resigned from the army.

CAREER BEFORE THE PRESIDENCY: Jackson practiced law in Martinsville and Jonesboro, North Carolina, and, from 1788, at Nashville, where he served as public prosecutor for what was then the western district of North Carolina. In 1796 he was a delegate to the convention at Knoxville that drafted the Tennessee Constitution.

U.S. Representative, 1796–1797. Elected without opposition as Tennessee's first U.S. representative, Jackson generally supported the Democratic-Republicans.

U.S. Senator, 1797–1798. Elected by the state legislature, Senator Jackson generally opposed the administration of John Adams. He grew impatient with the sluggish pace of Congress and resigned after just five months.

Justice of Tennessee Superior Court, 1798–1804. Elected to Tennessee's highest court by the state legislature, Judge Jackson won high marks for dispensing swift, impartial justice, despite his lack of judicial scholarship.

Duel with Charles Dickinson, 1806. Jackson challenged Charles Dickinson, a lawyer, to a duel for having maligned the character of Mrs. Jackson and for a misunderstanding following cancellation of an important horse race. The two squared off with pistols at eight paces in a poplar forest clearing at Harrison's Mills, Kentucky. Dickinson got off the first shot, a direct hit into Jackson's breast that raised dust from his coat as it entered. Jackson remained so stiffly erect that Dickinson stumbled back in disbelief. At the insistence of Jackson's second, Dickinson returned to his mark. Although it was commonplace for a man in Jackson's position to spare his opponent by firing into the air, Jackson chose otherwise. He fired once; the hammer failed to fall home. He fired again. The ball penetrated Dickinson's abdomen and exited the other side, killing him. Jackson walked off the field, his feet sloshing in blood that had drained from his chest. Dickinson's bullet had lodged too close to Jackson's heart to be removed safely. He carried it to his grave.

U.S. Senator, 1823–1825. Elected by the Tennessee legislature over the incumbent Senator John Williams, Jackson served as chairman of the Military Affairs Committee. He voted for internal improvements and a protective tariff. In 1824 he ran unsuccessfully for president (see "John Quincy Adams, 6th President," for presidential campaign of 1824). He resigned in 1825 in order to remain aloof of Washington politics as he prepared a second campaign for the presidency in 1828.

DEMOCRATIC PRESIDENTIAL NOMINATION, 1828: Within months after the inauguration of John Quincy Adams in 1825, the Tennessee legislature re-nominated Jackson for president, thus setting the stage for a rematch between these two very different politicians three years hence. No nominating caucus was held. Jackson accepted the incumbent vice president John C. Calhoun as his running mate. Jackson's supporters called themselves Democrats, thus marking the evolution of Jefferson's Republicanism into the modern Democratic party.

OPPONENT: President John Quincy Adams (1767–1848), of Massachusetts, Adams was renominated on the endorsement of state legislatures and partisan rallies. No nominating caucus was held. Adams accepted Richard Rush of Pennsylvania as his vice presidential running mate. Adams supporters called themselves National Republicans, antecedents of the Whig and later the Republican parties.

CAMPAIGN AND THE ISSUES, 1828: The campaign turned more on personality than on issues. Both men supported, in varying degrees, a protective tariff and a program of internal improvements. The contest pitted the erudite, experienced, reserved John Quincy Adams against a national war hero whose humble origins stood him in good stead with the swelling ranks of frontier settlers and manual laborers. For many Americans, Jackson embodied the democratic spirit that was anathema to the eastern aristrocracy. Campaigning was left to supporters, for it still was considered improper for the candidates themselves to stump for votes. However, Jackson did attend a gala celebration at New Orleans marking the thirteenth anniversary of his heroic victory there, an event carefully orchestrated to remind voters of his war record. Both camps resorted to ad hominem attacks: Democrats continued to charge Adams with striking a "corrupt bargain" with Henry Clay to steal the 1824 election from Jackson. Adams forces raked up charges of adultery against Jackson for having lived with Rachel before her divorce was final, rank mudslinging that contributed to the sudden death of Mrs. Jackson just weeks after the election. They also charged Jackson with murder for having approved the execution of soldiers for minor offenses during the War of 1812. The West supported Jackson without reservation. The South, although disturbed by his vote for the tariff while in the Senate, took comfort in his running mate, John C. Calhoun of South Carolina, and voted overwhelmingly for the Democratic ticket. Martin Van Buren, a leader of the Albany Regency political machine in New York State, was instrumental in winning for Jackson a majority of that state's vote. New England and the manufacturing interests supported Adams.

ELECTION AS PRESIDENT, FIRST TERM, 1828:

Popular Vote: Jackson (Democrat), 647,292 (56%); Adams (National Republican), 507,730 (44%).

Electoral Vote: Jackson, 178; Adams, 83.

States Carried: Jackson won the majority of electoral votes in 15 states—Alabama, Georgia, Illinois, Indiana, Kentucky, Louisiana, Mississippi, Missouri,

New York, North Carolina, Ohio, Pennsylvania, South Carolina, Tennessee, Virginia. Adams won the majority of electoral votes in 9 states—Connecticut, Delaware, Maine, Maryland, Massachusetts, New Hampshire, New Jersey, Rhode Island, Vermont. John C. Calhoun of South Carolina was elected vice president, having received 171 electoral votes, to 83 for Richard Rush of Pennsylvania and 7 for William Smith of South Carolina.

DEMOCRATIC NOMINATION FOR REELECTION AS PRESIDENT, 1832: In this the first presidential election in which candidates were chosen at national party conventions, Democrats met at Baltimore in May 1832 to endorse Jackson for reelection. Although there was substantial opposition within the party to Jackson's choice of Martin Van Buren of New York as his running mate, delegates nevertheless nominated him for vice president by an overwhelming margin. The convention adopted a rule requiring a two-thirds majority to nominate a candidate; it remained in force at Democratic conventions until 1936.

OPPONENT: Henry Clay (1777–1852) of Kentucky, National Republican. A presidential candidate in 1824 (see "John Quincy Adams, 6th President," "Opponents"), Clay emerged the leader of the anti-Jackson forces. He was nominated for president at a convention of National Republicans in Baltimore in December 1831. John Sergeant of Pennsylvania was nominated for vice president.

CAMPAIGN AND THE ISSUES, 1832: The dominant issue was the fate of the Bank of the United States (see "Administration"). Clay charged that in destroying the bank Jackson not only hurt the moneyed interests but also threatened the financial security of small borrowers. But most common people applauded Jackson's attack on the bank, long a symbol of special privilege and manipulation. Clay supporters, denouncing Jackson for instituting the spoils system and for his liberal use of the veto to thwart the will of Congress, dubbed the president King Andrew I. The Democratic press painted Clay as a dissolute gambler. The West and South continued to support Jackson overwhelmingly, and he improved his standing in New England. Anti-Masons formed a third party to oppose Jackson, himself a Mason, and in some states collaborated with Clay supporters.

ELECTION AS PRESIDENT, SECOND TERM, 1832:

> **Popular Vote:** Jackson (Democrat), 687,502 (55%); Clay (National Republican), 530,189 (42%).

> **Electoral Vote:** Jackson, 219; Clay, 49; others, 18.

> **States Carried:** Jackson won the majority of electoral votes in 16 states—Alabama, Georgia, Illinois, Indiana, Louisiana, Maine, Mississippi, Missouri, New Hampshire, New Jersey, New York, North Carolina, Ohio, Pennsylvania, Tennessee, Virginia. Clay won the majority of electoral votes in six states—Connecticut, Delaware, Kentucky, Maryland, Massachusetts, Rhode Island. South Carolina's 11 electors voted for John Floyd, Independent Democrat of Virginia. Vermont's 7 electors voted for William Wirt, Anti-Mason of Maryland. Martin Van Buren of New York was elected vice president, receiving 189 electoral votes, to 49 for John Sergeant of Pennsylvania, and 48 divided among three other candidates.

INAUGURAL ADDRESS (FIRST): March 4, 1829. ". . . Considering standing armies as dangerous to free governments in time of peace, I shall not seek to enlarge our present establishment, nor disregard that salutary lesson of political experience which teaches that the military should be held subordinate to the civil power. . . . The bulwark of our defense is the national militia, which in the present state of our intelligence and population must render us invincible. As long as our Government is administered for the good of the people, and is regulated by their will; as long as it secures to us the rights of person and of property, liberty of conscience and of the press, it will be worth defending; and so long as it is worth defending a patriotic militia will cover it with an impenetrable aegis. Partial injuries and occasional mortifications we may be subjected to, but a million of armed freemen, possessed of the means of war, can never be conquered by a foreign foe. . . ."

INAUGURAL ADDRESS (SECOND): March 4, 1833. ". . . Without union our independence and liberty would never have been achieved; without union they never can be maintained. Divided into twenty-four, or even a smaller number, of separate communities, we shall see our internal trade burdened with numberless restraints and exactions; communication between distant points and sections obstructed or cut off; our sons made soldiers to deluge with blood the fields they now till in peace; the mass of our people borne down and impoverished by taxes to support armies and navies, and military leaders at the head of their victorious legions becoming our lawgivers and judges. The loss of liberty, of all good government, of peace, plenty, and happiness, must inevitably follow a dissolution of the Union. . . ."

VICE PRESIDENT:

John C. Calhoun (1782–1850), of South Carolina, served 1825–1832. He had served as vice president under President John Quincy Adams. He fell out of favor with Jackson over Mrs. Calhoun's role in the Peggy Eaton affair and finally broke with the president over nullification and states' rights (see "Administration"). He resigned in December 1832, the only vice president besides Spiro Agnew to do so, in order to accept election to the Senate. After serving as secretary of state 1844–1845 under President Tyler, he resumed his seat in the Senate, where he was a principal spokesman for states' rights and ardent defender of slavery until his death in 1850.

Martin Van Buren (1782–1862), of New York, served 1833–1837. See "Martin Van Buren, 8th President."

CABINET:

Secretary of State. (1) Martin Van Buren (1782–1862), of New York, served 1829–1831 (see "Martin Van Buren, 8th President," "Career before the Presidency"). (2) Edward Livingston (1764–1836), of Louisiana, served 1831–1833. He drafted Jackson's proclamation against nullification. (3) Louis McLane (1786–1857), of Delaware, served 1833–1834. Transferred from Treasury secretary, he reorganized the State Department into seven distinct bureaus. (4) John Forsyth (1780–1841), of Georgia, served 1834–1841. He helped obtain reparations from France for U.S. commercial losses suffered during the Napoleonic Wars. He stayed on in the Van Buren administration.

Secretary of the Treasury. (1) Samuel D. Ingham (1779–1860), of Pennsylvania, served 1829–1831. He was chosen for his moderate position on the tariff. (2) Louis McLane served 1831–1833. For refusing Jackson's order to transfer federal deposits from the Bank of the United States to state banks, McLane was transferred to secretary of state. (3) William J. Duane (1780–1865), of Pennsylvania, served June–September 1833. An Irish immigrant, he also refused Jackson's order to transfer federal deposits from the Bank of the United States and was dismissed. (4) Levi Woodbury (1789–1851), of New Hampshire, served 1834–1841; he was transferred from secretary of the navy. In him, Jackson at last found a vigorous supporter of his campaign against the Bank of the United States. He stayed on in the Van Buren administration.

Secretary of War. (1) John H. Eaton (1790–1856), of Tennessee, served 1829–1831. He resigned amid the social ostracism of his wife (see "Administration: Peggy Eaton Affair"). (2) Lewis Cass (1782–1866), of Michigan, served 1831–1836. He directed the Black Hawk War (see "Administration"). He was the Democratic presidential nominee in 1848 (see "Zachary Taylor, 12th President," "Opponent").

Attorney General. (1) John M. Berrien (1781–1856), of Georgia, served 1829–1831. He was active in preparations for removal of Indians from Georgia to the West. (2) Roger B. Taney (1777–1864), of Maryland, served 1831–1833. He urged Jackson to veto renewal of the bank's charter and drafted much of the veto message. Jackson later appointed him to the Supreme Court. (3) Benjamin F. Butler (1795–1858), of New York, served 1833–1838. He stayed on in the Van Buren administration.

Secretary of the Navy. (1) John Branch (1782–1863), of North Carolina, served 1829–1831. He was an outspoken critic of the tariff. (2) Levi Woodbury served 1831–1834. He resigned to become Treasury secretary. (3) Mahlon Dickerson (1770–1853), of New Jersey, served 1834–1838. He stayed on in the Van Buren administration.

Postmaster General. (1) William T. Barry (1785–1835), of Kentucky, served 1829–1835. He was the first postmaster general of cabinet rank. (2) Amos Kendall (1789–1869), of Kentucky, served 1835–1840. He tightened accounting procedures and extended railroad mail service. He stayed on in the Van Buren administration.

ADMINISTRATION: March 4, 1829–March 3, 1837. More than any of his predecessors, Jackson exercised executive authority to implement his policies and thwart the opposition. He vetoed a dozen bills, more than had all previous presidents combined, and was the first chief executive to exercise the pocket veto, by which a bill passed within 10 days (excluding Sundays) before Congress adjourns does not become law if the president does not sign it. He grew powerful in office through effective use of the spoils system, domination of the party convention, and appeals to the common people. He was a founder of the modern presidency.

Kitchen Cabinet. Displeased with most of his official cabinet, largely because of their behavior in the Peggy Eaton affair (see below), Jackson abandoned regular cabinet meetings and instead began discussing and formulating policy with an informal group of advisers at the White House. Among the members of what came to be called the Kitchen Cabinet were Amos Kendall, partisan journalist and later postmaster general; Francis P. Blair, editor of the Washington *Globe*; Andrew Jackson Donelson, the president's nephew and secretary; William B. Lewis, longtime Jackson confidant; Secretary of State Martin Van Buren, and Secretary of War John H. Eaton.

Spoils System. Although the practice of rewarding supporters with government jobs had long been in use, the Jackson administration's abrupt turnover in personnel drew charges of abuse from the opposition. He ascribed to the maxim "To the victor belong the spoils," but, in practice, President Jackson replaced only about 15 percent of the federal work force during his two terms.

Peggy Eaton Affair. According to widespread gossip, Mrs. Peggy O'Neale Timberlake was having an affair with John Eaton, a close friend of Andrew Jackson, when her husband, a civilian navy employee, died at sea, reportedly from suicide, in 1828. Soon thereafter she married Eaton, who two months later became Jackson's secretary of war. Much of Washington society, most notably the wife of Vice President John C. Calhoun, ostracized Mrs. Eaton. In this rapidly escalating social feud, Jackson saw disturbing parallels with the slanderous attacks leveled against his late wife. He rushed to Mrs. Eaton's defense and demanded that the cabinet wives treat her with due courtesy and respect. All refused. Only Secretary of State Martin Van Buren, a widower, socialized with her, thereby ingratiating himself further with President Jackson at the expense of Calhoun. The episode distracted the administration until Secretary Eaton resigned in 1831.

Tariff and Nullification. President Jackson confronted head-on the growing sectional crisis, ostensibly over the tariff question, but fundamentally over the issue of states' rights vis-à-vis the federal Union. At a dinner in 1830 marking the eighty-seventh anniversary of Thomas Jefferson's birth, Jackson offered a toast: "Our Federal Union—it must be preserved!" Vice President Calhoun, who was to be a principal advocate of the South's right to nullify federal laws, responded with a counter-toast: "The Union—next to our liberty, the most dear!"[7] Thus the lines were drawn. In 1832 Jackson signed into law a moderate tariff, less exacting than the Tariff of Abominations (see "John Quincy Adams, 6th President," "Administration"). This failed to satisfy South Carolina, which quickly enacted the Ordinance of Nullification declaring the tariff null and void in that state. Within weeks Jackson responded with a strongly worded proclamation warning South Carolina to comply with the tariff law and denouncing the doctrine of nullification as "uncompatible with the existence of the Union." To those entertaining thoughts of secession in order to avoid the tariff or any other federal law, he issued this reminder: "Disunion by armed force is *treason*. Are you really ready to incur its guilt? If you are, on the heads of the instigators of the act be the dreadful consequences; on their heads be the dishonor, but on yours may fall the punishment."[8] To further demonstrate his determination, Jackson obtained from Congress the power to use armed force to collect import duties. The crisis ended with passage of the Tariff of 1833, a compromise bill sponsored by Senator Henry Clay and acceptable to both Jackson and the South.

Internal Improvements. In 1830 President Jackson disappointed his western supporters in vetoing the Maysville Road bill, which would have authorized federal funds for the construction of a highway wholly within Kentucky. He objected to the measure on the ground that it benefited a single state rather than the nation as a whole and therefore was unconstitutional. However, he supported genuinely national internal improvements, among them the extension of the National Road.

Jackson versus the Bank of the United States. In 1832 President Jackson vetoed the recharter of the second Bank of the United States because he believed that Congress lacked constitutional authority to create it and because, like many westerners, he considered the bank, under the direction of Nicholas Biddle, an elitist institution that monopolized the banking industry and favored eastern manufacturing interests at the expense of common working people. With the veto sustained, the bank was dissolved on the expiration of its charter in 1836. Meanwhile Jackson hastened its demise by withdrawing the approximately $11 million in federal funds on deposit at the bank and distributing it to various state banks, or "pet" banks. For this act, the Senate voted to censure Jackson in 1834 but expunged the censure three years later. With the dissolution of the bank went its conservative monetary policy. State banks extended easy credit and issued paper money freely, touching off a round of western land speculation and inflation. In 1836 Jackson sought to restore economic order by issuing the Specie Circular, which required buyers of public land to pay in gold or silver. The order effectively dried up credit and ended the feverish land speculation, but it also precipitated the panic of 1837 (see "Martin Van Buren, 8th President," "Administration").

Indian Policy. President Jackson adopted a paternalistic attitude toward the Indians. Dismissing Indian claims of sovereignty in the Southeast, he supported Georgia in its effort to remove the Cherokees from their homeland in that state. He encouraged various tribes to accept a federal offer of land west of the Mississippi where, he promised, they would enjoy complete sovereignty forever. Acting under the authority of the Indian Removal Act of 1830, the Jackson administration coerced numerous tribes to abandon some 100 million acres of Indian lands and settle in the West. In *Worcester v. Georgia* (1832), the Supreme Court ruled that the Cherokee nation was a distinct community within which the laws of Georgia had no force. Georgia flagrantly disregarded the ruling, and Jackson made no effort to enforce it. During 1838–1839 federal troops led some 15,000 Cherokees on a forced march from Georgia to their new home in what is now Oklahoma. One out of every four Indians died enroute. Cherokees referred bitterly to the journey as the Trail of Tears.

Black Hawk War, 1832. U.S. military forces under General Henry Atkinson defeated the Sac and Fox Indians under Chief Black Hawk in Illinois and Wisconsin. Among those fighting was 23-year-old militia captain Abraham Lincoln.

Assassination Attempt, January 30, 1835. As Jackson was leaving the U.S. Capitol Building, Richard Lawrence, 32, a mentally disturbed house painter, approached to within a distance of about 13 feet and fired a single-shot derringer at the president. Although the percussion cap exploded properly, the gunpowder failed to ignite. Jackson lunged forward to strike the would-be assassin with his cane. Lawrence then fired a second derringer, this one at point-blank range. It, too, did not fire. At his trial, Lawrence was found not guilty by reason of insanity. He was confined to a mental institution until his death in 1861. Soon after the assault, Lawrence's derringers were examined and found to be in working order. The odds of two such weapons malfunctioning in succession were put at one in 125,000.

States Admitted to the Union. Arkansas (1836), Michigan (1837).

SUPREME COURT APPOINTMENTS: (1) John McLean (1785–1861), of Ohio, served as associate justice 1829–1861. His dissent in *Dred Scott v. Sandford* (1857; see Taney, below) was hailed by antislavery forces. (2) Henry Baldwin (1780–1844), of Pennsylvania, served as associate justice 1830–1844. His flashes of temper and erratic behavior at times bordered on madness. His opinions lacked consistency. (3) James M. Wayne (1790–1867), of Georgia, served as associate justice 1835–1867. During the Civil War, he renounced his state's participation in the Confederacy and remained on the Supreme Court. He delivered notable opinions in admiralty law. (4) Philip P. Barbour (1783–1841), of Virginia, served as associate justice 1836–1841. A staunch states' right advocate, he delivered the majority opinion in *New York City* v. *Miln* (1837), upholding a state law designed to check the increasing numbers of destitute immigrants entering New York. Barbour asserted the absolute right of a state "to advance the safety, happiness and prosperity of its people" through such legislation. (5) Roger B. Taney (1777–1864), of Maryland, served as chief justice 1836–1864. He succeeded John Marshall. In *Charles River Bridge* v. *Warren Bridge* (1837), Chief Justice Taney handed down a landmark opinion that anticipated the federal antitrust policy of the early twentieth century. The ruling broke a monopoly enjoyed by a construction company operating a toll bridge in Boston and thus made possible cheaper transportation. For the first time the Court placed the public interest above private property rights. But Taney is best remembered for his controversial opinion in *Dred Scott* v. *Sandford* (1857). Speaking for the majority, he ruled that Congress had no constitutional authority to outlaw slavery in the territories, a decision that voided the Missouri Compromise (see "James Monroe, 5th President," "Administration"). He went on to assert that blacks, whether slave or free, were not "citizens" as defined in the Constitution. They were, Taney wrote, "beings of an inferior order; and altogether unfit to associate with the white race, either in social or political relations; and so far inferior that they had no rights which the white man was bound to respect."[9] The decision drew widespread criticism outside the South and seriously undermined the prestige of the Court for many years. (6) John Catron (1786–1865), of Tennessee, served as associate justice 1837–1865. He generally supported Chief Justice Taney. During the Civil War he renounced his state's participation in the Confederacy and remained on the Supreme Court.

RANKING IN 1962 HISTORIANS POLL: Jackson ranked sixth of 31 presidents; best of the 6 "near great" presidents. He ranked above Theodore Roosevelt, below Jefferson.

RETIREMENT: March 4, 1837–June 8, 1845. After attending the inaugural of his handpicked successor Martin Van Buren, Jackson retired to his 1,200-acre plantation, the Hermitage, near Nashville, Tennessee. During the economic depression that followed the panic of 1837, Jackson found little market for cotton, his cash crop, and was forced to borrow from friends to meet operating expenses. Covering the debts of his adopted son Andrew Jackson, Jr. further reduced his finances. From the Hermitage, he maintained a keen interest in national politics. He actively campaigned in Tennessee on behalf of President Van Buren's unsuccessful bid for reelection in 1840. He promoted the career of James K. Polk, nicknamed Young Hickory after his mentor. And he lobbied for the annexation of Texas.

DEATH: June 8, 1845, about 6 P.M., the Hermitage, Nashville. Jackson's last years were spent in great discomfort, eased only slightly by opiates. Chronic tuberculosis left him with just one functioning lung, and that one was impaired. His right eye went blind from a cataract. Dropsy puffed his features. Diarrhea sapped his strength. Near the end he could no longer lie flat but instead slept propped up in bed. On June 2, 1845, Dr. Esleman of Nashville performed an operation to drain water that had built up in his abdomen. Soon after waking up on the morning of June 8, Jackson fell unconscious. House servants sent up the cry, "Oh, Lord! Old Massa's dead!" Although a touch of brandy revived him, he and those around him realized he was slipping fast. His dying wish was that he one day would meet all his friends again on the other side—"Both white and black," he emphasized. To the sounds of wailing outdoors, Jackson said, "Oh, do not cry. Be good children, and we shall all meet in Heaven."[10] These were his last words. Late that afternoon, while holding the hand of his daughter-in-law, Mrs. Sarah Yorke Jackson, he shuddered, dropped his mouth open, and died. He was 78. Soon after, Sam Houston arrived, too late to see his old friend alive one last time. The towering Texan sank to his knees and openly wept over the body. According to Jackson's instructions, he was buried in a simple ceremony next to Rachel in the Hermitage garden. In his last will and testament, executed in June 1843, Jackson first instructed that his debts, totaling $16,000 plus interest, be paid from the disposition of his real and personal property. He distributed three ceremonial swords among his nephew Andrew Jackson Donelson, his grandnephew Andrew Jackson Coffee, and his grandson Andrew Jackson III— with the injunction that they use them, if necessary, to protect the Union and preserve the Constitution. He left the bulk of the residue of his estate, including his home, the Hermitage, and its contents, to his adopted son, Andrew Jackson, Jr.

JACKSON PRAISED: "A man of intelligence, and one of those prompt, frank, ardent souls whom I love to meet."[11]—Aaron Burr, 1805

"Faults he had, undoubtedly; such faults as often belong to an ardent, generous, sincere nature—the weeds that grow in rich soil. Notwithstanding this, he was precisely the man for the period in which he well and nobly discharged the duties demanded of him by the times. If he was brought into collision with the mercantile classes, it was more their fault than his own."[12]— William Cullen Bryant, editor of *New York Evening Post*, 1836

"The way a thing should be done struck him plainly. . . . If he had fallen from the clouds into a city on fire, he would have been at the head of the extinguishing host in an hour, and would have blown up a palace to stop the fire with as little misgiving as another would have torn down a board shed."[13]— Supreme Court Justice John Catron, 1845

"I never knew a man more free from conceit, or one to whom it was to a greater extent a pleasure, as well as a recognized duty, to listen patiently to what might be said to him upon any subject."[14]—Martin Van Buren

JACKSON CRITICIZED: "His passions are terrible. When I was President of the Senate, he was Senator, and he could never speak on account of the rashness of his feelings. I have seen him attempt it repeatedly, and as often choke with rage. His passions are, no doubt, cooler now; he has been much tried since I knew him, but he is a dangerous man."[15]—Thomas Jefferson

"[Jackson] spent the prime of his life in gambling, in cock-fighting, in horseracing . . . and to cap all tore from a husband the wife of his bosom."[16]— Thomas D. Arnold, candidate for Congress from Tennessee, 1828

"Ignorant, passionate, hypocritical, corrupt and easily swayed by the base men who surround him."[17]—Senator Henry Clay

"[Jackson's veto of the bank bill] manifestly seeks to influence the poor against the rich. It wantonly attacks whole classes of the people, for the purpose of turning against them the prejudices and resentments of other classes."[18]— Senator Daniel Webster, 1832

"A barbarian who could not write a sentence of grammar and hardly could spell his own name."[19]—John Quincy Adams, 1833

JACKSON QUOTES: "I know what I am fit for. I can command a body of men in a rough way; but I am not fit to be President."[20]—1821

"I . . . believe . . . that just laws can make no distinction of privilege between the rich and poor, and that when men of high standing attempt to trample upon the rights of the weak, they are the fitest objects for example and punishment. In general, the great can protect themselves, but the poor and humble, require the arm and shield of the law."[21]—1821

"Distinctions in society will always exist under every just government. Equality of talents, of education, or of wealth can not be produced by human institutions. In the full enjoyment of the gifts of Heaven and the fruits of superior industry, economy, and virtue, every man is equally entitled to protection by law; but when the laws undertake to add to these natural and just advantages artificial distinctions . . . to make the rich richer and the potent more powerful, the humble members of society—the farmers, mechanics, and laborers—who have neither the time nor the means of securing like favors to themselves, have a right to complain of the injustice of their Government."[22]— 1832

BOOKS ABOUT JACKSON: Curtis, James C. *Andrew Jackson and the Search for Vindication*. Boston: Little, Brown, 1976.

James, Marquis. *The Life of Andrew Jackson*. Indianapolis: Bobbs-Merrill, 1938.

Latner, Richard B. *The Presidency of Andrew Jackson: White House Politics 1829–1837*. Athens, Ga.: The University of Georgia Press, 1979.

Remini, Robert V. *Andrew Jackson and the Course of American Empire, 1767–1821. Andrew Jackson and the Course of American Freedom, 1822– 1832. Andrew Jackson and the Course of American Democracy, 1833–1845.* New York: Harper & Row, 1977, 1981, 1984.

Schlesinger, Arthur M., Jr. *The Age of Jackson*. Boston: Little, Brown, 1946.

NOTES:

1 Robert V. Remini, *Andrew Jackson and the Course of American Empire 1767–1821*, New York: Harper & Row, 1977, p. 378.

2 Marquis James, *The Life of Andrew Jackson*, Indianapolis: Bobbs-Merrill, 1938, p. 383.

3 Ibid., p. 28

4 Ibid., p. 578.

5 Ibid., p. 35.

6 Ben Truman, *The Field of Honor*, 1884, p. 283.

7 James, pp. 539–540.

8 Henry Steele Commager, *Documents of American History*, New York: Crofts, 1943, Doc. no. 144, p. 268.

9 Ibid., Doc. no. 185, p. 342.

10 James, p. 785.

11 Remini, p. 147.

12 *New York Evening Post*, Dec. 3, 1836.

13 Arthur M. Schlesinger, Jr., *The Age of Jackson*, Boston: Little, Brown, 1946, p. 448.

14 Martin Van Buren, *Autobiography of Martin Van Buren*, J. C. Fitzpatrick, ed., Washington: American Historical Society, 1920, p. 312.

15 Remini, p. 109.

16 James, p. 464.

17 Alfred Steinberg, *The First Ten: The Founding Presidents and Their Administrations*, Garden City, N.Y.: Doubleday, 1967, p. 265.

18 *Register of Debates*, 22nd Congress, First Session, p. 1240.

19 John T. Morse, Jr., *John Quincy Adams*, Boston: Houghton, Mifflin, 1891, p. 242.

20 James Parton, *A Life of Andrew Jackson*, Boston: Houghton, Mifflin, 1859–1860, vol. II, p. 354.

21 Remini, p. 414.

22 James D. Richardson, comp., *Messages and Papers of the Presidents*, Washington: Government Printing Office, 1897, vol. II, p. 590.

MARTIN VAN BUREN

8TH PRESIDENT

NAME: Martin Van Buren. He was named after his paternal grandfather, Marten Van Buren.

PHYSICAL DESCRIPTION: A small, though sturdily built, figure, Van Buren stood a bit under 5 feet 6 inches tall. He had a fair complexion, deeply set blue eyes, and a classic Roman nose. His high forehead became increasingly prominent as his sandy curls receded with age. By the the time he became president, he was distinguished by a crown of unruly white hair and great sidewhiskers. He spoke rapidly with crisp enunciation, but when he became excited, it is said, a touch of Dutch accent crept into his speech. He dressed impeccably. Indeed, his natty appearance often was the subject of scorn in the press.

PERSONALITY: Van Buren basically was optimistic, cheerful, quick to smile and laugh. His charm, courtesy, and fine manners made him a much-sought-after party guest. From an early age he was an engaging conversationalist. In politics, however, he preferred to let others talk about specific issues rather than to expound his own views. In drawing others out while keeping his own opinions closely guarded, he gained a reputation as a crafty partisan who, as one colleague asserted, "rowed to his object with muffled oars."[1] His rather unflattering nicknames, the Red Fox of Kinderhook and the Little Magician, reflected this image. He spoke cautiously, often in carefully worded phrases that left listeners in doubt about his true feelings. Van Buren was ambitious, but he was also a man of principle.

ANCESTORS: Van Buren was of Dutch ancestry. In 1631 his great[3]-grandfather Cornelius Maesen emigrated as an indentured servant from Buurmalsen in the Gelderland province of the Netherlands to the upper Hudson region of New Netherlands, near present-day Albany, New York. In America he recorded his native village Buurmalsen erroneously as Buren Malsen, and thus his children took the surname Van Buren. Having worked out his bond of indenture,

Cornelius in 1646 bought his own "house and plantation" on Manhattan; his property was roughly coextensive with what is now Greenwich Village.

FATHER: Abraham Van Buren (1737–1817). He was a farmer, owner of a handful of slaves, and tavern keeper in Kinderhook, N.Y. He supported the American Revolution and later the Jeffersonian Republicans. He died when his most famous son was a New York state senator.

MOTHER: Maria Hoes Van Alen Van Buren (1747–1818). Born Maria Hoes, of Dutch ancestry, she married Johannes Van Alen, who died and left her with three children. In 1776 she married Abraham Van Buren. She never got over the loss of her second husband in 1817; she died less than a year after burying him, while Martin was a New York state senator.

SIBLINGS: By his mother's first marriage to Johannes Van Alen, Martin Van Buren had one half sister and two half brothers, one of whom, James Van Alen, practiced law with Van Buren for a time and served as a Federalist member of Congress 1807–1809. By his mother's second marriage, Van Buren had two older sisters, Dirckie (Derike) and Jannetje (Hannah), and two younger brothers Lawrence and Abraham. Lawrence Van Buren served as an officer in the New York militia during the War of 1812 and later was active in the Barnburners, New York Democrats opposed to slavery.

COLLATERAL RELATIVE: Van Buren was a third cousin twice removed to Theodore Roosevelt.

CHILDREN: Van Buren had four sons.

Abraham Van Buren (1807–1873). A West Point graduate, he served as an infantry officer in the West. He rose to captain before resigning his commission in 1837 to serve as secretary to his father during his term as president. His wife, the former Angelica Singleton of South Carolina, served as official hostess at the White House during the Van Buren years. At the outbreak of the Mexican War, Abraham Van Buren rejoined the army as a major and saw action as an aide to General Zachary Taylor at Monterrey. For his bravery at Contreras and Churubusco, he was promoted to lieutenant colonel. He retired from the army in 1854.

John Van Buren (1810–1866). A lawyer, he was secretary of the American legation in London while his father was minister-designate to Great Britain. Returning to the United States, he opened a law practice in Albany. While his father was president, he visited England and was royally received. The appearance of his name beside those of nobility in press accounts of his reception prompted anti–Van Buren papers in the United States to dub him Prince John. In 1841 he became a Democratic member of the U.S. House, where he opposed the impeachment of President Tyler and the spread of slavery. He emerged a prominent abolitionist in New York, a Barnburner opposed to all compromise with the South on the question of slavery. An eloquent, passionate advocate, he once spent 24 hours in jail for getting into a fistfight with an opposing attorney in open court.

Martin Van Buren, Jr. (1812–1855). "Mat" Van Buren, a student of political science and history, served as a political aide to his father. He compiled information used by the former president in writing his memoirs. He died suddenly while visiting Europe with his father.

Smith Thompson Van Buren (1817–1876). Also a political aide to his father, he drafted some of his speeches and, as literary executor of the president's estate, edited the Van Buren papers. Following the death of his first wife, he married a niece of Washington Irving.

BIRTH: Van Buren was born on December 5, 1782, at Kinderhook, New York. He was the first president born an American citizen. His predecessors all were born prior to the Declaration of Independence and thus were born British subjects.

CHILDHOOD: Van Buren grew up familiar with Old World customs. The family spoke Dutch at home. Although they were not destitute, the Van Burens were relatively poor. Little Mat, as the future president was then called, delivered produce after school and helped out in his father's tavern. The Van Buren tavern was a favorite watering hole for passing lawyers and politicians, including rivals Aaron Burr and Alexander Hamilton, and the lad relished listening to the political conversations that took place there. He observed well his father's studied habit of remaining neutral on controversial issues. Privately, however, Abraham Van Buren was an ardent Anti-Federalist, a political philosophy his son came to share. At 15, Martin Van Buren was dismayed to learn of the victory of the Hamiltonian Federalists in the state elections. An older friend, taking the boy aside, counseled him to join the Federalist party for the good of his career. No, Van Buren replied, he would sink or swim with the Republicans. During the election of 1800 he campaigned for Thomas Jefferson and was elected a delegate to the Republican congressional caucus in Troy. At 18, he thus already was a practicing politician.

EDUCATION: Van Buren learned the basics at a dreary, poorly lit schoolhouse in his native village and later studied Latin briefly at the Kinderhook Academy. He excelled in composition and speaking. His formal education ended before he reached 14, when he began studying law at the office of Francis Sylvester, a prominent Federalist attorney in Kinderhook. Besides reading law, his apprenticeship duties included sweeping out the office, tending the fireplace, and making copies of documents. But he quickly developed a flair for legal argument and at 15 was allowed to sum up a routine case before his first jury. After six years under Sylvester, from whom he also acquired a taste for fine clothes, he spent a final year of apprenticeship in the New York City office of William P. Van Ness, a political lieutenant of Aaron Burr. (A few years later Van Ness served as Burr's second during his fateful duel with Hamilton.) Van Buren was admitted to the bar in 1803.

RELIGION: Van Buren was not overtly religious; he rarely quoted scripture. He did attend church regularly, however, and during hymnody invariably drowned out the voices of those around him. In Washington, he worshipped at St. John's Episcopal Church, because the capital had no Dutch Reformed church.

RECREATION: From early adulthood Van Buren enjoyed the theater and eventually developed a taste for opera. He fished often. He took wine regularly with meals, commonly a fine Madeira or the Italian Montepulciano. He gambled modestly, usually on the outcome of elections.

MARRIAGE: Martin Van Buren, 24, married Hannah Hoes, 23, his childhood sweetheart, on February 21, 1807, at the home of the bride's sister in Catskill, New York. Born in Kinderhook on March 8, 1783, the daughter of a farmer, Hannah Hoes was distantly related to Van Buren through his mother. Like Van Buren, she was raised in a Dutch home and never did lose her distinct Dutch accent. Van Buren was devoted to his shy, blue-eyed bride, whom he always called Jannetje, Dutch for Hannah. Unfortunately, after about 10 years of marriage, Mrs. Van Buren contracted tuberculosis. She died on February 5, 1819, at 35. Van Buren never remarried.

POSTMARITAL ROMANCE:

Ellen Randolph. According to widespread reports, never confirmed by the principals, Van Buren discreetly courted, some say proposed to, Ellen Randolph, a granddaughter of Thomas Jefferson, prior to her marriage to Joseph Coolidge of Boston in 1825. Van Buren was a middle-aged U.S. senator; she was in her mid-twenties. Van Buren characteristically was very tight-lipped about such matters. In his memoirs he referred to Miss Randolph simply as "a very interesting young lady . . . and my warm friend."[2]

Margaret Sylvester. In 1851 Van Buren proposed marriage to Margaret Sylvester, daughter of Francis Sylvester, under whom he had studied law a half century before. He was 68, she 40. Although flattered by the attentions of the former president, she declined, saying that she had remained single all these years and intended to continue so. The two remained friends.

MILITARY SERVICE: None:

CAREER BEFORE THE PRESIDENCY: On his admission to the New York bar in 1803, Van Buren joined the law practice of his half brother James Van Alen in Kinderhook. In 1808 he was appointed to his first public office, surrogate of Columbia County; he succeeded his half brother in that post. He was ousted for partisan reasons in 1813.

New York State Senator, 1812–1820. Van Buren narrowly defeated Federalist incumbent Edward P. Livingston for a state senate seat from the middle District (Dutch counties plus the Catskill region) of New York and was reelected in 1816. A Democratic-Republican, he was a leading supporter of the War of 1812, speaking eloquently in favor of state war measures. He championed the debtor class and was among the first politicians in the nation to advocate the abolition of imprisonment for debt. He condemned the system that jailed people, he said, "not for crimes which they have committed; not for frauds which they have practiced on the credulous and unwary . . . but for the misfortune of being poor; of being unable to satisfy the all-digesting stomach of some ravenous creditor."[3] He also campaigned against fradulent bank practices. In 1815 Van Buren was appointed state attorney general, a post he held for four years while continuing to serve as state senator. During his eight years in Albany, Van Buren emerged the leader of the Bucktail faction, mostly Tammany men, who opposed DeWitt Clinton and his followers. With Benjamin F. Butler, William Marcy, and others, Van Buren forged the Albany Regency, an efficient political machine that dominated New York State politics for many years. At a state constitutional convention in 1821, Van Buren led the effort to break down antiquated barriers to popular suffrage and otherwise to reform state law.

U.S. Senator, 1821–1828. Van Buren handily defeated the incumbent, Senator Nathan Sanford, in 1821 and was reelected six years later. During his maiden speech on the floor in 1822, in which he charged fraud in a Louisiana land transaction, he was so nervous that midway through it he suddenly froze, unable to continue. He fell back to his seat thoroughly embarrassed. In the weeks ahead he regained his self-confidence and went on to become a prominent member of the Senate and architect of the modern Democratic party, successor of the Jeffersonian Republican party. Senator Van Buren opposed President Monroe's attempts to lure Federalists to the Republican party. He cherished Jeffersonian democracy untainted by such Federal programs as internal improvements and a strong central government at the expense of states' rights. He believed in strict party discipline and worked tirelessly, though in vain, to preserve the congressional caucus as the vehicle for nominating presidential candidates. As chairman of the Senate Judiciary Committee, he was an outspoken critic of the Supreme Court, finding particularly offensive its practice of judicial review. During the presidential campaign of 1824, Van Buren supported William H. Crawford and remained loyal to his candidacy even after the Georgian suffered a paralytic stroke. Over the next four years, Van Buren emerged the leader of Senate opposition to the nationalism of President John Quincy Adams. In a particularly persuasive floor speech against U.S. participation in the Panama Congress (see "John Quincy Adams, 6th President," "Administration"), Van Buren declared, "I am against all alliances, against all army confederacies, or confederacies of any sort."[4] During the presidential campaign of 1828, Van Buren supported Andrew Jackson, whom he had only recently befriended in the Senate, because he believed the Tennessee war hero to be the only man able to unite the country behind a program based on Jeffersonian principles. He campaigned vigorously for Jackson, recruiting former supporters of Crawford and John C. Calhoun, forging a North-South alliance committed to his candidacy, and steering to passage the Tariff of Abominations (see "John Quincy Adams," "Administration").

Governor of New York, January–March 1829. Van Buren ran for governor in 1828 solely to improve Andrew Jackson's presidential chances in that state. During his brief tenure in Albany, Governor Van Buren sponsored the Safety Fund Plan, a landmark reform that helped curb the abuses of the banking industry in New York. Under its terms, banks were required to contribute a fixed percentage of their capital to a reserve fund to be used to redeem the outstanding paper currency of any bank that collapsed. He resigned to become secretary of state under President Jackson.

Secretary of State, 1829–1831. Secretary Van Buren exerted great influence within the administration. He encouraged the president to make use of the spoils system (see "Andrew Jackson, 7th President," "Administration"), a practice the Albany Regency had perfected in New York. As the only cabinet member to obey Jackson's order to pay courtesy calls on Peggy Eaton (see "Andrew Jackson," "Administration"), he cemented his already-close relationship with the president. He also was a prominent member of Jackson's Kitchen Cabinet. In 1830 Secretary Van Buren negotiated a commercial treaty with Turkey that granted the United States navigational rights on the Black Sea. In a treaty with Great Britain that same year, the United States renewed trade with the West Indies. Van Buren also helped win reparations from France for losses incurred during the Napoleonic Wars. At Van Buren's suggestion, Jackson reluctantly agreed to accept his resignation as part of a general cabinet shakeup in 1831. The president promptly appointed Van Buren minister to Great Britain, but the Senate, for purely political reasons, rejected the nomination.

Vice President, 1833–1837. Because of substantial opposition within the Democratic party to Van Buren's nomination as vice president, Jackson forces imposed the "two-thirds rule" on the 1832 nominating convention, confident that only Van Buren and none of his rivals could muster such a majority. Democrats continued to require a two-thirds vote for convention nominations until 1936. Jackson chose Van Buren as vice president specifically so that Van Buren would be well placed to succeed him as president. In fact, Jackson seriously considered resigning from office to enable Van Buren to assume the presidency without having to endure the rigors of an election campaign. Van Buren convinced him, however, that such an unprecedented maneuver would draw widespread criticism and cripple his presidency at birth. As vice president, Van Buren publicly supported Jackson on all issues and continued as his closest adviser. Although Van Buren had misgivings about Jackson's plan to withdraw federal funds from the Bank of the United States (see "Andrew Jackson," "Administration"), he supported it once the decision was made.

DEMOCRATIC PRESIDENTIAL NOMINATION, 1836: Democrats convened in Baltimore in May 1835, more than a year before the election, to nominate unanimously on the first ballot Martin Van Buren for president. Richard M. Johnson of Kentucky was nominated for vice president. Both choices were dictated by retiring president Andrew Jackson.

OPPONENTS: Opposition to President Andrew Jackson coalesced into a new party, the Whigs, in 1834. The Whigs, however, united only in their hatred of the chief executive they derisively called King Andrew I, were far too disorganized to hold a convention and rally behind a single candidate. Instead, party leaders adopted a strategy whereby each of various Whig candidates was to stand for president in the region where he was most popular. In this way they hoped to deny Van Buren a majority and thus throw the election into the House. To this end, then, a Pennsylvania state convention nominated William Henry Harrison (1773–1841), of Ohio, the Whig candidate of the West; the Massachusetts state legislature nominated Daniel Webster (1782–1852), of that state, the Whig candidate of the Northeast; and the Tennessee legislature and various southern rallies nominated Hugh Lawson White (1773–1840), of Tennessee, the Whig candidate of the South. Whig candidates for vice president were Francis Granger of New York and John Tyler of Virginia.

CAMPAIGN AND THE ISSUES, 1836: Van Buren's objective was to maintain the Albany-Richmond axis, the coalition of northern and southern political machinery that was the basis of Democratic strength from the Jacksonian era to the Civil War. To do this, he had to satisfy North and South alike on such divisive issues as economic policy and slavery. Pressed for his position on whether Congress had the power to abolish slavery in the nation's capital, as northern abolitionists were urging, Van Buren issued a statement conceding, albeit in carefully hedged terms, that Congress did indeed have such authority. But he then quickly added that he personally opposed abolition and pledged to resist interference with slavery in the South. Although Van Buren enjoyed the vigorous support of retiring president Andrew Jackson, the endorsement was a mixed blessing. Jackson's destruction of the Bank of the United States and his opposition to certain internal improvements (see "Andrew Jackson," "Administration") were extremely unpopular in the Northeast and West, respectively. Tennessee, though Jackson's home state, turned its back on Van Buren. Neither Daniel Webster nor Hugh Lawson White were regarded as serious national candidates. Van Buren's principal opponent, William Henry Harrison, favored distributing the federal surplus and the proceeds from the sale of public land directly to the states with no strings attached. Van Buren opposed this early form of revenue sharing. Harrison was willing to revive the national bank if the economy got out of control. Van Buren opposed the bank under any circumstances. Harrison reflected western sentiment in calling for internal improvements. Van Buren pledged federal support only for those construction projects that were truly national in scope. In the end, it was superior political organization, more than popular sentiment, that elected Van Buren.

ELECTION AS PRESIDENT, 1836:

Popular Vote. Van Buren (Democrat), 762,678 (51%); Harrison (Whig), 548,007 (36%); White (Whig), 145,396 (10%); Webster (Whig), 42,247 (3%)

Electoral Vote. Van Buren, 170; Harrison, 73; White, 26; Webster, 14. Willie P. Mangum of North Carolina, not a declared candidate, received 11 electoral votes.

States Carried. Van Buren won the electoral votes of 15 states—Alabama, Arkansas, Connecticut, Illinois, Louisiana, Maine, Michigan, Mississippi, Missouri, New Hampshire, New York, North Carolina, Pennsylvania, Rhode Island, and Virginia. Harrison won the electoral votes of 7 states—Delaware, Indiana, Kentucky, Maryland, New Jersey, Ohio, and Vermont. White won the electoral votes of 2 states—Georgia and Tennessee. Webster won the electoral vote of 1 state—Massachusetts. Mangum won the electoral vote of 1 state— South Carolina. Virginia electors, while supporting Van Buren, refused to vote for his running mate, Richard M. Johnson of Kentucky, and instead cast their vice presidential ballots for William Smith of Alabama. This defection deprived Johnson of a majority and thus threw the vice presidential race into the Senate for the only time in history. In February 1837 the Senate elected Johnson vice president over Francis Granger of New York, 33–16.

INAUGURAL ADDRESS: March 4, 1837. ". . . The last, perhaps the greatest, of the prominent sources of discord and disaster supposed to lurk in our political condition was the institution of domestic slavery. Our forefathers were deeply impressed with the delicacy of this subject, and they treated it with a forebearance so evidently wise that in spite of every sinister foreboding it never until the present period disturbed the tranquility of our common country. Such a result is sufficient evidence of the justice and the patriotism of their course; . . . I must go into the Presidential chair the inflexible and uncompromising opponent of every attempt on the part of Congress to abolish slavery in the District of Columbia against the wishes of the slaveholding States, and also with a determination equally decided to resist the slightest interference with it in the States where it exists. . . ."

VICE PRESIDENT: Richard Mentor Johnson (1780–1850), of Kentucky, served 1837–1841. Born in present-day Louisville, Kentucky, Johnson became a lawyer in 1802 and two years later was elected to the state legislature. A Democrat, he served in the U.S. House 1807–1819 and 1829–1837 and Senate 1819–1829. During the War of 1812, he took a leave of absence from Congress to command a Kentucky regiment under General William Henry Harrison. He took part in the Battle of the Thames (1813), where he was seriously wounded. According to his own account, it was he who killed Tecumseh there. Returning to Congress, he was a leader in the campaign to abolish imprisonment for debt and was an ardent supporter of Andrew Jackson. For his loyalty, Jackson chose him to run for vice president with Van Buren in 1836, a choice he dictated to the Democratic convention in Baltimore. Johnson was extremely unpopular in the South because he had taken a slave as his common-law wife and raised and educated their mulatto children as free persons. Democrats declined to nominate him or anyone else for vice president in 1840. At the end of his term in 1841, Johnson returned to Kentucky, where he served briefly in the state legislature before retiring from public life.

CABINET:

Secretary of State. John Forsyth (1780–1841), of Georgia, served 1834–1841. A holdover from the Jackson administration, he threatened to resign over a minor misunderstanding with the new president but went on to work harmoniously with him. He was a candidate for the Democratic vice presidential nomination in 1840.

Secretary of the Treasury. Levi Woodbury (1789–1851), of New Hampshire, served 1834–1841. A holdover from the Jackson administration, he continued a hard-money policy. He later was appointed to the Supreme Court by President Polk.

Secretary of War. Joel R. Poinsett (1779–1851), of South Carolina, served 1837–1841. He had served as minister to Mexico under President John Quincy Adams. As war secretary, he sought to strengthen the national defense in the wake of the Caroline affair and the Aroostook War (see "Administration"). His plan to create a federally supervised regional draft system to fill the militia drew such intense national criticism that President Van Buren was forced to scuttle it. An accomplished botanist, he introduced to the United States the ornamental tropical plant that bears his name, the poinsettia.

Attorney General. (1) Benjamin F. Butler (1795–1858), of New York, served 1833–1838. A holdover from the Jackson administration, he wanted to return to private life at the close of Jackson's term, but President Van Buren, a longtime friend and former law partner, convinced him to stay on. (2) Felix Grundy (1777–1840), of Tennessee, served 1838–1839. He resigned to resume his career in the Senate. (3) Henry D. Gilpin (1801–1860), of Pennsylvania, served 1840–1841. A native of England, he was a loyal Jacksonian Democrat and historian; he edited the papers of James Madison.

Secretary of the Navy. (1) Mahlon Dickerson (1770–1853), of New Jersey, served 1834–1838. He was a holdover from the Jackson administration. His age and failing health hampered his performance. (2) James K. Paulding (1778–1860), of New York, served 1838–1841. He dispatched explorers on a four-year expedition to the Oregon coast and Antarctica. He was known chiefly as an author of satirical novels, among them *The Diverting History of John Bull and Brother Jonathan* (1812).

Postmaster General. (1) Amos Kendall (1789–1869), of Kentucky, served 1835–1840. A holdover from the Jackson administration and member of his Kitchen Cabinet (see "Andrew Jackson," "Administration"), he resigned to resume full time his career as a newspaper editor. (2) John M. Niles (1787–1856), of Connecticut, who served 1840–1841, was a journalist and founder of the Hartford *Times*.

ADMINISTRATION: March 4, 1837–March 3, 1841.

Panic of 1837. Just two months after Van Buren's inaugural, banks in New York City and, subsequently, elsewhere suspended converting paper money into gold and silver, touching off a nationwide panic that gave way to a severe economic depression lasting until 1843. The panic was brought about chiefly by three converging factors: promulgation of the Specie Circular (see "Andrew Jackson," "Administration") and the resultant credit crunch, successive crop failures, and an unfavorable balance of trade with England. As conditions worsened, some 900 banks around the country collapsed and the growing numbers of unemployed conducted food riots in some cities. Van Buren, blaming the banks for much of the problem, set out to divorce the federal Treasury from private banking interests. He proposed a system of independent subtreasuries, operated by the government, where federal funds could be deposited safely without fear that the money would be loaned out on easy terms to fuel another round of speculation. After much delay in Congress, the Independent Treasury Act finally became law in July 1840. It was repealed the following year but restored in 1846. The economic slump was a major factor in Van Buren's defeat in 1840.

Caroline Affair, 1837. Canadian insurgents led by William L. Mackenzie of Ontario had been waging revolution against British rule. Thwarted in an attempt to capture Toronto, the rebels fell back to Navy Island in the Niagara River, where they established a government-in-exile committed to an independent Canada. Americans sympathetic to the revolution transported supplies to the island on the steamship *Caroline*. In December 1837 Canadian militia, on orders from Britain, seized the *Caroline* in U.S. waters, set it afire, and sent it hurtling over Niagara Falls in flames. One American was killed and several injured. In a message to Congress, President Van Buren denounced the incident as "an outrage of a most aggravated character . . . producing the strongest feelings of resentment on the part of our citizens in the neighborhood and on the whole border line."[5] Although he ordered American forces to the region, he resisted cries for war with Britain and issued a proclamation of neutrality regarding the Canadian rebellion. In 1840 a Canadian, Alexander McLeod, was arrested in New York for the murder of the American killed in the *Caroline* affair but was later acquitted. British-American relations, aggravated further by the Aroostook War (see below), remained strained until the signing of the Webster-Ashburton Treaty (see "John Tyler, 10th President," "Administration") in 1842.

Aroostook War, 1839. The border between Maine and the Canadian province of New Brunswick had never been defined. Both the United States and Canada claimed some 12,000 square miles along the Aroostook River. The "war," though bloodless, heated up in February 1839 when Canadian authorities arrested American Rufus McIntire for attempting to expel Canadians from the disputed region. McIntire had been acting on orders from Maine officials. Both sides immediately massed their militias along the frontier and sought support from their parent governments. As in the *Caroline* affair (see above), President Van Buren resisted cries for war and instead dispatched General Winfield Scott on a peace mission to the region. Scott arranged a truce, effectively defusing the crisis pending the settlement of the border issue by the Webster-Ashburton Treaty (see "John Tyler," "Administration") in 1842.

The Texas Question. Having won its independence from Mexico at the end of a bloody revolution in 1836, Texas applied for U.S. statehood. Northerners generally opposed annexation, fearing the national consequences of adding yet another slave state to the Union. Southerners and westerners favored annexation. President Van Buren, who had long agreed with the South that the issue of slavery was a wholly parochial matter unfit for national debate, this time sided with the North. He opposed the annexation of Texas because it threatened to exacerbate the debate over slavery and deepen sectional divisions within the country. Texas was finally admitted to the Union in 1845.

Second Seminole War. During the second term of the Jackson administration, Seminoles under Chief Osceola had gone to war against forced removal from Florida to the West. Van Buren drew criticism for continuing Jackson's Indian policy. The last Seminole resistance was stamped out in 1842.

SUPREME COURT APPOINTMENTS: (1) John McKinley (1780–1852), of Alabama, served as associate justice 1837–1852. A Jacksonian Democrat, he promoted states' rights over federalism and opposed, with limited success, the right of corporations to operate outside the states in which they were chartered. (2) Peter V. Daniel (1784–1860), of Virginia, served as associate justice 1841–1860. Van Buren rushed this appointment through the lame duck Democratic Senate during the last days of his administration. On the bench Justice Daniel maintained his longstanding commitment to states' rights.

RANKING IN 1962 HISTORIANS POLL: Van Buren ranked seventeenth of 31 presidents; sixth of 12 "average" presidents. He ranked above Monroe, below Taft.

RETIREMENT: March 4, 1841–July 24, 1862. After being defeated for reelection (see "William Henry Harrison, 9th President," for the election of 1840) Van Buren was nominated for president for the 1844 election by the Missouri legislature soon after the inaugural of his successor, William Henry Harrison. As others rallied to his candidacy, he was the front-runner going into the 1844 Democratic convention. He had come out anew against the annexation of Texas, a position that cost him the support of southern Democrats, but he still controlled a majority of the delegates. He led on the first four ballots but was unable to muster the two-thirds vote required for nomination and ultimately lost to dark-horse James K. Polk. Van Buren subsequently declined President Polk's offer of appointment as minister to Great Britain. He preferred to remain in New York as patronage chief for that state. Polk looked to others for advice in making appointments there, however, and the two soon fell out. Van Buren moved increasingly toward an antislavery position, going so far as to support the Wilmot Proviso, which would have banned slavery in the territories, in 1846. He drew the support of abolitionist Democrats and the antislavery, or "Conscience," Whigs—the forces that combined to form the Free Soil party in 1848. At its founding convention in Buffalo that year, the Free Soil party nominated Van Buren for president and Charles Francis Adams, son of John Quincy Adams, for vice president. Although the ticket carried no state, it drew enough votes away from the Democratic nominee, Lewis Cass, in New York to give that state, and with it the election, to Whig Zachary Taylor. It was for Van Buren, at 66, one last hurrah. He retired from public life to the serenity of Lindenwald, his 30-room brick mansion and 200-acre farm at Kinderhook, New York. Since leaving Washington in 1841, he had relished the life of country squire even while plotting his political comeback. He enjoyed tending his potato crop, fishing, and passing the time of day with old friends in Kinderhook. During 1853–1855 he toured Europe, where he had audiences with Queen Victoria and Pope Pius IX and began writing his memoirs, which he never completed. Politically, Van Buren returned to the Democratic fold soon after losing his third-party bid for the presidency. He was an elector for Franklin Pierce in 1852 and James Buchanan in 1856. And, unlike most Free Soilers, who supported the new Republican party and its nominee Abraham Lincoln in 1860, Van Buren endorsed Stephen A. Douglas. With the outbreak of the Civil War—a conflict he did not live to see resolved—he wholeheartedly supported Lincoln and the Union cause.

DEATH: July 24, 1862, 2 A.M., Lindenwald estate, Kinderhook, New York. During his last months, Van Buren suffered a severe attack of bronchial asthma and weakened steadily. After exchanging a few last words with his sons, he fell unconscious and, in the early morning hours of July 24, 1862, died of heart failure. At his request, no bells rang at his funeral, conducted at the Dutch Reformed Church in Kinderhook by the Reverend Alonzo Potter, Episcopal bishop of Pennsylvania, and the Reverend Benjamin Van Zandt, retired pastor of the church. From the church, a long funeral procession of some 80 carriages under escort of the Kinderhook fire department slowly made its way to the village cemetery, where the rosewood coffin was placed in a protective wooden container and lowered to a grave beside that of his wife in the enclosed Van Buren family plot. In his last will and testament, executed in 1860, Van Buren divided his estate, valued at about $225,000, among his three surviving sons.

VAN BUREN PRAISED: "I . . . believe him not only deserving of *my* confidence but the confidence of the *Nation.* . . . He . . . is not only well qualified, but desires to fill the highest office in the gift of the people, who in him, will find a true friend and safe repository of their rights and liberty."[6]—President Andrew Jackson, 1829

"The more I see of Mr. V. B., the more I feel confirmed in a strong personal regard for him. He is one of the gentlest and most amiable men I have ever met with."[7]—author Washington Irving, 1832

"Van Buren, like the Sosie of Moliere's Amphitryon, is '*l'ami de tout le monde*.' This is perhaps the great secret of his success in public life, and especially against the competitors with whom he is now struggling for the last step on the ladder of his ambition . . . Van Buren's principle is the talisman of democracy, which, so long as this Union lasts, can never fail."[8]—John Quincy Adams, 1836

"His purity of character, his marked ability as a statesman, his exalted patriotism, and his distinguished public service, which extended over nearly half a century, have given his name deserved prominence in the history of our country."[9]—Mayor Gegre Opdyke of New York City, 1862

VAN BUREN CRITICIZED: "Van Buren is as opposite to General Jackson as dung is to a diamond. . . . he is what the English call a dandy. When he enters the senate-chamber in the morning, he struts and swaggers like a crow in the gutter. He is laced up in corsets, such as women in town wear, and, if possible, tighter than the best of them. It would be difficult to say, from his personal appearance, whether he was man or woman, but for his large . . . whiskers."[10]—Representative Davy Crockett of Tennessee, 1835

"This democratic President's house is furnished in a style of magnificence and regal splendor that might well satisfy a monarch. . . . This is that plain, simple, humble, hard-handed democrat whom [the people] have been taught to believe is at the head of the democratic party. . . . He may call himself a democrat—such, no doubt, he professes to be—but then there is a great difference between names and things."[11]—Representative Charles Ogle of Pennsylvania, 1840

"Mr. Van Buren became offended with me at the beginning of my administration, because I chose to exercise my own judgment in the selection of my own Cabinet, and would not be controlled by him and suffer him to select it for me."[12]—President James K. Polk, 1847

VAN BUREN QUOTES: "All communities are apt to look to government for too much. . . . But this ought not to be. The framers of our excellent Constitution and the people who approved it with calm and sagacious deliberation . . . wisely judged that the less government interferes with private pursuits the better for the general prosperity. It is not its legitimate object to make men rich or to repair by direct grants of money or legislation in favor of particular pursuits losses not incurred in the public service. . . . Its real duty . . . is to enact and enforce a system of general laws commensurate with, but not exceeding, the objects of its establishment, and to leave every citizen and every interest to reap under its benign protection the rewards of virtue, industry, and prudence."[13]—1837

"There is a power in public opinion in this country—and I thank God for it: for it is the most honest and best of all powers—which will not tolerate an incompetent or unworthy man to hold in his weak or wicked hands the lives and fortunes of his fellow-citizens."[14]

BOOKS ABOUT VAN BUREN: Curtis, James C. *The Fox at Bay: Martin Van Buren and the Presidency 1837–41.* Lexington, Ky.: University of Kentucky Press, 1970.

Lynch, Denis Tilden. *An Epoch and a Man: Martin Van Buren and His Times.* Reprint ed. Port Washington, N.Y.: Kennikat Press, 1971 (originally published 1929).

Niven, John. *Martin Van Buren: The Romantic Age of American Politics.* New York: Oxford University Press, 1983.

Remini, Robert V. *Martin Van Buren and the Making of the Democratic Party.* New York: Columbia University Press, 1959.

NOTES

1 Arthur M. Schlesinger, Jr., *The Age of Jackson*, Boston: Little, Brown, 1946, p. 49.
2 Denis Tilden Lynch, *An Epoch and a Man: Martin Van Buren and His Times*, Port Washington, N.Y.: Kennikat Press, 1971 (originally published 1929), pp. 236–237.
3 Ibid., p. 125.
4 Robert V. Remini, *Martin Van Buren and the Making of the Democratic Party*, New York: Columbia University Press, 1959, p. 111.
5 James D. Richardson, comp., *Messages and Papers of the Presidents*, Washington: Government Printing Office, 1897, vol. III, p. 401ff.
6 Sol Barzman, *Madmen & Geniuses: The Vice Presidents of the U.S.*, Chicago: Follett, 1974, p. 61.
7 Pierre Munro Irving, *The Life and Letters of Washington Irving*, New York: Putnam, 1863, vol. II, p. 482.
8 Lynch, p. 391.
9 *New York Times*, July 28, 1862, p. 4.
10 Lynch, p. 386.
11 Ibid., pp. 445–446.
12 Allan Nevins, ed., *Polk: Diary of a President*, New York: Capricorn, 1968, p. 247.
13 Irving J. Sloan, ed., *Martin Van Buren: Chronology, Documents, Bibliographical Aids*, Dobbs Ferry, N.Y.: Oceana, 1969, pp. 51–52.
14 Lynch, p. 302.

WILLIAM HENRY HARRISON

NAME: William Henry Harrison.

PHYSICAL DESCRIPTION: Harrison was slim, of average height, with thin brown hair that had grayed by the time he became president and that he combed rather carelessly straight down over his forehead or sloping slightly to the right. He had a long, thin, angular face, of fair complexion, distinguished by a long, sharp-bridged nose, closely set eyes, thin lips, and a strong jaw. A female observer once described his expression as "serene and engaging."[1]

PERSONALITY: A plain-spoken man, Harrison was good-humored, affable, and accessible. The Reverend Timothy Flint, a frequent visitor to his home at North Bend, Ohio, described him as urbane, hospitable, kind, and utterly unpretentious.

ANCESTORS: Through his paternal grandmother, Anne Carter Harrison, Harrison descended from King Henry III (1207–1272) of England. In his direct paternal line, he was preceded by five Benjamin Harrisons in succession. Benjamin Harrison I, the president's great[3]-grandfather emigrated from England (exact place unknown) and by 1632 had settled in Virginia, where he served as clerk of the Virginia Council and became one of the largest landowners in the colony. Benjamin Harrison II, the president's great-great-grandfather, served in the House of Burgesses sporadically from 1680 to 1698 and on the Virginia Council during 1698–1712. Benjamin Harrison III, the president's great-grandfather, was attorney general of Virginia 1702–1705, speaker of the House of Burgesses 1705, and treasurer of the colony 1705–1710. Benjamin Harrison IV, the president's grandfather, served as a colonel in the militia, county sheriff, and, sporadically during 1734–1744, in the House of Burgesses. He was struck and killed by lightning.

FATHER: Benjamin Harrison V (1726–1791), known as the Signer. Born at Berkeley plantation, Charles City County, Virginia, he served in the House of Burgesses 1748–1775, where he opposed British colonial policy, notably the

Stamp Act. As a member of the Continental Congress 1774–1777, he was one of seven Virginians to sign the Declaration of Independence and was the official draftsman of congressional dispatches to General George Washington in the field. He resigned from Congress to take a seat in the Virginia House of Delegates; he was Speaker during 1778–1781. After serving as governor of Virginia 1781–1784, he again ran for the state legislature but was defeated by John Tyler, father of the future president. He was elected from a neighboring district, however, and served until his death. He died when his most famous son was a medical student.

MOTHER: Elizabeth Bassett Harrison (1730–1792). Born at Eltham plantation, New Kent County, Virginia, she married Benjamin Harrison V in 1748. Little is known of her. She died when Harrison was an army ensign stationed at Fort Washington (now Cincinnati), Ohio.

SIBLINGS: The youngest of seven children, Harrison had four sisters and two brothers—Mrs. Elizabeth Rickman Edmondson, whose first husband, Dr. William Rickman, was director-general of a hospital in Richmond during the Revolutionary War; Mrs. Anna Coupland, wife of Judge David Coupland of Cumberland County, Virginia; Benjamin Harrison VI, a paymaster general with the Continental army during the Revolution; Mrs. Lucy Randolph Singleton, whose first husband, Peyton Randolph, was aide-de-camp to the Marquis de Lafayette during the Revolution; Carter Bassett Harrison, member of the Virginia House of Delegates 1784–1786 and 1805–1808 and the U.S. House 1793–1799; and Mrs. Sarah Minge.

CHILDREN: Harrison had five sons and four daughters to live to maturity.

Elizabeth "Betsey" Bassett Harrison (1796–1846). Born at Fort Washington (now Cincinnati), Ohio, she married cousin Judge John Cleves Short in 1814. They settled at North Bend on a farm given them by her father.

John Cleves Symmes Harrison (1798–1830), public official. Born at Fort Washington, Ohio, he married Clarissa Pike, daughter of explorer Zebulon Pike, in 1819. Appointed receiver of the Vincennes (Indiana) Land Office by President James Monroe, he was charged with embezzling some $12,000 and was dismissed by President Andrew Jackson. He died soon thereafter of typhoid fever. His father assumed his debts as well as care and responsibility for his widow and six children.

Lucy Singleton Harrison (1800–1826). Born at Richmond, Virginia, she married David K. Este, a lawyer of Cincinnati and later a judge, in 1819.

William Henry Harrison, Jr. (1802–1838), lawyer, farmer. Born at Vincennes, Indiana, he practiced law for a time in Cincinnati but soon fell to alcoholism. His father tried repeatedly to reform him. "I must again exhort you," the elder Harrison scolded his 26-year-old namesake, "to abandon the lounging and procrastinating mode of life which for sometime you have followed. In the morning go to your office and stay there until dinner and if you have no other business read professional books and never open any other book in those hours devoted to business."[2] It fell on deaf ears. The young man abandoned his practice to take up farming but continued to drink heavily. He died an alcoholic at 35. His father assumed responsibility for his wife and children. His widow, Jane Irwin Harrison, served as official hostess at the White House during Harrison's brief term.

John Scott Harrison (1804–1878), farmer, congressman. The only man to be both the son of one president and father of another, John Scott Harrison, a native of Vincennes, Indiana, married Lucretia K. Johnson in 1824. Following her death, he married Elizabeth Ramsey in 1831. He had 13 children, including, by his second wife, Benjamin Harrison, the twenty-third president. He prospered as a farmer at North Bend, Ohio, and was widely respected for his antislavery views. Elected as a Whig to the U.S. House, he served during 1853–1857. He opposed all measures designed to permit the extension of slavery. In his only floor speech, he denounced the Kansas-Nebraska bill. He disliked politics for its intrigue and back-room deals and retired happily to his farm after two terms. Soon after his death at 73, grave robbers stole his body and sold it to the Ohio Medical College at Cincinnati. School officials, who regularly bought cadavers on the black market for use in training medical students, did not realize that they had Harrison's body until one of his sons, John Harrison, turned up at school on other business and to his horror accidentally discovered it dangling by the neck at the end of a rope.

Benjamin Harrison (1806–1840), doctor. A native of Vincennes, Indiana, he was wounded and taken prisoner briefly by Mexican forces during the Texas war of independence (1836). A doctor, he had established a modest practice by the time he died at 34.

Mary Symmes Harrison (1809–1842). Born at Vincennes, Indiana, she married Dr. John H. Fitzhugh Thornton in 1829 and settled in Cleves, Ohio.

Carter Bassett Harrison (1811–1839), lawyer. Born at Vincennes, Indiana, he married Mary A. Sutherland in 1836. At 17 he was an attaché at the U.S. legation in Colombia while his father was serving as minister there. He went on to practice law, but his career was cut short by his untimely death at 27.

Anna Tuthill Harrison (1813–1845). Born at North Bend, Ohio, she married cousin William Henry Harrison Taylor in 1836.

SUBSEQUENT DESCENDANTS:

Benjamin Harrison (1833–1901). The president's grandson, he was elected the twenty-third president in 1888.

Lytle Harrison (1876–1956). The president's great-grandson, he served as paymaster of the U.S. Navy during the Spanish-American War.

BIRTH: Harrison was born February 9, 1773, at Berkeley plantation, Charles City County, Virginia. He was the last president born a British subject.

CHILDHOOD: Harrison grew up during the American Revolution. When he was nearly eight years old, a unit of Hessian troops and American loyalists under the command of Brigadier General Benedict Arnold attacked the Harrison home at Berkeley. Although the Harrisons had learned of their advance in time to flee to safety, their home was stripped of its furnishings, livestock were slaughtered, and slaves and horses were carried off. That same year the family settled in Richmond while Benjamin Harrison V was governor. At an early age Harrison decided to become a doctor.

EDUCATION: With his brothers and sisters, Harrison learned the fundamentals from tutors in an outbuilding on Berkeley plantation and on other nearby estates owned by the Harrisons. Having decided on a career in medicine, Harrison at 14 was enrolled at Hampden-Sydney College in Prince Edward County for premedical instruction. There he studied classical languages, geography, history, mathematics, and rhetoric. He especially liked military history and was a founder of the campus literary society. An Episcopalian, he dropped out when the school took on a Methodist fervor. He transferred to an academy in Southampton County, where he remained briefly before becoming an apprentice to Dr. Andrew Leiper of Richmond in 1790. The next year he enrolled at the University of Pennsylvania Medical School in Philadelphia, where he studied under Benjamin Rush. On his arrival in the city he received word that his father had died. In obedience to his father's wishes, he continued his studies at Philadelphia for a time, but when his money ran out he abandoned the idea of becoming a doctor and, in August 1791, joined the army.

RELIGION: Episcopalian. A devout Christian, especially during the last two decades of his life, when he read the Bible daily, he attended church regularly and refused to discuss politics on Sunday. When in Washington he worshipped from Pew 45 at St. John's Episcopal Church. One of the last items he bought before his sudden death was a new Bible.

RECREATION: Harrison enjoyed brisk morning walks, horseback riding, social conversation, and reading the Bible. During his brief term as president he liked to rise early and do his own marketing before breakfast.

EARLY ROMANCE: Miss "M" of Philadelphia. Little is known of the mysterious Miss M, whom Harrison met and fell in love with while visiting Philadelphia as a young officer. In a letter to his brother Carter Bassett Harrison in 1794 he vowed to press his suit, though he feared that a lowly army officer might not stand much of a chance, thus hinting that the lady probably had some social standing. He further pledged to give her up if someone else came along who could give her more. "I love her so ardently," he gushed, "I would forego my own happiness forever to contribute to hers."[3]

MARRIAGE: William Henry Harrison, 22, married Anna Tuthill Symmes, 20, on November 25, 1795, at the home of Dr. Stephen Wood, treasurer of the Northwest Territory, at North Bend, Ohio. Born at Flatbrook, near Morristown, New Jersey, on July 25, 1775, Anna was the daughter of John Cleves Symmes, chief justice of the New Jersey Supreme Court and later a prominent landowner in southwestern Ohio, and Anna Tuthill Symmes. Mrs. Harrison was the only woman to be both the wife of one president and grandmother of another. When British forces occupied New Jersey during the Revolutionary War, Anna's father disguised himself as a redcoat and took infant Anna on horseback through enemy lines to her grandparents on Long Island. There she grew up, receiving an unusually broad education for a woman of the times. She attended Clinton Academy at Easthampton, Long Island, and the private school of Isabella Graham in New York City. When her father acquired some 500,000 acres of land in what is now the Cincinnati area, she joined him in settling there. While visiting relatives in Lexington, Kentucky, in the spring of 1795, she met Lieutenant William Henry Harrison, in town on military business. Symmes thoroughly disapproved of Harrison, largely because he wanted to spare his daughter the hardships of army camp life. Despite his decree that the two stop seeing each other, the courtship flourished behind his back. On a day that Symmes was away in Cincinnati on business, Anna and William hastily wed and spent their honeymoon at Fort Washington, as Harrison was still on duty. Two weeks later, at a farewell dinner for General "Mad" Anthony Wayne, Symmes confronted his son-in-law for the first time since the wedding. Addressing him sternly, he demanded to know how he intended to support his daughter. "By my sword, sir, and my good right arm."[4] Harrison shot back. Not until his son-in-law had achieved fame on the battlefield did Symmes come to accept him. The Harrisons apparently had a happy marriage despite a succession of tragedies in the untimely deaths of five of their grown children. With her husband's election as president, Mrs. Harrison did not accompany him to Washington but instead remained at their home in North Bend, making preparations to assume her duties as First Lady later in the spring. Because of the president's sudden death, she never occupied the White House. In June 1841 President John Tyler signed into law the first pension for a president's widow, a grant of $25,000 for Mrs. Harrison. In 1855 her home at North Bend burned down. She then moved in with her sole surviving child, John Scott Harrison. She died on February 25, 1864, at age 88 and was buried next to the president at North Bend.

MILITARY SERVICE: Harrison was a professional soldier 1791–1798 and 1812–1814, rising from ensign to major general. He served in the Indian wars in the Northwest Territory and the War of 1812 (see "Career before the Presidency").

CAREER BEFORE THE PRESIDENCY: Harrison joined the army in 1791 as an ensign with the First Infantry Regiment. After serving briefly as a recruiting officer in Philadelphia, he led 80 enlistees to Fort Pitt (now Pittsburg) and thence to Fort Washington (now Cincinnati). In 1792 he was promoted to lieutenant.

Indian wars in the Northwest Territory. In 1793 Harrison was appointed third aide-de-camp to Major General "Mad" Anthony Wayne, who had been ordered to the region to pacify the Ottawa, Chippewa, Shawnee, and Pottawatomie tribes. At the Battle of Fallen Timbers, August 20, 1794, the final engagement of the wars, Lieutenant Harrison was responsible for holding the ranks on the line. He received an official commendation from General Wayne for having "rendered the most essential service by communicating my orders in every direction, and by [his] conduct and bravery in exciting the troops to press for victory."[5] He was present at the signing of the Treaty of Greenville, 1795, concluding the wars. In 1797 he was promoted to captain but resigned from the army the next year.

Secretary of the Northwest Territory, 1798–1799. Appointed territorial secretary by President John Adams, Harrison welcomed the $1,200 annual salary but did not find the position challenging. As a Jeffersonian Republican, he did not get along well with the arch-Federalist governor of the territory, Arthur St. Clair.

Northwest Territory Delegate to the U.S. House, 1799–1800. Elected by the territorial legislature by a vote of 11–10 over Arthur St. Clair, Jr., son of the governor and then territorial attorney general, Harrison was a nonvoting delegate authorized only to introduce legislation and participate in debate. In the House he introduced and, with Representative Albert Gallatin of Pennsylvania, steered to passage the Harrison Land Act of 1800, opening the Northwest Territory to settlers of modest means. Under its terms government land was offered for sale in small, affordable tracts on easy credit terms.

Governor of Indiana Territory, 1800–1812. Appointed territorial governor by President John Adams, Harrison remained neutral in the presidential contest between Adams and Jefferson, although privately he favored the latter. He was successively reappointed by Presidents Jefferson and Madison. During his 12 years in that post, Governor Harrison negotiated Indian treaties, including the Sac and Fox Treaty (1804) and the Treaty of Fort Wayne (1809), opening to white settlement millions of acres in southern Indiana and Illinois. He also promoted the establishment of a circulating library at Vincennes, the territorial capital. Not all Indians acknowledged the validity of the treaties, however, and residents of isolated white settlements lived under a constant threat of attack.

In 1811, having received authorization from Washington, Harrison led a force of 300 regulars and 650 militia against the Indian confederacy under the Shawnee brothers Tecumseh and the Prophet. In the predawn hours of November 7, while most of Harrison's force were still alseep near Tippecanoe Creek, about 650 Indians, who had been convinced by the Prophet that they were impervious to the white man's weapons, attacked with chilling ferocity. Although taken completely by surprise, Harrison rallied his men and in more than two hours of intense fighting, some of it hand to hand, beat back the invaders. He suffered nearly 200 casualties and inflicted about an equal number. Harrison then burned down Prophetstown. The Indians were completely demoralized. The Battle of Tippecanoe, which earned Harrison the nickname Old Tippecanoe, put an end to the organized Indian resistance to white settlement in the region. Harrison resigned as governor to take part in the War of 1812.

War of 1812. Soon after the outbreak of the war in 1812, Harrison was commissioned a major general of Kentucky militia and then a brigadier general in command of the Northwest frontier and in 1813 was promoted to major general. On orders to recapture Detroit, Harrison got bogged down in the swamps of northwestern Ohio and was further hampered by insufficient supplies. But with Captain Oliver Hazard Perry's victory on Lake Erie in September 1813, he was able to ferry his forces across the lake from Put-in-Bay to Ontario and retake Detroit. On Canadian soil he issued strict orders against looting and other depredations against the local population. He then pursued the fleeing British and Indian forces up the Thames River, overtaking them near Chatham, Ontario, in October 1813. At the head of 2,100 Kentucky volunteers, 200 friendly Indians, and 120 other volunteers, he defeated a force of 1,700 British and Indians. Tecumseh was among those killed. The Americans took more than 600 prisoners and recaptured fieldpieces that the British had taken during the American Revolution. Victory at the Battle of the Thames secured the Northwest and made Harrison a national hero. In May 1814 he resigned from the army because of differences with Secretary of War John Armstrong.

U.S. Representative, 1816–1819. Harrison defeated four other candidates, burying his nearest opponent, T. R. Ross of Lebanon, Ohio, by a 2–1 margin, to win the Cincinnati seat (Hamilton, Butler, and Warren counties) in the U.S. House. As chairman of the militia committee, he pressed for universal military training. He also sponsored a relief bill for veterans and war widows. Aligning himself with Henry Clay, he voted for internal improvements and the censure of Andrew Jackson for his conduct in the First Seminole War. He joined southerners in opposing restrictions on the spread of slavery.

Ohio State Senator, 1819–1821. Harrison defeated William Gazley of Cincinnati for the state senate. In 1820 he stood as a presidential elector for James Monroe. The next year he was defeated 52–43 by Benjamin Ruggles for a seat in the U.S. Senate.

In a particularly bitter campaign for the U.S. House in 1822, in which the opposition ridiculed his war record, Harrison lost by 500 votes to William Gazley. In 1824 he stood as a presidential elector for Henry Clay.

U.S. Senator, 1825–1828. Harrison was elected to the Senate over Wyllis Silliman of Marietta and former Governor Thomas Worthington. As chairman of the Military and Militia committees, he advocated an increase in army pay and an expansion of the navy. He supported the program of internal improvements and protective tariffs of the John Quincy Adams administration.

U.S. Minister to Colombia, 1828–1829. Appointed by President John Quincy Adams, Minister Harrison arrived in Bogota in February 1829. He was recalled by President Andrew Jackson and returned to the United States in February 1830.

Harrison thereupon retired to his farm at North Bend, Ohio. In 1834 he was appointed clerk of the court of common pleas of Hamilton County, the post from which he was elected president.

Whig Presidential Nominee, 1836. In his first try for the presidency, Harrison was defeated by Martin Van Buren (see "Martin Van Buren, 8th President," for the presidential campaign of 1836).

WHIG PRESIDENTIAL NOMINATION, 1840: As Whigs convened in Harrisburg in December 1839, Henry Clay of Kentucky was the front-runner for the nomination, with Harrison second and Winfield Scott of Virginia third. But Clay, a prominent Mason, was bitterly opposed by powerful anti-Masonic elements present at the convention. In successive balloting Harrison gained support; the final tally read Harrison 148, Clay 90, and Scott 16. John Tyler of Virginia, a pro-Clay delegate, was nominated for vice president. The party declined to draft a platform.

OPPONENT: President Martin Van Buren (1782–1862) of New York; Democrat. At the Democratic national convention in Baltimore in May 1840, Van Buren was renominated unanimously. Opposition to Vice President Richard M. Johnson had grown so virulent, however, that delegates declined to nominate anyone for vice president. Johnson, therefore, ran as a de facto nominee for reelection. The convention produced the first national party platform. It called for limited exercise of federal authority and deposit of federal funds in independent banks and opposed federally funded internal improvements, a planned Treasury surplus, resurrection of the Bank of the United States, federal interference with slavery, and a protective tariff.

CAMPAIGN AND THE ISSUES, 1840: This was the first modern presidential campaign, complete with partisan songs, decorative objects advertising the candidates, and hoopla. Ironically, it was a Democratic newspaper, the Baltimore *American*, that provided the Whigs with their most memorable campaign theme. Intending to belittle Harrison for his presumed frontier manner, the paper editorialized: "Give him a barrel of hard cider and settle a pension of $2,000 a year on him and, my word for it, he will sit the remainder of his days in a log cabin by the side of a sea coal fire and study moral philosophy." Whigs were delighted with this image of their candidate. Pro-Harrison rallies were held in log cabins throughout the West, with hard cider served in generous proportions. Never mind that Harrison, far from being born in a log cabin, was raised on the grand Berkeley estate in Virginia or that his present home at North Bend, Ohio was a stately 22-room manor. In the eyes of the people, he was the candidate of the frontier, Van Buren, the nominee of the silk-stocking set. In one publicity stunt, a group of Harrison supporters rolled a huge paper ball from Kentucky to Baltimore touting the virtues of their candidate. The event gave rise to a catchy campaign ditty: "What has caused this great commotion, motion / Our Country through? / It is the ball a-rolling on, / For Tippecanoe and Tyler, Too / And with them we'll beat the little Van, Van, Van; / Van is a used up man." Substantively, the most damaging issue to Van Buren was the economic depression that accompanied the panic of 1837. Without specifying just how he would restore prosperity, Harrison nevertheless won the support of western settler and eastern banker alike. The extent of Van Buren's unpopularity was clearly demonstrated in Harrison's victories in New York, the president's home state, and in Tennessee, where that state's aging hero Andrew Jackson came out of retirement to stump for his former vice president. Henry Clay, though bitterly disappointed over having been passed over by his party, dutifully campaigned for the Whig ticket.

ELECTION AS PRESIDENT, 1840:

Popular Vote: Harrison (Whig), 1,275,017 (53%); Van Buren (Democrat), 1,128,702 (47%).

Electoral Vote: Harrison, 234; Van Buren, 60.

States Carried: Harrison won the electoral vote of 19 states—Connecticut, Delaware, Georgia, Indiana, Kentucky, Louisiana, Maine, Maryland, Massachusetts, Michigan, Mississippi, New Jersey, New York, North Carolina, Ohio, Pennsylvania, Rhode Island, Tennessee, Vermont. Van Buren won the electoral vote of 7 states—Alabama, Arkansas, Illinois, Missouri, New Hampshire, South Carolina, Virginia.

INAUGURAL ADDRESS: March 4, 1841. (The longest inaugural address, it took an hour and 40 minutes to deliver.) ". . . The great danger to our institutions does not appear to me to be in a usurpation by the Government of power not granted by the people, but by the accumulation in one of the departments of that which was assigned to others. Limited as are the powers which have been granted, still enough have been granted to constitute a despotism if concentrated in one of the departments. . . .

"There is no part of the means placed in the hands of the Executive which might be used with greater effect for unhallowed purposes than the control of the public press. The maxim which our ancestors derived from the mother country that 'the freedom of the press is the greatest bulwark of civil and religious liberty' is one of the most precious legacies which they have left us. We have learned, too, from our own as well as the experience of other countries, that golden shackles, by whomsoever or by whatever pretense imposed, are as fatal to it as the iron bonds of despotism. The presses in the necessary employment of the Government should never be used 'to clear the guilty or to varnish crime.' A decent and manly examination of the acts of the Government should be not only tolerated, but encouraged. . . ."

VICE PRESIDENT: John Tyler (1790–1862), of Virginia, served March–April 1841. He succeeded to the presidency on the death of President Harrison.

CABINET:

Secretary of State. Daniel Webster (1782–1852), of Massachusetts, served 1841–1843. Harrison first offered the post to his chief rival within the party, Henry Clay, who declined. He then offered Webster his choice of state or Treasury, and he accepted the premier post. Webster edited Harrison's lengthy inaugural address. He stayed on in the Tyler administration.

Secretary of the Treasury. Thomas Ewing (1789–1871), of Ohio, served March–September 1841. He was recommended for the post by Daniel Webster. He stayed on in the Tyler administration.

Secretary of War. John Bell (1797–1869), of Tennessee, served March–September 1841. He stayed on in the Tyler administration.

Attorney General. John J. Crittenden (1787–1863), of Kentucky, served March–September 1841. He stayed on in the Tyler administration.

Secretary of the Navy. George E. Badger (1795–1866), of North Carolina, served March–September 1841. He stayed on in the Tyler administration.

Postmaster General. Francis Granger (1792–1868), of New York, served March–September 1841. A Whig candidate for vice president in 1836, he stayed on in the Tyler administration.

ADMINISTRATION: March 4–April 4, 1841 Harrison, of course, accomplished little during his brief term. What little time he had was spent fending off an army of office seekers. At times his pockets literally bulged with petitions, and the first floor of the White House was thick with job hunters. He sincerely hoped to end the spoils system practiced by previous administrations. He ordered that incumbent officeholders be removed only for dereliction of duty.

SUPREME COURT APPOINTMENTS: None.

RANKING IN 1962 HISTORIANS POLL: Because of the brevity of his administration, Harrison was not ranked.

DEATH IN OFFICE: April 4, 1841, 12:30 A.M., White House, Washington, D.C. Although he was at 68 the oldest man before Ronald Reagan to be inaugurated president, he insisted on delivering an inaugural address lasting one hour and 40 minutes outdoors in a brisk March wind without hat, gloves, or overcoat. Sometime later he got caught in a downpour while out strolling and returned to the White House drenched. He came down with a cold, which grew progressively worse. He called Dr. Thomas Miller, who diagnosed his condition as "bilious pleurisy." The president remained in bed several days and seemed to rally but on April 3 conceded, "I am ill, very ill, much more so than they think me." More physicians had been called in by this time, but it was too late. He began drifting in and out of reality. He seemed to be sensing that he was losing his battle against the office seekers, for he muttered at one point, "These applications, will they never cease?" Then, shortly before succumbing to pneumonia, he uttered his last words: "I wish you to understand the true principles of the government. I wish them carried out. I ask nothing more."[6] On April 7, Episcopal funeral services were read in the East Room, where the president's body, face visible, rested. After lying in state at the Capitol, Harrison's body, accompanied by 26 pallbearers and a procession of 10,000 mourners, was buried in Washington. In June his remains were removed to his home at North Bend, Ohio, for permanent burial.

HARRISON PRAISED: "No military man in the U. States combines more general confidence in the West."[7]—Henry Clay, 1812

"He has the confidence of the forces without a parallel in our History except in the case of General Washington in the revolution."[8]—Major Richard M. Johnson, later vice president, 1812

"I believe him to be one of the first military characters I ever knew; and, in addition to this, he is capable of making greater personal exertions than any officer with whom I have ever served."[9]—Governor Isaac Shelby of Kentucky, 1814

"It is true, the victory of 1840 did not produce the happy results anticipated; but it is equally true, as we believe, that the unfortunate death of General Harrison was the cause of the failure. It was not the election of General Harrison that was expected to produce happy effects, but the measures to be adopted by his administration. By means of his death, and the unexpected course of his successor, those measures were never adopted."[10]—Abraham Lincoln, 1843

HARRISON CRITICIZED: "The greatest beggar and the most troublesome of all the office seekers during my Administration was General Harrison."[11]—John Quincy Adams, 1840

"The Republic . . . may suffer under the present imbecile chief, but the sober second thought of the people will restore it at our next Presidential election."[12]—Andrew Jackson, 1841

"As unconscious as a child of his difficulties and those of his country, he seems to enjoy his election as a mere affair for personal vanity. It is really distressing to see him."[13]—Senator John C. Calhoun of South Carolina, 1841

"General Harrison was neither Whig nor Tory, but the Indignation President; and, what was not at all surprising in this puny generation, he could not stand the excitement of seventeen millions of people but died of the Presidency in one month."[14]—Essayist and poet Ralph Waldo Emerson, 1841

HARRISON QUOTES: "The American Backwoodsman—clad in his hunting shirt, the product of his domestic industry, and fighting for the country he loves, he is more than a match for the vile but splendid mercenary of an European despot."[15]—1812

"All the measures of the Government are directed to the purpose of making the rich richer and the poor poorer."[16]—1840

"The people are the best guardians of their own rights and it is the duty of their executive to abstain from interfering in or thwarting the sacred exercise of the lawmaking functions of their government."[17]

BOOKS ABOUT HARRISON: Cleaves, Freeman. *Old Tippecanoe: William Henry Harrison and His Time*. New York: Scribner's Sons, 1939.

Goebel, Dorothy Burne. *William Henry Harrison: A Political Biography*. Indianapolis: Indiana Library and Historical Department, 1926.

NOTES

1 Freeman Cleaves, *Old Tippecanoe: William Henry Harrison and His Times*, Port Washington, N.Y.: Kennikat Press, 1969 (originally published Scribner's Sons, 1939), p. 257.
2 Ibid., p. 264.
3 Ibid., p. 22.
4 Ross F. Lockridge, Jr., "The Harrisons," *U.S. House Document No. 154*, 77th Congress, 1st Session, Mar. 21, 1941, p. 48.
5 Dorothy Burne Goebel, *William Henry Harrison: A Political Biography*, Indianapolis: Indiana Library and Historical Department, 1926, p. 34.
6 Cleaves, p. 342.
7 Ibid., p. 114.
8 Ibid., p. 120.
9 Ibid., p. 223.
10 John G. Nicolay and John Hay, ed., *Complete Works of Abraham Lincoln*, New York: Century, 1894, vol. I, p. 257.
11 Samuel Flagg Bemis, *John Quincy Adams and the Union*, New York: Knopf, 1956, p. 419.
12 Marquis James, *The Life of Andrew Jackson*, Indianapolis: Bobbs-Merrill, 1938, p. 745.
13 Margaret Coit, *John C. Calhoun: American Portrait*, Boston: Houghton, Mifflin, 1950, p. 346.
14 *Journals and Miscellaneous Notebooks of Ralph Waldo Emerson*, Cambridge, Mass.: Harvard University Press, 1960–1976, vol. VII, p. 448.
15 Cleaves, p. 114.
16 Arthur M. Schlesinger, Jr., *The Age of Jackson*, Boston: Little, Brown, 1946, p. 292.
17 Dorothy Burne Goebel and Julius Goebel, Jr., *Generals in the White House*, Garden City, N.Y.: Doubleday, Doran, 1945, p. 116.

JOHN TYLER

☆ ☆ ☆ ☆ ☆ ☆

10TH PRESIDENT

NAME: John Tyler. He was named after his father.

PHYSICAL DESCRIPTION: Tall (just over 6 feet) and thin, Tyler had blue eyes, fine wavy brown hair, rather large ears, thin lips, and a prominent forehead. His drawn cheeks sloped severely from high cheekbones to a rather weak chin, giving him a somewhat triangular expression. But the dominant feature was his large Roman nose; its long, sharp ridge bore a distinctive bump. His health generally was poor. He caught cold easily and suffered frequently from indigestion and diarrhea.

PERSONALITY: Tyler had all the dignified charm and grace and the soft, warm manner typical of the well-bred southerner of the early nineteenth century. He mixed readily with strangers of his class. Around working people, however, he became a different person—ill at ease, aloof, unresponsive. Some took this for vanity. But, as biographer Robert Seager pointed out, "What appeared to be vanity was an ingrained shyness and discomfort in the presence of people with dirty fingernails. . . . He had never had any experience with these people, and he was too diffident to gain any."[1]

ANCESTORS: Tyler was of English ancestry. In 1653 his great[3]-grandfather Henry Tyler (c. 1604–1672) emigrated from Shropshire, England, and settled near Williamsburg, Virginia. According to his own account, the president descended from Wat Tyler (d. 1381), leader of the ill-fated peasant revolt against Richard II. However, there is no genealogical proof to support this relationship.

FATHER: John Tyler (1747–1813). A planter, owner of some 40 slaves, he was a friend and admirer of Thomas Jefferson and vigorously supported the American Revolution. After the war, he opposed the U.S. Constitution as a usurpation of states' rights, although the adoption of the Bill of Rights lessened his hostility somewhat. He served as governor of Virginia from 1809 to 1811, when he was appointed a U.S. Circuit Court judge for Virginia. He died when his most famous son was a member of the Virginia House of Delegates.

MOTHER: Mary Armistead Tyler (1761–1797). Little is known of her. She married John Tyler in 1776. She died when the future president was seven years old.

SIBLINGS: The sixth of eight children, Tyler had five sisters and two brothers— Mrs. Anne Contesse Semple, wife of Judge James Semple of the Virginia General Court; Mrs. Elizabeth Armistead Pryor; Mrs. Martha Jefferson Waggaman; Mrs. Maria Henry Seawell; Dr. Wat Henry Tyler; William Tyler, member of the Virginia House of Delegates; and Mrs. Christiana Booth Curtis.

COLLATERAL RELATIVE: Tyler was a great³-uncle of Harry S Truman.

CHILDREN: Tyler had 14 children to live to maturity, more than any other president. By his first wife, Tyler had four daughters and three sons to live to maturity.

Mary Tyler (1815–1848). In 1835 she married Henry Lightfoot Jones, a prosperous Tidewater planter.

Robert Tyler (1816–1877), lawyer, public official. Having served as his father's private secretary in the White House, he settled in Philadelphia, where he practiced law and served as sheriff's solicitor. He also was chief clerk of the state supreme court. He married Priscilla Cooper, an actress, who served as official hostess at the White House during the first three years of the Tyler administration. As a leader of the Democratic party in Pennsylvania, Robert Tyler promoted the career of James Buchanan. At the outbreak of the Civil War, he fled Philadelphia when an antisouthern mob attacked his home. He returned to Virginia, where he served as register of the Treasury of the Confederacy. Penniless after the war, he settled in Montgomery, Alabama, and there regained his fortunes as a lawyer, editor of the Montgomery *Advertiser*, and leader of the state Democratic party.

John Tyler, Jr. (1819–1896), lawyer, public official. Like his older brother, John Tyler, Jr., also became a lawyer, served as private secretary to his father, and campaigned for James Buchanan. During the Civil War, he served as assistant secretary of war of the Confederacy. After the war, he settled in Baltimore, where he practiced law. Under the Grant administration, he was appointed to a minor position in the Internal Revenue Bureau at Tallahassee, Florida.

Letitia Tyler (1821–1907), educator. In 1839 she married James Semple, whom her father appointed a purser in the U.S. Navy. The marriage was an unhappy one. At the close of the Civil War, she left her husband to open a school, the Eclectic Institute, in Baltimore.

Elizabeth Tyler (1823–1850). At a White House wedding in 1842 she married William N. Waller. She died from the effects of childbirth at 27.

Alice Tyler (1827–1854). In 1850 she married the Reverend Henry M. Denison, an Episcopal rector in Williamsburg. She died suddenly of colic at 27.

Tazewell Tyler (1830–1874), doctor. During the Civil War, he served as a surgeon in the Confederate army. After the war, he moved to California. By his second wife, Tyler had five sons and two daughters.

David Gardiner "Gardie" Tyler (1846–1927), lawyer, public official. During the Civil War, he dropped out of Washington College to join the Confederate army, serving in the Home Guard artillery defending Richmond. After the war, he resumed his studies in Germany and became a lawyer, practicing in Charles City County, Virginia. In between terms in the Virginia state senate 1891–1892 and 1899–1904, he served in the U.S. House 1893–1897. He was a circuit court judge in Virginia from 1904 until his death.

John Alexander "Alex" Tyler (1848–1883) engineer. Like his older brother Gardie, Alex Tyler dropped out of Washington College to join the Confederate army and, after the war, resumed his studies in Germany. There he joined the Saxon Army during the Franco-Prussian War and took part in the occupation of France in 1871. For his service he was decorated by the Prussian government. He became a mining engineer and, returning to the United States, was appointed U.S. surveyor of the Interior Department in 1879. While working in this capacity in New Mexico, he drank contaminated water and died at 35.

Julia Gardiner Tyler (1849–1871). In 1869 she married William H. Spencer, a debt-ridden farmer of Tuscarora, New York. She died from the effects of childbirth at 22.

Lachlan Tyler (1851–1902), doctor. He practiced medicine in Jersey City, New Jersey, and in 1879 became a surgeon in the U.S. Navy. From 1887 he practiced in Elkhorn, West Virginia.

Lyon Gardiner Tyler (1853–1935), educator. He practiced law a few years in the 1880s but earned his reputation as an educator and writer. In 1885 he published in two volumes *The Letters and Times of the Tylers*. In this and other works, he consistently sought to vindicate his father's career as well as the South in general. He was a professor of literature at the College of William and Mary and, during 1888–1919, president of that institution.

Robert Fitzwalter "Fitz" Tyler (1856–1927), farmer of Hanover County, Virginia.

Pearl Tyler (1860–1947). At 12, she converted to Roman Catholicism, together with her mother. She married William M. Ellis, a former member of the Virginia House of Delegates, and lived near Roanoke.

BIRTH: Tyler was born March 29, 1790, at Greenway, the family plantation on the James River in Charles City County, Virginia, between Richmond and Williamsburg. In 1979 the 1,200-acre estate was purchased for $1 million by Henrich Harling K. G., an international timber company headquartered in Eversen, West Germany.

CHILDHOOD: Little is known of Tyler's childhood at Greenway in Charles City County, Virginia, except two incidents, at least partly, perhaps wholly, apocryphal: As an infant he once gazed into a night sky and stretched his arms up to grab the shining moon. At this his mother is said to have remarked, "This child is destined to be a president of the United States, his wishes fly so high." As a young student, he led a classroom revolt against a cruel schoolmaster, William McMurdo. Motherless at seven, Tyler was close to his father, who entertained him with lively fiddle music and great tales of the American Revolution.

EDUCATION: At age 12, Tyler enrolled in the preparatory division of the College of William and Mary in Williamsburg. He progressed to the college level and graduated in 1807. Besides the classics, his studies included English literature, history, and economics. A good student, he especially liked economics and is said to have accepted Adam Smith's *Wealth of Nations* as his socioeconomic bible. On graduation at age 17, he returned home to Charles City County, where he studied law successively with his father, with his cousin Chancellor Samuel Tyler, and, finally, at the Richmond office of Edmund Randolph, the first U.S. attorney general. He was admitted to the bar in 1809.

RELIGION: Episcopalian. In practice Tyler could more properly be called a Deist. He believed in a divine creator, a prime mover, who set the universe on its present course. He believed that God loosed evil on the world so that man might appreciate the good. Tyler was tolerant of all faiths; he spurned the religious bigots who rose to political prominence in the Know-Nothing and other parties. A firm believer in strict separation of church and state, he saw great danger in mixing religion and politics. As government officials must not interfere in religious matters, Tyler maintained, so too must the clergy refrain from preaching on political questions. Even such moral issues as slavery and human equality were unfit subjects for sermons, Tyler believed.

RECREATION: From his father, Tyler learned to play the violin well. In retirement, he often performed for guests, at times accompanied by his wife on guitar. Among his favorite numbers was "Home Sweet Home." A good marksman, he hunted deer, fowl, and other wild game about his grounds. He also enjoyed the ritual of the fox hunt. He shared with his second wife a love for animals; the Tylers maintained a menagerie of pets, including a canary named Johnny Ty and an Italian greyhound dubbed Le Beau.

MARRIAGE: John Tyler, 23, married Letitia Christian, 22, on March 29, 1813, at Cedar Grove, home of the bride, in New Kent County, Virginia. Born at the Cedar Grove plantation on November 12, 1790, the daughter of Col. Robert Christian, a prosperous planter, and Mary Brown Christian, Letitia was shy, quiet, pious, and, by all accounts, utterly selfless and devoted to her family. She met Tyler, then a law student, in 1808. Their five-year courtship was so restrained that not until a few weeks before the wedding did Tyler kiss her—and even then it was on the hand. In his only surviving love letter to her, written a few months before the wedding, Tyler promised, "Whether I float or sink in the stream of fortune, you may be assured of this, that I shall never cease to love you."[2] He kept that pledge. Their 29-year marriage appears to have been a singularly happy one. Mrs. Tyler avoided the limelight during her husband's political rise, preferring domestic responsibilities to those of a public wife. During Tyler's congressional service, she remained in Virginia except for one visit to Washington during the winter of 1828–1829. In 1839 she suffered a paralytic stroke that left her an invalid. As First Lady she remained in the upstairs living quarters of the White House; she came down just once, to attend the wedding of her daughter Elizabeth in January 1842. Later that year she suffered a second stroke and died peacefully the following day, September 10, 1842. She was buried at her birthplace, Cedar Grove.

President John Tyler, 54, married Julia Gardiner, 24, on June 26, 1844, at New York City. Born on Gardiner's Island, off the eastern tip of Long Island, New York, in 1820, the daughter of David Gardiner, prominent landowner and New York state senator (1824–1828), and Juliana McLachlan Gardiner, Julia was raised at East Hampton, Long Island amid wealth and comfort. A lively, darkly beautiful brunette, she at 19 shocked polite society by posing for a department store advertisement that billed her as the Rose of Long Island. She was introduced to President Tyler at a White House reception early in 1842. They began seeing each other in January 1843, a few months after the death of the First Lady, Mrs. Letitia Tyler. The president proposed at the 1843 George Washington's Ball. Julia at first turned him down, but eventually gave in. Because her father had recently been killed (see "Administration: *Princeton Explosion*"), the couple agreed to marry with a minimum of celebration. Thus in June the president slipped into New York City, where the nuptials were performed by the Reverend Benjamin T. Onderdonk, fourth bishop of the

Episcopal Diocese of New York, at the Church of the Ascension. The bride's sister Margaret and brother Alexander were bridesmaid and best man. Only the president's son John Tyler, Jr., represented the groom's family. Indeed, Tyler was so concerned about maintaining secrecy that he did not confide his plans to the rest of his children. Although his sons readily accepted the sudden union, the Tyler daughters were shocked and hurt. It was awkward for the eldest daughter, Mary, to adjust to a new stepmother five years younger than herself. One daughter, Letitia, never did make peace with the new Mrs. Tyler. After a wedding trip to Philadelphia, a White House reception, and a stay at Sherwood Forest, the estate the president had recently acquired for his retirement, the newlyweds returned to Washington. Mrs. Tyler thoroughly enjoyed the duties of First Lady. In the last month of the Tyler administration, she hosted a grand White House ball that drew 3,000 guests. The Tylers retired to Sherwood Forest, where they lived tranquilly until the Civil War. Although a northerner by birth, Mrs. Tyler came to espouse the principles of the South. After her husband's death in 1862, she moved north to Staten Island, where her sympathy for the Confederates strained relations with her family. The depression that followed the panic of 1873 depleted her fortune. She sought solace in Roman Catholicism, to which she had converted in 1872. She returned to Virginia to live with the aid of her grown children and, in her last years, a federal pension provided to all presidential widows. She suffered a stroke while in Richmond and, on July 10, 1889, died there. She was buried beside the president at Hollywood Cemetery in Richmond.

MILITARY SERVICE: War of 1812. Following a British raid on Hampton, Virginia, in 1813, Tyler joined the militia as captain of the Charles City Rifles. Assigned to the defense of Richmond, the unit saw no action. For his brief, uneventful service, Tyler was awarded a veteran's bonus consisting of 160 acres of land in what is now Sioux City, Iowa.

CAREER BEFORE THE PRESIDENCY:

Member of Virginia House of Delegates, 1811–1816. Tyler was elected as a Jeffersonian Republican to represent Charles City County in the Virginia House. He led the effort to censure Virginia's two U.S. senators for supporting the Bank of the United States. The state legislature had instructed the senators to oppose the bank.

U.S. Representative, 1816–1821. Elected on a states' rights platform to represent the Richmond district of Virginia in the U.S. House, John Tyler opposed the Bank of the United States, high tariffs, and federally funded internal improvements. He argued unsuccessfully for the censure of General Andrew Jackson for his invasion of Florida in 1818. He was a leader in the opposition to the Missouri Compromise (see "James Monroe, 5th President," "Administration"). He condemned the package as unconstitutional because it granted Congress the power to restrict slavery, and he later blamed it for setting the nation on the course toward Civil War. In poor health and frustrated over finding himself consistently in the minority, he resigned his seat in January 1821.

Member of Virginia House of Delegates, 1823–1825. Tyler was again elected to the Charles City County seat in the state legislature. He first promoted the candidacy of William H. Crawford of Georgia for president in 1824. When Crawford was paralyzed by a stroke, he switched his allegiance to John Quincy Adams of Massachusetts.

Governor of Virginia, 1825–1827. Elected governor by the state legislature, Tyler proposed, without success, statewide improvements in education and transportation. He resigned to accept election to the U.S. Senate.

U.S. Senator, 1827–1836. He was elected to the Senate by a vote of 115–110 in the state legislature, upsetting the incumbent, Senator John Randolph. Although Tyler had supported John Quincy Adams in the election of 1824, he entered the Senate a foe of the administration because of Adams's call for a national program of internal improvements. He joined the antiadministration forces loyal to Andrew Jackson, whom Tyler supported for president in 1828. Initially, Tyler applauded the Jackson administration, taking great comfort in the president's vetoes of the Maysville Road bill and the recharter of the Bank of the United States (see "Andrew Jackson, 7th President," "Administration"). He supported Jackson's reelection in 1832. However, as the battle lines hardened between Jackson and the state of South Carolina over the issues of secession and nullification (see "Andrew Jackson," "Administration"), Tyler turned against the administration. He tried to stake out a middle position by upholding the right of secession while at the same time opposing nullification. But when Jackson requested congressional authority to use armed force to collect the tariff in South Carolina—the so-called force bill—Tyler objected strenuously. In an impassioned floor speech against the bill in 1833, he said: "Yes, sir, 'the Federal Union must be preserved.' But how? Will you seek to preserve it by force? Will you appease the angry spirit of discord by an oblation of blood?"[3] Opponents of the force bill, clearly outnumbered, either absented themselves during the vote or abstained—all but Tyler, that is. The measure passed 32–1, with Tyler casting the lone No vote. From this time on he grew increasingly hostile toward Jackson and drifted into the camp of Henry Clay and the fledgling Whig party. Tyler broke irrevocably with the administration over Jackson's withdrawal of federal funds from the bank for redeposit at various "pet" banks. He now came to view Jackson as a virtual dictator and in 1834 voted for the Senate censure of the president. When in 1836 the Virginia legislature instructed its senators to vote to expunge the censure from the congressional record, Tyler resigned his seat rather than comply.

During the presidential campaign of 1836, Tyler supported Hugh Lawson White of Tennessee, the Whig candidate of the South. However, it is unclear whether he voted for White or William Henry Harrison of Ohio, Whig candidate of the West. That year Tyler was a candidate for vice president, in some states on a ticket with White, in others with Harrison. He received 47 electoral votes for vice president, third behind Richard M. Johnson of Kentucky, the ultimate winner, and Francis Granger of New York.

Member of Virginia House of Delegates, 1838–1840. Tyler was elected as a Whig to represent the Williamsburg district of Virginia and was named Speaker of the House in January 1839.

Vice President, March–April 1841. As a Virginia delegate to the Whig National Convention in Harrisburg, Pennsylvania, in December 1839, Tyler supported the candidacy of Henry Clay. After the nomination of William Henry Harrison, Tyler was selected as the vice presidential nominee in order to gain southern support for the ticket. During the campaign that gave birth to the slogan "Tippecanoe and Tyler too," Tyler campaigned in Virginia, Pennsylvania, and Ohio. He was elected vice president over Democratic incumbent Richard M. Johnson of Kentucky by an electoral vote of 234–48. As vice president, Tyler was not kept informed of President Harrison's deteriorating health. Therefore he was stunned when Fletcher Webster, chief clerk of the State Department, woke him up at his Williamsburg home in the early morning hours of April 5, 1841, officially to notify him of the president's death the previous day. Tyler immediately left for Washington, where on April 6, 1841, he was sworn in as president by Chief Justice William Cranch of the U.S. Circuit Court of the District of Columbia.

CABINET:

Secretary of State. (1) Daniel Webster (1782–1852), of Massachusetts, served 1841–1843. He was the only holdover from the Harrison administration to remain during the mass cabinet resignation (see "Administration"). He concluded the Webster-Ashburton Treaty (see "Administration"). In the wake of the trial of Alexander McLeod for his alleged part in the *Caroline* affair (see "Martin Van Buren, 8th President," "Administration"), Secretary Webster won passage in 1842 of a law granting federal justices the power to free defendants accused of crimes committed on orders from a foreign government. The law was intended to avoid a diplomatic crisis such as that which arose between the United States and Great Britain when it appeared that McLeod might be found guilty in a local American court and executed for a crime for which Great Britain had accepted responsibility. (2) Abel P. Upshur (1790–1884), of Virginia, served 1843–1844. Transferred from navy secretary, he conducted negotiations for the annexation of Texas. He was among those killed in the explosion aboard the *Princeton* (see "Administration"). (3) John C. Calhoun (1782–1850), of South Carolina, served 1844–1845. He had served as secretary of war under President Monroe and vice president under Presidents John Quincy Adams and Andrew Jackson. He concluded the agreement providing for the annexation of Texas that had been substantially negotiated by his predecessor.

Secretary of the Treasury. (1) Thomas Ewing (1789–1871), of Ohio, served March–September 1841. A holdover from the Harrison administration, he broke with the president over the bank issue (see "Administration") and joined the mass cabinet resignation. He later served as the first secretary of interior (see "Zachary Taylor, 12th President," "Cabinet"). (2) Walter Forward (1786–1852), of Pennsylvania, served 1841–1843. Dissatisfied with his performance, Tyler encouraged his resignation. (3) John C. Spencer (1788–1855), of New York, served 1843–1844. Transferred from war secretary, he resigned because he opposed the administration's efforts to annex Texas. (4) George M. Bibb (1776–1859), of Kentucky, served 1844–1845. He shared Tyler's distrust of Jacksonian authoritarianism.

Secretary of War. (1) John Bell (1797–1869), of Tennessee, served March–September 1841. A holdover from the Harrison administration, he joined the mass cabinet resignation. In 1860 he was the presidential nominee of the Constitutional Union party (see "Abraham Lincoln, 16th President," "Opponents"). (2) John C. Spencer, served 1841–1843. He resigned to become Treasury secretary. (3) William Wilkins (1779–1865), of Pennsylvania, served 1844–1845. A Democrat, he was the lone northerner in the final Tyler cabinet.

Attorney General. (1) John J. Crittenden (1787–1863), of Kentucky, served March–September 1841. A holdover from the Harrison administration, he joined the mass cabinet resignation. He later served as attorney general under President Fillmore. (2) Hugh S. Legaré (1797–1843), of South Carolina, served 1841–1843. A South Carolinian opposed to Calhoun and the secessionists, he was widely respected for his legal brilliance. He died in office. (3) John Nelson (1791–1860), of Maryland, served 1843–1845. He had served as minister to Naples under President Jackson.

Secretary of the Navy. (1) George E. Badger (1795–1866), of North Carolina, served March–September 1841. A holdover from the Harrison administration, he joined the mass cabinet resignation. (2) Abel P. Upshur served 1841–1843. He resigned to become secretary of state. (3) Thomas W. Gilmer (1802–1844), of Virginia, served February 19–28, 1844. He was among those killed in the explosion aboard the *Princeton* (see "Administration"). (4) John Y. Mason (1799–1859), of Virginia, served 1844–1845. He stayed on in the Polk cabinet, first as attorney general and later again as navy secretary.

Postmaster General. (1) Francis Granger (1792–1868), of New York, served March–September 1841. A holdover from the Harrison administration, he joined the mass cabinet resignation. (2) Charles A. Wickliffe (1788–1869), of Kentucky, served 1841–1845.

ADMINISTRATION: April 6, 1841–March 3, 1845.

Right of Succession. As the first vice president to accede to the presidency on the death of a president, Tyler began his term amid great controversy regarding his status. The Constitution was ambiguous on the right of succession. Some interpreted it to mean that only the powers and duties of the president, not the presidency itself, devolved on the vice president. According to this narrow construction, Tyler was to be merely acting president—a notion Tyler flatly rejected. From the beginning, he regarded himself as president, his powers undiminished by the manner of his accession. To emphasize the point, he returned unopened all mail addressed to him as "acting president." Tyler's view ultimately prevailed as the precedent that has many times since elevated the vice president to the full status of president.

The Bank Issue and Mass Cabinet Resignation, 1841. Congressional Whigs led by Senator Henry Clay of Kentucky sought to resurrect the national bank that had been destroyed by President Andrew Jackson. Tyler refused to accede to the wishes of his own party and twice vetoed bills to create a third Bank of the United States. Both vetoes were sustained. To protest the president's abandonment of this cornerstone of Whig principles, the entire cabinet, except Secretary of State Daniel Webster, resigned in September 1841. The mass walkout was a political victory for Henry Clay and left Tyler a president without a party.

Preemption Act, 1841. President Tyler signed into law this bill recognizing squatters' rights to occupy public lands. Under its terms, those who settled on and improved unsurveyed public land were entitled to first-purchase rights of 160 acres of their property at $1.25 per acre.

Webster-Ashburton Treaty, 1842. This treaty between the United States and Great Britain fixed the present boundary between the state of Maine and the Canadian province of New Brunswick, resolving a dispute that had erupted in the Aroostook War (see "Martin Van Buren, 8th President," "Administration"). Under its terms, the United States obtained 7,000 of the disputed 12,000 square miles. The treaty also made minor territorial adjustments to complete the present U.S.-Canadian border from the East Coast to the Rockies, leaving the Oregon question to be settled later (see "James K. Polk, 11th President," "Administration"). In addition, the agreement established extradition procedures between the two countries for most crimes of violence as well as for forgery and called for a cooperative effort to suppress the slave trade. Negotiators of the treaty were U.S. Secretary of State Daniel Webster and Alexander Baring, First Lord Ashburton.

Princeton Explosion, 1844. On February 28, 1844, President Tyler and other dignitaries inspected the USS *Princeton*, an advanced warship, the first such steamer to be driven by a screw propeller, designed by Swedish engineer John Ericsson and commanded by Captain Robert Stockton. The itinerary called for the presidential party to cruise down the Potomac and back. The highlight of the day was to be the firing of the "Peacemaker," the ship's principal weapon and at the time the world's largest naval gun. The gun had been test fired successfully and twice that day thrilled the presidential party with its loud report. At its third firing, however, the "Peacemaker" exploded at the breech, killing or injuring those near it. Fortunately, President Tyler was below decks at the time, along with his future wife and others, and thus escaped injury. Those killed were Secretary of State Abel P. Upshur, Secretary of the Navy Thomas W. Gilmer, David Gardiner, father of the president's future wife, an American diplomat, a naval officer, and the president's black valet.

Treaty of Wanghia, 1844. Under its terms, the United States gained access to Chinese ports and won the right of extraterritoriality, or exemption from the jurisdiction of Chinese law, in China. Negotiators of the treaty were Caleb Cushing, the first U.S. commissioner to China, and Ch'i-ying, envoy of the emperor of China.

Annexation of Texas, 1845. (For background, see "Martin Van Buren," "Administration: The Texas Question.") In April 1844 President Tyler approved a treaty for the annexation of Texas. However, the Senate refused to ratify it. With the election of James K. Polk on a proannexation platform in November 1844, public opinion seemed so overwhelmingly in favor of admitting Texas to the Union that Congress passed a joint resolution to accomplish just that. Three days before the end of his term, Tyler signed the measure; it is the first instance in American history of an international agreement being brought into effect by a joint congressional resolution instead of by a treaty. Under its terms, the dividing line (36°30') separating slave and free territory under the Missouri Compromise was to be extended through Texas. Texas officially became a state in December 1845.

State Admitted to the Union. Florida (1845).

SUPREME COURT APPOINTMENT: Samuel Nelson (1792–1873), of New York, served as associate justice 1845–1872. He was chief justice of the New York Supreme Court at the time of his appointment. He concurred in the *Dred Scott* decision (1857; see "Andrew Jackson, 7th President," "Supreme Court Appointments," Roger B. Taney). A strict constructionist, however, he was the only justice to base his opinion on sufficiently narrow grounds to avoid passing on the constitutionality of the Missouri Compromise. It was the majority's gratuitous remarks voiding the Missouri Compromise in the *Dred Scott* case that so discredited the Court. In the Legal Tender cases (1870–1871), Justice Nelson voted to deny the federal government the right to issue paper money, a view that ultimately failed to command a majority. He drafted the majority opinion in *Collector* v. *Day* (1871), exempting salaries of state officials from federal income tax. Nelson feared that if the federal government could tax state officials, it might one day abuse that power to destroy them and, by extension, the states themselves.

RANKING IN 1962 HISTORIANS POLL: Tyler ranked twenty-fifth of 31 presidents; second of 6 "below average" presidents. He ranked above Fillmore, below Taylor.

RETIREMENT: March 4, 1845–January 18, 1862. Quite literally a man without a party, Tyler declined to make a third-party bid for election in his own right in 1844 because he feared that his presence would undermine the candidacy of James K. Polk, who shared his commitment to the annexation of Texas, and lead to the election of Henry Clay. "In 1840 I was called from my farm to undertake the administration of public affairs," President Tyler recalled as he approached retirement, "and I foresaw that I was called to a bed of thorns. I now leave that bed which has afforded me little rest, and eagerly seek repose in the quiet enjoyments of rural life."[4] Confident that history would vindicate him, Tyler retired to Sherwood Forest, his 1,200-acre plantation, worked by a few dozen slaves, located 30 miles east of Richmond and a few miles from his birthplace. There, with his young bride, he began a second family, fathering seven children in 14 years. The Tylers spent summers at a cottage in Hampton, Virginia. He continued to take an active interest in his alma mater, the College of William and Mary, and, during his last years, served as its chancellor. Politically, Tyler returned to the Democratic fold, supporting, though not actively campaigning for, the party's presidential nominees. In February 1861, on the eve of the Civil War, he returned to Washington as chairman of a convention of 21 states hastily called at the suggestion of Virginia to attempt a last-minute compromise between North and South. The peace mission, of course, failed to forestall the inevitable breech. As the North mobilized for war under the new president, Abraham Lincoln, Tyler urged his state to secede. He served as a member of the Provisional Congress of the Confederacy. In November 1861 he was elected to the Confederate House of Representatives but died before taking his seat.

DEATH: January 18, 1862, 12:15 A.M., Exchange Hotel, Richmond. As 1862, the first full year of the Civil War, began, Representative-elect Tyler prepared to take his seat in the Confederate House. He checked into the Exchange Hotel in Richmond, where on January 10 his wife joined him. Mrs. Tyler had not planned to come to the Confederate capital so soon but changed her plans after having a nightmare that depicted her husband very ill. She was relieved to find Tyler alive and well, but two days after her arrival, he began complaining of nausea and dizziness. He vomited and later that day fainted in the hotel dining room. His physician, Dr. William Peachy, diagnosing his condition as biliousness and bronchitis, prescribed morphine and ordered the patient home to rest. Plans were made to return to Sherwood Forest, but on the eve of their scheduled departure, Tyler woke up struggling to catch his breath. When Doctor Peachy arrived, Tyler said, "Doctor, I am going." "I hope not, Sir," the physician replied. "Perhaps, it is best,"[5] Tyler added. These were his last words. He took a last sip of brandy, his teeth chattering on the glass, smiled at his wife, and died quietly. He was 71. On January 20, 1862, Tyler's body lay in state at the Confederate Congress, his open casket draped in the Confederate flag. The funeral at St. Paul's Episcopal Church in Richmond was conducted by the Reverend Charles Minnegrode and the Reverend John Johns, bishop of Virginia. From the church, a 150-carriage cortege proceeded amid light rain to nearby Hollywood Cemetery, where Tyler was buried next to the tomb of President James Monroe. In the North, Tyler was regarded as a traitor for having joined the Confederacy—the only president to do so. No official notice was taken of his passing in Washington. Not until 1915, 50 years after the end of the Civil War, did the U.S. Congress erect a memorial stone over his grave. In his last will and testament, executed in October 1859, Tyler left his private papers to sons Robert Tyler, John Tyler, Tazewell Tyler, and David Gardiner Tyler and sons-in-law James A. Semple and William N. Waller, all of whom were appointed his literary executors. The entire residue of his estate, heavily encumbered by debt, he left to his wife and his second set of children by her.

TYLER PRAISED: "A kind and overruling providence has interfered to prolong our glorious Union, . . . for surely Tyler . . . [will], stay the corruptions of this clique who has got into power by deluding the people by the grossest of slanders."[6]—Andrew Jackson, on the sudden death of William Henry Harrison and the accession of Tyler, 1841

[Tyler deserves] the lasting gratitude of his country [for] arresting the dominant majority in Congress in their mad career, and saving his country from the dominion and political incubus of the money-power in the form of a National Bank."[7]—Governor James K. Polk of Tennessee, 1841

"His manner was remarkably unaffected. I thought that in his whole carriage he became his station well."[8]—Charles Dickens, after visiting the White House in 1842

"An honest, affectionate, benevolent, loving man, who had fought the battles of his life bravely and truly, doing his whole great duty without fear, though not without much unjust reproach."[9]—Confederate General Henry A. Wise, 1862

TYLER CRITICIZED: "Tyler is a political sectarian, of the slave-driving, Virginian, Jeffersonian school, principled against all improvement, with all the interests and passions and vices of slavery rooted in his moral and political constitution—with talents not above mediocrity, and a spirit incapable of expansion to the dimensions of the station upon which he has been cast by the hand of Providence."[10]—John Quincy Adams, 1841

"I could not believe that a man so commonplace, so absolutely inferior to many fifteen shilling lawyers with whom you may meet at every county court in Virginia, would seriously aspire to the first station among mankind."[11]—John H. Pleasants, editor of the Richmond *Whig*, 1841

"Who could have believed that the condemned and repudiated doctrines and practices of the worst days of Jackson's rule would have been revived within the first half year of a Whig administration?"[12]—Representative Samson Mason of Ohio, 1841

"John Tyler, the poor, miserable, despised imbecile, who now goes from the Presidential chair scorned of all parties, but for his profligate and disgraceful, though impotent efforts for a reelection, would have passed at least decently through his official course."[13]—Thurlow Weed, Whig leader, editor of Albany *Evening Journal*, 1845

TYLER QUOTES: "Popularity, I have always thought, may aptly be compared to a coquette—the more you woo her, the more apt is she to elude your embrace."[14]

"Patronage is the sword and cannon by which war may be made on the liberty of the human race. . . . Give the president control over the purse—the power to place the immense revenues of the country into any hands he may please, and I care not what you call him, he is 'every inch a king,'"[15]—1834

"If the tide of defamation and abuse shall turn, and my administration come to be praised, future Vice-Presidents who may succeed to the Presidency may feel some slight encouragement to pursue an independent course."[16]—1848

BOOKS ABOUT TYLER: Chidsey, Donald Barr. *And Tyler Too.* New York: Thomas, Nelson, 1978.

Morgan, Robert J. *A Whig Embattled: The Presidency under John Tyler.* Lincoln: University of Nebraska Press, 1954.

Seager, Robert II. *And Tyler Too: A Biography of John and Julia Gardiner Tyler.* New York: McGraw-Hill, 1963.

NOTES

1 Robert Seager II, *And Tyler, Too: A Biography of John and Julia Gardiner Tyler*, New York: McGraw-Hill, 1963, p. 62.

2 Ibid., p. 56.

3 Ibid., p. 94.

4 Ibid., p. 291.

5 Ibid., p. 471.

6 Marquis James, *The Life of Andrew Jackson*, Indianapolis: Bobbs-Merrill, 1938, p. 745.

7 Charles Grier Sellers, *James K. Polk: Jacksonian*, Princeton, N.J.: Princeton University Press, 1957, p. 449.

8 Hugh Russell Frazer, *Democracy in the Making: The Jackson-Tyler Era*, Indianapolis: Bobbs-Merrill, 1938, p. 163.

9 Seager, p. 472.

10 Robert J. Morgan, *A Whig Embattled: The Presidency under John Tyler*, Lincoln, Neb., University of Nebraska Press, 1954, p. 11.

11 Seager, p. 160.

12 Morgan, p. 45.

13 Rexford G. Tugwell, *How They Became President*, New York: Simon & Schuster, 1964, p. 140.

14 Seager, p. 61.

15 Ibid., p. 99.

16 Morgan, p. 185.

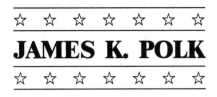

JAMES K. POLK

11TH PRESIDENT

NAME: James Knox Polk. He was named after his maternal grandfather, James Knox, a militia captain during the American Revolution.

PHYSICAL DESCRIPTION: A bit under medium height but sturdily built and erect in bearing, Polk had large, deeply set gray eyes, a high prominent forehead, high cheekbones, thin lips, and a rather large nose. His unruly black hair, which had grayed by the time he became president, was worn long and combed straight back. From childhood, his health generally was poor; he tired easily.

PERSONALITY: Polk was by nature an introvert but out of political necessity forced himself to mingle. He had few genuinely close friends. Still, he was generally well liked. A classic overachiever, he was very ambitious. Biographer Charles G. Sellers attributed his "feverish drive" to "early physical inferiority," "frustrations of his boyish aspirations," and "his mother's stern gospel of duty."[1] To compensate for a lack of brilliance and charisma, he, according to Sellers, "drove himself ruthlessly, exploiting the abilities and energies he did possess to an extent that few men can equal."[2] Yet he kept a firm rein on his ambition, never letting it threaten his career.

ANCESTORS: Polk was of Scoth-Irish ancestry. The name originally may have been spelled Pollok or Polke. His great[3]-grandfather Robert Bruce Polk emigrated from Ireland to Maryland's Eastern Shore about 1722. Subsequent generations moved near modern Cumberland County, Pennsylvania, west of Harrisburg, and later to the Mecklenburg region of North Carolina. Both his grandfathers were veterans of the American Revolution. Ezekiel Polk served as captain of a mounted regiment of the Mecklenburg militia. His maternal grandfather and namesake, James Knox, also a militia captain, fought with distinction at the Battle of Hanging Rock. Through his maternal line, Polk was a great[3]-grandnephew of John Knox, founder of Scottish Presbyterianism.

FATHER: Samuel Polk (1772–1827). A prosperous planter, surveyor, and land speculator, he in 1806 moved from his native Mecklenburg region of North Carolina to middle Tennessee. There he was a founding father of Maury County and Columbia, the county seat. He came to own thousands of acres of land and more than 50 slaves. Politically he was a Jeffersonian Republican and a friend and supporter of fellow Tennessean Andrew Jackson. He died in Columbia when his most famous son was a member of Congress.

MOTHER: Jane Knox Polk (1776–1852). A native of the Mecklenburg region of North Carolina, she married Samuel Polk in a double wedding ceremony (the other groom was Samuel's brother) on Christmas day, 1794. She impressed on her family the value of religion and education. She survived many of her 10 children, including the president. Polk was the first president who did not outlive his mother.

SIBLINGS: The eldest of 10 children, Polk had 5 brothers and 4 sisters—Mrs. Jane Maria Walker, wife of James Walker, prominent businessman of Columbia, Tennessee; Mrs. Lydia Eliza Caldwell, wife of Dr. Silas E. Caldwell of Columbia; Franklin Ezekiel Polk, who died an alcoholic at 28; Marshall Tate Polk, a lawyer of Charlotte, North Carolina, who died at 26; John Lee Polk, a Tennessee farmer who died at 24; Mrs. Naomi Tate Harris, wife of Adlai O. Harris, business partner of James Walker (see above) of Columbia; Mrs. Ophelia Clarissa Hays, wife of Dr. John B. Hays of Columbia, the president's personal physician; William Hawkins Polk, a lawyer who served as U.S. chargé d'affaires to the Kingdom of the Two Sicilies and as a member of Congress; and Samuel Polk, who was expelled from Yale for his part in a student riot and died from tuberculosis at 22.

CHILDREN: None; thus, no direct descendant of James K. Polk survives.

BIRTH: Polk was born about noon on November 2, 1795, on the family farm in Mecklenburg County, North Carolina.

CHILDHOOD: At age 10 Polk moved with his family from his native North Carolina to middle Tennessee. It was a grueling, though doubtless exciting, journey of nearly 500 miles by wagon over rugged terrain. In Tennessee they were met by Ezekiel Polk, James's grandfather, who had already purchased land and settled there. The lad helped his father clear a section for their new home in the fertile Duck River valley southwest of Nashville. But the rigors of frontier life were hard on the boy's generally weak constitution. He fared poorly in the rough-and-tumble sports common among Tennessee youth. On surveying trips with his father, Jimmy Polk usually kept close to camp, cooking and tending to the horses. He suffered from gallstones. The pain was so bad that at age 17 he was sent to Danville, Kentucky, to undergo what was then a very risky operation by Dr. Ephraim McDowell, a pioneer surgeon who a few years before had performed the first successful ovariotomy. With only liquor to dull the pain, Polk survived the operation to remove his gallstones (this before the value of sterilized instruments had become known) and returned to Tennessee with his health much improved.

EDUCATION: Having received informal basic instruction, Polk at 17 clerked briefly at a store in Columbia, Tennessee, in order to learn merchandising. He disliked it and quit after a few weeks. In 1813 he enrolled at a Presbyterian school run by the Reverend Robert Henderson outside Columbia. There he received his first formal education, grounded in the classics. He studied diligently and made such progress that after a year he transferred to a more demanding institution under Samuel P. Black at Murfreesboro. There he improved his Latin and Greek and studied mathematics, science, and philosophy. In 1816 he entered the University of North Carolina as a sophomore. In college he received a classical education, with emphasis on Greek, Latin, and philosophy. He especially liked mathematics and was among the best math students in his class. He also enjoyed public speaking and debate. He was chosen president of the Dialectic Society and joined regularly in its debates, arguing on one occasion against allowing foreigners to hold public office. Graduating with honors in 1818, he was selected to deliver the Latin welcoming address at commencement. His studies had so exhausted him that he was unable to travel home for several months. He had by this time decided upon a career in politics. To that end he in 1819 studied law under Felix Grundy, a prominent lawyer in Nashville and later attorney general under President Martin Van Buren. With Grundy's aid, Polk that same year became clerk of the state senate, in charge of directing the flow of legislative paperwork. The plum post paid $6 a day while the senate was in session. In 1820 Polk was admitted to the bar.

RELIGION: Presbyterian and Methodist. His parents had taken him as an infant to be baptized a Presbyterian, but the Reverend James Willis refused to perform the service unless both parents professed their faith, in accordance with Presbyterian custom. For Mrs. Polk, a devout worshiper, there was no problem. But Mr. Polk refused. An argument between Mr. Polk and the clergyman followed; the former stalked out with his wife and unbaptized child. Nevertheless, James Polk was raised a Presbyterian. He purchased a pew in the Presbyterian church in Columbia and attended regularly when in town. Then in 1833 he attended a religious camp meeting outside Columbia and was profoundly moved by the words of the Reverend John B. McFerrin. Thereafter he was actually a Methodist, privately affirming his devotion to that faith, although out of respect for his mother and wife, he continued to attend Presbyterian services. Occasionally, when his wife was unable to join him on Sunday, he worshiped at a Methodist church. On his deathbed he summoned Bishop McFerrin, who at last baptized him a Methodist.

RECREATION: From early adulthood Polk pursued politics with a singleness of purpose to the virtual exclusion of outside interests. "Politics had become his whole life," biographer Charles G. Sellers has written, "aside from which he had no aspirations, intellectual interests, recreation, or even friendships."[3]

MARRIAGE: James K. Polk, 28, married Sarah Childress, 20, on January 1, 1824, at the plantation home of the bride's parents near Murfreesboro, Tennessee. Born near Murfreesboro on September 4, 1803, the daughter of Joel Childress, a prominent planter, merchant, and land speculator, and Elizabeth Whitsitt Childress, Sarah was well educated for a woman of her time and place. She attended the exclusive Moravian Female Academy at Salem, North Carolina. She met Polk while both were receiving instruction from Samuel P. Black in Murfreesboro; he was 19, she 12. Several years later Polk began courting her, and in 1823 the two became engaged. In Washington as a congressman's wife during the administrations of John Quincy Adams, Jackson, and Van Buren, Mrs. Polk very much enjoyed her social duties. She risked a breech with Jackson, her husband's mentor, by taking part in the social ostracism of Peggy Eaton (see "Andrew Jackson, 7th President," "Administration"). Although not particularly attractive, Sarah Polk was lively, charming, intelligent, and a good conversationalist. President Polk at times discussed policy matters with her. A devout Presbyterian, she as First Lady banned dancing and hard liquor at official receptions. She hosted the first annual Thanksgiving dinner at the White House. She retired with the former president to Nashville, where she remained after his death in 1849. During the Civil War she supported the Confederacy. She died on August 14, 1891, at age 87. She was buried next to the president at their home in Nashville and was later reinterred with him at the state Capitol.

MILITARY SERVICE: In 1821 Polk was commissioned a captain of a militia cavalry regiment and later rose to colonel.

CAREER BEFORE THE PRESIDENCY:

Member of Tennessee House of Representatives, 1823–1825.
A Jeffersonian Republican, Polk was Governor William Carroll's chief lieutenant in the Tennessee House. He led the fight to resume specie payments, opposed with limited success the abuses of land speculators, and generally championed the common man in Tennessee. He broke with Governor Carroll temporarily to support Andrew Jackson for the U.S. Senate.

U.S. Representative, 1825–1839; Speaker of the House, 1835–1839.
In 1825 Polk was elected to the U.S. House from Tennessee's sixth Congressional District, comprised of Maury, Bedford, Lincoln, and Giles counties. He was reelected six times in succession. A staunch supporter of Andrew Jackson, he opposed the administration of John Quincy Adams, speaking out against U.S. participation in the Panama Congress (see "John Quincy Adams, 6th President," "Administration"), high tariffs, and the appropriation of federal funds for internal improvements, even those of direct benefit to his constituents. During the presidential campaign of 1828, he stumped vigorously for Andrew Jackson, who by this time had developed a warm personal affection for both Mr. and Mrs. Polk. During Jackson's first term, Polk remained aloof of the rivalry between Secretary of State Martin Van Buren and Vice President John C. Calhoun, but he continued to enjoy the complete confidence of the president. He led the administration forces in the House against the Maysville Road bill and supported the force bill requested by Jackson to deal with the nullification crisis (see "Andrew Jackson, 7th President," "Administration"). He was a principal advocate of economy in government, arguing in favor of lower taxes and elimination of the federal surplus. Polk helped lead the fight in the House against recharter of the Bank of the United States. In a hastily drafted, but incisive and well-documented, minority report, he exposed the financial weakness of the bank. Appointed chairman of the powerful House Ways and Means Committee in December 1833, he defended the administration's policy of hastening the bank's demise by withdrawing federal deposits (see "Andrew Jackson," "Administration"). If not destroyed, Polk warned, the bank one day would control national politics. Polk emerged from the struggle the administration's chief spokesman in the House. With Jackson's support, Polk sought the speakership in 1833 but lost narrowly to Representative John Bell of Tennessee. In a rematch in 1835, Polk was elected and was reelected two years later. He is the only House Speaker who became president. Polk supported the Van Buren administration and attempted to preside fairly during the bitter debates over the gag rule (see "John Quincy Adams, 6th President," "Retirement"). Polk retired from the House to run for governor of Tennessee.

Governor of Tennessee, 1839–1841.
Having narrowly ousted incumbent governor Newton Cannon, Governor Polk failed in his bid to institute state banking reforms. He ran unsuccessfully for the Democratic vice presidential

nomination in 1840; he received one electoral vote, from Virginia, for vice president in the general election. He campaigned for the reelection of Martin Van Buren. In 1841 Polk was defeated for reelection by James C. Jones, a Whig. Two years later he again ran for governor and again was defeated by Jones.

DEMOCRATIC PRESIDENTIAL NOMINATION, 1844: As Democrats convened in Baltimore in May 1844, former President Martin Van Buren was the frontrunner. He commanded a clear majority on the first ballot but failed to get the necessary two-thirds vote. Candidates Lewis Cass of Michigan, Richard M. Johnson of Kentucky, and James Buchanan of Pennsylvania steadily eroded Van Buren's margin in subsequent balloting, so that by the fifth tally Cass was in the lead, but he too fell short of nomination. Not until the eighth ballot did Polk receive a single delegate vote. Up to this time he had been considered a likely vice presidential candidate. On the ninth ballot the convention swung behind Polk, who received 233 votes, to 29 for Cass and 2 for Van Buren. Polk was the first dark-horse candidate to be nominated for president by a major party. Senator Silas Wright of New York was nominated for vice president, but he declined. George M. Dallas of Pennsylvania was nominated for vice president on the second ballot. The Democratic platform called for the annexation of Texas and "reoccupation" of Oregon and stood against federally funded internal improvements, resurrection of the Bank of the United States, planned surplus in the Treasury, and federal interference with slavery.

OPPONENT: Henry Clay (1777–1852) of Kentucky; Whig. He was a candidate for president in 1824 (see "John Quincy Adams, 6th President," "Opponents"), secretary of state under John Quincy Adams, and the Whig presidential nominee in 1832 (see "Andrew Jackson," 1832 "Opponent"). He was a candidate for the Whig nomination in 1836 and 1840 but lost both times to William Henry Harrison. Because John Tyler had abandoned traditional Whig principles (see "John Tyler, 10th President," "Administration"), party delegates convened in Baltimore in May 1844 united behind Clay, who was nominated without opposition on the first ballot. Theodore Frelinghuysen of New Jersey was nominated for vice president on the third ballot. The Whig platform, the first of this party to be adopted, supported a well-regulated currency, high tariffs, distribution of the proceeds from the sale of public lands, restrictions on the presidential veto, and a one-term presidency. This campaign was Clay's last hurrah. "I am the most unfortunate man in the history of parties," Clay once said, "always run by my friends when sure to defeated."[4] In 1849 Clay returned to the Senate, where he resumed his celebrated role in attempting to reconcile the increasingly divergent positions of North and South, a role that earned him the nickname the Great Compromiser. He was the chief architect of the Compromise of 1850 (see "Millard Fillmore, 13th President," "Administration").

CAMPAIGN AND THE ISSUES, 1844: As the campaign opened, it was widely believed that Clay, long a familiar figure in national politics, would have little trouble defeating Polk, the dark-horse compromise choice of Democrats. But Clay hurt his chances in the South by coming out against the annexation of Texas—a position that was interpreted in that region as an attempt to prevent the spread of slavery. Polk stood squarely for annexation. In the North, where Clay expected his view on Texas to win favor among the opponents of slavery, he was undercut by a third-party candidate, James G. Birney of Michigan, running on the Liberty-Abolitionist ticket. Because Clay, like Polk, was a slaveholder, Birney drew much of the abolitionist vote—not enough to carry any one state but sufficient to tip New York, and with it the election, to Polk. Clay also was damaged politically by his clash with the Tyler administration. Polk, having remained aloof of struggles within the Democratic party, had few enemies. Polk announced that if elected he would not seek a second term. The campaign itself, waged largely in the press as both candidates remained above the fray, relied heavily on personal attacks. Democratic papers denounced Clay as a gambler, a drunk, a shifty opportunist. The Whig press lambasted Polk as a puppet of Andrew Jackson and a coward for having once refused to take part in a duel. Polk had supported Jackson during his turbulent career with such consistency that he was nicknamed Young Hickory. Jackson now returned the favor by campaigning for Polk in Tennessee. It is a measure of Clay's enormous popularity in the West that he nevertheless carried Polk's home state. At 49, Polk became the youngest president up to that time.

ELECTION AS PRESIDENT, 1844:

   Popular Vote: Polk (Democrat), 1,337,243 (50%); Clay (Whig), 1,299,068 (48%); Birney (Liberty), 62,300 (2%).

   Electoral Vote: Polk, 170; Clay, 105.

   States Carried: Polk won the electoral vote of 15 states—Alabama, Arkansas, Georgia, Illinois, Indiana, Louisiana, Maine, Michigan, Mississippi, Missouri, New Hampshire, New York, Pennsylvania, South Carolina, and Virginia. Clay won the electoral votes of 11 states—Connecticut, Delaware, Kentucky, Maryland, Massachusetts, New Jersey, North Carolina, Ohio, Rhode Island, Tennessee, and Vermont.

INAUGURAL ADDRESS: March 4, 1845. ". . . The Republic of Texas has made known her desire to come into our Union, to form a part of our Confederacy and enjoy with us the blessings of liberty secured and guaranteed by our Constitution. . . .

   "I regard the question of annexation as belonging exclusively to the United States and Texas. . . . Foreign powers do not seem to appreciate the true character of our Government. Our Union is a confederation of independent States, whose policy is peace with each other and all the world. To enlarge its limits is to extend the dominions of peace over additional territories and increasing millions. The world has nothing to fear from military ambition in our Government. While the Chief Magistrate and the popular branch of Congress are elected for short terms by the suffrages of those millions who must in their own persons bear all the burdens and miseries of war, our Government can not be otherwise than pacific. Foreign powers should therefore look on the annexation of Texas to the United States not as the conquest of a nation seeking to extend her dominions by arms and violence, but as the peaceful acquisition of a territory once her own, by adding another member to our confederation, with the consent of that member, thereby diminishing the chances of war and opening to them new and ever-increasing markets for their products. . . ."

VICE PRESIDENT: George Mifflin Dallas (1792–1864), of Pennsylvania, served 1845–1849. Born in Philadelphia, the son of Alexander J. Dallas (secretary of the Treasury under President Madison), George M. Dallas, a lawyer and Democrat, served as mayor of Philadelphia 1819, U.S. Senator 1831–1833, attorney general of Pennsylvania 1833–1835, and U.S. minister to Russia 1837–1839. Although he had previously reflected the views of Pennsylvania in supporting a high protective tariff, Vice President Dallas demonstrated loyalty to Polk in casting the tie-breaking vote in the Senate in favor of the Walker Tariff of 1846, an administration-backed measure that curbed import duties. The vote, while winning him new friends in the South, so enraged the people of his home state that he was hung in effigy and was forced to remove his family from Philadelphia for their safety. As minister to Great Britain 1856–1861, he concluded the Dallas-Clarendon Convention (1856), the basis for settlement of difficulties in Central America, and convinced the British to drop their long-standing claim to the right to search foreign ships during peacetime. Dallas, Texas, was named for him.

CABINET:

Secretary of State. James Buchanan (1791–1868), of Pennsylvania, served 1845–1849 (see "James Buchanan, 15th President," "Career before the Presidency").

Secretary of the Treasury. Robert J. Walker (1801–1869), of Mississippi, served 1845–1849. A most able secretary, he drafted the Walker Tariff of 1846 (see "Administration"), raised private funds for the war with Mexico, and established the Independent Treasury system.

Secretary of War. William L. Marcy (1786–1857), of New York, served 1845–1849. It was Marcy who in 1832 had coined the phrase "to the victors belong the spoils," giving rise to the term *spoils system*. In directing the Mexican War, he came into conflict with General Winfield Scott and pressed for his removal. He later served as secretary of state in the Pierce administration.

Attorney General. (1) John Y. Mason (1799–1859), of Virginia, served 1845–1846. He had served as navy secretary in the Tyler administration. He resigned as attorney general again to become navy secretary. (2) Nathan Clifford (1803–1881), of Maine, served 1846–1848. In Mexico he helped conclude the Treaty of Guadalupe Hidalgo (1848) ending the Mexican War. He later was appointed to the Supreme Court by President James Buchanan. (3) Isaac Toucey (1792–1869), of Connecticut, served 1848–1849. He later served as navy secretary in the Buchanan administration.

Secretary of the Navy. (1) George Bancroft (1800–1891), of Massachusetts, served 1845–1846. The preeminent American historian of his day, he wrote the definitive *History of the United States* (10 vols., 1834–1874). As navy secretary he founded the U.S. Naval Academy at Annapolis. He directed the U.S. occupation of California and, as acting secretary of war, dispatched General Zachary Taylor across the border, touching off the Mexican War. He resigned to become U.S. minister to Great Britain. He later served as minister to Prussia and Germany under Presidents Andrew Johnson and Ulysses S. Grant. (2) John Y. Mason served 1846–1849. Transferred from attorney general, he disappointed the president in failing properly to direct naval support during the Mexican War. Later, as minister to France, he helped draft the Ostend Manifesto (see "Franklin Pierce, 14th President," "Administration").

Postmaster General. Cave Johnson (1793–1866), of Tennessee, served 1845–1849. He introduced the use of postage stamps.

ADMINISTRATION: March 4, 1845–March 3, 1849.

Oregon Treaty, 1846. Both Great Britain and the United States had long claimed the Oregon territory, the expanse west of the Rockies between 42° and 54°40' latitude. Polk at first would settle for nothing less than the entire region. "Fifty-four Forty or Fight!" was the Democrats' clarion call. But Polk soon agreed to the compromise that fixed the present boundary at the 49th parallel, thus granting the United States the present-day states of Washington and

Oregon. Vancouver Island, including the portion south of the 49th parallel, went to Britain.

Mexican War, 1846–1848. Manifest Destiny, a phrase popularized by Democrats to express the belief that the United States was divinely driven to rule from sea to sea, swept the nation, especially the West and South. President Polk wholeheartedly endorsed the concept. The annexation of Texas poisoned Mexican-American relations, and the border between the two countries remained in dispute. The United States claimed the Rio Grande as its southwest boundary; Mexico fixed the border at the Nueces River. In an attempt to resolve the issue peaceably while at the same time satisfying the American hunger for westward expansion, Polk in 1845 dispatched John Slidell to Mexico to offer that government compensation for its acceptance of the Rio Grande boundary as well as to offer to purchase New Mexico and California. With the failure of the Slidell mission, Polk prepared for war. He ordered U.S. forces under General Zachary Taylor into the disputed region.

The war: In April 1846 Mexican troops engaged Taylor's forces in the disputed region, thus providing Polk a concrete act of aggression on which to base his own request for a congressional declaration of war. "Mexico," Polk charged in his war message or May 11, 1846, "has passed the boundary of the United States, has invaded our territory and shed American blood upon the American soil."[5] Congress declared war two days later by a vote of 174–14 in the House and 40–2 in the Senate. Democrats enthusiastically supported the war effort. Whigs, however, were divided: Northern "Conscience" Whigs, among them Representative Abraham Lincoln of Illinois, denounced the conflict as an act of U.S. aggression, a device designed to spread slavery westward into captured territory. Southern and western "Cotton" Whigs supported the war. Twice the House passed the Wilmot Proviso barring slavery from any territory acquired in the war; twice the Senate defeated it.

Although Mexican forces outnumbered U.S. forces and enjoyed the advantage of fighting on familiar terrain, the United States utilized more sophisticated artillery and superior military skills to win the war. General Taylor pressed south, defeating the enemy at Palo Alto and Resaca de la Palma in May 1846 and capturing after intense fighting the stronghold of Monterrey in September. In February 1847 he defeated the Mexican army under Santa Anna at Buena Vista. U.S. forces led by General Winfield Scott took Veracruz in March 1847, routed Santa Anna at Cerro Gordo in April, and occupied Mexico City, the capital, in September. Meanwhile, to the north Commodore John D. Sloat had seized Monterey and San Francisco. Troops under General Stephen W. Kearny had captured Santa Fe and marched west to California. There with naval forces led by Commodore Robert F. Stockton and aided by an American insurrection against Mexican rule engineered by John C. Frémont, Kearny crushed the Mexicans. With the U.S. victory at San Gabriel in January 1847, California fell into American hands.

Treaty of Guadalupe Hidalgo, February 1848: Under the terms of the Treaty of Guadalupe Hidalgo, ending the war, (1) the border between the United States and Mexico was fixed at the Rio Grande; Mexico thus relinquished all or part of modern California, Nevada, Utah, Wyoming, Colorado, Texas, New Mexico, and Arizona; (2) Mexicans residing in the ceded territory were free to remain or to move to Mexico at any time without loss of personal or real property; (3) the United States was to pay Mexico $15 million for the ceded territory; (4) the

United States agreed to assume all claims lodged against Mexico by American citizens, a sum that totaled more than $3 million. Nicholas P. Trist negotiated the treaty for the United States after Polk had ordered his recall. Polk nevertheless accepted its terms. Ratified 38–14 by the Senate in March 1848, the treaty took effect in July.

Results: The United States acquired more than 500,000 square miles in the Southwest, the largest single annexation since the Louisiana Purchase. Mexico was reduced to about one-half its former size. Mexican resentment of the United States for what it regarded as a blatant land seizure still lingers. In the United States, whether to permit slavery in the newly won territory became the focus of national debate.

Walker Tariff, 1846. A longtime advocate of free trade, Polk signed into law a significant reduction in the tariff rates drawn up by Secretary of the Treasury Robert J. Walker. The law instituted the practice of storing imported goods in warehouses pending payment of duties.

Independent Treasury Act, 1846. A Polk-supported measure, this act restored the system of independent subtreasuries created by President Martin Van Buren in 1840 and repealed the following year by the newly elected Whig majority. It required that all federal funds be deposited in treasuries independent of private banks and that all debts due the government be paid in gold and silver coin or in federal Treasury notes.

States Admitted to the Union: Texas (1845), Iowa (1846), Wisconsin (1848).

SUPREME COURT APPOINTMENTS: (1) Levi Woodbury (1789–1851), of New Hampshire, served as associate justice 1845–1851. He had served as navy secretary in the Jackson administration and Treasury secretary in the Van Buren administration. A strict constructionist and defender of states' rights, he generally sided with Chief Justice Roger B. Taney. Although personally opposed to slavery, he nevertheless felt bound to uphold the constitutionality of the 1793 Fugitive Slave Law in speaking for the Court in *Jones* v. *Van Zandt* (1847). (2) Robert C. Grier (1794–1870), of Pennsylvania, served as associate justice 1846–1870. His first choice, George W. Woodward of Pennsylvania, having been rejected by the Senate and his second choice, James Buchanan, the future president, having declined the appointment, Polk turned to Grier, a Democrat and district court judge of Allegheny County. Grier concurred in the *Dred Scott* decision (see "Andrew Jackson, 7th President," "Supreme Court Appointments," Roger B. Taney). Speaking for a divided court in the Prize Cases (1863), he upheld the right of President Abraham Lincoln to blockade southern ports during the Civil War. He grew senile in his last years on the bench.

RANKING IN 1962 HISTORIANS POLL: Polk ranked eighth of 31 presidents; third of 6 "near great" presidents. He ranked above Truman, below Theodore Roosevelt. He was the greatest one-term president, according to the poll.

RETIREMENT: March 4–June 15, 1849. Polk early announced his intention to retire at the end of one term. "I feel exceedingly relieved that I am now free from all public cares," Polk confided to his diary on the day he left office. "I am sure I shall be a happier man in my retirement than I have been during the four years I have filled the highest office in the gift of my countrymen."[6] Unfortunately, he was to enjoy barely three months of retirement, the least of any former president. Leaving Washington following the inaugural of his successor, Zachary Taylor, Polk embarked on an extensive month-long southern tour that took him down the Atlantic seaboard, west along the Gulf states, and up the

Mississippi to Tennessee. The festivities enroute sorely taxed his energy. For his retirement he had recently purchased the home of Senator Felix Grundy in Nashville, a residence he named Polk Place. He spent his final weeks there sorting his papers and overseeing the remodeling of the estate.

DEATH: June 15, 1849, Polk Place, Nashville. During his southern tour, Polk fell ill, possibly from cholera that had broken out in New Orleans, one of his stops. He complained of "a derangement of the stomach and bowels,"[7] weakness, and fatigue. The diarrhea that often plagued him during his presidency returned. He grew progressively weaker and died on June 15, 1849. He was 53. He was buried at Polk Place. In 1893 his and his wife's remains were removed to a tomb at the state Capitol in Nashville. In his last will and testament, Polk left the bulk of his estate to his wife, requesting that she make provision to free their slaves on her death, a plea obviated by the Emancipation.

POLK PRAISED: "James K. Polk, of Tennessee—an able, honest, and incorruptible champion of the People's rights, in the Congress of the United States."[8]—toast of Philadelphia Democrats, 1834

"No man and no administration was ever more assailed, and none ever achieved more. . . . The United States were never in a more proud, peaceful, and prosperous condition than at present."[9]—*New York Sun*, 1849

"James K. Polk . . . proved an excellent embodiment of the principles of the Democrats. He had been well known in the House of Representatives, over which he had presided as Speaker, and where he had served most honorably, if without distinction. He was a southerner, and fully committed in favor of annexation. Though in no sense a man of brilliant parts, he may be said to have been a thoroughly representative man of his class, a sturdy, upright, straightforward party man. He believed in the policy for which his party had declared, and he meant, if elected, to carry it out."[10]—Professor Woodrow Wilson of Princeton University, 1902

"James K. Polk, a great president. Said what he intended to do and did it."[11]—former president Harry S Truman, 1960

POLK CRITICIZED: "He has no wit, no literature, no point of argument, no gracefulness of delivery, no elegance of language, no philosophy, no pathos, no felicitous impromptus; nothing that can constitute an orator, but confidence, fluency, and labor."[12]—Representative John Quincy Adams of Massachusetts, 1834

"Jas. K. Polk is an artful, cunning, intriguing man. He will talk soft words to you; he has a smooth tongue; but, mind, he is a snake in the grass; he will steal around you and win you away ere you are apprised of it."[13]—Paris *West Tennessean*, 1838

"I more than suspect that he is deeply conscious of being in the wrong,—that he feels the blood of this [the Mexican] war, like the blood of Abel, is crying to Heaven against him. . . . He is a bewildered, confounded, and miserably perplexed man."[14]—Representative Abraham Lincoln of Illinois, 1848

"Polk's appointments all in all are the most damnable set that was ever made by any President since the government was organized. . . . He has a set of interested *parasites* about him, who flatter him until he does not know himself. He seems to be acting upon the principle of hanging an old friend for the purpose of making two new ones."[15]—Representative Andrew Johnson of Tennessee

POLK QUOTES: "Public opinion: May it always perform one of its appropriate offices, by teaching the public functionaries of the State and of the Federal

Government, that neither shall assume the exercise of powers entrusted by the Constitution to the other."[16]—1830

"I would keep as much money in the treasury as the safety of the Government required, and no more. I would keep no surplus revenue there to scramble for, either for internal improvements, or for any thing else. I would bring the Government back to what it was intended to be—a plain economical Government."[17]—1830

"The passion for office and the number of unworthy persons who seek to live on the public is increasing beyond former example, and I now predict that no President of the United States of either party will ever again be reelected. The reason is that the patronage of the government will destroy the popularity of any President, however well he may administer the government."[18]—1847

BOOK BY POLK: *The Diary of James K. Polk during His Presidency, 1845 to 1849.* 4 vols., ed. Milo M. Quaife. Chicago: McClurg, 1910.

BOOK ABOUT POLK: McCormac, Eugene I. *James K. Polk: A Political Biography.* New York: Russell, 1965 (originally published 1922).

Sellers, Charles Grier, Jr. *James K. Polk, Jacksonian.* Princeton, N.J.: Princeton University Press, 1957.

NOTES

1 Charles Grier Sellers, Jr., *James K. Polk: Jacksonian*, Princeton, N.J.: Princeton University Press, 1957, pp. 40–41.

2 Ibid., pp.355–356.

3 Ibid., p. 355.

4 Irving Stone, *They Also Ran: The Story of the Men Who Were Defeated for the Presidency*, Garden City, N.Y.: Doubleday, 1966, p. 54.

5 Henry Steele Commager, ed., *Documents of American History*, New York: Crofts, 1945, Doc. no. 168, p. 311.

6 Allan Nevins, ed., *Polk: Diary of a President 1845–1849*, New York: Capricorn, 1968, p. 388.

7 Ibid., p. 400.

8 Sellers, p. 218.

9 Martha McBride Morrel, *Young Hickory: The Life and Times of President James K. Polk*, New York: Dutton, 1949, p. 368.

10 Woodrow Wilson, *Epochs of American History: Division and Reunion*, New York: Longman's Green, 1902, p. 146.

11 Robert H. Ferrell, ed., *Off the Record: The Private Papers of Harry S. Truman*, New York: Harper & Row, 1980, p. 390.

12 Sellers, p. 217.

13 Ibid., p. 357.

14 Carl Sandburg, *Abraham Lincoln: The Prairie Years and the War Years*, New York: Harcourt, Brace & World, 1954, p. 96.

15 Richard Kenin and Justin Wintle, eds., *Dictionary of Biographical Quotation*, New York: Knopf, 1978, p. 603.

16 Sellers, p. 148.

17 Ibid., p. 152.

18 Nevins, p. 184.

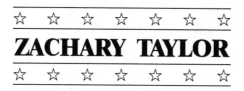

☆ ☆ ☆ ☆ ☆ ☆ ☆

ZACHARY TAYLOR

☆ ☆ ☆ ☆ ☆ ☆ ☆

12TH PRESIDENT

NAME: Zachary Taylor. He was named after his paternal grandfather.

PHYSICAL DESCRIPTION: Taylor stood about 5 feet 8 inches tall and weighed about 170 pounds in his prime, about 200 pounds as president. A disproportionate figure, he had long, gangling arms, a thickly set torso, and short, bowed legs. His long thin face was dominated by a high forehead and long nose. He had brown hair and hazel eyes. Farsighted and walleyed, he wore reading glasses and often squinted. He dressed sloppily, wearing whatever was most comfortable, and even as a soldier typically appeared in a hodgepodge of civilian and military dress. He often walked or stood with one hand behind his back. His health generally was sound.

PERSONALITY: By all accounts, Taylor was genuinely warm, open, and plainspoken. He was said to be a bit shy before new acquaintances but warmed readily. He stammered occasionally and thought carefully before speaking. Far from being the unmannerly boor that his long years in the military and careless dress led many to expect, he was, according to biographer Holman Hamilton, "a gentleman, inherently gracious, even gallant where women were concerned, and an affable and agreeable host . . . true to the Virginia-Kentucky tradition of unstudied gentlemanliness."[1]

ANCESTORS: Taylor was of English ancestry. He was a direct descendant of William Brewster, the Pilgrim leader who arrived on the *Mayflower.* His great-great-grandfather James Taylor emigrated from Carlisle, England, in the mid-seventeenth century and settled in St. Stephen's Parish, New Kent County (later King and Queen County), Virginia. His great-grandfather James Taylor (1673–1729), among the largest landowners in Virginia in his time, served in the House of Burgesses; he also was the great-grandfather of James Madison.

FATHER: Richard Taylor (1744–1829), planter, public official. He served in the Continental army during the American Revolution, rising to lieutenant colonel and participating in the battles of White Plains (1776) and Brandywine (1777).

During 1784–1785 he moved his family from his native Virginia to near Louisville, Kentucky. He came to own more than 10,000 acres of land in various parts of Kentucky. He served as justice of the peace, county magistrate, state legislator, and, by appointment of President George Washington, collector of the port of Louisville. Politically he was a Democratic-Republican; he supported Presidents Jefferson, Madison, and Monroe. In 1824 he supported Henry Clay. He died when his most famous son was a lieutenant colonel in the army. He bequeathed Zachary Taylor a farm in Jefferson County, Kentucky.

MOTHER: Sarah "Sally" Dabney Strother Taylor (1760–1822). Raised in Culpeper County, Virginia, she was well educated for a woman of her time and place. In 1779 she married Richard Taylor, at 35 nearly twice her age. Her hands were permanently disfigured in an accident when molten lead was spilled on her while she was making bullets. She died when Taylor was a lieutenant colonel in the army.

SIBLINGS: The third of eight children to live to maturity, Taylor had four brothers and three sisters—Hancock Taylor, manager of the Taylor lands in Kentucky while Zachary Taylor was absent and quartermaster's sergeant during the War of 1812; William Dabney Strother Taylor, a lieutenant of artillery in the army who was killed by Indians while stationed at Fort Pickering, Tennessee, in 1808; George Taylor, veteran of the War of 1812; Mrs. Elizabeth Lee Taylor of Jefferson County, Kentucky; Joseph Pannill Taylor, career military officer who rose to brigadier general and a political aide and confidant of Zachary Taylor; Mrs. Sarah Baily Gray, who had an unhappy marriage and went blind; Mrs. Emily Richard Allison, wife of John Stadler Allison wholesale merchant of Louisville, Kentucky, and financial counselor to Zachary Taylor.

COLLATERAL RELATIVES: Taylor was a second cousin of President James Madison, a fourth cousin once removed of Robert E. Lee, and a fourth cousin three times removed of President Franklin D. Roosevelt.

CHILDREN: Taylor had three daughters and a son to live to maturity.

Ann Mackall Taylor (1811–1875). Born near Louisville, she married Dr. Robert C. Wood, an army surgeon, in 1829.

Sarah Knox Taylor (1814–1835). Born at Vincennes, Indiana, she in 1835 married Jefferson Davis, the future president of the Confederacy, whom she had met while he was serving as an officer under her father. Zachary Taylor had adamantly opposed the union. "I will be damned if another daughter of mine will marry into the Army," he fumed. "I know enough of the family life of officers."[2] He forebad Davis to see her. The two men at one point considered settling their differences with a duel. Still, the young couple continued courting secretly and finally married in Kentucky; the bride's parents did not attend the wedding. The newlyweds settled at Davis's plantation on Palmyra Island in the lower Mississippi River. While visiting a Davis relative in West Feliciana Parish, Louisiana, they both contracted malaria. Jefferson Davis recovered; Sarah Taylor Davis, 21, died.

Mary Elizabeth "Betty" Taylor (1824–1909). Born near Louisville, Kentucky, she was the loveliest of the Taylor girls. She married William Wallace Smith Bliss, her father's adjutant general. She served as official White House hostess during the Taylor administration, because the First Lady was chronically ill.

Richard "Dick" Taylor (1826–1879), planter, military leader. Born near Louisville, he was educated in Scotland and France before attending Harvard and graduating from Yale in 1845. He served as a military aide to his father during the Mexican War and as his private secretary while he was president. He maintained a sugar plantation in Louisiana, where he settled after his father's death. Elected to the state senate in 1856, he served four years and in 1860 was a delegate to the Democratic national convention in Charleston, South Carolina. As a member of the Louisiana state convention called to consider secession, he joined the majority in voting for withdrawal from the Union. During the Civil War he served in the Confederate army, rising from colonel to lieutenant general. He fought under Stonewall Jackson in the Shenandoah Valley campaign, helped defeat General Nathaniel Banks at Sabine Crossroads, and from 1864 was commander of Confederate forces west of the Mississippi. In May 1865 he surrendered to General Edward Canby; he was the last Confederate general to lay down his arms. As his property was confiscated during the war, he returned to Louisiana virtually penniless. He represented American business interests abroad for a time and spent his final years writing *Destruction and Reconstruction*, about the impact of the Civil War on the South.

SUBSEQUENT DESCENDANTS:

John Taylor Wood (1830–1904). The president's grandson, he served as a lieutenant in the Confederate army and was aboard the *Merrimac* during its historic encounter with the *Monitor.*

Lillian Gish (1896–1993). The actress claimed in her autobiography (1969) to be a descendant of Zachary Taylor.

BIRTH: Taylor was born on November 24, 1784, in Orange County, Virginia. Most historians agree that he was born at Montebello, home of one of his mother's relatives, where the Taylors had stopped temporarily enroute from Hare Forest, their home in Orange County, to their new residence near Louisville, Kentucky. It is possible, however, that the birth took place at Hare Forest prior to the Taylor's departure. In 1979 a British farmer purchased Montebello for $400,000.

CHILDHOOD: Taylor was eight months old when the family settled in Springfield on Beargrass Creek just east of Louisville. Here he grew up, on the edge of the western frontier, at a time when settlers still lived under the threat of Indian attack. At 17 he swam the breadth of the Ohio River to Indiana and back again in the chill of early spring.

EDUCATION: Taylor received only the most basic education. His first teacher, Elisha Ayer, pronounced him "quick in learning and still patient in study."[3] He also apparently studied under one Lewis Wetsel. His last instructor was Kean O'Hara, an Irish Catholic immigrant and classical scholar. All his life Taylor was a poor speller.

RELIGION: Episcopalian. Although Taylor worshiped at Episcopal services, he never formally joined the church.

RECREATION: A rugged individualist of simple pleasures, Taylor belonged to no fraternal organizations but instead enjoyed the informal company of friends. He neither smoked nor drank. He chewed tobacco and reportedly was an unusually gifted marksman with a spittoon.

MARRIAGE: Lieutenant Zachary Taylor, 25, married Margaret "Peggy" Mackall Smith, 21, on June 21, 1810, at the home of the bride's sister, Mrs. Mary Chew, near Louisville, Kentucky. Born in Calvert County, Maryland, on September 21, 1788, the daughter of Walter Smith, a prosperous Maryland planter and veteran officer of the American Revolution, and Ann Mackall Smith, Peggy was raised amid refinement and wealth. Although no portrait of her survives, she was said to have been slender, about average in height, and amiable. While visiting her sister in Kentucky in 1809, she was introduced to Lieutenant Zachary Taylor, then home on leave, by Dr. Alexander Duke. Their marriage appears to have been a happy one. A devout Episcopalian, Mrs. Taylor prayed regularly for her soldier husband. She became somewhat reclusive because, it is said, she had promised God to give up the pleasures of society if her husband returned safely from war. With the rise in Taylor's political fortunes, she literally prayed for his defeat, for she dreaded the personal consequences of his becoming president. By the time she became First Lady, the hardships of following her husband from fort to fort and the birth of several children had taken their toll. A semiinvalid, she remained in seclusion on the second floor of the White House, leaving the duties of official hostess to her daughter Mrs. Betty Bliss. On the sudden death of the president, her health deteriorated rapidly. She died two years later, in August 1852, at Pascagoula, Mississippi. She was buried next to her husband near Louisville.

MILITARY SERVICE: Taylor was a career military officer 1808–1848, rising from first lieutenant to major general. He served in the War of 1812 and the Black Hawk, Second Seminole, and Mexican wars (see "Career before the Presidency").

CAREER BEFORE THE PRESIDENCY: In 1808 Taylor was commissioned a first lieutenant and assigned to the Seventh Infantry Regiment. His pay was $30 a month plus a subsistence allowance of $12 a month. He served as an army recruiter in Kentucky (1808), temporary commandant of Fort Pickering (1809) at present-day Memphis, and, after brief service under General James Wilkinson in New Orleans, was assigned to Washington Village near Natchez, Mississippi. He was promoted to captain in 1810 and the following year was appointed commandant of Fort Knox at Vincennes, Indiana Territory. His swift restoration of order at that post won him the admiration of William Henry Harrison.

War of 1812. In 1812 Captain Taylor successfully defended Fort Harrison on the Wabash River against a determined Indian assault. For this he was breveted a major, the first brevet rank ever conferred in the U.S. Army. In 1814 he led about 350 troops against the enemy at Credit Island in Illinois Territory. Surprised by the presence of British soldiers and artillery among the Indian forces there, he chose to retreat in order to accomplish his primary mission, construction of Fort Johnson at Des Moines.

In January 1815 Taylor was promoted to major, but months later, with the general demobilization following the end of the War of 1812, he was reduced again to captain. In June 1815 he resigned his commission and for a year devoted his energies to raising corn and tobacco at Springfield, his plantation near Louisville, Kentucky. In 1816 he rejoined the army as a major, assigned to Fort Howard at modern Green Bay, Wisconsin. In 1819 he was promoted to lieutenant colonel. Having established Fort Jesup, Louisiana (1822), he was appointed commandant at Baton Rouge (1823), a member of the Militia Board in Washington (1826), commandant of Fort Snelling at what is now Minneapolis, Minnesota (1828), and commandant of Fort Crawford at present-day Prairie du Chien, Wis. (1829). In 1832 he was promoted to colonel. He had by this time removed his permanent residence from Kentucky to Louisiana.

Black Hawk War, 1832. Colonel Taylor commanded the First Infantry at Fort Armstrong, constructed Fort Dixon, and arrived at the Battle of Bad Axe, the final engagement, in time to help rout the Sac and Fox warriors. After the war he was appointed commandant of Fort Crawford.

Second Seminole War. Colonel Taylor took part in this conflict from 1837 to 1840. As commander of the Army South of the Withlacoochee in Florida, he defeated the Seminoles at the Battle of Okeechobee (December 25, 1837), at a cost of 26 men killed and 112 wounded. For this in 1838 he was breveted a brigadier general and made commander of all U.S. forces in Florida with headquarters at Tampa Bay. Under his command, 53 new posts were erected, 848 miles of wagon road were cut, and 3,643 feet of bridges and causeways were constructed. Although he was unable completely to stamp out Seminole resistance before leaving Florida in 1840, War Secretary Joel Poinsett commended him for accomplishing all that could be expected under very trying circumstances.

In 1841 General Taylor became commander of the Second Department, Western Division, with headquarters at Fort Smith, Arkansas, and, in 1844, commander of the First Department at Fort Jesup, Louisiana.

Mexican War, 1846–1848. In early 1846 Taylor received orders to advance "on or near" the Rio Grande. He took up a position opposite Matamoros. Although outnumbered two to one at Palo Alto on May 8, 1846, he made good use of superior artillery to defeat a force of Mexicans under General Mariano Arista. The next day he again drove the Mexicans from the field at Resaca de la Palma. For this he was promoted to major general. In September 1846 Taylor advanced on heavily fortified Monterrey. At the end of three days of intense fighting, during which some 800 Americans were killed or wounded, Taylor accepted a proposal from General Pedro de Ampudia, Mexican commander in the city: In exchange for surrendering Monterrey to Taylor, the Mexican forces stationed there were permitted to march out of the city with their firearms and with six fieldpieces of artillery and 21 rounds of ammunition. In addition, Taylor agreed not to pursue the Mexicans for eight weeks. Taylor conceded that the terms were liberal but considered it fitting for the United States to act magnanimously in victory. President James K. Polk, however, was not so generously disposed. Furious over Taylor's acceptance of a two-month armistice, he ordered the immediate resumption of hostilities. In addition, he stripped Taylor of the bulk of his troops, placing them under the command of General Winfield Scott. Taylor deeply resented this action, which he believed was politically motivated and designed to goad him into resigning his command. Instead, Taylor vowed privately "to remain and do my duty no matter under what circumstances."[4] He chose to interpret as advice, and not binding orders, dispatches from Washington pointing out the necessity of his maintaining a defensive posture while Scott conducted his campaign at Veracruz and Mexico City. With the remnant of his command, totaling some 4,600 men, General Taylor proceeded to Buena Vista, where he encountered a large force of Mexicans under General Antonio Lopez de Santa Anna. Sizing up the situation, Santa Anna sent a condescending note to Taylor, warning that the Americans must surrender or else face certain slaughter. Taylor declined. On February 23, 1847, the two armies locked in pitched battle. Taylor himself narrowly escaped injury as one shot tore through his sleeve, just grazing the inner part of his upper left arm, and another passed through the front of his coat, taking off a button but sparing his flesh. In the end the Americans suffered 673 casualties, the Mexicans about 1,800. Again, superior U.S. artillery carried the day, and

Santa Anna was forced to withdraw from the field. When news of the American victory reached the United States, Zachary Taylor, or Old Rough and Ready as he was known affectionately to his men, became a national hero.

WHIG PRESIDENTIAL NOMINATION, 1848: As Whigs convened in Philadelphia in June 1848, Taylor was the front-runner. Veteran candidate Henry Clay of Kentucky, now over 70, was his closest competitor, with Winfield Scott of New Jersey running third but gaining momentum, and Daniel Webster of Massachusetts a distant and fading fourth. Taylor won the nomination on the fourth ballot as follows: Taylor, 171; Scott, 63; Clay, 32; Webster, 14. Millard Fillmore of New York was nominated for vice president on the second ballot. The Whig platform confined itself to extolling Taylor's virtues and recounting his military record. After the nomination, the president of the convention sent the nominee a letter of notification, without postage, a frequent practice of the period, which required the recipient to pay the amount due. Taylor, who had been receiving a large volume of such mail from admirers around the country, informed his local postmaster that he would henceforth accept only postage-paid letters. Thus the communication notifying him of his nomination languished in the dead-letter office for weeks before the president of the convention realized what had happened and sent Taylor a second, prepaid notice.

OPPONENT: Lewis Cass (1782–1866) of Michigan; Democrat. Born in Exeter, New Hampshire, and raised there and in Marietta, Ohio, Cass became a lawyer and, at 24, the youngest member of the Ohio legislature. During the War of 1812, he fought under General William Henry Harrison and rose to brigadier general. As governor of the Michigan Territory 1813–1831, appointed by President James Madison, he improved education and transportation, kept peace with the Indians, created a judicial system, encouraged residents of other states to settle in the territory, and promoted statehood for Michigan. He served as secretary of war, 1831–1836 in the Jackson administration. Appointed minister to France in 1836, he resigned in 1842 in protest over the Webster-Ashburton Treaty. In 1844 he was a major candidate for the Democratic presidential nomination, losing finally to dark-horse James K. Polk. During his first term in the Senate, 1845–1848, he supported the Mexican War and westward expansion. At the Democratic national convention in Baltimore in May 1848, Cass was the clear favorite of most of the delegates, with James Buchanan of Pennsylvania and Levi Woodbury of New Hampshire a distant second and third, respectively. Cass won the nomination on the fourth ballot. William O. Butler of Kentucky was nominated for vice president. The Democratic platform praised the Polk administration for its conduct of the Mexican War, a conflict the platform described as "just and necessary." After his defeat by Taylor, Cass was returned to the Senate 1849–1857, where he joined Henry Clay in putting together the Compromise of 1850. At 75 Cass capped his career as secretary of state 1857–1860 in the Buchanan administration. Openly critical of the president for his failure to deal more sternly with threats of rebellion in the South, he is said to have wept on hearing of the secession of South Carolina.

CAMPAIGN AND THE ISSUES, 1848: The dominant issue of the campaign was slavery, in particular the Wilmot Proviso, a bill to ban slavery from any territory acquired as a result of the Mexican War. Taylor did not comment directly on the issue, but that he owned more than 100 slaves was enough to win him substantial southern support. Cass came out against the Wilmot Proviso. As an alternative, he proposed "squatter sovereignty," allowing the residents of the new territories to decide whether to permit slavery. (The concept would later be co-opted by Senator Stephen Douglas of Illinois and renamed popular sovereignty.) Cass warned against federal interference with the practice of slavery. "If the relation of master and servant may be regulated or annihilated," he argued, "so may the relation of husband and wife, or parent and child, and of any other conditions which our institutions and the habits of our society recognize."[5] Although Whigs had been concerned that Taylor had no record of support for their party's principles—indeed, he had never held office or even voted in a presidential election before 1848—the candidate assured them that he shared their concerns. The Cass campaign was fatally handicapped by the third-party candidacy of former president Martin Van Buren, running on the Free Soil ticket. Antislavery Democrats abandoned Cass, whom they derisively dubbed Doughface, to rally behind Van Buren and the Free Soil banner. Although he failed to carry a single state, Van Buren drew enough votes, particularly in his native New York, to tip the election to Taylor.

ELECTION AS PRESIDENT, 1848: (This is the first presidential election in which voting took place nationwide on the same day.)

Popular Vote: Taylor (Whig), 1,360,101 (47%); Cass (Democrat), 1,220,544 (43%); Van Buren (Free Soil), 291,263 (10%).

Electoral Vote. Taylor, 163; Cass, 127.

States Carried. Taylor won the electoral vote of 15 states—Connecticut, Delaware, Florida, Georgia, Kentucky, Louisiana, Maryland, Massachusetts, New Jersey, New York, North Carolina, Pennsylvania, Rhode Island, Tennessee, and Vermont. Cass won the electoral vote of 15 states—Alabama, Arkansas, Illinois, Indiana, Iowa, Maine, Michigan, Mississippi, Missouri, New Hampshire, Ohio, South Carolina, Texas, Virginia, and Wisconsin.

INAUGURAL ADDRESS: March 5, 1849. ". . . As American freemen we can not but sympathize in all efforts to extend the blessings of civil and political liberty, but at the same time we are warned by the admonitions of history and the voice of our own beloved Washington to abstain from entangling alliances with foreign nations. In all disputes between conflicting governments it is our interest not less than our duty to remain strictly neutral, while our geographical position, the genius of our institutions and our people, the advancing spirit of civilization, and, above all, the dictates of religion direct us to the cultivation of peaceful and friendly relations with all powers. . . ."

VICE PRESIDENT: Millard Fillmore (1800–1874), of New York, served 1849–1850. See "Millard Fillmore, 13th President."

CABINET:

Secretary of State. John M. Clayton (1796–1856), of Delaware, served 1849–1850. Taylor's first choice, John J. Crittenden of Kentucky, having declined the post, the president turned to Clayton, a jurist and, more recently, a senator with no diplomatic experience and little grounding in foreign affairs. His unfamiliarity with protocol, compounded by the president's own inexperience in foreign affairs, led to a misunderstanding over two trivial incidents with France, which nearly brought about a break in relations between the two governments. His most significant contribution was the controversial Clayton-Bulwer Treaty (see "Administration"), for which he was widely criticized.

Secretary of the Treasury. William M. Meredith (1799–1873), of Pennsylvania, served 1849–1850. Taylor's first choice had been Horace Binney of

Pennsylvania; he next turned to Meredith, a proponent of a high protective tariff. He came to be one of Taylor's closest advisers in the cabinet. He was widely criticized for paying interest on the Galphin claim (see "Administration").

Secretary of War. George W. Crawford (1798–1872), of Georgia, served 1849–1850. He was the chief southern spokesman in the cabinet. At Taylor's direction, he exercised restraint on hearing what turned out to be exaggerated accounts of a Seminole uprising in Florida and thus avoided needless bloodshed. He was widely criticized for permitting payment of interest on the Galphin claim (see "Administration") without disclosing his own interest in the matter.

Attorney General. Reverdy Johnson (1796–1876), of Maryland, served 1849–1850. An outstanding constitutional lawyer, Johnson labored tirelessly in the post. He later argued successfully against Dred Scott in that controversial Supreme Court case (see "Andrew Jackson, 7th President," Supreme Court Appointments," Roger B. Taney). Although long committed to states' rights, he was instrumental in preventing Maryland's secession during the Civil War. He was minister to Great Britain during 1868–1869.

Secretary of the Navy. William B. Preston (1805–1862), of Virginia, served 1849–1850. Originally slated to become attorney general, he was switched to navy out of concern for his lack of legal experience. Although a southerner he opposed slavery and advocated gradual abolition.

Postmaster General. Jacob Collamer (1791–1865), of Vermont, served 1849–1850.

Secretary of Interior. Thomas Ewing (1789–1871), of Ohio, served 1849–1850. He had served as Treasury secretary in the Harrison and Tyler administrations. He was the first interior secretary, responsible for Indian affairs, patents, pensions, and public land.

ADMINISTRATION: March 5, 1849–July 9, 1850.

Clayton-Bulwer Treaty, 1850. This pact between the United States and Great Britain stipulated that (1) any canal constructed across Central America was to be neutral, with neither government exercising absolute control over it; (2) neither side was to "erect or maintain any fortifications" at the canal; (3) neither side was to "occupy, or fortify, or colonize, or assume, or exercise any dominion over . . . any part of Central America." This last clause, deliberately vague and interpreted differently by the two governments, drew widespread criticism in the United States, especially from Democrats, who complained that it sanctioned British claims to Honduras and other colonies already established. Indeed, Britain interpreted the treaty as a bar only to further colonization of the region without retroactive force. The Taylor administration, however, read the pact as a ban on all colonization, past as well as future. Negotiating the agreement were U.S. Secretary of State John M. Clayton and Henry Lytton Bulwer, British minister to the United States. The treaty was abrogated by the Hay-Pauncefote Treaty (1901; see "Theodore Roosevelt, 26th President," "Administration").

Galphin Claim. The principal of a long-standing claim against the United States by the Galphin family of Georgia had been paid before Taylor took office, but the family was now pressing for payment of $191,000 in interest. Treasury Secretary William M. Meredith, on the advice of Attorney General Reverdy Johnson, paid the full amount. During the whole time the matter was under consideration by the president and his cabinet, War Secretary George W.

Crawford never disclosed that he had long represented the Galphin family in the matter and, by previous arrangement, stood to receive half of whatever the government awarded them. When news of his interest leaked out, a firestorm of criticism broke over the administration. Although Taylor, Meredith, and Johnson all denied knowledge of Crawford's role, the opposition party charged conflict of interest and threatened impeachment of the president. Taylor was so upset over the episode that he decided to reorganize his cabinet. He died, however, before removing a single member.

Slavery. Although a slaveholder himself and elected with significant southern support, Taylor opposed the extension of slavery. He was committed to the Union above all and steadfastly denied the right of secession. He opposed what came to be known as the Compromise of 1850 (see "Millard Fillmore, 13th President," "Administration"). Although he favored California's admission to the Union as a free state, as called for under the compromise, he rejected those aspects of the measure favorable to the South. He referred to the package derisively as the Omnibus Bill, for its many disparate provisions, and made clear his willingness to exercise the veto. Prospects for the compromise were dim until the sudden death of Taylor and the accession of Millard Fillmore, who approved it.

SUPREME COURT APPOINTMENTS: None.

RANKING IN 1962 HISTORIANS POLL: Taylor ranked twenty-fourth of 31 presidents; best of 6 "below average" presidents. He ranked above Tyler, below Andrew Johnson.

DEATH IN OFFICE: July 9, 1850, 10:35 P.M., White House, Washington, D.C. On a hot Fourth of July, Taylor attended outdoor festivities at the Washington Monument, then under construction, where he sat through two hours of patriotic addresses. Afterward he went for a stroll, further exposing himself to the simmering rays of the sun. By the time he returned to the White house he was hungry and thirsty. Reports of precisely what he ate vary, but, according to the traditional account, he wolfed down a large bowl of cherries and a pitcher of ice milk. Later that day he developed severe cramps. Dr. Alexander S. Wotherspoon diagnosed his condition as cholera morbus, a gastrointestinal upset common in Washington, where poor sanitation made it risky to eat any raw fruit or fresh dairy product during the summer. He gave the president calomel and opium and was pleased to find him well enough the next day to conduct some business. Joining Dr. Wotherspoon on the case were Dr. Richard Coolidge, an army physician; Dr. James C. Hall of Washington, D.C.; and the president's son-in-law Dr. Robert C. Wood. During the next few days Taylor grew weaker from the effects of diarrhea and vomiting. He became depressed, convinced that he would never recover. On July 8 doctors reported that the president was running a fever and was seriously ill. The next day he coughed up green bile, his pulse faded. More calomel and a dose of quinine were ministered; the remedies of raising blisters and drawing blood were tried. But the president continued to decline. Realizing his fate, Taylor that evening spoke his last words: "I am about to die. I expect the summons very soon. I have tried to discharge my duties faithfully. I regret nothing, but I am sorry that I am about to leave my friends."[6] He died soon thereafter at 65. The distraught First Lady refused to permit mortician Samuel Kirby to embalm the body. Nor would she allow a death mask to be taken. However, Giuseppe Fagnani, an Italian artist, was allowed to sketch Taylor's features from death. The president lay in state in the East Room of the White House, where on July 13 Episcopal funeral services were conducted by the Reverend Smith Pyne. Pallbearers included Henry Clay, Daniel Webster, and Lewis Cass. Afterward, a funeral procession of more than 100 carriages, including Taylor's faithful war horse "Old Whitey," accompanied the lead and mahogany coffin to the Congressional Burial Ground. In October the president's remains were removed for permanent burial at his childhood home near Louisville, Kentucky. In his last will and testament, Taylor left his entire estate to his wife and children. He had made its provisions contingent on his death in combat, however, and because he died at peace from no war-related cause, his will was inadmissible for probate. William W.S. Bliss, Taylor's son-in-law, was appointed administrator. He then distributed the estate more or less equally among the former First Lady and the three Taylor children—Mrs. Anne Wood, Mrs. Betty Bliss, and Dick Taylor. The estate, valued at more than $130,000, included Cypress Grove plantation near New Orleans, warehouses and other property in Louisville, more than 100 slaves, and stock in the Bank of Louisville, the Western Bank of Baltimore, and the Northern Bank of Kentucky.

TAYLOR PRAISED: "We do not know which to admire most, his heroism in withstanding the assaults of the enemy in the most hopeless fields of Buena Vista . . . or in giving in the heat of battle, terms of merciful capitulation to a vanquished foe at Monterrey, and not being ashamed to avow that he did it to spare women and children, helpless infancy, and more helpless age."[7]—Whig Party Platform, 1848

"It did not happen to General Taylor, once in his life, to fight a battle on equal terms, or on terms advantageous to himself—and yet he was never beaten, and he never retreated. . . . General Taylor's battles were not distinguished for brilliant military maneuvers; but in all he seems rather to have conquered by the exercise of a sober and steady judgment, coupled with a dogged incapacity to understand that defeat was possible."[8]—Abraham Lincoln, 1850

"His death was a public calamity. No man could have been more devoted to the Union, or more opposed to the slavery agitation."[9]—Thomas Hart Benton of Missouri

TAYLOR CRITICIZED: "Old Zack is a good old soul but don't know himself from a side of sole leather in the way of statesmanship."[10]—Horace Greeley, 1849

"Zachary Taylor is dead and gone to hell, and I am glad of it!"[11]—Governor Brigham Young of Utah Territory, 1850

"Any allusion to literature much beyond good old Dilworth's Spelling Book, on the part of one wearing a sword, was evidence, [to Taylor] of utter unfitness for heavy marchings and combat. In short, few men have ever had a more comfortable, labor-saving contempt for learning of every kind."[12]—General Winfield Scott

"He really is a most simple-minded old man. He has the least show or pretension about him of any man I ever saw; talks as artlessly as a child about affairs of state, and does not seem to pretend to a knowledge of anything of which he is ignorant. He is a remarkable man in some respects; and it is remarkable that such a man should be President of the United States."[13]—Educator Horace Mann

TAYLOR QUOTES: "The power given by the Constitution to the Executive to interpose his veto is a high conservative power: but in my opinion it should never be exercised except in cases of clear violation of the Constitution, or manifest haste and want of due consideration by Congress."[14]—1848

"For more than half a century, during which kingdoms and empires have fallen, this Union has stood unshaken. The patriots who formed it have long since descended to the grave; yet still it remains, the proudest monument to their memory. . . . In my judgment, its dissolution would be the greatest of calamities. . . . Upon its preservation must depend our own happiness and that of countless generations to come. Whatever dangers may threaten it, I shall stand by it and maintain it in its integrity to the full extent of the obligations imposed and the power conferred upon me by the Constitution."[15]—1849

BOOKS ABOUT TAYLOR: Bauer, Karl Jack. *Zachary Taylor: Soldier, Planter, Statesman of the Old Southwest*. Baton Rouge: Louisiana State University Press, 1985.

Hamilton, Holman. *Zachary Taylor: Soldier in the White House*. 2 vols. Indianapolis: Bobbs-Merrill, 1941, 1951.

McKinley, Silas Bent, and Bent, Silas. *Old Rough and Ready: The Life and Times of Zachary Taylor*. New York: Vanguard Press, 1946.

Nichols, Edward J. *Zach Taylor's Little Army*. Garden City, N.Y.: Doubleday, 1963.

NOTES:

1 Holman Hamilton, *Zachary Taylor: Soldier in the White House*, Indianapolis: Bobbs-Merrill, 1951, vol. II, p. 218.

2 Ibid., vol. I, p. 101.

3 Ibid., p. 28.

4 Ibid., p. 226.

5 Andrew C. McLaughlin, *Lewis Cass* (American Statesman series, no. 24), Cambridge, Mass.: Riverside Press, 1891, p. 232.

6 Silas Bent McKinley and Silas Bent, *Old Rough and Ready: The Life and Times of Zachary Taylor*, New York: Vanguard Press, 1946, p. 287.

7 Kirk H. Porter and Donald Bruce Johnson, compilers, *National Party Platforms*, Urbana, Ill.: University of Illinois Press, 1961, p. 15.

8 McKinley and Bent, pp. 293–294.

9 Hamilton, vol. II, p. 410.

10 Allan Nevins, *Ordeal of the Union: Fruits of Manifest Destiny*, New York: Scribner's, 1947, p. 229.

11 Hamilton, vol. II, p. 411.

12 Ibid., vol. I, p. 116.

13 Richard Kenin and Justin Wintle, *Dictionary of Biographical Quotation*, New York: Knopf, 1978, p. 726.

14 Hamilton, vol. II, p. 80.

15 McKinley and Bent, p. 262.

☆ ☆ ☆ ☆ ☆ ☆ ☆ ☆

MILLARD FILLMORE

☆ ☆ ☆ ☆ ☆ ☆ ☆ ☆

13TH PRESIDENT

NAME: Millard Fillmore. He was named after his mother, Phoebe Millard Fillmore.

PHYSICAL DESCRIPTION: As a young man, Fillmore was strikingly handsome, 6 feet tall, well built, with wavy, somewhat unruly hair, light complexion, a high forehead, blue eyes, and determined expression. With age, however, he became heavy, and his hair had turned white by the time he became president. He dressed meticulously. His health generally was sound.

PERSONALITY: Fillmore was a likable fellow. He mixed readily. He was most persuasive in small groups; his stolid style did not play well before large audiences. He spoke slowly, deliberately, usually using simple expressions and short sentences. His speeches lacked the flourish typical of the great orators of the day. A practical, unemotional man, he relied on logic and common sense to make a point in argument. He appealed to the mind rather than to the heart. Although basically a pragmatist, he was capable of genuine idealism if the cause struck his sense of righteousness. "A spark of idealism smouldered in his mind," biographer Robert J. Rayback has written. "Because his whole training had been aimed toward making or improving his livelihood, nothing could ever ignite the spark that would place him in that class of complete idealists who steadfastly cling to their visions no matter how inimical to their interests. But the trait was there, seldom dominating, yet always helping to shape his values."[1]

ANCESTORS: Fillmore was of English ancestry. His paternal grandfather, Nathaniel Fillmore, was a veteran of the American Revolution.

FATHER: Nathaniel Fillmore (1771–1863), farmer. Weary of trying to coax crops from the rocky soil near Bennington, Vermont, Nathaniel Fillmore succumbed to the sales pitch of a land speculator who in 1799 sold him title—a faulty title— to a patch of wilderness in Cayuga County, New York. He cleared the land, raised a crude cabin, and set out his seeds, only to find out that crops fared little better in the dense clay of central New York than in stony Vermont. When the flaws in his title were exposed, he lost the property and took his family north to present-day Niles, near Lake Skaneateles, one of the Finger Lakes. Here he struggled as a tenant farmer for 17 years before moving southwest to Montville. In 1821 he continued west, settling at Aurora, near Buffalo. He was the first father of a president to visit his son in the White House. He died at age 92.

MOTHER: Phoebe Millard Fillmore (1780–1831). A native of Pittsfield, Massachusetts, she married Nathaniel Fillmore about 1796. She died when her most famous son was a New York State assemblyman.

SIBLINGS: The second of nine children, Fillmore had five brothers and three sisters—Mrs. Olive Armstrong Johnson, Cyrus Fillmore, Almon Hopkins Fillmore, Calvin Turner Fillmore, Mrs. Julia Harris, Darius Ingraham Fillmore, Charles DeWitt Fillmore, and Phoebe Maria Fillmore.

CHILDREN: By his first wife, Fillmore had a son and a daughter.

Millard Powers Fillmore (1828–1889). He studied law at his father's office in Buffalo and at Harvard. After serving as private secretary to his father in the White House, he practiced law in Buffalo and later was appointed a federal court clerk.

Mary Abigail Fillmore (1832–1854). A native of Buffalo, she studied at a private school in Lenox, Massachusetts, and graduated from New York State Normal School. She spoke French fluently and was conversant in Spanish, German, and Italian. She taught briefly in the Buffalo public schools until her father became president in 1850. She performed many of the social duties at the White House as the First Lady was ill. An accomplished musician, she played the piano, harp, and guitar and performed at White House functions. Her sudden death from cholera at 22, coming barely a year after the death of her mother, is thought to have contributed to former president Fillmore's decision to come out of retirement and resume his political career.

Neither of Fillmore's children married; thus, he has no direct descendants.

BIRTH: Fillmore was born in a log cabin in Locke Township, Cayuga County, New York, on the morning of January 7, 1800.

CHILDHOOD: Fillmore grew up on a farm carved from the lush wilderness of the Finger Lakes region of New York. A husky lad, he bore his share of farm chores, clearing fields, plowing, harvesting, and chopping wood. In his spare time he enjoyed hunting in the nearby woods and fishing at Lake Skaneateles. From his youth he determined to one day leave the farm for the outside world and, he dreamed, a career of distinction. When he was 14, his father apprenticed him to a clothmaker, Benjamin Hungerford of Sparta, New York. He disliked it there and quit after four months. Next his father sent him to clothmakers Zaccheus Cheney and Alvan Kellogg in New Hope, New York. He remained there several years.

EDUCATION: Until he was 17, Fillmore had received only basic instruction in reading, writing, and math. He had read little besides the Bible. When a circulating library was formed in the community, Fillmore discovered the world of ideas. He also discovered how little he really knew. His vocabulary was so weak that he had trouble understanding what he read. He bought a dictionary and, in idle moments at the cloth mill, mastered new words regularly. At 19 he enrolled at an academy recently erected at New Hope. An eager student, he was a favorite of the teacher, Abigail Powers, whom he later married. In 1819 his father arranged for him to study law at the office of County Judge Walter Wood in Montville. Fillmore was so ecstatic at the news that he wept openly. At the end of a two-month trial period, Judge Wood invited Fillmore to continue as his clerk on a permanent basis provided he was able to free himself of his indenture to the clothmaker. Realizing that the boy had little money, Wood offered to lend him funds and find him extra work. Fillmore taught school a few months to earn some cash and promptly bought up his indenture for $30. Among his duties at the law office was to oversee the judge's tenant farms, a task he disliked because at times he was expected to evict poor families. In 1821 he abruptly left Judge Wood following an argument over Fillmore's having done some minor legal work outside the firm. He then joined his parents at Aurora, where he again taught school briefly. The next year he accepted a teaching position in nearby Buffalo and in his spare time studied law at the office of Asa Rice and Joseph Clary. Fillmore was admitted to the bar in 1823.

RELIGION: Unitarian. Before becoming a charter member of Buffalo's Unitarian Church in 1831, Fillmore apparently belonged to no church. Just why he chose the Unitarian faith is unknown, for a Fillmore cousin in town was a Methodist minister and Fillmore's wife was a Baptist. Unlike many other politicians of the period, Fillmore rarely quoted the Bible in addresses. As a state assemblyman he fought unsuccessfully to abolish a New York law requiring witnesses in court to swear belief in God.

RECREATION: An avid bibliophile, Fillmore amassed a personal library of some 4,000 volumes and as president encouraged creation of the first permanent White House library. His literary tastes ran to practical works, rather than the belles-lettres. He was long active in the civic affairs of Buffalo, helping establish the city's first high school, an adult self-improvement organization known as the Lyceum, the Young Men's Association, the Buffalo Mutual Fire Insurance Company, the Buffalo Fine Arts Academy, the Buffalo Historical Society, the University of Buffalo, and Buffalo General Hospital. Fillmore did not smoke, drink, or gamble.

MARRIAGE: Millard Fillmore, 26, married Abigail Powers, 27, on February 5, 1826, at the home of the bride's brother Judge Powers, in Moravia, New York. Born in Stillwater, New York, on March 13, 1798, the daughter of the Reverend Lemuel Powers, a Baptist minister, and Abigail Newland Powers, Abigail grew up in Moravia, not far from the Fillmore farm. In 1819 she took a teaching post at the new academy in New Hope, where her oldest pupil was 19-year-old Millard Fillmore. The world of knowledge and Fillmore's steady progress in it drew them together, and gradually the relationship of teacher and student evolved into romantic attachment. After a long courtship, they were married by the Reverend Orsanius H. Smith. Without a honeymoon they settled at East Aurora, New York. Mrs. Fillmore continued to teach school until the birth of her son and maintained a lifelong interest in education. She shared her husband's love of books and helped build their personal library. As First Lady she prodded Congress to provide funds for the first permanent library at the White House. Frequently ill during her husband's term as president, she left much of the entertaining chores to her daughter. At the outdoor inaugural ceremonies for Franklin Pierce in 1853, she caught cold and next day came down with a fever. She developed pneumonia and died weeks later, on March 30, 1853, at the Willard Hotel in Washington. She was buried at Forest Lawn Cemetery in Buffalo.

On February 10, 1858, Fillmore married Caroline Carmichael McIntosh at Albany, New York. The widow of a prominent Albany businessman, Ezekiel C.

McIntosh, she signed a prenuptial agreement making Fillmore administrator of her fortune. The couple purchased a mansion on Niagara Square in Buffalo, where they settled. She remained there after the former president's death in 1874. She died on August 11, 1881.

MILITARY SERVICE: At the outbreak of the Civil War, former president Fillmore organized the Union Continentals, a Buffalo home guard comprised of men over 45, many of them retired state militiamen. He held the rank of major. The unit spent much of its time seeing groups of young volunteers off at the train station, taking part in funeral services for Buffalo's fallen heroes, and marching in patriotic parades.

CAREER BEFORE THE PRESIDENCY: In 1823 Fillmore began practicing law in East Aurora, New York. He became active in politics as an Anti-Mason and supported John Quincy Adams for president in 1824.

New York State Assemblyman, 1829–1831. Elected to three one-year terms as an Anti-Mason, Fillmore represented Erie County in the state assembly. He joined colleagues in denouncing the Masonic Order. In 1828 he supported President John Quincy Adams in his unsuccessful bid for reelection. As chairman of a special committee in 1831, he sponsored and helped steer to passage bills abolishing imprisonment for debt and establishing a state bankruptcy law. During this time he moved to Buffalo.

U.S. Representative, 1833–1835, 1837–1843. Elected to Congress in 1832, Fillmore helped found the Whig party in western New York and from 1836 was reelected as a Whig to three successive terms. He at first supported Justice John McLean as a candidate for president in 1836 but switched his allegiance to William Henry Harrison, voting for him at the state Whig convention in Albany. He opposed President Van Buren's Independent Treasury system. In 1840 he directed the presidential campaign of William Henry Harrison in western New York. He opposed Henry Clay's efforts to assume control of national policy during the Harrison and Tyler administrations, trying to prevent a split between congressional Whigs and President Tyler. Failing in that, however, he joined Clay forces in encouraging the mass resignation of Tyler's cabinet. As chairman of the powerful House Ways and Means Committee 1841–1843, Fillmore drafted and steered to passage the Tariff Act of 1842. He also supported the National Bankruptcy Act of 1841 and an emergency measure authorizing the president to borrow funds to compensate for dwindling Treasury reserves. He favored distribution to the states of funds realized from the sale of federal land.

In 1844 Fillmore was a candidate for the Whig vice presidential nomination, running third behind Theodore Frelinghuysen of New Jersey, the eventual nominee, and John Davis of Massachusetts. The Whig nominee for governor of New York that same year, Fillmore was defeated 241,090–231,057 by Democrat Silas Wright.

Comptroller of New York State, 1848–1849. Elected comptroller by a large margin over incumbent Democrat Azariah C. Flagg, Fillmore promoted expansion of the Erie Canal and a sound currency system.

Vice President, 1849–1850. At the Whig national convention in Philadelphia in 1848, John A. Collier, a pro-Clay delegate from New York, proposed Fillmore as a candidate for vice president on the ticket with Zachary Taylor. Fillmore was nominated on the second ballot, defeating Abbot Lawrence of Massachusetts 173–83. Fillmore and Taylor had never met, and they did not meet until after their election in 1848. As vice president, Fillmore was largely ignored by the Taylor administration. He played no part in shaping the cabinet or formulating policy. Despite his experience on Capitol Hill, he was not enlisted to promote administration programs. Indeed, Fillmore was even denied a say in the dispensation of patronage in his home state of New York. Vice President Fillmore presided over the great Senate debate on the Compromise of 1850 (see "Administration"). Although Taylor opposed it, Fillmore informed the president that should the Senate deadlock, he was prepared to cast the tie-breaking vote in favor of the measure, not, he assured Taylor, because of hostility to the administration, but because he believed it to be in the nation's best interest. On July 9, 1850, Fillmore visited the ailing president and realized, as did others, that he was dying. It thus came as no real surprise when a White House messenger appeared at his room at the Willard Hotel in Washington late that same evening to inform him that President Taylor had just passed away. Fillmore did not sleep a wink that night.

At noon on July 10, 1850, Fillmore was sworn in as president by Judge William Cranch, chief justice of the U.S. Circuit Court for the District of Columbia, before a joint session of the Congress.

CABINET:

Secretary of State. (1) Daniel Webster (1782–1852), of Massachusetts, served 1850–1852. Having served as secretary of state in the Harrison and Tyler administrations, he became the first man to hold the post twice. He was Fillmore's first cabinet appointment and acted as intermediary in feeling out other prospective appointees before the president formally offered the posts. Secretary Webster championed the right of the United States to express sympathy for oppressed peoples around the world in their struggle for independence from authoritarian regimes. He made no apologies for U.S. encouragement of the ill-fated Hungarian revolt led by Louis Kossuth. Rather, he used the occasion to deliver to the Austrian government a turgid, jingoistic note, written largely for domestic consumption, which he hoped would focus American attention on the national character of the United States and thus help blur sectional differences between North and South. Within the department, Webster promoted the merit system and urged creation of the office of assistant secretary. He died in office. (2) Edward Everett (1794–1865), of Massachusetts, served 1852–1853. During his brief four-month tenure, Everett presented a convincing case to Britain and France explaining why the United States declined their invitation to sign a pact renouncing forever the acquisition of Cuba. Citing the proximity and strategic location of the island, he pointed out that neither Britain nor France would promote the tripartite agreement if Cuba "guarded the entrance to the Thames or the Seine."

Secretary of the Treasury. Thomas Corwin (1794–1865), of Ohio, served 1850–1853. He opposed the Compromise of 1850.

Secretary of War. Charles M. Conrad (1804–1878), of Louisiana, served 1850–1853. He also served briefly as acting secretary of state immediately following Daniel Webster's death. Conrad drafted the administration's instructions to Commodore Matthew Perry (see "Administration").

Attorney General. John J. Crittenden (1787–1863), of Kentucky, served 1850–1853. He had served as attorney general in the Harrison and Tyler administrations. Fillmore chose him because he was a national Whig who promoted compromise between North and South. Asked for a legal opinion of the proposed fugitive slave bill (see "Administration: Compromise of 1850"), he pronounced it constitutional. Following the election of Abraham Lincoln in 1860, he put forth the Crittenden Compromise, a doomed last-minute bid to avert the Civil War.

Secretary of the Navy. (1) William A. Graham (1804–1875), of North Carolina, served 1850–1852. A moderate southerner committed to compromise, he resigned to accept the 1852 Whig nomination for vice president on the ticket with Winfield Scott. In 1856 he campaigned for Fillmore for president on the Know-Nothing ticket. He opposed secession but ultimately supported the South, serving as a member of the Confederate Senate. (2) John P. Kennedy (1795–1870), of Maryland, served 1852–1853. He was Fillmore's fourth choice for the post after Jared R. Ingersoll of Pennsylvania, John Bell of Tennessee, and E. P. Chambers of South Carolina. A popular novelist of the period, he had written *Horse-shoe Robinson* and other works. He introduced Fillmore to Washington Irving; the two became good friends.

Postmaster General. (1) Nathan K. Hall (1810–1874), of New York, served 1850–1852. He had studied law as a clerk in Fillmore's office in East Aurora, New York, and later was made a partner in the firm. (2) Samuel D. Hubbard (1799–1855), of Connecticut, served 1852–1853.

Secretary of Interior. (1) Thomas M. T. McKennan (1794–1852), of Pennsylvania, served August 1850. (2) Alexander H. H. Stuart (1807–1891), of Virginia, served 1850–1853. He organized the department.

ADMINISTRATION: July 10, 1850–March 3, 1853.

Compromise of 1850. The compromise represented Senator Henry Clay's final attempt to resolve the slavery issue and forestall civil war. President Zachary Taylor had opposed it, urging the admission of California as a free state without regard to the proslavery elements of the package. President Fillmore reversed that policy and embraced all aspects of the compromise, which consisted of five acts, signed into law separately during September 9–20, 1850: (1) California was admitted to the Union as a free state. Residents of other states created from territory acquired from Mexico were to decide for themselves whether to permit slavery. (2) The borders of Texas were defined, and Texas received $10 million to pay off its debts. The territory of New Mexico was established. (3) The territory of Utah was established. (4) The Fugitive Slave Act, clearly the most controversial element of the compromise, required the federal government to take an active part in returning fugitive slaves to their masters. Suspected fugitives were denied the right to trial or to defend themselves at a judicial proceeding. As a result, many free blacks residing legitimately in the North were turned over to white southerners claiming them as runaway slaves. Those aiding and abetting fugitive slaves along the Underground Railroad were subject to stiff criminal and civil penalties. The law was thoroughly repugnant to the northern antislavery faction of the Whig party. (5) The slave trade, though not slavery itself, was abolished in the District of Columbia.

The compromise achieved its intended purpose of averting civil war. It satisfied moderates in the North, and it temporarily mollified the increasingly militant South. Only South Carolina was prepared to secede rather than to accept the compromise, but it ultimately acquiesced, realizing the futility of trying to maintain its independence alone. However, the package fatally divided the Whig party.

Perry's Mission to Japan, 1852–1854. To open up trade in the Far East, President Fillmore dispatched four warships under Commodore Matthew C. Perry to Japan with instructions to obtain from that government pledges to assist shipwrecked American sailors, to provide U.S. vessels with coal and other supplies, and to open at least one port to U.S. trade. Perry won these concessions in the Treaty of Kanagawa (1854), which opened two Japanese ports for commerce.

States Admitted to the Union: California (1850).

Fillmore's approval of the Fugitive Slave Law cost him the support of the northern Whigs, without which he was unable to win his party's presidential nomination in 1852 (see "Franklin Pierce, 14th President," "Opponent").

SUPREME COURT APPOINTMENT: Benjamin R. Curtis (1809–1874), of Massachusetts, served as associate justice 1851–1857. Fillmore's first choice, Rufus Choate of Massachusetts, declined the appointment. On the recommendation of Daniel Webster, he then named Curtis. Justice Curtis wrote one of two dissenting opinions in the *Dred Scott* case (see "Andrew Jackson, 7th President," "Supreme Court Appointments," Roger B. Taney). In it he criticized the majority for denying to the slave, Dred Scott, standing in court and then compounding the error by deciding the merits against Scott anyway and declaring the Missouri Compromise unconstitutional. Curtis abruptly resigned following a heated written exchange with Chief Justice Taney over the procedure each followed in publishing their opinions in the Scott case. Curtis later served as chief defense counsel for President Andrew Johnson during his impeachment trial.

RANKING IN 1962 HISTORIANS POLL: Fillmore ranked twenty-sixth of 31 presidents; third of 6 "below average" presidents. He ranked above Coolidge, below Tyler.

RETIREMENT: March 4, 1853–March 8, 1874. Denied renomination, Fillmore retired to Buffalo in April 1853 after attending the inaugural of his successor, Franklin Pierce, and after the death of his wife. The loss of his wife and daughter during the first 16 months of his retirement was a great emotional strain on the former president. In the spring of 1854 he undertook an extensive tour of the South and Midwest. The next year he embarked on a 13-month excursion of Europe. In London at the same time as Martin Van Buren, the two former presidents appeared together at the House of Commons. In Paris Fillmore bailed Horace Greeley out of jail; the New York editor had been imprisoned there for failing to pay a debt. In Rome Fillmore reluctantly had an audience with Pope Pius IX, despite misgivings about how the meeting would be received in the United States and fears that he would be expected to genuflect and kiss the pope's hand, according to custom. (The pope spared his Protestant guest such displays.) While in Europe, Fillmore received word that he had been nominated for president by the American, or Know-Nothing, party, a nativist organization violently opposed to Roman Catholicism whose platform sought to exclude immigrants from holding public office in the United States and to lengthen the residency requirement for citizenship to 21 years. Fillmore mailed his acceptance and returned to the United States in June 1856. He was subsequently endorsed by the remnants of the Whig party, many of whose northern members had joined in forming the Republican party and supported its standard-bearer John C. Frémont. Fillmore polled 21 percent of the vote, third behind Frémont and the winner James Buchanan. He carried just one state,

Maryland (see also "James Buchanan, 15th President," "Opponent"). He thereafter was active in the civic affairs of Buffalo (see "Recreation"). In February 1861 he hosted Abraham Lincoln in Buffalo; the president-elect was enroute to his inaugural in Washington. Although Fillmore supported the Union cause during the Civil War, he came under attack for his support of the Fugitive Slave Law and other prewar attempts to appease the South. Following Lincoln's assassination, a mob vandalized the exterior of his home.

DEATH: March 8, 1874, 11:10 P.M., Buffalo. Fillmore enjoyed excellent health until a few weeks before his death. On February 13, 1874, while shaving, he suffered a stroke that paralyzed his left side. Under the care of his personal physician, Dr. James P. White, and a consulting physician, Dr. Gray of Utica, he recovered partial use of the affected muscles, but a second stroke on February 26 destroyed whatever chance he had for recovery. Because his throat muscles were affected, he had difficulty swallowing even liquids. He fell unconscious on the evening of March 8 and died peacefully a couple hours later. He was buried at Forest Lawn Cemetery in Buffalo. In his last will and testament, Fillmore directed that his personal property be invested in bonds of the U.S. government, New York State, and the New York Central railroad; he provided annuities totaling $1,700 for his surviving siblings, left sums to the Buffalo Orphan Asylum and other charities, and bequeathed the remainder of his estate to his second wife and son.

FILLMORE PRAISED: "I cannot forbear to express here my regret at [Fillmore's] retirement in the present emergency from [Congress]. There, or elsewhere, I hope and trust he will soon return for whether to the nation or to the state, no service can be or ever will be rendered by a more able or a more faithful public servant."[2]—John Quincy Adams, 1843

"When he had carefully examined a question and had satisfied himself that he was right, no power on earth, could induce him to swerve from what he believed to be the line of duty."[3]—Interior Secretary Alexander H. H. Stuart

"This president of ours is a very remarkable man. We have now been in daily intercourse with him for nearly three years, yet I doubt if either of us can say that we ever heard him utter a foolish or unmeaning word, in all that time!"[4]—Attorney General John J. Crittenden

"The long-continued and useful public service and eminent purity of character of the deceased ex-President will be remembered."[5]—President Ulysses S. Grant, 1874

FILLMORE CRITICIZED: "Providence has at last led the man of hesitations and double opinions where decision and singleness are indispensable."[6]—Senator William H. Seward of New York, 1850

"Fillmore lacks pluck. He wants backbone. He means well, but he is timid, irresolute, uncertain and loves to lean."[7]—Horace Greeley, c. 1851

"It must always be regretted that such a man as Millard Fillmore had not a mind comprehensive enough to properly meet a great crisis. . . . It was, moreover, his misfortune to see in slavery a political and not a moral question. Upon this one issue, which, it is true, was one of transcendent importance, he was a politician and not a statesman."[8]—*New York Times*, 1874

"Mr. Fillmore was . . . a man more amenable to the control of the leaders of Congress and of his party than the sturdy soldier had been whom he succeeded."[9]—Professor Woodrow Wilson of Princeton University

FILLMORE QUOTES: "The government of the United States is a limited government. It is confined to the exercise of powers expressly granted, and such others as may be necessary for carrying those powers into effect; and it is at all times an especial duty to guard against any infringement on the just rights of the States."[10]—1850

"It is a national disgrace that our Presidents . . . should be cast adrift, and perhaps be compelled to keep a corner grocery for subsistence. . . . We elect a man to the presidency, expect him to be honest, to give up a lucrative profession, perhaps, and after we have done with him we let him go into seclusion and perhaps poverty."[11]

BOOK ABOUT FILLMORE: Rayback, Robert J. *Millard Fillmore: Biography of a President.* Buffalo: Stewart, 1959.

NOTES

1 Robert J. Rayback, *Millard Fillmore: Biography of a President.* Buffalo, N.Y.: Stewart, 1959, p. 10.
2 Ibid., p. 147.
3 Ibid., p. 334.
4 Ibid., p. 335.
5 David C. Whitney, *The American Presidents: Biographies of Chief Executives from Washington through Nixon,* Garden City, N.Y.: Doubleday, 1967, p. 117.
6 Allan Nevins, *Ordeal of the Union: Fruits of Manifest Destiny,* New York: Scribner's Sons, 1947, p. 335.
7 Henry Luther Stoddard, *Horace Greeley: Printer, Editor, Crusader,* New York: Putnam's Sons, 1946, p. 148.
8 *New York Times,* March 10, 1874, p. 4.
9 Woodrow Wilson, *History of the American People,* New York: Harper & Bros., 1901, vol. IV, p. 140.
10 James D. Richardson, comp., *Messages and Papers of the Presidents,* Washington: Government Printing Office, 1897, vol. V, p. 79.
11 Rayback, p. 416.

FRANKLIN PIERCE

14TH PRESIDENT

NAME: Franklin Pierce.

PHYSICAL DESCRIPTION: Perhaps the most handsome president, Pierce was a trim 5 feet 10 inches tall and had a classic Roman nose, gray eyes, and thin lips. His most distinctive feature was the mass of curly dark hair that he combed on a deep slant over the side of his broad forehead. While president, he was only slightly gray at the temples. He suffered often from respiratory ailments. As president, he had a persistent cough due to chronic bronchitis. Heavy drinking over many years also undermined his health.

PERSONALITY: Pierce was open, congenial, and pliant. He mixed readily and won friends easily. However, he suffered from periodic bouts of depression. He also fought a longtime battle against alcoholism. Pierce found it hard to say No. "He lacked a sustained feeling of self-confidence and was desirous of approbation," according to biographer Roy Franklin Nichols. "Consequently he endeavored to be gracious and accommodating to all who sought [favors]. His graciousness was interpreted by many to mean approval of their requests."[1]

ANCESTORS: Pierce was of English ancestry. His great[3]-grandfather Thomas Pierce emigrated from England to settle at Charleston, Massachusetts, about 1634.

FATHER: Benjamin Pierce (1757–1839), public official. A native of Chelmsford, Massachusetts, he was plowing his field when word reached him of the Battle of Lexington (1775), the opening guns of the American Revolution. He promptly halted his team and walked off the field to war. He served until 1784, rising from private to lieutenant and company commander. He fought at Bunker Hill (1775) and Saratoga (1777) and survived the rigors of Valley Forge (1777–1778). After the war, he settled at Hillsborough, New Hampshire, where he married Elizabeth Andrews in 1787 and, following her death, Anna Kendrick (the president's mother) in 1790. Benjamin Pierce organized and commanded the militia of Hillsborough County 1786–1807, rising from brigade major to brigadier general. He was a delegate to the state constitutional convention in 1791. He served in the New Hampshire legislature 1789–1802, on the governor's council 1803–1809 and 1814–1818, as sheriff of Hillsborough County 1809–1813 and 1818–1827, and as governor of New Hampshire 1827 and 1829. A staunch Anti-Federalist and supporter of Thomas Jefferson, Pierce turned down an appointment as regimental commander in the standing army being raised by President John Adams. Later Pierce supported the policies of Andrew Jackson. He stood as a Democratic presidential elector in 1832. Pierce died when his most famous son was a U.S. senator.

MOTHER: Anna Kendrick Pierce (1768–1838). "She was a most affectionate and tender mother," Franklin Pierce said of her, "strong in many points and weak in some but always weak on the side of kindness and deep affection."[2] Two of her weaknesses—a tendency to mental depression and alcoholism—Pierce inherited. A native of Amherst, New Hampshire, she reportedly had an effervescent personality and a yen for flashy clothes. She grew senile in later years. She died when Pierce was a U.S. senator.

SIBLINGS: By his father's first marriage, Pierce had one half sister, Mrs. Elizabeth "Betsey" McNeil of Boston. By his father's second marriage, Pierce had four brothers and two sisters to live to maturity—Benjamin Kendrick Pierce, a veteran of the War of 1812; Mrs. Nancy McNeil; John Sullivan Pierce, a veteran of the War of 1812; Mrs. Harriet Jameson of Boston; Charles Pierce; and Henry Pierce.

CHILDREN: Pierce had one son to reach the age of reason.

Benjamin Pierce (1841–1853). Their first child, Franklin Pierce, having died in infancy and their second, Frank Robert Pierce, having died at four, the Pierces focused their ambitions on their sole surviving offspring, Bennie. On January 6, 1853, barely two months before Pierce's inauguration as president, a tragedy occured as the family traveled by train from Andover, Massachusetts, to Concord, New Hampshire, where they had planned to attend the funeral of a family friend. Minutes after departure, their passenger car broke loose from the train and rolled down an embankment. The only fatality was Bennie Pierce. His sudden death worked a crushing, enduring psychological hardship on President-elect and Mrs. Pierce. No direct descendant of Franklin Pierce survives.

BIRTH: Pierce was born November 23, 1804, in a log cabin on the Contoocook River at Hillsborough, New Hampshire.

CHILDHOOD: Soon after Pierce's birth, the family moved out of their cramped log cabin into a spacious home built by Benjamin Pierce in Hillsborough Lower Village. Growing up during the War of 1812, the lad thrilled to tales of combat from his older brothers, who served in that conflict, and from troops passing through Hillsborough. Pierce was a robust, active, and devilish youngster, quick to pick a fight or pull a prank.

EDUCATION: Pierce learned to read and write at a brick schoolhouse at Hillsborough. He was a quick, bright student and, according to legend, often spent his recess time tutoring slow learners. In 1818 he enrolled at the Hancock (New Hampshire) Academy and in the spring of 1820 transferred to Francestown (New Hampshire) Academy, where he took college preparatory instruction from Simeon I. Bard. That fall he passed an entrance examination—requiring Latin composition, Greek translation, and knowledge of geography and math—to gain admission to Bowdoin College at Brunswick, Maine. During his sophomore year he met an incoming freshman named Nathaniel Hawthorne, the future author, with whom he formed a lifelong friendship. Another classmate was Henry Wadsworth Longfellow, also a year behind Pierce. An indifferent student until his junior year, Pierce was absent often and slumped to the very bottom of his class. Eventually he applied himself and graduated fifth of 14 students in the class of 1824. In addition to classical languages and math, he also studied history, chemistry, mineralogy, and philosophy. He developed an intense interest in John Locke, finding particularly useful his "Essay on the Human Understanding." Also in his junior year, Pierce took on the duty of chapel monitor and, during spring break, taught briefly at a rural elementary school at Hebron, Maine. Returning for the third trimester, he delivered the Latin dissertation, "De triumphis Romanorum." In political discussions on campus, Pierce argued as a Jacksonian Democrat. He supported Greek rebels in their struggle for independence from the Turks. He was elected captain of the Bowdoin cadets, a march and drill club. At commencement in 1824 he was chosen to deliver a seven-minute disquisition on "The Influence of Circumstances on the Intellectual Character." On graduation he studied law successively under John Burnham in Hillsborough; Levi Woodbury, the future Supreme Court justice, in Portsmouth, New Hampshire; Samuel Howe in Northampton, Massachusetts; and Edmund Parker in Amherst, New Hampshire. Pierce was admitted to the bar in September 1827.

RELIGION: Episcopalian. Pierce first expressed deep faith in God in college; he and his roommate Zenas Caldwell knelt nightly to pray. Still, Pierce never formally professed his faith until late in life. When his son Bennie died in a train accident, Pierce feared that he was being punished for never having publicly affirmed his faith. In his grief he turned closer to God. As president he attended church regularly, read each morning from Thornton's *Family Prayers*, said grace at meals together with the First Lady and the servants, and observed the Sabbath so strictly that he refused even to read his mail on Sunday. After leaving the White House, Pierce in 1865 was at last formally baptized into St. Paul's Episcopal Church in Concord, New Hampshire, by the Reverend James H. Eames. The next year he was confirmed by Bishop Carlton Chase. "My mind has long been impressed," Pierce once wrote, "with the fact that if our present life is not probationary in its character, if we are not placed here, as the blessed word of God teaches, to prepare for another and more exalted state of being, we are destined to waste our energies upon things that are unsubstantial, fleeting, passing away and that can bring no permanent peace—can give no calm hope that is as an anchor to the soul."[3]

RECREATION: Pierce was an avid fisherman.

MARRIAGE: Franklin Pierce, 29, married Jane Means Appleton, 28, on November 19, 1834, at the home of the bride's maternal grandparents in Amherst, New Hampshire. Born in Hampton, New Hampshire, on March 12, 1806, the daughter of the Reverend Jesse Appleton, a Congregationalist minister, and Elizabeth Means Appleton, Jane was a petite, frail, shy, melancholy figure. After the death of her father, who had served as president of Bowdoin College not long before Pierce enrolled there, she at 13 moved into the mansion of her wealthy maternal grandparents in Amherst. Just how she met Pierce is unknown, but her brother-in-law Alpheus S. Packard was one of Pierce's instructors at Bowdoin. Theirs was a small wedding, conducted by her brother-in-law the Reverend Silas Aiken. The couple honeymooned six days at the boardinghouse of Sophia Southurt near Washington, D.C. The Pierces apparently had genuine affection for one another, but they quarreled often and gradually drifted apart. She opposed Pierce's decision to run for president, for she much preferred private life. When her son Bennie was killed in a train accident (see "Children"), she interpreted it as an act of God designed to rid the president-elect of all distractions as he assumed the burdens of office. She never recovered from the tragedy. She grew depressed, reclusive, resentful of her husband's ambition. For nearly two years she remained in the upstairs living quarters of the White House, spending her days writing maudlin letters to her dead son. She left the social chores to her aunt Abby Kent Means and her close friend Varina Davis, wife of War Secretary Jefferson Davis. Mrs. Pierce made her first official appearance as First Lady at a New Year's Day reception in 1855 and thereafter served as White House hostess intermittently. She died of tuberculosis at Andover, Massachusetts, on December 2, 1863. She was buried at Old North Cemetery in Concord, New Hampshire, where she later was joined by the former president.

MILITARY SERVICE: Mexican War 1846–1848. In May 1846 Pierce enlisted as a private in the volunteers at Concord, New Hampshire. He was commissioned a colonel in the regular army in February 1847 and was promoted to brigadier general the next month. He led 2,500 men from Veracruz to Puebla, Mexico, to become part of the Third Division of Major General Gideon Pillow. Enroute to Mexico City, he was injured at the Battle of Contreras (August 1847); his horse lurched from fright, slamming Pierce hard against the pommel of the saddle. The pain was so excruciating that he passed out. He also wrenched his knee in the fall. Later that month he joined in hot pursuit of the enemy at Churubusco but reinjured his knee there and again fainted in the field. He was among those appointed by Major General Winfield Scott to negotiate an armistice, which ultimately proved unacceptable. Bedridden with dysentery during the Battle of Chapultepec and the fall of Mexico City, he recovered sufficiently to take part in the occupation of the Mexican capital in September 1847. He resigned from the army in 1848.

CAREER BEFORE THE PRESIDENCY: Admitted to the bar in 1827, Pierce began practicing law in Hillsborough, New Hampshire.

Member of New Hampshire Legislature, 1829–1833; Speaker, 1831–1832. He served as chairman of the education committee and as a Jacksonian Democrat took an active part in the partisan struggles in the state. In 1832 he campaigned in New Hampshire and Massachusetts, for the reelection of President Jackson.

U.S. Representative, 1833–1837. Elected without formal opposition in 1833 and reelected handily two years later, Democratic Representative Pierce served on the Judiciary Committee. He steadfastly supported the policies of President Jackson, notably his campaign against the Bank of the United States. Pierce consistently opposed federally sponsored internal improvements and denounced abolitionists as "reckless fanatics." He supported the gag rule preventing consideration of antislavery petitions (see "John Quincy Adams, 6th President," "Retirement")

U.S. Senator, 1837–1842. Elected as a Democrat to the U.S. Senate by the New Hampshire legislature in 1836, Pierce at 32 was the youngest member in the upper chamber when he took his seat in March 1837. He generally supported the financial program of President Martin Van Buren, notably the creation of the Independent Treasury system. However, he bolted party ranks to join Whigs in opposing, unsuccessfully, a motion that went beyond the gag rule (preventing consideration of antislavery petitions) to prohibit the House from even accepting such petitions. He feared that failure to acknowledge the antislavery sentiments of constituents would be exploited by abolitionists to inflame passions further. Pierce opposed federal attempts to curb slavery in the District of Columbia or in the territories. He continued to vote against federally funded internal improvements. He voted to postpone consideration of the annexation of Texas. As chairman of the Senate pension committee, he devoted much time to the tedious task of sorting through a flood of pension bills. In 1840 he campaigned vigorously in New Hampshire and Massachusetts for the reelection of President Van Buren. With the Whig takeover in Congress, Pierce, now in the minority, began to lose interest in Senate business. Because of this and other factors, including his wife's repeated insistence that he give up politics, a desire to earn more money, and a longing to leave the unhealthy atmosphere of Washington for the wholesome air of New Hampshire, Senator Pierce resigned his seat in February 1842.

The Pierces had by this time moved their permanent residence to Concord, New Hampshire. Here the former senator resumed the practice of law and was active in party affairs. As chairman of the state Democratic party in 1844, he directed the presidential campaign of James K. Polk in New Hampshire; he was rewarded with appointment as U.S. district attorney for the state. In 1848 Pierce supported Levi Woodbury as a candidate for the Democratic presidential nomination. However, he endorsed the eventual nominee, Lewis Cass.

DEMOCRATIC PRESIDENTIAL NOMINATION, 1852: As Democrats convened in Baltimore in June 1852, four major candidates vied for the nomination— Lewis Cass of Michigan, the nominee in 1848, who had the backing of northerners in support of the Compromise of 1850; James Buchanan of Pennsylvania, popular in the South as well as in his home state; Stephen Douglas of Illinois, candidate of the expansionists and the railroad interests; and William L. Marcy of New York, whose strength was centered in his home state. Cass led on the first 19 ballots, with Buchanan second, and Douglas and Marcy exchanging third and fourth places. Buchanan took the lead on the twentieth ballot and retained it on each of the next nine tallies. Douglas managed a narrow lead on the thirtieth and thirty-first ballots. Cass then recaptured first place through the forty-fourth tally. Marcy carried the next four ballots. Pierce did not get on the board until the thirty-fifth ballot, when the Virginia delegation brought him forward as a compromise choice. He consolidated his support in subsequent voting and was nominated nearly unanimously on the forty-ninth ballot. Senator William R. King of Alabama was nominated for vice president. The Democratic platform supported the Compromise of 1850 (see "Millard Fillmore, 13th President," "Administration"), including the controversial Fugitive Slave Law.

OPPONENT: Winfield Scott (1786–1866), of New Jersey; Whig. Born at Petersburg, Virginia, Scott, a towering 6 feet 5 inches tall, began his military career in 1808. During the War of 1812 he was captured and held briefly as a prisoner of war, was wounded at Lundy's Lane, and rose to brigadier general and brevet major general. He also took part in the Black Hawk War (1832), the Second Seminole War (1835–1837), and the bloodless Aroostook War (1839). In 1841 he was appointed general in chief of the U.S. Army. As commander of U.S. forces during the Mexican War (1846–1848), he became a national hero at Veracruz and the occupation of Mexico City. Among his subordinates in the field was Brigadier

General Franklin Pierce. Scott was nicknamed Old Fuss and Feathers for his scrupulous attention to military form and tradition. At the Whig national convention in Baltimore in June 1852, Scott was an antislavery candidate, whereas incumbent president Millard Fillmore had the backing of the southern delegates, and Daniel Webster, a distant third in delegate strength, was supported in his native New England. Fillmore and Scott exchanged the lead five times in the first eight ballots and tied on the ninth. From the tenth ballot, Scott maintained an edge, which he widened gradually to win the nomination on the fifty-third tally. The final vote was Scott 159, Fillmore 112, and Webster 21. Navy Secretary William A. Graham of North Carolina was nominated for vice president. The Whig platform supported the Compromise of 1850, including the Fugitive Slave Law, a plank anathema to many rank-and-file Whigs. Scott, although opposed to slavery, endorsed the platform without reservation. After his defeat by Pierce, Scott remained in the army and in 1855 became the first commander since George Washington to hold the rank of lieutenant general. Soon after the outbreak of the Civil War, he retired from the service, having first impressed on President Lincoln the value of maintaining a naval blockade against the South.

CAMPAIGN AND ISSUES, 1852: The "Cotton" Whigs, those advocating appeasement of the slavery interests, wholeheartedly supported both the pro-Compromise platform and nominee Scott. Some "Conscience" Whigs, those opposed to slavery, among them Horace Greeley and William H. Seward, denounced the platform but endorsed Scott, hoping that once in office he would stand up to the South. The Democrats suffered no such divisions; Pierce enjoyed support from all segments of the party and even attracted some business support, traditionally a source of Whig strength. In a bid for the German and Irish vote, Scott proposed automatic citizenship for immigrants on completion of one year of military service. Whig campaigners reminded Catholic voters that Scott's daughter had become a nun. Democrats attempted to crucify Scott on the issue by playing on the fears of anti-Catholic nativist elements while at the same time charging before immigrant audiences that during the Mexican War General Scott had executed Irish Catholic soldiers for desertion. Whigs, of course, touted the military record of General Scott, while charging that Pierce had ducked the real fighting. Both sides called the other candidate a drunk. Pierce, brought forward as another Jackson, took on the nickname Young Hickory of the Granite Hills. Pierce's good friend Nathaniel Hawthorne contributed a flattering campaign biography. Perhaps the cleverest slogan of the campaign came from the Democrats: "We Polked you in 1844; we shall Pierce you in 1852!" In the end voters overwhelmingly opted for the dark-horse Pierce over war hero Scott. The election marked the demise of the Whig party, which thereafter fatally divided over the slavery issue.

ELECTION AS PRESIDENT, 1852:

Popular Vote. Pierce (Democrat), 1,601,474 (51%); Winfield Scott (Whig), 1,386,578 (44%).

Electoral Vote. Pierce, 254; Scott, 42.

States Carried. Pierce won the electoral vote of 27 states—Alabama, Arkansas, California, Connecticut, Delaware, Florida, Georgia, Illinois, Indiana, Iowa, Louisiana, Maine, Maryland, Michigan, Mississippi, Missouri, New Hampshire, New Jersey, New York, North Carolina, Ohio, Pennsylvania,

Rhode Island, South Carolina, Texas, Virginia, and Wisconsin. Scott won the electoral vote of 4 states—Kentucky, Massachusetts, Tennessee, and Vermont.

INAUGURAL ADDRESS: March 4, 1853. Pierce recited his inaugural address from memory without notes. ". . . With the Union my best and dearest earthly hopes are entwined. Without it what are we individually or collectively? . . . It is with me an earnest and vital belief that as the Union has been the source, under Providence, of our prosperity to this time, so it is the surest pledge of a continuance of the blessings we have enjoyed and which we are sacredly bound to transmit undiminished to our children. . . . To every theory of society or government, whether the offspring of feverish ambition or of morbid enthusiasm, calculated to dissolve the bonds of law and affection which unite us, I shall interpose a ready and stern resistance. I believe that involuntary servitude, as it exists in different States of this Confederacy, is recognized by the Constitution. I believe that it stands like any other admitted right, and that the States where it exists are entitled to efficient remedies to enforce the constitutional provisions. . . . I fervertly hope that the question is at rest, and that no sectional or ambitious or fanatical excitement may again threaten the durability of our institutions or obscure the light of our prosperity. . . ."

VICE PRESIDENT: William Rufus DeVane King (1786–1853), of Alabama, served March–April 1853. A native of Sampson County, North Carolina, King became a lawyer in 1806 and soon thereafter entered the North Carolina legislature. He served in the U.S. House 1811–1816, resigning his seat to act as secretary of the U.S. legation in Russia 1816–1818. On his return to the United States, he settled in Alabama to become one of that newly admitted state's first two senators. During nearly three decades in the Senate, 1819–1844, 1848–1852, and as president pro tem 1850–1852, King was a staunch Jacksonian Democrat and expansionist. As U.S. minister to France 1844–1846, he worked to dissuade that government from protesting U.S. annexation of Texas. In 1852 he supported James Buchanan, a close personal friend and fellow bachelor, for president. King's selection as vice president was a nod to the Buchanan camp. However, King was by this time terminally ill with tuberculosis. After his election, he sought relief in Cuba, where, because he was too weak to return for the inaugural ceremonies, he took his oath of office. He is the only nationally elected public official to be sworn in on foreign soil. He rallied sufficiently to travel to his home at Cahaba, Alabama, where he died without ever having assumed his duties as vice president.

CABINET:

Secretary of State. William L. Marcy (1786–1857), of New York, served 1853–1857. He had served as war secretary in the Polk administration. Pierce withdrew the nomination of his first choice, John A. Dix of New York, in the face of southern opposition. His second choice, Senator Robert M.T. Hunter of Virginia, declined the appointment. The president then settled on Marcy. Although lacking in diplomatic experience, Marcy surrounded himself with knowledgeable aides and presided skillfully over U.S. foreign policy. His accomplishments included the Gadsden Purchase (see "Administration") and a trade agreement with Canada. A committed expansionist, he favored annexation of Cuba at all costs. His instructions to the U.S. minister to Spain contributed to the Ostend Manifesto (see "Administration"), which he was forced to repudiate. Within the department, Marcy instituted a simple dress code for U.S. diplomats abroad. The rigors of the post drained him; he died three months after leaving office.

Secretary of the Treasury. James Guthrie (1792–1869), of Kentucky, served 1853–1857. He used the Treasury surplus to reduce the national debt and deposited federal revenues in strict compliance with the Independent Treasury Act. For his efforts to root out corruption in the department, he earned the nickname The Prairie Plow.

Secretary of War. Jefferson Davis (1808–1889), of Mississippi, served 1853–1857. Although inclined to turn down the appointment for health and other reasons, Davis relented at Pierce's insistent plea. An able secretary, he modernized the army, shaping it into a more efficient war machine that, ironically, a decade later would crush the rebellion Davis led as president of the Confederate States of America. Secretary Davis dispatched the survey teams that laid out the routes of the future transcontinental railroads.

Attorney General. Caleb Cushing (1800–1879), of Massachusetts, served 1853–1857. Because he was a former Whig, his appointment drew protests from long-standing Democrats who questioned his party credentials. He was among Pierce's closest advisers. As attorney general he cleared a formidable backlog of legal matters from the previous administration. His recommendations for reorganization of the judicial branch and creation of a department of law were not acted on by Congress. He later switched to the Republican party and served as minister to Spain under President Grant.

Secretary of the Navy. James C. Dobbin (1814–1857), of North Carolina, served 1853–1857. He sought to strengthen and streamline the navy. Although he failed to persuade Congress to increase substantially the size of the navy, he was successful in purging its officer corps of deadwood. On the basis of the findings of an investigative board he set up, Secretary Dobbin, with the president's concurrence, dismissed 7 percent of the naval officers as incompetent and retired at reduced pay another 21 percent.

Postmaster General. James Campbell (1812–1893), of Pennsylvania, served 1853–1857. He was placed in the cabinet at the suggestion of Pennsylvania Democratic leader James Buchanan.

Secretary of Interior. Robert McClelland (1807–1880), of Michigan, served 1853–1857. He was placed in the cabinet at the suggestion of Michigan Democratic leader Lewis Cass. Secretary McClelland cracked down on corruption in the sale of public lands and in dealings with the Indians.

ADMINISTRATION: March 4, 1853–March 3, 1857.

Gadsden Purchase, 1853. Under its terms, the United States bought from Mexico a 45,535-square-mile strip of land, now southernmost Arizona and New Mexico, for $10 million. The land was purchased because it lay on the proposed route for a southern transcontinental railroad. The acquisition completed the modern outline of the 48 contiguous states. Negotiating the treaty for the United States was the minister to Mexico, James Gadsden.

Kansas-Nebraska Act, 1854. Sponsored by Senator Stephen Douglas, Democrat of Illinois, ostensibly to promote settlement of the West and facilitate construction of a northerly transcontinental railroad, the bill repealed the Missouri Compromise (see "James Monroe, 5th President," "Administration") by permitting settlers in the newly organized territories of Kansas and Nebraska to decide for themselves whether to permit slavery—the concept of popular sovereignty. Critics charged that Douglas introduced the measure solely to promote his chances for the Democratic presidential nomination in 1856. Whatever the senator's motives, the bill opened with renewed vigor the bitter sectional debate over slavery that culminated in the Civil War. It prompted such prominent abolitionists as Salmon Chase and Charles Sumner to issue the Appeal of the Independent Democrats in January 1854, denouncing the bill as a southern device to open all the territories to slavery. In February 1854 opponents of the measure met at Ripon, Wisconsin, a gathering that gave birth to a new political force—the Republican party. President Pierce wholeheartedly supported the Kansas-Nebraska bill as a fair, practical compromise between the competing interests of North and South; he lobbied strenuously for its passage. The introduction of popular sovereignty in Nebraska was of no significance, for residents there overwhelmingly opposed slavery. But in Kansas the issue was bitterly and violently joined. Northern abolitionists settled in Kansas to promote its admission as a free state. "Border ruffians" poured into Kansas from the slave state of Missouri. The bloody encounters that followed included the infamous raid of John Brown in which five proslavery men were slaughtered at Pottawatomie Creek May 24, 1856. Casualties in the struggle known as Bleeding Kansas numbered some 200.

Ostend Manifesto, 1854. President Pierce had hoped to extend the southern boundary of the United States by annexing Cuba. To that end, he authorized Secretary of State Marcy to negotiate the acquisition of the island from Spain. Marcy, in turn, instructed U.S. Minister to Spain Pierre Soulé to negotiate its purchase in Madrid and added that if Spanish authorities refused to sell, "you will then direct your efforts to the next most desirable object, which is to detach that island from the Spanish dominion."[4] Marcy also suggested that Soulé meet with U.S. Minister to France John Y. Mason and U.S. Minister to Great Britain James Buchanan to consider how best to undertake the acquisition. Meeting at Ostend, Belgium, and Aix la Chapelle, Prussia, the three drew up what came to be called the Ostend Manifesto. It urged that the United States offer to purchase Cuba for as much as $120 million. If Spain should refuse to sell, the ministers continued, then the United States "shall be justified in wresting it from Spain." The manifesto supported such blatant aggression with the assertion that "Cuba is as necessary to the North American republic as any of its present members, and that it belongs naturally to that great family of States of which the Union is the providential nursery." Technically, the document was not a manifesto but an internal government communication written for the president's and the war secretary's eyes only. Its contents somehow were leaked, however, to the *New York Herald*, which published it. That Pierce was even considering going to war to take Cuba drew a firestorm of criticism from administration opponents, who denounced the policy as a scheme to extend slavery. Thus exposed, Pierce and Marcy were compelled formally to repudiate the Ostend Manifesto. Soulé, feeling betrayed, promptly resigned in protest. Although discredited for its disregard for international law, the manifesto contained one sentence that seems prophetic in light of the Cuban Missile Crisis more than a century later: "the Union can never enjoy repose, nor possess reliable security, as long as Cuba is not embraced within its boundaries."[5]

Nicaragua. In 1855 William Walker, a proslavery soldier of fortune, led a band of adventurers to Nicaragua to foment rebellion there. The revolution succeeded, Walker emerged as president of Nicaragua in 1856, and Pierce recognized the new government.

Because of his prominent role in securing passage of the controversial Kansas-Nebraska Act and his failure to maintain order in Bleeding Kansas, Pierce was deemed unelectable by members of his own party and thus was denied renomination in 1856 (see "James Buchanan, 15th President," "Democratic Presidential Nomination").

SUPREME COURT APPOINTMENT: John A. Campbell (1811–1889), of Alabama, served as associate justice 1853–1861. Appointed by Pierce on the recommendation of the other justices, Campbell was a strict constructionist highly regarded in the North as well as in the South. As the nation drifted to civil war, he urged compromise and opposed secession. With the outbreak of hostilities, however, he resigned from the Court and served as assistant secretary of war of the Confederacy 1862–1865. For this service, he was sentenced to four months in prison after the South's defeat.

RANKING IN 1962 HISTORIANS POLL: Pierce ranked twenty-eighth of 31 presidents; fifth of 6 "below average" presidents. He ranked above Buchanan, below Coolidge.

RETIREMENT: March 4, 1857–October 8, 1869. After attending the inaugural of his successor, James Buchanan, Pierce retired to Concord, New Hampshire, where he spent his final years in financial security but suffered great emotional strain. With his wife he traveled to Europe and the Bahamas, trying in vain to pull Mrs. Pierce out of the chronic depression she had slumped into on the death of their son Bennie. As civil war approached, Pierce spoke out in favor of the South and warned the federal government not to attempt to curb slavery. He denounced the war policy of President Lincoln, though he was careful to support the Union and oppose secession. In a Fourth of July address in 1863, the day after the Battle of Gettysburg, he lamented what he called the "fearful, fruitless, fatal civil war . . . prosecuted . . . upon the theory of emancipation, devastation, subjugation." Appalled by the carnage on both sides, he wondered, "How futile are all our efforts to maintain the Union by force of arms."[6] Such antiwar sentiments publicly expressed made Pierce very unpopular in his native New England. He was denounced as a traitor and abandoned by former friends and neighbors. On Lincoln's assassination, an angry mob threatened his home. In retirement Pierce began drinking heavily again.

DEATH: October 8, 1869, 4:40 A.M., Concord, New Hampshire. During the summer of 1869 Pierce's health steadily deteriorated from dropsy and inflammation of the stomach. Funeral services were held on October 11 at St. Paul's Episcopal Church in Concord, after the body had lain in state at the New Hampshire capitol. He was buried at Concord. In his last will and testament, Pierce left the bulk of his estate to his nephew and namesake Frank H. Pierce. The remainder was distributed among numerous friends, relatives, and charities.

PIERCE PRAISED: "It is his peculiar distinction, above all other public men within my knowledge, that he has never had occasion to take a single step backwards. What speech, vote, or sentiment of his whole political career has been inconsistent with the purest and strictest principles of Jeffersonian Democracy? . . . Our candidate, throughout his life, has proved himself to be peculiarly unselfish. The offices and honors which other men seek with so much eagerness, have sought him only to be refused. . . . Indeed, the public character of General Pierce is so invulnerable that it has scarcely been seriously assaulted."[7]—James Buchanan, 1852

"He has in him many of the chief elements of a great ruler. His talents are administrative, he has a subtle faculty of making affairs roll onward according to his will, and of influencing their course without showing any trace of his action. There are scores of men in the country that seem brighter than he is, but [he] has the directing mind, and will move them about like pawns on a chess-board, and turn all their abilities to better purpose than they themselves could do."[8]—Nathaniel Hawthorne, 1852

PIERCE CRITICIZED: "He has got round him so many whigs that democrats are crowded out of an organisation pretending to the democratic name. . . . This bastard race . . . controls the organisation, this unproductive hybrid [was] begot by southern arrogance upon northern subserviency."[9]—George Bancroft, historian and statesman, 1856

"A vain, showy, and pliant man . . . [who] by his errors and weakness broke down his administration, and his party throughout the country."[10]—Gideon Welles, 1868

"[Pierce was] a small politician, of low capacity and mean surroundings, proud to act as the servile tool of men worse than himself but also stronger and abler. He was ever ready to do any work the slavery leaders set him."[11]—Theodore Roosevelt

"Pierce was the best looking President the White House ever had—but as President he ranks with Buchanan and Calvin Coolidge."[12]—President Harry S Truman, 1952

PIERCE QUOTES: "A Republic without parties is a complete anomaly. The history of all popular Governments show how absurd is the idea of their attempting to exist without parties."[13]—1825

"In a body [Congress] where there are more than one hundred talking lawyers . . . you can make no calculation upon the termination of any debate and frequently the more trifling the subject the more animated and protracted the discussion."[14]

"We have to maintain inviolate the great doctrine of the inherent right of popular self-government; . . . to render cheerful obedience to the laws of the land, to unite in enforcing their execution, and to frown indignantly on all combinations to resist them; . . . to preserve sacred from all touch of usurpation, as the very palladium of our political salvation, the reserved rights and powers of the several States and of the people."[15]—1854

BOOK ABOUT PIERCE: Nichols, Roy Franklin. *Franklin Pierce: Young Hickory of the Granite Hills.* Philadelphia: University of Pennsylvania Press, 1931.

NOTES

1 Roy Franklin Nichols, *Franklin Pierce: Young Hickory of the Granite Hills*, Philadelphia: University of Pennsylvania Press, 1931, pp. 257–258.
2 Ibid., p. 10.
3 Ibid., p. 124.
4 Ibid., p. 370.
5 Henry Steele Commager, ed., *Documents of American History*, New York: Crofts, 1945, Doc. no. 181.
6 Nichols, p. 522.
7 George Ticknor Curtis, *Life of James Buchanan*, New York: Harper & Bros., 1883, vol. I, p. 44.
8 Nichols, p. 217.

9 Arthur M. Schlesinger, Jr., *The Age of Jackson*, Boston: Little, Brown, 1946, p. 482.

10 Nichols, p. 533.

11 Richard Kenin and Justin Wintle, eds., *Dictionary of Biographical Quotation*, New York: Knopf, 1978, p. 600.

12 Robert H. Ferrell, ed., *Off the Record: The Private Papers of Harry S. Truman*, New York: Harper & Row, 1980, p. 266.

13 Nichols, p. 30.

14 Ibid., p. 104.

15 Ibid., p. xii.

JAMES BUCHANAN

15TH PRESIDENT

NAME: James Buchanan. He was named after his father.

PHYSICAL DESCRIPTION: An imposing, handsome figure, Buchanan stood a bit over 6 feet tall and had broad shoulders and a sizable paunch. He had a very fair complexion and large blue eyes. His massive forehead receded to silky gray hair, which he wore swept up and back. He had rather small feet for his size and took quick steps. His most distinctive feature was a wryneck; his head was habitually cocked to the left. Unlike most victims of wryneck, his was not caused by muscular malfunction. Rather, it was a result of a peculiar eye disorder. One eye was nearsighted, the other farsighted; also, the left eyeball was pitched higher in the socket than was the right. To compensate, Buchanan early developed the habit of cocking his head and closing one eye. If he were talking to someone or examining something close up, he would wink shut the farsighted eye; if gazing in the distance, he closed the nearsighted one. For reading he found it easier to focus with a candle in front of his eyes. He apparently coped well with the disorder, for he read much throughout his career and did not wear glasses until near the end of his life. His health otherwise generally was sound. Buchanan dressed carefully, commonly in a black suit and white neckwear.

PERSONALITY: According to biographer George Ticknor Curtis, Buchanan's personality was marked by "strong family affections," "engaging social qualities," "fidelity to friends," a "forgiving temper towards those who had injured him,"[1] and generosity. He freely loaned money to friends in need and gave funds to the poor. He bought slaves in Washington and freed them in Pennsylvania without any guarantee of reimbursement. He was scrupulous to avoid even the appearance of conflict of interest. He declined all offers of free transportation passes and, as president, turned gifts over to the Patent Office. Buchanan carried himself with an air of dignity and was at all times graceful and courteous. He was not an especially gifted speaker.

ANCESTORS: Buchanan was of Scotch-Irish ancestry. His great[3]-grandfather George Buchanan (b. 1648) emigrated from Scotland to County Tyrone, Ireland. His grandfather John Buchanan was a farmer in County Donegal, Ireland.

FATHER: James Buchanan, Sr. (c. 1761–1821), merchant. Born in County Donegal, Ireland, he emigrated to the United States in 1783. He lived briefly with a maternal uncle in York County, Pennsylvania, until he was able to support himself. He worked as a trading post clerk in Stony Batter, Pennsylvania, and in 1788 went into business for himself in that community. A decade later he moved his business to Mercersburg, where he prospered as both merchant and farmer. He also was a justice of the peace. He died at Mercersburg when his son was a U.S. congressman-elect.

MOTHER: Elizabeth Speer Buchanan (1767–1833). A native of Lancaster County, Pennsylvania, she married James Buchanan, Sr., in 1788. Largely self-educated, she read much, especially the Bible and poetry; she was able to recite from memory large passages of John Milton and Alexander Pope. She encouraged the education of her children and regularly tested their powers of reason by engaging them in argument. Buchanan attributed to her responsibility for his success. In her old age, she tried without success to dissuade Buchanan from accepting appointment as minister to Russia, realizing that she would not live to see his return. She died at Greensburg, Pennsylvania, while her son was at his post in St. Petersburg.

SIBLINGS: The oldest of eight children to live to maturity, Buchanan had four sisters and three brothers—Mrs. Jane Lane, mother of Harriet Lane, official White House hostess during the Buchanan administration; Mrs. Maria Magaw Johnson Yates of Meadeville, Pennsylvania; Mrs. Sarah Huston; Mrs. Harriet Henry, wife of the Reverend Robert Henry of Greensburg (Pennsylvania) Presbyterian Church; William Speer Buchanan, a lawyer, who died at 22; George Washington Buchanan, a lawyer, who at 22 was appointed by President Andrew Jackson U.S. attorney for western Pennsylvania and died at 24; the Reverend Edward Young Buchanan, rector of Trinity Episcopal Church in Philadelphia, who married Ann Eliza Foster, sister of famed composer Stephen Collins Foster.

CHILDREN: None; thus, no direct descendant of Buchanan survives.

BIRTH: Buchanan was born on April 23, 1791, in a log cabin at Cove Gap, a few miles outside Mercersburg, Pennsylvania.

CHILDHOOD: At age five Buchanan moved with his family from the log cabin of his birth to Mercersburg, where he spent the remainder of his childhood.

EDUCATION: Buchanan learned the fundamentals at common schools and studied Latin and Greek at Old Stone Academy in Mercersburg, Pennsylvania, in preparation for admission as a junior to Dickinson College in Carlisle in 1807. Although he studied hard, taking a special interest in logic and metaphysics, he also found time to get into trouble. Just what he did is unknown, but school officials clearly considered him a discipline problem. "But for the respect which the faculty entertained for my father," Buchanan later recalled, "I would have been expelled from college on account of disorderly conduct."[2] Indeed, the administration wrote his father at the end of the first year urging him to keep his devilish son home. Buchanan thereupon pledged to reform and behaved himself during his senior year. His improved conduct did not completely satisfy the administration, however, for they pointedly denied Buchanan a scholastic honor due him. Mortified and disappointed, Buchanan considered boycotting commencement, but he relented and received his degree with the rest of the class of 1809. In December 1809, Buchanan moved to Lancaster to study law under James Hopkins. He applied himself diligently, reading law during the day and taking walks at night to contemplate what he had learned. He early developed a facility for putting arcane legal concepts into everyday language. Buchanan was admitted to the bar in 1812.

RELIGION: Presbyterian. "I can say sincerely for myself that I desire to be a Christian," Buchanan wrote to his brother, the minister, from his post in Russia in 1832, "and I think I could withdraw from the vanities and follies of the world without suffering many pangs. I have thought much upon the subject since my arrival in this strange land, and sometimes almost persuade myself that I am a Christian; but I am often haunted by the spirit of skepticism and doubt. My true feeling upon many occasions is: 'Lord, I would believe; help Thou mine unbelief.' Yet I am far from being an unbeliever."[3] His doubts persisted for many years. Then in August 1860, while vacationing at Bedford Springs, Pennsylvania, he poured out all his misgivings to the Reverend William M. Paxton, pastor of the First Presbyterian Church of New York City, in a private meeting that lasted more than two hours. He questioned the preacher closely on every religious matter that had been troubling him. At the end of the discussion, he pronounced himself satisfied on all points. Free of doubt at last, he felt ready formally to join a church for the first time. He postponed the ceremony, however, until after he had left the White House, fearing that such a sudden public display of religious sentiment would invite charges of hypocrisy. Soon after stepping down as president, he joined the Presbyterian church of Lancaster, Pennsylvania.

Despite his doubts, Buchanan had been an active Christian all his life. He recited daily prayers, read regularly from *Jay's Exercises*, a collection of scriptural commentary, and was thoroughly familiar with the Bible. He was particularly fond of the sermons of French clergyman Jean Baptiste Massillon. He scrupulously observed the Sabbath; while minister to Russia, he refused to dance at the official court balls held on Sunday in St. Petersburg.

RECREATION: Buchanan enjoyed reading and entertaining friends at his home. He read extensively, despite his eye disorder (see "Physical Description"), until late in life, when he suddenly lost all interest in books. He also like playing cards.

EARLY ROMANCE: During the summer of 1819 Buchanan, 28, became engaged to Anne C. Coleman, 23, daughter of millionaire Robert Coleman of Lancaster, Pennsylvania. By all accounts, Miss Coleman was a lovely woman, shy, sensitive, and attractive. The couple quarreled; she abruptly broke off the engagement and went to visit relatives in Philadelphia. There on December 9, 1819, she died suddenly, possibly of suicide. "I have lost the only earthly object of my affections," Buchanan commented in his grief, "without whom life now presents to me a dreary blank. My prospects are all cut off, and I feel that my happiness will be buried with her in the grave."[4] That her father held him responsible for her death was made clear when he returned unopened Buchanan's request to be permitted to take part in the funeral services. Just what caused the quarrel is unknown. According to rumor, Miss Coleman called off the wedding because she came to suspect that Buchanan was marrying her for her money. In later years, Buchanan let it be known that he had placed under seal certain materials that, when examined, would explain the trivial matter over which they quarreled. On his death, however, the sealed materials were discovered with a note ordering that they be destroyed unexamined; executors of his estate complied. Before his fiancée's death, Buchanan had intended to build quietly his law practice. But with his future now unsettled, he acceded to requests that he run for Congress, largely as a distraction from his grief.

MARRIAGE: None. Buchanan was the only president to remain a bachelor. His orphaned niece Harriet Lane, whom he raised from childhood, served as official White House hostess during the Buchanan administration.

MILITARY SERVICE:

War of 1812. At first Buchanan opposed the War of 1812 as unjustified. But with the British burning of Washington, D.C., in 1814, he emerged a leading voice at a war rally at Lancaster, Pennsylvania. He was among the first in the town to volunteer for the special company of dragoons led by Judge Henry Shippen. With the unit he marched to Baltimore to serve under Major Charles S. Ridgely of the Third Cavalry. After the British withdrawal from that city, the men of Shippen's company were honorably discharged.

CAREER BEFORE THE PRESIDENCY: Admitted to the bar in 1812, Buchanan began practicing law in Lancaster, Pennsyvlania.

Member of Pennsylvania House of Representatives, 1815–1816. Elected in October 1814 and reelected a year later to represent Lancaster in the state legislature, Buchanan, a Federalist, spoke out against a state draft during the War of 1812. He denounced the conscription bill under consideration, because he believed that it fell hardest on the poor. He favored instead a volunteer force with proper inducements. Buchanan also opposed the Bank of the United States. At the end of two terms, after losing a race for the U.S. House, he resumed his law practice in Lancaster.

U.S. Representative, 1821–1831. Elected as a Federalist in October 1820, Buchanan represented Pennsylvania's Lower Susquehanna District, comprised of Lancaster, York, and Dauphin counties. He was reelected three times in succession. With the disappearance of the Federalist party, he became associated with the Jacksonian Democrats. In 1822 he opposed liberalizing bankruptcy laws, fearing it would encourage financial irresponsibility. He was a moderate on the tariff question. In 1824 he supported Andrew Jackson in his unsuccessful bid for president. Buchanan emerged a leader of the opposition to the administration of President John Quincy Adams. Although he had supported extension of the Cumberland Road in 1822, when President James Monroe vetoed it, Buchanan now opposed it, unsuccessfully, as part of the Adams administration's policy of internal improvements. Buchanan spoke out in favor of relief for the aging officers of the American Revolution. In 1828 he campaigned actively in Pennsylvania for Jackson for president. As chairman of the House Judiciary Committee during 1829–1831, Buchanan demonstrated a broad knowledge of the court system and constitutional law and was largely responsible for defeating an attempt to remove from the Supreme Court appellate jurisdiction in matters involving constitutional questions, treaties, and federal law. He also was a manager for the prosecution in the impeachment trial of U.S. District Court Judge James H. Peck. Buchanan declined to stand for reelection in 1830, having decided to resume his law practice in Lancaster.

U.S. Minister to Russia, 1832–1833. Appointed by President Jackson in 1831 and overwhelmingly confirmed by the Senate in January 1832, Buchanan took up his duties at St. Petersburg in June with instructions to conclude commercial and maritime treaties with Russia. With Count Nesselrode, Buchanan successfully negotiated the commercial treaty but failed to persuade the Russian government to accept the U.S. maritime policy that free ships make free goods. It also fell to Minister Buchanan to explain to St. Petersburg officials, upset over anti-Russian commentary in American newspapers, that under the U.S. form of government the president was powerless to muzzle the press.

U.S. Senator, 1834–1845. Buchanan was elected as a Democrat to the Senate by the Pennsylvania legislature on the fourth ballot over Joel B. Sutherland, James Clarke, and Amos Ellmaker. He was reelected in 1837 and again in 1843. Senator Buchanan consistently supported the administration of President Andrew Jackson. He promoted improved national defense, defended Jackson's campaign against the Bank of the United States, opposed efforts to curb the president's power to remove subordinates, and argued forcefully in favor of expunging from the record the Senate's censure of Jackson (see "Andrew Jackson, 7th President," "Military Service"). In 1836 he supported Martin Van Buren for president. The next year he became chairman of the Senate Foreign Relations Committee. He endorsed the Independent Treasury system put forward by the Van Buren administration. He declined Van Vuren's offer of appointment as attorney general. In 1840 he campaigned for Van Buren's unsuccessful bid for reelection. During the administration of President John Tyler, he opposed the Bankruptcy Act and the Webster-Ashburton Treaty. In 1844 he was a candidate for the Democratic presidential nomination but campaigned for the eventual nominee, James K. Polk. He supported the annexation of Texas.

Secretary of State, 1845–1849. Buchanan's direction of foreign policy was limited, as President Polk largely served as his own secretary of state. Buchanan made final arrangements for the annexation of Texas and negotiated the Oregon Treaty (see "James K. Polk, 11th President," "Administration") with Great Britain.

In 1848 Buchanan was a candidate for the Democratic presidential nomination; he supported the eventual nominee, Lewis Cass, in the general election. With the end of Polk's term, he retired to Wheatland, the estate at Lancaster, Pennsylvania, he had recently purchased. In 1852 he was a candidate for the Democratic presidential nomination, losing to Franklin Pierce, for whom he campaigned in the general election.

Minister to Great Britain, 1853–1856. Appointed by President Pierce, Minister Buchanan in 1854 joined U.S. Minister to Spain Pierre Soulé and U.S. Minister to France John Y. Mason in drawing up the Ostend Manifesto (see "Franklin Pierce, 14th President," "Administration"), justifying U.S. acquisition of Cuba by any means necessary. Although the Pierce administration repudiated the document, the manifesto boosted Buchanan's popularity in the South, whose leaders looked to Cuba as fertile soil for the extension of slavery.

DEMOCRATIC PRESIDENTIAL NOMINATION, 1856: As Democrats convened in Cincinnati in June 1856, Buchanan was the front-runner for the nomination, ahead of incumbent President Franklin Pierce and Senator Stephen Douglas of Illinois. All three candidates had demonstrated concern for southern principles and upheld the constitutionality of slavery, but Buchanan enjoyed the advantage of having been abroad during the bitter debate over the Kansas-Nebraska bill (see "Franklin Pierce, 14th President," "Administration") and thus appeared above the political fray. Moreover, his part in drafting the Ostend Manifesto, repudiated by the Pierce administration, made him especially popular in the

South. Through the skillful efforts of his floor manager Colonel John W. Forney, Buchanan staked out a narrow lead on the first ballot, with 135 votes to 122 for Pierce, 33 for Douglas, and 5 for Lewis Cass of Michigan, and steadily increased his margin in subsequent balloting. Pierce's support gradually eroded, to the benefit of Douglas, but such a shift did not impede the Buchanan drive. Rather than deadlock the convention further, Douglas withdrew after 16 ballots, and Buchanan was nominated unanimously on the next tally. John C. Breckinridge of Kentucky was nominated for vice president. The Democratic platform opposed distribution among the states of proceeds from the sale of public land, rejected resurrection of the national bank, supported the Independent Treasury system and retention of the presidential veto, cricitized the antiforeign and anti-Catholic activities of the Know-Nothings, opposed federal interference with slavery, endorsed the Compromise of 1850 and the Kansas-Nebraska Act, and supported expansionism and a transcontinental railroad.

OPPONENTS: John C. Frémont (1813–1890) of California; Republican. Born in Savannah, Georgia, the illegitimate son of a refugee from the French Revolution, Frémont gained fame as the Pathfinder of the West for his many successful surveying expeditions. With the J. N. Nicollett party he helped map the region between the Mississippi and Missouri rivers during 1838–1839. He explored along the Des Moines River in 1841. Subsequent adventures included three great expeditions that contributed significantly to geographical knowledge of the West and facilitated settlement of the region. Assisted at times by scout Kit Carson, he explored the Oregon Trail (1842), trekked across the Sierra Nevadas into the Sacramento Valley (1843–1844), and returned (1845) to California in time to take part in the Mexican War. In the command dispute between Commodore Robert F. Stockton and General Stephen W. Kearney, Frémont sided with the former and for that was court-martialed and convicted in 1848. His sentence suspended by President Polk, he resigned from the army and settled in California, where he promptly struck gold. During 1850–1851 he served as one of California's first two U.S. senators. At the first national convention of Republicans in Philadelphia in June 1856, Frémont was the favorite of the delegates because he had no political record to defend—although his antislavery views were well known—he was acceptable to all factions, and he was a national hero for his daring expeditions. Frémont was nominated on the first ballot with 359 votes to 196 for Justice John McLean of Ohio. William L. Dayton of New Jersey was nominated for vice president on the first ballot, having defeated a large field, including Abraham Lincoln of Illinois, his nearest competitor. The Republican platform opposed the extension of slavery into the territories, held the Pierce administration responsible for the tragedy known as Bleeding Kansas, called for the admission of Kansas as a free state, denounced the Ostend Manifesto, supported a transcontinental railroad, and opposed the bigotry of the Know-Nothings. After his defeat by Buchanan, Frémont served as a major general during the early part of the Civil War and subsequently lost his fortune in a railroad venture. During 1878–1883 he was territorial governor of Arizona.

Millard Fillmore (1800–1874) of New York; American, or Know-Nothing, and Whig (see "Millard Fillmore, 13th President"). The American, or Know-Nothing, party consisted of nativist elements opposed to immigration and Catholic influence. At the party convention in New York in June 1856, Fillmore was nominated for president on the second ballot with 179 votes to 24 for George

Law of New York, his nearest competitor. Andrew J. Donelson of Tennessee, nephew of former President Andrew Jackson, was nominated for vice president on the first ballot. The American party platform favored restricting all public officers to native-born non-Catholic citizens—"Americans must rule America," it said—proposed extending to 21 years the residency requirement for naturalization, and opposed federal interference with slavery. The Whig party, convening at Baltimore in September, endorsed the Fillmore-Donelson ticket.

CAMPAIGN AND THE ISSUES, 1856: In this spirited campaign waged by party workers as the candidates remained aloof, the new Republican party shouted its first presidential slogan—"Free Speech, Free Press, Free Soil, Free Men, Frémont and Victory!" Democrats warned that a Republican victory would not be tolerated in the South and would lead to civil war. Democrats promised continued conciliation and economic stability, a posture that earned them the support of the financial community. Republicans responded that the sectional conflict would persist as long as Democrats continued to appease the South in its demands to spread slavery into the territories. They pointed to Bleeding Kansas (see "Franklin Pierce, 14th President," "Administration") and the assault by Democratic Representative Preston Brooks of South Carolina on abolitionist Senator Charles Sumner of Massachusetts as proof of southern savagery. The charge that Republicans were too radical for the times undermined the party's strength among moderates, notably Democratic Senator Thomas Hart Benton of Missouri, Frémont's father-in-law, who endorsed Buchanan. In a bid to court nativist elements, Democratic campaigners spread the lie that Frémont was privately a Catholic. He had married in the church and sent his adopted daughter to a Catholic school, but he was in fact an Episcopalian. He declined openly to deny the charge during the campaign, however, for fear of alienating the Catholics, whose support he was counting on. The election was decided in the hotly contested swing states of Pennsylvania, Illinois, and Indiana. Voters in all three chose Buchanan and stability over Frémont and the threat of civil war.

ELECTION AS PRESIDENT, 1856:

Popular Vote: Buchanan (Democrat), 1,838,169 (45%); Frémont (Republican), 1,335,264 (33%); Fillmore (American, or Know-Nothing, and Whig), 874,534 (22%).

Electoral Vote: Buchanan, 174; Frémont, 114; Fillmore, 8.

States Carried: Buchanan won the electoral votes of 19 states—Alabama, Arkansas, California, Delaware, Florida, Georgia, Illinois, Indiana, Kentucky, Louisiana, Mississippi, Missouri, New Jersey, North Carolina, Pennsylvania, South Carolina, Tennessee, Texas, and Virginia. Frémont won the electoral votes of 11 states—Connecticut, Iowa, Maine, Massachusetts, Michigan, New Hampshire, New York, Ohio, Rhode Island, Vermont, and Wisconsin. Fillmore won the electoral votes of 1 state—Maryland.

INAUGURAL ADDRESS: March 4, 1857. "All agree that under the Constitution slavery in the States is beyond the reach of any human power except that of the respective States themselves wherein it exists. May we not, then, hope that the long agitation on this subject is approaching its end, and that the geographical parties to which it has given birth, so much dreaded by the Father of his Country, will speedily become extinct? . . . Throughout the whole progress of this agitation, which has scarcely known any intermission for more than twenty years, whilst it has been productive of no positive good to any human being it has been the prolific source of great evils to the master, to the slave, and to the

218 / JAMES BUCHANAN

whole country. It has alienated and estranged the people of the sister States from each other, and has even seriously endangered the very existence of the Union. . . . should the agitation continue it may eventually endanger the personal safety of a large portion of our countrymen where the institution exists. In that event no form of government, however admirable in itself and however productive of material benefits, can compensate for the loss of peace and domestic security around the family altar. Let every Union-loving man, therefore, exert his best influence to suppress this agitation. . . ."

VICE PRESIDENT: John Cabell Breckinridge (1821–1875), of Kentucky, served 1857–1861. At 36, he was the youngest vice president. Born near Lexington, Kentucky, Breckinridge, a lawyer, served in the Mexican War and at 28 was elected as a Democrat to the Kentucky legislature. During two terms in the U.S. House 1851–1855, he emerged a national figure, defending slavery and upholding the right of secession, but opposing extension of slavery into the territories. As vice president he urged compromise to avert civil war. In 1860 he accepted the presidential nomination of the National Democratic party (see "Abraham Lincoln, 16th President," "Opponents").

CABINET:

Secretary of State. (1) Lewis Cass (1782–1866), of Michigan, served 1857–1860. He had served as war secretary in the Jackson administration and ran as the Democratic presidential nominee against Zachary Taylor in 1848. Now in his mid-70s, the venerable secretary pressed Buchanan to reinforce the federal installation at Fort Moultrie, South Carolina, in the face of southern threats on it. When the president refused, Cass resigned in protest, just 12 days before South Carolina forces took the fort. Cass derided the president for failing to stand up to secessionists. Buchanan, in turn, thought little of Cass's abilities as secretary. "So timid was he," the president said, "and so little confidence had he in himself that it was difficult for him to arrive at any decision of the least consequence."[5] (2) Jeremiah S. Black (1810–1883), of Pennsylvania, served 1860–1861. Transferred from attorney general, he urged President Buchanan to protect federal property in the South. He championed the right of naturalized U.S. citizens to visit their native lands without being subjected to the military draft there. As civil war loomed, he ordered diplomats abroad to dissuade foreign governments from recognizing the Confederacy as an independent state.

Secretary of the Treasury. (1) Howell Cobb (1815–1868), of Georgia, served 1857–1860. A moderate southerner, he had supported compromise and preservation of the Union until the election of Abraham Lincoln. He then promptly resigned from the cabinet to return to Georgia and press for secession. In 1861 he was chairman of the convention at Montgomery, Alabama, that organized the Confederacy. During the Civil War, he served as a major general in the Confederate army. (2) Philip F. Thomas (1810–1890), of Maryland, served 1860–1861. Although a Confederate sympathizer, he took no active part in the Civil War. (3) John A. Dix (1798–1879), of New York, served January–March 1861. During his brief tenure he took the first steps in preparing the Treasury for the demands to be placed on it during the Civil War. With the accession of Abraham Lincoln, he was commissioned a major general of Union volunteers. He later served as minister to France under President Andrew Johnson. Fort Dix New Jersey is named after him.

Secretary of War. (1) John B. Floyd (1807–1863), of Virginia, served 1857–1860. A moderate southerner, he at first opposed secession. Floyd came into conflict with Buchanan when the president overruled his decision to recall Major Robert Anderson from Fort Sumter. Financial irregularities in War Department accounts further undermined Buchanan's confidence in him, and he was dismissed. Thereafter, he supported secession and served as a brigadier general in the Confederate army. (2) Joseph Holt (1807–1894), of Kentucky, served January–March 1861. He was transferred from postmaster general. He had supported southern principles, but as civil war approached he maintained a strong unionist position. With the accession of Abraham Lincoln, he was appointed judge advocate general of the U.S. Army, serving 1862–1875.

Attorney General. (1) Jeremiah S. Black served 1857–1860. He exposed land-title fraud in California. It was at his counsel that Buchanan decided that in the face of secession he was constitutionally authorized only to enforce laws and to protect federal property in the South, but was powerless to use force of arms to preserve the Union. He resigned to become secretary of state. (2) Edwin M. Stanton (1814–1869), of Ohio, served 1860–1861. During his brief tenure following Lincoln's election, he counseled President Buchanan to deal sternly with secessionists and privately criticized him for failing to do so. He later served as war secretary in the Lincoln and Johnson administrations.

Secretary of the Navy. Isaac Toucey (1792–1869), of Connecticut, served 1857–1861. He had served as attorney general in the Polk administration. He counseled conciliation in the face of secession.

Postmaster General. (1) Aaron V. Brown (1795–1859), of Tennessee, served 1857–1859. He improved overland mail service. He died in office. (2) Joseph Holt (1807–1894), of Kentucky, served 1859–1860. He inaugurated Pony Express service. He resigned to become war secretary. (3) Horatio King (1811–1897), of Maine, served February–March 1861.

Secretary of Interior. Jacob Thompson (1810–1885), of Mississippi, served 1857–1861. With Mississippi's secession, he resigned from the cabinet to serve the Confederacy, first as an inspector general of the army and later as a secret agent in Canada.

ADMINISTRATION: March 4, 1857–March 3, 1861.

The Kansas Question. Soon after Buchanan was sworn in as president, the Supreme Court handed down the *Dred Scott* decision (see "Andrew Jackson, 7th President," "Supreme Court Appointments," Roger B. Taney), which buttressed Buchanan's view that slavery was rooted in the Constitution and therefore could not be legislated out of existence, even in the newly emerging territories. Kansas Territory had become a bloody battleground over slavery, as abolitionists worked to bring the region into the Union as a free state, while southerners promoted admission as a slave state. Although personally opposed to slavery on moral grounds, Buchanan felt constitutionally bound to uphold it and favored the admission of Kansas as a slave state. He appointed a southerner, Robert J. Walker of Mississippi, territorial governor. Under Walker's leadership, a state constitutional convention held at Lecompton was boycotted by antislavery elements. With proslavery forces firmly in command, then, the resulting Lecompton constitution called for the admission of Kansas as a slave state. Although Buchanan urged its adoption by Congress, Democratic Senator Stephen A. Douglas of Illinois led opposition forces in rejecting it on the ground that the people of Kansas had been denied the chance to vote for it. In 1858 a referendum was held, and the Lecompton constitution was overwhelmingly rejected. Buchanan still persisted, and Congress ordered a second referendum, with the same results. Opponents of slavery thereafter gained the initiative; Kansas was admitted as a free state in 1861.

Panic of 1857. The proximate cause of the panic was the failure of the Ohio Life Insurance Company of Cincinnati in August 1857. The sudden demise of a once-solid institution touched off a wave of bank runs across the country and plunged the nation into an economic depression that lasted until the Civil War. The underlying causes of the decline were (1) overexpansion of the railroads; (2) rapid growth of state banks operating, for the most part, under flimsy state banking laws; (3) end of the Crimean War in Europe, prompting governments abroad to cut back imports of U.S. foodstuffs; (4) drop in the price of gold in the wake of the California Gold Rush. The North and West were hit hardest; the South managed well, as the European demand for cotton continued unabated. President Buchanan, following the conventional wisdom of the period, took no federal action to relieve the victims of the depression.

Secession. With the election of Abraham Lincoln as president in November 1860, the South, led by South Carolina, prepared to secede from the Union. Before Buchanan stepped down, seven states—Alabama, Florida, Georgia, Louisiana, Mississippi, South Carolina, and Texas—joined in forming the Confederate States of America under President Jefferson Davis (see also "Abraham Lincoln, 16th President," "Administration"). Buchanan took the position that although secession was illegal, the federal government lacked the constitutional authority to force any state to remain in the Union. He was prepared to stand by as the Union dissolved, taking only such action as was necessary to protect federal property. Moreover, he adopted a conciliatory attitude toward the secessionists, fearing that to confront them would inevitably lead to civil war. In January 1861 he dispatched the *Star of the West* to reinforce the isolated garrison of Major Robert Anderson at Fort Sumter in Charleston harbor. As the unarmed merchant ship approached the harbor, Confederate shore batteries opened fire, forcing it to abandon its mission. Buchanan overlooked this act of aggression and made no further attempt to save Fort Sumter, which subsequently fell to the South, marking the beginning of the Civil War. Buchanan denounced northern antislavery elements for needlessly pushing the nation toward fratricide. "All that is necessary to [settle the slavery question]," Buchanan asserted in his last annual message to Congress in December 1860, "and all for which the slave States have ever contended, is to be let alone and permitted to manage their domestic institutions in their own way. As sovereign States, they, and they alone, are responsible before God and the world for the slavery existing among them. For this the people of the North are not more responsible and have no more right to interfere than with similar institutions in Russia or in Brazil." In this same address, however, he also warned the South that secession was unconstitutional. "In order to justify secession as a constitutional remedy," he declared, "it must be on the principle that the Federal Government is a mere voluntary association of States, to be dissolved at pleasure by any one of the contracting parties. If this be so, the [Union] is a rope of sand, to be penetrated and dissolved by the first adverse wave of public opinion in any of the States." He conceded that the states had an inalienable, extralegal right to resist federal oppression by force of arms but chastised the South for hiding behind the Constitution. "Let us look the danger fairly in the face," he urged. "Secession is neither more nor less than revolution. It may or it may not be a justifiable revolution, but still it is revolution."[6]

Unable to resolve the sectional differences leading to the Civil War and bereft of support from northern Democrats, Buchanan declined to seek a second term.

States Admitted to the Union: Minnesota (1858), Oregon (1859), Kansas (1861).

SUPREME COURT APPOINTMENT: Nathan Clifford (1803–1881), of Maine, served as associate justice 1858–1881. He had served as attorney general in the Polk administration. His appointment was criticized as being a reward for faithful party service rather than one based on merit; Clifford was narrowly confirmed, 26–23. On the bench, he voted, ultimately in the minority, to strike down the Legal Tender Act and joined the majority in narrowly construing the Fourteenth Amendment in the Slaughterhouse Case (1873). He presided over the electoral commission that decided the disputed presidential election of 1876 in favor of Republican Rutherford B. Hayes over Democrat Samuel J. Tilden. He believed that the commission acted incorrectly in nullifying Tilden's apparent victory at the polls and never accepted Hayes as the lawful president.

RANKING IN 1962 HISTORIANS POLL: Buchanan ranked twenty-ninth of 31 presidents; last of 6 "below average" presidents. His was the worst full-term administration to be untouched by major scandal, according to the poll. He ranked above Grant, below Pierce.

RETIREMENT: March 4, 1861–June 1, 1868. After attending the inaugural of his successor, Abraham Lincoln, Buchanan returned to Lancaster, Pennsylvania, where citizens afforded him a grand reception. He led a very private retirement, rarely commenting publicly on current events. He was content to carry on a voluminous correspondence with former associates and to entertain friends at Wheatland, the 16-room brick mansion he had purchased while he was secretary of state. He loyally supported the Union and the Lincoln administration during the Civil War and approved of the Reconstruction policy of President Andrew Johnson. In his own defense, he wrote *Mr. Buchanan's Administration on the Eve of the Rebellion*, published in 1866. He also served on the Board of Trustees of Franklin and Marshall College in Lancaster.

DEATH: June 1, 1868, Wheatland estate, Lancaster, Pennsylvania. Buchanan suffered recurring attacks of rheumatic gout during his retirement. These attacks, in addition to bouts of dysentery, weakened his resistence to infection. He died of pneumonia and inflammation of the lining of the heart. Following a simple funeral conducted by the Reverend John W. Nevin on June 4, he was buried at Woodward Cemetery near Lancaster. In his last will and testament, executed in January 1866, with a codicil added in August 1867, Buchanan left an estate, valued at about $300,000 as follows: The Wheatland estate at Lancaster to niece Harriet Lane Johnson in exchange for $12,000; all books, plate, and furniture to be divided among Harriet Lane Johnson, his brother the Reverend Edward Y. Buchanan, nephew J. Buchanan Henry, and housekeeper Esther Parker; cash bequests to various relatives, employees, and charities, including $2,000 to the Lancaster City Council in trust for the city's poor; all his personal papers plus $1,000 to William B. Reed of Philadelphia for the purpose of writing his biography, as well as $5,000 to Reed's wife, Mary. (Reed was unable to complete the biography. The Buchanan papers then were turned over to Judge John Cadwallader of Philadelphia, who died before undertaking the project. Finally his papers were given to George Ticknor Curtis, who wrote a biography published in 1883.) The residue of his estate was divided, 25 percent to Harriet

Lane Johnson, 25 percent to the Reverend Edward Y. Buchanan, and 50 percent among numerous other relatives.

BUCHANAN PRAISED: "In the course of a long, useful and consistent life, filled with exercise of talents of a fine order and uniform ability, he had made the Constitution of his country the object of his deepest affection, the constant guide of all his public acts."[7]—George Ticknor Curtis, lawyer, historian, and Buchanan biographer, 1883

"Buchanan was not a magnetic man, not a popular man in the common acceptation of the term, but he was respected by all not only for his ability, but for his integrity and generally blameless reputation."[8]—A. K. McClure, journalist and Pennsylvania Republican leader, 1902

"In 1856 . . . I preferred the success of a candidate whose election would prevent or postpone secession, to seeing the country plunged into a war the end of which no man could foretell. With a Democrat elected by the unaminous vote of the Slave States, there could be no pretext for secession for four years. . . . I therefore voted for James Buchanan for President."[9]—Ulysses S. Grant, 1885

BUCHANAN CRITICIZED: "There is no such person running as James Buchanan. *He is dead of lockjaw.* Nothing remains but a platform and a bloated mass of political putridity."[10]—Thaddeus Stevens of Pennsylvania

"The present Democratic Administration has far exceeded our worst apprehensions, in its measureless subserviency to the exactions of a sectional interest, as especially evinced in its desperate exertions to force the infamous Lecompton Constitution upon the protesting people of Kansas; in construing the personal relations between master and servant to involve an unqualified property in persons."[11]—Republican party platform, 1860

"In 1860 the rebels were encouraged by the contempt they felt for the incumbent of the presidency. . . . Mr. Buchanan's policy had, I think, rendered collision inevitable, and a continuance of that policy will not only bring it about, but will go far to produce a permanent division of the Union."[12]—Postmaster General Montgomery Blair, 1861

BUCHANAN QUOTES: "I believe [slavery] to be a great political and a great moral evil. I thank God, my lot has been cast in a State where it does not exist. But, while I entertain these opinions, I know it is an evil at present without a remedy . . . one of those moral evils, from which it is impossible for us to escape, without the introduction of evils infinitely greater. There are portions of this Union, in which, if you emancipate your slaves, they will become masters. There can be no middle course."[13]—1826

To his successor, Abraham Lincoln: "My dear, sir, if you are as happy on entering the White House as I on leaving, you are a very happy man indeed."[14]—1861

BOOK BY BUCHANAN: *Mr. Buchanan's Administration on the Eve of the Rebellion* (1866).

BOOKS ABOUT BUCHANAN: Curtis, George Ticknor. *Life of James Buchanan: Fifteenth President of the United States.* New York: Harper & Bros., 1883. Klein, Philip S. *President James Buchanan.* University Park, Pa.: Pennsylvania State University Press, 1962.

NOTES

1 George Ticknor Curtis, *Life of James Buchanan: Fifteenth President of the United States,* New York: Harper & Bros., 1883, vol. II, p. 664ff.
2 Ibid., vol. I, p. 4.
3 Ibid., p. 159.
4 Ibid., p. 18.
5 Graham H. Stuart, *The Department of State,* New York: Macmillan, 1949, p. 127.
6 Henry Steele Commager, ed., *Documents of American History,* New York: Crofts, 1945, Doc. no. 195.
7 Curtis, vol. II, p. 502.
8 A.K. McClure, *Our Presidents and How We Make Them,* New York: Harper & Bros., 1902, p. 146.
9 *Personal Memoirs of U.S. Grant,* New York: Webster, 1885, vol. I, p. 215.
10 Richard Kenin and Justin Wintle, eds., *Dictionary of Biographical Quotation,* New York: Knopf, 1978, p. 111.
11 Kirk H. Porter and Donald Bruce Johnson, *National Party Platforms,* Urbana, Ill., University of Illinois Press, 1961, p. 32.
12 John G. Nicolay and John Hay, eds., *Complete Works of Abraham Lincoln,* New York: Century, 1894, vol. VI, pp. 215–216.
13 Curtis, vol. I, p. 68.
14 John G. Nicolay and John Hay, *Abraham Lincoln: A History,* New York: Century, 1890, vol. II, p. 394ff.

ABRAHAM LINCOLN

16TH PRESIDENT

NAME: Abraham Lincoln. He was named after his paternal grandfather.

PHYSICAL DESCRIPTION: Lincoln, the tallest president, stood 6 feet 4 inches tall, weighed about 180 pounds, and had long, gangling limbs and a rather sunken chest. His coarse black hair was gray at the temples while he was president. His eyes were gray, the left one being slightly higher than the right. He began wearing reading glasses at age 48. He had a wart on his right cheek above the corner of his mouth. He also had a white scar on his thumb from an accident with an ax and a scar over his right eye from a fight with a gang of thieves. Long hours swinging an ax had given him muscular arms and shoulders. By conventional standards, Lincoln was homely; to some, downright ugly. "His cheekbones were high, sharp and prominent," wrote his law partner William Herndon, "his eyebrows cropped out like a huge rock on the brow of a hill; his long sallow face was wrinkled."[1] But to his private secretary John G. Nicolay, Lincoln's features were too complex to be recorded accurately by photographers, painters, or sculptors. "Graphic art," he commented, "was powerless before a face that moved through a thousand delicate gradations of line and contour, light and shade, sparkle of the eye and curve of the lip, in the long gamut of expression from grave to gay, and back again from the rollicking jollity of laughter to that far-away look."[2] For his part, Lincoln was comfortable with his homely appearance and readily poked fun at himself. His careless dress habits further detracted from his appearance.

During his term as president, Lincoln complained of frequent fatigue, severe headaches, and cold hands and feet. This and other evidence gathered over the course of 20 years of research into Lincoln's medical history has led Dr. Harold Schwartz of the University of Southern California School of Medicine to conclude that at the time of his assassination Lincoln was dying of heart disease. Writing in the *Western Journal of Medicine* in 1978, Dr. Schwartz asserted that Lincoln suffered from Marfan's syndrome, a hereditary disease that affects bone growth and heart function. Dr. Schwartz noted that Lincoln had disproportionately long arms and legs, unusually long middle fingers, and a sunken chest—all typical of Marfan sufferers. Moreover, Dr. Schwartz observed, Lincoln once commented that his left foot vibrated involuntarily when he sat with his left leg crossed over his right. This, said Dr. Schwartz, undoubtedly was caused by aortic regurgitation, a Marfan-related disorder in which the valves of the great artery leading from the heart do not close properly, causing blood to flow in spurts with enough force to wiggle a dangling foot. Lincoln also struggled with chronic constipation through much of his life.

PERSONALITY: By all accounts, Lincoln was disarmingly unpretentious, a plain-spoken man genuinely interested in people and their problems. A good listener, he typically sat in silence rubbing his chin while a visitor explained his point of view. He was at his best in relaxed conversation with small groups. His ready wit, down-home logic, and seemingly endless store of anecdotes delighted those present. "His custom of interspersing conversation with incidents, anecdotes, and witticisms," commented on observer, "are well calculated to impress his hearers with the kindheartedness of the man. And they are so adroitly and delicately mingled in the thread of his discourse that one hardly notices the digression."[3] For all his good humor, however, Lincoln had a dark side; he wrestled with severe bouts of mental depression. Longtime friend Joshua Speed recalled that when he first met Lincoln, then a young lawyer, "I looked up at him, and I thought then, as I think now, that I never saw so gloomy and melancholy a face in my life." Lincoln himself once complained, "If what I feel were equally distributed to the whole human family, there would not be one cheerful face on the earth. Whether I shall ever be better I cannot tell; I awfully forebode I shall not. To remain as I am is impossible; I must die or be better, it appears to me."[4] Lincoln spoke in a high-pitched voice with a marked frontier accent, pronouncing such words as *get, there,* and *chair* as *git, thar,* and *cheer* and saying *haint* for *haven't.*

ANCESTORS: Lincoln was of English ancestry. His great[4]-grandfather Samuel Lincoln emigrated from Norfolk, England, arriving at Hingham, Massachusetts, about 1637. Subsequent generations migrated to New Jersey, Pennsylvania, and Virginia. His paternal grandfather and namesake, Abraham Lincoln, served as a captain in the Virginia militia during the American Revolution. Hearing his friend Daniel Boone talk of cheap land in Kentucky, he moved in 1782 to Jefferson County east of Louisville. Four years later, while working his fields, he was shot and killed by an Indian.

FATHER: Thomas Lincoln (1778–1851), farmer, carpenter. Born in Rockingham County, Virginia, he was raised there and in Kentucky. He served in the Kentucky militia. He settled first in Hardin (now Larue) County, Kentucky, and later in Spencer County, Indiana, and Coles County, Illinois. He could neither read nor write but was able to sign his name. A year after the death of his first wife (the president's mother), he married Sarah Bush Johnston, a widow with three children. He and son Abraham do not seem to have been very close. Thomas Lincoln died in Coles County when Abraham was a lawyer in Springfield. Abraham did not attend his funeral.

MOTHER: Nancy Hanks Lincoln (1784–1818). Apparently of illegitimate birth, she married Thomas Lincoln in 1806. She reportedly was bright, though illiterate, pious, and close with her children. "All I am or hope to be," her son once said, "I owe to my sainted mother."[5] She died at 34, of "milk sickness," in

Spencer County, Indiana, when Abe was nine years old. Her husband cut her coffin from spare logs left over from construction of their cabin; young Abe whittled wooden pegs with which to fasten the planks together. Her unmarked grave was neglected long after her son achieved fame. A stone was finally erected in 1879. No portrait of her survives.

SIBLING: Lincoln had one older sister to live to maturity—Mrs. Sarah Grigsby, who died in childbirth at 21.

CHILDREN: Lincoln had three sons to survive infancy.

Robert Todd Lincoln (1843–1926), lawyer, diplomat, businessman. Born in the Globe Tavern in Springfield, Illinois, Robert Lincoln was the president's only son to live to maturity. Having failed the Harvard entrance exam, he attended Phillips Academy at Exeter, New Hampshire, and won admission to Harvard on his second try in 1860. Following graduation in 1864, he entered Harvard Law School but dropped out to join the Union army during the latter weeks of the Civil War. Commissioned a captain, he was assistant adjutant general of volunteers on the staff of General Ulysses S. Grant. He was present at Appomattox. After his father's assassination, he resigned his commission, resumed his law studies in Chicago, and was admitted to the Illinois bar in 1867. The following year he married Mary Harlan, daughter of James Harlan, interior secretary in the Lincoln and Johnson administrations. He earned distinction as a corporation lawyer, most notably as counsel for railroad interests. He served as war secretary during 1881–1885 in the Garfield and Arthur administrations. He was appointed minister to Great Britain 1889–1893 by President Benjamin Harrison. He was president of the Pullman Company during 1897–1911. At his instruction his father's personal papers were not made public until 1947. In 1985 Robert's grandson, the last direct descendant of Abraham Lincoln, died.

William "Willie" Wallace Lincoln (1850–1862). Born in Springfield, Illinois, he was a bookish child and especially close to his father. He was the only child of a president to die in the White House.

Thomas "Tad" Lincoln (1853–1871). Born in Springfield, Illinois, he had a cleft palate and lisped. He was a great comfort to the president following Willie's death. After Lincoln's assassination, he accompanied his mother to Europe, where he attended schools in England and Germany. He died at 18.

BIRTH: Lincoln was born at dawn on February 12, 1809, in a dirt-floor, one-room log cabin three miles south of Hodgenville in Hardin (now Larue) County, Kentucky.

CHILDHOOD: Recalling his childhood, Lincoln once said, "It can all be condensed into a single sentence . . . in Gray's Elegy—'The short and simple annals of the poor.'"[6] When Abe was two, the Lincolns moved 10 miles northeast of his birthplace to a 230-acre farm on Knob Creek, the first home he remembered. There he helped with light chores, toting wood and water and hoeing vegetables. In 1816 the Lincolns moved to Spencer County, Indiana, where seven-year-old Abe helped his father erect the 360-square-foot log cabin that was to be his home for the rest of his childhood. Although the loss of his mother when Abe was nine came as a crushing blow, he instantly took a liking to his step-mother, Sarah Bush Johnston Lincoln. She was kind to him and encouraged him to read and learn. Lincoln apparently was closer to his stepmother than to his father. With the addition of her and her children from a previous marriage, the small Lincoln cabin was made to accommodate eight residents. As a frontier youth Lincoln did his share of clearing, plowing, and planting. His father at times hired him out to neighboring farms. He became adept with an ax and was a skilled, swift rail-splitter. At 17, he operated a ferryboat for James Taylor. Two years later he built his own flatboat and ran farm produce down the Mississippi to New Orleans for James Gentry for $24, which he dutifully turned over to his father on his return. In 1830, soon after Abe turned 21, the Lincolns moved west to Illinois, throwing up a cabin on the Sangamon River west of Decatur. After surviving a brutal winter, the Lincolns moved on to Coles County, but Abe stayed behind to prepare another haul down the Mississippi, this time to transport goods belonging to Denton Offut. Thereafter Lincoln was independent of his family.

EDUCATION: Lincoln estimated that altogether he had about one year of formal education. The crude frontier schoolhouses were open whenever a literate person happened to pass through and could be persuaded to stay long enough to give a few lessons. In Kentucky Lincoln learned to read and write from Zachariah Riney, a Catholic, and Cabel Hazel. In Indiana he was taught successively by Andrew Crawford, James Swaney, and Azel Dorsey. As a youth Lincoln read voraciously. He regularly dipped into the family Bible and borrowed books whenever he could. Among his favorites were Parson Weems's fanciful biography of George Washington, *Pilgrim's Progress*, and *Robinson Crusoe*.

RELIGION: Although his father and stepmother belonged to a Baptist church, Lincoln never formally joined. In Springfield and Washington he attended Presbyterian services. During his campaign for Congress in 1846, he was charged with being "an open scoffer at Christianity." Lincoln responded after the election in a statement published in the *Illinois Gazette*, acknowledging that he belonged to no church but adding: "I have never spoken with intentional disrespect of religion in general, or of any denomination of Christians in particular. It is true that in early life I was inclined to believe in what I understand is called the 'Doctrine of Necessity'—that is, that the human mind is impelled to action, or held in rest by some power, over which the mind itself has no control; and I have sometimes (with one, two or three, but never publicly) tried to maintain this opinion in argument. The habit of arguing thus however, I have entirely left off for more than five years. . . .

"I do not think I could myself, be brought to support a man for office, whom I knew to be an open enemy of, and scoffer at, religion. Leaving the higher matter of eternal consequences, between him and his Maker, I still do not think any man has the right thus to insult the feelings, and injure the morals, of the community in which he may live."[7]

RECREATION: As president, Lincoln found it difficult to escape the burdens of office. "Nothing touches the tired spot,"[8] he complained. Unlike most boys raised on the frontier, Lincoln detested hunting. He was throughout his life an avid reader, becoming at times so engrossed in a book that he was utterly oblivious to his surroundings. "My best friend," he once said, "is the man who'll git me a book I ain't read."[9] He liked Shakespeare, especially *Macbeth* and *Hamlet*, and surprised White House visitors by reciting whole passages from memory with such emotion that at least one observer remarked that perhaps the president had missed his calling. Among his favorite poems were Edgar Allan Poe's "The Raven" and Oliver Wendell Holmes's "The Last Leaf." He also valued the verse of Robert Burns and Lord Byron. Lincoln enjoyed the theater and whenever possible slipped into the audience unannounced. He also played chess. But perhaps his favorite pastime was swapping jokes with friends.

EARLY ROMANCE: According to his stepmother, Lincoln was not very fond of girls. As a youngster in Indiana, however, he was attracted to a little girl passing through with her family in a wagon that had broken down near the Lincoln homestead. After the vehicle was fixed and the family continued their journey, young Abe began to fantasize about riding after them and eloping with the little girl on horseback. "I think that was the beginning of love with me,"[10] Lincoln later recalled.

Ann Rutledge. It is not known for certain if Lincoln was romantically involved with Ann Rutledge, the petite, blue-eyed, auburn-haired daughter of a tavern keeper in New Salem, Illinois. It is known that he visited the family often and that he grieved at her death, probably from typhoid fever, in 1835. According to legend—fostered first by John Hill, son of a New Salem businessman, in the story "A Romance of Reality" published in 1862 and later supported by William H. Herndon, Lincoln's law partner—Ann was the only girl Lincoln ever loved, and he never completely got over her death. Some believe that he was nearly suicidal in the days following her funeral.

Mary Owens. In 1833 Lincoln met Mary Owens, the blue-eyed, brunette daughter of a prosperous farmer in Green County, Kentucky, while she was visiting her sister Mrs. Bennett Abel in New Salem, Illinois. They courted for a time and corresponded when she returned to Kentucky. In 1836 she again visited New Salem, but by this time she had gained weight and lost some teeth. A refined young lady, Miss Owens frequently criticized Lincoln for his coarse backwoods manner. When they again parted in 1837 without becoming engaged, Lincoln wrote her a letter offering her the opportunity to break off the relationship. Miss Owens did not respond; they never saw each other again. Lincoln later referred to her in disparaging terms and professed to be much relieved to be done with her. In a satirical account of the affair, he depicted her as an ugly, toothless hulk. "Nothing," he wrote of her, "could have commenced at the size of infancy, and reached her present bulk in less than 35 or 40 years."[11]

MARRIAGE: Abraham Lincoln, 33, married Mary Todd, 23, on November 4, 1842, at the home of the bride's sister Mrs. Ninian Edwards in Springfield, Illinois. Born in Lexington, Kentucky, December 13, 1818, the daughter of Robert Smith Todd, a banker, and Elizabeth Parker Todd, Mary was raised in comfort and refinement. She attended fine schools, spoke French fluently, and studied dance, drama, and music. Although a bit too portly to be very attractive, she had a ready wit and sparkling personality that made her quite popular. She had an explosive temper and a quarrelsome nature, however, and was mentally unstable. She suffered from agonizing migraine headaches. After visiting her sister in Springfield in 1837, she returned to Lexington but apparently found it impossible to get along with her stepmother (her mother had died when she was seven). In 1839 she took up permanent residence with Mrs. Edwards in Springfield, where she met Lincoln at a dance. In 1840 they became engaged and, two years later, following a rather hesitant courtship, they wed. The Lincolns apparently had a comfortable marriage before the pressures of public life began to threaten her fragile mind. She became paranoid, irrationally jealous of those around the president. As First Lady she went on spending sprees that by 1864 totaled $27,000. In one four-month period alone she purchased 300 pairs of gloves. She yelled at her husband at the least provocation. Rather than argue back, Lincoln invariably walked away. The Civil War worked a crushing emotional burden on this former southern belle. While her husband was placing armies in the field to smash the Confederacy, her brother and three half brothers were fighting for the South. Congressional charges, never proved and vehemently denied by the Lincolns, that she was a Confederate sympathizer or, worse, a spy further drove Mrs. Lincoln to the emotional brink. The death of her son Willie in the White House in 1862 seems to have been the breaking point. She was thereafter noticeably disturbed. Lincoln's assassination only unhinged her further. In 1871 she experienced still more tragedy with the death of son Tad. She began hallucinating and spoke of plots to have her murdered. She became so uncontrollable that in 1875 son Robert had her committed to a mental institution at Batavia, Illinois. After three months she was released into the custody of her sister Mrs. Edwards in Springfield and in 1876 was once again declared competent to manage her own affairs. After a tour of Europe she returned to Springfield, where she died on July 16, 1882. An autopsy revealed evidence of "cerebral disease." She was buried next to the president at Oak Ridge Cemetery in Springfield.

MILITARY SERVICE: Black Hawk War, 1832. Responding to the governor's call for volunteers in this conflict (see "Andrew Jackson, 7th President," "Administration: Black Hawk War"), Lincoln enlisted in April 1832 and was promptly elected captain of a company of volunteers, an honor he was to cherish more than being nominated for president. Captain Lincoln marched his company to the mouth of the Rock River and joined a force of regulars under Colonel Zachary Taylor. Lincoln was reprimanded twice during his service, once for failing to restrain his men from stealing army liquor and getting drunk and a second time for discharging a weapon in camp. At the end of his 30-day hitch, Lincoln reenlisted for 20 days as a private in a company of the mounted Independent Rangers under Captain Elijah Iles. When this duty ran out, he re-uped again, this time for 30 days as a private in the Independent Spy Corps under Captain Jacob M. Early. During this service he attempted without success to track down Chief Black Hawk in the wilderness of what is now southern Wisconsin. Lincoln was mustered out in July, having seen no action. He later joked that the only blood he lost in defense of his country was to mosquitoes. He was paid $125 for his wartime service.

CAREER BEFORE THE PRESIDENCY: In 1831 Lincoln settled in New Salem, Illinois, where he worked as a clerk at the general store of Denton Offut for $15 a month plus sleeping quarters in the back. When Offut decided to close down the store, Lincoln volunteered to serve in the Black Hawk War (see "Military Service"). In 1832 he ran for the state legislature on a platform advocating internal improvements, improved education, and a legal limit on interest rates. Although he carried his hometown with more than 92 percent of the vote, he placed eighth of 13 candidates in district-wide voting. He supported Henry Clay for president in 1832. He was briefly a partner in a general store that failed.

Postmaster of New Salem, Illinois 1833–1836. Appointed by President Andrew Jackson, Lincoln earned about $55 per month plus personal franking privileges and free delivery of one daily newspaper. During this time he supplemented his income with such odd jobs as rail-splitting and surveying.

Member of Illinois Legislature, 1834–1842. Elected with bipartisan support and reelected as a Whig to three successive terms, Lincoln supported a system of improved transportation for the state and creation of a state bank. He served as Whig floor leader from 1836 and was chairman of the Finance Committee. Meanwhile he continued his law studies and was admitted to the bar in 1836. The next year he moved to Springfield. In 1840 he campaigned for William Henry Harrison for president and stood as a Whig presidential elector.

Lincoln practiced law in Springfield in partnership with Stephen T. Logan and, from 1844, with William H. Herndon. A candidate for the Whig nomination for Congress in 1843, Lincoln lost to John J. Hardin. In 1844 he campaigned in Illinois and Indiana for Henry Clay for president.

U.S. Representative, 1847–1849. Whig Congressman Lincoln served on the Post Office and Post Roads Committee and the War Department Expenditures Committee. He opposed U.S. involvement in the Mexican War (see "James K. Polk, 11th President," "Administration") and supported Whig measures blaming President Polk for starting the conflict. However, Lincoln supported appropriations to continue to supply the army in the field. He promoted federally sponsored internal improvements and worked unsuccessfully to abolish the slave trade in the District of Columbia. As a delegate to the 1848 Whig national convention in Philadelphia, he supported the candidacy of Zachary Taylor and later campaigned for him in Illinois, Maryland, and Massachusetts. Lincoln did not seek reelection to Congress. He resumed his law practice in Springfield, having declined appointments as secretary and governor of the Oregon Territory in 1849. He emerged one of the best-known lawyers in the state. In 1854 he was again elected to the state legislature but promptly resigned in order to run for the U.S. Senate. He led on the first six ballots for senator but ultimately lost to Lyman Trumbull. Lincoln's intense opposition to the extension of slavery into the territories prompted him to abandon the Whig party, which was fatally divided over the issue, and join the new Republican party in 1856. That year Lincoln was a favorite-son candidate for the Republican vice presidential nomination; he campaigned in Illinois for John C. Frémont for president.

"House Divided" Speech and the Lincoln-Douglas Debates, 1858. Nominated to run for the U.S. Senate at the Illinois Republican convention, Lincoln delivered his acceptance speech on June 17, 1858, in an address that popularized the Biblical phrase "A house divided against itself cannot stand" in reference to the growing sectional conflict. The speech read, in part: "We are now far into the fifth year since a policy was initiated with the avowed object and confident promise of putting an end to slavery agitation. Under the operation of that policy, that agitation has not only not ceased, but has constantly augmented. In my opinion, it will not cease until a crisis shall have been reached and passed. 'A house divided against itself cannot stand.' I believe this government cannot endure permanently half slave and half free. I do not expect the Union to be dissolved; I do not expect the house to fall; but I do expect it will cease to be divided. It will become all one thing, or all the other. Either the opponents of slavery will arrest the further spread of it, and place it where the public mind shall rest in the belief that it is in the course of ultimate extinction, or its advocates will push it forward till it shall become alike lawful in all the States, old as well as new, North as well as South."[12]

Lincoln and his opponent, incumbent senator Stephen A. Douglas, joined in a series of seven debates in towns across Illinois—Ottawa and Freeport in August, Jonesboro and Charleston in September, Galesburg, Quincy, and Alton in October. Lincoln and Douglas agreed on several issues: continued white supremacy, the right to hold slaves in the South, the right to retrieve runaway slaves, the paramount importance of preserving the Union. The main issue dividing them was the morality of slavery and whether it should be permitted to spread into the territories. Douglas advocated squatter, or popular, sovereignty, leaving the decision to permit or ban slavery to the residents themselves. Lincoln opposed the extension of slavery under any circumstances, although he had no objection to its continuance in those southern states where it already existed. At the second debate Lincoln focused on Douglas's inconsistency in supporting both squatter sovereignty and the *Dred Scott* decision (see "Andrew Jackson, 7th President," "Supreme Court Appointments," Roger B. Taney), which struck down as unconstitutional laws banning slavery from the territories. Pressed to reconcile his position, Douglas enunciated what came to be called the Freeport Doctrine, asserting that if territorial residents opposed slavery, they simply could decline to enforce it, a view that would cost Douglas crucial southern support in the presidential campaign of 1860. Douglas pointed to Lincoln's "house divided" speech as evidence that he was at heart an abolitionist, a dangerous radical who would promote racial equality. Lincoln responded by asserting his commitment to white supremacy. "I have no purpose to introduce political and social equality between the white and the black races," he declared at the opening debate. "There is a physical difference between the two, which, in my judgment, will probably forever forbid their living together upon the footing of perfect equality; and inasmuch as it becomes a necessity that there must be a difference, I, as well as Judge Douglas, am in favor of the race to which I belong having the superior position." But, Lincoln continued, "there is no reason in the world why the Negro is not entitled to all the natural rights enumerated in the Declaration of Independence—the right to life, liberty, and the pursuit of happiness."[13] Lincoln returned to the same theme in the fourth debate, declaring his opposition to granting blacks the right to vote, sit on juries, hold office, or intermarry with whites. In the final debate Lincoln scored Douglas for failing to concede that slavery was morally wrong. "That is the real issue," Lincoln concluded. "That is the issue that will continue in this country when these poor tongues of Judge Douglas and myself shall be silent. It is the eternal struggle between these two principles—right and wrong—throughout the world. They are the two principles that have stood face to face from the beginning of time; and will ever continue to struggle. The one is the common right of humanity, and the other the divine right of kings. It is the same principle in whatever shape it develops itself. It is the same spirit that says, 'You toil and work and earn bread, and I'll eat it.' No matter in what shape it comes, whether from the mouth of a king who seeks to bestride the people of his own nation and live by the fruit of their labor, or from one race of men as an apology for enslaving another race, it is the same tyrannical principle."[14]

Although Republicans edged Democrats in statewide voting for the legislature that would choose the next senator, districts had been drawn in the Democrats' favor, and that party retained its majority. Douglas thus defeated Lincoln, 54–46.

REPUBLICAN PRESIDENTIAL NOMINATION, 1860: As Republicans convened in Chicago in May 1860, William H. Seward of New York was the front-runner for the nomination. Delegates were looking for a candidate, however, who would run well in the crucial states of Indiana and Pennsylvania, a circumstance that favored Lincoln. On the first ballot Lincoln trailed Seward, 173½–102. He narrowed the gap to 184–181½ on the next tally and won the nomination on the third ballot. Hannibal Hamlin of Maine was nominated for vice president. The Republican platform denounced as treason all schemes for disunion, called for an end to slavery in the territories but upheld slavery in the South, condemned the Buchanan administration for its "measureless subservience to the exactions" of southern interests, denounced the *Dred Scott* decision, supported statehood for Kansas and a federal homestead law, opposed stricter naturalization laws and the abridgement of the rights of naturalized citizens, and endorsed federally sponsored river and harbor improvements and construction of a railroad to the West Coast.

OPPONENTS:

Stephen A. Douglas (1813–1861) of Illinois; Democrat. Born in Brandon, Vermont, Douglas settled in Illinois, where he was admitted to the bar in 1834. He entered politics as a Jacksonian Democrat. He held various local offices and in 1841 was appointed judge of the state supreme court. As a member of the U.S. House 1843–1847, he supported the Mexican War and westward expansion. In the U.S. Senate 1847–1861, he authored the Kansas-Nebraska Act (see "Franklin Pierce, 14th President," "Administration") and was a leading proponent of squatter, or popular, sovereignty, leaving the matter of slavery to local choice. He joined Henry Clay in promoting the Compromise of 1850. He was a leading candidate for the Democratic presidential nominations in 1852 and 1856 but lost to Franklin Pierce and James Buchanan, respectively. He was by this time nicknamed the Little Giant, for his diminutive stature and superior oratorical skills. During his successful campaign for reelection to the Senate in 1858, he engaged in a series of historic debates with his Republican opponent, Abraham Lincoln (see "Career before the Presidency"). Douglas hoped that his opposition to the proslavery Lecompton constitution in Kansas (see "James Buchanan, 15th President," "Administration"), balanced against his long-standing support of popular sovereignty, would broaden his appeal across sectional lines. Instead, he lost support in both the North and the South. At the Democratic national convention in Charleston, South Carolina, in April 1860, Douglas led on each of 57 ballots, with R.M.T. Hunter of Virginia and James Guthrie of Kentucky far behind exchanging second and third places. Southern extremists, angered over the convention's refusal to include in the platform a plank calling for federal protection of slavery in the territories, walked out in protest. With the convention deadlocked, Democrats adjourned to meet again in Baltimore in June. There Douglas was nominated on the second ballot. Senator Benjamin Fitzpatrick of Alabama was nominated for vice president, but he declined. Herschel V. Johnson of Georgia then was nominated in his place. After his defeat by Lincoln, Douglas vigorously supported the president and the Union. After a grueling speaking tour on behalf of the Union, he died from typhoid fever in 1861.

John C. Breckinridge (1821–1875) of Kentucky; National Democrat. Breckinridge was vice president under James Buchanan during 1857–1861. Southern Democrats who had bolted the convention that ultimately nominated Stephen Douglas convened as National Democrats in Baltimore in June to adopt the platform rejected by regular Democrats calling for federal protection of slavery in the territories. Breckinridge was nominated for president unanimously. Senator Joseph Lane of Oregon was nominated for vice president. After his defeat by Lincoln, Breckinridge returned to the Senate and worked to avert civil war through compromise. After Kentucky opted to remain in the Union, however, he fled south to join the Confederacy, first as a general in the army and, in the last weeks of the conflict, as secretary of war. With the South's surrender, he took refuge abroad; he returned to the United States under the general amnesty of 1868.

John Bell (1797–1869) of Tennessee; Constitutional Union party. Born near Nashville, Bell, a lawyer, entered politics as a Jacksonian Democrat but because of his support for the national bank joined the Whigs. He served in the U.S. House 1827–1841 and as Speaker in 1836, as war secretary in 1841 in the Harrison and Tyler administrations, and in the Senate 1847–1859. Although a southerner who supported slavery, he opposed its extension into the territories and supported the Union. The Constitutional Union party, consisting of old-line Whigs unwilling to join the new Republican party and remnants of the defunct American, or Know-Nothing, party, held its convention in Baltimore in May. Bell was nominated on the second ballot over Governor Sam Houston of Texas. Edward Everett of Massachusetts was nominated for vice president. After his defeat by Lincoln, Bell tried to keep Tennessee in the Union. Following its secession, he took no part in the Civil War.

CAMPAIGN AND THE ISSUES, 1860: The Republicans were united behind Lincoln. His chief opponent at the convention, William H. Seward, campaigned actively for him, and journalist and reformer Carl Schurz stumped the German community on Lincoln's behalf. Democrats, on the other hand, were regionally divided, with southerners for Breckinridge and northerners for Douglas. Douglas's campaign was further jeopardized by the presence of Bell and the short-lived Constitutional Union party, which drained from the Democratic nominee the votes of border-state Whigs and Know-Nothings unwilling to support Lincoln or Breckinridge. Neither Lincoln, nor Breckinridge, nor Bell campaigned actively. Standing by his previous statements on slavery, Lincoln refused to comment further on the issue. Only Douglas took to the stump. Campaigning across the country, even in the South where his chances were remote, the Little Giant denounced threats of secession but warned that Lincoln's election would inevitably lead to that tragic end.

ELECTION AS PRESIDENT, FIRST TERM, 1860:

Popular Vote: Lincoln (Republican), 1,866,352 (40%); Douglas (Democrat), 1,375,157 (29%); Breckinridge (National Democrat), 845,763 (18%); Bell (Constitutional Union), 589,581 (13%).

Electoral Vote: Lincoln, 180; Breckinridge, 72; Bell, 39; Douglas, 12.

States Carried: Lincoln won the majority of electoral votes in 18 states— California, Connecticut, Illinois, Indiana, Iowa, Maine, Massachusetts, Michigan, Minnesota, New Hampshire, New Jersey, New York, Ohio, Oregon, Pennsylvania, Rhode Island, Vermont, and Wisconsin. Breckinridge won the electoral votes of 11 states—Alabama, Arkansas, Delaware, Florida, Georgia, Louisiana, Maryland, Mississippi, North Carolina, South Carolina, and Texas. Bell won the electoral votes of 3 states—Kentucky, Tennessee, and Virginia. Douglas won the majority of electoral votes in 1 state—Missouri.

REPUBLICAN NOMINATION FOR REELECTION AS PRESIDENT, 1864: Republicans adopted the National Union party label to accommodate Democrats who had supported the Union war effort. With the outcome of the Civil War still in doubt, some party leaders, including Salmon Chase, Benjamin Wade, and Horace Greeley, opposed Lincoln's renomination on the ground that he could not win. Lincoln himself conceded as much in a private memorandum written in August 1864: "it seems exceedingly probable that this administration will not be reelected. Then it will be my duty to so cooperate with the President-elect as to save the Union between the election and the inauguration."[15] But Lincoln was still popular with rank-and-file Republicans, and he was renominated without opposition at the convention in Baltimore in June. Although Hamlin desired renomination as vice president, Lincoln prevailed on the convention to replace him with Andrew Johnson of Tennessee, a southern Democrat who had remained loyal to the Union. The Republican platform vowed to crush the Confederacy and punish rebel leaders, demanded an unconditional surrender, proposed a constitutional amendment banning slavery to buttress the Emancipation Proclamation, promised aid to disabled Union veterans, encouraged further immigration, and warned European governments to remain neutral in the Civil War.

OPPONENT: George B. McClellan (1826–1885) of New Jersey; Democrat. Born in Philadelphia, McClellan graduated valedictorian from West Point in 1846 and served in the Mexican War. He resigned his commission in 1857 to become a railroad executive. With the outbreak of the Civil War he was commissioned a major general and in July 1861 took command of the Department of the Potomac following the Union debacle at the first Battle of Bull Run. He demonstrated outstanding organizational talent and won genuine respect from his men. In November 1861 he was appointed general in chief of the Union armies. However, McClellan was a cautious commander, wary of the South's presumed strength and reluctant to take the war to the enemy. At Antietam in 1862 he ignored an opportunity to pursue the retreating forces of General Robert E. Lee. For such timidity President Lincoln relieved him of command. At the Democratic national convention in Chicago in August 1864, McClellan overwhelmed by a vote of 174–38 his nearest challenger, Thomas H. Seymour of Connecticut. Representative George H. Pendleton of Ohio was nominated for vice president. The Democratic platform condemned the Union war effort as a failure, blasted Lincoln for extraordinary wartime measures curbing civil liberties, and called for immediate cessation of hostilities and a negotiated settlement. After his defeat by Lincoln, McClellan served as chief engineer for the New York City Department of Docks 1870–1872 and governor of New Jersey 1878–1881. His autobiography, *McClellan's Own Story*, appeared posthumously in 1887.

CAMPAIGN AND THE ISSUES, 1864: As the campaign got underway, General McClellan was widely regarded as the favorite. But with General William T. Sherman's capture of Atlanta in September and other Union successes, the tide of the war decidedly turned in the North's favor. With victory now in sight, Democrats found themselves shackled by a platform calling for an immediate armistice. In a futile attempt to salvage his campaign, McClellan repudiated the platform, saying, "The Union must be preserved at all hazards. I could not look into the face of my gallant comrades and tell them that we had abandoned that Union for which we have so often periled our lives."[16] A Democratic slogan promised, "Mac Will Win the Union Back." Republicans warned, "Don't swap horses in the middle of the stream."

REELECTION AS PRESIDENT, 1864:

    Popular Vote: Lincoln (Republican), 2,216,067 (55%); McClellan (Democrat), 1,808,725 (45%).

Electoral Vote: Lincoln, 212; McClellan, 21.

States Carried: Lincoln won the electoral votes of 22 states—California, Connecticut, Illinois, Indiana, Iowa, Kansas, Maine, Maryland, Massachusetts, Michigan, Minnesota, Missouri, Nevada, New Hampshire, New York, Ohio, Oregon, Pennsylvania, Rhode Island, Vermont, West Virginia, and Wisconsin. McClellan won the electoral votes of 3 states—Delaware, Kentucky, and New Jersey. The 11 states of the Confederacy did not take part in the election.

INAUGURAL ADDRESS (FIRST): March 4, 1861. ". . . Apprehension seems to exist among the people of the Southern States that by the accession of a Republican Administration their property and their peace and personal security are to be endangered. There has never been any reasonable cause for such apprehension. . . .

"I have no purpose, directly or indirectly, to interfere with the institution of slavery in the States where it exists. I believe I have no lawful right to do so, and I have no inclination to do so. . . .

"I hold that in contemplation of universal law and of the Constitution the Union of these States is perpetual. Perpetuity is implied, if not expressed, in the fundamental law of all national governments. It is safe to assert that no government proper ever had a provision in its organic law for its own termination. . . .

"Physically speaking, we can not separate. We can not remove our respective sections from each other nor build an impassable wall between them. A husband and wife may be divorced and go out of the presence and beyond the reach of each other, but the different parts of our country can not do this. They can not but remain face to face, and intercourse, either amicable or hostile, must continue between them. . . .

"In *your* hands, my dissatisfied fellow-countrymen, and not in *mine*, is the momentous issue of civil war. The Government will not assail *you*. You can have no conflict without being yourselves the aggressors. *You* have no oath registered in heaven to destroy the Government, while *I* shall have the most solemn one to 'preserve, protect, and defend it.' . . ."

INAUGURAL ADDRESS (SECOND): March 4, 1865. ". . . Fondly do we hope, fervently do we pray, that this mighty scourge of war may speedily pass away. Yet, if God wills that it continue until all the wealth piled by the bondsman's two hundred and fifty years of unrequited toil shall be sunk, and until every drop of blood drawn with the lash shall be paid by another drawn with the sword, as was said three thousand years ago, so still it must be said 'the judgments of the Lord are true and righteous altogether.'

"With malice toward none, with charity for all, with firmness in the right as God gives us to see the right, let us strive on to finish the work we are in, to bind up the nation's wounds, to care for him who shall have borne the battle and for his widow and his orphan, to do all which may achieve and cherish a just and lasting peace among ourselves and with all nations."

VICE PRESIDENTS: Hannibal Hamlin (1809–1891), of Maine, served 1861–1865. Born in Paris Hill, Maine, Hamlin, a laywer, entered politics as a Democrat but broke ranks over the slavery issue and in 1856 joined the fledging Republican party. He served in the Maine legislature 1836–1841 and in the U.S. House 1843–1847. In between terms in the U.S. Senate 1848–1857 and 1857–1861 he was briefly the first Republican governor of Maine. Because of his swarthy complexion, false rumors spread during the 1860 presidential campaign that he was part black. As vice president he spent little time presiding over the Senate. A staunch abolitionist, he supported vigorous prosecution of the war. In 1864 Vice President Hamlin, then 55, enlisted as a private in the Maine Coast Guard and served two months as a cook. Much to Hamlin's chagrin, Lincoln dumped him from the ticket in 1864 to make room for the War Democrat Andrew Johnson. Hamlin returned to the Senate 1869–1881, supporting radical Reconstruction, and was appointed minister to Spain 1881–1882 by President Chester A. Arthur.

Andrew Johnson (1808–1875), of Tennessee, served March–April 1865. He succeeded to the presidency on the assassination of President Lincoln.

CABINET:

Secretary of State. William H. Seward (1801–1872), of New York, served 1861–1869. Seward saw his role as crucial to the survival of the Union. "It seems to me," he wrote, "that if I am absent only three days, this Administration, the Congress, and the District would fall into consternation and despair. I am the only *hopeful, calm,* and *conciliatory* person here."[17] Through his minister in London, Charles Francis Adams, Seward was able to dissuade Britain from recognizing or otherwise overtly aiding the Confederacy. He also skillfully defused the threat to British-American relations in the wake of the Trent Affair, in which a U.S. warship illegally seized a British steamer bearing two Confederate emissaries. He pressed for French withdrawal from Mexico. Within the department Seward demanded a loyalty oath of all employees and dismissed those with Confederate sympathies. Those professing loyalty to the Union were retained without regard to political affiliation. On the evening of Lincoln's assassination Seward suffered knife wounds about the face and neck from a co-conspirator. He recovered and stayed on in the Johnson administration.

Secretary of the Treasury. (1) Salmon P. Chase (1808–1873), of Ohio, served 1861–1864. He performed well the formidable task of directing the nation's finances during the Civil War. Under the Legal Tender Act of 1862, he issued fiat currency, or greenbacks, to help finance the war. He established the national banking system in 1863. A frequent critic of Lincoln within the administration, he submitted his resignation several times before the president finally accepted it in 1864. Lincoln later appointed him to the U.S. Supreme Court. His portrait appears on the $10,000 bill. (2) William P. Fessenden (1806–1869), of Maine, served 1864–1865. Fessenden generally continued Chase's monetary policy. He resigned to resume his seat in the Senate. (3) Hugh McCulloch (1808–1895), of Indiana, served 1865–1869. He had been serving as the first U.S. comptroller of the currency 1863–1865; he stayed on in the Johnson administration.

Secretary of War. (1) Simon Cameron (1799–1889), of Pennsylvania, served 1861–1862. At the Republican national convention, Cameron, as party boss of Pennsylvania, had thrown his support to Lincoln in exchange for a promise of a cabinet post. Unaware of the quid pro quo at the time, Lincoln reluctantly made good the pledge his lieutenants had made in his name. As secretary, Cameron tolerated widespread corruption in the awarding of army contracts. To rid him from the cabinet, Lincoln appointed him minister to Russia. Cameron defined an honest politician as "a man who, when he's bought, stays bought." (2) Edwin M. Stanton (1814–1869), of Ohio, served 1862–1868. He had served as attorney general in the Buchanan administration. He restored honesty and efficiency to the department. Stanton said at Lincoln's passing, "Now he belongs to the ages." He stayed on in the Johnson administration.

Attorney General. (1) Edward Bates (1793–1869), of Missouri, served 1861–1864. He was the first cabinet member from west of the Mississippi. As attorney general, Bates upheld Lincoln's authority to suspend habeas corpus during the Civil War. (2) James Speed (1812–1887), of Kentucky, served 1864–1866. The brother of Lincoln's longtime friend Joshua Speed, he stayed on in the Johnson administration.

Secretary of the Navy. Gideon Welles (1802–1878), of Connecticut, served 1861–1869. He undertook a major shipbuilding program that increased the Union fleet seven-fold and introduced iron-clad vessels, including the famous *Monitor*. He directed the effective blockade of southern ports. He stayed on in the Johnson administration.

Postmaster General. (1) Montgomery Blair (1813–1883), of Maryland, served 1861–1864. He introduced free city mail delivery. A moderate, he was forced from the cabinet by Radical Republicans. (2) William Dennison (1815–1882), of Ohio, served 1864–1866. He stayed on in the Johnson administration.

Secretary of the Interior. (1) Caleb B. Smith (1808–1864), of Indiana, served 1861–1862. Smith had been promised the post by Lincoln lieutenants at the 1860 Republican national convention in exchange for delivering the Indiana delegation. Smith resigned to accept a judgeship in his home state. (2) John P. Usher (1816–1889), of Indiana, served 1863–1865. He was promoted from assistant secretary of interior. He stayed on in the Johnson administration.

ADMINISTRATION: March 4, 1861–April 15, 1865.

Civil War, 1861–1865. Causes: The slavery question, long a source of sectional conflict, was the overriding cause of the war. The issue pitted abolitionists in the North who viewed it as a moral evil to be eradicated everywhere as soon as practicable against southern extremists who fostered the spread of slavery into the territories and new states carved therefrom. In the middle were moderates, like Lincoln, who believed slavery to be wrong but nevertheless protected by the Constitution and who were content to contain it in the South, where changing economic conditions would eventually destroy it. Publication of Harriet Beecher Stowe's *Uncle Tom's Cabin* (1852) had excited antislavery sentiment. The tariff question and the doctrines of nullification and secession, issues that had divided North and South for decades, also were contributing factors.

The War: Eleven states seceded from the Union in 1861—Alabama, Arkansas, Florida, Georgia, Louisiana, Mississippi, North Carolina, South Carolina, Tennessee, Texas, and Virginia—to form the Confederate States of America. Jefferson Davis became its president in February 1861. The Confederate capital was located at Montgomery, Alabama, and, from June 1861, at Richmond, Virginia. The North enjoyed a great advantage over the South in having twice as many people and the bulk of the nation's industry. It was able to undertake an effective naval blockade of southern ports, preventing the Confederacy from obtaining much-needed supplies from abroad. The South, on the other hand, had many of the nation's finest military leaders and the advantage of fighting for the most part on familiar terrain and the tenacity of resistance commonly found in troops defending their homeland. Moreover, the South won sympathy abroad, for its cotton was vital to European mills.

On April 12, 1861, Confederate forces under General Pierre G. T. Beauregard fired on Fort Sumter at Charleston harbor, forcing its commander, Major Robert Anderson, to surrender. The incident signaled the beginning of the Civil War. The first open engagement at Bull Run in July drew an audience of northern civilians who observed the scene from high ground amid great merriment, for it was widely believed that the Union army would make short work of the Confederate rabble. Instead, the rebels under Generals Beauregard, Joseph E. Johnston, and Stonewall Jackson routed the Yankee troops of General Irvin McDowell. Stunned by the setback, the North dug in for a long war. For the first time the United States found it necessary to turn to a military draft to fill the ranks. Lincoln replaced McDowell with Major General George B. McClellan as commander of the Army of the Potomac. McClellan was a brilliant military organizer but an overly cautious commander in the field. Ordered by Lincoln to move south on Richmond, he took 100,000 men by sea to the Virginia shore in 1862 and proceeded so deliberately up the peninsula toward Richmond that Confederate General Johnston was able to amass his forces in time to turn McClellan back, saving the capital. Confederate General Robert E. Lee sought to follow up this defensive victory with a bold offensive thrust north through Maryland to Harrisburg, Pennsylvania. Enroute he defeated superior Union forces under General John Pope at the Second Battle of Bull Run in August 1862 and proceeded across the Potomac River to Maryland, where he engaged General McClellan at Antietam Creek in September, a bloody encounter that checked Lee's advance and sent him southward in retreat. It is widely believed that Antietam would have signaled the end of the war if McClellan had pursued Lee. President Lincoln replaced McClellan with General Ambrose E. Burnside, who tried repeatedly without success to reach Richmond. Meanwhile, in the West, Union forces under General Ulysses S. Grant scored victories in Tennessee and the Mississippi Valley and Admiral David G. Farragut secured New Orleans in April 1862.

In September 1862 President Lincoln issued the Emancipation Proclamation with effect from January 1, 1863. Lincoln had postponed issuing the document until the Union had scored a significant victory, such as that at Antietam, because he feared that premature release would be misinterpreted as an act of desperation. The historic proclamation freed slaves only in those Confederate states still at war on its effective date. Exempted from its provisions were Delaware, Kentucky, Maryland, Missouri, and Tennessee, as well as portions of Louisiana and Virginia under Union occupation.

In May 1863 Confederates under Lee dispersed superior numbers of Union forces under General Joseph Hooker at Chancellorsville, Virginia, but lost one of their best commanders, Stonewall Jackson, there. Lee again turned north, making it as far as Gettysburg, Pennsylvania, where during July 1–3, 1863, he locked in historic combat with General George G. Meade. By the time the smoke cleared, one-fourth of the 75,000 Confederates and one-fifth of the 90,000 Union men at Gettysburg had fallen in action. Failing to penetrate Union defenses, Lee again was forced to retreat south. Meanwhile in the West, Grant took Vicksburg and secured the entire lower Mississippi Valley in July 1863.

In 1864 President Lincoln promoted Grant to commander of all Union armies. While Grant pursued the elusive Lee in the Wilderness campaign, General William T. Sherman marched on Atlanta, sacking that city in September, and undertook his famous "march to the sea," a scorched-earth trek southeast to Savannah. Sherman then wheeled north to join Grant in closing in on Lee. In early April 1865 Richmond fell, and on April 9 Lee surrendered at Appomattox. Grant allowed lenient terms—Confederate officers were allowed to return home with their sidearms, mounted forces were permitted to keep their horses, all were treated with dignity.

Effects: Union casualties were 365,000 dead, 282,000 wounded; the number of Confederate casualties is unknown. The war ended slavery forever. The prostrate South remained under direct northern rule for more than a decade and under its domination for many years after that. Not until 1977 did a man from the deep South again become president. That president, Jimmy Carter, in 1978 restored citizenship to Confederate President Jefferson Davis.

Extraordinary Wartime Measures: During the Civil War, President Lincoln undertook extraordinary measures curbing civil liberties. He suspended the writ of habeas corpus, permitted military arrest and court-martial of civilian antiwar activists, notably Clement L. Vallandigham, and spent war funds prior to congressional appropriation. His actions were subsequently approved by Congress.

Homestead Act, 1862. Under this act, the first federal law granting public lands to squatters, a citizen, or one about to become a citizen, was granted free title to 160 acres after having settled on it for five years. The law was responsible for the rapid settlement of the Great Plains following the Civil War.

Morrill Act, 1862. The government granted to each state, proportionate to its representation in Congress, public lands, which were to be sold to finance agricultural and mechanical arts colleges. The bill was sponsored by Republican Representative Justin S. Morrill of Vermont.

States Admitted to the Union: West Virginia (1863), Nevada (1864).

SUPREME COURT APPOINTMENTS: (1) Noah H. Swayne (1804–1884), of Ohio, served as associate justice 1862–1881. He joined the majority in sustaining President Lincoln's constitutional right to undertake extraordinary measures during the Civil War. Speaking for the Court in *Hickman* v. *Jones* (1869), he ruled that in law the Confederacy never existed but granted to the rebels "certain belligerent rights" that protected them from being prosecuted simply as traitors. In *Springer* v. *United States* (1881), he delivered a unanimous opinion upholding the constitutionality of the federal income tax imposed during the Civil War and the insistence by the government that it be paid on time. Although the decision was reversed in 1895, its spirit was incorporated in the Sixteenth Amendment, establishing the federal income tax. (2) Samuel F. Miller (1816–1890), of Iowa, served as associate justice 1862–1890. A doctor-turned-lawyer, Miller was a dominant liberal force on the bench following the Civil War. He wrote more than 700 opinions, many of them in dissent. He consistently opposed special privileges for business. In the Slaughterhouse Case (1873), his most significant majority opinion, he spoke for a divided Court in limiting the privileges and immunities clause of the Fourteenth Amendment. Although hailed by liberals at the time for its immediate effect, that of permitting a state to grant a monopoly to promote the health and welfare of its citizens, it also limited the federal government's authority to protect minorites from state discrimination. The decision paved the way for the Jim Crow laws that continued to oppress blacks in the South well into the twentieth century. (3) David Davis (1815–1886), of Illinois, served as associate justice 1862–1877. A longtime friend of Lincoln, he nevertheless ruled in *Ex Parte Milligan* (1866), his most significant opinion, that the president had acted illegally in authorizing courts-martial of civilians during the Civil War in places where the civil courts were open. "The Constitution of the United States," he wrote, "is a law for rulers and people, equally in war and in peace, and covers with the shield of its protection all classes of men, at all times, and under all circumstances. No doctrine involving more pernicious consequences was ever invented by the wit of man than that any of its provisions can be suspended during any of the great exigencies of government."[18] (4) Stephen J. Field (1816–1899), of California, served as associate justice 1863–1897. The brother of Cyrus W. Field, developer of the transatlantic cable, Field was a longtime conservative force on the bench, consistently voting to uphold property rights over human rights. In opposing the income tax as unconstitutional for taking more money from the rich than from the poor, he warned that its institution would bring on class warfare. Field grew senile in his last years. (5) Salmon P. Chase (1808–1873), of Ohio, served as chief justice 1864–1873. His great contribution was the fairness with which he presided over the impeachment trial of President Andrew Johnson in 1868. He dismissed irregular motions from Radical Republicans designed to speed Johnson's removal. Although as Treasury secretary during the Civil War he had administered the Legal Tender Act as a means of raising funds for the war effort, as chief justice he held the law unconstitutional in *Hepburn* v. *Griswold* (1870). He admitted that the excitement of wartime had clouded his judgment and that, on reflection, the government did not have the right to issue paper money. Ultimately, however, the Legal Tender Act was upheld. Chase dissented in the Slaughterhouse Case (1873), which narrowly construed the Fourteenth Amendment.

RANKING IN 1962 HISTORIANS POLL: Lincoln ranked first of 31 presidents; best of the 5 "great" presidents. He ranked above Washington.

ASSASSINATION: April 14, 1865, 10:15 P.M., Ford's Theater, Washington, D.C.; Death, April 15, 1865, 7:22 A.M., Peterson House, Washington, D.C. President and Mrs. Lincoln joined Major Henry Rathbone and Miss Clara Harris in the presidential box of Ford's Theater to see a Good Friday evening performance of the comedy *Our American Cousin* starring Laura Keene. The curtain had already risen by the time the Lincolns arrived, and the performance was suspended briefly to acknowledge their presence. The play resumed for another 90 minutes, when in act three, scene two, the character of Asa Trenchard remained alone on stage to deliver the line that never failed to get a big laugh: "Well, I guess I know enough to turn you inside out, you sockdologizing old man trap." These were the last words Lincoln was known to have heard. As the theater rocked in laughter, a shot rang out from behind the president. John Wilkes Booth, 27, a deranged actor sympathetic to the South, had slipped into the presidential box while Lincoln's bodyguard John F. Parker was away from his post and shot the president in the back of the head with a .44 single-shot derringer. The bullet, made of brittomia, an alloy of tin, copper, and antimony, split in two on impact, one piece stopping in the middle of the brain, the other continuing through the brain to the bone of the right eye socket. Dr. Charles Leale, who happened to be in the house that night, examined the president, removed a blood clot to relieve fluid pressure on the brain, and pronounced the wound fatal. Lincoln was carried across the street to the Peterson boardinghouse, where, because of his size, he was placed diagonally on a bed. There he died without regaining consciousness. An autopsy was performed in a guestroom of the White House. Because Lincoln's body lay in state in 14 different cities over a two-and-a-half week period, his decomposed face had blackened and withered by the time he was buried in Springfield.

The contents of Lincoln's pockets on the night of his assassination remained under seal until February 12, 1976. They contained two pairs of spectacles; a chamois lens cleaner; an ivory and silver pocketknife; a large white Irish linen handkerchief, slightly used, with "A. Lincoln" embroidered in red; a gold quartz watch fob without a watch; a new silk-lined, leather wallet containing a pencil, a Confederate five-dollar bill, and news clippings of unrest in the Confederate army, emancipation in Missouri, the Union party platform of 1864, and an article on the presidency by John Bright. Lincoln left an estate, valued at $111,000 at final administration, divided among his wife and two surviving sons.

After the shooting, John Wilkes Booth lept onto the stage below, catching his right foot on the flag marking the presidential box and crying, "Sic semper tyrannis! The South is avenged!" His leg broken in the fall, he hobbled offstage before a stunned cast of players and made his way to a farm near Bowling Green, Virginia. He was hiding in a tobacco barn when federal troops tracked him down. Co-conspirator David E. Herold surrendered at once. Booth held out as the soldiers set fire to the barn. One of the soldiers, Boston Corbett, later claimed that he shot Booth; however, the assassin may have shot himself. In whatever manner he was wounded, he was dragged from the barn and soon thereafter died, on April 26, 1865.

Four others were convicted and hanged for taking part or having foreknowledge of Booth's plot: David E. Herold, who escaped to Virginia with Booth and surrendered to authorities, had conspired to assassinate Secretary of State William H. Seward simultaneously with Lincoln's murder; Lewis Paine, who stabbed Seward that night; George A. Atzerodt, who conspired to assassinate Vice President Andrew Johnson but failed to go through with it; and Mrs. Mary Surratt, who knew about the conspiracy but whose active involvement in it was never proved.

LINCOLN PRAISED: "He is the strong man of his party—full of wit, facts, dates— and the best stump speaker, with his droll ways and dry jokes, in the West."[19]— Senator Stephen A. Douglas, 1858

"Although he cared little for simple facts, rules and methods, it was on the underlying principle of truth and justice that Lincoln's will was firm as steel and tenacious as iron. . . . When justice, right, liberty, the government, the Constitution, the Union, humanity were involved, then you may all stand aside. No man can move him. No set of men can."[20]—William H. Herndon, Lincoln's law partner.

"Next to the destruction of the Confederacy, the death of Abraham Lincoln was the darkest day the South has ever known."[21]—Jefferson Davis

"He was not a born king of men . . . but a child of the people, who made himself a great persuader, therefore a leader, by dint of firm resolve, patient effort and dogged perseverance. He slowly won his way to eminence and fame by doing the work that lay next to him—doing it with all his growing might— doing it as well as he could, and learning by his failure, when failure was encountered, how to do it better."[22]—Horace Greeley

LINCOLN CRITICIZED: "A horrid looking wretch he is, sooty and scoundrelly in aspect, a cross between the nutmeg dealer, the horse-swapper and the night-man. . . . He is a lank-sided Yankee of the uncomeliest visage and of the dirtiest complexion. Faugh! After him what white man would be President?"[23]—*Charleston Mercury*, 1860

"I never did see or converse with so weak and imbecile a man; the weakest man I ever knew in high place. If I wanted to paint a despot, a man perfectly regardless of every constitutional right of the people, I would paint the hideous, apelike form of Abraham Lincoln."[24]—Democratic Senator Willard Saulsbury of Delaware

"[Lincoln] is to the extent of his limited ability and narrow intelligence [the abolitionists'] willing instrument for all the woe which [has] thus far been brought upon the Country and for all the degradation, all the atrocity, all the desolation and ruin."[25]—former president Franklin Pierce

"The president is nothing more than a well-meaning baboon. He is the original gorilla. What a specimen to be at the head of our affairs now!"[26]—General George B. McClellan

LINCOLN QUOTES: "You can fool some of the people all of the time, and all of the people some of the time, but you can't fool all of the people all of the time."[27]— 1856

"Four score and seven years ago our fathers brought forth on this continent, a new nation, conceived in Liberty, and dedicated to the proposition that all men are created equal.

"Now we are engaged in a great civil war, testing whether that nation or any nation so conceived and so dedicated, can long endure. We are met on a great battlefield of that war. We have come to dedicate a portion of that field, as a final resting place for those who here gave their lives that that nation might live. It is altogether fitting and proper that we should do this.

"But, in a larger sense, we can not dedicate—we can not consecrate—we can not hallow—this ground. The brave men, living and dead, who struggled here, have consecrated it far above our poor power to add or detract. The world will little note, nor long remember what we say here, but it can never forget what they did here. It is for us the living, rather, to be dedicated here to the unfinished work which they who fought here have thus far so nobly advanced. It is rather for us to be here dedicated to the great task remaining before us—that from these honored dead we take increased devotion to that cause for which they gave the last full measure of devotion—that we here highly resolve that these dead shall not have died in vain—that this nation, under God, shall have a new birth of freedom—and that government of the people, by the people, for the people, shall not perish from the earth."[28]—Gettysburg Address, 1863

BOOKS ABOUT LINCOLN: Charnwood, Lord. *Abraham Lincoln.* Garden City, N.Y.: Garden City Publishing Co., 1917.

Hertz, Emanual. *Lincoln Talks: A Biography in Anecdote.* New York: Viking Press, 1939.

Sandburg, Carl. *Abraham Lincoln: The Prairie Years and the War Years.* 6 vols. New York: Harcourt, Brace, and World, 1926–1939.

Thomas, Benjamin P. *Abraham Lincoln.* New York: Knopf, 1952.

NOTES:

1 Victor Searcher, *The Farewell to Lincoln*, New York: Abingdon, 1965, p. 132.

2 Carl Sandburg, *Abraham Lincoln: The Prairie Years and the War Years*, New York: Harcourt, Brace, & World, 1954, pp. 401–402.

3 Benjamin P. Thomas, *Abraham Lincoln*, New York: Knopf, 1952, p. 459.
4 Ibid., p. 88.
5 Emanual Hertz, *Lincoln Talks: A Biography in Anecdote*, New York: Viking, 1939, p. 3.
6 Thomas, p. 4.
7 Ibid., pp. 108–109.
8 Charles M. Segal, ed., *Conversations with Lincoln*, New York: Putnam's Sons, 1961, p. 272.
9 Sandburg, p. 13.
10 Ibid., p. 40.
11 Ibid., p. 59.
12 Henry Steele Commager, ed., *Documents of American History*, New York: Crofts, 1945, Doc. no. 186, p. 345.
13 Philip Van Doren Stern, ed., *The Life and Writings of Abraham Lincoln*, New York: Random House, 1940, pp. 463–464.
14 Ibid., p. 530.
15 Ibid., p. 823.
16 Irving Stone, *They Also Ran*, Garden City, N.Y.: Doubleday, 1966, p. 171.
17 Graham Stuart, *The Department of State*, New York: Macmillan, 1949, p. 130.
18 Commager, Doc. no. 256, p. 23.
19 Thomas, p. 182.
20 Searcher, p. 166.
21 A. K. McClure, *Our Presidents and How We Make Them*, New York: Harper & Bros., 1902, p. 201.
22 Thomas, p. 497.
23 Coley Taylor and Samuel Middlebrook, *The Eagle Screams*, New York: Macauley, 1936, p. 106.
24 Arthur T. Hadley, *Power's Human Face*, New York: Morrow, 1965, p. 74.
25 Roy Franklin Nichols, *Franklin Pierce*, Philadelphia: University of Pennsylvania Press, 1931, p. 521.
26 Stone, p. 159.
27 Hertz, p. 138.
28 Commager, Doc. no. 228.

ANDREW JOHNSON

17TH PRESIDENT

NAME: Andrew Johnson. According to one theory, he was named after Andrew Jackson; according to another, he was given the name of a maternal uncle.

PHYSICAL DESCRIPTION: Stocky though well proportioned, Johnson stood 5 feet 10 inches tall and had a swarthy complexion, broad forehead, thick dark hair that was graying when he became president, piercing deeply set black eyes guarded by protruding bushy eyebrows, a square jaw with a cleft chin, and a large nose. His health generally was sound, though as president he suffered from kidney stones. He began wearing reading glasses in his fifties. He dressed neatly, usually in black.

PERSONALITY: Johnson was simple and direct in manner. He spoke bluntly and to some appeared cold. He was generally reserved and sober but went out of his way to remain on friendly terms with old acquaintances and often loaned money to people down on their luck. "I found him kind and helpful," recalled one Tennessee neighbor, "especially to poor young men, and he was entirely without condescension."[1] Because of his own common roots, he throughout his life identified with the underdog. He shunned Washington society, preferring the company of old friends. Yet he was ever polite and carried himself with great dignity. Possessed of a strong, clear voice, Johnson was a gifted orator.

ANCESTORS: Johnson was of English, Scottish, and Irish heritage.

FATHER: Jacob Johnson (1778–1812). A poor, though well-respected, citizen of Raleigh, North Carolina, he eked out a living as a porter at Casso's Inn, janitor at the bank run by Colonel William Polk (a cousin of President James K. Polk), and sexton of the Presbyterian church. He also for a time was town constable and captain of Raleigh's Muster Division No. 20 of the state militia. In December 1811 he rescued Colonel Thomas Henderson, editor of the *Raleigh Star*, and another man from drowning in Hunter's Mill Pond outside Raleigh. Chilled from the icy waters and exhausted from dragging the pair to shore, Johnson never regained his health. While tolling the church bells for a funeral the next month, he collapsed and soon thereafter died. Andrew Johnson thus was left fatherless at age three.

MOTHER: Mary "Polly" McDonough Johnson (1783–1856). After the death of her husband, Jacob Johnson, whom she had married in 1801, Mrs. Johnson took in work as a weaver and spinner. A few years later she married Turner Dougherty. She died when Andrew Johnson was governor of Tennessee.

SIBLING: Johnson had one older brother—William Johnson, a carpenter, settled in Texas, where he opposed secession.

CHILDREN: Johnson had three sons and two daughters, all born in Greeneville, Tennessee.

Martha Johnson (1828–1891). She married David T. Patterson, who after the Civil War served as U.S. senator from Tennessee. During the Johnson administration, she presided as official White House hostess in place of her invalid mother. "We are plain people from the mountains of Tennessee called here for a short time by a national calamity," she remarked on taking up her social duties at the White House. "I trust too much will not be expected of us."[2] The Pattersons maintained a farm outside Greeneville.

Charles Johnson (1830–1863), doctor and pharmacist. At the outbreak of the Civil War he remained loyal to the Union. While recruiting Tennessee boys for the Union army, he became the object of an intense Confederate manhunt. He joined the Middle Tennessee Union Infantry as an assistant surgeon; he was thrown from his horse and killed.

Mary Johnson (1832–1883). She married Dan Stover, who served as colonel of the Fourth Tennessee Union Infantry during the Civil War. The Stovers lived on a farm in Carter County, Tennessee. Following the death of her husband in 1864, she married W. R. Brown.

Robert Johnson (1834–1869), lawyer. He served for a time in the Tennessee state legislature. During the Civil War he was commissioned colonel of the First Tennessee Union Cavalry. He was private secretary to his father during his tenure as president. He died an alcoholic at 35.

Andrew Johnson, Jr. (1852–1879), journalist. He founded the weekly *Greeneville Intelligencer*, but it failed after two years. He died soon thereafter at 27.

BIRTH: Johnson was born December 29, 1808, in a one-story log cottage on the grounds of Casso's Inn in Raleigh, North Carolina.

CHILDHOOD: Fatherless at age three, Johnson grew up in Raleigh amid extreme poverty. When he was 14, his mother bound him and his older brother as apprentice tailors to James J. Selby of Raleigh. The boys were indentured servants, bound by law to work for Selby in return for which he was to provide food and clothing and teach them the tailoring trade. After two years, however, the Johnson brothers fled, breaking their contract. Selby then ran an ad in the *Raleigh Gazette* of June 24, 1824, which read: "Ran away from the Subscriber, on the night of the 15th instant, two apprentice boys, legally bound, named William and Andrew Johnson. . . . I will pay the above Reward [$10] to any person who will deliver said apprentices to me in Raleigh, or I will give the above Reward for Andrew Johnson alone." Johnson took refuge in Carthage, North Carolina, about 75 miles southwest of Raleigh, where he earned money tailoring. He then proceeded south to Laurens, South Carolina. A year later, in 1826, he returned to Raleigh briefly before heading west with his mother and stepfather in a one-horse cart crammed with all their belongings. The Johnsons settled in Greeneville, Tennessee, where on learning that the town tailor was retiring, the 17-year-old lad opened his own shop under the sign "A. Johnson, Tailor."

EDUCATION: Johnson did not attend a single day of school. While he was an apprentice tailor, shop foreman James Litchford and one Dr. Hill would read aloud to him from a collection of the world's great orations. Johnson was fascinated by the stirring speeches, especially those of the English statesmen, the younger William Pitt and Charles James Fox. Johnson demonstrated such an appetite for knowledge that Dr. Hill gave him the book as a present. Leafing through its pages late into the night, Johnson painstakingly taught himself to read.

RELIGION: Johnson belonged to no church. He at times attended Methodist services with his wife. He liked best the administrative structure of the Baptist faith, in which each church was an autonomous unit. He also greatly admired Roman Catholicism for its democratic policy of worship. He occasionally attended Catholic services and took special note that the faithful filled pews on a first-come-first-serve basis. He found repulsive the Protestant practice of selling fancy private pews to the wealthy and relegating the poor to a less desirable section of the church. As a congressman, he defended Catholicism from its critics and championed religious freedom.

RECREATION: Johnson enjoyed playing checkers and puttering in his vegetable garden. He also liked the circus and minstrel shows.

EARLY ROMANCE: During 1824–1825 Johnson, 16, fell in love with Sara Word, a young girl of Laurens, South Carolina, where he had fled after breaking his bond of indenture (see "Childhood"). Summoning his newly acquired tailoring skills, Johnson joined her in making a cotton quilt. Her parents objected to the match, and she dutifully broke off the relationship.

MARRIAGE: Andrew Johnson, 18, married Eliza McCardle, 16, on May 17, 1827, at the home of the bride's mother in Greeneville, Tennessee. Born at Leesburg, Tennessee, on October 4, 1810, the only child of John McCardle, a shoemaker, and Sarah Phillips McCardle, Eliza lost her father when she was still a small child. She was raised by her widowed mother in Greeneville. One day in September 1826, Eliza was chatting with classmates from Rhea Academy when she spotted Andrew Johnson and his family pull into town with all their belongings (see "Childhood"). They took an instant liking to each other and were married the following spring by Mordecai Lincoln, a distant relative of Abraham Lincoln. At 16 she married at a younger age than any other First Lady. Mrs. Johnson was rather tall and had hazel eyes, brown hair, and a good figure. She was better educated than Johnson, who by this time had barely taught himself to read and spell a little. She patiently tutored him, teaching him to write and to figure math and greatly improved his reading and spelling. While he labored in the tailor shop, she often read aloud to him. In middle age she developed "slow consumption" and was thereafter a semi-invalid. During the Civil War, Confederate authorities ordered her to evacuate her home in Greeneville; she took refuge in Nashville. A few months after her husband became president, she joined him in the White House but was too ill to preside as First Lady. She remained confined to a room on the second floor, leaving the social chores to her daughter Mrs. Martha Patterson. Mrs. Johnson appeared publicly as First Lady on only two occasions—at a reception for Queen Emma of the Sandwich (Hawaiian) Islands in 1866 and at a birthday party for the president in 1867. She died on January 15, 1876, at age 65, having survived her husband by just six months. She was buried beside him in Greeneville, Tennessee.

MILITARY SERVICE: Civil War. On March 4, 1862, President Abraham Lincoln appointed Johnson military governor of Tennessee with the rank of brigadier general. He served until 1865 (see "Career before the Presidency").

CAREER BEFORE THE PRESIDENCY:

Alderman of Greeneville, Tennessee, 1828–1830; Mayor of Greeneville, 1830–1833. He promoted the interests of the town's free laboring class.

Member of Tennessee House of Representatives, 1835–1837, 1839–1841. Elected as a Democrat over Matthew Stevenson, a Whig, in 1835, to represent Washington and Greene counties in the state legislature, Johnson supported economy in government and spoke out against nullification. He opposed, unsuccessfully, a popular program of internal improvements. On this issue, he was defeated for reelection in 1837. He was returned to the legislature in 1839, however. He supported Hugh Lawson White, Whig of Tennessee, for president in 1836. In 1840 he campaigned in Tennessee for the reelection of President Martin Van Buren and stood as a Van Buren elector.

Tennessee State Senator, 1841–1843. Elected to represent Greene and Hawkins counties in the state senate, Johnson continued to champion the rights of free laborers. He proposed repeal of the state law that provided greater representation to slaveholders than to nonslaveholders. He steered the bill through the senate, but it failed to become law. He also proposed, again without success, carving a new state, to be named Frankland, from the mountain regions of eastern Tennessee, Virginia, North Carolina, and Georgia.

U.S. Representative, 1843–1853. In 1843 Johnson was elected as a Democrat over Colonel John Aiken, a Democrat supported by the Whigs, to represent Tennessee's First Congressional District in the U.S. House. He was reelected biennially four times in succession, defeating by turns the Reverend William Brownlow, a Whig known as the "Fighting parson"; Judge O. P. Temple, a Whig; Colonel N. G. Taylor, a Whig; and Landon C. Haynes, a Democrat supported by the Whigs. A Jacksonian Democrat, Congressman Johnson supported the Constitution and the Union over states' rights and quickly fell out with a majority of his southern colleagues. During his decade in the House, he opposed a high protective tariff, attacked anti-Catholic prejudice, favored the admission of both Texas and Oregon, promoted homestead legislation, supported the Mexican War, voted generally in support of the gag rule preventing the consideration of antislavery petitions, voted for the Compromise of 1850 (see "Millard Fillmore, 13th President," "Administration"), defended the use of the presidential veto, and denounced as extravagant expenditures for the Smithsonian Institution and enlargement of certain federal buildings. Because his district had been gerrymandered to his disadvantage following the 1850 census, Johnson did not seek reelection in 1852.

Governor of Tennessee, 1853–1857. In a spirited campaign in 1852, Johnson was elected governor over Gustavus A. Henry, the Eagle Orator and descendant of Patrick Henry. He was reelected two years later, defeating Meredith P. Gentry, candidate of the Know-Nothing, or American, party. During his two terms, Governor Johnson instituted a state public school system, a state library, and a regular program of agricultural and mechanical fairs. Nationally, he supported Stephen A. Douglas and the Kansas-Nebraska Act (see "Franklin Pierce, 14th President," "Administration").

U.S. Senator, 1857–1862. Elected unanimously to the Senate as a Democrat by the Tennessee legislature, Johnson promoted economy in government, defended slavery, supported the Fugitive Slave Law, and opposed as unconstitutional proposed federal construction of a transcontinental railroad. A longtime advocate of granting free public land to settlers, he was the chief architect of the Homestead Act (1862; see "Abraham Lincoln, 16th President," "Administration"). In 1860 he was a favorite-son candidate for president; in the general election he supported John C. Breckinridge, nominee of the National Democrats. As civil war loomed, Johnson was the only southern senator to denounce secession and uphold the Union. He criticized his own party's president, James Buchanan, for failing to deal more sternly with the rebels. In stirring addresses that electrified the galleries, Johnson lambasted both abolitionists and secessionists alike as enemies of the Union. "Though I fought against Lincoln I love my country," he declared in December 1860. "I love the Constitution and swear that it and the Union shall be saved as 'Old Hickory' Jackson did in 1832. Senators, my blood, my existence, I would give to save this Union."[3] On the eve of South Carolina's secession, he warned that such a rift would lead to the utter dissolution of the United States, with the Union "divided into 33 petty governments, with a little prince in one, a little potentate in another, and a republic somewhere else . . . with quarreling and warring amongst the little petty powers which would result in anarchy."[4] He struggled unsuccessfully to keep Tennessee in the Union; with its secession he broke with his home state to become the only southern senator to spurn the Confederacy and retain his seat in the Senate. He vigorously defended the Lincoln administration, upholding the president's right to suspend habeas corpus and undertake other emergency measures in the midst of rebellion. He opposed last-minute compromise proposals as long as the South remained in a state of rebellion. Senator Johnson was regarded as a traitor in his native South. His life, and that of his family, were threatened. He was hung in effigy in Tennessee. But in the North his stature grew to heroic proportions.

Military Governor of Tennessee, 1862–1864. In March 1862 President Lincoln appointed Johnson military governor of Tennessee with the rank of brigadier general. His orders were to reestablish federal authority in the state and maintain peace and security pending restoration of civil government. Fully empowered to discharge executive, legislative, and judicial functions, Governor Johnson moved forcefully to rid the state of Confederate influence. He dismissed officeholders unwilling to take an oath of allegiance to the federal government, closed down anti-Union newspapers, arrested clergymen for promoting the Confederacy from the pulpit, seized the railroads, and levied taxes. He constructed and guarded from sabotage the railroad extending from Nashville to the Tennessee River, a vital link in the Union supply line. At Johnson's intercession, President Lincoln agreed to exempt Tennessee from the Emancipation Proclamation; it was the only rebel state to be wholly exempt. He shared Lincoln's belief that the emancipation of slaves was of secondary importance to preservation of the Union. In a valiant show of resistance, Governor Johnson remained in Nashville as the capital city several times nearly fell under a determined Confederate siege. "I am no military man," he vowed at one point during the ordeal, "but any one who talks of surrender I will shoot."[5] By war's end he had restored civil government to the state.

Vice President, March–April 1865. In June 1864, President Lincoln prevailed on delegates to the National Union (Republican) national convention to replace Vice President Hannibal Hamlin with Andrew Johnson in order to balance the ticket with a pro-Union southern Democrat. As he prepared to take the oath as vice president, Johnson was recovering from typhoid fever. Feeling weak on entering the stuffy Senate chamber, he fortified himself with a few shots of whiskey. After being sworn in, he gave a rambling, incoherent speech, a performance that convinced many in the audience that he was drunk. As part of the plot to assassinate President Lincoln in April 1865, co-conspirator George Atzerodt was assigned the task of murdering Johnson. He stalked the vice president for a time, but his courage failed at the last minute. Johnson, awakened from a sound sleep and told that Lincoln had been shot, rushed to Lincoln's bedside to see for himself that he was beyond recovery.

On the morning of April 15, 1865, Johnson was sworn in as president by Chief Justice Salmon P. Chase at the Kirkwood House in Washington, where the vice president had been residing.

CABINET:

Secretary of State. William H. Seward (1801–1872), of New York, served 1861–1869. A holdover from the Lincoln administration, he defended Johnson against the Radical Republicans. An ardent expansionist, he negotiated the purchase in 1867 of Alaska from Russia—an acquisition quickly dubbed Seward's Folly by those blind to its potential value—and annexed in 1867 the Midway Islands in the Pacific.

Secretary of the Treasury. Hugh McCulloch (1808–1895), of Indiana, served 1865–1869. A holdover from the Lincoln administration, he conducted a deflationary policy to cool down the economy in the wake of the Civil War. Through the sale of bonds he raised funds to retire greenbacks and return to specie, or hard money. By 1868 he had cut federal taxes nearly in half. That same year, however, Congress repealed authorization for the deflationary program amid an economic slump. He later served as Treasury secretary in the Arthur administration.

Secretary of War. (1) Edwin M. Stanton (1814–1869), of Ohio, served 1862–1868. A former attorney general in the Buchanan administration and a holdover from the Lincoln administration, he worked with Radical Republicans in Congress to impose on the South a harsh Reconstruction instead of Johnson's more tolerant policy. He was dismissed by Johnson in February 1868, but, claiming protection under the recently enacted Tenure of Office Act, refused to give up the office. He barricaded himself within the War Department until the Senate acquitted the president of House impeachment charges (see "Administration"). He then resigned in May 1868. (2) John M. Schofield (1831–1906), of Missouri, served 1868–1869. In presiding over Reconstruction, he opposed enfranchisement of blacks.

Attorney General. (1) James Speed (1812–1887), of Kentucky, served 1864–1866. A holdover from the Lincoln administration, he ruled that the co-conspirators in the Lincoln assassination could be tried in a military court. He joined Radical Republicans in opposition to Johnson's Reconstruction policy. (2) Henry Stanbery (1803–1881), of Ohio, served 1866–1868. He resigned in order to defend Johnson at his impeachment trial. (3) William M. Evarts (1818–1901), of New York, served 1868–1869. He was a member of Johnson's defense team in the impeachment trial. He later served as secretary of state in the Hayes administration.

Secretary of the Navy. Gideon Welles (1802–1878), of Connecticut, served 1861–1869. A holdover from the Lincoln administration, he supported Johnson against the Radical Republicans.

Postmaster General. (1) William Dennison (1815–1882), of Ohio, served 1864–1866. A holdover from the Lincoln administration, he supported the Radical Republicans against Johnson. (2) Alexander W. Randall (1819–1872), of Wisconsin, served 1866–1869. He was promoted from first assistant postmaster general.

Secretary of the Interior. (1) John P. Usher (1816–1889), of Indiana, served 1863–1865. A holdover from the Lincoln administration, he served only briefly under Johnson until his successor, appointed by Lincoln before the assassination, was able to take office. (2) James Harlan (1820–1899), of Iowa, served 1865–1866. A Lincoln appointee, he supported the Radical Republicans against Johnson. He resigned from the cabinet and entered the Senate in time to vote for impeachment. (3) Orville H. Browning (1806–1881), of Illinois, served 1866–1869. He supported Johnson against the Radical Republicans. His diary is a valuable, detailed source of information on the Lincoln and Johnson administrations.

ADMINISTRATION: April 15, 1865–March 3, 1869.

Reconstruction. President Johnson sought to carry out the lenient Reconstruction of the South envisioned by President Abraham Lincoln. Taking the position that, technically, the rebel states had never left the Union because constitutionally it is indissoluble, Johnson set out to restore their legal status swiftly, without recrimination, and with the least possible disruption in the lives of his fellow southerners. His plan was to appoint a local provisional governor, who was to call a state constitutional convention, which, in turn, would draft a new constitution repudiating secession, slavery, and Confederate war debts. Full rights of citizenship were to be restored to southerners on swearing a simple oath of allegiance to the federal government. Once these objectives were accomplished, according to Johnson's policy, the people of the southern states were to be free to govern themselves and send men of their own choosing to Congress. As for the recently emancipated slaves, it was Johnson's hope that the South would recognize the value of giving the vote to literate, responsible blacks. But the Lincoln-Johnson program of mild Reconstruction was not given a chance. The South had no intention of sharing political power with former slaves; Radical Republicans in the North, led by Thaddeus Stevens in the House and Charles Sumner in the Senate, were determined to punish the South and to prevent a resurgence of the southern Democratic power base that had dominated national affairs prior to the Civil War. The southern states enacted Black Codes, restricting the rights of former slaves. Under them, blacks were denied the right to vote, to serve on juries or testify against whites in court, to marry a white person, or to contract for their labor on an equal basis with whites. Radical Republicans in Congress responded by passing the Civil Rights Act (1866) to protect blacks in the South and incorporated this protection in the Constitution with the Fourteenth Amendment. In an attempt to thwart the Radical Republicans from imposing their stern brand of Reconstruction, Johnson exercised 29 vetoes, 15 of which were overridden. In addition to the Civil Rights Act, bills passed over his veto included (1) Freedmen's Bureau Act

(1866), extending the life of the bureau that provided education, medical services, land, and jobs to hundreds of thousands of blacks in the South before being abolished in 1872; (2) District of Columbia Suffrage Act (1867), enfranchising residents of the District of Columbia; (3) four Reconstruction Acts (1867–1868), dividing the South into five military districts, each commanded by a general empowered to organize civil government within guidelines set by Congress in preparation for readmission to the Union; under these guidelines, blacks were able to vote whereas many whites were disfranchised, and elected representatives were required to take an "ironclad oath" swearing that they had never willingly collaborated with the Confederacy. As a precondition to readmission to the Union, the errant states were required to ratify the Fourteenth Amendment and adopt a new constitution granting black suffrage. Meanwhile federal troops maintained the peace. Reconstruction was bitterly opposed by most white southerners, who referred derisively to northern officials administering the program as Carpetbaggers and the southern whites who collaborated with them Scalawags. The Ku Klux Klan was founded in Pulaski, Tennessee, in 1866 to promote white supremacy and resist Reconstruction by terrorism.

Impeachment, 1868. In 1867 Congress passed over Johnson's veto the Tenure of Office Act, forbidding the president to remove certain public officials without consent of the Senate. In February 1868 Johnson dismissed Secretary of War Stanton, who as a staunch Radical Republican had been undermining the president's policies. On February 24, 1868, the House voted 126–47 to impeach Johnson for "high crimes and misdemeanors." Johnson requested 40 days to prepare for the trial in the Senate but was allowed just 10 days. Chief Justice Salmon P. Chase presided over the Senate trial. The House had lodged 11 articles of impeachment against the president, most of which dealt with Johnson's alleged violation of the Tenure of Office Act. The eleventh article, an umbrella item encompassing the rest of the charges, was approved on May 16 by a vote of 35–19, just 1 vote short of the two-thirds necessary for conviction and removal. Ten days later, Johnson was acquitted of two other articles by the same vote. The remainder of the articles were never brought to a vote. Johnson's acquittal was owing to the courage of seven Republican senators who risked their political careers to bolt party ranks and join Democrats in exonerating the president. They were Edmund G. Ross of Kansas, William P. Fessenden of Maine, John B. Henderson of Missouri, Peter Van Winkle of West Virginia, Lyman Trumbull of Illinois, Joseph S. Fowler of Tennessee, and James W. Grimes of Iowa.

Purchase of Alaska, 1867. The United States purchased Alaska from Russia for $7.2 million. Residents were granted three years in which to decide whether to remain in Alaska as Americans or move to Russia to retain their Russian citizenship.

Constitutional Amendments Ratified: Thirteenth Amendment (1865). "Neither slavery nor involuntary servitude, except as a punishment for crime whereof the party shall have been duly convicted, shall exist within the United States, or any place subject to their jurisdiction." Fourteenth Amendment (1868). ". . . No State shall make or enforce any law which shall abridge the privileges or immunities of citizens of the United States; nor shall any State deprive any person of life, liberty or property, without due process of law; nor deny to any person within its jurisdiction the equal protection of the laws." It also provided that if any state denied the right to vote to any of its adult males, except for participation in rebellion, that state's representation in Congress would be reduced proportionately. It barred from office all who actively supported the Confederacy. It declared null and void all debts incurred by the Confederacy.

State Admitted to the Union: Nebraska (1867).

SUPREME COURT APPOINTMENTS: None confirmed.

RANKING IN 1962 HISTORIANS POLL: Johnson ranked twenty-third of 31 presidents; worst of 12 "average" presidents. He ranked above Taylor, below Eisenhower.

RETIREMENT: March 4, 1869–July 31, 1875. Johnson was denied renomination in 1868 (see "Ulysses S. Grant, 18th President," "Opponent"). Without attending the inauguration of his successor, Ulysses S. Grant, Johnson retired to Greeneville, Tennessee, where he was welcomed amid great festivity. The president's hometown, which just eight years before had strung a banner reading "Andrew Johnson Traitor" across its main street for his decision to remain loyal to the Union during the Civil War, now hoisted a friendlier message above the center of town—"Andrew Johnson, Patriot." He remained active in the Democratic party throughout his last years. He ran unsuccessfully for the Senate in 1871 and the House in 1872. He campaigned for Horace Greeley for president against President Grant in 1872. He stumped for various Democratic candidates in the congressional elections of 1874. In 1875 Johnson was elected to the U.S. Senate on the fifty-fifth ballot of the state legislature. He was the only former president to serve in the Senate. In his only floor speech (March 1875), he denounced the Grant administration's Reconstruction policy. He died in office.

DEATH: July 31, 1875, about 2 A.M., Carter County, Tennessee. "All seems gloom and despair," Johnson wrote in June 1873 in a memorandum discovered among his effects after his death. "I have performed my duty to my God, my country, and my family. I have nothing to fear in approaching death. To me it is the mere shadow of God's protecting wing. . . . Here I will rest in quiet and peace beyond the reach of calumny's poisoned shaft, the influence of envy and jealous enemies, where treason and traitors or State backsliders and hypocrites in church can have no place."[6] Johnson was among the victims of the cholera epidemic of 1873. He survived it but never recovered completely. On July 28, 1875, he visited his daughter Mrs. Mary Brown near Carter's Station in Carter County. After lunch, about 4 P.M., while talking with his granddaughter, he collapsed from a stroke and was left paralyzed on one side. Regaining consciousness, he ordered that no doctor or minister be called. The next day he suffered a second stroke. He lingered two more days before expiring. At his request his body was wrapped in an American flag, his head rested on a copy of the Constitution. On August 2 he lay in state at the Greeneville court house. The casket was closed because the body had begun to decompose. Following Masonic funeral services on August 3 he was buried on land he owned outside Greeneville at a spot he had marked with a willow tree, taken as a shoot from a tree grown at Napoleon's tomb on St. Helena.

JOHNSON PRAISED: "His record and character had much to attract the patriotic respect of the country. The vigor and boldness with which, though a Southern Senator, he had denounced secession at the beginning of the outbreak, had taken hold of the popular heart, the firmness and unyielding loyalty he had displayed as military governor of Tennessee greatly deepened the favorable impression."[7]—James G. Blaine

"No man has a right to judge Andrew Johnson in any respect who has not suffered as much and done as much as he for the Nation's sake."[8]—President Abraham Lincoln, 1864

"One of the people by birth, he remained so by conviction, continually referring to his origin. . . . He was indifferent to money and careless of praise or censure."[9]—Jefferson Davis, 1865

"If you could meet his straightforward honest look and hear the hearty tone of his voice, as I did, I am well assured you would believe with me, that although he may not receive personal assaults with the equanimity and forbearance Mr. Lincoln used to show, there is no need to fear that Andrew Johnson is not hearty and sincere in his adhension to the principles upon which he was elected."[10]— Governor Jacob D. Cox of Ohio, 1866

JOHNSON CRITICIZED: "Professing to be a Democrat, he has been politically if not personally hostile to me during my whole term [as president]. He is very vindictive and perverse in his temper and conduct. If he had the manliness or independence to manifest his opposition openly, he knows he could not be again elected by his constituents."[11]—President James K. Polk, 1849

"To think that one frail life stands between this insolent, clownish creature and the presidency! May God bless and spare Abraham Lincoln!"[12]—*New York World*, 1865

"Johnson is an insolent drunken brute in comparison with which Caligula's horse was respectable."[13]—Senator Charles Sumner of Massachusetts

"The President is pursuing and resolved to pursue a course in regard to reconstruction that can result in nothing but consigning the great Union or Republican party, bound hand and foot to the tender mercies of the rebels we have so lately conquered in the field and their copperhead allies of the North."[14]—Senator Ben Wade of Ohio, 1865

JOHNSON QUOTES: "There are no good laws but such as repeal other laws."[15]— 1835

"If the rabble were lopped off at one end and the aristocrat at the other, all would be well with the country."[16]

"There are some who lack confidence in the integrity and capacity of the people to govern themselves. To all who entertain such fears I will most respectfully say that I entertain none. . . . If man is not capable, and is not to be trusted with the government of himself, is he to be trusted with the government of others. . . . Who, then, will govern? The answer must be, Man—for we have no angels in the shape of men, as yet, who are willing to take charge of our political affairs."[17]—1853

BOOKS ABOUT JOHNSON: Lomask, Milton. *Andrew Johnson: President on Trial*. New York: Farrar, Straus, 1960.

Stryker, Lloyd Paul. *Andrew Johnson: A Study in Courage*. New York: Macmillan, 1929.

Trefousse, Hans L. *Andrew Johnson: A Biography*. New York: Norton, 1989.

Winston, Robert W. *Andrew Johnson: Plebian and Patriot*. New York: Henry Holt & Co., 1928.

NOTES

1 Robert W. Winston, *Andrew Johnson: Plebian and Patriot*, New York: Holt, 1928, p. 472.
2 Lloyd Paul Stryker, *Andrew Johnson: A Study in Courage*, New York: Macmillan, 1929, p. 218.
3 Winston, p. 167.
4 Stryker, p. 66.
5 Winston, p. 236.
6 *New York Times*, August 3, 1875, p. 5.
7 Stryker, p. 123.
8 Winston, p. 243.
9 Ibid., p. 100 n8.
10 Stryker, p. 283.
11 Allan Nevins, ed., *Polk: The Diary of a President*, New York: Capricorn, 1968, p. 362.
12 Sol Barzman, *Madmen & Geniuses: The Vice Presidents of the U.S.*, Chicago: Follett, 1974, p. 112.
13 Howard K. Beale, *The Critical Year*, New York: Ungar, 1958, p. 370.
14 Stryker, p. 228.
15 Winston, p. 30.
16 Ibid., p. 53.
17 Ibid., p. 77.

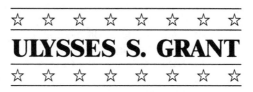

ULYSSES S. GRANT

18TH PRESIDENT

NAME: Hiram Ulysses Grant. He remained nameless for a month after his birth. His mother considered naming him Albert. But in the end he was named Hiram, after his maternal grandfather, and Ulysses, after the hero of Greek mythology. The prospect of entering West Point with the initials H.U.G. emblazoned on his trunk embarrassed him, so as a new cadet he began signing his name Ulysses H. Grant, or U. H. Grant. But soon he learned that Representative Thomas L. Hamer, who had arranged for his appointment, had enrolled him erroneously under the name Ulysses Simpson Grant. Grant went along with the change, finding nothing objectionable in the initials U.S.G. Classmates began calling him U.S., or Uncle Sam, Grant. Thereafter he was known to friends as Sam.

PHYSICAL DESCRIPTION: Grant stood 5 feet 7 inches tall and, though rather slightly built, was muscular. On entering West Point at 17, he was just 5 feet 1 inch tall, a scant 1 inch above the academy's minimum height requirement, but sprouted 6 inches by graduation. He had soft blue eyes, wavy brown hair, thin lips, and delicate hands with long, slim fingers. He sported a full beard and mustache. He wore false teeth. He suffered from migraine headaches all his life. At West Point, he developed the nagging cough, hoarseness, and abrupt weight loss typical of tuberculosis, a disease prevalent in the Grant family.

PERSONALITY: Ironically, the man who achieved fame on the battlefield was particularly squeamish. Grant could not stomach the sight of animal blood. Rare steak nauseated him; he insisted that his meat be well done. He never touched fowl. "I could never eat anything that went on two legs,"[1] he explained. He did not hunt, even as a boy in rural southern Ohio where shooting game was a favorite youthful pastime. Grant was modest, self-effacing, soft-spoken, and mild-mannered. One biographer, W. E. Woodward, went so far as to suggest that he was a bit effeminate. "Young Grant had a girl's primness of manner and modesty of conduct," he wrote. "There was a broad streak of the feminine in his personality. He was almost half-woman, but this strain was buried in the depths of his soul; it never came to the surface, except indirectly, and he was probably not aware of it himself."[2] Grant was somewhat prudish. He seldom used foul language. He disliked dirty jokes. And in the field he always bathed alone in a closed tent, never allowing even his aides to glimpse him naked. A serious, well-disciplined soldier, Grant spurned military pomp and pageantry. He was loyal to friends. A superstitious man, he believed it bad luck to retrace one's steps. If he inadvertently walked beyond his destination, for example, he would not simply turn around and walk back down the same street, but rather would keep going further away from the place and return via another road.

ANCESTORS: Grant was of English and Scotch heritage. His great[5]-grandfather Matthew Grant emigrated from Plymouth, England, to Dorchester, Massachusetts, in 1630. He settled in Windsor, Connecticut, where he long served as town clerk. His great-grandfather Captain Noah Grant was killed in action in 1756 during the French and Indian War. His grandfather, also Captain Noah Grant, served in the Continental army during the entire American Revolution; he fought at Bunker Hill. He migrated from Windsor, Connecticut, to Westmoreland County, Pennsylvania, and finally settled at Deerfield, Ohio.

FATHER: Jesse Root Grant (1794–1873), tanner. A native of Westmoreland County, Pennsylvania, he followed his father in the tanning business and prospered, amassing a small fortune, estimated at $150,000. He owned tanneries and leather goods stores in Ohio, Kentucky, Illinois, and Wisconsin. Blunt, quarrelsome, and boastful, he was the very antithesis of his shy, sensitive son. He was an outspoken abolitionist at a time when residents of southernmost Ohio, where he settled, were tolerant of slavery, practiced just across the river in Kentucky. Politically he supported the Whigs, though he had voted for Democrat Andrew Jackson. He served as mayor of Bethel, Ohio, and postmaster of Covington, Kentucky. In 1866 he distributed most of his wealth to his children, except for Ulysses, who declined his share, explaining that he did not help earn the money and therefore did not feel entitled to it. Jesse Grant did not attend his son's inauguration as president but frequently visited him at the White House. He died during Grant's second term.

MOTHER: Hannah Simpson Grant (1798–1883). A native of Montgomery County, Pennsylvania, she married Jesse Grant in 1821. Reserved, somewhat withdrawn, and diffident, she found comfort in religion, first as a Presbyterian and later as a Methodist. Ulysses was much closer to her than to his father and sorely missed her when he went away to West Point. "I seem alone in the world without my mother," he wrote her from the academy. "There have been so many ways in which you have advised me."[3] She did not attend her son's inauguration as president. She never visited the White House. Grant was the first president whose parents both lived to see him enter office.

SIBLINGS: The oldest of six children, Grant had three sisters and two brothers— Simpson Grant, who helped operate his father's leather goods store in Galena, Illinois; Clara Grant, who died unmarried at 36; Mrs. Virginia P. Corbin, wife of Abel R. Corbin, who served as go-between for Fisk and Gould in the gold conspiracy (see "Administration: Scandals"); Orvil L. Grant, who helped operate his father's leather goods store in Galena, Illinois; Mrs. Mary F. Cramer, wife of the Reverend Michael J. Cramer, U.S. minister to Denmark under President Hayes.

COLLATERAL RELATIVES: Grant was a fourth cousin once removed of Franklin D. Roosevelt and a sixth cousin once removed of Grover Cleveland. According to Mickey Deans's and Ann Pinchot's biography of Judy Garland (*Weep No More, My Lady*), the famed singer was a first cousin three times removed of Ulysses S. Grant.

CHILDREN: Grant had three sons and a daughter.

Frederick Dent Grant (1850–1912), soldier, public official. Born at St. Louis, Missouri, he as a youth accompanied his father during the Civil War and was wounded in the leg at Vicksburg. He graduated from West Point in 1871 and within a few short years rose to lieutenant colonel and aide to General Philip Sheridan. Resigning from the army a colonel in 1881, he was president of a utility company in Massachusetts for a time and suffered severe financial loss with the failure of Grant and Ward (see "Retirement"). Defeated as the Republican candidate for secretary of state of New York in 1887, he served as U.S. minister to Austria-Hungary under President Benjamin Harrison. On his return to the United States he was appointed to the New York City Board of Police Commissioners and in 1897 succeeded Theodore Roosevelt as police commissioner. He served as assistant war secretary in the McKinley administration. With the outbreak of the Spanish-American War, he reentered the army as a brigadier general and served in Cuba, Puerto Rico, and the Philippines.

Ulysses S. "Buck" Grant, Jr. (1852–1929), lawyer. Born at Bethel, Ohio, he was educated at Harvard (class of 1874), the University of Göttingen in Germany, and Columbia Law School (class of 1876). He served for a time as personal secretary to his father while he was president and as assistant U.S. district attorney in New York. With his father he formed the brokerage house of Grant and Ward (see "Retirement"). After its failure, he practiced law in New York and eventually settled in San Diego, California. He was a delegate to the Republican national convention in 1896. He ran unsuccessfully for U.S. senator from California in 1899.

Ellen "Nellie" Wrenshall Grant (1855–1922). Born near St. Louis, Missouri, she married Algernon C.F. Sartoris, a wealthy Englishman, singer, and nephew of actress Fanny Kemble, in a grand White House ceremony on May 21, 1874. They lived together in England for a time but later separated. He proved dissolute and a disappointment to his parents, who made it clear that they did not blame Nellie for the breakup. Sartoris died in 1890, leaving Nellie a wealthy young widow.

Jesse Root Grant (1858–1934), engineer. Born near St. Louis, Missouri, he studied engineering at Cornell University. He settled in California and in the 1890s was an early developer of Tia Juana (now Tijuana), Mexico, as a gambling resort. He abandoned the party of his father to become a Democrat and in 1908 was a candidate for the Democratic presidential nomination. He wrote *In the Days of My Father General Grant* (1925).

SUBSEQUENT DESCENDANT: Ulysses S. Grant III (1881–1968). The president's grandson, he served in the engineering corps from 1903 until his retirement in 1945, rising to the rank of major general. During World War I, he was secretary of the American section of the Supreme War Council in France. During World War II, he was chief of the protection branch of the Office of Civilian Defense. He married Edith Root, daughter of Elihu Root, secretary of state under Theodore Roosevelt. His biography of his grandfather, *Ulysses S. Grant: Warrior and Statesman*, appeared posthumously in 1968.

BIRTH: Grant was born about 5 A.M., April 27, 1822, in a two-room cabin in Point Pleasant, Ohio, on the Ohio River about 25 miles upstream from Cincinnati.

CHILDHOOD: While Ulysses was still an infant, the Grants moved east from Point Pleasant to the next county, settling at Georgetown, Ohio, where he was raised. From an early age he demonstrated a marked talent for handling horses and assumed all the chores requiring their use. He hauled wood, cleared and plowed fields, brought in the harvests, and transported passengers for a fee. The one chore he avoided whenever possible was work in his father's tannery, for the blood-caked hides nauseated him. One telling anecdote of Grant's youthful honesty, or naiveté, was substantiated as "nearly true" by Grant himself in his memoirs: When he was about eight years old, his father authorized him to negotiate for the purchase of a horse, instructing him to offer $20 but to pay as high as $25 if necessary. Grant approached the seller and told him exactly what his father had said. Naturally, he ended up paying the full $25 for the animal. Despite the burdensome chores, the rigors of the West in those times, and his innate shyness, Grant seems to have had a happy childhood. "I have no recollection of ever having been punished at home, either by scolding or by the rod,"[4] he once commented. At age nine he was saved from drowning in a swift creek by a friend, Daniel Ammen. His ambition was to be either a farmer or a down-the-river trader.

EDUCATION: Grant learned the fundamentals at subscription schools in Georgetown, Ohio, under the instruction of John D. White and others. During 1836–1837 he attended Maysville (Kentucky) Seminary, operated by Messrs. Richeson and Rand, where he was on the debating team. During 1838–1839 he attended the Presbyterian Academy at Ripley, Ohio. Grant was an above-average student with a marked aptitude for mathematics. In 1838, without Grant's knowledge, his father arranged for Representative Thomas L. Hamer to appoint him to West Point. Grant was horrified at the news, fearful that he would flunk out. He entered the academy in May 1839. At West Point, Cadet Grant excelled at math and horsemanship, setting a high-jump record on horseback, but found more difficult such subjects as French, English, military tactics, political science, geology, engineering, geography, and the sciences. He also accumulated a long list of demerits for a variety of minor, though frequently committed, offenses, including missing church on Sunday, tardiness, and sloppy dress. He was elected president of the Dialectic (literary) Society. "A military life had no charms for me," Grant later said of his attitude as a cadet, "and I had not the faintest idea of staying in the Army even if I should be graduated, which I did not expect."[5] Grant graduated twenty-first of 39 cadets in the class of 1843. He requested assignment to the dragoons (cavalry). The administration did not believe that his fine horsemanship sufficiently compensated for his lackluster class standing, however, and therefore relegated him to the infantry with the rank of brevet second lieutenant.

RELIGION: Methodist. As a youth Grant rarely went to church and had never been baptized. He began attending Methodist services irregularly with his wife. During Grant's final struggle with cancer, the Reverend John Phillip Newman of the Metropolitan Methodist Church of Washington, D.C., called on Grant regularly, urging him to confirm his faith in God and the church. After one such visit, Reverend Newman announced to the press that he had baptized the former president at his request. Family members later disputed this, however, saying that Grant had tolerated Newman's visits and bedside prayers only because they comforted Mrs. Grant and he did not wish to be rude to the minister. Indeed, Grant had little use for organized religion. However, he many times expressed belief in God, the Bible, and an afterlife.

RECREATION: Grant enjoyed smoking—a lot. He began smoking a pipe, but when a war correspondent described him with a cigar in his teeth, people from all over the country sent him some 10,000 cigars. He gave many away, but the rest he smoked himself at the rate of 20 cigars a day, a habit that likely contributed to the mouth cancer he developed in later years. Grant also liked to draw and paint and drive fast horses. As president he once was stopped and cited for speeding and paid a $20 fine.

EARLY ROMANCE: The identity of any girlfriend Grant may have had as a youth is unknown. Biographer W. E. Woodward suggested that he was not sexually active. "It is as certain as any historical fact can be," wrote Woodward, "that Grant was never immersed in love in the manner of the great lovers; that he never gave himself wholly, at any time, to its ardors. With him love was a function rather than a passion."[6]

MARRIAGE: Ulysses S. Grant, 26, married Julia Boggs Dent, 22, on August 22, 1848, at the bride's home in St. Louis. Born at White Haven plantation west of St. Louis on January 26, 1826, the daughter of Colonel Frederick Dent, a slaveholding planter and merchant, and Ellen Wrenshall Dent, Julia attended a private school in St. Louis, where she excelled in art and voice. She was rather plain in appearance and squinted through crossed eyes. She met Grant through her brother, a classmate of his at West Point. During a visit to White Haven in 1844 Grant was driving her in a buggy when they came to a bridge flooded by a suddenly swollen creek. Julia was reluctant to attempt the crossing, but Grant assured her it was safe. Still unconvinced, she grasped his arm, warning, "I'm going to cling to you no matter what happens." After successfully negotiating the bridge, Grant turned to her and asked, "How would you like to cling to me for the rest of your life?"[7] With that proposal and its acceptance, the couple embarked on a four-year engagement during which they saw each other only once. Neither of their fathers approved of the match—hers because as a career soldier Grant's prospects seemed bleak; his because the Dents were slaveholders. In fact, Grant's parents refused to attend the wedding, though they did come to accept Julia. As First Lady, Mrs. Grant entertained lavishly; the social highlight of the Grant years was the White House wedding of their daughter in 1874. Following her husband's death in 1885, Mrs. Grant lived in New York City, where she found comfort in her friendship with Varina Davis, wife of Jefferson Davis. She died on December 14, 1902, in Washington, D.C. She was buried at Grant's Tomb in New York City.

MILITARY SERVICE: Grant was a professional soldier. He served in the army during 1843–1854 and 1861–1869, rising from second lieutenant to general. He fought in the Mexican War and Civil War (see "Career before the Presidency").

CAREER BEFORE THE PRESIDENCY: On graduation from West Point in 1843, Grant was commissioned a brevet second lieutenant and assigned to the Fourth Infantry at Jefferson Barracks, Missouri. His commission was made permanent in 1845.

    Mexican War, 1846–1848. Grant privately opposed the war, believing the United States to be the aggressors. "I have never altogether forgiven myself for going into that," he later wrote. "I do not think there was ever a more wicked war than that waged by the United States on Mexico. I thought so at the time, when I was a youngster, only I had not moral courage enough to resign."[8]

Serving under General Zachary Taylor and later under General Winfield Scott, he took part in the battles of Palo Alto and Resaca de la Palma (both May 1846), the capture of Monterrey (September 1846) and Veracruz (March 1847), and engagements at Cerro Gordo (April 1847), Churubusco (August 1847), and Molino del Rey (September 1847). On the occupation of Mexico City (September 1847), he was promoted to first lieutenant. He was regimental quartermaster and commissary at Tacubaya during 1847–1848.

Returning to the United States, he was assigned to posts at Sacketts Harbor, New York (1848–1849, 1851–1852), Detroit (1849–1851), San Francisco (1852), and Vancouver, Oregon Territory (1852–1853). In 1853 he was promoted to captain and made company commander at Humboldt Bay, California. He reportedly was drinking heavily during this period. In 1854 he resigned from the army and joined his wife and children on a farm outside St. Louis. He cast his first vote for president in 1856. Fearing that the election of John C. Frémont would lead to secession, he voted for Democrat James Buchanan. He struggled for four years to make a go at raising crops and livestock and supplemented his income by selling wood in St. Louis. But in 1858 he fell ill with "fever and ague" and was forced to sell out. That winter he joined Harry Boggs, a cousin-in-law, in forming a real estate agency in St. Louis, but that too proved unprofitable. While in St. Louis he ran unsuccessfully for county engineer and worked a couple months at the U.S. customhouse. In 1860 he moved to Galena, Illinois, where he clerked in his father's leather goods store.

Civil War, 1861–1865. With the outbreak of the Civil War, Grant requested recommission in the army but never received a reply. Meanwhile he helped organize Galena volunteers and served as mustering officer under the Illinois adjutant general. In June 1861 he was appointed colonel of the Twenty-first Illinois Infantry, stationed in Missouri, and in August was promoted to brigadier general. As commander of the southeast Missouri district, he captured Fort Donelson, Tennessee in February 1862, the first major Union victory and one that launched Grant's national reputation. There he uttered his famous ultimatum to Confederate General Simon B. Buckner, "No terms except an unconditional and immediate surrender can be accepted," earning him the nickname Unconditional Surrender Grant. For this victory, Grant was promoted to major general. At Shiloh, near Pittsburg Landing, Tennessee in April 1862, Grant, reinforced by Generals D. C. Buell and Lew Wallace, took heavy casualties but succeeded in loosening the Confederate grip on Tennessee. In laying siege to Vicksburg May–July 1863, he starved into submission this last rebel bastion on the Mississippi and thus cut the Confederacy in two. Soon thereafter he was made commander of the military division of Mississippi. After victories at Lookout Mountain and Missionary Ridge, Tennessee, in November 1863, he was promoted to lieutenant general and commander of all Union armies in March 1864. Possessed of superior numbers of forces, Grant doggedly waged a war of attrition against the army of General Robert E. Lee. Withstanding tens of thousands of casualties himself, he whittled away at irreplaceable Confederate ranks in the Wildnerness campaign May–June 1864. Lee formally surrendered to Grant at Appomattox, Virginia, on April 9, 1865. In victory Grant was magnanimous, exacting lenient terms of surrender: Confederate officers were permitted to return home with their sidearms; mounted forces were permitted to keep their horses; all were treated with dignity. In July 1866 Grant was promoted to general of the army, the first commander since Washington to hold that rank. He served as secretary of war ad interim during 1867–1868.

REPUBLICAN PRESIDENTIAL NOMINATION, 1868: As Republicans convened in Chicago in May 1868, Grant had no serious opposition for the nomination; he was nominated unanimously on the first ballot. House Speaker Schuyler Colfax of Indiana was nominated for vice president on the sixth ballot, beating out the early favorite, Senator Benjamin F. Wade of Ohio. The Republican platform supported black suffrage in the South but agreed to let northern states decide for themselves whether to enfranchise blacks, opposed using greenbacks to redeem U.S. bonds, encouraged immigration and endorsed full rights for naturalized citizens, and favored Radical Reconstruction as distinct from the more lenient policy of President Andrew Johnson.

OPPONENT: Horatio Seymour (1810–1886) of New York; Democrat. Born at Pompey Hill, New York, Seymour was admitted to the New York bar in 1832 and soon became active in local Democratic party affairs. He settled in Utica and was elected its mayor in 1842. As a New York state assemblyman 1842 and 1844–1845, he promoted canal development. Elected governor of New York in 1852, he undertook reforms in education and prisons but was defeated for reelection in 1854 largely because he vetoed a state prohibition bill, invoking the wrath of the powerful temperance forces. With the outbreak of the Civil War, he loyally supported the Union and the war effort of President Lincoln, whose election he had opposed. However, he denounced the suspension of habeas corpus and other emergency measures undertaken by the administration. Returned to the governorship in 1862, he put down the New York City draft riots of 1863, but many believed that his outspoken opposition to conscription had touched off the disturbance in the first place. He also opposed Emancipation and called for a negotiated settlement of the war. He was defeated for reelection in 1864. At the Democratic national convention in New York City in July 1868, Seymour was a delegate, keynote speaker, and convention chairman. He supported Chief Justice Salmon P. Chase for the nomination and genuinely discouraged his own candidacy. The front-runner in early balloting was George H. Pendleton of Ohio, who led on the first 15 tallies, followed in varying order by incumbent president Andrew Johnson, Winfield S. Hancock of Pennsylvania, Sanford E. Church of New York, Asa Packer of Pennsylvania, Joel Parker of New Jersey, James E. English of Connecticut, James R. Doolittle of Wisconsin, and Thomas A. Hendricks of Indiana. The unpopular Johnson, having narrowly survived impeachment, reached his peak strength of 65 votes on the first ballot, less than one-third of the total necessary for nomination, thus losing his bid for election as president in his own right. Meanwhile, Seymour made it on the board only once, garnering just 9 votes on the fourth ballot. On the sixteenth ballot, Hancock took the lead and held it through the twenty-first tally. On the next vote Hendricks surged ahead, and Seymour picked up 21 Ohio delegates. Seymour continued to insist that he was not a candidate, but before the results of the twenty-second ballot could be announced, the convention stampeded to nominate him unanimously. He reluctantly answered the call. Francis P. Blair of Missouri was nominated for vice president. The Democratic platform called for amnesty for all former rebels, vowed to leave it to the southern states to decide whether to grant black suffrage, endorsed the use of greenbacks to redeem bonds, favored dismantling the Freedmen's Bureau and other vestiges of Radical Reconstruction, and supported full rights for naturalized citizens. After his defeat by Grant, Seymour remained active in party affairs and joined reformers in breaking the Tweed Ring in New York.

CAMPAIGN AND THE ISSUES, 1868: Grant took no part in the campaign and made no promises. A line in his letter of acceptance of the nomination became the Republican campaign theme—"Let us have peace." After four years of civil war, three years of wrangling over Reconstruction, and the attempted impeachment of a president, the nation craved the peace Grant pledged to achieve. Francis P. Blair, the Democratic vice presidential nominee, was the most active of the candidates. But his prosouthern speeches alienated many moderate voters, and Seymour took to the stump to try to undo the damage. Seymour ignored the Democrats' soft-money plank, which advocated the use of greenbacks to redeem government bonds, and thus the issue was not a factor in the campaign. The main issue was Reconstruction: Republicans pledged to continue the radical programs enacted over President Andrew Johnson's veto. Seymour promised a lenient policy designed to reintegrate the southern states into the Union without recrimination. On the low road, Republicans alleged that insanity ran through the Seymour family, citing as evidence the suicide of his father. Republicans waged a "bloody shirt" campaign, tagging the opposition as the party of secession and treason—an image that was to haunt Democrats for many years to come. Seymour enjoyed the support of white southerners, but Radical Reconstruction had disfranchised many former rebels while giving the vote to former slaves, who voted overwhelmingly for Grant and the party of Lincoln. But Grant's greatest asset was his enormous popularity as a war hero. Although Seymour gave him a good race in the popular voting, he was buried in the electoral college.

ELECTION AS PRESIDENT, FIRST TERM, 1868:

Popular Vote: Grant (Republican), 3,012,833 (53%); Seymour (Democrat), 2,703,249 (47%).

Electoral Vote: Grant, 214; Seymour, 80.

States Carried: Grant won the electoral votes of 26 states—Alabama, Arkansas, California, Connecticut, Florida, Illinois, Indiana, Iowa, Kansas, Maine, Massachusetts, Michigan, Minnesota, Missouri, Nebraska, Nevada, New Hampshire, North Carolina, Ohio, Pennsylvania, Rhode Island, South Carolina, Tennessee, Vermont, West Virginia, and Wisconsin. Seymour won the electoral votes of 8 states—Delaware, Georgia, Kentucky, Louisiana, Maryland, New Jersey, New York, and Oregon. Three states of the defunct Confederacy—Mississippi, Texas, and Virginia—had not yet been readmitted to the Union and thus were excluded from the election.

REPUBLICAN NOMINATION FOR REELECTION AS PRESIDENT, 1872: Grant's renomination was assured as Republicans convened in Philadelphia in June 1872. Vice President Colfax was denied renomination, largely for his part in the Crédit Mobilier scandal. Senator Henry Wilson of Massachusetts was nominated in his place. The Republican platform denounced racial and religious discrimination, applauded women's "admission to wider spheres of influence," and advocated the abolition of the franking privilege, a continued hard-money policy, and expanded foreign trade and shipbuilding.

OPPONENT: Horace Greeley (1811–1872) of New York; Liberal Republican, also endorsed by the Democrats. Born in Amherst, New Hampshire, Greeley was raised amid poverty and had little formal education, although he was a brilliant child, able to read at age three. He was apprenticed to a printer in his youth and thus learned the rudiments of journalism. Moving to New York City, he founded the *New Yorker* in 1834 and seven years later the *New York Tribune*, destined to become under his guidance among the most influential dailies of the nineteenth century. In its pages Greeley editorially championed the rights of workingmen, promoted a protective tariff, opposed slavery, denounced the Mexican War, and criticized big business. He also encouraged development of the frontier, summarizing his philosophy in a famous bit of advice—"Go West, young man, and grow up with the country." He helped establish the Republican party in 1854. As civil war loomed, Greeley at first advocated letting the South secede. But with the outbreak of hostilities, he urged vigorous prosecution of the war and pressed for immediate emancipation of slaves. After the war he offered limited support to Radical Reconstruction but also pleaded for amnesty for the rebels and was among those to sign a bail bond for the release of former Confederate president Jefferson Davis. Greeley supported Grant in 1868 but, disappointed in his performance, joined Liberal Republicans in seeking to deny his reelection. At a convention of this anti-Grant faction held in Cincinnati in May 1872, Greeley vied for the nomination with Charles Francis Adams of Massachusetts, the son of President John Quincy Adams. The two exchanged the lead on the first several ballots; Greeley was nominated on the sixth tally. B. Gratz Brown of Missouri was nominated for vice president. The Liberal Republican platform denounced the corruption of the Grant administration and called for reform of the civil service, universal amnesty for former rebels, restoration of home rule in the southern states, a one-term presidency, and resumption of specie payments. Democrats were in such disarray that they offered no candidate. Instead, at their convention in Baltimore in July 1872, delegates endorsed the Greeley-Brown ticket as their only chance to defeat Grant—this despite Greeley's long-standing antipathy to Democratic principles. Within weeks after his defeat by Grant, Greeley died in Pleasantville, New York.

CAMPAIGN AND THE ISSUES, 1872: "Never in American history have two more unfit men been offered to the country for the highest office,"[9] wrote Eugene H. Rooseboom of this contest in his history of presidential elections. Grant remained aloof, allowing subordinates to explain away the scandals that had rocked the administration. Greeley opened his campaign in August with a speech in Portland, Maine, and carried the fight for clean, honest government across the country. Despite Greeley's long-standing opposition to slavery, white southerners reluctantly rallied to him rather than face four more years of Radical Reconstruction under Grant, whereas former slaves remained loyal to the president and the party of Lincoln. Business interests and veterans supported Grant; the major nonpartisan newspapers endorsed Greeley. In the end, Grant's prestige as a war hero and the belief that he personally had not been involved in the scandals carried the day for Republicans.

REELECTION AS PRESIDENT, 1872:

Popular Vote: Grant (Republican), 3,597,070 (56%); Greeley (Liberal Republican, Democrat), 2,834,079 (44%).

Electoral Vote. Grant, 286; Greeley, 0. Greeley died after the general election but before the electoral votes were cast. The 66 votes that were expected to go to Greeley were divided as follows: Thomas A. Hendricks of Illinois, 42; B. Gratz Brown of Missouri, 18; Charles J. Jenkins of Georgia, 2; David Davis of Illinois, 1; not counted, 3.

States Carried: Grant won the electoral votes of 29 states—Alabama, California, Connecticut, Delaware, Florida, Illinois, Indiana, Iowa, Kansas, Maine, Massachusetts, Michigan, Minnesota, Mississippi, Nebraska, Nevada, New Hampshire, New Jersey, New York, North Carolina, Ohio, Oregon, Pennsylvania, Rhode Island, South Carolina, Vermont, Virginia, West Virginia, and Wisconsin. Greeley, having died, won the electoral vote of no state. The 6 states that were expected to go to Greeley were divided as follows: Hendricks won the majority of electoral votes in 4 states—Kentucky, Maryland, Pennsylvania, and Texas. Brown won the majority of electoral votes in 2 states—Georgia and Missouri.

INAUGURAL ADDRESS (FIRST): March 4, 1869. ". . . The country having just emerged from a great rebellion, many questions will come before it for settlement in the next four years which preceding Administrations have never had to deal with. In meeting these it is desirable that they should be approached calmly, without prejudice, hate, or sectional pride, remembering that the greatest good to the greatest number is the object to be attained.

"This requires security of persons, property, and free religious and political opinion in every part of our common country, without regard to local prejudice. All laws to secure these ends will receive my best efforts for their enforcement. . . ."

INAUGURAL ADDRESS (SECOND): March 4, 1873. ". . . The effects of the late civil strife have been to free the slave and make him a citizen. Yet he is not possessed of the civil rights which citizenship should carry with it. This is wrong, and should be corrected. To this correction I stand committed, so far as Executive influence can avail.

"Social equality is not a subject to be legislated upon, nor shall I ask that anything be done to advance the social status of the colored man, except to give him a fair chance to develop what there is good in him, give him access to the schools, and when he travels let him feel assured that his conduct will regulate the treatment and fare he will receive . . ."

VICE PRESIDENTS: Schuyler Colfax (1823–1885), of Indiana, served 1869–1873. Born in New York City, Colfax as a youth moved with his family to New Carlisle, Indiana. He studied law for a time but settled on a career in journalism. He acquired the *South Bend Free Press* in 1845, changed its banner to the *St. Joseph Valley Register*, and developed it into a leading Whig organ. Having helped organize the Republican party in Indiana in 1854, he was elected to the U.S. House for 1855–1869; he served his last six years as Speaker. In 1872 it was revealed that, when Speaker, Colfax had purchased at a deep discount from market value 20 shares of stock in the Crédit Mobilier company, which constructed the Union Pacific Railroad. The shares were sold cheaply to Colfax and other members of Congress to help head off an investigation of corruption in the construction of the railroad. Although he was never formally charged with bribery, his reputation suffered irreparable damage, and he was dumped from the ticket in 1872. Colfax retired to the lecture circuit. Enroute to a speaking engagement he stepped off a train at Minkato, Minnesota, into 30-below-zero weather and fell dead of a heart attack.

Henry Wilson (1812–1875), of Massachusetts, served 1873–1875. Born Jeremiah Jones Colbath in Farmington, New Hampshire, he changed his name to Henry Wilson, after the subject of an obscure biography he had read. Raised in poverty, he was indentured to a farmer for 11 years, during which time he educated himself by reading virtually every book he was able to find. Having worked off his bond at 21, he learned the shoemaker's trade in Natick, Massachusetts, and by 1839 had acquired his own shoe factory. His purse now secure, he entered politics, serving as a Whig in both houses of the state legislature 1840–1846 and 1850–1852. He helped found the short-lived Free Soil party in 1848 and, with its demise, drifted into the American, or Know-Nothing, party, attracted by its potential as a force to oppose slavery rather than by its nativist philosophy. His antislavery sentiment ultimately found expression in the new Republican party. As U.S. senator 1855–1873, he served as chairman of the Military Affairs Committee during the Civil War and generally supported Radical Reconstruction. While vice president he suffered a pair of strokes and died in office.

CABINET:

Secretary of State. (1) Elihu B. Washburne (1816–1887), of Illinois, served March 5–16, 1869. He resigned to become minister to France, remaining in Paris amid the siege of that city during the Franco-Prussian War. (2) Hamilton Fish (1808–1893), of New York, served 1869–1877. He reorganized and streamlined the department, adhered to the merit system as the basis for promotion, negotiated the Treaty of Washington (see "Administration"), and averted war with Spain by persuading Grant to remain neutral in Cuba's struggle for independence.

Secretary of the Treasury. (1) George S. Boutwell (1818–1905), of Massachusetts, served 1869–1873. Grant's first choice, A. T. Stewart, prominent merchant of New York, was duly appointed and confirmed but was barred from taking office on discovery of an obscure 1789 conflict-of-interest law disqualifying from the office of Treasury secretary anyone involved in trade or commerce. Boutwell ordered the release of federal gold to thwart the attempt of Fisk and Gould to corner the gold market (see "Administration: Scandals"). He resigned to enter the U.S. Senate. (2) William A. Richardson (1821–1896), of Massachusetts, served 1873–1874. He was held responsible for the misdeeds of his appointee John D. Sanborn, collector of delinquent taxes (see "Administration: Scandals"), and was forced to resign. (3) Benjamin H. Bristow (1832–1896), of Kentucky, served 1874–1876. He purged corrupt officials and exposed the Whiskey Ring scandal (see "Administration"). When his investigation threatened to implicate Orville E. Babcock, Grant's private secretary, Bristow was forced to resign. He was a candidate for the Republican presidential nomination in 1876. (4) Lot M. Morrill (1812–1883), of Maine, served 1876–1877. He had served as chairman of the Senate appropriations committee.

Secretary of War. (1) John A. Rawlins (1831–1869), of Illinois, served March–September 1869. A friend of Grant from Galena, Illinois, he had served as Grant's assistant adjutant general during the Civil War and later as his chief of staff. He died in office of tuberculosis. (2) William T. Sherman (1820–1891), of Ohio, served September–October 1869. (3) William W. Belknap (1829–1890), of Iowa, served 1869–1876. In 1876 the House voted to impeach Belknap on charges of accepting bribes from traders at Indian posts. As the Senate prepared for his trial, he hastily resigned. The Senate trial proceeded anyway; the vote for his conviction was 35–25, a majority but less than the two-thirds needed to find him guilty. Many senators voting for acquittal did so not because they believed him innocent but because they believed the Senate lacked jurisdiction to impeach an official after he had resigned. (4) Alphonso Taft

(1810–1891), of Ohio, served March–May 1876. He resigned to become attorney general (see also "William Howard Taft, 27th President," "Father"). (5) James D. Cameron (1833–1918), of Pennsylvania, served 1876–1877. He was the son of Simon Cameron, war secretary in the Lincoln administration.

Attorney General. (1) Ebenezer R. Hoar (1816–1895), of Massachusetts, served 1869–1870. A capable administrator who rewarded merit rather than political loyalty, he filled nine newly created federal judgeships with men of distinction and thus alienated congressional Republicans, who had hoped to place partisans on the enlarged federal bench. The Senate had its revenge in refusing to confirm Hoar as Grant's nominee for the Supreme Court. In 1871 the president appointed Hoar to the commission negotiating the *Alabama* claims (see "Administration: Treaty of Washington"). (2) Amos T. Akerman (1821–1880), of Georgia, served 1870–1871. He opposed the railroad interests, who prevailed on Grant to dismiss him. In asking for his resignation, Grant paid tribute to Akerman's "zeal, integrity, and industry" and offered as compensation a judgeship or diplomatic post, which Akerman refused. (3) George H. Williams (1820–1910), of Oregon, served 1872–1875. He suppressed an investigation of election fraud in his home state, which activity was revealed while he was awaiting Senate confirmation as Grant's nominee for chief justice; his nomination was withdrawn. (4) Edwards Pierrepont (1817–1892), of New York, served 1875–1876. A lifelong Democrat, he nevertheless had supported Grant. He prosecuted those involved in the Whiskey Ring conspiracy (see "Administration: Scandals"). He resigned to become minister to Great Britain. (5) Alfonso Taft served 1876–1877. Transferred from war secretary, he helped arrange the electoral commission to settle the disputed presidential election of 1876.

Secretary of the Navy. (1) Adolph E. Borie (1809–1880), of Pennsylvania, served March–June 1869. A wealthy entrepreneur with neither political experience nor knowledge of the navy, he soon resigned, explaining, "I am only a figurehead; the department is managed by Admiral Porter."[10] (2) George M. Robeson (1829–1897), of New Jersey, served 1869–1877. Charges of waste and favoritism prompted a congressional investigation, but nothing came of it. He sent out Charles F. Hall on the North Polar Expedition of 1871; Robeson Channel is named for him.

Postmaster General. (1) John A. J. Creswell (1828–1891), of Maryland, served 1869–1874. He introduced penny postcards and reorganized the department. His proposals for the creation of a postal savings system and the postal telegraph were later adopted. (2) James W. Marshall (1822–1910), of Virginia, served July–August 1874. (3) Marshall Jewell (1825–1883), of Connecticut, served 1874–1876. (4) James N. Tyner (1826–1904), of Indiana, served 1876–1877.

Secretary of the Interior. (1) Jacob D. Cox (1828–1900), of Ohio, served 1869–1870. He rewarded merit within the department and successfully resisted patronage. He resigned over a policy dispute with the president. (2) Columbus Delano (1809–1896), of Ohio, served 1870–1875. He presided over an investigation of fraud in the Bureau of Indian Affairs. (3) Zachariah Chandler (1813–1879), of Michigan, served 1875–1877. Grant first met Chandler in 1851 in Detroit, where he was stationed in the army and Chandler operated a dry goods store: Grant slipped on the ice in front of his store and swore out a summons against him. Chandler was convicted but was fined just six cents.

ADMINISTRATION: March 4, 1869–March 3, 1877.

Scandals. Though rigidly incorruptible himself, Grant was the first president whose administration was marked by major scandal: (1) Black Friday. Speculators James Fisk and Jay Gould set out to corner the gold market. To ensure that the administration would not foil their scheme by dumping federal gold reserves onto the market, Fisk and Gould employed the president's brother-in-law Abel R. Corbin to exercise his influence with the White House. They also arranged to be seen entertaining the president aboard Fisk's yacht, thus encouraging speculation that Grant was in their corner. The pair then began to purchase gold aggressively, driving its price up from $140 to $163½ in four days. Finally realizing that he had been duped, Grant ordered Treasury Secretary Boutwell to sell off immediately $4 million in federal gold. Its price nosedived, ending the crisis, but not before many investors and some businesses were ruined—on Black Friday, September 24, 1869. (2) Crédit Mobilier. News of this scandal broke during the 1872 presidential campaign. Officers of the Crédit Mobilier holding company had skimmed off huge profits in the federally subsidized construction of the Union Pacific Railroad. They sought to head off an investigation of their practices by selling shares of stock at a deep discount from market value to selected members of Congress. Serving as the company's agent in the bribery scheme was Republican Representative Oakes Ames of Massachusetts. Among those accused of accepting the stock were House Speaker (later vice president) Schuyler Colfax and Representative (later president) James A. Garfield of Ohio. (3) Delinquent tax corruption. Treasury Secretary William A. Richardson appointed John D. Sanborn as special agent in charge of collecting delinquent taxes under an arrangement that allowed Sanborn to retain as his fee a whopping 50 percent of all revenue collected. A House investigation in 1874 revealed that he had collected more than $400,000 in back taxes, half of which he kept. Exposure of the scandal forced the resignation of Secretary Richardson. (4) Whiskey Ring. Hundreds of distillers and federal officials were suspected of diverting millions of dollars in liquor taxes into their own pockets in a conspiracy uncovered by Treasury Secretary Benjamin H. Bristow in 1875. Grant at first called for swift retribution. "Let no guilty man escape,"[11] he instructed prosecutors. But when the scandal reached to his own personal secretary, Orville E. Babcock, Grant interceded on his behalf. Still, 110 conspirators were convicted. (5) Belknap bribery. In 1876 it was revealed that War Secretary W. W. Belknap had been taking annual kickbacks from traders at Indian posts. At first, such payments went to his wife, but on her death he took the bribes directly. He was acquitted of impeachment charges only because he resigned before the Senate trial got underway.

Treaty of Washington, 1871. The United States and Great Britain agreed to submit to international arbitration of the *Alabama* claims, that is, the U.S. suit against Britain for damages inflicted during the Civil War on Union vessels by the *Alabama* and other Confederate warships constructed in British ports. Meeting in Geneva during 1871, the arbitration panel, consisting of Charles Francis Adams of the United States and one member each from Great Britain, Italy, Switzerland, and Brazil, awarded the United States $15.5 million.

Reconstruction. Grant continued federal occupation of the South. In 1872 he signed legislation dismantling the Freedman's Bureau, which had aided blacks in their transition from slavery to independence. Empowered by a series of so-called force bills (1870–1871), the administration threatened the use of armed force against states denying the vote to blacks and against terrorist organizations, notably the Ku Klux Klan, which attempted to intimidate blacks into submission. In parts of South Carolina, where the Klan was particularly active, Grant suspended habeas corpus and authorized mass arrests. The Civil Rights Act of 1875 assured blacks "full and equal enjoyment of the accommodations, advantages, facilities, and privileges of inns, public conveyances on land or water, theaters, and other places of public amusement." The Supreme Court, however, declared the law unconstitutional in 1883.

Panic of 1873. The failure of Jay Cooke and Company in September 1873 precipitated a financial panic that led to a five-year depression, the worst up to that time. Contributing causes of the slump included a European depression touched off by the crash of the Vienna stock market earlier in the year, overextension of the railroads, and the depressed state of the insurance industry in the wake of the great Chicago fire of 1871 and a rash of lesser blazes in other cities. Some three million were unemployed; business failures totaled $500 million.

Resumption of Specie Act, 1875. A proponent of hard money, President Grant signed into law this act, which directed the Treasury secretary to accumulate gold reserves sufficient to redeem in gold all greenbacks tendered after January 1, 1879. Although denounced by soft-money advocates in the West, the act strengthened public confidence in U.S. currency.

Constitutional Amendment Ratified: Fifteenth Amendment (1870). "The right of citizens of the United States to vote shall not be denied or abridged by the United States or by any State on account of race, color, or previous condition of servitude."

State Admitted to the Union: Colorado (1876).

SUPREME COURT APPOINTMENTS: (1) William Strong (1808–1895), of Pennsylvania, served as associate justice 1870–1880. Appointed to one of two seats created by congressional expansion of the Court from seven to the present-day nine justices, Strong wrote the majority (5–4) opinion in the Legal Tender Case (1871), upholding the constitutionality of the 1862 Legal Tender Act. (2) Joseph P. Bradley (1813–1892), of New Jersey, served as associate justice 1870–1892. Appointed the same day as Justice Strong, he voted with him to uphold the 1862 Legal Tender Act. Because the votes of Strong and Bradley were the deciding factors in overturning Chief Justice Salmon P. Chase's opinion in *Hepburn* v. *Griswold* (1870), which had declared the Legal Tender Act unconstitutional, critics charged, though never proved, that Grant had packed the Court specifically to sustain the wartime currency measure. In *The Collector* v. *Day* (1871), in which the Supreme Court held that the salaries of state officials must be exempt from federal income taxes, Bradley dissented, in what has since become the prevailing view, arguing, "No man ceases to be a citizen of the United States by being an officer under the state government,"[12] Bradley spoke for the majority in the Civil Rights cases (1883), which struck down the Civil Rights, or Public Accommodations, Act of 1875 (see "Administration: Reconstruction"). In his opinion, the law interjected the federal government into social matters—an area, he claimed, not contemplated by the Thirteenth or Fourteenth amendments. Bradley was the swing member of the electoral commission that awarded the 1876 presidential election to Rutherford B. Hayes. (3) Ward Hunt (1810–1886), of New York, served as associate justice 1873–1882. A virtual nonentity on the Court, he was disabled within a few years of his appointment but refused to step down until Congress enacted special legislation allowing him to retire at full pay. (4) Morrison R. Waite (1816–1888), of Ohio, served as chief justice 1874–1888. A relatively obscure Toledo attorney without judicial experience, Waite was Grant's fourth choice to lead the Court, his first three nominees having either declined or been withdrawn. Yet once on the bench, Waite proved an able administrator and hardworking jurist, writing more than 1,000 opinions in 14 years. Although basically a strict constructionist and social conservative, he construed the due process clause of the Fourteenth Amendment to permit states to regulate businesses "affected with a public interest." This ruling in *Munn* v. *Illinois* (1877) and others of the so-called Granger cases offered relief to farmers long victimized by the artificially high prices charged by railroad and grain elevator monopolies; it forms the constitutional basis of modern regulatory agencies. In *Minor* v. *Happersett* (1875), Waite sustained the right of states to deny women the vote. In *Reynolds* v. *United States* (1878), Waite delivered the majority opinion in upholding the antipolygamy laws directed against the Mormons.

RANKING IN 1962 HISTORIANS POLL: Grant ranked thirtieth of 31 presidents, better of the 2 "failures." He ranked above Harding, below Buchanan.

RETIREMENT: March 4, 1877–July 23, 1885. After attending the inaugural of his successor, Rutherford B. Hayes, Grant prepared for an extensive global tour. From the spring of 1877 to the fall of 1879 Mr. and Mrs. Grant and their son Jesse traveled throughout Europe, Asia, and Africa, meeting such dignitaries as Pope Leo XIII and Queen Victoria. His adventures abroad were chronicled in John Russell Young's *Around the World with General Grant* (1879). Less than a year after his return he visited Cuba, the West Indies, and Mexico. Retiring to Galena, Illinois, in 1880, he was that year the leading candidate for the Republican nomination. He led on each of the first 35 ballots, coming within 66 votes of becoming the first president to be nominated for a third term. He supported the eventual nominee, James A. Garfield. In 1881 Grant moved to New York City, where he invested all his money in creating the brokerage firm of Grant and Ward, a partnership between his son Ulysses S. Grant, Jr., and Ferdinand Ward. Grant borrowed still more money from William H. Vanderbilt to put at the firm's disposal. In 1884 Grant and Ward went bankrupt; Ward had kept the enterprise afloat by juggling the books and other illegal practices, for which he subsequently went to prison. Grant was left virtually penniless. Taking pity on the aging general, veteran showman P. T. Barnum offered to pay him $100,000 plus a percentage of gate receipts if Grant would permit him to put on public display his war trophies and the gifts he had received from world leaders. Grant declined the offer and instead gave these valuables to Vanderbilt as repayment of his loan. Grant earned some cash by writing a series of highly popular articles on the Civil War for *Century* magazine. Author Mark Twain, then part owner of Webster and Company, publishers, offered Grant a $25,000 advance against 20 percent royalties for his memoirs. From the fall of 1884, he raced against terminal cancer to complete the memoirs that would provide his widow financial security. Not long before he died, Congress also came to his aid in restoring to him his rank as general with full pay.

DEATH: July 23, 1885, about 8 A.M., Mount McGregor, New York. In the spring of 1884 Grant noted pain in his throat. Attended by Dr. Fordyce Barker and throat specialist Dr. John H. Douglas, Grant was given medicinal mouthwashes and ordered to stop smoking. By the next year he was beginning to lose his voice from time to time and was unable to talk or swallow without pain. A biopsy revealed cancer at the root of the tongue and spreading down the throat. In April 1885 the malignancy ate through an artery, causing severe hemorrhaging. His neck became so swollen that he wore a muffler to hide his disfigurement. Unable to swallow much food, he lost weight rapidly, falling from a hearty 200 pounds to the 130–145 range. To ease the pain, his throat was swabbed with cocaine solution, and he was given morphine injections. Eventually he became addicted to cocaine. In late June 1885 he moved to Mount McGregor, near Sarasota Springs, New York, where he put the finishing touches on his memoirs. He had lost his voice completely by now and was forced to communicate by notes. Realizing that the end was near, he wrote, "My life is precious of course to my family and would be to me if I could entirely recover. There never was one more willing to go than I am."[13] On July 22 he failed rapidly. His pulse faded, his breathing became shallow, and his hands and feet were cold. Asked if he wanted anything, he replied, "Water," his last word, and a sponge was touched to his lips. He died shortly thereafter. Mrs. Grant refused to authorize an autopsy. For several days his body lay in state in Albany and New York City. On August 8, 1885, an estimated one million persons turned out for the funeral procession to a temporary burial site in the city. In 1897 President William McKinley formally dedicated Grant's Tomb, the imposing monument overlooking the Hudson River from Riverside Drive, where he was finally laid to rest. Once a popular tourist attraction, Grant's Tomb has more recently been neglected.

GRANT PRAISED: "Grant had come out of the war the greatest of all. It is true that the rebels were on their last legs, and that the Southern ports were pretty effectually blockaded and that Grant was furnished with all the men that were needed or could be spared after he took command of the army of the Potomac. But Grant helped more than any one else to bring about this condition. His great victories at Donelson, Vicksburg, and Missionary Ridge all contributed to Appomattox. . . . Grant has treated me badly; but he was the right man in the right place during the war, and no matter what his faults were or are, the whole world can never write him down."[14]—President Andrew Johnson

"I have carefully searched the military records of both ancient and modern history, and have never found Grant's superior as a general."[15]—Former Confederate General Robert E. Lee

"Faithful and fearless as a volunteer soldier, intrepid and invincible as commander-in-chief of the Armies of the Union and confident as President of a reunited and strengthened nation, which his genius has been instrumental in achieving, he has our homage and that of the world; but brilliant as was his public character, we love him all the more for his homelife and homely virtues."[16]— President William McKinley, 1897

GRANT CRITICIZED: "Our noble army of the Mississippi is being wasted by the foolish, drunken, stupid Grant. He can't organize or control or fight an army. . . . There is not among the whole list of retired major-generals a man who is not Grant's superior."[17]—Murat Halstead, editor of *Cincinnati Gazette*, 1863

"He has used the public service of the Government as a machinery of corruption and personal influence, and has interfered with tyrannical arrogance in the political affairs of States and municipalities."[18]—Preamble of Liberal Republican party platform, 1872

"He has done more than any other President to degrade the character of

Cabinet officers by choosing them on the model of the military staff, because of their pleasant personal relation to him and not because of their national reputation and the public needs."[19]—Republican Representative James A. Garfield of Ohio, 1874

"The honest, simple-hearted soldier had not added prestige to the presidential office. He himself knew that he had failed . . . that he ought never to have been made President."[20]—Professor Woodrow Wilson of Princeton University, 1902

GRANT QUOTES: "Some of our generals failed because they worked out everything by rule. They knew what Frederick did at one place and Napoleon at another. They were always thinking about what Napoleon would do. Unfortunately for their plans the rebels would be thinking about something else."[21]

"It was my fortune, or misfortune, to be called to the office of Chief Executive without any previous political training. . . . Mistakes have been made, as all can see and I admit, but it seems to me oftener in the selections made of the assistants appointed to aid in carrying out the various duties of administering the Government."[22]—1876

"The truth is I am more of a farmer than a soldier. . . . I never went into the army without regret and never retired without pleasure."[23]—1878

BOOK BY GRANT: *Personal Memoirs of U. S. Grant* (2 vols., 1885–1886).

BOOKS ABOUT GRANT: Catton, Bruce. 3 works published by Little, Brown of Boston: *U.S. Grant and the American Military Tradition*, 1954; *Grant Moves South*, 1960; *Grant Takes Command*, 1969.

Goldhurst, Richard. *Many Are the Hearts: The Agony and the Triumph of Ulysses S. Grant*. New York: Reader's Digest Press, 1975.

Grant, Major General Ulysses S., III. *Ulysses S. Grant: Warrior and Statesman*. New York: Morrow, 1968.

Woodward, W. E. *Meet General Grant*. New York: Liveright, 1928.

NOTES

1 Richard Goldhurst, *Many Are the Hearts: The Agony and the Triumph of Ulysses S. Grant*, New York: Reader's Digest Press, 1975, pp. 33–34.

2 W. E. Woodward, *Meet General Grant*, New York: Liveright, 1928, p. 25.

3 Major General Ulysses S. Grant III, *Ulysses S. Grant: Warrior and Statesman*, New York: Morrow, 1968, p. 14.

4 *Personal Memoirs of U. S. Grant*, New York: Webster, 1885, p. 31.

5 Ibid., p. 38.

6 Woodward, p. 26.

7 Sol Barzman, *The First Ladies*, New York: Cowles, 1970, p. 162.

8 Woodward, p. 77.

9 Eugene H. Roseboom, *A History of Presidential Elections*, New York: Macmillian, 1957, p. 231.

10 Fletcher Pratt, *The Navy: A History*, Garden City, N.Y.: Garden City Publishing, 1938, p. 347.

11 Thomas A. Bailey, *The American Pageant: A History of the Republic*, Boston: Heath, 1966, p. 493.

12 Henry Steele Commager, ed., *Documents of American History*, New York: Crofts, 1945, Doc. no. 282, p. 70.

13 Goldhurst, pp. 226–227.

14 Lloyd Paul Stryker, *Andrew Johnson: A Study in Courage*, New York: Macmillan, 1929, p. 759.

15 Major General Ulysses S. Grant III, pp. 269–270.

16 Ibid., p. 457.

17 Woodward, p. 292.

18 A. K. McClure, *Our Presidents and How We Make Them*, New York: Harper & Bros., 1902, p. 232.

19 Harry James Brown and Frederick D. Williams, eds., *Diary of James A. Garfield*, East Lansing, Michigan.: Michigan State University Press, 1967, vol. II, p. 389.

20 Woodrow Wilson, *A History of the American People*, New York: Harper & Bros., 1902, vol. V, p. 112.

21 Dorothy Burne Goebel and Julius Goebel, Jr., *Generals in the White House*, Garden City, N.Y.: Doubleday, Doran, 1945, p. 26.

22 James D. Richardson, comp., *Messages and Papers of the Presidents*, Washington: Government Printing Office, 1897, Vol. VII, pp. 399–400.

23 Major General Ulysses S. Grant III, p. 367.

RUTHERFORD B. HAYES

19TH PRESIDENT

NAME: Rutherford Birchard Hayes. He was named after his father, Rutherford Hayes, and his mother, Sophia Birchard.

PHYSICAL DESCRIPTION: A robust, broad-shouldered, handsome figure, Hayes stood 5 feet 8½ inches tall and usually weighed 170–180 pounds. He had a large head with a high forehead, deeply set blue eyes, a straight nose, firm lips, and sound, straight teeth. The auburn hair of his youth turned a dark brown and then white. From his service in the Civil War until his death, he wore a full beard. His health generally was sound. He dressed simply, often in ill-fitting clothes.

PERSONALITY: "Hayes was never a solitary, a boy of moods," wrote biographer H. J. Eckenrode. "He had no seasons of exaltation followed by depression. . . . All his life he liked society and shone in it in a modest way—not sparkling, not brilliant, but pleasing, satisfying. He had a gift of friendship and most of those he loved in youth he loved in age."[1] As a young man, however, Hayes went through a period of great inner tension, which he himself attributed to a fear that he would one day lose his mind, as some relatives, on both sides of his family, had done. Overcoming this fear, he matured into a relaxed, easygoing fellow, a good conversationalist, and a keen observer of human nature. He genuinely loved people and was interested in their thoughts and problems. When traveling by train, he invariably sat in the smoking car, eager to strike up a conversation. He had a remarkable memory for the names and faces of the most casual acquaintances. As a politician he respected the opposition and welcomed constructive criticism. Although not regarded as a great orator in his day, he delivered well-planned, reasoned addresses in a clear, pleasant voice.

ANCESTORS: Hayes was of Scotch and English ancestry. His great[3]-grandfather George Hayes emigrated from Scotland in 1680 and settled first at Windsor and later at Salmon Brook, Connecticut. His great-great-grandfather Daniel Hayes was kidnapped by Indians and held seven years before a missionary secured his release. Both his grandfathers, Rutherford Hayes and Roger Birchard, fought in the American Revolution, as did three of his four great-grandfathers.

FATHER: Rutherford Hayes (1787–1822), merchant, farmer. Born in Brattleboro, Vermont, redheaded Rutherford Hayes began as a store clerk in Wilmington, Vermont, and became a partner in Noyes, Mann, and Hayes, merchants of Dummerston, Vermont. In 1817 he opened his own store at Delaware, Ohio, where he quickly prospered. Five years later, however, he contracted a fever and died suddenly, 11 weeks before the birth of his son.

MOTHER: Sophia Birchard Hayes (1792–1866). A native of Wilmington, Vermont, she married Rutherford Hayes in 1813. After the death of her husband, she supported her family by renting out a farm for one-third the crops and one-half the fruit it yielded. Her brother Sardis Birchard also lent her support. She died at Columbus, Ohio, when her son was a member of Congress.

SIBLING: Hayes had one older sister to live to maturity—Mrs. Fanny A. Platt of Columbus, Ohio. She worked a profound influence on Hayes as he grew up. "The confidante of all my life," he called her. The unusually close bond between them continued even after each married. "She loved me," he commented, "as an only sister loves a brother whom she imagines almost perfect, and I loved her as an only brother loves a sister who is perfect."[2] She died in 1856 shortly after delivering stillborn twins. Her death crushed Hayes.

CHILDREN: Hayes had four sons and a daughter to live to maturity.

Sardis Birchard (known as Birchard Austin) Hayes (1853–1926), lawyer. Born in Cincinnati, he graduated from Cornell University (1874) and Harvard Law School (1877). He settled in Toledo, Ohio, where he prospered as a real estate and tax attorney.

James Webb (known as Webb Cook) Hayes (1856–1934), businessman, soldier. Born in Cincinnati, he followed his older brother to Cornell and on graduation became presidential secretary during his father's term. His unofficial duties included escorting single ladies at White House functions and tactfully closing parties that dragged on too long. He later helped found a small business that eventually grew into Union Carbide. During the Spanish-American War, he was commissioned a major and served in Cuba, Puerto Rico, and the Philippines. He was awarded the Congressional Medal of Honor "for distinguished gallantry" in slipping through enemy lines in the Philippines alone at night to get assistance for his beleaguered force and was promoted to lieutenant colonel. During the Boxer Rebellion, he was with the American relief force that marched into Peking to escort Americans to safety. Prior to U.S. entry into World War I, Hayes volunteered for service with British and French forces in Italy.

Rutherford Platt Hayes (1858–1931), library official. Born in Cincinnati, he attended the University of Michigan, graduated from Cornell University (1880), and did post graduate work at Boston Institute of Technology. He worked as a bank clerk in Fremont, Ohio, for a time but devoted most of his life to promoting libraries. He also helped develop Asheville, North Carolina, into a health and tourist resort.

Frances "Fanny" Hayes (1867–1950). Born in Cincinnati, she was educated at a private girls school in Farmington, Connecticut. In 1897 she married Ensign Harry Eaton Smith of Fremont, Ohio, later an instructor at the U.S. Naval Academy.

Scott Russell Hayes (1871–1923), businessman. Born in Columbus, he was still a youngster during his father's term as president. At six he and his sister played host to other Washington area children in the first Easter egg roll conducted on the White House lawn. He was an executive with railroad service companies in New York City.

BIRTH: Hayes was born posthumously about 9:30 P.M. October 4, 1822, in a west room of the family home on Williams Street in Delaware, Ohio. He was delivered by Dr. Reuben Lamb for a fee of $3.50. He was baptized at the Presbyterian meetinghouse in Delaware in June 1823.

CHILDHOOD: Having never known his father, Hayes was raised by his mother and his maternal uncle Sardis Birchard, a bachelor, in Delaware, Ohio. He developed an unusually close bond with his older sister Fanny; the two were inseparable playmates. He especially liked the trips out to the family farm, where he joined in the rural rituals of making sugar and cider. The highlight of his childhood was a trip to Vermont to visit relatives. His ambition was for the law and public affairs. "I have always been ambitious," he reflected at 19, "dreaming of future glory, of performing some virtuous or patriotic action, but it has been all dreams, and no reality. From my earliest recollection, I have thought I had great power in me, yet at the same time I was fully satisfied of my present insignificance and mental weakness. I have imagined that at some future time I could do considerable, but the more I learn, the more I feel my littleness."[3]

EDUCATION: Hayes learned the fundamentals from Daniel Granger, a harsh schoolmaster, at Delaware, Ohio. At 14 he attended the Norwalk (Ohio) Academy, a Methodist school run by Jonah Chaplin. The next year he entered the college preparatory academy of Isaac Webb in Middletown, Connecticut. In a progress report to Hayes's mother, Webb described the boy as industrious, well informed, polite, and respected by his peers. At 16, Hayes enrolled at Kenyon College in Gambier, Ohio. There he continued as a good student, taking a special interest in philosophy and debate but detesting science. As a senior, he took part in a class revolt, refusing to take a chemistry exam. Politically he already had identified with the Whig party; though still too young to vote, he supported William Henry Harrison for president in 1840. He graduated class valedictorian in 1842, choosing for his valedictory address the theme "college life." He then studied law for 10 months at the office of Thomas Sparrow in Columbus, Ohio. In 1843 he entered Harvard Law School, where his instructors included Supreme Court Justice Joseph Story, legal scholar Simon Greenleaf, and historian Jared Sparks. He graduated in January 1845 and was admitted to the Ohio bar two months later.

RELIGION: Hayes was baptized a Presbyterian, attended Episcopal services while single, and after his marriage accompanied Mrs. Hayes, a Methodist, to the church of her faith. Although Hayes attended church regularly, he never became a communicant. "I am not a subscriber to any creed," he wrote in later years. "But in a sense satisfactory to myself and believed by me to be important, I try to be a Christian. Or rather I want to be a Christian and help do Christian work."[4] He gave freely, both money and his time, to various denominations. He contributed 25 percent of the construction costs of a new Methodist church and bore another 25 percent of its reconstruction after it burned down. He spoke on behalf of the Catholic church, conceding his disagreement with Rome on certain matters of faith and morals but commending the church for its assistance to the poor and blacks and its protemperance activity. As president, Hayes introduced the practice of conducting group hymn sings at the White House on Sunday evenings.

RECREATION: Hayes was an outdoorsman, an avid hunter and fisherman. He kept in shape with a morning regimen of exercise followed by a brisk walk. He neither smoked nor drank. He played chess. He also enjoyed landscaping his own grounds. His literary tastes ran to American and Ohio history, biography, fiction, and poetry. His favorite authors included Emerson, novelists Hawthorne and Scott, and poets Byron and Browning. He was long an admirer of Shakespeare, Milton, and Spenser.

EARLY ROMANCE: As a young man Hayes was quite popular with girls. At one point he so wearied of several who were constantly contriving to run into him that he spread the lie that he had a girl in Columbus. He vowed to marry by age 25. "Uppermost in the medley of ideas that are rolling about under my hair," he wrote at age 24, "is that before a year rolls around I'll get me a wifey, or at least a sweetheart, if I can find one who agrees with me that I am one of the sunniest fellows in the world."[5]

Fanny G. Perkins. Hayes offered his first proposal of marriage to Fanny G. Perkins of New London, Connecticut, whom he met while she was visiting relatives in Sandusky City, Ohio, in 1846. He called on her often but was reluctant at first to press his suit because she was already involved with J. A. Camp, a Harvard student. When she returned his attentions, however, and made it clear that she was not engaged to Camp, Hayes began contemplating marriage. He followed her back to Connecticut and there proposed. She was agreeable, but before any plans were made the couple quarreled over where they would settle. She insisted that they remain in Connecticut; Hayes was set on returning to Ohio. "I could not get her without more feeling and trouble than was to my taste,"[6] Hayes sniffed as he returned home unwed. Ironically, Miss Perkins subsequently married J. A. Camp and settled in Ohio.

MARRIAGE: Rutherford B. Hayes, 30, married Lucy Ware Webb, 21, on December 30, 1852, at the home of the bride's mother in Cincinnati. Born in Chillicothe, Ohio, on August 28, 1831, the daughter of James Webb, a physician, and Maria Cook Webb, Lucy was descended from seven veterans of the American Revolution. Her father died when she was an infant. With her mother she moved to Delaware, Ohio, where in 1847 she met Rutherford B. Hayes. Later that year she enrolled at Wesleyan Women's College (class of 1850) in Cincinnati; she was the first First Lady to have graduated from college. Hayes was by this time practicing law in Cincinnati, and the two began dating seriously. He proposed in June 1851. After the wedding, performed by Dr. L. D. McCabe of Delaware, the couple honeymooned at the home of the groom's sister and brother-in-law in Columbus. A vigorous opponent of slavery, Mrs. Hayes contributed to her husband's decision to abandon the Whigs for the antislavery Republican party. During the Civil War, she visited Hayes often in the field. While her husband was governor of Ohio, she helped establish the state Home for Soldiers' Orphans at Xenia. As First Lady, she brought her zeal for temperance to the White House. She banned all alcoholic beverages at state functions, excepting only the reception for Grand Duke Alexis Alexandrovitch of Russia in 1877, at which wine was served. Detractors dubbed her Lemonade Lucy, but the Women's Christian Temperance Union hailed her policy and in gratitude commissioned a full-length portrait of her, which now hangs in the

White House. She also instituted the custom of conducting an Easter egg roll on the White House lawn. A devout Methodist, she joined the president in saying prayers after breakfast and conducting group hymn sings with the cabinet and congressmen on Sunday evenings. The social highlight of the Hayes years was their twenty-fifth wedding anniversary celebration, at which the president and First Lady repeated their vows at a White House ceremony before many of the same guests who had attended the original nuptials in Cincinnati. In 1881 she retired with the president to Spiegel Grove in Fremont, Ohio. She died of a stroke on June 25, 1889, and was buried at Spiegel Grove.

MILITARY SERVICE: Civil War. Hayes served with the Twenty-third Ohio Volunteer Infantry Regiment from June 1861 to June 1865, rising from major to major general. He took part in some 50 engagements and was wounded several times, once seriously, and had his horse shot out from under him four times. In July 1861 he marched with his unit into present-day West Virginia, where it clashed sporadically with Confederates. In September Hayes was appointed judge advocate general of the Ohio Department and in October was promoted to lieutenant colonel and deputy commander of the regiment. In 1862, now acting commander of the Twenty-third, Hayes took part in the campaign that culminated at Antietam. At the battle of South Mountain on September 14, 1862, he was severely wounded in the left arm. Although faint from loss of blood, he continued to give direction to his troops and succeeded in scattering the rebels. At one point in the engagement a tactical maneuver left him temporarily exposed to the Confederate line. Flat on his back from his wound, he cried out for help and was hastily carried to safety. In October 1862 he was promoted to colonel and commander of the Twenty-third. As a brigade commander he engaged Morgan's Raiders in the summer of 1863 along the Ohio River and fought under General Philip Sheridan in the Shenandoah campaign in 1864. At Cedar Creek in October 1864 he wrenched his ankle as his horse was shot out from under him. After this engagement he was promoted to brigadier general of volunteers. In March 1865 he was breveted major general of volunteers. He resigned from the army in June 1865.

CAREER BEFORE THE PRESIDENCY: On his admission to the bar in 1845, Hayes opened practice in partnership with Ralph D. Buckland in Lower Sandusky (now Fremont), Ohio. He campaigned for Zachary Taylor for president in 1848. The next year he moved to Cincinnati, where he continued to practice, eventually forming the firm of Corwine, Hayes, and Rogers. He supported Whig Winfield Scott for president in 1852 and Republican John C. Frémont in 1856.

Cincinnati City Solicitor, 1858–1861. The Cincinnati City Council appointed Hayes to fill the office of city solicitor left vacant by the death of the incumbent. It took 13 ballots for the council to choose Hayes over the early favorite, Caleb B. Smith, later interior secretary in the Lincoln administration. Hayes was elected city solicitor in his own right in 1859 but was denied reelection two years later.

He supported Abraham Lincoln for president in 1860. He served in the Civil War (see "Military Service").

U.S. Representative, 1865–1867. Still in uniform when informed of his Republican nomination for one of the Hamilton County seats in Congress, Hayes rejected suggestions from supporters that he return to Cincinnati to campaign. In a famous letter that boosted his prospects when publicized, he remarked, "An officer fit for duty who at this crisis would abandon his post to electioneer for a seat in Congress ought to be scalped."[7] He was elected handily and reelected in 1866. Congressman Hayes generally supported the Radical Republicans in their struggle against President Andrew Johnson to impose a harsh Reconstruction policy on the vanquished South. He took no active part in the debates, however. He voted for Johnson's impeachment. As chairman of the Joint Library Committee, Hayes steered to passage a bill that expanded and modernized the Library of Congress. It transferred the books and papers of the Smithsonian Institution to the Library, enlarged the facility, purchased the extensive Peter Force collection of Americana, and opened its shelves to more people.

Governor of Ohio, 1868–1872, 1876–1877. Running on a platform of universal manhood suffrage in Ohio, Hayes was elected governor over Democrat Allen G. Thurman in 1867. He was reelected in 1869 over Democrat George Pendleton in a campaign advocating sound money and ratification of the Fifteenth Amendment, guaranteeing equal rights for blacks. As governor, he encouraged merit appointments, trimmed the state debt by 20 percent, and promoted education, prison reform, and better treatment for the insane and indigent. He supported Ulysses S. Grant for president in 1868. Unwilling to break the precedent of a two-term limit for governor, he declined renomination for a third term. He was an Ohio delegate to the 1872 Republican national convention in Philadelphia and campaigned vigorously for Grant's reelection. Although he had decided to return to private law practice, he agreed to stand for Congress in 1872 after being informed of his nomination. He was defeated by Henry B. Banning, running on a combined Democrat and Liberal Republican ticket. He turned down President Grant's offer of appointment as assistant U.S. treasurer for Cincinnati. In 1875 he won the Republican gubernatorial nomination over Alphonso Taft. Running on a campaign of sound money and separation of church and state, he ousted incumbent governor William Allen in the general election.

REPUBLICAN PRESIDENTIAL NOMINATION, 1876: As Republicans convened in Cincinnati in June 1876, the clear front-runner for the nomination was James G. Blaine of Maine, first dubbed the Plumed Knight by Robert G. Ingersoll in a stirring nominating speech at this convention. Blaine came within 27 votes of the nomination. Through the first four ballots, Hayes trailed Blaine, Oliver P. Morton of Indiana, Benjamin H. Bristow of Kentucky, and Roscoe Conkling of New York. On the fifth tally Hayes surged to third place and on the next vote overtook second place, though he still lagged far behind Blaine, 308–113. But a stop-Blaine movement rallied to Hayes, putting him over the top on the seventh ballot with 384 votes, a scant 6 votes more than was needed, to 351 for Blaine. Representative William A. Wheeler of New York was nominated for vice president. The Republican platform promised "permanent pacification" of the South, continued sound-money policy, and civil service reform; opposed federal aid to Catholic or other sectarian schools and land grants to railroads or other corporations; called for a congressional investigation of the effects of Oriental immigration "upon the moral and material interest of the country"; and vowed to eradicate polygamy, "that relic of barbarism," in Utah.

OPPONENT: Samuel J. Tilden (1814–1886) of New York; Democrat. Born at New Lebanon, New York, the son of a Democratic party worker, Tilden from his youth was active in party affairs, supporting the Jackson and Van Buren administrations. Admitted to the bar in 1841, he quickly prospered as an able corporate attorney. He early opposed slavery, joining the Barnburners, the Free Soil faction of New York Democrats. As chairman of the New York Democratic committee 1866–1874, he brought down the notorious Tweed Ring and encouraged the election of reform Democrats. His campaign against corruption earned him the governorship, 1874–1876, and a national reputation as a champion of reform. At the Democratic convention in St. Louis, the first held west of the Mississippi, in June 1876, Tilden organizers dominated the proceedings from the start. He was nominated on the second ballot with 535 votes, to 60 for Thomas A. Hendricks of Indiana, 59 for Winfield S. Hancock of Pennsylvania, and 54 for William Allen of Ohio. Hendricks was nominated for vice president. The Democratic platform pledged to replace the corruption of the Grant administration with honest, efficient government and to end "the rapacity of carpetbag tyrannies" in the South; called for treaty protection for naturalized U.S. citizens visiting their homeland, restrictions on Oriental immigration, and tariff reform; and opposed land grants to railroads. Despite having his apparent victory at the polls negated by an electoral commission voting strictly along party lines, Tilden restrained his supporters from challenging the results. "I can retire to private life," he said in acknowledging defeat, "with the consciousness that I shall receive from posterity the credit of having been elected to the highest position in the gift of the people, without any of the cares and responsibilities of the office."[8] On his death in Yonkers, New York, he left the bulk of his estate to establish what evolved into the New York Public Library.

CAMPAIGN AND THE ISSUES, 1876: Each candidate drew support from reformers. Carl Schurz stumped for Hayes; Charles Francis Adams and James Russell Lowell endorsed Tilden. Tilden supporters lambasted Republicans for the corruption of the Grant administration, and Hayes backers waved the "bloody shirt," labeling Democrats the party of treason and rebellion. Although Republicans still were the dominant party nationwide, the backlash against the Grant scandals, Tilden's sterling record against the Tweed Ring in New York, and the resurgence of white control in the South encouraged Democrats. But they made one tactical blunder, which, as it turned out, cost them the election: The Democratically controlled House promoted the admission of Colorado to the Union in 1876, believing that it was a safe state for Tilden. Instead, the new state voted for Hayes, giving him three electoral votes, without which no amount of tinkering by the electoral commission could have denied Tilden the presidency. Still, Tilden was regarded as the favorite in the final days of the campaign. Each candidate went to bed on election night believing Tilden the winner. Many newspapers heralded a Democratic victory the next morning.

ELECTION AS PRESIDENT, 1876: Soon after the election, Hayes conceded to a reporter that he thought he had lost to Tilden. Althought Tilden won the popular vote and was ahead in electoral votes, the returns of three states—South Carolina, Louisiana, and Florida, all controlled by Republicans—were in confusion. One electoral vote in Oregon also was under challenge. Not counting the disputed electoral votes, Tilden led 184–166, just 1 vote shy of a majority. To win, Hayes needed every vote in dispute. Hayes appeared to be ahead in South Carolina, but Tilden led in Florida and Louisiana until Republican officials there ruled numbers of Democratic ballots invalid. To resolve the issue Congress established a 15-man electoral commission of five senators, three Republican and two Democrat; five representatives, three Democrat and two Republican;

and five Supreme Court justices, two Democratic appointees, two Republican appointees, and one chosen by the other four. The fifth justice chosen was Joseph P. Bradley, a Grant appointee and nominal Republican but one respected for his independence. In February 1877 the commission voted 8–7 strictly along party lines to award all disputed states, and with them the election, to Hayes. Some southern Democrats threatened open rebellion rather than to submit to what they regarded as rank usurpation. But Tilden restrained his followers, and Hayes further mollified them with the Compromise of 1877, by which he agreed to end military occupation of the South, to support genuine reconstruction of education and transportation in the South, and to bring at least one southern Democrat into his cabinet.

Popular Vote: Samuel J. Tilden (Democrat), 4,284,757 (51%); Hayes (Republican), 4,033,950 (48%).

Electoral Vote: Hayes, 185; Tilden, 184.

States Carried: Hayes won the electoral votes of 21 states—California, Colorado, Florida, Illinois, Iowa, Kansas, Louisiana, Maine, Massachusetts, Michigan, Minnesota, Nebraska, Nevada, New Hampshire, Ohio, Oregon, Pennsylvania, Rhode Island, South Carolina, Vermont, and Wisconsin. Tilden won the electoral votes of 17 states—Alabama, Arkansas, Connecticut, Delaware, Georgia, Indiana, Kentucky, Maryland, Mississippi, Missouri, New Jersey, New York, North Carolina, Tennessee, Texas, Virginia, and West Virginia.

INAUGURAL ADDRESS: March 5, 1877. ". . . The permanent pacification of the country upon such principles and by such measures as will secure the complete protection of all its citizens in the free enjoyment of all their constitutional rights is now the one subject in our public affairs which all thoughtful and patriotic citizens regard as of supreme importance. . . .

"Let me assure my countrymen of the Southern States that it is my earnest desire to regard and promote their truest interest—the interests of the white and of the colored people both and equally—and to put forth my best efforts in behalf of a civil policy which will forever wipe out in our political affairs the color line and the distinction between North and South, to the end that we may have not merely a united North or a united South, but a united country . . ."

VICE PRESIDENT: William Almon Wheeler (1819–1887), of New York, served 1877–1881. Born in Malone, New York, Wheeler, a lawyer and banker, had entered public affairs as a teenager, serving as clerk of his hometown. A Whig and later a Republican, he served as district attorney of Franklin County, New York, 1846–1849 and in the state assembly 1850–1851, the state senate 1858–1859, and the U.S. House 1861–1863 and 1866–1877. He also presided over the state constitutional convention 1867–1868. He stood out as an incorruptible politician at a time when misconduct in office seemed rampant. He was virtually unknown outside New York on his nomination for vice president in 1876, however. He had attained national notice only briefly with sponsorship of the Wheeler Compromise resolving a disputed election in Louisiana in 1874. His term as vice president was uneventful.

CABINET:

Secretary of State. William M. Evarts (1818–1901), of New York, served 1877–1881. He had served as attorney general under President Andrew Johnson. He negotiated the Treaty of 1880, curbing Chinese immigration without alienating the Chinese government. He also promoted foreign trade.

Secretary of the Treasury. John Sherman (1823–1900), of Ohio, served 1877–1881. Eminently qualified for this post, having served as chairman of the Senate Finance Committee for the previous decade, he administered the Resumption of Specie Act, redeeming greenbacks with gold. He later served as secretary of state in the McKinley administration.

Secretary of War. (1) George W. McCrary (1835–1890), of Iowa, served 1877–1879. Hayes at first considered fulfilling his pledge to name a southerner to the cabinet by appointing former Confederate General Joseph E. Johnston to this post. But, persuaded that the nomination would never clear the Senate, he tapped McCrary, who subsequently resigned to accept a federal judgeship. (2) Alexander Ramsey (1815–1903), of Minnesota, served 1879–1881.

Attorney General. Charles Devens (1820–1891), of Massachusetts, served 1877–1881. He had served on the Massachusetts supreme court.

Secretary of the Navy. (1) Richard W. Thompson (1809–1900), of Virginia, served 1877–1880. Indifferent to the appearance of conflict of interest, he, while secretary, accepted a salaried appointment as chairman of the American Advisory Committee of the Panama Canal Company of France. Hayes dismissed him. (2) Nathan Goff (1843–1920), of West Virginia, served January–March 1881.

Postmaster General. (1) David M. Key (1824–1900), of Tennessee, served 1877–1880. His appointment was the fulfillment of Hayes's pledge to appoint a southern Democrat to the cabinet. Key resigned to accept a federal judgeship. (2) Horace Maynard (1814–1882), of Tennessee, served 1880–1881.

Secretary of the Interior. Carl Schurz (1829–1906), of Missouri, served 1877–1881. A leader of the German-American community and a lifelong reformer, Schurz plunged into his duties determined to carry out in his own department the civil service reforms promised by Hayes. He introduced competitive examinations as the basis of appointments and promotions. He urged adoption of a national forest policy to curb the wasteful practices of the logging industry. He won passage of the Timber and Stone Act (1878), requiring timber firms to pay for trees cut on public land. Schurz also encouraged more sympathetic treatment of American Indians.

ADMINISTRATION: March 4, 1877–March 3, 1881.

End of Reconstruction, 1877. As promised by the Compromise of 1877 (see "Election as President"), Hayes withdrew the last federal troops from the South, thus ending Reconstruction and effectively restoring white supremacy to the region.

Bland-Allison Act, 1878. Passed over President Hayes's veto, this "soft money" measure sponsored by Democratic Representative Richard Bland of Missouri and Republican Senator William B. Allison of Iowa required the federal government to purchase $2–$4 million worth of silver monthly for coinage. It was intended to inflate the currency and thus aid farmers, debtors, and, of course, silver miners. It was superseded by the Sherman Silver Purchase Act (1890; see "Benjamin Harrison, 23d President" "Administration").

Resumption of Specie Act, 1879. A proponent of hard money, President Hayes eagerly enforced this act passed under the Grant administration. Under its terms Treasury Secretary Sherman was directed to redeem in gold all greenbacks tendered after January 1, 1879. Although denounced by soft-money advocates in the West, the act strengthened public confidence in U.S. currency.

Civil Service Reform. In June 1877 President Hayes issued an executive order barring federal employees from taking part in political activities. He repeatedly called for comprehensive civil service reform and funding of a civil service commission, but Congress failed to act. He looked with favor on competitive examinations conducted in the Interior Department and the Post Office. "I am convinced," he said in his third annual message to Congress in 1879, "that if a just and adequate test of merit is enforced for admission to the public service and in making promotions such abuses as removals without good cause and partisan and official interference with the proper exercise of the appointing power will in large measure disappear."

Chinese Immigration. For many years Chinese had been emigrating to the U.S. West Coast, constituting by 1880 some 9 percent of the population of California. At first they were welcomed as a source of cheap labor to build the railroads. But as the railroad boom waned, Chinese immigrants began competing for other jobs and thus posed a serious threat to the constituents of western politicians. In 1879 Congress passed a bill unilaterally abrogating the Burlingame Treaty of 1868, which recognized the right of Chinese to emigrate to the United States. Hayes vetoed the measure because it jeopardized relations with China and instead authorized Secretary of State Evarts to negotiate a new pact, the Treaty of 1880, restricting, but not banning altogether, future Chinese immigration. The treaty was supplanted by the Chinese Exclusion Act (1882; see "Chester A. Arthur, 21st President," "Administration").

Panama Canal. The French at this time were attempting to build a canal across Central America. In a special message to Congress in March 1880, President Hayes set down the policy that was carried out a quarter century later: "The policy of this country is a canal under American control. The United States can not consent to the surrender of this control to any European power or to any combination of European powers."

SUPREME COURT APPOINTMENTS: (1) John Marshall Harlan (1833–1911), of Kentucky, served as associate justice 1877–1911. Known as the Great Dissenter, Harlan objected to the Court's disregard for black civil rights and otherwise bucked the conservative trend of a majority of his colleagues. Of 380 written dissents, many of which later prevailed, perhaps the most striking was that in *Plessy* v. *Ferguson* (1896), which perpetuated racial segregation in upholding the constitutionality of the doctrine of separate-but-equal facilities for blacks. As the lone dissenter in that case, Justice Harlan wrote, prophetically, "The destinies of the two races in this country are indissolubly linked together and the interests of both require that the common government of all shall not permit the seeds of race hatred to be planted under the sanction of law. What can more certainly arouse race hatred . . . than state enactments, which, in fact, proceed on the ground that colored citizens are so inferior and degraded that they cannot be allowed to sit in public coaches occupied by white citizens."[9] His view ultimately was vindicated in *Brown* v. *the Board of Education* (1954; see "Dwight D. Eisenhower, 34th President," "Supreme Court Appointments," Earl Warren). Harlan also dissented from Court decisions that struck down the federal income tax, weakened antitrust laws, and denied territorial residents full protection of the Constitution. (2) William B. Woods (1824–1887), of Georgia, served as associate justice 1881–1887. The first southerner appointed to the Court since the Civil War, he wrote more than 200 opinions, most in complicated equity and patent cases. In *U.S.* v. *Harris* (1883), he spoke for the majority in ruling against federal attempts to combat the Ku Klux Klan.

RANKING IN 1962 HISTORIANS POLL: Hayes ranked fourteenth of 31 presidents, third of 12 "average" presidents. He ranked above McKinley, below John Quincy Adams.

RETIREMENT: March 4, 1881–January 17, 1893. Having renounced a second term in his letter of acceptance of the Republican presidential nomination four years before, Hayes retired happily, after attending the inauguration of his successor, James A. Garfield, to Spiegel Grove, the estate at Fremont, Ohio, that he had inherited from his Uncle Sardis Birchard. Enroute his train collided with another, killing 2 and injuring 20; Hayes was jostled but unhurt. The former president remained interested in public affairs. He loyally supported Republican presidential nominees, opposed women's suffrage, encouraged temperance, and as a director of the George Peabody Educational Fund and the John F. Slater Fund, promoted black education. Among those to whom he personally awarded scholarships was future black activist W.E.B. DuBois. He also served as a trustee of Ohio State University and other Ohio colleges. As president of the National Prison Association, he advocated greater emphasis on rehabilitation.

DEATH: January 17, 1893, 11 P.M., Spiegel Grove estate, Fremont, Ohio. Enroute from Columbus to Cleveland in January 1893, Hayes sat in a draft on the train and caught cold. After conducting some business in his capacity as a trustee of Western Reserve University, he proceeded to the Cleveland train station, where he suffered a heart attack. Dismissing suggestions that he be taken to the home of a relative in Cleveland, Hayes sipped some brandy and continued by train for his home at Fremont. There he was attended by Dr. F. S. Hilbish, who ordered complete bedrest. Hayes rallied at times over the next couple days, but his heart suddenly gave out. He died in the arms of his son Webb. His last recorded words were "I know that I am going where Lucy [his late wife] is."[10] A brief funeral service was conducted at Spiegel Grove by the Reverand J. L. Albritton of the local Methodist church. Pallbearers were veterans of his Civil War regiment. The funeral was notable for the presence of President-elect Grover Cleveland. Observers commented that his attendance marked the Democratic party's final concession of the disputed election of 1876. His remains were deposited temporarily at Oakwood Cemetery in Fremont. In 1915 the bodies of Mr. and Mrs. Hayes were reinterred together at Spiegel Grove. In his last will and testament, Hayes left the Spiegel Grove estate at Fremont, as well as all the personal property contained therein, to his children, to be held in common by them. Nothing was to be divided or sold. The children in turn offered the property to the Ohio Archaeological and Historical Society, provided that it would raise sufficient money in advance to guarantee its proper maintenance. The society was unable to do so, and the Hayes family withdrew the offer. The president's son Webb C. Hayes acquired the estate in the final settlement in 1899. In 1910 he deeded Spiegel Grove to the state of Ohio.

HAYES PRAISED: "He was a patriotic citizen, a lover of the flag and of our free institutions, an industrious and conscientious civil officer, a soldier of dauntless courage, a loyal comrade and friend, a sympathetic and helpful neighbor, and the honored head of a happy Christian home. He has steadily grown in the public esteem, and the impartial historian will not fail to recognize the conscientiousness, the manliness, and the courage that so strongly characterized his whole public career."[11]—President Benjamin Harrison, 1893

"President Hayes . . . stood firmly by his principles. The Southern policy was maintained, the resumption of specie payments successfully effected, and the financial honor of the country preserved. It is true that the practical reform of the civil service fell short of the original programme; but considering that his predecessor had abandoned the whole system, that President Hayes and the heads of departments under him had to work without any appropriations for the purpose, and were at every step obstructed and assailed by a hostile Congress, it is remarkable, not that not more, but that so much of permanent value was accomplished."[12]—Carl Schurz, interior secretary under Hayes, 1893

HAYES CRITICIZED: "The great fraud of 1876–77, by which, upon a false count of the electoral votes of two States, the candidate defeated at the polls was declared to be President, and for the first time in American history, the will of the people was set aside under a threat of military violence, struck a deadly blow at our system of representative government."[13]—Democratic party platform, 1880

"The policy of the President has turned out to be a give-away from the beginning. He has nulled suits, discontinued prosecutions, offered conciliation everywhere in the South, while they have spent their time in whetting their knives for any Republican they could find."[14]—Representative James A. Garfield of Ohio

"Mr. Hayes had as little political authority as Mr. Johnson had had. . . . He had no real hold upon the country. His amiable character, his lack of party heat, his conciliatory attitude towards the South alienated rather than attracted the members of his party in Congress. . . . The Democrats did not like him because he seemed to them incapable of frank, consistent action."[15]—Professor Woodrow Wilson of Princeton University, 1902

HAYES QUOTES: "Fighting battles is like courting girls: those who make the most pretensions and are boldest usually win."[16]

"I am not liked as a President by the politicians in office, in the press, or in Congress. But I am content to abide the judgment—the sober second thought—of the people."[17]—1878

"There can be no complete and permanent reform of the civil service until public opinion emancipates Congressmen from all control and influence over government patronage. . . . No proper legislation is to be expected as long as members of Congress are engaged in procuring offices for their constituents."[18]—1879

BOOKS ABOUT HAYES: Barnard, Harry. *Rutherford B. Hayes and His America.* New York: Russell & Russell, 1967 (originally published 1954).

Eckenrode, H. J. *Rutherford B. Hayes: Statesman of Reunion.* New York: Dodd, Mead, 1930.

Williams, Charles Richard. *The Life of Rutherford Birchard Hayes: Nineteenth President of the United States.* 2 vols. Columbus: Ohio State Archaeological and Historical Society, 1928.

Williams, T. Harry, editor. *Hayes: Diary of a President 1875–1881.* New York: McKay, 1964.

NOTES

1 H. J. Eckenrode, *Rutherford B. Hayes: Statesman of Reunion*, New York: Dodd, Mead, 1930, p. 41.
2 Charles Richard Williams, *The Life of Rutherford Birchard Hayes, Nineteenth President of the United States*, Columbus: Ohio State Archaeological and Historical Society, 1928, vol. I, pp. 83–84.
3 Ibid., p. 22.
4 John Sutherland Bonnell, *Presidential Profiles: Religion in the Life of American Presidents*, Philadelphia: Westminster, 1971, p. 133.
5 Eckenrode, p. 42.
6 Harry Barnard, *Rutherford B. Hayes and His America*, New York: Russell & Russell, 1967, p. 159.
7 Eckenrode, p. 72.
8 Irving Stone, *They Also Ran*, Garden City, N.Y.: Doubleday, 1966, p. 210.
9 Frank Latham, *The Great Dissenter: Supreme Court Justice John Marshall Harlan*, New York: Cowles, 1970, p. 123.
10 Eckenrode, p. 341.
11 Charles Richard Williams, vol. II, pp. 401–402.
12 Ibid., p. 403.
13 Kirk H. Porter and Donald Bruce Johnson, compilers, *National Party Platforms*, Urbana, Ill., University of Illinois Press, 1961, p. 56.
14 Richard Kenin and Justin Wintle, eds., *Dictionary of Biographical Quotation*, New York: Knopf, 1978, p. 369.
15 Woodrow Wilson, *A History of the American People*, New York: Harper & Bros., 1902, vol. V, p. 149.
16 Dorothy Burne Goebel and Julius Goebel, Jr., *Generals in the White House*, Garden City, N.Y., Doubleday, Doran, 1945, p. 206.
17 Arthur B. Tourtellot, *The Presidents on the Presidency*, New York: Russell and Russell, 1964, p. 44.
18 T. Harry Williams, ed., *Hayes: The Diary of a President*, New York: McKay, 1964, p. 187.

JAMES A. GARFIELD

20TH PRESIDENT

NAME: James Abram Garfield. He was named after his older brother James Garfield, who had died in infancy, and his father, Abram Garfield.

PHYSICAL DESCRIPTION: A muscular, robust, handsome figure, Garfield stood 6 feet tall and weighed about 185 pounds. He had a disproportionately large head, a prominent forehead, light brown hair, blue eyes, and an aquiline nose. He wore a beard from young adulthood. He was left-handed. His health generally was sound, except during periods of overwork, when he complained of body aches and indigestion.

PERSONALITY: Although a pugnacious youth, Garfield matured into a good-natured, amiable, and gregarious fellow. Extremely tactile, he liked to hug and stroke friends and characteristically slung an arm around the shoulders of whomever he was talking to. He was a gifted orator, among the most popular and persuasive of his day. He was most ambitious but did little to promote his own fortunes. "I so much despise a man who blows his own horn," he commented, "that I go to the extreme of not demanding what is justly my due."[1] To refrain from self-aggrandizement became the guiding principle of his life. "He was convinced that he was destiny's child," biographer Allan Peskin has written, "marked out for some special purpose. Secure in this faith, he placed his career in the hands of his destiny, preferring to drift with the tide of fortune rather than take the initiative and oppose it."[2] As a young adult he experienced a prolonged period of mental depression, a period he later referred to as his "years of darkness." Similarly after his election as president but before the inauguration, he was overcome with a sense of foreboding. He complained of severe headaches. He began having nightmares of being naked and lost. Throughout his life, his self-confidence was fragile.

ANCESTORS: Garfield was of English and French Huguenot ancestry. His great[5]-grandfather Edward Garfield emigrated from Chester, England, to Massachusetts in 1630; he served as selectman and tax collector for Watertown,

Massachusetts. His great[4]-grandfather Benjamin Garfield, too, was selectman there and also served as town clerk. His great-grandfather Solomon Garfield moved west to Cooperstown, New York, and was killed falling from the rafters of his barn about 1806.

FATHER: Abram Garfield (1799–1833), farmer. A native of Worcester, New York, he was known far and wide as a champion wrestler. According to legend, "he could take a barrel of whiskey by the chime, and drink out of the bung hold."[3] He fell in love with Mehitabel Ballou, but after she went off with another, he ended up marrying her sister Eliza in 1820. The couple settled in a log house he built on the Cuyahoga River near Cleveland, Ohio. He worked for a time as a supervisor in the construction of the Ohio and Erie Canal but relied mainly on farming for his livelihood. He caught cold while struggling to put out a forest fire and soon thereafter died, when his most famous son was 18 months old.

MOTHER: Eliza Ballou Garfield (1801–1888). A native of Richmond, New Hampshire, she grew up in New York and Muskingham County, Ohio. Garfield credited his success to her steady influence. "At almost every turning point in my life," he wrote of her, "she has been the molding agent."[4] After the death of her husband, she struggled to make a go of the farm and keep the family together. In 1842 she married Alfred Belden but left him after a few years; he divorced her for desertion in 1848. Garfield thoroughly detested his stepfather and even in his later years recalled him with indignation. Mrs. Garfield was the first mother of a president to attend her son's inauguration. She lived at the White House during his term. She survived President Garfield by nearly seven years.

SIBLINGS: The youngest of four children to live to maturity, Garfield had two sisters and a brother—Mrs. Mehitabel "Hitty" Trowbridge of Solon, Ohio; Thomas Garfield, farmer, of Jamestown, Michigan; and Mrs. Mary Larabee of Solon.

CHILDREN: Garfield had four sons and a daughter to live to maturity.

Harry Augustus Garfield (1863–1942), lawyer, educator, public official. He graduated from Williams College and Columbia Law School and was admitted to the bar in 1888. He opened practice in Cleveland in partnership with his brother James. He taught contract law at Western Reserve University during 1891–1897. He was the first professor of politics at Princeton University, teaching there during 1903–1908 under Dean Woodrow Wilson. In 1908 he returned to Williams College as its president. During World War I, President Wilson appointed him chairman of the price committee of the U.S. Food Administration and promoted him to fuel administrator. In the latter post, he instituted "gasless Sundays," "heatless days," and other rationing measures, which earned him the Distinguished Service Medal in 1921. After the war he resumed the presidency of Williams College, where he created the Institute of Politics, a forum for the discussion of world sociopolitical problems. He retired in 1934.

James Rudolph Garfield (1865–1950), lawyer, public official. He graduated from Williams College and Columbia Law School in the same class with his older brother, Harry, and was admitted to the bar in 1888. After practicing law with Harry in Cleveland for a time, he served in the Ohio state senate 1896–1900, on the U.S. Civil Service Commission 1902–1903, and as commissioner of corporations in the Department of Commerce and Labor 1903–1907. In the latter post he was instrumental in carrying out the antitrust policy of President Theodore Roosevelt. In 1907 Roosevelt appointed him secretary of the interior. "His administration of the Interior Department," Roosevelt later wrote of him, "was beyond comparison the best we have ever had. It was based primarily on the conception that it is as much the duty of public land officials to help the honest settler get title to his claim as it is to prevent the looting of public lands."[5] President Taft's unwillingness to retain Garfield in his cabinet contributed to the rift between Taft and Roosevelt. In 1912 Garfield bolted the Republican party to support Roosevelt's unsuccessful third-party bid for president. During World War I he was active in the Red Cross. In 1932 he was a leader in President Herbert Hoover's doomed reelection campaign. He thereafter practiced law in Cleveland.

Mary "Mollie" Garfield (1867–1947). Educated at private schools in Cleveland and Connecticut, she in 1888 married Joseph Stanley-Brown, presidential secretary during Garfield's term, later an investment banker. She lived in New York and Pasadena, California.

Irvin McDowell Garfield (1870–1951), lawyer. He followed his older brothers to Williams College and Columbia Law School. He settled in Boston, where he prospered as partner in the firm of Warren and Garfield and served on the boards of directors of several corporations.

Abram Garfield (1872–1958), architect. A graduate of Williams College and Massachusetts Institute of Technology, he settled in Cleveland, where he worked as an architect from offices in the James A. Garfield Building. He served as chairman of the Cleveland Planning Commission 1929–1942 and was active in the American Institute of Architects.

BIRTH: Garfield was born November 19, 1831, in a log cabin built by his father in Orange, Cuyahoga County, Ohio, southeast of Cleveland. "The largest Babe I ever had," his mother said of him, "he looked like a red Irishman."[6] Indeed, he weighed 10 pounds at birth. He also was markedly disproportionate, having a massive head and torso and short, stubby legs.

CHILDHOOD: Having never known his father, Garfield grew up amid poverty in rural Orange Township southeast of Cleveland under the influence of his mother and Uncle Amos Boynton. A precocious tot, he walked at 9 months, climbed ladders at 10 months, and was reading at three years. Despite his later success, Garfield was convinced that being poor had held him back. Although as the baby of the family he was doted on at home, the outside world was much less friendly. "I was made the ridicule and sport of boys that had fathers and enjoyed the luxuries of life,"[7] he recalled. From such experience he became aggressive, belligerent, and good with his fists. He was a rather dreamy child, often lost in his own thoughts, oblivious to the world around him. He was accident prone, several times gashing himself with an ax or falling down while doing his chores. He read voraciously, especially American history and sea adventures. From an early age he dreamed of becoming a sailor. Over his mother's objections, he at 16 hiked to the Cleveland docks and tried to sign on one of the ships. Turned away, he settled for work on the *Evening Star*, a canal boat, owned by his cousin Amos Letcher, which shuttled between Cleveland and Pittsburgh, ports considerably less exotic than those of his dreams. During his six-week stint on the canal he fell overboard 14 times, a dangerous habit for a boy who had never learned to swim. He came down with a fever and returned home, where he convalesced for several months. He had planned to return to the canal with hopes of one day making it to sea, but his mother and Samuel Bates, a local teacher, convinced him to resume his education instead.

EDUCATION: Garfield learned the fundamentals at a district school near home in Orange Township, Ohio. During 1849–1850 he attended Geauga Academy at Chester, Ohio, where his studies included algebra, English grammar, Latin and Greek, botany, and geography. He worked his way through school doing carpentry work and teaching at a district school in Solon, Ohio. In 1851 he enrolled at the Eclectic Institute at Hiram, Ohio. During his three years there, he was a good student and became a skilled debater. He worked his way through as a janitor and teacher at district schools in Warrensville and Blue Rock, Ohio. In 1854 he entered Williams College in Williamstown, Massachusetts, as a junior. There he blossomed intellectually. A speech by Ralph Waldo Emerson greatly impressed him, prodding him to a life of study and self-improvement. Another significant influence on Garfield's intellectual development at that time was college president Mark Hopkins. Many years later Garfield offered the noted educator this tribute: "The ideal college is Mark Hopkins on one end of a log and a student on the other."[8] At Williams, Garfield enjoyed nearly all his subjects, except chemistry. The oldest student on campus, he was respected and admired by the others. He was the school's debating champion and was active in a variety of extracurricular activities, as president of both the Philologian (literary) Society and the Mills Theological Society, editor of the *Williams Quarterly*, and a member of the Equitable Fraternity. Politically he identified with the new Republican party; he campaigned in Ohio for John C. Frémont for president in 1856. He graduated with honors in the class of 1856. At commencement he delivered the Metaphysical Oration, choosing for his subject "Matter and Spirit." He considered taking up the ministry but decided to teach instead.

RELIGION: Disciples of Christ. Moved by the preaching of W. A. Lillie, a Disciples of Christ evangelist, Garfield was baptized into the faith in 1850. He believed in literal interpretation of the scriptures, providence, and life after death. He was for a time a lay preacher; while a student at Williams College, he spoke often at a community of Disciples at Poestenkill, New York. Something of a zealot in his early days, he agonized over having occasional impure thoughts and his inability to get close to God. He concluded that the only course for a Christian was to make religion a personal matter of constant practice.

RECREATION: Garfield enjoyed hunting and fishing. He was a skilled player of chess, euchre, and whist. He also shot billiards regularly. A moderate social drinker, he rejected pleas from temperance groups that he take the pledge. He was an avid reader all his life; he found the novels of Jane Austen particularly entertaining.

EARLY ROMANCE:

    Mary Hubell. Miss Hubell was one of Garfield's students at Warrensville (Ohio) district school and later attended the Eclectic Institute with him. There in 1852 they dated so regularly that friends assumed they were engaged. But Garfield never actually proposed and in the end decided that they were just friends. She, however, was heartbroken at having lost him. In 1858 she married William Taylor and died seven years later.

    Rebecca J. "Rancie" Selleck. While a student at Williams College, Garfield met this pretty, witty young lady at the home of a mutual friend Mrs. Maria Learned in Poestenkill, New York, where he frequently preached to Disciples of Christ congregations. Miss Selleck also was a Disciple. Garfield dated her at the same time that he was courting his future wife. Both women attended his graduation in 1856. In the end he dropped Rebecca to wed Lucretia Rudolph, but the suspicion that he may have had a lingering attachment for Rancie disturbed Mrs. Garfield during the first few years of their marriage. Miss Selleck, who never married, died in 1909.

MARRIAGE: James A. Garfield, 26, married Lucretia "Crete" Rudolph, 26, November 11, 1858, at the home of the bride's parents in Hiram, Ohio. Born in Hiram April 19, 1832, the daughter of Zebulon Rudolph, a farmer and co-founder of the Eclectic Institute at Hiram, and Arabella Mason Rudolph, Lucretia met Garfield in 1849 when they were classmates at Geauga Seminary in Chester, Ohio, and followed him to the Eclectic Institute, where they began dating. She was somewhat plain in appearance, but Garfield was attracted to her keen intellect and appetite for knowledge. While Garfield went on to Williams College, she taught school in Cleveland and Bayou, Ohio. They had planned to marry on his graduation in 1856 but decided to postpone the wedding for a couple of years until he was earning more money. Although both were Disciples of Christ, the nuptials were performed by Henry Hitchcock, a Presbyterian minister. The newlyweds did not take a honeymoon but instead set up housekeeping immediately at Hiram. As First Lady Mrs. Garfield researched the history of White House furnishings with a view to restoring it to its former glory, but she contracted malaria and was unable to pursue the project. The president was on his way to visit his ailing wife in Elberon, New Jersey, when he was assassinated. With his death, she fled to England and anonymity but eventually settled at Lawnfield, the estate Garfield had purchased at Mentor, Ohio. She lived comfortably on a $350,000 trust fund raised for her and the Garfield children by financier Cyrus W. Field. She spent winters at South Pasadena, California, where she died March 14, 1918. She was buried next to the president at Lake View Cemetery in Cleveland.

EXTRAMARITAL AFFAIR: Mrs. Calhoun. According to biographer Allan Peskin, Garfield had a brief love affair with one Mrs. Calhoun in New York City in October 1862. Somehow his wife learned of it and charged Garfield with yielding to "lawless passion." He apologized for his indiscretion and was forgiven. In 1867 he retrieved from Mrs. Calhoun certain letters he had written to her. Because these letters, referred to in his diary, are no longer extant, it is believed that he destroyed them.

MILITARY SERVICE: Civil War. Garfield served in the Union army from August 1861 to December 1863, rising from lieutenant colonel to major general. Commissioned a lieutenant colonel with the Ohio Forty-second Regiment, Garfield was promoted to full colonel in November 1861. As commander of the Eighteenth Brigade he defeated superior numbers of Confederates under General Humphrey Marshall at the battle of Middle Creek in January 1862, successfully checking the rebel advance into the Sandy Valley of eastern Kentucky. For this he was promoted to brigadier general. Soon after taking part in the battle of Shiloh in April 1862, he contracted camp fever and convalesced two months at Hiram, Ohio. Appointed chief of staff under Major General William S. Rosecrans, commander of the Army of the Cumberland, in January 1863, Brigadier General Garfield saw action at Chickamauga in September 1863. In a daring ride under enemy fire, during which his horse was wounded, he conveyed vital information from flank to flank. For this he was promoted to major general. "I feel much indebted to him for both counsel and assistance in the administration of this army," Rosecrans said of his chief of staff. "He

298/ JAMES A. GARFIELD

possesses the instinct and energy of a great commander."[9] Having been elected to Congress in September 1862, Garfield resigned his commission to take his seat in December 1863.

CAREER BEFORE THE PRESIDENCY: On graduation from Williams College in 1856, Garfield returned to the Eclectic Institute at Hiram, Ohio, as an instructor in classical languages from 1856 to 1857 and president of the institute from 1857 to 1861. Campus life lacked sufficient stimulation, however, for the ambitious Garfield. He studied law on his own for two years and was admitted to the Ohio bar in 1860.

Ohio State Senator, 1859–1861. Joining the antislavery bloc, State Senator Garfield praised abolitionist John Brown as a hero whose execution "shall be the dawn of a better day";[10] however, he did not condone his bloody raid. He campaigned in Ohio for Abraham Lincoln for president in 1860. With the outbreak of the Civil War, he became an ardent hawk. He welcomed the Union defeat at Fort Sumter as an event that would galvanize Northern sentiment for war against the South. He joined the Union army (see "Military Service").

U.S. Representative, 1863–1880. Garfield was first elected to Congress as a Republican in 1862, while still in uniform, handily defeating his Democratic opponent, D. B. Woods, by a margin of more than two to one to represent Ohio's Nineteenth Congressional District, the Ashtabula-Youngstown-Akron region. He was reelected eight times in succession. As a member of the Military Affairs Committee, he sponsored the draft bill and criticized the Lincoln administration for failing to prosecute the war more vigorously. Among the most radical Republicans in Congress during the Civil War, he called for confiscation of rebel property and execution or exile of Confederate leaders. He reluctantly supported the reelection of President Lincoln after a Republican movement to deny him renomination failed to produce an alternative candidate. He declined to campaign for Lincoln, however. After the war Garfield's radicalism cooled. He attempted to reconcile the Radical Republican call for harsh Reconstruction with the more lenient policy of President Andrew Johnson. Ultimately, however, he sided with the Radicals and voted for Johnson's impeachment. In 1866 he made his first courtroom appearance as a lawyer—before the Supreme Court as counsel for Lambdin P. Milligan in *Ex Parte Milligan* (see "Abraham Lincoln, 16th President," "Supreme Court Appointments," David Davis). He was the first attorney to argue his first case before the U.S. Supreme Court. Garfield supported without enthusiasm Ulysses S. Grant for president in 1868 and 1872. During the Grant administration he emerged a leading congressional spokesman on financial matters, serving variously as chairman of the Banking and Currency Committee, chairman of the Appropriations Committee, and a member of the Ways and Means Committee. A proponent of hard money despite the soft-money views of his home district, he opposed the inflationary policy of redeeming bonds with greenbacks. He attempted to stake out middle ground on the tariff issue: "I am for a protection which leads to ultimate free trade. I am for that free trade which can be achieved only through protection."[11] He opposed federally funded relief projects during the depression of the 1870s. In 1873 Garfield was implicated in the Crédit Mobilier scandal (see "Ulysses S. Grant, 18th President," "Administration"). He was accused of accepting 10 shares of Crédit Mobilier stock and a loan of $300. Garfield denied any wrongdoing. Called before a congressional investigative committee, Garfield testified that he was offered the right to purchase the stock but turned it down. He admitted accepting the loan but insisted that he repaid it in full and that the transaction in no way influenced his votes. The scandal temporarily eroded his support back home, but he won reelection anyway. He supported Rutherford B. Hayes for president in 1876 and served on the electoral commission that decided the disputed election in his favor. During the Hayes administration, Garfield was the leader of the Republican minority in the House. In 1880 he was elected to the U.S. Senate; he declined the seat following his election as president.

REPUBLICAN PRESIDENTIAL NOMINATION, 1880: Incumbent president Rutherford B. Hayes kept his pledge to retire at the end of one term. As Republicans convened in Chicago in June 1880, the clear front-runner for the nomination was former president Ulysses S. Grant, seeking an unprecedented third term. Anti-Grant forces coalesced around James G. Blaine of Maine and John Sherman of Ohio. Grant was the candidate of the Stalwarts, or conservative Republicans. Sherman and Blaine divided the support of the Half Breeds, the moderate faction of the party. Garfield was head of the Ohio delegation, chairman of the Rules Committee, and leader of the Sherman forces. As Rules Committee chairman, Garfield was instrumental in getting the convention to reject the unit rule, a victory for the anti-Grant forces, for without it the former president had little chance to attain a majority. Roscoe Conkling of New York nominated Grant in a bombastic address that rocked the convention. Garfield followed with the nominating speech for Sherman, by contrast a low-key, yet equally moving, address that convinced some delegates that Garfield would make an ideal compromise candidate. The convention deadlocked through 33 ballots, with Grant in the lead with just over 300 votes, more than 70 votes shy of the nomination, followed by Blaine, whose vote ranged from 270 to 285, and Sherman, hovering around 100. Garfield, meanwhile, had been receiving 1 or 2 scattered courtesy votes. But as the convention dragged on, he came under increasing pressure to break with Sherman and declare his own candidacy. This he refused to do. Then on the thirty-fourth ballot Wisconsin suddenly cast 16 votes for Garfield, who promptly reaffirmed his loyalty to Sherman. On the next tally Garfield received 50 votes, and on the thirty-sixth ballot the Blaine and Sherman forces rallied to his banner. The final vote was Garfield, 399; Grant, 306; Blaine, 42; Elihu Washburne of Illinois, 5; and Sherman, 3. To observers, Garfield seemed genuinely stunned by it all. To placate the Stalwarts, Chester A. Arthur of New York was nominated for vice president. The Republican platform largely reiterated the platform of 1876.

OPPONENT: Winfield S. Hancock (1824–1886) of Pennsylvania; Democrat. Born in Montgomery County, Pennsylvania, the son of a lawyer, Hancock graduated from West Point in 1844 and served in the Mexican War and the Seminole War. He made his reputation during the Civil War, earning the nickname "Superb" Hancock for his valiant stands in battle. He was promoted to major general of volunteers after taking part in the Peninsular campaign and the bloody fighting at Antietam. At Gettysburg he blunted Pickett's Charge and was seriously wounded. He recovered to take part in the Wilderness campaign. After the war Major General Hancock was assigned briefly to Indian territory in Kansas before taking up his duties as military governor of Louisiana and Texas. In that post he attempted to restore civilian control without recrimination and thereby ran afoul of Radical Republicans in Washington. At his own request he was transferred to the command of the Dakota Territory in 1869; he became commander of the Atlantic division in 1872. As early as 1868 Hancock was being mentioned as a presidential contender. At the Democratic national convention in Cincinnati in June 1880, Hancock emerged the leading candidate after Samuel J. Tilden of New York withdrew his name from consideration. On the first ballot Hancock led with 171 votes to 153½ for Thomas F. Bayard of Delaware, 81 for Henry B. Payne of Ohio, 68½ for Allen G. Thurman of Ohio, and the rest scattered. On the next tally, Tilden supporters pushed Samuel J. Randall of Pennsylvania to second place with 128½ votes, but Hancock held such a commanding lead with 320 votes that masses of delegates bolted to him before the second ballot was recorded, giving him 705 votes and the nomination. William H. English of Indiana was nominated for vice president. The Democratic platform condemned centralization of power in Washington, promised hard money and a tariff for revenue only, called for civil service reform, opposed monopolies, encouraged the labor movement, and called for "No more Chinese immigration." After his defeat by Garfield, Hancock resumed his military career with the Atlantic division. He died at his post on Governor's Island, New York.

CAMPAIGN AND THE ISSUES, 1880: In this lackluster campaign, the candidates differed little on the issues. Only the tariff question divided them. Republicans supported a high tariff; Democrats favored one "for revenue only." The tariff became a source of embarrassment to Democrats when Hancock, asked by a reporter for his position on the issue, dismissed it as "a local question." The gaffe only reinforced his image as a career military officer with little grounding in politics or affairs of state. Garfield, by contrast, could point to his long service in the House. His record proved a mixed blessing, however, as Democrats lambasted him for his part in the Crédit Mobilier scandal. Incumbent president Rutherford B. Hayes wholeheartedly endorsed Garfield but warned him to keep a low profile during the campaign. This Garfield did, calmly receiving delegations of supporters at his home in Mentor, Ohio, while leaving the politicking to others. To win, Garfield needed the Stalwarts, the pro-Grant conservatives led by New York party boss Roscoe Conkling. For some time Conkling refused to lift a finger for the nominee. But in a meeting with Conkling subordinates in New York, Garfield reportedly agreed to consult with them on patronage for the state, something President Hayes had refused to do. The meeting, later dubbed the Treaty of Fifth Avenue, brought about Conkling's active support. Hancock, working from a solid base of support in the South, sought to woo northern reformers by pledging genuine civil service reform. The business community, fearful of Hancock's antitariff policy, contributed heavily to the Garfield campaign. Labor, too, was wary of Hancock, because as a military officer he had helped break a railroad strike.

ELECTION AS PRESIDENT, 1880:

Popular Vote: Garfield (Republican), 4,454,416 (48.3%); Hancock (Democrat), 4,444,952 (48.2%).

Electoral Vote: Garfield, 214; Hancock, 155.

States Carried: Garfield won the majority of electoral votes in 19 states— Colorado, Connecticut, Illinois, Indiana, Iowa, Kansas, Maine, Massachusetts, Michigan, Minnesota, Nebraska, New Hampshire, New York, Ohio, Oregon, Pennsylvania, Rhode Island, Vermont, and Wisconsin. Hancock won the majority of electoral votes in 19 states—Alabama, Arkansas, California, Delaware, Florida, Georgia, Kentucky, Louisiana, Maryland, Mississippi, Missouri, Nevada, New Jersey, North Carolina, South Carolina, Tennessee, Texas, Virginia, and West Virginia.

INAUGURAL ADDRESS: March 4, 1881. ". . . The elevation of the negro race from slavery to the full rights of citizenship is the most important political change we have known since the adoption of the Constitution of 1787. No thoughtful man can fail to appreciate its beneficent effect upon our institutions and people. It has freed us from the perpetual danger of war and dissolution. It has added immensely to the moral and industrial forces of our people. It has liberated the master as well as the slave from a relation which wronged and enfeebled both. It has surrendered to their own guardianship the manhood of more than 5,000,000 people, and has opened to each one of them a career of freedom and usefulness. It has given new inspiration to the power of self-help in both races by making labor more honorable to the one and more necessary to the other. The influence of this force will grow greater and bear richer fruit with the coming years. . . ."

VICE PRESIDENT: Chester A. Arthur (1829–1886), of New York, served March–September 1881. He succeeded to the presidency on Garfield's assassination.

CABINET:

    Secretary of State. James G. Blaine (1830–1893), of Maine, served March–December 1881. Garfield rewarded Blaine, a leader of the moderate Republicans, with this post for his support during the campaign. The appointment outraged New York party boss Roscoe Conkling, leader of the conservative Stalwarts. Blaine stayed on briefly in the Arthur administration.

    Secretary of the Treasury. William Windom (1827–1891), of Minnesota, served March–November 1881. Garfield resisted pressure from New York party boss Roscoe Conkling to name Levi P. Morton of New York to this post, insisting that it was important to choose a secretary far removed from the nation's money center. Instead, he chose William B. Allison of Iowa, who at first accepted but changed his mind. He next turned to Windom, who stayed on briefly in the Arthur administration.

    Secretary of War. Robert T. Lincoln (1843–1926), of Illinois, served 1881–1885. The son of Abraham Lincoln, he was chosen for the prestige of his name and his acceptability to the Stalwarts in Illinois. He was the only cabinet member to remain to the end of the Arthur administration.

    Attorney General. I. Wayne MacVeagh (1833–1917), of Pennsylvania, served March–October 1881. He was chosen as a representative of the Independent, or radical reform, faction of the Republican party. He clashed with Secretary of State Blaine. He prosecuted perpetrators of the Star Route fraud (see "Administration"). He stayed on briefly in the Arthur administration.

    Secretary of the Navy. William H. Hunt (1823–1884), of Louisiana, served 1881–1882. The token southerner in the cabinet, he stayed on in the Arthur administration.

    Postmaster General. Thomas L. James (1831–1916), of New York, served March–December 1881. He was postmaster of New York City. Though a Stalwart, he remained independent of boss Roscoe Conkling. He exposed the Star Route scandal (see "Administration"). He stayed on briefly in the Arthur administration.

    Secretary of the Interior. Samuel J. Kirkwood (1813–1894), of Iowa, served 1881–1882. Garfield first offered this post to William B. Allison of Iowa, who declined. Kirkwood stayed on in the Arthur administration.

ADMINISTRATION: March 4–Sept. 19, 1881. During his brief term, Garfield was preoccupied with the struggle over patronage with New York Republican boss

Roscoe Conkling. In bitter intraparty wrangling, Garfield succeeded in placing his own man, William H. Robertson, as collector of the Port of New York despite Conkling's strenuous efforts to thwart Senate confirmation of the appointment. The president's victory broke Conkling's grip on the party and marked the end of his career.

Star Route Scandal. In the first week of his presidency, Garfield ordered Postmaster General James to investigate charges that mail route contracts were being awarded fraudulently. James's preliminary investigation turned up evidence of bribery involving members of the president's own party. To James's request to press the investigation and expose the scandal, Garfield replied, "Go ahead regardless of where or whom you hit. I direct you not only to probe this ulcer to the bottom, but to cut it out."[12] Republican Senator Stephen W. Dorsey of Arkansas, Second Assistant Postmaster General Thomas Brady, and others were implicated in the scheme, which prosecutors estimated cost taxpayers $4 million. Although no one was convicted, revelation of the scandal led to subsequent adoption of civil service reform.

SUPREME COURT APPOINTMENT: Stanley Matthews (1824–1889), of Ohio, served as associate justice 1881–1889. Matthews had been appointed by President Hayes several weeks before Garfield took office, but the Senate refused to act. As a courtesy to Hayes, Garfield resubmitted the appointment. Although the Senate Judiciary Committee recommended that Matthews be rejected, the full Senate confirmed him by a one-vote margin. In *Yick Wo* v. *Hopkins* (1886), Matthews ruled for the Court that the discriminatory administration of otherwise just laws violated the equal protection clause of the Fourteenth Amendment.

RANKING IN 1962 HISTORIANS POLL: Because of the brevity of his administration, Garfield was not ranked.

ASSASSINATION: July 2, 1881, 9:30 A.M., Washington, D.C.; Death, September 19, 1881, 10:35 P.M., Elberon, New Jersey. Charles J. Guiteau, 39, had been stalking the president for weeks. Three times before, he was armed and within firing range of the president, and each time he backed down. Finally, on July 2, 1881, he fired a .44 British Bulldog (a relatively expensive pistol he had picked out specifically for the assassination because he thought it would look attractive in a museum) at the back of the president as he strolled arm in arm with Secretary of State Blaine across the waiting room of the Baltimore and Potomac railroad station in Washington. He was promptly arrested by District of Columbia policeman Patrick Kearney, who had rushed into the station at the first sound of gunfire. Ironically, Guiteau, a Stalwart, had supported Garfield in the election of 1880. When Guiteau came to Washington seeking a diplomatic post as his reward, however, he was politely but firmly rebuffed. Thereafter, the disappointed office seeker, mentally unstable for some time, came to believe that Garfield must die. "The President's tragic death," Guiteau wrote on the morning of the assassination, "was a sad necessity, but it will unite the Republican party and save the Republic. . . . I had no ill-will toward the president. His death was a political necessity."[13]

Garfield received two gunshot wounds. One grazed his right arm, doing no permanent damage. The other entered the lower back, deflected off a rib, and lodged near the pancreas. Dr. Smith Townshend was the first physician on the scene, arriving just a few minutes after the shooting. After his removal to the White House, Garfield was under the care of Dr. D. W. Bliss, assisted by a team of surgeons—J. K. Barnes, J. J. Woodward, Robert Reyburn, D. H. Agnew, and F. H. Hamilton. Three separate operations were performed to drain abscesses and to remove bone fragments. Meanwhile, doctors repeatedly probed the wound with bare fingers and unsterilized instruments, a common practice of the period. It was this probing that led to blood poisoning, the immediate cause of the president's death. On September 6, at his own request, Garfield was transferred by special train to Elberon, New Jersey. There he seemed to rally, but by September 17 he had developed bronchopneumonia and was drifting in and out of consciousness. He died two days later. His last words were to his chief of staff David G. Swaim: "Swaim, can't you stop this [pain]? Oh, Swaim!"[14] An autopsy was performed by Dr. D. S. Lamb of the Army Medical Museum. Garfield was buried at Lake View Cemetery in Cleveland.

On the day Garfield died, Guiteau wrote to the new president, Chester A. Arthur, "My inspiration is a God send to you and I presume that you appreciate it. . . . It raises you from a political cypher to the president of the United States. . . . Never think of Garfield's removal as murder. It was an act of God, resulting from a political necessity for which he was responsible."[15] He then proceeded to advise Arthur on the selection of a new cabinet. At his trial, November 1881–January 1882, Guiteau, defended by his brother-in-law George Scoville, pleaded not guilty by reason of insanity. He told the court that God had ordered him to kill the president. The jury deliberated an hour before returning a verdict of guilty. Judge Walter Cox sentenced him to be hanged. On June 30, 1882, Guiteau climbed the scaffold before a crowd of spectators, to whom he read aloud from the Bible, and sang a hymn he had composed for the occasion, which began, "I am going to the Lordy, I am so glad."

GARFIELD PRAISED: "There is a great deal of strength in Garfield's life and struggles as a self-made man. . . . From poverty and obscurity, by labor at all avocations, he became a great scholar, a statesman, a major general, a Senator, a Presidential candidate. . . . The truth is, no man ever started so low that accomplished so much, in all our history. Not Franklin or Lincoln even."[16]—President Rutherford B. Hayes, 1880

"As far as knowledge of public questions and experience of public business go, no President since the younger Adams has been so well prepared to get along with second-rate men as Mr. Garfield. He does not, like Lincoln, or Grant or Hayes, need cabinet officers to teach him, or 'keep him straight,' on any point whatever. There is not one of the departments of which he is not himself fully competent to take charge."[17]—*The Nation*, 1881

"He was earnestly seeking some practical way of correcting the evils arising from the distribution of overgrown and unwieldy patronage,—evils always appreciated and often discussed by him, but whose magnitude had been more deeply impressed upon his mind since his accession to the Presidency. Had he lived, a comprehensive improvement in the mode of appointment and in the tenure of office would have been proposed by him, and with the aid of Congress no doubt perfected."[18]—James G. Blaine, 1882

GARFIELD CRITICIZED: "Garfield has shown that he is not possessed of the backbone of an angle-worm."[19]—Former president Ulysses S. Grant, 1881

"He has been in office now for two months trying to restore 'harmony' and satisfy 'claims,' and recognize 'wings' and 'sections' by making appointments without regard . . . to fitness, and he has simply produced deadlock and confusion and disappointment among politicians, and disgust among the taxpayers."[20]—E. L. Godkin, Journalist and champion of reform, 1881

"He was not executive in his talents—not original, not firm, not a moral force. He leaned on others—could not face a frowning world; his habits suffered from Washington life. His course at various times when trouble came betrayed weakness."[21]—Former president Rutherford B. Hayes, 1883

"His will power was not equal to his personal magnetism. He easily changed his mind and honestly veered from one impulse to another."[22]—John Sherman, 1895

GARFIELD QUOTES: "A brave man is a man who dares to look the Devil in the face and tell him he is a Devil."[23]

"I would rather believe something and suffer for it, than to slide along into success without opinions."[24]—1871

"The people are responsible for the character of their Congress. If that body be ignorant, reckless, and corrupt, it is because the people tolerate ignorance, recklessness, and corruption. If it be intelligent, brave, and pure, it is because the people demand these high qualities to represent them in the national legislature."[25]—1877

BOOKS ABOUT GARFIELD: Conwell, Russell H. *The Life, Speeches and Public Services of James A. Garfield.* Portland, Maine: Stinson & Co., 1881.

Leech, Margaret, and Brown, Harry J. *The Garfield Orbit: The Life of President James A. Garfield.* New York: Harper & Row, 1978.

Peskin, Allan. *Garfield.* Kent, Ohio: Kent State University Press, 1978.

Taylor, John M. *Garfield of Ohio: The Available Man.* New York: Norton, 1970.

NOTES

1 Allan Peskin, *Garfield*, Kent, O.: Kent State University Press, 1978, p. 301.

2 Ibid., p. 322.

3 John M. Taylor, *Garfield of Ohio: The Available Man*, New York: Norton, 1970, p. 31.

4 Harry James Brown and Frederick D. Williams, eds., *Diary of James A. Garfield*, East Lansing, Mich.: Michigan State University Press, 1967, vol. I, p. 277.

5 *Theodore Roosevelt: An Autobiography*, New York: Scribner's Sons, 1920, p. 412.

6 Peskin, p. 6.

7 Ibid., p. 9.

8 Taylor, p. 156.

9 Brown and Williams, p. xxxvii.

10 Taylor, p. 59.

11 Peskin, p. 266.

12 Ibid., p. 580.

13 Robert J. Donovan, *The Assassins*, New York: Harper & Bros., 1952, p. 46.

14 Theodore C. Smith, *The Life and Letters of James Abram Garfield*, New Haven, Yale University Press, 1925, p. 1200.

15 Taylor, p. 283.

16 Dorothy Burne Goebel and Julius Goebel, Jr., *Generals in the White House*, Garden City, N.Y.: Doublebay, Doran, 1945, pp. 241–242.

17 Brown and Williams, vol. I, p. lx.

18 James G. Blaine, *Eulogy on James A Garfield*, Boston: Osgood, 1882, p. 43.

19 Adam Badeau, *Grant in Peace*, Hartford: Scranton, 1887, p. 534.

20 *Nation*, May 12, 1881, p. 329.

21 Charles Richard Williams, *The Life of Rutherford Birchard Hayes*, Columbus, O.: Ohio State Archaeological and Historical Society, 1928, vol. I, pp. 364–365n.

22 John Sherman, *Recollections of Forty Years in the House, Senate and Cabinet*, New York: Werner, 1895, vol. II, p. 807.

23 Bill Adler, *Presidential Wit: From Washington to Johnson*, New York: Trident Press, 1966, p. 76.

24 Peskin, p. 323.

25 James A. Garfield, "A Century of Congress," *Atlantic*, July 1877.

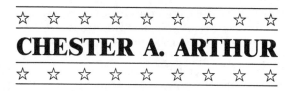

CHESTER A. ARTHUR

21ST PRESIDENT

NAME: Chester Alan (pronounced Alán) Arthur. He was named after Dr. Chester Abell, the physician who delivered him, and his paternal grandfather, Alan Arthur.

PHYSICAL DESCRIPTION: A sturdily built, handsome figure, Arthur stood 6 feet 2 inches tall and had a chubby, round face, high forehead, fleshy nose, black eyes, and wavy brown hair. As a young man he was trim, weighing perhaps 175–185 pounds, but a penchant for late-night feasts brought him up to 225 pounds by the time he became president. His most distinctive feature was the side-whiskers and mustache he wore throughout most of his career. A fastidious dresser, he had an extensive wardrobe that is said to have included 80 pairs of pants and changed clothes for every occasion, often several times a day. He was nicknamed Elegant Arthur. While he was president his health steadily eroded from terminal Bright's disease (see "Death").

PERSONALITY: Arthur was an amiable, easy-going fellow, an accomplished raconteur, a careful observer of social amenities, a man of charm, grace, and polish. Yet, observes biographer Thomas C. Reeves, "Though few would have guessed it of this urbane politician, Arthur was a deeply emotional, even romantic person, capable of great loyalties and easily brought to tears."[1] Reeves notes further that Arthur spent considerable effort to conceal that he retained much of the romanticism of his youth.

ANCESTORS: Arthur was of Scotch-Irish and English heritage.

FATHER: The Reverend William Arthur (1796–1875). A native of Dreen, County Antrim, Ireland, he graduated from Belfast College and emigrated to Dunham, Quebec, as a young man. There he taught school for a time and in 1821 eloped with Malvina Stone. He walked with a limp from a childhood accident. In 1828 he became a Baptist preacher. From that time until his retirement he successively tended 11 parishes in Vermont and New York. A fiery, tempestuous, often quarrelsome preacher, he was not always popular with his congrega-

307

tion. He spoke out vociferously for abolition and was a co-founder of the New York Antislavery Society. He edited the *Antiquarian and General Review* and wrote *The Derivation of Family Names*. He died at Newtonville, New York, when his most famous son was collector of the Port of New York.

MOTHER: Malvina Stone Arthur (1802–1869). A native of Berkshire, Vermont, she as a child moved with her family to Quebec, where she met and married William Arthur. She shared her husband's deep faith and, like him, was deeply disappointed that their son never chose to be baptized. She died in Newtonville, New York, when Arthur was a leading Republican in the state.

SIBLINGS: The fifth of eight children to live to maturity, Arthur had six sisters and a brother—Mrs. Regina Caw, widow of William G. Caw, merchant of Cohoes, New York, was an active Baptist and prohibitionist; Jane Arthur, died at 18; Mrs. Almeda Masten; Ann Eliza Arthur, schoolteacher in South Carolina; Mrs. Malvina Haynesworth, schoolteacher, wife of Henry Haynesworth, Confederate civil servant during the Civil War; Major William Arthur, Jr., career military officer, was struck deaf from a gunshot wound received at Ream's Station during the Civil War; Mrs. Mary McElroy, widow of the Reverend John E. McElroy, served as official White House hostess during the Arthur administration.

CHILDREN: Arthur had a son and a daughter to live to maturity.

Chester Alan Arthur, Jr. (1864–1937). He graduated from Princeton University in 1885 and went on to Columbia Law School, but rather than follow in his father's footsteps, he chose instead to become a gentlemen of leisure. President Arthur on his deathbed warned his son not to go into politics. Alan Arthur, as he was known, traveled extensively, maintained a fine stable of horses, and relied on polo for exercise. A celebrated playboy, he at 36 finally settled down, marrying Myra Townsend, a California heiress. The couple separated after 16 years and divorced in 1927. Eventually he settled in Colorado Springs, Colorado. In 1934 he married Rowena Graves, a real estate and insurance businesswoman.

Ellen "Nell" Herndon Arthur (1871–1915). Still a child while her father was president, she was shielded from the press. She married Charles Pinkerton and lived in New York City.

SUBSEQUENT DESCENDANT: Arthur had one grandchild, who died without having children. Thus no direct descendant of Arthur survives.

BIRTH: Arthur was born October 5, 1829, in the parsonage in North Fairfield, Vermont, according to entries in the Arthur family Bible. He weighed nine pounds at birth; he was delivered by Dr. Chester Abell, his namesake. In middle age Arthur began giving his year of birth erroneously as 1830, the year still listed in some reference books. Political opponents alleged that he was born across the Vermont border in Canada and, therefore, as a native foreigner, was constitutionally disqualified from becoming either vice president or president. Arthur denied the charge, and no proof of his Canadian birth has ever surfaced.

CHILDHOOD: Arthur underwent a rather rootless childhood, moving no fewer than seven times as his preacher father transferred from parish to parish. He grew up in the Vermont towns of North Fairfield, Williston, and Hinesburg and the New York communities of Perry, York, Union Village (now Greenwich), Schenectady, and Hoosick.

EDUCATION: Having learned the fundamentals from his father at home, Arthur attended the academy in Union Village (now Greenwich), New York. At 15 he enrolled at the Lyceum in Schenectady. There he was an editor of the school newspaper, the *Lyceum Review,* and took part in campus demonstrations in support of Henry Clay for president. In 1845 he entered Union College in Schenectady as a sophomore, choosing the classical curriculum. He engaged in his share of campus pranks, among them dumping the school bell in the Erie Canal. During winter vacations he taught school at Schaghticoke, New York. Admitted to Phi Beta Kappa his senior year, he graduated in the top third of the class of 1848. He went on to study law at Ballston Spa, New York, while teaching part time. After a brief teaching career, he in 1853 resumed his law studies in the office of E. D. Culver in New York City. He was admitted to the bar in 1854.

RELIGION: Episopalian. Much to the disappointment of his parents, Arthur never formally joined a church. As president, he attended St. John's Episocopal Church in Washington, to which he donated a window in memory of his late wife.

RECREATION: President Arthur often invited friends to late-night suppers at the White House followed by relaxed conversation lasting well past midnight. Sometimes he took guests on a stroll through the streets of Washington as late as three or four o'clock in the morning. He rarely retired before 2 A.M. An avid fisherman, he belonged to the Restigouche Salmon Club, a group of New York anglers who fished in Canada. He also liked to hunt.

EARLY ROMANCE: Although he dated various women as a young man, Arthur was not seriously involved with any woman before meeting his wife. By age 25, he began to fear that he would never marry.

MARRIAGE: Chester A. Arthur, 30, married Ellen "Nell" Lewis Herndon, 22, on October 25, 1859, at Calvary Episcopal Church in New York City. The bride was born in Culpepper Court House, Virginia, on August 30, 1837, the daughter of William L. Herndon, a naval officer who gained national attention in 1857 when he calmly went down with his ship after having safely evacuated passengers and crew of the *Central America* amid a storm off Cape Hatteras, and Frances Hansbrough Herndon. Miss Herndon and Arthur were introduced in 1856 by her cousin Dabney Herndon, a friend of Arthur, in New York City. Arthur proposed to her on the porch of the United States Hotel in Saratoga Springs, New York. After the wedding, the couple resided for a time with the bride's mother in New York. A talented soprano, Mrs. Arthur sang with the Mendelssohn Glee Club and performed at benefits around New York. The Arthurs apparently had a strong marriage, but one strained both by the political activities that consumed so much of his time and the Civil War. While Arthur was serving in the New York militia during the conflict, his wife privately sympathized with the Confederacy, for which many of her Virginia kinfolk were fighting. In January 1880 Mrs. Arthur came down with a cold from waiting outdoors for a carriage after an evening concert. Always frail in health, she quickly developed pneumonia and died two days later, on January 10, 1880, at age 42. She was buried in the Arthur family plot in Albany, New York. Away on business at the time, Arthur arrived home too late to see his wife conscious again. For weeks he was unconsolable; he never fully recovered from her death. He often privately expressed the regret that she did not live to see him become president. President Arthur ordered fresh flowers placed daily before her portrait in the White House.

MILITARY SERVICE: Civil War. Arthur served in the New York State militia from February 1858 to December 1862, rising from brigade judge advocate to quartermaster general. In January 1861 he was appointed engineer in chief with the rank of brigadier general. Three months later he was promoted to acting assistant quartermaster general, headquartered in New York City. In February 1862 he became inspector general and, after five months, quartermaster general. In the spring of 1862 he inspected New York troops at Fredericksburg and on the Chickahominy River. War Governor Edwin D. Morgan said of his service: "He was my chief reliance in the duties of equipping and transporting troops and munitions of war. In the position of Quarter Master General he displayed not only great executive ability and unbending integrity, but great knowledge of Army Regulations. He can say No (which is important) without giving offense."[2]

CAREER BEFORE THE PRESIDENCY: Arthur taught school at North Pownall, Vermont, during 1851–1852 and was principal of the academy at Cohoes, New York, during 1852–1853. In 1852 he cast his first presidential vote for Winfield Scott. Admitted to the bar in 1854, he became the junior partner in the New York City law firm of Culver, Parker, and Arthur. The next year he successfully represented a black woman, Lizzie Jennings, in her suit against a Brooklyn streetcar company for forcibly ejecting her from a whites-only car—a landmark case that led to desegregation of public transportation in New York City. In 1856 he formed a law partnership with Henry D. Gardiner and with him the next year moved to Kansas, then popularly known as Bleeding Kansas for the struggle there between slaveholders and abolitionists. After three months in the West the two returned to New York. In 1856 Arthur campaigned for the first Republican ticket as a member of the Young Men's Frémont Vigilance Committee. In 1860 he supported Abraham Lincoln for president. During the Civil War he served in the New York State militia (see "Military Service"). He became associated with the Stalwarts, the Republican party's conservative wing led in New York by Roscoe Conkling. At the party's national convention in 1864, Arthur supported President Lincoln's renomination and promoted the candidacy of Andrew Johnson for vice president. In 1867 he was named to the executive committee of New York City Republicans and the next year emerged as chairman of the state executive committee. During the presidential campaign of 1868, Arthur was chairman of the Central Grant Club of New York. He served as counsel to the New York City tax commission 1869–1870 at a salary of $10,000 a year.

Collector of the Port of New York, 1871–1878. Appointed by President Grant to this lucrative post at the suggestion of outgoing collector Thomas Murphy, Arthur was responsible for collection of about 75 percent of the nation's duties from ships that landed within his jurisdiction, which included the entire coast of New York State, the Hudson River, and parts of New Jersey. In 1872 Arthur supported Grant's reelection, raising contributions for the Republican ticket from customhouse employees. At the Republican national convention in 1876, he backed New York party boss Roscoe Conkling for president but on the final ballot joined the Conkling forces in backing Rutherford B. Hayes over James G. Blaine. He unsuccessfully supported Stewart Woodford for the vice presidential nomination. He campaigned for Hayes in the general election, again assessing customhouse employees to fill party coffers. Once elected, President Hayes made it clear that his policy of civil service reform would extend to Arthur's bailiwick. The Jay Commission, created in 1877 to investigate charges of corruption in the New York customhouse, called Arthur as its leadoff witness. In six hours of testimony, Arthur was unable to deter the commission from its ultimate findings—that merit appointments had been neglected to make room for political hacks and that employees were expected to kick back part of their salaries to the party. President Hayes accepted the commission's recommendation that the customhouse undergo a thorough housecleaning and reduction in force. In the interests of party unity, the president agreed to ease Arthur out with an appointment as consul in Paris. When Arthur refused, Hayes, on July 11, 1878, suspended him and appointed Edwin A. Merritt in his place. Arthur then resumed his law practice as senior partner in the New York firm of Arthur, Phelps, Knevels, and Ransom.

Vice President, March–September 1881. This was Arthur's first elective office. Arthur attended the Republican national convention in 1880 as a pro-Grant delegate and lieutenant of Stalwart boss Roscoe Conkling. The eventual nominee, James A. Garfield, sought to placate party conservatives by naming a New York Stalwart as vice president. His first choice, Representative Levi P. Morton, declined. Garfield then agreed to share the ticket with Arthur, who ignored Conkling's advice that he decline the offer. "The office of the Vice President is a greater honor than I ever dreamed of attaining,"[3] he is said defiantly to have informed an angry Conkling. Arthur was nominated on the first ballot, defeating Elihu Washburne of Illinois, his nearest rival, 468–199. With the Senate evenly divided, 37–37, between the two parties, Vice President Arthur's tie-breaking vote as presiding officer was crucial in winning for Republicans the right to organize the Senate and secure committee chairmanships. Arthur broke with President Garfield to side with Conkling in their bitter struggle over patronage (see "James A. Garfield, 20th President," "Administration"). On July 2, 1881, Arthur and Conkling stepped off a steamer in New York to learn that Garfield had been shot; the first report to reach them erroneously stated that the president had been killed. At the request of the cabinet, Arthur went to Washington to await developments. As the president's condition improved, Arthur returned to New York and prayed for his recovery. He was visibly shaken by the assassination attempt and was horrified to hear rumors that he or other Stalwarts had hired Guiteau to shoot the president. When Garfield's condition began to deteriorate, Arthur this time refused to go to Washington, fearing that he might appear to be eagerly mounting a deathwatch. At 11:30 P.M. September 19, 1881, a messenger arrived at Arthur's home to inform him that the president had died about an hour before.

At 2:15 A.M. on Spetember 20, 1881, Arthur was sworn in as president by New York Supreme Court Justice John R. Brady at Arthur's home, 123 Lexington Avenue, New York City. At that moment there was no vice president, no president pro tem of the Senate or Speaker of the House (neither had been selected yet), and, therefore, no constitutional line of succession. If Arthur had then been assassinated or otherwise died suddenly, there would have been an interregnum for the first time in U.S. history. To preclude such a catastrophe, Arthur that day drafted a proclamation calling the Senate into special session and mailed it to the White House. Once in Washington he could then safely destroy the letter and call the Senate into session himself. On September 22, 1881, Arthur took a second oath administered by Chief Justice Morrison R. Waite at the U.S. Capitol Building.

CABINET:

Secretary of State. (1) James G. Blaine (1830–1893), of Maine, served March–December 1881. A holdover from the Garfield administration, he agreed to remain in the cabinet until Congress convened. He promoted Pan-American-ism, calling for an International American Conference, and sought to ensure U.S. control over the proposed canal across Central America. He went on to become the Republican presidential nominee in 1884 (see "Grover Cleveland, 22d President," "Opponent"). He again served as secretary of state under President Benjamin Harrison. (2) Frederick T. Frelinghuysen (1817–1885), of New Jersey, served 1881–1885. He canceled his predecessor's plans for the International American Conference but took part in the International Red Cross Conference and the Berlin Conference for the African Congo. The Senate failed to ratify the treaty he concluded with Nicaragua providing for joint control of a proposed canal across Central America.

Secretary of the Treasury. (1) William Windom (1827–1891), of Minnesota, served March–November 1881. A holdover from the Garfield administration and conspicuous opponent of Arthur, he resigned and ran for the Senate. He served again as Treasury secretary under President Benjamin Harrison. (2) Charles J. Folger (1818–1884), of New York, served 1881–1884. Arthur first offered the post to Edwin D. Morgan, the New York governor he had served under during the Civil War, but Morgan declined for health reasons. Arthur next turned to Folger, a fellow Conkling lieutenant. Secretary Folger instituted the civil service system in the department. He died in office. (3) Walter Q. Gresham (1832–1895), of Indiana, served September–October 1884. Transferred from postmaster general, he resigned to accept a seat on the U.S. Circuit Court. He later served as secretary of state during Grover Cleveland's second term. (4) Hugh McCulloch (1808–1895), of Indiana, served 1884–1885. He had served as Treasury secretary in the Lincoln and Johnson administrations.

Secretary of War. Robert T. Lincoln (1843–1926), of Illinois, served 1881–1885. He was the only Garfield appointee to remain to the end of Arthur's term. He was the son of Abraham Lincoln.

Attorney General. (1) I. Wayne MacVeagh (1833–1917), of Pennsylvania, served March–October 1881. A holdover from the Garfield administration and an Independent Republican long committed to reform in government, he refused to serve in a Stalwart administration, despite Arthur's repeated pleas that he stay on. He later served as ambassador to Italy under President Cleveland and was chief counsel for the Unites States in the Venezuela Claims (1903) dispute. (2) Benjamin H. Brewster (1816–1888), of Pennsylvania, served 1882–1885. It was on Brewster's advice that Arthur refused a stay of execution pending a psychiatric exam for Garfield assassin Charles J. Guiteau.

Secretary of the Navy. (1) William H. Hunt (1823–1884), of Louisiana, served 1881–1882. A holdover from the Garfield administration, he encouraged a naval buildup. He resigned to become minister to Russia. (2) William E. Chandler (1835–1917), of New Hampshire, served 1882–1885. Appointed at the recommendation of James G. Blaine, Chandler mounted an extensive shipbuilding program for the navy and merchant marine, cut waste, reduced the bloated ranks of officers through attrition and a mandatory retirement program, encouraged the merit system, and established the Naval War College.

Postmaster General. (1) Thomas L. James (1831–1916), of New York, served March–December 1881. A holdover from the Garfield administration, he resigned despite Arthur's plea that he stay on. (2) Timothy O. Howe (1816–1883), of Wisconsin, served 1882–1883. A longtime Stalwart Republican, he died in office. (3) Walter Q. Gresham served 1883–1884. An Independent, or reform,

Republican, he was transferred to Treasury secretary. (4) Frank Hatton (1846–1894), of Iowa, served 1884–1885. A Stalwart Republican, he was promoted from first assistant postmaster general. He was a leader of the Arthur forces at the 1884 Republican convention.

Secretary of the Interior. (1) Samuel J. Kirkwood (1813–1894), of Iowa, served 1881–1882. He was a holdover from the Garfield administration and a conspicuous opponent of Arthur. (2) Henry M. Teller (1830–1914), of Colorado, served 1882–1885. A Stalwart Republican, he nevertheless enjoyed support from reformers. He defended the interests of western homesteaders against cattlemen, speculators, and Indians. He promoted vocational education among the Indians and established the court of Indian offenses.

ADMINISTRATION: September 20, 1881–March 4, 1885.

Chinese Exclusion Act, 1882. Circumventing the spirit if not the letter of the Treaty of 1880 (see Rutherford B. Hayes, 19th President," "Administration: Chinese Immigration"), which authorized restriction or temporary suspension of, but not an outright ban on, Chinese immigration, Congress passed a bill suspending Chinese immigration for 20 years. Arthur vetoed it but signed a subsequent measure, the Chinese Exclusion Act, which shortened the term of suspension to 10 years. The law applied to "both skilled and unskilled laborers and Chinese employed in mining." It also forbade U.S. courts to grant citizenship to Chinese already residing in the United States. The law was renewed in 1892 and 1902 and repealed in 1943.

River and Harbors Act, 1882. Arthur vetoed this bill appropriating $19 million for various internal improvements because he deemed it rank pork barrel legislation. Although Congress promptly overrode his veto, Arthur drew widespread praise for having attempted to thwart what many regarded as a Treasury raid.

Pendleton Act, 1883. This bill created the modern civil service system. Reformers had been calling for an end to the spoils system for more than a decade, but not until President Garfield was gunned down by a disappointed office seeker did national sentiment prod Congress to action. President Arthur, himself a product and long a practitioner of the spoils system, angered his old friends and delighted his former critics in signing the measure and enforcing it in good faith. The measure, sponsored by Democratic Senator George H. Pendleton of Ohio, created a bipartisan three-man Civil Service Commission to oversee the system. Arthur made clear his commitment by appointing three men long identified with civil service reform, notably its chairman, Dorman B. Eaton, a leader of the reform movement in New York and author of the Pendleton Act. The new law provided for open, competitive exams for applicants for government jobs classified under civil service, banned the practice of exacting political contributions from civil servants or otherwise pressing them into partisan service, excluded alcoholics from the civil service, and curbed nepotism.

Mongrel Tariff, 1883. In 1882 Arthur created a tariff commission, which after study recommended that duties be cut sharply. Protectionists and free-traders alike then descended on Capitol Hill to lobby members as they set about the task of tariff reform. Buffeted from all sides, Congress delivered a patchwork bill, the so-called Mongrel Tariff, which reduced duties overall by less than 1.5 percent. Arthur signed the measure, but it satisfied no one. It marked the beginning of the struggle over the tariff along distinct party lines, however, as Republicans became the party of protection, Democrats the champions of freer trade.

Arthur sought election as president in his own right in 1884, but his sudden conversion to governmental reform had alienated the conservative Stalwarts, his natural base of support, while failing to win over the Independents, or reformers, who continued to distrust him. He thus was denied his party's presidential nomination (see "Grover Cleveland, 22d President," "Opponent").

SUPREME COURT APPOINTMENTS: (1) Horace Gray (1828–1902), of Massachusetts, served as associate justice 1882–1902. A state supreme court chief justice and legal scholar, he brought to the bench a broad knowledge of past decisions. Speaking for the majority in *Julliard* v. *Greenman* (1884), he sustained the right of the federal government to issue greenbacks as legal tender in times of peace as well as war. (2) Samuel Blatchford (1820–1893), of New York, served as associate justice 1882–1893. Arthur first nominated and the Senate confirmed his former political boss Roscoe Conkling, who declined to serve. Blatchford, a former circuit court judge, wrote hundreds of opinions and was notable for his expertise in patent law. Speaking for the majority in *Chicago, Milwaukee, and St. Paul* v. *Minnesota* (1889), he ruled that corporations whose rates were subject to state regulation were entitled, under the due process clause of the Constitution, to seek relief in the courts.

RANKING IN 1962 HISTORIANS POLL: Arthur ranked twenty-first of 31 presidents; tenth of 12 "average" presidents. He ranked above Eisenhower, below Benjamin Harrison.

RETIREMENT: March 4, 1885–November 18, 1886. After attending the inaugural of his successor, Grover Cleveland, Arthur retired to his home in New York City. He resumed practicing law with S. W. Knevals and R. S. Ransom, but declining health prevented him from doing much to earn his $12,000-a-year salary. He also served as president of the New York Arcade Railway Company. His last public appearance in December 1885 was at a testimonial for Charles P. Daly, retiring chief justice of the New York City Court of Common Pleas.

DEATH: November 18, 1886, 5:00 A.M., at his home, 123 Lexington Avenue, New York City. As president, Arthur knew that he was suffering from Bright's disease, a then-fatal kidney ailment. He had occasional debilitating attacks but denied the reports of serious illness that appeared in the press from time to time. His health steadily deteriorated after his term as president. In February 1886 he underwent an acute attack. Retained fluids gave him a puffy appearance, and his urine became cloudy as the kidney malfunction progressed. He also was suffering from an enlarged heart, probably the result of high blood pressure caused by Bright's disease, and a nagging malarial infection contracted as president. He was attended by his personal physician, Dr. George A. Peters. Bedridden in his final months, he cheerily assured visitors that he would be fine. Meanwhile, at his direction, public and private papers in his possession were burned. Sometime during the night of November 16–17, he suffered a stroke that paralyzed his left side. He never fully regained consciousness and died the next day. The funeral was conducted on November 22 at the Church of the Heavenly Rest in New York; pallbearers included Robert T. Lincoln, General Philip H. Sheridan, Charles L. Tiffany, and Cornelius Vanderbilt. He was buried next to his wife at the Arthur family plot in Rural Cemetery, Albany, New York. In his last will and testament, Arthur divided his estate into two trusts, one for his son, Chester Alan Arthur, then 22, and the other for his daughter, Ellen

Herndon Arthur, then 15. The principal was to be turned over to his son at age 30 and his daughter at age 23.

ARTHUR PRAISED: "He was wise in statesmanship and firm and effective in administration. Honesty in national finance, purity and effectiveness in the civil service, the promotion of commerce, the re-creation of the American navy, reconciliation between North and South and honorable friendship with foreign nations received his active support. Good causes found in him a friend and bad measures met in him an unyielding opponent."[4]—Elihu Root, 1899

"If his conduct of affairs be criticized as lacking aggressiveness, it may confidently be replied that aggressiveness would have been unfortunate, if not disastrous. Rarely has there been a time when an indiscreet president could have wrought more mischief. It was not a time for showy exploits of brilliant experimentation. Above all else, the people needed rest from the strain and excitement into which the assassination of their president had plunged them. The course chosen by President Arthur was the wisest and most desirable that was possible."[5]—William Chandler, navy secretary under Arthur

ARTHUR CRITICIZED: "I have but one annoyance with the administration of President Arthur, and that is, that, in contrast with it, the administration of Hayes becomes respectable, if not heroic."[6]—New York Republican party boss Roscoe Conkling

"On [the civil service question] he evidently has no faith in the reform, but in deference to public sentiment, he yields so far as to recommend an appropriation of $25,000 to carry it out and express a readiness to [do] so."[7]—former president Rutherford B. Hayes, 1881

"Mr. Arthur's temperament is sluggish. He is indolent. It requires a great deal for him to get to his desk and begin the dispatch of business. Great questions of public policy bore him. No President was ever so much given to procrastination as he is."[8]—*Chicago Tribune*, 1882

ARTHUR QUOTES: "Men may die, but the fabrics of our free institutions remain unshaken. No higher or more assuring proof could exist of the strength and permanence of popular government than the fact that though the chosen of the people be struck down his constitutional successor is peacefully installed without shock or strain except the sorrow which mourns the bereavement."[9]—1881

"I may be President of the United States, but my private life is nobody's damned business."[10]

BOOKS ABOUT ARTHUR: Howe, George F. *Chester A. Arthur, A Quarter-Century of Machine Politics.* New York: Dodd, Mead, & Co., 1934.

Reeves, Thomas. *Gentleman Boss: The Life of Chester A. Arthur.* New York: Knopf, 1975.

NOTES

1 Thomas Reeves, *Gentleman Boss: The Life of Chester A. Arthur*, New York: Knopf, 1975, p. 51.
2 Ibid., p. 30.
3 Ibid., p. 180.
4 Ibid., p. 419.
5 Ibid., p. 421.

6 Richard Kenin and Justin Wintle, eds., *Dictionary of Biographical Quotation*, New York: Knopf, 1978, p. 32.

7 Charles Richard Williams, ed., *Diary and Letters of Rutherford B. Hayes*, Columbus, O.: Ohio State Archaeological and Historical Society, 1922, vol. IV, p. 52.

8 Reeves, p. 275.

9 Ibid., p. 248.

10 Ibid., p. 275.

GROVER CLEVELAND

22D PRESIDENT

NAME: Stephen Grover Cleveland. He was named after the Reverend Stephen Grover, whom Cleveland's father had succeeded as minister in Caldwell, New Jersey. By age 19 he began signing his name S. Grover Cleveland and a couple years later dropped the initial.

PHYSICAL DESCRIPTION: A massive, hulking figure, at 250 pounds the heaviest president up to that time, Cleveland stood 5 feet 11 inches tall and had a great bull neck, strong jaw, double chin, and ham-like fists. His hair, quite thin by middle age, was brown, his eyes blue, and his complexion fair. He wore a great bushy mustache. He spoke crisply in a strong resonant voice. His health generally was sound. In 1893, at the beginning of his second term as president, a malignant tumor was discovered in his mouth. In a secret hour-long operation performed aboard a yacht owned by Commodore E. C. Benedict as it cruised the East River off Manhattan, a team of doctors led by Dr. Joseph Bryant removed the president's left upper jaw and part of his palate and fitted him with a vulcanized rubber prosthesis that retained the natural contour of his jawline. In this operation and in a second one performed to remove suspicious tissue nearby, all surgery was done from within the mouth to avoid an external scar. The cancer never recurred. Although speculation that Cleveland was seriously ill arose in the press, the White House categorically denied it. The operation remained a secret until 1917, when Dr. W. W. Keen, one of the physicians present, described it in detail for the *Saturday Evening Post.*

PERSONALITY: In his Pulitzer-prize-winning biography, Allan Nevins observed that Cleveland had a dual personality. "To the end of his life," wrote Nevins, "his intimates were struck by the gulf which separated the exuberant, jovial Cleveland of occasional hours of carefree banter, and the stern, unbending Cleveland of work and responsibility, whose life seemed hung round by a pall of duty."[1] He had a quick temper and spoke bluntly.

ANCESTORS: Cleveland was mostly of English and Irish heritage. The immigrant ancestor of his paternal line, Moses Cleveland of Ipswich, England, arrived at Plymouth, Massachusetts, as an indentured carpenter's apprentice in 1635. Aaron Cleveland, the president's great-great-grandfather, was a noted Puritan-turned-Anglican minister and friend of Benjamin Franklin, in whose home he died in 1757. His son, also Aaron Cleveland, the president's great-grandfather, served in the Connecticut legislature during the American Revolution and later was ordained a Congregational minister.

FATHER: The Reverend Richard Falley Cleveland (1804–1853). A native of Norwich, Connecticut, he graduated with honors from Yale in 1824, studied briefly at Princeton Theological Seminary, and was ordained in 1829. After serving at the Congregational church in Windham, Connecticut, he successively ministered to Presbyterians in Portsmouth, Virginia, Caldwell, New Jersey and Fayetteville, New York. During 1850–1853 he was district secretary of the Central New York Agency of the American Home Missionary Society in Clinton, New York. Forced by illness to resign, he accepted the Presbyterian pastorate in Holland Patent, New York, but died soon after taking up the post, when Grover Cleveland was 16.

MOTHER: Ann Neal Cleveland (1806–1882). A native of Baltimore, daughter of a prosperous law book publisher, she married Richard F. Cleveland in 1829. She died in Holland Patent, New York, when her most famous son was mayor of Buffalo.

SIBLINGS: The fifth of nine children, Cleveland had five sisters and three brothers—Mrs. Anna N. Hastings, wife of the Reverend Eurotas P. Hastings, missionary and president of Jaffna College in Ceylon; the Reverend William N. Cleveland, Presbyterian minister; Mrs. Mary A. Hoyt, housekeeper for Cleveland during his term as governor of New York and assistant White House hostess during his term as president; Richard Cecil Cleveland, a bachelor, with his younger brother Lewis operated the Royal Victoria hotel, Nassau, the Bahamas, and was lost at sea in 1872; Mrs. Margaret L. Bacon; Lewis Frederick Cleveland, a bachelor and hotel owner, with his older brother Richard was lost at sea in 1872; Mrs. Susan S. Yeomans; Rose E. Cleveland, teacher, author of *George Eliot's Poetry and Other Studies* (1885), and White House hostess during Cleveland's bachelor days as president.

COLLATERAL RELATIVE: Cleveland was a sixth cousin once removed of Ulysses S. Grant.

CHILDREN: Cleveland had three daughters and two sons.

> **Ruth Cleveland (1891–1904).** Born in New York City, she was referred to as Baby Ruth in the press. Her sudden death from diptheria at age 12 crushed the former president.

> **Esther Cleveland(1893–1980).** The only child of a president to be born in the White House itself, she did volunteer work in England during World War I. There she met and married British Captain William Bosanquet. They settled in Yorkshire, where Bosanquet was an iron executive. Following his death she in 1971 returned to the United States and settled in Tamworth, New Hampshire.

> **Marion Cleveland (1895–1977).** Born in Buzzard's Bay, Massachusetts, she attended Columbia University Teachers College and married first Stanley Dell and second, in 1926, John Amen, a New York lawyer. During 1943–1960 she was community relations adviser for the Girl Scouts of America at its headquarters in New York.

Richard Folsom Cleveland (1897–1974), lawyer. Born in Princeton, New Jersey, he served as an officer in the Marines during World War I, graduated from Princeton University in 1919, receiving a master's degree in 1921, and from Harvard Law School in 1924. He practiced law in Baltimore. At the Democratic national convention in 1932, he seconded the nomination of Governor Albert C. Ritchie of Maryland. During 1934–1935 he served as general counsel to the Public Service Commission in Baltimore. An anti–New Deal Democrat, he opposed the reelection of President Franklin D. Roosevelt and was active in the American Liberty League.

Francis Grover Cleveland (1903–1995), actor. Born in Buzzard's Bay, Massachusetts, he graduated from Harvard University with a degree in drama. After teaching for a time in Cambridge, Massachusetts, he went to New York to enter the theater. Eventually he settled in Tamworth, New Hampshire, where he served as selectman and operated a summer stock company, the Barnstormers.

For Cleveland's alleged illegitimate son, see "Premarital Affair."

BIRTH: Cleveland was born March 18, 1837, at the Presbyterian manse in Caldwell, New Jersey.

CHILDHOOD: When Cleveland was four years old, the family moved from his birthplace to Fayetteville, New York, and 10 years later moved to Clinton, New York. A burly, fun-loving, yet responsible lad, Cleveland took time out from such chores as chopping wood, cultivating the garden, and babysitting for his younger siblings to fish in Green Lake, take a dip in Limestone Creek, or pull off an occasional nocturnal prank, typically ringing the school bell or unhinging a neighbor's front gate. Still, he learned early the value of using his time well. In an essay written when he was nine, Cleveland declared, "If we expect to become great and good men and be respected and esteemed by our friends we must improve our time when we are young."[2] He pointed to George Washington and Andrew Jackson as ideal role models of this precept. To earn spare cash, Cleveland picked up odd jobs around the Erie Canal. At 15 he left his family in Clinton to work as a clerk in the store of John McVicar in Fayetteville for $50 a year plus room and board. The next year he moved with his family to Holland Patent, New York.

EDUCATION: Having learned the basics at home from his parents, Cleveland at age 11 entered the Fayetteville, New York, academy. He attended the Clinton (New York) Liberal Institute 1850–1851 and then returned to the Fayetteville academy, where he organized a debating society. He was a hardworking, though not particularly brilliant, student. He had hoped to go on to college, but his father's death in 1853 abruptly ended his formal education, for it became necessary for him to go to work. His older brother William arranged for his appointment as an assistant teacher in the literary department of the New York Institute for the Blind in New York City, where during 1853–1854 he taught reading, writing, arithmetic, and geography. He disliked the job and quit after one year to join his family in Holland Patent. Although he longed to continue his education, he turned down an offer from a benefactor who had agreed to send him through college if he would enter the ministry. He decided instead in 1855 to strike out for the growing lakeport of Cleveland, Ohio. Enroute, however, he stopped off at Buffalo to visit his Uncle Lewis F. Allen, who persuaded him to settle there. Allen, a prominent Buffalo resident and stock breeder, hired Cleveland at $10 a month plus room and board to edit the *American Shorthorn*

Handbook. He also arranged for him to study law at the Buffalo office of Rogers, Bowen, and Rogers. Cleveland was admitted to the bar in 1859.

RELIGION: Presbyterian. As a minister's son, Cleveland was imbued with religious training as a child. Playing was absolutely forbidden on the Sabbath. He was expected to attend church twice on Sundays as well as to go to Sunday school and midweek prayer meetings. Although he grew lax in observing the Sabbath as an adult, Cleveland retained a deep faith in God and Providence and never regretted his strict religious upbringing. "I have always felt that my training as a minister's son," he once reflected, "has been more valuable to me as a strengthening influence than any other incident in my life."[3] He also believed that his mother's regular prayers were largely responsible for his political success. In Washington he attended the First Presbyterian Church.

RECREATION: Cleveland's favorite recreation was fishing, and his favorite spot was Saranac Lake and other fishing resorts in the Adirondacks. He also hunted with his trusty rifle dubbed "Death and Destruction." As president he often took a morning walk and an afternoon carriage ride. He played euchre, cribbage, pinochle, and poker. He smoked cigars and drank liquor, mostly beer. As a young bachelor he was a regular at various Buffalo saloons and beer gardens. As his size evidenced, he loved to eat, especially German food.

PREMARITAL AFFAIR: Maria C. Halpin. In 1871 Mrs. Maria Halpin, a 33-year-old widow, left her two children behind in Jersey City, New Jersey, to seek a new life in Buffalo, where she found work first as a collar maker and then as a department store clerk, rising at the latter establishment to manager of the cloak department. In Buffalo she kept company with various men, among them Grover Cleveland. In September 1874 she gave birth to a son, whom she named Oscar Folsom Cleveland, after Oscar Folsom (father of the president's future bride) and Grover Cleveland. She named Cleveland as the father. Although Cleveland was unsure of the child's paternity, he accepted responsibility rather than burden the other potential fathers, all of whom were married. As a bachelor, he reasoned, he had the least to lose from such an admission. He agreed to pay child support but chose not to marry the mother. As she nursed the infant, Mrs. Halpin began drinking heavily. Out of concern for the child's welfare, Cleveland sought guidance from his friend Judge Roswell L. Burrows, who placed Mrs. Halpin in an insane asylum temporarily and the child in an orphanage. Cleveland paid the child's expenses—$5 a week—at the orphanage. On Mrs. Halpin's release from the asylum, Cleveland set her up in a small business in Niagara Falls, New York. Soon, however, Mrs. Halpin petitioned to regain custody of the child. Rebuffed in the courts, she took matters into her own hands and in 1876 kidnapped him. The child was quickly recovered and returned to the orphanage; eventually he was adopted by a prominent New York family and became a doctor. Mrs. Halpin accepted $500 from Cleveland and left town. She later remarried and settled in New Rochelle, New York. The episode, made public in lurid headlines in 1884, nearly scotched Cleveland's bid for the presidency (see "Campaign and the Issues, 1884").

MARRIAGE: President Grover Cleveland, 49, married Frances Folsom, 21, on June 2, 1886, at the White House. Cleveland was the only president to be married in the White House itself (Tyler had married while president but in New York). The bride was born in Buffalo, New York, on July 21, 1864, the daughter of Oscar Folsom, a lawyer, and Emma Harmon Folsom. A longtime close friend of Oscar Folsom, Cleveland at 27 met his future wife shortly after she was born.

He took an avuncular interest in the child, buying her a baby carriage and otherwise doting on her as she grew up. When her father died in a buggy accident in 1875 without having provided a will, the court appointed Cleveland administrator of his estate. This brought Cleveland into still more contact with Frances, then 11. She attended Central High School in Buffalo and went on to Wells College in Aurora, New York. Sometime while she was in college, Cleveland's feelings for her took a romantic turn. He proposed by letter in August 1885, soon after her graduation. They did not announce their engagement, however, until just five days before the wedding. President Cleveland worked as usual on his wedding day. The ceremony, a small affair attended by relatives, close friends, and the cabinet and their wives, was performed at 7 P.M. in the Blue Room of the White House by the Reverend Byron Sunderland, assisted by the Reverend William Cleveland, the president's brother. The words "love, honor, and keep" were substituted for "love, honor, and obey." John Philip Sousa and the Marine Band provided the music. The couple spent a five-day honeymoon at Deer Park in the Cumberland Mountains of Maryland. The youngest First Lady ever, Mrs. Cleveland was the subject of intense interest in the press. Baseless gossip that she was unhappy and at times physically abused by the president wounded the Clevelands deeply, but they bore it in silence. After Cleveland's defeat at the polls in 1888, she warned the White House staff that she would return in four years. She proved correct, becoming the only First Lady to preside at two nonconsecutive administrations. After Cleveland's death in 1908, she remained in Princeton, New Jersey. In 1913 she married Thomas J. Preston, professor of archaeology at Princeton University; she was the first presidential widow to remarry. During the Depression of the 1930s she led the Needlework Guild of America in its clothing drive for the poor. She died on October 29, 1947, in Baltimore and was buried next to the president at Princeton.

MILITARY SERVICE: None. Cleveland was drafted during the Civil War but chose to purchase a substitute, a legal option under the terms of the Conscription Act of 1863. He paid $150 to George Brinske (or Benninsky), a 32-year-old Polish immigrant, to serve in his place.

CAREER BEFORE THE PRESIDENCY: Admitted to the bar in 1859, Cleveland practiced with the Buffalo firm of Rogers, Bowen, and Rogers. He had by this time already become associated with the Democratic party, attracted by its conservatism and stability in contrast to the fledgling Republican party. He supported Stephen A. Douglas for president in 1860. But with the outbreak of the Civil War, he approved Lincoln's war policy, including suspension of habeas corpus and other emergency measures. He even may have bolted party ranks in 1864 to vote for Lincoln's reelection. On the local level, however, he remained a loyal Democrat. In 1862 he was elected ward supervisor. During 1863–1865 he was assistant district attorney for Erie County. In 1865 he ran unsuccessfully for district attorney. He then returned to private practice, at first in partnership with Isaac K. Vanderpoel and later with Albert P. Lanning and Oscar Folsom.

Sheriff of Erie County, New York, 1871–1873. As sheriff he ended routine graft in the department, thereby alienating many politicians of his own party. He earned a reputation, however, for fearlessness and incorruptibility, which he retained throughout his career. Among his duties was that of public executioner. Although he anguished at the prospect of taking a man's life, he refused to slough off the task on subordinates. Cleveland personally sprang the trap on two men—Patrick Morrissey, convicted of stabbing his mother to death, and Jack Gaffney, found guilty of shooting a man over a card game. After his term as sheriff, he again returned to private practice in partnership with Lyman K. Bass and Wilson S. Bissell. In 1876 he supported Thomas F. Bayard for the Democratic presidential nomination but endorsed the eventual nominee, Samuel J. Tilden. In 1880 he backed Winfield S. Hancock for president.

Mayor of Buffalo, New York, 1882. Elected on a reform ticket over Republican Milton C. Beebe, Cleveland became known as the "veto mayor" for his repeated efforts to block inflated contracts with firms doing business with the city. He drew widespread praise for vetoing an overpriced street-cleaning contract. To ensure that city funds were spent prudently, he insisted on competitive bidding for even the smallest projects. He also took steps to check the rising number of typhoid-related deaths by improving the city's sewage system. His honest, efficient administration at City Hall prompted the *Buffalo Sunday Times* in June 1882 to suggest Cleveland for governor.

Governor of New York, 1883–1885. Elected overwhelmingly (58%–37%) over the Republican candidate, Treasury Secretary Charles J. Folger, Governor Cleveland strengthened his reputation by standing up to Tammany Hall and its boss, John Kelly. He turned back requests for patronage, insisting that merit, not party service, be the sole consideration for appointment. He vetoed numerous private bills and other treasury grabs. He promoted and signed into law the state civil service bill sponsored by a brash young assemblyman named Theodore Roosevelt and appointed distinguished reformers to the newly created civil service commission. He instituted closer scrutiny of state banking practices. He took steps to preserve some 1.5 million acres around Niagara Falls. "Public office is a public trust" became his slogan.

DEMOCRATIC PRESIDENTIAL NOMINATION, 1884: As Democrats convened in Chicago in July 1884, Cleveland was the clear front-runner, the candidate of northern reformers and sound-money men. Although Tammany Hall bitterly opposed his nomination, the machine represented a minority of the New York delegation. Its only chance to block Cleveland was to break the unit rule, and this it failed to do. Daniel N. Lockwood of New York placed Cleveland's name in nomination. But this rather lackluster address was eclipsed by a seconding speech by Edward S. Bragg of Wisconsin, who roused the delegates with a memorable slap at Tammany. "They love him, gentleman," Bragg said of Cleveland, "and they respect him, not only for himself, for his character, for his integrity and judgment and iron will, but they love him most of all for the enemies he has made."[4] As the convention rocked with cheers, Tammany boss John Kelly lunged at the platform, screaming that he welcomed the compliment. On the first ballot Cleveland led the field with 392 votes, more than 150 votes short of the nomination. Trailing him were Thomas F. Bayard of Delaware, 170; Allen G. Thurman of Ohio, 88; Samuel J. Randall of Pennsylvania, 78; and Joseph E. McDonald of Indiana, 56; with the rest scattered. Randall then withdrew in Cleveland's favor. This move, together with the southern bloc scrambling aboard the Cleveland bandwagon, was enough to put him over the top of the second ballot, with 683 votes, to 81½ for Bayard and 45½ for Thomas Hendricks of Indiana. Hendricks was nominated for vice president. The Democratic platform supported tariff revisions ("not . . . to injure any domestic industries, but rather to promote their healthy growth"), taxing luxuries more severely than necessities, a hard-money policy, Pan-Americanism, the rights of organized labor, expansion of the merchant marine, and continued curbs on Chinese immigration.

OPPONENT: James G. Blaine (1830–1893) of Maine; Republican. Born in West Brownsville, Pennsylvania, the son of a county clerk, Blaine graduated near the top of his class at Washington and Jefferson College in 1847 and taught school for a time. In 1854 he settled in his wife's hometown, Augusta, Maine, where he edited the *Kennebec Journal* and helped found the Republican party in that state. He served in the state legislature 1858–1862 and the U.S. House 1863–1876, serving as Speaker 1869–1875. He supported Radical Reconstruction and the impeachment of President Andrew Johnson. He was a leading presidential candidate at the 1876 Republican national convention, at which he was first dubbed the Plumed Knight (see "Rutherford B. Hayes, 19th President," "Republican Presidential Nomination"). Disclosure of the so-called Mulligan letters implicating Blaine in graft from railroad interests doomed his candidacy, however. Elected to the Senate 1876–1881, he in 1880 again vied for the Republican presidential nomination as candidate of the Half Breeds, the moderately conservative faction of the party, but lost to James A. Garfield. He served as secretary of state briefly, in 1881 in the Garfield and Arthur administrations. At the Republican national convention in Chicago in June 1884, Blaine had little opposition. Incumbent president Chester A. Arthur was a candidate, but his sudden conversion to governmental reforms alienated the conservative Stalwarts, his natural base of support, while failing to win over the Independents, or reformers, who continued to distrust him. Only the popular war hero General William T. Sherman had a chance to snatch the nomination from Blaine. When anti-Blaine elements took steps to bring him forward, however, the veteran soldier deflated the boomlet with a statement that has since become the ultimate political disclaimer: "If nominated, I will not accept. If elected, I will not serve." On the first ballot, Blaine led with 334½ votes, 76 votes short of the nomination, to 278 for President Arthur, 93 for George F. Edmunds of Vermont, 63½ for John A. Logan of Illinois, and the rest scattered. Blaine steadily increased his strength in subsequent balloting and won the nomination on the fourth tally with 541 votes to 207 for Arthur. Logan, who had withdrawn after the third ballot in favor of Blaine, was nominated for vice president. The Republican platform supported a high tariff, "not for revenue only, but . . . to afford security to our diversified industries and protection to the rights and wages of the laborers," and called for regulation of the railroads, creation of a bureau of labor, enforcement of the eight-hour day, extension of the civil service, expansion of the navy, and continued curbs on Chinese immigration. After his defeat by Cleveland, Blaine retired to complete his memoirs, *Twenty Years in Congress* (2 vols., 1884–1886). With the accession of President Benjamin Harrison, he was again appointed secretary of state, serving 1889–1892.

CAMPAIGN AND THE ISSUES, 1884: The campaign turned less on issues than on the personal morality of the candidates. Democrats assailed Blaine for long-standing charges that he had profited from association with railroad interests while in Congress. "Blaine! Blaine! James G. Blaine! Continental liar from the state of Maine!" was the Democratic battlecry. Republicans spotted a chink in Cleveland's moral armor, as the *Buffalo Evening Telegraph*, under the banner headline "A Terrible Tale—Dark Chapter in Public Man's History," exposed Cleveland's liaison with Maria C. Halpin (see "Premarital Affair"). Asked by his political handlers how to respond to the charges, Cleveland boldly instructed them to tell the truth. His candid admission caught the fancy of the electorate and did much to defuse the issue. A popular chant of the campaign was "Ma, Ma, where's my Pa? Gone to the White House, Ha, Ha, Ha!" Despite attacks on his character, Cleveland retained the support of most reformers, including Carl Schurz, Henry Ward Beecher, and other anti-Blaine Republicans known as the Mugwumps. Some Republican reformers, however, notably young Theodore Roosevelt, chose not to bolt the party. The race was exceedingly close, especially in New York, the outcome of which would decide the election. Two events fatally damaged Blaine's campaign: At a meeting with Protestant ministers in New York, Blaine listened passively as the Reverend Samuel D. Burchard declared, "We are Republicans, and don't propose to leave our party and identify ourselves with the party whose antecedents have been Rum, Romanism, and Rebellion."[5] The remark, left unchallenged by Blaine, cost the Republican candidate New York's crucial Irish Catholic vote. Blaine then lost labor when he was seen at a time of high unemployment dining at a sumptuous feast in the company of John Jacob Astor, Jay Gould, and other tycoons.

ELECTION AS PRESIDENT, FIRST TERM, 1884:

Popular Vote: Cleveland (Democrat), 4,911,017 (49%); Blaine (Republican), 4,848,334 (48%).

Electoral Vote: Cleveland, 219; Blaine, 182.

States Carried: Cleveland won the electoral votes of 20 states—Alabama, Arkansas, Connecticut, Delaware, Florida, Georgia, Indiana, Kentucky, Louisiana, Maryland, Mississippi, Missouri, New Jersey, New York, North Carolina, South Carolina, Tennessee, Texas, Virginia, and West Virginia. Blaine won the electoral votes of 18 states—California, Colorado, Illinois, Iowa, Kansas, Maine, Massachusetts, Michigan, Minnesota, Nebraska, Nevada, New Hampshire, Ohio, Oregon, Pennsylvania, Rhode Island, Vermont, and Wisconsin.

INAUGURAL ADDRESS: March 4, 1885. ". . . He who takes the oath today to preserve, protect, and defend the Constitution of the United States only assumes the solemn obligation which every patriotic citizen—on the farm, in the workshop, in the busy marts of trade, and everywhere—should share with him. The Constitution which prescribes his oath, my countrymen, is yours; the Government you have chosen him to administer for a time is yours; the suffrage which executes the will of freemen is yours; the laws and the entire scheme of our civil rule, from the town meeting to the State capitals and the national capital, is yours. . . . Every Citizen owes to the country a vigilant watch and close scrutiny of its public servants and a fair and reasonable estimate of their fidelity and usefulness. Thus is the people's will impressed upon the whole framework of our civil polity—municipal, State, and Federal; and this is the price of our liberty and the inspiration of our faith in the Republic. . . ."

VICE PRESIDENT: Thomas Andrews Hendricks (1819–1885), of Indiana, served March–November 1885. Born in Muskingum County, Ohio, Hendricks grew up in Shelby County, Indiana, graduating from Hanover College in 1841. A lawyer, he was elected to the Indiana legislature in 1848 and served in the U.S. House 1851–1855 and Senate 1863–1869. He opposed Emancipation and supported President Andrew Johnson's Reconstruction goals. Elected governor of Indiana 1873–1877, he was the first Democratic governor to take office in the North after the Civil War. In 1876 he ran unsuccessfully for vice president on the ticket with Samuel J. Tilden. In 1880 he was a candidate for the Democratic presidential nomination. In 1884 he again ran for the presidential nomination but settled for the number-two spot. He died of a stroke in Indianapolis less than nine months after becoming vice president. For 12 days, from Hendricks's death until John Sherman was elected president pro tem of the Senate, no one stood in the line of presidential succession.

CABINET:

Secretary of State. Thomas F. Bayard (1828–1898), of Delaware, served 1885–1889. A leading Democrat from a distinguished political family, Bayard took up his duties conscientiously. He attempted to resolve the North Atlantic fisheries dispute with Canada and Britain, but the Senate refused to ratify the treaty. He also sought a peaceful resolution of the dispute with Germany over Samoa but drew criticism for failing to deal sternly with German aggression against the islands. Still, he retained the president's complete confidence. He later served as the first ambassador to Great Britain, 1893–1897, previous U.S. personnel abroad having held the rank of minister.

Secretary of the Treasury. (1) Daniel Manning (1831–1887), of New York, served 1885–1887. Rewarded for his efforts on behalf of Cleveland at the convention and in the campaign, Manning, in poor health, only reluctantly accepted this post but proved an able, hardworking secretary, committed to a sound-money policy. Although an advocate of a reduced tariff, he vigorously enforced the law, ending the long-standing practice of undervaluing imported goods, a practice that had benefited foreign manufacturers and American importers at the expense of the federal Treasury. He collapsed from a stroke while in office. (2) Charles S. Fairchild (1842–1924), of New York, served 1887–1889. Promoted from assistant secretary, Fairchild, long a champion of government reform, was an able, efficient secretary.

Secretary of War. William C. Endicott (1826–1900), of Massachusetts, served 1885–1889. The Endicott Board of Fortifications layed out the coastal defense of cities along the Eastern Seaboard. He came under intense criticism for a proposal to return captured Confederate flags to the southern states.

Attorney General. Augustus H. Garland (1832–1899), of Arkansas, served 1885–1889. He had served in both houses of the Confederate Congress during the Civil War. As attorney general he drew widespread criticism when it was disclosed that he owned 10 percent of the stock of the Pan-Electric Company, then involved in patent litigation before the federal government.

Secretary of the Navy. William C. Whitney (1841–1904), of New York, served 1885–1889. He undertook a major shipbuilding program, completed by his successor Benjamin F. Tracy.

Postmaster General. (1) William F. Vilas (1840–1908), of Wisconsin, served 1885–1888. He was transferred to interior secretary. (2) Donald M. Dickinson (1846–1917), of Michigan, served 1888–1889.

Secretary of the Interior. Lucius Q. C. Lamar (1825–1893), of Mississippi, served 1885–1888. A veteran officer of the Confederate army, he had been a force for reconciliation since the Civil War. He resigned to accept appointment to the Supreme Court. (2) William F. Vilas served 1888–1889. Transferred from postmaster general, he won praise for his administration of the burgeoning western bureaus of the department.

Secretary of Agriculture. Norman J. Colman (1827–1911), of Missouri, served February–March 1889. Having promoted creation of this new cabinet post, he was named the department's first secretary.

ADMINISTRATION: March 4, 1885–March 3, 1889.

Presidential Succession Act, 1886. Superseding the presidential succession act of 1792, this law provided that on the death, incapacity, or resignation of both the president and vice president, the line of succession to the presidency was to fall to the cabinet in the chronological order of the creation of each department. The law was superseded by the Presidential Succession Act of 1947 (see "Harry S Truman, 33d President," "Administration") and ultimately by the Twenty-fifth Amendment (see "Lyndon Johnson, 36th President," "Administration").

Pension and Private Relief Bills. President Cleveland vetoed hundreds of pension and private relief bills as unwarranted drains on the Treasury. His action drew fire from the powerful Grand Army of the Republic, the Civil War veterans organization. "Public money appropriated for pensions," Cleveland insisted, ". . . should be devoted to the indemnification of those who in the defense of the Union and in the nation's service have worthily suffered, and who in the day of their dependence resulting from such suffering are entitled to the benefactions of their Government."[6]

Interstate Commerce Act, 1887. This law created the Interstate Commerce Commission (ICC), the first federal regulatory agency. The ICC was to see that interstate railroad rates were "reasonable and just" and to put an end to rebates and other discriminatory practices by which railroads had long favored large corporations over small businessmen and farmers. The commission lacked enforcement powers, however, until the advent of the Theodore Roosevelt administration.

Dawes Severalty Act, 1887. Prodded by Helen Hunt Jackson's *A Century of Dishonor*, criticizing U.S. treatment of the Indians, Congress passed and President Cleveland approved this law, which granted citizenship and full title to defined parcels of reservation land to Indians willing to renounce tribal allegiance.

Hatch Act, 1887. A compliment to the Morrill Act (1862; see "Abraham Lincoln, 16th President," "Administration"), it provided federal funds for the establishment of agricultural experiment stations under the direction of agricultural colleges in the various states.

Tariff. In his third annual message to Congress, December 1887, President Cleveland argued strenuously for a reduction in the tariff. Calling the current rates "indefensible extortion and a culpable betrayal of American fairness and justice" as well as a "vicious, inequitable, and illogical source of unnecessary taxation," Cleveland staked out the position on which he was to wage his campaigns for reelection. Republicans responded by defending the high tariff as a protection of domestic manufactures and the wages of labor. No action was taken during his term.

SUPREME COURT APPOINTMENTS: (1) Lucius Q. C. Lamar (1825–1893), of Mississippi, served as associate justice 1888–1893. He resigned as secretary of the interior to accept the seat. Strong opposition to his appointment arose over his age, 62, and his service to the Confederacy during the Civil War, but the Senate narrowly (32–28)confirmed him. He died five years later without having made a significant impact on the Court. (2) Melville W. Fuller (1833–1910), of Illinois, served as chief justice 1888–1910. Succeeding Chief Justice Waite, Fuller proved an efficient administrator of the Court's clogged docket. At his urging, Congress created the Circuit Court of Appeals, which relieved the

Supreme Court of half its work load. Fuller strove for a consensus among the brethren, believing that the Court spoke with greater authority in the absence of written dissent. He was basically conservative, committed to states' rights and free enterprise unfettered by government interference. Speaking for the barest majority in *Pollock* v. *Farmer's Loan and Trust Co.* (1895), he struck down the federal income tax law: "The Constitution prohibits any direct tax, unless in proportion to numbers as ascertained by the census." The ruling drew a firestorm of criticism and threats of impeachment, but it stood until ratification of the Sixteenth Amendment in 1913. Fuller generally opposed the interests of the labor movement, voting to sustain the yellow dog contract, whereby job applicants were required to swear that they would not join a union; and to overturn state laws restricting the work week to 60 hours. In *Fong Yue Ting* v. *U.S.* (1893), Fuller dissented from the Court's ruling that Chinese aliens in the United States could be summarily deported without due process. "The general government . . . cannot . . . arbitrarily deal with persons lawfully within the place of its dominion," he argued.

RANKING IN 1962 HISTORIANS POLL: Cleveland ranked eleventh of 31 presidents, last of 6 "near great" presidents. He ranked above Madison, below John Adams.

TEMPORARY RETIREMENT: 1889–1893. Having been defeated for reelection (see under "Benjamin Harrison, 23d President," for election of 1888), Cleveland attended the inauguration of his successor and returned to the practice of law with the firm of Bangs, Stetson, Tracy, and MacVeagh in New York City. He also spent much time at his summer home, Gray Gables, at Buzzard's Bay, Massachusetts. In a letter to the Reform Club in February 1891, Cleveland broke with congressional Democrats in declaring his opposition to the free coinage of silver, calling it a "dangerous and reckless experiment."[7] The letter marked his commitment to the conservative eastern wing of the party.

See also "Grover Cleveland, 24th President."

NOTES:

1 Allan Nevins, *Grover Cleveland: A Study in Courage*, New York: Dodd, Mead, 1932, pp. 57–58.

2 Robert McElroy, *Grover Cleveland: The Man and the Statesman*, New York: Harper & Bros., 1923, vol. I, p. 9.

3 John Sutherland Bonnell, *Presidential Profiles: Religion in the Life of American Presidents*, Philadelphia: Westminster, 1971, p. 147.

4 Denis Tilden Lynch, *Grover Cleveland: A Man Four-Square*, New York: Horace Liveright, 1932, p. 198.

5 Eugene H. Roseboom, "A History of Presidential Elections, New York: Macmillan, 1957, p. 272.

6 Henry Steele Commager, ed., *Documents of American History*, New York: Crofts, 1945, Doc. no. 312, p. 120.

7 Ibid., Doc. no. 322, p. 138.

☆ ☆ ☆ ☆ ☆ ☆ ☆ ☆ ☆

BENJAMIN HARRISON

☆ ☆ ☆ ☆ ☆ ☆ ☆ ☆ ☆

23D PRESIDENT

NAME: Benjamin Harrison. He was named after his paternal uncle Dr. Benjamin Harrison and his great-grandfather Benjamin Harrison, signer of the Declaration of Independence.

PHYSICAL DESCRIPTION: A stocky figure with a large paunchy torso set atop short stubby legs, Harrison stood about 5 feet 6 inches tall and had a fair complexion, blue eyes, and light brown hair that had been corn-silk blond in his youth. He was among the last of the nineteenth-century statesmen to wear a full beard; Harrison's had a reddish tinge. He spoke in a high, soft voice. He dressed fashionably. His health generally was sound, except for a brief physical breakdown in 1867 brought on from overwork.

PERSONALITY: Known as the "human iceberg," Harrison was stiff and formal in dealing with people. He disliked small talk. He could not tolerate inefficiency or incompetence in subordinates. He tackled problems through mastery of detail. Although he lacked both charisma and the common touch, he was widely respected for his intelligence, honesty, attention to duty, and diligence. "Integrity formed the backbone of Harrison's character," according to biographer Harry J. Sievers. "His active intellect firmly backed by moral courage, he was regarded as a bulwark of political decency."[1] He was among the best extemporaneous speakers of his day.

ANCESTORS: Harrison was a grandson of President William Henry Harrison (see also "William Henry Harrison, 9th President," "Ancestors").

FATHER: John Scott Harrison (1804–1878). The only man to be both the son of one president and father of another, he was a member of the U.S. House 1853–1857 (see "William Henry Harrison," "Children").

MOTHER: Elizabeth Irwin Harrison (1810–1850). Born of Scotch heritage in Mercersburg, Pennsylvania, she was raised amid strict Presbyterian principles and in 1831 married, as his second wife, John Scott Harrison. She died in childbirth a few days before her most famous son's seventeenth birthday.

SIBLINGS: By his father's first marriage, Harrison had two older half sisters to live to maturity—Mrs. Elizabeth "Betsie" Eaton of Cincinnati and Mrs. Sarah "Sallie" Devin of Ottumwa, Iowa. Harrison had three full brothers and two full sisters to live to maturity—Lieutenant Colonel (Archibald) Irwin Harrison, distinguished veteran of the Civil War; Mrs. Mary Jane "Jennie" Morris; Carter Harrison, farmer and federal assessor of Murfreesboro, Tennessee; Mrs. Anna Morris; and John Scott Harrison, Jr., of Kansas City, Missouri.

CHILDREN: By his first wife, Harrison had a son and a daughter.

Russell Benjamin Harrison (1854–1936), engineer, soldier, lawyer, state legislator. Born in Oxford, Ohio, he graduated with a degree in mechanical engineering from Lafayette College in Easton, Pennsylvania, in 1877 and, after brief employment with an Indianapolis gas company, was appointed assistant assayer at the U.S. Mint in New Orleans and later assayer at Helena, Montana Territory. In 1884 he married May Saunders, daughter of Senator Alvin Saunders of Nebraska. A man of varied interests, he also raised livestock and published the *Helena Daily Journal.* He served as private secretary to his father during Harrison's term as president. Subsequently he was president of a streetcar company in Terre Haute, Indiana. During the Spanish-American War, he rose from major to lieutenant colonel of U.S. volunteers. At its conclusion, he prematurely hoisted the American flag over Morro Castle, Cuba, in violation of the surrender terms and thereby drew an official reprimand. He nevertheless was appointed inspector general for Santiago Territory and provost martial for Puerto Rico. Discharged from the army in 1900, he became a lawyer and served as Mexico's legal representative in the United States for many years. He also served in both houses of the Indiana state legislature.

Mary Scott "Mamie" Harrison (1858–1930). Born in Indianapolis, she in 1884 married J. Robert McKee, later a founder and vice president of General Electric Company. She was assistant hostess at the White House during the Harrison administration.

By his second wife, Harrison had a daughter.

Elizabeth Harrison (1897–1955), lawyer. Born in Indianapolis, she graduated from New York University law school in 1919. In 1922 she married James Blaine Walker, grandnephew of her father's secretary of state, James G. Blaine. She was founder and publisher of *Cues on the News,* an investment newsletter for women.

SUBSEQUENT DESCENDANT: William Henry Harrison (1896–1990) The president's grandson, Harrison, a Republican, was Wyoming's congressman-at-large during 1951–1955, 1961–1965, and 1967–1969.

BIRTH: Harrison was born August 20, 1833, at the home of his paternal grandfather William Henry Harrison in North Bend, Ohio.

CHILDHOOD: Soon after Harrison's birth, the family settled at The Point, a 600-acre farm at North Bend, Ohio, given them by William Henry Harrison, who was elected president when Ben was seven years old. Here Ben grew up a typical antebellum farmboy. His chores included hauling wood and water, dishwashing, and feeding livestock. For recreation he hunted, fished, swam, and visited his grandfather's estate nearby. He thoroughly enjoyed country life, free from what he regarded as the foul, unwholesome air of Cincinnati. At 16 he came up with this insight: "The manner by which women are treated is good criterion to judge of the true state of society. If we knew but this one feature in a character of a nation, we may easily judge the rest, for as society advances, the true character of woman is discovered."[2] His ambitions were divided between the ministry and the law.

EDUCATION: Harrison learned the basics from tutors at home and in a one-room log schoolhouse nearby. His first teacher, Harriet Root, pronounced him "the brightest of the family . . . determined to go ahead in everything," but, she added, "terribly stubborn about many things."[3] Subsequent local instructors were Joseph Porter, Mr. Skinner, and Thomas Lynn. In addition, young Harrison apparently had free run of grandfather William Henry Harrison's library. During 1847–1850 he attended Farmers' College, a preparatory school in Cincinnati, where under the liberal instruction of Dr. Robert H. Bishop, Harrison developed a lifelong interest in history, politics, and sociology. He wrote papers on such topics as the North American explorers, the Puritans, the American Revolution and the War of 1812, and societal contrasts between primitive and advanced civilizations. In September 1850 Harrison was admitted as a junior to Miami University in Oxford, Ohio. An outstanding public speaker, his idol being Patrick Henry, he was elected president of the Union Literary Society and joined the Phi Delta Theta fraternity. He graduated near the top of his class in 1852. At commencement he delivered the third address, "The Poor of England"; he suffered the indignity of having his name misspelled on the commencement program. Having by this time decided to become a lawyer rather than a minister, he studied at the Cincinnati office of Storer and Gwynne during 1852–1854. He was admitted to the bar in 1854.

RELIGION: Presbyterian. Brought up in a devout Presbyterian home, Harrison formally joined the church while a student at Miami University after hearing a sermon by the Reverend Dr. Joseph Claybaugh. In Indianapolis, he regularly attended the First Presbyterian Church; he became a deacon in 1857, an elder in 1861. He taught Sunday school, attended prayer meetings regularly, and organized Bible classes. As president he held a pew at the Presbyterian Church of the Covenant in Washington. He conducted no state business on Sunday. Harrison believed firmly that the end of all human activity is to serve God and took great personal comfort in prayer.

RECREATION: In pleasant weather President Harrison enjoyed a brisk afternoon walk of three or four miles along the streets of Washington or a carriage ride into Maryland or Virginia, sometimes taking up the reins himself. He was an avid duck hunter. Indoors he liked to shoot billiards. From his youth Harrison smoked cigars.

MARRIAGE: Benjamin Harrison, 20, married Caroline Lavinia Scott, 21, on October 20, 1853, at the home of the bride in Oxford, Ohio. The bride was born in Oxford, October 1, 1832, the daughter of the Reverend John W. Scott, a Presbyterian minister and educator, and Mary Neal Scott. Her father was professor of chemistry and physics at Farmers' College while Harrison was a student there. Through Reverend Scott, Ben and "Carrie" met in 1848; he was 14, she 15. While Harrison attended Miami University in Oxford, Carrie was a student at the Oxford Female Institute, a school founded by her father. Over the next two years Harrison spent so many evenings with her that he became known on campus as "the pious moonlight dude." By the time he graduated in 1852, they had become secretly engaged. They decided to postpone the wedding while he studied law in Cincinnati and she finished school at Oxford and taught music. At her request the wedding, performed by her father, was small and simple. The newlyweds honeymooned at North Bend and settled in Indianapolis. As First Lady, Mrs. Harrison secured $35,000 in appropriations from Congress to renovate the White House. She purged the mansion of its growing rodent and insect population, laid new floors, installed new plumbing, painted and wallpapered, and added more bathrooms. In 1891 she installed electricity but was so frightened of it that she refused to handle the switches; instead, she left the lights on all night until the engineer came in to turn them off in the morning. In 1889 she put up the first Christmas tree in the White House. She also introduced the custom of using orchids as the official floral decoration at state receptions. A talented artist herself, she conducted china-painting classes in the White House. She served as the first president-general of the Daughters of the American Revolution. During her husband's campaign for reelection, Mrs. Harrison contracted tuberculosis and on October 25, 1892, died, just two weeks before election day. She was buried at Crown Hill cemetery in Indianapolis.

Former President Benjamin Harrison, 62, married Mary Scott Lord Dimmick, 37, a widow, on April 6, 1896, at St. Thomas Episcopal Church in New York City. The bride was born in Honesdale, Pennsylvania, April 30, 1858, the daughter of Farnham Lord, an engineer, and Elizabeth Scott Lord. In 1882 Mary Lord married Walter E. Dimmick, who died soon after the wedding. A niece of Caroline Harrison, she in 1889 moved into the White House to serve as assistant to the First Lady. Sometime after Mrs. Harrison's death in 1892, the former president and Mrs. Dimmick fell in love and late in 1895 announced their engagement. Harrison's grown children from his first marriage, horrified at the news, did not attend the wedding. Harrison's vice president, Levi P. Morton, and several former cabinet members were among the three dozen guests; former navy secretary Benjamin F. Tracy was best man. Without a honeymoon, the couple settled in Indianapolis. Mrs. Harrison survived the former president by nearly half a century. She died in New York on January 5, 1948, and was buried in Indianapolis.

MILITARY SERVICE: Civil War. Harrison served with the seventieth Indiana Infantry Regiment from July 1862 to June 1865, rising from second lieutenant to brigadier general. "I am not a Julius Caesar, nor a Napoleon," he wrote of his lack of taste for military life, "but a plain Hoosier colonel, with no more relish for a fight than for a good breakfast and hardly so much."[4] Still, he performed admirably on the battlefield. As a brigade commander under Major General Joseph Hooker during the Atlanta campaign, Colonel Harrison exhorted his men to penetrate Confederate defenses at Peach Tree Creek, Georgia, in July 1864 and held fast against a determined enemy effort to throw them back. The victory made possible Major General William T. Sherman's continued advance on Atlanta. Harrison was among the Union forces to march into the city when it finally fell on September 1, 1864. For his part in the Atlanta campaign, General Hooker recommended him for promotion to brigadier general, citing his foresight, discipline, and fighting spirit.

CAREER BEFORE THE PRESIDENCY: Admitted to the bar in 1854, Harrison that year settled in Indianapolis, where he formed a law partnership with William Wallace. In 1856 he joined the new Republican party and campaigned for its first presidential nominee, John C. Frémont. The following year he was elected Indianapolis city attorney at a salary of $400 a year. During 1858–1860 he was secretary of the Republican state central committee. In 1860 he supported Abraham Lincoln for president. He served briefly during 1861–1862 as supreme court reporter of Indiana before taking up arms in the Civil War (see "Military

Service"). In 1864, while still in uniform, he made speeches in support of the reelection of President Lincoln. After the war he resumed his post as supreme court reporter and the practice of law in partnership with Albert G. Porter and William P. Fishback, the latter later replaced by Cyrus C. Hines. He supported Ulysses S. Grant for president in 1868. In 1871 Grant appointed him defense counsel for army personnel being sued for civil damages by Lambdin P. Milligan, who, the U.S. Supreme Court had ruled in *Ex parte Milligan* (1866), had been illegally arrested and tried by court-martial during the Civil War. With Milligan's right to recover damages already established, it fell to Harrison to convince the jury to limit the reward to a token sum. Largely as a result of his persuasive oratory, the court awarded Milligan just $5 of the $100,000 he had requested. In 1872 Harrison ran unsuccessfully for the Republican gubernatorial nomination, losing to Thomas M. Browne, and campaigned in Indiana for Grant's reelection. In 1876 a Harrison-for-president boomlet arose in Ohio and Indiana but quickly faded. That year he received the Republican nomination for governor but in a hard-fought race was narrowly defeated by Democrat James D. "Blue Jeans" Williams. He stumped in the East and Midwest for Rutherford B. Hayes for president. In 1879 Hayes appointed him to the Mississippi River Commission. As chairman of the Indiana delegation to the Republican national convention in 1880, Harrison helped secure the nomination for dark horse James A. Garfield and campaigned vigorously for the ticket in the East and Midwest.

U.S. Senator, 1881–1887. Elected as a Republican to the U.S. Senate by the Indiana legislature in January 1881, Harrison declined President-elect Garfield's offer of a cabinet post. Senator Harrison became known as the "soldier's legislator" for his steadfast support of pensions for Civil War veterans. As chairman of the Territories Committee, he pressed unsuccessfully for Dakota statehood. He supported the high tariff, declaring himself to be "a protectionist for every interest which I am sent here by my constituents to protect."[5] With some misgivings he voted for the Mongrel Tariff (1883; see "Chester A. Arthur, 21st President," "Administration"). He voted against the Chinese Exclusion Act (1882; see "Chester A. Arthur," "Administration") and for the Pendleton Act (1883; see "Chester A. Arthur," "Administration"). One of the first national leaders to recognize the need for conservation, Harrison recommended setting aside land along a stretch of the Colorado River, a proposal adopted decades later in the creation of Grand Canyon National Park. He also supported expansion of the navy. In 1884 Harrison led the uncommitted Indiana delegation to the Republican national convention but withdrew when he learned that supporters planned to nominate him; however, the Harrison campaign never got off the ground. He stumped Indiana for the eventual nominee, James G. Blaine. In February 1887 Harrison was defeated for reelection in the Democrat-controlled state legislature, losing his Senate seat on the sixteenth ballot to David Turpie.

In February 1888 Harrison announced his candidacy for the Republican presidential nomination in an address before the Michigan Club in Detroit. "I am a dead statesman," he conceded in reference to his lack of a power base, "but I am a living and a rejuvenated Republican."[6] "Rejuvenated Republicanism" became the slogan of the Harrison campaign.

REPUBLICAN PRESIDENTIAL NOMINATION, 1888: By the time Republicans convened in Chicago in June 1888, front-runner James G. Blaine of Maine had withdrawn from the race because he believed that only a harmonious convention and uncontested nomination would produce a Republican candidate strong enough to upset incumbent president Grover Cleveland and he realized that the party was unlikely to choose him without a bitter struggle. In withdrawing, Blaine expressed confidence in the prospects of both Harrison and John Sherman of Ohio. The Harrison forces, led by Indiana attorney general Louis T. Michener, conducted a strategy to make their candidate everyone's second choice. After maintaining a low profile in early balloting, they hoped to pick up the support of the other candidates as they dropped out. Governor Albert G. Porter of Indiana delivered Harrison's nominating speech, seconded by Representative Jacob Gallinger of New York and E. H. Terrell of Texas. John Sherman, enjoying the broadest support under the direction of Mark Hanna, led through the first four ballots but stalled in the 240s, some 170 votes short of the nomination. Judge Walter Q. Gresham of Indiana, candidate of the Mugwumps (Republican reformers who had bolted the party in 1884) and labor, peaked on the third ballot with 123 votes. Chauncey Depew, president of the New York Central Railroad, whose support was limited to his home state and eastern money men, reached 99 votes and withdrew after the third tally. Governor Russell A. Alger of Michigan, popular in the South, rose to 142 votes on the fifth ballot before fading. At a meeting following the third ballot, most party leaders seemed ready to avoid a prolonged deadlock by settling for William B. Allison of Iowa. The conspicuous holdout to such a compromise was Chauncey Depew, who favored Harrison. Behind the scenes, James G. Blaine also was promoting Harrison. Other leaders eventually fell in line. On the fourth ballot, then, Harrison spurted to second place, just 18 votes behind Sherman, closed the gap to 11 on the next tally, surged to first place on the seventh ballot, and went over the top on the eighth count. The final vote read Harrison, 544; Sherman, 118; Alger, 100; Gresham, 59; Blaine, 5; William McKinley of Ohio, 4. Levi P. Morton of New York was nominated for vice president over Walter W. Phelps of New Jersey, his nearest rival. The Republican platform supported the protective tariff, reduction or elimination of internal taxes whenever a surplus accumulated in the Treasury, repeal of taxes on tobacco and alcohol used in the arts and for mechanical purposes, antitrust laws, expansion of the navy and merchant marine, federal aid to education, pension relief for veterans, civil service reform, and statehood for the western territories; it also denounced the power and influence of the Mormon church.

OPPONENT: Incumbent President Grover Cleveland (1837–1908) of New York; Democrat. The Democratic national convention held in St. Louis in June 1888 was harmonious. President Cleveland was renominated unanimously without a formal ballot. Allen G. Thurman of Ohio was nominated for vice president. The Democratic platform largely confined itself to a defense of the Cleveland administration, while supporting reduction in the tariff and taxes generally as well as statehood for the western territories.

CAMPAIGN AND THE ISSUES, 1888: "I cannot recall another presidential contest that was conducted on both sides with greater dignity and decency than that between Cleveland and Harrison in 1888,"[7] remarked veteran political observer A. K. McClure. President Cleveland remained aloof of the contest, making just one appearance, to accept renomination. Harrison, at the direction of Republican campaign manager Matthew S. Quay of Pennsylvania, confined his activity to carefully worded addresses before a steady stream of delegations to his home in Indianapolis. James G. Blaine, still a strong force in Republican affairs, campaigned vigorously and effectively for Harrison. The tariff issue dominated the campaign. Cleveland pledged a reduction while making it clear that he opposed absolute free trade. Harrison promised a strong protective tariff as a safeguard to domestic industry. The contest was extremely close. In fact Cleveland outpolled Harrison in the popular vote. But, ironically, Cleveland lost the election by failing to carry his home state. Tammany Hall, a longtime bitter foe of the reform-minded Cleveland, undermined his campaign in New York, thereby denying him the state's 36 electoral votes that would have assured his reelection.

ELECTION AS PRESIDENT, 1888:

Popular Vote: Cleveland (Democrat), 5,540,329 (49%); Harrison (Republican), 5,439,853 (48%).

Electoral Vote: Harrison, 233; Cleveland, 168.

States Carried: Harrison won the electoral votes of 20 states—California, Colorado, Illinois, Indiana, Iowa, Kansas, Maine, Massachusetts, Michigan, Minnesota, Nebraska, Nevada, New Hampshire, New York, Ohio, Oregon, Pennsylvania, Rhode Island, Vermont, and Wisconsin. Cleveland won the electoral votes of 18 states—Alabama, Arkansas, Connecticut, Delaware, Florida, Georgia, Kentucky, Louisiana, Maryland, Mississippi, Missouri, New Jersey, North Carolina, South Carolina, Tennessee, Texas, Virginia, and West Virginia.

INAUGURAL ADDRESS: March 4, 1889. ". . . If our great corporations would more scrupulously observe their legal limitations and duties, they would have less cause to complain of the unlawful limitations of their rights or of violent interference with their operations. The community that by concert, open or secret, among its citizens denies to a portion of its members their plain rights under the law has severed the only safe bond of social order and prosperity. . . .

"An unlawful expedient can not become a permanent condition of government. If the educated and influential classes in a community either practice or connive at the systematic violation of laws that seem to them to cross their convenience, what can they expect when the lesson that convenience or a supposed class interest is a sufficient cause for lawlessness has been well learned by the ignorant classes? A community where law is the rule of conduct and where courts, not mobs, execute its penalties is the only attractive field for business investments and honest labor. . . ."

VICE PRESIDENT: Levi Parsons Morton (1824–1920), of New York, served 1889–1893. Born in Shoreham, Vermont, Morton, with little formal education, operated a dry goods store first in Hanover, New Hampshire, and then in Boston before settling in New York City in 1854. In 1863 he went into the banking business as founder of L. P. Morton and Company. Through this and its successor firm, Morton, Bliss, and Company, established in 1869, he became one of the most influential of the eastern bankers. Politically he associated with Republican party boss Roscoe Conkling, leader of the conservative Stalwarts, and served a term in the U.S. House 1879–1881. President Garfield appointed him minister to France 1881–1885. After his term as vice president he was governor of New York 1895–1897 and in 1899 founded the Morton Trust Company. A favorite-son candidate for president at the 1896 Republican national convention, he received 58 votes to place fourth on the ballot that nominated William McKinley. He died in Rhinebeck, New York, on his ninety-sixth birthday.

CABINET:

Secretary of State. (1) James G. Blaine (1830–1893), of Maine, served 1889–1892. He had served as secretary of state in the Garfield and Arthur administrations and was the 1884 Republican presidential nominee (see "Grover Cleveland, 22d President," "Opponent"). Long a champion of closer ties among the Western Hemisphere nations, Blaine presided as chairman of the First Pan-American Conference, 1889–1890, in Washington and promoted, with limited success, reciprocity tariff agreements with Latin American nations. He also took steps to save Pribilof Island seals from extinction at the hands of Canadian hunters. (2) John W. Foster (1836–1917), of Indiana, served 1892–1893. A veteran diplomat, he had served as minister to Mexico 1873–1880, to Russia 1880–1881, and to Spain 1883–1885. As secretary, he tacitly encouraged the American-led coup against Queen Liliuokalani of Hawaii and negotiated a treaty of annexation in 1893, which was later withdrawn (see "Grover Cleveland, 24th President," "Administration: Hawaii"). His writings include *A Century of American Diplomacy* (1900) and *Diplomatic Memoirs* (1909).

Secretary of the Treasury. (1) William Windom (1827–1891), of Minnesota, served 1889–1891. He had served as Treasury secretary in the Garfield and Arthur administrations. Windom, one of Harrison's closest advisers, died in office, collapsing at the end of a speech in New York City. (2) Charles Foster (1828–1904), of Ohio, served 1891–1893. A longtime friend of Harrison, he conducted a sound-money policy.

Secretary of War. (1) Redfield Proctor (1831–1908), of Vermont, served 1889–1891. Rewarded for his early support of Harrison at the convention, Proctor resigned to enter the U.S. Senate. (2) Stephen B. Elkins (1841–1911), of West Virginia, served 1891–1893. A wealthy industrialist and founder of Elkins, West Virginia, he later gained fame in the Senate as author of the Elkins Act of 1903, barring railroads from giving rebates to preferred customers.

Attorney General. William H. H. Miller (1840–1917), of Indiana, served 1889–1893. He was highly regarded for his resistance to partisan pressures in the selection of candidates for the federal judiciary. William Howard Taft, who served under him as solicitor general, praised him for giving subordinates a free rein.

Secretary of the Navy. Benjamin F. Tracy (1830–1915), of New York, served 1889–1893. He is known as the father of the modern American navy for his ambitious shipbuilding program and general naval expansion and modernization, a program begun by his predecessor, William C. Whitney.

Postmaster General. John Wanamaker (1838–1922), of Pennsylvania, served 1889–1893. Harrison rewarded the famed Philadelphia department store owner for his work as chief Republican fundraiser during the campaign. He advocated three important innovations that eventually were adopted by his successors: rural free delivery, parcel post, and the postal savings bank.

Secretary of the Interior. John W. Noble (1831–1912), of Missouri, served 1889–1893. At his urging, Congress passed and President Harrison signed into law a rider to the General Land Law Revision Act of 1891 making it possible to set aside timberlands by presidential proclamation. Thus empowered, Harrison created numerous forest reserves totaling 13 million acres. Noble also organized the Oklahoma Territory, 1890.

Secretary of Agriculture. Jeremiah M. Rusk (1830–1893), of Wisconsin, served 1889–1893. He instituted federal inspection of meat exports.

ADMINISTRATION: March 4, 1889–March 3, 1893.

Dependent and Disability Pensions Act, 1890. A longtime champion of his fellow veterans, Harrison heartily approved this law, which extended compensation to veterans disabled from nonmilitary causes and to veterans' dependents.

Sherman Anti-Trust Act, 1890. The first of the antitrust laws to attempt to curb the abuses of monopolies made it a misdemeanor, punishable by up to one year in prison and a $5,000 fine, to take part in a "contract, combination in the form of trust or otherwise, or conspiracy, in restraint of trade or commerce among the several States, or with foreign nations." Sponsored by Republican Senator John Sherman of Ohio, the law was deliberately vague about what in fact constituted a "trust" or "restraint." As interpreted by the U.S. Supreme Court in *U.S.* v. *E. C. Knight Co.* (1895), the law was enforceable only against purely commercial interests, as distinct from manufacturers. The act thus lost much of its effectiveness but was reinvoked with some success by the administrations of Theodore Roosevelt and William Howard Taft. The law was strengthened by the Clayton Anti-Trust Act (1914; see "Woodrow Wilson, 28th President," "Administration").

Sherman Silver Purchase Act, 1890. Sponsored by Senator John Sherman of Ohio, this act represented the Harrison administration's concession to the western silver interests in return for their support of the McKinley tariff bill. Under its terms, the U.S. Treasury was required to purchase at market price 4.5 million ounces of silver per month, nearly the entire output of the nation's mines at that time. The silver was to be bought with notes redeemable in gold or silver. Many holders of the notes promptly redeemed them for gold, seriously depleting federal reserves. The law was repealed in 1893 (see "Grover Cleveland, 24th President," "Administration").

McKinley Tariff Act, 1890. Sponsored by Republican Representative William McKinley of Ohio, this severely protectionist measure set the average tariff rate at a whopping 48 percent, the highest in peacetime up to that time. Although its intention was to protect domestic industry, its excessive rates proved prohibitive in some cases. Duties were placed on some items not manufactured domestically and on agricultural products that the farm-rich United States had no need to import anyway. Sugar was placed on the duty-free list, but a 2¢-per-pound bounty was levied on domestic raw sugar to compensate producers. The net effect was a marked increase in consumer prices. Voters responded by turning against Republicans in the 1890 congressional elections. The McKinley Tariff was superseded by the Wilson-Gorman Tariff (1894; see "Grover Cleveland, 24th President," "Administration").

States Admitted to the Union: North Dakota (1889), South Dakota (1889), Montana (1889), Washington (1889), Idaho (1890), Wyoming (1890).

SUPREME COURT APPOINTMENTS: (1) David J. Brewer (1837–1910), of Kansas, served as associate justice 1889–1910. Born in Turkey of American parents, he was a nephew of Justice Stephen J. Field. Brewer generally was conservative in judicial outlook. In *Regan* v. *Farmers' Loan and Trust Co.* (1894), he ruled that state railroad rates were subject to judicial review. Speaking for the majority in *In Re Debs* (1895), he upheld the use of injunction against labor strikes. In a noteworthy decision, *Muller* v. *Oregon* (1908), regarded as progressive in its day, Brewer let stand a state law limiting the workday for some female employees to 10 hours. Brewer held that a woman's "physical structure and a proper discharge of her maternal functions . . . justify legislation to protect her from the greed as well as the passion of man." During 1895–1897 he headed the U.S. commission investigating the boundary dispute between Venezuela and British Guiana. (2) Henry B. Brown (1836–1913), of Michigan, served as associate justice 1891–1906. He was highly regarded as an expert on admiralty law. In a notable dissent in *Pollock* v. *Farmers' Loan and Trust Co.* (1895), Brown criticized the majority opinion, which struck down the federal income tax law, calling it "nothing less than a surrender of the taxing power to the moneyed classes." (3) George Shiras (1832–1924), of Pennsylvania, served as associate justice 1892–1903. He was among the top corporation lawyers in Pittsburgh at the time of his appointment, though his lack of judicial experience prompted considerable opposition to his confirmation. He is most remembered as the probable swing justice in *Pollock* v. *Farmers' Loan and Trust Co.* (1895), which struck down the federal income tax law. (4) Howell E. Jackson (1832–1895), of Tennessee, served as associate justice 1893–1895. A Confederate civil servant during the Civil War, Jackson was a renowned federal circuit court judge at the time of his appointment. Harrison chose Jackson, a Democrat, at least partly to avoid criticism that he was attempting to ram a last-minute partisan appointment through Congress just one month before his Democratic successor took office. Soon after assuming his seat on the bench, Jackson contracted tuberculosis and died two years later.

RANKING IN 1962 HISTORIAN POLL: Harrison ranked twentieth of 31 presidents, ninth of 12 "average" presidents. He ranked above Arthur, below Hoover.

RETIREMENT: March 4, 1893–March 13, 1901. Having been defeated for reelection (see under "Grover Cleveland, 24th President," for election of 1892) largely because of the unpopular McKinley Tariff (see "Administration"), Harrison attended the inauguration of his successor and retired to Indianapolis. It was terribly difficult for the former president to contemplate life without his wife, who had died just a few months before. But he soon shook off his despair and undertook a very active retirement. He resumed the practice of law and wrote articles for national magazines. In the spring of 1894 he delivered a series of lectures on constitutional law at Stanford University. In 1896 he remarried (see "Marriage"). Under pressure to run again for president, he in February 1896 formally renounced any intention to seek the Republican nomination. He campaigned actively for the eventual nominee, William McKinley. During 1897–1899 he served as counsel for Venezuela in its boundary dispute with British Guiana before an international arbitration panel in Paris. In a prodigious display of energy and mastery of detail, Harrison filed an 800-page written brief and presented 25 hours of oral argument over the course of five days. Nevertheless, the tribunal awarded Britain 90 percent of the disputed territory. After a brief European tour, Harrison returned to the United States in November 1899. A year later President McKinley appointed him to the newly established Permanent Court of Arbitration, but he took no active part in its proceedings.

DEATH: March 13, 1901, 4:45 P.M., Indianapolis. Earlier in the month Harrison came down with the flu, which developed into pneumonia. He failed to respond to vapor inhalation and other treatment and steadily declined. He lapsed into unconsciousness on March 12 and died quietly the next day. On March 16 his body lay in state at the Indiana statehouse. Funeral services were conducted the next day at the First Presbyterian Church in Indianapolis. Hoosier poet James Whitcomb Riley delivered the eulogy. He was buried beside his first wife at Crown Hill Cemetery in Indianapolis. In his last will and testament, executed in February 1901, Harrison left the bulk of his estate, valued at about $400,000, to his second wife and their four-year-old daughter, Elizabeth. Having become estranged from his two older children following his remarriage, he left a small sum to his daughter, Mrs. Mary McKee, and a like amount in trust for the education of the children of his son, Russell.

HARRISON PRAISED: "[Harrison] is a man with whom nothing is gained by argument or urgency at the wrong time. I have learned that lesson well. He is a very true and a very sincere man. He gains in my regard I may say daily."[8]— James G. Blaine, 1889

"One of the characteristics of General Harrison always commanded my profound respect—his fearless independence and stand for what he believed to be right and just. . . . A fearless man inwardly commands respect, and above everything else Harrison was fearless and just."[9]—James Whitcomb Riley, 1901

"Mr. Harrison was an excellent President, a man of ability and force; perhaps the best President the Republican party had put forward since Lincoln's death."[10]—Henry Adams, 1918

"Harrison . . . brought to leadership in American politics the incarnate nobility of what his party would have been, were it not for its partisans."[11]— journalist William Allen White, 1946

HARRISON CRITICIZED: "Benjamin Harrison is . . . at the close of the first year of his administration, in a pitiful position. . . . To many of the members of Congress he seems contemptible, others smile at his insignificance, no one troubles himself about what he says or does. The absolute indifference with which the recommendations or suggestions contained in his first message were received is without parallel in American history. In a word, favoritism and nepotism are the distinctive characteristics of the first year of Harrison government."[12]—*New York Staats-Zeitung*, 1890

"Damn the President! He is a cold-blooded, narrow-minded, prejudiced, obstinate, timid old psalm-singing Indianapolis politician."[13]—U.S. Civil Service Commissioner Theodore Roosevelt, 1890

"Four years ago our civil service reformers in Indiana were all supporting the Republican party . . . were all active supporters of Mr. Harrison. After four years' experience of his Administration they are now for Cleveland."[14]—Indiana reformer William Dudley Foulke, 1892

HARRISON QUOTES: "Two presidents or three, with equal powers, would as surely bring disaster as three generals of equal rank and command in a single army. I do not doubt that this sense of single and personal responsibility to the people has strongly held our Presidents to a good conscience, and to a high discharge of their duties."[15]—1897

"The indiscriminate denunciation of the rich is mischievous. It perverts the mind, poisons the heart and furnishes an excuse to crime. No poor man was ever made richer or happier by it. It is quite as illogical to despise a man because he is rich as because he is poor. Not what a man has, but what he is, settles his class. We can not right matters by taking from one what he has honestly acquired to bestow upon another what he has not earned."[16]—1898

BOOKS BY HARRISON: *This Country of Ours* (1897); *Views of an Ex-President* (1901).

BOOK ABOUT HARRISON: Sievers, Harry J. *Benjamin Harrison*. Vols. 1–2, New York: University Publishers, 1952, 1959; Vol. 3, Indianapolis: Bobbs-Merrill, 1968.

NOTES

1 Harry J. Sievers, S.J. *Benjamin Harrison*, vols. I–II, New York: University Publishers, 1952, 1959, vol. III, Indianapolis: Bobbs-Merrill, 1968, vol. III, p. 4.
2 Ibid., vol. I, p. 37.
3 Ibid., p. 25.
4 Ibid., p. 264.
5 Ibid., vol. II, p. 212.
6 Ibid., p. 321.
7 A. K. McClure, *Our Presidents and How We Make Them*, New York: Harper & Row, 1902, p. 332.
8 Sievers, vol. III, p. 89.
9 Ibid., p. 276.
10 Henry Adams, *The Education of Henry Adams*, Boston: Houghton Mifflin, 1918, p. 320.
11 *The Autobiography of William Allen White*, New York: Macmillan, 1946, p. 358.
12 James E. Pollard, *The Presidents and the Press*, New York: Macmillan, 1947, pp. 545–546.
13 Edmund Morris, *The Rise of Theodore Roosevelt*, New York: Coward, McCann & Geoghegan, 1979, p. 426.
14 *New York Times*, October 7, 1892, p. 4.
15 Benjamin Harrison, *This Country of Ours*, New York: Scribner's, 1897, p. 72.
16 Benjamin Harrison, *Views of an Ex-President*, Indianapolis: Bowen-Merrill, 1901, p. 336.

☆ ☆ ☆ ☆ ☆ ☆ ☆ ☆ ☆

GROVER CLEVELAND

☆ ☆ ☆ ☆ ☆ ☆ ☆ ☆ ☆

24TH PRESIDENT

See also "Grover Cleveland, 22d President."

DEMOCRATIC PRESIDENTIAL NOMINATION, 1892: As Democrats convened in Chicago in June 1892, Cleveland was the front-runner for the nomination but faced formidable opposition. He had come out against the free coinage of silver, thereby earning the enmity of western and southern Democrats. Most damaging of all was the opposition of his home state; the New York delegation, packed with Tammany men, frequently demonstrated their hostility to Cleveland's candidacy on the convention floor. Governor Leon Abbett of New Jersey delivered the nominating address for Cleveland, calling him "the nominee of the people, the plain, blunt, honest citizen, the idol of the Democratic masses."[1] In a narrow first-ballot victory, Cleveland received 617⅓ votes, barely 10 more than needed, to 114 for Governor David B. Hill of New York, the candidate of Tammany Hall, 103 for Governor Horace Boies of Iowa, a populist and former Republican; the rest scattered. Although the Cleveland forces preferred Isaac P. Gray of Indiana for vice president, they accepted the convention favorite, Adlai E. Stevenson of Illinois. The Democratic platform promised a lower tariff, calling the Republican-sponsored McKinley Tariff "the culminating atrocity of class legislation,"[2] straddled the currency issue, supported antitrust laws, condemned the oppression of Lutherans and Jews in czarist Russia, expressed sympathy for Ireland's struggle for home rule, and advocated improvement of inland waterways, construction of a canal across Central America, federal aid to education, and statehood for New Mexico and Arizona.

OPPONENTS: Incumbent president Benjamin Harrison (1833–1901) of Indiana; Republican. Although Tom Platt and other disaffected party leaders mounted a dump-Harrison movement coalescing around veteran candidate James G. Blaine of Maine, the president's forces had the nomination locked up by the time delegates assembled in Minneapolis in June 1892. Richard Thomas of Indiana delivered Harrison's nominating speech. Harrison was nominated on the first ballot with 535⅙ votes to 182⅚ for Blaine, 182 for William McKinley of Ohio; the rest scattered. The strength of McKinley, nominally a favorite-son candidate, surprised many observers. Whitelaw Reid of New York, editor of the New York *Tribune* and recent U.S. minister to France, was nominated for vice president. The Republican platform supported the high tariff, bimetallism, stiffer immigration laws, free rural mail delivery, and a canal across Central America; and expressed sympathy for Ireland's struggle for home rule and the plight of Jews under persecution in czarist Russia.

James B. Weaver (1833–1912) of Iowa; People's (Populist) party. A native of Dayton, Ohio, Weaver, a lawyer, settled in Bloomfield, Iowa. After military service during the Civil War, he served as district attorney and a federal tax assessor in Iowa. Abandoning the Republican party, he joined the Greenback party and under its banner served in the U.S. House 1879–1881 and 1885–1889. In 1880 he was the party's nominee for president. The Greenback party evolved into the Populist party. At the first Populist national convention in Omaha in July 1892, Weaver was nominated for president on the first ballot. James G. Field of Virginia was nominated for vice president. The Populist platform called for nationalization of the telegraph, telephone, and railroads, free coinage of silver, a graduated income tax, and creation of postal savings banks. After his defeat by Cleveland, Weaver led the Populist movement into the Democratic party in support of William Jennings Bryan. He was mayor of Colfax, Iowa, 1904–1906.

CAMPAIGN AND THE ISSUES, 1892: The tariff issue dominated this rather lackluster campaign. Harrison defended the protectionist McKinley Tariff passed during his term: Cleveland, assuring voters that he opposed absolute free trade, continued his campaign for a reduction in the tariff. William McKinley campaigned extensively for Harrison, setting the stage for his own run four years later. The campaign took a somber turn when, in October, First Lady Caroline Harrison died suddenly. The candidates ceased campaigning. Populist James B. Weaver, calling for free coinage of silver and an inflationary monetary policy, won surprisingly strong support in the West to become the only third-party nominee between 1860 and 1912 to carry a single state.

ELECTION AS PRESIDENT, 1892:

Popular Vote: Cleveland (Democrat), 5,556,918 (46%); Harrison (Republican), 5,176,108 (43%); Weaver (People's, or Populist), 1,041,028 (9%).

Electoral vote: Cleveland, 277; Harrison, 145; Weaver, 22.

States Carried: Cleveland won the majority of electoral votes in 23 states—Alabama, Arkansas, California, Connecticut, Delaware, Florida, Georgia, Illinois, Indiana, Kentucky, Louisiana, Maryland, Mississippi, Missouri, New Jersey, New York, North Carolina, South Carolina, Tennessee, Texas, Virginia, West Virginia, and Wisconsin. Harrison won the majority of electoral votes in 16 states—Iowa, Maine, Massachusetts, Michigan, Minnesota, Montana, Nebraska, New Hampshire, Ohio, Oregon, Pennsylvania, Rhode Island, South Dakota, Vermont, Washington, and Wyoming. Weaver won the majority of electoral votes in 4 states—Colorado, Idaho, Kansas, and Nevada. The three electoral votes of North Dakota were divided evenly among the three candidates; thus, none carried the state.

INAUGURAL ADDRESS: March 4, 1893. ". . . Manifestly nothing is more vital to our supremacy as a nation and to the beneficent purposes of our Government than a sound and stable currency. Its exposure to degradation should at once arouse to activity the most enlightened statesmanship, and the danger of depreciation in the purchasing power of the wages paid to toil should furnish the strongest incentive to prompt and conservative precaution. . . .

"Closely related to the exaggerated confidence in our country's greatness which tends to a disregard of the rules of national safety, another danger confronts us not less serious. I refer to the prevalence of a popular disposition to expect from the operation of the Government especial and direct individual advantages. . . ."

"The lessons of paternalism ought to be unlearned and the better lesson taught that while the people should patriotically and cheerfully support their Government its functions do not include the support of the people. . . ."

VICE PRESIDENT: Adlai Ewing Stevenson (1835–1914), of Illinois, served 1893–1897. Born in Christian County, Kentucky, the son of a slaveholding farmer, he was raised there and in Bloomington, Illinois. Admitted to the bar in 1857, he had by this time become associated with the Democratic party as a supporter of Stephen A. Douglas. He served in the U.S. House 1875–1877 and 1879–1881. Appointed assistant postmaster general 1885–1889 by President Cleveland, he dismissed some 40,000 Republican postmasters to make room for Democratic appointees, thereby earning the lasting enmity of the opposition party and the nickname the Headsman. Republicans got even by refusing to confirm Cleveland's nomination of Stevenson to a federal court seat in 1889. Stevenson was nominated for vice president in 1892 for his soft-money views, thus balancing Cleveland's hard-money policy. He again ran for the office in 1900, this time unsuccessfully, on the ticket with William Jennings Bryan. In 1908 he was defeated in the race for governor of Illinois. His grandson and namesake was the Democratic presidential nominee in 1952 and 1956.

CABINET:

Secretary of State. (1) Walter Q. Gresham (1832–1895), of Indiana, served 1893–1895. He had served as postmaster general and Treasury secretary under President Arthur. A candidate for the Republican presidential nomination in 1888, he in 1892 joined other Mugwumps in bolting the party to support Cleveland. As secretary, he opposed imperialist influences in American foreign policy. He denounced U.S. participation in the overthrow of Queen Liliuokalani of Hawaii and urged Cleveland to withdraw from the Senate the Harrison administration's treaty to annex the islands. He died in office. (2) Richard Olney (1835–1917), of Massachusetts, served 1895–1897. Transferred from attorney general, he proved a forceful, at times belligerent, secretary of state. In compelling Britain to arbitrate the Venezuelan boundary dispute (see "Administration"), he issued, with the president's wholehearted endorsement, the Olney Corollary to the Monroe Doctrine: "Today the United States is practically sovereign on this continent, and its fiat is law upon the subjects to which it confines its interposition, . . . because in addition to all other grounds, its infinite resources combined with its isolated position render it master of the situation and practically invulnerable as against any or all powers."[3] He also took steps to place the consular service on the merit system.

Secretary of the Treasury: John G. Carlisle (1835–1910), of Kentucky, served 1893–1897. He had been Speaker of the House 1883–1889. A champion of reduced tariffs and a sound-money policy, he was anathema to the increasingly influential free-silver wing of the party. Maintaining his commitment to the gold standard in the face of severe economic depression, he was bitterly assailed in his native region, where he became known as the Judas of Kentucky.

Secretary of War. Daniel S. Lamont (1851–1905), of New York, served 1893–1897. Formerly Cleveland's private secretary, he was among the president's closest advisors. "Lamont is a wonderful man," Cleveland once said of him. "I never saw his like. He has no friends to gratify or reward and no enemies to punish."[4]

Attorney General. (1) Richard Olney served 1893–1895. He interposed the full weight of his office to break the Pullman strike in 1894, securing an injunction against the strikers, calling in federal troops, and vigorously prosecuting strikers in the courts. He resigned to become secretary of state. (2) Judson Harmon (1846–1927), of Ohio, served 1895–1897. He undertook antitrust suits against railroad and iron pipe monopolies.

Secretary of the Navy. Hilary A. Herbert (1834–1919), of Alabama, served 1893–1897. A disabled Confederate veteran, he had long supported a naval buildup and as secretary oversaw construction of battleships and torpedo boats.

Postmaster General. (1) Wilson S. Bissell (1847–1903), of New York, served 1893–1895. (2) William L. Wilson (1843–1900), of West Virginia, served 1895–1897.

Secretary of the Interior. (1) Hoke Smith (1855–1931), of Georgia, served 1893–1896. At his urging, Congress created the National Forest Commission to determine the status of American forests in 1896. He resigned to support William Jennings Bryan for president. (2) David R. Francis (1850–1927), of Missouri, served 1896–1897. At his urging, the president set aside 20 million acres in forest reserves in California, Washington, Utah, Montana, and Wyoming. He later was ambassador to Russia during the Russian Revolution.

Secretary of Agriculture. J. Sterling Morton (1832–1902), of Nebraska, served 1893–1897. A celebrated advocate of forestation, he had founded Arbor Day in 1872. As secretary he was hardworking, efficient, and cost conscious. He established the Foreign Markets section to promote agricultural exports.

ADMINISTRATION: March 4, 1893–March 3, 1897.

Hawaii. In 1893 Cleveland condemned American complicity in the overthrow of Queen Liliuokalani of Hawaii and withdrew from Senate consideration the treaty for the annexation of the islands submitted by President Benjamin Harrison.

Panic of 1893. Touched off by the failure of the Philadelphia and Reading Railroad in February 1893, the panic was followed by a four-year depression. Underlying causes of the depression were rapidly dwindling gold reserves, industrial overexpansion, poor crop harvests in the South and West, and an economic slump in Europe. Thousands of businesses (including a quarter of the nation's railroads)worth hundreds of millions of dollars went bankrupt during this period. Riots broke out in Chicago. In Massillon, Ohio, Jacob Coxey organized 100 area jobless for a march on Washington. Coxey's Army swelled to 500 by the time it reached the nation's capital in May 1894 to petition, unsuccessfully, for a $500 million public works program.

Repeal of the Sherman Silver Purchase Act, 1893. Convinced that the Sherman Silver Purchase Act (see "Benjamin Harrison, 23d President," "Administration") was largely responsible for the alarming drain on federal gold reserves, President Cleveland called Congress into special session to urge its repeal. Congress consented, but only after acrimonious debate that divided the

Democratic party into two hostile camps—the eastern "goldbugs" and the silver wing of the West and South that was to propel young William Jennings Bryan to the fore in 1896. "The people of the United States," Cleveland asserted in his message to Congress, "are entitled to a sound and stable currency and to money recognized as such on every exchange and in every market of the world."[5] Only maintenance of the gold standard, Cleveland believed, could guarantee such a stable currency. When gold reserves continued to decline even after repeal of the Silver Purchase Act, Cleveland in 1895 sold gold bonds at a discount to J. P. Morgan and other Wall Street bankers in return for their cooperation in checking the withdrawal of gold from the treasury. The arrangement further alienated Cleveland from Populist elements in the party.

Wilson-Gorman Act, 1894. As it emerged from the House under the sponsorship of Democratic Representative William L. Wilson of West Virginia, the bill provided for a genuine reduction in the McKinley Tariff (see "Benjamin Harrison, 23d President," "Administration"), but Senate forces led by Democrat Arthur P. Gorman of Maryland added duties on a variety of goods. Cleveland, long committed to a low tariff, denounced the package as "party perfidy and party dishonor"[6] but allowed it to become law without his signature. The result was to shave the average 48 percent rate of the McKinley Tariff to 41 percent. The act also provided for a federal income tax, a provision declared unconstitutional by the Supreme Court in 1895. It was replaced by the Dingley Tariff Act (1897; see "William McKinley, 25th President," "Administration").

Pullman Strike, 1894. In response to deteriorating economic conditions in the wake of the Panic of 1893, the Pullman Palace Car Company sharply reduced employee wages while maintaining rents and prices of goods workers were forced to buy in the company stores. A strike followed and quickly spread to other railroad companies. Under the direction of Eugene V. Debs, who had recently formed the American Railway Union, strikers managed to cripple rail traffic between Chicago and the West Coast. When violence broke out, railroad executives appealed to the federal government. On the advice of Attorney General Olney, Cleveland secured an injunction against the strikers and, over the objections of Governor John P. Altgeld, dispatched federal troops to Illinois on the ground that the interruption in rail service unlawfully obstructed the mails. The strike thus was broken. Debs was arrested for violating the injunction.

Venezuela Boundary Dispute. Cleveland supported Secretary of State Olney's aggressive policy in attempting to compel Great Britain to submit to arbitration the boundary dispute between its colony of Guiana and Venezuela. Partly at U.S. insistence, then, and partly for other foreign policy considerations, Great Britain agreed to arbitration by an international tribunal, which in 1899 decided the question largely in Britain's favor.

State Admitted to the Union: Utah (1896).

SUPREME COURT APPOINTMENTS: (1) Edward D. White (1845–1921), of Louisiana, served as associate justice 1894–1910 and chief justice 1910–1921. Generally conservative in judicial outlook, he upheld court injunctions against labor (*In Re Debs*, 1895), sustained the yellow dog contract (*Adair* v. *United States*, 1904), and narrowly construed the Sherman Anti-Trust Act (*United States* v. *E. C. Knight Co.*, 1895). Promoted to chief justice by President William Howard Taft in 1910, he was the first associate justice to be so elevated and the first southern chief justice since the Civil War. In *Standard Oil of New Jersey et* *al.* v. *United States* (1911), Chief Justice White for the first time applied the "rule of reason" to the Sherman Anti-Trust Act, barring only those contracts in "unreasonable" restraint of trade. In *Wilson* v. *New* (1917) he spoke for the Court in upholding the Adamson Act, which established the eight-hour day for railroad workers. (2) Rufus W. Peckham (1838–1909), of New York, served as associate justice 1896–1909. A conservative jurist, he delivered the majority opinion in *Lochner* v. *New York* (1905), striking down a state law that limited the number of hours certain employees could work. "Statutes of the nature of that under review," he wrote, "limiting the hours in which grown and intelligent men may labor to earn their living are mere meddlesome interferences with the rights of the individual."

RETIREMENT: March 4, 1897–June 24, 1908. In 1896 Cleveland bolted party ranks to support John M. Palmer, nominee of the National, or gold, Democrats, a conservative splinter group opposed to the free-silver platform of the regular Democratic party and its nominee, William Jennings Bryan. After attending the inaugural of his successor, William McKinley, he settled in Princeton, New Jersey, at an estate he named Westland. In 1899 he was appointed Henry Stafford Little Lecturer in Public Affairs at Princeton University. In 1901 he joined the university's board of trustees and was elevated to board president three years later. An active president, he clashed over school policy with university president Woodrow Wilson. During 1900–1906 he wrote numerous articles for the *Saturday Evening Post*. In 1904 he campaigned for Alton B. Parker for president. In 1906 he was hired as a consultant to reorganize the Equitable Life Assurance Society. The following year he accepted a $25,000-a-year position as president of the Association of Presidents of Life Insurance Companies.

DEATH: June 24, 1908, 8:40 P.M., at home, Princeton, New Jersey. In his last years, Cleveland suffered from rheumatism and was bedridden for weeks at a time. He also underwent acute attacks of indigestion, relieved only with the use of a stomach pump, which he learned to operate on himself. Chronic nephritis impaired his kidneys. In April 1908 he experienced severe abdominal and chest pains. Thereafter his health steadily declined. On the evening of June 23 he lapsed into a stupor and died of heart failure the next morning. His last words were "I have tried so hard to do right."[7] Simple funeral services were conducted in his home by the Reverend Henry Van Dyke. Venezuela, in tribute to his services in settling its boundary dispute with Britain, flew flags at half-mast. Cleveland was buried in Princeton on June 26. He left an estate of an estimated $250,000 in personal and real property.

CLEVELAND PRAISED: "Your patriotic virtues have won for you the homage of half the nation and the enmity of the other half. This places your character upon a summit as high as Washington's. . . . When the votes are all in a public man's favor the verdict is against him. It is sand, and history will wash it away. But the verdict for you is rock, and will stand."[8]—Mark Twain, 1906

"As president, Mr. Cleveland enforced the laws and did not truckle to organized violence or crouch before public clamor. The man who taught the Chicago labor lords that there was a Government at Washington, the man who wrote the Venezuela message, is sure of an honorable place in history and of the final approval of his countrymen."[9]—*New York Sun*, 1907

"In the midst of the shifting scene Mr. Cleveland personally came to seem the only fixed point. He alone stood firm and gave definite utterance to principles intelligible to all."[10]—Woodrow Wilson, 1907

CLEVELAND CRITICIZED: "We do not believe the American people will knowingly elect to the Presidency a coarse debauchee who would bring his harlots with him to Washington and hire lodgings for them convenient to the White House."[11]—Charles Dana, editor and publisher of New York *Sun*, 1884

"What in the world has Grover Cleveland done? Will you tell me? You give it up? I have been looking for six weeks for a Democrat who could tell me what Cleveland has done for the good of his country and for the benefit of the people, but I have not found him. . . . He says himself . . . that two thirds of his time has been uselessly spent with Democrats who want office. . . . Now he has been so occupied in that way that he has not done anything else."[12]—Republican Representative William McKinley of Ohio, 1885

"Two names stand out as meaning all that can be said of treachery and infamy. They are Judas Iscariot and Benedict Arnold. A third should be added, that of Grover Cleveland."[13]—Democratic leader Champ Clark, c. 1897

CLEVELAND QUOTES: "This office-seeking is a disease—I am entirely satisfied of that. It is even catching. Men get it, and they lose the proper balance of their minds. I've known men to come here to Washington on other business, with no thought of office, but when they had been here a couple of weeks they had caught it."[14]—1885

"I mistake the American people if they favor the odious doctrine that there is no such thing as international morality; that there is one law for a strong nation and another for a weak one."[15]

BOOKS BY CLEVELAND: *Presidential Problems* (1904); *Fishing and Shooting Sketches* (1906); *Good Citizenship* (1908).

BOOKS ABOUT CLEVELAND: Lynch, Denis Tilden. *Grover Cleveland: A Man Four-Square*. New York: Horace Liveright, 1932.

McElroy, Robert. *Grover Cleveland: The Man and the Statesman: An Authorized Biography*. New York: Harper & Bros., 1923.

Nevins, Allan. *Grover Cleveland: A Study in Courage*. New York: Dodd, Mead, 1932.

Tugwell, Rexford G. *Grover Cleveland*. New York: Macmillan, 1968.

NOTES:

1 Herbert Eaton, *Presidential Timber: The Study of How Presidential Candidates Are Nominated*, New York: Free Press of Glencoe, 1964, p. 146.

2 Kirk H. Porter and Donald Bruce Johnson, compilers, *National Party Platforms*, Urbana, Ill.: University of Illinois Press, 1961, p. 87.

3 Graham Stuart, *The Department of State*, New York: Macmillan, 1949, p. 186.

4 Allan Nevins, *Grover Cleveland: A Study in Courage*, New York: Dodd, Mead, 1932, p. 109.

5 Henry Steele Commager, ed., *Democrats of American History*, New York: Crofts, 1945, Doc. no. 327, p. 148.

6 Denis Tilden Lynch, *Grover Cleveland: A Man Four-Square*, New York: Horace Liveright, 1932, p. 446.

7 Ibid., p. 541.

8 Ibid., p. 533.

9 Robert McElroy, *Grover Cleveland: The Man and the Statesman*, New York: Harper & Bros., 1923, p. 379.

10 Arthur S. Link, *Wilson*, Princeton, N.J.: Princeton University Press, 1947–1965, vol. I, pp. 112–113.

11 *New York Sun*, August 7, 1884.

12 *Speeches and Addresses of William McKinley*, New York: Appleton, 1893, pp. 192–193.

13 Asa Martin, *After the White House*, State College, Pa.: Penns Valley, 1951, p. 328.

14 Arthur B. Tourtellot, *The Presidents on the Presidency*, New York: Russell & Russell, 1964, p. 166.

15 McElroy, vol. II, p. 45.

WILLIAM McKINLEY

25TH PRESIDENT

NAME: William McKinley, Jr. He was named after his father. He dropped the "junior" on his father's death.

PHYSICAL DESCRIPTION: A brawny figure, with a barrel chest, broad shoulders, and, with advancing years, a swelling paunch, McKinley stood 5 feet 7 inches tall and weighed up to nearly 200 pounds. His handsome features were marked by deeply set blue-gray eyes guarded by bushy eyebrows, a fair complexion, a strong jaw punctuated by a cleft chin, and a rather large nose. He spoke in a strong, clear voice. He had good posture and walked briskly. He was the only clean-shaven president between Andrew Johnson and Woodrow Wilson. He wore reading glasses. He dressed conservatively, typically in a white vest, and refused to be photographed unless he was impeccably groomed. During political campaigns he wore a red carnation in his buttonhole for good luck, a practice that prompted the Ohio legislature to designate the scarlet carnation the state flower. His health generally was sound except for a brief physical breakdown in college, perhaps brought on by overwork.

PERSONALITY: By all accounts, McKinley was open, friendly, even tempered, cheerful, optimistic, and universally well liked. "McKinley was more than popular," according to historian Margaret Leech, "he was beloved. . . . Even his political opponents were attracted by the peculiar sweetness of his personality."[1] Biographer Charles S. Olcott concluded, similarly, "His uniform courtesy and fairness commanded the admiration of Democrats as well as Republicans. . . . The general public found him free from vanity or affectation."[2]. Yet he did not gush with emotion. Rather, he worked a subtle charm effective with people from all walks of life. He enjoyed having lots of people around. Although not a particularly gifted storyteller, he had a dry wit and enjoyed a good, clean joke but bristled at off-color remarks.

ANCESTORS: McKinley was of Scotch-Irish heritage. The name is said to have evolved from MacIanla to MacKinlay to McKinley. His paternal ancestors were

355

from Perthshire, Scotland, and eventually settled in Ireland. The first of the line to emigrate to America was David McKinley, a weaver, the president's great[3]-grandfather, who in 1743 settled in York County, Pennsylvania. John McKinley, the president's great-great-grandfather, and David McKinley, his great-grand-father, both served in the York County militia during the American Revolution. His grandfather James S. McKinley fought under General William Henry Harrison in the War of 1812 and settled in New Lisbon, Ohio, where he operated a blast furnace in the manufacture of pig iron.

FATHER: William McKinley, Sr. (1807–1892), pig iron manufacturer. A native of Mercer County, Pennsylvania, he at 16 followed his father into the iron foundry at New Lisbon, Ohio, and later went into business for himself. He married Nancy Allison in 1829. He died in Canton, Ohio, when his most famous son was governor of Ohio.

MOTHER: Nancy Allison McKinley (1809–1897). A native of New Lisbon, Ohio, she was a pious, tidy, loving mother, who had hoped that son Bill would enter the ministry. Throughout her life she maintained a close relationship with him. On the evening of his election as president, Mother McKinley, as she was called, summoned her son and his wife to her bedroom for prayer, asking God to keep the new chief executive humble. She attended the inauguration. As her health began to fail, President McKinley installed a special wire between the White House and her home in Canton, Ohio. He sped back by special train to be with her when she died.

SIBLINGS: The seventh of eight children to live to maturity, McKinley had four sisters and three brothers—David A. McKinley, of California, served as U.S. consul in Honolulu and as Hawaiian consul general in San Francisco; Anna McKinley, schoolteacher of Canton, Ohio; James McKinley, of California; Mrs. Mary May, of Poland, Ohio; Helen McKinley, of Canton and Cleveland; Mrs. Sarah E. Duncan, of Cleveland; Abner McKinley, lawyer of Canton and New York City.

CHILDREN: McKinley had two daughters—Katherine "Katie" McKinley and Ida McKinley, both of whom died in infancy. Thus, no direct descendant of McKinley survives.

BIRTH: McKinley was born January 29, 1843, in a small frame house in Niles, Ohio.

CHILDHOOD: McKinley spent his early years in Niles, Ohio, where he was known as a spritely, fun-loving youth. During the Mexican War, he and his playmates delighted in drilling like soldiers. He enjoyed such outdoor sports as fishing, camping, ice skating, horseback riding, and swimming. Once he nearly drowned in Mosquito Creek; as he went down for the third time, he was rescued by Jacob Shealer. When he was age nine, the McKinleys moved about 10 miles south to Poland, Ohio, where he spent the remainder of his childhood.

EDUCATION: McKinley learned the fundamentals at a Niles, Ohio, public school run by Alva Sanford. At Poland, Ohio, he attended the local public school and in 1852 enrolled at the Poland Seminary, a Methodist institution administered by B. F. Lee. There he studied under Miss E. M. Blakeless, a gifted instructor, who more than any other woman outside his family influenced his life. His favorite subject was speech. A naturally gifted orator, he helped organize and served as first president of the school's Everett Literary and Debating Society. At 17 McKinley entered Allegheny College at Meadville, Pennsylvania, as a junior but within the year was forced by illness (apparently physical exhaustion from studying too hard) to drop out. He had planned to resume his studies after a period of convalescence at home, but family finances suffered during the depression following the Panic of 1857, and he had to go to work. He taught for a term during 1860–1861 at the Kerr District School in Poland and then clerked at the town post office before taking part in the Civil War (see "Military Service"). After the war he studied law at the Youngstown office of Judge Charles E. Glidden. During 1866–1867 he attended Albany (New York) Law School but dropped out before graduation. He was admitted to the Ohio bar in March 1867.

RELIGION: Methodist. Brought up in a devout Methodist home, McKinley at 10 years old publicly professed his faith at a revival meeting in Poland, Ohio, and at 16 became a communicant in the church. He was throughout his life a devout, active Methodist and a regular churchgoer. In Canton, Ohio, he belonged to the First Methodist Church, where he was superintendent of the Sunday school. He also was president of the local Y.M.C.A. In Washington he attended the Metropolitan Methodist Church. At his inaugural he kissed the Bible opened to 2 *Chronicles* 1:10: "Give me now wisdom and knowledge, that I may go out and come in before this people: for who can judge this thy people, that is so great?" As president he often invited guests to sing hymns with him in the Blue Room on Sunday evenings; among his favorites were "Nearer My God, to Thee" and "Lead, Kindly Light." In 1899 he summarized his credo in a personal memorandum: "My belief embraces the Divinity of Chirst and a recognition of Christianity as the mightiest factor in the world's civilization."[3] Maintaining his faith to the end, he was overheard softly reciting the Lord's Prayer as he was being prepared for surgery after being shot.

RECREATION: President McKinley got very little exercise. Occasional strolls around the White House grounds and an afternoon carriage ride with his wife were virtually his only exposure to fresh air. He enjoyed the opera and the theater. His favorite plays included Shakespeare productions and *Rip Van Winkle*. In the evenings he often played euchre or cribbage with his wife and friends. He smoked cigars and sometimes bit them in two and chewed them. He drank an occasional glass of wine or scotch.

MARRIAGE: William McKinley, 27, married Ida Saxton, 23, on January 25, 1871, at the First Presbyterian Church, then still under construction, in Canton, Ohio. The bride was born in Canton on June 8, 1847, the daughter of James Saxton, prominent Canton banker, and Catherine DeWalt. Her grandfather John Saxton in 1815 had founded the Canton *Repository*, the city's first and now its only newspaper. A graduate of Brook Hall Seminary, a finishing school in Media, Pennsylvania, Miss Saxton was refined, charming, and strikingly attractive when she met Bill McKinley at a picnic in 1867. They did not begin courting until after she returned from a European tour in 1869. While single, she worked for a time as a cashier in her father's bank, a position then usually reserved for men. Following the wedding, performed by the Reverend E. Buckingham and the Reverend Dr. Endsley, the couple attended a reception at the home of the bride's parents and left on an eastern wedding trip. Possessed of a fragile, nervous temperament, Mrs. McKinley broke down under the loss of her mother and two infant daughters within a short span of time. She developed epilepsy and became totally dependent on her husband. Her seizures at times occured in public; she had one at McKinley's inaugural ball as governor. Although an invalid the rest of her life, she kept busy with her hobby, crocheting slippers, making gifts of literally thousands of pairs to friends and acquaintances. President McKinley took great care to accommodate her condition. In a break with tradition, he insisted that his wife be seated next to him at state dinners rather than at the other end of the table. At receiving lines, she alone remained seated. And many of the social chores normally assumed by the First Lady fell to Mrs. Garret Hobart, wife of the vice president. Guests noted that whenever Mrs. McKinley was about to undergo a seizure, the president would gently place a napkin or handkerchief over her face to conceal her contorted features. When it passed, he would remove it and resume whatever he was doing as if nothing had happened. The president's patient devotion and loving attention was the talk of the capital. "President McKinley has made it pretty hard for the rest of us husbands here in Washington,"[4] remarked Mark Hanna. With the assassination of her husband, Mrs. McKinley lost much of her will to live. Although she bore up well in days between the shooting and the president's death, she could not bring herself to attend his funeral. Her health eroded as she withdrew to the safety of her home and memories in Canton. She survived the president by less than six years, dying on May 26, 1907. She was buried next to him in Canton.

MILITARY SERVICE: Civil War. McKinley served with the Twenty-third Ohio Volunteer Infantry from June 1861 to July 1865, rising from private to brevet major. Throughout his hitch he neither was wounded nor fell ill. Enlisting at Camp Chase near Columbus, Ohio, with Company E, he first saw action at Carnifex Ferry, West Virginia, in September 1861. The following April he was promoted to commissary sergeant and took part in engagements at Clark's Hollow and Princeton, West Virginia, in May 1862 and South Mountain in September 1862. At Antietam in September 1862 he demonstrated marked valor in transporting under fire much-needed rations to troops at the front. For this act he was promoted to second lieutenant in command of Company D and appointed to the staff of Colonel Rutherford B. Hayes. In February 1863 he was promoted to first lieutenant. He clashed with Morgan's Raiders at Buffington's Island, Ohio, in July 1863 and fought at Clay's Mountain in May 1864. At Winchester, Virginia, in July 1864, he carried orders to the front under fire and against risked his life to retrieve heavy artillery. The day after this engagement he was promoted to captain of Company G. He saw action at Opequon and Cedar Creek in September 1864 and Fisher's Hill, Virginia, in October 1864 and served on the staffs of Generals George Crook and Winfield S. Hancock. While in uniform he cast his first vote for the reelection of President Abraham Lincoln in 1864. In March 1865 he was promoted to brevet major. His commander, Rutherford B. Hayes, said of his wartime services: "Young as he was, we soon found that in the business of a soldier, requiring much executive ability, young McKinley showed unusual and unsurpassed capacity, especially for a boy of his age. When battles were fought or service was to be performed in warlike things, he always filled his place."[5]

CAREER BEFORE THE PRESIDENCY: Admitted to the bar in 1867, McKinley set up practice in Canton, Ohio, and became associated with the local Republican party. So quickly did he gain in local esteem that he was elected Stark County prosecutor in 1869 despite the county's Democratic majority. Narrowly defeated for reelection in 1871, he resumed private practice.

U.S. Representative, 1877–1883, 1885–1891. Elected in 1876 as a Republican over Democrat Leslie L. Sanborn, McKinley represented Ohio's Eighteenth District, which, until subsequently gerrymandered, comprised Stark, Mahoning, Columbiana, and Carroll counties. He was reelected over Aquila Wiley in 1878 and Leroy D. Thoman in 1880. In 1882 he appeared to edge out Jonathan H. Wallace by eight votes, but under challenge the seat was awarded to Wallace. Returned to Congress over D. R. Paige in 1884, McKinley was reelected over Wallace H. Phlelps in 1886 and George P. Ikert in 1888. Although fundamentally in favor of sound currency, Congressman McKinley pleased westerners by voting for the Bland-Allison Act (1878; see "Rutherford B. Hayes, 19th President," "Administration") and the Sherman Silver Purchase Act (1890; see "Benjamin Harrison, 23d President," "Administration"). He earned his national reputation as the foremost champion in the House of protectionism. He considered a high tariff a necessary means of national self-defense against cheap labor and goods abroad. Having campaigned for Representative James A. Garfield for president in 1880, he succeeded him on the Ways and Means Committee, rising to chairman in 1889. From this position, then, he drafted and steered to passage the McKinley Tariff (1890; see "Benjamin Harrison, 23d President," "Administration"). This severely protectionist measure brought about a marked increase in consumer prices. In the 1890 congressional elections angry voters turned against Republicans, including McKinley, who was upset by Lieutenant Governor John G. Warwick. Among Republican leaders, however, McKinley remained very popular. He had been named chairman of the state party convention in 1884, and as a delegate-at-large to the national convention that year he helped secure the nomination of James G. Blaine of Maine. Again a delegate to the national convention in 1888, this time pledged to John Sherman of Ohio, he remained loyal to the candidate and quickly quashed a McKinley-for-president boomlet. In 1889 he was narrowly defeated for Speaker of the House by Republican Representative Thomas B. Reed of Maine. Although ousted from Congress in 1890 over the tariff issue, he left Washington convinced that he one day would be vindicated, that protection was what Americans wanted and needed.

Governor of Ohio, 1892–1896. McKinley was elected governor of Ohio over Democrat James E. Campbell in October 1891 and reelected two years later over Lawrence T. Neal. He was a candidate for the Republican presidential nomination in 1892 and campaigned for the eventual nominee, Benjamin Harrison. As governor, McKinley called out the National Guard to put down labor-related disturbances in Akron, Cleveland, and elsewhere in the state. He imposed an excise tax on corporations, secured safety legislation for transportation workers, and restricted antiunion practices of employers.

REPUBLICAN PRESIDENTIAL NOMINATION, 1896: As Republicans convened in St. Louis in June 1896, McKinley was the clear front-runner, his campaign for the nomination ably directed by Mark Hanna. Opposition to McKinley centered around the candidacy of House Speaker Thomas B. Reed of Maine. Joseph Foraker of Ohio placed McKinley's name in nomination. McKinley was nominated on the first ballot with 661½ votes to 84½ for Reed, 61½ for Matthew S. Quay of Pennsylvania, 58 for Levi P. Morton of New York, and 35½ for William B. Allison of Iowa. Garret A. Hobart of New Jersey was nominated for vice president over Henry Clay Evans of Tennessee, his nearest rival. The Republican platform supported the gold standard but, in a nod to the western silverites, left the door open to the free coinage of silver if part of "an international agreement with the leading commercial nations of the world." The plank still failed to satisfy some western delegates, who walked out of the convention on its adoption. The platform also supported acquisition of Hawaii and part of the Danish West Indies, approved construction of a canal across Central America and naval expansion, expressed sympathy for revolutionaries in Cuba and Armenians suffering at the hands of the Turks, called for exclusion of all illiterate immigrants, applauded gains in women's rights and pledged "equal pay for equal work," and encouraged creation of a national board of arbitration to settle labor disputes.

OPPONENT: William Jennings Bryan (1860–1925) of Nebraska; Democrat. Born in Salem, Illinois, the son of a circuit court judge, Bryan graduated from Illinois College in 1881 and Union College of Law in 1883, practiced law for a time in Jacksonville, Illinois, and in 1887 settled in Lincoln, Nebraska, where he became active in politics as a Democrat. Elected to the U.S. House for 1891–1895, he championed free silver and the federal income tax. Following his defeat for the senate in 1894 he was editor in chief of the *Omaha World-Herald* from 1894–1896. As a delegate to the Democratic national convention in Chicago in July 1896, Bryan was determined to write a free-silver plank into the platform. In perhaps the most memorable address ever delivered before a political convention, Bryan rocked the hall with a blistering attack on the gold standard, concluding: "Having behind us the producing masses of this nation and the world, supported by the commercial interests, the laboring interests and the toilers everywhere, we will answer their demand for a gold standard by saying to them: You shall not press down upon the brow of labor this crown of thorns, you shall not crucify mankind upon a cross of gold."[6] The silver plank carried, 628–301. With this speech Bryan was catapulted into the front ranks of candidates for the nomination. The leading contender was Representative Richard "Silver Dick" Bland of Missouri. Other candidates were Robert E. Pattison of Pennsylvania, Governor Horace Boies of Iowa, Joseph S.C. Blackburn of Kentucky, and John R. McLean of Ohio. Bland maintained his lead through the first three ballots but never came within 220 votes of the total needed for nomination. Bryan overtook him on the fourth tally. Then Illinois's defection from Bland touched off a stampede to Bryan, putting him over the top on the fifth ballot. Arthur Sewall of Maine was nominated for vice president. Besides calling for free silver, the Democratic platform opposed the protective tariff, condemned the Supreme Court for overturning the federal income tax law, called for "prevention of foreign pauper labor," favored arbitration of labor disputes, demanded a stronger Interstate Commerce Commission, denounced the use of the injunction to end strikes, favored statehood for the western territories, and expressed sympathy for revolutionaries in Cuba. After his defeat by McKinley, Bryan retained control of the party and was again nominated for president in 1900.

CAMPAIGN AND THE ISSUES, 1896: The currency issue dominated this campaign, blurring party lines. Eastern Democrats, unable to accept the party's free-silver platform and unwilling to support McKinley for his tariff views, nominated their own candidate, John M. Palmer of Illinois and called themselves the National, or Gold, Democrats. Meanwhile silver Republicans in the West bolted their party to support Bryan. The Populist party found itself in the curious position of seeing the Democrats co-opt virtually every issue that had given rise to the third party. At their convention in July, then, Populists endorsed Bryan. The candidates themselves were a study in contrast. Bryan, a vigorous 36, crisscrossed the nation in the most strenuous campaign conducted up to that time. Relying on just a few hours sleep a night, he traveled 18,000 miles in three months to address an estimated five million people. McKinley, on the other hand, remained in the comfort of his home in Canton, Ohio, venturing only as far as the front porch to address delegations that streamed into the city daily. Meanwhile some 1,400 surrogate speakers stumped for McKinley nationwide, supplemented by tens of millions of pieces of Republican campaign literature, much of it in foreign languages to attract the immigrant vote. Republicans painted Bryan as a radical, a demagogue, a socialist. Democrats denounced McKinley as a tool of the capitalists. Influential eastern newspapers, like the *Boston Globe, New York World,* and *Baltimore Sun,* which had been friendly to Grover Cleveland and other sound-money Democrats, could not stomach Bryan. Of the major New York dailies, only Hearst's *Journal* endorsed him. But it was in campaign fundraising that Republicans far ourstripped the Democrats. Under the direction of campaign manager Mark Hanna, the McKinley campaign tapped more than $3 million from industrialists fearful of Bryan's populist notions. The Bryan effort raised only about one-fifth as much, largely from silver mine owners. Mayor Tom Johnson of Cleveland summed up the campaign as "the first great protest of the American people against monopoly—the first great struggle of the masses in our country against the privileged classes."[7]

ELECTION AS PRESIDENT, FIRST TERM, 1896:

Popular Vote: McKinley (Republican), 7,035,638 (51%); Bryan (Democrat; Populist), 6,467,946 (47%).

Electoral Vote: McKinley, 271; Bryan, 176.

States Carried: McKinley won the majority of electors in 23 states—California, Connecticut, Delaware, Illinois, Indiana, Iowa, Kentucky, Maine, Maryland, Massachusetts, Michigan, Minnesota, New Hampshire, New Jersey, New York, North Dakota, Ohio, Oregon, Pennsylvania, Rhode Island, Vermont, West Virginia, and Wisconsin. Bryan won the majority of electoral votes in 22 states—Alabama, Arkansas, Colorado, Florida, Georgia, Idaho, Kansas, Louisiana, Mississippi, Missouri, Montana, Nebraska, Nevada, North Carolina, South Carolina, South Dakota, Tennessee, Texas, Utah, Virginia, Washington, and Wyoming.

REPUBLICAN NOMINATION FOR REELECTION AS PRESIDENT, 1900:

McKinley's renomination was assured as Republicans convened in Philadelphia in June 1900. His renomination speech was delivered by Joseph Foraker of Ohio and seconded by Governor Theodore Roosevelt of New York, among others. Vice President Hobart having died in office, attention focused on the selection of a new running mate. Privately, President McKinley preferred Senator William B. Allison of Iowa, but Allison withdrew himself from consideration. The president announced his readiness to accept the will of the convention. The clear favorite of delegates was Theodore Roosevelt, who at first protested that he was reluctant to give up the governorship of New York for the boring, low-profile duties of vice president. But with encouragement from Senator Henry Cabot Lodge, who sincerely believed that the office might serve as a springboard to the presidency, and New York boss Tom Platt, who was eager to get the reform-minded Roosevelt out of his state, he consented. The Republican platform pointed with pride to McKinley prosperity in contrast to the Cleveland depression, approved the administration's conduct of the Spanish-American War and expansionism, reaffirmed its faith in the gold standard and the protective tariff, favored further restrictions on immigration, called for raising the age limit for child labor, comdemned southern laws designed to keep blacks from the polls, and supported statehood for the western territories, construction of a canal across Central America, and the Open Door policy toward China.

OPPONENT: William Jennings Bryan (1860–1925) of Nebraska; Democrat. He had been the Democratic presidential nominee in 1896. At the party's national convention in Kansas City, Missouri, in July 1900, Bryan was nominated without opposition. The only disagreement arose over the silver plank of the platform. Party strategists wanted to omit specific mention of free silver on the ground that recent prosperity had made it no longer relevant and therefore a needless slap at eastern Gold Democrats, whom they hoped to woo back into the party. Bryan, however, insisted on complete reiteration of the strong silver plank of 1896. Without it, he said, he would not accept the nomination. The silver plank carried narrowly. For vice president Bryan privately preferred Charles A. Towne of Minnesota, leader of the silver Republicans, but agreed to accept the convention's choice, Adlai E. Stevenson of Illinois, former vice president under Grover Cleveland. Besides maintaining its stance on the currency issue, the Democratic platform denounced as imperialism the McKinley administration's acquisition of territory at the end of the Spanish-American War and demanded immediate independence for Cuba and eventual independence for the Philippines. It called for stricter antitrust laws, reduction in the tariff, direct election of senators, arbitration rather than the injunction to settle labor disputes, construction of a canal across Central America, and statehood for the western territories. After his second defeat by McKinley, Bryan published the *Commoner*, a weekly paper that provided him a forum from which to speak out on current events. He again ran for president in 1908 (see "William Howard Taft, 27th President," "Opponent").

CAMPAIGN AND THE ISSUES, 1900: In the McKinley-Bryan rematch, the currency issue was shunted aside, for gold discoveries in Alaska and elsewhere had inflated the currency and eased credit, and a return to prosperity during McKinley's first term removed much of the discontent that had given rise to the populist fervor. The dominant issue in this campaign was imperialism. Democrats charged that under McKinley the United States was becoming an imperial power, bent on acquiring far-flung colonies and abandoning its traditional role as a champion of local autonomy. Republicans countered that as an emerging world power the United States had a responsibility to bring civilization and American ideals to backward peoples. Bryan again stumped the nation, calling for independence of the lands acquired at the end of the Spanish-American War. President McKinley remained aloof, leaving the campaigning to his vigorous running mate Theodore Roosevelt, who everywhere stressed the Republican campaign slogan, "Four Years More of the Full Dinner Pail." McKinley increased his margin of victory from four years before. Bryan's support was limited to the traditionally Democratic South and isolated pockets in the West. Even Nebraska, his home state, went for McKinley.

REELECTION AS PRESIDENT, 1900:

    Popular Vote. McKinley (Republican), 7,219,530 (52%); Bryan (Democrat), 6,358,071 (46%).

    Electoral Vote: McKinley, 292; Bryan 155.

    States Carried: McKinley won the electoral votes of 28 states—California, Connecticut, Delaware, Illinois, Indiana, Iowa, Kansas, Maine, Maryland, Massachusetts, Michigan, Minnesota, Nebraska, New Hampshire, New Jersey,

New York, North Dakota, Ohio, Oregon, Pennsylvania, Rhode Island, South Dakota, Utah, Vermont, Washington, West Virginia, Wisconsin, and Wyoming. Bryan won the electoral votes of 17 states—Alabama, Arkansas, Colorado, Florida, Georgia, Idaho, Kentucky, Louisiana, Mississippi, Missouri, Montana, Nevada, North Carolina, South Carolina, Tennessee, Texas, and Virginia.

INAUGURAL ADDRESS (FIRST): March 4, 1897. ". . . It has been the policy of the United States since the foundation of the Government to cultivate relations of peace and amity with all the nations of the world, and this accords with my conception of our duty now. . . . We want no wars of conquest; we must avoid the temptation of territorial aggression. War should never be entered upon until every agency of peace has failed; peace is preferable to war in almost every contingency. Arbitration is the true method of settlement of international as well as local or individual differences. . . ."

INAUGURAL ADDRESS (SECOND): March 4, 1901. ". . . We face at this moment a most important question—that of the future relations of the United States and Cuba. With our near neighbors we must remain close friends. The declaration of the purposes of this Government in the resolution of April 20, 1898, must be made good. . . . The Principles which led to our intervention require that the fundamental law upon which the new government rests should be adapted to secure a government capable of performing the duties and discharging the functions of a separate nation, of observing its international obligations of protecting life and property, insuring order, safety, and liberty, and conforming to the established and historical policy of the United States in its relation to Cuba. . . ."

VICE PRESIDENTS: Garret Augustus Hobart (1844–1899), of New Jersey, served 1897–1899. Born in Long Branch, New Jersey, Hobart graduated from Rutgers College in 1863 and began practicing law in Paterson, New Jersey, where he became active in Republican politics. He served in the state assembly 1873–1875 and the state senate 1877–1882 and as state party chairman 1880–1891. Meanwhile he served on the boards of dozens of railroads, utilities, and banks. Although little known outside his home state, he proved an asset to the ticket; for the first time since 1872, New Jersey went Republican. Vice President Hobart cast the tie-breaking vote in the Senate in support of McKinley's decision to retain the Philippines at the conclusion of the Spanish-American War. He died in office in Paterson.

Theodore Roosevelt (1858–1919), of New York, served March–September 1901. He succeeded to the presidency on McKinley's assassination. See "Theodore Roosevelt, 26th President."

CABINET:

Secretary of State. (1) John Sherman (1823–1900), of Ohio, served 1897–1898. He had served as Treasury secretary in the Hayes administration. As senator he had sponsored the Sherman Anti-Trust Act and the Sherman Silver Purchase Act (both 1890; see "Benjamin Harrison, 23d President," "Administration"). His appointment drew widespread criticism because it was generally acknowledged that it was designed to free his Senate seat for Mark Hanna, McKinley's campaign manager. Moreover, Sherman was ill and unable to discharge fully his duties as secretary, duties that fell to Assistant Secretary William R. Day. Sherman disapproved of going to war with Spain. (2) William R. Day (1849–1923), of Ohio, served April –September 1898. Having served as de facto secretary of state under the ill John Sherman, Day was promoted to secretary at the outbreak of the Spanish-American War. He resigned to lead the American delegation to Paris to negotiate the peace treaty. He privately opposed annexation of the Philippines but acceded to McKinley's decision to acquire the islands. He convinced the president, however, to pay Spain $20 million in compensation. He later was appointed to the Supreme Court by President Theodore Roosevelt. (3) John M. Hay (1838–1905) of Washington, D.C., served 1898–1905. Former assistant private secretary to President Abraham Lincoln, Hay only reluctantly relinquished his post as ambassador to Great Britain to join McKinley's cabinet. As secretary, he approved annexation of the Philippines and pursued the Open Door policy toward China (see "Administration"). In 1900 he dispatched a relief expedition to rescue Americans in China during the Boxer Rebellion (see "Administration"). It was Hay who first described the Spanish-American conflict as a "splendid little war." He stayed on in the Roosevelt administration.

Secretary of the Treasury. Lyman J. Gage (1836–1927), of Illinois, served 1897–1902. He was president of the First National Bank of Chicago. A Gold Democrat, he had bolted the party to support McKinley in 1896. As secretary, he maintained a sound-money policy and eased restrictions on national banks. He stayed on in the Roosevelt administration.

Secretary of War. (1) Russell A. Alger (1836–1907), of Michigan, served 1897–1899. He resigned amid reports of gross inefficiency, including the so-called embalmed beef scandal in which tainted meat had been supplied to U.S. troops during the Spanish-American War. An investigation, however, cleared Alger of any criminal activity. He wrote *The Spanish American War* (1901). (2) Elihu Root (1845–1937), of New York, served 1899–1904. Among the most efficient administrators ever to head the department, he took charge of territories acquired at the end of the Spanish-American War. He appointed General Leonard Wood military governor of Cuba, promoted economic development in Puerto Rico, and put down unrest in the Philippines. He reorganized the department, improved military preparedness, and established the Army War College. He stayed on in the Roosevelt administration.

Attorney General. (1) Joseph McKenna (1843–1926), of California, served 1897–1898. He reluctantly gave up his seat on the Ninth U.S. Circuit Court to join McKinley's cabinet, but only after receiving assurances that he would be appointed to the first vacancy on the Supreme Court. (2) John W. Griggs (1849–1927), of New Jersey, served 1898–1901. He resigned as governor of New Jersey to join the cabinet. (3) Philander C. Knox (1853–1921), of Pennsylvania, served 1901–1904. He undertook antitrust action against the Northern Securities Company. He stayed on in the Roosevelt administration.

Secretary of the Navy. John D. Long (1838–1915), of Massachusetts, served 1897–1902. He directed naval operations during the Spanish-American War. He stayed on in the administration of Theodore Roosevelt, who had served under him as assistant secretary of the navy.

Postmaster General. (1) James A. Gary (1833–1920), of Maryland, served 1897–1898. He urged establishment of a postal savings bank. (2) Charles Emory Smith (1842–1908), of Pennsylvania, served 1898–1902. He curbed fraudulent use of the mails and extended rural free delivery. He stayed on in the Roosevelt administration.

Secretary of the Interior. (1) Cornelius N. Bliss (1833–1911), of New York, served 1897–1898. Bored by the office, he resigned to return to private business.

(2) Ethan A. Hitchcock (1835–1909), of Missouri, served 1898–1907. He gave up his post as minister to Russia to join the cabinet. An ardent conservationist, he stayed on in the Roosevelt administration.

Secretary of Agriculture. James Wilson (1835–1920), of Iowa, served 1897–1913. A Scottish immigrant, he was professor of agriculture at Iowa Agricultural College. As secretary, he promoted scientific farming and established experimental stations around the country. He stayed on in the Roosevelt administration.

ADMINISTRATION: March 4, 1897–September 14, 1901.

Dingley Tariff Act, 1897. Sponsored by Republican Representative Nelson R. Dingley of Maine, the bill redeemed Republican campaign promises to restore the high protective tariff and provided for an average rate of 46 percent. It replaced the Wilson-Gorman Act (1894; see "Grover Cleveland, 24th President," "Administration"). It was replaced by the Payne-Aldrich Tariff (1909; see "William Howard Taft, 27th President," "Administration").

Annexation of Hawaii, 1898. Reversing the policy of the previous administration (see "Grover Cleveland, 24th President," "Administration"), President McKinley in July 1898 signed a joint congressional resolution annexing the Hawaiian Islands.

Spanish-American War, 1898. Causes: Many Americans were eager for the conflict. Sympathy for Cubans struggling for independence from Spain, a natural antipathy toward a European power trying desperately to maintain its colonies in the Western Hemisphere, reports of Spanish atrocities against Cubans—all stirred Americans to battle. The so-called yellow press whipped the nation into a frenzy with lurid accounts, often exaggerated, of conditions in Cuba. President McKinley had hoped to resolve the Cuban conflict without U.S. military intervention. Through diplomatic channels he urged the Spanish government to adopt a more humane policy toward Cuban civilians and to reach a negotiated settlement with the rebels. But as the insurgency dragged on, McKinley succumbed to the growing clamor for war. Two events of February 1898 forced his hand: (1) William Randolph Hearst, among the most vociferous of the war hawks, published in his *New York Journal*, a private letter written by Enrique Dupuy de Lôme, Spanish minister to the Unites States, stolen from the mails by Cuban revolutionaries, and leaked to the *Journal*. In it de Lôme characterized McKinley as "weak and a bidder for the admiration of the crowd, besides being a would-be politician who tries to leave a door open behind himself while keeping on good terms with the jingoes of his party." Its publication gave rise to a fresh outpouring of anti-Spanish sentiment. (2) A week later, on February 15, 1898, the U.S. battleship *Maine* exploded and sank in Havana harbor; 266 of the 350-man crew were killed. The cause of the explosion has never been determined. But many in the United States, convinced that Spanish mines had destroyed the ship, joined in the war cry "Remember the *Maine*! To Hell with Spain!"

The war: On April 11, 1898, President McKinley dismissed Spain's offer to suspend hostilities in Cuba and asked Congress for authorization "to take measures to secure a full and final termination of hostilities between the Government of Spain and the people of Cuba, and to secure in the island the establishment of a stable government . . . and to use the military and naval forces of the United States as may be necessary for these purposes." Congress granted the authorization on April 20 and formally declared war April 25. The vote was 310–6 in the House, 42–35 in the Senate. To reassure such dovish critics as House Speaker Thomas B. Reed, author Mark Twain, and industrialist Andrew Carnegie, who denounced intervention as blatant imperialism, Congress in a joint resolution known as the Teller Amendment asserted, "That the United States hereby disclaims any disposition or intention to exercise sovereignty, jurisdiction, or control over [Cuba] except for the pacification thereof, and asserts its determination when that is accomplished, to leave the government and control of the Island to its people." On May 1, 1898, Commodore George Dewey, with a fleet of six vessels, handily destroyed Spain's 10-ship Pacific fleet under Admiral Montojo in Manila Bay without losing a single man. Spanish casualties in the encounter totaled 381. In August U.S. troops captured Manila itself and took possession of the Philippines. Meanwhile in Cuba, U.S. troops under General William Shafter, including the Rough Riders of Colonel Theodore Roosevelt, overcame stiff Spanish resistance to capture Santiago in July. That same month Admiral William T. Sampson destroyed Spain's Atlantic fleet under Admiral Cervera in waters between Cuba and Jamaica. Later in July, U.S. forces under General Nelson A. Miles captured Puerto Rico. Spain sued for peace. A cease fire was declared on August 12. Americans killed in action during the war numbered less than 400, but thousands more died from malaria, yellow fever, and other diseases.

Paris Peace Treaty, signed December 10, 1898; ratified February 6, 1899: U.S. negotiators were William R. Day, Cushman K. Davis, William P. Frye, George Gray, and Whitelaw Reid. Under its terms Spain relinquished its claim to Cuba and ceded Puerto Rico, Guam, and, for $20 million, the Philippine Islands to the United States.

Effects: With the acquisition of the Philippines, the United States joined the ranks of the world's colonial powers. President McKinley saw in it a chance to "educate . . . and uplift and civilize and Christianize"[8] the Filipinos. But Filipino nationalists under Emilio Aguinaldo rose up in armed rebellion against American rule in 1899. U.S. forces crushed the insurrection but only after more than two years of bloody encounters. Retention of the Philippines as the anchor of the U.S. presence in the Pacific emboldened the McKinley administration to pursue its Open Door policy toward China. Cuba remained under U.S. military occupation until local government was established in 1902 and was virtually a U.S. protectorate until 1934.

Open Door Policy and the Boxer Rebellion, 1899–1900. Responding to European concern that Japanese aggression threatened to close Chinese ports to Western commerce, President McKinley authorized Secretary of State John Hay to set forth the Open Door policy, 1899–1900, in which the United States expressed its desire to have all commercial nations on an equal footing in China, unfettered by discriminatory tariffs or other restrictions. Soon thereafter, in June 1900, Chinese nationalists of the I-ho T'uan (Righteous and Harmonious Society), popularly known as the Boxers for their pugilistic-like ritual of battle preparation, advanced on Peking, after having massacred numerous Western missionaries and Chinese converts to Christianity, and laid siege to the foreign community in that city. In August a relief expedition of American, British, French, German, Russian, and Japanese forces dispersed the Boxers and rescued their foreign hostages. Under the terms of the Boxer Protocol of 1901, the Chinese government agreed to pay the foreign governments $333 million in compensation for the incident. Much of the U.S. share of $25 million was used for scholarships for Chinese students.

Gold Standard Act, 1900. Under its terms, the United States formally placed its money on the gold standard. All currency was fully backed by gold. Its price was fixed at $20.67 an ounce.

SUPREME COURT APPOINTMENT: Joseph McKenna (1843–1926), of California, served as associate justice 1898–1925. He was attorney general when nominated. In *German Alliance Insurance Co.* v. *Kansas* (1914), he upheld state regulation of the insurance industry. In *Bunting* v. *Oregon* (1917) he spoke for the majority in letting stand a state law limiting the normal workday in factories to 10 hours and mandating time-and-a-half pay for overtime.

RANKING IN 1962 HISTORIANS POLL: McKinley ranked fifteenth of 31 presidents, fourth of 12 "average" presidents. He ranked above Taft, below Hayes.

ASSASSINATION: September 6, 1901, 4:07 P.M., Buffalo, New York; Death, September 14, 1901, 2:15 A.M., Buffalo. In his last public address at the Pan American Exposition in Buffalo on September 5, 1901, President McKinley appeared to break with his long-standing commitment to a high protective tariff, arguing for greater reliance on reciprocal trade agreements. "The Period of exclusiveness is past," he asserted. "The expansion of our trade and commerce is the pressing problem. Commercial wars are unprofitable. A policy of good will and friendly trade relations will prevent reprisals. Reciprocity treaties are in harmony with the spirit of the times; measures of retaliation are not."[9] The next day he stood in a receiving line at the Temple of Music on the Exposition grounds. Leon F. Czolgosz, 28, a Detroit native of Polish heritage and an unemployed wire millworker, queued up with others waiting to shake the president's hand. His right hand was wrapped in a bandage, which concealed a .32 Iver Johnson revolver. As McKinley stretched to greet him, Czolgosz fired two shots at point-blank range. The first apparently struck a button near the breastbone and failed to penetrate the skin. Startled by the shot, the president rose up on his toes and turned his body slightly to the right in time to take the second round in the abdomen between the naval and the left nipple. The bullet passed through the stomach, nipped the top of the left kidney, and lodged in the pancreas. The president doubled over and fell backward into the arms of a Secret Service agent. Seeing his assailant being pummeled to the ground, he cried out, "Don't let them hurt him." Moments later he turned to his secretary and said, "My wife, be careful, Cortelyou, how you tell her—oh, be careful."[10] The president was rushed to a hospital on the Exposition grounds. Principal attending physicians were Dr. P. M. Rixey, McKinley's personal physician; surgeons Roswell Park, Herman Mynter, Matthew D. Mann, and John Parmenter; and Dr. Eugene Wasdin, who administered the anesthesia. Two operations were performed. During the first, lasting one hour, doctors searched in vain for the bullet, closed the bullet holes in the stomach walls, rinsed the abdominal cavity with a saline solution, and sewed shut the surface wound. A second, minor operation, performed four days later, removed a small fragment of clothing that the bullet had carried into the abdomen. The president was removed to the home of Exposition president John G. Milburn for postoperative recovery. At first doctors were optimistic. By September 11 his temperature, which had been running at 102°, eased to 100°. He felt so fit that he asked for a cigar (denied) and solid food (granted). The next day, however, he suffered a relapse. Digitalis was administered, but his heart failed to respond. On September 13, he continued to sink and died early the following morning. His last words were: "It is God's way. His will, not ours, be done."[11] An autopsy revealed the proximate cause of death to be gangrene, which had developed around the bullet holes and along the track of the bullet. A plaster death mask was taken by Edward L.A. Pausch of Hartford, Connecticut. His body lay in state in Buffalo, Washington, and Canton, Ohio. Private funeral services were held at the Milburn home in Buffalo; public services were performed at Canton's Methodist Church. He was buried temporarily at Westlawn Cemetery in Canton. In 1907 his remains were transferred to the McKinley National Memorial in Canton.

In his last will and testament, executed in McKinley's own hand in October 1897, the president left the bulk of his estate, valued at more than $200,000, to his wife. He provided a $1,000 lifetime annuity for his mother; because she had already died, the annuity fell to his sister Helen.

Czolgosz, a self-avowed anarchist, admitted the shooting. "I killed President McKinley," he informed Buffalo authorities, "because I done my duty. I don't believe one man should have so much service and another man should have none."[12] At his trial on September 23, 1901, Czolgosz pleaded guilty, but in New York defendants accused of capital crimes must enter a plea of not guilty; the plea was so changed. Czolgosz declined to retain counsel, because as an anarchist he did not acknowledge the right of the court to try him. The court appointed Loran L. Lewis and Robert C. Titus, both former state supreme court justices, to represent him. After nine hours the case went to the jury, which took another 34 minutes to find him guilty. Judge Truman C. White sentenced him to death by electrocution. On October 29, 1901, Czolgosz took the electric chair at Auburn State Prison, after telling onlookers, "I killed the president because he was the enemy of the people—the good working people. I am not sorry for my crime."[13] Sulfuric acid was then poured over his corpse to accelerate decomposition.

MCKINLEY PRAISED: "William McKinley has left us a priceless gift in the example of a useful and pure life, in his fidelity to public trusts and in his demonstration of the value of kindly virtues that not only ennoble but lead to success."[14]—former president Grover Cleveland, 1901

"Under his rule Hawaii has come to us, and Tutuila; Porto Rico and the vast archipelago of the East. Cuba is free. Our position in the Caribbean is assured beyond the possibility of future question. The doctrine called by the name Monroe, so long derided and denied by alien publicists, evokes now no challenge or contradiction when uttered to the world. . . . In dealing with foreign powers, he will take rank with the greatest of our diplomatists."[15]—Secretary of State John Hay, 1902

"There have been people who suggest my ideas would take us back to the days of McKinley. Well, what's wrong with that? Under McKinley, we freed Cuba."[16]—Ronald Reagan, 1976

MCKINLEY CRITICIZED: "McKinley keeps his ear to the ground so close that he gets it full of grasshoppers much of the time."[17]—Representative Joe Cannon of Illinois

"McKinley has no more backbone than a chocolate eclair."[18]—Assistant Secretary of the Navy Theodore Roosevelt, 1897

"We earnestly condemn the policy of the present National Administration in the Philippines. It seeks to extinguish the spirit of 1776 in those islands. We deplore the sacrifice of our soldiers and sailors, whose bravery deserves admiration even in an unjust war. We denounce the slaughter of the Filipinos as a needless horror. We protest against this extension of American sovereignty by Spanish methods."[19]—American Anti-Imperialist League, 1899

"[McKinley] used too many hackneyed phrases, too many stereotyped forms. He shook hands with exactly the amount of cordiality and with precisely the lack of intimacy that deceived men into thinking well of him, too well of him."[20]— Journalist William Allen White

MCKINLEY QUOTES: "Unlike any other nation, here the people rule, and their will is the supreme law. It is sometimes sneeringly said by those who do not like free government, that here we count heads. True, heads are counted, but brains also. And the general sense of 63 millions of free people is better and safer than the sense of any favored few, born to nobility and ruling by inheritance."[21]— 1891

"Business life, whether among ourselves or with other people, is ever a sharp struggle for success. It will be none the less so in the future. Without competition we would be clinging to the clumsy antiquated processes of farming and manufacture and the methods of business of long ago, and the twentieth would be no further advanced than the eighteenth century."[22]—1901

BOOK BY MCKINLEY: *The Tariff in the Days of Henry Clay and Since* (1896).
BOOKS ABOUT MCKINLEY: Gould, Lewis L. *The Presidency of William McKinley.* Lawrence, Kansas: Regents Press of Kansas, 1980.
Leech, Margaret. *In the Days of McKinley.* New York: Harper & Bros., 1959.
Olcott, Charles S. *The Life of William McKinley.* 2 vols. Boston: Houghton, Mifflin, 1916.
Spielman, William Carl. *William McKinley: Republican Stalwart.* New York: Exposition Press, 1954.

NOTES

1 Margaret Leech, *In the Days of McKinley*, New York: Harper & Bros., 1959, p.23.
2 Charles S. Olcott, *The Life of William McKinley*, Boston: Houghton, Mifflin, 1916, vol. I, pp. 265–266.
3 John Sutherland Bonnell, *Presidential Profiles: Religion in the Life of American Presidents*, Philadelphia: Westminster, 1971, p. 175.
4 Olcott, vol. I, p. 64.
5 Ibid., p. 36.
6 Henry Steele Commager, ed., *Documents of American History*, New York: Crofts, 1945, Doc. no. 342, p. 178.
7 John D. Hicks et al., *A History of American Democracy*, Boston: Houghton, Mifflin, 1966, p. 456.
8 Olcott, vol. II, p. 111.
9 Commager, Doc. no. 354.
10 Olcott, vol. II, p. 316.
11 Ibid., p. 324.
12 John Mason Potter, *Plots against the Presidents*, New York: Astor-Honor, 1968, p. 172.
13 Ibid., p. 184.
14 Edward T. Roe, *The Life of William McKinley*, Laird & Lee, 1901, p. 169.
15 Charles Ulysses Gordon, compiler, *William McKinley Commemorative Tributes*, Waterloo, Wis.: Courier, 1942, pp. 77–78.

16 Jules Witcover, *Marathon: Pursuit of the Presidency 1972–1976*, New York: Viking, 1977, p. 432.

17 Leech, p. 49.

18 William Carl Spielman, *William McKinley: Republican Stalwart*, New York: Exposition, 1954, p. 127.

19 Commager, Doc. no. 351, p. 192.

20 *The Autobiography of William Allen White*, New York: Macmillan, 1946, p. 251.

21 *Speeches and Addresses of William McKinley*, New York: Appleton, 1893, p. 537.

22 Louis Filler, ed., *The President Speaks*, New York: Putnam's Sons, 1964, p. 27.

THEODORE ROOSEVELT

26TH PRESIDENT

NAME: Theodore Roosevelt, Jr. He was named after his father. The toy teddy bear was named for him after a cartoon depicted him sparing the life of a cub while hunting. Often referred to as TR in news headlines, he was the first president to be known popularly by his initials.

PHYSICAL DESCRIPTION: Spindly, pale, asthmatic as a boy, Roosevelt, through rigorous exercise and sheer force of will, matured into a brawny, robust man of action. He stood about 5 feet 8 inches tall, weighed about 200 pounds, and had a great barrel chest, bull neck, cleft chin, closely cropped brown hair, wide-set blue eyes, a bushy drooping mustache, a rather large nose, and small ears and feet. His most distinctive feature was a wide toothsome grin. He spoke in a rather high-pitched voice. He wore pince-nez to correct severe myopia. As president he suffered a hard blow to his left eye during a boxing match; he developed a detached retina and lost virtually all vision in that eye. Roosevelt characteristically stood with his shoulders back and his head pitched slightly forward. He dressed fashionably.

PERSONALITY: It was often said that Roosevelt craved the limelight, that he set out to be, as one observer put it, "the bride at every wedding, the corpse at every funeral."[1] The youngest man to become president, he was also the most visibly energetic, zestful chief executive up to that time. Unlike many of his predecessors, he delighted in being president and was sorry to see his term end. He was fearless, decisive, ambitious, proud, and irresistibly charming to men and women alike. He loved children and often took the time to romp with them or gather them round for a story. A gifted raconteur, he captivated listeners with tales of his adventures out West. He detested dirty jokes, however, and typically walked away in the middle of a story as soon as he detected its off-color nature. Whether delivering speeches before large crowds or engaged in a private conversation, Roosevelt spoke forcefully in crisp, clipped tones and gesticulated constantly, his fist pounding the air to emphasize a point, his head jerking to and fro virtually with each word. But he was also a good listener, capable of remaining stock still for extended periods totally engrossed in the words of others. He had a prodigious, apparently photographic memory. He often stunned visitors by reciting whole passages of a book he had read decades before. He explained that with concentration the page seemed to appear in his mind's eye and he simply read from it.

ANCESTORS: Roosevelt was mostly of Dutch, Scotch, Huguenot, and English heritage. The first of the paternal line to emigrate from Holland was his great[5]-grandfather Claes Maertenszen van Rosenvelt (also the immigrant ancestor of Franklin D. Roosevelt), a farmer, who settled in New Netherland about 1644. His great[4]-grandfather Nicholas Roosevelt was alderman of New York (1698–1701). On his mother's side, his great-great-grandfather, Archibald Bulloch, was the first president of Georgia during the American Revolution.

FATHER: Theodore Roosevelt, Sr. (1831–1878), merchant. "My father," the president wrote, "was the best man I ever knew." He added, "I never knew anyone who got greater joy out of living . . . who more wholeheartedly performed every duty."[2] A native of New York City, he was a partner in the importing firm of Roosevelt and Son. He also devoted much of his time to charitable causes, working with the poor children of New York City and helping to found the New York Orthopedic Hospital, the Metropolitan Museum of Art, and other worthy institutions. A Republican, he supported Abraham Lincoln and the Union during the Civil War, a conflict that worked a special hardship on the Roosevelt household because of his wife's southern roots and sympathies. To avoid the draft, he purchased a substitute but served as a civilian allotment commissioner. In this capacity he toured army camps encouraging the troops to send part of their military pay back home. After the war, he supported Republican reformers against the party bosses. In 1877 President Rutherford B. Hayes, in his struggle against the Roscoe Conkling machine, named Roosevelt collector of the Port of New York in place of the incumbent, Chester A. Arthur. The Senate rejected the nomination, 31–25, however. Soon thereafter Roosevelt died of intestinal cancer, when his more famous son was a student at Harvard. Young Roosevelt inherited $125,000 from his father's estate.

MOTHER: Martha "Mittie" Bulloch Roosevelt (1834–1884). "My mother," the president wrote, "was a sweet, gracious, beautiful Southern woman, a delightful companion, and beloved by everybody. She was entirely 'unreconstructed' to the day of her death."[3] Raised on a Georgia plantation, she was at the time of her marriage to Theodore Roosevelt, Sr., in 1853 a typical southern belle. As she set up housekeeping in New York, she felt utterly disjointed without slaves at her elbow. During the Civil war, she did not hide her southern sympathies. While two of her brothers served in the Confederate Navy, she donated food and clothing to the cause through Confederate agents in New York. She died of typhoid fever on the same day and in the same house as her son's first wife, when he was a New York State assemblyman. Roosevelt inherited $62,500 on his mother's death.

SIBLINGS: The second of four children, Roosevelt had two sisters and a brother—Mrs. Anna "Bamie" Cowles, wife of Rear Admiral William Sheffield Cowles, whom she met while serving as hostess of the American Legation in London at the invitation of legation secretary, J. Roosevelt "Rosie" Roosevelt, half brother of Franklin D. Roosevelt; Elliot Roosevelt, father of Eleanor Roosevelt; and Mrs. Corinne Robinson, a member of the Republican National Committee

Executive Council, active in the Red Cross, author of *My Brother Theodore Roosevelt* (1921), and wife of Douglas Robinson, great-grandnephew of President James Monroe.

COLLATERAL RELATIVES: Theodore Roosevelt was a third cousin twice removed of President Martin Van Buren, a fifth cousin of President Franklin D. Roosevelt, an uncle of Eleanor Roosevelt, and a great-uncle of journalists Joseph Alsop and Stewart Alsop.

CHILDREN: By his first marriage Roosevelt had one daughter.

Alice Roosevelt (1884–1980). "I can do one of two things," Roosevelt once said, "I can be President of the United States, or I can control Alice. I cannot possibly do both."[4] Dubbed Princess Alice in the press, she was from her youth until her death at 96 as outspoken and spirited as her father. She made her society debut in 1902 and four years later married Republican Representative Nicholas Longworth of Ohio, later Speaker of the House, in the East Room of the White House. After her husband's death in 1931, she remained in the nation's capital to become "Washington's other Monument," a popular society hostess famous for her biting wit.

By his second marriage Roosevelt had four sons and a daughter.

Theodore Roosevelt, Jr. (1887–1944), public official, soldier. The spitting image of his father in mannerisms and features, TR, Jr., graduated from Harvard before being commissioned a major in 1917. During World War I he was promoted to lieutenant colonel, was wounded and gassed at the Battle of Soissons, and commanded an infantry regiment at the Argonne. He was awarded a Purple Heart, the U.S. Distinguished Service Medal, and the Distinguished Service Cross. After the armistice, he served in the New York State assembly in 1919 and was appointed assistant secretary of the navy, 1921–1925, by President Warren G. Harding. He was an unwitting accomplice in the Teapot Dome scandal (see "Warren G. Harding, 29th President," "Administration") as he facilitated transfer of oil reserves from the Navy to the Interior Department. In 1924 he ran as a Republican for governor of New York but lost to Democrat Al Smith. He was appointed governor of Puerto Rico, 1929–1932, by President Calvin Coolidge and governor-general of the Philippines, 1932–1933, by President Herbert Hoover. During World War II he served as a brigadier general and commander of the Twenty-sixth Infantry in Africa, Italy, and Normandy. He was part of the first assault wave to land at Normandy on D-Day. Soon thereafter he died of natural causes. For his part in the Normandy invasion he was awarded posthumously the Congressional Medal of Honor.

Kermit Roosevelt (1889–1943), businessman, soldier. A Harvard graduate, he accompanied his father on his celebrated African safari in 1909–1910 and on his trek through the Brazilian jungle in 1913–1914. During World War I he served as a captain in the British Army in the Middle East and, with U.S. entry into the war, as a major of artillery in the U.S. Army. After the war he became a steamship executive. In the early days of World War II, he again joined the British Army, this time as a major serving in Norway and Egypt. He subsequently joined the U.S. Army. He died of natural causes on duty in Alaska.

Ethel Carow Roosevelt (1891–1977). In 1913 she married Dr. Richard Derby. During World War I she served as a nurse at the American Ambulance Hospital in Paris while her husband was a doctor there.

Archibald Bulloch Roosevelt (1894–1979), financier, soldier. A Harvard graduate, he served as a captain in the army during World War I and was severely wounded in France. He was awarded the Croix de Guerre and discharged as disabled. After the war he prospered as a Wall Street investment banker. During World War II he again served in the army, this time as a lieutenant colonel in the Pacific. He was severely wounded by shrapnel on Biak Island and again was discharged as disabled.

Quentin Roosevelt (1897–1918). An Army Air Corps pilot during World War I, he was shot down and killed by German fighters over France.

BIRTH: Roosevelt was born on October 27, 1858, at 7:45 P.M., at the family brownstone, 28 East 20th Street, New York City. He was the only president born in New York City. His mother described his appearance as "a cross between a terrapin and Dr. Young,"[5] but his grandmother pronounced him sweet and pretty. He weighed 8½ pounds.

CHILDHOOD: Roosevelt was a sickly boy. Indeed he choked so severely from asthma that for much of his early childhood he had to sleep propped up in bed or slouching in a chair. Despite this and frequent bouts with diarrhea, coughs, colds, and other maladies, he was a hyperactive, often mischievous youngster. Once he was chased down by his father for biting his sister's arm. At age seven, he first developed his lifelong interest in animals, when he spotted a dead seal on a slab of wood at a local market. "That seal," he later recalled, "filled me with every possible feeling of romance and adventure." He somehow acquired the seal's head and, with the aid of two cousins, established what he called the Roosevelt Museum of Natural History. Determined to become a zoologist, he snared countless creatures great and small, stored their prepared carcasses all about the house, and examined and catalogued them. At age nine he wrote a precociously learned paper "The Natural History of Insects," based on personal observation. At his father's urging, he set out to strengthen his scrawny physique. At Wood's Gym and with equipment in his home he exercised rigorously. After a couple of young fellows beat him up, he began taking boxing lessons. He benefited from two trips abroad with his family: During 1869–1870 he toured Europe, spent Christmas in Rome, and kissed the hand of Pope Pius IX. Not yet sensitized to the victims of poverty, 11-year-old "Teedie" thought it great sport to toss bits of cake at a crowd of Italian beggars and watch them scramble for crumbs. During 1872–1873 he toured Egypt, climbing to the top of the pyramids, and the Holy Land, before spending several months in Dresden, Germany. On their return to the United States in 1873 the Roosevelts settled in a newly built mansion at 6 West 57th Street in New York City.

EDUCATION: Too sickly to attend school, except for a few month's stint at Professor McMullen's school near his home, Roosevelt learned the fundamentals from his maternal aunt Annie Bulloch, who imbued him with a sense of history with tales of the antebellum south. Other tutors followed, including a teacher of taxidermy to encourage his affinity for natural history. In Dresden, Germany, in the summer of 1873 he studied German and French under Fraulein Anna Minkwitz, who predicted of her pupil, "He will surely one day be a great professor, or who knows, he may become president of the United States."[6] Returning to New York later that year, he underwent intensive tutoring under Arthur Hamilton Cutler to prepare for the Harvard entrance examination, which he passed in 1875. As a freshman at Harvard in 1876 he took part in a torchlight campus demonstration for Rutherford B. Hayes for president. He excelled in the sciences, German, rhetoric, and philosophy but fell down in the ancient languages. He was librarian of the Porcellian Club, secretary of the

Hasty Pudding Club, vice president of the Natural History Club, editor of the *Advocate*, and founder of the Finance Club and still found time to write and lecture before the Nuttall Ornithological Club. He also was runner-up for the campus lightweight boxing championship, losing the title to C. S. Hanks. Although outclassed by Hanks in a particularly bloody slugfest, Roosevelt was long remembered for his sportmanship during the bout. At the end of one round, Hanks bloodied Roosevelt's nose after the bell had rung, drawing a chorus of jeers from ringside. Roosevelt turned to the crowd and called for quiet, explaining that Hanks had not heard the bell. Thereupon he walked over to his opponent and shook his hand, to the pleasure of the fans. Roosevelt graduated Phi Beta Kappa and magna cum laude, twenty-first of 177 students of the class of 1880. At the urging of Professor J. Laurence Laughlin and Alice Lee, Roosevelt's girlfriend, he gave up his ambition to become a naturalist and decided instead to attend law school with a view to entering public life. He entered Columbia Law School in 1880 but dropped out the following year to run for the state assembly. He never sought admission to the bar.

RELIGION: Dutch Reformed. At 16, Roosevelt joined the Dutch Reformed church. As a child, however, he attended Madison Square Presbyterian Church, because no Dutch Reformed church was accessible. At Oyster Bay, Long Island, he attended Episcopal services; his wife was of that faith. In Washington he worshipped at Grace Reformed Church. At Harvard he taught Sunday school at Christ's Church until the rector discovered that he was not Episcopalian and dismissed him. He was well versed in the Bible. Among his favorite passages was James 1:22, "Be ye doers of the word, and not hearers only." He opposed the Lutheran and Calvinist doctrines of salvation by faith and the Roman Catholic doctrines of papal infallibility, confession of sins, and priest celibacy. A firm believer in separation of church and state, he considered it both unconstitutional and sacrilegious to stamp In God We Trust on U.S. coins and as president tried unsuccessfully to have the legend removed.

RECREATION: A proponent of "the strenuous life," Roosevelt found diversion in a wide variety of athletic as well as intellectual pursuits. While governor of New York he grappled with a middleweight champion wrestler several times a week. As president he boxed regularly with sparring partners until being severely injured (see "Physical Description"). He thereupon took up jiujitsu. Other favorite sports included horseback riding, tennis, hiking over rough terrain, and, in winter, skinny-dipping in the icy waters of the Potomac River. He also enjoyed hunting, polo, and rowing. Among his more sedentary hobbies were the study of animals, especially birds, and reading history, biography, poetry, and fiction. "I find it a great comfort to like all kinds of books," he remarked as president, "and to be able to get half an hour or an hour's complete rest and complete detachment from the fighting of the moment."[7] He especially liked the novels of Scott, Thackeray, and Dickens and the poetry of Poe and Longfellow. He also kept a diary and wrote numerous books (see "Books by Roosevelt"). He did not smoke and seldom drank.

MARRIAGE: Theodore Roosevelt, 22, married Alice Hathaway Lee, 19, on October 27, 1880, at the Unitarian Church in Brookline, Massachusetts. Born July 29, 1861, in Chestnut Hill, Massachusetts, the daughter of George Cabot Lee, a prominent banker, and Caroline Haskell Lee, Alice was tall (5 feet 7 inches), charming, pretty, and intelligent. She met Roosevelt on October 18, 1878 at the home of her next-door neighbors, the Saltonstalls; Theodore was a classmate of young Richard Saltonstall at Harvard. By Thanksgiving Roosevelt had resolved to marry her, and the following June he proposed. She put him off, however, taking another six months before saying yes. Their engagement was announced on Valentine's Day, 1880. Among the guests at the wedding and at the reception at the home of the bride's parents was Edith Carow, later to become Roosevelt's second wife. The couple spent their wedding night in Springfield, Massachusetts, and honeymooned two weeks at the Roosevelt home in Oyster Bay, New York. Tragically, Mrs. Roosevelt died in New York on February 14, 1884, on the fourth anniversary of their engagement, from Bright's disease and childbirth complications. She was 22. (On the same day and in the same house, Theodore Roosevelt's mother also died.) She was buried at Cambridge, Massachusetts.

Theodore Roosevelt, 28, married secondly Edith Kermit Carow, 25, on December 2, 1886, at St. George's Church of Hanover Square, in London, England. Born on August 6, 1861, in Norwich, Connecticut, the daughter of Charles Carow, a merchant, and Gertrude Tyler Carow, Edith grew up next door to Theodore in New York and was best friends with his younger sister Corinne. She was his first real playmate outside his family. In adolescence a mutual love of books and nature evolved into romantic attachment, but after Theodore went off to Harvard and met Alice Lee, they drifted apart. The year after his first wife's death, Roosevelt ran into Miss Carow at his sister's house. They began seeing each other again; on November 17, 1885, he proposed and she accepted. However, for appearance's sake, the young widower delayed the announcement. On the day of the wedding, a quiet affair with few guests, the London fog was so thick that it filled the church. The groom was visible, however, for he wore bright orange gloves. His best man was Cecil Arthur Spring-Rice, later British ambassador to the United States during World War I. After a 15-week honeymoon tour of Europe, the newlyweds settled in New York City. Mrs. Roosevelt, reserved and efficient, managed the household budget. As First Lady she converted the traditional weekly levees to musicales, remodeled the White House at a cost of $475,000 into what the president described as "a simple and dignified dwelling for the head of a republic," and arranged the White House wedding of her stepdaughter, Alice. On her husband's death, she traveled abroad extensively. She died at 87 on September 30, 1948, at Oyster Bay, New York, where she was buried next to the president.

MILITARY SERVICE: Roosevelt was a member of the New York national guard during 1882–1885, rising from second lieutenant to captain.

Spanish-American War. Roosevelt served as commander of the First U.S. Volunteer Cavalry Regiment, popularly known as the Rough Riders, from May to September 1898, rising from lieutenant colonel to colonel. The unit first saw action at Las Guásimas, Cuba, on June 24, beating back an enemy ambush. At San Juan on July 1 Roosevelt and his Rough Riders distinguished themselves and, through press reports, electrified the nation in a valiant charge up Kettle Hill (San Juan was the name of a group of hills nearby, but it was Kettle Hill that Roosevelt took). His commanding officer Major General Leonard Wood described his heroism in a report (December 30, 1898) to Washington: "Colonel Roosevelt, accompanied only by four or five men, led a very desperate and extremely gallant charge on San Juan Hill, thereby setting a splendid example to the troops and encouraging them to pass over the open country intervening between their position and the trenches of the enemy. In leading this charge, he started off first, as he supposed, with quite a following of men, but soon discovered that he was alone. He then returned and gathered up a few men and led them to the charge. . . . Everybody finally went up the hill in good style. . . . During the assault, Colonel Roosevelt was the first to reach the trenches in his part of the line and killed one of the enemy with his own hand."[8] Promoted to colonel, Roosevelt took part in the occupation of Santiago. It was largely at his prodding that his disease-ravaged troops were recalled to the United States in August. Said Roosevelt of his service, "I would rather have led that charge and earned my colonelcy than served three terms in the United States Senate. It makes me feel as though I could now leave something to my children which will serve as an apology for my having existed."[9]

During World War I, Roosevelt offered to raise a force of volunteers, but President Wilson denied his request.

CAREER BEFORE THE PRESIDENCY:

New York State Assemblyman, 1882–1884. Elected as a Republican in 1881 and reelected in 1882 and 1883, Roosevelt at 23 was the youngest member of the assembly when he took his seat in Albany in January 1882. His energy and persistent struggle against machine politics earned him the nickname the Cyclone Assemblyman. Crossing party lines to align himself with Governor Grover Cleveland, he sponsored the civil service reform act and secured passage of a bill reforming the method of electing aldermen. In 1883 he served as minority leader but was defeated for speaker. As a New York delegate to the Republican national convention in 1884, Roosevelt supported Senator George F. Edmunds of Vermont for president and joined others in attempting, unsuccessfully, to prevent the nomination of James G. Blaine of Maine. After the convention he at first refused to endorse Blaine but eventually did so. In failing to join the Mugwumps (Republican reformers who backed the Democratic nominee, Grover Cleveland), Roosevelt drew widespread criticism from former supporters and in the press.

From June 1884 to October 1886, Roosevelt worked as a cattle rancher in the Dakota Territory and was for a time deputy sheriff of Billings County. In November 1886 he was defeated for mayor of New York City by Abram S. Hewitt. He then concentrated on his writing. In 1888 he campaigned in the Midwest for Benjamin Harrison for president.

Member of U.S. Civil Service Commission, 1889–1895. Appointed commissioner by President Benjamin Harrison at a salary of $3,500 a year and reappointed by President Grover Cleveland, Roosevelt vigorously pressed for strict enforcement of the civil service laws, much to the chagrin of party professionals. During his term the number of jobs to come under civil service classification more than doubled. In 1892 he supported the reelection of President Harrison.

President of New York City Police Board, 1895–1897. He rooted out corruption in the Police Department, which he described as "utterly demoralized" and steeped in "venality and blackmail." In a highly visible campaign that won him favorable press notice as far away as Europe, he strictly enforced the Sunday Excise Law, banning the sale of alcohol on the Sabbath. Although personally opposed to the statute because of its overwhelming unpopularity and widespread violation, he dutifully closed down offending saloons in the city and fined proprietors. "I do not deal with public sentiment," he explained, "I deal with the law. How I might act as a legislator, or what kind of legislation I should advise, has no bearing on my conduct as an executive officer charged with administering the law."[10] In 1896 he supported House Speaker Thomas B. Reed of Maine for the Republican presidential nomination but campaigned in the Midwest and East for the eventual nominee, William McKinley.

Assistant Secretary of the Navy, 1897–1898. Appointed by President William McKinley at an annual salary of $4,500, Roosevelt emerged a principle advocate of expansionism and war with Spain. He often served as acting secretary during the prolonged absences of ailing Navy Secretary John D. Long. Although Long came to agree with his brash assistant regarding the need for a rapid naval buildup, he nevertheless was exasperated by his whirlwind administrative techniques. "He is full of suggestions," Long conceded, "many of which are of great value, and his spirit and forceful habit is a good tonic; but the very devil seems to possess him—distributing ships, ordering ammunition which there is no means to move to places where there is no means to store it; sending messages to Congress for immediate legislation authorizing the enlistment of an unlimited number of seamen."[11] After the explosion of the *Maine* in Havana harbor in 1898, an act he blamed on Spanish agents, Roosevelt set out to put the navy on full alert. In a cable wholly unauthorized by his superiors, Roosevelt instructed Commodore George Dewey in the Pacific that, in the event of war, he was to bottle up the Spanish squadron on the Asiatic coast and then undertake offensive operations in the Philippines. Roosevelt was also among the first to foresee the military potential of airplanes. At his urging, a naval panel was formed to study the new "flying machine" of Samuel P. Langley. Roosevelt resigned to volunteer for the Spanish-American War (see "Military Service").

Governor of New York, 1898–1900. With the support of state Republican party boss Thomas C. Platt, Roosevelt narrowly defeated, 661,715–643,921, Judge Augustus van Wyck for governor. Although Governor Roosevelt regularly consulted with Boss Platt on state policy, to the disappointment of reformers, it was largely an empty exercise, for Roosevelt routinely ignored Platt's advice. He obtained laws further to remove the civil service from politics, limit the number of hours women and children could work, and curb sweatshop abuses. In his most significant confrontation with Platt, Roosevelt promoted and signed into law state taxation of corporations.

Vice President, March–September 1901. With the death in office of Vice President Garret Hobart, Boss Platt began promoting Roosevelt to fill his place on the ticket with President McKinley in 1900, principally in order to remove him and his reformist influence from New York politics. Roosevelt at first protested that he was reluctant to give up the governorship for the boring, low-profile duties of vice president. But with added encouragement from Senator Henry Cabot Lodge, who earnestly believed that the office might serve as a springboard to the presidency, he consented. As a New York delegate to the Republican national convention in 1900, Roosevelt delivered a seconding speech for the renomination of President McKinley. Because he abstained from voting for himself for vice president, Roosevelt was nominated with 925 of 926 possible votes. During the campaign, McKinley remained aloof while Roosevelt stumped the country, delivering 673 speeches in 567 cities and towns in 24 states. Vice President Roosevelt was lunching with the Vermont Fish and Game League on Isle La Motte in Lake Champlain on September 6, 1901, when he received word that President McKinley had been shot at Buffalo, New York. He rushed to the president's bedside but, assured that McKinley was recovering, joined his family for a vacation at Camp Tahawus, New York, in the Adirondacks. While lunching on the edge of Lake Tear-of-the-Clouds on September 13, he received news that McKinley was dying. By the time he returned to Buffalo, the president had passed away.

On September 14, 1901, Roosevelt was sworn in as president at the home of Ansley Wilcox in Buffalo by U.S. District Court Judge John R. Hazel. At age 42 he was the youngest man ever to become president. (John F. Kennedy was the youngest ever elected president.)

REPUBLICAN PRESIDENTIAL NOMINATION, 1904: As Republicans convened in Chicago in June 1904, President Roosevelt's nomination was assured. A dump-Roosevelt movement had centered around the candidacy of Senator Mark Hanna of Ohio, but Hanna's death earlier in the year had removed this obstacle. Roosevelt's nomination speech was delivered by former governor Frank Black of New York and seconded by Senator Albert Beveridge of Indiana. Roosevelt was nominated unanimously with 994 votes. Senator Charles W. Fairbanks of Indiana was nominated for vice president. The Republican platform insisted on maintenance of the protective tariff, called for increased foreign trade, pledged to uphold the gold standard, favored expansion of the merchant marine, promoted a strong navy, and praised in detail Roosevelt's foreign and domestic policy.

OPPONENT: Alton B. Parker (1852–1926) of New York; Democrat. Born in Cortland, New York, Parker graduated from Albany Law School in 1873 and began practice at Kingston, New York. He was elected surrogate of Ulster County, 1877–1885; appointed to the New York Supreme Court, 1885–1889, the state appeals court, 1889–1896, and the appellate division of the state supreme court, 1896–1897; and elected chief justice of the New York Court of Appeals, 1898–1904. Although a gold Democrat, he nevertheless endorsed William Jennings Bryan in 1896 and 1900, an act of party loyalty that enhanced his prospects of wooing disaffected free-silver Democrats to his standard. In 1904 both Bryan and former president Grover Cleveland declined to run for president. Parker, too, refused to work actively for the nomination but did nothing to restrain his conservative supporters, among them the sachems of Tammany Hall. Former president Cleveland endorsed Parker. Inheriting Bryan's support was publisher, now congressman, William Randolph Hearst of California. At the Democratic national convention in St. Louis in July, Parker handily won the nomination on the first ballot with 679 votes to 181 for Hearst and the rest scattered. Former senator Henry G. Davis of West Virginia was nominated for vice president; at 81, he was the oldest major party candidate ever nominated for national office. The Democratic platform pointedly omitted reference to the monetary issue. To make his position clear, Parker, after his nomination, informed the convention by letter that he supported the gold standard. The platform called for reduction in government expenditures and a congressional investigation of the executive departments "already known to teem with corruption," condemned monopolies and pledged an end to government contracts with companies violating antitrust laws, opposed imperialism and insisted upon independence for the Philippines, and opposed the protective tariff. It favored strict enforcement of the eight-hour day, construction of a Panama Canal, the direct election of senators, statehood for the western territories, the extermination of polygamy, reciprocal trade agreements, cuts in the army, and enforcement of the civil service laws. It condemned the Roosevelt administration in general as "spasmodic, erratic, sensational, spectacular, and arbitrary." After his defeat by Roosevelt, Parker practiced law in New York City, where he died.

CAMPAIGN AND THE ISSUES, 1904: President Roosevelt and Judge Parker agreed on the fundamental issues: both stood solidly behind the gold standard, favored eventual independence for the Philippines, championed the rights of labor and consumers, and condemned monopoly. Thus, the campaign turned largely on personality, a situation ideally suited to the flamboyant, popular style of the president, as contrasted with the colorless, sober demeanor of Judge Parker. Neither candidate took to the stump. Roosevelt remained in the White House, tending to business. Parker, although the underdog, was content to conduct a passive front-porch campaign. Despite Roosevelt's strong antitrust record, much of big business remained staunchly Republican. Of the $2 million GOP war chest, railroad magnate Edward H. Harriman contributed $50,000 and financier J. P. Morgan $150,000. Parker's support was confined to the traditionally Democratic South.

ELECTION AS PRESIDENT, NOVEMBER 8, 1904:

Popular Vote: Roosevelt (Republican), 7,628,834 (56%); Parker (Democrat), 5,084,401 (38%); Eugene V. Debs (Socialist), 402,714 (3%).

Electoral Vote: Roosevelt, 336; Parker, 140.

States Carried: Roosevelt won the majority of electoral votes of 32 states—California, Colorado, Connecticut, Delaware, Idaho, Illinois, Indiana, Iowa, Kansas, Maine, Massachusetts, Michigan, Minnesota, Missouri, Montana, Nebraska, Nevada, New Hampshire, New Jersey, New York, North Dakota, Ohio, Oregon, Pennsylvania, Rhode Island, South Dakota, Utah, Vermont, Washington, West Virginia, Wisconsin, Wyoming. Parker won the majority of electoral votes in 13 states—Alabama, Arkansas, Florida, Georgia, Kentucky, Louisiana, Maryland, Mississippi, North Carolina, South Carolina, Tennessee, Texas, Virginia.

INAUGURAL ADDRESS: March 4, 1905. ". . . We have become a great nation, forced by the fact of its greatness into relations with the other nations of the earth, and we must behave as beseems a people with such responsibilities. Toward all other nations, large and small, our attitude must be one of cordial and sincere friendship. We must show not only in our words, but in our deeds, that we are earnestly desirous of securing their good will by acting toward them in a spirit of just and generous recognition of all their rights. But justice and generosity in a nation, as in an individual, count most when shown not by the weak but by the strong. While ever careful to refrain from wronging others, we must be no less insistent that we are not wronged ourselves. We wish peace, but we wish the peace of justice, the peace of righteousness. We wish it because we think it is right and not because we are afraid. No weak nation that acts manfully and justly should ever have cause to fear us, and no strong power should ever be able to single us out as a subject for insolent aggression. . . ."

VICE PRESIDENT: Charles Warren Fairbanks (1852–1918), of Indiana, served 1905–1909. Born in a one-room log cabin in Unionville Center, Ohio, Fairbanks graduated from Ohio Wesleyan University in 1872, was admitted to the bar in 1874, and began practice in Indianapolis, where he became a prominent railroad attorney. In 1896 he was temporary chairman and keynote speaker at the Republican national convention. As a U.S. senator 1897–1905 he supported the policies of President William McKinley. In 1904 he actively sought the vice presidential nomination on the ticket with Roosevelt, enlisting the editorial aid of several Indiana newspapers he owned to tout his candidacy. As vice president he disagreed with Roosevelt's progressive policies and at times collaborated with congressional conservatives against administration programs. In 1912 he turned his back on Roosevelt's third-party candidacy to support the reelection of President Taft. In 1916 Fairbanks again ran for vice president, this time unsuccessfully, on the ticket with Charles Evans Hughes.

CABINET:

Secretary of State. (1) John M. Hay (1838–1905), of Washington, D.C., served 1898–1905. A holdover from the McKinley administration, he concluded treaties with Britain and Panama making possible construction of the Panama Canal. Hay died in office. (2) Elihu Root (1845–1937), of New York, served 1905–1909. He had served as war secretary in the McKinley and Roosevelt administrations. For his efforts to improve Latin American relations and his part in numerous arbitration treaties with European powers, including the settlement of a long-standing dispute with Great Britain over fishing rights off Newfoundland, Root was awarded the 1912 Nobel Peace Prize. Within the department, he established the Division of Far Eastern Affairs. He resigned to enter the Senate. (3) Robert Bacon (1860–1919), of New York, served January–March 1909. He had been Root's assistant. He later was appointed ambassador to France by President Taft.

Secretary of the Treasury. (1) Lyman J. Gage (1836–1927), of Illinois, served 1897–1902. He was a holdover from the McKinley administration. (2) Leslie M. Shaw (1848–1932), of Iowa, served 1902–1907. He loosened credit restraints. (3) George B. Cortelyou (1862–1940), of New York, served 1907–1909. He was transferred from postmaster general. Amid the panic of 1907 (see "Administration"), he shored up vulnerable banks with federal deposits.

Secretary of War. (1) Elihu Root served 1899–1904. A holdover from the McKinley administration, he expanded and reorganized the army, adopting the general staff system, and established the Army War College. He resigned to resume his law practice but was quickly recalled as secretary of state. (2) William Howard Taft (1857–1930), of Ohio, served 1904–1908. See "William Howard Taft, 27th President," "Career before the Presidency." (3) Luke E. Wright (1846–1922), of Tennessee, served 1908–1909. He had served under Roosevelt as ambassador to Japan 1906–1907.

Attorney General. (1) Philander C. Knox (1853–1921), of Pennsylvania, served 1901–1904. A holdover from the McKinley administration, he successfully concluded antitrust action against the Northern Securities Company in 1904 and took part in gaining clear title to land for construction of the Panama Canal. He resigned to enter the Senate. He later served as secretary of state in the Taft administration. (2) William H. Moody (1853–1917), of Massachusetts, served 1904–1906. Transferred from navy secretary, he successfully brought antitrust action against the meat-packing industry and other combinations. He resigned to accept appointment to the Supreme Court. (3) Charles J. Bonaparte (1851–1921), of Maryland, served 1906–1909. Transferred from navy secretary, he continued Moody's vigorous prosecution of antitrust violations, notably against the tobacco industry.

Secretary of the Navy. (1) John D. Long (1838–1915) of Massachusetts, served 1897–1902. A holdover from the McKinley administration, he had been Roosevelt's boss when the latter was assistant secretary of the navy. He wrote

The New American Navy (1903). (2) William H. Moody served 1902–1904. He had first gained national attention as prosecutor in the sensational murder trial of Lizzie Borden in 1893. He gave up a U.S. House seat to join the cabinet. He was transferred to attorney general. (3) Paul Morton (1857–1911), of Illinois, served 1904–1905. He took steps to expand the navy. (4) Charles J. Bonaparte served 1905–1906. A grandnephew of Napoleon and longtime champion of civil service reform, he was transferred to attorney general. (5) Victor H. Metcalf (1853–1936), of California, served 1906–1908. Transferred from commerce and labor secretary, he expanded the fleet and increased manpower. (6) Truman H. Newberry (1864–1945), of Michigan, served 1908–1909. A veteran naval officer of the Spanish-American War, he was promoted from assistant secretary of the navy.

Postmaster General. (1) Charles E. Smith (1842–1908), of Pennsylvania, served 1898–1902. He was a holdover from the McKinley administration. (2) Henry C. Payne (1843–1904), of Wisconsin, served 1902–1904. He died in office. (3) Robert J. Wynne (1851–1922), of Pennsylvania, served 1904–1905. (4) George B. Cortelyou served 1905–1907. He had served as commerce and labor secretary under Roosevelt. He improved the efficiency of the post office and relied on the merit system for appointments and promotions. He was transferred to Treasury secretary. (5) George von L. Meyer (1858–1918), of Massachusetts, served 1907–1909. He had served as ambassador to Italy under Presidents McKinley and Roosevelt and ambassador to Russia under Roosevelt. He later served as navy secretary in the Taft administration.

Secretary of the Interior. (1) Ethan A. Hitchcock (1835–1909), of Missouri, served 1898–1907. A holdover from the McKinley administration, he promoted conservation of natural resources and established the Bureau of Reclamation. (2) James R. Garfield (1865–1950), of Ohio, served 1907–1909. Promoted to cabinet rank from commissioner of corporations in the Department of Commerce and Labor, he, too, aggressively promoted conservation. See also "James A. Garfield, 20th President," "Children."

Secretary of Agriculture. James Wilson (1835–1920), of Iowa, served 1897–1913. A holdover from the McKinley administration, he established the Bureaus of Statistics, Entomology, and Biological Survey. He stayed on in the Taft administration.

Secretary of Commerce and Labor. (1) George B. Cortelyou served 1903–1904. Personal secretary to Presidents McKinley (he was present at the assassination) and Roosevelt, he was promoted by the latter to become the first secretary of commerce and labor. He resigned to manage Roosevelt's presidential campaign in 1904. The following year he was appointed postmaster general. (2) Victor H. Metcalf served 1904–1906. He checked Japanese poaching of Alaskan salmon and organized the Bureau of Manufacturers. He was transferred to navy secretary. (3) Oscar S. Straus (1850–1926), of New York, served 1906–1909. A German immigrant, he was the first Jewish cabinet member. He also was minister (later ambassador) to Turkey under Presidents Cleveland, McKinley, and Taft.

ADMINISTRATION: September 14, 1901–March 3, 1909.

Panama Canal. Under the terms of the Hay-Pauncefote Treaty (1901), which supplanted the Clayton-Bulwer Treaty (1850, see "Zachary Taylor, 12th President," "Administration"), Great Britain conceded to the United States the right to construct and exclusively operate and police a canal across Central

America, provided that the canal remain free and open to all commercial and war vessels of all nations without discriminatory fees. Having determined to build the canal across Panama, rather than across Nicaragua, as the Walker Commission and others had proposed, President Roosevelt instructed Secretary of State Hay to negotiate purchase of a canal zone from Colombia, then in possession of Panama. Colombia balked at the terms offered, however. During the stalemate, Panama revolted from Colombia and, with U.S. aid, succeeded in establishing its independence. In November, 1903, three days after the revolution, the United States officially recognized the new nation and proceeded to conclude with it virtually the same canal treaty rejected by Colombia. Under its terms, Panama granted to the United States in perpetuity the use of a 10-mile-wide canal zone in exchange for $10 million plus an annual sum that has been steadily increased. In 1904 Colonel William C. Gorgas was appointed chief sanitary officer for the project. It was his success in eradicating yellow fever from the region by 1906 and reducing by 90 percent the incidence of malaria that made construction of the canal possible. At a cost of $380 million, 43,000 laborers under the direction of Colonel George W. Goethals of the U.S. Army Corps of Engineers constructed the canal from Colón on the Atlantic to Balboa on the Pacific. It was completed in 1914 and opened to traffic in 1920. Amid great controversy, the Canal Zone was transferred to Panama in 1979 (see "Jimmy Carter, 39th President," "Administration").

Roosevelt Corollary and Big Stick Diplomacy. As set forth in annual messages to Congress in December 1904 and December 1905, President Roosevelt asserted that it was the obligation of the United States to enforce the Monroe Doctrine (see "James Monroe, 5th President," "Administration") and to intervene anywhere in Latin America to maintain stability. "Chronic wrongdoing," he declared in what is known as the Roosevelt Corollary, "or an impotence which results in a general loosening of the ties of civilized society, may in America, as elsewhere, ultimately require intervention by some civilized nation, and in the Western Hemisphere the adherence of the United States to the Monroe Doctrine may force the United States, however reluctantly, in flagrant cases of such wrongdoing or impotence, to the exercise of an international police power." But, he added, "we would interfere with them only in the last resort, and then only if it became evident that their inability or unwillingness to do justice at home and abroad had violated the rights of the United States or had invited foreign aggression." Roosevelt's insistence on U.S. hegemony in the Western Hemisphere was part of what came to be called Big Stick Diplomacy, after Roosevelt's comment, "Speak softly and carry a big stick; you will go far."

Russo-Japanese War, 1904–1905. For his success in mediating peace, in the Treaty of Portsmouth, between Russia and Japan in their struggle over control of Manchuria and Korea, President Roosevelt was awarded the 1906 Nobel Peace Prize. He was the first American to win the award. With the prize money of $36,735, Roosevelt created a trust fund to promote industrial peace. On U.S. entry into World War I, however, he diverted the trust, which had appreciated to $45,000, to aid war victims.

Antitrust Policy. In his first annual message to Congress, December 1901, President Roosevelt set forth his antitrust policy on a note that attempted to strike a balance between free enterprise and corporate responsibility: "The captains of industry . . . have on the whole done great good to our people. Without them the material development of which we are so justly proud could never have taken place. . . . Yet it is also true that there are real and great evils. . . . There is a widespread conviction in the minds of the American people that the great corporations known as trusts are in certain of their features and tendencies hurtful to the general welfare. This . . . is based upon sincere conviction that combination and concentration should be, not prohibited, but supervised and within reasonable limits controlled; and in my judgment this conviction is right." The administration brought suit under the antitrust laws against the railroad, beef, oil, tobacco, and other combinations. The Elkins Act (1903) and the Hepburn Act (1906) strengthened the Interstate Commerce Commission in regulating the railroads. Roosevelt's antitrust policy and advocacy of labor and consumer rights constituted what he called the Square Deal.

Anthracite Coal Strike, 1902. During May–October 1902, 150,000 coal miners in Pennsylvania went on strike for union recognition, higher pay, and shorter hours. Mine owners declined to negotiate with strikers and at first refused to submit to arbitration, but they relented after President Roosevelt threatened to seize the mines. An arbitration panel settled the strike largely in the union's favor except for union recognition.

Meat Inspection Act, Pure Food and Drug Act, 1906. Prompted by publication of Upton's Sinclair's *The Jungle*, exposing unsanitary conditions in the meatpacking industry, these laws, heartily approved by President Roosevelt, provided for government inspection of meat and barred "adulterated or misbranded or poisonous or deleterious foods, drugs, medicines, and liquors" from interstate commerce.

Conservation. "To waste, to destroy, our natural resources," President Roosevelt warned in his seventh annual message to Congress, December 1907, "to skin and exhaust the land instead of using it so as to increase its usefulness, will result in undermining in the days of our children the very prosperity which we ought by right to hand down to them amplified and developed." During his term he did much to earn the nickname the Great Conservationist. The Reclamation Act of 1902 channeled funds from the sale of western lands into the construction of great dams to irrigate the arid regions of the West. He reserved some 125 million acres in national forests, 68 million acres of coal lands, and 2,500 water-power sites. He established the first national wildlife refuge at Pelican Island, Florida, in 1903 and designated Devils Tower in Wyoming the first national monument in 1906.

Panic of 1907. Touched off by the failure of the Knickerbocker Trust Company of New York in October 1907, the panic brought on the collapse of a dozen other banks and some railroads. Stock prices plummeted. Administration critics blamed Roosevelt's antitrust and prolabor policies for squeezing corporate profits; the president, in turn, blamed big business for the slump. To help curb the decline, he assured U.S. Steel that the government would not direct antitrust action against its proposed acquisition of the failing Tennessee Coal and Iron Company. The administration also deposited federal funds with ailing banks. Recovery began in the spring of 1908.

Gentleman's Agreement, 1907. In response to growing hostility in California toward Japanese immigrants, President Roosevelt reached a private understanding with Tokyo officials, whereby Japan promised to curb emigration of laborers and the United States would refrain from enacting an outright exclusion law, similar to that directed against the Chinese (see "Chester A. Arthur, 21st President," "Administration").

State Admitted to the Union: Oklahoma (1907).

SUPREME COURT APPOINTMENTS: (1) Oliver Wendell Holmes (1841–1935), of Massachusetts, served as associate justice 1902–1932. Holmes combined a deep sense of judicial restraint regarding the acts of legislatures with a finely wrought literary style to become, often in dissent, perhaps the most highly regarded associate justice in the Court's history. In *Northern Securities Co.* v. *United States* (1904), Holmes surprised President Roosevelt and others who had expected him to be a consistent exponent of progressive ideals in dissenting from the majority opinion that dissolved the railroad holding company for its activities in restraint of trade. In other dissents, Holmes voted to permit states to regulate working hours (*Lochner* v. *New York*, 1905), to uphold a federal ban against the yellow dog contract (*Adair* v. *United States*, 1908), to allow Congress to ban from interstate commerce the products of child labor (*Hammer* v. *Dagenhart*, 1918), to sustain the right of harmless free speech during wartime (*Abrams* v. *United States*, 1919, "the ultimate good desired is better reached by free trade in ideas . . . the best test of truth is the power of the thought to get itself accepted in the competition of the market"), to permit a congressionally created panel to fix a minimum wage for women (*Adkins* v. *Children's Hospital*, 1923), and to uphold the Tenure of Office Act forbidding a president from removing cabinet officers without Senate approval (*Meyers* v. *United States*, 1926). In perhaps his most memorable majority opinion (*Schenck* v. *United States* , 1919), Holmes defined the limits of free speech in wartime in sustaining the conviction of draft protestors during World War I: "The most stringent protection of free speech would not protect a man in falsely shouting fire in a theatre and causing a panic. . . . The question in every case is whether the words used are used in such circumstances and are of such a nature as to create a clear and present danger that they will bring about the substantive evils that Congress has a right to prevent. It is a question of proximity and degree. When a nation is at war many things that might be said in time of peace are such a hindrance to its efforts that their utterance will not be endured so long as men fight and that no Court could regard them as protected by any constitutional right." (2) William R. Day (1849–1923), of Ohio, served as associate justice 1903–1922. He had served as secretary of state under President McKinley. Day was often a swing vote between the conservatives clinging to laissez-faire and the progressives favoring greater regulation of big business. Generally, he supported strict enforcement of the antitrust laws, narrowly construed the powers of the federal government, and more loosely construed the powers of state government. Speaking for the majority in *Hammer* v. *Dagenhart* (1918), he struck down the Keating-Owen Child Labor Law of 1916 as an unconstitutional interference with a state's authority over local trade and manufacture. In *Coppage* v. *Kansas* (1915), he joined Justices Holmes and Hughes in dissenting from the majority opinion that struck down a state ban on yellow dog contracts. "The right of contract is not absolute and unyielding," Day wrote, "but is subject to limitation and restraint in the interests of public health, safety, and welfare." (3) William H. Moody (1853–1917), of Massachusetts, served as associate justice 1906–1910. He had served as navy secretary and attorney general under President Theodore Roosevelt. Roosevelt had offered the seat first to William Howard Taft, who declined. Illness limited Moody's influence and prompted his resignation after just four years on the bench.

RANKING IN 1962 HISTORIANS POLL: Theodore Roosevelt ranked seventh of 31 presidents, second of 6 "near great" presidents. He ranked above Polk, below Jackson.

RETIREMENT: March 4, 1909–January 6, 1919. In seeking election as president in his own right in 1904, Roosevelt pledged that he would retire at the end of a single full term. After attending the inauguration of his handpicked successor, William Howard Taft, Roosevelt retired to Sagamore Hill, his country estate at Oyster Bay, New York, to prepare for an African safari. During the year-long expedition, 1909–1910, accompanied by taxidermists and naturalists from the Smithsonian Institution, his son Kermit, and more than 200 porters, Roosevelt and his party killed 5 elephants, 7 hippos, 9 lions, and 13 rhinos and collected hundreds of specimens of plants and animals for the Smithsonian. After a tour of Europe, he returned to the United States in June 1910 to a hero's welcome. He grew disturbed over the conservative direction of the Taft administration and quickly emerged as the leader of the progressive wing of the party. Despite his long-standing pledge not to seek a third term as president, Roosevelt in February 1912 declared his candidacy for the Republican nomination. Losing to Taft (see "Woodrow Wilson, 28th President," "Opponents, 1912"), he bolted the party to run on the Progressive, or Bull Moose ticket, thus fatally dividing the Republicans and tossing the election to Woodrow Wilson (see "Woodrow Wilson," "Campaign and the issues, 1912"). On October 14, 1912, John N. Schrank, 36, a German immigrant bartender, shot Roosevelt once with a .38 Colt revolver as he was enroute to address a crowd in Milwaukee. The bullet passed through the doubled-over pages of his prepared speech in his breast pocket, then through a metal spectacle case, and finally into the chest about an inch below and to the right of the right nipple, traveling about four inches upward and inward to fracture the fourth rib. No vital organs were affected. In a dramatic, if foolhardy, display of courage, Roosevelt insisted on delivering his speech as planned before going to the hospital. He spoke for nearly an hour. At an examination afterward at Mercy Hospital in Chicago, doctors treated the wound but decided not to remove the bullet. Roosevelt recovered completely with no complications. As for Schrank, he explained to authorities that the ghost of William McKinley had appeared to him in a dream and told him to avenge his assassination by killing his successor. He was judged insane and committed to an institution, where he died in 1943.

In 1913 Roosevelt sued the editor of *Iron Age* magazine for libel for calling him a drunk in print. Roosevelt won the suit and the token damages (6¢) that he had requested. During 1913–1914 he undertook a seven-month, 1,500-mile expedition through Brazil, where he explored the River of Doubt and collected more plant and animal specimens. Enroute he was beset by malaria and was at times delirious with fever that ran as high as 105°. He also suffered a gash in the leg, which became infected. In his honor, Brazil renamed the river, Rio Roosevelt. During his retirement Roosevelt also found time to write books (see "Books by Roosevelt") and magazine articles. During 1910–1914 he was associate editor of *Outlook* magazine. From 1917 he was a regular editorial contributor to the *Kansas City Star*. In 1916 he campaigned for Charles Evans Hughes for president. Upon U.S. entry into World War I he offered to organize and lead a group of volunteers, but President Wilson rejected his request.

DEATH: January 6, 1919, shortly after 4 A.M., at home, Sagamore Hill estate, Oyster Bay, New York. During his last years Roosevelt was plagued by recurrences of the malaria and leg infection contracted in Brazil (see "Retirement"), painful inflammatory rheumatism, and an ear infection that developed into mastoiditis, leaving him deaf in one ear. For these ailments, he underwent treatment at Roosevelt Hospital in New York City (February 5–March 4, November 11–December 25, 1918). On January 5, 1919, he wrote an editorial for the *Kansas City Star* critical of President Wilson's proposal for a League of Nations. He went to bed at 11 P.M., after telling his valet James Amos, "Please put out the light."[12] These were his last words. In his sleep he suffered a coronary embolism and died. At his request, simple funeral services, without music, were conducted at the Episcopal church in Oyster Bay. He was buried at Young's Memorial Cemetery in Oyster Bay. In his last will and testament, executed in December 1912, Roosevelt left the bulk of his estate, valued at $500,000, to his wife. A $60,000 trust fund was to be divided among his children.

ROOSEVELT PRAISED: "Men say he is not safe. He is not safe for the men who wish to prosecute selfish schemes to the public detriment . . . who wish government to be conducted with greater reference to campaign contributions than to the public good . . . who wish to draw the President of the United States into a corner and make whispered arrangements which they dare not have known by their constituents."[13]—Elihu Root, 1904

"President Roosevelt of all the Presidents, best understood the uses of publicity. He had a genius for it. He had his favorites among the reporters, but he played fair with all."[14] Gus J. Karger, veteran Washington reporter, 1919

"I am sorry to learn of his death. He was a great American. His loss will be a great one for the country."[15]—John N. Schrank, Roosevelt's would-be assassin, 1919

"I had never known such a man as he, and never shall again. He overcame me. . . . He poured into my heart such visions, such ideals, such hopes, such a new attitude toward life and patriotism and the meaning of things, as I had never dreamed men had."[16]—William Allen White, journalist

ROOSEVELT CRITICIZED: "Now look! That damned cowboy is President of the United States."[17]—Republican Senator Mark Hanna of Ohio, 1901

"Well, the mad Roosevelt has a new achievement to his credit. He succeeded in defeating the party that furnished him a job for nearly all of his manhood days after leaving the ranch, and showed his gratitude for the presidency, at that party's hands. The eminent fakir can now turn to raising hell, his specialty, along other lines."[18]—Warren G. Harding, on Roosevelt's Bull Moose candidacy, 1912

"My judgment is that the view of . . . Mr. Roosevelt, ascribing an undefined residuum of power to the president is an unsafe doctrine, and that it might lead under emergencies to results of an arbitrary character, doing irremediable injustice to private right."[19]—William Howard Taft

"Theodore Roosevelt was always getting himself in hot water by talking before he had to commit himself upon issues not well-defined."[20]—former president Calvin Coolidge, 1932

ROOSEVELT QUOTES: "The men with the muckrakes are often indispensable to the well being of society; but only if they know when to stop raking the muck, and to look upward to the celestial crown above them, to the crown of worthy endeavor."[21]—1906

"To announce that there must be no criticism of the President, or that we are to stand by the President, right or wrong, is not only unpatriotic and servile, but is morally treasonable to the American public."[22]—1918

"A man who has never gone to school may steal from a freight car; but if he has a university education, he may steal the whole railroad."[23]

BOOKS BY ROOSEVELT: *The Naval War of 1812* (1882); *Hunting Trip of a Ranchman* (1885); *Life of Thomas Hart Benton* (1887); *Gouverneur Morris* (1888); *Ranch Life and the Hunting Trail* (1888); *The Winning of the West 1769–1807* (4 vols., 1889–1896); *New York* (1891); *Hero Tales from American History* (1895); *Rough Riders* (1899); *African Game Trails* (1910); *The New Nationalism* (1910); *History as Literature, and Other Essays* (1913); *Theodore Roosevelt, An Autobiography* (1913); *Through the Brazilian Wilderness* (1914); *Life Histories of African Game Animals* (1914); *America and the World War* (1915); *Fear God and Take Your Own Part* (1916); *The Foes of Our Own Household* (1917); *National Strength and International Duty* (1917).

BOOKS ABOUT ROOSEVELT: Chessman, G. Wallace. *Theodore Roosevelt and the Politics of Power.* Boston: Little, Brown, 1969.

Hagedorn, Hermann. *The Roosevelt Family of Sagamore Hill.* New York: Macmillan, 1954.

McCullough, David. *Mornings on Horseback.* New York: Simon and Schuster, 1981.

Morris, Edmund, *The Rise of Theodore Roosevelt.* New York: Coward, McCann, and Geoghegan, 1979.

Pringle, Henry F. *Theodore Roosevelt: A Biography.* New York: Harcourt, Brace Jovanich, 1956.

Roosevelt, Nicholas. *Theodore Roosevelt: The Man as I Knew Him.* New York: Dodd, Mead, 1967.

NOTES:

1 Nicholas Roosevelt, *Theodore Roosevelt: The Man as I Knew Him,* New York: Dodd, Mead, 1967, p. 71.
2 *Theodore Roosevelt: An Autobiography,* New York: Scribner's Sons, 1920, pp. 7, 9.
3 Ibid., p. 11.
4 Hermann Hagedorn, *The Roosevelt Family of Sagamore Hill,* New York: Macmillan, 1954, p. 186.
5 Doris Faber, *The Presidents' Mothers,* New York: St. Martin's, 1978, p. 175.
6 Edmund Morris, *The Rise of Theodore Roosevelt,* New York: Coward, McCann, & Geoghegan, 1979, p. 73.
7 Nicholas Roosevelt, p. 53.
8 Theodore Roosevelt, pp. 262–263.
9 Lord Charnwood, *Theodore Roosevelt,* Boston: Atlantic Monthly Press, 1923, p. xii.
10 Morris, pp. 497–498.
11 Fletcher Pratt, *The Navy: A History,* Garden City, N.Y.: Garden City Publishing, 1941, p. 360.
12 Joseph B. Bishop, *Theodore Roosevelt and His Time: Shown in His Own Letters,* New York: Scribner's Sons, 1920, vol. II, p. 475.
13 Nicholas Roosevelt, p. 66.
14 James E. Pollard, *The Presidents and the Press,* New York: Macmillan, 1947, p. 583.
15 John Mason Potter, *Plots Against the Presidents,* New York: Astor-Honor, 1968, p. 200.
16 *The Autobiography of William Allen White,* New York: Macmillan, 1946, p. 297.
17 Donald Young, *American Roulette: The History and Dilemma of the Vice Presidency,* New York: Holt, Rinehart and Winston, 1965, p. 120.

18 Francis Russell, *The Shadow of Blooming Grove: Warren G. Harding in His Times*, New York: McGraw-Hill, 1968, p. 236.
19 Norman J. Small, *Some Presidential Interpretations of the Presidency*, Baltimore: Johns Hopkins Press, 1932, p. 42.
20 Pollard, p. 733.
21 William Safire, *The New Language of Politics*, New York: Random House, 1968, p. 270.
22 Arthur B. Tourtellot, *The Presidents on the Presidency*, New York: Russell & Russell, 1964, p. 56.
23 Bill Adler, *Presidential Wit*, New York: Trident, 1966, p. 94.

WILLIAM HOWARD TAFT

27TH PRESIDENT

NAME: William Howard Taft. His middle name was after his paternal grandmother, Sylvia Howard. Friends called him Will. Because of his size, he earned the nickname Big Lub in school.

PHYSICAL DESCRIPTION: Taft stood 6 feet 2 inches tall, had chestnut hair, blue eyes, and a rather high, soft voice, and wore a great handlebar mustache. The heaviest president, he struggled all his adult life with a weight problem. He graduated from college a pudgy 243 pounds, and by 1904 he was up to 326 pounds. He then went on a diet, losing 75 pounds in two years. But as president his weight soared to 332 pounds. He had grown so bulky that he got stuck in the White House bathtub and had to have an outsized model brought in for his use. After stepping down as president he again began to watch his calories. By 1929 he, at 244 pounds, had regained the relatively trim figure of his youth. Except for the strain that his weight placed on his heart, Taft generally was in good health. However, in the Philippines in 1901 he nearly died from dengue fever.

PERSONALITY: Taft was cheerful, friendly, a typical hail-fellow-well-met with an infectious chuckle. Always popular, he had many friends, but, surprisingly, few intimates. "One of the astonishing things about Taft's four years in the White House," wrote biographer Henry F. Pringle, "was the almost total lack of men, related or otherwise, upon whom he could lean. . . . For the most part he faced his troubles alone."[1] He was not happy as president. The break with his predecessor and former mentor, Theodore Roosevelt, weighed heavily on his mind; he was often irritable, depressed, at least once in tears. He regained his good spirits in retirement and as chief justice.

ANCESTORS: Taft was of English heritage. His great[4]-grandfather Robert Taft, a carpenter, left England for Braintree, Massachusetts in 1678. His great-great-grandfather Peter Taft reportedly fought at Bunker Hill. In 1985 President Taft was expelled posthumously from the Mayflower Society after a review of his application exposed flaws in his claim to direct descent from the Pilgrims.

FATHER: Alphonso Taft (1810–1891), lawyer, cabinet officer, diplomat. A native of Townshend, Vermont, he graduated Phi Beta Kappa from Yale in 1833, studied law there, and in 1839 settled in Cincinnati. He married Fanny Phelps, who died of tuberculosis at 29, and then Louise Torrey, the president's mother, in 1853. Taft helped found the Republican party in Cincinnati; he was a delegate to the national convention in 1856 and an alternate delegate in 1860. He served as judge of Cincinnati Superior Court for three terms, 1866–1872. President Ulysses S. Grant appointed him secretary of war, March–May 1876, and attorney general, 1876–1877. President Chester A. Arthur named him minister to Austria-Hungary, 1882–1884, and Russia, 1884–1885. While in St. Petersburg he fell ill and returned to the United States. He retired to San Diego, California, where he died when his most famous son was U.S. solicitor general.

MOTHER: Louisa "Louise" Maria Torrey Taft (1827–1907). Born in Boston, the daughter of a merchant, she reportedly was strong willed and efficient. Taft once remarked that she would have made a good railroad president. She discouraged Taft from seeking the White House. Shortly before her death, she endorsed Elihu Root for president in 1908. She died at Millbury, Massachusetts, when her son was secretary of war.

SIBLINGS: By his father's first marriage, Taft had two half brothers to live to maturity—Charles Phelps Taft, publisher of the *Cincinnati Times-Star* and member of the U.S. House, 1895–1897; Peter Rawson "Rossy" Taft, brilliant but unstable, he suffered a physical breakdown and died prematurely in a sanitarium. By his father's second marriage, Taft had two brothers and a sister to live to maturity—Henry Waters Taft, lawyer of New York; Horace Dutton Taft, founder of the Taft School in Watertown, Connecticut; Mrs. Frances L. Edwards, wife of Dr. William A. Edwards, of San Diego, California.

COLLATERAL RELATIVES: Taft was a seventh cousin twice removed of Richard Nixon and a distant relative of Ralph Waldo Emerson.

CHILDREN: Taft had two sons and a daughter.

Robert Alphonso Taft (1889–1953), political leader. He graduated from Yale in 1910 and first in his class from Harvard Law School in 1913. Poor eyesight kept him from the army during World War I, but he served in a civilian capacity as assistant general counsel to the food administrator. After the war he was elected as a Republican to the Ohio house, 1920–1926 and the Ohio senate, 1931–1932. He was a favorite-son candidate at the Republican national convention in 1936. Two years later he was elected to the U.S. Senate, 1939–1953, where he emerged the leader of the conservative wing of the party, earning the nickname Mr. Republican. He opposed the New Deal programs of President Franklin D. Roosevelt as well as the Fair Deal of President Harry Truman. He was an outspoken isolationist until the Japanese attack on Pearl Harbor in December 1941. He opposed U.S. participation in NATO and the United Nations. He was the principal American critic of the Nuremberg trials of Nazi war criminals. "The trial of the vanquished by the victors," he said, "cannot be impartial no matter how it is hedged about with the forms of justice. . . . About this whole judgment there is the spirit of vengeance, and vengeance is seldom justice. The hanging of the eleven men convicted will be a blot on the American record which we shall long regret."[2] From 1946 he was chairman of the Republican policy committee. In 1947 he sponsored the Taft-Hartley Act (see "Harry S Truman, 33d President," "Administration") restricting the activities of organized labor. He endorsed the anti-Communist campaign of Senator Joseph McCarthy. In

1952 he was a leading candidate for the Republican presidential nomination but, in a bitter convention struggle, lost to Dwight D. Eisenhower. He died months after becoming Senate majority leader.

Helen Herron Taft Manning (1891–1987), educator. After earning a doctorate in history from Yale, she became dean of Bryn Mawr College in 1917 and later head of the history department, too. In 1920 she married Frederick Manning, also a history professor.

Charles Phelps Taft (1897–1983), civic leader. He dropped out of Yale to serve as a first lieutenant in the army during World War I and then returned to graduate in 1918 and earn his law degree in 1921. He practiced law in Cincinnati and became active in local politics. He emerged a leading opponent of municipal corruption and helped introduce the home-rule charter to the city in 1925, making Cincinnati the first major U.S. city to adopt the city manager form of government. He was Hamilton County prosecutor during 1927–1928. Although a Republican, he did not always share his brother's conservative views. He at times supported and served in the Franklin Roosevelt administration. During World War II he was director of U.S. community war services for the Federal Security Agency and director of economic affairs at the State Department. After the war he was named the first layman president of the Federal Council of the Churches of Christ in America, 1947–1948. In 1952 he ran for governor of Ohio but lost to Democrat Frank J. Lausche. He was long active in Cincinnati politics, serving as city councilman 1938–1942, 1948–1951, and 1955–1977 and as mayor 1955–1957. He wrote *City Management: The Cincinnati Experiment* (1933) and *You and I and Roosevelt* (1936).

BIRTH: Taft was born September 15, 1857, at home in the Mount Auburn section of Cincinnati, Ohio. He was described as "well and hearty." Both parents had hoped for a girl.

CHILDHOOD: Taft grew up in Cincinnati a fun-loving, active, well-behaved child. An avid baseball player, he was a good second baseman and power hitter but, because of his size, a poor base runner. He and his friends enjoyed swimming and ice-skating in an idle canal. He joined other Mount Auburn youths in stone-throwing warfare against a rival gang from Walnut Hills. At nine he fractured his skull in a carriage accident. He characteristically acted as referee in fights between his brothers.

EDUCATION: Taft learned the fundamentals at the Sixteenth District public school in the Mount Auburn section of Cincinnati. He was a good student, invariably placing at or near the top of his class. He also took dancing lessons twice a week and, despite his bulk, was relatively light on his feet. At Woodward High School 1870–1874 he took the college preparatory curriculum; he graduated second in the class of 1874 with a four-year grade average of 91.5. At Yale University 1874–1878 he likewise performed well in class and was popular but took part in few extracurricular activities. His father had warned him that sports would only divert him from study. He did represent the freshman class, however, in an intramural wrestling match with sophomore E. C. Cook, whom he pinned. He also joined the Skull and Bones society and was elected junior class orator. He later credited Yale for shaping much of his character and singled out Professor William Graham Sumner for stimulating his intellect. Taft won a math prize his junior year, composition prizes his senior year. He graduated second, salutatorian, of 132 students of the class of 1878. While attending the University of Cincinnati law school 1878–1880, he worked part time as a courthouse reporter for the *Cincinnati Commercial*. He was admitted to the bar in May 1880 before his graduation from law school that year.

RELIGION: Unitarian. "I am a Unitarian," Taft declared in a private letter written in 1899 but not made public until after he was president. "I believe in God. I do not believe in the divinity of Christ, and there are many other of the postulates of the orthodox creed to which I cannot subscribe. I am not however a scoffer at religion but on the contrary recognize, in the fullest manner, the elevating influence that it has had and always will have in the history of mankind."[3] During the 1908 presidential campaign, he refused to engage in "a dogmatic discussion of creed" with religious critics who charged him with atheism. Although he did not accept the articles of faith of Roman Catholicism, he praised that church as a bulwark against socialism and anarchy.

RECREATION: Taft was the first president to take up golf. He followed baseball and inaugurated the custom for the president to toss out the first ball at the beginning of the professional season. He enjoyed the theater, especially musical comedies. He frequently spent summer vacations at Murray Bay on the St. Lawrence River. He seldom drank.

MARRIAGE: William Howard Taft, 28, married Helen "Nellie" Herron, 25, on June 19, 1886, at the home of the bride's parents in Cincinnati. Born June 2, 1861, in Cincinnati, the daughter of Judge John W. Herron, a law partner of Rutherford B. Hayes, and Harriet Collins Herron, Nellie graduated from the Cincinnati College of Music and taught school briefly before her marriage. With her parents she attended the twenty-fifth wedding anniversary celebration of President and Mrs. Rutherford B. Hayes at the White House in 1877. Two years later she met Taft at a bobsledding party in Cincinnati; he was 22, she 18. He asked her out for the first time in February 1880, but they did not date regularly until 1882. He proposed in April 1885, she accepted in May. The wedding was performed by the Reverend D.N.A. Hoge of Zanesville, Ohio. Taft's younger brother Horace was best man. The couple honeymooned one day in New York City and four days at Sea Bright, New Jersey, before setting off on a three-month tour of Europe. On their return, they settled in Cincinnati. Mrs. Taft encouraged her husband's political career despite his oft-stated preference for the judiciary. As First Lady, she was the first wife of a president to ride alongside her husband down Pennsylvania Avenue on Inauguration Day (heretofore the outgoing chief executive had accompanied the new president). Two months after entering the White House, Mrs. Taft suffered a stroke, impairing her speech; she never fully recovered. With the help of her sisters, however, she entertained moderately. She received guests three afternoons a week in the Red Room. The social highlight of the Taft administration was the silver wedding anniversary gala (June 19, 1911) for some 8,000 guests. In her most lasting contribution as First Lady, Mrs. Taft arranged for the planting of the 3,000 Japanese cherry trees that grace the Washington Tidal Basin; with the wife of the Japanese ambassador, she personally planted the first two saplings in ceremonies on March 27, 1912. The Tafts were divided over Prohibition; the former president was a Dry, Mrs. Taft a Wet. With Taft's appointment to the Supreme Court, Mrs. Taft became the only woman to be both First Lady and wife of a chief justice. She died on May 22, 1943, and was buried next to the president at Arlington National Cemetery.

MILITARY SERVICE: None.

CAREER BEFORE THE PRESIDENCY: By dint of his father's prominence and his own political connections, Taft became assistant prosecutor of Hamilton County, Ohio, 1881–1882, at an annual salary of $1,200, having turned down an offer of $1,500 a year to stay on as a full-time reporter at the *Cincinnati Commercial*, and became collector of internal revenue for Ohio's First District, 1882–1883. During 1883–1884 he practiced law in Cincinnati in partnership with Harlan Page Lloyd. In 1884 he supported the nomination of President Chester A. Arthur but campaigned for the eventual Republican nominee, James G. Blaine. He was assistant solicitor of Hamilton County during 1885–1887. Taft early discovered that he was best suited temperamentally for the judiciary and set his sights on the U.S. Supreme Court. He was appointed judge of Cincinnati Superior Court, 1887–1890, U.S. solicitor general, 1890–1892, and judge of the Sixth U.S. Circuit Court and ex officio member of the Sixth U.S. Circuit Court of Appeals, 1892–1900, with jurisdiction over Ohio, Michigan, Kentucky, and Tennessee. While on the bench he abstained from partisan political activity. Meanwhile he also was professor of law and dean of the University of Cincinnati Law School, 1896–1900.

Commissioner, 1900–1901, and Governor-General, 1901–1904, of the Philippines. Appointed by President William McKinley to establish civil government in the Philippines, recently acquired in the Spanish-American War, Taft clashed over policy with U.S. military governor General Arthur McArthur, whom he criticized in reports to Washington for his public disdain for the natives. Taft was instrumental in drafting the islands' governing document, which, although failing to promise independence, called for eventual creation of a national legislature and the abolition of slavery and included a Bill of Rights virtually identical to the first 10 amendments to the U.S. Constitution, with the notable absence of the right to trial by jury. During his four years in the Philippines, Taft converted the U.S. presence from military to civil rule, suppressed an insurrection led by Emilio Aguinaldo, established a civil service system, reformed a corrupt judicial system, opened English-language public schools, began harbor and road improvements, and upgraded health standards. He also negotiated with Vatican officials for the purchase of some 390,000 acres of church property in the Philippines for $7.5 million. The land was then distributed at low-cost mortgages to tens of thousands of Filipino peasants. To see his program through to completion, Governor Taft twice, October 1902 and January 1903, declined President Theodore Roosevelt's offer to appoint him to the Supreme Court.

Secretary of War, 1904–1908. He was appointed by President Roosevelt to succeed Elihu Root. In 1904 Taft defended the Roosevelt administration in a series of campaign speeches. As secretary he supervised preparations for construction of the Panama Canal; he personally inspected the site in November–December 1904. In July 1905 he met in Tokyo with Japanese Premier Count Taro Katsura. Without instructions from Washington, Taft assured Katsura that the United States would not oppose imposition of Japanese suzerainty over Korea, provided that it was not a prelude to aggression against the Philippines. Katsura denied any interest in the Philippines. President Roosevelt promptly approved the arrangement, but it was not immediately made public. Taft continued to oversee developments in the Philippines, revisiting the islands in July–September 1905. That year he also served as acting secretary of state during the illness of Secretary John Hay. He was provisional governor of Cuba during September–October 1906. In January 1906 Taft for the third time reluctantly declined appointment to the Supreme Court. Ostensibly, he turned down President Roosevelt's offer, he said, in order to complete his duties in the War Department. But he was by this time a leading contender for the 1908 Republican nomination, and both his wife and Roosevelt were urging him to run for president. In a celebrated incident, Roosevelt is said to have playfully fallen into a mock trance before Secretary and Mrs. Taft one evening in the White House library, intoning, "I am the seventh son of a seventh daughter and I have clairvoyant powers. I see a man weighing 350 pounds. There is something hanging over his head. I cannot make out what it is. . . . At one time it looks like the presidency, then again it looks like the chief justiceship." "Make it the presidency," piped up Mrs. Taft. "Make it the chief justiceship," said Secretary Taft.[4]

REPUBLICAN PRESIDENTIAL NOMINATION, 1908: In December 1905 Taft declared that his ambition was for a seat on the Supreme Court not the White House but conceded that he would accept a draft and, once nominated, would campaign vigorously against his Democratic opponent. Incumbent president Theodore Roosevelt in 1904 had pledged not to run again in 1908, explaining that he regarded as two full terms the seven and one-half years he served following the assassination of President McKinley. By the time Republicans convened in Chicago in June 1908, Taft, with Roosevelt's enthusiastic endorsement had the nomination locked up. After Senator Theodore E. Burton of Ohio delivered Taft's nominating speech, he was nominated on the first ballot with 702 votes to 68 for Senator Philander Knox of Pennsylvania, 67 for Governor Charles Evans Hughes of New York, 58 for House Speaker Joe Cannon of Illinois and the rest scattered. For vice president, Taft privately preferred a progressive westerner, Senator J. P. Dolliver of Iowa, but left the choice up to the convention, which nominated Representative James S. Sherman of New York. The Republican platform pointed with pride to the accomplishments of the Roosevelt administration and called for tariff revision, creation of a national monetary commission to develop a permanent currency system, establishment of a postal savings bank system, stricter antitrust laws, more stringent regulation of the railroads, improved labor safety, collective U.S. citizenship for all inhabitants of Puerto Rico, and statehood for New Mexico and Arizona.

OPPONENT: William Jennings Bryan (1860–1925) of Nebraska; Democrat. He was the Democratic presidential nominee in 1896 and 1900. After the overwhelming defeat of conservative Alton B. Parker by President Theodore Roosevelt in 1904, control of the Democratic party reverted to the progressives under Bryan, whose supporters dominated the party's national convention in Denver in July 1908. So enthusiastic were his delegates that a Bryan demonstration lasted a record 87 minutes. Bryan was nominated on the first ballot with 892½ votes to 50½ for Judge George Gray of Delaware and 46 for Governor John A. Johnson of Minnesota. John W. Kern of Indiana was nominated for vice president. The Democratic platform blamed the Roosevelt administration for bloated bureaucracy, wasteful spending, and misuse of patronage; objected to the "absolute domination" of the House by the Speaker; called for making public the names of campaign contributors and the amount of their contributions, an end to corporate campaign contributions, and a limit on private contributions; and favored tariff reduction, stricter antitrust laws, curbs on interlocking corporate directorships, federal charters for interstate corporations, strengthening the Interstate Commerce Commission better to regulate railroads, a bank deposit insurance program, an income tax, restrictions on the use of the labor injunction, the eight-hour day on all government work, workmen's compensation insurance, creation of a national bureau of public health, direct election of senators, statehood for Arizona and New Mexico, federal regulation of telegraph and telephone companies, conservation of natural resources, and independence for the Philippines. After his defeat by Taft, Bryan was secretary of state 1913–1915 in the Wilson administration and became a leading defender of religious fundamentalism against the theory of evolution. As prosecutor and witness in the famous Scopes trial in Dayton, Tennessee, in 1925, he contrasted unfavorably with defense attorney Clarence Darrow. He died days after the trial.

CAMPAIGN AND THE ISSUES, 1908: This rather lackluster contest centered around a single theme: Which candidate could most effectively carry on the popular policies of President Theodore Roosevelt. Although Taft was the president's handpicked candidate and thus seemed the obvious choice to continue his program, Bryan claimed that Roosevelt had largely co-opted the Democratic platform and that he, not Taft, would more effectively carry on the battle against the trusts and the despoilers of the nation's natural resources. But Bryan undermined his claim to the Roosevelt mantle by coming out in favor of nationalization of the railroads: "Public ownership is necessary where competition is impossible,"[5] he said. Both Roosevelt and Taft denounced the proposal as rank socialism. Bryan backpedaled on the issue, conceding that the country might not be ready for nationalization, but the incident only reinforced Bryan's image as a radical and drove Wall Street and the business community deeper into the Taft camp. Taft also attacked as unsound Bryan's proposal for a federal deposit insurance program, an idea later enacted under President Franklin Roosevelt. Although Taft ran on Roosevelt's record and pledged to carry through his policies, he warned the nation not to expect another whirlwind term. The country needed a rest, a period of consolidation, after the breathless Roosevelt years, he maintained.

ELECTION AS PRESIDENT, NOVEMBER 3, 1908:

Popular Vote: Taft (Republican), 7,679,006 (52%); Bryan (Democrat), 6,409,106 (43%); Eugene V. Debs (Socialist) 420,858 (3%).

Electoral Vote: Taft, 321; Bryan, 162.

States Carried: Taft won the majority of electoral votes in 29 states—California, Connecticut, Delaware, Idaho, Illinois, Indiana, Iowa, Kansas, Maine, Massachusetts, Michigan, Minnesota, Missouri, Montana, New Hampshire, New Jersey, New York, North Dakota, Ohio, Oregon, Pennsylvania, Rhode Island, South Dakota, Utah, Vermont, Washington, West Virginia, Wisconsin, and Wyoming. Bryan won the majority of electoral votes in 17 states—Alabama, Arkansas, Colorado, Florida, Georgia, Kentucky, Louisiana, Maryland, Mississippi, Nebraska, Nevada, North Carolina, Oklahoma, South Carolina, Tennessee, Texas, and Virginia.

INAUGURAL ADDRESS: March 4, 1909. ". . . The progress which the negro has made in the last fifty years, from slavery, when its statistics are reviewed, is marvelous, and it furnishes every reason to hope that in the next twenty-five years a still greater improvement in his condition as a productive member of society, on the farm, and in the shop, and in other occupations may come.

"The negroes are now Americans. Their ancestors came here years ago against their will, and this is their only country and their only flag. They have shown themselves anxious to live for it and to die for it. Encountering the race feeling against them, subjected at times to cruel injustice growing out of it, they may well have our profound sympathy and aid in the struggle they are making. We are charged with the sacred duty of making their path as smooth and easy as we can. . . ."

VICE PRESIDENT: James Schoolcraft Sherman (1855–1912), of New York, served 1909–1912. Born in Utica, New York, Sherman was admitted to the bar in 1880 and began practice in his native city. A Republican, he in 1884 was elected mayor of Utica. During 20 years in the U.S. House, 1887–1891 and 1893–1909, Sherman demonstrated party loyalty and parliamentary skill and rose to chairman of the Indian Affairs Committee. His genial nature earned him the nickname Smiling Jim. He was renominated for vice president on the ticket with Taft in 1912 but died of Bright's disease days before the election.

CABINET:

Secretary of State. Philander C. Knox (1853–1921), of Pennsylvania, served 1909–1913. He was attorney general under President Theodore Roosevelt. He undertook a major reorganization of the department that included creation of the offices of counselor, resident diplomatic officer, and director of the consular service; political-geographic divisions for Western European, Near Eastern, and Latin American affairs; and the division of information. In foreign policy, he implemented Dollar Diplomacy (see "Administration").

Secretary of the Treasury. Franklin MacVeagh (1837–1934), of Illinois, served 1909–1913. On his advice, Taft overruled his attorney general to permit subsidiaries of bank holding companies to invest in the stock market.

Secretary of War. (1) Jacob M. Dickinson (1851–1928), of Tennessee, served 1909–1911. He had served as assistant attorney general under President Cleveland. He dispatched 20,000 troops to police the Mexican border in 1911 as Mexico drifted toward revolution. (2) Henry L. Stimson (1867–1950), of New York, served 1911–1913. He later served as secretary of state in the Hoover administration and war secretary in the Franklin Roosevelt administration.

Attorney General. George W. Wickersham (1858–1936), of New York, served 1909–1913. He undertook antitrust action against dozens of combinations, most notably the American Tobacco Company and the Standard Oil Company, and was instrumental in securing passage of the Mann-Elkins Act (1910; see "Administration"). He later was chairman of the Wickersham Commission (1929) investigating Prohibition.

Secretary of the Navy. George von L. Meyer (1858–1918), of Massachusetts, served 1909–1913. He had served as postmaster general under President Theodore Roosevelt. He counseled intervention in the Mexican revolution in 1912, but Taft resisted.

Postmaster General. Frank H. Hitchcock (1869–1935), of Massachusetts, served 1909–1913. He had served as assistant postmaster general under President Theodore Roosevelt. He established the postal savings bank and parcel post and promoted development of air mail service.

Secretary of the Interior. (1) Richard A. Ballinger (1858–1922), of Washington, served 1909–1911. He had served as commissioner of public lands under President Theodore Roosevelt. In a highly publicized dispute with Gifford Pinchot, chief of the Forest Service, Secretary Ballinger was accused of collaborating with coal interests to plunder federal reserves in Alaska. Taft stood by Ballinger and fired Pinchot. A congressional investigation cleared Ballinger of any wrongdoing, but the incident polarized the Republican party, widening the gulf between the conservatives under President Taft and the progressives loyal to Roosevelt. Ballinger resigned for health and financial reasons. In accepting his resignation, Taft regretted that he had become "the object of one of the most unscrupulous conspiracies for the defamation of character that history can show." (2) Walter L. Fisher (1862–1935), of Illinois, served 1911–1913. He encouraged development of Alaska, creation of national parks, and conservation of natural resources. He wrote *Alaskan Coal Problems* (1911).

Secretary of Agriculture. James Wilson (1835–1920), of Iowa, served 1897–1913. A holdover from the McKinley and Roosevelt administrations, he was popular with farmers, but Taft became disappointed with his administrative ability.

Secretary of Commerce and Labor. Charles Nagel (1849–1940), of Missouri, served 1909–1913. At his urging, Taft vetoed a bill requiring a literacy test for the admission of immigrants. "This exclusion," Nagel wrote in a letter appended to Taft's veto message, "would embrace probably in large part undesirable but also a great many desirable people, and the embarrassment, expense, and distress to those who seek to enter would be out of all proportion to any good that can possibly be promised for this measure."[6]

ADMINISTRATION: March 4, 1909–March 3, 1913.

Payne-Aldrich Tariff Act, 1909. It replaced the Dingley Tariff (1897; see "William McKinley, 25th President," "Administration"). Sponsored by Republican Representative Sereno E. Payne of New York and Republican Senator Nelson W. Aldrich of Rhode Island, the law trimmed the overall rate from 46 to 41 percent but raised rates on such items as coal, iron ore, and animal hides. In a speech at Winona, Minnesota, in September 1909, Taft defended the new tariff against Democratic and progressive Republican charges that it was a token revision representing little departure from the conservative Republicans' long-standing commitment to protection. "I am bound to say," he told the crowd, "that I think the Payne tariff bill is the best tariff bill that the Republican party ever passed. . . . If the country desires free trade, and the country desires a revenue tariff and wishes the manufacturers all over the country to go out of business, and to have cheaper prices at the expense of the sacrifice of many of our manufacturing interests, then it ought to say so and ought to put the Democratic party in power."[7] In 1910 Democrats directed their congressional campaign against the tariff law, ridiculing Taft's Winona speech, and succeeded in recapturing the House. The Payne-Aldrich Tariff was replaced by the Underwood Tariff (1913; see "Woodrow Wilson, 28th President," "Administration").

Mann-Elkins Act, 1910. Sponsored by Republican Representative James R. Mann of Illinois and Republican Senator Stephen B. Elkins of West Virginia and supported by President Taft, the law extended the authority of the Interstate Commerce Commission (ICC) to fix on its own accord maximum rates charged by railroads and banned the practice of charging more for short hauls than for longer ones. It also for the first time placed the telephone and telegraph industries under the regulatory supervision of the ICC.

Dollar Diplomacy. President Taft authorized Secretary of State Knox to pursue what became known as Dollar Diplomacy, marshaling military might and diplomatic influence to promote American business interests abroad. Taft encouraged American investor participation in the construction of railroads in China, but the deal fell through. In the Caribbean he invited American bankers to rescue financially troubled Honduras and establish a major financial stake in Haiti. In 1912 he dispatched marines to Nicaragua to crush a local rebellion against a government friendly to American business interests. In his last annual message to Congress, December 1912, Taft defended Dollar Diplomacy as an extension of the Monroe Doctrine (see "James Monroe, 5th President," "Administration"). Its goal was to protect Central American nations, he said, "from the jeopardy involved by heavy foreign debt and chaotic national finances and from the ever present danger of international complications due to disorder at home." He added, "Hence the United States has been glad to encourage and support American bankers who were willing to lend a helping hand to the financial rehabilitation of such countries because this financial rehabilitation and the protection of their customhouses from being the prey of would-be dictators would remove at one stroke the menace of foreign creditors and the menace of revolutionary disorder."

Antitrust Policy. Taft enforced the antitrust laws as faithfully and as vigorously as his predecessor. His most significant victory was the dismantling of both the American Tobacco Company and the Standard Oil Company in 1911.

Webb-Kenyon Interstate Liquor Shipments Act, 1913. Passed over President Taft's veto, the law barred the interstate transportation of liquor into dry states.

States Admitted to the Union: New Mexico (1912), Arizona (1912). Taft was the first president of the 48 contiguous states.

Constitutional Amendment Ratified: Sixteenth Amendment, 1913. "The Congress shall have the power to lay and collect taxes on incomes, from whatever source derived, without apportionment among the several States, and without regard to any census or enumeration."

SUPREME COURT APPOINTMENTS: (1) Horace H. Lurton (1844–1914), of Tennessee, served as associate justice 1910–1914. Taft had long admired Lurton since they served together on the Sixth U.S. Circuit Court of Appeals. Taft dismissed objections from Attorney General Wickersham and others that at 66 Lurton was too old to begin a term on the Court and later called the appointment "the chief pleasure of my administration."[8] Lurton died four years later, having established a conservative record, but leaving little mark on the Court. (2) Charles Evans Hughes (1862–1948), of New York, served as associate justice 1910–1916. He was governor of New York and regarded as a likely candidate for president at the time of his appointment. In offering the seat, President Taft suggested, but was careful not to promise, that he would elevate Hughes to chief justice if the vacancy arose during his term. Hughes joined the Court's liberal bloc. In *Bailey* v. *Alabama* (1911), he overturned the conviction of a black man sentenced to more than four months' hard labor for failing to return a $15 advance on an uncompleted labor contract. In *Truax* v. *Reich* (1915), he struck down an Arizona law reserving four out of five jobs in the state for U.S. citizens. Hughes resigned in 1916 to run for president (see "Woodrow Wilson, 28th President," "Opponent"). He returned as chief justice in 1930 (see "Herbert Hoover, 31st President," "Supreme Court Appointments"). (3) Edward D. White (1845–1921), of Louisiana, served as associate justice 1894–1910 and as chief justice 1910–1921. He was the first associate justice to be elevated to chief justice. See "Grover Cleveland, 24th President," "Supreme Court Appointments." (4) Willis Van Devanter (1859–1941), of Wyoming, served as associate justice 1911–1937. He was a federal circuit court judge. Although he wrote very few opinions himself, he reportedly was influential in conference. Taft, who as chief justice served with him for 16 years, praised him for his unusually broad knowledge of the law and influence on the Court. Ultraconservative during his last years on the bench, he bitterly opposed as unconstitutional the New Deal legislation of the Franklin Roosevelt administration. (5) Joseph R. Lamar (1857–1916), of Georgia, served as associate justice 1911–1916. He had helped compile *The Code of the State of Georgia* (1896) and served on the Georgia Supreme Court. He died after just five years, having left little mark on the high court. (6) Mahlon Pitney (1858–1924), of New Jersey, served as associate justice 1912–1922. He had served as a member of the New Jersey supreme court. He most often voted with the conservatives and was especially hostile to organized labor. He spoke for the Court in *Duplex Printing Press Co.* v. *Deering* (1921), which crippled the Clayton Anti-Trust Act (1914; see "Woodrow Wilson," "Administration") in limiting strike activity to employees of a particular plant, thus denying them the aid of the parent union. Taft, who as chief justice served briefly with him, was unimpressed with his work.

RANKING IN 1962 HISTORIANS POLL: Taft ranked sixteenth of 31 presidents, fifth of 12 "average" presidents. He ranked above Van Buren, below McKinley.

CAREER AFTER THE PRESIDENCY: Having been defeated for reelection (see under "Woodrow Wilson, 28th President," for the election of 1912), Taft attended the inaugural of his successor and accepted appointment as Kent professor of law at Yale University, 1913–1921, where he lectured on government and taught international law. During this time he also spoke around the country and contributed articles to national magazines. In 1916 he campaigned for Charles Evans Hughes for president, but he supported Wilson's attempts to keep the United States out of World War I. In 1918 he reconciled with former president Theodore Roosevelt when the two bumped into each other in a Chicago restaurant, embraced, and chatted at length, to the delight of onlookers. In 1918 Wilson appointed Taft co-chairman of the National War Labor Board. Taft supported Prohibition and U.S. participation in the League of Nations. In 1920 he endorsed Warren G. Harding for president.

Chief Justice of the United States, 1921–1930. Appointed by President Harding in June 1921, Taft at long last attained the office he had sought for decades and thus became the only man to serve both as president and as chief justice. Having three times declined, for various reasons, President Theodore Roosevelt's offer to name him to the Court, Taft now eagerly took up his duties as chief justice. Taft proved an efficient judicial administrator, swiftly dispatching the court's clogged docket. During his nine years on the bench, he wrote 253 opinions, about one sixth of all the decisions handed down during his term. In *Truax* v. *Corrigan* (1921), he struck down the provision of the Clayton Anti-Trust Act (1914; see "Woodrow Wilson," "Administration") that barred injunctions against peaceful labor picketing. Taft held that even peaceful picketing, when it causes financial loss to a business, violates the 14th Amendment in depriving the entrepreneur of his property without due process of law. In *Bailey* v. *Drexel Furniture Co.* (1922), Taft denied the right of Congress to attempt to discourage child labor by levying an excise tax on goods manufactured by children. In thus declaring invalid the Child Labor Tax Act of 1919 as a congressional usurpation of states' rights, Taft warned, "The good sought in unconstitutional legislation is an insidious feature because it leads citizens and legislators of good purpose to promote it without thought of the serious breach it will make in the ark of our covenant or the harm which will come from breaking down recognized standards." Dissenting in *Adkins* v. *Children's Hospital* (1923), which struck down a minimum wage law for women in the District of Columbia, Taft reminded the majority that "it is not the function of this court to hold Congressional acts invalid simply because they are passed to carry out economic views which the court believes to be unwise or unsound." Speaking for the majority in *Myers* v. *United States* (1926), Taft invalidated the Tenure of Office Act of 1867, which limited the power of the president to remove subordinates. (It was the violation of this act that had formed the basis of the impeachment charges against President Andrew Johnson.) Taft resigned from the Court in failing health in February 1930.

DEATH: March 8, 1930, late afternoon, at home, Washington, D.C. When Taft retired from the Supreme Court, he was suffering from arteriosclerotic heart disease, high blood pressure, and inflammation of the bladder. Taft failed rapidly, eating little and failing to recognize familiar faces. In early March he drifted in and out of consciousness and finally passed away in his sleep. His was the first presidential funeral broadcast on radio. His body lay in state at the U.S. Capitol Building. Simple services, conducted at All Soul's Church, included his favorite hymns, "Lead Kindly Light" and "Abide With Me" and readings of Wordsworth's "Happy Warrior" and Tennyson's "Ode on the Death of the Duke of Wellington." He was buried at Arlington National Cemetery near the grave of Robert Todd Lincoln, son of Abraham Lincoln. Taft and Kennedy are the only presidents buried at Arlington. In his last will and testament, executed in June 1925, Taft left the bulk of his estate, valued at $475,000, to his wife.

TAFT PRAISED: "I do not believe there can be found in the whole country a man so well fitted to be President. He is not only absolutely fearless, absolutely disinterested and upright, but he has the widest acquaintance with the nation's needs without and within and the broadest sympathies with all our citizens. He would be as emphatically a President of the plain people as Lincoln, yet not Lincoln himself would be freer from the least taint of demagogy, the least tendency to arouse or appeal to any class hatred of any kind."[9]—President Theodore Roosevelt, 1908

"[Taft is] as wise and patient as Abraham Lincoln, as modest and dauntless as Ulysses S. Grant, as temperate and peace-loving as Rutherford B. Hayes, as patriotic and intellectual as James A. Garfield, as courtly and generous as Chester A. Arthur, as learned in the law as Benjamin Harrison, as sympathetic and brave as William McKinley, as progressive as his predecessor."[10]—Warren G. Harding, 1912

"Mr. Taft's service to our country has been of rare distinction and was marked by a purity of patriotism, a lofty disinterestedness, and a devotion to the best interests of the nation that deserve and will ever command the grateful memory of his countrymen."[11]—President Herbert Hoover, 1930

TAFT CRITICIZED: "For the first time in the history of the country a President of the United States has openly proclaimed himself the friend of thieves and the enemy of honest men. . . . Many Republican Presidents have by indirection through the protective policy proclaimed themselves the friend of robbery under the forms of law; Mr. Taft becomes the first to depart from the process of licensed robbery, and to announce that the debts of his party are in future to be paid out of the people's domain."[12]—*Louisville Courier-Journal*, on the Ballinger-Pinchot controversy (see "Cabinet: Secretary of Interior"), 1910

"Taft, who is such an admirable fellow, has shown himself such an utterly commonplace leader, good-natured, feebly well-meaning, but with plenty of small motive; and totally unable to grasp or put into execution any great policy."[13]—former president Theodore Roosevelt

"Taft was a man of real intelligence, great working power, abundant physical courage, high legal attainments and immense personal charm. Weak rather than wicked, he was one of those genial men who are everything that fancy paints until a showdown comes along that demands real toughness of moral fiber."[14]—Gifford Pinchot, forester and public official

TAFT QUOTES: "Don't sit up nights thinking about making me President for that will never come and I have no ambition in that direction. Any party which would nominate me would make a great mistake."[15]—1903

"The diplomacy of the present administration has sought to respond to modern ideas of commercial intercourse. This policy has been characterized as substituting dollars for bullets. It is one that appeals alike to idealistic humanitarian sentiments, to the dictates of sound policy and strategy, and to legitimate commercial aims."[16]—1912

"I have come to the conclusion that the major part of the President is to increase the gate receipts of expositions and fairs and bring tourists into the town."[17]

BOOKS BY TAFT: *Four Aspects of Civic Duty* (1906); *Our Chief Magistrate and His Powers* (1916).

BOOKS ABOUT TAFT: Anderson, Donald F. *William Howard Taft: A Conservative's Conception of the Presidency*. Ithaca, N.Y.: Cornell University Press, 1973.

Anderson, Judith Icke. *William Howard Taft: An Intimate History*. New York: Norton, 1981.

Pringle, Henry. *The Life and Times of William Howard Taft*. 2 vols. New York: Farrar & Rinehart, 1939.

NOTES

1 Henry F. Pringle, *The Life and Times of William Howard Taft*, New York: Farrar & Rinehart, 1939, p. 385.

2 John F. Kennedy, *Profiles in Courage*, New York: Harper & Bros., 1955, p. 218.

3 Edmund Fuller and David E. Green, *God in the White House: The Faiths of American Presidents*, New York: Crown, 1968, p. 170; Pringle, p. 45.

4 Pringle, pp. 312–313.

5 Ibid., p. 345.

6 Henry Steele Commager, ed., *Documents of American History*, New York: Crofts, 1945, Doc. no. 387, p. 257.

7 Ibid., Doc. no. 374, p. 235.

8 Pringle, p. 531.

9 Ibid., p. 356.

10 William Safire, *The New Language of Politics*, New York: Random House, 1968, p. 457.

11 Ishbell Ross, *An American Family: The Tafts*, Cleveland: World, 1964, p. 361.

12 Pringle, p. 472.

13 Elting E. Morison, ed., *The Letters of Theodore Roosevelt*, Cambridge, Mass.: Harvard University Press, 1951–1954, vol. VII, p. 112.

14 Frank Graham, Jr., *Man's Dominion: The Story of Conservation in America*, New York: Evans, 1971, p. 140.

15 Pringle, p. 102.

16 Louis Filler, ed., *The President Speaks*, New York: Putnam's Sons, 1964, p. 90.

17 Bill Adler, *Presidential Wit*, New York: Trident, 1966, p. 100.

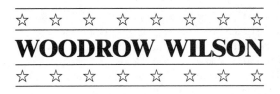

WOODROW WILSON

28TH PRESIDENT

NAME: Thomas Woodrow Wilson. He was named after his maternal grandfather, the Reverend Thomas Woodrow, a Presbyterian minister. After graduating from Princeton he began going by T. Woodrow Wilson and soon thereafter dropped the first initial.

PHYSICAL DESCRIPTION: "For beauty I am not a star / There are others more handsome by far / But my face I don't mind it / For I am behind it / It's the people in front that I jar." Thus in composing this self-deprecatory limerick did Wilson humorously acknowledge his rather homely features. He had a long, drawn face, blue-gray eyes, brown hair, a high forehead, oversized ears, and a thrusting jaw. He stood about 5 feet 11 inches tall and weighed 175–185 pounds. His health generally was poor. From childhood he was plagued by indigestion; as president he at times used a stomach pump on himself. The strain of overwork severely undermined his health; in college and as a professor at Princeton University he nearly collapsed under the load. Thereafter he learned to pace himself better. He wore glasses from age eight. In 1895 a retinal hemorrhage left him with poor vision in his right eye. He was virtually blind in his last years.

PERSONALITY: Wilson was an emotionally complex man. According to his principal biographer Arthur S. Link, Wilson craved affection and demanded unquestioned loyalty. "He had few intimates," wrote Link, "and broke sooner or later with most of them . . . [and] his most enduring friends were admiring, uncritical women."[1] Wilson once described his own nature as a struggle between his Irish blood, "quick, generous, impulsive, passionate, anxious always to help and to sympathize with those in distress," and his Scotch blood, "canny, tenacious, cold, and perhaps a little exclusive."[2] In another instance he compared himself to a dormant volcano, placid on the outside, a boiling caldron within. Before large crowds Wilson was expansive, supremely self-confident, a gifted, moving orator. In small groups of strangers, however, he often appeared shy and awkward.

ANCESTORS: Wilson was of Scotch-Irish heritage. His paternal grandfather, James Wilson, a native of Strabane, northern Ireland, emigrated to Philadelphia in 1807 and in 1815 settled at Steubenville, Ohio. He was editor of the *Western Herald and Steubenville Gazette*, served as a Democrat in the state legislature and as associate judge of the Court of Common Pleas, and converted to the Whig party in 1840. His maternal grandfather and namesake, the Reverend Thomas Woodrow, a native of Paisley, Scotland, and alumnus of the University of Glasgow, emigrated in 1835 and was pastor of various churches in Ohio and Kentucky, the last being the Scioto Presbyterian Church in Columbus during 1862–1865.

FATHER: Joseph Ruggles Wilson (1822–1903), Presbyterian minister. A native of Steubenville, Ohio, he graduated valedictorian from Jefferson College in 1844 and attended Western Theological Seminary 1845–1846 and Princeton Theological Seminary 1846–1847. Ordained in 1849, he was pastor of Presbyterian churches in Staunton, Virginia, 1855–1857, Augusta, Georgia, 1857–1870, and Wilmington, North Carolina, 1874–1885. He taught theology at Columbia Theological Seminary 1870–1874 and Southwestern Presbyterian University 1885–1893. A staunch supporter of the South during the Civil War, he helped organize the Presbyterian church of the Confederate States of America. He worked a profound influence in the development of Woodrow Wilson's character and intellect, prodding him on with such aphorisms as, "The roast beef of hard industry gives blood for climbing the hills of life." He died at Princeton, New Jersey, when his most famous son was president of Princeton University.

MOTHER: Janet "Jessie" Woodrow Wilson (1830–1888). A native of Carlisle, England, she at age four emigrated with her family to America and grew up mostly in Chillicothe, Ohio, where she attended the Female Seminary. She married Joseph Ruggles Wilson in 1849. Although she was said to be quarrelsome with outsiders, she was warm and giving to her family; son Woodrow was devoted to her. "I remember how I clung to her (a laughed-at 'mama's boy') till I was a great big fellow," he once said, "but love of the best womanhood came to me and entered my heart through those apron strings."[3] She died in Clarksville, Tennessee, when Wilson was an associate professor at Bryn Mawr College.

SIBLINGS: The third of four children, Wilson had two older sisters and a younger brother—Mrs. Marion W. Kennedy, wife of the Reverend Anderson R. Kennedy; Mrs. Annie J. Howe, wife of Dr. George Howe, of Columbia, South Carolina; Joseph R. Wilson, Jr., journalist for the *Nashville Banner*, later an insurance executive of Baltimore.

CHILDREN: Wilson had three daughters by his first marriage.

    Margaret Woodrow Wilson (1886–1944), singer, businesswoman. Born in Gainesville, Georgia, she attended Goucher College in Baltimore, studied voice and piano for a year at the Peabody Institute of Music in Baltimore, and took singing lessons under various instructors for many years. In 1915 Miss Wilson, a soprano, made her singing debut with the Chicago Symphony Orchestra in Syracuse, New York. During World War I, she performed at army camps and at benefits for the Red Cross. In 1923 she gave up her singing career to work as a consultant and writer for an advertising agency. She later speculated in stocks and bonds. She became interested in Indian mysticism and in 1940 settled at Pondicherry, India, to study the religious teachings of Sri Aurobondo. Taking the name Dishta, she lived as a virtual recluse in the isolated religious community until her death by uremia four years later.

Jessie Woodrow Wilson (1887–1933). Born in Gainesville, she attended Goucher College in Baltimore and worked three years at a settlement house in Philadelphia before marrying Francis B. Sayre in a White House wedding on November 25, 1913. They eventually settled at Cambridge, Massachusetts, when Mr. Sayre joined the faculty of Harvard Law School. Jessie Sayre was active in the League of Women Voters, served on the national board of the Y.W.C.A., and, at the time of her death following an appendix operation, was secretary of the Massachusetts Democratic Committee.

Eleanor Randolph Wilson (1889–1967). Born in Middletown, Connecticut, she was said to have been the closest to the president in temperament, physical constitution, and ideology. On May 7, 1914, she married Treasury Secretary William G. McAdoo, a widower, in a White House wedding. They divorced in 1934. She wrote *The Woodrow Wilsons* (1937). She settled at Montecito, California, where she died.

BIRTH: Wilson was born December 28, 1856, at the Presbyterian manse in Staunton, Virginia. He was baptized the following April by the Reverend J. H. Smith of Charlottesville, Virginia.

CHILDHOOD: When Wilson was less than a year old, the family moved from his native Staunton, Virginia, to Augusta, Georgia. "My first recollection," said Wilson, "is of standing at my father's gateway in Augusta, Georgia, when I was four years old, and hearing someone pass and say that Mr. Lincoln was elected and there was to be war."[4] He saw General Robert E. Lee pass under Union guard through Augusta in 1865. His earliest impressions, then, were of the Civil War, the devastation of the South, and the humiliation of Reconstruction. Although he left the region as a young adult, he throughout his life regarded himself as a southerner. He believed that the South was fully justified in seceding from the Union; he believed in white supremacy. In 1870 the Wilsons moved to Columbia, South Carolina, and in 1874 to Wilmington, North Carolina. In reading international publications to which his father subscribed, Wilson early developed an interest in British politics and greatly admired Prime Minister William Gladstone. His ambition was for a career in politics. In college he had cards printed to read, "Thomas Woodrow Wilson, Senator from Virginia."

EDUCATION: Wilson was thought to be a slow learner as a young child. He was unable to read until age nine; he had trouble grasping fundamental arithmetic. His weak eyes and frail health undermined his efforts at improvement. Having learned the basics at home from his parents, he at 12 attended the school of Charles Heyward Barnwell in Columbia. In 1873 he entered Davidson College, but poor health forced him to drop out at the end of his freshman year. He performed well there, however, earning averages of 97 in English, 96 in composition, 95 in logic and rhetoric, 94 in Latin, 92 in declamation, 88 in Greek, and 81 in math; he especially enjoyed debating in the Eumenean Society. His health restored, he enrolled at the College of New Jersey (now Princeton) in 1875. Science and math continued to pull his grades down, but he still managed to graduate with a 90 average, thirty-eighth of some 167 students of the class of 1879. In extracurricular activities, he contributed historical articles to the *Nassau Literary Magazine* and an incisive piece on "Cabinet Government in the United States" to the *International Review* and was editor of the *Princetonian*, joined the American Whig Society debating club and organized the Liberal Debating Club for discussion of "political questions of the present century," was president of the baseball association and secretary of the football association, and played Marc Antony in the satirical sketch "The Sanguinary Tragedy of Julius Sneezer." In 1879 he entered the University of Virginia law school but dropped out, again for health reasons, in his second year. He was bored with legal study, pursuing it only as a means to enter politics. He much preferred extracurricular activities at the Charlottesville campus. He was president of the Jefferson Literary Society debating club. He won the orator's prize in arguing the negative of "Is the Roman Catholic Church a menace to American institutions?" but lost the debate to William Cabell Bruce, later U.S. senator from Maryland. He also sang tenor in the glee club and the college quartet. While recuperating at home in Wilmington, North Carolina, Wilson continued to study law on his own and was admitted to the bar in October 1882. He settled briefly in Atlanta, where he practiced law in partnership with Edward I. Renick. In 1883 he decided to give up law and, he thought, his dream of a career in politics, to become an educator. He enrolled as a graduate student at Johns Hopkins University in Baltimore, where he earned a Ph.D. in political science in 1886. There he wrote *Congressional Government* (1885), a critically acclaimed work in which he condemned congressional domination of the other two branches of government and the diffusion of power and responsibility in American democracy and recommended adoption of the British parliamentary system. He also organized the Johns Hopkins glee club. Wilson was the only president to earn a doctorate.

RELIGION: Presbyterian. "My life," Wilson asserted, "would not be worth living if it were not for the driving power of religion, for faith, pure and simple. I have seen all my life the arguments against it without ever having been moved by them. Never for a moment have I had one doubt about my religious beliefs."[5] He believed in providence and predestination and that God had foreordained him president. In the White House he read the Bible daily, said grace before meals, and prayed on his knees each morning and night. He was an elder of the Central Presbyterian Church in Washington and often attended Wednesday evening prayer meetings.

RECREATION: As president, Wilson golfed regularly for exercise on the recommendation of his physician but took little pleasure in the game he defined as "an ineffectual attempt to put an elusive ball into an obscure hole with implements ill-adapted to the purpose."[6] His average for 18 holes was about 115 strokes. He also took up horseback riding as president; his mount was a bay named *Arizona*. On weekends he occasionally cruised Chesapeake Bay aboard the presidential yacht *Mayflower*. He enjoyed the theater, especially vaudeville and musical comedies. A gifted mimic, he delighted in telling dialect jokes in English, Irish, Scottish, and black accents or imitating a drunk. With his daughters he liked to sing or play billiards. He was fond of the poetry of Shelley, Keats, Tennyson, Browning, and Swinburne, the novels of Jane Austen and Sir Walter Scott, and the essays of Lamb and G. K. Chesterton.

MARRIAGE: Woodrow Wilson, 28, married first Ellen Louise Axson, 25, on June 24, 1885, at the home of the bride's paternal grandfather in Savannah, Georgia. Born in Savannah on May 15, 1860, the daughter of the Reverend Samuel E. Axson, a Presbyterian minister, and Margaret Hoyt Axson, Ellen was a lady of refined tastes with a fondness for art, music, and literature. She met Wilson in

April 1883 at the home of his cousin Jesse Woodrow Bones in Rome, Georgia. They were engaged five months later but postponed the wedding while he did postgraduate work at Johns Hopkins and she nursed her ailing father. The wedding was performed jointly by his father, the Reverend Joseph R. Wilson, and her grandfather, the Reverend I.S.K. Axson. They honeymooned at Waynesville, a mountain resort in western North Carolina. As First Lady Mrs. Wilson painted and drew sketches in a studio set up on the third floor of the White House, donating much of her work to charity. She arranged the White House weddings of two of her daughters. She lobbied Congress to fund slum clearance in the District of Columbia. She died of Bright's disease in the White House on August 6, 1914, and was buried with her parents in Rome, Georgia. President Wilson was so devastated at her loss that he confided to aide E. M. House that he hoped to be assassinated.

President Woodrow Wilson, 58, then married Mrs. Edith Bolling Galt, 43, a widow, on December 18, 1915, at the home of the bride in Washington, D.C. Born October 15, 1872, in Wytheville, Virginia, the daughter of William Bolling, a circuit court judge, and Sallie White Bolling, Edith was a great[7]-granddaughter of Pocahontas. She attended private girls schools in Virginia and in 1896 married Norman Galt, a jeweler of Washington, D.C. He died in 1908. In March 1915 she was introduced to President Wilson at the White House by Helen Bones, the president's cousin and official White House hostess since the death of Mrs. Wilson. Wilson invited her to stay to tea and instantly took a liking to the attractive, intelligent widow. The president proposed in May, she consented in July, but the engagement remained secret until October. As news of the courtship became public, there followed much malicious gossip of the president's lack of respect for the memory of his first wife and even rumors that he and Mrs. Galt had murdered the First Lady. A typographical error in a *Washington Post* article drew snickers. "The president spent much of the evening entering [entertaining] Mrs. Galt," said the report of one of their evenings out together. *Post* editors frantically recalled the edition from newsstands but not before some hit the streets. Complicating matters were rumors, apparently groundless, that Wilson had been cheating on his first wife with one Mrs. Peck. Distressed at the effect all this might be having on his fiancé, Wilson offered Mrs. Galt the opportunity to back out of their engagement. She spurned the offer, replying that she would stand by him not for duty, pity, or honor, but for love. The wedding, a small affair attended by some 40 relatives and close friends, was performed jointly by the Reverend Dr. James H. Taylor of Central Presbyterian Church and the Reverend Dr. Herbert Scott Smith of St. Margaret's Episcopal Church, pastors of the groom and bride, respectively. The couple honeymooned two weeks at Hot Springs, Virginia. As First Lady during World War I, Mrs. Wilson observed gasless Sundays, meatless Mondays, and wheatless Tuesdays to set an example for the federal rationing effort. Similarly, she set sheep to graze on the White House lawn rather than waste manpower in mowing it and auctioned off their wool for the benefit of the Red Cross. But her most significant contribution was her service as steward of the executive branch following the president's stroke in September 1919. She carefully screened all matters of state and decided which were important enough to bring to the bedridden president. "I studied every paper sent from the different Secretaries or Senators," she wrote later of her role, "and tried to digest and present in tabloid form the things that, despite my vigilance, had to go to the President. I, myself, never made a single decision regarding the disposition of public affairs. The only decision that was mine was what was important and what was not, and the *very* important decision of when to present matters to my husband."[7] In 1921 Mrs. Wilson retired with the former president to their home on S Street in Washington, nursing him until his death three years later. She later served as director of the Woodrow Wilson Foundation. Her memoir appeared in 1938. In 1961 she attended the inaugural of President Kennedy. She died of congestive heart failure on December 28, 1961, on what would have been Wilson's one-hundred-fifth birthday. She was buried next to the president at the Washington Cathedral.

MILITARY SERVICE: None.

CAREER BEFORE THE PRESIDENCY: During 1885–1888, Wilson taught political economy and public law at Bryn Mawr (Pennsylvania) College for a salary of $1,500 a year. Growing restless in the classroom, he in 1887 applied, unsuccessfully, for a federal vacancy as first assistant secretary of state. During 1888–1890, he was professor of history at Wesleyan University in Middletown, Connecticut, where he also organized a debating society and coached the football team. At the same time he commuted to Baltimore weekly to deliver a series of lectures at Johns Hopkins University. During 1890–1902 he was professor of jurisprudence and political economy at Princeton University. Meanwhile he wrote political and historical works (see "Books by Wilson"), earning a national reputation for sound, insightful scholarship. He opposed the nomination of Democrat William Jennings Bryan in 1896 and bolted the party to vote for John M. Palmer, the National, or "gold" Democrat nominee for president.

President of Princeton University, 1902–1910. The first layman ever to head Princeton, Wilson embarked on an ambitious program to transform the venerable New Jersey university into a vital model of higher education, one emulated by other institutions in the years to come. He discarded the impersonal lecture-hall method for the preceptorial concept in which instructors guided the reading of small groups of students. He also reorganized university departments and redesigned the curriculum. He was less successful, however, in his attempts to abolish the social cliques on campus. His proposal to replace the eating clubs with quadrangles where masses of students from all classes would reside and take meals together under one roof ran into bitter opposition and was rejected. During this time Wilson's political views evolved from conservative to progressive. He voted for Williams Jennings Bryan for president in 1908. In 1909 he was elected the first president of the Short Ballot association, a municipal reform group.

Governor of New Jersey, 1911–1913. At the urging of George Harvey, editor and publisher of the *North American Review*, Wilson in July 1910 agreed to run for governor provided that the nomination came to him unsought and with no strings attached. With the support of the state Democratic machine, Wilson was nominated for governor on the first ballot in September and already was being talked about as a likely candidate for president in 1912. In his acceptance speech, he impressed progressives, who had opposed his nomination, in declaring his independence of the party bosses. He was elected 233,933–184,573 over Republican Vivian M. Lewis in November. Governor Wilson declared war on the bosses, vowing to lance them like warts from the body politic, and secured passage of four significant pieces of reform legislation: (1) the Geran

Law mandated direct party primaries for all elected officials in the state and delegates to national conventions and reformed voting procedures; (2) a corrupt practices act required candidates to file campaign financial statements, limited campaign expenditures, and banned corporate contributions to political campaigns; (3) a state public utility commission empowered to fix utility rates was created; (4) the state's first workmen's compensation law was enacted. Wilson unsuccessfully urged the state legislature to ratify the 16th Amendment, providing for a federal income tax. He brought about enactment of state antitrust laws, but they were repealed after he left office.

DEMOCRATIC PRESIDENTIAL NOMINATION, 1912: Wilson began his campaign for the nomination on a speaking tour of the West in 1911. As Democrats convened in Baltimore in June 1912, progressives were divided in their support of Wilson and House Speaker Champ Clark of Missouri. Southern conservatives were behind Representative Oscar W. Underwood of Alabama. The majority of conservative delegates favored Governor Judson Harmon of Ohio. The key to the nomination lay in the hands of William Jennings Bryan, not a candidate himself but as titular head of the party a great influence at the convention. Wilson's candidacy nearly derailed on publication of a private letter he had written to Princeton trustee Adrian H. Joline in April 1907, in which he said, "Would that we could do something, at once dignified and effective, to knock Mr. Bryan, once and for all, into a cocked hat."[8] But Bryan chose to overlook the insult and let it be known that either Wilson or Clark was acceptable to him. Judge John W. Westcott of New Jersey placed Wilson's name in nomination, calling him "the ultimate Democrat, the genius of liberty, and the very incarnate of progress." On the first ballot, Clark received 440½ votes, Wilson 324, Harmon 148, and Underwood 117½. The figures changed little until the tenth tally, when Tammany Hall forces, heretofore behind Harmon, swung to Clark, giving him 556 votes, a majority but still 170 votes shy of the necessary two thirds. Wilson was now prepared to release his delegates, conceding the nomination to Clark, but at the urging of William G. McAdoo of New York, he agreed to stay in the race a while longer. Meanwhile, Bryan became distressed at Clark's apparent collaboration with Tammany and Wall Street forces. On the fourteenth ballot Bryan endorsed Wilson, thereby checking Clark's momentum. Wilson gained steadily, capturing the lead on the twenty-eighth ballot and climbing to 633 votes on the forty-fifth tally, touching off a stampede that led to his nomination on the next ballot with 990 votes. For vice president Wilson preferred Oscar W. Underwood, who declined. Wilson then agreed to accept the convention favorite, Thomas R. Marshall of Indiana. The Democratic platform favored a lower tariff; enforcement of criminal as well as civil antitrust laws; protection of states' rights; constitutional amendments providing for a federal income tax, direct election of senators, and a single presidential term; extension of the presidential primary system; a ban against corporate campaign contributions and limits on individual contributions; regulation of the railroads, express companies, telegraph, and telephone; banking and currency reform, a workmen's compensation law; stricter pure food and public health laws; and an immediate declaration of intent to recognize the independence of the Philippines.

OPPONENTS: President William Howard Taft (1857–1930) of Ohio; Republican. Although as the incumbent President Taft commanded the support of party professionals, he faced a formidable challenge to his renomination in the candidacy of former president Theodore Roosevelt. Roosevelt, who had handpicked Taft as his successor, returned from his celebrated African safari displeased with what he regarded as the conservative course of Taft's administration. In a major speech at Osawatomie, Kansas in August 1910, Roosevelt called for a New Nationalism that included enforcement of antitrust laws, a ban on corporate campaign contributions, workmen's compensation, and other progressive measures. On February 21, 1912, Roosevelt declared his candidacy with the now-famous phrase "My hat is in the ring." Reminded that as president he had pledged not to seek a third term, Roosevelt explained that he had meant to say no *consecutive* third term. At the party's convention in Chicago in June 1912, bitterness between the two camps erupted into sporadic fights on the floor. Concealed barbed wire guarded the rostrum. With the Taft forces clearly in command, Roosevelt's only chance was to stage a credentials fight, challenging the Taft delegates. But the credentials committee awarded Taft more than 90 percent of the contested seats, thereby ensuring his renomination. Roosevelt then accused Taft of steamroller tactics and ordered his people to take no further part in the convention. Warren G. Harding of Ohio delivered Taft's renomination speech amid jeers from progressives. Robert M. LaFollette of Wisconsin also was placed in nomination, but Roosevelt was not. Thus, Taft was renominated handily on the first ballot with 561 votes to 107 for Roosevelt, 41 for LaFollette, and 348 abstentions. Vice President James S. Sherman of New York also was renominated. The Republican platform pointed with pride to the accomplishments of the Taft administration and favored creation of a federal trade commission with quasi-judicial powers, retention of the protective tariff, banking and currency reform, extension of civil service protection, a ban on corporate campaign contributions, conservation of natural resources consistent with the rights of settlers, prospectors, and miners, and further restrictions on immigration.

Theodore Roosevelt (1858–1919) of New York; Progressive (Bull Moose). Progressive Republicans met in Chicago in August 1912 to nominate Theodore Roosevelt. Governor Hiram Johnson of California was nominated for vice president. The Progressive platform favored primaries for all state and national offices; direct election of senators; ballot initiative, referendum, and recall; an easier method of amending the Constitution; women's suffrage; limits on individual campaign contributions and campaign financial disclosure laws; registration of lobbyists; opening congressional committee hearings to the public and recording committee votes; permitting Supreme Court decisions to be reversed by national referendum; a ban on labor injunctions; national occupational safety standards; prohibition of child labor; a minimum wage for women; a six-day workweek and an eight-hour day; workmen's compensation insurance; a social security system; improved educational standards; creation of a national health service; strengthening the Interstate Commerce Commission; currency reform; maintenance of the protective tariff only to the extent that it benefits labor; graduated inheritance and income taxes; greater assimilation of the immigrant population away from the central cities; and a federal securities commission to supervise public offerings of stocks and bonds.

CAMPAIGN AND THE ISSUES, 1912: With Republicans divided between Taft and Roosevelt, Wilson was virtually assured of election. Still, it proved a spirited campaign as Roosevelt and Wilson stumped the country while the president, after making a few speeches, retired to the White House. Wilson offered voters the New Freedom, pledging to end monopoly, restore free competition, and establish the right of labor to bargain collectively for its welfare. He denounced the trusts as "a great incubus on the productive part of American brains."[9] Roosevelt's New Nationalism went further, promising federal regulation of business on an unprecedented scale and comprehensive social welfare legislation, as embodied in the Progressive platform. The campaign was interrupted in October with an assassination attempt on Roosevelt (see "Theodore Roosevelt, 26th President," "Retirement"). As Wilson realized that he was headed for victory, he succeeded in shifting the focus of the campaign to the election of a Democratic majority in Congress. A week before the election New York bookmakers were giving odds of 6–1 for Wilson. Wilson owed his success less to personal popularity than to the split in Republican ranks, for he was to win with fewer votes than Bryan received in each of his three defeats in 1896, 1900, and 1908.

ELECTION AS PRESIDENT, FIRST TERM, NOVEMBER 5, 1912:

Popular Vote. Wilson (Democrat), 6,286,820 (42%); Roosevelt (Progressive, or Bull Moose), 4,126,020 (27%); Taft (Republican), 3,483,922 (23%); Eugene V. Debs (Socialist), 901,255 (6%).

Electoral Vote: Wilson, 435; Roosevelt, 88; Taft, 8.

States Carried: Wilson won the majority of electoral votes in 40 states— Alabama, Arizona, Arkansas, Colorado, Connecticut, Delaware, Florida, Georgia, Idaho, Illinois, Indiana, Iowa, Kansas, Kentucky, Louisiana, Maine, Maryland, Massachusetts, Mississippi, Missouri, Montana, Nebraska, Nevada, New Hampshire, New Jersey, New Mexico, New York, North Carolina, North Dakota, Ohio, Oklahoma, Oregon, Rhode Island, South Carolina, Tennessee, Texas, Virginia, West Virginia, Wisconsin, and Wyoming. Roosevelt won the majority of electoral votes in 6 states—California, Michigan, Minnesota, Pennsylvania, South Dakota, and Washington. Taft won the electoral votes of two states—Utah and Vermont.

DEMOCRATIC NOMINATION FOR REELECTION AS PRESIDENT, 1916:

Wilson's renomination was ensured as Democrats convened in St. Louis in June 1916. Judge John W. Westcott of New Jersey again delivered Wilson's nominating speech. Wilson was renominated on the first ballot, 1092–1. Vice President Marshall also was renominated. The Democratic platform coined the party's campaign theme, "He kept us out of war." The platform also favored military preparedness, a world association of nations to secure peace and maintain national and individual rights, Pan-American unity, health and safety standards and a retirement system for federal employees, a ban on child labor, creation of a federal bureau of safety, strengthening the bureau of mines, establishment of federal tuberculosis sanitariums for the needy, women's suffrage, and prison reform.

OPPONENT: Charles Evans Hughes (1862–1948) of New York; Republican. Born in Glen Falls, New York, the son of a Baptist preacher, Hughes graduated from Brown University in 1881 and Columbia University law school in 1884. He taught law briefly at Cornell University and served as legal counsel in investigations of the utility and insurance industries. Elected governor of New York, 1907–1910, over William Randolph Hearst, he established the state Public Service Commission to regulate the utilities and railroads. He was appointed to the Supreme Court in 1910 (see "William Howard Taft, 27th President," "Supreme Court Appointments"). He did not seek the Republican nomination in

1916 and as a supreme court justice had not commented on public issues for six years. Nevertheless, he was the front-runner at the party's convention in Chicago in June. On the first ballot Hughes led with 253½ to 105 for Senator John W. Weeks of Massachusetts and 103 for Elihu Root of New York. Hughes picked up another 70 votes on the next tally, sparking a rush to his banner that gave him 949½ votes and the nomination, to 37½ for all others, on the third ballot. Former vice president Charles W. Fairbanks of Indiana was nominated for vice president. The Republican platform condemned Wilson's failure to protect U.S. interests abroad and called for "a strict and honest neutrality." It also favored establishment of a world court, restoration of friendly relations with Mexico, closer ties with Latin America, retention of the Philippines, stronger national defense, a higher tariff, a ban on child labor, workmen's compensation insurance, and women's suffrage. After his defeat by Wilson, Hughes served as secretary of state in the Harding and Coolidge administrations, a member of the Hague Tribunal 1926–1930, judge of the World Court 1928–1930, and U.S. chief justice 1930–1941 (see "Herbert Hoover, 31st President," "Supreme Court Appointments").

CAMPAIGN AND THE ISSUES, 1916: The war in Europe dominated the campaign. "He kept us out of war" was the successful Democratic slogan. Republican Hughes criticized the president for failing to assert American neutral rights in the conflict. Organized labor supported Wilson for his efforts on their behalf. Theodore Roosevelt, who advocated U.S. participation in the war, endorsed Hughes, bringing many Progressives with him. Catholics lined up behind Hughes in protest against Wilson's hostile policy toward Catholic Mexico. Hughes was the odds-on favorite as election day drew near. Some news sources even projected Hughes the winner. But late returns tipped California, and with it the election, to Wilson.

REELECTION AS PRESIDENT, NOVEMBER 7, 1916:

Popular Vote: Wilson (Democrat), 9,129,606 (49%); Hughes (Republican), 8,538,221 (46%).

Electoral Vote: Wilson, 277; Hughes, 254.

States Carried: Wilson won the majority of electoral votes in 30 states— Alabama, Arizona, Arkansas, California, Colorado, Florida, Georgia, Idaho, Kansas, Kentucky, Louisiana, Maryland, Mississippi, Missouri, Montana, Nebraska, Nevada, New Hampshire, New Mexico, North Carolina, North Dakota, Ohio, Oklahoma, South Carolina, Tennessee, Texas, Utah, Virginia, Washington, and Wyoming. Hughes won the majority of electoral votes in 18 states— Connecticut, Delaware, Illinois, Indiana, Iowa, Maine, Massachusetts, Michigan, Minnesota, New Jersey, New York, Oregon, Pennsylvania, Rhode Island, South Dakota, Vermont, West Virginia, and Wisconsin.

INAUGURAL ADDRESS (FIRST): March 4, 1913. ". . . Our life contains every great thing, and contains it in rich abundance.

"But the evil has come with the good, and much fine gold has been corroded. With riches has come inexcusable waste. We have squandered a great part of what we might have used, and have not stopped to conserve the exceeding bounty of nature, without which our genius for enterprise would have been worthless and impotent, scorning to be careful, shamefully prodigal as well as admirably efficient. We have been proud of our industrial achievements, but we have not hitherto stopped thoughtfully enough to count the human cost, the cost of lives snuffed out, of energies overtaxed and broken, the fearful physical and spiritual cost to the men and women and children upon whom the dead weight and burden of it all has fallen pitilessly the years through. The groans and agony of it all had not yet reached our ears, the solemn, moving undertone of our life, coming up out of the mines and factories and out of every home where the struggle had its intimate and familiar seat. With the great Government went many deep secret things which we too long delayed to look into and scrutinize with candid, fearless eyes. The great Government we loved has too often been made use of for private and selfish purposes, and those who used it had forgotten the people. . . .

"There has been something crude and heartless and unfeeling in our haste to succeed and be great. Our thought has been 'Let every man look out for himself, let every generation look out for itself,' while we reared giant machinery which made it impossible that any but those who stood at the levers of control should have a chance to look out for themselves. . . ."

INAUGURAL ADDRESS (SECOND): March 5, 1917. ". . . We are provincials no longer. The tragic events of the thirty months of vital turmoil through which we have just passed have made us citizens of the world. There can be no turning back. Our own fortunes as a nation are involved whether we would have it so or not. . . .

"These, therefore, are the things we shall stand for, whether in war or in peace:

That all nations are equally interested in the peace of the world and in the political stability of free peoples, and equally responsible for their maintenance; that the essential principle of peace is the actual equality of nations in all matters of right or privilege; that peace cannot securely or justly rest upon an armed balance of power; that governments derive all their just powers from the consent of the governed and that no other powers should be supported by the common thought, purpose or power of the family of nations; that the seas should be equally free and safe for the use of all peoples, under rules set up by common agreement and consent, and that, so far as practicable, they should be accessible to all upon equal terms; that national armaments shall be limited to the necessities of national order and domestic safety; that the community of interest and of power upon which peace must henceforth depend imposes upon each nation the duty of seeing to it that all influences proceeding from its own citizens meant to encourage or assist revolution in other states should be sternly and effectually suppressed and prevented. . . ."

VICE PRESIDENT: Thomas Riley Marshall (1854–1925), of Indiana, served 1913–1921. Born in North Manchester, Indiana, Marshall graduated from Wabash College in 1873, was admitted to the bar in 1875, and practiced law successfully in Columbia City, Indiana. As governor of Indiana 1909–1913, he established a child labor law and prison reform. As vice president he at first opposed U.S. entry into World War I but loyally supported the administration and spurned suggestions that he assume the presidency following Wilson's disabling stroke in 1919. He is best remembered for his ready wit. Listening to Senator Joseph L. Bristow of Kansas drone on in a floor speech on "What This Country Needs," Marshall, from his perch as presiding officer, interjected, "What this country needs is a really good five-cent cigar." On the significance of his office, he commented, "Once there were two brothers. One ran away to sea, the other was elected vice president, and nothing was ever heard of either of them again." After leaving office he practiced law in Indianapolis.

CABINET:

Secretary of State. (1) William Jennings Bryan (1860–1925), of Nebraska, served 1913–1915. He had run for president three times (see "William McKinley, 25th President," "Opponent, 1896, 1900"; "William Howard Taft, 27th President," "Opponent, 1908"). As secretary he negotiated arbitration treaties with various nations. Committed to U.S. neutrality during the early years of World War I, he objected to what he regarded as the pro-British policy of the administration and resigned in protest against Wilson's belligerent note to Germany following the sinking of the *Lusitania*. (2) Robert Lansing (1864–1928), of New York, served 1915–1920. Promoted from counselor of the State Department, Lansing was an early advocate of U.S. entry into World War I. He arranged for the purchase from Denmark of what is now the U.S. Virgin Islands for $25 million. He concluded the Lansing-Ishii Agreement of 1917, in which the United States adjusted the Open Door policy in recognizing Japan's special interests in China; the agreement was abrogated in 1923. He tried in vain to dissuade President Wilson from attending the Paris Peace Conference. Lansing also attended but took little part in the proceedings. He had grave reservations about the Treaty of Versailles and the proposed League of Nations. As reports of Lansing's dissatisfaction reached the press, Wilson began to question his loyalty to the administration. The final break came when, while the president was bedridden from a stroke, Lansing convened cabinet meetings on his own authority. Wilson asked for and received his resignation. Lansing's accounts of the Versailles proceedings, *The Big Four and Others at the Peace Conference* and *The Peace Negotiations: A Personal Narrative*, appeared in 1921. (3) Bainbridge Colby (1869–1950), of New York, served 1920–1921. Denouncing as "agitators of dangerous revolt" the Bolshevik leaders who came to power in the wake of the Russian Revolution in 1917, Colby set forth the U.S. policy of refusing to recognize the new government; the United States did not recognize the Soviet Union until 1933.

Secretary of the Treasury. (1) William G. McAdoo (1863–1941), of New York, served 1913–1918. He was the first chairman of the Federal Reserve Board. During World War I, he ran the nation's railroads, taken over by the government for the duration, and directed Liberty Bond drives. He married the president's daughter Eleanor Wilson in a White House ceremony in 1914. He was a leading candidate for the Democratic presidential nomination in 1920 and 1924. (2) Carter Glass (1858–1946), of Virginia, served 1918–1920. He had served as chairman of the House Banking and Currency Committee and cosponsored the Glass-Owen Act of 1913 creating the Federal Reserve system. He resigned as secretary to enter the Senate. (3) David F. Houston (1866–1940), of Missouri, served 1920–1921. He was transferred from agriculture secretary. He wrote *Eight Years with Wilson's Cabinet* (2 vols., 1926).

Secretary of War. (1) Lindley M. Garrison (1864–1932), of New Jersey, served 1913–1916. He favored a strong military buildup, a stern policy toward Mexico, and retention of the Philippines. He resigned following Wilson's refusal to insist that Congress authorize a substantial increase in the size of the regular army and creation of a reserve force. (2) Newton D. Baker (1871–1937), of Ohio, served 1916–1921. He directed the U.S. expedition against the guerrillas of Pancho Villa along the Mexican border. A pacifist, he was slow to prepare for World War I, but once hostilities began he instituted the draft and quadrupled the size of the army to four million men. Bureaucratic and logistical inefficiences in the department drew criticism, however.

Attorney General. (1) James C. McReynolds (1862–1946), of Tennessee, served 1913–1914. He vigorously enforced the antitrust laws, notably against American Telephone and Telegraph, the U.S. Thread Association, the National Wholesale Jewelers Association, and the New Haven Railroad. He resigned to accept appointment to the Supreme Court. (2) Thomas W. Gregory (1861–1933), of Texas, served 1914–1919. At the president's direction, he reluctantly suspended antitrust action against industries vital to the war effort. (3) A. Mitchell Palmer (1872–1936), of Pennsylvania, served 1919–1921. He was promoted from alien property custodian. On the basis of the Espionage Act of 1917 and the Sedition Act of 1918, he launched a controversial attack against dissidents and aliens designed to thwart what he believed to be Bolshevik-inspired anarchy. The so-called Palmer Raids drew heated protest from some quarters for a disregard of basic civil liberties. He was a candidate for the Democratic presidential nomination in 1920.

Secretary of the Navy. Josephus Daniels (1862–1948), of North Carolina, served 1913–1921. He directed the naval effort during World War I with the aid of Assistant Secretary Franklin D. Roosevelt, who later as president appointed him ambassador to Mexico, 1933–1942. He wrote *Our Navy at War* (1922), *Life of Woodrow Wilson* (1924), and *The Wilson Era* (1944–1946).

Postmaster General. Albert S. Burleson (1863–1937), of Texas, served 1913–1921. He was chairman of the House Post Office and Post Roads Committee. He was extremely unpopular with postal workers because of his hostility toward their attempts to unionize. During World War I he vigorously enforced mail censorship, banning leftist literature and hiring an army of censors to examine the contents of some 125,000 pieces of suspicious mail daily.

Secretary of the Interior. (1) Franklin K. Lane (1864–1921), of California, served 1913–1920. He was chairman of the Interstate Commerce Commission. He promoted conservation, greater autonomy for Indians, and development of Alaska. He was instrumental in the establishment of the National Park Service in 1916 and named noted conservationist Stephen Tyng Mather as its first director. (2) John B. Payne (1855–1935), of Illinois, served 1920–1921. He developed national parks and protected naval oil reserves.

Secretary of Agriculture. (1) David F. Houston (1866–1940), of Missouri, served 1913–1920. He established the federal farm loan system and the cooperative extension service. He resigned to become Treasury secretary. (2) Edwin T. Meredith (1876–1928), of Iowa, served 1920–1921. A publisher of farming periodicals, he later founded what became *Better Homes and Gardens* magazine.

Secretary of Commerce. (1) William C. Redfield (1858–1932), of New York, served 1913–1919. He was the first secretary of commerce. He championed business interests within the cabinet but exerted little influence on the president. (2) Joshua W. Alexander (1852–1936), of Missouri, served 1919–1921.

Secretary of Labor. William B. Wilson (1862–1934), of Pennsylvania, served 1913–1921. A founder of the United Mine Workers, he as chairman of the House Labor Committee had been instrumental in creating the Department of Labor and drafting prolabor legislation. As the first labor secretary, he established the U.S. Employment Service.

ADMINISTRATION: March 4, 1913–March 3, 1921.

Underwood Tariff, 1913. This act replaced the Payne-Aldrich Tariff (1909; see "William Howard Taft, 27th President," "Administration"). To redeem campaign pledges to reduce the tariff, President Wilson addressed Congress in person (the last president to do so had been John Adams) to urge immediate action. Congress responded with the Underwood Tariff, sponsored by Democratic Representative Oscar W. Underwood of Alabama, which reduced the average rate from 41 to 27 percent and placed on the free list such items as iron, steel, and raw wool. It also provided for a federal income tax in accordance with the 16th Amendment, placing a 1 percent tax on individual incomes above $3,000 and an additional graduated surtax of 1–6 percent on incomes above $20,000. It was replaced by the Emergency Tariff Act of 1921 and the Fordney-McCumber Act of 1922 (see "Warren G. Harding, 29th President," "Administration").

Federal Reserve Act, 1913. Sponsored by Democratic Representative Carter Glass of Virginia and Democratic Senator Robert L. Owen of Oklahoma, this law created the modern Federal Reserve system. Designed to make the nation's money supply more elastic in order to cope with changing economic conditions and curb banking abuses, it established a system of 12 regional banks, governed by a board appointed by the president, which in turn were to serve as bankers' banks. All national banks, as well as those state banks willing to participate, were required to keep a portion of their capital on deposit at a federal reserve. The "Fed" also loaned money to member banks and by varying the interest rate, known as the discount rate, it was now able to control credit, tightening it in boom times, relaxing it in periods of economic contraction, and thus smoothing out the wild fluctuations typical of past business cycles.

Federal Trade Commission, 1914. President Wilson urged its creation so as to allow small business better to compete with big business and "to kill monopoly in the seed." The quasi-judicial body, appointed by the president, was authorized to investigate the business practices of interstate corporations (except banks and the common carriers already provided for in other legislation) and order an end to "unfair methods of competition." Its powers were limited by subsequent Supreme Court rulings, however.

Clayton Anti-Trust Act, 1914. Sponsored by Democratic Representative Henry DeLamar Clayton of Alabama, it is known as the labor Magna Carta for its provisions exempting labor and agricultural associations from the antitrust laws, curbing the use of the labor injunction, and legalizing such tools of collective bargaining as strikes, pickets, and boycotts. Its other provisions barred corporations from acquiring stock in a competitor and otherwise sought to curb the monopolistic tendencies of big business.

Child Labor Laws. The Keating-Owen Act, 1916, barred the interstate shipment of goods manufactured by children but was struck down by the Supreme Court (*Hammer* v. *Dagenhart*, 1918). Congress responded with the Child Labor Act, 1919, placing a 10 percent tax on the profits of companies employing children. This, too, was declared unconstitutional (*Bailey* v. *Drexel Furniture Co.*, 1922).

Adamson Act, 1916. To avert a threatened railroad strike on the advent of U.S. entry into World War I, President Wilson persuaded Congress to enact this bill, sponsored by Democratic Representative William C. Adamson of Georgia, fixing the eight-hour day for trainmen. It paved the way for general acceptance of the eight-hour day.

Relations with Mexico. The rapidly shifting forces of the Mexican Revolution brought to power the reactionary Victoriano Huerta in 1913. President Wilson refused to recognize his government and instead adopted a policy of "watchful waiting." To answer hawkish critics calling for a U.S. invasion of Mexico, Wilson set forth the Mobile Doctrine in October 1913 in a speech before the Southern Commercial Congress in Alabama, in which he declared that the United States never again would acquire territory by conquest. Relations with Mexico continued to deteriorate, however, in the wake of the Tampico incident in April 1914, in which Mexican authorities arrested U.S. sailors at Tampico. Although the sailors were quickly released, the United States demanded a 21-gun salute to the American flag as an appropriate apology. When Huerta refused, Wilson dispatched Marines to occupy Vera Cruz. War seemed inevitable, but at the intercession of Argentina, Brazil, and Chile, tempers cooled. Unable to consolidate his grip on the country, Huerta resigned in July 1914. In his place arose Venustiano Carranza, whose government the United States recognized in 1915. But Carranza, too, failed to maintain order in the country, as revolutionaries under Pancho Villa controlled much of northern Mexico. In March 1916 Villa crossed the border and raided the town of Columbus, New Mexico, killing 17 Americans. Wilson responded by dispatching 6,000 troops under General John J. Pershing to round up Villa and his men. Pershing penetrated hundreds of miles into Mexico in pursuit of the elusive Villa but succeeded only in arousing the ire of Carranza for invading Mexican soil. Wilson called off the expedition in February 1917. That same month Wilson received from British intelligence an intercepted message from German Foreign Minister Arthur Zimmerman to the German minister in Mexico. In this note Germany proposed an alliance with Mexico in the event that the United States entered World War I. "We shall give general financial support," read the Zimmerman telegram, "and it is understood that Mexico is to reconquer the lost territory in New Mexico, Texas, and Arizona." Release of the message in March 1917 galvanized U.S. public opinion against Germany.

World War I, 1914–1918. The immediate cause of the war was the assassination of Archduke Francis Ferdinand of Austria-Hungary by Gavrilo Princip, a 19-year-old Serbian nationalist, in Sarajevo in June 1914. The chief underlying cause was the militant nationalism that had been mounting in Europe for decades. The conflict pitted the Central Powers (Germany, Austria-Hungary, Turkey, and Bulgaria) against the Allied Powers (Great Britain, France, Russia, Italy, Japan, Portugal, certain Latin American nations, China, Greece, and, from 1917, the United States). With the outbreak of the war in August 1914, President Wilson appealed to Americans to remain strictly neutral. Eventually, however, German submarine warfare and the Americans' natural affinity for the British prodded the United States to join the Allies. In May 1915 a German submarine torpedoed the British liner *Lusitania* off the coast of Ireland, killing 1,200, including more than 120 American passengers. The incident raised a clamor for war in the United States, but still Wilson resisted. Speaking before a group of newly naturalized citizens days after the sinking, he said, "There is such a thing as a man being too proud to fight. There is such a thing as a nation being so right that it does not need to convince others by force that it is right."[10] American protests prompted Germany to suspend unrestricted submarine warfare for a time, but sinkings still occured, and in February 1917 Germany officially resumed the practice. Meanwhile Wilson placed U.S. defenses on a war footing while pressing for a negotiated settlement. In an address before the Senate in January 1917 he called on the belligerents to accept "peace without victory." The effort inevitably failed. Following Germany's resumption of unrestricted submarine warfare and publication of the Zimmerman telegram (see "Administration: Relations with Mexico"), Wilson appeared before a joint session of Congress on April 2, 1917, to ask for a declaration of war against Germany. "The present German submarine warfare against commerce," he said, "is a war against mankind. It is a war against all nations. . . . We are accepting this challenge of hostile purpose because we know that in such a Government, following such methods, we can never have a friend; and that in the presence of its organized power, always lying in wait to accomplish we know not what purpose, there can be no assured security for the democratic Governments of the world. . . . We are glad . . . to fight thus for the ultimate peace of the world and for the liberation of its peoples, the German peoples included. . . . The world must be made safe for democracy. Its peace must be planted upon the tested foundations of political liberty. We have no selfish ends to serve. We desire no conquest, no dominion. We seek no indemnities for ourselves, no material compensation for the sacrifices we shall freely make. We are but one of the champions of the rights of mankind." On April 4 the Senate voted 82–6 to declare war; the House concurred 373–50 on April 6.

The American Expeditionary Force, led by General John J. Pershing, fought overseas independent of Allied control. As such, it was instrumental in turning the tide against the Central Powers, taking part in engagements at Chateau-Thierry and Belleau Wood in June 1918, the Second Battle of the Marne in July 1918, Saint-Mihiel in September 1918, and the Meuse-Argonne offensive during September–November 1918. Meanwhile, in January 1918, President Wilson set forth the Fourteen Points, the only basis, he insisted, on which a lasting peace could be made: (1) open treaties, openly arrived at; (2) absolute freedom of navigation on the seas in peace and war; (3) removal of all economic barriers and establishment of equal trade conditions among all parties to the peace; (4) multilateral arms reductions; (5) adjustment of colonial claims based on the interests of the populations concerned; (6) evacuation of all Russian territory; (7) evacuation and restoration of Belgium; (8) all French territory to be freed and restored and Alsace-Lorraine to be awarded to France; (9) realignment of Italian frontiers along lines of nationality; (10) peoples of Austria-Hungary to be accorded opportunity for autonomous development; (11) evacuation and restoration of Rumania, Serbia, and Montenegro; (12) sovereignty for the Turkish portion of the Ottoman Empire but autonomy for other nationalities then under Turkish rule and free access to the Dardanelles for ships of all nations; (13) an independent Poland with access to the sea; (14) a general association of nations to guarantee political independence and territorial integrity for all members. The Armistice was signed on November 11, 1918. U.S. casualties numbered more than 300,000, including 53,000 killed in action and 63,000 dead from war-related disease or accident.

President Wilson personally led the American delegation to the Paris Peace Conference, proceedings dominated by the Big Four—Wilson, Premier Georges Clemenceau of France, Prime Minister David Lloyd George of Great Britain, and Premier Vittorio Orlando of Italy. The Treaty of Versailles, 1919, placed full blame for the war on Germany. It stripped Germany of all colonial possessions, awarded the Saar basin coal lands and Alsace-Lorraine to France, the Sudentenland to Czechoslovakia, certain regions to Belgium, and the Polish corridor to Poland; demilitarized the Rhineland, virtually abolished the German armed forces, and imposed war reparations of $15 billion plus an indeterminate future sum. It also provided for the establishment of the League of Nations. Wilson marshaled the full weight of his office on behalf of U.S. participation in the League. He embarked on a national speaking tour in September 1919 to promote it. After delivering dozens of speeches in 29 cities in three weeks, he suffered a physical breakdown in Pueblo, Colorado, and hastily returned to Washington. Days later he suffered a stroke from which he never fully recovered. Because neither the Constitution nor precedent provided guidance in coping with the disability of a president, the nation faced a real crisis of leadership. During his convalescence Wilson chose not to relinquish, even temporarily, the office and duties of the president to the vice president; no one challenged his authority to do so. Although he continued to make decisions from his sickbed, Mrs. Wilson decided which matters were important enough to bring to his attention (see "Marriage"). Meanwhile Republican Senator Henry Cabot Lodge of Massachusetts, chairman of the Senate Foreign Relations Committee, led the fight to add relatively minor reservations to the treaty, reservations Wilson stubbornly refused to accept. As a result, the Senate failed to ratify the treaty. The United States never joined the League. For his efforts to achieve world peace and establish the League, Wilson was awarded the 1919 Nobel Peace Prize. A separate peace treaty with Germany was concluded in 1921 (see "Warren G. Harding, 29th President," "Administration"). The result of World War I was to sow the seeds of resentment and revenge among the German people, conditions that contributed to the rise of Adolf Hitler. Of all the belligerents, only the United States and Japan emerged from the war more powerful. The United States had become a major world power. Much of its industry, particularly the chemical industry, had grown dynamically during the war and would continue to flourish in the years ahead.

Constitutional Amendments Ratified. Seventeenth Amendment, 1913. It provided for the election of U.S. senators directly by the people. Heretofore senators were elected by state legislatures. Eighteenth Amendment, 1919. Prohibition of alcoholic beverages. Nineteenth Amendment, 1920. Extended the right to vote to women.

SUPREME COURT APPOINTMENTS: (1) James C. McReynolds (1862–1946), of Tennessee, served as associate justice 1914–1941. Generally regarded at the time of his appointment as a liberal because of his prosecution of the antitrust laws as special counsel to the attorney general 1907–1912 and as attorney general 1913–1914, Justice McReynolds became increasingly conservative, joining the majority that in the 1930s invalidated much of the early New Deal program of President Franklin Roosevelt. (2) Louis D. Brandeis (1856–1941), of Massachusetts, served as associate justice 1916–1939. His appointment drew strong, often emotional, criticism, both because he would be the first Jewish Supreme Court justice and for his reputation as "the people's attorney" espousing what some regarded as radical causes. His abilities, however, were never at issue; he characteristically employed what came to be called the "Brandeis brief," copious documentation of economic and sociological data to buttress legal argument. On the bench, he was known chiefly for his dissents from the conservative majority. He argued repeatedly that the acts of legislatures attempting to cope with changing social and economic conditions deserve a presumption of constitutionality. Typical of his philosophy was his dissent in *New State Ice Co.* v. *Liebmann* (1932), which struck down Oklahoma's attempt to regulate the ice industry in that state. "It is one of the happy incidents of the federal system," wrote Brandeis, "that a single courageous state may, if its citizens choose, serve as a laboratory, and try novel social economic experiments without risk to the rest of the country. This Court has the power to prevent an experiment. . . . But, in the exercise of this high power, we must ever be on our guard, lest we erect our prejudices into legal principles. If we would guide by the light of reason, we must let our minds be bold." (3) John H. Clarke (1857–1945), of Ohio, served as associate justice 1916–1922. He was a U.S. district court judge. He often joined Oliver Wendell Holmes and Brandeis in dissent from the conservative majority. In perhaps his most significant majority opinion (Hardwood Lumber case, 1921), he applied the antitrust laws to the price-fixing practices of trade associations.

RANKING IN 1962 HISTORIANS POLL: Wilson ranked fourth of 31 presidents, fourth of 5 "great" presidents. He ranked above Jefferson, below Franklin Roosevelt.

RETIREMENT: March 4, 1921–February 3, 1924. Wilson rode to the Capitol with his successor, Warren G. Harding, but did not stay for the Inaugural. The Wilsons retired to their recently acquired red brick house on S Street in Washington, where the former president spent his final years in failing health. He tried practicing law in partnership with Bainbridge Colby, his former secretary of state, but was unable to do more than discuss legal matters at home. He could read only with the aid of a magnifying glass and eventually was virtually blind. He attended the funeral of President Harding in Washington in August 1923. On November 10, 1923, he delivered his only radio address. Unfamiliar with the device, he concluded his remarks on the significance of Armistice Day and then said, within range of his still-live microphone, "That's all, isn't it?" Next day he uttered his last public words to a crowd gathered outside his home, concluding, "I am not one of those that have the least anxiety about the triumph of the principles I have stood for. I have seen fools resist Providence before, and I have seen their destruction, as will come upon these again, utter destruction and contempt. That we shall prevail is as sure as that God reigns."[11]

DEATH: February 3, 1924, 11:15 A.M., at home, Washington, D.C. As president, Wilson had contracted influenza during the epidemic of 1918 and thereafter suffered acute asthma attacks that deprived him of sleep and sapped his strength. On October 2, 1919, he suffered a stroke paralyzing his left side and slurring his speech. He recovered sufficiently to walk haltingly with a cane. On January 31, 1924, he experienced acute indigestion and grew steadily weaker. Dr. Cary Grayson was summoned from a vacation to discover the former president near death. On February 1 Wilson said falteringly, "I am a broken piece of machinery. When the machinery is broken. . . ." He fell silent, then added, "I am ready."[12] These were his last words except for a cry for his wife the next day. He fell unconscious but opened his eyes for 10 minutes shortly before he died, his right hand held by his wife, his left by daughter Margaret. There was no state funeral. The Reverend James Taylor of Central Presbyterian Church, the Reverend Sylvester Beach of Princeton University, and Bishop James Freeman of the Washington Cathedral conducted simple services at the home before the funeral at the Bethlehem Chapel of the Washington Cathedral, then still under construction, where he was buried. He is the only president buried in Washington. In his last will and testament, Wilson left his estate to his wife, except for an annuity amounting to about $2,500 a year for his daughter Margaret as long as she remained unmarried.

WILSON PRAISED: "[Wilson] is a clean, learned, honorable, and patriotic man."[13]—Warren G. Harding, 1912

"Mr. Wilson is a fine, humorous, cultivated American gentleman. . . . Here at last we have a president whose real interest in life centers around the common man, and on whom we can count to serve that man so far as his ability goes."[14]—Ida M. Tarbell, journalist and author, 1916

"Mr. Wilson's mind was richly stored and disciplined to almost perfect precision. . . . His 'single track mind' was never deflected to long consideration of any question that did not head up in how government should be best administered and made to advance the common weal."[15]—Josephus Daniels, Wilson's navy secretary, 1924

"Three qualities of greatness stood out in Woodrow Wilson. He was a man of staunch morals. He was more than just an idealist; he was the personification of the heritage of idealism of the American people. He brought spiritual concepts to the peace table. He was a born crusader."[16]—Herbert Hoover, 1958

WILSON CRITICIZED: "I regard him as a ruthless hypocrite, and as an opportunist, who has not convictions that he would not barter at once for votes. . . . He surrenders a conviction, previously expressed, without the slightest hesitation, and never even vouchsafes to the public the arguments upon which he was induced to change his mind."[17]—William Howard Taft, 1916

"For Heaven's sake never allude to Wilson as an idealist or militaire or altruist. He is a doctrinaire when he can be so with safety to his personal ambition. . . . He hasn't a touch of idealism in him. His advocacy of the League of Nations no more represents idealism on his part than his advocacy of peace without victory. . . . He is a silly doctrinaire at times and an utterly selfish and cold-blooded politician always."[18]—Theodore Roosevelt, 1919

"The President is the most prejudiced man I ever knew and likes but few people."[19]—Colonel E. M. House, Wilson adviser, 1919

"He thinks he is another Jesus Christ come upon the earth to reform men."[20]—French President Georges Clemenceau, 1919

WILSON QUOTES: "It is not men that interest or disturb me primarily; it is ideas. Ideas live; men die."[21]

"If you think too much about being reelected, it is very difficult to be worth reelecting."[22]—1913

"The President is a superior kind of slave, and must content himself with the reflection that the *kind* is superior!"[23]

"The Americans who went to Europe to die are a unique breed. Never before have men crossed the seas to a foreign land to fight for a cause which they did not pretend was peculiarly their own, which they knew was the cause of humanity and mankind. These Americans gave the greatest of all gifts, the gift of life and the gift of spirit."[24]

BOOKS BY WILSON: *Congressional Government: A Study in American Politics* (1885); *The State: Elements of Historical and Practical Politics* (1889); *George Washington* (1893); *An Old Master, and Other Political Essays* (1893); *More*

Literature and Other Essays (1896); *A History of the American People* (5 vols., 1902); *President Wilson's Case for the League of Nations* (1923).

BOOKS ABOUT WILSON: Baker, Ray Stannard, *Woodrow Wilson: Life and Letters.* 8 vols. New York: Doubleday, Doran & Co., 1927–1939.

Link, Arthur S. *Wilson.* 5 vols. Princeton, N.J.: Princeton University Press, 1947–1965.

Link, Arthur S., et al. *The Papers of Woodrow Wilson.* Princeton, N.J.: Princeton University Press, 1966– .

Smith, Gene. *When the Cheering Stopped: The Last Years of Woodrow Wilson.* New York: Morrow, 1964.

Tribble, Edwin, ed. *A President in Love: The Courtship Letters of Woodrow Wilson and Edith Bolling Galt.* Boston: Houghton, Mifflin, 1981.

Walworth, Arthur. *Wilson and His Peacemakers: American Diplomacy at the Paris Peace Conference.* New York: Norton, 1986.

NOTES:

1 Arthur S. Link, *Wilson*, Princeton, N.J.: Princeton University Press, 1947–1965, vol. II, p. 67.
2 Joseph P. Tumulty, *Woodrow Wilson as I Know Him*, New York: AMS Press, 1921, p. 457.
3 Sigmund Freud and William C. Bullitt, *Thomas Woodrow Wilson: A Psychological Study*, Boston: Houghton, Mifflin, 1966, p. 10.
4 Link, vol. I, p. 1.
5 Arthur Walworth, *Woodrow Wilson: American Prophet*, New York: Longmans, Green, 1958, p. 417.
6 Frank Cormier, *Presidents Are People Too*, Washington: Public Affairs Press, 1966, p. 124.
7 Edith Bolling Wilson, *My Memoir*, Indianapolis: Bobbs-Merrill, 1938, p. 289.
8 Josephus Daniels, *The Wilson Era 1910–1917*, Chapel Hill, N.C.: University of North Carolina Press, 1944, p. 31.
9 Link, vol. I, p. 520.
10 Louis Filler, ed., *The President Speaks*, New York: Putnam's Sons, 1964, p. 108.
11 Gene Smith, *When the Cheering Stopped: The Last Years of Woodrow Wilson*, New York: Morrow, 1964, p. 232.
12 Ibid., pp. 237–238.
13 Francis Russell, *The Shadow of Blooming Grove: Warren G. Harding in His Times*, New York: McGraw-Hill, 1968, p. 236.
14 Link, vol. V, p. 117.
15 Josephus Daniels, *The Life of Woodrow Wilson*, [n.p.]: Will H. Johnston, 1924, p. 14.
16 Herbert Hoover, *The Ordeal of Wilson*, New York: McGraw-Hill, 1958, p. viii.
17 Link, vol. V, p. 141.
18 Joseph B. Bishop, *Theodore Roosevelt and His Time*, New York: Scribners, 1920, vol. II, p. 470.
19 Louis W. Koenig, *The Invisible Presidency*, New York: Rinehart, 1960, p. 246.
20 Edmund Fuller and David E. Green, *God in the White House: Faiths of American Presidents*, New York: Crown, 1968, p. 178.
21 Link, vol. I, p. 94.
22 Bill Adler, *Presidential Wit*, New York: Trident, 1966, p. 107.
23 Walworth, p. 310.
24 Alden Hatch, *Edith Bolling Wilson: First Lady Extraordinary*, New York: Dodd, Mead, 1961, p. 185.

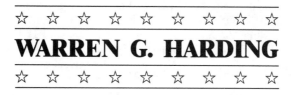

WARREN G. HARDING

NAME: Warren Gamaliel Harding. He was named after his great-uncle the Reverend Warren Gamaliel Bancroft, a Methodist chaplain at the Wisconsin State Prison. Warren's mother had wanted to name him Winfield but deferred to her husband's wishes. She called him "Winnie," however.

PHYSICAL DESCRIPTION: Six feet tall, large-boned, and full-chested, he was darkly handsome with a thick head of gleaming white hair, bushy black eyebrows above soft, gray eyes, a classic Roman nose, and a rich, pleasant voice. He dressed impeccably. His health generally was poor. At 24 he suffered a nervous breakdown and spent several weeks in a sanitarium in Battle Creek, Michigan, run by Dr. J. P. Kellogg of the breakfast-cereal Kelloggs. Four years later, and sporadically thereafter, he returned to Battle Creek for rest. Besides frazzled nerves, Harding also suffered frequently from heartburn and indigestion.

PERSONALITY: Harding genuinely liked people. His relaxed managerial style in running his newspaper in Marion, Ohio, made for good labor relations. In his more than three decades as publisher he never fired a single employee. As a legislator, he was well liked by members of both parties and although he voted the Republican line, his aversion to confrontation kept him above brute political infighting. In campaigning he always took the high road, pointing out the positive aspects of his candidacy rather than resorting to personal attacks on his opponent. Harding was truly humble, a humility that sprang from a candid awareness of his own limitations. "Harding desperately sought approval all his life," wrote biographer Andrew Sinclair. "He hated to be forced to decide on matters that might antagonize people. At any given moment of his career, he was prepared to trim his sails in order to please."[1] Harding himself acknowledged his pliable nature in a revealing anecdote he recounted before the National Press Club in 1922: His father said to him ruefully one day, "Warren,

431

it's a good thing you wasn't born a gal." When the boy asked why, Mr. Harding responded, "Because you'd be in the family way all the time. You can't say No."[2]

ANCESTORS: Harding was of English, Scotch, Irish, and Dutch heritage. His great[8]-grandfather Richard Harding, a Puritan fisherman, emigrated from England in 1623 and settled in Braintree, Massachusetts. His great[4]-grandfather Abraham Harding of New York served as a second lieutenant in the Continental army during the American Revolution. The Hardings settled as pioneers at Blooming Grove, north of Columbus, Ohio, in 1818. Soon thereafter there arose gossip so widespread, so persistently whispered from one generation to the next, that it haunted Harding all the way to the White House—the rumor that the Hardings were of Negro blood. At school Warren and other Harding children were taunted as "niggers." Whenever he ran for office, the issue cropped up. During the 1920 presidential race, the black question exploded in racist literature written by William Estabrook Chancellor, a self-avowed white supremacist and professor of economics, politics, and social sciences at Wooster (Ohio) College. The circulars charged that Harding's great-great-grandfather Amos Harding was a West Indian black and that other blacks lurked in his family tree. The campaign infuriated Harding, but he left it to campaign manager Harry Daugherty to issue a denial that was itself racist. "No family in the state [of Ohio]," Daugherty declared proudly, "has a clearer, a more honorable record than the Hardings, a blue-eyed stock from New England and Pennsylvania, the finest pioneer blood."[3] As for how such a rumor could have begun at all, the official Harding family explanation is this: Shortly after settling in Ohio, Amos Harding caught a neighbor red-handed stealing his corn. In revenge, the neighbor spread the lie that the Hardings were black. For his part, President Harding was not so sure. "How do I know?" he once confided to a friendly reporter. "One of my ancestors may have jumped the fence."[4]

FATHER: George Tryon Harding (1843–1928), doctor. Born in Corsica, Ohio, he twice enlisted for service during the Civil War, once as a fifer with the Ninety-sixth Ohio Volunteer Infantry and again as a drummer boy with the Ohio National Guard but was discharged both times after coming down with pleurisy and typhoid fever, respectively. After the war he tried teaching but quit in 1869 to study medicine first under a doctor and during 1870–1873 at Western College of Homeopathy in Cleveland. From 1873 he maintained a marginal practice in and around Marion, Ohio. He married three times, first at age 20 to Warren's mother, then at age 68, and again at age 78. He survived the president by five years, making Warren G. Harding the first president not to outlive his father.

MOTHER: Phoebe Elizabeth Dickerson Harding (1843–1910), doctor. A deeply religious woman, she in middle age converted from Methodism to Seventh-Day Adventism. On the basis of her experience as a midwife and that gained from assisting her husband in his medical practice, she was granted a license to practice medicine from Ohio's newly created State Medical Board in 1896. She specialized in obstetrics and pediatrics. Her career nearly ended abruptly, however, when in 1897 a baby she had been treating for cholera infantum died suddenly after being given a medication she prescribed. The distraught father, having been told by a druggist that the prescription contained morphine, accused Mrs. Harding of malpractice. She protested innocence, her son defended her on the pages of his newspaper, but the child's death threatened to turn much of Marion against the Hardings. Finally, a respected local physican pronounced the death to be the natural consequence of cholera, thus exonerating Mrs. Harding. She died when Warren Harding was a candidate for governor.

SIBLINGS: The oldest of six children to live to maturity, Harding had four sisters and a brother—Mrs. Charity "Chat" Malvina Remsberg; Mary Clarissa Harding, who, virtually blind herself, taught kindergarten at the Institution for the Education of the Blind in Columbus, Ohio; Mrs. Abigail Victoria "Daisy" Lewis, English teacher at Harding High in Marion; George Tryon "Deacon" Harding, Jr., a physician specializing in mental disorders near Columbus; and Mrs. Phoebe Caroline "Carolyn" Votaw, by turns a missionary at the Seventh-Day Adventist mission in Rangoon, Burma, a Washington, D.C., policewoman, and, while her brother was president, a public health officer assigned to the Veterans Bureau.

CHILDREN: Harding had no legitimate children. He had one illegitimate child, Elizabeth Ann Christian, born in 1919. See "Extramarital Affairs: Nan Britton."

BIRTH: Harding was born the morning of November 2, 1865, at the family farmhouse in Corsica (Blooming Grove), Ohio. He weighed 10 pounds at birth.

CHILDHOOD: Throughout his life, Harding fondly remembered his childhood and credited his success to the virtues of village life. In Caledonia, Ohio, where the Hardings moved when Warren was a small boy, he kept up with his farm chores, milking cows, grooming horses, painting barns, and still found time to swim Whetstone Creek, form a secret club, the Stunners, with his pals to compete with the Chain Gang, and play cornet in the village band. As a hired hand, he helped grade the roadbed of the Toledo and Central Railroad. More importantly for his later career, he worked part time as a printer's devil at the weekly *Caledonia Argus* and gradually learned all phases of running a press. His boyhood heroes were Napoleon and Alexander Hamilton.

EDUCATION: His mother taught him to memorize and recite poetry even before sending him off to Blooming Grove's one-room schoolhouse and its McGuffey's Readers. From an early age he enjoyed standing up in front of the class to declaim excerpts from famous speeches or poems. At 15 he entered Ohio Central College, 1880–1882, at Iberia, Ohio. One of 60 students there, he studied such traditional subjects as Latin, math, history, and chemistry but excelled in debating and composition. Drawing on his printing background, he helped launch a campus newspaper, the *Iberia Spectator*, which he edited. He also played the alto horn in a brass band. He graduated with a B.S. degree in 1882 and delivered the commencement address.

RELIGION: Baptist. For a time Harding accepted his mother's Seventh-Day Adventism, but at Ohio Central College his study of Darwin caused him to doubt divine creation. He briefly flirted with atheism but settled on the Baptist faith. He believed in quiet prayer and as president felt that God was guiding his actions. He attended Calvary Baptist Church in Washington regularly.

RECREATION: Twice a week President Harding played golf, at least twice a week he played poker. He attended baseball games regularly, followed boxing, and occasionally sneaked off to a burlesque house in Washington. A regular at the Chevy Chase Country Club, he generally golfed in the low 100s and often broke into the 90s. In the White House, Harding played cards with what he called his "poker Cabinet," War Secretary Weeks, Attorney General Daugherty, Interior Secretary Fall, and others. Once he gambled away in a single hand of poker an entire set of White House china dating back to the administration of Benjamin Harrison. Although as senator he had voted, albeit reluctantly, for Prohibition,

Harding kept the White House well stocked with bootleg liquor. He also enjoyed auto trips, yachting, and fishing. He read little besides a daily news digest and personal correspondence.

EARLY ROMANCE: Prior to his marriage Harding apparently had no steady girlfriend.

MARRIAGE: Warren Harding, 25, married Florence "Flossie" Mabel Kling DeWolfe, 30, a divorcée with one son, at his home in Marion, Ohio, on July 8, 1891. Born in Marion on August 15, 1860, the daughter of Amos Kling, a prominent Marion banker, and Louisa Bouton Kling, Flossie was a headstrong, dowdy woman, somewhat masculine in manner, with a piercing voice and cold blue eyes. Pregnant at 19, she married the father, Henry "Pete" DeWolfe, in 1880 but divorced him six years later. She refused financial help from her wealthy father and supported herself and, for a time, her son by giving piano lessons; she had studied at the Cincinnati Conservatory of Music before her marriage. Eventually, she let her parents raise the boy, who, like his father, became a drifter and died young. From the moment she met "Wurr'n," as she pronounced his first name, in 1890, Flossie chased after him. Harding lazily ducked her advances at first, but his feeble defenses soon gave way, and he found himself engaged to be married. Mr. Kling opposed the union, however, and warned his daughter not to marry into what he called "the black-blooded Harding family." He even accosted his future son-in-law on the street, calling him a "nigger" and threatening his life if he did not leave his daughter alone. Theirs was an unhappy marriage. Harding neglected her and sought refuge from her shrill demands in the camaraderie of his poker pals and the arms of other women (see "Extramarital Affairs"). Still, her martial demeanor and managerial skills helped him build his newspaper into a financial success. As circulation manager of the *Marion Star* for 14 years, Mrs. Harding saw that the paper was distributed efficiently and subscriptions were paid up. "Mrs. Harding in those days ran the show," recalled one of her newsboys, Norman Thomas, later the Socialist presidential candidate. "Her husband was the front, . . . it was she who was the real driving power in the success that the *Marion Star* was unquestionably making in its community."[5] In Washington, Mrs. Harding became deeply interested in astrology. Early in 1920, when Harding was still a dark-horse contender for the Republican presidential nomination, she visited Madame Marcia, a noted clairvoyant in the capital, who predicted that her husband was a shoo-in, but added that he would die suddenly in office. As First Lady Mrs. Harding hosted elegant garden parties and mixed readily with guests. Following the president's sudden death, Mrs. Harding, herself weakened by kidney disease, returned to Marion, where she died less than 16 months later, on November 21, 1924. She was buried next to the president.

EXTRAMARITAL AFFAIRS:

Carrie Phillips. Harding's 15-year intermittent affair with Carrie Fulton Phillips, wife of his longtime friend James Phillips, did not come to light until 1963, when dozens of love letters written by Harding to her were discovered. A tall, attractive woman about 10 years younger than Harding, she never really loved her husband, a successful dry goods merchant in Marion, but married him to get out of the stifling society of her home town, Bucyrus, Ohio. The affair began in Marion in the spring of 1905 while Mrs. Harding was in Columbus undergoing treatment for a kidney ailment and Mr. Phillips was soothing his nerves at the Battle Creek sanitarium. For many years neither of their spouses suspected a thing, even though the two couples often met socially and even traveled as a foursome, sailing to Europe together in 1909 and to Bermuda in 1911. It seemed the perfect affair until Carrie began pressing Harding to leave his wife. When he refused, Carrie abruptly left her husband and, with her daughter, moved to Berlin, Germany. With the outbreak of World War I she returned to the United States and resumed the affair, but there was a distance between them now. During her stay abroad she had become very attached to Germany and on her return home became an outspoken advocate of German principles. As the United States moved closer to entering the conflict against Germany, Carrie threatened to expose their affair unless Harding, now a U.S. senator, voted against a declaration of war. Harding called her bluff and voted for the declaration anyway; Carrie backed down from her threat. She continued to speak out for Germany even after the United States declared war. Her activities attracted the attention of the Secret Service. Nevertheless, the affair continued until Harding won the Republican presidential nomination. To prevent a scandal from upsetting its potential landslide, the Republican National Committee sent Mr. and Mrs. Phillips (Jim Phillips had by this time discovered the affair) on a free, slow trip to Japan and gave them some $20,000 plus a guarantee of a more modest monthly payment in exchange for their cooperation. The affair thus ended. The monthly payoffs continued until Harding's death. The Phillips lost their fortune during the Depression. Carrie died a senile pauper in a state home for the aged in 1960.

Nan Britton. Even while seeing Carrie Phillips, Harding also was registering into hotels with his "niece" Nan Britton, a cute blonde from Marion, Ohio, more than 30 years younger than Harding and by whom he had a daughter. From her freshman year in high school in 1910, Nan had a crush on Harding and plastered his campaign posters on her bedroom walls. The affair began in 1917, when she wrote Senator Harding from New York, where she was attending secretarial school, for his help in finding a job. Harding obligingly got her a position as a stenographer at U.S. Steel Corporation. She expressed her gratitude on July 30, 1917, at a hotel in lower Manhattan. In January 1919 on a couch in his Senate office, Nan conceived Harding's child, born October 22, 1919, in Asbury Park, New Jersey, and christened Elizabeth Ann Christian. Harding apparently saw his daughter only in photographs but paid Nan generous child support, hand delivered by trustworthy Secret Service agents. The couple continued their intimacy while Harding was president, at times making love in a 25-square-foot closet near the president's office in the White House. Their last tryst occured in January 1923. After the deaths of President and Mrs. Harding, Nan tried unsuccessfully to extract from the Harding estate a trust fund for Elizabeth. Failing that, she wrote a sensational book *The President's Daughter* (1927), dedicated "to all unwed mothers, and to their innocent children whose fathers are usually not known to the world." A bestseller (90,000 copies sold), the 175,000-word exposé recounted in painstaking, convincing detail the logistics of the affair. In 1932 Nan Britton settled in Evanston, Illinois. As of 1964 the president's daughter reportedly was living in Glendale, California.

MILITARY SERVICE: None.

CAREER BEFORE THE PRESIDENCY: After graduating from Ohio Central College in 1882, Harding taught one term at the White Schoolhouse outside Marion. Drilling the three Rs for $30 a month was, Harding later confessed, the hardest job he ever had. At the end of the term, he strapped his belongings onto a mule and rode into Marion, where his family had recently settled. At his father's insistence, he studied law briefly but quit to become an insurance salesman, a career that ended abruptly when he wrote a fat policy for the Hotel Marion at rates below the minimum set by the home office. He next took a job as a reporter and jack-of-all-chores at the *Marion Mirror*. In 1884, together with John Warwick and John Sickle, he purchased for $300 the nearly defunct *Marion Star*. Calling themselves the Star Publishing Company, the trio announced confidently on the front page of the November 26 edition, "We have purchased the Star and we will stay." Harding soon acquired full ownership and slowly increased circulation and advertising while at the same time improving the quality of the paper. Harding instituted a profit-sharing plan at the *Star*, one of the first in Ohio, in which employees were entitled to own as much as 25 percent of the stock. From his arrival in Marion, Harding was an enthusiastic Republican. In his first bid for elective office, he ran for county auditor in 1892 even though he knew he had no chance in heavily Democratic Marion County.

Ohio State Senator, 1899–1903. During his first campaign for the Ohio state senate in 1899, Harding met Harry Daugherty, already a power broker in Ohio politics, who over the next 21 years would steer him to the White House. It was at their first encounter, at a rally in Richwood, Ohio, that Daugherty said to himself, "Gee, what a great-looking president he'd make."[6] During the second of his two terms in the statehouse, Harding served as majority floor leader.

Lieutenant Governor of Ohio, 1903–1905. In 1903 Harding was elected lieutenant governor of Ohio under Governor Myron T. Herrick. In 1910 he tried to oust incumbent governor Judson Harmon but was buried in a Democratic sweep. Two years later he campaigned hard for the reelection of President Taft. A delegate to the Republican convention in Chicago in 1912, Harding was chosen to place Taft's name in nomination. As he mounted the podium to deliver his address, his first opportunity for national exposure, progressive supporters of Theodore Roosevelt jeered him down. Through the din Harding shouted from his prepared text, but every tribute to Taft only invited louder catcalls. At the end of the speech, he scrambled offstage to a chorus of "We Want Teddy!"

U.S. Senator, 1915–1921. In 1914 Harding won (41–35%) the Ohio Republican primary for senator, thus denying a comeback bid by former senator Joseph Foraker. The general election against state Attorney General Timothy Hogan, a Catholic, was marked by an intensely bitter campaign of religious bigotry. Although Harding carefully maintained the high road, never mentioning the religion of his opponent, he did little to discourage the virulently anti-Catholic propaganda of such sheets as *The Menace*, which warned that the election of a Catholic senator would somehow deliver Ohio to the pope. The religious issue so poisoned Ohio politics that year that Harding won handily (52–42%) without having to address the hot issues of Prohibition and women's suffrage. Harding's Senate career was undistinguished. Present for less than a third of the roll-call votes, he had one of the poorest attendance records in the upper chamber. He even missed the vote on the critical measure to send the Nineteenth Amendment, enfranchising women, to the states for ratification, although having remained uncommitted through much of the debate, he ultimately agreed to have his absentee vote paired *for* the bill. Similarly, he remained aloof of the debate over the Eighteenth Amendment, establishing Prohibition. In the end, he voted with the Drys. He introduced 134 bills during his term, none significant. His boldest effort was to join Senator Henry Cabot Lodge in destroying the League of Nations. Senator Harding blasted the League, the forerunner of the United Nations, as a world body either that would create "a supergovernment of the nations which enter it or it will prove the colossal disappointment of the ages." Harding was keynote speaker and chairman of the 1916 Republican national convention.

REPUBLICAN PRESIDENTIAL NOMINATION, 1920: "I don't expect Senator Harding to be nominated on the first, second, or third ballot," Harry Daugherty, Harding's campaign manager, predicted several months before the Republican convention opened in Chicago, "but I think about 11 minutes after two o'clock on Friday morning of the convention, when 15 or 20 men, bleary-eyed and perspiring profusely from the heat, are sitting around a table some one of them will say: 'Who will we nominate?' At that decisive time the friends of Senator Harding can suggest him."[7] That is what happened. Harding arrived in Chicago in June the darkest of dark horses. On the first ballot General Leonard Wood, former army chief of staff, Governor Frank Lowden of Illinois, and Senator Hiram Johnson of California all garnered more votes than Harding's meager 65½. And Harding even slipped some in the next three ballots. But, more significantly, Wood, the front-runner, was unable to shake enough delegates loose from the other candidates to generate any momentum. Apparently deadlocked, the convention adjourned until the next morning. During the recess, Daugherty worked tirelessly promoting Harding as a logical compromise. That night party leaders huddled in suite 404–6 on the thirteenth floor of the Blackstone Hotel—a meeting that inspired the phrase "smoke-filled room." The group settled on Harding because, unlike others in the field, he had no real strikes against him: he had no political enemies, he was popular, he represented a state crucial to Republicans, he had voted "right," that is, *for* Prohibition and women's suffrage. One thing bothered the bosses. Did Harding have any skeletons in his closet? To find out, they summoned the candidate to the Blackstone about 2 A.M. and asked him point-blank. After examining his conscience for ten minutes, he replied, simply, no, he had nothing to hide. On the tenth ballot, Pennsylvania put Harding over the top. The final tally read Harding, 692⅕; Wood, 156; Johnson, 80⅕; Wisconsin favorite-son Robert LaFollette, 24; and Lowden, 11. Governor Calvin Coolidge of Massachusetts was nominated for vice president. The Republican platform condemned the Wilson administration for unpreparedness in war as well as peace, opposed U.S. entry into the League of Nations on Wilson's terms, and advocated a federal budget system, a protective tariff, stricter immigration requirements, annual registration of aliens, and "equal pay for equal service" for women.

OPPONENT: James M. Cox (1870–1957) of Ohio; Democrat. Born in Butler County, Ohio, north of Cincinnati, Cox, like Harding, began his career as a newspaperman, first as a reporter for the *Cincinnati Enquirer* and later as publisher of the *Dayton Daily News*. Cox, a liberal Democrat, served in the U.S. House 1900–1913 and as governor of Ohio 1913–1915 and 1917–1921. Governor Cox instituted many long-lasting reforms. He created the first state budget system in the nation, pressed for a workmen's compensation law, reorganized the state judicial system, regulated utilities, reformed the tax structure, required lobbyists to register, licensed stockbrokers, built modern schools, and improved transportation. At the Democratic national convention in San Francisco in June–July 1920, the forces of Treasury Secretary William G. McAdoo and Attorney General A. Mitchell Palmer deadlocked, making it possible for Cox to emerge a compromise choice on the forty-fourth ballot. Franklin D. Roosevelt of New York was nominated for vice president. The Democratic platform looked to the League of Nations "as the surest, if not the only, practicable means of maintaining the permanent peace of the world" and advocated tax reform, maintenance of the tariff "for revenue only," adoption of a federal budget system, and federal efforts to eradicate illiteracy.

CAMPAIGN AND THE ISSUES, 1920: The election was a referendum on the Wilson administration and the League of Nations, which Cox supported wholeheartedly. Despite his Senate record against the League, Harding straddled the issue, speaking only in platitudes that led both pro- and anti-League advocates to believe that he was on their side. Cox opposed Prohibition; Harding had voted for it. While Harding conducted a front-porch campaign in Marion, Cox traveled 22,000 miles to deliver nearly 400 speeches. Cox challenged war-weary Americans to remain active in world affairs and to tackle their domestic problems. He decried the 17 percent illiteracy rate in the United States and the existence of poverty in a land of plenty. Entertainer Al Jolson stumped for Harding, belting out the campaign song he had written, which ended, "We need another Lincoln / To do the country's thinkin' / Mist-ter Hard-ding / You're the man for us!"

ELECTION AS PRESIDENT, NOVEMBER 2, 1920:

Popular Vote. Harding (Republican), 16,152,200 (61%); Cox (Democrat), 9,147,353 (35%); Eugene V. Debs (Socialist), 915,490 (3%). This was the first election in which women were allowed to vote nationwide.

Electoral Vote: Harding, 404; Cox, 127.

States Carried: Harding won the electoral votes of 37 states—Arizona, California, Colorado, Connecticut, Delaware, Idaho, Illinois, Indiana, Iowa, Kansas, Maine, Maryland, Massachusetts, Michigan, Minnesota, Missouri, Montana, Nebraska, Nevada, New Hampshire, New Jersey, New Mexico, New York, North Dakota, Ohio, Oklahoma, Oregon, Pennsylvania, Rhode Island, South Dakota, Tennessee, Utah, Vermont, Washington, West Virginia, Wisconsin, and Wyoming. Cox won the electoral votes of 11 states—Alabama, Arkansas, Florida, Georgia, Kentucky, Louisiana, Mississippi, North Carolina, South Carolina, Texas, and Virginia.

INAUGURAL ADDRESS: March 4, 1921. ". . . A world supergovernment is contrary to everything we cherish and can have no sanction by our Republic. This is not selfishness, it is sanctity. It is not aloofness, it is security. It is not suspicion of others, it is patriotic adherence to the things which made us what we are. . . ."

VICE PRESIDENT: Calvin Coolidge (1872–1933), of Massachusetts, served 1921–1923. He succeeded to the presidency on Harding's death. See "Calvin Coolidge, 30th President."

CABINET:

Secretary of State. Charles Evans Hughes (1862–1948), of New York, served 1921–1925. He surrounded himself with top-notch career diplomats and did his best to insulate the department from patronage. In his most significant contribution, he organized and chaired the Washington Conference for the Limitation of Armament (see "Administration"). Commented one British officer on his efforts to halt the naval arms race, "Secretary Hughes sank in 35 minutes more ships than all the admirals of the world have sunk in a cycle of centuries."[8] Hughes also improved relations with Latin America. He stayed on in the

WARREN G. HARDING / **439**

Coolidge administration. See also "William Howard Taft, 27th President," "Supreme Court Appointments"; "Woodrow Wilson, 28th President," "Campaign, 1916," and "Opponent"; and "Herbert Hoover, 31st President" "Supreme Court Appointments".

Secretary of the Treasury. Andrew Mellon (1855–1937), of Pennsylvania, served 1921–1932. An arch–fiscal conservative and proponent of the trickle-down theory of economics, he pressed for a reduction of the national debt, lower income taxes, and a more favorable climate for business. He stayed on in the Coolidge and Hoover administrations.

Secretary of War. John W. Weeks (1860–1926), of Massachusetts, served 1921–1925. He stayed on in the Coolidge administration.

Attorney General. Harry M. Daugherty (1860–1941), of Ohio, served 1921–1924. In one of his first acts, he requested and obtained from the president sole responsibility over alien property, that is, property in the United States owned by German nationals that had been confiscated during World War I. Although indicted for conspiracy to defraud the government in connection with misuse of such property, he survived two hung juries to claim vindication. He was strongly antilabor, using his influence whenever possible to break strikes and preserve the open shop. A bill of impeachment was filed against him with the House Judiciary Committee, charging him with, among other things, failure to enforce antitrust, war-profiteering, and prohibition laws; abuse of the pardon privilege; hiring undesirables; use of undue influence in breaking strikes; and spying on unfriendly members of Congress. Harding professed confidence in his attorney general. The impeachment movement failed. Daugherty stayed on in the Coolidge administration. He defended his activities in *The Inside Story of the Harding Tragedy* (with Thomas Dixon, 1932).

Secretary of the Navy. Edwin Denby (1870–1929), of Michigan, served 1921–1924. A basically honest man out of his depth, he naively agreed to relinquish federal oil reserves from his department to the Interior Department and thus became an unwitting accomplice in the Teapot Dome scandal. He stayed on in the Coolidge administration.

Postmaster General. (1) Will Hays (1879–1954), of Indiana, served 1921–1922. Popular with postal workers, he improved morale in the department. He left the cabinet to become president of the Motion Picture Producers and Distributors of America, in which post he acted as chief censor of the moral content of American films. (2) Hubert Work (1860–1942), of Colorado, served 1922–1923. He also served as Secretary of the Interior. (3) Harry S. New (1858–1937), of Indiana, served 1923–1929. He stayed on in the Coolidge administration.

Secretary of the Interior. (1) Albert B. Fall (1861–1944), of New Mexico, served 1921–1923. An archfoe of conservationists, he persuaded Harding, with the acquiescence of Navy Secretary Denby, to transfer federal oil reserves to his control. He then secretly allowed the Mammoth Oil Company to tap the Teapot Dome reserve in Wyoming in exchange for $308,000 and a herd of cattle. Similarly, he accepted $100,000 from the Pan-American Petroleum and Transport Company for access to the Elk Hills reserve in California. Fall denied any wrongdoing, calling the bribes "loans," but a jury in 1929 decided otherwise. He served 10 months of a one-year sentence in New Mexico State Prison. (2) Hubert Work served 1923–1928. He stayed on in the Coolidge administration.

Secretary of Agriculture. Henry C. Wallace (1866–1924), of Iowa, served 1921–1924. In 1922 he sponsored the President's National Agricultural Conference to consider ways to improve the earnings of the nation's farmers, especially hard hit by postwar inflation. He stayed on in the Coolidge administration.

Secretary of Commerce. Herbert Hoover (1874–1964), of California, served 1921–1928. He stayed on in the Coolidge administration. See "Herbert Hoover, 31st President," "Career before the Presidency."

Secretary of Labor. James J. Davis (1873–1947), of Pennsylvania, served 1921–1930. A Welsh immigrant and former steelworker, he had more recently served as director general of the Loyal Order of the Moose. He stayed on in the Coolidge administration.

ADMINISTRATION: March 4, 1921–August 2, 1923.

Teapot Dome and Other Scandals. Harding surrounded himself with many distinguished, capable men (Hughes at state, Mellon at Treasury, Hoover at commerce), but he also brought to town a thoroughly unsavory lot of grafters: Secretary of Interior Albert Fall sold for personal gain the nation's oil reserves at Wyoming's Teapot Dome (see "Cabinet"). Thomas Miller, the alien property custodian, was convicted of accepting bribes. Jess Smith, bagman for the operation and personal aide to Attorney General Daugherty, destroyed his papers and committed suicide shortly after Harding demanded his resignation. Another suicide victim, Charles Cramer, was an aide to Charles Forbes, the corrupt director of the Veterans Bureau who skimmed the proceeds from the sale of war surplus goods, earned fat kickbacks for purchasing government supplies at exorbitant prices, and diverted alcohol and drugs from Veterans hospitals to bootleggers and narcotics dealers. Convicted of fraud, conspiracy, and bribery, Forbes drew a two-year sentence. No evidence found to date suggests that Harding personally profited from such crimes. He apparently had a vague notion that friends had betrayed him, however, and may even have learned enough before his death to realize that his presidency was about to collapse.

League of Nations. "The League Covenant can have no sanction by us," President Harding informed Congress in April 1921. The statement ended the suspense over whether the president ultimately would support or oppose U.S. entry into the League of Nations. In refusing to join the world body, Harding ensured its ultimate failure. He did advocate American participation in the World Court, created by the League to arbitrate international legal disputes, but could not marshal the Senate votes necessary for ratification.

Formal Conclusion of World War I. Because the Republicans had rejected Wilson's Treaty of Versailles, it fell to President Harding formally to conclude World War I. He did so with none of the pomp and ceremony usually spent on such occasions. On July 2, 1921, he was summoned off a golf course in New Jersey by a White House aide who was to hand deliver the document for the president's signature. At the home of a friend, Senator Joseph Frelinghuysen, where he had been visiting, the president perused the joint resolution ending "the state of war between the Imperial German government and the United States of America" while the Frelinghuysens' dog sniffed his shoes. Still dressed in his golf clothes, he then signed the treaty on a mahogany table in his host's living room. "That's all,"[9] he said. The war was over. Harding sped back to the links.

Arms Limitation. With the United States and Great Britain jockeying for naval supremacy, Great Britain locked into an uneasy alliance with Japan, and China defenseless against potential Japanese aggression, Harding authorized Secretary of State Hughes to convene the Washington Conference for the Limitation of Armament, November 1921–February 1922. The United States, Great Britain, Japan, France, and Italy agreed to limit their fleets of battleships, cruisers, and carriers to an aggregate tonnage ratio of 5:5:3:1.75:1.75 for the five nations, respectively. The conference led the United States, Great Britain, France, and Japan to conclude the Four Power Pact, in which they agreed to respect one another's holdings in the Pacific and to arbitrate any disputes peacefully. The conference also made possible the Nine Power Pact (United States, Great Britain, France, Belgium, Netherlands, Portugal, Italy, China, and Japan), which for a decade forestalled Japanese aggression against China and preserved the Open Door policy.

Budget Bureau. In 1921 President Harding established the Bureau of the Budget, which for the first time placed formal budgetary restraints on federal expenditures. He got the bureau off to a strong start with the appointment of Charles G. Dawes (see "Calvin Coolidge, 30th President," "Vice President"), a no-nonsense administrator, as its first director.

Debs Pardon. Although Harding refused to grant a general amnesty to those convicted of nonviolent antiwar activities during World War I, he ordered the Justice Department to review clemency petitions on a case-by-case basis and pardoned the period's most celebrated wartime protestor, Eugene V. Debs, the leader of the Socialist party who by then had served nearly 3 years of a 10-year sentence at the federal penitentiary in Atlanta. Moreover, Harding hastened Debs's release, scheduled for the end of 1921, so that he could spend Christmas with his family.

Civil Rights. Harding was the first president since the Civil War to speak out on southern soil for the rights of blacks. On October 26, 1921, in Birmingham, Alabama, where he had gone to accept an honorary degree from the University of Alabama, he lectured a segregated audience of 20,000 whites and 10,000 blacks on the virtues of racial equality. "I want to see the time come," he declared, "when black men will regard themselves as full participants in the benefits and duties of American citizenship. . . . We cannot go on, as we have gone on for more than half a century, with one great section of our population, numbering as many people as the entire population of some significant countries of Europe, set off from real contribution to solving national issues, because of a division on race lines."[10]

Tariff. The Emergency Tariff Act of 1921 and the Fordney-McCumber Tariff Act of 1922 raised duties to an average rate of 38 percent and singled out for special protection the chemical, drug, and other American industries that had arisen during the war. These tariffs replaced the Underwood Tariff (1913; see "Woodrow Wilson, 28th President," "Administration"). They were replaced by the Hawley-Smoot Tariff (1930; see "Herbert Hoover, 31st President," "Administration").

SUPREME COURT APPOINTMENTS: (1)William Howard Taft (1857–1930), of Ohio, served as chief justice 1921–1930. See "William Howard Taft, 27th President," "Career after the Presidency." (2) George Sutherland (1862–1942), of Utah, served as associate justice 1922–1938. A native of England, he was a staunch strict-constructionist who consistently held that most social welfare legislation violated the Constitution. The right of individuals to enter into contracts, he asserted for the Court in *Adkins* v. *Children's Hospital* (1923), rendered unconstitutional the minimum wage law in the District of Columbia. He joined the Court's conservative majority in nullifying early New Deal attempts to grapple with the Depression, which, Sutherland asserted, was "nothing new" and did not call for emergency measures. "If the provisions of the Constitution be not upheld when they pinch as well as when they comfort," he said, "they may as well be abandoned." (3) Pierce Butler (1866–1939), of Minnesota, served as associate justice 1922–1939. In *Morehead* v. *Tipaldo* (1936), the last decision in which conservatives were able to muster a majority in striking down legislation designed to regulate the economy, Butler overturned the New York minumum wage law, writing for the majority, "Parties have equal rights to obtain from each other the best terms they can by private bargaining." (4) Edward T. Sanford (1865–1930), of Tennessee, served as associate justice 1923–1930. He had served as assistant attorney general under President Theodore Roosevelt and more recently as district court judge. He left little impact on the high court.

RANKING IN 1962 HISTORIANS POLL: Harding ranked last of 31 presidents, the worse of the 2 "failures," the other being Grant.

DEATH IN OFFICE: August 2, 1923, 7:30 P.M., Palace Hotel, San Francisco, California. On June 20, 1923, Harding set out on a cross-country Voyage of Understanding, a strenuous undertaking in which he hoped to get out and meet ordinary folks and explain his administration's policies. He was suffering from high blood pressure and an enlarged heart. The dozens of public appearances he made enroute exhausted him. He seemed to enjoy himself in Alaska (he was the first president to visit here), but on the return trip south, on the evening of July 27, he went to bed with severe cramps and indigestion. Surgeon General Charles Sawyer dismissed it as a touch of food poisoning. Harding's schedule was cleared, and the presidential train continued to San Francisco, where on July 29 he was checked into room 8064 of the Palace Hotel. He soon developed pneumonia, but by August 1 his 102° fever had lifted, his accelerated pulse had slowed, and he was breathing more comfortably. The next day he was even making plans to do some fishing off Catalina Island. That evening Mrs. Harding sought to cheer him up by reading him "A Calm View of a Calm Man," a flattering profile of the president written by Samuel Blythe for the *Saturday Evening Post*. "That's good. Go on; read some more,"[11] he said at one point. These were his last words. Mrs. Harding finished reading the article and left the president, eyes closed, to bask contentedly in the shower of compliments he had just heard. During her absence Nurse Ruth Powderly entered the room. As she approached the sickbed, she noticed the president's face twitch, his mouth drop open and his head roll lifelessly to one side. Doctors concluded that he had suffered a stroke. Mrs. Harding, alone beside his brown metal casket in the East Room of the White House, spoke for more than an hour into the face of her dead husband. He was buried at Marion, Ohio. In 1930 Gaston Means, a convicted swindler, published a sensational book, *The Strange Death of President Harding*, in which he suggested that Mrs. Harding had poisoned the president, possibly as punishment for cheating on her or to spare him the indignity of impeachment, or both. Because Mrs. Harding had refused permission for an autopsy of the president, Means's charge could not be disproved, but historians generally discount it. In his last will and testament, executed in June 1923,

President Harding left the income from the bulk of his estate, valued at $850,000, to his wife. He left his father the interest from $50,000 worth of government bonds. The principal, after the deaths of his wife and father, was to go to the president's brother and three sisters, except for the following specific bequests: $25,000 to the Marion Park Commission, $10,000 to each of his nieces and nephews, $4,000 to each of his wife's two grandchildren, $2,000 to the Trinity Baptist Church, and $1,000 to Episcopal St. Paul's Church.

HARDING PRAISED: "He caught the ear of a war-tired world. He called our country back to paths of peace and gladly it came. He beckoned the nations to come and sit in council. . . . He sought for men and nations a peace, the only true and lasting peace, based on justice and right. . . . So he led the way to the monumental accomplishments of the Washington Conference on Limitation of Armament."[12]—President Calvin Coolidge, 1923

"Warren G. Harding gave his life for his country. No one can do more than that. He exhausted himself in service, a martyr in fidelity to the interests of the people for whom he labored with a passionate devotion. He was a man of the people, indulging no consciousness of superiority, incapable of arrogance, separated from neither by experience nor by pride nor by eccentricity."[13]— Secretary of State Charles Evans Hughes, 1924

"It is yet too early to see him in true, full perspective—a modern Abraham Lincoln whose name and fame will grow with time."[14]—Harry Daugherty, Harding's attorney general, 1932

HARDING CRITICIZED: "His speeches leave the impression of an army of pompous phrases moving over the landscape in search of an idea."[15]—William G. McAdoo

"I like Harding. I like him very much, but I can't conceive of his being President of the United States. He's done nothing to deserve it."[16]—Republican senator Hiram Johnson of California, 1920

"Senator Harding is the kind of man who, on his way to the legislature, would empty his pockets to some poor creature, and then vote with the conservative Republicans for a bill that would maintain the conditions making possible the suffering of the recipient."[17]—James M. Cox, 1920 Democratic presidential nominee

"I have just read the President's treaty message. I thought it was the best speech Secretary Hughes ever wrote."[18]—Will Rogers, 1922

"Harding was not a bad man. He was just a slob."[19]—Alice Roosevelt Longworth, daughter of President Theodore Roosevelt.

"He was not a man with either the experience or the intellectual quality that the position [of president] needed."[20]—Herbert Hoover

HARDING QUOTES: "It is my conviction that the fundamental trouble with the people of the United States is that they have gotten too far away from Almighty God."[21]—1920

"I don't know what to do or where to turn in this taxation matter. Somewhere there must be a book that tells all about it, where I could go to straighten it out in my mind. But I don't know where the book is, and maybe I couldn't read it if I found it!"[22]—1923

"My God, this is a hell of a job! I have no trouble with my enemies. . . . But my damn friends, they're the ones that keep me walking the floor nights."[23]— 1923

BOOKS ABOUT HARDING: Adams, Samuel Hopkins. *Incredible Era: The Life and Times of Warren Gamaliel Harding.* Boston: Houghton, Mifflin, 1939.
Russell, Francis. *The Shadow of Blooming Grove: Warren G. Harding in His Times.* New York: McGraw-Hill, 1968.
Sinclair, Andrew. *The Available Man: The Life Behind the Mask of Warren Gamaliel Harding.* New York: Macmillan, 1965.

NOTES

1 Andrew Sinclair, *The Available Man: The Life Behind the Mask of Warren Gamaliel Harding,* New York: Macmillan, 1965, p. 65.

2 Samuel Hopkins Adams, *Incredible Era: The Life and Times of Warren Gamaliel Harding,* Boston: Houghton, Mifflin, 1939, p. 8.

3 Francis Russell, *The Shadow of Blooming Grove: Warren G. Harding in His Times,* New York: McGraw-Hill, 1968, p. 404.

4 Ibid., p. 40.

5 Adams, p. 25.

6 Russell, p. 109.

7 Ibid., pp. 341–342.

8 Graham Stuart, *The Department of State,* New York: Macmillan, 1949, p. 266.

9 Russell, p. 461.

10 Ibid., pp. 471–472.

11 Ibid., p. 591.

12 *Congressional Memorial Services and Tributes of Respect to the Late President of the U.S. Warren G. Harding,* Washington: Government Printing Office, 1924, pp. 63–64.

13 Ibid., p. 28.

14 Harry M. Daughterty, *The Inside Story of the Harding Tragedy,* New York: Churchill, 1932, p. 300.

15 Adams, p. 115.

16 Russell, p. 383.

17 Adams, p. 178.

18 Donald Day, *Will Rogers: A Biography,* New York: McKay, 1962, p. 121.

19 Frank Freidel, *America in the Twentieth Century,* New York: Knopf, 1965, p. 231.

20 *Memoirs of Herbert Hoover,* New York: Macmillan, 1951–1952, vol. II, p. 47.

21 Adams, p. 194.

22 Russell, p. 559.

23 *The Autobiography of William Allen White,* New York: Macmillan, 1946, p. 619.

CALVIN COOLIDGE

30TH PRESIDENT

NAME: John Calvin Coolidge. He was named after his father but was always called Calvin or Cal at home to avoid confusion. He dropped the first name after graduating from college.

PHYSICAL DESCRIPTION: Coolidge stood about 5 feet 9 inches tall and was slightly built. He had finely chiseled features, a narrow pointed nose, cleft chin, small deeply set blue eyes, and thin pursed lips. The red hair of his youth turned sandy in maturity. He spoke with a New England nasal twang. He walked in short, quick steps. He suffered from chronic respiratory and digestive ailments. As president he underwent frequent attacks of asthma, hay fever, bronchitis, and stomach upset. He relied on nasal sprays to relieve his swollen sinuses and took a variety of pills for other symptoms. He coughed so often that he feared he had tuberculosis. He tired easily and usually slept about 11 hours a day, 9 hours at night and a 2-hour nap in the afternoon. He dressed fashionably in suits tailor-made in Vermont. He slicked down his hair with petroleum jelly. Curiously, he insisted on wearing baggy underwear.

PERSONALITY: Coolidge was shy, undemonstrative, restrained, cautious, wholly self-reliant, and a man of few friends. "When I was a little fellow," Coolidge recalled, "as long ago as I can remember, I would go into a panic if I heard strange voices in the kitchen. I felt I just couldn't meet the people and shake hands with them. . . . The hardest thing in the world was to have to go through the kitchen door and give them a greeting. I was almost ten before I realized I couldn't go on that way. And by fighting hard I used to manage to get through that door. I'm all right with old friends, but everytime I meet a stranger, I've got to go through the old kitchen door, back home, and it's not easy."[1] Coolidge was frugal but no sponger. When he sent an aide out for a magazine, for example, he expected his change, even if it was just a nickel, and complained if he did not get it promptly. Whenever he borrowed a minor sum, he quickly repaid it to the penny. His reputation as a man of few, but witty, words was legend. A typical exchange involved the hostess who came up to him and said, "You must talk to me, Mr. President. I made a bet today that I could get more than two words out of you." Coolidge replied, "You lose."[2]

ANCESTORS: Coolidge was of English, Scotch, and Welsh heritage. He also had a trace of Indian blood, he believed. His great[7]-grandfather John Coolidge emigrated from Cambridgeshire, England, about 1630 and settled at Watertown, Massachusetts. His great-great-grandfather John Coolidge fought at Lexington during the American Revolution and settled in Vermont. His paternal grandfather, Calvin Galusha "Galoosh" Coolidge, served in the Vermont legislature and on his death left six-year-old Calvin 40 acres of land and some livestock.

FATHER: John Calvin Coolidge (1845–1926), farmer, storekeeper, local public official. A native of Plymouth, Vermont, he attended Black River Academy in Ludlow, Vermont, and in 1868 married Victoria Josephine Moor, the president's mother. He prospered as a farmer and storekeeper at Plymouth Notch, Vermont. He served six years in the Vermont House of Representatives and a term in the Vermont Senate. He also held a variety of offices, including that of selectman, tax collector, and constable. From him Calvin inherited thrift, taciturnity, and interest in public affairs. In 1891, six years after the death of his wife, Mr. Coolidge married Carrie A. Brown, a schoolteacher in Plymouth. As a notary public and justice of the peace, Mr. Coolidge administered the presidential oath of office to his son in 1923 (see "Career before the Presidency"); he was the only father of a president to do so. President Coolidge invited his father to live at the White House, but he declined. Mr. Coolidge died during his son's term as president.

MOTHER: Victoria Josephine Moor Coolidge (1846–1885). Born near Pinney Hollow, Vermont, she was a frail, sensitive woman devoted to her family. "There was a touch of mysticism and poetry in her nature," Coolidge observed of his mother, "which made her love to gaze at the purple sunsets and watch the evening stars."[3] Coolidge inherited her delicate features. She died, probably of tuberculosis, when Calvin was 12 years old. Life never seemed the same without her, he later recalled. Throughout his life Coolidge carried a picture of her in his watchcase and daydreamed of her often.

SIBLING: The older of two children, Coolidge had a sister, Abigail "Abbie" Gratia Coolidge, who died, probably of appendicitis, at age 15.

CHILDREN: Coolidge had two sons.

 John Coolidge (1906–2000), retired railroad and print company executive. Born in Northampton, Massachusetts, he was a trainee at a citizens military camp at Fort Devens, Massachusetts, when his father became president. He graduated from Mercersburg (Pennsylvania) Acadamy in 1924 and Amherst College in 1928. Uncomfortable in the limelight, he spent little time in the White House. In 1929 he married Florence Trumbull, daughter of Governor Robert H. Trumbull of Connecticut. He was an executive with the New York, New Haven, and Hartford Railroad until 1941, when he became president of a printing company in Hartford, Connecticut. Now retired, he lives in Farmington, Connecticut. In a communication to the author, Coolidge asserted that historians have failed to evaluate the Coolidge presidency fairly. "I do not believe they have thoroughly researched the administration's accomplishments in the context of the time," he said. He regrets that President Coolidge's "philosophy of thrift and the role of government are no longer in vogue" but adds, hopefully, "perhaps they will become more so in the Reagan administration." Coolidge believes that his father would view today's world "dimly and sorrowfully." Calvin Coolidge probably would not run for president today, Coolidge believes, and even if he did, he probably would be defeated.

Calvin Coolidge, Jr. (1908–1924). Born in Northampton, Massachusetts, he was picking tobacco during summer vacation from Mercersburg (Pennsylvania) Academy when his father became president. In a tragic accident, he blistered a toe playing tennis in sneakers without socks, developed an infection, and at 16 died. His freak death during the 1924 presidential campaign devastated Coolidge. "When he went," he said, "the power and the glory of the Presidency went with him."[4]

BIRTH: Coolidge was born July 4, 1872, at the family home adjoining the Coolidge general store in Plymouth, Vermont.

CHILDHOOD: Coolidge grew up in Plymouth, Vermont. At age three he was taken to Montpelier to watch his father take part in the state legislature. His early ambition was to be a storekeeper, like his father. A sober, dependable lad, he helped out with such chores as plowing, planting, stacking wood, and picking fruit. His favorite work was tapping and processing maple sugar. He earned spare cash selling apples and popcorn balls at town meetings and, while a student in Ludlow, Vermont, making toys at a local carriage shop. He disliked team sports, preferring the solitary pasttime of horseback riding. At 19 he accompanied his father to Bennington, Vermont, to hear President Benjamin Harrison speak.

EDUCATION: From age 5 to 13, Coolidge attended the local elementary school in Plymouth. He was a fair student and behaved satisfactorily. In 1886 he enrolled at the Black River Academy at Ludlow. He continued to receive average marks and was class secretary at the time of his graduation in the nine-member class of 1890. At commencement he delivered the "Oratory in History." Having failed the entrance examination to Amherst College, he in 1891 took college preparatory instruction at the St. Johnsbury Academy in Ludlow, where he earned a college entrance certificate qualifying him for automatic acceptance at Amherst. At Amherst 1891–1895 Coolidge continued an average student during his first two years but from his junior year improved markedly, taking a special interest in declamation, rhetoric, history, and philosophy. He also studied modern and ancient languages, becoming quite proficient in Greek, math through calculus, and literature. His worst grade was a D in physics. His favorite instructor was philosophy professor Charles E. Garman, who greatly influenced Coolidge's social values and encouraged his interest in public service. Coolidge was something of a loner on campus. He did not participate in sports and took part in few extracurricular activities. He remained an "ouden," or nonfraternity man, until his senior year, when he was asked into Phi Gamma Delta. In 1892 he joined the Republican Club and supported the renomination of President Benjamin Harrison. For his senior essay "The Principles Fought for in the American Revolution," Coolidge won first prize, a $150 gold medal, in a national contest sponsored by the Sons of the American Revolution. Coolidge graduated cum laude with a 79 percent cumulative grade average in the 76-student class of 1895. The outstanding graduate of the year was Dwight Morrow, later ambassador to Mexico under Coolidge. Having earned a reputation as the campus wit, Coolidge was chosen by his fellow students to deliver the Grove Oration, traditionally an irreverent, satirical address. After graduation, Coolidge studied law at the office of John C. Hammond and Henry P. Field in Northampton, Massachusetts. He supported William McKinley for president in 1896. Coolidge was admitted to the bar in July 1897.

RELIGION: Congregationalist. Although he usually attended Sunday services, Coolidge did not formally join a church until after he became president because he doubted his ability to lead the examplary life expected of church members. Moreover, he did not actually join the church, but rather was inducted. Attending services at the First Congregational Church on his first Sunday in Washington as president, Coolidge responded to the Reverend Dr. Jason Noble Pierce's invitation to all celebrants, members and nonmembers alike, to take communion. Reverend Pierce considered Coolidge's action that day as sufficient profession of faith for admission, and the church voted him a member. Coolidge accepted the honor but conceded that had he been asked beforehand, he would have hesitated out of fear that such action might seem hypocritical. In Northampton, he attended Edwards Congregational Church.

RECREATION: President Coolidge usually went out walking twice daily, weather permitting. He loved to window-shop; he said it relaxed his mind. He enjoyed horseback riding but as president gave it up for a mechanical horse. Occasionally he even whooped it up like a real cowboy astride his electric steed. As president he also took up fishing and skeet shooting. An inveterate prankster, he relished playing practical jokes on his staff. One of his favorites was to press the buzzer in the Executive Office Building to warn the servants that the president was about to leave for the living quarters—and then go out for a walk. He was very fond of animals and at times could be seen strolling through the White House with a kitten or raccoon clinging about his neck. He cared little for the theater or musical entertainment but did enjoy the circus. He often spent weekends aboard the presidential yacht *Mayflower*. He spent summer vacations at various retreats, including those at Swampscott, Massachusetts; White Pines Camp, New York; Black Hills, South Dakota; Cedar Island, Wisconsin; and Sapelo Island, Georgia. Coolidge seldom drank and, as president during Prohibition, abstained completely. He smoked cigars; his favorite brand was Fonesca Corona Fines de Luxe, a 21¢ black Havana.

MARRIAGE: Calvin Coolidge, 33, married Grace Anna Goodhue, 26, on October 4, 1905, at the home of the bride's parents in Burlington, Vermont. Born in Burlington on January 3, 1879, the only child of Andrew I. Goodhue, a mechanical engineer and steamboat inspector, and Lemira Barrett Goodhue, Grace graduated from the University of Vermont in 1902 and joined the faculty of the Clarke Institute for the Deaf in Northampton, Massachusetts, as a lip reading instructor. While watering the flowers outside the school one day in 1903, she happened to look up at the open window of Robert N. Weir's boardinghouse and caught a glimpse of Coolidge, shaving in front of a mirror, with nothing on but long underwear and a hat. She burst out laughing at the sight; he heard the noise and turned to look at her. It was their first meeting. After a more formal introduction sometime later, the two were quickly attracted to each other. Grace's vivacity and charm proved a perfect complement to Coolidge's reserved manner. In the summer of 1905 Coolidge proposed in the form of an ultimatum: "I am going to be married to you."[5] Grace readily consented, but her mother objected and did everything she could to postpone the wedding. Coolidge never reconciled with his mother-in-law, who later insisted that Grace had been largely responsible for Coolidge's political success.

The small wedding, attended by 15 guests, was performed by the Reverend Edward A. Hungerford. The newlyweds planned a two-week honeymoon to Montreal, Canada, but at Coolidge's suggestion cut it short at the end of one week and settled at Northampton. Mrs. Coolidge, although raised a Democrat, adopted the party of her husband. As First Lady, she was a popular hostess. The social highlight of the Coolidge years was the party for Charles Lindbergh following his transatlantic flight in 1927. The Coolidges were a particularly devoted couple, although the president never discussed state matters with her. She did not even know that he had decided not to seek reelection in 1928 until he announced it to the press. After Coolidge's death in 1933, Mrs. Coolidge continued her work on behalf of the deaf. During World War II, she was active in the Red Cross, civil defense, and scrap drives. She died at Northampton on July 8, 1957, and was buried next to the president at Plymouth, Vermont.

MILITARY SERVICE: None.

CAREER BEFORE THE PRESIDENCY: Admitted to the bar in 1897, Coolidge opened a law office in Northampton, Massachusetts, and became active in local Republican affairs. He was elected to the Northampton City Council, 1899–1900, an unpaid position; he pressed for construction of an armory in the city. The city council named him city solicitor, 1900–1902, at a salary of $600 a year. He served briefly as Hampshire County clerk of courts in 1903 to fill the remainder of an unexpired term. In 1904 he was named chairman of the local Republican party organization. In 1905 he was defeated for a seat on the Northampton School Board, his only loss at the polls in his career.

Member of Massachusetts General Court, 1907–1908. During his two terms in the state legislature, Coolidge established a progressive record in support of the six-day workweek, women and child labor laws, and ratification of constitutional amendments for the direct election of senators and women's suffrage. He worked unsuccessfully on behalf of bills to ban the use of the labor injunction and unfair price-cutting practices designed to destroy competition. He also helped codify state banking laws.

Mayor of Northampton, Massachusetts, 1910–1911. During his two terms as mayor, Coolidge cut taxes and partially retired the city's debt while at the same time expanding the police and fire departments and upgrading sidewalks and streets.

Massachusetts State Senator, 1912–1915; Senate President, 1914–1915. During his four terms in the state senate, Coolidge established a moderately progressive record. As chairman of the Special Conciliation Committee, he mediated an end to the Lawrence textile strike of 1912. As chairman of the Railroad Committee he steered to passage over the governor's veto a bill to extend rail service in his district. He supported a minimum wage for women, workmen's compensation, and the legalization of labor picketing as well as women's suffrage, a state income tax, and the direct election of senators. He opposed attempts by the insurance industry to strip savings banks of the authority to underwrite life insurance, a program popular with labor. In 1912 he supported the reelection of President William Howard Taft.

Lieutenant Governor of Massachusetts, 1916–1918. During his three terms as lieutenant governor, Coolidge was ex officio chairman of the governor's Council, with a voice in appointments and pardons. He also headed a commission to bail out the financially troubled Boston Elevated Street Railway. In 1916 he campaigned actively for Charles Evans Hughes for president. During World

War I he stumped the state on behalf of various activities in support of the war effort.

Governor of Massachusetts, 1919–1920. Elected narrowly over Democrat Richard H. Long, a shoe manufacturer of Framingham, in 1918, Governor Coolidge took steps to ease the postwar housing shortage, approved cost-of-living pay increases for public employees, limited the workweek for women and children to 48 hours, regulated outdoor advertising, and established a state budget system. He gained national attention for his handling of the Boston police strike of 1919. To protest the police commissioner's refusal to recognize their union, about 75 percent of the Boston police force walked off the job, sparking a crime wave in the city. Mayor Andrew J. Peters requested state assistance, but Governor Coolidge hesitated. Peters then called out state troops under his jurisdiction in Boston to meet the emergency. The next day Coolidge sent additional state forces into the city and upheld the police commissioner's decision not to rehire the strikers. When American Federation of Labor President Samuel Gompers urged him to reconsider, Governor Coolidge refused, saying, "There is no right to strike against the public safety by anybody, anywhere, any time."[6] Coolidge's firm stand for law and order drew widespread praise, especially from those who believed the strike to be inspired by anarchists. Coolidge was reelected handily, again over Richard H. Long, in 1919.

Vice President, 1921–1923. Coolidge was a favorite-son candidate for the Republican presidential nomination in 1920. At the party's convention in Chicago, he received 34 votes, mostly from Massachusetts, on the first ballot. His support eroded in subsequent tallies, and he was not among the list of candidates under consideration by policital leaders who met at the Blackstone Hotel to agree on the nomination of Warren G. Harding. The front-runner for the vice presidential nomination was Senator Irvine Lenroot of Wisconsin. But during Lenroot's nomination speech, scattered cries of "Coolidge! Coolidge!" went up from the floor. The chair recognized Wallace McCamant of Oregon, apparently in the belief that he was about to second the Lenroot nomination. Instead, McCamant nominated Coolidge, touching off a stampede to the Massachusetts governor. Coolidge won the nomination on the first ballot with 674 votes to 146 for Lenroot and the rest scattered. During the contest, Coolidge campaigned moderately, mostly in New England and the South. As vice president, he attended cabinet meetings but took little part in the proceedings. He presided loosely over the Senate, rarely interjecting from the chair. He ran afoul of Progressives in failing to follow agreed-on procedures during Senate consideration of a farm relief bill. Coolidge was vacationing at his father's home in Plymouth Notch, Vermont, when on August 2, 1923, President Harding died. Because the Coolidge home had no telephone, three men— Coolidge's stenographer Erwin C. Geisser, his chauffeur Joseph N. McInerney, and reporter William H. Crawford—set out by car in the middle of the night from Bridgewater, where they had received by wire news of the president's death, to notify the vice president. They first roused John Coolidge, the vice president's father, who in turn woke his son. Stunned but not shaken by the news, Calvin Coolidge, together with his wife and father, knelt down to say a brief prayer before going downstairs to take the oath of office.

At 2:47 A.M. on August 3, 1923, Calvin Coolidge was sworn into office as president by his father, in his capacity as justice of the peace and notary public, in the sitting room of his father's home. He then went back to sleep.

REPUBLICAN PRESIDENTIAL NOMINATION, 1924: As Republicans gathered in Cleveland in June 1924 for the first national party convention to be broadcast on radio, Coolidge's nomination was ensured. Marion L. Burton, president of the University of Michigan, delivered his nomination speech. Coolidge was nominated on the first ballot with 1,165 votes to 34 for Senator Robert M. LaFollette of Wisconsin and 10 for Senator Hiram Johnson of California. For vice president Coolidge preferred Senator William E. Borah of Idaho, but he declined. On the second ballot the convention nominated Governor Frank Lowden of Illinois, who stunned everybody by sending word of his refusal just as delegates were making the vote unanimous. Charles G. Dawes of Illinois was then nominated for vice president on the third ballot. The Republican platform favored tax reduction, extension of civil service protection to postmasters and Prohibition-enforcement field forces, collection of foreign debts, the protective tariff, U.S. participation in the World Court but not in the League of Nations, aid to farmers by broadening export markets and establishing a federal organization for cooperative marketing of farm products, a constitutional amendment banning child labor, the eight-hour workday, creation of a cabinet-level department of education and relief, federal encouragement of commercial aviation, and a federal antilynching law.

OPPONENTS: John W. Davis (1873–1955) of West Virginia; Democrat. Born in Clarksburg, West Virginia, the son of a lawyer and active Democrat, Davis graduated from Washington and Lee University law school in 1895 and taught there briefly before joining his father in practice in Clarksburg. In 1899 he was elected to the state legislature. During his single term in the U.S. House, 1911–1913, he helped draft the Clayton Anti-Trust Act (1914; see "Woodrow Wilson, 28th President," "Administration"). Appointed solicitor general, 1913–1918, by President Wilson, he pleased Progressives with his arguments on behalf of administration programs. As ambassador to Great Britain 1918–1921, he helped prepare the Treaty of Versailles of 1919 ending World War I. Davis was a minor candidate for the Democratic presidential nomination in 1920. He was president of the American Bar Association during 1922–1924. The Democratic national convention held in New York during June–July 1924 was a protracted struggle between the forces of former Treasury secretary William G. McAdoo of California, the candidate of the rural South and West, the Drys, and the Ku Klux Klan, and Governor Alfred E. Smith of New York, supported by Tammany Hall, the eastern cities, and the Wets. Franklin D. Roosevelt, attempting to make a political comeback after being stricken by polio, electrified the convention with a speech nominating Smith, dubbing him the Happy Warrior. The aging warhorse William Jennings Bryan, a McAdoo backer, rose to the rostrum to defend the Ku Klux Klan, thus helping to defeat an anti-Klan plank in the platform by a wafer-thin margin. On the first ballot McAdoo led with 431½ votes, 300 short of the necessary two thirds, to 241 for Smith. There followed the longest deadlock of any major party convention in U.S. history. Through 100 ballots McAdoo and Smith forces slugged it out, neither able to gain significant ground. Both then withdrew, clearing the way for Davis to emerge as a compromise choice on the one-hundred-third ballot. Governor Charles W. Bryan of Nebraska, brother of William Jennings Bryan, was nominated for vice president. The Democratic platform favored a reduction in the tariff, a graduated income tax, relief for farmers, land reclamation, federal regulation of the coal industry, extending civil service protection to Internal Revenue officers, public financing of political campaigns and limits on individual campaign contributions, enforcement of Prohibition, independence for the Philippines, multilateral disarmament, a national referendum to decide whether the United States should join the League of Nations, rigorous enforcement of antitrust laws, development of government and commercial aviation, and public works projects in times of high unemployment. After his defeat by Coolidge, Davis resumed his law practice. He frequently appeared before the Supreme Court, notably in opposition to President Truman's seizure of the steel mills and in defense of segregated school systems in the South.

Robert M. LaFollette (1855–1925) of Wisconsin; Progressive. Born in Primrose, Wisconsin, LaFollette graduated from the University of Wisconsin in 1879, was admitted to the bar in 1880, and became active in politics as an independent Republican. He served in the U.S. House 1885–1891, as governor of Wisconsin 1900–1906, and as U.S. senator 1906–1925. He emerged the leading progressive Republican in the country but was eclipsed by former president Theodore Roosevelt in his third-party bid for president in 1912. Senator LaFollette crossed party lines to support President Wilson's progressive domestic policies but voted against the U.S. declaration of war in 1917 and opposed U.S. participation in the League of Nations and the World Court. He sponsored the resolution calling for an investigation of the Teapot Dome scandal (see "Warren G. Harding, 29th President," "Administration"). At the Progressive national convention in Cleveland in July 1924, LaFollette was nominated for president. Senator Burton K. Wheeler of Montana was nominated for vice president. The Progressive platform favored marshaling the powers of the federal government to crush private monopoly, public ownership of water resources and the railroads, an increase in the inheritance tax, an excess-profits tax, relief for farmers, abolition of the labor injunction, election of all federal judges, ratification of the child labor amendment and a federal law to protect children in industry, an end to sex discrimination, a deep waterway from the Great Lakes to the sea, and multinational agreements to outlaw war, abolish conscription, and disarm. LaFollette died in Washington less than a year after his defeat by Coolidge.

CAMPAIGN AND THE ISSUES, 1924: With the country prosperous, the nation at peace, and the integrity of the executive branch restored in the wake of the Harding scandals, the Republican slogan "Keep Cool with Coolidge" caught the popular mood. The president let others campaign for him until the last week of the contest, when he delivered a probusiness address to a receptive audience of the U.S. Chamber of Commerce. Davis endorsed the Democratic platform but went beyond it in denouncing the Ku Klux Klan and advocating U.S. participation in the League of Nations. Although his chances of ousting a popular incumbent were all but destroyed by the divisive convention that nominated him, Davis nevertheless campaigned vigorously against both LaFollette and the Republican administration, which he blamed for corruption favoritism, and impotence. To his distress, few voters were prepared to blame Coolidge for the sins of Harding. William Jennings Bryan campaigned for the Democratic nominee, but even his oratorical skills did little to broaden Davis's base outside the South. LaFollette campaigned moderately, delivering 20 speeches in 13 states. Yet, for a third-party candidate, he drew surprisingly strong support, his cause aided by the endorsement of the Socialist party and the American Federation of Labor. But his strength was so diffuse that, although he netted one sixth of the popular vote, he carried only his home state, for just 2 percent of the electoral votes.

ELECTION AS PRESIDENT, NOVEMBER 4, 1924:

Popular Vote: Coolidge (Republican), 15,725,016 (54%); Davis (Democrat), 8,385,586 (29%); LaFollette (Progressive), 4,822,856 (17%).

Electoral Vote: Coolidge, 382; Davis, 136; LaFollette, 13.

States carried: Coolidge won the electoral votes of 35 states—Arizona, California, Colorado, Connecticut, Delaware, Idaho, Illinois, Indiana, Iowa, Kansas, Kentucky, Maine, Maryland, Massachusetts, Michigan, Minnesota, Missouri, Montana, Nebraska, Nevada, New Hampshire, New Jersey, New Mexico, New York, North Dakota, Ohio, Oregon, Pennsylvania, Rhode Island, South Dakota, Utah, Vermont, Washington, West Virginia, and Wyoming. Davis won the electoral votes of 12 states—Alabama, Arkansas, Florida, Georgia, Louisiana, Mississippi, North Carolina, Oklahoma, South Carolina, Tennessee, Texas, and Virginia. LaFollette won the electoral votes of 1 state— Wisconsin.

INAUGURAL ADDRESS: March 4, 1925. ". . . The method of raising revenue ought not to impede the transaction of business; it ought to encourage it. I am opposed to extremely high rates, because they produce little or no revenue, because they are bad for the country, and, finally, because they are wrong. We can not finance the country, we can not improve social conditions, through any system of injustice, even if we attempt to inflict it upon the rich. Those who suffer the most harm will be the poor. This country believes in prosperity. It is absurd to suppose that it is envious of those who are already prosperous. The wise and correct course to follow in taxation and all other economic legislation is not to destroy those who have already secured success but to create conditions under which every one will have a better chance to be successful. . . ."

VICE PRESIDENT: Charles Gates Dawes (1865–1951), of Illinois, served 1925– 1929. Born in Marietta, Ohio, Dawes took a degree in engineering from Marietta College in 1884 and in law from the University of Cincinnati in 1886. Admitted to the bar in 1886, he set up practice in Lincoln, Nebraska, and from 1894 in the Chicago area. He was appointed comptroller of the currency, 1897–1901, by President McKinley. In 1902 he founded the Central Trust Company of Illinois and prospered. During World War I, he rose from a major in the Engineering Corps to brigadier general and purchasing agent for the American Expeditionary Force under General John J. Pershing. Testifying after the war before a congressional committee investigating charges of overpayment for military supplies, Dawes caught the nation's fancy by lashing back: "Sure we paid. We didn't dicker. . . . We would have paid horse prices for sheep if sheep could have pulled artillery to the front. . . . Hell and Maria, we weren't trying to keep a set of books, we were trying to win the war!"[7] Thereafter he was nicknamed Hell and Maria Dawes. He was appointed the nation's first director of the Budget Bureau, 1921–1922, by President Harding. As chairman of the reparations committee in 1924 examining the financial condition of Germany, he devised the Dawes Plan, reducing reparations payments and otherwise stabilizing the German economy. For this he was awarded the 1925 Nobel Peace Prize. As vice president Dawes did not get along well with President Coolidge. Coolidge took umbrage at Dawes's letter informing him that he did not wish to attend cabinet meetings. And on Inauguration Day, Dawes stole the spotlight from the president in taking the occasion to denounce Congress and demand repeal of the filibuster rule. The final break came when Coolidge's nominee for attorney general failed to gain confirmation by a tie vote, while Dawes, who as presiding officer of the Senate could have broken the tie in the administration's favor, was napping at the Willard Hotel. Dawes later served as ambassador to Great Britain 1929–1932 and president of the Reconstruction Finance Corporation in 1932 under President Hoover. Dawes also was a talented musician and composer. His most notable work, "Melody in A Major" (1911), achieved some success as a violin piece in the 1920s and even wider fame as the music of the 1952 popular song "It's All in the Game." Dawes's writings include *A Journal of the Great War* (1921) and *Notes as Vice President* (1935).

CABINET:

Secretary of State. (1) Charles Evans Hughes (1862–1948), of New York, served 1921–1925. A holdover from the Harding administration, he resigned to return to private practice. See also "William Howard Taft, 27th President," "Supreme Court Appointments"; "Woodrow Wilson, 28th President," "Campaign, 1916," and "Opponent"; "Herbert Hoover, 31st President," "Supreme Court Appointments." (2) Frank B. Kellogg (1856–1937), of Minnesota, served 1925–1929. Promoted from ambassador to Great Britain, he negotiated the Kellogg-Briand Pact of 1928 (see "Administration"), which earned him the 1929 Nobel Peace Prize.

Secretary of the Treasury. Andrew W. Mellon (1855–1937), of Pennsylvania, served 1921–1932. A holdover from the Harding administration, he administered a probusiness policy that coincided perfectly with President Coolidge's philosophy of government. He persuaded Congress to cut taxes (see "Administration"), especially among the wealthy. He stayed on in the Hoover administration.

Secretary of War. (1) John W. Weeks (1860–1926), of Massachusetts, served 1921–1925. A holdover from the Harding administration, he clashed with General Billy Mitchell over the role of aviation in defense. (2) Dwight F. Davis (1879–1945), of Missouri, served 1925–1929. He was promoted from assistant secretary of war. A tennis player in his youth, he in 1900 had donated the Davis Cup as an international tennis trophy.

Attorney General. (1) Harry M. Daugherty (1860–1941), of Ohio, served 1921–1924. A holdover from the Harding administration, he was the subject of a congressional investigation for alleged participation in criminal activity. When he refused to open Justice Department files to congressional investigators, President Coolidge dismissed him. (2) Harlan Fiske Stone (1872–1946), of New York, served 1924–1925. He had been a classmate of Coolidge at Amherst College. He restored integrity to the department in the wake of the scandals in the Harding administration. He reorganized the Bureau of Investigation, appointing as its director a 29-year-old lawyer, J. Edgar Hoover. Stone resigned to accept appointment to the Supreme Court. (3) John G. Sargent (1860–1939), of Vermont, served 1925–1929. He grappled with enforcement of Prohibition.

Secretary of the Navy. (1) Edwin Denby (1870–1929), of Michigan, served 1921–1924. A holdover from the Harding Administration, he had been an unwitting participant in the Teapot Dome scandal. He resigned following passage of a Senate resolution calling on him to do so. In accepting his resignation, President Coolidge affirmed his faith in his honesty and integrity.

(2) Curtis D. Wilbur (1867–1954), of California, served 1924–1929. He encouraged greater use of aircraft.

Postmaster General. Harry S. New (1858–1937), of Indiana, served 1923–1929. A holdover from the Harding administration, he improved and extended air mail service.

Secretary of the Interior. (1) Hubert Work (1860–1942), of Colorado, served 1923–1928. A holdover from the Harding administration, he restored integrity in the department in the wake of the criminal involvement of his predecessor, Albert Fall, in the Teapot Dome scandal. He resigned to direct Herbert Hoover's presidential campaign. (2) Roy O. West (1868–1958), of Illinois, served 1928–1929. His appointment was controversial because of his close ties with Chicago utilities magnate Samuel Insull.

Secretary of Agriculture. (1) Henry C. Wallace (1866–1924), of Iowa, served 1921–1924. A holdover from the Harding administration, he argued unsuccessfully for farm relief as embodied in the McNary-Haugen bill (see "Administration") and clashed with Commerce Secretary Hoover over food policy. He died in office. (2) Howard M. Gore (1877–1947), of West Virginia, served 1924–1925. Promoted from assistant secretary of agriculture, he resigned after four months to become governor of West Virginia. (3) William M. Jardine (1879–1955), of Kansas, served 1925–1929. President of the Agricultural College in Manhattan, Kansas, at the time of his appointment, he encouraged the formation of farm cooperatives.

Secretary of Commerce. (1) Herbert Hoover (1874–1964), of California, served 1921–1928. He was a holdover from the Harding administration. See "Herbert Hoover, 31st President," "Career before the Presidency." (2) William Whiting (1864–1936), of Massachusetts, served 1928–1929.

Secretary of Labor. James J. Davis (1873–1947), of Pennsylvania, served 1921–1930. A holdover from the Harding administration, he stayed on in the Hoover administration.

ADMINISTRATION: August 3, 1923–March 3, 1929.

Immigration Act of 1924. This law cut the immigration quota in two ways: reducing it from 3 percent to 2 percent of foreign nationals resident in the United States, and changing the base on which these percentages were applied from the 1910 census figures to those of 1890. Because much of the immigration between 1890 and 1910 had stemmed from southern and eastern Europe, the law sharply reduced quotas for such peoples as Italians and Jews while favoring those from northern Europe. The law also placed a ceiling of 150,000 immigrants annually from all sources with effect from 1927 and excluded the Japanese altogether.

Tax Reduction. Revenue acts of 1924 and 1926, skewed in favor of the wealthy, sharply reduced income and inheritance taxes and abolished the gift tax and most of the excise taxes imposed during World War I. In freeing up funds for private investment, it contributed to the dizzying round of speculation later in the decade that led to the stock market crash and Great Depression (see "Herbert Hoover, 31st President," "Administration").

Veterans Bonus, 1924. Passed over President Coolidge's veto, the bill awarded World War I veterans paid-up insurance redeemable in 20 years, the amount to be determined by length of service and whether served at home or abroad. It was veterans' insistence on immediate payment of the bonus during the Great Depression that led to the Bonus March (see "Herbert Hoover," "Administration").

Commercial Aviation. In 1926 the Coolidge administration won passage of the Air Commerce Act, placing civil aviation under the direction of the commerce department, and approved the first two commercial air routes: The Transcontinental Airway was to link New York and Los Angeles/San Francisco via Cleveland, Chicago, Iowa City, Des Moines, North Platte, Cheyenne, and Salt Lake City. The Southwestern Airway connected Chicago and Dallas via Fort Wayne, Moline, St. Joseph, Kansas City, Wichita, Tulsa, and Oklahoma City. Three other routes were promised between Boston and Miami, southern California and Portland, and St. Louis and New Orleans, as well as feeder routes to service Detroit and Minneapolis–St. Paul.

Farm Relief Vetoes, 1927–1928. Under the McNary-Haugen Bill, Congress hoped to support farm prices by setting up a government corporation to buy certain surplus crops for resale abroad, either storing them until prices rose on the world market or dumping them at a loss. The bill passed twice and was vetoed each time. In the first veto message President Coolidge condemned the bill as rank price fixing. "Nothing is more certain," he warned, "than that such price fixing would upset the normal exchange relationships existing in the open market and that it would finally have to be extended to cover a multitude of other goods and services. Government price fixing, once started, has alike no justice and no end. It is an economic folly from which this country has every right to be spared."[8]

Kellogg-Briand Pact, 1928. Under its terms, 15 countries—the United States, France, Germany, Belgium, Great Britain, Ireland, Canada, Australia, New Zealand, India, South Africa, Italy, Japan, Poland, and Czechoslovakia—agreed to renounce war as a means of settling international disputes. Eventually another 47 nations joined in the pact, virtually the entire civilized world except for Argentina, Bolivia, Uruguay, El Salvador, and Yemen. The pact was drawn up by Secretary of State Frank B. Kellogg and French Foreign Minister Aristide Briand. It is also known as the Pact of Paris or the Pact of Peace.

SUPREME COURT APPOINTMENTS: Harlan Fiske Stone (1872–1946), of New York, served as associate justice 1925–1941 and as chief justice 1941–1946. He was attorney general at the time of his appointment. He generally joined liberals on the bench, at first in minority and later in majority, in upholding social welfare legislation and civil liberties. Dissenting from the majority in *United States* v. *Butler* (1936), which struck down the Agricultural Adjustment Act of the Franklin Roosevelt administration, Stone reminded his brethren, "Courts are concerned only with the power to enact statutes, not with their wisdom. . . . While the unconstitutional exercise of power by the executive and legislative branches of the government is subject to judicial restraint, the only check upon our own exercise of power is our own exercise of self-restraint." With a change of personnel and climate of opinion on the Court, Stone was able to deliver the unanimous opinion in *United States* v. *Darby Lumber* (1940), upholding the Fair Labor Standards Act of 1938, which fixed a minimum wage and maximum hours in interstate commerce. But although Stone afforded a presumption of constitutionality to legislation restricting business, he presumed laws limiting individual freedom to be unconstitutional until proven otherwise. He applied this doctrine of "preferred freedoms" to a series of cases, including *Minersville School District* v. *Gobitis* (1940), in which he stood alone in dissent against a state law compelling Jehovah's Witness children to salute the flag in public schools. "If only popular causes are entitled to enjoy the benefit of constitutional guarantees," he said, "they serve no purpose and could as well not have been written." Stone's position was vindicated in a subsequent ruling. Appointed chief justice by President Franklin Roosevelt in 1941, Stone presided loosely over the Court, encouraging full and open discussion of cases. Stone suffered a stroke while reading a dissent in open court and died shortly thereafter.

RANKING IN 1962 HISTORIANS POLL: Coolidge ranked twenty-seventh of 31 presidents, fourth of 6 "below average" presidents. He ranked above Pierce, below Fillmore.

RETIREMENT: March 4, 1929–January 5, 1933. On August 2, 1927, Coolidge surprised the nation with a terse announcement of his retirement: "I do not choose to run for President in 1928." He did not explain why. Some observers have speculated that he turned down almost certain reelection out of concern for his health and that of his wife. According to Mrs. Coolidge, he once commented that he was best suited to directing tight-fisted governmental policy and that perhaps the next four years were a time for greater federal spending, a policy he believed could best be administered by a less frugal president. Still others believe that Coolidge retired because he was farsighted enough to see the coming economic crash and got out before his reputation for fostering prosperity became tarnished. After attending the inauguration of his successor, Herbert Hoover, he retired to Northampton, Massachusetts. He wrote his autobiography as well as articles for such national magazines as the *Saturday Evening Post* and *Collier's*. During 1930–1931 he wrote a daily column, *Thinking Things Over with Calvin Coolidge*, for the McClure Newspaper Syndicate. He also served on the board of directors of the New York Life Insurance Company. In October 1931 he spoke on radio warning listeners to beware of insurance agents who frequently attempt to alter their policies. Lewis B. Tibbett, an insurance salesman of St. Louis, sued Coolidge for $100,000, claiming that he had lost business because of the speech. Anxious to avoid the publicity of a trial, Coolidge settled out of court for $2,500. Coolidge campaigned for the reelection of President Hoover in 1932.

DEATH: January 5, 1933, about 12:45 P.M., at home, Northampton, Massachusetts. During his last months, Coolidge complained often of difficulty in breathing, indigestion, and listlessness. On January 5, 1933, he spent about 90 minutes at his office in town and returned home about 10 A.M. He worked on a jigsaw puzzle of George Washington for a time and about noon went upstairs. Little more than an hour later Mrs. Coolidge discovered him in his shirtsleeves sprawled on his back on the floor, dead. He had suffered a coronary thrombosis. Funeral services were held at Edwards Congregational Church in Northampton. He was buried at the Coolidge family plot at Plymouth, Vermont. Characteristically, Coolidge's last will and testament, executed in December 1926, was just 23 words in length: "Not unmindful of my son John, I give all my estate, both real and personal, to my wife, Grace Coolidge, in fee simple." His estate was valued at about $700,000.

COOLIDGE PRAISED: "He is very self-contained, very simple, very direct and very shrewd in his observations."[9]—Chief Justice William Howard Taft, 1923

"Mr. Coolidge belongs rather in the class of Presidents who were distinguished for character more than for heroic achievement. His great task was to restore the dignity and prestige of the Presidency when it had reached the lowest ebb in our history, and to afford, in a time of extravagance and waste, a shining public example of the simple and homely virtues which came down to him from his New England ancestors."[10]—Alfred E. Smith, 1928 Democratic presidential nominee, 1933

"You hear a lot of jokes every once in a while about 'Silent Cal Coolidge.' The joke is on the people who make the jokes. Look at his record. He cut the taxes four times. We had probably the greatest growth and prosperity that we've ever known. I have taken heed of that because if he did that by doing nothing, maybe that's the answer."[11]President Ronald Reagan, 1981

COOLIDGE CRITICIZED: "He is a timid man frightened into conventionality."[12]—E. M. House, former aide to President Wilson

"He believes in machine politics. . . . He possesses no outstanding ability."[13]—Republican Senator George W. Norris of Nebraska, 1924

"Mr. Coolidge's genius for inactivity is developed to a very high point. It is far from being an indolent inactivity. It is a grim, determined, alert inactivity which keeps Mr. Coolidge occupied constantly. . . . Inactivity is a political philosophy and a party program with Mr. Coolidge."[14]—Journalist Walter Lippman, 1926

"In what manner he would have performed himself if the holy angels had shoved the Depression forward a couple of years—this we can only guess, and one man's hazard is as good as another's. My own is that he would have responded to bad times precisely as he responded to good ones—that is, by pulling down the blinds, stretching his legs upon his desk, and snoozing away the lazy afternoons."[15]—Journalist H. L. Mencken, 1933

COOLIDGE QUOTES: "Do the day's work. If it be to protect the rights of the weak, whoever objects, do it. If it be to help a powerful corporation better to serve the people, whatever the opposition, do that. Expect to be called a stand-patter, but don't be a stand-patter. Expect to be called a demagogue, but don't be a demagogue. Don't hesitate to be as revolutionary as science. Don't hesitate to be as reactionary as the multiplication table. Don't expect to build up the weak by pulling down the strong. Don't hurry to legislate. Give administration a chance to catch up with legislation."[16]—1914

"The chief business of America is business."[17]—1924

"Four-fifths of all our troubles in this life would disappear if we would only sit down and keep still."[18]

BOOK BY COOLIDGE: *The Autobiography of Calvin Coolidge* (1929).

BOOKS ABOUT COOLIDGE: McCoy, Donald R. *Calvin Coolidge: The Quiet President.* New York: Macmillan, 1967.

White, William Allen. *A Puritan in Babylon: The Story of Calvin Coolidge.* New York: Macmillan, 1938.

NOTES

1 Claude M. Fuess, *Calvin Coolidge: The Man from Vermont*, Hamden, Conn.: Archon Books, 1965, p. 25.
2 Donald R. McCoy, *Calvin Coolidge: The Quiet President*, New York: Macmillan, 1967, pp. 160–161.
3 *The Autobiography of Calvin Coolidge*, New York: Cosmopolitan Book Corp., 1929, p. 13.
4 Ibid., p. 190.
5 Ishbel Ross, *Grace Coolidge and Her Era*, New York: Dodd, Mead, 1962, p. 17.

6 McCoy, p. 94.

7 Donald Young, *American Roulette: The History and Dilemma of the Vice Presidency*, New York: Holt, Rinehart and Winston, 1965, p. 155.

8 Henry Steele Commager, ed., *Documents of American History*, New York: Crofts, 1945, Doc. no. 462, p. 394.

9 Henry Pringle, *The Life and Times of William Howard Taft*, New York: Farrar and Rinehart, 1939, p. 1019.

10 Edward Connery Lathem, ed., *Meet Calvin Coolidge: The Man behind the Myth*, Brattleboro, Vt.: Stephen Green Press, 1960, pp. 219–220.

11 *Cleveland Plain Deale-*, May 29, 1981, p. 8–D.

12 William Allen White, *A Puritan in Babylon: The Story of Calvin Coolidge*, New York: Macmillan, 1938, p. 236.

13 Burl Noggle, *Teapot Dome: Oil and Politics in the 1920s*, New York: Norton, 1965, p. 149.

14 Lathem, p. 52.

15 Ibid., p. 57.

16 McCoy, p. 55.

17 Frank Freidel, *America in the Twentieth Century*, New York: Knopf, 1965, p. 244.

18 Arthur M. Schlesinger, Jr., *The Crisis of the Older Order 1919–1933*, Boston: Houghton, Mifflin, 1957, p. 58.

HERBERT HOOVER

☆ ☆ ☆ ☆ ☆ ☆ ☆ ☆

31st PRESIDENT

NAME: Herbert Clark Hoover. From his youth he was known as Bert to friends.

PHYSICAL DESCRIPTION: Hoover stood 5 feet 11 inches tall and had straight brown hair, parted just to the left of center, hazel eyes, a round fleshy face, ruddy complexion, and a husky build. He was slightly round-shouldered. As a young man he wore a beard and mustache to look older. He dressed simply.

PERSONALITY: Hoover was hardworking, incorruptible, self-assured and self-reliant. But he was also aloof, shy, wary of crowds, awkward at superficial social relations, and extremely sensitive to criticism. "It was," biographer David Burner has written, "perhaps the private man's shrinkage from rough political contact, the predilection for working by himself, and the habit of perceiving problems as requiring rational, impersonal solutions that made Hoover uncomfortable with the rude, demanding Congress as well as with the press."[1] Hoover often was curt with subordinates. A model of efficiency himself, he expected the same of others. Characteristically, he concentrated on detail rather than on the broader significance of a problem. He was a dull speaker, rarely lifting his eyes from the prepared text.

ANCESTORS: Hoover was of Swiss-German and English heritage. His great[4]-grandparents Jonas and Anna Huber emigrated from Switzerland to Ellerstadt in the German Palatinate in the seventeenth century. His great[3]-grandfather Andreas Huber sailed to Philadelphia in 1738, anglicized his name to Andrew Hoover, and eventually operated a grist mill on the Uwharrie River in Randolph County, North Carolina.

FATHER: Jesse Clark Hoover (1846–1880), blacksmith, farm equipment salesman. A native of West Milton, Ohio, he grew up there and at West Branch, Iowa. He prospered first as a blacksmith and later selling farm equipment in the closely knit Quaker community at West Branch, where he also served as town assessor and councilman. He died at 34 of heart trouble when his most famous son was six years old. Herbert Hoover had only a dim memory of his father.

MOTHER: Huldah Minthorn Hoover (1848–1883). A native of Burgersville, Ontario, Canada, she grew up there and on a farm near West Branch, Iowa. She attended the University of Iowa and taught school briefly before her marriage to Jesse Hoover in 1870. After her husband's death she took in sewing, carefully saving his life insurance money for her children's education. She became a Quaker minister and preached at various Friends meetings around Iowa. She advocated women's rights. Returning from a Quaker meeting one day, she was overly·exposed to the winter chill, developed pneumonia, and at 35 died. Thus orphaned at age nine, Herbert Hoover was to remember his mother chiefly as "a sweet-faced woman who for two years kept the little family of four together."[2]

SIBLINGS: The second of three children, Hoover had an older brother and a younger sister—Theodore Jesse Hoover, dean of the Stanford University School of Engineering; and Mrs. Mary "May" Leavitt.

COLLATERAL RELATIVE: Hoover was an eighth cousin once removed of Richard Nixon.

CHILDREN: Hoover had two sons.

Herbert Hoover, Jr. (1903–1969), engineer, diplomat. Born in London, he by age two had been around the world twice with his globe-trotting parents. He graduated from Stanford University in 1925 and began working as an aircraft engineer. He taught briefly, 1928–1929, at the Harvard Business School. Eventually he turned to geophysical engineering, founding the United Geophysical Company in 1935 and developing new electronic instruments to discover oil. During 1953–1954 he mediated the oil dispute between Britain and Iran that provided for the latter to nationalize its petroleum. He was appointed undersecretary of state for Middle Eastern affairs 1954–1957 by President Eisenhower. He died in Pasadena, California.

Allan Hoover (1907–1994), mining engineer. Born in London, he graduated from Stanford University in 1929 with a degree in economics and earned a master's degree from Harvard Business School in 1931. He went into banking and operated a ranch in California for a time, but eventually he, too, became a mining engineer. A private man, he shunned publicity throughout his career. He lived in Greenwich, Connecticut.

BIRTH: Hoover was born around midnight of August 10–11, 1874, in a small cottage on Downey Street in West Branch, Iowa. According to church records and Hoover's own account in 1915, the date of birth was August 11. But in his memoirs, Hoover fixed his birthday at August 10. He was delivered by his Aunt Ellen, a midwife. Another aunt, Agnes Minthorn, described the infant as "sweet," "round and plump," and "cordial." His father spoke prophetically of the new arrival, "Well, we have another General Grant at our house."[3]

CHILDHOOD: Hoover grew up in West Branch, Iowa, and, from age 10, in Oregon. At about 2 years of age, Hoover nearly died of the croup. His vital signs were imperceptible to his parents, who gave him up for dead, placing pennies over his eyes and drawing a sheet over his face. Fortunately, his uncle, Dr. John Minthorn, arrived in time to revived him. He subsequently contracted such typical childhood diseases as measles, mumps, and chicken pox. Among his earliest memories was stepping barefoot on a hot iron chip in his father's blacksmith shop; the incident permanently scarred the sole of his foot. At 6, he hurled a flaming stick into a hot cauldron of tar, sending billows of thick black smoke all over town. That same year he marched in the town's torchlight parade in support of James A. Garfield for president. At 10 he joined the Bank of Hope, a children's Prohibitionist club. With his father's death in 1880, Herbert from time to time was sent to stay with relatives in order to ease the burden on his mother. He lived briefly with Uncle Pennington Minthorn in his pioneer sod house in Sioux County, Iowa. At 7, he spent an exciting eight months living with Uncle Laban Miles, superintendent of the Osage Indian reservation at Pawhuska, Oklahoma Territory. There Herbert played with Indian children and learned how to hunt with bow and arrow and other native survival skills. As a child, Hoover dreamed of becoming a railroad engineer, but he also showed an early interest in geology, as he often examined the stone collection of Dr. William Walker, a West Branch dentist. He earned spare cash picking strawberries and collecting scrap iron. With the death of their mother in 1883, the three Hoover orphans were divided among the relatives. Nine-year-old Herbert was taken by Uncle Allan Hoover, who had a farm outside West Branch. But the next year the boy was passed to Dr. John Minthorn, the uncle who had saved his life as an infant and whose own son had recently died, in Newberg, Oregon. Uncle John was a stern, nonpacifist Quaker, who paraphrased a Biblical admonition to instruct the lad. "Turn your cheek once, but if he smites you again then punch him."[4] About 1888 Herbert and the Minthorn moved to Salem, Oregon. Now in his teens, he helped with many of the chores, clearing fields, chopping wood, tending the horses. He also hired out to work the nearby onion fields and was an office boy for the Oregon Land Company.

EDUCATION: From age five, Hoover learned the fundamentals at the West Branch Free School. An average student, he later recalled that the only part of school he liked was recess. After moving to Oregon, he attended Friends Pacific Academy 1885–1887 in Newberg, where he continued to receive average marks in most subjects but excelled in math, and a business school in Salem. He never graduated from high school. A Miss Jennie Gray of Salem introduced him to English literature. Robert Brown, an engineer from the East, encouraged him to take up engineering. Having failed in all areas, except math, the entrance examination for the newly established Stanford University, he in 1891 took college preparatory instruction at Palo Alto, California. Tested again, he passed but was admitted "conditioned" in English, a condition removed during his senior year. At 17 he was the youngest student in Stanford's first class in 1891. Under the university's pass-fail system of evaluation, Hoover, a geology major, received passing marks in all subjects except German. In extracurricular activities, he was elected junior class treasurer and treasurer of the student body, played shortstop on the freshman baseball team, and was manager of the baseball and football teams. He was a campus "barbarian," or nonfraternity man. During his junior year, former president Benjamin Harrison arrived at Stanford to deliver a series of lectures. One day he attended a college baseball game and inadvertently slipped past the student ticket takers. Hoover, who as baseball manager was responsible for gate receipts, went after the former president and respectfully asked for the 25¢ admission. Harrison promptly paid up and bought three more advance tickets. The incident was, Hoover later recalled, "my first contact with a great public man."[5] Hoover worked his way through Stanford as a newsboy and clerk in the registration office and started up a student laundry service. During the summer between his freshman and sophomore years, he worked as an assistant on the Geological Survey of Arkansas, mapping out the north side of the Ozarks. The next two summers he worked with the U.S. Geological Survey in California and Nevada. Hoover graduated with an A.B. in geology in May 1895. He had decided to become a mining engineer.

RELIGION: Quaker. Hoover was the first Quaker president. Raised amid strong religious influence, he had read the entire Bible by age 10. As president he attended the Friends Meeting House in Washington. He believed the most important Quaker tenet to be "individual faithfulness." Unable to accept absolute pacifism, he regarded war as a morally justifiable last resort when all attempts at peace fail. In his later years, he came to regard the Cold War as a religious struggle. In 1950 he called on the God-fearing nations of the world to unite "against this tide of Red agnosticism . . . against the hideous ideas of the police state and human slavery."[6]

RECREATION: As president, Hoover exercised by tossing a medicine ball around for 30 minutes every morning before breakfast. An avid fisherman, he liked to escape the White House on weekends for the headwaters of the Rapidan River in what is now Shenandoah National Park in Virginia. He enjoyed reading mysteries. He drank moderately. As commerce secretary during Prohibition he reportedly stopped off at the Belgian Embassy for drinks on his way home; because embassies technically are foreign territory, the practice was legal. After repeal of Prohibition, he enjoyed martinis in his own home.

MARRIAGE: Herbert Hoover, 24, married Lou Henry, 24, on February 10, 1899, at the home of the bride's parents in Monterey, California. Born on March 29, 1874, in Waterloo, Iowa, the daughter of Charles D. Henry, a banker, and Florence Weed Henry, Lou grew up something of a tomboy in Waterloo, and in Whittier, and Monterey, California. She attended San Jose Normal School and in 1894 enrolled at Stanford University as the school's only female geology major. That year she met Hoover, then a senior. By the time he graduated the following June, they had reached an understanding but put off wedding plans while she continued her education and he pursued his engineering career in Australia. From there in 1898, the year she graduated from Stanford, Hoover cabled a marriage proposal, which she promptly accepted by return wire. Although raised an Episcopalian, Miss Henry decided to become a Quaker. But because there was no Quaker meeting in Monterey, they were married in a civil ceremony performed by Father Ramon Mestres, a Roman Catholic priest of the San Carlos Borromeo Mission. Soon after the wedding they sailed for Tientsin, China, and Hoover's new job. She was present with her husband during the Boxer Rebellion. Possessed of a natural ear for languages, Mrs. Hoover became quite proficient in Chinese. In the White House the Hoovers at times conversed in Chinese to foil eavesdroppers. Also well versed in Latin, she collaborated with her husband in translating Agricola's *De Re Metallica*, a sixteenth-century encyclopedia of mining and metallurgy; the Hoover translation was published in 1912. During World War I, she assisted her husband in providing relief for Belgian refugees. For her work she was decorated in 1919 by King Albert of Belgium. While Hoover served in the cabinet of Presidents Harding and Coolidge, she was active as national president of the Girl Scouts. As First Lady, she entertained frequently and at times threw together informal dinners on the spur of the moment, placing an unwelcome strain on the White House staff. She discontinued the New Year's Day reception, the annual open house observance begun by Mrs. John Adams in 1801. Mrs. Hoover died of a heart attack, in New York City on January 7, 1944. She was buried in Palo Alto, California, and reinterred at West Branch, Iowa, next to the president, following his death in 1964.

MILITARY SERVICE: None.

CAREER BEFORE THE PRESIDENCY:

Mining Engineer, 1896–1914. On graduation from Stanford University in 1895, Hoover, failing to find work as a surveyor, pushed ore carts 70 hours a week at a gold mine near Nevada City, California. Soon, however, he landed a modest office job in San Francisco and in 1896 was hired by Bewick, Moreing and Company as a mining engineer at Coolgardie, Australia, where he was responsible for inspecting and evaluating prospective mines prior to purchase. Transferred to China in 1899, he both represented the company's interest there and served as China's mining engineer in Chihli and Jehol provinces. There he developed vast coal deposits. During the Boxer Rebellion in 1900, he helped defend the foreign community in Tientsin. In 1902 he returned to Australia to develop highly lucrative zinc mines. It was with the Bawdwin silver mine in Burma that Hoover made much of his fortune; by 1914 he was worth an estimated $4 million. In 1908 he formed his own engineering firm, which aided in unearthing resources all over the globe, including important oil deposits in Russia. Politically, he identified with the Progressive wing of the Republican party. He contributed $1,000 to Theodore Roosevelt's third-party bid for president in 1912.

Relief Efforts during World War I. Hoover gained international attention during World War I with his highly efficient distribution of food and supplies to war-ravaged Europe. In 1914 he headed the American Relief Committee, lending assistance to some 120,000 Americans stranded in Europe at the opening of hostilities. As head of the Commission for the Relief of Belgium, 1914–1919, and as director of the American Relief Administration, 1919–1920, he distributed some 34 million tons of American food, clothing, and supplies valued at $5.2 billion in addition to supplies provided by other countries. Meanwhile, as U.S. food administrator 1917–1918, he exhorted the nation to observe wheatless and meatless days to conserve supplies for the war effort; the new verb *to hooverize* meant voluntarily to ration one's goods. During this same time, the peripatetic Hoover served on the War Trade Council, 1917–1920, chaired the Sugar Equalization Board, 1918–1919, and the European Coal Council, 1919, and was economic director of the Supreme Economic Council, 1918–1919, and economic advisor to President Woodrow Wilson at the Versailles Peace Conference. In 1919 he founded at Stanford University the Hoover Institution on War, Revolution, and Peace as a repository for records of World War I. He supported American participation in the League of Nations and blamed President Wilson's intransigence for its failure. He was mentioned as a presidential possibility as early as 1920.

Secretary of Commerce, 1921–1928. Having supported Warren G. Harding for president in 1920, Hoover was appointed secretary of commerce and stayed on in the Coolidge administration. He expanded the Bureau of Standards into a testing facility for a wide range of products, increased the amount of data collected by the Census Bureau to provide more useful information to business, authorized the Bureau of Fisheries to upgrade the nation's fish stocks through selective breeding, and used the Foreign and Domestic Commerce Bureau to seek new markets abroad. Under the Radio Act of 1927, he undertook regulation of the air waves. Under the Air Commerce Act of 1926, he established the Aeronautics Board for the development of commercial aviation. He sponsored the Conference on Unemployment in 1921, which recommended greater local efforts to aid the jobless and urged more farsighted economic planning. Often at odds with Agriculture Secretary Henry C. Wallace, he opposed the McNary-Haugen bill (see "Calvin Coolidge, 30th President," "Administration"); Hoover's solution to the American farm surplus was to expand food exports, cut food transportation costs by improving the nation's inland waterways, and erect a stiffer tariff barrier against foreign foodstuffs. He also encouraged the growth of trade associations. A longtime advocate of improved working conditions, he was instrumental in persuading the steel industry to abandon the 12-hour workday in 1923. As head of the commission studying the feasibility of linking the Great Lakes to the Atlantic, he encouraged construction of the St. Lawrence Seaway. As chairman of the Colorado River Commission, he pressed for construction of Boulder Dam, later renamed Hoover Dam. He also supported the Dawes Plan, which eased the war-reparations schedule on Germany in an effort to stablilize that nation's war-ravaged economy. A strong Germany, Hoover believed at this time, was the best defense against the spread of Bolshevism. Hoover was a candidate for the Republican vice presidential nomination in 1924, losing to Charles G. Dawes. He campaigned in California for President Calvin Coolidge in the general election that year.

REPUBLICAN PRESIDENTIAL NOMINATION, 1928: When President Calvin Coolidge declared "I do not choose to run in 1928," he opened the way for Hoover aggressively to pursue the nomination. Although Coolidge declined to endorse anyone, he did nothing to impede Hoover, who emerged the clear front-runner by the time Republicans convened in Kansas City in June. On the basis of the primaries, Hoover already had 450 votes. He was supported by women's groups, the former Progressive supporters of Theodore Roosevelt, and ethnics. A stop-Hoover movement was divided between the supporters of Senator Charles Curtis of Kansas and those hoping to draft President Coolidge. The opposition melted away after Treasury Secretary Andrew Mellon, the dominant figure in the Pennsylvania delegation, endorsed Hoover. John L. McNab delivered Hoover's nominating address. Hoover was nominated on the first ballot with 837 votes to 72 for former governor Frank Lowden of Illinois, 64 for Curtis, and the rest scattered. Curtis was nominated for vice president. In his acceptance speech Hoover declared, in words that were to haunt him four years later, "We in America today are nearer to the final triumph over poverty than ever before in the history of any land. The poorhouse is vanishing from among us. . . . We shall soon with the help of God be in sight of the day when poverty will be banished from this nation."[7] The Republican platform was cautious, praising Coolidge prosperity and favoring reduction in the national debt, lower taxes, maintenance of the protective tariff, creation of a federal farm board "to prevent and control surpluses through orderly distribution," the right of collective bargaining, improvement of inland and intracoastal waterways, "observance and vigorous enforcement" of Prohibition, disclosure of campaign finances, and drafting material resources as well as manpower in times of war.

OPPONENT: Alfred E. Smith (1873–1944), of New York; Democrat. Smith was the first Roman Catholic to be nominated for president by a major party. Born amid poverty on the Lower East Side of New York City, the son of a teamster, Smith had little formal education and worked at the Fulton Fish Market and at other odd jobs as a young man. He early became associated with Tammany Hall and at 30 was elected to the state assembly, 1903–1915, rising to majority floor leader, 1911–1913, and speaker, 1913–1915. Radicalized by the Triangle Shirt-waist Factory fire of 1911 in which 146 women were killed for lack of adequate fire escapes, he emerged a champion of improved safety standards and working conditions. After serving as sheriff of New York County 1915–1917 and president of the New York City Board of Aldermen in 1917, he was four times elected governor of New York, 1919–1920 and 1923–1928. An active, progressive governor, he brought about such labor reforms as the eight-hour workday, minimum wage, workmen's compensation, and a state labor arbitration commis-sion. He also promoted the rights of women and immigrants, cleared slums, extended medical services to rural areas, built schools, hospitals, prisons, and parks, and established a state budget system. He was a leading candidate for the Democratic presidential nomination in 1924 (see "Calvin Coolidge, 30th President," "Opponents"). At the party's convention in Houston in June 1928, the Smith forces dominated the proceedings. Again, as in 1924, Franklin D. Roosevelt delivered Smith's nominating speech. On the first ballot Smith received 724⅔ votes, just 10 short of the necessary two thirds, against scattered favorite-son opposition. Before the second roll call, Ohio switched to Smith, putting him over the top. Other delegations followed to give Smith the nomination on a revised first ballot with 849⅔ votes. Senator Joseph T. Robinson of Arkansas was nominated for vice president; he was the first southerner to be nominated on the national ticket of a major party since the Civil War. In a bid to unite Wet and Dry Democrats behind Smith, who had long opposed Prohibition, the Democratic platform promised "an honest effort to enforce" Prohibition while taking no position for or against it. The platform also dropped the party's traditional call for a lower tariff and favored reduced taxes, creation of a federal farm board to assist farmers and stock raisers in marketing their products, international disarmament agreements, abolition of executive agreements with foreign powers that circumvent the constitutional requirement of Senate ratification, improved waterways and flood control projects, exemp-tion of labor from antitrust laws, public works projects in times of high unemployment, public disclosure of campaign finances, and federal aid to education. After his defeat by Hoover, Smith again sought the Democratic presidential nomination in 1932 but lost in a bitter contest to his former protégé Franklin D. Roosevelt. The two never fully reconciled. Smith grew increasingly conservative and joined the Liberty League, a right-wing organization violently opposed to the New Deal. In 1936 he bolted the party to support Republican Alf Landon for president.

CAMPAIGN AND THE ISSUES, 1928: Religion and Prohibition dominated the campaign. Smith defended his Catholicism in a major address in Oklahoma City, but his appeal for religious tolerance did little to allay fears that a Catholic president would become a tool of the pope. Scurrilous pamphlets distributed without Hoover's knowledge predicted that as president Smith would annul Protestant marriages and make Catholicism the state religion. The issue especially hurt Smith in the traditionally Democratic South, where Protestant fundamentalism ran deep and the Ku Klux Klan campaigned for Hoover. Smith's long-standing opposition to Prohibition also alienated the South and West, while Hoover defended the law as "a great social and economic experiment noble in motive and farreaching in purpose."[8] Hoover campaigned on the record of

Republican prosperity. A GOP circular, though apparently not Hoover himself, promised "a chicken in every pot and a car in every garage."[9] Smith lashed out against the corruption of the Harding administration and the probusiness policy of the Coolidge administration. Republicans condemned Smith for his Tammany Hall connections and lack of foreign policy experience. Both candidates agreed on the need to provide relief to farmers, develop waterpower, maintain the protective tariff, and conduct a noninterventionist foreign policy. On the stump, Smith was colorful and quick-witted, celebrated for his brown derby and cigar. Hoover in contrast was lackluster. Smith's campaign theme song, "The Sidewalks of New York," heralded the Democrat's humble origins, although observers noted that he enjoyed the support of Herbert Lehman and other Wall Street executives far removed from the Lower East Side. The Republican slogan "Let's Keep What We've Got" warned voters not to tamper with economic success. One notable Republican defector was Senator George W. Norris of Nebraska, who endorsed Smith for his support of federal development of hydroelectric power at Muscle Shoals, Alabama. Noted social worker Jane Addams endorsed Hoover for his record against poverty and for labor. Labor divided its support between the two candidates. Hoover closed his campaign with a speech in New York City October 22, 1928, in which he declared that the election offered voters a critical choice between "the American system of rugged individualism" set in place by Republicans after World War I and "doctrines of paternalism and state socialism" popular in Europe and espoused by some Democrats.

ELECTION AS PRESIDENT, NOVEMBER 6, 1928:

Popular Vote: Hoover (Republican), 21,392,190 (58%); Smith (Democrat), 15,016,443 (41%). This was Hoover's only elective office.

Electoral Vote: Hoover, 444; Smith, 87.

States Carried: Hoover won the electoral votes of 40 states—Arizona, California, Colorado, Connecticut, Delaware, Florida, Idaho, Illinois, Indiana, Iowa, Kansas, Kentucky, Maine, Maryland, Michigan, Minnesota, Missouri, Montana, Nebraska, Nevada, New Hampshire, New Jersey, New Mexico, New York, North Carolina, North Dakota, Ohio, Oklahoma, Oregon, Pennsylvania, South Dakota, Tennessee, Texas, Utah, Vermont, Virginia, Washington, West Virginia, Wisconsin, and Wyoming. Smith won the electoral votes of 8 states—Alabama, Arkansas, Georgia, Louisiana, Massachusetts, Mississippi, Rhode Island, South Carolina.

INAUGURAL ADDRESS: March 4, 1929. ". . . There would be little traffic in illegal liquor if only criminals patronized it. We must awake to the fact that this patronage from large numbers of law-abiding citizens is supplying the rewards and stimulating crime. . . .

"Our whole system of self-government will crumble either if officials elect what laws they will enforce or citizens elect what laws they will support. The worst evil of disregard for some law is that it destroys respect for all law. For our citizens to patronize the violation of a particular law on the ground that they are opposed to it is destructive of the very basis of all that protection of life, of homes and property which they rightly claim under other laws. If citizens do not like a law, their duty as honest men and women is to discourage its violation; their right is openly to work for its repeal. . . ."

VICE PRESIDENT: Charles Curtis (1860–1936), of Kansas, served 1929–1933. One-quarter Kaw Indian, Curtis was born on Indian land at North Topeka,

Kansas, and grew up for a time on an Indian reservation. Admitted to the bar in 1881, he practiced law in Topeka and in 1885 was elected county attorney for Shawnee County. He served as a Republican in the U.S. House, 1893–1907, and Senate, 1907–1913 and 1915–1929. A conservative and faithful party regular, he advanced to Republican whip in 1915 and majority leader in 1924. He was a candidate for the Republican presidential nomination in 1928 but settled for the number-two spot. His term as vice president was uneventful. He was renominated in 1932. With the Republican defeat that year he resumed practicing law in Washington, where he died.

CABINET:

Secretary of State. Henry L. Stimson (1867–1950), of New York, served 1929–1933. He had served as war secretary in the Taft administration. He headed the American delegation to the London Naval Conference in 1930 and the Geneva Disarmament Conference in 1932. In response to Japan's invasion of Manchuria in 1931, he set forth the Stimson Doctrine, by which the United States refused to recognize territorial changes brought about by aggression. He later served as war secretary in the Franklin Roosevelt administration.

Secretary of the Treasury. (1) Andrew W. Mellon (1855–1937), of Pennsylvania, served 1921–1932. A holdover from the Harding and Coolidge administrations, he continued his probusiness policy, popular during the boom years but called into question amid the Great Depression (see "Administration"). He grossly underestimated the depths of the Depression and was among those predicting imminent recovery. Under the Tariff Act of 1930, Mellon relaxed obscenity laws regarding the importation of foreign literature. Under the new guidelines, works generally regarded as classics were to be admitted regardless of content. Among the books legalized for import were *The Arabian Nights*, *Memoirs of Casanova*, and Boccaccio's *The Decameron*. Mellon later donated his vast art collection to the United States; with it was founded the National Gallery of Art in Washington. (2) Ogden L. Mills (1884–1937), of New York, served 1932–1933. Promoted from undersecretary of the Treasury, he helped draft the Emergency Banking Act of 1933 curbing speculative banking practices and establishing a temporary deposit insurance program.

Secretary of War. (1) James W. Good (1866–1929), of Illinois, served March–November 1929. He had been Hoover's western campaign manager in 1928. He died in office. (2) Patrick J. Hurley (1883–1963), of Oklahoma, served 1929–1933. Promoted from undersecretary of war, he directed the military confrontation with the Bonus Army in 1932 (see "Administration"). He dedicated the Tomb of the Unknown Soldier in 1932 at Arlington National Cemetery. He later served as minister to New Zealand, 1942, and ambassador to China, 1944–1945.

Attorney General. William D. Mitchell (1874–1955), of Minnesota, served 1929–1933. He had served as solicitor general in the Coolidge administration. He reorganized the federal prison system and attempted to enforce Prohibition.

Secretary of the Navy. Charles Francis Adams (1866–1954), of Massachusetts, served 1929–1933. A great-grandson of President John Quincy Adams, he was a delegate to the 1930 London Naval Conference.

Postmaster General. Walter F. Brown (1869–1961), of Ohio, served 1929–1933. He expanded air mail service. He was derisively dubbed High Hat Brown when it was revealed that he had ordered a government limousine custom-made with sufficient headroom for him to wear a tall silk hat.

Secretary of the Interior. Ray Lyman Wilbur (1875–1949), of California, served 1929–1933. He upgraded health care and education among the Indians. He also promoted conservation and founded the Save the Redwoods League.

Secretary of Agriculture. Arthur M. Hyde (1877–1947), of Missouri, served 1929–1933. He attempted with little success to control surpluses through the short-lived Federal Farm Board.

Secretary of Commerce. (1) Robert P. Lamont (1867–1948), of Illinois, served 1929–1932. He dismissed the stock market crash of 1929 as a temporary correction that would do little more than "curtail the buying power, especially of luxuries, of those who suffered losses."[10] (2) Roy D. Chapin (1880–1936) of Michigan, served 1932–1933. He tried unsuccessfully to persuade industrialist Henry Ford to maintain his deposits in threatened Michigan banks. The subsequent closure of banks in that state prompted runs in other states near the end of Hoover's term.

Secretary of Labor. (1) James J. Davis (1873–1947), of Pennsylvania, served 1921–1930. A holdover from the Harding and Coolidge administrations, he encouraged collective bargaining. (2) William N. Doak (1882–1933), of Virginia, served 1930–1933. Long active in the Brotherhood of Railroad Trainmen, he pressed for a crackdown on illegal aliens competing for American jobs.

ADMINSTRATION: March 4, 1929–March 3, 1933.

Agricultural Marketing Act, 1929. Redeeming his pledge to provide relief to farmers, President Hoover signed this measure, which created a Federal Farm Board to encourage the formation of farm cooperatives and to control farm surpluses. The limited authority of the board, however, was insufficient to handle the severe glut in agricultural products. The board was abolished in 1933.

Hawley-Smoot Tariff, 1930. It replaced the Emergency Tariff Act of 1921 and the Fordney-McCumber Act of 1922 (see "Warren G. Harding, 29th President," "Administration"). With some misgivings, Hoover signed this protectionist measure because he hoped, in vain, that it would aid hard-pressed farmers by protecting them from foreign competition. Instead, a global tariff war ensued, and all trade suffered. Sponsored by Republican Senator Reed Smoot of Utah and Republican Representative Willis C. Hawley of Oregon, the bill raised the general level of duties to 42 percent, the highest in the nation's history. The protective tariff policy was abandoned with the adoption of reciprocal trade agreements from 1934.

Prohibition. Alarmed at the soaring crime rate and widespread disregard for Prohibition, President Hoover in 1929 appointed the National Commission on Law Observance and Law Enforcement, popularly known as the Wickersham Commission, after its chairman, former attorney general George W. Wickersham. Although it examined law enforcement in general, it was its findings on Prohibition that attracted most attention; the commission concluded that enforcement had failed but nevertheless opposed its repeal.

Stock Market Crash and the Great Depression. There were warning signs—building starts and consumer spending had been slipping, inventories had been building up—but few were prepared to heed them as prices on Wall Street climbed steadily. Then on Black Thursday, October 24, 1929, stock prices, after falling off sharply the day before, continued to slide in heavy trading. A group of investment bankers hastily agreed to shore up confidence by ostentatiously buying large blocks of stock, but the tactic only temporarily checked the collapse. On October 29, 1929, came the crash as stock losses for the day totaled in the billions of dollars amid then-record volume of more than 16 million shares. The Dow-Jones Industrial Average, having peaked in 1929 at 381, a level not attained again until the mid-1950s, bottomed out at 41 in 1932.

The causes of the Great Depression that followed were many including: (1) A chronic surplus in agricultural products had been depressing farm prices. (2) Lack of credit restraints, especially in the securities industry, where stocks could be purchased on 25 percent margin, spurred a dizzying round of speculation. (3) High tariffs discouraged world trade. (4) Acceleration of corporate profits at the expense of higher wages stunted purchasing power.

By the spring of 1930 four million were unemployed; the figure more than tripled by 1933, the worst year of the Depression. The national unemployment rate peaked at 25 percent in 1933. Some 25 percent of all banks in the United States failed during 1929–1932. Farmers were among the hardest hit as crop prices, already depressed, fell another 30 percent during 1930–1931. Compounding the problem were dust storms in the Midwest and Southwest that literally blew away the topsoil of entire farms, forcing thousands to abandon their barren fields in an aimless exodus movingly portrayed in John Steinbeck's *The Grapes of Wrath.*

President Hoover and his advisers at first failed to grasp the enormity of the Depression. "All the evidences indicate that the worst effects of the crash upon unemployment will have passed during the next 60 days,"[11] the president declared in March 1930. And again two months later, he expressed confidence that the worst was over. Hoover limited government assistance to business, believing that such aid would eventually trickle down to the people. He refused to engage in a massive program of direct federal aid to the unemployed. Instead, he established in 1932 the Reconstruction Finance Corporation, which by the time Hoover left office had loaned nearly $2 billion to ailing banks, insurance companies, and other financial institutions as well as to businesses and state governments. As the crisis deepened, Hoover himself became a symbol of the Depression. At public appearances the man once hailed as the Great Humanitarian for his war-relief efforts drew rude jeers. The homeless huddled in makeshift dwellings of cardboard and scrap metal and called their collection of shanties, "Hoovervilles." Newspapers came to be called "Hoover blankets." Empty pants pockets turned inside out were dubbed "Hoover flags." Jackrabbits slaughtered for food were "Hoover hogs."

Bonus March, 1932. In May 1932 some 15,000 veterans descended on Washington to lobby for immediate payment of the bonus awarded them in 1924 (see "Calvin Coolidge, 30th President," "Administration") but not due until 1945. The bonus marchers, as they came to be called, pitched camp near the capitol. When Congress voted down the bonus bill, many demonstrators drifted away, but thousands remained, a squalid reminder of the Depression and its effect on those who once had risked their lives for their country. In July President Hoover ordered the bonus camp cleared. General Douglas MacArthur, aided by Major Dwight Eisenhower and Major George Patton, lead four cavalry troops with drawn sabers, an infantry column with fixed bayonets and tear gas bombs, and six tanks against the ragged band of veterans and their families. Bernard Myers, an infant recently born in the camp, died from tear gas inhalation. A small boy was bayoneted in the leg as he scrambled to save a pet rabbit. In short order, federal troops dispersed the "enemy" and set fire to their shacks. Hoover's use of armed force to defeat the Bonus Army drew widespread criticism and reinforced the image of a heartless president insensitive to the suffering of the Depression's victims.

London Naval Treaty, 1930. It revised the Washington Conference agreement of 1922 (see "Warren G. Harding, 29th President," "Administration: Arms Limitation") to permit Japan to increase its fleet relative to that of the United States and Great Britain. In 1934 Japan renounced the treaty with effect from 1936. A naval arms race ensued, culminating in World War II.

Norris-LaGuardia Act, 1932. Sponsored by Republican Senator George Norris of Nebraska and Republican Representative Fiorello LaGuardia of New York and signed by President Hoover, the law restricted the use of the labor injunction to strikes that threaten public safety and banned the yellow dog contract denying workers the right to unionize and binding them to a no-strike clause.

Constitutional Amendment Ratified. Twentieth Amendment, 1933. The so-called lame-duck amendment, it moved the presidential inauguration date up to January 20 (from March 4) and authorized each new Congress to convene on January 3.

SUPREME COURT APPOINTMENTS: (1) Charles Evans Hughes (1862–1948), of New York, served as chief justice 1930–1941. He had served on the Court during 1910–1916 (see "William Howard Taft, 27th President," "Supreme Court Appointments") and resigned to run for president (see "Woodrow Wilson, 28th President," "Opponent, 1916"). As chief justice he generally was a centrist. He wrote the majority opinions sustaining such New Deal programs as abandonment of the gold standard (Gold Clause cases, 1935), the Tennessee Valley Authority (*Ashwander* v. *TVA*, 1936), and the National Labor Relations Act (*NLRB* v. *Jones & Laughlin Steel*, 1937). But he also spoke for the Court in striking down the National Industrial Recovery Act (NIRA), a cornerstone of the early New Deal. Constitutional objections to the NIRA, Hughes wrote in *Schechter Poultry Corp.* v. *United States* (1935), were twofold: It delegated legislative powers to the executive branch and sought to regulate intrastate commerce. Hughes actively opposed Roosevelt's court-packing plan. (2) Owen J. Roberts (1875–1955), of Pennsylvania, served as associate justice 1930–1945. Hoover turned to Roberts after the Senate rejected his original nominee, John J. Parker of North Carolina. Like Hughes a centrist, Roberts opposed much of the early New Deal but became more tolerant as the sentiment of the Court shifted. Speaking for the majority, he struck down the Agricultural Adjustment Act (*United States* v. *Butler et al*, 1936) as a congressional usurpation of state and local authority. He also voted with the majority in outlawing the National Industrial Recovery Act (*Schechter Poultry Corp.* v. *United States*, 1935). Similarly he negated the Railroad Retirement Act (*Railroad Retirement Board* v. *Alton Railroad*, 1935), declaring that congressional authority to promote efficiency in interstate commerce did not include creation of a compulsory pension system. But Roberts upheld the Wagner National Labor Relations Act (*Associated Press* v. *National Labor Relations Board*, 1937), dismissing print media arguments that the law's restraints violated First Amendment guarantees of press freedom. "The publisher of a newspaper has no special immunity from the application of general laws," Roberts wrote. (3) Benjamin N. Cardozo (1870–1938), of New York, served as associate justice 1932–1938. Joining the liberal bloc on the Court, Cardozo regarded the Constitution as a living document subject to changing interpretations as society evolves. He voted to uphold much New Deal legislation, with the notable exception of the National Industrial Recovery Act (*Schechter Poultry Corp.* v. *United States*, 1935). In sustaining the Social Security system, Cardozo expressed his philosophy of evolutionary law. "Needs that were narrow or parochial a century ago," he wrote in *Helvering et al.* v. *Davis* (1937), "may be interwoven in our day with the well-being of the nation. What is critical or urgent changes with the times." His books, lucid expositions on law and society, include *The Nature of the Judicial Process* (1921), *The Growth of the Law* (1924), and *The Paradoxes of Legal Science* (1928).

RANKING IN 1962 HISTORIANS POLL: Hoover ranked nineteenth of 31 presidents, eighth of 12 "average" presidents. He ranked above Benjamin Harrison, below Monroe.

RETIREMENT: March 4, 1933–October 20, 1964. Defeated for reelection (see under "Franklin D. Roosevelt, 32d President," for election of 1932), Hoover attended the inauguration of his successor and retired to his home in Palo Alto, California. In later years he resided mostly at the Waldorf-Astoria Hotel in New York City. He spoke out in harsh terms against the New Deal, condemning many of its programs as "fascistic." He especially criticized President Roosevelt's decisions to go off the gold standard, recognize the Soviet Union, and attempt to pack the Supreme Court. Still, he refused to join the Liberty League, a conservative organization opposed to the New Deal. He campaigned for Alf Landon for president in 1936. In 1938 he toured Europe as it drifted toward war. He met with Adolf Hitler, whom he found "partly insane" but intelligent and well informed. He opposed U.S. entry into World War II until the Japanese attack on Pearl Harbor. During the war he served as chairman of relief organizations for Poland, Finland, and Belgium. He opposed dropping the atomic bomb on Japan in 1945. After the war President Truman appointed him coordinator of the Food Supply for World Famine 1946–1947. His most prominent activity in retirement was as chairman of the Commission on Organization of the Executive Branch of the Government, popularly known as the Hoover Commission, 1947–1949, and of the Commission on Government Operations, the so-called second Hoover Commission, 1953–1955. The first commission made 273 recommendations to streamline government, about three fourths of which were adopted; the second commission turned in 314 recommendations, about two thirds of which were adopted. Significant changes included a consolidation of functions into new cabinet-level Departments of Defense and Health, Education and Welfare and tighter lines of authority from the office of the president to the rest of the executive branch. Hoover opposed U.S. participation in the Korean War. Shortly before his death he endorsed Barry Goldwater for president.

DEATH: October 20, 1964, 11:35 A.M., New York City. At 84 Hoover underwent his first operation, for removal of his gallbladder. He developed intestinal cancer and in 1962 had a tumor removed. Thereafter he was plagued by sporadic gastrointestinal hemorrhages. He was virtually deaf and blind near the end. On October 17, 1964, he was struck with massive internal bleeding and lapsed into coma two days later. He died the following morning without regaining consciousness. A simple funeral without eulogies, as befitted his Quaker faith, was conducted at St. Bartholomew's Episcopal Church in New York City. After the service, his body lay in state for two days at the Capitol Rotunda in

Washington. He was buried at West Branch, Iowa. In his last will and testament, executed in August 1964, Hoover left the bulk of his estate, believed to be worth millions of dollars, to a trust fund established in 1961 for the benefit of his heirs. He also left specific bequests totaling $140,000 to six female secretaries.

HOOVER PRAISED: "He is certainly a wonder and I wish we could make him President of the United States. There could not be a better one."[12]—Assistant Secretary of the Navy Franklin D. Roosevelt, 1920

"I never reflected on the personal character or integrity of Herbert Hoover. I never doubted his probity or his patriotism. In many ways he was superbly equipped for the Presidency. If he had been President in 1921 or 1937 he might have ranked with the great Presidents."[13]—former vice president John Nance Garner, 1948

"Like all presidents, Mr. Hoover made his mistakes. But for years his political opponents unjustly held him responsible for the depression of the thirties. His distinguished career of public service was forgotten in a storm of insult and criticism. A lesser man of lesser faith might well have grown bitter."[14]—*Collier's Weekly*, 1949

"In the light of history, I believe he was a great President; and I think future historians will bear out that statement."[15]—Democratic Senator Mike Mansfield of Montana, 1962

HOOVER CRITICIZED: "I have the feeling that he would rather see a good cause fail than succeed if he were not the head of it."[16]—President Woodrow Wilson

"That man has offered me unsolicited advice for the past six years, all of it bad."[17]—President Calvin Coolidge

"I accuse the present administration of being the greatest spending administration in peacetime in all our history. It is an administration that has piled bureau on bureau, commission on commission, and has failed to anticipate the dire needs of and the reduced earning power of the people."[18]—Democratic presidential nominee Franklin D. Roosevelt, 1932

"Mr. Hoover has long since abandoned his old faith in rugged individualism. His platform is a document of indefatigable paternalism. Its spirit is that of the Great White Father providing help for all his people. Every conceivable interest which has votes is offered protection, or subsidies, or access of some kind to the Treasury."[19]—journalist Walter Lippmann, 1932

HOOVER QUOTES: "War is a losing business, a financial loss, a loss of life and an economic degeneration. . . . It has but few compensations and of them we must make the most. Its greatest compensation lies in the possibility that we may instill into our people unselfishness."[20]—1917

"Many years ago I concluded that a few hair shirts were part of the mental wardrobe of every man. The President differs only from other men in that he has a more extensive wardrobe."[21]—1929

"True Liberalism is found not in striving to spread bureaucracy but in striving to set bounds to it."[22]

BOOKS BY HOOVER: *Principles of Mining* (1909); *American Individualism* (1922); *The New Day* (1929); *The Challenge to Liberty* (1934); *America's First Crusade* (1943); *The Problems of Lasting Peace* (with Hugh Gibson, 1943); *The Basis of Lasting Peace* (with Hugh Gibson, 1944); *The Memoirs of Herbert Hoover* (3 vols., 1951–1952); *The Ordeal of Wilson* (1958); *An American Epic* (3 vols., 1959–1961; *On Growing Up* (1962); *Fishing for Fun* (1963).

BOOKS ABOUT HOOVER: Burner, David. *Herbert Hoover: A Public Life.* New York: Knopf, 1979.

Hinshaw, David. *Herbert Hoover: American Quaker.* New York: Farrar, Straus & Co., 1950.

Lyons, Eugene. *Herbert Hoover: A Biography.* New York: Doubleday, 1964.

Nash, George H. *The LIfe of Herbert Hoover: The Engineer.* New York: Norton, 1983.

Smith, Richard Norton. *An Uncommon Man: The Triumph of Herbert Hoover.* New York: Simon and Schuster, 1984.

NOTES:

1 David Burner, *Herbert Hoover: A Public Life*, New York: Knopf, 1979, p. 256.

2 *Memoirs of Herbert Hoover*, New York: Macmillan, 1951–1952, vol. I, p. 4.

3 Burner, pp. 5–6.

4 Ibid., p. 19.

5 *Memoirs*, vol. I, p. 21.

6 Robert S. Alley, *So Help Me God: Religion and the Presidency*, Richmond, Va.: John Knox Press, 1972, p. 56.

7 Burner, P. 201.

8 Ibid., p. 218.

9 William Safire, *The New Language of Politics*, New York: Random House, 1968, p. 74.

10 Arthur M. Schlesinger, Jr., *The Age of Roosevelt: The Crisis of the Old Order 1919–1933*, Boston: Houghton Mifflin, 1957, p. 162.

11 *New York Times*, March 8, 1930.

12 Nathan Miller, *F.D.R.: An Intimate History*, Garden City, N.Y.: Doubleday, 1983, p. 167.

13 Asa Martin, *After the White House*, State College, Pa.: Penns Valley, 1951, p. 449.

14 David Hinshaw, *Herbert Hoover: American Quaker*, New York: Farrar, Straus, 1950, p. 369.

15 Eugene Lyons, *Herbert Hoover: A Biography*, New York: Doubleday, 1964, p. 440.

16 Burner, p. 151.

17 Herbert Eaton, *Presidential Timber: The Story of How Presidential Candidates Are Nominated*, New York: Free Press of Glencoe, 1964, p. 316.

18 Lyons, p. 295.

19 Richard Oulahan, *The Man Who . . . . : The Story of the 1932 Democratic Convention*, New York: Dial, 1971, p. 64.

20 Burner, p. 99.

21 Arthur B. Tourtellot, *The Presidents on the Presidency*, New York: Russell & Russell, 1964, p. 368.

22 Anne Emery, *American Friend: Herbert Hoover*, Chicago: Rand McNally, 1967, p. 215.

FRANKLIN D. ROOSEVELT

32D PRESIDENT

NAME: Franklin Delano Roosevelt. He was named after a great-uncle, Franklin Hughes Delano. His father wanted to name him Isaac, but his mother objected. His mother wanted to name him Warren Delano, but her brother had just lost an infant by that name and in his grief persuaded her to choose another name. The indecision left the infant nameless for seven weeks.

PHYSICAL DESCRIPTION: Roosevelt stood 6 feet 1 inch tall and as president generally weighed in the 180s. Strikingly handsome, lean, and athletic as a young man, he had blue eyes, underscored by dark circles as he grew older, dark wavy hair, and a strong thrusting jaw. He was nearsighted and from age 18 wore eyeglasses. He contracted polio in 1921. After a day of sailing and fishing with his boys on Campobello Island, Roosevelt helped some local residents fight a forest fire and then took a cold dip in the Bay of Fundy. He jogged the mile back home, where, still in his wet trunks, he went through his mail. That night he went to bed with the chills. Two days later he could not move his legs. Dr. W. W. Keen (who had taken part in the cancer operation on President Grover Cleveland in 1893) of Philadelphia diagnosed some sort of temporary paralysis. Dr. Robert S. Lovett of Boston recognized the signs of poliomyelitis. Through rigorous exercise Roosevelt eventually learned to stand with braces and to walk briefly with crutches or canes. In deep water he was able to stand without braces. Except for polio and chronic sinus trouble, Roosevelt was strong and healthy. Although his lower limbs withered, he was muscular from the waist up.

PERSONALITY: Roosevelt was ebullient, charming, persuasive, gregarious, and genuinely interested in people and their problems. To some he seemed snooty as a young man; his habit of carrying his head back and literally looking down his nose at others through pince-nez reinforced this early image. According to his wife, being stricken with polio made him more sensitive to the feelings of other people. He was not the least bit sensitive about his handicap, however. While onlookers typically shifted about in discomfort as he was lifted in and out of automobiles or struggled with his ungainly braces, he invariably eased the tension with a joke or simply carried on a conversation as if nothing unusual were going on. As president during 12 of the most difficult years in American history, Roosevelt worked well under pressure. "His composure under stress was remarkable," commented biographer James MacGregor Burns. "The main reason for Roosevelt's composure was his serene and absolute assurance as to the value and importance of what he was doing."[1] A common complaint about Roosevelt, even among his admirers, was his devious nature. Interior Secretary Harold Ickes complained that he never spoke with complete frankness even to his most loyal supporters.

ANCESTORS: Roosevelt was mostly of Dutch and French Huguenot heritage, with traces of Swedish, Finnish, and English blood. The first of the paternal line to emigrate from Holland was his great[5]-grandfather Claes Maertenszen van Rosenvelt (also the immigrant ancestor of Theodore Roosevelt), a farmer who settled in New Netherland about 1644. His great[4]-grandfather Nicholas Roosevelt was alderman of New York 1698–1701. His great-great-grandfather Isaac Roosevelt, "the Patriot," prospered as a sugar refiner and during the American Revolution helped draft New York's first constitution; a Hamiltonian Federalist after the war, he attended the state convention to vote for ratification of the U.S. Constitution and later served in the New York State Senate. His great-grandfather James Roosevelt (1760–1847), also an active Federalist, served in the New York State Assembly. The immigrant ancestor on his mother's side was Philippe de la Noye (subsequent generations transformed the name to Delano), a French Huguenot of Holland who reportedly rivaled Pilgrim John Alden for the affections of Priscilla Mullens; he emigrated to Plymouth in 1621.

FATHER: James Roosevelt (1828–1900), lawyer, financier. A native of Hyde Park, New York, he attended New York University briefly and in 1847 graduated from Union College in Schenectady. During 1847–1849 he toured Europe, then in the throes of revolutionary fervor. He took time off from a walking tour of Italy to serve a one-month hitch with Garibaldi's Red Shirts. Returning to the United States, he graduated from Harvard Law School and practiced law in New York City briefly but lived much of his life as a country squire at Hyde Park while undertaking financial ventures from time to time. He was a founder and director of the Consolidated Coal Company, president of the Southern Railway Security Company, and a director of the Delaware and Hudson Railroad. He suffered significant losses in the panics of 1873 and 1893 but remained financially comfortable. He maintained his own private railroad car and spurned the nouveaux riches. He once turned down an invitation to dine with the lowly Vanderbilts out of fear that he would have to invite them to his house. Politically he was a conservative Democrat, a proponent of sound currency. He married Rebecca Howland in 1853; she died in 1876. He then married his sixth cousin Sara Delano, the president's mother, in 1880. He died of heart disease at 72 when son Franklin was a freshman at Harvard.

MOTHER: Sara "Sallie" Delano Roosevelt (1854–1941). Born near Newburgh, New York, the daughter of a merchant who made his fortune in trade with China, she traveled abroad extensively before her marriage to James Roosevelt, a widower old enough to be her father. After her husband's death in 1900, Mrs. Roosevelt concentrated all her energies on son Franklin. She opposed his decision to enter politics. Instead, she encouraged him to become a country squire like his father. After he was stricken with polio, she again appealed to him to withdraw to the comforts of Hyde Park. A strong-willed, forceful personality, she wholly dominated her daughter-in-law Eleanor Roosevelt during the first years of her marriage to Franklin. She died at 86 during his third term as president. On her death, Roosevelt inherited $920,000.

SIBLING: By his father's first marriage, Roosevelt had a half brother. James Roosevelt "Rosy" Roosevelt married into the Astor fortune and served as first secretary of the U.S. Embassy in Vienna during Grover Cleveland's first administration and in the same position in London during Cleveland's second administration. Franklin was his mother's only child.

COLLATERAL RELATIVES: Roosevelt was a fourth cousin once removed of President Ulysses S. Grant, a fourth cousin three times removed of President Zachary Taylor, a fifth cousin of President Theodore Roosevelt, a fifth cousin once removed of his wife, Eleanor Roosevelt, and a seventh cousin once removed of Winston Churchill.

CHILDREN: Roosevelt had a daughter and four sons to live to maturity.

Anna Eleanor Roosevelt (1906–1975), journalist, public relations officer. Born in New York City, she attended Cornell University in 1925, was women's page editor of the *Seattle Post Intelligencer* 1936–1943 and private secretary to her father 1943–1945, during which time she accompanied him to the Yalta Conference, and co-hosted a radio show in 1948 with her mother. From 1952 she was a public relations officer for hospitals in various U.S. cities and during 1958–1960 helped establish a medical school in Iran.

James Roosevelt (1907–1991), businessman, congressman, author. Born in New York City, he attended Harvard 1926–1930 but did not graduate. He was an insurance executive until 1937, when he became secretary to his father in the White House. During World War II he served in the Marines, rising from captain to colonel. He was decorated for saving the lives of Marines whose boats had capsized while evacuating Makin Island. After the war he settled in California, where he was the unsuccessful Democratic nominee for governor in 1950. Elected to the U.S. House, 1955–1966, he rose to prominence on the Education and Labor Committee and established a liberal voting record. His writings include *Affectionately, FDR* (with Sidney Shalett, 1959) and *My Parents* (with Bill Libby, 1976).

Elliott Roosevelt (1910–1990), businessman, mayor, author. Born in New York City, he graduated from Groton in 1929 and was for a time a radio executive for Hearst stations in Texas. During World War II he served in the Army Air Corps, rising from captain to brigadier general, a meteoric advance that drew unfavorable press comment. He was most severely criticized in January 1945 when, without his knowledge, three soldiers on emergency leave were bumped from a military aircraft to make room for a large mastiff dog he had ordered sent home to his wife. He flew numerous reconnaissance missions, photographing at close range enemy targets in North Africa and Italy. For his service he was awarded the Distinguished Flying Cross and also was decorated by Britain and France. He accompanied his father to the Casablanca and Teheran conferences. After the war he ran an import-export business in Florida and served as mayor of Miami Beach in the 1960s. He later was chairman of Grow Force Fertilizer in Bellevue, Vermont. The third of his five wives was actress Faye Emerson. He edited *FDR: His Personal Letters* (4 vols., 1947–1950). He wrote *An Untold Story: The Roosevelts of Hyde Park* (1974), a sensational account denounced by the other Roosevelt children, *Mother R* (with James Brough, 1977), and several murder mysteries in the 1980s.

Franklin D. Roosevelt, Jr. (1914–1988), businessman, congressman, farmer. Born on Campobello Island, New Brunswick, Canada, he graduated from Harvard in 1937 and the University of Virginia law school in 1940. During World War II, he served as a ship commander in the navy and was decorated. He accompanied his father to the Teheran Conference. After the war he practiced law in New York City and helped found the American Veterans Committee. He was elected as a Democrat to the U.S. House 1949–1954, where he established a liberal voting record. He was defeated for the New York Democratic gubernatorial nomination in 1954. A close friend and early backer of John F. Kennedy, he was appointed undersecretary of commerce, 1963–1965, and was chairman of the Equal Employment Opportunity Commission, 1965–1966. He ran unsuccessfully for governor of New York on the Liberal party ticket in 1966. He later was national distributor of Fiat automobiles in the United States. FDR, Jr., believed that on the whole historians have fairly evaluated his father's administration. In a communication to the author, he claimed that being a presidential son did not influence his life. "We don't have royal families in America," he added, "only prominent families." He believed that each generation must have "the guts and talent to succeed on its own."

John Aspinwall Roosevelt (1916–1981), merchant, stockbroker. Born in Washington, D.C., he graduated from Harvard in 1938 and worked briefly as a clerk at Filene's department store in Boston for $18.50 a week. During World War II, he served in the navy as a logistics officer aboard the carrier *Wasp*, rising from lieutenant to lieutenant commander. After the war he operated the Grayson-Robinson department store in Los Angeles and in 1956 entered Wall Street as a partner in Bache and Company, later becoming senior vice president. The only one of the Roosevelt children to become a Republican, he was chairman of Citizens for Eisenhower in 1952 and later supported Richard Nixon and Ronald Reagan.

BIRTH: Roosevelt was born at 8:45 P.M. January 30, 1882, in an upstairs bedroom of the family home in Hyde Park, New York. He weighed 10 pounds at birth. It was a difficult delivery that nearly killed both mother and child. When after long hours of labor the baby would not come, Dr. Edward H. Parker of Poughkeepsie administered chloroform, an overdose as it turned out, to the mother. She fell unconscious and turned blue for a time. Then came the baby, also unconscious and blue, too stuporous to be aroused by several cracks on the rump. Only with mouth-to-mouth resuscitation did Dr. Parker breathe life into the infant.

CHILDHOOD: Roosevelt grew up in the protective atmosphere of Hyde Park and the Roosevelt Summer place on Campobello Island. As a child he accompanied his parents abroad frequently. At age 2½ he bit off the lip of a water glass. After his mother frantically fished the jagged shard from his mouth, he purposely bit down on a second goblet. He wore dresses until he was 5, then was clad in kilts and, finally, at 8 began wearing pants. At 8 he was permitted to take his first unsupervised bath. At 4 he was given a pony, at 11 his own hunting rifle, at 16 a 21-foot sailboat. In 1887 his father took him to the White House, where he met Grover Cleveland. The weary president patted 5-year-old Franklin on the head and said, "My little man, I am making a strange wish for you. It is that you may never be president of the United States."[2] In 1893 he accompanied his parents in their private railroad car to the World's Columbian Exposition in Chicago. In

1897 he spent the Fourth of July weekend at the Oyster Bay estate of cousin Theodore Roosevelt. His early ambition was to attend Annapolis and become a career naval officer, but his father encouraged him to take up law.

EDUCATION: Roosevelt learned the basics from a series of private tutors. The most influential of these was Mlle. Jeane Sandoz, a Swiss native. He attended just one public school, at Bad Nauheim, Germany, where in 1891 Franklin studied six weeks while abroad with his parents. He was conversant in French and German. He liked taking dance lessons but detested his drawing and piano lessons. At Groton 1896–1900 he was an above-average, although far from brilliant, student, generally performing in the 75th–80th percentile. He later credited headmaster Endicott Peabody, however, with having shaped his character more than anyone else besides his parents. In extracurricular activities he sang soprano in the choir, set a school record in the high kick (over seven feet), played seventh-string football, boxed as a lightweight, managed the baseball team, and was dormitory prefect. As a member of the Groton Missionary Society, he directed a summer camp for disadvantaged youth. He played Uncle Bopaddy, an aging country bumpkin, in W. S. Gilbert's *The Wedding March.* He won the Latin Prize. His final report card read: "He has been a thoroughly faithful scholar and a most satisfactory member of this school throughout his course." Governor Theodore Roosevelt spoke at his graduation in June 1900. At Harvard 1900–1904 Roosevelt was an average (mostly low Bs and Cs) student, majoring in political history and government. Class generally bored him, but he attended regularly. He did join other students, however, in cutting the lecture of one myopic professor by slipping out a window at the rear of the classroom. He later compared his Harvard education to an electric lamp without a cord. In extracurricular activities, he was captain of the third crew of the Newell Boating Club, secretary of the Glee Club, librarian of Alpha Delta Phi (Fly Club) and the Hasty Pudding Club, permanent chairman of the class committee, and a member of the Harvard Union library committee. His big disappointments were failure to make the football team (he was too light) and the prestigious Porcellian Club. His favorite activity was as editor-in-chief of the Harvard *Crimson.* In fact, he had the credits to graduate in 1903 but continued his studies an extra year just to work on the *Crimson,* work he later described as very useful in preparing him for public service. That last year he took graduate courses in history and economics but did not earn a master's degree. In 1900 he joined the Harvard Republican Club and took part in a torchlight parade in Boston for the McKinley-Roosevelt ticket. He formally graduated with the class of 1904. At Columbia Law School 1904–1907 Roosevelt continued an average student. He failed two courses—contracts as well as pleading and practice. He dropped out on passing the bar exam in 1907; thus, he never graduated from law school. Although he considered himself a Democrat, he cast his first presidential vote in 1904 for a Republican, cousin Theodore Roosevelt, because he regarded him as a better Democrat than the Democratic candidate.

RELIGION: Episcopalian. Roosevelt rarely spoke about his faith. His wife and others close to him maintained that he believed in God and divine guidance but had little patience for complex dogma. He was well versed in the Bible and believed that a succinct guide to life could be found in the Sermon on the Mount. He was a lifelong member of St. James Episcopal Church in Hyde Park, where he was vestryman and senior warden. In Washington he worshipped at St. John's Episcopal Church but also liked to attend Baptist and Methodist services.

He attended special services every year on the anniversary of his first inaugural. He resented tourists ogling him in church. "I can do almost everything in the goldfish bowl of the president's life," he once said, "but I'll be hanged if I can say my prayers in it."[3]

RECREATION: As president Roosevelt exercised by swimming in the White House pool and found the waters of Warm Springs, Georgia, especially soothing. He was a skilled birdwatcher. He maintained an extensive stamp collection, which by the 1930s had grown to 40 albums of 25,000 stamps. As president he received the first sheet of each new commemorative issue and had a State Department officer regularly send him unusual foreign stamps. Occasionally he made suggestions for the design of new commemoratives. He also enjoyed sailing, fishing, and watching motion pictures in the White House with friends. He liked to play cards, especially small-stakes poker. A moderate drinker, Roosevelt preferred a dry martini at the end of the day. Occasionally he concocted what he called "my Haitian libation," a cocktail of rum, brown sugar, and orange juice. He smoked more than a pack of cigarettes a day.

EARLY ROMANCE: Roosevelt was popular with girls as a youth but, according to his mother, was not serious about anybody before Eleanor. His sons James and Elliot, however, claimed that in college he had fallen in love with Frances Dana, granddaughter of author Richard Henry Dana and Henry Wadsworth Longfellow, but was discouraged from pressing his suit by his mother because the girl was Catholic.

MARRIAGE: Franklin D. Roosevelt, 23, married (Anna) Eleanor Roosevelt, 20, his fifth cousin once removed, on March 17, 1905, at the townhouse of the bride's aunt Mrs. E. Livingston Ludlow on East 76th Street in New York City. Born in New York City on October 11, 1884, the daughter of Elliott Roosevelt, the dissolute younger brother of Theodore Roosevelt, and Anna Hall Roosevelt, Eleanor grew up a painfully shy, insecure child. So sober a girl was she that her mother nicknamed her Granny. Her mother passed away when she was eight and her father, an alcoholic confined to a sanitarium, died soon thereafter. Thus, she was raised from adolescence by her maternal grandmother. She was tutored privately and at 15 was sent to Allenswood, a girls finishing school outside London, where for three years she flourished under the guidance of head-mistress Mlle. Souvestre. Returning to New York, she made her society debut in 1902 and became a social worker in the East Side slums. That same year she met Franklin Roosevelt and was overwhelmed when the dashing Harvard student demonstrated affection for her. She brought Franklin along on her rounds of the squalid tenements, a walking tour that profoundly moved the heretofore sheltered young man. Franklin proposed in November 1903; Eleanor accepted. Franklin's mother opposed the union, however. "I know what pain I must have caused you," Franklin wrote his mother of his decision. But, he added, "I know my own mind, have known it for a long time, and know that I could never think otherwise."[4] Mrs. Roosevelt took her son on a cruise in 1904 hoping that the separation would squelch the romance, but Franklin returned to Eleanor with renewed ardor. The wedding date was fixed to accommodate President Theodore Roosevelt, who agreed to give away the bride, his niece. His presence focused national attention on the wedding. The Reverend Dr. Endicott Peabody, Franklin's headmaster at Groton, performed the service. Lathrop Brown, the groom's roommate at college, was best man. The couple spent a preliminary honeymoon of one week at Hyde Park, then set up housekeeping at an apartment in New York. That summer they went on their formal honeymoon, a three-month tour of Europe. Returning to the United States, Mrs. Roosevelt deferred to her mother-in-law in virtually all household matters. She did not gain a measure of independence until Franklin was elected to the state senate and the couple moved to Albany. When Roosevelt was stricken with polio in 1921, it was Eleanor who patiently nursed and prodded him to return to active life. To compensate for his lack of mobility, she overcame her shyness to make public appearances on his behalf and thereafter served him as a listening post and barometer of popular sentiment. She was the first First Lady to become significantly involved in matters of substance. She was active in the National Youth Administration, served as co-chairman of the Office of Civilian Defense, and spoke out for black civil rights. In a celebrated incident in 1939, she resigned from the Daughters of the American Revolution to protest that organization's refusal to permit black singer Marian Anderson to perform at Constitution Hall. Also while First Lady she wrote a daily syndicated column, *My Day*. The social highlight of the Roosevelt years was the 1939 visit of King George VI and Queen Elizabeth, the first British monarchs to set foot on U.S. soil. Mrs. Roosevelt was criticized in some quarters for serving hot dogs to the royal couple during a picnic at Hyde Park. After her husband's death, Mrs. Roosevelt reflected on her contribution: "He might have been happier with a wife who was completely uncritical. That I was never able to be, and he had to find it in some other people. Nevertheless, I think I sometimes acted as a spur, even though the spurring was not always wanted or welcome."[5] She remained active the rest of her life. Appointed by President Truman to the first U.S. delegation to the United Nations, 1946–1952, she was chairman of the U.N. Commission on Human Rights, which drafted the International Declaration of Human Rights, and championed the creation of Israel. Politically, she supported Adlai Stevenson for president in 1952 and 1956 and urged his renomination in 1960. Although she had misgivings about John F. Kennedy for his failure to condemn McCarthyism, she supported him for president against Richard Nixon. President Kennedy in turn reappointed her to the United Nations, 1961–1962. She died of bone marrow tuberculosis in New York City on November 7, 1962, and was buried next to the president at Hyde Park. Her writings include *This Is My Story* (1937), *On My Own* (1958), and *The Autobiography of Eleanor Roosevelt* (1961).

EXTRAMARITAL AFFAIR: Lucy Page Mercer. After Roosevelt was appointed assistant secretary of the navy in 1913, his wife hired Miss Mercer, 22, as her social secretary. Just when the affair began is unknown, but Eleanor learned of it in 1918 when she discovered love letters between the two. Eleanor confronted Franklin and reportedly issued an ultimatum that either he must stop seeing Lucy or she would divorce him. Franklin agreed to end the relationship. Eleanor emerged from the episode a changed, more independent woman. In 1920 Lucy Mercer married Winthrop Rutherfurd, a wealthy widower. Despite his promise, Roosevelt sometime later resumed the affair. Lucy frequently visited the White House when Eleanor was out of town. He even shared diplomatic and military secrets with her, writes Joseph Alsop in *FDR, 1882–1945: A Centenary Remembrance* (1982). She was with the president when he was fatally stricken at Warm Springs, Georgia, but was quickly hustled away before Eleanor arrived.

MILITARY SERVICE: None. In April 1898, while a student at Groton, Roosevelt and two classmates laid plans to sneak off to Boston to enlist in the navy for the Spanish-American War. But the boys all came down with scarlet fever and gave up their scheme. During World War I, he requested active duty, but President Wilson insisted that he remain assistant secretary of the navy.

CAREER BEFORE THE PRESIDENCY: Admitted to the bar in 1907, Roosevelt joined the law firm of Carter, Ledyard, and Milburn in New York City.

New York State Senator, 1911–1913. During his two terms in the state senate, Roosevelt emerged the leader of insurgent Democrats in revolt against Tammany Hall. He established a progressive voting record in support of farmer and labor issues. He also favored local-option Prohibition, a federal uniform divorce law, the direct election of senators, and women's suffrage.

Assistant Secretary of the Navy, 1913–1920. An early supporter of Woodrow Wilson for the 1912 Democratic presidential nomination, Roosevelt was rewarded with the appointment of assistant secretary of the navy. He ran for the Democratic nomination for the U.S. Senate from New York in 1914 but was defeated by James Gerard, U.S. ambassador to Germany. As assistant secretary he proposed expansion of the navy, drew up war contingency plans as early as 1913, and was among the early advocates of U.S. entry into World War I. During the war he directed the mining of waters between Scotland and Norway and undertook two inspection tours, July–September 1918 and January–February 1919, of naval bases and war zones in Europe. He resigned to accept the Democratic vice presidential nomination on the ticket with James M. Cox in 1920.

During the campaign Roosevelt stressed his support for the League of Nations. After being defeated in the Harding-Coolidge landslide that year, he resumed the practice of law as junior partner in the firm of Emmet, Marvin, and Roosevelt in New York City. Roosevelt was struck with polio in 1921 (see "Physical Description"). After three painstaking years of convalescence, he began one of the most remarkable political comebacks in American history with a speech nominating Alfred E. Smith ("the Happy Warrior," Roosevelt dubbed him) for president in 1924. He again placed Smith's name in nomination four years later. In 1924 he began practicing law in partnership with D. Basil O'Conner in New York City.

Governor of New York, 1929–1933. Elected narrowly, 2.13 million–2.10 million, over state attorney general Albert Ottinger in 1928 and reelected overwhelmingly, 1.8 million–1.0 million, over U.S. Attorney Charles H. Tuttle in 1930, Roosevelt established a progressive record as governor. He eased credit to hard-pressed farmers and created a Temporary Emergency Relief Administration to aid the growing numbers of unemployed. He reduced the workweek for women and children to 48 hours, extended workmen's compensation, and restricted use of the labor injunction. He also campaigned for a state project to harness the waterpower of the St. Lawrence River, a feat accomplished many years later. It was as governor that Roosevelt first delivered fireside chats, informal radio addresses that were to become a hallmark of his presidency. In January 1932 he announced his candidacy for the Democratic presidential nomination.

DEMOCRATIC PRESIDENTIAL NOMINATION, 1932: As Democrats convened in Chicago in June 1932, Roosevelt was the front-runner for the nomination. His chief rivals were 1928 nominee Alfred E. Smith of New York and House Speaker

John Nance Garner of Texas. On the basis of the primaries, Roosevelt had more than 400 of the 770 votes needed for the nomination. A stop-Roosevelt movement led by Smith counted on the favorite sons holding firm and deadlocking the convention. But the Roosevelt forces led by Louis Howe and James Farley skillfully overcame this strategy. Judge John E. Mack of New York delivered Roosevelt's nominating address. On the first ballot Roosevelt received 666¼ votes to 201¾ for Smith, 90¼ for Garner, and the rest scattered. By the third ballot Roosevelt picked up another 16 votes but still lacked 87. The suspense ended when Garner withdrew in favor of Roosevelt, who won the nomination on the next ballot with 945 votes to 190½ for Smith and the rest scattered. Roosevelt in turn chose Garner as his running mate. In an unprecedented gesture, Roosevelt flew to Chicago to deliver his acceptance speech in person. "I pledge you," he told the enthusiastic delegates, "I pledge myself, to a new deal for the American people. Let us all here assembled constitute ourselves prophets of a new order of competence and of courage. This is more than a political campaign; it is a call to arms. Give me your help, not to win votes alone, but to win in this crusade to restore America to its own people."[6] The phrase "new deal" went largely unnoticed until it appeared in a political cartoon by Rollin Kirby. The Democratic platform blamed the Republicans for the Depression and favored cutting federal expenditures by 25 percent or more, a balanced budget, sound currency, reciprocal trade agreements, shorter working hours, public works projects, unemployment and old age insurance, aid to farmers, stronger antitrust laws, federal regulation of securities and utility rates, banking restrictions, international disarmament agreements, and repeal of Prohibition.

OPPONENT: President Herbert Hoover (1874–1964) of California; Republican. In June 1932 Republicans gloomily gathered in Chicago to renominate President Herbert Hoover on the first ballot without significant opposition. To have repudiated the incumbent would have destroyed what little chance of victory the party had amid the worst economic depression in U.S. history. Former senator Joseph I. France of Maryland attempted to engineer a draft-Coolidge movement, but the former president expressed no interest in the nomination. Senator Joseph Scott of California delivered Hoover's nominating address, praising him as the man who taught the nation to resist the temptations of governmental paternalism. Vice President Charles Curtis of Kansas also was renominated. The Republican platform blamed the Depression on European events but failed to propose any meaningful remedy. It favored "drastic reduction in public expenditure," retention of the gold standard and protective tariff, supervision of banking practices, shorter working hours, a crackdown on organized crime, and revision of Prohibition to permit individual states to exercise local option while maintaining federal enforcement of Prohibition in states choosing to remain Dry.

CAMPAIGN AND THE ISSUES, 1932: The Great Depression and the federal government's response to it dominated the campaign. Before the nomination Roosevelt had assembled a group of policy advisers, popularly known as the Brain Trust, recruited by Raymond Moley and including Rexford G. Tugwell, A. A. Berle, and Samuel Rosenman. The group was responsible solely for proposing policy. Politics was left to James Farley, whose comprehensive strategy and mastery of detail set the pattern for modern presidential campaigns. The Republican effort, directed by former Indiana congressman

Everett Sanders, concentrated its attack on Roosevelt's record as governor, which was criticized as experimental and dangerous if extended on a national level in a time of crisis. Beneath the surface were doubts that an invalid would be able to withstand the rigors of the presidency. To reassure voters, Roosevelt undertook a strenuous campaign, delivering nearly 60 speeches, including 27 major addresses, around the nation. Before large, enthusiastic audiences Roosevelt set forth, albeit in rather vague terms, his plan to combat the Depression. To farmers he promised government aid in stabilizing prices. For the jobless he proposed immediate relief and public works projects. To worried businessmen he pledged to increase benefits under Hoover's Reconstruction Finance Corporation. Skeptics wondered how all this could be done within a balanced budget, which Roosevelt also promised to achieve. President Hoover remained in Washington until the last few weeks of the campaign. He then set out to deliver 10 major speeches in defense of his administration. But unlike the Roosevelt crowds, his were small and often hostile. Visibly shaken by the hatred in the faces of some in the crowd and exhausted from four years in the White House, Hoover was at times unsteady on the platform, the text of his speech frequently trembled in his grip. Sounding increasingly like a desperate challenger rather than a confident incumbent, Hoover began swinging wildly. In his final speech of the campaign he warned that if Roosevelt were elected, "The grass will grow in the streets of a hundred cities, a thousand towns; the weeds will overrun the fields."[7] Meanwhile several prominent Republican senators had deserted Hoover's sinking ship to endorse Roosevelt; they included George Norris of Nebraska, Hiram Johnson of California, Bronson Cutting of New Mexico, and Robert M. LaFollette, Jr., of Wisconsin. Republican campaign buttons fell flat with the slogan "Play Safe with Hoover." Roosevelt buttons prodded people to "Kick Out Depression with a Democratic Vote." Roosevelt's campaign theme song "Happy Days Are Here Again" captured his spirit of confidence. In the end Roosevelt swept seven out of eight counties nationwide and every major city except Philadelphia.

ELECTION AS PRESIDENT, NOVEMBER 8, 1932:

Popular Vote: Roosevelt (Democrat), 22,821,857 (57%); Hoover (Republican), 15,761,841 (40%).

Electoral Vote: Roosevelt, 472; Hoover, 59.

States Carried: Roosevelt won the electoral votes of 42 states—Alabama, Arizona, Arkansas, California, Colorado, Florida, Georgia, Idaho, Illinois, Indiana, Iowa, Kansas, Kentucky, Louisiana, Maryland, Massachusetts, Michigan, Minnesota, Mississippi, Missouri, Montana, Nebraska, Nevada, New Jersey, New Mexico, New York, North Carolina, North Dakota, Ohio, Oklahoma, Oregon, Rhode Island, South Carolina, South Dakota, Tennessee, Texas, Utah, Virginia, Washington, West Virginia, Wisconsin, and Wyoming. Hoover won the electoral votes of 6 states—Connecticut, Delaware, Maine, New Hampshire, Pennsylvania, and Vermont.

DEMOCRATIC NOMINATION FOR REELECTION AS PRESIDENT, 1936: As

Democrats convened in Philadelphia in June 1936, Roosevelt's renomination was ensured. Judge John E. Mack of New York again delivered Roosevelt's nominating speech, followed by 56 seconding speeches. Vice President John Nance Garner also was renominated. The most significant event of the convention was the abolition of the two-thirds rule; since then a simple majority has been sufficient for nomination. A dramatic moment occured when just before delivering his acceptance speech Roosevelt toppled off balance on his braces and fell to the floor. Restored to his feet and brushed off, he addressed the convention: "There is a mysterious cycle in human events. To some generations much is given. Of other generations much is expected. This generation of Americans has a rendezvous with destiny."[8] The Democratic platform largely confined itself to praise of the New Deal.

OPPONENT: Alf M. Landon (1887–1987), of Kansas; Republican. Born in West Middlesex, Pennsylvania, the son of an oil promoter, he at 17 moved with his family to Independence, Kansas, and in 1908 took a law degree from the University of Kansas. He worked briefly as a bookkeeper and then followed his father into the oil business as a wildcatter. Joining the Progressive wing of the Republican party, he campaigned for Theodore Roosevelt in his third-party presidential bid in 1912. During World War I he served as a lieutenant in the chemical warfare division but entered on duty too late to see action. After the war he emerged a popular party figure in the state, serving briefly as secretary to Governor Henry J. Allen of Kansas in 1922. In 1932 Landon was elected governor, a feat that drew national attention in the year Roosevelt Democrats were swept into office across the country. Two years later he was reelected, the only Republican incumbent governor to be returned to office in 1934. As governor, Landon established a moderately progressive record. Although he insisted on a balanced budget despite the Depression, he supported government relief efforts and won high marks for diligence and accessibility. At the Republican national convention in Cleveland in June 1936, Landon was nominated on the first ballot with 984 votes to 19 for Senator William Borah of Idaho. Landon offered the vice presidential nomination to Senator Arthur Vandenberg of Michigan, but he declined. Newspaper publisher Frank Knox of Illinois was then nominated for vice president. The Republican platform condemned the New Deal, which, it said, "has dishonored American traditions," and urged that federal recovery programs be turned over to the states. It also favored repeal of reciprocal trade agreements and called for a balanced budget and collection of foreign debts. After his defeat by Roosevelt, Landon retired to Kansas. In 1938 he was appointed by the president as the U.S. delegate to the Pan-American Conference at Lima, Peru. His daughter Nancy Landon Kassebaum was elected as a Republican to the U.S. Senate in 1978.

CAMPAIGN AND THE ISSUES, 1936: The dominant issue was the administration's program of economic recovery. Landon, who approved of the goals of the New Deal, concentrated his early attack on the president's methods. He claimed that waste, inefficiency, and an antibusiness philosophy were combining to impede recovery. Landon conducted four national campaign tours. Only during the last one did he take off the gloves to charge Roosevelt with violating the Constitution and declaring the election to be a battle to save the American system of government. His sudden attack on the New Deal programs themselves blurred his image among voters and weakened his credibility. Roosevelt's strategy was to ignore the opposition. He largely confined his remarks to a defense of the New Deal and blasts at the Republicans as the party of economic disaster. Roosevelt reminded voters that it was his administration that saved the systems of private property and free enterprise from the ruins of the Hoover administration. The National Association for the Advancement of Colored People endorsed Roosevelt, marking a decisive shift of the black vote from the party of Lincoln to the Democrats. Republican slogans that year were

"Life, Liberty, and Landon" and "Off the Rocks with Landon and Knox." Democrats countered with "Follow Through with Roosevelt." A notable feature of the campaign was the inaccurate Literary Digest Poll. Drawing its sample from telephone listings, the Literary Digest predicted that Landon would win by a landslide. But because many of those hardest hit by the depression did not own a phone, the sample was skewed in favor of the wealthy, likely Republican voters. Instead of a landslide victory, Landon suffered the worst electoral college defeat in modern times, carrying just two New England states.

REELECTION AS PRESIDENT, SECOND TERM, NOVEMBER 3, 1936:
    Popular Vote: Roosevelt (Democrat), 27,751,597 (61%); Landon (Republican), 16,679,583 (37%).

    Electoral Vote: Roosevelt, 523; Landon, 8.

    States Carried: Roosevelt won the electoral votes of 46 states—Alabama, Arizona, Arkansas, California, Colorado, Connecticut, Delaware, Florida, Georgia, Idaho, Illinois, Indiana, Iowa, Kansas, Kentucky, Louisiana, Maryland, Massachusetts, Michigan, Minnesota, Mississippi, Missouri, Montana, Nebraska, Nevada, New Hampshire, New Jersey, New Mexico, New York, North Carolina, North Dakota, Ohio, Oklahoma, Oregon, Pennsylvania, Rhode Island, South Carolina, South Dakota, Tennessee, Texas, Utah, Virginia, Washington, West Virginia, Wisconsin, and Wyoming. Landon won the electoral votes of 2 states—Maine and Vermont.

DEMOCRATIC NOMINATION FOR REELECTION AS PRESIDENT, 1940: As Democrats convened in Chicago in July 1940, delegates still were uncertain whether Roosevelt would seek an unprecedented third term. His longtime campaign strategist Postmaster General James Farley as well as Vice President John Nance Garner opposed a third term largely because they themselves wanted the nomination. Farley had specifically asked Roosevelt for his blessing to launch his own campaign. When Roosevelt told him to go ahead, Farley believed that the president had decided to retire at the end of his second term. Instead, Roosevelt maneuvered to be drafted by the convention. Through Senator Alben Barkley of Kentucky he delivered a statement to the convention that he had no desire or purpose to serve another term and urged the delegates to vote for whomever they pleased. Delegates got the message. After having his name placed in nomination by Senator Lister Hill of Alabama, Roosevelt was renominated on the first ballot with 946 votes to 72 for Farley and 61 for Garner. For vice president Roosevelt dumped Garner for Agriculture Secretary Henry A. Wallace of Iowa. Many delegates objected to Wallace for his leftist views, but Roosevelt insisted that without him on the ticket he would decline renomination. Wallace was nominated for vice president with 626 votes to 330 for House Speaker William Bankhead of Alabama. The Democratic platform recounted the accomplishments of the New Deal and pledged to keep out of World War II while maintaining a strong defense as a deterrent to aggression.

OPPONENT: Wendell Willkie (1892–1944) of Indiana; Republican. Born in Elwood, Indiana, Willkie graduated from Indiana University in 1909, received a law degree in 1916, and trained as an artillery officer during World War I but came on duty too late to see action. After the war he settled in Akron, Ohio, where he practiced law and became active in Democratic party affairs. He campaigned for the Cox-Roosevelt ticket in 1920. As a delegate to the party's national convention four years later, he fought for platform planks supporting the League of Nations and condemning the Ku Klux Klan. In 1929 he became counsel to the newly formed Commonwealth and Southern utility company and rose to president four years later. Still a Democrat in 1932, he contributed $150 to Roosevelt's first campaign. He broke with the New Deal over the Tennessee Valley Authority, which competed with Willkie's utility company. Having switched parties, Willkie attacked the Roosevelt administration in speeches that began drawing national attention by the time Republicans convened in Philadelphia in June 1940. A Willkie boom had been building across the country, but he was still a dark horse behind front-runners Senator Robert Taft of Ohio and New York District Attorney Thomas Dewey. Senator Arthur Vandenberg of Michigan also was a candidate. On the first ballot Dewey led with 360 votes (140 short of nomination) to 189 for Taft, 105 for Willkie, and 76 for Vandenberg. On the third ballot Willkie surged to second place, at the expense of Dewey, who at age 38 was regarded by some as too young to provide a serious challenge to Roosevelt. On the fourth ballot Willkie took the lead as the galleries rocked with chants of "We Want Willkie! We Want Willkie!" Then the party's titular leader, Alf Landon, heretofore a Dewey supporter, switched Kansas's 13 votes to Willkie, and, after the fifth ballot, Vandenberg released his delegates to him, touching off a stampede that led to Willkie's unanimous nomination on the sixth ballot. Senator Charles McNary of Oregon was nominated for vice president. The Republican platform blasted the New Deal for its "regimentation" and "shifting, contradictory and overlapping administrations and policies." It also criticized the administration both for military unpreparedness and "explosive utterances . . . which serve to imperil our peace." The platform called for passage of two constitutional amendments—to provide equal rights for women and to limit a president to two terms. After his defeat by Roosevelt, Willkie was dispatched by him to visit Allied countries during World War II. He ran again for the Republican presidential nomination in 1944 but lost to Thomas Dewey. His book *One World* (1943) became a bestseller.

CAMPAIGN AND THE ISSUES, 1940: Two issues dominated the campaign—the war in Europe and the third term. Willkie abandoned the dominant isolationism of his party to pledge a strong stand against Hitler and to favor a military draft. On domestic issues, he supported much of the New Deal, except the Tennessee Valley Authority, promising only to make programs more cost efficient. He concentrated his attack on Roosevelt's violation of the two-term precedent established by George Washington. He stumped 30,000 miles, delivering more than 500 speeches in 34 states but failed to offer voters sufficient reason for ousting the incumbent. Still he won support from such disaffected Democrats as Al Smith and former Brain Trust member Raymond Moley. He ran strong in rural America, carrying 57 percent of farmers in the Midwest, and also was popular in villages, towns, and small cities. Roosevelt, confident of victory, remained in Washington until the last two weeks of the campaign. Then he largely ignored his opponent to concentrate his attack on the Republican party in general. Like Wilson before him, Roosevelt campaigned for reelection on a pledge to keep the United States out of the world war. Independents for Roosevelt, led by Senator George Norris of Nebraska and Mayor Fiorello LaGuardia of New York City, rallied to his standard. The president ran strongest in urban areas, carrying every city of more than 400,000 except Cincinnati. Prizefighter Joe Louis campaigned for Willkie, Jack Dempsey for Roosevelt. Some 78 percent of the nation's newspapers endorsed Willkie, barely 9 percent came out for Roosevelt. According to tape recordings of conversations in the Oval Office during the campaign, made public in 1982, Roosevelt considered putting out the story that Willkie was having an affair with another woman. The smear campaign was never put into effect.

REELECTION AS PRESIDENT, THIRD TERM, NOVEMBER 5, 1940:

Popular Vote: Roosevelt (Democrat), 27,243,466 (55%); Willkie (Republican), 22,304,755 (45%).

Electoral Vote: Roosevelt, 449; Willkie, 82.

States Carried: Roosevelt won the electoral votes of 38 states—Alabama, Arizona, Arkansas, California, Connecticut, Delaware, Florida, Georgia, Idaho, Illinois, Kentucky, Louisiana, Maryland, Massachusetts, Minnesota, Mississippi, Missouri, Montana, Nevada, New Hampshire, New Jersey, New Mexico, New York, North Carolina, Ohio, Oklahoma, Oregon, Pennsylvania, Rhode Island, South Carolina, Tennessee, Texas, Utah, Virginia, Washington, West Virginia, Wisconsin, and Wyoming. Willkie won the electoral votes of 10 states—Colorado, Indiana, Iowa, Kansas, Maine, Michigan, Nebraska, North Dakota, South Dakota, and Vermont.

DEMOCRATIC NOMINATION FOR REELECTION AS PRESIDENT, 1944: As Democrats convened in Chicago in July 1944, Roosevelt's renomination was ensured. Senator Alben W. Barkley of Kentucky delivered his renomination address. He was renominated on the first ballot with 1,086 votes to 89 for Senator Harry Byrd of Virginia. Because the president's health had visibly eroded during his third term, many delegates believed, correctly, that in choosing a running mate they were choosing the next president. Overwhelming opposition to Vice President Henry Wallace forced Roosevelt reluctantly to dump him from the ticket. He considered three men in his place—Senator Harry Truman of Missouri, Supreme Court Justice William O. Douglas, and War Mobilization Director James F. Byrnes. He narrowed it down to Truman and Douglas and finally chose the former. Truman balked but relented on hearing that the president had said, "Tell him if he wants to break up the Democratic party in the middle of a war, that's his responsibility."[9] Truman was nominated for vice president on the second ballot over stubborn opposition from diehard Wallace supporters. The Democratic platform praised the administration's conduct of the war and favored the creation of a Jewish state in Palestine, equal pay for equal work regardless of sex, and an equal rights amendment for women.

OPPONENT: Thomas E. Dewey (1902–1971) of New York; Republican. Born in Owosso, Michigan, the son of a Republican newspaper editor, he graduated from the University of Michigan in 1923, studied voice briefly at the Chicago Musical College, and took his law degree from Columbia University in 1925. He practiced law in New York City and gained national attention for his campaign against organized crime. During the 1930s, first as chief assistant to the U.S. attorney for the Southern District of New York, then as U.S. attorney, special investigator of organized crime, and finally as district attorney of New York County, he became known as the "racket buster" for dozens of convictions of crime figures, including Waxey Gordon and Lucky Luciano. As governor of New York 1943–1955, Dewey cracked down on graft in the state police department, improved conditions in mental institutions, established a conservative fiscal policy, and resisted federal regulation of business. In 1940 he was the early front-runner for the Republican presidential nomination but lost to dark-horse Wendell Willkie. In 1944 Willkie was knocked out of the race following a dismal showing in the Wisconsin primary. General Douglas MacArthur withdrew his name from consideration in May. Conservative opposition to Dewey coalesced briefly around Governor John W. Bricker of Ohio, but Dewey was the overwhelming favorite as the party's convention opened in Chicago in June. Before balloting began, Bricker withdrew in favor of Dewey, removing the last vestige of opposition. Dewey was nominated on the first ballot with 1,056 votes to 1 for MacArthur. Bricker was nominated for vice president. The highlight of the convention was a scathing attack on the Roosevelt administration by Representative Clare Boothe Luce of Connecticut. The Republican platform abandoned its longtime commitment to isolationism to advocate U.S. participation in a postwar organization of nations. It warned that four more years of the New Deal "would daily subject every act of every citizen to regulation by [Roosevelt's] henchmen." Yet at the same time it favored extension of Social Security and unemployment compensation. It also called for a two-term limit for president, an equal rights amendment and equal pay for women, and creation of a Jewish state in Palestine. Dewey ran for president again in 1948 (see "Harry S Truman, 33d President," "Opponent").

CAMPAIGN AND THE ISSUES, 1944: Amid World War II Dewey declined to attack the administration's foreign policy. Instead, he campaigned indirectly against the president's failing health, criticizing "the tired old men" who had been conducting the nation's affairs for three terms. Roosevelt, who was indeed exhausted and just months away from death, sought to reassure voters by trotting out his physician, Vice Admiral Ross McIntire, to give him a public clean bill of health and ostentatiously campaigning in bad weather. Dewey promised to build on some New Deal programs, such as Social Security, but lambasted Roosevelt for conducting what he called the most wasteful, extravagant and incompetent administration in the nation's history. Democrats pointed to Dewey's lack of foreign policy experience and, as World War II raged on, warned, "Don't change horses in midstream." The most memorable episode of the campaign came in the wake of Republican charges that Roosevelt had dispatched a Navy destroyer to the Aleutians to retrieve his pet dog, mistakenly left behind after an inspection tour. In a speech before the Teamsters Union, Roosevelt deftly blunted the charges with a witty retort: "These Republican leaders have not been content with attacks on me, or my wife, or on my sons. No, not content with that, they now include my little dog, Fala. Well, of course, I don't resent attacks, and my family doesn't resent attacks, but Fala does resent them."[10] In the end, voters again responded to Roosevelt's appeal but handed him the slimmest margin of victory of his four elections.

ELECTION AS PRESIDENT, FOURTH TERM, NOVEMBER 7, 1944:

Popular Vote: Roosevelt (Democrat), 25,602,505 (53%); Dewey (Republican), 22,006,278 (46%).

Electoral Vote: Roosevelt, 432; Dewey, 99.

States Carried: Roosevelt won the electoral votes of 36 states—Alabama, Arizona, Arkansas, California, Connecticut, Delaware, Florida, Georgia, Idaho, Illinois, Kentucky, Louisiana, Maryland, Massachusetts, Michigan, Minnesota, Mississippi, Missouri, Montana, Nevada, New Hampshire, New Jersey, New Mexico, New York, North Carolina, Oklahoma, Oregon, Pennsylvania, Rhode Island, South Carolina, Tennessee, Texas, Utah, Virginia, Washington, and West Virginia. Dewey won the electoral votes of 12 states—Colorado, Indiana,

Iowa, Kansas, Maine, Nebraska, North Dakota, Ohio, South Dakota, Vermont, Wisconsin, and Wyoming.

ASSASSINATION ATTEMPT: On February 15, 1933, Giuseppe Zangara, a 32-year-old Italian bricklayer, shouted, "Too many people are starving to death!"[11] as he fired five shots from a 32-caliber revolver at the president-elect's open motorcade in Miami, Florida. Four people were wounded. Mayor Anton Cermak of Chicago was killed. Roosevelt escaped unharmed. Zangara was found guilty of murder and electrocuted on March 20, 1933.

INAUGURAL ADDRESS (FIRST): March 4, 1933. ". . . First of all, let me assert my firm belief that the only thing we have to fear is fear itself—nameless, unreasoning, unjustified terror which paralyzes needed efforts to convert retreat into advance. . . .

"Our greatest primary task is to put people to work. This is no unsolvable problem if we face it wisely and courageously. It can be accomplished in part by direct recruiting by the Government itself, treating the task as we would treat the emergency of a war, but at the same time, through this employment, accomplishing greatly needed projects to stimulate and reorganize the use of our natural resources. . . ."

INAUGURAL ADDRESS (SECOND): January 20, 1937. ". . . In this nation I see tens of millions of its citizens—a substantial part of its whole population—who at this very moment are denied the greater part of what the very lowest standards of today call the necessities of life.

"I see millions of families trying to live on incomes so meager that the pall of family disaster hangs over them day by day.

"I see millions whose daily lives in city and on farm continue under conditions labeled indecent by a so-called polite society half a century ago.

"I see millions denied education, recreation, and the opportunity to better their lot and the lot of their children.

"I see millions lacking the means to buy the products of farm and factory and by their poverty denying work and productiveness to many other millions.

"I see one-third of a nation ill-housed, ill-clad, ill-nourished.

"It is not in despair that I paint you that picture. I paint it for you in hope—because the Nation, seeing and understanding the injustice in it, proposes to paint it out. . . ."

INAUGURAL ADDRESS (THIRD): January 20, 1941. ". . . Lives of nations are determined not by the count of years, but by the lifetime of the human spirit. The life of a man is three-score years and ten: A little more, a little less. The life of a nation is the fullness of the measure of its will to live.

"There are men who doubt this. There are men who believe that democracy, as a form of Government and a frame of life, is limited or measured by a kind of mystical and artificial fate—that, for some unexplained reason, tyranny and slavery have become the surging wave of the future—and that freedom is an ebbing tide.

"But we Americans know that this is not true.

"Eight years ago, when the life of this Republic seemed frozen by a fatalistic terror, we proved that this is not true. We were in the midst of shock—but we acted. We acted quickly, boldly, decisively. . . ."

INAUGURAL ADDRESS (FOURTH): January 20, 1945. ". . . Today, in this year of war, 1945, we have learned lessons—at a fearful cost—and we shall profit by them.

"We have learned that we cannot live alone, at peace; that our own well-being is dependent on the well-being of other nations far away. We have learned that we must live as men, not as ostriches, nor as dogs in the manger.

"We have learned to be citizens of the world, members of the human community.

"We have learned the simple truth, as Emerson said, that 'The only way to have a friend is to be one.' . . ."

VICE PRESIDENTS: John Nance Garner (1868–1967), of Texas, served 1933–1941. Born in Red River County, Texas, Garner dropped out of Vanderbilt University to study law at a private office and was admitted to the bar in 1890. He settled in Uvalde, Texas, where he practiced law and became active in Democratic party affairs. He was elected to the state legislature 1898–1902 and the U.S. House 1903–1933, rising to Speaker in 1931. During three decades in the House, he earned a reputation as a conscientious, outspoken party regular, attentive to the needs of his district, and popular with other members whom he regularly invited to his office "to strike a blow for liberty" with bourbon and branch water. He was a leading candidate for the Democratic presidential nomination in 1932 but settled for the number-two spot. He later regretted leaving the House for the vice presidency. Garner supported the New Deal but broke with the president over the Court-packing plan and the decision to seek a third term. Garner unsuccessfully challenged Roosevelt for the Democratic presidential nomination in 1940.

Henry Agard Wallace (1888–1965), of Iowa, served 1941–1945. Born in Adair County, Iowa, the son of Henry C. Wallace, agriculture secretary under Presidents Harding and Coolidge, he graduated with a degree in animal husbandry from Iowa State College in 1910 and conducted independent research into farm problems. He crossbred the first commercially practical hybrid corn. In 1921 he became editor of *Wallace's Farmer*, an agricultural journal founded by his grandfather, and began to speak out on behalf of hard-pressed farmers. Although he had been raised a Republican, he switched parties to support Al Smith for president in 1928 and Roosevelt in 1932. Roosevelt appointed him secretary of agriculture (see "Cabinet"). As vice president, his first elective office, Wallace was dispatched on goodwill tours to Latin America in 1943 and to Russia and China in 1944. After U.S. entry into World War II, he served as chairman of the Board of Economic Warfare, in which capacity he came into bitter conflict with Commerce Secretary Jesse Jones. He spoke out for postwar international cooperation, a comprehensive foreign aid program, and closer ties with the Soviet Union. Wallace's views, regarded as unrealistic by some, pro-Communist by others, drew heated criticism from many Democrats as well as Republicans. Party leaders persuaded Roosevelt to dump him from the ticket in 1944. Afterward the president named him secretary of commerce (see "Cabinet"). Dismissed from the cabinet by President Truman in 1946, Wallace became editor of the *New Republic* and an outspoken critic of the Cold War. In 1948 he ran for president on the Progressive party ticket and was endorsed by the Communist party; he won 1.16 million votes, 2.4 percent of the total. According to FBI records obtained by The *Des Moines Sunday Register* through the Freedom of Information Act and made public in 1983, Wallace was under FBI surveillance during and after his term as vice president.

Harry S Truman (1884–1972), of Missouri, served January–April 1945. He succeeded to the presidency on Roosevelt's death.

CABINET:

Secretary of State. (1) Cordell Hull (1871–1955), of Tennessee, served 1933–1944. A longtime advocate of a low tariff, he won passage of the Trade Agreement Act of 1934, authorizing the president to negotiate reciprocal trade agreements and grant most-favored-nation status. He implemented the administration's Good Neighbor policy toward Latin America (see "Administration"), attending Pan-American conferences at Montevideo in 1933, Buenos Aires in 1936, Lima in 1938, and Havana in 1940. He urged diplomatic recognition of Russia. During the early stages of World War II, he supported assistance to the Allies and concluded the Lend-Lease agreement with Britain. In a celebrated confrontation, he condemned Japanese deception in blistering language before two Japanese representatives who called on him on December 7, 1941, just after he had received word of the attack on Pearl Harbor. At the Dumbarton Oaks Conference in 1944 he was instrumental in setting the stage for the founding of the United Nations. He resigned for health reasons, having served longer than any other secretary of state. He was awarded the Nobel Peace Prize in 1945. His memoirs appeared in 1948. (2) Edward R. Stettinius, Jr. (1900–1949), of Virginia, served 1944–1945. Promoted from undersecretary of state, he attended the Yalta Conference in 1945 and led the U.S. delegation to the Inter-American Conference on the Problems of War and Peace in 1945. He wrote *Roosevelt and the Russians* (1949). He stayed on in the Truman administration.

Secretary of the Treasury. (1) William H. Woodin (1868–1934), of New York, served March–December 1933. A Republican industrialist and personal friend of Roosevelt, he was instrumental in restoring public confidence during the banking crisis of 1933. He resigned for health reasons. (2) Henry Morgenthau, Jr. (1891–1967), of New York, served 1934–1945. A longtime friend and neighbor of Roosevelt, he was promoted from undersecretary of the Treasury. He administered the revenue programs that funded the New Deal and during World War II directed the bond drive that raised more than $200 billion. He stayed on in the Truman administration.

Secretary of War. (1) George H. Dern (1872–1936), of Utah, served 1933–1936. He died in office. (2) Harry H. Woodring (1890–1967), of Kansas, served 1936–1940. Promoted from assistant secretary of war, he objected to military aid to the Allies during the early stages of World War II. (3) Henry L. Stimson (1867–1950), of New York, served 1940–1945. He had served as war secretary in the Taft administration and secretary of state in the Hoover administration. He supported Lend-Lease aid to Britain and mobilized the nation's defenses during World War II. He also was instrumental in the formulation of U.S. atomic policy. He stayed on in the Truman administration.

Attorney General. (1) Homer S. Cummings (1870–1956), of Connecticut, served 1933–1939. He played a key role in resolving the banking crisis in 1933, sought to establish the constitutionality of the New Deal, won from Congress greater federal authority to combat organized crime, and promoted the administration's ill-fated Court-packing scheme. (2) Frank Murphy (1890–1949), of Michigan, served 1939–1940. He established the civil rights section in the department and prosecuted political corruption in Missouri and Louisiana. He resigned to accept appointment to the Supreme Court. (3) Robert H. Jackson (1892–1954), of New York, served 1940–1941. He counseled that Lend-Lease aid to Britain was legal. He resigned to accept appointment to the Supreme Court.

(4) Francis Biddle (1886–1968), of Pennsylvania, served 1941–1945. He supervised the internment of 120,000 Japanese-Americans during World War II. In 1988 the U.S. formally apologized for the internment and awarded each of 60,000 surviving internees compensation of $20,000. He stayed on in the Truman administration.

Secretary of the Navy. (1) Claude A. Swanson (1862–1939), of Virginia, served 1933–1939. Regarded as an expert in naval affairs in the Senate, he as secretary undertook a major naval expansion program. He died in office. (2) Charles Edison (1890–1969), of New Jersey, served January–June 1940. The son of inventor Thomas Edison, he was promoted from assistant secretary of the navy. He saved from the scrap heap World War I destroyers that were given to Britain during World War II. (3) Frank Knox (1874–1944), of Illinois, served 1940–1944. He had run for vice president on the Republican ticket with Alf Landon in 1936 and had been an outspoken critic of the New Deal. He directed the massive naval buildup during World War II. He died in office. (4) James V. Forrestal (1892–1949), of New York, served 1944–1947. Promoted from undersecretary of the navy, he stayed on in the Truman administration and became the first secretary of defense.

Postmaster General. (1) James A. Farley (1888–1976), of New York, served 1933–1940. Roosevelt's campaign manager in 1932 and 1936, he broke with the president over his decision to seek a third term and challenged him for the nomination in 1940. As postmaster general he extended air mail service. He wrote *Jim Farley's Story: The Roosevelt Years* (1948). (2) Frank C. Walker (1886–1959), of Pennsylvania, served 1940–1945. He stayed on in the Truman administration.

Secretary of the Interior. Harold L. Ickes (1874–1952), of Illinois, served 1933-1946. A progressive Republican who had bolted to support Roosevelt for president in 1932, he brought many noted conservationists into the department, won passage of the Taylor Grazing Act in 1934 restricting private grazing on public land, and established the Soil Erosion Service in the department. He directed the Public Works Administration and during World War II was a fuel administrator. He wrote *My Twelve Years with FDR* (1948). He stayed on in the Truman administration.

Secretary of Agriculture. (1) Henry A. Wallace (1888–1965), of Iowa, served 1933–1940. With passage of the Agricultural Adjustment Act, Wallace geared up the department actively to assist farmers during the Depression. He implemented the domestic allotment plan, in which farmers were paid to reduce crop output. To deal with huge surpluses of cotton and pork, he compensated farmers who agreed to plow under cotton plants and slaughter pigs, an emergency measure that shocked many at a time of widespread hunger. Among other programs established by Wallace were the Soil Conservation Service in 1935, the Federal Crop Insurance Corporation in 1938, the food stamp program in 1939, and the school milk program in 1940. He resigned to run for vice president and later was commerce secretary. (2) Claude R. Wickard (1893–1967), of Indiana, served 1940–1945. Promoted from undersecretary of agriculture, he directed the effort to increase farm production during World War II until creation of the War Food Administration in 1943. He stayed on in the Truman administration.

Secretary of Commerce. (1) Daniel C. Roper (1867–1943), of South Carolina, served 1933–1938. He established a business advisory council and cut the department's budget. Roosevelt appointed him minister to Canada in 1939.

(2) Harry L. Hopkins (1890–1946), of New York, served 1938–1940. He had served as director of the Federal Emergency Relief Administration 1933–1935 and the Works Progress Administration 1935–1938. He resigned as commerce secretary for health reasons. (3) Jesse H. Jones (1874–1956), of Texas, served 1940–1945. He had been appointed chairman of the Reconstruction Finance Corporation by President Hoover and was retained in that post by Roosevelt. During World War II he also served on the War Production Board and other panels. (4) Henry A. Wallace (1888–1965), of Iowa, served 1945–1946. He had served as agriculture secretary and vice president. He stayed on in the Truman administration.

Secretary of Labor. Frances Perkins (1882–1965), of New York, served 1933–1945. The first woman cabinet officer, she was instrumental in the establishment of the Social Security system in 1935, and passage of the Fair Labor Standards Act of 1938. She also rooted out corruption in the Immigration Bureau. She stayed on in the Truman administration. She wrote *The Roosevelt I Knew* (1946).

ADMINISTRATION: March 4, 1933–April 12, 1945.

New Deal. Confronted with the worst economic depression in the nation's history, President Roosevelt launched the New Deal, an unprecedented program of direct federal relief and economic regulation that established the modern welfare state. It included:

Response to Banking Crisis, 1933. The day Roosevelt took office, the banking industry was in imminent danger of collapse as nervous depositors had been withdrawing their money from institutions across the country. More than half the national banks had either gone bankrupt or suspended withdrawal privileges. Roosevelt immediately declared a bank holiday while federal auditors went over the books. Those determined to be essentially sound were reopened. This act alone restored a measure of public confidence and helped check further bank runs. The administration followed with banking acts of 1933 and 1935, which barred banks from dealing in stocks and bonds and established the Federal Deposit Insurance Corporation. By executive orders in April 1933 Roosevelt called in all gold, forbade its export, and formally took U.S. currency off the gold standard.

Civilian Conservation Corps, 1933. The CCC hired more than three million young men aged 18–25 of poor families, mostly from cities, to build roads, plant trees, and work on flood control and other conservation projects. The youths were stationed in rural camps under military supervision. They were provided food, shelter, and $1 a day in wages, most of which was required to be sent home to their families.

Agricultural Adjustment Acts, 1933, 1938. The First AAA sought to reduce crop surpluses and thereby boost prices by paying farmers cash subsidies to limit production. The funds were derived from a tax on processors of farm products. Although the idea of paying farmers not to grow crops was ridiculed in some quarters, the program substantially raised national farm income by the time the Supreme Court declared it unconstitutional (*United States* v. *Butler et al.*, 1936). The second AAA sought to stabilize farm income with creation of the "ever normal granary," by which the government in times of surplus loaned money to farmers and stored their surplus; in times of scarcity farmers sold their stored surplus and repaid the loans.

Tennessee Valley Authority, 1933. To aid the depressed Tennessee Valley, the

TVA harnessed the floodwaters of the Tennessee River and its tributaries for conversion to electricity. With operations covering 41,000 square miles in seven states, the TVA also practiced soil conservation and forestation, and manufactured fertilizers at Muscle Shoals, Alabama. Over the next 50 years, the TVA developed into the nation's largest utility, providing more than $4 billion worth of power annually to 2.9 million consumers.

Federal Emergency Relief Administration, 1933. Administered by Harry Hopkins, the program provided assistance to the poor.

National Industrial Recovery Act, 1933. The cornerstone of the early New Deal, it created the Public Works Administration, under Interior Secretary Ickes, to provide grants-in-aid to states and cities for large construction projects, and the National Recovery Administration (NRA), led by Hugh Johnson, to revitalize business. The NRA suspended the antitrust laws to foster greater cooperation among businesses on the road to recovery; price fixing was no longer illegal. In return, participating businesses were required to improve working conditions and wages, reduce the workweek, end child labor, and recognize labor unions. Eventually 750 codes of fair competition were promulgated to cover 500 different types of businesses and 20 million workers. The program was launched with great fanfare, but problems soon arose. Small businessmen complained that giant corporations were price fixing them out of the marketplace. Consumer prices went up markedly. And some industrialists, most notably Henry Ford, refused to cooperate. A study commission in 1934 headed by Clarence Darrow determined that the NRA was fostering monopoly. In 1935 the Supreme Court declared the NRA unconstitutional *(Schechter Poultry Corp.* v. *United States).*

Securities and Exchange Commission, 1934. This agency was created to correct abuses that had led to the stock market crash of 1929. Virtually all stocks and bonds traded on the exchanges were to be registered with the SEC. The SEC was authorized to set margin requirements and otherwise regulate securities transactions on the exchanges. Roosevelt appointed Joseph P. Kennedy as its first chairman.

National Housing Act, 1934. To aid the moribund housing industry, this bill established the Federal Housing Authority, the Federal National Mortgage Association, and the Federal Savings and Loan Insurance Corporation. The FHA insured its first mortgage loan in 1934 on a home in Pompton Plains, New Jersey.

Works Progress Administration, 1935. Although critics charged that the WPA, administered by Harry Hopkins, amounted to a "make work" scheme, the program found useful employment for a wide range of skills. WPA employees constructed 125,000 public buildings, 650,000 miles of road, 75,000 bridges, and numerous other public facilities. Its Federal Arts Program hired writers, artists, actors, and musicians. The WPA was dissolved with the decline in unemployment during World War II.

Rural Electrification Administration, 1935. The REA provided funds to extend electric power to rural areas long neglected by the utility companies because such service was less profitable than in concentrated population areas.

Wagner Act, 1935. Sponsored by Democratic Senator Robert F. Wagner of New York following the Supreme Court's invalidation of the NRA, it established labor's right to organize and bargain collectively through representatives of their own choosing and barred employers from discriminating against union members or attempting to interfere with or dominate unions. It also required management to bargain in good faith with union representatives. It established the National Labor Relations Board to settle disputes arising from the act as well as jurisdictional disputes among the unions. The Supreme Court upheld the act (*NLRB* v. *Jones & Laughlin Steel Corp.*, 1937). The law was modified by the Taft-Hartley Act of 1947 (see "Harry S Truman, 33d President," "Administration").

Social Security Act, 1935. It created the modern Social Security system to provide retirement income for those over 65, financial assistance for the aged needy, unemployment and disability insurance, and survivors' benefits.

Court Packing Plan, 1937. Angered over the Supreme Court's invalidation of much of the early New Deal, Roosevelt sought to pack the Court in his favor with a bill enabling him to appoint one new justice, up to a maximum of six, for every sitting justice of 70 years of age or older with at least 10 years' service. The plan drew heated protest, even among Roosevelt supporters. Its chief sponsor in the Senate, Democrat Joseph Robinson of Arkansas, died during its consideration, and the bill died with him.

Hatch Act, 1939. Sponsored by Democratic Senator Carl A. Hatch of New Mexico, it barred federal employees from engaging in partisan political activity.

Recognition of the Soviet Union, 1933. In an exchange of notes between Roosevelt and Soviet Foreign Minister Maxim Litvinov, the United States agreed for the first time since the Russian Revolution to establish formal diplomatic relations with the Soviet Union. The Soviets in turn promised, in bad faith as it turned out, to cease propaganda and subversive activities in the United States and also pledged to guarantee religious freedom and the right to fair trials for Americans residing in the Soviet Union.

Good Neighbor Policy. Roosevelt replaced Dollar Diplomacy (see "William Howard Taft, 27th President," "Administration") with the Good Neighbor policy toward Latin America. He withdrew U.S. forces from Haiti, abrogated the Platt Amendment, by which the United States was authorized to intervene in Cuba's internal affairs, and increased payments to Panama for use of the Panama Canal. He personally attended a Pan-American conference at Buenos Aires in 1936 to pledge cooperation in hemispheric defense. The Good Neighbor policy laid the groundwork for the Western Hemisphere's strong stance against the Axis Powers during World War II.

World War II, 1939–1945; U.S. Participation, 1941–1945. The immediate cause of the war was Germany's invasion of Poland in September 1939. Chief among the underlying causes was the rise of fascism in Europe, made possible by the severe economic dislocation arising from the exacting peace terms at the end of World War I, the global economic depression of the 1930s, and the fear of Communism. The conflict pitted the Axis Powers (Germany, Italy, Japan, Rumania, Bulgaria, Hungary, and Finland) against the Allied Powers (United States, Great Britain, France [free French], Soviet Union, China, India, Canada, Australia, New Zealand, South Africa, and Brazil and much of the rest of Latin America). Early Axis occupation of the following countries denied the Allies their men and material: France, Belgium, Netherlands, Norway, Denmark, Greece, Yugoslavia, and Poland. At the outbreak of the war, Roosevelt reflected national sentiment in maintaining U.S. neutrality. The America First Committee, formed in 1940 to keep the United States out of the war, included such prominent figures as Charles Lindbergh, Senator Burton K. Wheeler, and

General Robert E. Wood of Sears, Roebuck. But with the fall of France and the Battle of Britain in 1940, the United States drifted ever closer to the Allies. In September 1940 Roosevelt announced plans to deliver 50 old destroyers to Britain in exchange for the use of certain naval and air bases abroad. Under the Lend-Lease Act of March 1941, the United States provided Britain, and later the Soviet Union and other Allies, military equipment and supplies valued at $50 billion. In August 1941 Roosevelt and British Prime Minister Winston Churchill concluded the Atlantic Charter, in which they looked forward to "the final destruction of Nazi Germany" and vowed to seek a peace in which "all the men in all the lands may live out their lives in freedom from fear and want." On December 7, 1941, Japanese carrier-based aircraft attacked Pearl Harbor, Hawaii, killing 2,300 Americans, wounding 1,200, and destroying much of the U.S. Pacific fleet at anchor there. The next day Roosevelt asked Congress for a declaration of war. Predicting that the date of the attack "will live in infamy," he declared, "Hostilities exist. There is no blinking at the fact that our people, our territory, and our interests are in grave danger." Congress unanimously voted for war. For much of 1942 the Axis Powers seemed invincible. Japanse forces swarmed over Southeast Asia and the Pacific islands. General Douglas MacArthur was driven from the Philippines. German troops advanced deep into the Soviet Union. German Field Marshal Erwin Rommel dominated North Africa. But by the end of the first year of U.S. participation, the Allies began to turn the tide, beginning with a naval victory at Midway in June 1942 and a U.S.-British counteroffensive in North Africa in November 1942. At the Casablanca Conference in January 1943 Roosevelt and Churchill agreed to insist on the unconditional surrender of Germany and laid plans for the aerial bombardment of that country. In 1943 British and American forces secured Sicily and proceeded up the Italian peninsula against stiff German resistance; the Italians meanwhile overthrew dictator Benito Mussolini in July and declared war on Germany in October 1943. In the Soviet Union that year Soviet forces broke the Nazi siege of Leningrad and relentlessly pushed German forces back west. Meanwhile in the Pacific, General MacArthur and Admiral Chester Nimitz launched an island-hopping offensive around Japanese strongholds. At the Battle of Leyte Gulf in October 1944, the Japanese Navy was virtually destroyed. In Europe Allied forces under the command of General Dwight D. Eisenhower landed at Normandy on June 6, 1944, D-Day. Withstanding heavy casualities, the force secured beachheads, enabling the Third Army under General George Patton to spearhead the drive inland. Paris was liberated on August 25, 1944. In the Battle of the Bulge, December 1944–January 1945, Germany made one last desperate attempt to throw back the Allies but only delayed the inevitable. With the end of the war in sight, Roosevelt, Churchill, and Soviet Premier Josef Stalin met at Yalta in February 1945 to consider postwar plans. In return for a Soviet pledge to enter the war against Japan after Germany's surrender, Churchill and Roosevelt granted certain concessions to Stalin in Europe and Asia that were to strengthen the Soviet hand in drawing postwar boundaries and spheres of influence. Roosevelt died two months later, during the final stages of the war. See also "Harry S Truman, 33d President," "Administration."

    Constitutional Amendment Ratified. Twenty-first Amendment, 1933. Repeal of Prohibition.

SUPREME COURT APPOINTMENTS: (1) Hugo L. Black (1886–1971), of Alabama, served as associate justice 1937–1971. While his confirmation was pending it was disclosed that he had been a member of the Ku Klux Klan briefly in the mid-1920s. Black defended himself in a radio address and was quickly confirmed. On the bench Black emerged a champion of civil liberties. His dissent in *Betts* v. *Brady* (1940), in which the majority held that a defendant too poor to hire a lawyer was not necessarily entitled to one at the court's expense, eventually formed the basis of the reversal of that opinion in *Gideon* v. *Wainright* (1963). No doubt with supreme satisfaction Black delivered the majority opinion in *Gideon*. In *Engel* v. *Vitale* (1962), he invalidated mandatory school prayers in New York. In *Youngstown Sheet and Tube* v. *Sawyer* (1952), he denied President Truman's authority to seize steel mills during the Korean War. But Black is best remembered for his relentless, consistent defense of free speech unrestricted by the "clear and present danger" test previously applied by Justice Oliver Wendell Holmes. A typical example was his minority opinion in *Barenblatt* v. *United States* (1959): "Our Constitution assumes that the common sense of the people in their attachment to their country will enable them, after free discussion, to withstand ideas that are wrong. To say that our patriotism must be protected against false ideas by means other than these is, I think, to make a baseless charge." (2) Stanley F. Reed (1884–1980), of Kentucky, served as associate justice 1938–1957. As solicitor general from 1935, he had defended much of the New Deal legislation before the Supreme Court. On the bench he generally was a centrist. He consistently voted with conservatives in curbing civil liberties during the McCarthy era but joined liberals in sustaining black civil rights. At 95 he lived longer than any other Supreme Court justice. (3) Felix Frankfurter (1882–1965), of Massachusetts, served as associate justice 1939–1962. Despite his longtime commitment to liberal causes, having been a charter member of the American Civil Liberties Union and a leading champion of Sacco and Vanzetti, on the bench Frankfurter was foremost a proponent of judicial restraint and often joined the conservative bloc in narrowly interpreting the First Amendment. He spoke for the majority in upholding a statute that required students to salute the flag in public schools (*Minersville School District* v. *Gobitis*, 1940). (4) William O. Douglas (1898–1980), of Connecticut, served as associate justice 1839–1975. A man of enormous energy, he served longer (36 years) and wrote more opinions (1,500) than any other justice in the Court's history. He emerged, with Justice Black, a champion of civil liberties. In a celebrated dissent (*Dennis et al.* v. *United States*, 1951), he wrote: "When ideas compete in the marketplace for acceptance, full and free discussion even of ideas we hate encourages the testing of our own prejudices and preconceptions. Full and free discussion keeps a society from becoming stagnant and unprepared for the stresses and strains that work to tear all civilizations apart." In 1953 Douglas stayed the execution of convicted spies Julius and Ethel Rosenberg, but his action was reversed by the full Court. In 1970 Republican Representative Gerald R. Ford of Michigan led an unsuccessful drive to impeach Douglas, ostensibly for his paid activities on behalf of the Parvin Foundation, a charitable organization with alleged ties to organized crime. His writings include the autobiographical *Go East, Young Man* (1974) and *The Court Years* (1980). (5) Frank Murphy (1890–1949), of Michigan, served as associate justice 1940–1949. He was attorney general. He generally joined the liberal bloc in voting to uphold civil liberties. He wrote the dissenting opinion in *Korematsu* v. *United*

States (1944), which upheld the internment of Japanese-Americans during World War II. (6) Harlan Fiske Stone (1872–1946), of New York, served as associate justice 1925–1941 and as chief justice 1941–1946. See "Calvin Coolidge, 30th President," "Supreme Court Appointments." (7) James F. Byrnes (1879–1972), of South Carolina, served as associate justice 1941–1942. He resigned from the Court at Roosevelt's request to become director of Economic Stabilization (later of War Mobilization) during World War II. He later served as secretary of state in the Truman administration. (8) Robert H. Jackson (1892–1954), of New York, served as associate justice 1941–1954. He was attorney general. He generally maintained a centrist position on the Court but joined conservatives in restricting the activities of Communists in the United States. His most significant contribution at this time, however, was off the bench as chief prosecutor of Nazi war criminals at Nuremberg in 1945–1946 (see "Harry S Truman, 33d President," "Administration"). (9) Wiley B. Rutledge (1894–1949), of Iowa, served as associate justice 1943–1949. He generally sided with the Court's liberal bloc.

RANKING IN 1962 HISTORIANS POLL: Roosevelt ranked third of 31 presidents, third of 5 "great" presidents, best of the twentieth-century presidents. He ranked above Wilson, below Washington.

DEATH IN OFFICE: April 12, 1945, 3:35 P.M., Warm Springs, Georgia. Roosevelt had been suffering from high blood pressure and arteriosclerosis. About 1 P.M., April 12, 1945, he was going over some papers at the "Little White House" at Warm Springs, while artist Elizabeth Shoumatoff was sketching his portrait and the president's cousin Margaret Suckley was crocheting nearby. Mrs. Lucy Rutherfurd (see "Extramarital Affair") also was present. Suddenly he pressed his hand to his temple and then over his forehead and said, "I have a terrific headache."[12] These were his last words. Moments later he slumped into unconsciousness, the victim of a cerebral hemorrhage. Two servants carried him to bed and dressed him in pajamas. Dr. Howard G. Bruenn, acting physician to the president, and Dr. James E. Paullin, an Atlanta internist, agreed that his condition was irreversible. Roosevelt died without regaining consciousness. No autopsy was performed. His arteries had grown so severly sclerotic that morticians had great difficulty embalming the body. Dr. Harry S. Goldsmith, of Dartmouth Medical School, believes that Roosevelt may have been suffering from cancer at the time of his death. Writing in *Surgery, Gynecology, and Obstetrics* (December 1979), the journal of the American College of Surgeons, Dr. Goldsmith observed that the president apparently had a growth removed from his left temple in the early 1940s, tissue that he believes may have been malignant. Funeral services were conducted in the East Room of the White House by Bishop Angus Dun of the Episcopal diocese of Washington. He was buried at Hyde Park, New York. In his last will and testament, Roosevelt named the Warm Springs Foundation beneficiary of insurance policies totaling $560,000. He left the residue of his estate, valued at $1.9 million, to his wife and, on her death, to his children.

ROOSEVELT PRAISED: "He has great imagination . . . if he had been president at the time when the Treasury was overflowing, he would have gone down in history as the greatest builder since the world began."[13]—Interior Secretary Harold L. Ickes, 1934

"He was the one person I ever knew, anywhere, who was never afraid."[14]—Democratic Representative Lyndon B. Johnson of Texas, 1945

"The Democratic Party took over when the nation was almost in a state of receivership in 1933. Fortunately, we had a great and revered leader, Franklin Roosevelt. Under his leadership the Democratic Party dedicated itself to improving opportunity and security for all our citizens."[15]—Adlai E. Stevenson, 1952

"With some of Mr. Roosevelt's political acts I could never possibly agree. But I knew him solely in his capacity as leader of a nation at war—and in that capacity he seemed to me to fulfill all that could possibly be expected of him."[16]—General Dwight D. Eisenhower, 1948

ROOSEVELT CRITICIZED: "Franklin D. Roosevelt proposes to destroy the right to elect your own representatives, to talk politics on street corners, to march in political parades, to attend the church of your faith, to be tried by jury, and to own property."[17]—Republican presidential nominee Alf Landon, 1936

"Along with currency manipulation, the New Deal introduced to Americans the spectacle of Fascist dictation to business, labor and agriculture."[18]—former president Herbert Hoover, 1952

"It is regrettable that Giuseppe Zangara hit the wrong man when he shot at Roosevelt in Miami. Roosevelt made many decisions in favor of Soviet Russia, beginning with his recognition of the Soviet Government. Thereafter he permitted the whole bureaucracy to be infested with spies."[19]—journalist Westbrook Pegler

"If [President Roosevelt] became convinced tomorrow that coming out for cannibalism would get him the votes he so sorely needs, he would begin fattening a missionary in the White House backyard come Wednesday."[20]—journalist H. L. Mencken

ROOSEVELT QUOTES: "A radical is a man with both feet firmly planted—in the air. A conservative is a man with two perfectly good legs who, however, has never learned to walk forward. A reactionary is a somnambulist walking backwards. A liberal is a man who uses his legs and his hands at the behest of his head."[21]

"The Presidency is not merely an administrative office. That's the least of it. It is more than an engineering job, efficient or inefficient. It is pre-eminently a place of moral leadership."[22]—1932

"We look forward to a world founded upon four essential human freedoms. . . . freedom of speech and expression . . . freedom of every person to worship God in his own way . . . freedom from want . . . freedom from fear."[23]—1941

BOOK BY ROOSEVELT: *The Happy Warrior,* Alfred E. Smith (1928).

BOOKS ABOUT ROOSEVELT: Alsop, Joseph. *FDR, 1882–1945: A Centenary Remembrance.* New York: Viking, 1982.

Bishop, Jim. *FDR's Last Year.* New York: Morrow, 1974.

Burns, James MacGregor. *Roosevelt: The Lion and the Fox.* New York: Harcourt, Brace and World, 1956.

Burns, James MacGregor. *Roosevelt: Soldier of Freedom.* New York: Harcourt Brace Jovanovich, 1970.

Davis, Kenneth. *FDR: The Beckoning of Destiny.* New York: Putnam, 1972; *The New York Years, The New Deal Years.* New York: Random House, 1985, 1986.

Freidel, Frank. *Franklin D. Roosevelt.* 4 vols. Boston: Little, Brown, 1952–1973.

Ward, Geoffrey C. *Before the Trumpet: Young Franklin Roosevelt*. New York: Harper & Row, 1985.

NOTES:

1 James MacGregor Burns, *Roosevelt: The Lion and the Fox*, New York: Harcourt, Brace and World, 1956, p. 152.
2 Arthur M. Schlesinger, Jr., *The Age of Roosevelt: The Crisis of the Old Order 1919–1933*, Boston: Houghton Mifflin, 1957, pp. 319–320.
3 Frances Perkins, *The Roosevelt I Knew*, New York: Viking, 1946, p. 144.
4 James Roosevelt and Sidney Shalett, *Affectionately FDR: A Son's Story of a Lonely Man*, New York: Harcourt, Brace, 1959, pp. 31–32.
5 Eleanor Roosevelt, *This I Remember*, New York: Harper & Bros., 1949, pp. 348–349.
6 Lloyd Robinson, *The Hopefuls: Ten Presidential Campaigns*, Garden City, N.Y.: Doubleday, 1966, p. 49.
7 Schlesinger, p. 435.
8 Burns, *Lion and the Fox*, p. 275.
9 Donald Young, *American Roulette: The History and Dilemma of the Vice Presidency*, New York: Holt, Rinehart and Winston, 1965, p. 230.
10 James MacGregor Burns, *Roosevelt: The Soldier of Freedom*, New York: Harcourt Brace Jovanovich, 1970, p. 523.
11 Burns, *Lion and the Fox*, p. 147.
12 Jim Bishop, *FDR's Last Year*, New York: Morrow, 1974, p. 531.
13 *The Secret Diary of Harold L. Ickes: The First Thousand Days*, New York: Simon & Schuster, 1953, p. 206.
14 Bishop, p. 556.
15 Bert Cochran, *Adlai Stevenson: Patrician among the Politicians*, New York: Funk & Wagnalls, 1969, p. 217.
16 Dwight D. Eisenhower, *Crusade in Europe*, Garden City, N.Y.: Doubleday, 1948, pp. 409–410.
17 Irving Stone, *They Also Ran*, Garden City, N.Y.: Doubleday, 1966, pp. 315–316.
18 *Memoirs of Herbert Hoover*, New York: Macmillan, 1951–1952, vol. III, p. 408.
19 Marcus Cunliffe, *American Presidents and the Presidency*, New York: McGraw-Hill, 1968, pp. 166–167.
20 Coley Taylor and Samuel Middlebrook, *The Eagle Screams*, New York: Macauley, 1936, p. 171.
21 Bill Adler, *Presidential Wit*, New York: Trident, 1966, p. 165.
22 Sidney Warren, *The President as World Leader*, Philadelphia: Lippincott, 1964, p. 171.
23 Henry Steele Commager, ed., *Documents of American History*, New York: Crofts, 1945, Doc. no. 537, p. 634.

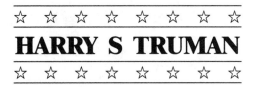

HARRY S TRUMAN

33D PRESIDENT

NAME: Harry S Truman. He was named after a maternal uncle Harrison Young. "S" was his full middle name. Undecided whether to give him the middle name Shippe, after his paternal grandfather, Anderson Shippe Truman, or Solomon, after his maternal grandfather, Solomon Young, his parents affixed the initial to represent both.

PHYSICAL DESCRIPTION: Truman stood 5 feet 10 inches tall and weighed 185 pounds when he became president, 175 pounds during his last year in office. He had blue eyes, brown hair that was mostly gray by the time he became president, a droopy nose, and a round full face. He had a slow heartbeat and chronic low blood pressure. He was extremely nearsighted and wore eyeglasses from age six. Otherwise his health generally was sound. He dressed fashionably in tailor-made suits; he was named one of the 10 best-dressed senators.

PERSONALITY: "To really understand Harry S Truman," wrote his daughter, "you must grasp the importance of humility in his thinking." To brag about himself or claim credit for something in public was anathema to him. "But," Margaret Truman added, "this *practice* of humility never meant that Dad downgraded his worth, his accomplishments, in his own mind."[1] Indeed, he was supremely confident of his own judgment. He acted boldly, decisively. Once he made a decision, he forgot about it and went on to something else. He was earnest, incorruptible, and blunt in speech. Like Andrew Jackson, he was notorious for his explosive temper and salty language. To some it was refreshing to see a president honest enough to blow off steam in public. It disturbed others, like David Lilienthal, chairman of the Atomic Energy Commission, who worried that his temper might set off World War III. Although irascible, Truman was not moody or prone to depression. He thrived on the rough and tumble of politics. "If you can't stand the heat, stay out of the kitchen," was his much-heralded philosophy. Truman delivered prepared addresses poorly in a flat voice marked by a distinct Missouri twang. But out on the stump, he fired up crowds with off-the-cuff speeches, characteristically of simple, straightforward language and short sentences.

ANCESTORS: Truman was of English, Irish, and German ancestry. The first Truman to arrive in America was Joseph Truman, who emigrated from Nottingham, England, in 1666 and settled at New London, Connecticut. Subsequent generations moved to Shelby County, Kentucky. In the 1840s, all four of Truman's grandparents left Kentucky for Westport Landing (now Kansas City), Missouri.

FATHER: John Anderson Truman (1851–1914) farmer, livestock salesman. A native of Jackson County, Missouri, he earned the nickname Peanuts for his size, about 5 feet 4 inches, 140 pounds, but was feisty and stood his own in numerous brawls with bigger men. He worked his father's farm until at age 30 he married and established his own spread at Lamar, Missouri. He prospered as a farmer and livestock trader but suffered severe financial loss speculating in commodities futures in 1901. He found work as a nightwatchman in Kansas City before turning again to farming near Clinton, Missouri, in 1904. Two years later he settled on his mother-in-law's farm near Grandview, Missouri. A self-educated man, he saved up change to buy a complete set of Shakespeare's works and read *Plutarch's Lives* aloud to son Harry. As an active Democrat, he served for a time as an election judge at Grandview. Late in life he was appointed a road overseer for Jackson County. He strained himself rolling a boulder off the road and died soon thereafter, when son Harry was a farmer. Truman later said of his father, "His code was honesty and integrity. His word was good. . . . He was not a talker. He was a doer."[2]

MOTHER: Martha Ellen Young Truman (1852–1947). Born on a farm within the present city limits of Kansas City, Missouri, she grew up in a pro-Confederate household during the Civil War and never overcame her resentment at the indignities her family suffered at the hands of Yankees. Arriving as a guest at the White House during the Truman years, she refused to sleep in Lincoln's bed. She studied art and music at the Baptist Female College in Lexington, Missouri, before her marriage in 1881. She followed Harry's career closely; while he was in the Senate, she read the *Congressional Record* faithfully every day. She died at age 94 during Truman's unelected term as president.

SIBLINGS: The oldest of three children, Truman had a brother and a sister— Vivian Truman, a farmer, and Mary Jane Truman, both of Grandview, Missouri.

COLLATERAL RELATIVE: Truman was a great[3]-nephew of President John Tyler.

CHILD: Truman had one daughter.

(Mary) Margaret Truman (1924–   ) singer, author. Born in Independence, Missouri, she earned a degree in history and international relations from George Washington University in 1946 and studied voice. She marked her singing debut as a coloratura soprano with Carl Krueger and the Detroit Symphony Orchestra before a national radio audience in March 1947. She performed the rest of the year on tour, mostly in cities in the South and Southwest. In 1948 she suspended her career to campaign for her father's election. She returned to the concert tour in 1949 and the following year made her television debut on Ed Sullivan's *Toast of the Town.* In a review of her performance at Constitution Hall at the end of her 1950 tour, Paul Hume, music critic for the *Washington Post*, wrote, "She is flat a good deal of the time. She cannot sing with anything approaching professional finish. . . . She communicates almost nothing of the music she presents."[3] An enraged President Truman wrote out in longhand and personally mailed a celebrated letter lambasting Hume. "I have just read your lousy review buried in the back pages," wrote Truman. "You sound like a frustrated old man who never made a success, an eight-ulcer man on a four-ulcer job and all four ulcers working. I never met you, but if I do you'll need a new nose and a supporter below."[4] In 1956 Margaret Truman married Clifton Daniel, Jr., a journalist for the *New York Times*. Her writings include *Harry S. Truman* (1973), *Bess W. Truman* (1986), and several murder mysteries set in Washington.

BIRTH: Truman was born May 8, 1884, at the family home in Lamar, Missouri.

CHILDHOOD: Truman's first memory was that of chasing a frog around the back yard. He grew up on farms near Harrisonville, 1885–1887, and Grandview, 1887–1890, before settling with his family in Independence, Missouri. Because he wore thick, expensive glasses, Truman was under strict orders not to roughhouse or take part in contact sports. He umpired baseball games rather than take his turn at bat. He apparently never got into a fistfight. "To tell the truth," Truman later admitted, "I was kind of a sissy. If there was any danger of getting into a fight, I always ran."[5] He was a fringe member of the Waldo Street gang in Independence but stayed out of trouble. Other boys teased him for taking piano lessons. He helped in the kitchen and cared for his baby sister, braiding her hair and singing her to sleep. An accident-prone youngster, he broke his collar bone in a fall from a chair while combing his hair, nearly chocked to death on a peach pit (his mother saved his life by forcing the seed down his throat with her fingers), and slammed the cellar door on his left foot, shearing off the tip of his big toe (a doctor reattached it successfully). At 9 he contracted diptheria. The disease temporarily paralyzed his arms and legs; he was pushed around in a baby carriage for several months until he regained the use of his limbs. A voracious reader, he at 10 received a four-volume set of Charles Francis Horne's *Great Men and Famous Women*. It awakened in him an interest in biography, history, and the principles of leadership and government. His early heroes included Hannibal and Robert E. Lee. He turned against such warriors as Alexander the Great and Napoleon because he felt they fought for the sake of conquest rather than from principle. Politically, he early followed his father into the Democratic party. He wore a Cleveland-Stevenson hat during the campaign of 1892. He worked as a page at the 1900 Democratic national convention in Kansas City.

EDUCATION: At five Truman was taught to read by his mother. He attended Noland and Columbia grade schools in Independence. In 1901 he graduated from Independence High School, where, according to English teacher Tillie Brown, he was a hardworking, though not a particularly brilliant, student. Valedictorian of the class was Charlie Ross, later President Truman's press secretary. His favorite subjects were history and Latin. He wanted to apply to West Point or Annapolis, but his poor eyesight made it impossible. Meanwhile he had become an accomplished pianist under the direction of Mrs. E. C. White of Kansas City. In 1900 she introduced the boy to Ignace Paderewski, who was in Kansas City on a concert tour. He gave young Truman a spot lesson on how to play his famed "Minuet in G." Mrs. White encouraged him to pursue a musical career, but when his father went broke in 1901, he dropped his lessons and any plans for college and went to work as a timekeeper. When later he decided to make a career of politics, he enrolled at Kansas City Law School, 1923–1925. He scored an 86 average for his two years there; his best subject was Blackstone's *Commentaries*, 96; his worst, sales, 77.

RELIGION: Baptist. Although raised in a Baptist family, Truman as a child attended the Presbyterian church and Sunday school in Independence, because it was near home. At 18 he formally joined the Baptist church. As president he worshipped irregularly at the First Baptist Church of Washington. An avid student of the Bible all his life, he singled out the Sermon on the Mount as its greatest passage. He favored ecumenism among the faiths and blamed much of the world's troubles on religious differences. He believed in the power of prayer. After being sworn in as president he asked members of the press to pray for him. He proclaimed July 4, 1952, the first annual day of prayer. From his school days to the presidency, Truman regularly recited the following prayer: "Oh, Almighty and Everlasting God, Creator of Heaven, Earth and the Universe— Help me to be, to think, to act what is right, because it is right; make me truthful, honest and honorable in all things, make me intellectually honest for the sake of right and honor and without thought of reward to me. Give me the ability to be charitable, forgiving and patient with my fellowmen—help me to understand their motives and their shortcomings—even as Thou understandest mine!"[6]

RECREATION: For exercise President Truman walked two miles every morning at a rapid clip of 128 steps per minute. He enjoyed playing small-stakes poker. A talented pianist himself, he often attended concerts. His favorite pieces included Mozart's "Fifth Sonata," Beethoven's *Symphony Number Five*, and Strauss's "Blue Danube Waltz." He also liked Chopin's waltzes, especially "Opus 42," and Bach's preludes and fugues. He appreciated fine art; among his favorite painters were Holbein, Rubens, and Leonardo da Vinci. But he detested the work of Picasso and other modern artists. "Any kid," said Truman, "can take an egg and a piece of ham and make more understandable pictures."[7] He was especially fond of equestrian statues; his favorite was Charles Keck's "Stonewall Jackson" in Charlottesville, Virginia. Truman did not smoke. He drank moderately, usually bourbon or white wine.

MARRIAGE: Harry S. Truman, 35, married Elizabeth "Bess" Virginia Wallace, 34, on June 28, 1919, at Trinity Episcopal Church in Independence, Missouri. Born in Independence on February 13, 1885, the daughter of David W. Wallace, a local public official who committed suicide in 1903, and Madge Gates Wallace, Bess grew up a tomboy. She played basketball and tennis, covered third base on the baseball field, fenced well, and took part in shot put competition—all the things Truman was unable to do because of his glasses. The two met in Sunday school when he was six, she five. "I only had one sweetheart from the time I was six,"[8] Truman said of his early attachment for the blue-eyed blonde who was his classmate from the fifth grade through high school. But they did not begin dating seriously until 1913, long after Bess had returned to Independence from Barstow's finishing school for girls in Kansas City. Judging from the content of hundreds of love letters, made public in 1983, Truman was a shy suitor. They became engaged in 1917 and married two years later. Following a brief honeymoon to Chicago and Detroit, they settled in Independence. While Truman was in the Senate, he hired his wife as secretary at a salary of $4,500 a year. According to her daughter's 1986 biography of her, Bess resented Truman's decision to accept the vice presidency and detested her years in the White House. An "emotional separation" developed between the President and

Mrs. Truman, Margaret Truman wrote. Mrs. Truman discontinued the First Lady press conferences initiated by Eleanor Roosevelt. Official entertaining during the Truman years was limited while the White House was under repair, 1948–1952, during which time the First Family resided at Blair House. She died of congestive heart failure on October 18, 1982. At 97 she was the longest living First Lady.

MILITARY SERVICE: Truman served in the Missouri National Guard during 1905–1911 and rejoined in May 1917. With U.S. entry into World War I, his unit became part of the regular army. Truman served with the 129th Field Artillery from August 1917 to May 1919, rising from lieutenant to major. He was neither wounded nor decorated. In basic training at Camp Doniphan, Fort Sill, Oklahoma, he was regimental canteen officer. In March 1918 he shipped overseas to artillery school in France. Promoted to captain in April 1918, he was appointed commander of the 129th's Battery D, made up mostly of Irish toughs from Kansas City. In its first encounter, in September 1918, the unit withstood a German barrage on its position at Mount Herrenberg in the Vosges Mountains. When some of the men panicked under first fire, Truman rallied them back to position. Battery D also saw action at St. Mihiel in September and in the Meuse-Argonne offensive in September–November 1918. Truman fired one of the last rounds of the war on a village northeast of Verdun minutes before the beginning of the Armistice. On a three-day pass to Paris in December 1918 he took in the Folies Bergère; "a disgusting performance,"[9] he said of it. Truman was discharged with the rank of major at Camp Funston, Fort Riley, Kansas. Truman later credited his wartime service and associates for his successful political career.

CAREER BEFORE THE PRESIDENCY: After graduation from high school in 1901, Truman held various jobs. He was a timekeeper for a railroad contractor at a salary of $35 a month in 1901–1902, a mailroom clerk at the *Kansas City Star* for $7 a week in 1902–1903, a clerk at the National Bank of Commerce in Kansas City for $35, later $60, a month in 1903–1904, and a bookkeeper at the Union National Bank in Kansas City for $75 a month in 1904–1906. He roomed for a time at a boardinghouse in Kansas City with Arthur Eisenhower, brother of Dwight D. Eisenhower. In 1906, at his father's request, he returned home to help run the family farm near Grandview, Missouri, where he remained until volunteering for World War I (see "Military Service"). Meanwhile, he lost money in a lead and zinc venture in 1915 and in oil exploration in 1916. After the war he established a haberdashery in Kansas City, in partnership with Eddie Jacobson, who had served under him as canteen manager at Camp Doniphan. The store at first prospered but went under in the recession of 1922. To avoid bankruptcy, Truman repaid his creditors in installments over the next 12 years. He lost about $28,000 on the venture.

Judge of Jackson County, Missouri, 1922–1924. Presiding Judge of Jackson County, 1926–1934. With the backing of the Democratic machine of Thomas J. Pendergast, Truman in November 1922 was elected judge for the Eastern District of Jackson County, an administrative post tantamount to county executive. He cut waste, reduced the county debt, and improved roads. Defeated for reelection in 1924, Truman worked for a time selling memberships for the Kansas City Automobile Club. In 1926 he was elected presiding judge of the county and was reelected four years later. In this post as chief executive of the county, Judge Truman won bond issues for the construction of roads, a county hospital for the elderly, and a new courthouse and insisted on competitive bidding and on-site inspection for all construction contracts. He also cut deadwood from the county payroll and curbed expense-account abuse. In 1929 Truman became leader of the Democratic party for the Eastern District of the county. In 1930 he was named president of the Greater Kansas City Plan Association and director of the National Conference on City Planning. In 1933 he was recruited by President Roosevelt's Federal Emergency Relief Administration to serve as a dollar-a-year reemployment director for Missouri.

U.S. Senator, 1935–1945. Elected as a Democrat to the Senate from Missouri over Republican incumbent Roscoe Conkling Patterson in November 1934 and reelected six years later over Manvel Davis, Truman entered Congress handicapped by the prevailing notion that he was, as some called him, "the senator from Pendergast." Although the Kansas City boss was indeed responsible for his political advancement, Truman carefully remained above the corruption on which the machine was based. "Pendergast never asked me to do a dishonest deed," Truman maintained. "He knew I wouldn't do it if he asked it."[10] Assigned to the Appropriations and Interstate Commerce committees, Truman loyally voted in support of New Deal programs and even stood by President Roosevelt in his controversial plan to pack the Supreme Court. He helped draft the Civil Aeronautics Act of 1938 to regulate the airline industry and the Transportation Act of 1940 to strengthen the regulatory powers of the Interstate Commerce Commission. He generally supported prolabor legislation. He pleased blacks with votes for a federal antilynching bill, an end to poll taxes, and creation of the Fair Employment Practices Committee. But it was as chairman of the Special Committee to Investigate the National Defense Program during World War II that Truman gained national attention. His investigation in 1941–1944 exposed waste totaling an estimated $15 billion in the military-industrial complex.

Vice President, March–April 1945. In 1944 President Roosevelt gave in to pressure from party leaders to dump Vice President Henry A. Wallace from the ticket. He considered three men in his place—War Mobilization Director James F. Byrnes, Supreme Court Justice William O. Douglas, and Truman. He narrowed it down to the latter two and finally chose Truman. Truman balked but relented on hearing that the president had said, "Tell him if he wants to break up the Democratic party in the middle of a war, that's his responsibility."[11] In 1986 Truman's daughter revealed that he was reluctant to accept the vice presidency, because he feared that in the mudslinging of a national campaign, the 1903 suicide of his father-in-law might be exposed, and he wanted to spare Mrs. Truman that humiliation. Truman was nominated on the second ballot in the face of stubborn opposition from diehard Wallace supporters. During his brief term as vice president, an office he once described as "about as useful as a cow's fifth teat,"[12] Truman was not privy to atomic bomb development or other vital matters. He was instrumental in winning Senate confirmation of Henry A. Wallace as commerce secretary and cast the tie-breaking vote against an anti-administration proposal, sponsored by Republican Senator Robert Taft of Ohio, that would have dismantled the Lend-Lease program immediately after the end of the war. On April 12, 1945, Truman was having a drink at the office of House Speaker Sam Rayburn when he was summoned to the White House. He went immediately, unaware that President Roosevelt had been stricken. He was greeted by Mrs. Eleanor Roosevelt, who said, "Harry, the President is dead."

Truman replied, "Is there anything I can do for you?" Mrs. Roosevelt shook her head and said, "Is there anything we can do for you? For you are the one in trouble now."[13]

At 7:09 P.M. on April 12, 1945, Truman was administered the presidential oath by Chief Justice Harlan Fiske Stone beneath the portrait of President Woodrow Wilson in the White House Cabinet Room. The next day Truman told reporters, "I don't know whether you fellows ever had a load of hay fall on you, but when they told me what had happened, I felt like the moon, the stars, and all the planets had fallen on me."[14]

DEMOCRATIC PRESIDENTIAL NOMINATION, 1948: As Democrats convened in Philadelphia in July 1948, many believed that Truman had little chance to be elected in his own right. Liberals, including Senator Claude Pepper of Florida and the sons of the late President Roosevelt, set out to dump Truman for the popular General Dwight D. Eisenhower, whose political affiliation was not yet established, or Supreme Court Justice William O. Douglas. When both Eisenhower and Douglas withdrew their names from consideration, the insurgency petered out. Southern conservatives deserted Truman to rally around the candidacy of Senator Richard Russell of Georgia. Governor Phil M. Donnelly of Missouri placed Truman's name in nomination. Truman was nominated on the first ballot with 947½ votes to 263 for Russell. Senator Alben Barkley of Kentucky was nominated for vice president. It was 2 A.M. by the time Truman mounted the podium to deliver his acceptance speech. Delegates, weary from the day's proceedings and sullen about their prospects in the fall, settled in for what they thought was to be another lackluster Truman address. But the president brought them to their feet with a two-fisted attack on the opposition. In a surprise announcement that electrified the hall, Truman vowed to call Congress into special session later that month to enact bills for slum clearance, low-cost housing, extension of Social Security, and other liberal measures Republicans claimed to favor in their platform. The struggle over the Democratic platform brought national attention to the young mayor of Minneapolis, Hubert Humphrey, and a regional split in party ranks. Humphrey led the successful fight for a civil rights plank, which asserted "that racial and religious minorities must have the right to live, the right to work, the right to vote, the full and equal protection of the laws, on a basis of equality with all citizens as guaranteed by the Constitution." In protest, 35 southerners (Mississippi and half the Alabama delegation) walked out. The Democratic platform also favored arms control, recognition of Israel, comprehensive housing legislation, repeal of the Taft-Hartley Act, an increase in the minimum wage from 40¢ to 75¢ an hour, extension of Social Security coverage, and a national health program.

OPPONENTS: Thomas E. Dewey (1902–1971) of New York; Republican. Dewey was the Republican presidential nominee in 1944. As titular head of the party, Dewey had been considered the odds-on favorite for the nomination in 1948. But in April former Governor Harold Stassen of Minnesota won a decisive victory over General Douglas MacArthur in the Wisconsin primary. Jolted out of complacency, Dewey abandoned his strategy of remaining aloof and engaged Stassen directly in the primaries. The showdown came in Oregon, where the candidates debated on radio Stassen's proposal to outlaw the Communist party. Observers agreed that Dewey outperformed Stassen on the air; largely as a result of the debate Dewey went on to win the Oregon primary. Dewey's most formidable potential opponent, General Dwight D. Eisenhower, already had announced in January that he was not a candidate. At the Republican national convention in Philadelphia in June, Dewey led on the first ballot with 434 votes to 224 for Senator Robert Taft of Ohio, 157 for Stassen, 62 for Senator Arthur Vandenberg of Michigan, 59 for Governor Earl Warren of California, and the rest scattered. Dewey picked up additional support on the next tally and was nominated unanimously on the third ballot. Earl Warren was nominated for vice president. The Republican platform favored reduction of the public debt, federal aid to states for slum clearance and low-cost housing, extension of Social Security benefits, a federal antilynching law, federal civil rights legislation, abolition of the poll tax, a crackdown on Communist influence in the United States, recognition of Israel, and international arms control, "on a basis of reliable disciplines against bad faith." After his defeat by Truman, Dewey resumed his duties as governor of New York, 1943–1955. In 1952 he was instrumental in securing the Republican presidential nomination for Dwight D. Eisenhower.

Strom Thurmond (1903–2003) of South Carolina; States' Rights (Dixiecrat). Southern conservative Democrats upset over the party's civil rights plank convened in Birmingham in July 1948 to found the States' Rights, or Dixiecrat, party and nominate Governor Thurmond for president, Governor Fielding L. Wright of Mississippi for vice president. The Dixiecrat platform favored racial segregation and states' rights.

Henry A. Wallace (1888–1965) of Iowa; Progressive, endorsed by the Communist party. Leftist Democrats upset over Truman's hardline policy toward the Soviet Union convened as the Progressive party in Philadelphia in July 1948 to nominate former vice president Wallace for president, Senator Glenn H. Taylor of Idaho for vice president. The Communist party endorsed the ticket in August. The Progressive platform condemned "big business control of our economy and government," criticized the Marshall Plan as a means "to subjugate the economies of the European countries to American big business," and called for rapprochement with the Soviet Union, an end to the peacetime draft, and other pacifist measures.

CAMPAIGN AND THE ISSUES, 1948: Virtually everyone had written off Truman as a caretaker president doomed to defeat—everyone except Harry Truman. His strength was undermined on the left by Progressive Henry Wallace, on the ballot in 45 states, and on the right by Dixiecrat Strom Thurmond, on the ballot in the South as well as in Minnesota and North Dakota. Wallace hurt Truman most in New York, where he drained off 8 percent of the vote, enough to tip the state to Dewey. Thurmond deprived him of part of the traditionally Democratic South. Despite the odds, the president confidently undertook a 30,000-mile whistlestop campaign in which he delivered more than 300 speeches to an estimated six million people. His spunky stump style and plain, blunt speech played well with average voters. "Give 'em Hell, Harry!" yelled a man at a rally in Seattle. Truman replied that he never deliberately gave anybody hell; he just told the truth, he said, and the opposition thought it was hell. When the special session of Congress he had called adjourned without accomplishing anything of substance, Truman tagged it the "Do Nothing 80th Congress" and condemned the Republican majority for failing to enact reforms recommended in their own platform. He warned that the true aim of the GOP was to dismantle the New Deal. He lashed out against the Taft-Hartley Act, which Dewey generally supported. He called for a national health insurance program, which Dewey opposed. Dewey, confident of victory, campaigned on a theme of national unity and vaguely promised an end to the waste and inefficiency of 16 years of Democratic rule. Referring to Dewey's cautious campaign, Truman quipped, "He has given GOP another meaning . . . Grand Old Platitudes."[15] Labor turned out in force for Truman. His desegregation of the armed forces increased his popularity among blacks. His pledge of higher farm price supports improved his standing in the agricultural Midwest. As election day approached, however, the national pollsters were unanimous in predicting Truman's defeat. Gallup expected Dewey to win 49–44 percent, Roper read it 52–37 percent, Crossley predicted 50–45 percent. Political statistician Louis Bean was among the few correctly to foresee the Truman upset. The *Chicago Tribune* sent out its early edition with the headline "Dewey Defeats Truman," a copy of which the president triumphantly held aloft for photographers after learning that California and Ohio had fallen into the Democratic column, ensuring his election.

ELECTION AS PRESIDENT, NOVEMBER 2, 1948:

Popular Vote: Truman (Democrat), 24,105,812 (49%); Dewey (Republican), 21,970,065 (45%); Thurmond (States' Rights, or Dixiecrat), 1,169,063 (2%); Wallace (Progressive), 1,157,172 (2%).

Electoral Vote: Truman, 303; Dewey, 189; Thurmond, 39; Wallace, 0.

States Carried: Truman won the majority of electoral votes in 28 states— Arizona, Arkansas, California, Colorado, Florida, Georgia, Idaho, Illinois, Iowa, Kentucky, Massachusetts, Minnesota, Missouri, Montana, Nevada, New Mexico, North Carolina, Ohio, Oklahoma, Rhode Island, Tennessee, Texas, Utah, Virginia, Washington, West Virginia, Wisconsin, Wyoming. Dewey won the electoral votes of 16 states—Connecticut, Delaware, Indiana, Kansas, Maine, Maryland, Michigan, Nebraska, New Hampshire, New Jersey, New York, North Dakota, Oregon, Pennsylvania, South Dakota, and Vermont. Thurmond won the majority of electoral votes in 4 states—Alabama, Louisiana, Mississippi, and South Carolina.

INAUGURAL ADDRESS: January 20, 1949. ". . . The United States and other like-minded nations find themselves directly opposed by a regime with contrary aims and a totally different concept of life.

"That regime adheres to a false philosophy which purports to offer freedom, security, and greater opportunity to mankind. Misled by this philosophy, many peoples have sacrificed their liberties only to learn to their sorrow that deceit and mockery, poverty and tyranny, are their reward.

"That false philosophy is communism.

"Communism is based on the belief that man is so weak and inadequate that he is unable to govern himself, and therefore requires the rule of strong masters.

"Democracy is based on the conviction that man has the moral and intellectual capacity, as well as the inalienable right, to govern himself with reason and justice. . . ."

VICE PRESIDENT: Alben William Barkley (1877–1956), of Kentucky, served 1949–1953. Born amid poverty in Graves County, Kentucky, the last national officeholder to be born in a log cabin, Barkley worked his way through Marvin College, 1897, studied law at Emory College and the University of Virginia, and was admitted to the bar in 1901. He practiced law in Paducah, Kentucky, and entered politics. He was elected prosecutor of McCracken County, 1905–1909, and county judge, 1909–1913, before entering the U.S. House, 1913–1927, and Senate, 1927–1949. In Congress he generally supported the liberal programs of Presidents Wilson and Franklin D. Roosevelt. As Senate majority leader from 1937 he was instrumental in steering to passage the later New Deal and wartime measures. As vice president he was briefed regularly on policy matters, a practice instituted by President Truman, mindful of his own isolation in the Roosevelt administration. Barkley sat ex officio on the newly established National Security Council. He was the first to be dubbed the Veep, a contraction coined by his 10-year-old grandson. In 1949 Vice President Barkley, 71, married Jane Hadley, a 38-year-old widow. In 1952 he was briefly a candidate for the Democratic presidential nomination. After his term, he was returned to the Senate, 1955–1956. While speaking at Washington and Lee University he suffered a fatal heart attack.

CABINET:

Secretary of State. (1) Edward R. Stettinius, Jr. (1900–1949), of Virginia, served 1944–1945. A holdover from the Roosevelt administration, he was chairman of the San Francisco Conference of 1945, at which was drafted the United Nations charter. He resigned to become U.S. representative at the UN. (2) James F. Byrnes (1879–1972), of South Carolina, served 1945–1947. He had served on the Supreme Court at the appointment of President Franklin Roosevelt. He attended the Potsdam Conference in 1945. He abandoned an early willingness to cooperate with the Soviet Union to become one of the architects of the Cold War. He won passage of the Foreign Service Act of 1946, upgrading standards for U.S. diplomats. (3) George C. Marshall (1880–1959), of Pennsylvania, served 1947–1949. He devised the European Recovery Program, or Marshall Plan (see "Administration"), for which he was awarded the 1953 Nobel Peace Prize. He established the policy-planning staff within the department. He resigned for health reasons but later returned as defense secretary. (4) Dean Acheson (1893–1971), of Connecticut, served 1949–1953. The architect of the Communist-containment policy, he nevertheless came under Republican fire for being "soft on Communism" largely because he was secretary when the United States "lost" China to the Red forces of Mao Tse-tung. He implemented the Marshall Plan and helped found the International Bank for Reconstruction and Development and the United Nations Relief and Rehabilitation Administration. He was instrumental in forging the North Atlantic Treaty Organization and fostered close relations between a free West Germany and the West. His memoir *Present at the Creation* (1969) won a Pulitzer Prize.

Secretary of the Treasury. (1) Henry Morgenthau, Jr. (1891–1967), of New York, served 1934–1945. A holdover from the Roosevelt administration, he resigned in disagreement with Truman's postwar plans for Germany. *From the Morgenthau Diaries* appeared in 1959. (2) Frederick M. Vinson (1890–1953), of Kentucky, served 1945–1946. He had been serving as director of War Mobilization. He resigned to become U.S. chief justice. (3) John W. Snyder (1896–1985), of Missouri, served 1946–1953. He had been serving as director of War Mobilization and Reconversion. A longtime friend of Truman, he launched a major campaign to promote U.S. savings bonds.

Secretary of War. (1) Henry L. Stimson (1867–1950), of New York, served 1940–1945. A holdover from the Roosevelt administration, he recommended use of the atomic bomb against Japan. His autobiography *On Active Service in Peace and War* appeared in 1948. (2) Robert P. Patterson (1891–1952), of New

York, served 1945–1947. Promoted from undersecretary of war, he pressed for the unification of the armed forces. (3) Kenneth C. Royall (1894–1971), of North Carolina, served July–September 1947. Promoted from undersecretary, he was the last secretary of war before its integration into the new Department of Defense. He became the first secretary of the army, 1947–1949.

Secretary of Defense. (1) James V. Forrestal (1892–1949), of New York, served 1947–1949. He was secretary of the navy when it was integrated into the new Department of Defense. His administration was hampered by intense interservice rivalries. Despondent at least in part over his failure to achieve greater cooperation among the armed forces, he committed suicide. (2) Louis A. Johnson (1891–1966), of West Virginia, served 1949–1950. Truman's chief fund raiser during the 1948 campaign, Johnson pressed for unification of the armed forces but was unpopular with Pentagon personnel for failing to fight for a bigger defense budget. He resigned shortly after the outbreak of the Korean War. (3) George C. Marshall (1880-1959), of Pennsylvania, served 1950–1951. He had served as secretary of state. Congress exempted him from the law barring military men from the post of defense secretary. He improved morale at the Pentagon and directed the war effort in Korea. (4) Robert A. Lovett (1895–1986), of New York, served 1951–1953. Promoted from deputy secretary of defense, he directed the war effort in Korea.

Attorney General. (1) Francis Biddle (1886–1968), of Pennsylvania, served 1941-1945. A holdover from the Roosevelt administration, he was upset that Truman did not choose to retain him but accepted appointment as the U.S. judge at the Nuremberg trials. His memoirs *In Brief Authority* appeared in 1962. (2) Thomas C. Clark (1889–1977), of Texas, served 1945–1949. Promoted from head of the criminal division of the Justice Department, Clark oversaw the crackdown on alleged subversives and Communists in the United States and supported the FBI in that effort. He resigned to accept appointment to the Supreme Court. (3) J. Howard McGrath (1903–1966), of Rhode Island, served 1949–1952. Truman dismissed him for refusing to cooperate with an investigation of corruption in the department. (4) James P. McGranery (1895–1962), of Pennsylvania, served 1952–1953. He conducted the investigation thwarted by his predecessor and dismissed numerous employees for wrongdoing. He approved prosecution of Communists in the United States under the Smith Act.

Secretary of the Navy. James V. Forrestal (1892–1949), of New York, served 1944–1947. A holdover from the Roosevelt administration, he integrated the navy into the new defense department, of which he became the first secretary.

Postmaster General. (1) Frank C. Walker (1886–1959), of Pennsylvania, served 1940–1945. A holdover from the Roosevelt administration, he retired in poor health. (2) Robert E. Hannegan (1903–1949), of Missouri, served 1945–1947. He introduced the use of helicopters in the transport of mail from airport to downtown. He resigned for health reasons. (3) Jesse M. Donaldson (1885–1970), of Missouri, served 1947–1953. A career postal employee, he had worked his way up through the ranks from letter carrier. He cut residential mail delivery from twice to once daily.

Secretary of the Interior. (1) Harold L. Ickes (1874–1952), of Illinois, served 1933–1946. A holdover from the Roosevelt administration, he resigned in protest over Truman's appointment of Edwin Pauley as undersecretary of the navy. (2) J. A. Krug (1907–1970), of Wisconsin, served 1946–1949. He was involved in contract negotiations during railroad and coal strikes. (3) Oscar L.

Chapman (1896–1978), of Colorado, served 1949–1953. He was promoted from assistant secretary.

Secretary of Agriculture. (1) Claude R. Wickard (1893–1967), of Indiana, served 1940–1945. He was a holdover from the Roosevelt administration. (2) Clinton P. Anderson (1895–1975), of New Mexico, served 1945–1948. He directed postwar food relief for refugees and established the production and marketing administration within the department. (3) Charles F. Brannan (1903–1992), of Colorado, served 1948–1953. Promoted from assistant secretary, he won a greater role for agricultural experts in the foreign service.

Secretary of Commerce. (1) Henry A. Wallace (1888–1965), of Iowa, served 1945–1946. A holdover from the Roosevelt administration, he was dismissed by Truman for publicly criticizing the administration's policy toward the Soviet Union. (2) W. Averell Harriman (1891–1986), of New York, served 1946–1948. He had been serving as ambassador to Great Britain. He promoted the Business Advisory Board. He later served as chief U.S. negotiator at the Paris peace talks on Vietnam, 1968–1969. (3) Charles Sawyer (1887–1979), of Ohio, served 1948–1953. He established the maritime administration within the department.

Secretary of Labor. (1) Frances Perkins (1882–1965), of New York, served 1933–1945. She was a holdover from the Roosevelt administration. (2) Lewis B. Schwellenbach (1894–1948), of Washington, served 1945–1948. He opposed legislation curbing union activities and proposed outlawing the Communist party. He died in office. (3) Maurice J. Tobin (1901–1953), of Massachusetts, served 1948–1953. He attempted unsuccessfully to win repeal of the Taft-Hartley Act (see "Administration").

ADMINISTRATION: April 12, 1945–January 20, 1953.

Conclusion of World War II. See also "Franklin D. Roosevelt, 32d President," "Administration". Soon after Truman became president, the war in Europe ended with the surrender of Germany in May 1945, and the Allies began to close in on Japan. At the Potsdam Conference, July–August 1945, Truman, Soviet Premier Josef Stalin, and British Prime Minister Winston Churchill (replaced in mid-conference by the new prime minister, Clement Atlee), discussed postwar administration of Germany and reiterated demands for the unconditional surrender of Japan. Meanwhile, Truman learned that his predecessor had authorized development of the atomic bomb. According to notes written by Truman at the time he made the decision to use the weapon and made public in 1980 by historian Robert Ferrell, who discovered them, the president feared that its use might lead to the end of the world. Nevertheless, to avoid hundreds of thousands of Allied casualties in an invasion of Japan, Truman ordered the atomic bombing of Hiroshima, August 6, 1945; some 250,000 were either incinerated instantly or died of radioactivity within a year. When Japan still refused to surrender, Truman ordered a second atomic strike, on Nagasaki, August 9, 1945. Japan sued for peace the next day and formally surrendered on September 2, 1945. U.S. casualties in World War II were 292,000 killed in action, 115,000 other deaths, and 672,000 wounded. Of the Allies, the Soviets suffered the heaviest losses, an estimated 7.5 million killed in action. Of the Axis Powers, Germany suffered the most, an estimated 3.5 million killed in action.

Nuremberg Trials, 1945–1946. Local war-crimes trials held in various countries resulted in the conviction of thousands of Axis leaders, including that of Japanese Premier Tojo in 1948. But it was the Nuremberg International Military Tribunal that attracted the most attention. Led by U.S. Supreme

Court Justice Robert H. Jackson, the prosecution put to trial 22 Nazi leaders for war crimes that fell into three categories: waging aggressive war, violating long-established rules of war (e.g., care of prisoners of war), and crimes against humanity, specifically the Holocaust, the wholesale slaughter of Jews. Dismissing defense claims that actions taken under orders from higher authority during wartime are justifiable, the eight judges from the United States, Britain, France, and Soviet Union found 19 of the 22 defendants guilty, sentenced 12 to death (including Reichsmarshal Hermann Göring and German Foreign Minister Joachim von Ribbentrop), 3 to life imprisonment (including Hitler deputy Rudolf Hess), and 4 to terms of 10–20 years.

United Nations. Spurning the isolationism that guided U.S. foreign policy in the wake of the First World War, Truman led the United States in helping to create the United Nations. Its charter was drafted at the San Francisco Conference in 1945. It met for the first time in London in October 1946. Its present site in Manhattan was donated by John D. Rockefeller, Jr. Through the UN Truman promoted creation of the state of Israel, 1948, and conducted the Korean War, 1950–1953.

Truman Doctrine and the Cold War. With the end of World War II, the Soviet Union set out to install Communist regimes in countries occupied by the Red Army and neighboring lands where a Communist minority might exploit postwar confusion to seize power. An "iron curtain," Winston Churchill said, was descending over Europe. To counter the threat, Truman in March 1947 enunciated the doctrine that bears his name: "I believe that it must be the policy of the United States to support free peoples who are resisting attempted subjugation by armed minorities or by outside pressures."[16] With bipartisan support fostered by Senate Foreign Relations Committee Chairman Arthur Vandenberg, Truman won from Congress appropriations for aid to Greece and Turkey. During 1948–1949 the United States undertook jointly with Great Britain a massive airlift of more than 2 million tons of supplies to West Berlin to break a Soviet blockade of that isolated city. To form a united front against future Soviet aggression, the United States in 1949 led in the establishment of the North Atlantic Treaty Organization, a military alliance of the United States, Belgium, Canada, Denmark, France, Great Britain, Iceland, Italy, Luxembourg, the Netherlands, Norway, Portugal, and later Greece and Turkey. Under Truman, the United States sought not to liberate countries already in the grip of Communism, but rather to check its spread—a so-called policy of containment. Meanwhile, in the Far East U.S. attempts to mediate the struggle between the Communists and Nationalists in China failed. In 1949 the Red forces of Mao Tse-tung succeeded in driving Chiang Kai-shek and the Nationalists off the mainland to Formosa.

Marshall Plan (or European Recovery Program). Truman approved Secretary of State Marshall's plan to rebuild Europe from the ashes of World War II. During 1948–1952 the United States spent some $13 billion on reconstruction projects and set the European economy on the path to unprecedented prosperity.

Creation of Israel, 1948. With the end of the British mandate in Palestine, Jews proclaimed the state of Israel. The United States promptly recognized the new nation.

Point Four Program, 1949. In outlining his administration's program for peace and freedom, Truman listed four courses of action. Point four was "a bold new program for making the benefits of our scientific advances and industrial progress available for the improvement and growth of underdeveloped areas."[17] It marked the beginning of the U.S. commitment to provide technical assistance to Third World nations in Latin America, Asia, and Africa.

Korean War, 1950–1953. The immediate cause of the war was the invasion of South Korea by North Korean Communist forces in June 1950. In the larger sense it represented the inevitable collision of the Sino-Soviet impulse to extend Communism and the U.S. policy of containment. President Truman won a United Nations mandate to expel the North Koreans from the South. Ostensibly, then, it was a UN force under General Douglas MacArthur that launched a counteroffensive during September–October 1950 in Korea, but in fact more than 90 percent of the forces were either American or South Korean. With a daring amphibious landing at Inchon in September 1950, MacArthur seized the initiative and pursued the Communists back north across the 38th parallel. However, he misread the intentions of Red China. As U.S. forces approached the Yalu River, hundreds of thousands of Chinese poured across the border in January 1951 and drove MacArthur back south. MacArthur now called for all-out war against China. When Truman refused to extend the conflict for fear of touching off World War III and a possible nuclear exchange with the Soviet Union, MacArthur publicly criticized U.S. policy. Unwilling to tolerate such insubordination, Truman in April 1951 relieved the popular general of his command and replaced him with General Matthew Ridgway—a decision that drew a firestorm of criticism from the political opposition. Peace talks began in June 1951 but dragged on beyond the end of Truman's term. See also "Dwight D. Eisenhower, 34th President" "Administration."

Seizure of the Steel Mills, 1952. To head off an impending strike during the Korean War, Truman in April 1952 ordered the federal seizure of the nation's steel mills. In June the Supreme Court, in *Youngstown Sheet and Tube Co.* v. *Sawyer*, negated his order, declaring that he had exceeded his constitutional authority.

H-bomb. In October 1952 the United States detonated the first hydrogen bomb at Eniwetok, Marshall Islands, Truman had authorized its development.

Red Scare and the Rise of McCarthyism. As early as 1946 President Truman established a Temporary Commission on Employee Loyalty to facilitate the removal of security risks from sensitive federal jobs. But with Communism on the march around the world, the Republican Congress criticized the administration for not going far enough. The McCarran Internal Security Act of 1950, passed over Truman's veto, required Communists in the United States to register with the Justice Department and restricted their activities. Sensational espionage trials contributed to the impression that Washington was thick with traitors. In 1950 suspected spy Alger Hiss was convicted of perjury. In 1951 Julius and Ethel Rosenberg were convicted of passing atomic secrets to the Soviets. Preying on national fears of Communist influence in the government, Republican Senator Joseph McCarthy of Wisconsin in February 1950 claimed to have a list of 205 (the number changed in later speeches) names of known Communists in the State Department. Although he failed to produce a shred of evidence to substantiate the charge, he rose to prominence on the issue, denouncing the Roosevelt and Truman administrations for "20 years of treason." He continued to lash out against Communists in the executive branch even after a Republican entered the White House (see "Dwight D. Eisenhower," "Administration").

Presidential Succession Act, 1947. This law superseded the 1886 Succession Act (see "Grover Cleveland, 22d President," "Administration") to place the Speaker of the House and the president pro tempore of the Senate in direct line of succession behind the vice president and ahead of the cabinet. Presidential succession law was further refined with ratification of the Twenty-fifth Amendment (see "Lyndon B. Johnson, 36th President," "Administration").

Taft-Hartley Act, 1947. Passed over President Truman's veto, this law curbed labor rights provided by the Wagner Act of 1935 (see "Franklin D. Roosevelt, 32d President," "Administration"). Sponsored by Republican Senator Robert A. Taft of Ohio and Republican Representative Fred A. Hartley of New Jersey, it outlawed the closed shop, thereby sustaining a worker's right not to join a union, empowered the attorney general to secure an injunction of 80 days in strikes affecting the national health or safety, and barred unions from contributing to political campaigns.

Fair Deal. Truman's domestic policy, popularly known as the Fair Deal, achieved the Housing Act of 1949 (federal funds for slum clearance and urban renewal), an increase in the minimum wage, extension of Social Security coverage, and desegregation of the armed forces. However, other parts of his program, notably national health insurance and repeal of the Taft-Hartley Act, failed to pass.

Assassination Attempt, 1950. On November 1, 1950, armed Puerto Rican nationalists Oscar Collazo, 36, and Griselio Torresola, 25, attacked Blair House, the temporary residence of President Truman. In an exchange of gunfire with White House guards in the street, Torresola was killed, Collazo wounded. Private Leslie Coffelt was fatally wounded, two other guards were less seriously injured. Truman, who observed the disturbance from an upstairs window, was unharmed. Collazo was convicted of murder, assault, and attempted assassination of the president and sentenced to death. In July 1951 Truman commuted his sentence to life imprisonment. President Jimmy Carter freed Collazo in 1979.

Constitutional Amendment Ratified. Twenty-second Amendment, 1951. It limited future presidents to two terms in office.

SUPREME COURT APPOINTMENTS: (1) Harold H. Burton (1888–1964), of Ohio, served as associate justice 1945–1958. He generally joined conservatives except in cases involving black civil rights. He voted to sustain loyalty oaths and other antisubversive measures. Speaking for the majority in *Henderson* v. *United States* (1950), he struck down the practice of some railroads of maintaining segregated dining cars. "The curtains, partitions, and signs," he wrote, "emphasize the artificiality of a difference in treatment which serves only to call attention to racial classification of passengers holding identical tickets and using the same public dining facility." (2) Frederick M. Vinson (1890–1953), of Kentucky, served as chief justice 1946–1953. He had been serving as Treasury secretary. Vinson generally voted to sustain antisubversive legislation and uphold black civil rights. A consistent supporter of the actions of the Truman administration, he wrote the dissenting opinion in *Youngstown Sheet and Tube* v. *Sawyer* (1952), which invalidated Truman's seizure of the steel mills. (3) Thomas C. Clark (1899–1977), of Texas, served as associate justice 1949–1967. Truman told author Merle Miller that his biggest mistake as president was naming Clark to the Court. Clark had been serving as attorney general. He generally voted to sustain loyalty oaths and other government antisubversive measures. In a controversial opinion (*School District of Abington* v. *Schempp*, 1963), he spoke for the Court in banning prayer in public schools. In *Mapp* v. *Ohio* (1961), he extended the constitutional freedom from unlawful search and seizure to defendants in state courts. He retired when his son Ramsey Clark was appointed attorney general. (4) Sherman Minton (1890–1965), of Indiana, served as associate justice 1949–1956. He generally aligned himself with Chief Justice Vinson in sustaining antisubversive legislation and upholding black civil rights. He wrote the majority opinion in *Barrows* v. *Jackson* (1953), striking down racial covenants in real estate deeds. Ill health hampered his performance.

RANKING IN 1962 HISTORIANS POLL: Truman ranked ninth of 31 presidents, fourth of 6 "near great" presidents. He ranked above John Adams, below Polk.

RETIREMENT: January 20, 1953–December 26, 1972. As early as 1949 President Truman decided not to seek reelection for a third term but did not disclose his decision until March 1952. He did so, he said, because he wanted to restore the custom of the two-term presidency in the wake of the long Roosevelt administration. His personal choice as successor, Chief Justice Frederick Vinson, declined to run; Truman campaigned for Adlai Stevenson for president in 1952. After attending the inaugural of his successor, Dwight D. Eisenhower, he retired to Independence, Missouri. In 1954 he underwent emergency surgery following a gallbladder attack. He came through the operation nicely only to suffer a near-fatal reaction to antibiotics administered in the hospital. He supported Averell Harriman for the Democratic presidential nomination in 1956 but campaigned for the eventual nominee, Adlai Stevenson. In 1960 he promoted Senator Stuart Symington of Missouri for the Democratic presidential nomination in opposition to John F. Kennedy, whom he regarded as too inexperienced; he campaigned for Kennedy in the general election. In 1964 he represented the United States at the funeral of King Paul I of Greece. In 1965 he welcomed President Lyndon B. Johnson to Independence for the signing of the Medicare Act; Johnson paid this tribute to Truman for his early advocacy of national health insurance.

DEATH: December 26, 1972, 7:50 A.M., Research Hospital, Kansas City, Missouri. Truman had been in failing health for several years. He was hospitalized for gastrointestinal ailments repeatedly after 1966. On December 4, 1972, he was admitted to Research Hospital for lung congestion. Kidney malfunction and other complications weakened him further. He lapsed into unconsciousness on Christmas Day and died the next morning of what was officially termed "organic failures causing a collapse of the cardiovascular system." Funeral services were conducted by the Reverend John H. Lembcke, Jr., rector of Trinity Episcopal Church of Independence, at the Truman Library in Independence. He was buried in the courtyard behind the library. In his last will and testament, executed in January 1959, Truman divided the bulk of his estate, valued at about $600,000, between his wife and daughter. He also left a plot of land in Grandview, Missouri, to his Masonic Lodge there and $15,000 divided among numerous nieces and nephews and their children.

TRUMAN PRAISED: "President Truman is beloved by the American people because of his candor, honesty, frankness, and principle. He received the support of the American people because he represented in the minds of the

American citizens the bold principles of the New Deal and the Fair Deal."[18]— Democratic Senator Hubert Humphrey of Minnesota, 1952

"There never has been a decision made under this man's administration . . . that has not been made in the best interest of his country. It is not only the courage of these decisions that will live, but the integrity of them."[19]— former secretary of state George Marshall

"When the death of President Franklin Delano Roosevelt thrust him suddenly into the Presidency in April of 1945 at one of the most critical moments of our history, he met that moment with courage and vision. His farsighted leadership in the postwar era has helped ever since to preserve peace and freedom in the world."[20]—President Richard M. Nixon, 1972

TRUMAN CRITICIZED: "Mr. Truman is not performing, and gives no evidence of his ability to perform, the functions of the Commander-in-chief. At the very center of the Truman administration . . . there is a vacuum of responsibility and authority."[21]—Walter Lippmann

"[Truman] is vastly concerned with being right; he does not seem sufficiently concerned with getting the right things done. The great thing about Mr. Roosevelt was his sense of urgency. . . . One misses this in Mr. Truman."[22]— columnist Samuel Grafton, 1949.

"This country today is in the hands of a secret inner coterie which is directed by agents of the Soviet Union. We must cut this whole cancerous conspiracy out of our Government at once. Our only choice is to impeach President Truman and find out who is the secret invisible government which has so cleverly led our country down the road to destruction."[23]– Republican Senator William Jenner of Indiana, 1951

"It defies all common sense to send that roughneck ward politician back to the White House."[24]— Republican Senator Robert A. Taft of Ohio, 1952

TRUMAN QUOTES: "The Soviet Union does not have to attack the United States to secure domination of the world. It can achieve its ends by isolating us and swallowing up all our allies."[25]—1951

"Within the first few months, I discovered that being a President is like riding a tiger. A man has to keep on riding or be swallowed."[26]

"I sit here all day trying to persuade people to do the things they ought to have sense enough to do without my persuading them. . . . That's all the powers of the President amount to."[27]

"Three things can ruin a man—money, power, and women. I never had any money, I never wanted power, and the only woman in my life is up at the house right now."[28]

BOOKS BY TRUMAN: *Year of Decisions* (1955); *Years of Trial and Hope* (1956); *Mr. Citizen* (1960).

BOOKS ABOUT TRUMAN: Cochran, Bert. *Harry Truman and the Crisis Presidency.* New York: Funk & Wagnalls, 1973.

Donovan, Robert J. *Tumultuous Years: The Presidency of Harry S Truman.* New York: Norton, 1982.

Ferrell, Robert H., ed. *Off the Record: The Private Papers of Harry S Truman.* New York: Harper & Row, 1980.

Miller, Merle. *Plain Speaking: An Oral Biography of Harry S Truman.* New York: Berkley, 1973.

Miller, Richard Lawrence. *Truman: The Rise to Power.* New York: McGraw-Hill, 1986.

Poen, Monte M. *Strictly Personal and Confidential: The Letters Harry Truman Never Mailed.* Boston: Little, Brown, 1982.

Steinberg, Alfred. *The Man from Missouri: Life and Times of Harry S Truman.* New York: Putnam's Sons, 1962.

Truman, Margaret. *Harry S Truman.* New York: Morrow, 1973.

NOTES:

1 Margaret Truman, *Harry S Truman*, New York: Morrow, 1973, p. 3.

2 William Hillman, *Mr. President*, New York: Farrar, Straus and Young, 1952, p. 153.

3 Margaret Truman, p. 502.

4 Merle Miller, *Plain Speaking: An Oral Biography of Harry S Truman*, New York: Berkley, 1973, p. 88.

5 Bert Cochran, *Harry Truman and the Crisis Presidency*, New York: Funk & Wagnalls, 1973, p. 29.

6 Hillman, unnumbered page following Table of Contents.

7 Robert H. Ferrell, ed., *Off the Record: The Private Papers of Harry S Truman*, New York: Harper & Row, 1980, p. 299.

8 Ibid., p. 43.

9 Hillman, p. 172.

10 Frank McNaughton and Walter Hehmeyer, *This Man Truman*, New York: McGraw-Hill, 1945, p. 69.

11 Donald Young, *American Roulette: The History and Dilemma of the Vice Presidency*, New York: Holt, Rinehart and Winston, 1965, p. 230.

12 Frank Cormier, *Presidents Are People Too*, Washington: Public Affairs Press, 1966, p. 64.

13 Margaret Truman, pp. 208–209.

14 *New York Times*, April 14, 1945.

15 Alonzo Hamby, *Beyond the New Deal: Harry S. Truman and American Liberalism*, New York: Columbia University Press, 1973, p. 253.

16 Harry S. Truman, *Years of Trial and Hope 1946–1952*, Garden City, N.Y.: Doubleday, 1956, p. 106.

17 Ibid., p. 230.

18 *Memorial Services in the Congress of the United States and Tributes in Eulogy of Harry S Truman*, Washington: U.S. Government Printing Office, 1973, p. 134.

19 Alfred Steinberg, *The Man from Missouri: The Life and Times of Harry S Truman*, New York: Putnam's Sons, 1962, p. 429.

20 *Memorial Services*, p. 2.

21 Cabell Phillips, *The Truman Presidency*, New York: Macmillan, 1966, pp. 160–161.

22 Hamby, pp. 316–317.

23 John W. Spanier, *The Truman-MacArthur Controversy and the Korean War*, Cambridge, Mass.: Belknap Press, 1959, p. 212.

24 William Manchester, *The Glory and the Dream: A Narrative History of America 1932–1972*, Boston: Little, Brown, 1973, p. 576.

25 *New York Times*, January 9, 1951.

26 James David Barber, *The Presidential Character*, Englewood Cliffs, N.J.: Prentice-Hall, 1972, p. 271.

27 Marcus Cunliffe, *American Presidents and the Presidency*, New York: American Heritage Press, 1968, p. 326.

28 Hope Ridings Miller, *Scandals in the Highest Office*, New York: Random House, 1973, p. 245.

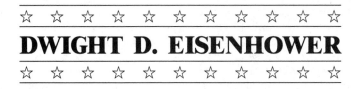

DWIGHT D. EISENHOWER

34TH PRESIDENT

NAME: David Dwight Eisenhower. He was named after his father but from childhood was called by his middle name to avoid confusion between the two. By the time he entered West Point, he was signing his name Dwight David Eisenhower. All six Eisenhower boys were at one time or another nicknamed Ike.

PHYSICAL DESCRIPTION: Eisenhower stood 5 feet 10 inches tall and weighed 178 pounds on becoming president. He had a fair complexion, blue eyes, light brown hair, although he was almost completely bald as president, square shoulders, and large hands. His most distinctive feature was his broad grin. He wore reading glasses. He had a trick knee, the result of a football injury. He caught cold easily and suffered from bursitis and ileitis from time to time. While president, he in 1955 suffered a heart attack, described by doctors as "moderate," underwent an intestinal bypass operation in 1956, and had a slight stroke in 1957 that impaired his speech for 24 hours.

PERSONALITY: By all accounts, Eisenhower was affable, gregarious, and a decent, honorable man who quietly inspired confidence and commanded respect. "Eisenhower wanted to like people," biographer Peter Lyon has written, "he wanted people to like him; he was distressed when it failed to happen so. His need for a friendly rapport was one reason for his reluctance, so often marked by journalists, to speak ill of anyone."[1] Another reason was a lesson learned in childhood: Angry because he was not allowed to go out on Halloween with the older boys, young Ike beat his knuckles bloody against a tree trunk. That night his mother nursed his hands and, in what he called one of the most valuable moments in his life, explained how futile was the emotion of hatred. Thereafter, he sought to avoid hating or publicly bad-mouthing anyone. The famous Eisenhower smile reflected his generally sunny, optimistic disposition. At times he grew depressed or exploded in anger, but never for extended periods. A bit superstitious, he carried in his pocket three lucky coins, a silver dollar, a five-guinea gold piece, and a French franc. Eisenhower was a rather poor speaker, notorious for his fractured syntax. Sometimes, however, he hid behind this reputation when he wanted to avoid responding directly to a question.

ANCESTORS: Eisenhower was of Swiss-German heritage. His great[3]-grand-father Hans Nicholas Eisenhauer (subsequent generations adopted the present spelling), born in the Palatinate, emigrated to Philadelphia in 1741 and settled as a farmer in Lebanon County, Pennsylvania. In 1878 his great-grandfather Frederick Eisenhower, grandfather Jacob F. Eisenhower, and his father left Pennsylvania for Abilene, Kansas.

FATHER: David Jacob Eisenhower (1863–1942), mechanic, gas company manager. A native of Elizabethville, Pennsylvania, he moved with his family to Abilene, Kansas, in 1878. Finding farming distasteful, he studied engineering at Lane University but dropped out to marry Ida Stover in 1885 and went into partnership in a general store in Hope, Kansas. Three years later his partner absconded with the store's cash, leaving David Eisenhower to face creditors. The humiliation of bankruptcy haunted him long after; he paid cash for everything and forbade his wife and sons to charge anything. He found work on the railroad in Texas but soon returned to Abilene, where he regained a measure of financial security first as a mechanic in a creamery and later as manager for a gas company. He died in Abilene, when General Eisenhower was overseas as deputy to General George C. Marshall. "He was a just man, well liked, a thinker,"[2] Eisenhower said of his father.

MOTHER: Ida Elizabeth Stover Eisenhower (1862–1946). A native of Mount Sidney, Virginia, she met Jacob Eisenhower while visiting her brother in Topeka in 1883 and married him two years later. She was deeply religious and as a pacifist wept when her son went off to West Point. In later years she became a Jehovah's Witness. She died in Abilene when General Eisenhower was chief of staff of the U.S. Army. "She was a worker, an administrator, a teacher and guide, a truly wonderful woman,"[3] Eisenhower said of her.

SIBLINGS: The third of six children to live to maturity, Eisenhower had five brothers—Arthur Eisenhower, banker of Kansas City, Missouri; Edgar Eisenhower, lawyer of Tacoma, Washington; Roy Eisenhower, pharmacist of Kansas City; Earl Eisenhower, electrical engineer of Charleroi, Pennsylvania; Milton Eisenhower, president of Johns Hopkins University and unofficial adviser to President Eisenhower.

CHILD: Eisenhower had one son to live to maturity.

John Sheldon Doud Eisenhower (1922–   ), soldier, diplomat, author. Born in Denver, Colorado, he graduated from West Point in 1944 and earned a master's degree in English literature from Columbia University in 1950. During his military career, 1944–1963, he served with the Army of Occupation 1945–1947 and in the Korean War 1952–1953, rising from second lieutenant to lieutenant colonel; he later rose to general in the Army Reserve. Having served as chairman of Pennsylvania Citizens for Nixon during the 1968 presidential campaign, he was appointed ambassador to Belgium, 1969–1971. He has written an account of the Battle of the Bulge, *The Bitter Woods* (1969), *Strictly Personal* (1974), and *Allies: Pearl Harbor to D-Day* (1982). He now lives in Valley Forge, Pennsylvania. In a communication to the author, Mr. Eisenhower expressed concern that succeeding presidents have eroded the most important achievements of the Eisenhower administration. "Eisenhower left a strong military establishment and strong American economy," he wrote. "Unfortunately, beginning with Kennedy, presidents since have frittered these assets away so that they now need rebuilding." Mr. Eisenhower believes that historians have unfairly evaluated his father's administration. He adds, however, "Historians seem to be developing some understanding other than the 'accepted wisdom' they have indulged in over 20 years. So much went on behind the scenes—and historians like to be entertained by government—that publication of Eisenhower's papers makes a great difference." Mr. Eisenhower believes that his father would not run for president today. "He would not be asked to," he asserts. "A country has to win its wars before they elect generals as presidents."

BIRTH: Eisenhower was born on the night of October 14, 1890, in a rented room near the railroad tracks in Denison, Texas.

CHILDHOOD: In 1891, when Ike was still an infant, the Eisenhowers moved from Denison, Texas, to Abilene, Kansas. Eisenhower's first memory, at age four, was that of fighting off a charging gander with a broomstick. He grew up in a family poorer than most in Abilene. Teased by other children for wearing hand-me-downs that included their mother's old shoes, the Eisenhower boys were scrappers, quick to settle a score with their fists and to stick up for one another. To earn spare cash, Dwight peddled produce from the family garden and worked in the local creamery, hauling ice and shoveling coal. At age six he marched in a torchlight parade for Republican presidential nominee William McKinley. In the most traumatic experience of his childhood, he at 15 developed blood poisoning after scraping his knee. The doctor recommended amputation, but Eisenhower protested so vehemently, arguing that he would rather die than be crippled, that his parents agreed to less radical treatment. He early developed an interest in military history; his childhood heroes were Hannibal and George Washington. His early ambition was to become a railroad engineer.

EDUCATION: A mediocre student, Eisenhower attended Lincoln school, grades one through six, Garfield school, grades seven and eight, and Abilene High School, in the class of 1909, in Abilene, Kansas. His favorite subjects were history and plane geometry. In extracurricular activities, he organized the high school athletic association and played football and baseball. Of his performance as Shylock's servant Gobbo in a senior class spoof of *A Merchant of Venice*, a local reviewer wrote, "He was the best amateur humorous character seen on the Abilene stage in this generation."[4] Attracted by the opportunity for a free college education, Eisenhower took the entrance exam for the U.S. Naval Academy but was informed that having passed his twentieth birthday he was too old for admission. He settled for the U.S. Military Academy at West Point, 1911–1915. Still an average student, Eisenhower placed fifty-seventh of 212 plebes at the end of his first year, eighty-first of 177 cadets his second year, sixty-fifth of 170 the third year, and graduated sixty-first of 164 with a four-year score of 2,084 out of a possible 2,525. His best subjects were engineering, ordnance, gunnery, and drill regulation. In deportment he graduated ninety-fifth of 164 cadets. He received numerous demerits for various minor infractions, such as smoking or tardiness. Once he was busted from sergeant to private for ignoring a warning that he refrain from whirling his dance partner so vigorously around the ballroom. Eisenhower blamed his misbehavior on a lack of interest in anything but athletics. Indeed, by his second year he was well on his way to becoming a star halfback. But in the game against Tufts in 1912, he injured his knee so badly that he was barred permanently from play. It was a crushing blow. He grew despondent and even considered dropping out of the academy but stayed on to coach the junior varsity squad. On graduating in 1915, Eisenhower was commissioned a second lieutenant and assigned to the Nineteenth Infantry. He later attended the Command and General Staff School 1925–1926 at Fort Leavenworth, Kansas, graduating first in a class of 275 officers, and the Army War College 1928–1929.

RELIGION: Presbyterian. Eisenhower was raised in a strict religious environment of the River Brethren faith and joined in family Bible-reading daily but did not formally join a church until he became president. He was baptized into the National Presbyterian Church in Washington in 1953. "I am the most intensely religious man I know," Eisenhower asserted in 1948. "Nobody goes through six years of war without faith."[5] He believed in the power of prayer and divine guidance. He once said that all free government boils down to an attempt to translate religious faith into a political world. He composed a prayer that he recited before delivering his inaugural address, asking God for the power to discern clearly right from wrong. As president, he instituted the interdenominational White House Prayer Breakfast and the practice of opening cabinet meetings with prayer.

RECREATION: Eisenhower's favorite pastime was golf. The U.S. Golf Association installed a putting green for him near the Rose Garden, and he practiced chip shots on the south lawn of the White House. He usually scored in the 80s. He also enjoyed dry-fly fishing and hunting. Besides sports, his favorite recreation was landscape painting; he maintained a studio in the White House. Although some of his work was quite good, he dismissed his landscapes as mere "daubs, born of my love of color and in my pleasure in experimenting."[6] From his youth he was a shrewd poker player. For years he was able to supplement his army pay with poker winnings. But he gave up the game in middle age, because, he said, fellow officers were losing more than they could afford. He turned to bridge and canasta. A skilled chef, Eisenhower was famous for his vegetable soup, charcoal-broiled steaks, and cornmeal pancakes. As president he also relaxed reading westerns (favorite author, Luke Short) and watching "The Fred Waring Show" on television. Of the many films screened for him at the White House, his favorite was *The Big Country* with Gregory Peck and Charlton Heston. At West Point he began smoking cigarettes, rolling his own Bull Durham, and built up to a four-pack-a-day habit. On the advice of his doctor, he quit cold turkey in 1949. He drank moderately, usually a Scotch, martini, or old fashioned before dinner.

MARRIAGE: Lieutenant Dwight D. Eisenhower, 25, married Marie "Mamie" Geneva Doud, 19, on July 1, 1916, at the home of the bride's parents in Denver, Colorado. Born on November 14, 1896, in Boone, Iowa, the daughter of John Sheldon Doud, a prosperous meat packer, and Elvira Carlson Doud, Mamie grew up in relative comfort in Cedar Rapids, Iowa, Colorado Springs, Denver, and the Doud winter home in San Antonio, Texas. It was soon after completing her education at Miss Wolcott's finishing school that she met Eisenhower at San Antonio in October 1915. Introduced by Mrs. Lulu Harris, wife of a fellow officer at Fort Sam Houston, the two hit it off at once, as Eisenhower, officer of the day, invited Miss Doud to accompany him on his rounds. Eisenhower found her vivacious, attractive, and saucy. Because of Eisenhower's meager salary, they went on cheap dates, usually a Mexican dinner at the Original and a movie or a vaudeville show. They became engaged on Valentine's Day, 1916. Following the wedding, performed by Reverend Williamson of the Central Presbyterian Church in Denver, the newlyweds honeymooned a couple days at Eldorado

Springs, a resort near Denver, and then visited the groom's parents in Abilene before settling into the lieutenant's crude living quarters at Fort Sam Houston. Although accustomed to more creature comforts than that afforded at military posts, Mamie adjusted readily and joined her husband in moving 28 times before their retirement at the end of his term as president. As First Lady, she was a gracious hostess but carefully guarded her privacy. A victim of Meniere's disease, an inner-ear disorder that affects equilibrium, Mrs. Eisenhower was at times unsteady on her feet, a spectacle that fed baseless rumors that she had a drinking problem. In 1961 she retired with the former president to Gettysburg, Pennsylvania, their first permanent home. She suffered a stroke in September 1979 and died on November 11. She was buried next to the president at Abilene. In 1980 her birthplace in Boone, Iowa, was dedicated a historic site; Mrs. John Adams is the only other First Lady to be so honored.

EXTRAMARITAL AFFAIR: Kay Summersby? In May 1942 Kay Summersby, 24, a native of Ireland, was assigned to drive Generals Eisenhower and Mark Clark during their 10-day visit to London. When Eisenhower assumed command of the European Theater of Operation in London the next month, he requested Summersby as his personal driver. At this time she was engaged to Colonel Richard Arnold, an American, but he was soon killed in North Africa. She joined the Women's Army Corps, rose to captain, and was promoted from driver to personal secretary and military aide to General Eisenhower. In her wartime memoir *Eisenhower Was My Boss* (1948), she did not mention having an affair with the general. But in *Past Forgetting: My Love Affair with Dwight D. Eisenhower* (1975), written while she was dying of cancer, she asserted that they had fallen in love during the war. In *Plain Speaking: An Oral Biography of Harry S Truman*, author Merle Miller quoted Truman as saying that he had seen and destroyed correspondence between Eisenhower and General George C. Marshall, in which Eisenhower announced his intention to divorce his wife and marry Summersby. Marshall responded in blistering language that as his superior officer he would, according to Truman, bust him out of the Army and make his life miserable thereafter. The Eisenhower family has denied that Ike ever contemplated divorce. After Eisenhower left Europe at the end of the war, he never saw Summersby again. She was hurt, she wrote, but had no regrets about the affair. Summersby later married Reginald Morgan. She was fashion consultant for the film *The Stepford Wives* shortly before her death in 1975.

MILITARY SERVICE: Eisenhower was a professional soldier. He served in the army during 1915–1948 and 1951–1952, rising from second lieutenant to five-star general. See "Career before the Presidency."

CAREER BEFORE THE PRESIDENCY: On graduation from West Point in 1915, Eisenhower was commissioned a second lieutenant and assigned to the Nineteenth Infantry at Fort Sam Houston, Texas. He was promoted to first lieutenant in July 1916 and captain in May 1917. During World War I he requested overseas assignment but was ordered to remain stateside as a training instructor at Fort Ogelthorpe, Georgia, organizer of the Sixty-fifth Battalion Engineers at Camp Meade, Maryland, and finally as commander of the Tank Corps Training Center at Camp Colt, Pennsylvania. Meanwhile, he received temporary wartime promotions to major in June and lieutenant colonel in October 1918. After the war he resumed the permanent rank of captain and was promoted to major in June 1920. During 1921–1922 he was a tank commander at Camp Dix, New Jersey, Fort Benning, Georgia, and Camp

Meade. Following assignment to the Panama Canal Zone, 1922–1924, he attended Command and General Staff School 1925–1926 at Fort Leavenworth, Kansas, and the Army War College 1928–1929 and was special assistant to the assistant secretary of war 1929–1932 in Washington. In 1932 he joined the staff of General Douglas MacArthur and that year was present as his aide in clearing the Bonus Marchers (see "Herbert Hoover, 31st President," "Administration") from the capital. In 1935 he accompanied MacArthur to the Philippines, where he served as his senior military assistant until 1939. While there he was promoted to lieutenant colonel in July 1936. Reassigned to Fort Lewis, Washington, he served as executive officer of the Fifteenth Regiment of the Third Infantry Division, January–November 1940, chief of staff to infantry commander General Charles F. Thompson, November 1940–March 1941, and, with promotion to colonel, as chief of staff to General Kenyon A. Joyce of IX Corps, March–June 1941. When the United States entered World War II, Eisenhower was chief of staff to III Corps Commander General Walter Krueger at Fort Sam Houston, June–December 1941. Following his impressive direction of large-scale training maneuvers, he was promoted to brigadier general in September 1941.

World War II. Soon after the Japanese attack on Pearl Harbor, General Eisenhower was summoned to Washington to become assistant chief of staff in charge of war plans. In March 1942 he was promoted to major general and named chief of the general staff's operations division. In June 1942 he was appointed commander of U.S. forces in Europe and the next month was promoted to lieutenant general. He was Allied commander in chief for the invasions of North Africa, November 1942, Sicily, July 1943, and Italy, September 1943. Meanwhile, in February 1943 he was promoted to general. In December 1943 President Franklin Roosevelt named him Supreme Allied Commander with orders to mount an invasion of Europe aimed at Germany; code name for the operation was Overlord. To take advantage of favorable tides, moon phase, and time of sunrise, Eisenhower selected June 5 for D-Day, but bad weather forced him to postpone it 24 hours. Although the weather forecast for June 6 also appeared threatening, he gave the go-ahead nevertheless because the tides would not be favorable again for another two weeks. Luckily the skies cleared, and the Allies landed successfuly at Normandy and proceeded to fight their way inland. Promoted to five-star general of the army in December 1944, he directed the final assault on Germany and on May 7, 1945, accepted that country's surrender in ceremonies at Rheims. In November 1945 he returned to the United States to succeed General George C. Marshall as army chief of staff. Although horrified by the destruction of the atomic bomb, he emerged from the war hopeful that the dreadful new weapon might serve as a deterrent to World War III. General Eisenhower resigned from the army in February 1948.

President of Columbia University, 1948–1950. With little in his background to prepare him for this position, Eisenhower was largely a figurehead president. He was wooed by both major political parties to run for president in 1948 but declined; he voted for Republican Thomas Dewey.

Supreme Commander of the North Atlantic Treaty Organization, 1951–1952. Appointed by President Truman in December 1950, General Eisenhower assumed his duties as chief of NATO in April 1951. He resigned from NATO in May 1952 and from the army in July following his nomination for president.

REPUBLICAN PRESIDENTIAL NOMINATION, 1952: As Republicans gathered in Chicago in July 1952, Senator Robert Taft of Ohio, the candidate of conservatives, was the front-runner. Eisenhower had shown remarkable strength in the primaries (he won in New Hampshire without campaigning there and ended Harold Stassen's candidacy by running a strong second as a write-in candidate in Stassen's home state of Minnesota), but Taft had actively campaigned for the nomination and seemed to have it within his grasp. The Eisenhower forces, however, crying, "Taft Can't Win," mounted a successful credentials challenge against Taft's southern delegates and turned the tide to their candidate. That the credentials fight was bitter and emotional became evident to television viewers when from the podium Senator Everett Dirkson of Illinois, a Taft delegate, glared down at Governor Thomas Dewey of New York, leader of the draft-Eisenhower movement and twice-defeated candidate for president, and with contempt bellowed, "We followed you before and you took us down the path to defeat!" Other highlights of the convention were a slashing anti-Communist speech by Senator Joseph McCarthy of Wisconsin, condemning "Red Dean [Acheson]'s State Department," and the keynote address by General Douglas MacArthur. Governor Theodore R. McKeldin of Maryland placed Eisenhower's name in nomination. Eisenhower was nominated on the first ballot with 845 votes to 280 for Taft, 77 for Governor Earl Warren of California, and 4 for General MacArthur. At Dewey's suggestion, Eisenhower chose Senator Richard M. Nixon of California as his running mate. The Republican platform condemned the Truman administration for "appeasement of Communism at home and abroad" and favored elimination of "the hordes of loafers" and "incompetents" from the State Department, a strong national defense, a balanced budget, lower taxes, retention of the Taft-Hartley Act, and reorganization of the government in accordance with recommendations of the Hoover Commission.

OPPONENT: Adlai E. Stevenson (1900–1965) of Illinois; Democrat. Born in Los Angeles, the grandson of Vice President Adlai E. Stevenson (see "Grover Cleveland, 24th President," "Vice President"), Stevenson grew up from age six in Bloomington, Illinois, graduated from Princeton University in 1922, attended Harvard Law School, and received his law degree from Northwestern University in 1926. He practiced law in Chicago until 1933, when he was hired by the New Deal's Agricultural Adjustment Administration. Although he returned to private practice in 1935, he thereafter was frequently summoned to public service. He was legal assistant to the secretary of the navy during World War II. As special assistant to the secretary of state after the war, he took part in the creation of the United Nations and served as senior adviser to the first U.S. delegation in 1946. As governor of Illinois 1949–1952, he purged political deadwood from the payrolls, insulated the state police from patronage, prosecuted elements of organized crime, increased aid to education, upgraded mental institutions, and constructed new roads. President Truman urged Stevenson to run for president in 1952, promising him his full support. When Stevenson demurred, Truman promoted Vice President Alben Barkley until labor leaders objected to him because of his age. Rivaling Stevenson for the nomination were liberals W. Averell Harriman of New York and Senator Estes Kefauver of Tennessee, the latter the front-runner in delegate strength on the basis of the primaries, and conservative Senator Richard Russell of Georgia. In his welcoming address to the party convention in Chicago in July 1952, Stevenson sparked the hall with a literate attack on the recent Republican convention: "For almost a week pompous phrases marched over this landscape in search of an idea. . . . Our [Republican] friends were out of patience, out of sorts, and, need I add, out of office." On the first ballot Kefauver led with 340 votes, far from the 616 needed to win, to 273 for Stevenson, 268 for Russell, and 123½ for Harriman. After the second tally President Truman persuaded Harriman to withdraw in favor of Stevenson, who was then nominated on the third ballot with 617½ votes to 275½ for Kefauver and 261 for Russell. In his acceptance speech, Stevenson promised a campaign of candor: "Let's talk sense to the American people. Let's tell them the truth, that there are no gains without pains, that this is the eve of great decisions, not easy decisions." Senator John J. Sparkman of Alabama was nominated for vice president. The Democratic platform pointed with pride to the achievements of the New Deal and Fair Deal and favored a strong national defense, collective security against Communist aggression, multilateral disarmament, repeal of the Taft-Hartley Act, equal employment opportunities for women, minorities, and the handicapped, increased public assistance for the aged, children, blind, and disabled, expansion of the school lunch program, and continued efforts to eradicate racial discrimination. Stevenson was again the Democratic presidential nominee in 1956.

CAMPAIGN AND THE ISSUES, 1952: Both candidates campaigned extensively: Eisenhower traveled 50,000 miles to deliver 228 speeches; Stevenson 32,000 miles for 203 speeches. Eisenhower vowed to "clean up the mess in Washington" but refrained from personal attacks. It was left to Nixon, his running mate, and others to lash out against the Democrats. Republican literature labeled the opposition the party of "Communism, Corruption, and Korea." Nixon was brought up short by reports that he had maintained an $18,000 slush fund but managed to defuse the issue in a tense television address known as the Checkers speech (see "Richard M. Nixon, 37th President," "Career before the Presidency"). Republican Joseph McCarthy of Wisconsin caused problems for both candidates. Eisenhower, sickened by the senator's attack on the patriotism of George C. Marshall, tried, unsuccessfully, to avoid appearing on the same platform with him in Wisconsin. Stevenson drew blasts from McCarthy for having appeared as a character witness for suspected spy Alger Hiss. In a television address attacking Stevenson, McCarthy coyly began sentences, "Alger, I mean, Adlai. . . ." Stevenson countered with swipes at the Republican party for having "to be dragged kicking and screaming into the twentieth century." In a speech in Detroit in October, Eisenhower scored a masterful stroke by promising that if elected, "I shall go to Korea" to break the deadlock in the peace negotiations. Television, for the first time a vital force in a presidential election, helped the Republicans as Stevenson's erudition and formality paled before Eisenhower's folksiness and smiling benevolence. In fact, Stevenson's brilliance hurt him at a time when intellectuals were derisively dubbed "eggheads," an epithet that first appeared in a Stewart Alsop column in September. "I like Ike" was the most famous slogan of the campaign. And many people did, as Eisenhower swept the nation outside the South.

ELECTION AS PRESIDENT, FIRST TERM, NOVEMBER 4, 1952:

Popular Vote: Eisenhower (Republican), 33,936,234 (55%); Stevenson (Democrat), 27,314,992 (44%).

Electoral Votes: Eisenhower, 442; Stevenson, 89.

States Carried: Eisenhower won the electoral votes of 39 states—Arizona, California, Colorado, Connecticut, Delaware, Florida, Idaho, Illinois, Indiana,

Iowa, Kansas, Maine, Maryland, Massachusetts, Michigan, Minnesota, Missouri, Montana, Nebraska, Nevada, New Hampshire, New Jersey, New Mexico, New York, North Dakota, Ohio, Oklahoma, Oregon, Pennsylvania, Rhode Island, South Dakota, Tennessee, Texas, Utah, Vermont, Virginia, Washington, Wisconsin, and Wyoming. Stevenson won the electoral votes of 9 states—Alabama, Arkansas, Georgia, Kentucky, Louisiana, Mississippi, North Carolina, South Carolina, West Virginia.

REPUBLICAN NOMINATION FOR REELECTION AS PRESIDENT, 1956: As Republicans gathered in San Francisco in August 1956, Eisenhower's renomination was ensured. Harold Stassen of Minnesota led a movement to dump Nixon from the ticket in favor of Governor Christian Herter of Massachusetts, but Eisenhower chose to retain his running mate. The Republican platform confined itself largely to praise for Eisenhower's first term and reiteration of the 1952 platform.

OPPONENT: Adlai E. Stevenson (1900–1965), of Illinois; Democrat. Stevenson was the Democratic presidential nominee in 1952. After overcoming a surprisingly strong challenge from Senator Estes Kefauver of Tennessee in the primaries, Stevenson appeared to be virtually unopposed for renomination. But shortly before delegates convened in Chicago in August, former president Truman came out for Governor Averell Harriman of New York. Former First Lady Eleanor Roosevelt lobbied strenuously for Stevenson among delegates. Senator John F. Kennedy of Massachusetts placed Stevenson's name in nomination. Stevenson was renominated on the first ballot with 905½ votes to 210 for Harriman, 80 for Texas favorite son Senator Lyndon B. Johnson, and the rest scattered. Stevenson then surprised delegates by throwing the vice presidential choice open to the convention. A struggle ensued between John F. Kennedy and Estes Kefauver. Kennedy led in early balloting, coming within 39 votes of the nomination, but Kefauver rallied, winning 755½–589. The Democratic platform condemned Republicans as "political amateurs, dominated by representatives of special privilege," and favored greater reliance on the United Nations, increased efforts at mutual disarmament, more spending for social welfare and agricultural programs, repeal of the Taft-Hartley Act, "a full and integrated program of development, protection, management, and conservation of all of our natural resources," greater peaceful use of nuclear power, voting rights and equal employment opportunities for minorities, and school desegration. After his defeat by Eisenhower, Stevenson declined to run again in 1960. In 1961 President Kennedy appointed him U.S. ambassador to the United Nations, a post he held until he was fatally stricken by a heart attack in London in 1965.

CAMPAIGN AND THE ISSUES, 1956: Stevenson faced an uphill struggle against the popular incumbent president. The Democrats' strongest issue, one addressed indirectly, was the state of Eisenhower's health following his heart attack. To quiet rumors, Eisenhower undertook a reasonably active campaign schedule, covering 14,000 miles and 13 states. Stevenson called for an end to the draft in favor of an all-volunteer army and a halt to atmospheric testing of nuclear weapons. Eisenhower opposed both as serious threats to national security. It was Stevenson who coined the phrase "quality of life" in this campaign. The impoverished state of the Stevenson campaign was depicted in a candid news photograph of the candidate with a hole in his shoe. Republicans reproduced the photo over the caption, "Don't let this happen to you! Vote for

Ike!" Republicans this year sought to woo back the black vote lost to Democrats during the New Deal. Pointing to Eisenhower's efforts to enforce school desegregation orders in Little Rock, the GOP launched Task Force '56 to campaign in black neighborhoods. Prominent among blacks for Eisenhower was Democratic Representative Adam Clayton Powell of New York. As a result, Eisenhower garnered 40 percent of the black vote, more than any other Republican presidential nominee since. Ironically, at the same time, he cracked the traditionally Democratic South, becoming the first Republican since Rutherford B. Hayes to carry Louisiana. The Suez Crisis erupted late in the campaign, reinforcing in voters' minds the need for experience in the White House at a time of international tension.

ELECTION AS PRESIDENT, SECOND TERM, NOVEMBER 6, 1956:
   Popular Vote: Eisenhower (Republican), 35,590,472 (57%); Stevenson (Democrat), 26,031,322 (42%).
   Electoral Vote: Eisenhower, 457; Stevenson, 73.
   States Carried: Eisenhower won the electoral votes of 41 states—Arizona, California, Colorado, Connecticut, Delaware, Florida, Idaho, Illinois, Indiana, Iowa, Kansas, Kentucky, Louisiana, Maine, Maryland, Massachusetts, Michigan, Minnesota, Montana, Nebraska, Nevada, New Hampshire, New Jersey, New Mexico, New York, North Dakota, Ohio, Oklahoma, Oregon, Pennsylvania, Rhode Island, South Dakota, Tennessee, Texas, Utah, Vermont, Virginia, Washington, West Virginia, Wisconsin, and Wyoming. Stevenson won the majority of electoral votes in 7 states—Alabama, Arkansas, Georgia, Mississippi, Missouri, North Carolina, and South Carolina.

INAUGURAL ADDRESS (FIRST): January 20, 1953. ". . . In pressing our labor for world peace, we shall be guided by certain fixed principles. These principles are:
1. . . . we hold it to be the first task of statesmanship to develop the strength that will deter the forces of aggression and promote the conditions of peace. . . .
2. . . . we shall never try to placate an aggressor by the false and wicked bargain of trading honor for security. . . .
3. . . . we view our nation's strength and security as a trust, upon which rests the hope of free men everywhere. . . .
4. . . . we shall never use our strength to try to impress upon another people our own cherished political and economic institutions.
5. . . . we shall strive to help [our friends] to achieve their own security and well-being. . . .
6. . . . the impoverishment of any single people in the world means danger to the well-being of all other peoples.
7. . . . we hope, within the framework of the United Nations, to help strengthen [regional groupings of free peoples] the world over. . . .
8. . . . we reject any insinuation that one race or another, one people or another, is in any sense inferior or expendable.
9. . . . we shall strive to make [the United Nations] not merely an eloquent symbol but an effective force. . . ."

INAUGURAL ADDRESS (SECOND): January 21, 1957. ". . . No people can live to itself alone. The unity of all who dwell in freedom is their only sure defense. . . . Not even America's prosperity could long survive if other nations did not prosper. No nation can longer be a fortress, lone and strong and safe.

And any people, seeking such shelter for themselves, can now build only their own prison. . . ."

VICE PRESIDENT: Richard M. Nixon (1913–1994), of California, served 1953–1961. See "Richard M. Nixon, 37th President."

CABINET:

Secretary of State.   (1) John Foster Dulles (1888–1959), of New York, served 1953–1959. A conspicuous critic of the Truman administration's policy of Communist containment, Dulles sought, unsuccessfully, to liberate "captive nations" from the Communist bloc. To meet the Sino-Soviet challenge, he forged mutual defense pacts, the southeast Asia Treaty Organization in 1954 and the Central Treaty Organization in 1959 in the Middle East. In January 1954 he set forth the policy that the United States would rely more on the "deterrent of massive retaliatory power" than on conventional forces. He fostered the art of brinksmanship in diplomacy. Responding to the pressures of McCarthyism, he purged the department of many Chinese specialists blamed for "losing" China in 1949, dismissed more than 400 others as security risks, and banned books containing "Communist propaganda" from the shelves of U.S. libraries overseas. Dulles resigned for health reasons. (2) Christian A. Herter (1895–1967), of Massachusetts, served 1959–1961. Promoted from undersecretary of state, he was involved in the delicate diplomacy following the U-2 incident (see "Administration: Cold War").

Secretary of the Treasury.   (1) George M. Humphrey (1890–1970), of Ohio, served 1953–1957. He consistently sought to reduce spending and taxes. Alarmed at the administration's budget for 1957, he warned, "If we don't [cut spending], over a long period, I will predict that you will have a depression that will curl your hair."[7] (2) Robert B. Anderson (1910–1989), of Connecticut, served 1957–1961. He had served as navy secretary. A proponent of tight money, he pressed Eisenhower to apply budget surpluses against the national debt rather than to cut taxes. In 1987 he was sentenced to a month in prison for income tax evasion.

Secretary of Defense.   (1) Charles E. Wilson (1890–1961), of Michigan, served 1953–1957. President of General Motors prior to his appointment, he is best remembered for his statement at his confirmation hearing: "What was good for our country was good for General Motors, and vice versa."[8] In the wake of the Korean War he cut the defense budget significantly. (2) Neil H. McElroy (1904–1972), of Ohio, served 1957–1959. He had been president of Proctor and Gamble. (3) Thomas S. Gates, Jr. (1906–1983), of Pennsylvania, served 1959–1961. Promoted from deputy secretary of defense, he established a task force to set nuclear target priorities and authorized the U-2 reconnaissance flight of Francis Gary Powers.

Attorney General.   (1) Herbert Brownell, Jr. (1904–1996), of New York, served 1953–1957. He established the Internal Security Division and required numerous organizations with alleged Communist ties to register with the attorney general. He filed the first desegregation suits in compliance with the 1954 Supreme Court decision *Brown v. Board of Education of Topeka*. (2) William P. Rogers (1913–2001), of Maryland, served 1957-1961. Promoted from deputy attorney general, he established the Civil Rights Division and counseled the president on the decision to send troops to enforce desegregation at Little Rock. He prosecuted numerous electric equipment companies for price fixing. He later served as secretary of state under President Nixon.

Postmaster General. Arthur E. Summerfield (1899–1972), of Michigan, served 1953–1961. As part of a campaign to purge obscene literature from the mails, he sought to ban D. H. Lawrence's *Lady Chatterly's Lover* but was rebuffed in the courts. He decentralized postal operations and modernized accounting procedures.

Secretary of the Interior. (1) Douglas McKay (1893–1959), of Oregon, served 1953–1956. He drew criticism from conservationists for granting numerous oil and mineral leases on land administered by the Fish and Wildlife Service. (2) Frederick A. Seaton (1909–1974), of Nebraska, served 1956–1961. He promoted a project to extract drinking water from the sea and led administration efforts to win statehood for Alaska and Hawaii.

Secretary of Agriculture. Ezra Taft Benson (1899–1994), of Utah, served 1953–1961. He sought to reduce federal regulations of agriculture and promoted increased exports of farm products. His opposition to fixed price supports made him unpopular with farmers.

Secretary of Commerce. (1) Sinclair Weeks (1893–1972), of Massachusetts, served 1953–1958. He expanded the merchant marine fleet and increased trade on nonstrategic goods to Communist bloc countries in Europe. (2) Frederick H. Mueller (1893–1976), of Michigan, served 1959–1961. He was promoted from undersecretary of commerce following Senate rejection of secretary-designate Lewis L. Strauss of New York. Mueller implemented the trade embargo against Cuba.

Secretary of Labor. (1) Martin P. Durkin (1894–1955), of Illinois, served January–September 1953. He resigned in protest over the administration's refusal to seek revision of the Taft-Hartley Law. (2) James P. Mitchell (1900–1964), of New Jersey, served 1953–1961. A Democrat-for-Eisenhower in 1952, he was dubbed "the social conscience of the Republican party" for his efforts on behalf of migrant workers, to extend unemployment compensation coverage, and other liberal labor measures.

Secretary of Health, Education and Welfare. (1) Oveta Culp Hobby (1905–1995), of Texas, served 1953–1955. She had been administrator of the Federal Security Agency. As the first HEW secretary, she organized the department. She was the second woman cabinet official. (2) Marion B. Folsom (1893–1976), of New York, served 1955-1958. He had been director of the New York Federal Reserve Board. He promoted medical research and antipollution measures. (3) Arthur S. Flemming (1905–1996), of Ohio, served 1958–1961. He was also chairman of Eisenhower's advisory committee on government organization.

ADMINISTRATION: January 20, 1953–January 20, 1961.

Korean War, Conclusion, 1953. See also "Harry S. Truman, 33rd President," "Administration." As he had promised during the campaign President-elect Eisenhower went to Korea in December 1952 to revive the stalled peace talks. Under the terms of the Armistice signed at Panmunjom in July 1953, the two Koreas were separated by a demilitarized zone at the 38th parallel, roughly the same border that existed prior to the war. The war was seen as proof that the UN could be counted on to resist aggression and that modern warfare could be conducted without resort to nuclear weapons. Casualties for the war totaled some 150,000 Americans, including 34,000 killed in action, 900,000 Chinese, and two million Koreans.

Cold War and the Eisenhower Doctrine. The Eisenhower administration undertook a nuclear missile buildup and adopted the stategy of massive retaliation as a deterrent. The Soviets spoke of "peaceful coexistence" with the West but gave no sign of lifting the Iron Curtain, as they kept pressure on Berlin and crushed the Hungarian revolt of 1956. In January 1959 Fidel Castro seized power in Cuba and at length fell into the Soviet camp. After Castro expropriated nearly $2 billion of American property there, Eisenhower placed a tight embargo on Cuba and in January 1961 severed diplomatic relations. With the establishment of the Southeast Asia Treaty Organization in 1954, the United States agreed to come to the aid of Pakistan, the Philippines, and Thailand in the event of Communist aggression. When the French asked for U.S. air support during their last stand against the Vietnamese at Dienbienphu in 1954, Eisenhower refused but expressed concern about the consequences of a Communist takeover there."You have a row of dominoes set up," Eisenhower said in enunciating what came to be called the domino theory, "and you knock over the first one, and what will happen to the last one is the certainty that it will go over very quickly. So you have a beginning of a disintegration that would have the most profound influences."[9] He provided aid and U.S. military advisers to the Diem regime in South Vietnam. To prevent the Soviet Union from filling the power vacuum left in the Middle East following the Suez Crisis of 1956–1957, the president enunciated the Eisenhower Doctrine, by which the United States asserted the right to aid any country in the area threatened by Communist aggression or subversion. On the basis of this doctrine, Eisenhower dispatched Marines to Lebanon in 1958 to shore up the pro-Western government in Beirut. Less than two weeks before the scheduled opening of an East-West summit meeting in Paris in 1960, it was learned that a U-2, a U.S. spy plane piloted by Francis Gary Powers, had been shot down from deep within Soviet air space. After some dissembling about the true nature of the spy mission, Eisenhower defended U.S. reconnaissance flights as necessary for national security and repeated a call for mutual air inspection of defense installations, the so-called Open Skies proposal he had put forth in 1955. The U-2 incident strained Soviet-American relations as Eisenhower prepared to turn over the government to his successor, John F. Kennedy. Powers, convicted of espionage in a Soviet court, was exchanged for Soviet spy Colonel Rudolf Abel in 1962.

Fall of McCarthy, 1954. Republican Senator Joseph McCarthy of Wisconsin continued his witch-hunt for Communists in government during Eisenhower's term (see also "Harry S. Truman, 33rd President," "Administration"). His campaign culminated in the Army-McCarthy hearings, called to investigate charges of Communist infiltration of the U.S. defense establishment. McCarthy's tactic of bullying witnesses to mask a dirth of evidence was exposed during the nationally televised proceedings, and he quickly fell into disgrace. The Senate voted 67–22 to censure him. Eisenhower long was criticized for failing to confront McCarthy directly. However in *The Hidden-Hand Presidency* (1982), author Fred I. Greenstein, drawing on recently declassified papers, asserted that Eisenhower maneuvered behind the scenes to help bring down McCarthy.

Civil Rights. In the wake of the Supreme Court's desegration decision (*Brown* v. *Board of Education of Topeka*, 1954), violence erupted in Little Rock, Arkansas. In 1957 Eisenhower dispatched federal troops to the scene to ensure the safety of black students attempting to enroll at formerly all-white Central High. The Civil Rights Act of 1960 provided for federal sanctions against local officials obstructing the registration and voting rights of blacks.

Interstate Highway System. In 1956 Eisenhower signed into law the bill authorizing construction of a 42,000-mile interstate highway system, which as of 1981 was about 95 percent complete. The remainder is scheduled to be open by 1990. Total cost for the network, originally put at $27 billion, is expected to be $130 billion. The idea for an interstate highway system is said to have originated with General John J. Pershing as early as 1918.

St. Lawrence Seaway, Opened 1959. In 1954 Eisenhower signed into law the St. Lawrence Seaway Act providing for joint construction, with Canada, of waterway improvements to open the Great Lakes to ocean-going vessels.

States Admitted to the Union: Alaska (1959), Hawaii (1959).

SUPREME COURT APPOINTMENTS: (1) Earl Warren (1891–1974), of California, served as chief justice 1954–1969. A consistent supporter of the civil rights of minorities and criminal defendants, he led the Court in handing down a body of liberal opinion that had much to do with making the 1960s a decade of turmoil and progress. In *Brown* v. *Board of Education of Topeka* (1954), he reportedly exerted personal influence to amass a unanimous opinion mandating desegregation of public schools "with all deliberate speed." "To separate [black children] from others of similar age and qualifications solely because of their race," Warren wrote, "generates a feeling of inferiority as to their status in the community that may affect their hearts and minds in a way unlikely ever to be undone. . . . We conclude that in the field of education the doctrine of 'separate but equal' has no place. Separate educational facilities are inherently unequal." He also spoke for the Court in *Miranda* v. *Arizona* (1966), requiring criminal suspects to be advised of their rights on apprehension. He was chairman of the Presidential Commission to Investigate the Assassination of John F. Kennedy. (2) John Marshall Harlan (1899–1971), of New York, served as associate justice 1955–1971. Grandson of Justice John M. Harlan (see "Rutherford B. Hayes, 19th President," "Supreme Court Appointments"), he was a strict constructionist often at odds with the Warren Court majority. In *Barenblatt* v. *United States* (1959), Harlan spoke for the Court in upholding the authority of the House Un-American Activities Committee to compel testimony from college educators. Academic freedom is important, Harlan conceded, but Congress is not precluded from interrogating a witness simply because he is a teacher. In *Yates* v. *United States* (1957), however, Harlan joined liberals on the bench in narrowly construing the Smith Act, the basis on which the government had been prosecuting Communists in the United States. The Smith Act, Harlan wrote, bars "advocacy and teaching of *concrete action* for the forcible overthrow of the government" and not just abstract principle. (3) William J. Brennan (1906–1997), of New Jersey, served as associate justice 1956–1990. He has generally voted with the liberal bloc. He wrote the majority opinion in *Jencks* v. *United States* (1957), granting a defendant access to confidential FBI reports pertaining to his case. In *Baker* v. *Carr* (1962), he laid the groundwork for the principle of "one man, one vote" in congressional apportionment. (4) Charles E. Whittaker (1901–1973), of Missouri, served as associate justice 1957–1962. He generally voted with the conservative bloc. He resigned for health reasons. (5) Potter Stewart (1915–1985), of Ohio, served as associate justice 1959–1981. He was generally moderate-to-conservative in his rulings. He alone dissented in *Engel* v. *Vitale* (1962), which banned prayer in public schools. "I cannot see," he wrote, "how an 'official religion' is established by letting those who want to say a prayer say it." However, he is perhaps best remembered for his remark concerning the nettlesome question of what constitutes pornography. He was unable to define the term himself, he conceded, but added, "I know it when I see it."

RANKING IN 1962 HISTORIANS POLL: Eisenhower ranked twenty-second of 31 presidents, eleventh of 12 "average" presidents. He ranked above Andrew Johnson, below Arthur.

RETIREMENT: January 20, 1961–March 28, 1969. Eisenhower had supported Richard Nixon for president in 1960. After attending the inauguration of his successor, John F. Kennedy, Eisenhower retired to Gettysburg, Pennsylvania, and wrote his memoirs (see "Books by Eisenhower"). Despite arthritis, he golfed regularly and scored a hole-in-one in 1968. He supported the Vietnam War. He reluctantly endorsed Barry Goldwater for president in 1964 and, breaking his long-standing rule against endorsing candidates before the convention, came out for Richard Nixon for the Republican presidential nomination in 1968.

DEATH: March 28, 1969, 12:35 P.M., Walter Reed Army Medical Center, Washington, D.C. Having survived a heart attack in office, Eisenhower suffered several more in retirement, two in November 1965, one in March 1968, another in June 1968, and two more in August 1968. Each time he rallied, but with a progressively weaker heart. In February 1969 he contracted pneumonia following surgery for the removal of a scar-tissue obstruction of the intestine. From March 15, he steadily declined from congestive heart failure. "I've always loved my wife," he said from his deathbed, "I've always loved my children. I've always loved my grandchildren. I've always loved my country."[10] His last words, according to his son, were, "I want to go; God take me."[11] He was buried in military uniform in an army coffin at Abilene, Kansas. In his last will and testament, executed in May 1965, he left the bulk of his estate, valued at nearly $3 million, in trust to his wife. He also left varying sums, totaling $11,500, to four military aides.

EISENHOWER PRAISED:: "Putting political considerations before world peace and security seemed to Eisenhower not only the height of false economy but ridiculously dangerous."[12]—Presidential Assistant Sherman Adams

"He was a far more complex and devious man than most people realized, and in the best sense of those words. Not shackled to a one-track mind, he always applied two, three, or four lines of reasoning to a single problem and he usually preferred the indirect approach where it would serve him better than the direct attack on a problem. His mind was quick and facile."[13]—Richard M. Nixon

"I knew Ike casually; and I liked him as a human being. His smile and simple frontier approach to complex problems made him as American as apple pie."[14]— Supreme Court Justice William O. Douglas

"The sturdy and enduring virtues—honor, courage, integrity, decency, all found eloquent expression in the life of this good man and noble leader."[15]— former president Lyndon B. Johnson, 1969

EISENHOWER CRITICIZED: "General Eisenhower employs the three monkeys standard of campaign morality: see no evil—if it's Republican; hear no evil— unless it is Democratic; and speak no evil—unless Senator Taft says it's all right."[16]—Democratic presidential nominee Adlai Stevenson, 1952

"I think that when the President stops being President the best job we could give him in our country would be as director of a children's home. He would not harm children. But as head of a mighty state he is more dangerous and might do a lot of harm. . . . I saw the way he behaved at the Geneva conference in 1955 and I felt sorry for the President. . . . One shuddered at the thought of what a great force was in such hands."[17]—Soviet Premier Nikita Khrushchev, 1960

"Ike didn't know anything, and all the time he was in office he didn't learn a thing. . . . In 1959, when Castro came to power down in Cuba, Ike just sat on his ass and acted like if he didn't notice what was going on down there, why, maybe Castro would go away or something."[18]—former president Harry S. Truman, 1961

EISENHOWER QUOTES: "In the councils of government, we must guard against the acquisition of unwarranted influence, whether sought or unsought, by the military-industrial complex. The potential for the disastrous rise of misplaced power exists and will persist."[19]—1961

"The United States never lost a soldier or a foot of ground in my administration. We kept the peace. People ask how it happened—by God, it didn't just happen, I'll tell you that."[20]

"I have no patience with extreme Rightists who call everyone who disagrees with them a Communist, nor with the Leftists who shout that the rest of us are heartless moneygrubbers."[21]—1962

BOOKS BY EISENHOWER: *Crusade in Europe* (1948); *The White House Years* (2 vols.); *Mandate for Change, 1953–1956* (1965); *Waging Peace, 1956–1961* (1966); *At Ease: Stories I Tell to Friends* (1967).

BOOKS ABOUT EISENHOWER: Ambrose, Stephen E. *Eisenhower.* 2 vols. New York: Simon & Schuster, 1983, 1984.

Greenstein, Fred I. *The Hidden-Hand Presidency: Eisenhower as Leader.* New York: Basic Books, 1982.

Lyon, Peter. *Eisenhower: Portrait of the Hero.* Boston: Little, Brown, 1974.

Neal, Steve. *The Eisenhowers: Reluctant Dynasty.* Garden City, N.Y.: Doubleday, 1978.

NOTES:

1 Peter Lyon, *Eisenhower: Portrait of the Hero*, Boston: Little, Brown, 1974, p. 295.

2 Dwight D. Eisenhower, *At Ease: Stories I Tell to Friends*, Garden City, N.Y.: Doubleday, 1967, p. 304.

3 Ibid., p. 306.

4 Ibid., p. 101.

5 Robert S. Alley, *So Help Me God: Religion and the Presidency*, Richmond, Va.: John Knox Press, 1972, p. 83.

6 Dwight D. Eisenhower, *At Ease*, p. 341.

7 Lyon, p. 735.

8 William Safire, *The New language of Politics*, New York: Random House, 1968, p. 486.

9 *New York Times*, April 8, 1954.

10 Lyon, p. 858.

11 John S. D. Eisenhower, *Strictly Personal: A Memoir*, Garden City, N.Y.: Doubleday, 1974, p. 336.

12 Sherman Adams, *First-Hand Report: The Story of the Eisenhower Administration*, New York: Harper & Bros., 1961, p. 20.

13 Richard M. Nixon, *Six Crises*, Garden City, N.Y.: Doubleday, 1962, p. 161.

14 William O. Douglas, *The Court Years 1939–1975: The Autobiography of William O. Douglas*, New York: Random House, 1980, p. 293.

15 *New York Times*, March 29, 1969, p. 22.

16 Richard Kenin and Justin Wintle, eds., *Dictionary of Biographical Quotation*, New York: Knopf, 1978, p. 266.

17 *New York Times*, June 4, 1960, pp. 1, 6–7.
18 Merle Miller, *Plain Speaking: An Oral Biography of Harry S. Truman*, New York: Berkley, 1973, p. 343.
19 Louis Filler, ed., *The President Speaks*, New York: Putnam's Sons, 1964, p. 368.
20 Lyon, p. 854.
21 *Saturday Evening Post*, April 21, 1962, p. 19.

JOHN F. KENNEDY

35TH PRESIDENT

NAME: John Fitzgerald Kennedy. He was named after his maternal grandfather, John F. "Honey Fitz" Fitzgerald. He was Jack to friends.

PHYSICAL DESCRIPTION: Kennedy stood 6 feet ½ inch tall and weighed 170 pounds at the time of his death. Strikingly handsome and youthful in appearance, he had sensitive blue eyes, a mass of reddish-brown hair, and sound straight teeth. He wore reading glasses from age 13. His right leg was ¾ inch longer than his left; he wore corrective shoes to compensate. Although he was muscular and athletic, his health generally was poor. He suffered from chronic backache and was in pain much of his adult life. Injury in World War II (see "Military Service") aggravated his back condition. In 1954 he underwent spinal fusion surgery, following which he developed a nearly fatal infection and received the last rites of the Catholic church. He rallied, but his back plagued him for the rest of his life. He wore a canvas back brace for support and found some relief in treatments administered by Dr. Janet Travell of New York. From 1946 Kennedy also suffered from an adrenal insufficiency, an ailment akin to Addison's disease. With cortisone and later corticosteroid tablets, the disease was controlled. In 1951 Kennedy contracted a fever in Japan and was near death with a 106° temperature. Kennedy dressed fashionably but had an aversion to hats.

PERSONALITY: Kennedy described himself as "an idealist without illusions"[1] and considered his best quality to be curiosity, his worst irritability. Kennedy's charm, grace, and wit were to a great extent responsible for his immense popularity as president. He seemed distant to some, but, according to historian and Kennedy aide Arthur M. Schlesinger, he remained a bit detached in order to counter his extremely sensitive nature. For the most part he controlled his temper. Kenneth P. O'Donnell and other longtime associates report that he exploded in anger only twice as a national figure, once over a scheduling foul-up near the end of the 1960 presidential campaign and again during the confrontation with the steel industry (see "Administration"). The Kennedy style, idealized after his death as the romance of the mythical Camelot, was, according to Schlesinger, simply "the triumph, hard-bought and well-earned, of a gallant and collected human being over the anguish of life."[2]

ANCESTORS: Kennedy was of Irish heritage. His great-grandfather Patrick Kennedy, a cooper, emigrated from Dunganstown, County Wexford, Ireland, in 1848 and settled in Boston. His paternal grandfather, Patrick J. Kennedy, served in the Massachusetts House 1886–1890 and Senate 1892–1893 and was Boston wire commissioner 1902–1905 and fire commissioner in 1905. His maternal grandfather and namesake, John F. "Honey Fitz" Fitzgerald, served in the Massachusetts Senate 1893 and 1894 and the U.S. House 1895–1901 and 1919 and was mayor of Boston 1906, 1907, and 1910–1914.

FATHER: Joseph Patrick Kennedy (1888–1969) businessman, public official, diplomat. Born in Boston, he graduated from Harvard in 1912 and at 25 became the youngest bank president in the state. He handily achieved his goal of becoming a millionaire by age 35. He amassed much of his fortune in the stock market during the raging bull market of the 1920s and shrewdly sold out his holdings just months before the crash of 1929. On the eve of the end of Prohibition he formed Somerset Importers, sole U.S. distributor for certain Scotch and gin distillers, on an investment of $100,000. He sold the firm for $8 million in 1946. He also made money in real estate; the principal Kennedy property is the Merchandise Mart of Chicago. Kennedy earned another $5 million as a Hollywood movie producer in the late 1920s. It was at this time that he had an affair with Gloria Swanson, according to the actress's autobiography *Swanson on Swanson* (1980). Having been an early supporter of Franklin D. Roosevelt for president in 1932, he was appointed chairman of the newly created Securities and Exchange Commission, 1934–1935. In this post he put an end to many of the speculative and manipulative practices that he had so skillfully employed himself. He also served as chairman of the U.S. Maritime Commission in 1937. As ambassador to Great Britain 1937–1940, he publicly opposed U.S. involvement in World War II and broke with president Roosevelt on the issue. Kennedy instilled in his children a fierce competitive spirit, a compelling drive to win, and a moral obligation to contribute to a society that had given much to them. "My father," President Kennedy once said, "wasn't around as much as some fathers when I was young; but, whether he was there or not, he made his children feel that they were the most important things in the world to him. He was so terribly interested in everything we were doing. He held up standards for us, and he was very tough when we failed to meet those standards."[3] Kennedy was the only father of a president to attend his son's inaugural in Washington. He suffered a paralytic stroke in 1961. Tragically, he lived to see sons John and Robert slain.

MOTHER: Rose Fitzgerald Kennedy (1890–1995). Born in Boston, she was educated at the Convent of the Sacred Heart in Boston and the Blumenthal convent school in the Netherlands. She also studied piano at the New England Conservatory of Music. During her father's term as mayor of Boston, she served as hostess for the city. She married Joseph P. Kennedy on October 7, 1914. The matriarch of a remarkable political family, she took an active part in her sons' campaigns. She was returning from a round of golf when she learned of President Kennedy's assassination. She has long been active on behalf of mentally retarded children. In 1980, at age 90, she led a grandparents' parade in

Hyannis, Massachusetts, for the Special Olympics. She lives in Hyannis Port, Massachusetts. Her memoir *Times to Remember* appeared in 1974.

SIBLINGS: The second of nine children, Kennedy had five sisters and three brothers—Lieutenant Joseph P. Kennedy, Jr., killed in action over Suffolk, England, during World War II; Rosemary Kennedy, mentally retarded; Mrs. Kathleen "Kick" Cavendish, killed in an air crash in 1948; Mrs. Eunice M. Shriver, wife of R. Sargent Shriver, director of the Peace Corps 1961–1966 and 1972 Democratic vice presidential nominee; Mrs. Patricia Lawford, former wife of actor Peter Lawford; Robert F. Kennedy, U.S. attorney general 1961–1964, U.S. senator from New York, 1965–1968, assassinated while a candidate for the 1968 Democratic presidential nomination; Mrs. Jean Smith; and Edward M. Kennedy, U.S. senator from Massachusetts 1962–   , and candidate for the 1980 Democratic presidential nomination.

CHILDREN: Kennedy had a daughter and a son to live to maturity.

Caroline Kennedy (1957–   ). Just six years old when her father was killed, she has vague memories of the White House. Between graduation from Radcliffe in 1980 and Columbia University Law School in 1988, she worked for several years as a film curator at the Metropolitan Museum of Art. In 1987 she married Edwin Schlossberg, a designer.

John F. Kennedy, Jr. (1960–1999). He was educated at Brown University and New York University Law School. He was interested in non-elective public service and ran a political magazine entitled *George*. America's favorite bachelor for years, he married Carolyn Bessette in 1996. On July 16, 1999, the couple, along with Bessette's sister, died in a plane crash in his private plane.

BIRTH: Kennedy was born at home, 83 Beals Street, Brookline, Massachusetts, on May 29, 1917. He was the first president born in the twentieth century.

CHILDHOOD: Kennedy grew up in comfort in Brookline, Massachusetts, 1917–1926, New York City, 1926–1929, and Bronxville, New York, from 1929, as well as at the Kennedy summer home in Hyannis Port, Cape Cod, and the family's winter vacation quarters at Palm Beach, Florida. He spent much of his childhood recuperating from a host of ailments, including scarlet fever, whooping cough, measles, chicken pox, bronchitis, tonsilitis, appendicitis, jaundice, and a bad back. His brothers used to joke that Jack was so sickly that a mosquito took a big risk in biting him. Still, he was an active child, a scrapper who took a lot of pounding from big brother Joe. On turning 21, Kennedy came into a $1 million trust fund established by his father.

EDUCATION: Kennedy learned the fundamentals at the Dexter School in Brookline, Massachusetts, then attended the Riverdale Country Day School in New York for the fourth to sixth grades. He studied briefly at the Canterbury (Catholic) school in New Milford, Connecticut, until an attack of appendicitis forced his withdrawal in the spring of 1931. At Choate prep school 1931–1935, he showed signs of promise but was more interested in pranks than study. "Jack has a clever, individual mind," reported his headmaster. "When he learns the right place for humor and learns to use his individual way of looking at things as an asset instead of handicap, his natural gift of an individual outlook and witty expression are going to help him. . . . Jack is not as able academically as his high IQ might lead us to think."[4] At Choate he was nicknamed "rat face" for his scrawny appearance. He graduated a lackluster sixty-fourth of 112 students but nevertheless was voted "most likely to succeed." During the summer of 1935 he studied at the London School of Economics. While there he contracted jaundice.

That fall he enrolled at Princeton University, but a recurrence of jaundice forced his withdrawal in December. At Harvard University 1936–1940, Kennedy majored in political science with emphasis on international relations. It was not until his junior year, however, that he began to take his studies seriously. He toured Europe at the end of his sophomore year and spent the second semester of his junior year working as secretary to his father, the ambassador to Great Britain. In this capacity he was sent to Glasgow to care for American survivors of the torpedoed liner *Athenia*. He turned in an insightful senior thesis, entitled "Appeasement at Munich: The Inevitable Results of the Slowness of the British Democracy to Change from a Disarmament Policy." Later published as *Why England Slept* (1940), it won wide acceptance and earned the young author $40,000, the English royalties of which he donated to the bombed town of Plymouth, England. In extracurricular activities, Kennedy played end on the freshman and junior varsity football team and held a place on the 1938 champion sailing crew. He also was on the freshman swim and golf teams and took part in intramural softball and hockey. He was on the staff of the Harvard *Crimson* and was a member of the Hasty Pudding Club. He graduated cum laude in June 1940. He studied briefly, 1940–1941, at the Stanford Business School before touring South America.

RELIGION: Roman Catholic. Kennedy, the only Roman Catholic president, rarely spoke of his religious beliefs. He did not accept completely the teachings of the Catholic church. He supported, for example, the use of birth control devices and opposed federal aid to parochial schools. To many, the religious issue seemed an insuperable barrier to the Kennedy candidacy in 1960. Kennedy confronted the issue in a speech before the Greater Houston Ministerial Association during the campaign. "I believe," he said, "in an America where the separation of Church and State is absolute, where no Catholic prelate would tell the President (should he be a Catholic) how to act and no Protestant minister would tell his parishioners for whom to vote." He went on to say that he was prepared to accept defeat on the basis of the issues. "But," he added on behalf of his co-religionists, "if this election is decided on the basis that 40 million Americans lost their chance of being president on the day they were baptized, then it is the whole nation that will be the loser in the eyes of Catholics and non-Catholics around the world, in the eyes of history, and in the eyes of our own people." As president, Kennedy declined to raise relations with the Vatican to the ambassadorial level and attended Protestant services from time to time.

RECREATION: Kennedy enjoyed sailing, swimming, golf, and an occasional touch-football game with family and friends. As president he swam 20–30 minutes before lunch and again in the early evening in the White House pool, heated to 90° to soothe his chronically ailing back. He also performed a daily regimen of exercises to strengthen his back muscles. He was a superb golfer, generally shooting in the high 70's or low 80's. He had a strong drive and was a good putter but was less adept at chip shots. He maintained a winter retreat, Glen Ora, in Middleburg, Virginia. After dinner he often had movies screened in the White House. Unless the film was very good, however, he usually left in the middle. His favorites included *Bad Day at Black Rock* with Spencer Tracy and *Casablanca*. He also attended the theater frequently. His favorite music included such standards as "Stardust" and "Stormy Weather." He read newspapers voraciously every morning. He smoked cigars.

EARLY ROMANCE: Kennedy was extremely successful with women and dated countless beauties before meeting his wife. Ralph "Rip" Horton, Jr., a close friend from his student days at Choate, revealed to authors Joan and Clay Blair (*The Search for JFK*, 1976) that Kennedy lost his virginity at 17 in a Harlem brothel. Among his serious girlfriends were:

Frances A. Cannon. A member of the Cannon Mills family, she dated Kennedy while he was a student at Harvard. The Kennedy family expected them to marry eventually. But in 1939 she announced her engagement to journalist John Hersey. Kennedy reportedly was dejected at having lost her. She divorced Hersey in 1956 and remarried.

Charlotte McDonnell. The daughter of a wealthy New York stockbroker and sister-in-law of Henry Ford II, she met Kennedy through his sister Kathleen, her best friend. Kennedy and she were rumored to have been engaged for a time in 1940, but she later said that Kennedy never proposed. She married one Richard Harris in 1943 and lived in New York City.

Harriet "Flip" Price. A San Francisco girl, she dated Kennedy while he was a student at Stanford. She was, she later recalled, very much in love with him and believed that he loved her, too. They talked of marriage but made no definite plans. The romance, she said, fizzled out when he left Stanford. She married James D. Fullerton and settled in Pasadena.

Inga Arvad. A voluptuous Dane and former Miss Europe four years older than Kennedy, she had acted in German films and befriended Hitler and other Nazi leaders before coming to Washington. She was a feature columnist for the *Washington Times Herald* during her liaison with Kennedy in 1941–1942. Kennedy's pet name for her was Inga Binga. Their relationship was strained because of her Nazi connections. She was under surveillance by the FBI, whose files reportedly contain wiretapped phone conversations between her and Kennedy. She married former cowboy film star Tim McCoy in 1947 and settled in Arizona. She died of cancer in 1973.

MARRIAGE: Senator John F. Kennedy, 36, married Jacqueline L. Bouvier, 24, on September 12, 1953, at St. Mary's Church in Newport, Rhode Island. Born on July 28, 1929, at Southampton, New York, the daughter of John V. Bouvier III, a stockbroker, and Janet Lee Bouvier, Jackie was raised among wealth and refinement. Her parents divorced in 1940; her mother married Hugh Auchincloss in 1942. Jackie lived with her mother in Newport but also remained close to her father. She was educated at the Holton-Arms school in Washington 1942–1944, Miss Porter's School in Farmington, Connecticut, 1944–1947, Vassar College 1947–1948, and the Sorbonne in Paris in 1949. She earned a degree in art from George Washington University in 1951. When she made her society debut in 1947, a Hearst columnist dubbed her "Queen Deb of the Year." On graduation from college, she was hired as the "Inquiring Camera Girl" for the *Washington Times Herald* at a weekly salary of $42.50. She met Kennedy, then a congressman, at a dinner party of a mutual friend, Charles Bartlett, Washington correspondent for the *Chattanooga Times*, in May 1951. They began dating sporadically; together they attended Eisenhower's Inaugural Ball in 1953. They delayed announcing their engagement until June of that year as a courtesy to the *Saturday Evening Post*, which was about to run an article entitled "Jack Kennedy—The Senate's Gay Young Bachelor." The wedding, attended by some 800 persons, was performed by Archbishop Richard J. Cushing, who read a special blessing on the marriage from Pope Pius XII. Robert F. Kennedy was best man. Following a honeymoon in Acapulco, the couple settled in McLean, Virginia. Mrs. Kennedy was among the most popular of the First Ladies. Her hairdo, the "Jackie Look," became fashionable. Under her direction, the White House was remodeled with many of the original furnishings restored. In February 1962 she conducted a televised tour of the refurbished rooms. She invited cellist Pablo Casals and other talented artists to perform at the White House. She was with President Kennedy at the time of his assassination and bore the ordeal of his grisly death and period of national mourning with great dignity. In 1968 she married Greek tycoon Aristotle Onassis, who died in 1975. A book editor for Doubleday publishers since 1975, she brought out a number of bestsellers, including Michael Jackson's *Moonwalk*. She divided her time among residences in Manhattan, New Jersey and Martha's Vineyard. After the death of President Kennedy, she closely guarded her privacy, going to court to legally restrain veteran Jackie watchers from following her too closely. Jacqueline Kennedy Onassis died in 1994.

EXTRAMARITAL AFFAIRS: After the assassination there arose a spate of allegations that President Kennedy routinely cheated on his wife. Women claiming to have been intimate with Kennedy include stripper Blaze Starr, painter Mary Pinchot Meyer, who died mysteriously in 1964, and Judith Campbell Exner, lover to reputed Mafia boss Sam Giancana. It also has been charged that he had an affair with actress Marilyn Monroe.

MILITARY SERVICE:

World War II. Kennedy served in the navy from September 1941 to April 1945, rising from ensign to lieutenant. He had volunteered for the army but was rejected because of his bad back. Through his father's influence he was able to get a sea command as skipper of the *PT-109*. While on patrol in Blackett Strait off the Solomon Islands on August 2, 1943, his boat was rammed in two by the Japanese destroyer *Amagiri*. Two U.S. sailors were killed. Lieutenant Kennedy and the rest of the crew were thrown into the water aflame with burning gasoline. Despite his weak back, Kennedy not only managed to swim four hours to safety but also towed an injured crewman by the life jacket strap with his teeth. Days later they were discovered on Olasana Island by two natives. Biuku Gasa and Eroni Kumana. Kennedy scratched a message on a coconut shell with his knife: "Native knows posit. He can pilot. alive need small boat." The natives delivered the shell to Allied personnel and the crew was picked up August 8. The incident earned Kennedy a purple heart and the Navy and Marine Corps medal. The citation signed by Admiral W.F. (Bull) Halsey read, in part, "His courage, endurance, and excellent leadership contributed to the saving of several lives and was in keeping with the highest traditions of the United States Naval Service." The episode first gained national attention in an article, "Survival," written by John Hersey for the *New Yorker* (June 17, 1944) and was reported in detail in Robert J. Donovan's *PT 109: John F. Kennedy in World War II* (1961). The ordeal aggravated his back trouble; he was rotated home in December 1943, hospitalized, and finally discharged.

CAREER BEFORE THE PRESIDENCY: Following his discharge from the navy, Kennedy worked briefly as a journalist. He covered the United Nations Conference on International Organization in San Francisco, April–June 1945, for the *Chicago Herald-American* and the Potsdam Conference, July–August 1945, for the International News Service.

U.S. Representative, 1947–1953. In the 1946 Democratic primary for the House seat from Massachusetts's Eleventh District (working-class wards of Boston plus Cambridge and part of Somerville), Kennedy topped a crowded field of 10 candidates with 42 percent of the vote, a primary victory tantamount to election in this heavily Democratic district. He handily defeated Republican Lester Bowen in the general election and was reelected twice. Congressman Kennedy maintained a moderately liberal voting record and served on the House Education and Labor Committee. He opposed the Taft-Hartley bill, spoke out for low-cost public housing, and supported the Truman Doctrine and the Marshall Plan. He joined Republicans, however, in denouncing the Truman administration for "losing" China to Communism. He remained aloof of the party structure in the House and won a reputation as something of an iconoclast. Angered over the American Legion's opposition to public housing, he stunned members by lashing out at the venerable veterans organization. "The leadership of the American Legion," Kennedy said on the floor, "has not had a constructive thought for the benefit of this country since 1918." Despite the urging of supporters, he refused to retract or apologize for the statement.

U.S. Senator, 1953–1961. Bucking the national Republican sweep that accompanied Eisenhower's landslide victory in 1952, Kennedy that year ousted incumbent Massachusetts Senator Henry Cabot Lodge by 70,000 votes. He was reelected in 1958 with 74% of the vote over Vincent J. Celeste of East Boston. Senator Kennedy served variously on the Government Operations Committee, Labor and Public Welfare Committee, Foreign Relations Committee, and the Joint Economic Committee. He was the only Massachusetts legislator to vote for President Eisenhower's proposal to develop the St. Lawrence Seaway, a project that threatened to divert foreign ships from Boston and other East Coast ports to inland cities on the Great Lakes. He consistently supported prolabor legislation. He was critical of the Cold War diplomacy of Secretary of State John Foster Dulles. But he warned of the "Red tide of Communism" threatening Southeast Asia. His most controversial position in the Senate was his passivism toward the reckless Red-baiting tactics of Republican Senator Joseph McCarthy. Because his brother Robert F. Kennedy had served on McCarthy's staff, because McCarthy was a personal friend of the Kennedy family, because McCarthy was popular in Massachusetts, Kennedy was loath to speak out against him. When the motion to censure McCarthy reached the floor, Kennedy was in the hospital recovering from spinal surgery and thus did not vote or request to be paired. Although it was expected that he would have joined the overwhelming majority, which included all voting Democrats, in censuring McCarthy, critics charged that he deliberately ducked the issue. During long months of convalescence, Kennedy wrote *Profiles in Courage* (1956), a collective biography of principled politicians distinguished for taking unpopular stands, for which he was awarded a Pulitzer Prize. In 1956 Kennedy was a candidate for the Democratic vice presidential nomination (see "Dwight D. Eisenhower, 34th President," "Opponent," 1956) but lost to Senator Estes Kefauver of Tennessee.

DEMOCRATIC PRESIDENTIAL NOMINATION, 1960: Kennedy won each of the seven primaries he entered. His victories in Wisconsin and West Virginia crippled the candidacy of Senator Hubert Humphrey of Minnesota. Kennedy's showing in West Virginia was especially critical in proving that a Catholic could win Protestant votes. The other leading contender for the nomination was

Senator Lyndon B. Johnson of Texas, and there lingered some sentiment for Adlai Stevenson of Illinois. As Democrats convened in Los Angeles in July 1960, Kennedy was the clear front-runner. He enjoyed a superb organization led by brother Robert F. Kennedy, who maintained direct contact with Kennedy forces on the floor via 60 telephone lines. Governor Orville Freeman of Minnesota placed Kennedy's name in nomination. Kennedy was nominated on the first ballot with 806 votes to 409 for Johnson and the rest scattered. To the chagrin of some of his most ardent liberal supporters, Kennedy chose Johnson as his running mate. One reason for doing so was to enhance his prospects in the South, especially in Texas, which, as it turned out, was crucial to his election. But, according to Kennedy aide Kenneth P. O'Donnell, another reason was to get Johnson out of the Senate, where he might sabotage the Kennedy program. In his acceptance speech Kennedy declared, "We stand today on the edge of a New Frontier—the frontier of the 1960s—a frontier of unknown opportunities and perils—a frontier of unfulfilled hopes and threats." The Democratic platform promised a strong stand on behalf of civil rights and favored increased defense spending while seeking agreements on arms control, more aid to underdeveloped nations, medical insurance for the elderly, increased medical research on cancer and other major diseases, disability insurance, conservation of natural recources and environmental protection, expansion of federal programs for slum clearance and other urban problems, acceleration of the space program, limitations on campaign contributions and expenditures, and creation of a consumer protection council.

OPPONENT: Richard M. Nixon (1913–1994) of California; Republican. By the time Republicans convened in Chicago in July 1960, Vice President Richard M. Nixon had no serious opposition for the nomination. Governor Nelson Rockefeller of New York had posed a threat, but in a celebrated midnight meeting at his New York City apartment on the eve of the convention, Rockefeller agreed to endorse Nixon and Nixon agreed to incorporate into the platform Rockefeller's liberal stand on civil rights and certain other issues. Nixon was nominated on the first ballot with 1,321 votes to 10 for Senator Barry Goldwater of Arizona. UN Ambassador Henry Cabot Lodge of Massachusetts was nominated for vice president. In his acceptance speech, Nixon called for action to meet the Soviet challenge. "When Mr. Khrushchev says our grandchildren will live under Communism," Nixon declared, "let us say his grandchildren will live in freedom." In addition to promising to uphold the civil rights of minorities, the Republican platform favored a strong anti-Communist foreign policy and continued exclusion of Red China from the UN, more defensive weapons with "no price ceiling on America's security," economic growth through increased productivity, extension of unemployment benefits, conservation of natural resources, a balanced budget, reduced national debt, and presidential authority to veto parts of bills.

CAMPAIGN AND THE ISSUES, 1960: In this pitched battle in which the lead, according to the polls, seesawed back and forth between the candidates, the dominant issues were the economy and the Communist challenge. Kennedy, hammering away at the theme "Let's get America moving again," vowed to close the so-called missile gap and denounced the Eisenhower-Nixon administration for permitting a Communist regime to come to power 90 miles from American shores in Cuba. Nixon, referring to Kennedy's youth and limited experience in government, warned that the presidency was no place for on-the-job training. He vowed to maintain a strong stand against Communism around the world. Although Nixon forbade his staff to raise the religious issue, some Protestant clergy publicly questioned whether Kennedy would be able to divorce his Catholicism from his secular duties as president. Kennedy masterfully defused the issue in a speech before the Greater Houston Ministerial Association (see "Religion") in September. Nixon's claim to superior governmental experience as the most active vice president in history was undermined by an offhand remark from President Eisenhower in August. Asked by a reporter to list the major decisions in which Nixon had participated as vice president, Eisenhower replied, "If you give me a week, I might think of one." Kennedy was aided by a well-organized voter registration drive led by Representative Frank Thompson, who sent some 200,000 volunteers into working-class and minority neighborhoods in all 50 states. At the beginning of the campaign Nixon promised to speak in every state. He kept his promise but in so doing wasted valuable time in areas that were hopelessly Democratic. To compound his troubles, Nixon banged his knee on a car door in Greensboro, North Carolina, and subsequently developed an infection. For nearly two crucial weeks, August 29–September 9, he lay on his back submitting to antibiotic treatments at Walter Reed Hospital. The main focus of the campaign, however, was the nationally televised debates of September 26 and October 7, 14, and 21; an estimated 115 million people watched at least one of them. The first was the most important, because it fixed perceptions of the two candidates and drew the largest audience, 70 million viewers. To most observers, on the basis of debating points the confrontation appeared to be a draw. Yet a draw was a plus for Kennedy, for it demonstrated that he had mastered the issues as well as his more experienced opponent. But it was the physical comparison of the two men that most hurt Nixon. Kennedy appeared tan, fit, composed; Nixon, having lost weight in the hospital, appeared haggard, pale, menacing. Kennedy himself believed that without the debates he would have lost the election. Kennedy enhanced his standing among blacks when in October civil rights leader the Reverend Martin Luther King, Jr., was arrested in Atlanta during a sit-in demonstration. Kennedy personally called Mrs. King to express sympathy and offer assistance, while brother Robert F. Kennedy interceded with a local judge to arrange for King's release on bail. Soon thereafter, the Reverend Martin Luther King, Sr., the civil rights leader's father, issued a statement saying that he had intended to vote for Nixon but was switching to the Democratic nominee because, "Jack Kennedy has the moral courage to stand up for what he knows is right." Vice presidential nominee Lyndon Johnson was instrumental in carrying Texas, where Nixon won a majority of the Anglo vote, but the Democratic ticket swept the Chicano barrios to carry the state by less than 50,000.

ELECTION AS PRESIDENT, NOVEMBER 8, 1960:

Popular Vote: Kennedy (Democrat), 34,227,096 (49.7%); Nixon (Republican), 34,108,546 (49.5%).

Electoral Vote: Kennedy, 303; Nixon, 219 (Senator Harry F. Byrd of Virginia, not a party candidate, received 15 electoral votes).

States Carried: Kennedy won the majority of electoral votes in 22 states— Arkansas, Connecticut, Delaware, Georgia, Hawaii, Illinois, Louisiana, Maryland, Massachusetts, Michigan, Minnesota, Missouri, Nevada, New Jersey, New Mexico, New York, North Carolina, Pennsylvania, Rhode Island, South Carolina, Texas, and West Virginia. Nixon won the majority of electoral votes in

26 states—Alaska, Arizona, California, Colorado, Florida, Idaho, Indiana, Iowa, Kansas, Kentucky, Maine, Montana, Nebraska, New Hampshire, North Dakota, Ohio, Oklahoma, Oregon, South Dakota, Tennessee, Utah, Vermont, Virginia, Washington, Wisconsin, and Wyoming. Senator Harry F. Byrd of Virginia received the majority of electoral votes in 2 states—Alabama and Mississippi.

INAUGURAL ADDRESS: January 20, 1961. ". . . Let the word go forth from this time and place, to friend and foe alike, that the torch has been passed to a new generation of Americans—born in this century, tempered by war, disciplined by a hard and bitter peace, proud of our ancient heritage—and unwilling to witness or permit the slow undoing of those human rights to which this Nation has always been committed, and to which we are committed today at home and around the world.

"Let every nation know, whether it wishes us well or ill, that we shall pay any price, bear any burden, meet any hardship, support any friend, oppose any foe in order to assure the survival and success of liberty. . . .

"In the long history of the world, only a few generations have been granted the role of defending freedom in its hour of maximum danger. I do not shrink from this responsibility—I welcome it. I do not believe that any of us would exchange places with any other people or any other generation. The energy, the faith, the devotion which we bring to this endeavor will light our country and all who serve it—and the glow from that fire can truly light the world.

"And so, my fellow Americans: Ask not what your country can do for you— ask what you can do for your country. . . ."

VICE PRESIDENT: Lyndon B. Johnson (1908–1973), of Texas, served 1961–1963. He succeeded to the presidency on the assassination of President Kennedy.

CABINET:

Secretary of State. Dean Rusk (1909–1994), of New York, served 1961–1969. He had served as assistant secretary for Far Eastern affairs in the Truman administration. At the Geneva Conference in July 1962 he signed the agreement providing for the independence and neutrality of Laos. He sought to isolate Cuba diplomatically and commercially in the Western Hemisphere. During the Cuban missile crisis (see "Administration"), he marshaled the support of the Organization of American States for the arms quarantine of Cuba. He signed the nuclear test ban treaty of 1963 (see "Administration") for the United States. He stayed on in the Johnson administration.

Secretary of the Treasury. C. Douglas Dillon (1909–2003), of New Jersey, served 1961–1965. A Republican, he had served as ambassador to France and undersecretary of state for economic affairs in the Eisenhower administration. He promoted freer trade. He led the U.S. delegation to the first annual conference of the Alliance for Progress in Mexico City in 1962. He urged tax reduction as a spur to economic growth. In 1962 he joined in pressuring the steel industry to roll back a price hike. He stayed on in the Johnson administration.

Secretary of Defense. Robert S. McNamara (1916–   ), of Michigan, served 1961–1968. He abandoned the Eisenhower administration's policy of "massive retaliation" in favor of a flexible-response strategy that relied on increased U.S. capacity to conduct limited, nonnuclear warfare. Bringing to the Pentagon a zeal for efficiency, he streamlined defense operations and centralized authority. He created the Defense Intelligence Agency and the Defense Supply Agency. In 1962 he announced that the United States would train the forces of other countries threatened by Communist subversion. He stayed on in the Johnson administration.

Attorney General. Robert F. Kennedy (1925–1968), of Massachusetts, served 1961–1964. The appointment of the president's brother drew charges of nepotism. He directed the prosecution of labor racketeering and antitrust law violations. He emerged a champion of civil rights for his involvement in ensuring the admission of black students to the University of Mississippi in 1962 and the University of Alabama in 1963. He was a principal adviser during the Cuban missile crisis in 1962. He stayed on in the Johnson administration.

Postmaster General. (1) J. Edward Day (1914–1996), of California, served 1961–1963. He was the first postmaster general to recognize the postal unions. (2) John A. Gronouski (1919–1996), of Wisconsin, served 1963–1965. He was the first Polish-American cabinet officer. He stayed on in the Johnson administration.

Secretary of the Interior. Stewart L. Udall (1920–   ), of Arizona, served 1961–1969. He promoted conservation and environmental protection. He stayed on in the Johnson administration.

Secretary of Agriculture. Orville L. Freeman (1918–2003), of Minnesota, served 1961–1969. He increased food aid to the poor and conducted a food stamp pilot project in West Virginia that later was adopted nationwide. He stayed on in the Johnson administration.

Secretary of Commerce. Luther H. Hodges (1898–1974), of North Carolina, served 1961–1964. He argued for tax cuts to stimulate the economy and promoted foreign trade. He stayed on in the Johnson administration.

Secretary of Labor. (1) Arthur J. Goldberg (1908–1990), of Washington, D.C., served 1961–1962. He had been serving as counsel for the AFL-CIO. He played an active role in mediating strikes in auto, steel, airline, and other key industries. He resigned to accept appointment to the Supreme Court. (2) W. Willard Wirtz (1912–   ), of Illinois, served 1962–1969. Promoted from undersecretary of labor, he continued the active role in strike mediation begun by his predecessor. He stayed on in the Johnson administration.

Secretary of Health, Education and Welfare. (1) Abraham A. Ribicoff (1910–1998), of Connecticut, served 1961–1962. He won passage of a Social Security reform law omitting the requirement that recipients of Aid to Dependent Children be of single-parent homes. (2) Anthony J. Celebrezze (1910–1998), of Ohio, served 1962–1965. He stayed on in the Johnson administration.

ADMINISTRATION: January 20, 1961–November 22, 1963.

Bay of Pigs Invasion, 1961. On April 17, 1961, 1,500 Cuban exiles, trained and armed by the U.S. Central Intelligence Agency, invaded Cuba at Cochinos Bay (Bay of Pigs). Their mission was to establish a beachhead and spark a popular uprising that would topple the Communist regime of Fidel Castro. The invaders were led to believe that U.S. forces would follow in support if they met overwhelming resistance. The support never came. Castro's tanks and soldiers pinned them to the sea, making it impossible for them to establish themselves securely on shore. After three days of fighting, 1,100 survivors surrendered. The United States paid Cuba $53 million in food and medical supplies for their release in 1962. The invasion had been planned by the Eisenhower administration, but President Kennedy approved its execution and accepted full responsibility for its failure.

Alliance for Progress. Kennedy sought to build on the Good Neighbor policy of President Franklin Roosevelt by establishing the Alliance for Progress, in which the United States provided billions of dollars in aid to Latin America. The Alliance charter was signed at the Inter-American Conference at Punta del Este, Uruguay, in August 1961.

Peace Corps. The Peace Corps was established in March 1961 as an agency of the State Department to enlist volunteers in teaching and providing technical manpower to underdeveloped countries. Kennedy appointed his brother-in-law R. Sargent Shriver as its first director. Some 85,000 Americans served in the corps over the next 20 years. In 1971 it and other volunteer service agencies were merged to form an independent agency, Action. As of 1981, 6,000 Peace Corps volunteers were working in 63 countries.

Southeast Asia. In July 1962 representatives of the United States and 13 other nations agreed at the Second Geneva Conference to guarantee the independence and neutrality of Laos. Events in Vietnam, however, proved more intractable. Communist guerrillas were making headway in the Mekong Delta region of the South despite the Diem government's strategic-hamlet program, in which peasants were evacuated from their villages and herded into fortified camps in an attempt to isolate the insurgents from popular support. President Kennedy had little taste for the draconian methods of the Diem regime. After government forces opened fire on unarmed Buddhist demonstrators in Hue in May 1963 and conducted raids on pagodas in other cities, Kennedy tacitly supported a military coup in November 1963, led by Major General Duong Van "Big" Minh, which ended in Diem's murder. During the Kennedy administration, the number of U.S. military advisers in South Vietnam grew from less than 1,000 to more than 16,000. Still Kennedy refused to commit U.S. combat forces to the region. Some Kennedy aides, including Theodore Sorenson and Arthur Schlesinger, later contended that Kennedy had planned to end U.S. involvement in Vietnam after he was safely reelected in 1964. Indeed, less than two months before his death, Kennedy did seem to close the door on escalating the U.S. committment. "In the final analysis," he said, "it is their war. They are the ones who have to win it or lose it. We can help them, we can give them equipment, we can send them our men out there as advisers, but they have to win it, the people of Vietnam against the Communists."[5]

Steel Price Rollback, 1962. To combat inflation, the Kennedy administration established voluntary wage-price guidelines that it hoped labor and management would honor. In 1962 steelworkers agreed to a contract without a wage increase on the assumption that the steel industry would refrain from raising prices. Soon thereafter the U.S. Steel Corporation announced a 3.5% increase in steel prices; other steel producers quickly followed suit. A furious President Kennedy went on television in April 1962 to denounce the "tiny handful of steel executives whose pursuit of private power and profit exceeds their sense of public responsibility." Privately, Kennedy reportedly said, "My father always told me that all businessmen were sons-of-bitches, but I never believed it till now."[6] Under administration pressure, first Bethlehem Steel, then the others, rolled back the price hike.

Civil Rights. In 1962 black student James Meredith enrolled at the formerly all-white University of Mississippi under the protection of the National Guard. Governor Ross Barnett had physically attempted to bar his admission. Street rioting followed in which two people were killed, scores injured. Similarly, in

Alabama in 1963, Governor George Wallace stood defiantly at the door of the state university in an unsuccessful attempt to bar the admission of two black students. Meanwhile, "freedom riders" were traveling around the South challenging the segregation of public facilities. Violence erupted in April 1963 in Birmingham, Alabama, when Civil rights activists led by the Reverend Martin Luther King, Jr., protested segregation in that city. In August 1963 Reverend King, Roy Wilkins, and others led 200,000 peaceful demonstrators on a Freedom March on Washington. The Kennedy administration responded to black demands for civil rights with executive action, a legislative program, and moral leadership: Through executive action, President Kennedy in November 1962 ordered an end to discrimination in housing owned, operated, or financed by the federal government; established the President's Committee on Equal Employment Opportunity; and appointed numerous blacks to prominent federal positions. The Kennedy legislative program, calling for desegregation of public facilities and greater authority for the attorney general in bringing suits against segregated school systems, was fulfilled under President Johnson. President Kennedy exerted moral leadership on the race issue in a television address in June 1963, challenging the American people to live up to the promise of American ideals and abide by the Golden Rule. "If an American," he asked his audience, "because his skin is dark, cannot eat lunch in a restaurant open to the public, if he cannot send his children to the best public school available, if he cannot vote for the public officials who represent him, if in short, he cannot enjoy the full and free life which all of us want, then who among us would be content to have the color of his skin changed and stand in his place? Who among us would then be content with the counsels of patience and delay?" He added, "We preach freedom around the world, and we mean it, and we cherish our freedom here at home; but are we to say to the world and, much more importantly, to each other that this is a land of the free except for the Negroes; that we have no class or caste system, no ghettos, no master race except with respect to Negroes?"

Berlin Crisis. In August 1961 Berlin again (see "Harry S Truman, 33d President," "Administration") became the focus of East-West tensions, as East Germany erected a wall sealing off East Berlin from the free city of West Berlin. President Kennedy made it clear that he was prepared to go to war to keep West Berlin free, but because the wall had been built entirely on East German soil and appeared to be designed to keep East Berliners from escaping rather than as a threat to West Berlin itself, it was allowed to stand, a grim reminder of the isolation and vulnerability of that democratic enclave and the frustrated impulse of Iron Curtain peoples to seek freedom. In an emotional speech at the wall in June 1963, Kennedy stirred an audience of West Germans, concluding, "All free men, wherever they may live, are citizens of Berlin, and, therefore, as a free man, I take pride in the words '*Ich bin ein Berliner.*'"

Cuban Missile Crisis, 1962. In October 1962 U.S. intelligence learned that the Soviet Union was constructing offensive nuclear missile bases in Cuba capable of striking the eastern two thirds of the United States as well as much of Latin America. Although the Soviet Union steadfastly maintained that the weapons were defensive, aerial photographs proved otherwise. In a solemn television address on October 22, President Kennedy condemned the Soviet Union for lying about the nature of the buildup and ordered a quarantine of Cuba, in which, he said, "All ships of any kind bound for Cuba from whatever nation or port will, if found to contain cargoes of offensive weapons, be turned back." He then warned Moscow, "It shall be the policy of this nation to regard any nuclear missile launched from Cuba against any nation in the Western Hemisphere as an attack by the Soviet Union on the United States, requiring a full retaliatory response upon the Soviet Union." He also called for "the prompt dismantling and withdrawal of all offensive weapons in Cuba." Tense days followed as Soviet ships steamed toward the American blockade. Finally, in an exchange of notes that reflected indecision within the Kremlin, Soviet Premier Nikita Khrushchev agreed to dismantle the missile sites and return the weapons to the Soviet Union in exchange for a U.S. pledge not to invade Cuba. By the end of 1962 U.S. intelligence confirmed their removal.

Nuclear Test Ban Treaty, 1963. In July 1963 the United States, the Soviet Union, and Great Britain agreed to end atmospheric testing of nuclear weapons. Although underground testing was allowed to continue, the ban on nuclear explosions in the skies greatly reduced the danger from radioactive fallout. Eventually the treaty was ratified by more than 100 other nations, with the notable exceptions of Red China and France. In signing the treaty into effect in October, President Kennedy said, "Today the fear is a little less and the hope a little greater. For the first time we have been able to reach an agreement which can limit the dangers of this [nuclear] age."

Space Program. In May 1961 President Kennedy enunciated the U.S. objective to put a man on the moon by the end of the decade. During his term the U.S. National Aeronautics and Space Administration (NASA) undertook Project Mercury to determine the effects of high-gravity launch, weightlessness in space, and reentry on human pilots. In May 1961 Alan B. Shepard, Jr., became the first American in space, and in February 1962 John Glenn became the first American in orbit.

Constitutional Amendment Ratified: Twenty-third Amendment, 1961. It gave residents of the District of Columbia the right to vote in presidential elections.

SUPREME COURT APPOINTMENTS: (1) Byron R. White (1917–2002), of Colorado, served as associate justice 1962–1993. Byron "Whizzer" White had been an All-American football player for the University of Colorado and played professional ball briefly for the Pittsburgh and Detroit teams before becoming a lawyer. A longtime friend of John F. Kennedy, he was deputy attorney general under Robert Kennedy at the time of his appointment. Justice White has generally maintained a centrist position on the Court. In 1973 he dissented in the abortion cases, which upheld the right of abortion on demand during the first trimester of pregnancy. "The Court," wrote White, "apparently values the convenience of the pregnant mother more than the continued existence and development of the life or potential life that she carries." (2) Arthur J. Goldberg (1908–1990), of Illinois, served as associate justice 1962–1965. He had been serving as labor secretary. He wrote the opinion in *Escobedo* v. *Illinois* (1964), upholding a criminal suspect's right to counsel during pretrial questioning. He resigned to become U.S. ambassador to the United Nations.

ASSASSINATION: November 22, 1963, 12:30 P.M., Dallas Texas; Death, 1:00 P.M., Parkland Memorial Hospital, Dallas. President Kennedy had come to Texas to reconcile differences between opposing factions of the Democratic party in the state. The presidential party flew into Dallas's Love Field from Fort Worth at 11:37 A.M. President and Mrs. Kennedy and Governor and Mrs. John Connally then proceeded in an open limousine to the city for a scheduled luncheon address at the Dallas Trade Mart. As the motorcade made its way through Dallas, the reception from crowds lining the streets was enthusiastic. Mrs. Connally turned to Kennedy and said, "Mr. President, you can't say Dallas doesn't love you." The president replied, "That is very obvious."[7] Moments later, after the president's car passed by the Texas School Book Depository, shots rang out. One bullet passed through Kennedy's neck, a second, fatal bullet tore away the right side of the back of his head. Governor Connally also was wounded. The president was rushed to the hospital, where Dr. Malcolm Perry performed a tracheotomy and administered blood infusions and oxygen. The president's heart stopped; cardiac massage failed to revive him. According to the autopsy, performed by Navy Commander J. J. Humes at Bethesda Naval Hospital that evening, "the wound of the skull produced such extensive damage to the brain as to preclude the possibility of the deceased surviving this injury." The president's body lay in state at the Capitol Rotunda while an estimated 250,000 mourners filed by. Richard Cardinal Cushing of Boston performed the funeral mass at St. Matthew's Roman Catholic Cathedral in Washington. Kennedy was buried at Arlington National Cemetery. An eternal flame, lit by Mrs. Kennedy, marked the grave.

According to the Warren Commission, appointed by President Johnson to investigate the assassination, the president was shot by Lee Harvey Oswald, 24, a clerk at the book depository, a former Marine and self-avowed Marxist who lived for a time in the Soviet Union. The murder weapon was a 6.5 Mannlicher-Carcano Italian carbine with scope, which Oswald had purchased through the mail for $19.95. After the shooting, Oswald fled the book depository and was arrested about 45 minutes later at the Texas Theatre. Oswald denied shooting the president. On November 24, while being transferred under custody to the county jail, Oswald was shot to death at point-blank range by Jack Ruby, a Dallas nightclub owner, before live television cameras. Because Oswald did not live to stand trial, it was left to the Warren Commission to establish his guilt and to determine that he acted alone. From its publication, however, the Warren Report was criticized as incomplete and inaccurate by those contending that Kennedy was the victim of a conspiracy—a conspiracy, some believed, directed by Cuban leader Fidel Castro, or organized crime figures, or both. In 1979 the House Select Committee on Assassinations, called to reinvestigate the deaths of Kennedy and civil rights leader Martin Luther King, Jr., concluded an intensive two-year probe that relied heavily on complex acoustical analysis, technology unavailable in 1964. According to its final report, Oswald did indeed fire three shots (two hits and a miss), including the fatal one to the brain, from the book depository, as the Warren Report contended. But on the basis of analysis of a police tape recording of sounds picked up on the scene by a motorcycle patrolman's radio, acoustical experts concluded that there was a 95 percent probability that a fourth shot had been fired, not from behind where Oswald was perched, but from the grassy knoll in front of the presidential limousine. Thus, the committee concluded, a conspiracy was "likely." Moreover, the committee discovered that Oswald had associated with Carlos Marcello, reputed crime boss of New Orleans, and concluded that organized crime figures "probably" were involved in the conspiracy to assassinate the president. The FBI dismissed the committee's findings as "invalid," however, and stuck to its original conclusion that Oswald acted alone. A 1982 study by the National Research Council also disputed the committee's acoustical analysis. The committee's chief counsel, G. Robert Blakely, in his book *The Plot to Kill the President* (with Richard N. Billings, 1981), detailed a strong, though circumstantial case against Marcello and another reputed underworld figure Santo Trafficante as the masterminds behind the conspiracy. Once Oswald was arrested, Blakely contends, the mob hired Ruby to kill him.

Since Oswald's death, rumors persisted that he was not buried in the grave marked by his name at Rose Hill Burial Park in Fort Worth. Michael Eddowes, British author of *The Oswald File* (1977), contended that the body was that of a Russian spy, Alek James Hidell, who had been posing as Oswald. But exhumation and examination of the badly decomposed body at the Baylor University Medical Center in Dallas in 1981 disproved Eddowes's theory; the shape and placing of 10 fillings in the teeth of the corpse matched identically with dental X rays of Oswald while he was in the Marines.

In his last will and testament, executed in June 1954, Kennedy left $25,000 and all personal effects to his wife and divided the residue of his estate, estimated in the millions of dollars, into two equal trusts for his wife and children.

KENNEDY PRAISED: "More than any President before him, he committed the Presidency to achieving full civil rights for every American. He opposed prejudice of every kind. There was no trace of meanness in this man. There was only compassion for the frailties of others. If there is a supreme lesson we can draw from the life of John Kennedy, it is a lesson of tolerance, a lesson of conscience, courage, and compassion."[8]—Democratic Senator Abraham Ribicoff of Connecticut, 1963

"He was, perhaps, a step or two ahead of the people at times. But as an American who understood America, who brought form to its amorphous yearnings, who gave direction to its efforts, John Kennedy walked with the people."[9]—Democratic Senator Hubert H. Humphrey of Minnesota, 1963

"John Fitzgerald Kennedy [was] a great and good President, the friend of all people of good will; a believer in the dignity and equality of all human beings; a fighter for justice; an apostle of peace."[10]—Chief Justice Earl Warren, 1963

KENNEDY CRITICIZED: "I sincerely fear for my country if Jack Kennedy should be elected president. The fellow has absolutely no principles. Money and gall are all the Kennedys have."[11]—Republican Senator Barry Goldwater of Arizona

"During these first two weeks [of the 1960 campaign], Kennedy concentrated on building up what I characterized as a 'poor mouth' image of America. . . . He seized on every possible shortcoming and inequity in American life and promised immediate cure-alls."[12]—Richard M. Nixon

"Kennedy, in the supercilious arrogance which Harvard inculcates in lace-curtain Irish, doggedly mispronounced ordinary words. . . . This was the true Rooseveltian contempt for the common man. He seems afraid to be taken for a valid American."[13]—journalist Westbrook Pegler

"[The Kennedy administration's] difficulty appears to stem primarily from an inadequate understanding of our American system—of how it really works, of the psychological, motivational and economic factors that make it ebb and flow."[14]—former president Dwight D. Eisenhower, 1962

KENNEDY QUOTES: "What kind of peace do we seek? Not a *Pax Americana* enforced on the world by American weapons of war. Not the peace of the grave or the security of the slave. I am talking about genuine peace, the kind of peace that makes life on earth worth living, the kind that enables men and nations to grow and to hope to build a better life for their children—not merely peace for Americans, but peace for all men and women; not merely peace in our time, but peace for all time."[15]—1963

"It should be clear by now that a nation can be no stronger abroad than she is at home. Only an America which practices what it preaches about equal rights and social justice will be respected by those whose choice affects our future."[16]— undelivered speech, Dallas, 1963

BOOKS BY KENNEDY: *Why England Slept* (1940); *Profiles in Courage* (1956).

BOOKS ABOUT KENNEDY: Blair, Joan, and Blair, Clay, Jr. *In Search of JFK.* New York: Berkley/Putnam, 1976.

Goodwin, Doris Kearns. *The Fitzgeralds and the Kennedys: An American Saga.* New York: Simon & Schuster, 1987.

Manchester, William. *Portrait of a President: JFK in Profile.* Boston: Little, Brown, 1967.

O'Donnell, Kenneth P., *et al. Johnny, We Hardly Knew Ye: Memories of John F. Kennedy.* Boston: Little, Brown, 1970.

Schlesinger, Arthur M. *A Thousand Days: John F. Kennedy in the White House.* Boston: Houghton, Mifflin, 1965.

Sorensen, Theodore C. *The Kennedy Legacy.* New York: Macmillan, 1969.

Wills, Garry. *The Kennedy Imprisonment: A Meditation on Power.* Boston: Little, Brown, 1982.

NOTES:

1 Arthur M. Schlesinger, *A Thousand Days: John F. Kennedy in the White House*, Boston: Houghton, Mifflin, 1965, p. 95.
2 Ibid., p. 115.
3 Ibid., p. 79.
4 Joan Blair and Clay Blair, Jr., *In Search of JFK*, New York: Berkley/Putnam, 1976, p. 30.
5 Theodore C. Sorensen, *The Kennedy Legacy*, New York: Macmillan, 1969, p. 207.
6 Schlesinger, p. 635.
7 *The Warren Report: The Official Report on the Assassination of President John F. Kennedy*, New York: Associated Press, n.d., p. 21.
8 *John F. Kennedy Memorial Addresses Delivered in Congress*, Washington, D.C: Government Printing Office, 1964, p. 18.
9 Ibid., p. 177.
10 *The Memoirs of Earl Warren*, Garden City, N.Y.: Doubleday, 1977, p. 353.
11 Victor Lasky, *JFK: The Man and the Myth*, New York: Macmillan, 1963, p. 310.
12 Richard M. Nixon, *Six Crises*, Garden City, N.Y.: Doubleday, 1962, p. 336.
13 Lasky, p. 5.
14 *Facts on File Yearbook 1962*, p. 217.
15 Allan Nevins, ed., *The Burden and the Glory*, New York: Harper & Row, 1964, pp. 53–54.
16 Ibid., p. 276.

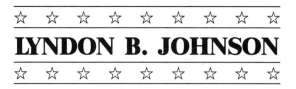

LYNDON B. JOHNSON

36TH PRESIDENT

NAME: Lyndon Baines Johnson. He was named after W. C. Linden, a lawyer and family friend. His mother altered the spelling to Lyndon. Baines was his mother's maiden name. He remained unnamed for the first three months, during which he was called, simply, Baby.

PHYSICAL DESCRIPTION: Johnson stood 6 feet 3 inches tall and weighed 210 pounds on becoming president. He had brown eyes and black hair, mixed with gray, which he combed straight back. His long, lined face was dominated by a rather large nose, a strong cleft chin, and oversized protruding ears. He wore reading glasses. In 1955 he suffered a severe heart attack but after six months' convalescence recovered to resume a full work schedule. He suffered periodically from kidney stones. While president he underwent surgery to repair a scar that had not healed properly from a previous gall bladder operation and had a polyp removed from his throat. Otherwise his health generally was sound. Johnson dressed fashionably but preferred western clothing while on the ranch in Texas.

PERSONALITY: By all accounts Johnson was a complex personality, fiercely competitive, "always in a rush," said his wife, a man who relished power, a master manipulator who harnessed his finely tuned political instincts to achieve lofty goals. Journalists Rowland Evans and Robert Novak said of him during his term, "He can be as gentle and solicitous as a nurse, but as ruthless and deceptive as a riverboat gambler."[1] The president's brother Sam Houston Johnson and others described him as secretive and stubborn. First Lady Lady Bird Johnson regrets that the public did not get to see the soft side of the president. "He was a warm and mellow man in so many ways, gentle, extremely loving," she said in an interview for *U.S. News and World Report* (December 24, 1973). "But he was not eager to get up in front of thousands or millions of people and act that way. He was that way with his neighbors, his friends and in his home."

ANCESTORS: Johnson was of English, Scotch, and German heritage. A great[4]-grandfather John Buntine emigrated from Scotland and settled in Rowan County, North Carolina, in 1758. The earliest known Johnson ancestor was the president's great-great-grandfather John Johnson of Georgia, a veteran of the American Revolution. The president's great-grandfather, Jesse Johnson moved to Texas in 1846. His paternal grandfather, Sam Ealy Johnson, Sr., a cattleman and Confederate veteran of the Civil War, founded Johnson City, Texas, and established the family ranch on the Pedernales River. His maternal grandfather Joseph W. Baines, also a Confederate veteran of the Civil War, was a lawyer, newspaper publisher, Texas secretary of state 1883–1887 and state representative 1903–1905.

FATHER: Sam Ealy Johnson, Jr. (1877–1937), farmer, trader, legislator. Born at Buda, Hays County, Texas, Sam Johnson, a high school graduate, taught school at Sandy and Hye, Texas, 1896–1898 before turning to farming. As a member of the Texas House of Representatives 1905–1909 and 1917–1925, he sponsored the Johnson Blue Sky law, a consumer protection measure directed against unscrupulous salesmen, cosponsored the bill to purchase the Alamo, and spoke out for tolerance toward German-Americans residing in Texas during World War I. He also opposed the Ku Klux Klan. Meanwhile, he dabbled in real estate and was a cotton broker. He suffered severe financial loss when the San Francisco earthquake destroyed his cotton holdings. During the 1930s he was an inspector for the state railroad commission. He died of a heart ailment at 60 when Lyndon was serving his first term in the U.S. House. President Johnson often repeated his father's advice to him: "If you can't come into a roomful of people and tell right away who is for you and who is against you, you have no business in politics."

MOTHER: Rebekah Baines Johnson (1881–1958). Born in McKinney, Texas, she worked her way through Baylor University as a journalism major by operating the college bookstore. She taught elocution for a time at Fredericksburg, Texas, before her marriage to Sam Johnson in 1907. She also edited a small local newspaper. She died of cancer at 77 when her son was majority leader of the Senate.

SIBLINGS: The oldest of five children, Johnson had three sisters and a brother—Mrs. Rebekah L. Bobbitt of Austin, Texas; Mrs. Josefa H. Moss; Sam Houston Johnson, lawyer of Austin; and Mrs. Lucia H. Alexander of Austin.

CHILDREN: Johnson had two daughters.

Lynda Bird Johnson (1944–   ). Born in Washington, D.C., she was a sophomore history major at the University of Texas when her father became president; she promptly transferred to George Washington University in the nation's capital. She dated actor George Hamilton but married Marine Captain Charles S. Robb in a White House ceremony in December 1967. She was for a time a contributing editor for the *Ladies Home Journal*. President Carter named her chairperson of the National Advisory Committee for Women. Robb, a conservative Democrat, was governor of Virginia 1982–1986, and in 1988 was elected to the U.S. Senate.

Luci Baines Johnson (1947–   ). Born in Washington, she was a student at the Episcopalian National Cathedral School for Girls in Washington when her father became president. She converted to Roman Catholicism and married Patrick Nugent in August 1966; a White House reception followed the church ceremony. They divorced in 1979. She married Ian Turpin, a Scottish-born investment banker, in 1984, and settled in Toronto.

BIRTH: Johnson was born in a three-room farmhouse on the Pedernales River between Stonewall and Johnson City, Texas, on the morning of August 27, 1908. He weighed about 10 pounds at birth.

CHILDHOOD: Johnson grew up amid hardship in and around Johnson City, Texas. Among his earliest memories is of comforting his mother while she was crying at the water pump. Besides doing household chores, Johnson earned spare cash as a hired hand on neighboring farms, a printer's devil on a local paper, and a shoeshine boy in a barbershop and trapped and sold animal skins. He was a crack marble shooter and used his lanky frame to good advantage as first baseman at area ballgames. The most thrilling experience of his childhood was a trip to the Alamo with his father. He was deeply moved by the valor of Jim Bowie, Davy Crockett, and others who died defending the mission. As president he often compared the U.S. role in Vietnam to the Texans at the Alamo. As a youngster Johnson enjoyed listening to his father talk politics with a steady stream of visitors to his home. In 1918 he went on the campaign trail with his father, who was running for reelection to the Texas House. Lyndon frequently attended sessions of the state legislature and followed the debate. Classmate Anna Itz later recalled that Lyndon early dreamed of a political career and once confided to her, "Someday I'm going to be president of the United States."[2]

EDUCATION: At his mother's coaching, Johnson learned the alphabet at age two and to read at four. He attended public elementary schools near his birthplace and in Johnson City. At the end of the first grade he was chosen to recite a poem, "I'd Rather Be Mamma's Boy." Although bright, he disliked schoolwork, especially math, and was often cited for misbehavior. He took dancing lessons for a time but quit after being spanked for teasing the girls. He also studied violin for several months. After graduating from the seventh grade at Junction school in 1920, he completed the eighth grade at the Stonewall and Albert schools. At Johnson City High School 1921–1924, he was on the two-man debating team that won the county title during his final year. He graduated the youngest of the six-member class of 1924. According to the class prophecy, he was to become governor of Texas. Despite his mother's pleas to go on to college, Johnson worked briefly as a clerk in Robstown, Texas, and in July 1924 set out with five friends to California in a used Model-T Ford. For two years he bummed around, finding work, by turns, as a fruit picker, dishwasher, and elevator operator. In 1926 he returned home flat broke. After working on a county road gang for several months, he finally agreed to try college. At Southwest Texas State Teachers College 1927–1930, Johnson scored well in history, political science, and education but poorly in science, math, and physical education. He worked his way through college as a trash collector, assistant janitor, and finally assistant secretary to the college president. In extracurricular activities, he was on the debating team, took part in campus politics as campaign manager for the White Stars faction, wrote editorials for the campus paper, joined the Harris Blair Literary Society, and was president of the Press Club, senior legislator of his class, and a member of the student council. He and some friends crashed the 1928 Democratic national convention in Houston. He also found time to direct the campaign of Welly Hopkins in his successful bid for the state senate in 1928. During 1928–1929 he taught at a predominantly Mexican-American school in Cotulla, Texas, while taking a few courses at the

Southwest Texas State extension there. He graduated in August 1930. Johnson studied law briefly, 1934–1935, at Georgetown Univesity.

RELIGION: Disciple of Christ. At 18 Johnson joined the Christian Church, or Disciple of Christ, in Texas. As president he worshiped at churches of various denominations. Since the assassination of President Kennedy he regularly said grace before dinner and prayed often in the White House. Late one night in June 1966, Johnson, worried that bombing raids over Hanoi and Haiphong might bring the Soviets into the Vietnam War, sneaked out with daughter Luci to pray at St. Dominic's Chapel. In 1966 Johnson conferred with Pope Paul VI; he was the first incumbent president to meet a pontiff.

RECREATION: President Johnson relaxed playing dominoes or an occasional hand of poker. He enjoyed life on the 415-acre LBJ Ranch in Texas. He was notorious for taking guests on 90-mph rides around the ranch in his Lincoln Continental. He also golfed but, unlike his two immediate predecessors, kept his score secret. He swam regularly in the White House pool. He read little besides daily newspapers and work-related material. He drank moderately, usually Cutty Sark and soda. Once a three-pack-a-day cigarette smoker, he quit following his heart attack in 1955.

EARLY ROMANCE: According to his brother, Sam Houston Johnson, Lyndon while a college student was informally engaged to the daughter of a prominent Ku Klux Klan leader in Texas. Because Lyndon's father had been an outspoken critic of the KKK, the girl's father objected to the union. "I won't have my daughter marrying into that no-account Johnson family," he reportedly said. "I've known that bunch all my life, one generation after another of shiftless dirt farmers and grubby politicians. Always sticking together and leeching onto one another so the minute one starts to make it, the other drags him down. None of them will ever amount to a damn."[3] When Johnson heard what her father had said, he dropped her.

MARRIAGE: Lyndon B. Johnson, 26, married Claudia Alta "Lady Bird" Taylor, 21, on November 17, 1934, at St. Mark's Episcopal Church in San Antonio, Texas. Born December 22, 1912, at Karnack, Texas, the daughter of Thomas Jefferson Taylor, rancher, storekeeper, and "dealer in everything," and Minnie Pattillo Taylor, she was nicknamed in infancy by a nursemaid, who exclaimed, "She's purty as a ladybird." Just five years old when her mother died, Lady Bird was raised by her father and Aunt Effie Pattillo. In 1934 she graduated near the top of her class from the University of Texas. That same year she met Johnson, then secretary to a congressman, at the home of a mutual friend Eugene Lasseter, in Austin. Johnson invited her to breakfast the following morning, poured out his life story to her there, and proposed marriage later in the day. Unsure of just what to make of such forward behavior, Lady Bird refused but confessed to having a "moth and flame" feeling about him. Returning to Washington, he sent her his photo, inscribed, "For Bird, a lovely girl with ideals, principles, intelligence, and refinement, from her sincere admirer, Lyndon." After much soul searching, she heeded the advice of her father, who wholeheartedly approved of Johnson, and agreed to marry him. Once engaged, Johnson rushed through the legal preliminaries and persuaded the Reverend Arthur E. McKinistry to skip his usual prenuptial consultation with the couple. A $2.50 wedding ring was hastily purchased at Sears, Roebuck. The groom's friend Dan Quill, later postmaster of San Antonio, was pressed into service as best man. The couple spent their wedding night at the Plaza Hotel in San Antonio, honeymooned in Mexico, and made it back to Washington in time for the opening of Congress. In 1942 Mrs. Johnson invested a portion of her inheritance in a small radio station, KTBC in Austin, which she parlayed into a multimillion-dollar communications empire. As First Lady, she traveled some 200,000 miles promoting a campaign to improve the landscape of America—the so-called beautification program, a term she disliked because it sounded cosmetic and trivial. She helped win passage of the Highway Beautification Act in 1965 restricting billboards and junkyards along major highways. In her honor the Lady Bird Johnson Grove of the Redwood National Park was dedicated in 1969. She also promoted the administration's war on poverty. Although she was very active, she has asserted that the primary obligation of a First Lady is to create in the White House "an island of peace" for the President. She had long urged President Johnson not to seek reelection in 1968 but did not know for certain that he had agreed until he read the surprise announcement on national television in March. She retired with the president to the LBJ Ranch in Texas. Since his death in 1973, she has spent much of her time in Austin, remaining active as board chairman of the LBJ Company, the radio and cable TV enterprise, a board member of the LBJ Library, regent of the University of Texas, and a member of the National Parks Advisory Board. She spoke out for the Equal Rights Amendment for women. In 1983 she founded the National Wildflower Research Center. In 1988 she moved into a new home in Austin.

EXTRAMARITAL AFFAIR: Alice Glass. In *The Years of Lyndon Johnson: The Path to Power* (1982), author Robert A. Caro asserts that Johnson had a longtime love affair with Alice Glass, companion of Texas newspaper publisher Charles E. Marsh. The relationship began in the late 1930s and ended in the 1960s. She reportedly broke it off because of her opposition to the Vietnam War.

MILITARY SERVICE:

World War II. Johnson served as a lieutenant commander in the navy from December 1941 to July 1942. He had joined the naval reserve in January 1940. He was sent on an observation mission to Australia and New Guinea. His plane survived an attack by Japanese aircraft over New Guinea. For this mission he was awarded the Silver Star. The citation from General Douglas MacArthur read, "His gallant action enabled him to obtain and return with valuable information." During his service, Johnson retained his House seat. He resigned his commission in 1942 in compliance with President Roosevelt's order that all congressmen in the service resume their legislative duties.

CAREER BEFORE THE PRESIDENCY: During 1930–1931 Johnson taught public speaking in Pearsall, Texas, and debate and public speaking at Sam Houston High School in Houston. He quit education to become secretary to Democratic Representative Richard M. Kleberg of Texas during 1931–1934. In 1933 he was elected speaker of the Little Congress, an organization of congressional secretaries.

Director of National Youth Administration in Texas, 1935–1937. Under Johnson the state NYA assisted colleges in providing part-time jobs for needy students and provided technical training and local public works jobs for young nonstudents. The program benefited tens of thousands of Texans during the Depression.

U.S. Representative, 1937–1949. In a special election for the House seat from Texas's Tenth District (Austin and environs), Johnson, running on a straight New Deal platform, topped a crowded field with 27 percent of the vote. He was reelected six times in succession, sometimes without opposition. In 1941 in a special election for the Senate he was defeated narrowly by Governor W. Lee "Pappy" O'Daniel. In the House, Johnson served on the Naval Affairs Committee and its successor the Armed Services Committee. He was chairman of the Naval Affairs special subcommittee investigating waste in the conduct of the naval war. President Roosevelt took an instant liking to the freshman congressman; Johnson in turn was one of the administration's most consistent supporters. He was less supportive of President Truman, however. Johnson voted to override Truman's veto of the Taft-Hartley bill and urged a larger defense budget than the administration thought prudent. He voted with his southern colleagues in opposing an antilynching bill, integration of the armed forces, and an end to the poll tax. He won numerous benefits for his district, including completion of the Colorado Dam project.

U.S. Senator, 1949–1961. In the Senate Democratic primary (then tantamount to election in Texas) in 1948, Johnson defeated Governor Coke Stevenson by just 87 votes out of 988,000 cast, thereby earning the nickname "Landslide Lyndon." He was reelected by nearly a 3–1 margin over conservative Democrat Dudley T. Dougherty in 1954. He served on the Armed Services (1949–1960), Interstate and Foreign Commerce (1949–1955), Finance (1955–1957), and Appropriations (1957–1960) committees. An early advocate of a national space program, he was the first chairman of the Senate Aeronautics and Space Sciences Committee, 1959–1960. As chairman of the Armed Services Defense Preparedness Subcommittee during the Korean War, he exposed waste in manpower and procurement. Senator Johnson opposed President Truman on several important issues. He criticized the administration's failure to make more effective use of air power in Korea, denounced Truman's seizure of the steel mills, and voted to override the president's veto of the McCarran-Walter bill restricting immigration. Johnson was elected Democratic whip in 1951, minority leader in 1953. With the Democratic takeover of the Senate in 1955, he became at 46 the youngest majority leader in that body's history. Although felled by a heart attack later that year, he recovered to emerge a dynamic, skilled parliamentarian with a keen instinct for workable compromise. Characteristically, he discouraged protracted debate, preferring instead to hammer out differences off the floor. Unlike his predecessors, he routinely kept the Senate in night session to conclude pressing business. During the Eisenhower years, Johnson drew criticism from some Democrats for failing to square off more directly and more often against the popular Republican president. In the 1950s Johnson opposed the admission of China to the UN as well as military support for the French in Indochina (Vietnam). Publicly he did little to challenge the Communist witch-hunt conducted by Senator Joseph McCarthy, but privately he pressed for television coverage of the Army-McCarthy hearings, believing, correctly, that such exposure would bring down the Wisconsin Republican. Johnson supported legislation benefiting the oil and gas interests of his state. He steered to passage extension of Social Security coverage and increases in the minimum wage. Until 1957 Johnson consistently voted with his southern colleagues against civil rights legislation. It was all the more remarkable, then, that he engineered passage of the Civil Rights acts of 1957 and 1960, which, though restrained, were the first civil rights laws enacted in the twentieth century. Crucial to their passage was Johnson's role in persuading southern senators not to filibuster. Johnson's leadership on the issue marked his departure from a regional political leader to a national statesman and fore-shadowed his strong civil rights position as president. A favorite-son candidate for president in 1956, he received 80 votes at the Democratic national convention that renominated Adlai Stevenson. He was a leading candidate for the Democratic presidential nomination in 1960, losing to John F. Kennedy, 806–409, on the first ballot.

Vice President, 1961–1963. Kennedy's choice of Johnson as his running mate in 1960 surprised and disappointed many liberals in the party (see "John F. Kennedy, 35th President," "Nomination"). Although Johnson had said that he was not interested in the number-two spot, and key supporters, most notably House Speaker Sam Rayburn, urged him to remain in the Senate, Johnson agreed to run. It is generally believed that without Johnson on the ticket, Kennedy probably would have failed to carry Texas, Louisiana, and the Carolinas, states crucial to his victory. Vice President Johnson served as chairman of the National Aeronautics and Space Council, the Peace Corps Advisory Council, and the President's Committee on Equal Employment Opportunity. Although he maintained good relations with the president person-ally, Johnson did not get along well with the young eastern liberals that dominated Kennedy's staff. Johnson undertook presidential missions and goodwill tours to more than 30 nations. In August 1961 he spoke in Berlin soon after the wall went up. In August–September 1962 he discussed foreign aid policy with officials in the Middle East and southern Europe.

Vice President Johnson was riding two cars behind President Kennedy when he was assassinated in Dallas on November 22, 1963. At 2:39 P.M. that day Johnson was administered the presidential oath by U.S. District Court Judge Sarah T. Hughes aboard Air Force One at Dallas's Love Field.

DEMOCRATIC PRESIDENTIAL NOMINATION, 1964: At the Democratic na-tional convention in Atlantic City in August 1964, President Johnson was nominated by acclamation. Governors John Connally of Texas and Pat Brown of California had placed his name in nomination. Johnson squelched speculation that he might choose Attorney General Robert F. Kennedy as his running mate by ruling out all members of his cabinet. He nevertheless pleased liberals in tapping Senator Hubert H. Humphrey of Minnesota for the number-two spot. The highlight of the convention was an emotional film tribute to the late President Kennedy. As Robert Kennedy attempted to introduce it, delegates applauded for 16 straight minutes. The Democratic platform pointed with pride to the accomplishments of the Kennedy-Johnson administrations and con-demned extremism, specifically the conduct of the Ku Klux Klan and the John Birch Society.

OPPONENT: Barry M. Goldwater (1909–1998), of Arizona; Republican. Born in Phoenix, Arizona Territory, the grandson of a Russian Jewish immigrant who founded a trading post that grew into a chain of Arizona department stores, Goldwater dropped out of the University of Arizona after his freshman year to join the family business. He rose to president of Goldwater's, Inc., in 1937. During World War II he was a pilot with the Army Air Corps in the China-India theater. He was served in the Phoenix City Council 1949–1953 and in the U.S. Senate 1953–1965 and 1969–1987. Following publication of his book *The Conscience of a Conservative* (1960), he emerged a champion of the right wing of the Republican party. At various times, Goldwater proposed a sharp reduction in the size of government, repeal of the graduated income tax, an end to federal aid for education and agricultural subsidies, and a voluntary form of Social Security. He was among a handful of Republicans to vote against the Civil Rights Act of 1964. He publicly questioned the utility of the United Nations and urged U.S. withdrawal from the world body if China were admitted. He advocated a tough stand against the Soviet Union and other Communist nations. He proposed granting field commanders the authority to use tactical nuclear weapons at their discretion. Such hawkish views alarmed many prominent Republicans, notably former president Eisenhower. But Goldwater skillfully organized a grass-roots campaign, staffed by a cadre of dedicated conservative volunteers, to nail down delegates prior to the July convention in San Francisco. His principal opponent, Governor Nelson Rockefeller of New York, was handicapped by his recent divorce and remarriage. A last-minute stop-Goldwater movement coalescing around Governor William Scranton of Pennsylvania failed to check the conservative's advance despite a convention-eve Gallup poll showing Scranton the favorite of 60 percent of Republicans, to 34 percent for Goldwater. Goldwater was nominated on the first ballot with 883 votes to 214 for Scranton, 114 for Rockefeller, and the rest scattered. Republican National Committee Chairman William E. Miller of New York, also a conservative, was nominated for vice president. In an acceptance speech that reinforced his image as a radical and one that would dog him throughout the campaign, Goldwater declared, "I would remind you that extremism in the defense of liberty is no vice. And let me remind you also that moderation in the pursuit of justice is no virtue." Conservatives controlled the platform, rejecting a civil rights plank and refusing to repudiate extremism. The platform reflected Goldwater's views of less government, states' rights, and greater freedom for the individual. When Rockefeller addressed the convention on behalf of the civil rights plank, Goldwater supporters drowned him out with a chorus of boos. Rockfeller interrupted his speech to remind his audience, "It's still a free country, ladies and gentlemen." Goldwater later resumed his career in the Senate, 1969–1987.

CAMPAIGN AND THE ISSUES, 1964: Goldwater kept his pledge to offer the people "a choice, not an echo." Throughout the campaign he continued to call for deep cuts in social programs and an increase in the defense budget. A longtime opponent of civil rights bills, he spurned bigotry but stressed the need to restore freedom in American life—"freedom of association," the right not to associate with minorities if one so chooses. "Our aim, as I understand it," Goldwater said "is neither to establish a segregated society nor to establish an integrated society as such. It is to preserve a free society. . . . One thing that will surely poison and embitter our relations with each other is the idea that some predetermined bureaucratic schedule of equality—and, worst of all, a schedule based on the concept of race—must be imposed."[4] Although Goldwater's hard core of right-wing supporters was gratified that he did not substantially temper his conservatism to suit a national campaign, his uncompromising position hurt him among certain blocs of voters. His proposal to sell the Tennessee Valley Authority undermined his strength in that region. His suggestion that Social Security be made voluntary frightened senior citizens. His opposition to civil rights legislation reduced his support among black voters to just 3 percent. But it was Goldwater's foreign policy statements that most alarmed the nation. He spoke casually of "conventional nuclear weapons" and raised the prospect of nuclear war. He denounced the administration's restrained policy in Vietnam and pledged to drive the Communists from the South. For his part, Johnson remained aloof of the campaign. He refused Goldwater's challenge to debate. Compared with Goldwater, he appeared to be the peace candidate and seemed to promise no wider war in Vietnam. "Some others are eager to enlarge the conflict," Johnson said in reference to his opponent. "They call upon us to supply American boys to do the job that Asian boys should do. They ask us to take reckless actions, which might risk the lives of millions and engulf much of Asia."[5] Democratic ads portrayed Goldwater as an apostle of war. One notorious TV commercial associated the Republican candidate with a tranquil scene suddenly obliterated by a rising mushroom cloud. Goldwater objected to such tactics but never managed to shake his hawkish image. His slogan "In Your Heart, You Know He's Right," was corrupted by Democrats to read "In Your Heart, You Know He Might." The principal Democratic slogan was "All the Way with LBJ." The Goldwater campaign got a brief lift when a breath of scandal touched the White House following the arrest of Johnson aide Walter Jenkins on a morals charge. Goldwater referred derisively to Johnson and his "curious crew," but the episode apparently had little effect at the polls. In the end voters repudiated Goldwater's call to the right. His support was limited to the Deep South and his home state.

ELECTION AS PRESIDENT, NOVEMBER 3, 1964:

Popular Vote: Johnson (Democrat), 43,126,506 (61%); Goldwater (Republican), 27,176,799 (39%).

Electoral Vote: Johnson, 486; Goldwater, 52.

States Carried: Johnson won the electoral votes of the District of Columbia and 44 states—Alaska, Arkansas, California, Colorado, Connecticut, Delaware, Florida, Hawaii, Idaho, Illinois, Indiana, Iowa, Kansas, Kentucky, Maine, Maryland, Massachusetts, Michigan, Minnesota, Missouri, Montana, Nebraska, Nevada, New Hampshire, New Jersey, New Mexico, New York, North Carolina, North Dakota, Ohio, Oklahoma, Oregon, Pennsylvania, Rhode Island, South Dakota, Tennessee, Texas, Utah, Vermont, Virginia, Washington, West Virginia, Wisconsin, and Wyoming. Goldwater won the electoral votes of 6 states—Alabama, Arizona, Georgia, Louisiana, Mississippi, and South Carolina.

INAUGURAL ADDRESS: January 20, 1965. ". . . I do not believe that the Great Society is the ordered, changeless, and sterile battalion of the ants.

"It is the excitement of becoming—always becoming, trying, probing, falling, resting, and trying again—but always trying and always gaining. . . .

"Our enemies have always made the same mistake. In my lifetime—in depression and in war—they have awaited our defeat. Each time, from the secret places of the American heart, came forth the faith they could not see or that they could not even imagine. It brought us victory. And it will again.

"For this is what America is all about. It is the uncrossed desert and the unclimbed ridge. It is the star that is not reached and the harvest sleeping in the unplowed ground. . . ."

VICE PRESIDENT: Hubert Horatio Humphrey (1911–1978), of Minnesota, served 1965–1969. Born in Wallace, South Dakota, Humphrey attended the Denver College of Pharmacy 1932–1933, graduated with a degree in political science from the University of Minnesota in 1939, and earned a master's degree from Louisiana State University in 1940. He worked as a pharmacist for several years in Huron, South Dakota, and taught political science at Macalester

College in St. Paul, Minnesota, before entering politics as an organizer of the Democratic Farmer-Labor party in 1944. The next year he was elected mayor of Minneapolis, 1945–1949, at 34 the youngest in the city's history. In 1947 he helped found the liberal Americans for Democratic Action. He gained national attention at the 1948 Democratic convention as champion of the strong civil rights plank in the party's platform. "The time has arrived," Humphrey declared, "for the Democratic party to get out of the shadow of states' rights and walk forthrightly into the bright sunshine of human rights." Later that year Humphrey was elected to the U.S. Senate, 1949–1965. He ran unsuccessfully for the Democratic presidential nomination in 1960. As Senate majority whip 1961–1965 he marshaled Democratic votes for the Nuclear Test Ban Treaty and the Civil Rights Act of 1964. Vice President Humphrey traveled extensively on behalf of the president and vigorously defended the administration's Vietnam War policy against a growing legion of liberal critics. Privately, however, he began to raise doubts about the war. Humphrey was the 1968 Democratic presidential nominee (see "Richard M. Nixon, 37th President," "Opponent").

CABINET:

Secretary of State. Dean Rusk (1909–1994), of New York, served 1961–1969. A holdover from the Kennedy administration, he staunchly supported U.S. involvement in Vietnam. In 1967 he asserted that the United States had begun to win the war. He proposed educational and scientific exchanges with China but opposed full diplomatic relations or its admission to the UN.

Secretary of the Treasury. (1) C. Douglas Dillon (1909–2003), of New Jersey, served 1961–1965. A holdover from the Kennedy administration, he resigned to return to private investment banking. (2) Henry H. Fowler (1908–2000), of Virginia, served 1965–1968. He was the administration's principal lobbyist in the protracted struggle to win the 10 percent tax surcharge in 1968 to help finance the Vietnam War. (3) Joseph W. Barr (1918–1996), of Indiana, served December 1968–January 1969. He was promoted from undersecretary.

Secretary of Defense. (1) Robert S. McNamara (1916–   ), of Michigan, served 1961–1968. A holdover from the Kennedy administration, he directed the escalation of the Vietnam War. In 1967 he opposed Pentagon recommendations, however, to escalate the bombing of North Vietnam and the numbers of U.S. troops in South Vietnam. He resigned to become president of the World Bank. (2) Clark M. Clifford (1906–1998), of Maryland, served 1968–1969. He had served as special counsel to President Truman. He emerged a principal dove within the administration. He was instrumental in President Johnson's decision, announced in March 1968, to limit the bombing in Vietnam and seek a negotiated settlement.

Attorney General. (1) Robert F. Kennedy (1925–1968), of Massachusetts, served 1961–1964. Personal relations between Johnson and the brother of the slain president, never cordial, grew strained in the wake of the assassination. In 1968 he publicly broke with the administration over the Vietnam War. (2) Nicholas deB. Katzenbach (1922–   ), of Illinois, served 1965–1966. He was promoted from deputy attorney general, in which capacity he had personally confronted Alabama governor George Wallace at the schoolhouse door and helped draft the Civil Rights Act of 1964. He drafted the Voting Rights Act of 1965 and promoted school desegregation. (3) Ramsey Clark (1927–   ), of Texas, served 1967–1969. The son of Supreme Court Justice Tom Clark, he was promoted from deputy attorney general. He restricted federal wiretapping and came into open conflict with FBI Director J. Edgar Hoover. Perceived by some to be overly concerned with the rights of the accused at the expense of law and order, he became a special target of Republican presidential candidate Richard Nixon in 1968.

Postmaster General. (1) John A. Gronouski (1919–1996), of Wisconsin, served 1963–1965. A holdover from the Kennedy administration, he resigned to become ambassador to Poland. (2) Lawrence F. O'Brien (1917–1990), Of Massachusetts, served 1965–1968. He had been serving as the president's congressional liaison. In 1966 he began phasing out door-to-door mail delivery, ordering that curbside boxes be erected in all new housing developments. He urged converting the department to a nonprofit public corporation, an idea adopted in 1970 under President Nixon. (3) W. Marvin Watson (1924–   ), of Texas, served 1968–1969. He had been serving as special assistant to the president.

Secretary of the Interior. Stewart L. Udall (1920–   ), of Arizona, served 1961–1969. A holdover from the Kennedy administration, he championed conservation and resisted attempts by private developers to encroach on the Grand Canyon region and other public land. He established the National Trails System in 1968. He also won last-minute approval from retiring President Johnson to set aside an additional 384,500 acres of national parkland.

Secretary of Agriculture. Orville L. Freeman (1918–2003), of Minnesota, served 1961–1969. A holdover from the Kennedy administration, he launched the food stamp program and was chairman of the Presidential Task Force on Agriculture and Rural Life.

Secretary of Commerce. (1) Luther H. Hodges (1898–1974), of North Carolina, served 1961–1965. The only holdover from the Kennedy administration to have supported Johnson for president in 1960, he retired because of age. (2) John T. Connor (1914–2000), of New Jersey, served 1965–1967. He helped settle the East Coast dock strike in 1965. (3) Alexander B. Trowbridge (1929–   ), of New York, served 1967–1968. Promoted from assistant secretary, he resigned to become president of the American Management Association. (4) C. R. Smith (1899–1990), of New York, served 1968–1969. He was chairman of the board of American Airlines at the time of his appointment.

Secretary of Labor. W. Willard Wirtz (1912–   ), of Illinois, served 1962–1969. A holdover from the Kennedy administration, he curbed racial discrimination among federal contractors. He came into conflict with President Johnson over proposed reorganization of the department.

Secretary of Health, Education and Welfare. (1) Anthony J. Celebrezze (1910–1998), of Ohio, served 1962–1965. A holdover from the Kennedy administration, he was instrumental in winning passage of the Elementary and Secondary Education Act of 1965. (2) John W. Gardner (1912–2002), of New York, served 1965–1968. He directed many of the programs of the administration's war on poverty and proposed streamlining the department. He later founded the citizens' lobby, Common Cause. (3) Wilbur J. Cohen (1913–1987), of Maryland, served 1968-1969. Promoted from undersecretary, he urged an expansion of social welfare programs beyond the limits of President Johnson's Great Society. He also proposed standardized welfare payments to stem the exodus of poor southerners to the North and West. He was chairman of the President's Committee on Mental Retardation in 1968.

Secretary of Housing and Urban Development. (1) Robert C. Weaver (1907-1997), of New York, served 1966-1969. The first black cabinet officer, he was promoted from administrator of the Housing and Home Finance Agency. As the first secretary of HUD, he organized the department to provide broad authority to regional directors. With passage of the Demonstration Cities and Metropolitan Development Act of 1966, he established the Model Cities program to assist local authorities in urban renewal. (2) Robert C. Wood (1923–   ), of Massachusetts, served January 1969. He was promoted from undersecretary.

Secretary of Transportation. Alan S. Boyd (1922–   ), of Florida, served 1967–1969. He was promoted from undersecretary of commerce for transportation to become the first secretary of transportation.

ADMINISTRATION: November 22, 1963–January 20, 1969. In a commencement address at the University of Michigan in May 1964, President Johnson declared, "We have the opportunity to move not only toward the rich society and the powerful society, but upward to the Great Society. The Great Society rests on abundance and liberty for all. It demands an end to poverty and racial injustice. . . . The Great Society is a place where every child can find knowledge to enrich his mind and to enlarge his talents. It is a place where leisure is a welcome chance to build and reflect, not a feared cause of boredom and restlessness. It is a place where the city of man serves not only the needs of the body and the demands of commerce but the desire for beauty and the hunger for community." The Great Society encompassed the war on poverty, civil rights legislation, Medicare and Medicaid, environmental protection, and consumerism.

War on Poverty. "Unfortunately," President Johnson said in his 1964 State of the Union address, "many Americans live on the outskirts of hope, some because of their poverty and some because of their color, and all too many because of both. Our task is to help replace their despair with unconditional war on poverty in America." The Economic Opportunity Act of 1964 created the Office of Economic Opportunity, which, under its first director R. Sargent Shriver, administered and/or funded several antipoverty programs: (1) The Job Corps provided vocational training in residence to disadvantaged youth aged 16–21. (2) Volunteers in Service to America (VISTA), a domestic Peace Corps, enlisted volunteers to work and teach in ghettos. (3) The Work-Study Program provided jobs to enable students of low-income families to work their way through college. (4) The Work Experience Program provided child day-care and other support services to poor heads of households. (5) The Community Action Program administered Head Start, instruction for disadvantaged preschoolers; Upward Bound, tutoring for disadvantaged high school students; Foster Grandparents, elderly volunteers to befriend institutionalized children; and legal aid services to the poor.

Civil Rights. The Civil Rights Act of 1964 barred discrimination in employment as well as in hotels, restaurants, and other public facilities and authorized the attorney general to initiate desegregation suits. The Voting Rights Act of 1965, Johnson's proudest achievement, outlawed discriminatory literacy tests and authorized the federal government to promote voter registration; it resulted in a marked increase in minority voting. The Civil Rights Act of 1968 barred discrimination in the sale and rental of housing and stiffened federal criminal penalties for civil rights violations. Accompanying these the greatest strides in civil rights since Reconstruction was a surge in black radicalism and violence. While the Reverend Martin Luther King Jr., and the NAACP remained committed to nonviolence, others grew more militant. The Black Panthers, founded in Oakland, California, in 1966, called for minority control of ghetto neighborhoods and armed rebellion against the white establishment. Stokely Carmichael, chairman of the Student Non-Violent Coordinating Committee, coined the phrase Black Power, an ambiguous term interpreted by such extremists as H. "Rap" Brown to mean armed revolt and by moderates like Floyd McKissick, national director of the Congress of Racial Equality, as simply an expression of ethnic pride. During 1964–1968 riots erupted sporadically in cities across the country. In 1967 alone disturbances broke out in more than 100 cities; about 100 people were killed, thousands were injured, some 12,000 were arrested. Hardest hit was Detriot, where after five days of rioting the damage totaled hundreds of millions of dollars. Urban violence erupted again in April 1968 following the assassination of Martin Luther King, Jr., in Memphis.

Medicare and Medicaid, 1965. Medicare, funded through the Social Security system, provided hospital insurance and, for a low monthly premium, medical insurance for those 65 years of age or older. Medicaid provided hospital and medical benefits for the poor of any age.

Environmental Protection. The Water Quality Act of 1965 required states to establish water quality standards subject to the approval of the Interior Department. The Clean Water Restoration Act of 1966 provided federal matching funds to states for the construction of sewage treatment plants. The Clean Air Act of 1965 set auto emission standards. The Air Quality Act of 1967 created an advisory board to assist states in setting and enforcing air quality standards.

Consumerism. The Fair Packaging and Labeling Act of 1966 required that contents and net quantity be listed on package labels. The National Traffic Safety Act of 1966 led to the adoption of mandatory safety standards for all cars from the 1968 model year. The Highway Safety Act of 1966 established a national highway safety program and required states to adopt similar local programs. The Wholesome Meat Act of 1967 in effect extended federal meat inspection standards to all processing plants, including those engaged solely in intrastate commerce.

Vietnam War. President Johnson escalated the U.S. role in Vietnam (see "John F. Kennedy, 35th President," "Administration"). In August 1964 North Vietnamese torpedo boats reportedly attacked the U.S. destroyer *Maddox* and, possibly, the *Turner Joy*, in the Gulf of Tonkin. The United States promptly retaliated with air strikes against naval installations in North Vietnam. In a televised address, President Johnson condemned North Vietnam for "open aggression on the high seas," defended the U.S. reprisals as "limited and fitting," but reassured his audience, "We still seek no wider war." Within days of the attack Johnson requested and received broad, open-ended congressional authority to "take all necessary measures to repel any armed attack against the forces of the United States and to prevent further aggression." The Gulf of Tonkin Resolution passed both houses of Congress with just two dissenting votes—those of Democratic Senators Wayne Morse of Oregon and Ernest Gruening of Alaska. In the absence of a formal declaration of war, the resolution became the legal basis on which the United States conducted the Vietnam War. In February 1965 the United States launched Operation Rolling Thunder, air raids over North Vietnam. The next month President Johnson dispatched the first contingent of 3,500 Marines to Danang, marking the beginning of eight years of U.S. ground combat in South Vietnam, a war of attrition that was to spark violent antiwar protests in the United States and end in Communist victory. The number of U.S. troops in Vietnam reached 180,000 by the end of 1965, 400,000 at the end of 1966, 470,000 by late 1967, and peaked at 550,000 in 1968. Even while escalating the war, the Johnson administration continued to press for a negotiated settlement, but the North Vietnamese refused to talk until the United States unconditionally stopped bombing the North. In January 1968 the North Vietnamese and the Viet Cong launched the Tet offensive. Although the campaign failed to topple the regime in Saigon, its intensity and scope dealt a severe psychological blow to an administration that had been predicting imminent victory. In March 1968 President Johnson, handicapped by the "credibility gap" between promise and performance, announced simultaneously an unconditional halt to the bombing of northern North Vietnam and his decision not to seek reelection in order, he said, to devote his full energies to achieving peace. In response Hanoi agreed to negotiate. As the Paris Peace Talks became bogged down in such trivia as the shape of the conference table, however, the promise of a rapid resolution of the conflict quickly evaporated. In what was interpreted by some as an attempt to aid the presidential campaign of Democrat Hubert Humphrey, Johnson ceased all bombing in the North days before the 1968 election. Meanwhile, the antiwar movement continued to grow. In 1967 demonstrators marched on the Pentagon; an antiwar rally in New York attracted 125,000 protesters. Young men openly burned their draft cards in defiance. Democratic Senators George McGovern of South Dakota, Eugene McCarthy of Minnesota, J. William Fulbright of Arkansas, and Frank Church of Idaho emerged as prominent doves. And while Democrats met in Chicago to choose a successor to Lyndon Johnson in 1968, 5,000 demonstrators clashed with police in the streets. See also "Richard M. Nixon, 37th President," "Administration."

Dominican Republic. In 1965 U.S. Marines were dispatched to the Dominican Republic following a military coup. President Johnson explained that intervention was necessary to protect American lives there.

***Pueblo* Incident, 1968.** In January 1968 North Korean forces seized the *Pueblo*, a U.S. electronic-intelligence-gathering vessel under Commander Lloyd Bucher, in waters off North Korea. One American seaman was killed. The United States maintained that the spy ship was in international waters; North Korean officials charged that it had penetrated the nation's 12-mile limit. After months of negotiation, the United States in December gave in to North Korean demands for a formal apology in exchange for the safe return of the crew. As prearranged, however, the United States repudiated the apology immediately after issuing it. The 82 crewmen were promptly released.

Constitutional Amendments Ratified. Twenty-fourth Amendment, 1964. Outlawed the poll tax. Twenty-fifth Amendment, 1967. Provided for presidential appointment, subject to congressional approval, to fill a vacancy in the vice presidency and detailed procedures to be followed in the event a president is disabled.

SUPREME COURT APPOINTMENTS: (1)Abe Fortas (1910–1982), of Tennessee, served as associate justice 1965–1969. He wrote the opinion in *In re Gault* (1967), extending to juvenile court defendants the same constitutional rights guaranteed to adults in criminal courts. While on the bench he remained a close adviser to President Johnson on a wide range of issues. In June 1968 Johnson sought to elevate him to chief justice but withdrew the appointment in the face of overwhelming conservative opposition in the Senate. In 1969 it was disclosed that in 1966 Fortas accepted but later returned $20,000 from a foundation established by an industrialist then under investigation by the Securities and Exchange Commission for stock manipulation. Fortas denied any wrongdoing but, amid the ensuing controversy over the propriety of such conduct, resigned from the bench. (2) Thurgood Marshall (1908–1993), of Maryland, served as associate justice 1967–1991. He was the first black justice of the Supreme Court. As legal counsel for the NAACP he had argued for the desegregation of public schools before the Court in *Brown* v. *Board of Education of Topeka* (1954). Since 1965 he had been serving as the first black solicitor general. Justice Marshall generally voted with the liberal bloc. He wrote opinions that upheld the right of labor unions to picket peacefully at privately owned shopping centers (*Food Employers Local 590* v. *Logan Valley Plaza,* 1968) and nullified as unconstitutionally vague a city ordinance banning films that depict "sexual promiscuity" (*Interstate Circuit, Inc.* v. *City of Dallas,* 1968).

RETIREMENT: January 20, 1969–January 22, 1973. After attending the inaugural of his successor, Richard Nixon, Johnson retired to the LBJ Ranch in Texas. He held a three-part series of televised interviews, December 1969–May 1970, with broadcaster Walter Cronkite. He wrote his memoirs and tended the day-to-day operations of the ranch. In his last public appearance six weeks before his death, he addressed a civil rights symposium at the LBJ Library in Austin, Texas.

DEATH: January 22, 1973, about 4 P.M., enroute from the LBJ Ranch to San Antonio, Texas. Johnson, plagued by arteriosclerosis, had been hospitalized for chest pains in March 1970 and survived a second heart attack (the first was in 1955) in April 1972. He was stricken by a third attack while napping about 3:30 P.M. on January 22, 1973. He groped for the telephone and summoned a Secret Service agent. He died enroute to the hospital. His body lay in state at the Capitol Rotunda. Funeral services were conducted by Dr. George Davis at the National City Christian Church in Washington; hymns were sung by opera soprano Leontyne Price. He was buried at the Johnson family plot near Johnson City, Texas. Graveside services were conducted by the Reverend Billy Graham; Anita Bryant sang "The Battle Hymn of the Republic." In his last will and testament, Johnson left his portion of property that he held jointly with his wife, an estate estimated to be worth $20 million, in two equal trusts for his daughters.

JOHNSON PRAISED: "He doesn't have the best mind on the Democratic side of the Senate; he isn't the best orator; he isn't the best parliamentarian. But he's the best combination of all those qualities."[6]—Democratic Senator Richard Russell of Georgia, 1953

"Millions of Americans will always remember a bitter day in November, 1963, when so many of our people doubted the very future of this Republic. . . . Lyndon Johnson rose above the doubt and the fear to hold this Nation on course until we rediscovered our faith in ourselves."[7]—President Richard Nixon, 1973

"Lyndon Johnson's public life was filled with controversy because he was a man who cared, a man of action, and a man of decision. He will be remembered most kindly not by the high and mighty, but rather by those whom society had forgotten or ignored."[8]—Democratic Senator Hubert Humphrey of Minnesota, 1973

"As President, his brilliant leadership on the Civil Rights Act of 1964 and the Voting Rights Act of 1965 has earned him a place in the history of civil rights alongside Abraham Lincoln."[9]—Democratic Senator Edward Kennedy of Massachusetts, 1973

JOHNSON CRITICIZED: "He hasn't got the depth of mind nor the breadth of vision to carry great responsibility. . . . Johnson is superficial and opportunistic."[10]—President Dwight D. Eisenhower, 1960

"The inspiration and commitment of the Great Society have disappeared. In concrete terms, the President simply cannot think about implementing the Great Society at home while he is supervising bombing missions over North Vietnam. There is a kind of madness in the facile assumption that we can raise the many billions of dollars necessary to rebuild our schools and cities and public transport and eliminate the pollution of air and water while also spending tens of billions to finance an 'open-ended' war in Asia."[11]—Democratic Senator J. William Fulbright of Arkansas, 1966

"We've got a wild man in the White House, and we are going to have to treat him as such."[12]—Democratic Senator Eugene McCarthy of Minnesota

"He tells so many lies that he convinces himself after a while he's telling the truth. He just doesn't recognize truth or falsehood."[13]—Robert F. Kennedy

JOHNSON QUOTES: "The battle against Communism must be joined in Southeast Asia with strength and determination to achieve success there—or the United States, inevitably, must surrender the Pacific and take up our defenses on our own shores."[14]—memo to President Kennedy, 1961

"I do not want to be the President who built empires, or sought grandeur, or extended dominion. I want to be the President who educated young children to the wonders of their world . . . who helped to feed the hungry and to prepare them to be taxpayers instead of tax-eaters . . . who helped the poor to find their own way and who protected the right of every citizen to vote in every election . . . who helped to end hatred among his fellow men and who promoted love among the people of all races and all regions and all parties . . . who helped to end war among the brothers of this earth."[15]—1965

BOOK BY JOHNSON: *The Vantage Point: Perspectives of the Presidency, 1963–1969* (1971).

BOOKS ABOUT JOHNSON: Caro, Robert A. *The Years of Lyndon Johnson: The Path to Power.* New York: Knopf, 1982.

Evans, Rowland, and Novak, Robert. *Lyndon B. Johnson: The Exercise of Power.* New York: New American Library, 1966.

Goldman, Eric F. *The Tragedy of Lyndon Johnson.* New York: Knopf, 1969.

Harwood, Richard, and Johnson, Haynes. *Lyndon.* New York: Praeger, 1973.

Kearns, Doris. *Lyndon Johnson and the American Dream.* New York: Harper & Row, 1976.

Steinberg, Alfred. *Sam Johnson's Boy: A Close-Up of the President from Texas.* New York: Macmillan, 1968.

NOTES

1 Rowland Evans and Robert Novak, *Lyndon B. Johnson: The Exercise of Power*, New York: New American Library, 1966, p. 4.

2 Alfred Steinberg, *Sam Johnson's Boy: A Close-up of the President from Texas*, New York: Macmillan, 1968, p. 30.

3 Sam Houston Johnson, *My Brother Lyndon*, New York: Cowles, 1969, p. 29.

4 Theodore H. White, *The Making of the President 1964*, New York: Atheneum, 1965, p. 349.

5 Arthur Schlesinger, Jr., "A Look at the Power of Defeat," *Cleveland Plain Dealer*, June 22, 1975, sect. 1, p. 4.

6 Evans and Novak, p. 50.

7 *Memorial Tributes Delivered in Congress: Lyndon Baines Johnson*, Washington, D.C.: Government Printing Office, 1973, p. 1.

8 Ibid., pp. 164–165.

9 Ibid., p. 192.

10 Fred I. Greenstein, *The Hidden-Hand Presidency: Eisenhower as Leader*, New York: Basic Books, 1982, p. 28.

11 Steinberg, pp. 788–789.

12 Ibid., p. 787,

13 Arthur M. Schlesinger, Jr., *Robert Kennedy and His Times*, Boston: Houghton Mifflin, 1978, p. 692.

14 Sol Barzman, *Madmen & Geniuses: The Vice Presidents of the United States*, Chicago: Follett, 1974, p. 279.

15 Evans and Novak, p. 497.

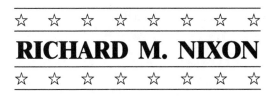

RICHARD M. NIXON

☆ ☆ ☆ ☆ ☆ ☆ ☆ ☆

37TH PRESIDENT

NAME: Richard Milhous Nixon. Milhous was his mother's maiden name.

PHYSICAL DESCRIPTION: Nixon was 5 feet 11½ inches tall and weighed 175 pounds. He had brown wavy hair, brown eyes guarded closely by thick eyebrows, a prominent ski nose, sagging jowls, and a slightly protruding jaw. From childhood he suffered from motion sickness and hay fever. Near the end of his term as president, he developed phlebitis in the leg. Nixon dressed conservatively, typically in dark suits.

PERSONALITY: The Nixon personality has become the subject of extensive psychology inquiry. In *Nixon vs. Nixon* (1977), Dr. David Abrahamsen, a psychoanalyst, described him as a man torn by inner conflict, lonely, hypersensitive, narcissistic, suspicious, and secretive. In *In Search of Nixon* (1972), Bruce Mazlish, a historian trained in psychoanalysis, concluded that the predominant characteristic of the "real" Nixon behind the public figure was a fear of passivity, of appearing soft, of being dependent on others. In *Richard Nixon: The Shaping of His Character* (1981), historian Fawn Brodie painstakingly sought to demonstrate that he was a compulsive liar and concluded: "Nixon lied to gain love, to shore up his grandiose fantasies, to bolster his ever-wavering sense of identity. He lied in attack, hoping to win. . . . And always he lied, and this most aggressively, to deny that he lied."

ANCESTORS: Nixon was of Scotch-Irish heritage on his father's side and German-English-Irish on his mother's side. Through his maternal grandfather, Franklin Milhous, Nixon descended from King Edward III (1312–1377) of England. His great[4]-grandfather James Nixon emigrated from Ireland and settled in New Castle County, Delaware, in 1753. His great[3]-grandfather George Nixon was among the troops to cross the Delaware with General George Washington during the American Revolution. His great-grandfather George Nixon III was killed at Gettysburg during the Civil War.

FATHER: Francis "Frank" Anthony Nixon (1878–1956), gas station owner, grocer. Born in Vinton County, Ohio, he dropped out of grade school to work as a farmhand and later as a house painter, telephone lineman, and at several other odd jobs. While he was working as a motorman on an open trolley in Columbus, Ohio, his toes were frostbitten and thereafter troubled him in cold weather. Seeking relief in a warmer climate, he settled in Southern California. In 1908 he met and married Hannah Milhous in Whittier, California. He converted to her faith, Quakerism. He tried growing lemons for a time at Yorba Linda, but failed and returned to Whittier, where he operated a gas station and Nixon's Market. He was described as outspoken, quarrelsome, and quick to anger. Politically, he started out as a Democrat. Then one day President William McKinley passed through his hometown in Ohio and complimented him on the fine horse he was riding. From then on he voted Republican, except in 1924, when the Teapot Dome scandal prompted him to support third-party candidate Robert M. LaFollette. In later years he lived on a farm at York, Pennsylvania, and named his cattle after movie stars. He died at 77 in La Habra, California, while his son was vice president.

MOTHER: Hannah Milhous Nixon (1885–1967). Born in Jennings County, Indiana, she was raised a devout Quaker there and in Whittier, California. She was a student at Whittier College before her marriage to Frank Nixon in 1908. She, too, was a Republican but angered her husband in bolting to support the reelection of Woodrow Wilson in 1916 because he had so far kept the United States out of World War I. Her ambition for son Richard was that he become a Quaker missionary. She died at 82 in Whittier, while Nixon was preparing to launch his second, and this time successful, bid for president. "My mother," Nixon once said of her, "is the gentlest, most considerate woman. She never turned a tramp away from the door."[1]

SIBLINGS: The second of five children, Nixon had four brothers—Harold S. Nixon, died of tuberculosis at 23; (Francis) Donald Nixon, businessman, who for a time operated a chain of drive-in restaurants that featured a triple-decker Nixonburger; Arthur B. Nixon, died of tuberculosis at age seven; Edward C. Nixon, telephone manager.

COLLATERAL RELATIVES: Nixon is a second cousin of author Jessamyn West, a seventh cousin twice removed of President William Howard Taft, and an eighth cousin once removed of President Herbert Hoover.

CHILDREN: Nixon has two daughters.

    Patricia 'Tricia' Nixon (1946–   ). A graduate of Finch College, she married Edward F. Cox in a White House Rose Garden ceremony in 1971. She and her husband settled in New York. She has rarely spoken publicly on matters of substance.

    Julie Nixon (1948–   ), author, editor. She married (Dwight) David Eisenhower II, grandson of President Eisenhower, in 1968. A graduate of Smith College, she wrote *Special People*, a collective profile of six famous persons she met during the Nixon administration and *Pat Nixon: The Untold Story* (1986), a biography of her mother. She and her husband lived in Southern California for a time and in 1980 settled in Chester County, Pennsylvania. A loyal and outspoken defender of her father's actions during the Watergate affair, she reportedly urged him not to resign.

BIRTH: Nixon was born the evening of January 9, 1913, in the small frame house his father had built in Yorba Linda, California. He weighed 11 pounds at birth.

Nurse Henrietta Shockney, who assisted Dr. Horace P. Wilson in the delivery, pronounced him, "roly-poly" and "good-natured."[2]

CHILDHOOD: Nixon grew up amid poverty in Yorba Linda, 1913–1922, and Whittier, California, from 1922. At age three he fell out of a buggy and gashed open his scalp on the wagon wheel. He nearly bled to death during the 25-mile trip to the nearest hospital. At four he again almost died, this time from pneumonia. He was a quiet, obedient child, dutifully helping out with chores and keeping out of mischief. Every morning before school he trucked produce in from Los Angeles, washed it, and mounted it for display in Nixon's Market. He also was especially good at mashing potatoes. At night he lay in bed listening to the trains pass by and dreamed of becoming a railroad engineer. When the Teapot Dome scandal engulfed the Harding administration, 10-year-old Richard looked up from the newspaper one day to tell his mother, "I would like to become a lawyer—an honest lawyer, who can't be bought by crooks."[3] The most traumatic experience of his childhood was the death of brother Arthur from tuberculosis. His mother later recalled that Richard set out to make up for the loss by becoming a success and making his parents proud of him. In a frantic though futile attempt to save her other tubercular son, Mrs. Nixon took Harold to a sanitarium in Arizona for two years. During summer vacations Richard joined them and found part-time work as a barker for the Wheel of Fortune at the Slippery Gulch Rodeo in Prescott.

EDUCATION: Nixon was a hardworking, serious, prompt student throughout his school years. He attended elementary schools in Yorba Linda and Whittier, California. He entered Fullerton High School and in his junior year transferred to Whittier High. At Fullerton he won the Constitutional Oratorical Contest and represented the West Coast in the National Oratorical Contest. "He had this ability," commented his Whittier High debate coach, "to kind of slide round an argument instead of meeting it head on, and he could take any side of a debate."[4] He graduated from Whittier High first in the class of 1930 and was presented the California Interscholastic Federation Gold Seal Award for scholarship and the Harvard Award for best all-around student. At Whittier College 1930–1934, he majored in history and was captain of the debating team. In extracurricular activities, he played second-string tackle on the football team, belonged to the drama and glee clubs, and helped found and was first president of the Orthogonians, also known as the Square Shooters, a club for students of modest background that competed with the elite Franklins. As a senior he was elected president of the student body on a platform promising "A Dance a Month." The college had barred dancing, but Nixon convinced school officials that campus mixers might keep students away from Los Angeles dance halls. He graduated from Whittier College second of 85 students in the class of 1934. He applied for and received a scholarship to Duke University Law School, 1934–1937. To help meet expenses he did research at the law library for 35¢ an hour under a program sponsored by the New Deal's National Youth Administration and shared a rundown off-campus farmhouse, without running water or electricity, with three other students. His sober demeanor and preoccupation with his studies earned him the nickname Gloomy Gus. He nevertheless was elected president of his graduating class. He was a member of the Order of Coif, the national scholastic fraternity for honor law students. He graduated from Duke Law School third of 25 students of the class of 1937. He was admitted to the California bar in November 1937.

RELIGION: Quaker. Nixon belonged to the Friends Meeting of East Whittier, California, but as president attended services of various denominations. He rejected the Quaker tenet of pacifism, enlisting in the navy during World War II. He also ignored the Quaker ban on swearing oaths on taking office as vice president and president. (Under the Constitution, he could have substituted the word *affirm* for *swear*, as Quaker Herbert Hoover had done in 1929.) Nixon cited religious and moral grounds in opposing abortion.

RECREATION: President Nixon played golf (low 90s), bowled (about 175 average), and swam occasionally. He especially like the seashore. He was from his navy days a sharp poker player. He reportedly won several thousand dollars in the service, money he used to help finance his first campaign for Congress. He enjoyed reading history. Among his favorite films was *Patton*. He smoked a pipe occasionally.

EARLY ROMANCE: Ola Florence Welch. The daughter of Whittier's police chief, Miss Welch met Nixon when the two played the title roles in *Aeneas and Dido*, a Whittier High stage production based on Virgil's *Aeneid*. They dated steadily for six years, from Nixon's senior year in high school to his first year at law school. Friends expected them to be married. She was described as pretty, vivacious, and popular, a contrast to Nixon's reserved, sober demeanor. She was attracted to Nixon most, she said, for his intelligence but also because she found him handsome, interesting, and worldly. Politically they were poles apart: she supported Franklin Roosevelt and the New Deal, Nixon opposed both. They argued often. Precisely when they broke up, however, remains unclear. She has said that they just drifted apart. In 1936 she married Gail Jobe, a college football teammate of Nixon.

MARRIAGE: Richard M. Nixon, 27, married Thelma Catherine "Pat" Ryan, 28, on June 21, 1940, at the Mission Inn in Riverside, California. Born on March 16, 1912, in Ely, Nevada, the daughter of William Ryan, a copper miner, and Kate Halberstadt Ryan, a native of Germany, she was nicknamed Pat because she was born on the eve of St. Patrick's Day, the day she celebrates as her birthday. During her infancy, the Ryans moved to Artesia, California, southeast of Los Angeles, where her father operated a truck farm. Pat was 13 when her mother died of cancer, 17 when her father died of silicosis, caused by his years in the mines. After graduating from Excelsior Union High School in 1929, she worked her way through one year at Fullerton Junior college as a bank clerk. In 1930 she hitched a ride to New York with an elderly couple and found work as a secretary, then as an X-ray technician at Seton Hospital. Two years later she used her savings to enroll as a merchandising major at the University of Southern California. She continued to work part time in a variety of jobs, including that of movie extra. In 1935 she was paid $25 for a walk-on and one-line speaking part (later cut from the final version) in *Becky Sharp*. She also appeared as an extra in *The Great Ziegfeld* (1936) and a few other films. Graduating cum laude from the University of Southern California in 1937, she taught typing and shorthand at Whittier High School and continued acting, as an amateur, at the Whittier Little Theater. Nixon, then a young lawyer, learned from friend Jack Drown that a pretty new teacher had come to town and was active in the local theater. Nixon auditioned and won a part opposite her in *The Dark Tower*. That same night he proposed. "I thought he was nuts or something," Mrs. Nixon later recalled. "I guess I just looked at him. I couldn't imagine anyone ever saying anything like that so suddenly."[5] She turned him down, but they dated for two years, and in the spring of 1940 she finally agreed to marry him. Although a Methodist, she consented to a Quaker service. Following a two-week honeymoon motor trip through Mexico, the couple settled into an apartment over a garage in Whittier. Mrs. Nixon continued teaching until World War II. While her husband was away in the navy, she worked in San Francisco as a stenographer and later as an economist for the Office of Price Administration. As First Lady, she promoted volunteerism but for the most part avoided publicity. Following Nixon's resignation she retired with him to San Clemente, and later to New York and New Jersey. She suffered mild strokes in 1976 and 1983, and died in 1993.

MILITARY SERVICE:

World War II. Nixon served in the navy from June 1942 to March 1946, rising from lieutenant junior grade to lieutenant commander. He underwent basic training at Quonset Point, Rhode Island, where he met William P. Rogers, later his secretary of state. He was an aide to the executive officer at the Naval Reserve air base at Ottumwa, Iowa, October 1942–May 1943, before shipping out to the Pacific. For his service as officer in charge of the South Pacific Combat Air Transport Command at Bougainville and Green Island, January–June 1944, he was cited for "meritorious and efficient performance." The citation, signed by Vice Admiral J. H. Newton, continued, "He established the efficient liasion which made possible the immediate supply by air of vital material and key personnel, and the prompt evacuation of battle casualties from these stations to rear areas." Rotated back to the United States in August 1944, he was assigned to Fleet Air Wing 8 at Alameda, California and from December 1944 to the Navy Department's Bureau of Aeronautics in Washington.

CAREER BEFORE THE PRESIDENCY: On admission to the California bar in November 1937, Nixon practiced law with the firm of Wingert and Bewley of Whittier and two years later rose to junior partner in Bewley, Knoop, and Nixon. In 1940 he joined with other Whittier businessmen in forming the Citra-Frost Company for the manufacture of frozen orange juice. With Nixon as company president, the business failed within two years. During January–June 1942, he worked in the tire-rationing section of the Office of Price Administration in Washington at a starting salary of $61 a week, later raised to $90. From this experience, he grew disillusioned about bureaucracy and the efficacy of government. He resigned to join the navy (see "Military Service").

U.S. Representative, 1947–1950. In 1946 Republican Nixon upset five-term incumbent Democrate Representative Jerry Voorhis, by a vote of 65,586–49,994, to represent California's Twelfth Congressional District, comprised of Whittier and certain other parts of Los Angeles County. He was reelected without opposition two years later. As a member of the House Education and Labor Committee, he helped draft the Taft-Hartley Act of 1947 (see "Harry S. Truman, 33rd President," "Aministration"). A member of the House Un-American Activities Committee, he cosponsored the Mundt-Nixon bill requiring the registration of Communist-front organizations and making it a crime to "aid the immediate or ultimate objectives of the world Communist movement." The bill passed the House but died in the Senate. Its basic provisions were incorporated in the McCarran Internal Security Act of 1950. Nixon emerged a national figure as chairman of the House Un-American Activities Special Subcommittee created to investigate changes by *Time* editor Whittaker Chambers, himself a former Communist party courier, that certain U.S. Government officials had operated as Communist spies in the 1930s. Among those fingered by Chambers was Alger Hiss, a former State Department official, who denied the charge in testimony before the committee. Nixon relentlessly grilled Hiss about his activities but failed to shake his assertion of innocence. President Truman dismissed the episode as a "red herring," but when Chambers produced incriminating evidence, including a dramatic display of microfilmed State Department documents stashed in a hollowed-out pumpkin on Chambers's farm, Hiss was indicted and in 1950 convicted of perjury. (The statute of limitations prevented prosecution for espionage.) "The Hiss case," Nixon later wrote, "for the first time, forcibly demonstrated to the American people that domestic Communism was a real and present danger to the security of the nation."[6] In other matters, Representative Nixon voted for the Marshall Plan, aid to Greece and Turkey, reciprocal trade agreements, a peacetime military draft, lower taxes, and an end to the discriminatory poll tax.

U.S. Senator, 1951–1953. In 1950 Nixon defeated Democratic Representative Helen Gahagan Douglas for the seat of retiring California senator Sheridan Downey by a margin of 680,000 votes. Nixon had flooded the state with 500,000 "pink sheets" that sought to link Mrs. Douglas's voting record in the House with the goals of the Communist party. Nixon himself referred to her as the Pink Lady. Such tactics prompted the *Independent Review*, a small Southern California newspaper, to dub him Tricky Dick, an epithet that has dogged him ever since. Nixon, at 38 the youngest senator to take his seat in 1951, served on the Government Operations Committee and its Permanent Investigations Subcommittee chaired by Republican Senator Joseph McCarthy of Wisconsin. An outspoken critic of the Truman administration, Nixon condemned its restraint in conducting the Korean War and the president's decision to fire General Douglas MacArthur. He continued to warn of the dangers of Communist influence in the government.

Vice President 1953–1961. Republican presidential nominee Dwight D. Eisenhower chose Nixon for his running mate in 1952 because of Nixon's conservative reputation as an anti-Communist crusader and because as a representative of a large western state he balanced the ticket geographically. During the campaign the *New York Post* broke the story, under the headline "SECRET NIXON FUND," that while a senator he had maintained an $18,000 slush fund, provided by private contributors, from which he drew to defray out-of-pocket expenses. Eisenhower, under intense pressure to dump Nixon, gave him time to answer the charges but made it clear that to remain on the ticket he must come through the ordeal "clean as a hound's tooth." On September 23, Nixon delivered an emotional 30-minute television address, the so-called Checkers speech, in which he conceded the existence of the fund but insisted that none of it went for his personal use, but only to "pay for political expenses that I did not think should be charged to the taxpayers of the United States." To assure the public that he had not enriched himself in office, he went on to list his assets—1950 Oldsmobile, $3,000 equity in California home, $20,000 equity in Washington home, $4,000 in life insurance, no stocks or bonds—and liabilities— $10,000 mortgage on California home, $20,000 mortgage on Washington home, $4,500 bank note, $3,500 debt to his parents, $500 due on life insurance. Near the end of the speech, he admitted accepting one gift—a cocker spaniel his six-year-old daughter Tricia had named Checkers. "I just want to say this, right now," he said in mock seriousness, "that regardless of what they say about it, we are going to keep it." Nixon left the television studio that night convinced that his performance had been a flop, that he probably would be forced from the ticket. But viewers inundated the Republican National Committee with letters of support. The next day Eisenhower beamed at Nixon, "You're my boy."[7] Vice President Nixon presided over cabinet meetings when Eisenhower was away from the capital and during his convalescence from a heart attack in 1955. He traveled extensively abroad. During a tour of South America in 1958, he was spat on in Lima, and a mob in Caracas stoned and rocked his car. During a trip to the Soviet Union in 1959, Nixon engaged in the celebrated Kitchen Debate with Soviet chairman Nikita Khrushchev. At the "typical American house" display at the U.S. exhibition in Moscow, the two leaders exchanged heated remarks about the relative merits of capitalist and communist societies.

Republican Presidential Nomination, 1960. Nixon received the Republican presidential nomination in 1960 but was defeated narrowly by Senator John F. Kennedy in the general election. (See under "John F. Kennedy, 35th President" for the election of 1960)

Defeated for Governor of California, 1962. Having won the gubernatorial primary over state assembly leader Joseph Shell in June 1962, Nixon was defeated, 52–47 percent in the general election by incumbent Democratic governor Edmund G. "Pat" Brown. In a celebrated postelection press conference, Nixon bitterly lashed out at reporters, who, he said, "are so delighted that I have lost." He added: "For 16 years, ever since the Hiss case, you've had a lot of —a lot of fun—that you've had an opportunity to attack me and I think I've given as good as I've taken. . . . But as I leave you I want you to know—just think how much you're going to be missing. You won't have Nixon to kick around anymore, because, gentlemen, this is my last press conference."

During 1963–1968 Nixon practiced law in New York. In 1964 he campaigned for Barry Goldwater for president.

REPUBLICAN PRESIDENTIAL NOMINATION, 1968: As Republicans gathered in Miami Beach in August 1968, Nixon was regarded as the front-runner with broad support among moderate conservatives in the party. Other major contenders were Governor Nelson Rockefeller of New York, popular among moderates, and Governor Ronald Reagan of California, strong among conservatives in the South and West. Senator Strom Thurmond of South Carolina was instrumental in wooing southern delegates from Reagan to Nixon. Governor Spiro T. Agnew of Maryland placed Nixon's name in nomination. With 667 votes needed to win, Nixon was nominated on the first ballot with 692 votes to 277 for Rockefeller, 182 for Reagan, and the rest scattered. Governor Agnew was nominated for vice president. In his acceptance speech Nixon deplored the state of the country: "When the strongest nation in the world can be tied down for four years in a war in Vietnam with no end in sight, when the richest nation in the world can't manage its own economy, when the nation with the greatest tradition of the rule of law is plagued by unprecedented racial violence, when the President of the United States cannot travel abroad or to any major city at home, then it's time for new leadership for the United States of America." The Republican platform was deliberately vague on major issues so as to avoid an open split between conservatives and moderates. It was a platform, commented Senator Everett Dirksen of Illinois, any Republican could run on. It promised peace in Vietnam without specifying how it was to be achieved but excluded "peace at any price" or "a camoflaged surrender of U.S. or Allied interests." It pledged a solution to the "crisis of the cities" but offered no specifics, except to insist that private enterprise be given a major role. It also vowed to restore "law and order" and allocate funds freed up by the end of the Vietnam War to strengthen the national defense, reduce taxes, and meet domestic needs.

OPPONENTS: Hubert H. Humphrey (1911–1978) of Minnesota; Democrat. He was vice president 1965–1969 under President Lyndon B. Johnson. The Democratic party was bitterly divided over the Vietnam War. Senator Eugene McCarthy of Minnesota, an early opponent of the war, nearly upset President Johnson in the New Hampshire primary. With Johnson now clearly vulnerable, Senator Robert F. Kennedy of New York, also a peace candidate, entered the race. The focus of the election shifted abruptly on March 31, when President Johnson declared that he would not seek reelection, thus paving the way for Vice President Humphrey to announce his candidacy. Humphrey's biggest handicap was his association with the administration's conduct of the war. But following the assassination of Robert Kennedy in June, he emerged the clear front-runner. At a raucous convention in Chicago in August, Humphrey was nominated on the first ballot with 1,760¼ votes (1,312 were needed) to 601 for McCarthy, and 146½ for Senator George McGovern of South Dakota, a last-minute candidate who inherited much of Kennedy's support. Senator Edmund Muskie of Maine was nominated for vice president. In a bid to unite the party's opposing factions behind him, Humphrey declared in accepting the nomination, "Let those who believe our cause in Vietnam has been right—and those who believe it has been wrong—agree here and now, neither vindication or repudiation will bring peace or be worthy of our country." Meanwhile, outside Convention Hall, 5,000 antiwar protestors clashed with police. An independent commission appointed to investigate the incident blamed Chicago police for an excessive use of force in maintaining order. Amid heated debate, the Democratic platform committee rejected a peace plank 65–35 and instead adopted a proadministration position that linked a bombing halt to concessions from Hanoi and withdrawal of U.S. forces to South Vietnam's ability to take up the slack. After his defeat by Nixon, Humphrey was elected to the Senate from Minnesota 1971–1978 and ran unsuccessfully for the Democratic presidential nomination in 1972.

George Wallace (1919–1998), of Alabama; American Independent. Born in Clio, Alabama, Wallace graduated from the University of Alabama law school in 1942, served as a flight engineer in the Pacific during World War II, and became active in state Democratic party affairs in the late 1940s. He was elected to the state legislature 1947–1953, as state judge 1953–1958, and governor of Alabama 1963–1966. He gained national attention in 1963, when he stood at the door of the University of Alabama to prevent the enrollment of blacks there. Although he gave way to National Guardsmen and admitted the students, his dramatic stand made him a hero in much of the white South. Running on a platform of victory in Vietnam, law and order at home, and against busing to achieve racial balance, he in 1968 mounted a third-party bid for president, under the banner of the American Independent Party, and got on the ballot in all 50 states. He chose former Air Force General Curtis LeMay of California as his running mate. After his defeat by Nixon, Wallace again was elected governor of Alabama 1971–1979. He ran for president in 1972 but was paralyzed by a gunshot wound while campaigning in Maryland. In 1982 he once again was elected governor.

CAMPAIGN AND THE ISSUES, 1968: Nixon, far ahead in early polls, carefully avoided offering specific solutions to the main issues. Said to have a "secret plan" to end the war in Vietnam, he promised an honorable peace settlement. He called for restoration of law and order while upholding the rights of minorities and dissidents, a crackdown on narcotics traffic, an end to the draft and creation of a volunteer army, and a reduction in taxes and inflation. Humphrey, beset by lack of funds, deep divisions within the party, and the lingering specter of violence in the streets of Chicago, set out to put some distance between himself and the unpopular Johnson administration on the war issue. "As president," he announced, "I would be willing to stop the bombing of North Vietnam as an acceptable risk for peace."[8] He repeated his long-standing commitment to civil rights and enjoyed the support of organized labor. Wallace, building from a strong base in the Deep South, pitched his law and order, antibusing campaign to blue-collar voters. Aided by a last-minute endorsement from Senator McCarthy and President Johnson's October 31 order to halt the bombing of North Vietnam, Humphrey rapidly closed the gap in the polls during the final days but failed to overcome Nixon's lead.

ELECTION AS PRESIDENT, FIRST TERM, NOVEMBER 5, 1968:

    Popular Vote: Nixon (Republican), 31,785,480 (43.4%); Humphrey (Democrat), 31,275,166 (42.7%); Wallace (American Independent), 9,906,473 (13.5%).

    Electoral Vote. Nixon, 301; Humphrey, 191; Wallace, 46.

    States Carried: Nixon won the majority of the electoral votes in 32 states—Alaska, Arizona, California, Colorado, Delaware, Florida, Idaho, Illinois, Indiana, Iowa, Kansas, Kentucky, Missouri, Montana, Nebraska, Nevada, New Hampshire, New Jersey, New Mexico, North Carolina, North Dakota, Ohio, Oklahoma, Oregon, South Carolina, South Dakota, Tennessee, Utah, Vermont, Virginia, Wisconsin, and Wyoming. Humphrey won the electoral votes of the District of Columbia and 13 states—Connecticut, Hawaii, Maine, Maryland, Massachusetts, Michigan, Minnesota, New York, Pennsylvania, Rhode Island, Texas, Washington, and West Virginia. Wallace won the majority of electoral votes in 5 states—Alabama, Arkansas, Georgia, Louisiana, and Mississippi.

REPUBLICAN NOMINATION FOR REELECTION AS PRESIDENT, 1972: Nixon faced only token opposition to his renomination—on the left from Representative Paul McCloskey of California and on the right from Representative John Ashbrook of Ohio. At the Republican national convention in Miami Beach in August 1972, Nixon's renomination speech was delivered by Governor Nelson Rockefeller of New York. He was renominated on the first ballot with 1,347 votes to 1 for McCloskey. Vice President Spiro T. Agnew also was renominated. In his acceptance speech Nixon reaffirmed his faith in America. "It has become fashionable in recent years to point up what is wrong with our . . . American system," he declared in a not-so-subtle slap at his opponent, Democrat George McGovern. "The critics contend it is so unfair, so corrupt, so unjust that we should tear it down and substitute something else in its place. I totally disagree, I believe in the American system." The Republican platform condemned the McGovernites as "a radical clique which scorns our nation's past and would blight her future" and favored creation of a volunteer army, arms control, and full employment while opposing busing to achieve racial balance, national health insurance, and complete withdrawal of U.S. forces from Vietnam without the return of the prisoners of war.

OPPONENT: George S. McGovern (1922–   ) of South Dakota; Democrat. Born in Avon, South Dakota, and raised there and in Mitchell, South Dakota, McGovern, a decorated combat pilot during World War II, graduated from Dakota Wesleyan University in 1945 and took his master's degree in 1949 and doctorate in 1953 in history from Northwestern University. After teaching history and political science at Dakota Wesleyan 1949–1953, he became active in Democratic party affairs in South Dakota. He served in the U.S. House 1957–1961, as director of President Kennedy's Food for Peace Program 1961–1962, and in the U.S. Senate 1963–1981. He was an early and outspoken opponent of the Vietnam War. In 1968 he waged a last-minute bid for the Democratic presidential nomination following the assassination of Robert Kennedy. In January 1971 he declared his candidacy for the 1972 Democratic presidential nomination. Although he began as a dark horse, he emerged a serious contender after placing a strong second behind front-runner Senator Edmund Muskie of Maine in the New Hampshire primary. Muskie's effort petered out soon thereafter. Governor George Wallace of Alabama, who rolled up impressive victories in southern primaries as well as in Maryland and Michigan, was shot by Arthur Bremer while campaigning at the Laurel (Maryland) Shopping Center and was left paralyzed below the waist. Senator Hubert Humphrey of Minnesota, the candidate of organized labor, emerged the most serious obstacle to McGovern's nomination but withdrew following his defeat in the California primary. The Democratic national convention in Miami Beach in July was notable for the large representation of women and minorities, the result of quotas adopted by the party following the debacle in Chicago four years before. With 1,509 votes needed to win, McGovern was nominated on the first ballot with 1,715 votes to 534 for Senator Henry Jackson of Washington, heir to Humphrey's labor support, 386 for Wallace, 152 for Representative Shirley Chisholm of New York, 78 for Governor Terry Sanford of North Carolina, and the rest scattered. McGovern's first three choices for vice president—Senator Edward M. Kennedy of Massachusetts, Senator Abraham Ribicoff of Connecticut, and Governor Reubin Askew of Florida—all declined. He then turned to Senator Thomas F. Eagleton of Missouri, who was nominated. Soon after the convention, however, it was disclosed that Eagleton had undergone electric shock therapy for mental depression. McGovern at first stood behind his running mate "1,000 percent." But under intense pressure from party leaders he dumped him from the ticket. He next chose, and the Democratic National Committee nominated, former Peace Corps director and Kennedy brother-in-law R. Sargent Shriver of Maryland. The Democratic platform called for "immediate total withdrawal of all Americans from Southeast Asia," reduced defense spending, congressional participation in decisions involving war and peace, full employment, tax reform, desegregation, including busing to achieve racial balance, an end to capital punishment, and a ban on handguns. After his defeat by Nixon, McGovern resumed his duties in the Senate; in 1980 he was defeated for reelection. He again ran for president in 1984.

CAMPAIGN AND THE ISSUES, 1972: McGovern never was able to shake his image as a radical leftist. His proposal that the government give everyone $1,000, offered during the primaries and in the face of harsh criticism from fellow Democrats largely abandoned, and his call for a minimum income floor and public-service jobs for the needy were ridiculed by Republicans as unsound. His cry for immediate withdrawal from Vietnam was derided as a "cut-and-run" strategy that would undermine U.S. prestige abroad and destroy chances for retrieving the prisoners of war. He also campaigned for tax reform and sharp cuts in defense spending. The AFL-CIO, long an important source of campaign strength for Democrats, this time declined to endorse either candidate for president. The Eagleton affair consumed valuable time at the beginning of the campaign and squandered McGovern's most precious asset, his reputation for refusing to compromise for political advantage, as he at first supported then dumped his beleaguered running mate. Many dismissed as campaign rhetoric McGovern's charge that the administration was deceiving the American public when, less than two weeks before the election, national security adviser Henry Kissinger announced that peace was "at hand" in Indochina. And although the most important facts of Watergate had already been disclosed, few listened when McGovern described the Nixon administration as "the most corrupt" in U.S. history and placed the blame where most eventually would agree it belonged, on the president himself. One measure of how low McGovern's credibility had sunk was a Time/Yankelovich Poll revealing that two thirds of those interviewed believed Nixon was more "open and trustworthy" than the Democratic candidate. For his part, President Nixon, far ahead in the polls throughout the campaign, confined his activity to a few carefully chosen personal appearances and television addresses. He relied on "surrogate" speakers, cabinet members and others, and Vice President Agnew to bear the brunt of the campaign. This was the first presidential election in which 18–20-year-olds were allowed to vote. Their participation, at first expected to be a boon to McGovern, had no effect on the outcome.

ELECTION AS PRESIDENT, SECOND TERM, NOVEMBER 7, 1972:
    Popular Vote: Nixon (Republican), 47,165,234 (61%); McGovern (Democrat), 29,168,110 (38%).
    Electoral Vote. Nixon, 520; McGovern, 17. John Hospers of California, nominee of the Libertarian party, received 1 electoral vote from Virginia.
    States Carried: Nixon won the majority of electoral votes in 49 states—Alabama, Alaska, Arizona, Arkansas, California, Colorado, Connecticut, Delaware, Florida, Georgia, Hawaii, Idaho, Illinois, Indiana, Iowa, Kansas, Kentucky, Louisiana, Maine, Maryland, Michigan, Minnesota, Mississippi, Missouri, Montana, Nebraska, Nevada, New Hampshire, New Jersey, New Mexico, New York, North Carolina, North Dakota, Ohio, Oklahoma, Oregon, Pennsylvania, Rhode Island, South Carolina, South Dakota, Tennessee, Texas, Utah, Vermont, Virginia, Washington, West Virginia, Wisconsin, and Wyoming. McGovern won the electoral votes of the District of Columbia and 1 state—Massachusetts.

INAUGURAL ADDRESS (FIRST): January 20, 1969. ". . . In these difficult years, America has suffered from a fever of words; from inflated rhetoric that promises more than it can deliver; from angry rhetoric that fans discontents into hatreds; from bombastic rhetoric that postures instead of persuading.
    "We cannot learn from one another until we stop shouting at each other—until we speak quietly enough so that our words can be heard as well as our voices. . . ."

INAUGURAL ADDRESS (SECOND): January 20, 1973. ". . . At every turn, we have been beset by those who find everything wrong with America and little that is right. But I am confident that this will not be the judgment of history on these remarkable times in which we are privileged to live.

"America's record in this century has been unparalleled in the world's history for its responsibility, for its generosity, for its creativity and for its progress.

"Let us be proud that our system has produced and provided more freedom and more abundance, more widely shared, than any other in the history of man.

"Let us be proud that in each of the four wars in which we have been engaged in this century, including the one we are now bringing to an end, we have fought not for selfish advantage, but to help others resist aggression. . . ."

VICE PRESIDENT: Spiro T. Agnew (1918–1996), of Maryland, served 1969–1973. Born in Baltimore, the son of Theofrastos Spiro Anagnostopoulis, a Greek immigrant who changed his name to Agnew, he dropped out as a chemistry major from Johns Hopkins University to work as an insurance claims adjuster while attending night classes at the University of Baltimore Law School. Interrupting his studies to serve as an officer in World War II, he graduated in 1947 and was admitted to the bar that year. He was elected Baltimore County executive 1963–1967 and governor of Maryland 1967–1969. Although regarded as a moderate on the race issue when he became governor, he won attention for his rigid law-and-order stand during the Baltimore riots that followed the assassination of Martin Luther King, Jr. Nixon chose him as his running mate for his acceptibility in the South and his appeal in the border states. Vice President Agnew emerged an outspoken defender of the administration and critic of the news media, dissidents, and liberals. His blunt style and affinity for alliteration brought forth several neologisms. He blasted newsmen as "nattering nabobs of negativism," protesting students and intellectuals as "an effete corps of impudent snobs." By 1972, however, Agnew was tiring of his controversial role and expressed pleasure at campaigning for reelection on a loftier plane. His contentment was short-lived. In August 1973 federal prosecutors disclosed that Agnew was the target of an investigation involving a kickback scheme allegedly conducted while he was county executive and governor. It was further charged that he continued to accept bribes while he was vice president. After weeks of complicated legal maneuvering, Agnew struck a deal with prosecutors: To avoid criminal prosecution, he resigned from office and pleaded no contest to one charge of income tax evasion; the prosecution published a 40-page document spelling out in detail Agnew's misdeeds over a 10-year period. Agnew was fined $10,000 and placed on three years' probation. Still, he continued to maintain his innocence. In *Go Quietly . . . Or Else* (1980), he claimed that he resigned not to avoid prosecution but because he believed that White House Chief of Staff Alexander Haig might have him murdered if he stayed on. Disbarred following his resignation, Agnew became an international business consultant. In 1983, in compliance with a court order, Agnew paid $268,000 to the state of Maryland as reimbursement and penalty for his misdeeds as governor.

Gerald R. Ford (1913–   ), of Michigan, served 1973–1974. He was the first vice president appointed under the provision of the Twenty-fifth Amendment. He succeeded to the presidency on the resignation of Richard Nixon (see "Gerald R. Ford, 38th President").

CABINET:

Secretary of State. (1) William P. Rogers (1913–2001), of Maryland, served 1969–1973. He was attorney general 1957–1961 under President Eisenhower. He accompanied President Nixon on his historic trip to China in 1972. He urged international cooperation to combat terrorism. He was overshadowed by National Security Adviser Henry Kissinger. (2) Henry Kissinger (1923–   ), of the District of Columbia, served 1973–1977. As national security adviser he had arranged for President Nixon's 1972 trips to China and the Soviet Union and negotiated with North Vietnamese officials an end to the war in Indochina. For the latter effort he was awarded, with North Vietnamese representative Le Duc Tho, the 1973 Nobel Peace Prize. He worked toward détente with the Soviet Union. In 1974 his widely heralded shuttle diplomacy eased tensions in the Middle East and led to resumption of U.S. diplomatic relations with Egypt and Syria. His memoirs of the Nixon term, *White House Years* (1979) and *Years of Upheaval* (1982), were well received. He stayed on in the Ford administration.

Secretary of the Treasury. (1) David M. Kennedy (1905–1996), of Illinois, served 1969–1971. He drew criticism for stating that a 4 percent unemployment rate was acceptable. (2) John B. Connally (1917–1993), of Texas, served 1971–1972. A Democrat and protégé of former president Johnson, he negotiated a devaluation of the dollar at the Group of Ten (finance ministers) meeting in 1971. He also served as chairman of the Cost of Living Council supervising wage and price controls. He resigned to head Democrats for Nixon during the 1972 campaign and eventually became a Republican. He later was tried and acquitted of charges of bribery, perjury, and conspiracy to obstruct justice in connection with the administration's decision to increase federal milk price supports in 1971. (3) George P. Shultz (1920–   ), of Illinois, served 1972–1974. He had served as labor secretary and was budget director at the time of his appointment. While Treasury secretary, he also served as chairman of the newly created President's Council on Economic Policy. He later served as secretary of state in the Reagan administration. (4) William E. Simon (1927–2000), of New Jersey, served 1974–1977. Transferred from federal energy administrator, he stayed on in the Ford administration.

Secretary of Defense. (1) Melvin R. Laird (1922–   ), of Wisconsin, served 1969–1973. He supervised the Vietnamization program, took steps to create an all-volunteer army, and strengthened civilian control of the intelligence community. He supported development of the antiballistic missile system but also encouraged progress in the strategic arms limitations talks. (2) Elliot L. Richardson (1920–1999), of Massachusetts, served January–May 1973. Transferred from secretary of health, education and welfare, he resigned to become attorney general. (3) James R. Schlesinger (1929–   ), of Virginia, served 1973–1974. Transferred from director of the Central Intelligence Agency, he opposed amnesty for draft dodgers and pressed for development of more sophisticated nuclear weapon systems. He stayed on in the Ford administration and later served as energy secretary under President Carter.

Attorney General. (1) John N. Mitchell (1913–1988), of New York, served 1969–1972. He spoke out for law and order, lending support to local law enforcement agencies and stepping up federal efforts against drug trafficking. He generally opposed busing to achieve racial balance. In 1971 he tried unsuccessfully to exercise prior restraint in preventing the *New York Times* and other newspapers from publishing excerpts from the so-called Pentagon Papers, a classified 47-volume government study of the origins of U.S. involvement in the Vietnam War. He resigned to become director of the Committee to Reelect the President (CREEP). He was convicted and served 19 months in prison for conspiracy, obstruction of justice, and perjury in connection with the Watergate scandal. (2) Richard G. Kleindienst (1923–2000), of Arizona, served 1972–1973. Promoted from deputy attorney general, he declared that the original, limited, grand jury probe of the Watergate break-in was the most extensive since the assassination of President Kennedy. He resigned amid the Watergate scandal and pleaded guilty to a misdemeanor of testifying falsely before a Senate panel investigating the administration's relationship with International Telephone and Telegraph. He received a 30-day suspended sentence. (3) Elliot L. Richardson served May–October 1973. Transferred from defense secretary, he appointed Archibald Cox as special Watergate prosecutor. He resigned during the so-called Saturday night massacre rather than obey Nixon's order to fire Cox for seeking access to tape recordings of presidential conversations. (4) William B. Saxbe (1916–   ), of Ohio, served 1974–1975. He stayed on in the Ford administration.

Postmaster General. Winton Blount (1921–2002), of Alabama, served 1969–1971. He negotiated settlement of the 1970 postal strike. He supervised conversion of the department into the U.S. Postal Service, an independent government agency, and was appointed its first director. He thus was the last cabinet-level postmaster general.

Secretary of the Interior. (1) Walter J. Hickel (1919–   ), of Alaska, served 1969–1970. Although environmentalists had opposed his appointment, he proved a strong advocate of conservation. He held oil companies accountable for oil spills, blocked construction of an airport in the Florida Everglades, and took steps to curb water pollution. He was dismissed for criticizing the administration's failure to address the concerns of young people. (2) Rogers C. B. Morton (1914–1979), of Maryland, served 1971–1975. He approved construction of the Alaska oil pipeline. He stayed on in the Ford administration.

Secretary of Agriculture. (1) Clifford M. Hardin (1915–   ), of Nebraska, served 1969–1971. He established the Food and Nutrition Service to administer food programs for the poor and the Office of Intergovernmental Affairs to coordinate efforts with state and local officials. He extended the food stamp program and began providing free stamps to those least able to afford them. (2) Earl L. Butz (1909–   ), of Indiana, served 1971–1976. He had served as assistant secretary for marketing and foreign agriculture under President Eisenhower. He stayed on in the Ford administration.

Secretary of Commerce. (1) Maurice H. Stans (1908–1998), of New York, served 1969–1972. He had served as budget director under President Eisenhower. He resigned as commerce secretary to serve as finance chairman of the Committee of Reelect the President. He pleaded guilty to five misdemeanor violations of campaign law and was fined $5,000. (2) Peter G. Peterson (1926–   ), of Illinois, served 1972–1973. He had served as presidential assistant for international economic affairs and executive director of the Council on International Economic Policy under Nixon. (3) Frederick B. Dent (1922–   ), of South Carolina, served 1973–1975. he stayed on in the Ford administration.

Secretary of Labor. (1) George P. Shultz served 1969–1970. He resigned to become budget director and was later secretary of the Treasury. (2) James D. Hodgson (1915–   ), of California, served 1970–1973. He was promoted from undersecretary. (3) Peter J. Brennan (1918–1996), of New York, served 1973–1975. As head of New York City's building and construction union, he had earned the nickname Mr. Hardhat for organizing his men in counterdemonstrations against antiwar protestors and in support of President Nixon's Vietnam policy. He stayed on in the Ford administration.

Secretary of Health, Education and Welfare. (1) Robert H. Finch (1925–), of California, served 1969–1970. A longtime associate of Richard Nixon, he resigned as secretary to become counselor to the president. (2) Elliot L. Richardson served 1970–1973. Transferred from undersecretary of state, he resigned to become defense secretary. (3) Caspar W. Weinberger (1917–), of California, served 1973–1975. Transferred from budget director, where he had earned the nickname of Cap the Knife for his sharp eye for waste, he served on the president's Cancer Advisory Panel, which proposed a crash research program to find a cure for the disease. He stayed on in the Ford administration.

Secretary of Housing and Urban Development. (1) George Romney (1907–1995), of Michigan, served 1969–1973. He had been governor of Michigan and a candidate for the Republican presidential nomination in 1968 prior to his appointment. (2) James T. Lynn (1927–), of Ohio, served 1973–1975. He stayed on in the Ford administration.

Secretary of Transportation. (1) John A. Volpe (1908–1994), of Massachusetts, served 1969–1973. To combat air piracy, he promoted development of airport security systems and established the sky marshal force. (2) Claude S. Brinegar (1926–), of California, served 1973–1975. He stayed on in the Ford administration.

ADMINISTRATION: January 20, 1969–August 9, 1974.

Vietnam War. President Nixon both steadily reduced U.S. involvement in the war and expanded the fighting beyond the borders of Vietnam into Cambodia and Laos—a policy critics dubbed "widening down" the war. Under the Vietnamization program, South Vietnamese forces were trained and equipped to take over for U.S. troops as they were withdrawn. From a 543,000-man contingent in 1969, U.S. forces in Vietnam were cut to 340,000 in 1970, 177,000 in 1971, and 25,000 in 1972. To coincide with Vietnamization, the president enunciated the Nixon Doctrine, which called for reduced presence of U.S. forces in Asia generally. On April 30, 1970, 70,000 U.S. and South Vietnamese forces invaded Cambodia to strike enemy sanctuaries along the border and disrupt supply lines. A main objective, to capture the Communist headquarters in Cambodia, failed. President Nixon justified the raid as necessary to protect the dwindling ranks of U.S. forces in Vietnam and to ensure the success of the Vietnamization program. But it drew a firestorm of protest in the United States, most dramatically on the campus of Kent State University, where Ohio National Guardsmen fired into a crowd of 2,000 demonstrators, killing four and wounding nine. To counter the growing wave of violent protests on campuses and in cities across the country, President Nixon considered but apparently never carried out the hiring of Teamster union "thugs" to "go in and knock their heads off," according to a transcript of a White House tape recording obtained by the *New York Times* in 1981. Meanwhile, doves in Congress stepped up pressure to end the war. In 1970 the Senate repealed the Gulf of Tonkin Resolution, which had been cited as tantamount to a congressional declaration of war. Peace forces failed to muster sufficient strength to enact the McGovern-Hatfield measure, however, which would have mandated withdrawal of all U.S. forces from Vietnam. Adding to the growing American distaste for the war was the disclosure of the My Lai massacre of March 1968, in which unarmed South Vietnamese civilians were slaughtered by U.S. troops.

In February 1971 the United States provided air and artillery support for a

South Vietnamese invasion of Laos, but Communist forces quickly threw them back. In March 1972 the North Vietnamese launched an offensive across the demilitarized zone into the South. President Nixon responded by resuming massive bombing of the North and mining Haiphong Harbor. In August 1972 the last U.S. ground combat troops were withdrawn, leaving behind only military support personnel. The main obstacle to complete U.S. withdrawal was the U.S. prisoners of war held in North Vietnam. This issue was finally resolved in protracted negotiations between U.S. National Security Adviser Henry Kissinger and North Vietnamese representative Le Duc Tho. The peace agreement, signed in Paris in January 1973, provided for the simultaneous withdrawal of all U.S. forces and the release of the prisoners, a cease fire in place, continued presence of U.S. civilian advisers in South Vietnam, and U.S. aid for the reconstruction of bomb-torn North Vietnam (this last provision never was carried out). Although the agreement enabled the United States to end its involvement and retrieve its prisoners, fighting between North and South quickly resumed eventually ending in Communist victory (see "Gerald R. Ford, 38th President," "Administration").

The Vietnam War cost the U.S. 58,000 dead, 304,000 wounded, and $110 billion.

New China Policy. In a dramatic departure in U.S. foreign policy, President Nixon set aside his long-standing hostility to Communist China to support Peking's admission to the United Nations in October 1971, while trying in vain to persuade the world body to permit Taiwan to retain its seat, too. In February 1972 he undertook what he called "a journey for peace," a widely publicized visit to China where he was received warmly by Chairman Mao Tse-tung and Premier Chou En-Lai. In a joint communiqué following the talks, the two governments agreed to broaden scientific, cultural, and trade contacts. Nixon was the first U.S. president to visit China and the first to visit a nation with which the United States had no formal diplomatic relations.

Seabed Treaty, 1970. The United States, Soviet Union, and other countries agreed with effect from 1972 to ban nuclear weapons from the ocean floor in international waters.

Chemical Weapons Treaty, 1971. The United States and the Soviet Union agreed with effect from 1972 to destroy stockpiles of chemical and biologial weapons and ban their further development.

SALT Agreement, 1972. In May 1972 President Nixon and Soviet leader Leonid Brezhnev signed two agreements concluded at the Strategic Arms Limitation Talks (SALT): (1) The United States and the Soviet Union were limited to two antiballistic missile (ABM) sites each—one to protect the capital city, the other to guard an offensive missile site at least 800 miles away. In addition, the number of ABM weapons were limited at each site. (2) The two countries agreed to freeze the number of strategic offensive ballistic missiles roughly at current levels. Neither agreement provided for on-site inspection to ensure compliance.

Wage-Price Controls, 1971–1973. To combat inflation, the Nixon administration in 1971 imposed a freeze on wages and prices, replaced after 90 days with a complex system of wage-price controls. Most controls were removed by the end of 1973.

Revenue Sharing, 1972. The Nixon administration adopted a program of revenue sharing, plowing back billions of dollars of taxes annually to state and local governments.

Law and Order. Redeeming his pledge to strengthen law enforcement, President Nixon won approval of three major crime bills in 1970: (1) The Organized Crime Control Act authorized more severe penalties for "dangerous special offenders" and barred the use of organized crime money in legitimate businesses. (2) The Drug Abuse Control Act reduced penalties for simple possession but increased penalties for trafficking; it also contained a controversial "no-knock" provision enabling authorities to break in unannounced to capture evidence that otherwise might be hastily destroyed. (3) The District of Columbia Criminal Justice Act, in addition to the "no-knock" provision, authorized "preventive detention," pretrial incarceration up to 60 days for defendants deemed dangerous; the law applied only to Washington, D.C.

Environmental Protection. (1) The Environmental Quality Policy Act of 1969 required the filing of an environmental impact statement for each new federal program. (2) The Environmental Protection Agency was established in 1970 to monitor, regulate, reduce, and control pollution. (3) The Water Quality Improvement Act of 1970 curbed water pollution from nuclear power plants and offshore oil rigs and tankers. (4) The National Air Quality Standards Act of 1970 restricted auto emissions and established federal clean air standards to be met by states. (5) The Resource Recovery Act of 1970 encouraged recycling. (6) The Water Pollution Act of 1972, passed over President Nixon's veto, provided federal funds for the construction of local waste treatment plants and sharply curtailed the discharge of industrial waste into the nation's waterways.

Consumer Product Safety Act, 1972. This law created the Consumer Product Safety Commission, an independent regulatory agency, empowered to set product safety standards and ban unsafe products from the marketplace.

Man on the Moon. On July 20, 1969, Astronaut Neil Armstrong, commander of Apollo 11, became the first man to set foot on the moon, saying, "That's one small step for a man, one giant leap for mankind." In the last of the moon-landing missions (Apollo 17, December 1972), astronauts Eugene Cernan and Harrison Schmitt spent a record 75 hours on the lunar surface and retrieved 250 pounds of moon samples.

Constitutional Amendment Ratified. Twenty-sixth Amendment, 1971. Lowered the voting age from 21 to 18.

Watergate and Other Scandals. On June 17, 1972, five agents of the Committee to Reelect the President (CREEP)—Bernard L. Barker, James McCord, Eugenio Martinez, Frank Sturgis, and Virgilio Gonzales—were arrested in the act of burglarizing the Democratic National Headquarters at the Watergate complex in Washington, D.C. What was dismissed by the White House as "a third-rate burglary attempt" touched off a chain of events that was to unravel the worst political scandal in U.S. history and for the first time force a president to resign in disgrace. Over the next two years numerous misdeeds committed by or in the name of President Nixon were disclosed by investigative reporters, notably Bob Woodward and Carl Bernstein of the *Washington Post*, and the Senate Select Committee on Watergate, chaired by Democratic Senator Sam Ervin of North Carolina: (1) Nixon campaign officials had installed eavesdropping devices inside Democratic headquarters at Watergate. (2) A Republican dirty tricks squad had attempted to sow dissension among Democratic candidates. (3) White House officials, apparently including the president, authorized payment of hush money to Watergate defendants and otherwise attempted to cover up criminal acts. (4) A White House "plumbers" unit, created to plug leaks of classified information, had burglarized the office of the psychiatrist of Daniel Ellsberg, the former government official who had distributed the Pentagon Papers, a top-secret study of the origins of the Vietnam War, to the press. (5) The Nixon administration had drawn up an Enemies List in order to, according to a White House memo, "use the available federal machinery to screw our political enemies." Included on the list were black Representative John Conyers of Michigan, with a notation "Has known weakness for white females"; CBS newsman Daniel Schorr, "a real media enemy"; show business celebrities Carol Channing, Bill Cosby, Jane Fonda, Paul Newman, and Tony Randall; businessmen and academics. President Nixon repeatedly denied any wrongdoing. His principal accuser, White House counsel John Dean, maintained that although the president may not have authorized the Watergate break-in, he did direct the cover-up that followed. The truth probably never would have been known were it not for the existence of an elaborate White House taping system installed by President Nixon, presumably as an aid in reconstructing the events of his administration for his memoirs. While vowing his innocence, Nixon at first refused to turn over the tapes to the Senate investigating committee, citing executive privilege. Only after the Supreme Court unanimously ordered him to release them did he do so. One tape arrived with a mysterious 18½-minute gap that sound experts concluded had been deliberately erased. The tapes generally supported Dean's version of events and thoroughly discredited the president. Nixon later regretted not having destroyed the tapes, to which the U.S. archivist granted limited public access in 1986. Meanwhile, special prosecutor Archibald Cox and successor Leon Jaworski proceeded with the prosecution of Nixon officials. Besides the original burglars and John Dean, those convicted of or pleading guilty to unlawful activity were presidential appointments secretary Dwight Chapin, special presidential counsel Charles Colson, chief domestic affairs adviser John D. Ehrlichman, presidential chief of staff H. R. "Bob" Haldeman, White House consultant E. Howard Hunt, personal attorney to the president and campaign fund raiser Herbert Kalmbach, White House aide and chief "plumber" Egil "Bud" Krogh, White House and campaign aide Frederick Larue, White House assistant and CREEP counsel G. Gordon Liddy, White House aide and CREEP deputy director Jeb Stuart Magruder, attorney general and CREEP chairman John Mitchell, White House aide and CREEP scheduling director Herbert Porter, CREEP dirty trickster Donald Segretti, commerce secretary and CREEP finance director Maurice Stans. President Nixon was named an unindicted co-conspirator.

Impeachment Proceedings. In televised proceedings in July 1974, the House Judiciary Committee, chaired by Democratic Representative Peter Rodino of New Jersey, approved three articles of impeachment against President Nixon: (1) Obstruction of justice—making false or misleading statements to investigators, withholding evidence, condoning and counseling perjury, interfering with lawful investigations, approving payment of hush money, attempting to misuse the Central Intelligence Agency, using Justice Department information to help subjects of investigation avoid criminal liability, making false or misleading statements to the public, holding out the prospect of favored treatment to those convicted in exchange for their silence. (2) Abuse of power—misusing the Internal Revenue Service, Federal Bureau of Investigation, Secret Service, and other executive personnel; maintaining an unlawful secret investigative unit (plumbers) within the office of president; failing to prosecute the criminal acts of subordinates; interfering with the Watergate investigation. (3) Failure to comply with congressional subpoenas. "In all of this," the committee concluded, "Richard M. Nixon has acted in a manner contrary to his trust as President and subversive of constitutional government, to the great prejudice of the cause of law and justice and to the manifest injury of the people of the United States. Wherefore, Richard M. Nixon by such conduct, warrants impeachment and trial, and removal from office."

Resignation. Realizing that he faced almost certain impeachment, Nixon resigned the office of president, effective soon, August 9, 1974. In his farewell address he admitted nothing but errors of judgment. He decided to quit, he said, because "to continue to fight through the months ahead for my personal vindication would almost totally absorb the time and attention of both the President and the Congress in a period when our entire focus should be on the great issues of peace abroad and prosperity without inflation at home."

SUPREME COURT APPOINTMENTS: (1) Warren E. Burger (1907–1995), of Minnesota, served as chief justice 1969–1986. Although he generally has been described as conservative, particularly by comparison with his predecessor, Earl Warren, Burger considers himself a moderate. Speaking for the majority in *Swann* v. *Mecklenburg Board of Education* (1971), he attempted to strike middle ground on school desegregation by ruling that busing was a valid tool to achieve racial balance but one not required in all cases. Burger pleased the Nixon administration in dissenting from the Pentagon Papers (1971), in which he argued that the government had a legitimate national security interest in seeking prior restraint against the *New York Times* and other newspapers to prevent publication of classified material. However, in *United States* v. *Richard Nixon* (1974), the Burger Court unanimously rejected administration claims of executive privilege and ordered the president to comply with a congressional subpoena to surrender tape recordings of certain White House conversations related to the Watergate scandal. Off the bench, Chief Justice Burger has urged creation of additional appellate courts to relieve the Supreme Court's clogged docket, enactment of comprehensive prison reform to include mandatory educational and vocational programs for prisoners, a factory system within prisons in which inmates would earn wages and pay room and board, and a national academy of corrections in train prison personnel. (2) Harry A. Blackmun (1908–1999), of Minnesota, served as associate justice 1970–1994. He was appointed to the Court following Senate rejection of Nixon nominees Clement Haynsworth of South Carolina and G. Harrold Carswell of Florida. Because of his long association with Chief Justice Burger (they had grown up together in St. Paul) and the similarity of their judicial views, the pair were dubbed the Minnesota twins. Blackmun wrote the Court's opinion in companion cases (*Roe* v. *Wade, Doe* v. *Bolton*, 1973) establishing the right to abortion on demand during the first trimester of pregnancy. (3) Lewis F. Powell, Jr. (1907–1998), of Virginia, served as associate justice 1972–1987. A Democrat, he emerged as a swing vote who sided with the conservative bloc about 75 percent of the time but joined liberals in striking down anti-abortion laws and federal aid to private schools. In *Regents of the University of California* v. *Bakke* (1978), he spoke for a badly divided Court in striking down racial quotas as a basis for college admissions. His opinion let stand, however, affirmative action programs not based on rigid quotas. (4) William H. Rehnquist (1924–   ), of Arizona, served as associate justice 1972–1986, chief justice 1986–   . Generally regarded as the Burger Court's most conservative member, he was named chief justice by President Ronald Reagan. He was confirmed by the Senate, 65–33, the largest negative vote ever recorded for a successful Supreme Court nominee. He spoke for the Court in sustaining the exclusion of women from the military draft (*Rostker* v. *Goldberg*, 1981).

RETIREMENT: August 9, 1974–April 22, 1994. Nixon retired to San Clemente, California, reportedly in deep depression. He later moved to New York City and, in 1981, to Saddle River, New Jersey. In September 1974 he accepted from his successor, President Gerald R. Ford, a "full, free and absolute pardon" for all federal crimes that he "committed or may have committed or taken part in" while president. He attempted to take possession of the White House tapes but was thwarted by an act of Congress. In 1980 he testified at the trial of two former FBI officials charged with ordering warrantless break-ins at the homes of friends and relatives of suspected terrorists; Nixon confirmed that he had authorized such break-ins. In 1985 he mediated a contract dispute between major league baseball and the umpire association. Still popular abroad, Nixon, during his first decade in retirement, traveled to eighteen foreign countries and met with sixteen heads of state. He conferred by telephone regularly with members of the Reagan administration, though rarely with the president.

DEATH: April 22, 1994.

NIXON PRAISED: "I am always struck by the President's breadth and depth of knowledge . . . and his ability to articulate significant considerations in so many fields."[9]—Housing and Urban Development Secretary George Romney

"The irony about Nixon is that his pre-Watergate record is a lot better than most liberals realize. It was Nixon, after all, who opened the door to China and who eventually brought American troops home from Vietnam."[10]—former House Speaker Thomas P. "Tip" O'Neill, 1987

"We need this man of action, this man of accomplishment, this man of experience, this man of courage, we need this man of faith in America . . . who has brought us to the threshold of peace."[11]—Governor Nelson Rockefeller of New York, 1972

"[Nixon is] a man of great reading, a man of great intelligence and a man of great decisiveness."[12]—former president Dwight D. Eisenhower, 1968

NIXON CRITICIZED: "[Nixon is] an indecisive man who lacks that inner conviction and self-confidence which are the mark of the natural leader and governor of men."[13]—columnist Walter Lippman, 1960

"Richard Nixon is a no-good lying bastard. He can lie out of both sides of his mouth at the same time, and if he ever caught himself telling the truth, he'd lie just to keep his hand in."[14]—Harry S. Truman

"The men who have collected millions in secret money, who have passed out special favors, who have ordered political sabotage, who have invaded our offices in the dead of night—all of these men work for Mr. Nixon. . . . Their power comes from him alone. They act on his behalf, and they all accept his orders."[15]—Democratic presidential nominee George S. McGovern, 1972

"In two hundred years of history, he's the most dishonest President we've ever had. I think he's disgraced the Presidency."[16]—Governor Jimmy Carter of Georgia, 1974

NIXON QUOTES: "Once a man has been in politics, once that's been in his life, he will always return if the people want him."[17]

"A man who has never lost himself in a cause bigger than himself has missed one of life's mountaintop experiences. Only in losing himself does he find himself. Only then does he discover all the latent strengths he never knew he had and which would otherwise have remained dormant."[18]

"Any culture which can put a man on the Moon is capable of gathering all the nations of the earth in peace, justice and concord."[19]—1969

BOOKS BY NIXON: *Six Crises* (1962); *The Memoirs of Richard Nixon* (1978); *The Real War* (1980); *Leaders* (1982); *Real Peace: Strategy for the West* (1984); *No More Vietnams* (1985); *1999: Victory Without War* (1988).

BOOKS ABOUT NIXON: DeToledano, Ralph. *One Man Alone: Richard Nixon.* New York: Funk & Wagnalls, 1969.

Ambrose, Stephen E. *Nixon: The Education of a Politician 1913–1962.* New York: Simon & Schuster, 1987.

Kornitzer, Bela. *The Real Nixon: An Intimate Biography.* New York: Rand McNally, 1960.

Lurie, Leonard. *The Running of Richard Nixon.* New York: Coward, McCann, & Geoghegan, 1971.

Mazo, Earl, and Hess. Stephen. *Nixon: A Political Portrait.* New York: Harper and Row, 1968.

White, Theodore. *Breach of Faith: The Fall of Richard Nixon.* New York: Atheneum, 1975.

Wills, Garry. *Nixon Agonistes.* Boston: Houghton, Mifflin, 1970.

NOTES:

1 Leonard Lurie, *The Running of Richard Nixon*, New York: Coward, McCann and Geoghegan, 1972, p. 18.

2 Earl Mazo, *Richard Nixon: A Political and Personal Portrait*, New York: Harper & Bros., 1959, p. 13.

3 Bela Kornitzer, *The Real Nixon: An Intimate Biography*, New York: Rand McNally, 1960, p. 19.

4 Lurie, p. 26.

5 Mazo, p. 31.

6 Richard M. Nixon, *Six Crises*, Garden City, N.Y.: Doubleday, 1962, p. 62.

7 Mazo, p. 134.

8 Lewis Chester *et al.*, *An American Melodrama: The Presidential Campaign of 1968*, New York: Viking, 1969, p. 649.

9 Allen Drury and Fred Maroon, *Courage and Hesitation: Notes and Photographs of the Nixon Administration*, Garden City, N.Y.: Doubleday, 1971, p. 318.

10 Thomas P. "Tip" O'Neill, *Man of the House*, New York: Random House, 1987, p. 240.

11 Theodore H. White, *The Making of the President 1972*, New York: Atheneum, 1973, p. 257.

12 *Facts on File Yearbook 1968*, p. 292.

13 Victor Lasky, *JFK: The Man and the Myth*, New York: Macmillan, 1963, p. 456.

14 Barbara Rowes, *The Book of Quotes*, New York: Dutton, 1979, p. 146.

15 Arthur Schlesinger, Jr., "A Look at the Power of Defeat," *Cleveland Plain Dealer*, June 22, 1975, sect. 1, p. 4.

16 Kandy Stroud, *How Jimmy Won: The Victory Campaign from Plains to the White House*, New York: Morrow, 1977, p. 16.

17 Earl Mazo and Stephen Hess, *Nixon: A Political Portrait*, New York: Harper & Row, 1968, back cover.

18 Nixon, p. xxviii.

19 Robert S. Alley, *So Help Me God: Religion and the Presidency*, Richmond, Va.: John Knox Press, 1972, p. 119.

GERALD R. FORD

NAME: Gerald Rudolph Ford, Jr. He was born Leslie Lynch King, Jr., named after his biological father. He was renamed after his adoptive father, Gerald Rudolf Ford, Sr. He later changed the spelling of his middle name. Except in formal signature, he signs his name Jerry Ford.

PHYSICAL DESCRIPTION: Ford is 6 feet tall and weighed about 195 pounds as president. He has blond hair, which he combs straight back, and small blue eyes. He has largely retained the trim, muscular figure of his youth. His handsome features are characterized by a square jaw, somewhat fleshy nose, and generous mouth. His broad grin reveals large, straight teeth. Except for weak knees, the result of football injuries, his health generally has been sound. Although he took a lot of kidding in the press and from comedians for lack of physical coordination, he described himself as "the most athletic president to occupy the White House in years."[1] Ford is a right-handed sportsman but writes and eats with his left hand. He dresses sporty.

PERSONALITY: By all accounts, Ford is open, friendly, forthright, honest, and considerate. He appears genuinely to like people and, although a 30-year veteran of the political wars, made remarkably few enemies along the way. "He never in his life tried to outsmart anybody," observed Bud Vestal, a Grand Rapids reporter and longtime Ford watcher. "But if from intellectual hubris a tormentor gave him a chance, Jerry would outdumb him, swiftly and deadpan. It might be days before the attacker would realize he'd been had."[2]

ANCESTORS: Ford is of English heritage.

BIOLOGICAL FATHER: Leslie Lynch King (1882–1941), wool merchant. A wool merchant of Omaha, Nebraska, he married Dorothy Gardner in 1912. The tempestuous marriage ended after three years. Ford remembers seeing his biological father only twice. The first time, Ford, then 17, was working at a restaurant in Grand Rapids when King walked in and introduced himself as his father. The two had lunch over awkward conversation, Ford checking an urge to

603

lash out at him for never having bothered to look him up before. King slipped the boy $25 and drove off in a shiny new Lincoln back to his home in Wyoming. He visited his son once again at Yale. King died in Tucson in 1941, the year his son graduated from law school. Ford bitterly resented him as a carefree man of wealth indifferent about the future of his first-born son.

ADOPTIVE FATHER: Gerald Rudolf Ford, Sr. (1890–1962), paint store owner. Dropping out of school after the eighth grade, he sold paint for the Grand Rapids Wood Finishing Company and in 1929 established the Ford Paint and Varnish Company in that city. He managed to keep the business afloat during the Depression and prospered moderately with the recovery. He married Dorothy Gardner King in 1916 and adopted her son, the future president, renaming him Gerald R. Ford, Jr. He was active in the local Republican party. He died in 1962, when his stepson was a congressman. Ford described his stepfather as a man of impeccable integrity who exerted the strongest influence on his life.

MOTHER: Dorothy Ayer Gardner Ford (1892–1967). A native of Harvard, Illinois, she married first Leslie L. King in 1912 and settled in Omaha, Nebraska. Reportedly beaten at times by her husband, she fled with her infant son, the future president, to the safety of her parents' home in Grand Rapids. In 1916, the year after her divorce, she married Gerald R. Ford. Although beset by numerous ailments, she was active in local church and civic affairs until her death in 1967, when her oldest son was House minority leader. Ford described her as selfless and solicitous of other people's problems.

SIBLINGS: Ford had no full siblings. From his father's second marriage, he has a half brother and two half sisters—Leslie H. "Bud" King, retail manager of Cookeville, Tennessee; Mrs. Marjorie Werner of Cumberland, Maryland; and Patricia King of Balboa Island, California. From his mother's second marriage he has three half brothers, all of Grand Rapids, Michigan—Thomas G. Ford, Republican member of the Michigan legislature 1964–1972; Richard A. Ford, manager of the Ford Paint and Varnish Company; and James F. Ford, optometrist.

CHILDREN: Ford has three sons and a daughter.

Michael Gerald Ford (1950–   ), minister. He was a student at the Gordon Conwell Theological Seminary in South Hamilton, Massachusetts, when his father became president. To the left of his father politically, he had opposed the Vietnam War and criticized President Nixon's conduct during the Watergate affair. In 1977 he joined the Coalition for Christian Outreach program at the University of Pittsburgh and in 1981 was appointed student affairs director at Wake Forest University. He married Gayle Brumbaugh in 1974.

John "Jack" Gardner Ford (1952–   ), journalist, public relations man. He was a summer park ranger at Yellowstone National Park between terms as a forestry student at Utah State University when his father became president. A rock music fan, he brought former Beatle George Harrison and other celebrities to the White House. He was for a time assistant to the publisher of *Outside* magazine. During 1978–1980 he was copublisher of the weekly *Del-Mar* (California) *News Press.* In 1982 he was working in public relations in San Diego and reportedly contemplating a move into politics.

Steven Meigs Ford (1956–   ), actor. He had recently graduated from high school when his father became president. Suddenly the object of intense media attention, he decided to postpone (permanently, as it turned out) college and his ambition for dentistry. He had been accepted at Duke University but instead worked for the next two years as a ranchhand in Utah, Montana, and Idaho. Later he signed on as a calf roper and bronco rider with the Los Angeles Rough Riders rodeo. His horsemanship landed him a bit part in the film *Cattle Annie and Little Britches*. He found that he enjoyed acting and began taking lessons. He won small roles on "Happy Days" and other television programs. For a time in the 1980s he was a regular player on the popular daytime soap opera "The Young and the Restless."

Susan Elizabeth Ford (1957–   ), photographer. She was a student at the Holton-Arms School in Bethesda, Maryland, when her father became president. She served as official White House hostess while Mrs. Ford was in the hospital. She accompanied President and Mrs. Ford to China in 1975. She studied photography under Ansel Adams and others. In 1977 she worked as a still photographer during production of the film *Jaws II*. She and her former husband Charles Vance, a Secret Service agent once assigned to President Ford, for a time operated a private security company in Washington, D.C.

BIRTH: Ford was born on July 14, 1913, in Omaha, Nebraska.

CHILDHOOD: From age two, Ford grew up in modest circumstances in Grand Rapids and East Grand Rapids, Michigan. He was a spirited, industrious, and athletic youngster. He helped out with chores, tending to the coal furnace, mowing the lawn, washing dishes. With the family he vacationed at Ottawa Beach on Lake Michigan and fished at the Little South Branch of the Pere Marquette River. As a teenager he drove a used Model T Ford with a rumble seat but one day threw a blanket atop the overheated engine and returned to find the car destroyed in flames. When he was 12 or 13 his parents told him he was adopted. The most traumatic experience of his youth was confronting his biological father (see "Ancestors") for the first time. The encounter left him shaken and in tears. Ford was an Eagle Scout.

EDUCATION: Ford attended Madison Elementary School for kindergarten, East Grand Rapids Elementary School for grades one through six, and South High School for seventh grade through senior year. At South High, he excelled in history and government, performed well in math and the sciences, but did poorly in Latin. At the end of his junior year he made the National Honor Society and ranked in the top 5 percent of his class. He also held down part-time jobs, working at an amusement park and frying burgers in Bill Skougis's restaurant. In a movie theater promotional contest, he won the title of most popular high school senior and his first trip to Washington, D.C. He also was a star center for the South High Trojans football team and was named to the all-city squad. Following his graduation in 1931, he entered the University of Michigan on a partial scholarship as a prelaw student majoring in economics and political science. Generally a B student, he earned As in four courses—money and credit, European history from the decline of Rome to 1648, organized labor, and American government. He helped work his way through college busing tables at the university hospital dining room and washing dishes at his fraternity, Delta Kappa Epsilon. He was named outstanding freshman on the Michigan Wolverines football team but played second string during his sophomore and junior years behind All-American center Chuck Bernard. As a senior he was named most valuable player and played center in the 1935 College All-Stars game against the Chicago Bears. Both the Detroit Lions and Green Bay Packers offered him a professional contract, but he turned them down to study law. He graduated in the top 25 percent of Michigan's class of 1935. That year he was hired at a salary of $2,400 a year to be assistant football coach and head boxing coach at Yale University. Among those he coached in football were future senators Robert Taft, Jr., of Ohio and William Proxmire of Wisconsin. Ford intended to begin taking law courses immediately, but because of his full-time coaching schedule, Yale officials denied him admission. At his repeated application, officials reluctantly accepted him on a trial basis in 1938. He surprised them by maintaining a B average and ranking in the top third of his class, which included such future notables as Supreme Court Justice Potter Stewart, Secretary of State Cyrus Vance, and Peace Corps Director Sargent Shriver. Ford's best subject was legal ethics. During the summer of 1936, Ford worked as a park ranger at Yellowstone National Park, feeding the bears and directing traffic. He also worked for a time as a male model (see "Early Romance"). Ford received his law degree in January 1941 and was admitted to the Michigan bar in June.

RELIGION: Episcopalian. President Ford attended St. John's Episcopal Church in Washington. As president he prayed for guidance in making particularly difficult decisions, notably the pardon of his predecessor, Richard Nixon.

RECREATION: President Ford enjoyed swimming, playing golf (18 handicap) and tennis, and skiing, usually at Vail, Colorado. Before breakfast he rode an exercise bike and lifted weights in the president's study. He followed football closely and remained a loyal fan of the Michigan Wolverines. He smoked a pipe, about eight bowls of Sir Walter Raleigh or other blends a day.

EARLY ROMANCE: Phyllis Brown. "My torrid four-year love affair with Phyllis Brown . . . matured me,"[3] Ford recalled of his first serious romance. They met when coach Ford took his Yale boxing team for a match against the U.S. Coast Guard Academy in New London, Connecticut, where she was a student at Connecticut College for Women. Slim, blond, beautiful, and outgoing, she swept Ford off his feet. She introduced him to skiing, the New York theater, and fashion modeling. Miss Brown, having dropped out of college to become a Powers model, persuaded Ford to invest as a silent partner in a modeling agency in New York and to model clothes himself. Together Jerry and Phyllis appeared in a winter sports spread for *Look* magazine in March 1940. They made the cover of *Cosmopolitan* in 1942, Ford resplendent in his crisp navy uniform. They talked of marriage, Ford brought her home to meet his parents, but they broke up over where to settle down. She wanted to continue her modeling career in New York; he wanted to return to Grand Rapids to practice law. Ford anguished over the breakup. Miss Brown went on to marry several times. Their paths crossed again in Nevada in 1970. Ford described the meeting as cordial.

MARRIAGE: Gerald R. Ford, 35, married Elizabeth Anne Bloomer, 30, on October 15, 1948, at Grace Episcopal Church in Grand Rapids, Michigan. Born on April 8, 1918, in Chicago, Illinois, the daughter of William S. Bloomer, an industrial supply salesman of rubber products, and Hortense Neahr Bloomer, Betty grew up from age three in Grand Rapids and early decided to become a dancer. She graduated from the Calla Travis Dance Studio in 1935 and attended the Bennington Vermont School of Dance during 1936–1937. She studied dance under Martha Graham, who invited her to join her New York Concert Group in 1939. Meanwhile, in New York, she also worked as a Powers model. At her mother's repeated urging, she in 1941 moved back home to Grand Rapids, where she became fashion coordinator for Herpolscheimer's department store and in 1942 married William C. Warren, a furniture salesman. They divorced amicably in 1947. That year she received a call from Jerry Ford, whom she knew only for his reputation on the football field. A mutual friend, Peg Neuman, had urged Ford to ask her out now that she was getting a divorce. With some hesitation, she agreed to have a drink with him at a nearby bar. They dated regularly thereafter, and in February 1948 Ford proposed and she accepted. Then embroiled in his first congressional election campaign, Ford attended a rally just before his wedding and traipsed down the aisle in muddy shoes. His college roommate Jack Beckwith was best man. In an unusual honeymoon, the newlyweds drove to Ann Arbor for the Michigan-Northwestern football game and that evening went on to Owosso to hear Republican presidential nominee Thomas Dewey address an outdoor rally, then spent one quiet day together in Detroit before returning to Grand Rapids. As First Lady, Mrs. Ford spoke out in favor of liberalized abortion laws and the Equal Rights Amendment and promoted the appointment of a woman to the Supreme Court. For her efforts on behalf of women's rights, she received the Anti-Defamation League's Human Relations Award in 1975. She also promoted aid to the handicapped and mentally retarded. Shortly after becoming First Lady, she underwent a radical mastectomy for the removal of cancerous tissue. Her public candor in discussing what for many women had been a private tragedy focused national attention on breast cancer and the importance of early detection. Similarly, she won praise for speaking freely of her struggle against alcohol and pain-killing drugs, on which she had become dependent in seeking relief from an inoperable pinched nerve. In *Betty: A Glad Awakening* (with Chris Chase, 1987), she revealed that both her father and brother were alcoholics and recounted in painful detail how in 1978 her family forced her to confront her own alcoholism and seek treatment. Following her recovery, she established the Betty Ford Clinic, a chemical dependency recovery center. In 1982 she received the American Cancer Society's Hubert Humphrey Award.

MILITARY SERVICE:

World War II. Ford served in the navy from April 1942 to February 1946, rising from ensign to lieutenant commander. After undergoing basic training at the Naval Academy in Annapolis, he was a physical fitness instructor at a preflight school in Chapel Hill, North Carolina. At his request he in 1943 was assigned to sea duty as athletic director and gunnery division officer aboard the USS *Monterey*, a light aircraft carrier that joined Admiral William "Bull" Halsey's Third Fleet in the South Pacific. As gunnery officer, Ford directed the firing of the 40-mm. antiaircraft gun. He later was made assistant navigator of the carrier. Once Ford nearly was thrown overboard during a typhoon. The *Monterey* took part in virtually all the major battles in the South Pacific, including the assaults on Wake Island and Okinawa and the recapture of the Philippines. Ford racked up 10 battle stars. Rotated home near the end of the war, he spent the remainder of his service attached to the Naval Reserve Training Command at Glenview, Illinois. At this time he narrowly survived a plane crash at the Chapel Hill airbase.

CAREER BEFORE THE PRESIDENCY: On admission to the bar in 1941, Ford practiced law in partnership with Philip A. Buchen (later White House counsel under President Ford) in Grand Rapids, Michigan, until U.S. entry into World

War II (see "Military Service"). After the war he joined the firm of Butterfield, Keeney, and Amberg in Grand Rapids.

U.S. Representative, 1949–1973; House Minority Leader 1965–1973. In 1948 Ford upset isolationalist incumbent Representative Bartel J. Jonkman in the Republican primary 23,632–14,341 and went on to defeat Democrat Fred J. Barr in the general election 74,191–46,972 to represent Michigan's Fifth Congressional District, comprised of Kent and Ottawa counties (redrawn in 1964 to consist of Kent and Ionia counties). Ford was reelected 12 times in succession, each time with more than 60 percent of the vote. His closest contest was in 1970, when he defeated Democrat Jean McKee 88,208–55,337. At first appointed to the Public Works Committee, Representative Ford gave it up in 1951 for a seat on the powerful Appropriations Committee and rose to prominence on the Defense Appropriations Subcommittee, becoming its ranking minority member in 1961. During the Truman administration, Ford established a moderately conservative record, internationalist in foreign affairs but conservative on domestic issues. He supported the Marshall Plan, Truman's Point Four program for aid to underdeveloped countries, and increases in the defense budget. He opposed repeal of the Taft-Hartley Act and a minimum-wage hike and voted to override Truman's veto of the McCarran Immigration bill. In 1952 he was an early supporter of Dwight D. Eisenhower for the Republican presidential nomination. In retrospect, his biggest regret of this period was having failed to speak out against the Communist witch-hunt of Republican Senator Joseph McCarthy of Wisconsin. A personal friend of Vice President Richard Nixon from their service together in the House in the late 1940s, Ford defended Nixon from Republican insurgents who sought to dump him from the ticket in 1956 and early backed Nixon for the 1960 Republican presidential nomination. In 1961 Ford received the American Political Science Association's Distinguished Service Award; the citation praised him for his "diligent application to committee work and mastery of highly complex defense matters" and called him a "Congressman's Congressman." In a 1963 revolt of the Young Turks in the party, Representative Charles Hoeven of Iowa was ousted as chairman of the House Republican Conference, and Ford was named in his place. President Johnson appointed Ford one of two House members on the Warren Commission investigating the assassination of President Kennedy. He fully endorsed the Warren Commission's conclusion that assassin Lee Harvey Oswald had acted alone. To help dispel the belief of many skeptics that Kennedy was the victim of a conspiracy, Ford, with Warren Commission special assistant John R. Stiles, published his conclusions in *Portrait of an Assassin* (1965). During the Kennedy-Johnson years, Ford drew criticism from black leaders for voting to weaken civil rights legislation, although he generally supported such measures on final passage. He opposed the establishment of Medicare and denounced the Johnson administration's war on poverty as "a lot of washed-up old programs."[4] At the 1964 Republican national convention, Ford nominated Governor George Romney of Michigan for president but supported the eventual nominee, Senator Barry Goldwater of Arizona. Since entering the House, Ford had set out to become Speaker. To that end he in January 1965 successfully challenged Representative Charles A. Halleck of Indiana for House minority leader, defeating the incumbent 73–67. In 1967 Ford delivered a major floor speech attacking the Johnson administration's conduct of the Vietnam War. In effect calling on the president to unleash American military might and win the war or get out, he asked, "why are we pulling our best punches in Vietnam? Is there no end, no other answer except more men, more men, more men?" He went on to charge, "What is especially dishonest is secretly to forbid effective strategic action and publicly portray it as an honest try."[5] From 1969, Representative Ford was among the Nixon administration's most consistent supporters, on the pursuit of "peace with honor" in Vietnam, on retrenchment of federal social welfare programs, and on détente with the Soviet Union and recognition of China. He even set aside his long-standing opposition to wage and price controls to endorse the administration's antiinflation program. In 1970, in what was regarded as a reaction to Senate rejection of Nixon Supreme Court nominees Clement Haynsworth and G. Harrold Carswell, both judicial conservatives, Ford launched a campaign to impeach Justice William O. Douglas, the high court's most liberal member. Citing Douglas's paid activities on behalf of the Parvin Foundation, a charitable organization with alleged ties to organized crime, as well as certain off-the-bench remarks, Ford argued that the same standard of judicial ethics by which the Senate rejected Nixon's nominees should now be applied to Douglas. But when pressed on whether Douglas's behavior warranted impeachment, he cast the proceedings in coldly pragmatic terms, which unsettled many members and came back to haunt him during the debate over the impeachment of President Nixon. "An impeachable offense," Ford declared, "is whatever the majority of the House of Representatives considers it to be at a given moment of history; conviction results from whatever offenses two-thirds of the [Senate] considers to be sufficiently serious to require removal of the accused from office."[6] Ford later was unwilling to apply that same standard to President Nixon during the Watergate scandal, arguing that impeachment of a president should require more conclusive evidence of wrongdoing than that for removal of a justice. With Democrats firmly in control in the House, Ford realized that his prospects of becoming Speaker were bleak. Thus, early in 1973 he decided to stand for reelection once more and retire at the end of that term in 1976. Events postponed his retirement.

Vice President, 1973–1974. Ford was the first vice president appointed under provision of the Twenty-fifth Amendment. Following Vice President Agnew's resignation in October 1973, President Nixon reportedly first considered former Treasury secretary John Connally of Texas for the vacancy but rejected him because his nomination was sure to invite protracted debate at his confirmation hearings. He next thought of turning to Governors Nelson Rockefeller of New York or Ronald Reagan of California but was concerned that their prominence in opposite wings of the party might undermine Republican unity. He settled on Ford as a moderate with broad support whose record could withstand the intense scrutiny of a full-field FBI check as well as the Democratic dominated confirmation hearings. Ford was confirmed in the Senate, 92–3, in November; in the House, 387–35, in December. He took the oath of office on December 6, 1973. Vice President Ford defended President Nixon against charges of personal involvement in the Watergate cover-up. Nixon had assured him that he was withholding subpoenaed tape recordings of pertinent White House conversations solely to maintain the principle of executive privilege, that in fact the recordings contained evidence that would clear him of suspicion, and offered Ford the opportunity to listen to them. Ford declined but urged Nixon to release any such exculpatory material immediately.

At 12:03 P.M., August 9, 1974, minutes after President Nixon resigned, Ford

610 / GERALD R. FORD

was sworn in as president by Chief Justice Warren Burger in the East Room of the White House. "Our long national nightmare is over," Ford said following the ceremony. "Our Constitution works; our great Republic is a government of laws and not of men."

VICE PRESIDENT: Nelson A. Rockefeller (1908–1979), of New York, served 1974–1977. Born in Bar Harbor, Maine, the grandson of industrialist John D. Rockefeller, he graduated Phi Beta Kappa from Dartmouth in 1930 and became active in the family financial empire, particularly Rockefeller Center in Manhattan. Although a Republican, he was appointed assistant secretary of state in the Franklin Roosevelt administration during World War II and head of the International Development Advisory Board in the Truman administration. President Eisenhower named him chairman of his Advisory Committee on Government Organization and undersecretary of health, education and welfare. Elected four times governor of New York, 1958–1973, he introduced numerous social programs and emerged a leading liberal spokesman in the party. Although he ran unsuccessfully for the Republican presidential nomination in 1960, his views dominated the party platform that year. He ran again in 1964 but was overwhelmed in the conservative tide of Barry Goldwater and suffered the indignity of being booed at the convention. He ran a third time in 1968, again losing to Richard Nixon. In his last years as governor, Rockefeller drew criticism from his traditional liberal supporters for his stern law-and-order policy and refusal to intervene in the five-day prison riot at Attica in 1971 in which dozens of persons were killed. In 1973 he resigned as governor to head the Commission on Critical Choices for America. President Ford nominated him for vice president under provision of the Twenty-fifth Amendment. At his confirmation hearings, Rockefeller revealed that his personal net worth was $62 million and estimated his total assets, mostly in trusts, at $218 million. He was sworn in as vice president in December 1974. He soon became the target of conservatives within the party, who called for his removal from the ticket in 1976. He spared President Ford the necessity of addressing the issue by announcing in 1975 that he would not be a candidate for vice president the following year.

CABINET:

Secretary of State: Henry Kissinger (1923–   ), of the District of Columbia, served 1973–1977. A holdover from the Nixon administration, Kissinger continued his shuttle diplomacy to ease tensions in the Middle East and southern Africa. He helped bring about the 1975 Sinai accord, an interim peace agreement between Egypt and Israel in which the two sides agreed to renounce war as a means of settling remaining differences and Israel pledged to withdraw partially from the Sinai and give back captured oil fields. In 1976 Kissinger met frequently with southern African leaders to discuss a timetable for black majority rule in Rhodesia and independence for South Africa–controlled Namibia.

Secretary of the Treasury. William E. Simon (1927–2000), of New Jersey, served 1974–1977. A holdover from the Nixon administration, he also headed Ford's Economic Policy Board in charge of coordinating the administration's overall economic policy. In 1974 he negotiated the Soviet purchase of U.S. grain. A vigorous proponent of reduced government spending, he argued for continuation of a tight-money policy to fight inflation despite rising unemployment.

Secretary of Defense. (1) James R. Schlesinger (1929–   ), of Virginia, served 1973–1974. A holdover from the Nixon administration, he was dismissed by Ford, who disliked what he called "his aloof, frequently arrogant manner." (2) Donald H. Rumsfeld (1932–), of Illinois, served 1975–1977. Transferred from White House chief of staff, he warned that the Soviet Union was attempting to achieve nuclear weapons superiority.

Attorney General. (1) William B. Saxbe (1916–), of Ohio, served 1974–1975. A holdover from the Nixon administration, he ruled that the Nixon White House tapes belonged to the former president and should be sent to him, a position overruled by Congress. He resigned to become ambassador to India. (2) Edward H. Levi (1911–2000), of Illinois, served 1975–1977. He restored confidence in the department in the wake of the Watergate scandal and tightened the attorney general's authority over the FBI.

Secretary of the Interior. (1) Rogers C. B. Morton (1914–1979), of Maryland, served 1971–1975. A holdover from the Nixon administration, he was Ford's transition team liaison with the federal departments and agencies. He was among those Ford considered for vice president. He resigned to become commerce secretary. (2) Stanley K. Hathaway (1924–), of Wyoming, served June–July 1975. He resigned because of ill health. (3) Thomas S. Kleppe (1919–), of North Dakota, served 1975–1977. He had been serving as director of the Small Business Administration.

Secretary of Agriculture. (1) Earl L. Butz (1909–), of Indiana, served 1971–1976. A holdover from the Nixon administration, he resigned under fire during the 1976 presidential campaign amid press reports of a racist joke he had told in private. In 1981 he pleaded guilty to income tax evasion. (2) John A. Knebel (1936–), of Oklahoma, served 1976–1977. He was promoted from undersecretary of agriculture.

Secretary of Commerce. (1) Frederick B. Dent (1922–), of South Carolina, served 1973–1975. A holdover from the Nixon administration, he resigned to accept appointment as special representative for trade negotiations at the General Agreement on Tariffs and Trade talks at Geneva. (2) Rogers C.B. Morton served April–December 1975. Transferred from interior secretary, he resigned because of ill health. (3) Elliot L. Richardson (1920–1999), of Massachusetts, served 1975–1977. He was ambassador to Great Britain at the time of his appointment and had served as secretary of health, education and welfare and of defense and as attorney general in the Nixon administration.

Secretary of Labor. (1) Peter J. Brennan (1918–1996), of New York, served 1973–1975. A holdover from the Nixon administration, he clashed with George Meany and other AFL-CIO leaders and thereby undermined Ford's confidence in his ability to represent labor's viewpoint in government. (2) John T. Dunlop (1914–2003), of Massachusetts, served 1975–1976. Director of the Cost of Living Council in the Nixon administration, he resigned as labor secretary in protest against Ford's veto of the common situs picketing bill, a measure drafted and promoted by Dunlop, which would have extended the picketing rights of striking construction workers. (3) W. J. Usery, Jr. (1923–), of Georgia, served 1976–1977. He was promoted from assistant secretary of labor, in which post he had become known as Nixon's labor troubleshooter. He helped mediate the Teamsters' strike against the auto companies in 1976.

Secretary of Health, Education and Welfare. (1) Caspar W. Weinberger (1917–), of California, served 1973–1975. A holdover from the Nixon administration, he resigned because of his wife's ill health. He later served as defense secretary in the Reagan administration. (2) F. David Matthews

(1935–   ), of Alabama, served 1975–1977. A Democrat, he was president of the University of Alabama at the time of his appointment.

Secretary of Housing and Urban Development. (1) James T. Lynn (1927–   ), of Ohio, served 1973–1975. A holdover from the Nixon administration, he won passage of the Housing and Community Development Act of 1974, which substituted block grants for categorical grants. He resigned to become budget director. (2) Carla A. Hills (1934–   ), of California, served 1975–1977. She had been serving as assistant attorney general in charge of the civil division. She was among the candidates Ford considered appointing to the Supreme Court to succeed Justice Douglas.

Secretary of Transportation. (1) Claude S. Brinegar (1926–   ), of California, served 1973–1975. He was a holdover from the Nixon administration. (2) William T. Coleman, Jr. (1920–   ), of Pennsylvania, served 1975–1977. He overruled objections from the Environmental Protection Agency and representatives of airport-area residents to permit the Anglo-French supersonic Concorde to service the United States.

ADMINISTRATION: August 9, 1974–January 20, 1977.

Nixon Pardon, 1974. In September 1974 President Ford granted "a full, free and absolute pardon" to former president Nixon "for all offenses against the United States which he . . . has committed or may have committed or taken part in" during his term in office. He did so, he said, because during the long period of delay and protracted litigation that would precede Nixon's trial, should he be indicted, "ugly passions would again be aroused. And our people would again be polarized in their opinions. And the credibility of our free institutions of government would again be challenged at home and abroad." The pardon drew a firestorm of criticism. Ford's press secretary, Jerald F. terHorst, resigned in protest. To those who believed that Ford had shown favoritism in pardoning Nixon before he was even indicted while his agents were tried, convicted, and sent to prison, Ford responded that the humiliation of resigning the presidency in disgrace was punishment enough, "the equivalent to serving a jail term,"[7] Ford argued.

Clemency for Draft Evaders and Deserters, 1974. In September 1974 President Ford offered clemency to the tens of thousands of Vietnam-War-era draft evaders, provided that they swear an oath of allegiance to the United States and perform two years of public service. Deserters also were required to swear allegiance and serve two years in the branch of the armed forces from which they fled. Veterans organizations denounced the program as too lenient. Many exiles, convinced that they had acted properly in refusing to participate in what they regarded as an unjust war, spurned the offer of clemency as tantamount to an admission of wrongdoing.

Communist Victory in Southeast Asia, 1975–1976. In 1974 Congress denied President Ford's request for more aid to South Vietnam. In April 1975 the Communist Pathet Lao gained power in Laos, ending that country's year-old coalition government, the Communist Khmer Rouge overthrew the government of Lon Nol in Cambodia, and Communist forces in Vietnam captured the capital of Saigon. During the fall of Saigon, the U.S. embassy was besieged by hordes of South Vietnamese rushing to flee the country ahead of the Communist advance. More than 5,000 such refugees managed to escape, some clinging to the runners of helicopters. More than 100,000 others fled to safety in boats or other means. By July 1976 the Communists had sufficiently consolidated their gains in the South to unify the two Vietnams into one nation, the Socialist Republic of Vietnam, with Hanoi as its capital. Saigon was renamed Ho Chi Minh City.

Mayaguez Incident, 1975. In May 1975 Cambodian gunboats seized the *Mayaguez*, a U.S. merchant ship enroute from Hong Kong to the Thai port of Sattahip, near Poulo Wai Island. In a daring rescue two days later, U.S. forces recovered the vessel and all 39 crewmen. In the preparation and execution of the rescue, however, 41 Americans were killed.

Helsinki Agreement, 1975. At the Conference on Security and Cooperation in Europe held in Helsinki in 1975, 35 nations, including the United States and the Soviet Union, reached agreements designed to ease East-West tensions: The West recognized the East European boundaries established after World War II and pledged noninterference in the internal affairs of the Communist nations of Eastern Europe. Communist-bloc nations, in turn, agreed to relax travel restrictions and otherwise improve East-West communications.

Whip Inflation Now, 1974. With great fanfare President Ford in October 1974 launched a Whip Inflation Now (WIN) campaign, complete with WIN buttons. The deepening recession of 1974–1975, however, forced him to abandon the program and stimulate the economy. Ford later conceded that the WIN effort was "probably too gimmicky."[8]

Consumerism. In 1975 four bills were passed to enable consumers to make informed decisions and provide equity in the marketplace: the Fair Credit Billing Act, the Real Estate Settlement Procedure Act, the Equal Credit Opportunity Act, and the Magnuson-Moss Warranty Act.

New York City Bail Out, 1975. President Ford at first refused to lend federal funds to financially strapped New York City. But in November 1975, after the city itself raised taxes and cut spending, Ford signed legislation extending $2.3 billion in short-term loans, enabling New York to avoid default.

Energy. In 1974 President Ford signed legislation creating the Energy Research and Development Administration and converting the Atomic Energy Commission to the Nuclear Regulatory Commission. In an effort to curb oil consumption, he in 1975 imposed a duty on imported oil and signed into law a bill to phase in over 40 months the decontrol of domestic oil prices.

Campaign Reform Law, 1974. A reaction to the campaign finance abuses of Watergate, the bill, signed by President Ford in October 1974, with effect from 1975, provided for public funding of presidential campaigns and strict limits on individual contributions to such campaigns as well as campaign expenditures. Funds for the program were to be derived from the $1 checkoff on federal income tax returns.

Extension of Voting Rights Act. In 1975 President Ford approved a seven-year extension of the 1965 Voting Rights Act and extended its benefits to Spanish-speaking and other language minorities.

Assassination Attempts. In separate incidents in September 1975, two women tried and failed to shoot President Ford. On September 5, Lynette "Squeaky" Fromme, 26, a disciple of mass-murder Charles Manson, drew a Colt .45 from her thigh holster and squeezed the trigger just as Ford reached to shake her hand in a crowd outside the Senator Hotel in Sacramento. The gun failed to fire because, although it contained a clip of ammunition, there was no bullet in the chamber. Secret Service agents quickly wrestled Miss Fromme to the ground. She was the first person convicted under the 1965 statute making attempted assassination of a president a federal offense punishable by life imprisonment. Sentenced to life, she is eligible for parole in 1990. In San Francisco, on September 22, Sara Jane Moore, 45, a political activist and one-time FBI informant pulled a .38 revolver from her purse and fired one shot at President Ford from about 40 feet away. An alert bystander spoiled her aim, and she was quickly subdued. The shot missed Ford by a few feet. Miss Moore was convicted and sentenced to life. In 1979 she was recaptured hours after escaping from the Federal Correctional Institution at Alderson, West Virginia. She is eligible for parole in 1985.

SUPREME COURT APPOINTMENT: John Paul Stevens (1920–   ), of Illinois, served as associate justice 1975–   . A U.S. Court of Appeals judge at the time of his appointment, he has maintained a centrist position on the high court.

RETIREMENT: January 20, 1977–   . Having been defeated for election in his own right (see "Jimmy Carter, 39th President," for the election of 1976), Ford attended the inaugural of his successor and retired to Rancho Mirage, California. He wrote his memoirs, maintained an active speaking schedule, earning a reported $10,000–$15,000 per appearance, and lectured on college campuses under a program sponsored by the American Enterprise Institute, a Washington-based think tank. He served on the boards of several corporations, including AMAX, GK Technologies, and Santa Fe International, and also earned liberal consulting fees. He became cochairman of People for the American Way, founded by television producer Norman Lear to counter the influence of the ultraconservative Moral Majority. He briefly considered running as vice president on the ticket with Ronald Reagan in 1980. In 1981 he joined former presidents Nixon and Carter in representing the United States at the funeral of slain Egyptian president Anwar Sadat.

FORD PRAISED: "In all the years I sat in the House, I never knew Mr. Ford to make a dishonest statement nor a statement part-true and part-false. He never attempted to shade a statement, and I never heard him utter an unkind word."[9]—Democratic Representative Martha W. Griffiths of Michigan, 1974

"The nicest thing about Jerry Ford is that he just doesn't have enemies."[10]— Republican Senator Robert P. Griffin of Michigan

"The way back to a healthy economy has been difficult and painful. But by refusing to resign us to the seductive panaceas of more government spending, President Ford has persisted, he has persevered—and he has prevailed. He has suffered abuse, he has endured accusations about his concern for the jobless; he has borne with patience those who have questioned his compassion for the poor, and he has put this economy back on the road to good health."[11]—Republican Senator Robert Dole of Kansas, 1976

"For myself and for our nation, I want to thank my predecessor for all he has done to heal our land."[12]—President Jimmy Carter, 1977

FORD CRITICIZED: "He's a nice fellow but he spent too much time playing football without a helmet."[13]—President Lyndon B. Johnson

"Under Messers. Kissinger and Ford this nation has become Number Two in military power in a world where it is dangerous—if not fatal—to be second best. . . . All I can see is what other nations the world over see: collapse of the American will and the retreat of American power. There is little doubt in my mind that the Soviet Union will not stop taking advantage of détente until it sees that the American people have elected a new President and appointed a new Secretary of State."[14]—Ronald Reagan, 1976

"I think this Republican administration has been almost all style and spectacular and not substance. . . . As far as foreign policy goes, Mr. Kissinger has been the President of this country. Mr. Ford has shown an absence of leadership, and an absence of a grasp of what this country is and what it ought to be."[15]—Democratic presidential nominee Jimmy Carter, 1976

FORD QUOTES: "I believe that truth is the glue that holds government together, not only our government but civilization itself. That bond, though strained, is unbroken at home and abroad. In all my public and private acts as your President, I expect to follow my instincts of openness and candor with full confidence that honesty is always the best policy in the end."[16]—1974

"Our inflation, our public enemy number one, will, unless whipped, destroy our country, our homes, our liberties, our property and finally our national pride as surely as will any well-armed wartime enemy."[17]—1974

BOOKS BY FORD: *Portrait of an Assassin* (with John R. Stiles, 1976); *A Time to Heal* (1979).

BOOKS ABOUT FORD: Sidey, Hugh, and (photos) Ward, Fred. *Portrait of a President*. New York: Harper & Row, 1975.

terHorst, Jerald F. *Gerald Ford and the Future of the Presidency*. New York: Third Press, 1974.

Vestal, Bud. *Jerry Ford, Up Close*. New York: Coward, McCann, & Geoghegan, 1974.

NOTES

1 Gerald R. Ford, *A Time to Heal*, New York: Harper & Row, 1979, p. 281.
2 Bud Vestal, *Jerry Ford, Up Close*, New York: Coward, McCann & Geoghegan, 1974, p. 18.
3 Ford, p. 61.
4 Jerald F. terHorst, *Gerald Ford and the Future of the Presidency*, New York: Third Press, 1974, p. 83.
5 Ibid., p. 106.
6 Ibid., p. 124.
7 Ford, p. 168.
8 Ibid., p. 199.
9 terHorst, p. xiv.
10 Ibid., p. 215.
11 *Facts on File Yearbook 1976*, p. 612.
12 Jimmy Carter's Inaugural Address, January 20, 1977.
13 terHorst, p. 99n1.
14 Jules Witcover, *Marathon: The Pursuit of the Presidency 1972–1976*, New York: Viking, 1977, p. 402.
15 Ibid., p. 596.
16 terHorst, p. 188.
17 Ford, p. 190.

☆ ☆ ☆ ☆ ☆ ☆

JIMMY CARTER

☆ ☆ ☆ ☆ ☆ ☆

39TH PRESIDENT

NAME: James Earl Carter, Jr. He was named after his father. He signs his name Jimmy Carter.

PHYSICAL DESCRIPTION: Carter is 5 feet 9½ inches tall and weighed about 155 pounds as president. He used to part his sandy hair on the right but changed to the left during his term as president. He has hazel eyes and wears a soft contact lens in his right eye for reading. His most distinctive feature is his broad, toothsome grin. He suffers from a bad knee and a permanently bent finger, the latter the result of a cotton gin accident. He speaks in a soft Georgia drawl. He dresses simply, often wearing his "lucky" red tie. He prefers his denim "peanut clothes," however.

PERSONALITY: Carter is introspective, always ready to confront his own shortcomings and seek self-improvement. He is industrious and self-disciplined and believes strongly in the power of positive thinking. He has said that his greatest strength is an inner peace. Disarmingly unpretentious, he brought an informality to the White House typified in photos of the president toting his own suit bag aboard Air Force One. Yet for all his outward simplicity, Carter is a complex personality. Bruce Mazlish, a historian trained in psychoanalysis, concluded that a "fusion of contradictions" runs deep in the Carter character and added, "The ambiguities that could tear another person apart are held together in Jimmy Carter."[1] Indeed, Carter has been described variously as shy yet supremely self-confident, compassionate and tender but also at times inconsiderate and steely. Only occasionally did he explode in anger in front of others. Usually he expressed displeasure with an icy stare or a searing bit of sarcasm.

ANCESTORS: Carter is of English heritage. The immigrant ancestor of his paternal line, Thomas Carter, Sr., left England for Isle of Wight County, Virginia in 1637. His great[4]-grandfather Kindred Carter (c. 1750–1800) was the first of the clan to settle in Georgia. His great-grandfather Littleberry Walker Carter, a Confederate veteran of the Civil War, was killed, according to some

618 / JIMMY CARTER

accounts, by his business partner in 1874 in a dispute over the proceeds of a merry-go-round. Similarly, his paternal grandfather, William A. "Billy" Carter, was killed in a dispute over the ownership of a desk. His maternal grandfather, Jim Jack Gordy, also a Confederate veteran of the Civil War, was active in the Democratic party and served as postmaster at Richland, Georgia, for many years. It is said that he originated the idea for rural free delivery, suggesting it to Democratic Representative Tom Watson of Georgia.

FATHER: (James) Earl Carter, Sr. (1894–1953), farmer, peanut broker, local public official. With a tenth-grade education, Carter prospered as a farmer and founded the Carter peanut warehouse business in Plains, Georgia. He also sold insurance. During World War I, he served as a lieutenant in the Quartermaster Corps. Eventually he owned 4,000 acres of farmland, worked by 200 black tenant farmers. He did not share his wife's enlightened racial views and reportedly used to leave the house whenever she entertained a black guest in the parlor. Still, he declined to join the Ku Klux Klan. Politically he was a conservative Democrat opposed to President Franklin Roosevelt. He served on the Sumter County School Board and in 1952 was elected to the Georgia legislature. He died of cancer at 59, when his older son was a naval officer. It was his death that prompted Jimmy Carter to resign his commission and move back to Georgia.

MOTHER: (Bessie) Lillian Gordy Carter (1898–1983), registered nurse, Peace Corps volunteer. A native of Richland, Georgia, she married Earl Carter in 1923. She advocated racial equality long before it was acceptable in the South and thus drew violent criticism from white neighbors. As a nurse she played midwife to black sharecropper mothers who could not afford a doctor. She encouraged Jimmy to read and instilled in him the value of a good education. After her husband died, she worked as a fraternity house mother at Auburn University. In 1964 she was cochairman of the Lyndon Johnson presidential campaign committee in Americus, Georgia. In 1966, at age 68, she volunteered for the Peace Corps. After a crash course in the Marathi language at the University of Chicago, she spent two years in India disseminating birth control information, an experience that moved her deeply. She attended her son's inaugural in 1977 and visited often at the White House, apparently relishing her role as "First Mother." In February 1977 she represented the United States at the funeral of President Fakhruddin Ali Ahmed of India and revisited the village of Vikhroli, where she had served with the Peace Corps. She died of cancer. Carter has described his mother as "an extrovert, very dynamic, inquisitive in her attitude about life, compassionate toward others."[2]

SIBLINGS: The oldest of four children, Carter had two sisters and a brother— Mrs. Gloria Spann of Plains, Georgia; Mrs. Ruth Carter Stapleton, a Baptist evangelist, author of *The Gift of Inner Healing* (1976); Billy Carter, former peanut broker and gas station owner of Plains, more recently marketing director for a mobil home manufacturer of Waycross, Georgia.

CHILDREN: Carter has three sons and a daughter.

John William 'Jack' Carter (1947–   ), lawyer. Born in Portsmouth, Virginia, he earned a degree in nuclear physics from Georgia Tech and a law degree from the University of Georgia. He practiced law in Calhoun, Georgia before taking a job with the Chicago Board of Trade.

James Earl 'Chip' Carter III (1950–   ), businessman. He worked in the Carter peanut business until his father became president. He then moved into the White House and became a paid staff member of the Democratic National Committee. He rejoined the family peanut business in Plains in 1978 and was deputy Southern coordinator for Walter Mondale's presidential campaign in 1984. He later co-founded Carter/Smith & Associates, a corporate consulting firm in Decatur, Georgia.

(Donnell) Jeffrey Carter (1952–), computer consultant. Born in New London, Connecticut, he studied city planning and urban geography at Georgia State College and graduated with honors from George Washington University with a degree in geography, specializing in computer cartography. In 1978 he and a partner founded Computer Mapping Consultants.

Amy Lynn Carter (1968–). A student activist, she was arrested for illegally protesting apartheid outside the South African embassy in 1985 and CIA recruitment at the University of Massachusetts in 1986. For the latter she was acquitted. In 1987 she was dismissed from Brown University for academic reasons.

BIRTH: Carter was born October 1, 1924, at Wise Hospital (now Plains Convalescent Home) in Plains, Georgia. He was the first president born in a hospital.

CHILDHOOD: When Carter was four years old the family moved from Plains, Georgia, to a farm at nearby Archery, a largely black community, where Jimmy spent the rest of his childhood. He early encountered racial discrimination as he was free to play with black children but attended segregated schools and church services. Although the Carters were well-off by community standards, they had neither electricity nor running water. Home entertainment was limited to reading or listening to a battery-operated radio. Jimmy was a well-behaved, industrious youngster. At age five he was selling boiled peanuts on the streets of Plains. He also helped work the fields. Still, he occasionally got into trouble and later recalled that between the ages of 4 and 15 he was whipped six times by his father, once for stealing a penny from the church collection plate, another time for shooting his sister with a BB gun. His hero as a child was his maternal uncle Thomas Watson Gordy, a navy radioman. It was his influence that prompted Carter to attend the naval academy. Carter's nickname as a youngster was Hot, short for Hot Shot.

EDUCATION: Carter attended public elementary and high school in Plains. His first-grade teacher, Eleanor Forest, remembered him as a model student, well behaved and eager to read. His favorite subjects included history and literature. The greatest educational influence on Carter was Julia Coleman, his English teacher. She encouraged his interest in literature, drew up reading lists for him, and, when he was 12, introduced him to *War and Peace*, a work that Jimmy was disappointed to learn was not about cowboys and Indians. President Carter paid tribute to Miss Coleman in his Inaugural Address. At Plains High School, Carter played on the basketball team. After graduation in 1941, he attended Georgia Southwestern College in Americus, Georgia. He applied to the U.S. Naval Academy at Annapolis and, after taking additional math courses at Georgia Institute of Technology in 1942, was admitted in 1943. At Annapolis, Plebe Carter underwent the traditional hazing. He was repeatedly whacked in the rear with serving spoons for failing to wipe that irrepressible smile off his face to the satisfaction of upperclassmen. He was singled out for particular ridicule for his southern accent. He withstood a torrent of verbal abuse and more spanking for refusing an upperclassman's order to sing "Marching through

Georgia," the Civil War battle hymn of General Sherman's scorched-earth campaign across the state. Carter's best subjects were electronics, gunnery, and naval tactics. He also took ballroom dancing and after-dinner speaking and ran cross-country. As part of the curriculum he in 1944 saw sea duty aboard the USS *New York* on East Coast–Caribbean patrol; Carter's assignment was to clean the toilet troughs. He graduated fifty-ninth of 820 midshipmen of the accelerated wartime class of 1947 in June 1946. His yearbook caption read: "Studies never bothered Jimmy. In fact the only times he opened his books were when his classmates desired help on problems." Carter intended to become a career naval officer; he aspired to be chief of naval operations.

RELIGION: Baptist. Baptized at age 11, Carter was what he called a superficial Christian until early 1967, when, in despair over his gubernatorial defeat, he communed with his sister Ruth Carter Stapleton, an evangelist, and became a born-again Christian. "I formed a very close, intimate personal relationship with God, through Christ," he said of the experience, "that has given me a great deal of peace, equanimity, and the ability to accept difficulty without unnecessarily being disturbed."[3] He subsequently volunteered for Baptist missionary work among the poor in New York and elsewhere. He became a deacon and taught Sunday school at Plains (Georgia) Baptist Church. President Carter taught Bible class at the First Baptist Church in Washington. He and the First Lady nightly took turns reading the Bible to each other in bed. He does not adhere to a completely literal interpretation of the Bible.

RECREATION: President Carter kept fit by jogging, hiking, bicycling, playing tennis, cross-country skiing, and bowling (about 160 average). He also was an avid fisherman. A speed-reader clocked at 2,000 words per minute with 95 percent comprehension, Carter regularly devoured three or four books a week in addition to work-related material. He especially enjoyed the writings of Reinhold Neibuhr and the poetry of Dylan Thomas. He had classical music (Bach, Vivaldi) piped into the Oval Office but appreciated such modern musicians as Bob Dylan, Paul Simon, and the Allman Brothers. With the First Lady he screened about two motion pictures a week at the White House. He drank moderately, usually Scotch. He smoked an occasional cigar.

MARRIAGE: Ensign Jimmy Carter, 21, married (Eleanor) Rosalynn Smith, 18, on July 7, 1946, at the Plains (Georgia) Methodist Church. Born in Plains on August 18, 1927, the daughter of Edgar Smith, a mechanic, and Allie Murray Smith, Rosalynn grew up amid hardship following the death of her father when she was 13 years old. To supplement her mother's income as a postal clerk and at-home seamstress, Rosalynn worked in the local beauty parlor and helped with the sewing. Meanwhile she maintained an excellent scholastic record, graduating valedictorian of her high school class. She went on to study interior decorating for two years at Georgia Southwestern College. From childhood she was best friends with Ruth Carter, Jimmy's sister, and often visited the Carter home. But Jimmy never showed any interest in her until 1945, when, home on leave from Annapolis, he suddenly asked his sister to fix him up with her. By the second date they knew they were in love and married soon after Carter's graduation from Annapolis. She is, Carter has said, the only woman he ever loved. Immediately after the wedding they drove to Norfolk, Virginia, for Carter's first tour of duty. Having led a very sheltered life in rural Georgia, Mrs. Carter relished the excitement and independence of being a navy wife far removed from their families. She adamantly opposed Carter's decision to resign his commission and return to Plains in 1953 but, after much heated argument, reluctantly agreed. She was bookkeeper for the Carter peanut business and helped build it into a prosperous enterprise. President Carter regularly discussed policy with the First Lady and valued her advice. Like Eleanor Roosevelt before her, Mrs. Carter painstakingly overcame her basic shyness to deliver speeches before large groups and actively promoted issues independent of the president. She was the first First Lady since Mrs. Roosevelt to testify before Congress—on behalf of more funds for mental health programs. She spoke out for the Equal Rights Amendment but opposed abortion. Her greatest anguish as First Lady, she has said, was the abortive mission to rescue the American hostages in Iran. Her memoir *First Lady From Plains* (1984) was a best-seller.

MILITARY SERVICE: Carter served in the navy from 1946 to 1953, rising from ensign to lieutenant senior grade. During 1946–1948 he was an electronics instructor aboard the *Wyoming* and the *Mississippi*. He attended submarine school in New London, Connecticut, graduating third of 52 seamen in December 1948. Aboard the submarine *Pomfret* out of Hawaii he was nearly washed overboard in a storm. In 1950 he was reassigned to the *K-1*, an antisub submarine. Then in 1951 he joined the nuclear submarine program. He studied nuclear physics at Union College in Schenectady, New York, and was chosen by Admiral Hyman Rickover to serve as engineering officer aboard the Sea Wolf, one of the first atomic submarines. Rickover's drive and insistence on excellence deeply impressed the young officer. When Rickover asked Carter if he had done his best at Annapolis, Carter confessed that he had not but vowed to put forth his best effort from then on. The incident inspired the title of Carter's campaign autobiography *Why Not the Best?* (1976). Carter resigned from the navy in 1953 to manage the family farming interests on the death of his father.

CAREER BEFORE THE PRESIDENCY: Carter returned to Plains, Georgia, in 1953 to take over the farm and peanut brokerage business left by his late father. With modern farming techniques learned from the local Agricultural Experiment Station, he steadily improved production and expanded the Carter peanut warehouse into a thriving commercial enterprise, which by 1979 had made him a millionaire. He became active in local civic affairs as chairman of the Sumter County Board of Education, church deacon, and a leader in regional planning and development organizations. Locally, amid bitter passions aroused by the Supreme Court's desegregation decision of 1954, Carter emerged a voice of reason calling for racial tolerance and spurned an invitation to join the Plains chapter of the segregationist White Citizens Council.

Georgia State Senator, 1963–1967. According to initial returns in 1962, Carter was narrowly defeated by Homer Moore in the Democratic primary for the state senate, but Carter was able to prove voter fraud and thus had the election overturned in his favor. He went on to win handily in the general election and was reelected two years later. State Senator Carter immersed himself in the legislative process, literally reading every word of the hundreds of bills that came up for a vote, and promoted improvements in education. In the Democratic gubernatorial primary in 1966, Carter ran third, behind Lester Maddox, the eventual winner, and Ellis Arnall.

Governor of Georgia, 1971–1975. Carter again ran for governor in 1970, this time against former Governor Carl E. Sanders, a moderate. Although a moderate himself, Carter waged a conservative campaign, coming out against busing to achieve racial balance and inviting archsegregationist Governor George Wallace of Alabama into the state to campaign for him. He scored points with simple rural folk in derisively referring to his well-dressed opponent as "Cufflinks Carl." Carter upset Sanders 59–41 percent and went on to defeat Republican Hal Suit, an Atlanta television newsman, in the general election by the same margin. Despite his conservative campaign, Governor Carter was soon heralded as a "New South" leader eager to throw off the shackles of racism. "I say to you quite frankly," he said in his Inaugural Address in January 1971, "that the time for racial discrimination is over." Following up on his promise, he equalized state school funding for rich and poor districts, appointed dozens of blacks to theretofore virtually all-white state boards and agencies, increased the number of black state employees by 40 percent, and opened the state capitol gallery to portraits of notable black Georgians, beginning with that of slain civil rights leader Martin Luther King, Jr. He also improved educational facilities for prison inmates and established community centers for the mentally retarded. In addition, Carter reorganized state government, streamlining and consolidating agencies and boards, instituted zero-base budgeting, and championed environmental protection. In national issues, he supported the Vietnam War and proclaimed April 5, 1971, "American Fighting Man's Day," in response to the court-martial of Lieutenant William Calley on charges of massacring unarmed Vietnamese civilians at My Lai. In 1972 he directed that national party effort to elect more Democratic governors and nominated Senator Henry Jackson of Washington for president at the Democratic national convention. In 1974 he headed the Democratic National Campaign Committee. That same year, just two years before he was elected president, Carter was still such an obscure political figure that he appeared as a guest on the television game show "What's My Line" and nearly stumped the panel.

DEMOCRATIC PRESIDENTIAL NOMINATION, 1976: A dark horse not even listed in early public opinion polls, Carter was the first to declare, in December 1974, his candidacy for the 1976 Democratic presidential nomination. He campaigned chiefly on the general theme of restoring trust in government in the wake of the Watergate scandals. He stunned observers with early victories in the Iowa caucuses and the New Hampshire primary. One by one he knocked out the other contenders in the areas of their strength. He stopped former Governor George Wallace of Alabama in Florida, Representative Morris Udall of Arizona in Wisconsin, and Senator Henry Jackson of Washington in Pennsylvania. Governor Jerry Brown of California, a late entry, upset Carter in the Maryland and California primaries, but by then it was too late to stop the Carter bandwagon. Carter sustained some damage from a speech in April, in which he defended the right of neighborhoods "to maintain their ethnic purity" provided that it is done without "discrimination against, say, a black family, or any other family, from moving into that neighborhood." To some blacks, the phrase "ethnic purity" smacked of racism. As Democrats convened in New York in July, Carter had more than the 1,054 delegates needed to win. He was nominated on the first ballot with 2,238½ votes to 329½ for Udall, 300½ for Brown, and the rest scattered. Senator Walter Mondale of Minnesota was nominated for vice president. The symbol of Carter as the candidate of unity was reinforced for television viewers with the spectacle of George Wallace and Coretta Scott King and other prominent blacks joining the nominee on the victory platform. In his acceptance speech, he continued to stress unifying themes: "It is time to honor and strengthen our families and our neighborhoods and our diverse cultures and customs. We need a Democratic President and Congress to work in harmony for a change, with mutual respect for a change, in the open for a change." The Democratic platform pledged to cut unemployment to 3 percent by 1980, opposed an antiabortion amendment, and favored tax reform, busing as a last resort to achieve racial balance, national health insurance, cuts in the defense budget, gun control, and a Panama Canal treaty that guarded U.S. interests while commanding broad Latin American support.

OPPONENT: President Gerald R. Ford (1913–   ) of Michigan; Republican. As Republicans convened in Kansas City, Missouri, in August 1976, President Ford appeared to be the front-runner for the nomination. Former Governor Ronald Reagan of California had mounted a strong challenge, defeating the incumbent president in the North Carolina, Texas, Indiana, California, and other primaries, and came to the convention with a sizable bloc of delegates. In a bold tactic to win over uncommitted moderates, Reagan broke precedent to announce in advance his choice for vice president, Senator Richard Schweiker of Pennsylvania. But Ford beat back the challenge from the right with endorsements from such prominent conservatives as Senator Barry Goldwater of Arizona and John Connally of Texas. With 1,130 votes needed to win, Ford was nominated on the first ballot with 1,187 votes to 1,070 for Reagan. Senator Robert Dole of Kansas was nominated for vice president. Aware that he lagged far behind his Democratic opponent in the polls, President Ford in his acceptance speech challenged Carter to debate; he was the first incumbent president to make such a challenge. The Republican platform, dominated by Reaganites, favored tax cuts to spur business and investment, increased defense spending, retention of the Panama Canal, and constitutional amendments to ban busing and abortion. It opposed national health insurance and gun control.

CAMPAIGN AND THE ISSUES, 1976: President Ford, the only man to enter the White House without having won a national election either as president or vice president, began the campaign more than 30 points behind in the polls. Capitalizing on the powers of incumbency and exploiting Carter's image as a man "fuzzy on the issues," he managed to close the gap by election day to "too close to call." The most damaging issue to Ford's campaign was his pardon of former president Richard Nixon for crimes relating to the Watergate scandals. The Carter campaign was sidetracked temporarily on publication of a controversial interview with *Playboy* magazine. In it Carter candidly confessed: "I've looked on a lot of women with lust. I've committed adultery in my heart many times." With Ford steadily gaining in the polls, the outcome seemed to depend on the debates. Most observers believed Ford outperformed Carter in the first debate, in Philadelphia September 23, limited to domestic issues, an encounter best remembered for a 20-minute loss of the audio portion of the program caused by a defective amplifier. In the second debate, in San Francisco October 7, on foreign policy, Ford stumbled badly, asserting that Eastern Europe was free of Soviet domination. Carter, pointedly addressing ethnic voters, responded, "I'd like to see Mr. Ford convince Polish-Americans that they're not under Russian domination." Carter continued to take the offensive in the third debate, in Williamsburg, Virginia, October 22, on general issues. Meanwhile, in the first nationally televised vice presidential debate, Senator Robert Dole, to the chagrin of his party, reinforced his image as the Republican hatchet man in blaming Democrats for all the wars of the twentieth century. In the end, Carter was able to combine support in the South, the industrial North, and among blacks, white ethnics, and labor to offset narrowly Ford's strength in the West and among upper-income white-collar voters. Carter was the first man from the Deep South elected president since Zachary Taylor in 1848.

ELECTION AS PRESIDENT, NOVEMBER 2, 1976:
   Popular Vote. Carter (Democrat), 40,825,839 (50%); Ford (Republican), 39,147,770 (48%).
   Electoral Vote. Carter, 297; Ford, 240. (Ronald Reagan of California, a noncandidate, received 1 electoral vote from Washington State.)
   States Carried. Carter won the electoral votes of the District of Columbia and 23 states—Alabama, Arkansas, Delaware, Florida, Georgia, Hawaii, Kentucky, Louisiana, Maryland, Massachusetts, Minnesota, Mississippi, Missouri, New York, North Carolina, Ohio, Pennsylvania, Rhode Island, South Carolina, Tennessee, Texas, West Virginia, and Wisconsin. Ford won the majority of electoral votes of 27 states—Alaska, Arizona, California, Colorado, Connecticut, Idaho, Illinois, Indiana, Iowa, Kansas, Maine, Michigan, Montana, Nebraska, Nevada, New Hampshire, New Jersey, New Mexico, North Dakota, Oklahoma, Oregon, South Dakota, Utah, Vermont, Virginia, Washington, and Wyoming.

INAUGURAL ADDRESS: January 20, 1977. ". . . You have given me a great responsibility—to stay close to you, to be worthy of you, and to exemplify what you are. Let us create together a new national spirit of unity and trust. Your strength can compensate for my weakness, and your wisdom can help to minimize my mistakes. . . ."

VICE PRESIDENT: Walter F. Mondale (1928–   ), of Minnesota, served 1977–1981. Born in Ceylon, Minnesota, the son of a Methodist minister, Mondale graduated in 1951 from the University of Minnesota and, after service in the army during the Korean War, took his law degree in 1956 there. Meanwhile, he already had gained political experience in helping to manage Hubert Humphrey's successful Senate bid in 1948. After serving as director of Governor Orville Freeman's 1958 reelection campaign, he was appointed, and later elected on his own, state attorney general, 1960–1964. Following Humphrey's election as vice president in 1964, Mondale was appointed to serve out his unexpired term in the Senate and was elected twice in his own right. In the Senate 1965–1977, Mondale established a solidly liberal voting record in support of civil rights, education, health, and welfare. He cosponsored the Open Housing Law of 1968. As chairman of the Senate Select Committee on Equal Education, he promoted busing to achieve racial balance. He was slower than most of his liberal colleagues, however, in turning against the Vietnam War. He was a candidate for the 1976 Democratic presidential nomination but dropped out early. As vice president, Mondale established a fine working relationship with President Carter and was involved in day-to-day policymaking to a degree not enjoyed by his predecessors. In 1979 he undertook a week-long goodwill trip to China. His advice for future vice presidents: "Don't wear a president down. . . . Give your advice once and give it well. You have a right to be heard, not obeyed."[4] He was the early frontrunner for the 1984 Democratic presidential nomination.

CABINET:
   Secretary of State. (1) Cyrus R. Vance (1917–2002), of New York, served 1977–1980. He had served as deputy defense secretary in the Johnson

administration. His shuttle diplomacy between Israel and Egypt helped lay the groundwork for the Camp David accords. He took part in the strategic arms negotiations with the Soviets and supported, unsuccessfully, ratification of the SALT II treaty. A longtime advocate of détente with the Soviet Union, he came into conflict with National Security Adviser Zbigniew Brzezinski. He resigned in protest of President Carter's ill-fated military raid to free the American hostages in Iran. (2) Edmund S. Muskie (1914–1996), of Maine, served 1980–1981. He was the Democratic vice presidential nominee in 1968. He resumed diplomatic appeals to win release of the hostages in Iran.

Secretary of the Treasury. (1) W. Michael Blumenthal (1926–   ), of Michigan, served 1977–1979. A German immigrant, he had served as deputy assistant secretary of state in the Kennedy administration. In March 1979 he signed an agreement in Peking settling long-standing U.S. claims for assets seized in the Communist takeover in 1949. He was dismissed in a general cabinet shake-up. (2) G. William Miller (1925–   ), of Oklahoma, served 1979–1981. He had been serving as chairman of the Federal Reserve Board. He supervised the federal bail out of the financially troubled Chrysler Corporation.

Secretary of Defense. Harold Brown (1927–   ), of California, served 1977–1981. He had served as air force secretary in the Johnson administration. A nuclear physicist, he was the first scientist to become defense secretary. He promoted, unsuccessfully, ratification of the SALT II treaty, testifying that compliance was verifiable even with the loss of electronic monitoring stations in Iran. He warned that the Soviet Union was seeking a first-strike capability and that the U.S. nuclear strike force was vulnerable. He supported the administration's strategic shift to target a U.S. nuclear response on Soviet military sites rather than on cities and industrial areas. The first U.S. defense secretary to visit Communist China, he discussed with Peking officials possible joint strategy against Soviet aggression in the Near East.

Attorney General. (1) Griffin B. Bell (1918—   ), of Georgia, served 1977–1979. A longtime Carter adviser, he supervised admission of Vietnamese refugees to the United States and appointed a special prosecutor to investigate charges of banking irregularities against Budget Director Bert Lance. His memoir *Taking Care of the Law* appeared in 1982. (2) Benjamin R. Civiletti (1935–   ), of Maryland, served 1979–1981. Promoted from assistant attorney general in charge of the civil division, he deported illegal Iranian aliens during the hostage crisis and argued for release of the hostages before the World Court.

Secretary of the Interior. Cecil D. Andrus (1931–   ), of Idaho, served 1977–1981. Although generally popular with environmentalists, he came under fire in 1979 for postponing implementation of strip-mining controls. He stood by small western farmers against agribusiness in limiting the size of farms eligible for irrigation water from federal projects.

Secretary of Agriculture. Robert S. Bergland (1928–   ), of Minnesota, served 1977–1981. In November 1978 he visited China to conduct preliminary talks that led to the October 1980 agreement for the Chinese purchase of tens of millions of metric tons of U.S. wheat and corn by 1984.

Secretary of Commerce. (1) Juanita M. Kreps (1921–   ), of North Carolina, served 1977–1979. She had been the first woman director of the New York Stock Exchange. She resigned for personal reasons. (2) Philip M. Klutznick (1907–1999), of Illinois, served 1980–1981. He supervised the ban on the sale of high-technology equipment to the Soviet Union following the country's invasion of Afghanistan.

Secretary of Labor. F. Ray Marshall (1928–   ), of Texas, served 1977–1981. At his urging, the United States in 1977 withdrew from the Soviet-dominated International Labor Organization.

Secretary of Health, Education and Welfare (changed in 1979 to Health and Human Services). (1) Joseph A. Califano Jr. (1931–   ), of the District of Columbia, served 1977–1979. He had served as chief domestic affairs adviser to President Johnson. Having kicked a three-pack-a-day cigarette habit himself, he launched a national antismoking campaign. He promoted, unsuccessfully, passage of the administration's national health insurance bill but later had second thoughts about it. He was dismissed in a general cabinet shake-up. His memoir *Governing America: An Insider's Report from the White House and the Cabinet,* an account critical of the Carter administration, appeared in 1981. (2) Patricia Roberts Harris (1924–1985), of the District of Columbia, served 1979–1981. Transferred from secretary of housing and urban development, she in December 1979 issued new department guidelines requiring colleges and universities receiving federal funds to upgrade sports programs for women.

Secretary of Housing and Urban Development. (1) Patricia R. Harris served 1977–1979. She had served as the first black woman ambassador, to Luxembourg, in the Johnson administration. She cracked down on racial discrimination in the sale and rental of housing and tightened HUD control over the operations of the Federal National Mortgage Association. She resigned to become secretary of health, education and welfare. (2) Moon Landrieu (1930–   ), of Louisiana, served 1979–1981. He had served as mayor of New Orleans and president of the U.S. Conference of Mayors prior to his appointment.

Secretary of Transportation. (1) Brock Adams (1927–   ), of Washington, served 1977–1979. He promoted auto safety and fuel efficiency. He was dismissed in a general cabinet shake-up. (2) Neil E. Goldschmidt (1940–   ), of Oregon, served 1979–1981. He promoted development of mass transit systems and deregulation of the transportation industries.

Secretary of Energy. (1) James R. Schlesinger (1929–   ), of Virginia, served 1977–1979. He had served as chairman of the Atomic Energy Commission, director of the Central Intelligence Agency, and defense secretary in the Nixon and Ford administrations. President Carter's assistant for energy affairs at the time of his appointment, he became the first cabinet-level energy secretary. He supervised establishment of the department, which absorbed the energy-related functions of some 50 government agencies, including the now-defunct Federal Power Commission and Federal Energy Administration. He was dismissed in a general cabinet shake-up. (2) Charles W. Duncan, Jr. (1926–   ), of Texas, served 1979–1981. He had been serving as deputy defense secretary. He encouraged energy conservation and in March 1980 concluded a price regulation agreement with Canada ending a U.S. freeze on the importation of Canadian natural gas.

Secretary of Education. Shirley M. Hufstedler (1925–   ), of California, served 1979–1981. As the first education secretary, she established the department, which absorbed some 150 programs from the former department of health, education and welfare and the defense department.

ADMINISTRATION: January 20, 1977–January 20, 1981.

Pardon of Draft Evaders, 1977. In his first full day as president, Carter redeemed his campaign pledge to pardon the estimated 10,000 draft evaders of the Vietnam War era. The pardon did not extend to wartime deserters. The act was condemned by the Veterans of Foreign Wars.

Deregulation. President Carter signed legislation providing for the deregulation of cargo airlines, 1977, commercial airlines, 1978, natural gas prices, 1978, and the trucking industry, 1980.

Energy. "Energy will be the immediate test of our ability to unite this nation," President Carter asserted in a major address in July 1979, "and it can also be the standard around which we rally. On the battlefield of energy we can win for our nation a new confidence and we can seize control again of our common destiny." In a protracted 18-month struggle with Congress, the Carter administration had won a watered-down version of its energy bill in November 1978, providing for decontrol of natural gas prices, tax credits for the installation of insulation and other fuel-conservation measures, and requirements for business and industry to convert from oil or gas to coal. In 1980 Congress enacted the administration-sponsored windfall-profits tax on oil companies. Carter also promoted development of synthetic fuels.

Three Mile Island. The future of nuclear power became clouded in the wake of the accident at the Three Mile Island (Pennsylvania) nuclear power plant in March 1979. A breakdown in the cooling system of the number two reactor was blamed on a combination of human, mechanical, and design error. A commission appointed by President Carter to investigate the incident and make recommendations urged suspension of nuclear plant construction pending adoption of stricter safety standards. The Nuclear Regulatory Commission concurred.

Environmental Protection. President Carter signed into law a ban on the dumping of raw sewage in the ocean in 1977, the Strip Mining Control and Reclamation Act of 1977, and the Alaska Land Act of 1980, setting aside 104 million acres in national parks, wildlife refuges, and wilderness areas.

Social Welfare. In 1977 President Carter approved legislation making food stamps free to those eligible. In 1978 he signed the Humphrey-Hawkins Full Employment Act. Sponsored by Democratic Senator Hubert Humphrey of Minnesota and Democratic Representative Augustus F. Hawkins of California, the measure set a goal of 4 percent unemployment by 1983 and required the president to establish five-year goals for unemployment, employment, inflation, and production.

Human Rights. The cornerstone of the Carter administration's foreign policy was a call for human rights around the world. Carter denounced the trials of Soviet dissidents, notably Anatoly Shcharansky and Alexander Ginzburg. In Warsaw in 1977 he spoke out for the rights of Eastern Europeans. He condemned racism in South Africa and endorsed black attempts to gain majority rule in Rhodesia. He criticized the repressive regimes of Castro in Cuba and Idi Amin in Uganda. He suspended foreign aid to Argentina, Uruguay, and Ethiopia.

Panama Canal Treaty, 1977. After 13 years of negotiations begun under the Johnson administration, the United States and Panama concluded a treaty in September 1977 providing for the return of the Panama Canal and the Canal Zone with effect from December 31, 1999. Panamanian voters ratified the treaty in referendum by a 2–1 majority. In the United States, however, there followed months of debate, during which prominent conservatives, among them former Governor Ronald Reagan of California and some retired military leaders, condemned the treaty as a giveaway that would undermine hemispheric security. Amid intense lobbying from the White House, the Senate ratified the treaty in two separate votes during March—April 1978, each by 68–32, just 1 vote to spare for the necessary two thirds. In October 1979 the United States relinquished the Canal Zone to Panama while retaining rights to operate and defend the canal itself until the end of the century.

Camp David Accords, 1978. The Middle East peace process, begun with a bold gesture by Egyptian president Anwar Sadat in his historic visit to Jerusalem in November 1977, had stalled in September 1978, when President Carter invited Sadat and Israeli Prime Minister Menachem Begin to Camp David. During 13 days of intense, highly personal negotiations in the seclusion of the Maryland retreat, the three heads of state hammered out two documents, signed amid great fanfare before television cameras—a Framework for Peace in the Middle East and a Framework for the Conclusion of a Peace Treaty between Egypt and Israel. Although snags later developed, chiefly over the issue of Palestinian autonomy, the Camp David accords led to a formal peace treaty in March 1979, ending a 31-year state of war between Egypt and Israel, and the return of occupied Sinai of Egypt, completed in stages by April 1982.

China. In 1979 the United States established diplomatic relations with China and withdrew its forces from Taiwan. Although trade and cultural exchanges with Taiwan were to continue, the United States had thus formally recognized Peking as the legitimate government of China. Also that year Deputy Premier Teng Hsiao-ping became the first Chinese Communist leader to visit the United States, and the two countries signed scientific, cultural, and trade agreements.

SALT II Treaty Defeated. In June 1979 President Carter and Soviet Premier Leonid Brezhnev signed the second treaty negotiated at the Strategic Arms Limitation Talks. Charging that the agreement was dangerously disadvantageous to the United States, Senate conservatives, led by Democrat Sam Nunn of Georgia, Republican John Tower of Texas, and Democrat Henry Jackson of Washington, mounted a successful campaign to kill the treaty. Chances for ratification, never good, were destroyed when the Soviet Union invaded Afghanistan in December 1979. The SALT II pact thus never was voted on.

Afghanistan. In 1979, in response to the slaying of U.S. Ambassador Adolph Dubs in Kabul, President Carter cut off all but humanitarian aid to Afghanistan. Later that year the Soviet Union invaded Afghanistan, marking the beginning of a futile, nine-year struggle to crush insurgents threatening the Soviet-backed regime of Babrak Karmal. Reportedly angrier than at anytime in his presidency, Carter mounted a global protest against the invasion: In 1980 the United States suspended sales of high-technology equipment and grain to the Soviets, won passage of a UN General Assembly resolution calling for the withdrawal of all foreign troops from Afghanistan, and joined 63 other nations in boycotting the Olympic Games in Moscow. President Reagan lifted the grain embargo in 1981. The Soviets withdrew in defeat in 1988 and 1989 after a loss of 13,000 dead and 35,000 wounded.

American Hostages in Iran, 1979–1981. On November 4, 1979, Iranian militants seized the U.S. embassy in Teheran and took more than 60 American hostages. For their safe return, the militants demanded that the deposed Shah Reza Pahlavi, then in New York undergoing medical treatment, be returned to Iran to stand trial. On the order of Iranian leader the Ayatollah Khomeini, nearly all the women and blacks plus one very ill hostage were released. The remaining 52 Americans were held captive for more than a year, pawns in a global war of nerves that outraged and frustrated the American government, provided an anti-American focus to the chaotic Islamic revolution in Iran, and contributed to the 1980 defeat of President Carter. Following the embassy takeover, the Carter administration undertook a massive diplomatic, economic, and, eventually, military offensive to win release of the hostages. In November 1979 President Carter suspended oil imports from Iran and froze Iranian assets in the United States. In December 1979 the UN Security Council called for the immediate release of the hostages, and President Carter expelled all 183 Iranian diplomats in the United States. Canadian embassy personnel hid six Americans who had eluded capture in the embassy takeover and in January 1980 arranged for them to slip out of Iran posing as Canadian diplomats. In early April 1980 Carter imposed more economic sanctions and barred all Americans except journalists from traveling to Iran. With no resolution in sight, Carter on April 24 dispatched a military force to rescue the hostages. The unit landed in Iran, but the malfunction of three helicopters caused the commander to abort the raid prior to the final assault on Teheran. During evacuation, two aircraft collided, killing eight servicemen. To foil any such future raids, the Iranians scattered the hostages among locations throughout Iran. The death of the shah in Cairo in July 1980 spurred hopes that the hostages might soon be freed, but Khomeini now demanded return of the late shah's assets, cancellation of all U.S. claims against Iran, unfreezing Iranian assets in the United States, and a U.S. pledge of noninterference in Iranian affairs. Meanwhile, war broke out between Iraq and Iran, making the latter now even more vulnerable to economic pressure. In November 1980 the militants relinquished the hostages to the Iranian government. With Algeria acting as intermediary, a deal was struck. Khomeini agreed to release the hostages in exchange for unfreezing Iranian assets in the United States, thus dropping his other demands. The hostages left Iran on January 20, 1981, ending 444 days of captivity, as President Carter turned over the government to Ronald Reagan.

Carter Doctrine, 1980. In his State of the Union address of January 1980, President Carter warned the Soviet Union not to exploit unrest in Iran and Afghanistan as a pretext for attaining a long-standing Soviet goal of obtaining a warm-water port. "Any attempt by an outside force," he declared in what was dubbed the Carter Doctrine, "to gain control of the Persian Gulf region will be regarded as an assault on the vital interests of the United States. It will be repelled by the use of any means necessary including military force."

SUPREME COURT APPOINTMENTS: None.

RETIREMENT: January 20, 1981–   . Having been defeated for reelection (see "Ronald Reagan, 40th President," for the election of 1980), Carter returned to Plains, Georgia. He established the Carter Presidential Center in Atlanta and took an active role in its projects, notably the effort to eradicate the Guinea worm parasite in Africa. As a member of Habitat for Humanity, he helped build homes in New York slums. He also lectured in political science at Emory University. He was awarded the Nobel Peace Prize in 2002 for his peacemaking between Egypt and Israel and his humanitarian works.

CARTER PRAISED: "I've known him for years. He's got courage. . . . He's got a religious tone in what he says and maybe we should have a little more religion in our community. . . . The man talks about true values."[5]—Mayor Richard Daley of Chicago, 1976

"He gave me a broader role and was kinder to me [as vice president] than any President in history."[6]—former vice president Walter Mondale, 1981

"When it came to understanding the issues of the day, Jimmy Carter was the smartest public official I've ever known. The range and extent of his knowledge were astounding; he could speak with authority about energy, the nuclear issue, space travel, the Middle East, Latin America, human rights, American history, and just about any other topic that came up."[7]—former House Speaker Thomas P. "Tip" O'Neill, 1987

CARTER CRITICIZED: "President Carter simply has failed to lead the nation in the direction it must go, and as a result, America is in dire jeopardy. Our foreign policy is confused."[8]—former president Gerald Ford

"The Carter administration has managed the extraordinary feat of having, at one and the same time, the worst relations with our allies, the worst relations with our adversaries, and the most serious upheavals in the developing world since the end of the Second World War."[9]—former secretary of state Henry Kissinger, 1980

"We must overcome something the present administration has cooked up: a new and altogether indigestible economic stew, one part inflation, one part high unemployment, one part recession, one part runaway taxes, one part deficit spending, seasoned by an energy crisis. It's an economic stew that has turned the national stomach!"[10]—Republican presidential nominee Ronald Reagan, 1980

CARTER QUOTES: "The passage of the civil rights acts during the 1960s was the greatest thing to happen to the South in my lifetime. It lifted a burden from the whites as well as the blacks."[11]

"Confidence has defined our course [as a nation] and has served as the link between generations. We've always believed in something called progress. We've always had a faith that the days of our children would be better than our own. Our people are losing the faith. Not only in government itself but in the ability as citizens to serve as the ultimate rulers and shapers of our democracy."[12]—1979

BOOKS BY CARTER: *Why Not the Best?* (1976); *Keeping Faith: Memoirs of a President* (1982). *Everything to Gain: Making the Most Out of the Rest of Your Life* (with Rosalynn Carter, 1987); *An Outdoor Journal* (1988).

BOOKS ABOUT CARTER: Glad, Betty. *Jimmy Carter: In Search of the Great White House.* New York: Norton, 1980.

Kucharsky, David. *The Man from Plains: The Mind and Spirit of Jimmy Carter.* New York: Harper & Row, 1976.

Mazlish, Bruce, and Diamond, Edwin. *Jimmy Carter: An Interpretive Biography.* New York: Simon & Schuster, 1979.

Stroud, Kandy. *How Jimmy Won. The Victory Campaign from Plains to the White House.* New York: Morrow, 1977.

Wooten, James. *Dasher: The Roots and Rising of Jimmy Carter.* New York: Summit Books/Simon & Schuster, 1978.

NOTES:

1 Bruce Mazlish and Edwin Diamond, *Jimmy Carter: An Interpretive Biography*, New York: Simon & Schuster, p. 16.
2 Bill Adler, ed., *The Wit and Wisdom of Jimmy Carter*, Secaucus, N.J.: Citadel, 1977, p. 46.
3 Ibid., p. 67.
4 Walter F. Mondale, "How a Vice President Should Handle His Leader," *Akron Beacon Journal*, March 15, 1981, p. G-5.
5 Jules Witcover, *Marathon 1972–1976: The Pursuit of the Presidency*, New York: Viking, 1977, pp. 349–350.
6 *Parade Magazine*, August 30, 1981, p. 6.
7 Thomas P. "Tip" O'Neill, *Man of the House*, New York: Random House, 1987, p. 297.
8 Gerald R. Ford, *A Time to Heal*, New York: Harper & Row, 1979, p. xiv.
9 Frank Van der Linden, *The Real Reagan*, New York: Morrow, 1981, p. 214.
10 *President Reagan*, compiled and published by Congressional Quarterly, 1981, p. 100.
11 Adler, p. 72.
12 Carter television address, July 15, 1979.

RONALD REAGAN

NAME: Ronald Wilson Reagan. Wilson was his mother's maiden name.

PHYSICAL DESCRIPTION: The oldest president in history, Reagan was just shy of his 78th birthday on leaving office. Yet throughout his term he was surprisingly vigorous and relatively youthful in appearance. He stood 6 feet 1 inch tall, weighed about 185 pounds, and had blue eyes and thick brown hair with only a touch of gray. Severely nearsighted since childhood, he began wearing contact lenses as early as the 1940s. He was hard of hearing ever since another actor fired a pistol near his head during the making of a motion picture. He began wearing a hearing aid in his right ear in 1983, his left ear in 1985. In 1947 he nearly died of viral pneumonia. At a celebrity baseball game a few years later, he shattered his right thigh bone in six places sliding into first base; he spent months in traction and never regained complete flexibility in the leg. As president, he suffered from hay fever, an enlarged prostate (corrected in 1987), and diverticulosis. In July 1985 President Reagan underwent surgery for colon cancer. In an operation lasting nearly three hours, doctors excised a two-foot section of the upper large intestine containing a malignant tumor about two inches in diameter that had grown into the intestinal wall but had not yet penetrated it. Small benign polyps appeared in the colon from time to time thereafter and were surgically removed. In 1985 and again in 1987, he had a small malignant growth, a basal-cell carcinoma, removed from the outside surface of his nose. Two weeks before he left office, he underwent surgery to correct Dupuytren's contracture of his left hand, a harmless but progressive condition that had left him unable to straighten his ring finger. President Reagan spoke in a soft, though clear, well-modulated voice developed during his years as a radio broadcaster.

PERSONALITY: The only professional actor to become president, Reagan earned the nickname the Great Communicator for his effective use of television in presenting the administration's program. He was a gifted raconteur with a seemingly endless store of anecdotes of his days in Hollywood. By all accounts, he was affable, cheerful, even-tempered, and forever optimistic. According to Hedrick Smith of the *New York Times*, "His aw-shucks manner and charming good looks disarm those who from a distance have thought of him as a far-right fanatic."[1] Anne Edwards, chronicler of Reagan's early years, described him as aloof, intensely private, and reluctant to reveal much about himself to those outside his family. In a rash of so-called kiss-and-tell books by such administration insiders as Budget Director David Stockman, press secretary Larry Speakes, White House chief of staff Donald Regan, deputy chief of staff Michael Deaver, and Secretary of State Alexander Haig, the president was portrayed as a remarkably passive figure, disengaged from day-to-day operations, timid about asserting his authority, inept at personal confrontation, and lacking at times even a basic understanding of major issues. His impatience for detail and his willingness to delegate much authority to his staff came in for sharp criticism in the wake of the Iran-contra affair (see "Administration"). As president, he permitted his schedule to be influenced by an astrologer consulted by Mrs. Reagan but denied that policy decisions were ever based on astrological forecasts. Reagan confessed to being claustrophobic.

ANCESTORS: Reagan is of Irish and Scotch-English heritage. The paternal line (originally O'Regan) hailed from Ballyporeen, County Tipperary, Ireland. His great-grandfather Michael Reagan fled the small village during the potato famine, lived in London for a decade, and in 1856 emigrated to the United States, settling on a farm near Fairhaven, Illinois.

FATHER: John Edward "Jack" Reagan (1883–1941), shoe salesman. Born in Fulton, Illinois, Jack Reagan was orphaned at six when his parents died of tuberculosis within a week of each other. He was raised by an aunt in Bennett, Iowa, and his paternal grandmother in Fulton. With a sixth-grade education, he eked out a modest living selling shoes in small Illinois towns and for a time at Marshall Field's in Chicago. His future brightened in the 1920s when in partnership with H. C. Pitney he operated the Fashion Boot Shop in Dixon, Illinois, but the enterprise folded during the Depression. His next job for a store in Springfield ended poignantly when he received his dismissal notice on Christmas Eve, 1931. Following the election of President Franklin D. Roosevelt, whom Jack Reagan, a liberal Democrat, staunchly supported, he was hired as a director of various New Deal public works projects in the area, chief among them the construction of the Dixon Airport. A Catholic, he abhorred bigotry of any kind; he refused to let his children see the motion picture *The Birth of a Nation* because it glorified the Ku Klux Klan and once walked out of a hotel when he learned that it barred Jews. He died of heart failure not long after attending the premiere of *Knute Rockne—All American* (1940), his son's first significant film. "He was a man who might have made a brilliant career out of selling," Ronald Reagan wrote of his father, "but he lived in a time—and with a weakness [alcoholism]—that made him a frustrated man."[2]

MOTHER: Nelle Wilson Reagan (1885–1962). Born in Fulton, Illinois, she, though a Protestant, married Jack Reagan in a Catholic ceremony in 1904. A warm-hearted, generous woman, she regularly visited prisoners and tubercular patients and took great care that her children realized that their father's alcoholism was a disease, for which they should not resent him. She organized local drama recitals, at which young Reagan got his first taste of the theater. During the Depression she supplemented the family's meager income by working as a salesclerk and seamstress at a local dress shop. With her husband she settled in California in 1939. She died at 77 when her son was a television personality.

SIBLING: Reagan has an older brother—(John) Neil "Moon" Reagan, retired advertising executive of Rancho Santa Fe, California.

CHILDREN: By his first wife, Reagan had one daughter to live to maturity. A second daughter, born prematurely, died the day after her birth in 1947.

    Maureen Reagan (1941–2001), businesswoman, political figure. Just seven years old when her parents divorced, Maureen grew up mostly in boarding schools. She graduated from Marymount High School in Tarrytown, New York, and attended Marymount College of Virginia. After a 16-year career in show business, which included separate stints as hostess of radio and television talk shows, she in 1977 helped found *Showcase, USA*, a magazine promoting American exports. Its success led to the establishment of Sell Overseas America, an association sponsored by numerous U.S. corporations to help American business overcome bureaucratic, linguistic, and other obstacles in marketing products abroad. Maureen Reagan served as executive director of the firm. She became a Republican, she said, when she was 11 years old, after watching televised coverage of the 1952 political conventions. Long active in California Republican affairs, she in 1982 ran unsuccessfully for the GOP nomination for the U.S. Senate; the president was cool to her candidacy, and her Uncle Neil Reagan served as campaign cochairman for her opponent and the eventual winner, Pete Wilson. Although she shared her father's economic conservatism and opposition to big government, she, unlike the president, promoted gun control, the Equal Rights Amendment, and comparable-worth pay for women. During her father's administration, she worked as a political consultant on women's issues for the Republican party and later as cochairman of the party. In 1984 she campaigned in all 50 states for the president's reelection. Although an effective campaigner, she raised eyebrows among party leaders when she insisted to skeptical reporters that she and her husband, political consultant Dennis Revell, had seen Lincoln's ghost in the White House. She wrote *First Father, First Daughter* (Little, Brown, 1989).

    With his first wife, Reagan in 1945 adopted a son.

    Michael Reagan (1945–), businessman, sportsman. He worked variously as a boat salesman, part-owner of a gasohol development firm, an executive with a Santa Ana title company, vice president of a defense contract plant in Burbank, bit-part actor, TV talk show host, and, most successfully, as a professional speedboat racer. He wrote of his troubled childhood in *On the Outside Looking In* (with Joe Hyams, Zebra Books, 1988).

    By his second wife, Reagan had a daughter and a son.

    Patti (Reagan) Davis (1952–), actress, novelist. Dropping out of Northwestern University at the end of her junior year, she embarked on a show business career under the stage name Patti Davis. Under a one-year $100,000 contract signed with NBC in 1980, she appeared in just one television film, *For Ladies Only*. She landed minor roles in other films and appeared in regional theater productions. She was active in opposition to the development of nuclear energy. In 1984 she married Paul Grilley, a yoga instructor. Her first novel, *Home Front* (with Maureen Strange Foster, Crown, 1986), was a best-seller.

    Ronald Prescott Reagan (1958–), dancer, journalist. He dropped out of Yale University at the end of his freshman year to study ballet. In 1982 he resigned from the Joffrey Ballet, complaining of low pay and poor working conditions. He contributed articles to a variety of national magazines and in 1985 joined ABC-TV as an entertainment reporter for *Good Morning America*.

BIRTH: Reagan was born February 6, 1911, in the family's five-room rented flat above a bakery on Main Street in Tampico, Illinois. He weighed 10 pounds at birth. Because of the difficult delivery, the attending physician, Dr. Harry Terry, advised Mrs. Reagan against having more children. Mr. Reagan, on seeing his bawling son for the first time, commented, "For such a little bit of a fat Dutchman, he makes a hell of a lot of noise, doesn't he."[3] The nickname Dutch stuck.

CHILDHOOD: Reagan was raised in a lower-middle-class environment in various Illinois communities. When he was two years old, the Reagans moved from his birthplace to the South Side of Chicago, thence to Galesburg and Monmouth (where he watched the 1918 Armistice parade), then back to Tampico. From age nine he grew up in Dixon. Ron once nearly was killed as he and his brother crawled under a steaming train just before departure. In another incident, he and a friend fired a hole in the ceiling with a shotgun. But his worst childhood experience, he recalls, was sorting potatoes, some of them rotten, in a stuffy boxcar on a hot summer's day. At 14, he took a summer job digging house foundations for 35¢ an hour and, when the Ringling Brothers Circus passed through Dixon that year, worked as a roustabout for 25¢ an hour. During the summers of 1926–1933 he was a lifeguard at Lowell Park on the Rock River. He rescued 77 people in all, very few of whom ever bothered to thank him. One grateful gentleman, however, tipped him $10 for retrieving his dentures from the river bottom. Young Reagan enjoyed sports, especially football. In his spare time, he collected bird eggs and butterflies, raised pigeons and rabbits, looked after his pet cat Guinevere, regularly visited an elderly couple who provided him with afternoon snacks and a 10¢ weekly allowance, tuned in to the nation's first radio station, KDKA Pittsburgh, on a crystal set, and caught the latest cowboy picture at the Family Theatre. He took an interest in acting after seeing the war play *Journey's End* during his freshman year in college. Despite the poverty of his youth and the anguish of coping with his father's alcoholism, Reagan recalls his childhood as the happiest time of his life.

EDUCATION: Reagan at five was taught to read by his mother. In grade school, he usually earned A's in reading and math, B's in other subjects. A low-B student at Dixion High School, class of 1928, he played right guard on the football team, made the basketball and track teams, was president of the student body, appeared in school plays, and wrote for the yearbook. His yearbook caption read, "Life is just one grand sweet song, so start the music." At Eureka (Illinois) College 1928–1932, Reagan majored in economics and sociology but spent most of his time away from the books. "I let football and other extracurricular activities eat into my study time," he admitted in a commencement address to Eureka graduates in 1982, "with the result that my grade average was closer to the C level required to maintain eligibility than it was to straight A's."[4] He was admitted on a partial football scholarship; he earned the rest of his tuition and expenses washing dishes in his fraternity house, Tau Kappa Epsilon, and at a girls dormitory and, during his last two years, as a lifeguard and swim coach. As a freshman he was a leader of a student strike in protest against curriculum cutbacks. The demonstration ended in victory for the students and the resignation of college president Bert Wilson.

Reagan played right guard on the Eureka Golden Tornadoes football team and was on the swimming and track teams. He also was a basketball cheerleader, president of the student council and booster club, feature editor of the yearbook, a reporter for the student newspaper *Pegasus*, and a member of the debating team and the drama club. As a junior he won special honors for his portrayal of the shepherd boy in Edna St. Vincent Millay's *Aria da Capo* at the Eva le Galliene one-act play competition sponsored annually by Northwestern University. Following his graduation in June 1932, Reagan decided to enter radio broadcasting.

RELIGION: Disciple of Christ, Presbyterian. Reagan often expressed a deep faith in God but as president rarely attended Sunday services. He believed in a divine plan in which everything happens for the best. Yet he also believed in free will. "We are given a certain control of our destiny because we have a chance to choose," he asserted. "We are given a set of rules or guidelines in the Bible by which to live and it is up to us to decide whether we will abide by them or not."[5]

RECREATION: Despite his age, President Reagan kept fit through regular strenuous exercise. He worked out daily in a makeshift White House gym equipped with a slant board, exercise bike, treadmill, and weight lifting apparatus. His favorite retreat was Rancho de Cielo, the 688-acre ranch in the Santa Ynez Mountains east of Santa Barbara, California, that he purchased in 1974. He liked to work the ranch himself, clearing brush, chopping wood, or building fences. There he also enjoyed horseback riding. An avid reader of newspapers from all over the country, he habitually turned first to the comic pages. Reagan did not smoke and drank little besides an occasional glass of wine.

EARLY ROMANCE: Margaret "Mugs" Cleaver. Dutch Reagan and Mugs Cleaver, the popular brunette daughter of the local minister, were classmate sweethearts in high school and college. They parted in the fall of 1932 as he went off to Chicago to try to break into broadcasting and she began teaching high school, but they still planned to marry one day. While visiting France, she fell in love with a foreign service officer at the U.S. Consular Service. They married in Glasgow in 1935 and eventually settled in Virginia. Reagan was crushed at receiving a Dear John letter from abroad.

MARRIAGES: Ronald Reagan, 28, married actress Jane Wyman, 26, on January 26, 1940, at the Wee Kirk o'Heather wedding chapel near Hollywood, California. Born Sarah Jane Fulks in St. Joseph, Missouri, on January 4, 1914, the daughter of Richard D. Fulks, a police detective and local public official, and Emme Reise Fulks, she grew up there and, following her father's death in 1928, in Los Angeles. She attended the University of Missouri briefly in 1935 but dropped out to become a radio singer under the name Jane Durrell. The following year she signed a film contract with Warner Brothers, at whose suggestion she adopted the name Jane Wyman. In 1937 she married Myron Futterman, a dress manufacturer of New Orleans; they divorced the next year. She met Reagan during the filming of *Brother Rat* (1938), in which they appeared together. In between takes of the shooting of the sequel *Brother Rat and a Baby* (1940), Reagan proposed and she accepted. Reagan gave her a 52-carat amethyst engagement ring. The engagement was announced during a national vaudeville tour of young Hollywood hopefuls sponsored by gossip columnist Louella Parsons. Following the wedding and a reception at Miss Parsons's home, they honeymooned at Palm Springs and settled in Beverly Hills. As Reagan's acting career began to flounder after his return from wartime service, hers soared. Her role in *The Lost Weekend* (1945) won favorable notices. She was nominated for an Academy Award for her work in *The Yearling* (1946). And in 1948 she won the Oscar for best actress for her portrayal of the deaf-mute in *Johnny Belinda*, a demanding role for which she studied six months at a school for the deaf and played with her ears plugged with wax. It was at this time that the Reagan-Wyman marriage, long portrayed as idyllic in fan magazines, was disintegrating. They separated, reconciled briefly, and in May 1948 separated permanently. Reagan never discussed the reasons for the break-up, but Wyman, in testimony at divorce proceedings in 1948, blamed it on his increasing political involvement with the Screen Actors Guild and his insistence that she share his interest. Contributing to the strain in their marriage was the death of their day-old daughter, born four months prematurely in June 1947, at a time when Reagan was near death himself from pneumonia. Reagan, who resisted the divorce, became despondent and withdrawn. He was seen weeping at a New Year's Eve party. Some nights he sat alone in a parked car outside Wyman's home. The divorce was granted initially on June 28, 1948, and finalized on July 18, 1949. The court awarded Wyman custody of their two children, $6,000 annual child support, and $6,000 annual alimony, the latter to be paid only if she were unable to work because of illness or injury. He was the first president to have been divorced. Jane Wyman married orchestra leader Freddie Karger in 1952, divorced, remarried him in 1961, and divorced again four years later. Meanwhile, during the 1950s she starred in her own television series. In 1981 she returned to television as the matriarch in the popular CBS series "Falcon Crest."

Ronald Reagan, 41, married actress Nancy Davis, 30, on March 4, 1952, at the Little Brown Church in the San Fernando Valley, California. Although Nancy Reagan officially lists her birth date as July 6, 1923, early records disclose 1921 as the year of her birth. Born Anne Frances Robbins in New York City, the only child of Kenneth Robbins, a used-car salesman, and Edith Luckett, a Broadway actress, she was nicknamed Nancy in infancy. Her godmother was famed Russian-American actress Alla Nazimova. She knew little of her biological father, who divorced her mother shortly after she was born. She was raised to age eight largely by a maternal aunt in Bethesda, Maryland, while her mother pursued a theatrical career. In 1929 her mother married Dr. Loyal Davis, a pioneer neurosurgeon of Chicago, who legally adopted Nancy eight years later. She was educated at the Girls' Latin School in Chicago and graduated with a degree in drama from Smith College in 1943. While she was in college, her steady boyfriend Frank Birney was killed by a train. She gained her first professional acting experience in summer stock with her mother's friend ZaSu Pitts and in 1946 landed the part of Si-tchun in the Broadway play *Lute Song* starring Yul Brynner and Mary Martin. In 1949 she signed a film contract with MGM, embarking on a career that included 11 films, among them *East Side West Side* (1950), *Night into Morning* (1951), and *It's a Big Country* (1952), and brought her together with Ronald Reagan. According to the Reagans, they first met in 1949, when Nancy, alarmed at finding her name on the mailing list of left-wing organizations, sought advice from director Mervyn LeRoy, who in turn referred the matter to Screen Actors Guild president Ronald Reagan. Reagan straightened out the matter and agreed to meet her for dinner to explain how she had been confused with another Nancy Davis. Although he had planned to make it an early evening, he was so taken with Miss Davis that after dinner he took her to see Sophie Tucker perform at Ciro's and they began seeing each other regularly. Following a simple wedding, at which actor William Holden was best man, they spent the night at the Mission Inn in Riverside, California, and honeymooned in Phoenix, where Reagan met his in-laws for the first time. The Reagans appeared together in *Hell Cats of the Navy* (1957) and in a teleplay "Money and the Minister" for "General Electric Theatre." Mrs. Reagan long promoted the Foster Grandparents Program. As First Lady, she overcame early criticism for spending nearly a million dollars to remodel the White House living quarters and to acquire 220 place settings of gilt-edged Lenox china at a time when the Reagan administration was calling for cutbacks in domestic programs. She emerged a leader in the national campaign against drug abuse among the young. In 1987 she was stung by unusually harsh criticism for her behind-the-scenes role in the ouster of White House chief of staff Donald Regan, who retaliated with a book, released on Mother's Day, 1988, in which he portrayed Mrs. Reagan as a cunning manipulator who arranged the president's daily schedule to conform to the advice of a San Francisco astrologer. Mrs. Reagan admitted that she turned to astrology for comfort following the attempted assassination of the president in 1981. According to Michael Deaver, a White House aide and long-time friend of the Reagans, she quietly and indirectly lobbied the president on a variety of issues. Whenever the president was adamant in opposition to her, said Deaver, she would retreat and urge others to confront him instead. She reportedly encouraged him to tone down his early anti-Soviet rhetoric, to curb increases in defense spending, and to seek a diplomatic solution in Nicaragua. In October 1988, Mrs. Reagan underwent a fresh round of criticism when *Time* magazine disclosed that she had been wearing expensive gowns on free loan from the world's most exclusive designers, despite a 1982 pledge to discontinue the practice and without reporting the loaners on financial-disclosure forms. In 1989 she was awarded the Council of Fashion Designers of America's Lifetime Achievement Award for her contribution to fashion.

MILITARY SERVICE:

World War II. Reagan had been serving as a second lieutenant in the Army Reserve. Called up to active duty following the Japanese attack on Pearl Harbor, he served in the U.S. Army from April 1942 to July 1945, rising from second lieutenant to captain. Because of poor eyesight he was barred from combat. At Fort Mason in San Francisco, he was in charge of loading convoys and attended war-bond rallies. Transferred to the Army Air Force First Motion Picture Unit, he narrated preflight training films for bomber pilots about to conduct raids over Japan. While in the service, he appeared in Irving Berlin's musical film *This Is the Army* (1943).

CAREER BEFORE THE PRESIDENCY:

Radio Announcer, 1932–1937. Following his graduation from college in 1932, Reagan applied for work at radio stations in Chicago but was turned away for lack of experience. He finally was hired as a weekend sportscaster at WOC, Davenport, Iowa, for $10 per game plus transportation. In 1934 he was promoted to staff announcer at an annual salary of $1,200. He had by this time decided to use radio as a stepping-stone to an acting career, despite advice from fellow announcer Hugh Hipple that he just did not have what it takes to make it in show business. (Hipple later became an actor himself, changing his name to

Hugh Marlowe, and appeared for many years in the daytime soap opera "Another World.") Transferred to sister station WHO, Des Moines, NBC's principal radio outlet in the Midwest, Reagan became something of a regional celebrity as the voice of major league baseball and Big Ten football. Relying only on a telegraph receiver to tell him the barest outline of each inning of a baseball game, he displayed a lively imagination in fleshing out the details for his listeners. Politically, he supported the Democratic party and cast his first presidential vote for Franklin D. Roosevelt in 1932.

Actor, 1937–1965. A friend, singer Joy Hodges, introduced Reagan to an agent who arranged for a screen test, a scene from Philip Barry's play *Holiday*, which impressed Warner Brothers enough to offer him a seven-year contract, with effect from June 1937, at a beginning salary of $200 a week. Reagan promptly quit radio and moved to Hollywood, where in some 50 motion pictures over a quarter-century he earned a reputation as a solid, dependable performer, often cast as the clean-cut boy-next-door type. He played the lead in B pictures, supporting roles in A pictures. He adopted as his trademark in films the wearing of a wristwatch with the face on the inside of the wrist near the palm. He made his screen debut, appropriately as a radio announcer, in the comedy melodrama *Love Is on the Air* (1937). He made seven other pictures his first year, none memorable. Subsequent films included *Sergeant Murphy* (1938), *Brother Rat*, (1938), *Dark Victory* (1939), and *Hell's Kitchen* (1939). His first enduring performance was in the supporting role of the terminally ill George Gipp in *Knute Rockne—All American* (1940), a part he desperately wanted to play and one for which he had to beat out John Wayne, Robert Young, and a dozen others who were up for the role. "Someday, when things are tough," Reagan tells Pat O'Brien in the classic deathbed scene, "maybe you can ask the boys to go in there and win just once for the Gipper." During filming, Reagan had to run an 80-yard touchdown scene three times before satisfying the director, an effort that caused Reagan to throw up the bacon and egg sandwich he had had for lunch. The next year Reagan turned in what is generally regarded as his finest performance, as Drake McHugh in *Kings Row*. In his key scene, the most challenging of his career, he awakens after surgery gradually, wordlessly to realize that his legs have been amputated. His cry, "Where's the rest of me?" became the title of his 1965 autobiography. During the shooting of that picture, actor Bob Cummings overheard Reagan talking politics with director Sam Wood and suggested that Reagan ought to run for president someday. With the film's success, Reagan's salary and prospects improved. In 1941 Warner Brothers announced that, except for Errol Flynn, Reagan was getting the largest volume of fan mail on the lot. But World War II (see "Military Service") intervened, and on his return Reagan again was relegated to a string of forgettable films. In 1946 he signed a second seven-year contract with Warners, this time at $3,500 a week. He was cast opposite Shirley Temple in her first adult role in *That Hagen Girl* (1947) and as the college professor who tries to raise a chimpanzee as a child in *Bedtime For Bonzo* (1951). *New York Times* critic Bosley Crowther enjoyed Reagan's performance opposite Virginia Mayo in *The Girl from Jones Beach* (1949), calling him "a fellow who has a cheerful way of looking at dames" and "is thoroughly capable of getting the most that's to be had out of the major comedy encounters that develop in this film."[6] To prepare for his role as the epileptic baseball pitcher Grover Cleveland Alexander in *The Winning Team* (1952), Reagan took pitching instruction from veteran hurlers Bob Lemon of the

Cleveland Indians and Jerry Priddy of the Detroit Tigers. In his last film, *The Killers* (1964), the only one in which he played a villain, he appeared "ill at ease as the criminal mastermind,"[7] observed critic Eugene Archer.

Meanwhile, Reagan was elected president of the Screen Actors Guild 1947–1952 and 1959–1960. In 1947 he testified as a friendly witness before the House Committee on Un-American Activities investigating Communist influence in Hollywood. According to FBI documents obtained under the Freedom of Information Act by the *San Jose Mercury News* in 1985, Reagan was an FBI informant, code-named T-10, during the 1940s and passed on names of those actors who he believed were Communists. Privately, the documents reveal, Reagan criticized Congress for its witch-hunting tactics in the conduct of its investigation. Reagan himself belonged to or was associated with several organizations that were labeled Communist fronts, including the Committee for a Democratic Far Eastern Policy and the Hollywood Independent Citizens Committee of the Arts, Sciences and Professions, but severed his ties as soon as he became convinced of their Communist sympathies. During the actors strike of 1959 Reagan negotiated a new contract with the motion picture studios that provided better pay and benefits for the members. Politically, Reagan underwent a transformation from what he called "a near hopeless hemophiliac liberal" Democrat who "bled for causes"[8] to a staunchly conservative Republican. Although actor Dick Powell and others had been urging him to switch parties as early as 1941, Reagan remained a loyal Democrat through the Truman administration and campaigned for Helen Gahagan Douglas for senator against Richard Nixon in 1950. But in 1952 and 1956 he joined Democrats-for-Eisenhower and in 1960 delivered 200 speeches for Republican presidential nominee Richard Nixon. He formally changed his voter registration to Republican in 1962.

With his film career fading, Reagan in 1954 reluctantly agreed to a two-week engagement in Las Vegas on a bill with the Continentals quartet, the Blackburn Twins, and show girls in Latin costume. In what he has described as the low point of his career, Reagan opened the show with a monologue, did slapstick sketches with the Continentals, and closed with poetry. Later that year he accepted a position as television host and sometime performer of "General Electric Theatre" at an annual salary of $125,000, later $165,000. His duties included speaking at GE factories around the country. According to reporter Lou Cannon, a veteran Reagan watcher, it was his experience as spokesman for GE more than anything else that converted him from a liberal adversary of big business into one of its most visible champions. When the program was discontinued in 1962, he became host of the television series "Death Valley Days."

In 1964 Reagan served as cochairman of California Republicans for Goldwater. In the final week of the campaign, he delivered a 30-minute television address on behalf of the Republican presidential nominee, which, according to the *New York Times*, drew more contributions than any other political speech in history.

Governor of California, 1967–1975. Elected in 1966 with 58 percent of the vote over Democratic incumbent Governor Pat Brown, who was seeking a third term, and reelected with 53 percent of the vote over Democratic speaker of the state assembly Jesse Unruh in 1970, Governor Reagan established a conservative record in restricting the size and cost of state government and erasing the deficit inherited from the Brown administration. He promptly imposed a hiring freeze on state employees and cut the budget of state agencies by 10 percent across the board. He won from the legislature an increase in the state income tax to help balance the budget and a welfare reform package that dropped hundreds of thousands of the less needy from the welfare rolls while increasing benefits to those meeting new, more stringent eligibility requirements. He took a hard line against Vietnam War protesters on the state's college campuses. He vetoed bills to decriminalize possession of small amounts of marijuana and to establish bilingual education. Not all his decisions displeased liberals, however. He signed a liberalized abortion law, created state antipollution agencies, helped establish the Redwood National Park, granted conjugal visitation rights to prison inmates, and helped defeat a state proposition that would have barred homosexual teachers from public schools. But it was restoration of solvency to the state budget and welfare reform that Reagan cited as his two greatest achievements as governor. As a candidate for the 1968 Republican presidential nomination, Reagan received 182 delegate votes, third behind Richard Nixon and Nelson Rockefeller. Later Reagan admitted, however, that he was relieved upon losing the nomination that year, because he felt that he was unprepared for the presidency. During the Watergate scandal (see "Richard Nixon, 37th President," "Administration"), Reagan was among the die-hard defenders of President Nixon.

After stepping down as governor in January 1975, Reagan commented on current events in a newspaper column, a five-minute syndicated radio broadcast, and on the lecture circuit, where he commanded as much as $5,000 per speech. In November 1975 he announced his decision to challenge President Gerald Ford for the 1976 Republican presidential nomination. At the GOP convention in Kansas City, Missouri, Reagan received 1,070 votes, falling just 60 votes short of becoming the first candidate in this century to deny an incumbent president the nomination of his party.

REPUBLICAN PRESIDENTIAL NOMINATION, 1980: As Republicans gathered in Detroit in July 1980, Reagan's nomination was ensured. He had dominated the primaries, early driving from the field Senate Minority Leader Howard Baker of Tennessee, former governor John Connally of Texas, Senator Robert Dole of Kansas, Representative Phillip Crane of Illinois, and Representative John Anderson of Illinois, who dropped out to run as an independent. George Bush of Texas posed the strongest challenge to Reagan with victories in the Pennsylvania and Michigan primaries, but it was not enough to turn the tide. Bush withdrew before arriving at the convention. After having his name placed in nomination by Senator Paul Laxalt of Nevada, Reagan was nominated on the first ballot with 1,939 votes to 37 for Anderson and 13 for Bush. In his acceptance speech, Reagan promised restrictions on the growth of government and a strong national defense and concluded with an emotional call for prayer. The highlight of the convention was the behind-the-scenes negotiations, reported on frantically by floor television reporters, to name former President Ford as the vice presidential nominee. Ford reportedly held out for a promise that his role in the administration would be something akin to a co-president. When the commitment was not forthcoming, Ford declined, and Reagan chose Bush as his running mate. The Republican platform, dominated by Reaganites, dropped the party's longstanding support for an equal rights amendment for women; called for steep tax cuts, a balanced budget, a constitutional amendment to ban abortion, decontrol of oil and gas prices, greater reliance on nuclear power, and increased defense spending; and opposed national health insurance and ratification of the SALT II treaty.

OPPONENTS: President Jimmy Carter (1924–   ) of Georgia; Democrat. Having defeated Senator Edward M. Kennedy of Massachusetts in 24 of 34 primaries, President Carter entered the party's convention in New York in August 1980 with 60 percent of the delegates pledged to him on the first ballot. After a futile last-ditch attempt by Kennedy to alter the rules to free delegates from that first-ballot pledge, Carter was renominated with 2,129 votes to 1,146 for Kennedy. Vice President Walter Mondale also was renominated. The highlight of the convention was Kennedy's stirring appeal to the party's liberal roots: "For all those whose cares have been our concern, the work goes on, the cause endures, the hope still lives and the dream shall never die." The speech touched off a spontaneous, emotional demonstration. Overshadowed was Carter's acceptance speech, in which the president warned that Reagan's conservatism posed a threat to world peace and progressive social welfare programs from the New Deal to the Great Society. In a conspicuous gaffe, Carter attempted to invoke the name of the 1968 presidential nominee Hubert Horatio Humphrey but called him instead Hubert Horatio Hornblower. Kennedy at length endorsed Carter and appeared briefly with him on the podium in a decidedly awkward show of unity. The Democratic platform opposed a constitutional amendment to ban abortion and called for ratification of the Equal Rights Amendment, a federal public jobs program, development of solar power and other safe and renewable energy sources while suspending construction of nuclear power plants, national health insurance, and ratification of the SALT II treaty.

John B. Anderson (1922–   ) of Illinois; Independent. In April 1980 Anderson, a moderate Republican 10-term congressman, dropped out of the race for his party's presidential nomination to run as an independent. He chose Governor Patrick J. Lucey, a Wisconsin Democrat, as his running mate. In New York the ticket was endorsed by the Liberal party. Anderson ran on a platform opposing a constitutional amendment to ban abortion and calling for lower Social Security taxes, a stiff gasoline tax to discourage use of imported oil, and ratification of the SALT II treaty.

CAMPAIGN AND THE ISSUES, 1980: President Carter knew from the outset that he was in trouble. Runaway inflation, the gasoline shortage, and the lingering hostage crisis in Iran all contributed to the perception of an administration lacking direction, helpless to impose its will on a Democratic Congress or to influence events abroad. Carter tried to focus the debate on what kind of president Ronald Reagan would make. Ironically, however, Carter had aided Republican efforts to keep the spotlight on the administration's record by compiling a list of 660 promises he made during the 1976 campaign. Republicans gleefully dug up the document and compared promise with performance. Carter's promise to trim the inflation rate to 4 percent seemed ludicrous with the cost of living galloping at a double-digit pace. Similarly, he raised defense spending after pledging to cut the Pentagon budget and tolerated severe deficits despite his vow to balance the budget by the end of his term. The issues dividing the candidates were sharp: President Carter called for greater research into synthetic fuels while maintaining the windfall-profits tax on oil companies; Reagan vowed to unleash the oil companies from government restraints and urged greater reliance on nuclear power; Anderson touted his controversial

50¢-a-gallon tax on gasoline to encourage conservation. Carter and Anderson supported the Equal Rights Amendment; Reagan opposed it. Reagan supported an antiabortion amendment; Carter and Anderson opposed it. Reagan called for supply-side economics (see "Administration: Reaganomics"); Carter accepted the party platform's $12 billion jobs bill; Anderson suggested limiting federal spending to 20 percent of the gross national product. Carter had won passage of peacetime draft registration; Reagan and Anderson opposed it. Reagan promised increased defense spending and opposed the SALT II treaty; Carter and Anderson supported SALT II and modest rises in the defense budget. Carter called for national health insurance; Reagan and Anderson supported only catastrophic health insurance. In a televised debate in Cleveland, October 28, between the two principal candidates, Carter lashed out at Reagan as a threat to world peace and long-established social programs. Reagan brushed aside such charges with a smile and a shake of the head, saying, in dismay, "There you go again." Observers agreed that Reagan scored well with viewers at the close of the debate in posing this question directly into the camera: "I think when you make that decision [on election day] it might be well if you could ask yourself, are you better off than you were four years ago?" In 1983 it was disclosed that the Reagan camp somehow had obtained Carter campaign strategy documents that were helpful in preparing the Republican nominee for the debate. As election day neared, most pollsters rated the race a toss-up. Among the few to foresee the Reagan electoral landslide was Pat Caddell, Carter's own pollster, who informed the president of his fate hours before the polls opened.

ELECTION AS PRESIDENT, FIRST TERM, NOVEMBER 4, 1980:

Popular Vote. Reagan (Republican), 43,899,248 (51%); Carter (Democrat), 35,481,435 (41%); Anderson (Independent), 5,719,437 (7%).

Electoral Vote. Reagan, 489; Carter, 49; Anderson, 0.

States Carried. Reagan won the electoral votes of 44 states—Alabama, Alaska, Arizona, Arkansas, California, Colorado, Connecticut, Delaware, Florida, Idaho, Illinois, Indiana, Iowa, Kansas, Kentucky, Louisiana, Maine, Massachusetts, Michigan, Mississippi, Missouri, Montana, Nebraska, Nevada, New Hampshire, New Jersey, New Mexico, New York, North Carolina, North Dakota, Ohio, Oklahoma, Oregon, Pennsylvania, South Carolina, South Dakota, Tennessee, Texas, Utah, Vermont, Virginia, Washington, Wisconsin, and Wyoming. Carter won the electoral votes of the District of Columbia and 6 states—Georgia, Hawaii, Maryland, Minnesota, Rhode Island, and West Virginia.

REPUBLICAN NOMINATION FOR REELECTION AS PRESIDENT, 1984:

Reagan faced no opposition for renomination. At the Republican national convention in Dallas in August 1984, Senator Paul Laxalt of Nevada again delivered Reagan's nominating speech. In a break with tradition, President Reagan and Vice President Bush were renominated together in a single roll-call vote. In his acceptance speech, Reagan blasted the Democrats as the party of high taxes and inflation and warned that returning them to power under Walter Mondale would mean a return to the economic distress of the 1970s. Despite warnings from Senator Lowell Weicker of Connecticut and other moderates that the party would be doomed to minority status if it did not reach out beyond its conservative ranks, the Republican platform retained its staunchly conservative tone. It called for constitutional amendments to ban abortion and to balance the federal budget, pledged to reform the internal revenue code to produce a "fair and simple tax," and flatly opposed any increase in taxes.

OPPONENT: Walter F. Mondale (1928–   ), of Minnesota; Democrat. He was vice president under Jimmy Carter. Mondale entered the primary season a confident front-runner with the support of organized labor and other important interest groups. But Senator Gary Hart of Colorado, stressing a theme of "new ideas" and independence of special-interest groups, scored an upset victory in the New Hampshire primary and jolted the Mondale forces out of complacency. The Reverend Jesse Jackson of Illinois, the first black candidate to reach a major party convention with a significant block of delegates, siphoned off black support from Mondale. Hart lacked the organization necessary to capitalize on his early primary victory and thus gave Mondale time to recover. Mondale at length succeeded in putting Hart on the defensive by charging that his theme of new ideas lacked substance; "Where's the beef?" asked Mondale, borrowing the tag line from a popular burger commercial. By the time Democrats convened in San Francisco in July, Mondale had the nomination locked up. Mondale received 2,191 votes; Hart, 1,200; Jackson, 458. In his acceptance speech, Mondale surprised many observers by calling for a tax hike. "Mr. Reagan will raise taxes," he warned bluntly, "and so will I. He won't tell you. I just did." The highlight of the convention was the nomination for vice president of Representative Geraldine Ferraro of New York, the first woman on a major party ticket. Also noteworthy was a stirring keynote address by Governor Mario Cuomo of New York and a passionate oration by Jesse Jackson. The Democratic platform, dominated by Mondale forces, pledged its commitment to affirmative action without mentioning quotas, promised to raise taxes on corporations and upper-income individuals and earmark those extra funds to reduce the deficit, called for a nuclear freeze and annual summit meetings, and opposed the MX missile, B-1 bomber, and the space-based nuclear defense system proposed by the Reagan administration.

CAMPAIGN AND THE ISSUES, 1984: Looking back on the campaign in an interview with the *New York Times* (March 4, 1987), Mondale conceded that within two days after the convention, he realized that he did not have a chance of upsetting Ronald Reagan. The Mondale campaign stepped off to a rocky start. His running mate, Geraldine Ferraro, got bogged down in a prolonged defense of her failure to disclose details of her husband's finances, as required of all House members under the Ethics in Government Act. Although she drew high marks for her poise and openness during a tense 90-minute press conference on the issue, the episode consumed valuable campaign time and diverted attention from Mondale's attack on the Reagan record. On two critical issues, the deficit and trade, the candidates seemed to reverse the traditional roles of their parties: (1) Deficit spending had been a feature of Democratic administrations since the New Deal, and Republicans invariably pledged to balance the budget. In 1984, however, President Reagan talked casually of deficits in the $200 billion range, predicting that sustained economic growth and unspecified cuts in domestic spending would balance the budget in due time. Mondale denounced the administration for amassing the largest deficits in history and proposed making up the shortfall with a minimum corporate tax, a 10 percent surcharge on family incomes above $100,000, and other specific measures aimed at the wealthy. Reagan promised never to raise taxes except as a last resort. (2) The struggle to reduce tariff barriers and bring about freer trade around the globe had been a Democratic issue since Grover Cleveland made the idea respectable in the 1880s. Now a century later Mondale, reflecting the view of organized labor, called for certain import quotas, subsidies for exporters trying to crack difficult foreign markets, and domestic-content legislation requiring a minimum of American parts or labor to be used in the manufacture of foreign cars sold in the United States. Reagan opposed most such protectionist measures and reminded voters that the Hawley-Smoot Tariff (see "Herbert Hoover, 31st president," "Administration") helped precipitate the Great Depression.

In foreign policy matters, Mondale criticized the Reagan administration for a wasteful military buildup and failure to negotiate arms reduction with the Soviets. He ridiculed Reagan's proposed space-based nuclear defense system as unreliable and a dangerous extension of the arms race. And he condemned the Reagan administration's covert efforts to destabilize the Sandinista regime in Nicaragua.

The age issue loomed over the campaign briefly following the first presidential debate on domestic issues in Louisville, during which President Reagan appeared befuddled at times and stammered noticeably in his closing remarks. His halting performance disturbed some who realized that Reagan already was a few years older than Eisenhower was when he left office. But Reagan deftly turned aside the issue during the second debate on foreign policy in Kansas City. Appearing alert, knowledgeable, and in control, he even drew an appreciative chuckle from Mondale when he quipped, "I'm not going to exploit for political purposes my opponent's youth and inexperience." A debate between the vice presidential candidates in Philadelphia was rather dull except for a brief tense exchange in which Ferraro upbraided Vice President Bush for addressing her in a condescending manner. Although Mondale was drawing increasingly large crowds, he made little progress in the polls. In every region of the country, voters of all age groups and nearly all blocs preferred Reagan over Mondale. Even with Ferraro on the ticket, Mondale failed to win a majority among women, Catholics, or New York's large Italian-American community. Blacks still voted 10–1 for the Democratic nominee, however, and Mondale remained popular among Jewish and Hispanic voters as well as the very poor. The Sierra Club supported Mondale; this was the first time the environmental group ever endorsed a presidential candidate. But it was not enough to offset Reagan's huge margins elsewhere. On the eve of the election, there was an unusually large disparity in public opinion poll predictions of Reagan's margin of victory. They ranged from the Roper projections of a 10-point victory margin for Reagan to the landslide proportions of 25 percent cited by *USA Today*. The Gallup Poll called it perfectly, Reagan by 18 percent.

ELECTION AS PRESIDENT, SECOND TERM, NOVEMBER 6, 1984:

Popular Vote. Reagan (Republican), 54,281,858 (59%); Mondale (Democrat), 37,457,215 (41%).

Electoral Vote. Reagan, 525; Mondale, 13. Reagan's electoral total was the largest in history.

States Carried. Reagan won the electoral votes of 49 states—Alabama, Alaska, Arizona, Arkansas, California, Colorado, Connecticut, Delaware, Florida, Georgia, Hawaii, Idaho, Illinois, Indiana, Iowa, Kansas, Kentucky, Louisiana, Maine, Maryland, Massachusetts, Michigan, Mississippi, Missouri, Montana, Nebraska, Nevada, New Hampshire, New Jersey, New Mexico, New York, North Carolina, North Dakota, Ohio, Oklahoma, Oregon, Pennsylvania,

Rhode Island, South Carolina, South Dakota, Tennessee, Texas, Utah, Vermont, Virginia, Washington, West Virginia, Wisconsin, and Wyoming. Mondale won the electoral votes of the District of Columbia and 1 state—Minnesota.

INAUGURAL ADDRESS (FIRST): January 20, 1981. ". . . Now, so there will be no misunderstanding, it's not my intention to do away with government.

"It is rather to make it work—work with us, not over us; to stand by our side, not ride on our back. Government can and must provide opportunity, not smother it; foster productivity, not stifle it. . . .

"It is time for us to realize that we are too great a nation to limit ourselves to small dreams. We're not, as some would have us believe, doomed to an inevitable decline. I do not believe in a fate that will fall on us no matter what we do. I do believe in a fate that will fall on us if we do nothing. . . ."

INAUGURAL ADDRESS (SECOND): January 21, 1985. ". . . We are creating a nation once again vibrant, robust and alive. But there are many mountains yet to climb. We will not rest until every American enjoys the fullness of freedom, dignity and opportunity as our birthright. It is our birthright as citizens of this great republic.

"And if we meet this challenge, these will be years when Americans have restored their confidence and tradition of progress; when our values of faith, family, work and neighborhood were restated for a modern age; when our economy was finally freed from government's grip; when we made sincere efforts at meaningful arms reductions . . . ; when America courageously supported the struggle for individual liberty, self-government and free enterprise throughout the world and turned the tide of history away from totalitarian darkness and into the warm sunlight of human freedom. . . ."

VICE PRESIDENT: George Bush (1924–   ), of Texas, served 1981–1989. See "George Bush, 41st President."

CABINET:

Secretary of State. (1) Alexander M. Haig, Jr. (1924–   ), of Pennsylvania, served 1981–1982. He drew widespread criticism on the day Reagan was shot for declaring himself, erroneously, "in control of the government." In 1982 he tried in vain to find a peaceful solution to the British-Argentine dispute over the Falkland Islands. Haig resigned abruptly, complaining that administration foreign policy was no longer clear or consistent. In *Caveat: Realism, Reagan and Foreign Policy* (Macmillan, 1984), he credited Reagan with having sound instincts but lamented that too often they were subjugated to the whims of the White House staff, which Haig portrayed as a collection of amateur diplomats more concerned with short-term political gain than long-term foreign policy objectives. He was a candidate for the Republican presidential nomination in 1988. (2) George P. Shultz (1920–   ), of California, served 1982–1989. He had served as labor secretary and treasury secretary in the Nixon administration. Long the target of conservative hard-liners who distrusted Shultz's eagerness to negotiate arms control with the Soviets, Shultz survived intense administration infighting with the full confidence of the president, who on at least three separate occasions refused to accept his resignation. He struggled with mixed success to assert State Department influence over foreign policy decision-making at the expense of White House operatives. He opposed the arms-for-hostages deal with Iran and was appalled to learn of the diversion of funds to the contras (see "Administration: Iran-Contra Scandal"). In 1988, he denied Palestine Liberation Organization Chairman Yasser Arafat an entry visa to speak to the United Nations on the ground that he countenanced terrorism, but in a stunning reversal of U.S. policy weeks later he urged, and the administration approved, the beginning of a dialogue with the PLO after Arafat explicitly renounced all forms of terrorism and for the first time acknowledged Israel's right to exist.

Secretary of the Treasury. (1) Donald T. Regan (1918–2003), of New York, served 1981–1985. He pressed for broad tax cuts, detailed reform of the federal income tax structure, and deregulation of the banking industry. He switched jobs with White House chief of staff James Baker. In *For the Record: From Wall Street to Washington* (Harcourt, Brace, Jovanovich, 1988), he revealed that White House scheduling was influenced by astrology. (2) James A. Baker. (1930–), of Texas, served 1985–1988. He helped steer to passage landmark income tax reform. He engineered a slide in the dollar in order to reduce the record U.S. trade deficit and head off mounting protectionism in Congress. He resigned to direct the presidential campaign of George Bush. He was appointed secretary of state in the Bush administration. (3) Nicholas F. Brady (1930–), of New Jersey, served 1988–1989. He stayed on in the Bush administration.

Secretary of Defense. (1) Caspar W. Weinberger (1917–), of California, served 1981–1987. He had served as health, education and welfare secretary in the Nixon and Ford administrations. Amid sharp cutbacks in social programs, he presided over the largest military buildup in U.S. peace-time history. He was a principal opponent of arms control talks with the Soviet Union. He vigorously pressed for the development of the Strategic Defense Initiative, the so-called Star Wars defense system. He opposed sending the Marines to Lebanon in 1982 and arms sales to Iran. (2) Frank C. Carlucci (1930–), of Pennsylvania, served 1987–1989. Unlike his predecessor, he enjoyed a good working relationship with Congress. He trimmed the defense budget by more than 10 percent by eliminating certain weapons systems. In 1988 he established a departmental task force to determine how to reform the weapons procurement system in the wake of the defense contracting bribery scandal.

Attorney General. (1) William French Smith (1917–1990), of California, served 1981–1985. Reagan's lawyer and long-time friend, he directed the legal battle to decertify striking air traffic controllers in 1981. He reversed the department's longstanding support for busing and affirmative action to achieve racial balance and eased antitrust enforcement. He stepped up efforts against organized crime and drug trafficking. (2) Edwin Meese (1931–), of California, served 1985–1988. His confirmation hearings dragged on for more than a year amid charges that while serving as counselor to the president, he found federal jobs for those who had assisted him financially. He was cleared by a special prosecutor and confirmed over determined Democratic opposition. In 1988 another special prosecutor, James McKay, cleared Meese of other criminal charges, including involvement with the Wedtech Corporation, a defense contractor at the center of an influence peddling scheme, and a bribery scandal involving the proposed construction of a Middle East oil pipeline. Although McKay concluded that Meese probably had violated the law, the evidence against him was insufficient to return an indictment. In March 1988, two of Meese's top aides, the deputy attorney general and the head of the criminal division, resigned reportedly over what they regarded as his unethical conduct. More visible and combative than his predecessor, Meese was a hero to hard-line conservatives as he pressed to bolster the rights of victims of crime at the expense of criminal defendants and carefully culled judicial appointments from a pool of like-minded conservatives. He undertook a campaign to educate the young about the dangers of drug abuse. Meese was severely criticized for his role in the Iran-contra affair. He advised the president that it was legal to authorize U.S. arms sales to Iran without notifying Congress and, many on the Iran-contra committee charged, directed a sloppy investigation of the diversion of funds to the contras. Meese surprised everyone, including President Reagan, in resigning abruptly the day the McKay report cleared him of criminal wrongdoing. In January 1989, the Justice Department's Office of Professional Responsibility, in a final review of the McKay probe, condemned Meese for "conduct which should not be tolerated of any government employee, especially not the attorney general" and declared that if Meese were still in office he would have been subject to disciplinary action. (3) Richard Thornburgh (1932–   ), of Pennsylvania, served 1988–1989. A former Pennsylvania governor who gained national attention for his calm leadership during the nuclear accident crisis at Three Mile Island, he was chosen for his integrity, broad bipartisan support, and ability to restore morale in the department in the wake of the Meese scandals. He stayed on in the Bush administration.

Secretary of the Interior. (1) James G. Watt (1938–   ), of Wyoming, served 1981–1983. Arguably the most controversial figure to head the department since Albert Fall in the Harding administration, Watt outraged environmentalists for his efforts to open public land and resources to private development. Frequently in hot water for his inflammatory rhetoric, Watt resigned under bipartisan attack for his reference to members of an advisory panel as "a black, a woman, two Jews, and a cripple." (2) William P. Clark (1930–   ), of California, served 1983–1985. He had been serving as national security advisor. Less abrasive than his predecessor, he improved relations with Congress and environmentalists. He renewed modest acquisition of parklands and scaled back Watt's plans for private development of federal lands. (3) Donald P. Hodel (1935–   ), of Oregon, served 1985–1989. Transferred from energy secretary, he attempted to find middle ground between conservationists and oil producers eager to drill federal lands.

Secretary of Agriculture. (1) John R. Block (1935–   ), of Illinois, served 1981–1986. A hog farmer himself, he struggled with limited success to free his fellow farmers from dependence on federal price and income supports. He argued successfully for an end to the grain embargo against the Soviet Union. (2) Richard E. Lyng (1918–2003), of California, served 1986–1989. He was Block's deputy and had served as California agriculture director under Governor Ronald Reagan. He recognized half of the nation's agricultural counties as disaster areas amid the 1988 drought.

Secretary of Commerce. (1) Malcolm Baldrige (1922–1987), of Connecticut, served 1981–1987. He sought middle ground between the administration's free trade policy and the rising tide of protectionism in Congress. He was killed in a horse-riding accident while in office. (2) C. William Verity, Jr. (1917–   ), of Ohio, served 1987–1989. He won administration support, over Pentagon objections, to expand trade with the Soviet Union in such areas as energy, medicine, and construction.

Secretary of Labor. (1) Raymond J. Donovan (1930–   ), of New Jersey, served 1981–1985. Dogged by persistent reports that while executive vice president of a New Jersey construction company he had taken part in bribery and had ties to organized crime, he was cleared in two separate special-prosecutor probes but in 1985 resigned after being indicted on charges of fraud and larceny in connection with a subway construction project before he joined the cabinet. He was the first cabinet member ever to be indicted while in office. He was acquitted of all charges at the end of an eight-month trial. (2) William E. Brock (1930–   ), of Tennessee, served 1985–1987. He improved relations with organized labor. He resigned to direct the presidential campaign of Senator Robert Dole. (3) Ann Dore McLaughlin (1941–   ), of Washington, D.C., served 1987–1989. She lifted a 1943 ban on the at-home manufacture of jewelry and certain apparel on the ground that such work no longer is performed under sweatshop conditions.

Secretary of Health and Human Services. (1) Richard S. Schweiker (1926–   ), of Pennsylvania, served 1981–1983. He had been Reagan's choice for vice president in 1976 (see "Jimmy Carter, 39th President," "Opponent"). He set out to hold down health-care costs and restore the Social Security system to solvency. (2) Margaret M. Heckler (1931–   ), of Massachusetts, served 1983–1985. She pressed for swifter collection of child-support from delinquent fathers and increased funding for AIDS research. Her ouster reportedly was engineered by White House chief of staff Donald Regan. (3) Otis R. Bowen (1918–   ), of Indiana, served 1985–1989. A retired physician, he in 1988 won an expansion of Medicare to cover certain catastrophic health costs. He predicted that the AIDS epidemic will reach the proportions of the Black Plague before a cure is found.

Secretary of Housing and Urban Development. Samuel R. Pierce, Jr. (1922–2000), of New York, served 1981–1989. The ranking black in the administration and the only member of the Reagan cabinet to serve throughout both terms in the same post, he earned the nickname Silent Sam for his low profile. He had been on the job for five months when President Reagan bumped into him at an official function and failed to recognize him. Pierce phased out construction of federally subsidized low-rent housing.

Secretary of Transportation. (1) Andrew "Drew" Lewis (1931–   ), of Pennsylvania, served 1981–1983. He implemented the administration's no-compromise policy during the 1981 air traffic controllers strike, cut federal operating subsidies for mass transit, pressed for voluntary curbs on Japanese auto imports, and won a boost in the federal gasoline tax to finance repair of the nation's highways and mass transit systems. (2) Elizabeth H. Dole (1936–   ), of Kansas, served 1983–1987. She instituted random drug testing for public transportation workers in safety-related positions, promoted air bags and other passive restraint systems in automobiles, and authorized a rash of mergers in the airline industry. She resigned to join the presidential campaign of her husband, Senator Robert Dole. She was appointed labor secretary in the Bush administration. (3) James H. Burnley (1948–   ), of North Carolina, served 1987–1989. He extended the random drug testing program to cover nearly 4 million private transportation employees, including pilots, truckers, and merchant mariners.

Secretary of Energy. (1) James B. Edwards (1927–   ), of South Carolina, served 1981–1982. As head of a department that candidate Reagan had promised to abolish, Edwards, an oral surgeon with little grounding in energy matters, served amid widespread skepticism of his influence within the administration. He promoted nuclear energy. (2) Donald P. Hodel (1935–   ), of Oregon, served 1982–1985. He resigned to become Interior secretary. (3) John S. Herrington (1939–   ), of California, served 1985–1989. He promoted closer ties with Iraq, predicting that it one day will become the world's largest oil producer. He also predicted that OPEC, the Middle East oil cartel, will continue to steadily decline in influence. In 1988 he chose Waxahachie, Texas, south of Dallas, as the site of the $4.4 billion superconducting supercollider atomic research facility, physically the largest scientific project ever constructed, which is scheduled for completion in 1996.

Secretary of Education. (1) Terrel H. Bell (1922–   ), of Utah, served 1981–1985. In time he came to oppose Reagan's campaign pledge to abolish the department. He advocated a system of merit pay for teachers and the master teacher concept. He created the National Commission on Excellence in Education, which in 1983 issued its alarming report, "A Nation at Risk: The Imperative for Educational Reform." In *The Thirteenth Man: A Reagan Cabinet Memoir* (Free Press, 1988), he revealed that he was bitterly disappointed to learn that President Reagan's campaign interest in implementing the costly recommendations of "A Nation at Risk" evaporated after the 1984 election, and he described his efforts to preserve federal funding for aid to handicapped students, civil rights enforcement in schools, and other educational programs in the face of the determined opposition of those whom Bell called "right-wing ideologues." (2) William J. Bennett (1943–   ), of New York, served 1985–1988. A Democrat, he supported cuts in the education budget and advocated a back-to-basics approach to teaching. When Bennett stepped down, President Reagan called him "the best thing to happen to American education since the McGuffey Reader." (3) Lauro F. Cavazos (1927–   ), of Texas, served 1988–1989. A Democrat, he was the first Hispanic cabinet member. He stayed on in the Bush administration.

ADMINISTRATION: January 20, 1981–January 20, 1989.

Assassination Attempt, 1981. At 2:35 P.M. on March 30, 1981, John W. Hinckley, Jr., a 25-year-old drifter from a wealthy family of Evergreen, Colorado, fired six Devastator explosive rounds from a .22 Röhm RG-14 revolver at President Reagan as he emerged from the Washington (D.C.) Hilton Hotel. One bullet ricocheted off the presidential limousine, entered Reagan's left side, bounced off the seventh rib, punctured and collapsed a lung, and lodged an inch from his heart. Another round penetrated the brain of Press Secretary James Brady, leaving him severely paralyzed. Policeman Thomas Delahanty and Secret Service agent Timothy McCarthy also were seriously wounded. Two rounds missed human targets. At the first sound of gunfire, Jerry Parr, senior Secret Service agent on the scene, slammed Reagan into the presidential limousine and pounced on top of him as a shield. Neither Parr nor Reagan realized at first that he had been injured. But when Reagan began coughing up bright red blood fresh from the lungs, agent Parr ordered the limousine to George Washington University Hospital, where an emergency team, already alerted, awaited the president's arrival. Reagan walked into the hospital on his own steam but suddenly grew weak from the loss of three pints of blood and complained of difficulty in breathing. Doctors later reported that his blood pressure had dropped so sharply that if treatment had been delayed just five minutes he probably would have died. "I forgot to duck," the president joked gamely just before undergoing two hours of surgery, in which Dr. Benjamin Aaron removed the bullet and sutured his tattered lung. Reagan's first words,

652 / RONALD REAGAN

scribbled on a pad after awakening, were borrowed from W. C. Fields: "All in all, I'd rather be in Philadelphia." Reagan later described being shot as a paralyzing pain similar to the effect of being hit with a hammer. Despite his 70 years, the president made a remarkably quick and complete recovery. Twelve days after the shooting, he returned to the White House.

Hinckley was charged with attempting to kill the president and with a dozen other counts of assault and illegal possession and use of a firearm. He pleaded not guilty by reason of insanity. It was clear to everyone, including Reagan himself, that Hinckley was deeply disturbed. Hinckley had become obsessed with the film *Taxi Driver*, in which an alienated young man is driven to murder by his love for a teenage prostitute, played by actress Jodie Foster. He saw the film 15 times, bought the sound track recording as well as the book on which it was based, and began writing love letters to Miss Foster. Less than two hours before the shooting, he wrote but did not mail a letter to the actress in which he stated that he was about to kill the president simply to impress her and that he would give up the idea only if she would agree to run away with him.

In June 1982, at the end of a seven-week trial in which defense counsel portrayed Hinckley as irrational and prosecutors sought to prove him troubled but sane, a federal jury deliberated four days and found him not guilty by reason of insanity, a controversial decision that prompted calls for revision of insanity plea rules. Judge Barrington Parker committed him to St. Elizabeth's Hospital, a mental institution in Washington. After the verdict Hinckley described the assassination attempt as the greatest love offering in history.

Reaganomics. The crowning economic achievements of the Reagan administration were taming inflation and creating new jobs. By other measures, the record was mixed. The economic expansion that began in November 1982 was the longest in peacetime since World War II, but it came on the heels of the worst recession since the Great Depression. The stock market soared to record levels in August 1987, but two months later crashed more sharply than in 1929. Federal income taxes were cut significantly, but state taxes rose at least in part to restore some services cut on the federal level, and other federal taxes, most notably Social Security and certain user fees, were up sharply, so that the Tax Foundation, a Washington-based private research group that monitors government fiscal policy, estimated that the overall tax burden on the average American worker was little changed or slightly worse during the Reagan years. Moreover, federal spending as a percentage of gross national product increased, creating budget deficits larger than those of all previous presidents combined. Every year the average American had more money to spend, as measured by real disposable personal income, but saved less and less, as measured by personal savings as a percentage of that income. And much of that spending went for foreign products, swelling the trade deficit. During the Reagan terms, the United States went from being the largest creditor nation to the largest debtor nation.

President Reagan adopted supply-side economics—the theory that tax cuts spur personal savings and investment, which in turn can be used to modernize industrial plants and equipment and thus strengthen the economy, improve productivity, provide more jobs, and generate sufficient revenue, which, in combination with spending cuts, will balance the budget and curb inflation. Aided by the Federal Reserve Board's tight-money policy and a drop in world oil prices, the administration made great strides against inflation, going a long way toward reversing the psychology of inflationary expectations that had fueled the wage-price spiral of the 1970s. The inflation rate, which stood at more than 13 percent when Reagan took office, was brought down below 2 percent in 1986 before settling in the 4–5 percent range. However, the high interest rates that helped check inflation also drove an already weak economy into severe recession, which, before bottoming out in November 1982, raised fears of another depression. The monthly unemployment rate, 7.5 percent when Reagan took office, climbed to 10.8 percent, the highest since the Great Depression. The number of bank failures was the highest since 1940, and bankruptcies and farm foreclosures reached record levels. As the economy expanded once again, however, unemployment dropped steadily to 5.3 percent by the end of Reagan's presidency, the lowest since the last months of the Nixon administration. During the Reagan years, a record 20 million new jobs were created, or five jobs for every minute he was in office. Upon his retirement, 118 million Americans were employed, more than at any time in history.

The budget deficit, however, proved less tractable than unemployment. Reagan repeatedly called for a constitutional amendment mandating a balanced budget but failed to submit a single balanced budget himself. The national debt surpassed a trillion dollars for the first time in history in October 1981 and more than doubled before Reagan left office. The annual interest on that debt surged to more than $150 billion to become the third largest item in the budget next to entitlement programs and defense. In 1982 the annual deficit soared beyond $100 billion for the first time in history; in three of the next four years it exceeded $200 billion. In December 1985 Reagan signed into law the Gramm-Rudman-Hollings Act setting deficit reduction targets designed to achieve a balanced budget by the early 1990s. Sweeping tax reform enacted in 1986 restricted the use of tax shelters, shifted more of the tax burden from individuals to corporations, and dropped millions of low-income people from the tax rolls, but also blunted the progressivity of the income tax and provided the greatest windfall for the wealthiest Americans. Although the Reagan administration slashed a total of $45 billion from selected social programs, the cuts were more than offset by increases elsewhere, particularly in defense. As he left office, Reagan cited as his major regret his failure to fulfill his 1980 campaign pledge to balance the budget. He blamed that failure, however, not on his administration but on what he called the "iron triangle" of Congress, special interests, and the media.

Social Security, 1983. After two years of partisan wrangling over the future of Social Security, President Reagan in 1983 signed into law a measure designed to ensure the retirement system's solvency beyond the year 2050. Its provisions included accelerated increases in the Social Security tax rate, taxing for the first time the Social Security benefits of relatively affluent retirees, a stabilizer formula to restrict cost-of-living increases whenever trust fund reserves dip to a dangerously low level, incentives to postpone retirement beyond age 65, mandatory enrollment for federal employees, and a gradual increase in the retirement age to 67 by the year 2027.

U.S.-Canadian Trade Pact, 1988. Promoted by President Reagan and Canadian Prime Minister Brian Mulroney over significant opposition, especially in Canada, the pact promised to establish virtual free trade between the two countries, abolishing tariffs on goods and services in stages until 1999.

Terrorism. In successfully campaigning against Jimmy Carter in 1980,

Reagan had promised swift retribution against international terrorism and vowed never to negotiate with terrorists. The Reagan administration found it difficult to redeem those pledges as more Americans were taken hostage in Lebanon by groups with ties to Iran and more Americans died from acts of terrorism around the globe.

• In April 1983, an explosion at the U.S. embassy in Beirut killed 16 Americans and dozens of other nationals.

• In October 1983, terrorists drove trucks packed with explosives into the U.S. Marine headquarters at Beirut airport, killing 241 servicemen, and into a French compound nearby, killing more than 50 there. Iranian radicals were linked to both incidents. The threat of renewed attack and a resumption of civil war between Lebanese Moslems and Christians prompted President Reagan in February 1984 to announce the redeployment of the Marines to ships offshore.

• In June 1985, Shiite Moslem extremists hijacked a TWA jetliner en route from Athens to Rome with 153 passengers aboard, including 104 Americans. The terrorists promptly murdered one of the passengers, a U.S. Navy diver. At the intercession of Syria, they released the remaining hostages but not before winning freedom for Shiite prisoners being held in Israel.

• In October 1985, members of the Palestine Liberation Front hijacked the *Achille Lauro*, an Italian cruise ship en route to Egypt, and murdered an elderly American confined to a wheelchair. The group surrendered on a pledge from Egyptian authorities to grant them safe conduct out of Egypt. As they were being transported out of the country in an Egyptian commercial airliner, U.S. Navy F-14 fighters, in a daring hijacking of their own, forced the Egyptian plane to land in Sicily, where Italian authorities arrested the PLO members.

• In December 1985, Palestinian terrorists opened fire in the Rome and Vienna airport terminals, killing 20, including an 11-year-old American girl and 4 other Americans.

• In April 1986, an American serviceman was killed and 60 other Americans were injured in an explosion at a West Berlin discotheque.

• In December 1988, a Pan Am passenger jet exploded over Scotland, killing all 259 aboard and several residents of Lockerbie on the ground. Authorities traced the blast to a bomb hidden in an audiocassette player.

The Reagan administration charged that five nations—Iran, Libya, North Korea, Cuba, and Nicaragua—routinely sponsored terrorist activities around the world. Reagan singled out Muammar Qaddafi of Libya as the world's principal terrorist, calling him "flakey" and a "barbarian." In May 1981, the Reagan administration expelled all Libyan diplomats in the United States and ordered closed that country's mission in Washington following charges that Libyan agents had attempted to murder Libyan dissidents residing in the United States. In August 1981, and again in January 1989, U.S. Navy jets shot down Libyan fighter planes engaged in threatening maneuvers off the Libyan coast. In January 1986, Reagan banned all trade with and travel to Libya, ordered all Americans out of that country for their own safety, and threatened military action against Libya if it continued to sponsor terrorism. In April 1986, in retaliation for the West Berlin discotheque bombing, U.S. F-111 fighter planes bombed the Tripoli area, striking Qaddafi's home and reportedly killing his adopted infant daughter. Also damaged in the 10-minute raid were military targets, civilian homes, and the French embassy. Many countries condemned the bombing as an act of terrorism itself; only Britain, Israel, and South Africa openly supported the air raid. To keep Qaddafi off balance and encourage dissent within Libya, the Reagan administration undertook a campaign of disinformation, planting false stories in the *Wall Street Journal* and other papers that the United States was about to strike Libya again soon. Exposure of the campaign touched off a firestorm of criticism in the media; State Department press spokesman Bernard Kalb resigned in protest. In December 1988, the Reagan administration warned of a possible second attack on Libya to take out what it charged was a nearly operational chemical warfare plant. Libya claimed that the heavily fortified plant produced only pharmaceutical products.

Iran-Contra Scandal. In 1985 President Reagan agreed to sell arms covertly to Iran amid its war with Iraq in exchange for the release of American hostages. Although a few hostages were freed, still more were taken. President Reagan had pledged repeatedly never to negotiate with terrorists or make concessions to them, because it would simply invite more terrorist acts. He also publicly pressured other nations to refrain from selling weapons to Iran. When the arms deal was exposed by a Lebanese periodical, Reagan insisted that he had never intended to trade arms for hostages but rather to renew ties with Iranian moderates. In the face of overwhelming evidence to the contrary, however, Reagan conceded that the United States had given the appearance of engaging in a direct arms-for-hostages swap. In *Perilous Statecraft* (Scribner's, 1988), Michael Ledeen, former consultant to the National Security Council, reported that the president had grown so frustrated at his inability to free the Americans that he once blurted out at a meeting, "I don't care if I have to go to Leavenworth; I want the hostages out." Private middlemen who arranged the sale of the arms grossly overcharged Iran; about one-fourth of those profits were diverted to the contras, the anti-Sandinista rebels fighting in Nicaragua. In a futile attempt to cover up the arms sales and the diversion of funds, some White House officials destroyed documents and drafted a false chronology of events.

President Reagan appointed a commission chaired by former Republican Senator John Tower of Texas to investigate the arms sales to Iran and the diversion of profits to the contras. The Tower Commission condemned the administration for secretly trading arms for hostages while publicly pressuring other nations not to deal with Iran. It placed primary responsibility on the president's staff, under the direction of Donald Regan, for "the chaos that descended upon the White House" following disclosure of the arms sales. It blamed the president for failing to oversee the implementation and consequences of his own policies.

A special joint congressional committee, chaired by Democratic Senator Daniel Inouye of Hawaii and Democratic Representative Lee Hamilton of Indiana, probed the affair during May–July 1987. In televised hearings, National Security Adviser John Poindexter admitted that he had approved the plan to divert the arms sales profits to the contras but did not inform the president, he said, because he wanted to provide him "plausible deniability" in case the diversion was exposed. Admiral Poindexter also admitted that he had destroyed the document by which Reagan authorized arms sales to Iran in order to protect the president from political embarrassment. Poindexter's subordinate, Lieutenant Colonel Oliver North, in six days of compelling testimony, admitted that he had lied and falsified and destroyed documents in an attempt to conceal the extent to which the Reagan administration had been dealing with Iran and aiding the contras but claimed that all his actions were authorized by his superiors, whom he kept fully informed. He testified that, with the approval of the late CIA director William Casey, he was putting together a secret, self-financed, "stand-alone" unit capable of conducting covert actions abroad unfettered by congressional oversight.

In a 690-page report, the committee concluded that the president apparently was unaware of the illegal diversion of arms sales profits to the contras, but agreed with the Tower Commission that his hands-off management style was to blame. "The President," the committee wrote, "created or at least tolerated an environment where those who did know of the diversion believed with certainty that they were carrying out the president's policies." The report cited several violations of law: failure to notify Congress of covert U.S. operations, diversion of federal funds for purposes unintended by Congress, lying to or misleading Congress, tampering with and destroying official documents, and providing illegal assistance to the contras. The committee condemned the arms-for-hostages swap as an utter fiasco. "The Iran initiative," the report charged, "succeeded only in replacing three American hostages with another three, arming Iran with 2,004 TOWs [missiles] and more than 200 vital spare parts for Hawk missile batteries, improperly generating funds for the Contras and other covert activities, . . . producing profits for the Hakim-Secord Enterprise [arms middlemen] that in fact belonged to the U.S. taxpayers, leading certain NSC [National Security Council] and CIA personnel to deceive representatives of their own government, undermining U.S. credibility in the eyes of the world, damaging relations between the executive and the Congress, and engulfing the president in one of the worst credibility crises of any administration in U.S. history."

In March 1988, Lawrence Walsh, the special prosecutor appointed by President Reagan to investigate criminal charges arising from the Iran-contra affair, secured indictments against North and Poindexter for conspiracy, fraud, and theft of government funds. Robert McFarlane, Poindexter's predecessor as national security adviser, pleaded guilty to misleading Congress and agreed to cooperate with the prosecution. In January 1989, Walsh dropped the central conspiracy charges against North, because the Reagan administration had refused to release classified documents central to the case.

At his final press conference in December 1988, President Reagan asserted that in order to free the remaining nine hostages, the United States ultimately must again negotiate with Iran.

Escort in the Persian Gulf. In January 1987, amid the Iran-Iraq War, the Reagan administration agreed to a Kuwaiti request to reflag and escort their ships through the treacherous waters of the Persian Gulf. In May 1987, Iraqi forces mistakenly fired on the U.S. frigate *Stark*, killing 37 crew members. In October 1987, Iranian forces launched a missile at a reflagged tanker, blinding its American captain and wounding 17 other crewmen; three days later the United States retaliated by destroying two Iranian oil platforms in the gulf. In the first direct engagement between U.S. and Iranian armed forces, touched off in April 1988 by a U.S. strike against two more oil platforms in the gulf in reprisal for Iranian mine damage to a U.S. frigate, U.S. naval forces sank or disabled two Iranian frigates, a missile gunship, and three attack boats. Four days later the United States offered protection to all neutral vessels under attack in the gulf. In July 1988, a U.S. warship shot down an Iranian passenger jet, mistaking it for an F-14 fighter plane; all 290 civilians aboard were reported killed.

Nicaragua and the Contra Resistance. Within days after taking office, President Reagan suspended U.S. aid to Nicaragua, charging that country with aiding leftist guerrillas in El Salvador. The administration provided covert aid to the contra rebels fighting to overthrow the Marxist-led Sandinista regime in Nicaragua. Following disclosure in 1984 that the CIA had directed the mining of Nicaraguan harbors, Congress enacted the Boland Amendment, suspending military aid to the contras. Reports that the CIA had prepared a manual for the contras demonstrating how to "neutralize," or murder, Sandinista officials despite a 1981 executive order barring federal employees from taking part in assassinations abroad further undermined congressional support for the contras. During the aid suspension, the administration sought to sustain the contras through private contributions. Under the direction of National Security Council aide Lieutenant Colonel Oliver North and with the approval of National Security Adviser John Poindexter, profits from the sale of arms to Iran also were diverted to the contras. President Reagan claimed and Poindexter confirmed that Reagan never authorized this diversion. In 1988 Congress approved humanitarian aid for the contras while rebel leaders attempted to negotiate their differences with the Sandinista regime.

Grenada Invasion, 1983. In October 1983, U.S. forces invaded the West Indies island of Grenada, the smallest nation in the western hemisphere, to rescue hundreds of Americans threatened amid a violent leftist military coup there. With the support of Grenadian residents, who welcomed the Americans as liberators, the United States succeeded in ridding the island of the Marxist regime and Cuban support personnel. President Reagan kept his pledge to withdraw U.S. combat troops by Christmas.

South Africa. Although the Reagan administration consistently deplored the system of apartheid that perpetuated white minority oppression of the black majority in South Africa, it opposed U.S. sanctions against that government on the ground that such punitive action would fall hardest on black workers. Nevertheless, more and more American corporations withdrew from South Africa. In September 1986, Congress overrode a presidential veto to enact sanctions, barring certain imports from and new investments in South Africa and suspending commercial air traffic between the two countries.

Relations with the Soviet Union. Amid exchanges of harsh rhetoric reminiscent of the 1950s, relations between the United States and the Soviet Union grew strained in the early 1980s. President Reagan condemned the Soviet system as "the focus of evil in the modern world." Relations between the two superpowers reached a low point in September 1983, when the Soviet Union shot down a South Korean airliner that had strayed into Soviet airspace, killing all 269 passengers and crew, including Democratic Representative Lawrence McDonald of Georgia. To counter a Soviet buildup of medium-range missiles aimed at Western Europe, the United States, with the approval of other NATO governments, began deploying Pershing and Cruise missiles in Europe in December 1983, despite protests from nuclear freeze advocates in the host countries. The Cold War began to thaw in 1985 with the emergence of Soviet leader Mikhail Gorbachev and the spirit of *glasnost*, or openness. With the Soviet economy a perennial shambles, Gorbachev seemed eager to reach an accommodation with the West. Nevertheless, summit meetings between Reagan and Gorbachev in Geneva in November 1985, and in Iceland in October 1986, produced little agreement. The main stumbling blocks to meaningful arms control was the Soviet military's unwillingness to permit on-site inspection to ensure treaty compliance and the Reagan administration's plans to go forward with a space-based missile defense system, the so-called Star Wars program, which its proponents asserted would serve as a celestial shield, destroying incoming missiles in outer space. Gorbachev at length agreed to accept mutual on-site inspection, paving the way for a landmark arms-control pact, which for the first time eliminated whole classes of nuclear weapons. Under the terms of the Intermediate-range Nuclear Forces (INF) Treaty, signed by the two leaders in December 1987, the United States and the Soviet Union agreed to destroy hundreds of medium- and short-range missiles, capable of striking targets up to 3,400 miles away, and to permit dozens of short-notice inspections by each side on the other's soil until the end of the century. Throughout that time, each side has the right to assign resident inspectors at a major military factory in the other country to monitor compliance continuously. Although hailed as a breakthrough agreement, the treaty promised to reduce the nuclear stockpiles of the superpowers by just 4 percent and affected neither long-range nor very-short-range nuclear weapons. In December 1988, during a visit to the United States that was cut short by an earthquake in Armenia, Gorbachev declared an unprecedented unilateral reduction in Soviet armed forces and vowed to withdraw significant numbers of tanks and troops from Eastern Europe. Soviet forces also were withdrawn from Afghanistan (see "Jimmy Carter, 39th President," "Administration").

SUPREME COURT APPOINTMENTS: (1) Sandra Day O'Connor (1930-   ), of Arizona, served as associate justice 1981-   . She was the first woman justice to serve on the Court. (2) William H. Rehnquist (1924-   ), of Arizona, served as associate justice 1972-1968 and as chief justice 1986-   . See "Richard Nixon, 37th President," "Supreme Court Appointments." (3) Antonin Scalia (1936-   ), of Virginia, served as associate justice 1986-   . He quickly emerged as the Court's principal defender of presidential power against congressional or judicial encroachment. (4)Anthony M. Kennedy (1936-   ), of California, served as associated justice 1988-   . Reagan's first nominee for the seat, Robert H. Bork, was rejected by the Senate as too radically conservative. His second choice, Douglas H. Ginsburg, withdrew following revelations that he had used marijuana during his tenure as a law professor.

RETIREMENT: January 20, 1989- . After attending the inaugural of his successor, George Bush, Reagan retired to Bel Air, California, as the most popular outgoing president since Eisenhower. Before moving into their retirement home on St. Cloud Road, the Reagans had the house number changed from 666, considered unlucky because of the Biblical reference as the devil's number, to 668. He vowed to continue to speak out for two constitutional amendments—to require a balanced budget and repeal the 22nd Amendment, which limits a president to two terms. He signed a book contract with Simon & Schuster for his memoirs, retaining movie and other dramatic rights to his story.

DEATH: June 5, 2004 at his home in the Bel Air section of Los Angeles. His wife, Nancy, and children, Patty and Ron, were at his bedside. President Reagan had revealed ten years earlier that he was suffering from Alzheimer's disease. A month before his death while attending a fund-raiser for Alzheimer's research, Nancy Reagan said, "Ronnie's long journey has finally taken him to a distant place where I can no longer reach him. Because of this I'm determined to do whatever I can to save other families from this pain." After lying in state in the Capitol Rotunda, where more than 100,000 people filed past his coffin, he was buried June 11 at the Ronald Reagan Presidential Library and Museum in Simi Valley, California.

REAGAN PRAISED: "He understands how to use the presidency as a tool of government. He may not be strong on some details, but he knows how to sketch out broad outlines of his objectives and to provide a sense of direction."9—Republican Representative Barber Conable of New York, 1981

"He has contributed greatly to the revival of America's confidence and pride in itself, and in the restoration of the economy and in beginning the process of rebuilding the nation's military strength. Thanks to the President's fundamental good judgment and his many acts of political courage, the United States is stronger now that it was in 1980, its voice is more clearly heard and on the whole better understood. . . ."10—former Secretary of State Alexander Haig, 1984

"Ronald Reagan brought to the presidency confidence in the American experience . . . The Reagan administration has restored the American economy. It is restoring our military strength. It has liberated the people of Grenada from terror and tyranny. With NATO, it has installed missiles to defend the cities of Europe."11—Ambassador Jeane Kirkpatrick, chief U.S. representative to the United Nations, 1984

"Let us above all thank President Reagan for ending the West's retreat from world responsibility, for restoring the pride and leadership of the United States, and for giving the West back its confidence. He has left America stronger, prouder, greater than ever before and we thank him for it."12—Prime Minister Margaret Thatcher of Great Britain, 1988

REAGAN CRITICIZED: "I know for a fact that Mr. Reagan is not clear about the difference between the Medici and Gucci. He knows that Nancy wears *one* of them."13—author Gore Vidal, 1982

"How can you take this man seriously? Perhaps even he doesn't know what he's talking about. . . . He is the biggest liar of all the American Presidents . . . the worst terrorist in the history of mankind . . . a madman, an imbecile and a bum. . . . His ideas are from the era of Buffalo Bill, not the nuclear age."14—President Fidel Castro of Cuba, 1985

"For years, we've heard courageous words about terrorists from a president who sends them missiles for ransom and then pleads amnesia when he's called to account. For years, we've heard patriotic words from an administration that compares the Nicaraguan contras to our own founding fathers—and then solicits sultans and Saudis and Swiss bankers to fund them behind our backs."15—former Governor Bruce Babbitt of Arizona, 1987

"Reaganites say that Reagan has lifted our 'spirits'—correct if they mean he led the nation in a drunken world-record spending binge while leaving millions of American workers, consumers, and pollution victims defenseless."16—consumer advocate Ralph Nader, 1989

REAGAN QUOTES: "Many Americans today, just as they did 200 years ago, feel burdened, stifled, and sometimes even oppressed by government that has grown too large, too bureaucratic, too wasteful, too unresponsive, too uncaring about people and their problems. I believe we can embark on a new age of reform in this country and an era of national renewal, an era that will reorder the relationship between citizen and government, that will make government again responsive to people, that will revitalize the values of family, work, and neighborhood, and that will restore our private and independent social institutions."[17]—1980

"What I'd really like to do is go down in history as the President who made Americans believe in themselves again."[18]—1981

"Freedom is not the sole prerogative of a chosen few; it is the universal right of all God's children. Look to where peace and prosperity flourish today. It is in homes that freedom built. Victories against poverty are greatest and peace most secure where people live by laws that insure free press, free speech, and freedom to worship, vote, and create wealth."[19]—State of the Union address, 1985

"The détente of the 1970s was based not on actions but promises. . . . This time so far it's different. . . . My view is that President Gorbachev is different from previous Soviet leaders. . . . I want the new closeness to continue . . . as long as they continue to act in a helpful manner. If and when they don't, then first pull your punches. If they persist, pull the plug. It's still trust but verify; it's still play but cut the cards."[20]—Farewell Address, 1989

BOOKS BY REAGAN: *Where's the Rest of Me? The Ronald Reagan Story* (with Richard G. Hubler, 1965); *An American Life: The Autobiography* (1990)

BOOKS ABOUT REAGAN: Barrett, Laurence I. *Gambling with History.* Garden City, N.Y.: Doubleday, 1983.

Boyarski, Bill. *Ronald Reagan: His Life and Rise to the Presidency.* New York: Random House, 1981.

Cannon, Lou. *Reagan.* New York: Putnam, 1982.

Dugger, Ronnie. *On Reagan: The Man and His Presidency.* New York: McGraw-Hill, 1983.

Edwards, Anne. *Early Reagan: The Rise to Power.* New York: Morrow, 1987.

Mayer, Jane, and McManus, Doyle. *Landslide: The Unmaking of the President 1984-1988.* Boston: Houghton Mifflin, 1988.

Van der Linden, Frank. *The Real Reagan.* New York: Morrow, 1981.

Wills, Garry. *Reagan's America: Innocents at Home.* Garden City, N.Y.: Doubleday, 1987.

NOTES:

1 Hedrick Smith et al., *Reagan: The Man, the President.* New York: Macmillan, 1980, p. 152
2 Ronald Reagan, with Richard G. Hubler, *Where's the Rest of Me? The Ronald Reagan Story,* New York: Duell, Sloan, and Pearce, 1965, p. 7.
3 Ibid., p. 3
4 *Vital Speeches,* June 1, 1982, p. 482
5 Frank Van der Linden, *The Real Reagan,* New York: Morrow, 1981, pp. 90-91.
6 *New York Times,* July 30, 1949, p. 9.
7 Ibid., July 18, 1964, p. 10.
8 Reagan, with Hubler, p. 139.
9 *Wall Street Journal,* December 16, 1981, p.6.
10 Alexander M. Haig, Jr., *Caveat: Realism, Reagan, and Foreign Policy,* New York: Macmillan, 1984, p. 353.
11 *Facts on File* 1984, p. 614.
12 *USA Today,* November 16, 1988, p. A-2.

13 *Newsweek,* April 26, 1982, p. 37.

14 *Washington Post,* July 10, 1985, p. A-16.

15 *Wall Street Journal,* March 11, 1987, p. 62.

16 *Washington Post,* January 18, 1989, p. A-21.

17 Smith, et al., p. 154.

18 Lou Cannon, *Reagan,* New York: Putnam, 1982, p. 320.

19 *Facts on File* 1985, p. 83.

20 Farewell Address, broadcast January 11, 1989.

GEORGE BUSH

41ST PRESIDENT

NAME: George Herbert Walker Bush. He was named after his maternal grandfather, George Herbert Walker, an investment banker. Because his grandfather was called "Pop," young George was soon nicknamed "Little Pop" and "Poppy"; the latter stuck through his college years.

PHYSICAL DESCRIPTION: Bush stands 6 feet 2 inches tall, weighs about 195 pounds, and has blue eyes and straight brown hair streaked with gray, which he keeps in place with styling mousse. His most distinctive feature is an uneven grin, a Bush family trademark borne by his father and eldest son. He bears a scar on his forehead from a prep school soccer accident and another on the back of the hand from a bluefish bite. He is left-handed. He has been slightly hard of hearing ever since he piloted noisy aircraft during World War II. He is allergic to bee stings and suffers from mild arthritis of the hips, a mild form of glaucoma and a slightly enlarged prostate. In 1960 he underwent surgery for an intestinal ulcer. In 1989 he had a benign cyst removed from the middle finger of his right hand. In May 1991 he was hospitalized for two days for an irregular heartbeat caused by Graves Disease, a disorder in which the immune system attacks the thyroid gland, which in turn becomes hyperactive. Mrs. Bush suffers from the same disease. Medical estimates of the odds of a husband and wife both coming down with Graves Disease ranged from one in 10,000 to one in three million. After undergoing radioactive treatments to destroy his thyroid, Bush was required to take thyroid hormone pills indefinitely.

Bush speaks with a slight lisp and tends to talk rapidly in a moderately high-pitched voice, which drops naturally when he forces himself to slow down. The spare syntax of his speech, commonly devoid of first-person pronouns and replete with phrases posing as complete sentences, was the object of widespread parody. Bush dresses conservatively.

PERSONALITY: "George is not John Wayne," observed Republican media consultant Roger Ailes. "He's more like Gary Cooper in *High Noon*. He's very gentle.

He would much rather talk than fight. But he's capable of taking care of himself."[1] After eight years of quiet loyalty to Ronald Reagan, during which he developed a reputation for reserve and deference, Bush emerged as a tough, tenacious campaigner in 1988 and as president earned grudging respect even from longtime critics for his resolute leadership in the Persian Gulf War. During such times of crisis, Bush pointedly hewed to a normal work and recreation schedule to avoid the appearance of a president under siege. In preparing for a televised wartime address to the nation, he had to delete certain references to civilian casualties, according to *Newsweek* (January 28, 1991), because he choked up with emotion on the lines during rehearsals and did not want to convey an image of weakness to Iraq. Bush adopted an informal diplomatic style, building personal relationships with other world leaders and keeping in frequent telephone contact with them. As president he was more accessible to the press and less scripted than his predecessor. He liked to hold impromptu news conferences with very little formal preparation. He was more persuasive in small groups than before large audiences. He maintained many of the friendships of his wartime and college years for the rest of his life. Longtime friends described him as warm, witty, engaging, generous, considerate, unpretentious, and unerringly polite, but also flighty at times. "He gets giddy when he's on a roll," noted John White, a friend from Texas and former Democratic national chairman. "George has always been kind of like popcorn on a hot griddle."[2] His awkward gestures, often restrained in public, were likened by one observer to those of an errant toy soldier from a Nutcracker ballet chorus. Bush described himself as practical, pragmatic, and down-to-earth. During his twenties and early thirties, Bush was a classic Type A personality, maintaining a breakneck schedule as an independent oilman and worrying constantly over business details. He changed his lifestyle only after a bleeding intestinal ulcer attack literally knocked him to the floor and Dr. Lillo Crain of the Texas Medical Center warned him that he was headed for an early grave. After that he learned to pace himself and ignore problems outside his control.

ANCESTORS: Bush is of English heritage. The immigrant Bush ancestors settled on Cape Cod, Massachusetts, in the mid-17th century. His great-great-grandfather James Smith Bush was one of the forty-niners who took part in the California gold rush; he died en route back East. His great-grandfather James Smith Bush was an Episcopal minister. His paternal grandfather Samuel P. Bush, a Democrat, was a mechanical engineer who became president of the Buckeye Steel Casting Company in Columbus, Ohio, 1906–1928, and during World War I served under Bernard Baruch on the War Industries Board. His maternal grandfather and namesake George Herbert Walker founded the investment banking firm of G. H. Walker and Company; he once was the amateur heavyweight boxing champion of Missouri, served as president of the U.S. Golf Association, 1921–1923, and established the Walker Cup competition for American and British amateur golfers.

FATHER: Prescott S. Bush (1895–1972), businessman, senator. Born and raised in Columbus, Ohio, Prescott Bush entered Yale University in 1913 but three years later interrupted his studies briefly to serve as a private with the Connecticut National Guard at the Mexican border as part of General John J. Pershing's expedition against Pancho Villa. Following his graduation from Yale in 1917, he served as a captain in the 158th Field Artillery Brigade during World War I. He saw action in the Meuse-Argonne offensive and was part of the Army of Occupation in Germany. After the war, he settled in St. Louis, where he worked as a salesman for the Simmons Hardware Company. A few years later he was hired to rebuild a failing floor-covering firm. In doing so he made the company an attractive acquisition target for the U.S. Rubber Company. After the merger was completed, he in 1924 was assigned to the U.S. Rubber office in Braintree, Massachusetts. Transferred to New York later that year, he settled in nearby Greenwich, Connecticut. In 1926 he was named a vice president of the Wall Street firm of W. A. Harriman and Company, which, after the stock market crash, merged with another investment banking firm to become Brown Brothers, Harriman and Company. As a partner in the new firm, Bush prospered over the next two decades. During World War II, he served as chief fundraiser for the U.S.O. After the war he became active in the Connecticut Republican party, and in 1950 he lost narrowly in a bid to unseat Democratic Senator William Benton. In 1952 he defeated Abraham Ribicoff in a special election to fill the Senate seat of the late Brien McMahon and four years later was reelected over Thomas Dodd. As a member of the moderate Eisenhower wing of the party, Senator Bush was fiscally conservative but internationalist in foreign policy and opposed the tactics of Senator Joseph McCarthy. Widely respected as an authority on economic matters, he served on the Joint Economic Committee as well as the Banking and Currency Committee, Public Works Committee, and Armed Services Committee. He coauthored the Federal Aid Highway Act of 1956, which created the modern interstate highway system. He was chairman of the platform committee of the 1956 Republican national convention. President Eisenhower included him in an undated handwritten list of the 10 best prospective candidates for the 1960 Republican presidential nomination. He served on the boards of several corporations, including the Columbia Broadcasting System, Dresser Industries, and Prudential Insurance. A longtime supporter of the United Negro College Fund, he served briefly as its Connecticut chairman. As president of the U.S. Golf Association in the 1930s, Bush pressed unsuccessfully for the elimination of the stymie rule, which required a golfer to putt around an opponent's ball if it blocked access to the cup; the rule eventually was dropped. Bush himself won the national senior golf championship in 1951 with a score of 66. Bush instilled in his children the tradition that people of wealth and privilege have an obligation to give something back to society. He died of lung cancer when his most famous son was ambassador to the United Nations.

MOTHER: Dorothy Walker Bush (1901–1992). Born in Kennebunkport, Maine, the daughter of a dry-goods wholesaler who later turned to investment banking, she was raised in St. Louis and became a remarkably versatile athlete, excelling in baseball, basketball, track, and tennis. She once was runner-up for the girls national tennis championship in Merion, Pennsylvania. She married Prescott Bush in Kennebunkport on August 6, 1921. Moments before leaving for the hospital to deliver her first child, she smacked a home run in a family softball game. She offered five dollars to the first of her sons to beat her in tennis, a prize George collected at age 16. A strict disciplinarian, she laid down house rules designed to prevent her children from being spoiled by the wealth around them and instilled in them an aversion to boasting or self-promotion. While her husband served in the Senate, she wrote "Washington Life of a Senator's Wife," a column that was distributed to 20 newspapers in Connecticut. She was so upset over Vice President Bush's tie-breaking vote in the Senate to resume the production of nerve gas that President Reagan phoned to reassure her that he believed that such resumption was necessary. She died two weeks after her son was defeated for reelection as president.

SIBLINGS: The second of five children, Bush has three brothers and a sister—Prescott Bush, a businessman of Connecticut; Mrs. Nancy Ellis of Lincoln, Massachusetts; Jonathan Bush, head of J. Bush & Company, a Wall Street investment firm; and William "Buck" Bush, senior partner of Bush & Kobusch, a management consulting and investment advisory firm in St. Louis.

COLLATERAL RELATIVES: According to the New England Historic Genealogical Society in Boston, Bush is a fourth cousin seven times removed of Benedict Arnold, a fifth cousin four times removed of President Franklin Pierce, a seventh cousin three times removed of President Theodore Roosevelt, a seventh cousin four times removed of President Abraham Lincoln, an eighth cousin once removed of Winston Churchill, a ninth cousin twice removed of actress Marilyn Monroe, a tenth cousin once removed of Vice President Dan Quayle, and an eleventh cousin once removed of President Gerald Ford.

CHILDREN: Bush has four sons and a daughter. A daughter, Robin, died of leukemia at age four.

George W. Bush (1946–   ), businessman, politician. He served as a pilot in the Texas National Guard during the Vietnam War. After graduating from Yale, he earned an M.B.A. from Harvard Business School in 1975. Three years later he ran as a Republican candidate for the U.S. House from Texas's 19th Congressional District, the Lubbock-Odessa region, but was defeated by Democrat Kent Hance. He helped form Spectrum 7 Energy Corporation, an oil and gas exploration firm in Midland, Texas, which prospered until the oil glut of the mid-1980s. In 1987, having sold his interest in the business to Harken Oil and Gas, he began campaigning full time for his father's presidential bid. During the 1988 campaign, he focused on carrying Texas, stumping 300 communities in 94 counties. In 1989 he purchased part interest in the Texas Rangers and became the baseball team's managing general partner, a position he held until he was elected Governor on November 8, 1994. In 1998, he was elected to a second term as governor. He was elected President of the United States in November, 2000.

John E. "Jeb" Bush (1953–   ), banker, real estate developer, politician. A graduate of the University of Texas at Austin, he was an executive with the Texas Commerce Bank in Houston and later in Caracas, Venezuela, before taking up real estate development in Miami. He became active in Florida politics, serving as chairman of the Dade County Republican party, 1984–1987, and Florida secretary of commerce under Governor Bob Martinez, 1987–1988. After his father's election, he resumed real estate sales in Miami. In December 1988, he and his Mexican-born wife, Columba (for whom he converted to Catholicism), were among those representing the United States at the inaugural of President Carlos Salinas in Mexico City. He headed his father's reelection campaign in Florida in 1992. He was elected governor of Florida in 1998.

Neil M. Bush (1955–   ), oilman. He overcame severe childhood dyslexia. A graduate of Tulane University, he settled in Denver, where he became president of JNB Exploration, an unsuccessful oil and gas firm. From 1989 to 1991, he worked for the Apex Energy Company of Denver. He met his wife, Sharon, while campaigning for his father in the 1980 presidential primary in New Hampshire, where she was a real estate agent. He was one of the eight presidential electors from Colorado pledged to his father in 1988. He came under widespread criticism for his activities as an outside director of the Silverado

Banking, Savings and Loan Association of Denver, which failed in late 1988 at a cost to taxpayers of $1 billion. In 1991 the Office of Thrift Supervision asserted that he had shown "evidence of personal dishonesty" in failing to disclose adequately his business relationship with developers who later defaulted on large loans and set forth rules of behavior he must follow if he ever joins the board of any other federally insured savings institution.

Marvin P. Bush (1956–   ), investment consultant. A 1981 graduate of the University of Virginia, he worked for a time for Shearson, Lehman Brothers before becoming director of new business development at John Stewart Darrell & Company, an investment firm in Charlottesville, Virginia, in June 1988. He has been active in the United Ostomy Association since 1986, when he developed intestinal ulcers and had his colon removed.

Dorothy W. 'Doro' Bush (1959–   ), businesswoman. Reportedly the first person publicly baptized in Communist China, she was christened in Beijing on her 16th birthday by Chinese Christian clergymen while her father was chief U.S. liaison there. A graduate of Boston College, she worked as a travel agent, a caterer, a bookkeeper for Eilder Investments (a construction business owned by her then-husband William LeBlond in Cape Elizabeth, Maine), and a promoter for the Maine tourist office, before taking a job in the communications and development office of the National Rehabilitation Hospital in Washington in 1991. In 1992 she married Robert Koch, who days before the private Camp David wedding resigned as an aide to House Democratic leader Richard Gephardt to manage the Washington office of the Wine Institute.

BIRTH: Bush was born June 12, 1924, in a makeshift delivery room of the family's Victorian home in Milton, Massachusetts. Bush was the first president born in June; presidents now have been born in all 12 months.

CHILDHOOD: While Bush was still an infant, the family moved from his birthplace to Greenwich, Connecticut, an exclusive suburb of New York City. Bush was raised on Grove Lane in a nine-bedroom Victorian-style home set on two acres of wooded property. When at age two he was given a toy car, he promptly offered to share it with his older brother Prescott and thus for some time thereafter was nicknamed "Have-Half." A pudgy toddler, he also was dubbed "Fatty McGee McGaw" by his father. Raised amid wealth and comfort, young George was driven to school and out on early dates by the family handyman/chauffeur, Alec. Agnes, the Scottish nanny, and Nina, the housekeeper, also tended to the family's needs. Spankings were administered with a squash racket or similar instrument. An early baseball fan, George took part in family ball games out on the lawn, often accompanied his father to Yankee Stadium, where he once caught a foul ball, and followed the Boston Red Sox in the sports pages. His childhood hero was Yankee first baseman Lou Gehrig. A versatile athlete and fierce competitor, George on rare occasions found his desire to win overtaking good sportsmanship. While playing in a tennis tournament at about age 10, he angrily ordered his aunt off courtside for making too much noise. Evenings often were spent on the living room floor listening to Jack Benny, Edgar Bergen and Charlie McCarthy, or other popular radio personalities. He also liked to catch the latest Marx Brothers film. His fondest childhood memories, however, are of the summer vacations spent at his maternal grandfather's rambling stone and shingle home on 11 acres at Walker's Point in Kennebunkport, Maine. There he combed the beach for starfish, learned to drive a motorboat, played tennis at the River Club, and fished for mackerel and pollack aboard his grandfather's boat, the *Tomboy*.

EDUCATION: Bush attended the Greenwich (Connecticut) Country Day School, where he covered first base on the baseball team, was a running back on the football team, and played soccer and tennis. At 13, he enrolled at Phillips Academy, a boys prep school in Andover, Massachusetts. As a "prep," or freshman, he underwent typical hazing rituals of that era, wearing a blue beanie and taking orders from seniors. Most teachers remember Bush as an unremarkable student who did little more than was expected of him. In extracurricular activities, he was president of his senior class, captain of the baseball and soccer teams, manager of the basketball team, president of the Society of Inquiry (which organized local charity drives), and an editor of the school paper *The Phillipian*. He was voted second most influential with the faculty, third best athlete, third most popular, and third most handsome. Like nearly half of the 215 students of the class of 1942, Bush decided to enter Yale University, but World War II intervened (see "Military Service"). He ignored the advice of the commencement speaker, Secretary of War Henry Stimson, who urged the Phillips graduates to go on to college before joining the armed forces. After the war, Bush, now married, enrolled in Yale's accelerated two-and-a-half-year program. He majored in economics, minored in sociology. As first baseman on the Yale baseball team, which included pitcher Frank Quinn, who later played for the Boston Red Sox, George "Poppy" Bush was known as an outstanding fielder but only a fair hitter often fooled by breaking pitches. He threw left-handed but batted right-handed, usually seventh or eighth in the lineup. In 51 games played during his two seasons on the team—which won the eastern regional championship both years, but lost to California and Southern Cal, respectively, in the NCAA College World Series of 1947 and 1948—Bush hit for a .251 average with two home runs and 23 runs batted in. While making 442 put-outs and 24 assists, he committed just nine errors. (President Bush keeps his Yale first-baseman's glove handy in a drawer of his Oval Office desk.) During a home game against Princeton in his senior year, Bush, the team captain, was chosen to take part in a pregame ceremony with Babe Ruth. In one of his last public appearances before succumbing to cancer that summer, Ruth presented the black-bound manuscript of his autobiography to Bush for donation to the Yale University Library. In an impromptu gesture greatly appreciated by his teammates, Bush led Ruth to the Yale dugout to meet the rest of the squad. Ruth joined 5,000 fans in watching Yale trounce the Princeton Tigers 14–2 on 16 hits, including a double by Bush. Bush also won a letter in soccer on a team that won the New England collegiate championship. He joined the Delta Kappa Epsilon fraternity. As a senior, Bush, like William Howard Taft 70 years earlier, was inducted into Skull and Bones, Yale's venerable secret society. Also during his senior year, he attended an organizational meeting of the United Negro College Fund; he has been a supporter ever since. Bush's grades improved markedly in college. He won the Francis Gordon Brown Prize as outstanding junior, made Phi Beta Kappa, and graduated with honors in the class of 1948.

RELIGION: Episcopalian. "I am guided by certain traditions," Bush declared in his acceptance speech at the convention. "One is that there's a God and He is good, and His love, while free, has a self-imposed cost: we must be good to one another." He was raised in a family that regularly read aloud from the Bible at the breakfast table. The president and Mrs. Bush attend Sunday services regularly, recite bedtime prayers aloud together nightly, and read the Bible daily. He has publicly professed faith in an afterlife and in Jesus Christ as his personal savior. He is a vestryman at St. Anne's Episcopal Church in Kennebunkport, Maine, where the family occupies the first three right rows of pews at the 10 A.M. Sunday service, and is a longtime member of St. Martin's Episcopal Church in Houston.

RECREATION: Bush's retreat is the main house at Walker's Point, in Kennebunkport, Maine, which his maternal grandfather built around the turn of the century and which Bush purchased from other family members while he was vice president. Except for his years in the service, he has spent a part of each year there. Bush stays fit taking part in a wide variety of outdoor activity. He has been jogging regularly since 1976. An avid tennis player from age five, he developed his game in group lessons from Czech pro Karel Kozeluh. Bush prefers men's doubles on grass courts. By his own assessment, his backhand strokes are poor, but he has a strong forehand and plays an aggressive net game. His golf game is decent but is hampered by poor putting and his enthusiasm for quick play, a style dubbed "aerobic golf." He also plays raquetball and pitches horseshoes. He annually hunts quail in Beeville, Texas. He enjoys fishing, especially for bluefish which he tracks off the Maine coast with the aid of an electronic fish finder that buzzes whenever his boat is over a school. He also likes to cast for bonefish and tarpon off Islamorada, Florida. Because he does not particularly like seafood, Bush releases much of his catch or gives it to his Secret Service detail or others. He is a quiet fisherman who uses his time on the water to think or clear his mind. He likes to take visitors on a breathtaking ride on his 28-foot speedboat, the *Fidelity,* named for the Fidelity Printing Corporation stock that he sold to buy it. A longtime baseball fan, he follows the Houston Astros and, since his days as ambassador at the United Nations, has rooted for the New York Mets, which was partly owned by one of his uncles. In 1985 Bush paid $300 to become a life member of the National Rifle Association. He belongs to three men's clubs—the Alfalfa Club, an organization of government officials and corporate executives founded in 1913; the Alibi Club, a select group of political figures and business leaders who meet in Washington; and the Bohemian Club, whose members gather at a secluded redwood grove north of San Francisco. Bush prefers Mexican and Chinese food and likes to snack on pork rinds doused with Tabasco sauce. He barred broccoli from the Air Force One menu. "I haven't liked it since I was a little kid and my mother made me eat it," he explained with mock petulance, as reported in the *New York Times* (March 23, 1990). "And I'm President of the United States, and I'm not going to eat any more broccoli!" A favorite way to spend an evening is a long, lingering dinner with friends at a restaurant. He sips an occasional beer or vodka martini. He enjoys the writings of C.S. Lewis and Tom Clancy. Among the few television programs, besides the news and sporting events, that he has watched regularly are "America's Funniest Home Videos" and "Murder, She Wrote." His favorite classic movie stars included Clark Gable and Greer Garson. He enjoys the action-adventure films of Clint Eastwood, Chuck Norris, Sylvester Stallone, and Arnold Schwarzenegger. He also liked *Chariots of Fire.* His musical tastes run from country-and-western to Broadway show tunes. Having never learned to dance well, Bush must be coaxed to circle the floor at state occasions.

MARRIAGE: Navy Lieutenant (j.g.) George Bush, 20, married Barbara Pierce, 19, on January 6, 1945, at the First Presbyterian Church in Rye, New York. The

First Lady was born in Rye on June 8, 1925, the daughter of Marvin Pierce, the publisher of *Redbook* and *McCall's* magazines, and Pauline Robinson Pierce. She attended the Milton public school in Rye and the private Rye Country Day School before graduating from the Ashley Hall prep school in Charleston, South Carolina in 1943. She then entered Smith College. She had met Bush, then on leave from the navy, at a Christmas dance in Greenwich, Connecticut, in 1942. He spotted her across the dance floor and quickly arranged for a mutual friend, Jack Wozencraft, to introduce them. Each of them has said that it was love at first sight. He was the first boy she ever kissed; Bush named his bomber plane "Barbara" after her. While visiting him at preflight training school in Chapel Hill, North Carolina, in August 1943, she agreed to a secret engagement. They announced their wedding plans to their families that December. She dropped out of Smith College during her sophomore year to marry Bush while he was home on leave. At the ceremony, performed by the Reverend Dr. John D. Gregory, the bride wore an ivory satin gown and a veil of rosepoint lace borrowed from her mother-in-law. The groom's elder brother, Prescott Bush, Jr., interrupted his own honeymoon to serve as best man. The couple honeymooned at the Cloisters Hotel on Sea Island, Georgia. Throughout their long marriage the Bushes never lived in one place long enough to put down roots, occupying 29 homes in 17 cities. As newlyweds they lived in an off-campus apartment while Bush attended Yale. She had mixed feelings about Bush's decision to give up the security of the East and strike out on his own in Texas. She had always assumed that she would raise a family in the familiar, comfortable surroundings she grew up in, but a part of her longed to escape the influence of their strong-willed families. One of their first homes in Texas was half of a cramped duplex on East 7th Street in Odessa with a common bathroom, which they shared with a mother-daughter team of prostitutes. While living in Bakersfield, California in 1949, she received word that her mother had been killed in a freak accident that made the front page of the *New York Times:* Her father had been driving along a familiar stretch of road when he noticed that a cup of coffee precariously perched on the seat next to him was about to spill toward his wife's lap. As he groped to save it, he lost control of the car, hurtled down an embankment, and slammed into a tree and a stone wall. Mrs. Pierce died crashing through the windshield; Mr. Pierce suffered a concussion and four broken ribs. The coffee cup of English bone china survived intact.

The most difficult time of the Bush marriage was the death of their four-year-old daughter Robin from leukemia in 1953. After that Mrs. Bush made a point of visiting young cancer patients during Christmas time. She revealed in an interview with David Frost in January 1991 that upon her return from Beijing following Bush's stint as chief U.S. liaison there in 1975, she underwent a period of mild depression but was "too proud" to seek treatment. It was at that time that she overcame an aversion to public speaking by touring the country with a slide show on China, the proceeds from which were donated to St. Martin's Episcopal Church in Houston. The First Lady has been described as direct, spirited, independent, tenacious, well-organized, and endearingly unpretentious. She dressed for comfort and thought nothing of revealing that she wore fake pearls to conceal a wrinkled neck. She grew weary of suggestions that she resume dying her hair, as she did between ages 35 and 45, preferring to age naturally. As First Lady, she was active in promoting adult literacy, an interest that sprang from her son Neil's dyslexia. In March 1989 she helped organize and was named honorary chairperson of the Barbara Bush Foundation for Family Literacy. She also has lent her support to such children's programs as Head Start and Chapter One. Her advocacy for the homeless included taking guest bars of soap and shampoo from hotel rooms for donation to women's shelters, an example that prompted at least one hotel chain to begin donating such items directly. A trustee, since 1983, of the Morehouse School of Medicine, a predominantly black institution in Atlanta, she promoted the nomination of its president, Dr. Louis Sullivan, as secretary of health and human services. She discussed issues candidly with the president over breakfast but refused to publicly disagree with him. In two rare exceptions, she came out in support of a ban on the sale of military assault weapons in 1989 and opposed the anti-abortion plank in 1992 Republican platform. As First Lady she was treated for Graves disease, a thyroid disorder, and resultant vision problems. In 1991 she broke her left leg sledding at Camp David. She wrote two humorous books from the points of view of the family's dogs—*C. Fred's Story* (Doubleday, 1984) and *Millie's Book* (Morrow, 1990). The latter was on the best-seller lists for nearly four months. Her children nicknamed her "the silver fox." The president called her "Bar."

MILITARY SERVICE:

World War II. On June 12, 1942, his 18th birthday, Bush enlisted in the navy as a seaman second class. He served until September 1945, rising to lieutenant (junior grade). He underwent preflight training at Chapel Hill, North Carolina, primary flight training at Minneapolis, Minnesota, flight training at Corpus Christi, Texas, advanced flight training at Charlestown, Rhode Island, torpedo bomber training at Fort Lauderdale, Florida, and aerial photography training at Chincoteague, Virginia. In June 1943 he earned his wings and a commission as an ensign, becoming the youngest pilot then in the navy. While stationed at Chincoteague in the fall of 1943, he was reprimanded for buzzing the nearby fairgrounds, frightening a circus elephant, which broke from its handlers and fled into town. From that episode he picked up another nickname, "Ellie the Elephant." During a training exercise at Chincoteague on November 1, 1943, his wheels collapsed, sending him into a belly-landing on the tarmac. Although he was unhurt, his $96,000 aircraft was destroyed.

Assigned to the VT-51 torpedo bomber squadron, Bush flew 58 combat missions in a three-man Grumman Avenger, a single-engine aircraft with a 2,000-lb. payload, off the carrier *San Jacinto* against Japanese strongholds in the Pacific, including Wake Island, Guam, and Saipan. He logged a total of 1,228 hours of flight time during his 39 months of service. He was one of just four pilots in his original 14-pilot squadron to survive the war. On June 19, 1944, he was forced to land at sea with a full payload and narrowly escaped before the crippled aircraft exploded; he was rescued by the *U.S.S. Bronson* a half hour later. His most harrowing wartime experience, occurred on September 2, 1944, while on a bombing mission against the Japanese radio center of Chichi Jima, one of the Bonin Islands. During his descent the plane was struck by enemy antiaircraft fire. Despite the smoke that was filling the cockpit and the flames eating away at the wings, Bush pressed toward the target, dropped his payload, and limped out to sea, where he yelled out the order to bail out and then bailed out himself. Tailgunner Ted White already was dead from gunfire. Radioman Jack Delaney was killed in the fall. Bush slammed into the tail of the aircraft during bailout, slicing open his scalp and slightly tearing his parachute,

672 / GEORGE BUSH

before splashing safely into the Pacific. He scrambled into his yellow seat-back rubber raft and hand-paddled against the currents that were carrying him toward the Japanese. He remained in the water for more than 3 hours, nursing his head wound and a fresh sting from a Portuguese man-of-war and thinking about his family, his faith, and, he later claimed, the separation of church and state, until rescued by the submarine *Finback*. He was shaken by the loss of his crewmen, especially White, who was not his regular tailgunner but an old family friend, who had pleaded with Bush to let him ride along on his first bombing run. Bush was awarded the Distinguished Flying Cross for completing the mission. Had he been captured at sea by the Japanese boats that were kept away from him by U.S. warplanes, it is likely that he would have fallen into the hands of Japanese authorities on the Bonin Islands, who after the war were convicted of war crimes, including the torture, decapitation, and even cannibalization of downed American airmen. Bush spent a month aboard the *Finback* while it engaged Japanese ships in the area. In December 1944, he was rotated home and later was assigned to the VT-153 torpedo bomber squadron at the Oceana Naval Air Station in Virginia in preparation for the final air assault on Japan itself. President Truman's decision to drop the atomic bomb on Japan, which Bush supported, obviated that final mission. Lieutenant and Mrs. Bush took part in V-J Day street celebrations in Virginia Beach.

CAREER BEFORE THE PRESIDENCY:

Oilman, 1948–1966. Upon his graduation from Yale in 1948, Bush declined to join the Brown Brothers, Harriman investment firm in New York, with which his father had been associated, in order to strike out on his own. After reading Louis Bromfield's *The Farm,* he considered going into agriculture, but he could not afford the substantial initial investment required and did not want to borrow from his family. He interviewed with Procter and Gamble but was not offered a suitable job. Finally he agreed to a proposition from Neil Mallon, a family friend and president of Dresser Industries, that he learn the oil business with the International Derrick and Equipment Company (Ideco), a Dresser subsidiary, in West Texas. Bush packed his belongings into his 1947 Studebaker and, together with his wife and young son, drove to Odessa, where he started out sweeping floors, monitoring inventory, painting oil rigs, and doing other field work for $375 a month. In the fall of 1948 he began selling oil drilling equipment. During his first Christmas Eve in Texas, he tried to keep up with the hard-drinking oil hands at the office party but ended up being carried home dead drunk with no memory of the evening. In 1949 he was transferred to Pacific Pumps, another Dresser subsidiary in Huntington Park, California, where he worked in assembly long enough to join the United Steelworkers Union, a membership that he later touted when speaking before blue-collar audiences. Reassigned later that year to Ideco sales in Bakersfield, he peddled drilling bits at rig sites in Southern California, traveling as much as 1,000 miles a week, and living by turns in Whittier, Ventura, and Compton. In 1950 he returned to Midland, Texas, where, after much thought and a little anguish, he resigned from Dresser to form the Bush-Overbey Oil Development Company, capitalized with $350,000 raised by his uncle G. Herbert Walker, Jr. His partner John Overbey was responsible for examining and selecting potential oil properties; Bush handled the people end of the business, talking to landowners and leaseholders, buying and selling parcels. In 1953 Bush-Overbey merged with another independent oil company owned by the Liedtke brothers, Bill and

Hugh. They decided to give the combined enterprise a name beginning with "Z" so it would fall last in the Yellow Pages and thus stand out among the long list of independent oil contractors in the area. They chose Zapata Petroleum Corporation, after the film *Viva Zapata,* starring Marlon Brando, which was then playing in Midland. Zapata soon struck it rich in the Jameson Field southwest of Abilene, a find that eventually supported more than 100 wells. In 1954 Bush established and became president of a subsidiary, the Zapata Off-Shore Company. Eventually he bought out the Liedtkes' share of Zapata Off-Shore for $800,000, a sum raised from family and friends, and in 1959 moved his headquarters to Houston. (The Liedtkes parleyed what was left of Zapata Petroleum into the Pennzoil Company.) With Bush as president, 1954–1964, and chairman of the board, 1964–1966, Zapata Off-Shore prospered as a pioneer in the construction of offshore drilling platforms and eventually produced ocean equipment for oil companies on five continents. Bush created a stock option plan for the benefit of his employees. The company suffered a serious setback in September 1965, when Hurricane Betsy destroyed the Maverick, Zapata's largest drilling barge, worth nearly $6 million. Although the rig was insured, the course of business was seriously disrupted. In February 1966, Bush sold his interest in Zapata Off-Shore to Texas businessman D. Doyle Mize for $1 million.

Meanwhile, Bush had become active in Republican party affairs. He campaigned in Midland for Dwight D. Eisenhower for president in 1952 and 1956. He served as chairman of the Harris County (Houston area) Republican party, 1963–1964, having been encouraged by moderates fearful that the ultraconservative John Birch society was threatening to take over the local party organization. He attended the 1964 Republican national convention as a Goldwater delegate. That year Bush defeated Jack Cox in a Republican primary runoff to earn the right to challenge the reelection of liberal Democratic Senator Ralph Yarborough. Bush ran as a conservative, speaking out against the Nuclear Test Ban Treaty (see "John F. Kennedy, 35th President," "Administration"), Medicare, and the Civil Rights Act of 1964 (see "Lyndon B. Johnson, 36th President," "Administration"). Although Bush was defeated 57–43 percent, he ran well ahead of Goldwater and most other Republican candidates in the state. His showing was all the more remarkable given the presence of Texan Lyndon Johnson at the top of the Democratic ticket. Bush later admitted privately, however, that his hard-right rhetoric was campaign posturing designed to fire up the state's Goldwater supporters.

U.S. Representative, 1967–1971. In 1966 Bush ran as a moderate, stumping in black neighborhoods and projecting a campaign of youthful vigor with the slogan "Elect George Bush and Watch the Action," to defeat, 57–42 percent, District Attorney Frank Briscoe, a conservative Democrat who stressed law and order, for the newly created 7th Congressional District seat, a predominantly Republican enclave in Houston. Coming into the district to campaign for him that year were two future presidents, former Vice President Richard Nixon and House Minority Leader Gerald Ford. Bush was one of two Texas Republicans elected to the House that year. He was reelected without opposition in 1968. He was only the third freshman congressman in the twentieth century to win a coveted seat on the House Ways and Means Committee. "I put him on," said Representative Wilbur Mills of Arkansas, then chairman of the committee. "I got a phone call from his father telling me how much it mattered to him."[3] During his two terms in the House, Bush supported the Vietnam War, favored lowering the voting age to 18, established a reputation as a fiscal conservative, headed a Republican task force on the environment, pressed unsuccessfully for a law requiring congressmen to disclose their personal finances, personally lobbied President Nixon to preserve tax incentives for independent oil operators, and otherwise guarded the interests of the oil industry. His most courageous vote was for the Civil Rights Act of 1968, barring discrimination in the sale and rental of housing. The bill was so unpopular in his conservative district that he began receiving threatening letters. Greeted by an angry white audience at Memorial High School in Houston days after the assassination of Martin Luther King, Jr., he called for an end to bigotry and challenged those present to justify denying equal housing opportunity to black soldiers returning from Vietnam. His impassioned plea turned the hall to his favor; he left to a standing ovation. He later described the incident as the most thrilling of his prepresidential public career. A delegate to the Republican national convention in 1968, Bush quietly lobbied for the vice presidential nomination, enlisting Representative Bill Steiger of Wisconsin and former presidential nominee Thomas Dewey to put in a good word for him with Richard Nixon. When Nixon passed him over for Governor Spiro Agnew of Maryland, he explained to Bush that he simply could not settle for a one-term congressman. "He was right," Bush later conceded, "I couldn't have brought anything more than a new, young face to the ticket, and that isn't enough in a national campaign."[4] (These words were written before his selection of Senator Dan Quayle for vice president.) Although a Republican, Congressman Bush went out of his way to cultivate friendly relations with President Lyndon Johnson, both during and after his terms in the White House. Johnson had served with Bush's father on the Senate Armed Services Committee and had gotten along well with him despite party differences. On the day Nixon was sworn in as president, Bush was the only Republican officeholder to pass up the inaugural parade in order to bid farewell to the retiring president at Andrews Air Force Base. Johnson reportedly was deeply moved by the gesture.

In April 1969, Bush visited Johnson at the LBJ Ranch in Texas to seek the former president's advice on whether he should give up a safe House seat to run again for the Senate against Yarborough or remain in the House and build seniority on the Ways and Means Committee. Bush, who was ambivalent about making the switch, was persuaded at least in part by Johnson's earthy assessment. "The difference between being a member of the Senate and a member of the House," Johnson told Bush, "is the difference between chicken *salad* and chicken *shit.*"[5] Bush entered the race in 1970 prepared to blast Yarborough for his liberal record, a strategy that had to be scrapped when Yarborough was upset in the primary by former congressman Lloyd Bentsen. The Nixon administration, which had urged Bush to enter the race to rid the Senate of one of Nixon's most outspoken critics, diverted its resources elsewhere once Yarborough was defeated. Bush was so repulsed by the bitter war waged by Vice President Agnew against the media and Democratic Senate candidates that year that he specifically requested that Agnew not campaign in Texas for him. White House aide Charles Colson complained privately that Bush lacked the stomach to wage a hardball negative campaign against Bentsen. Despite a last-minute campaign swing through Texas by President Nixon, Bush was defeated, 53–47 percent, in part because of an unusually large turnout from rural Democratic strongholds. He was so discouraged over this second loss for the Senate that he considered giving up politics for good.

U.S. Ambassador to the United Nations, 1971–1973. In urging Bush to give up his safe House seat to run for the Senate in 1970, President Nixon had promised to keep him in mind for an appointive office if he lost. Nixon considered him for head of the National Aeronautics and Space Administration, head of the Small Business Administration, undersecretary of commerce, and assistant to the president with unspecified general responsibilities, but Bush requested appointment as ambassador to the United Nations. According to a memo by White House Chief of Staff H.R. "Bob" Haldeman, Bush impressed upon the president that, besides his duties at the UN, he could be counted on to speak up for Nixon and his policies on the New York social circuit, where the president had few advocates. Nixon agreed to the appointment only after his first choice, White House aide Daniel Patrick Moynihan, at first accepted and then rejected it. Some criticized the appointment because Bush lacked diplomatic experience. Ambassador Bush led the fight for a two-China policy, admitting mainland China to the UN for the first time since the Communist takeover in 1949 while allowing Taiwan to retain its seat. Although Bush thought he had enough support to carry the measure in the General Assembly, he got blindsided on a procedural vote as several delegations reneged on promises to support the U.S. position. Bush's job was made more difficult by the surprise announcement that Nixon was preparing for a historic trip to China (see "Richard M. Nixon, 37th President," "Administration: New China Policy"). Bush has said that his 22 months at the UN made him more aware of the flaws and limitations of the world body but also more appreciative of its potential for humanitarian aid whenever ideological differences can be overcome or set aside.

Chairman of Republican National Committee, 1973–1974. With the reelection of President Nixon in 1972, Bush wanted to extend his foreign policy experience with a senior post in the State Department or, failing that, to consider an offer from Treasury Secretary George Shultz to be his chief deputy, but at a meeting in November 1972 Nixon persuaded Bush to become chairman of the Republican party. As the Watergate scandal (see "Richard Nixon, 37th President," "Administration") unfolded, Bush spent much of his time defending Nixon and shoring up party morale around the country. During his 20-month tenure, he held 84 press conferences, delivered 118 speeches, and logged 124,000 miles of flight. Among the last of the Republicans to desert Nixon, he sent a formal letter, dated August 7, 1974, calling on the president to resign; he did so two days later. Although Bush took some satisfaction in his efforts to streamline the party organization, he later called his term as party chairman "a political nightmare."[6]

Chief U.S. Liaison in China, 1974–1975. With Gerald Ford's accession to the presidency, Bush again quietly lobbied for the vice presidency. In a poll of congressional Republicans and other prominent party members commissioned by Ford, Bush was favored for vice president over former Governor Nelson Rockefeller of New York, 255–181. Ford nevertheless nominated Rockefeller and offered Bush his pick of ambassadorships. Bush passed over plum posts in London and Paris to choose China, where, because relations with the United States were not yet fully restored to permit the exchange of ambassadors, Bush's title was chief of the U.S. Liaison Office. During his 13 months in Beijing, Bush had little contact with ordinary Chinese besides an occasional tennis partner. His worst experience there occurred following the fall of Saigon in the spring of 1975, when days of street demonstrations celebrating the long-awaited Communist victory in Vietnam discomfited Bush and the rest of the small American contingent in Beijing.

Director of Central Intelligence Agency, 1976–1977. Although Bush was content to remain in China or, failing that, to obtain a Commerce Department post to round out his resume, President Ford persuaded him to accept appointment as CIA director after his first choice, Washington attorney Edward Bennett Williams, declined. Bush confided to Secretary of State Henry Kissinger that he was heartbroken at the appointment but accepted it because his father had advised him never to turn down a direct request from the president. Bush was reluctant to become CIA director because he still had his eye on the vice presidency, perhaps in 1976, and the CIA was widely regarded as a graveyard for political ambitions. Moreover, the appointment of a former national party leader to a sensitive intelligence post in the wake of the Watergate scandal alarmed many, including Senate Democrats, who wrung from President Ford a pledge to rule out Bush as a possible running mate in 1976. Bush was confirmed, 64–27. The first politician to head the agency, Bush carefully avoided even the appearance of partisanship during his 51-week tenure, declining all invitations to party affairs, including the Republican national convention in 1976. Director Bush restored agency morale, which had been battered by congressional investigations of CIA assassination plots against foreign leaders and other extreme covert activity. As a gesture of his loyalty to the troops, he made a point of taking the employee elevator to his office every morning instead of the director's private lift. But he also took seriously a congressional mandate to rein in the agency. He replaced three quarters of the CIA's top administrators and set in place safeguards designed to restrict the agency to lawful espionage. Bush also approved creation of Team B, a group of outside experts assigned to assess Soviet military capabilities as a check on the CIA's own assessment. He won increased funding for spy satellites and other high-tech innovations in espionage. He encouraged the sharing of intelligence information with U.S. allies, particularly Great Britain. He warned that terrorists were escalating their activities in Lebanon and urged the evacuation of Americans from that country. In December 1976, he confronted Attorney General Edward Levi over the prosecution of Edwin Gibbons Moore on spy charges. Bush granted Levi only limited access to classified documents pertaining to the Moore case, despite Levi's angry assertion that such action smacked of a cover-up and was jeopardizing the case against Moore. Bush stood firm; Moore was convicted on available evidence. The Democrat-controlled Senate Intelligence Committee praised Bush as one of the best of the 11 CIA directors to have served up to that time. During the 1976 presidential campaign, Bush provided regular intelligence briefings to Democratic candidate Jimmy Carter. With Carter's election, Bush expressed a willingness to stay on at the CIA, but Carter preferred to name his own man.

Vice President, 1981–1989. In 1977 Bush began organizing a presidential campaign, and on May 1, 1979, he announced his candidacy for the 1980 Republican nomination. Following an upset victory, 32–29 percent, over Ronald Reagan in the Iowa caucuses in January 1980, Bush emerged as Reagan's principal rival and went on to win key primaries in Michigan and Pennsylvania. While campaigning at Carnegie Mellon University in Pittsburgh on April 10, he ridiculed Reagan's proposed supply-side economic program as "voodoo economics," a phrase coined by aide Pete Teeley. Bush later repeatedly denied ever having used that phrase until an NBC News crew unearthed a film clip of his speech. In a gracious withdrawal speech, designed at least in part to enhance his chances for a spot on the ticket, Bush called on the convention to rally around Reagan. Bush received 13 courtesy votes for the nomination. Reagan's pollsters determined that Bush was the second strongest running mate after former President Gerald Ford. When negotiations with the Ford camp broke down (see "Ronald Reagan, 40th President," "Republican Presidential Nomination, 1980"), Reagan chose Bush. They were elected handily over President Jimmy Carter and Vice President Walter Mondale (see "Ronald Reagan, 40th President," "Campaign and the Issues, 1980"). Upon taking office, Bush sold his Houston home for $843,000 and purchased the main house at Walker's Point, the family's long-time summer residence in Kennebunkport, Maine.

On March 30, 1981, Vice President Bush was departing from Fort Worth, Texas, where he had unveiled a plaque at the site of the hotel in which President John F. Kennedy had spent his last night alive, when he received word that President Reagan had been shot (see "Ronald Reagan, 40th President," "Administration: Assassination Attempt"). He cancelled a scheduled speech to the state legislature in Austin and returned to Washington at once. He rejected as unseemly advice from aides that he land by helicopter on the South Lawn of the White House, as the president typically does, and instead touched down at the vice president's residence and motored to the White House. While Reagan recuperated, Bush presided over cabinet meetings routinely, never occupying the president's chair, and met with staff members, congressional leaders, and foreign dignitaries. He conducted no business in the Oval Office and deferred all policy decisions until Reagan's return nearly two weeks after the shooting. On July 13, 1985, presidential powers were transferred to Bush for eight hours while Reagan underwent surgery for intestinal cancer. Although the transfer conformed to the provisions of the 25th Amendment to the Constitution, Reagan did not invoke it specifically for fear of setting a precedent. Acting President Bush spent much of his brief tenure playing tennis and napping at the vice president's Naval Observatory residence in Washington.

Vice President Bush served as chairman of several presidential task forces:

• The task force on regulatory relief recommended the elimination or revision of hundreds of federal regulations.

• The key recommendation of the task force on combatting terrorism, that the government must never make concessions to terrorists, was ignored by the administration when it decided to trade arms for hostages (see "Ronald Reagan, 40th President," "Administration: Iran-Contra Affair").

• The South Florida antidrug task force fostered cooperation among competing government agencies but failed to stem the flow of cocaine and other narcotics into the United States.

In presiding over the Senate, Bush cast tie-breaking votes for a resumption of the production of nerve gas weapons in July 1983, against a proposal to delay production of the MX missile in June 1984, and against a plan to cut funding for the Star Wars antimissile defense system in September 1987. Bush enjoyed the extensive foreign travel expected of a vice president, logging more than a million miles in eight years. He represented the United States at the funerals of Soviet leaders Leonid Brezhnev and Yuri Andropov. In 1982 he returned to Beijing to reassure the Chinese that the Reagan administration was committed to improved relations despite the continued sale of American military spare parts to Taiwan. In 1983 he toured Europe to bolster support for the planned deployment of U.S. medium-range missiles there. That same year he ignored Secret Service concerns for his safety in confronting alone armed officers linked to the "death squads" in El Salvador. His most difficult overseas assignment, he said, was to inspect the damage to U.S. facilities in Beirut following the terrorist attack that killed 241 marines in October 1983.

Perhaps his lowest point as vice president was during the 1984 reelection campaign, in which Bush seemed off-stride. In his debate with Representative Geraldine Ferraro of New York, the Democratic vice presidential nominee, Bush gestured awkwardly and asserted repeatedly, albeit erroneously, that his opponent had declared that the marines killed in Lebanon "died in shame." Challenged to cite his source or apologize, Bush did neither. After the debate, he boasted to a crowd that he had "tried to kick a little ass." Although the Reagan-Bush ticket was reelected by a landslide, Bush was displeased, reportedly even despondent, over his own performance in the campaign.

Within the councils of government Vice President Bush maintained a low profile, rarely speaking up in cabinet or National Security Council meetings, avoiding off-the-record interviews and news leaks, and reserving any advice or criticism for his private Thursday lunches with the president. UN Ambassador Jeane Kirkpatrick said publicly that, despite having been in countless meetings with Bush in attendance, she had no idea where he stood on most foreign policy issues. Budget Director David Stockman asserted that Bush refused his invitation to join him in advocating strong deficit reduction measures. According to White House chief of staff Donald Regan, Bush's daily routine included helping him come up with a morning joke to start President Reagan's day. Bush reportedly was involved, however, in some backstage maneuvers: He urged President Reagan to reject Attorney General Edwin Meese's proposals to undercut affirmative action, sided with Secretary of State George Shultz in his outspoken protest against a proposed anti-leak policy requiring all senior staff to submit to periodic lie detector tests, and headed the crisis management team that recommended the invasion of Grenada (see "Ronald Reagan, 40th President," "Administration"). According to a sanitized summary of classified documents made public during the 1989 trial of Lieutenant Colonel Oliver North, Bush served as a secret emissary to President Roberto Suazo Cordova of Honduras in March 1985, informing Suazo that the United States was increasing and expediting economic and military aid to Honduras. Bush's mission may have been part of a Reagan administration effort to encourage Honduras to aid the contra rebels fighting the Sandinista regime in Nicaragua in a way that circumvented a congressional ban on direct U.S. military aid to them.

Bush's role in the Iran-contra affair (see "Ronald Reagan, 40th President," "Administration") is unclear. He claimed that he was "out of the loop." Although he admitted that he had known of efforts to sell arms to Iran and to secure the release of the hostages, he maintained that he did not realize until much later that the two were linked. He asserted that privately he expressed reservations about the sale of arms to Iran, which he conceded in retrospect was a mistake, but supported the decision once it was made. In a memo written by National Security Adviser John Poindexter, however, Bush was described as "solid" in support of selling the weapons. Bush refused to reveal the nature of his advice to President Reagan on the matter. Bush claimed that he was unaware of and opposed to the diversion of profits from such sales to the contras fighting the Nicaraguan government. According to Oliver North's private notebooks, which were made public in 1990, North met with Bush just hours after North had lied to Congress about his activities on behalf of the contras. The subject of the conversation was not mentioned in the notebooks. Bush administration officials asserted that the two discussed the arms sales to Iran and the plight of American hostages but did not deal with North's covert aid to the contras. In their book *Men of Zeal* (1988), Maine senators William S. Cohen, a Republican, and George J. Mitchell, a Democrat, both of whom served on the congressional committee investigating the Iran-contra affair, concluded that Vice President Bush endorsed the arms sales either out of loyalty to the president or concern for the hostages. The senators pointed out that Bush was present, and reportedly raised no objections, at no fewer than three separate White House meetings in January 1986, at which the plan to swap arms for hostages was discussed and approved, at times over the vigorous objections of Secretary of State George Shultz and Secretary of Defense Caspar Weinberger, and that in July 1986, Bush was briefed by an Israeli official who several times referred explicitly to an arms-for-hostages deal. According to a Shultz memo written in 1987 and disclosed in 1992, Weinberger, appalled at Bush's public denial of knowledge of their objections to the arms sales, reminded Shultz that Bush not only heard their objections but "was on the other side." A similar contemporaneous memo by Weinberger, also made public in 1992, said much the same thing. In 1992 Richard Secord, who worked with North in executing the secret deals, asserted his belief that Bush had been well-informed from the beginning. Classified Israeli documents revealed in 1992 also suggested that Bush knew more about the arms-for-hostages deal than he later admitted. In January 1988, Bush sought to put the Iran-contra question behind him in a live interview on the "CBS Evening News," which quickly degenerated into a shouting match with anchorman Dan Rather. "The worst time I've had in 20 years in public life," Bush afterwards complained angrily into a microphone that was live within the studio but no longer linked for broadcast. "That bastard didn't lay a glove on me. . . . You can tell your goddamned network that if they want to talk to me, raise their hands at a press conference. No more Mr. Inside stuff."[7] Although some observers believed that the confrontation with Rather was planned as a way to turn the issue back onto the media while at the same time dispelling the myth that Bush was a "wimp," the vice president, according to his wife, was so upset at his performance that he was unable to sleep that night. The next day Bush described the incident as "Tension City." On Christmas Eve, 1992, less than a month before he was to leave office, President Bush pardoned Weinberger and others facing criminal charges for their alleged roles in the Iran-Contra affair. Infuriated by the pardons, special prosecutor Lawrence Walsh disclosed that Bush had withheld from investigators his own relevant notes made while he was vice president and announced that Bush had become a target of his investigation.

REPUBLICAN PRESIDENTIAL NOMINATION, 1988: As Republicans gathered in New Orleans in August 1988, Bush's nomination was assured. In February, after a humiliating third-place showing in the Iowa caucuses behind Senator Robert Dole of Kansas and the Reverend Pat Robertson, Bush came back to win the New Hampshire primary with an intensely negative ad campaign directed against Dole's voting record, which left the senator embittered and visibly angry. From then on Bush gathered momentum as one by one his opponents withdrew from the race—former Governor Pierre "Pete" du Pont of Delaware, former

Secretary of State Alexander Haig, Representative Jack Kemp of New York, and, finally, Dole and Robertson. After having his name placed in nomination by Senator Phil Gramm of Texas, Bush was nominated without opposition on the first ballot. In his acceptance speech, a moving and at times poetic address crafted by Reagan speechwriter Peggy Noonan, Bush presented himself as a sincere civil servant whose life since World War II has been a series of missions completed and as a quiet man who hears "the quiet people others don't." He assailed those who exploited the prosperity of the Reagan years as a chance to pursue wealth as an end in itself and called on government and the private sector to bring about "a kinder, and gentler nation." In counterpoint to his gentler side, he went on to denounce his opponent as a symbol of the economic decline of the 1970s, deriding him as a "technocrat" who "makes the trains run on time but doesn't know where they're going," and pledged to stand up to a Democratic-controlled Congress, which, he predicted, would try repeatedly to raise taxes. He closed by inviting the hall to join him in reciting the Pledge of Allegiance, a pointed reminder that his opponent had once vetoed a Massachusetts bill requiring school teachers to lead students in the Pledge. Overshadowing the speech, however, was the furor surrounding Bush's selection of Senator Dan Quayle of Indiana as his running mate. Even longtime Bush supporters were dismayed at the way he rushed an obviously ill-prepared junior senator onto the national stage in the middle of an otherwise orderly and predictable convention, where the only outlet for news-hungry journalists was the background of the vice presidential nominee. Other highlights of the convention were President Reagan's farewell speech and a slashing attack on Governor Dukakis by former President Ford. The Republican platform opposed abortion and called for child-care tax credits, catastrophic health insurance for children, a reduction in the capital gains tax, the line-item veto, and constitutional amendments requiring a balanced budget and limiting the number of consecutive terms congressmen can serve.

OPPONENT: Michael S. Dukakis (1933–   ) of Massachusetts; Democrat. Born in Brookline, Massachusetts, the son of Greek immigrants, Dukakis graduated with a degree in political science from Swarthmore College in 1955 and, after army service in Korea, graduated with honors from Harvard Law School in 1960. Between his junior and senior years at Swarthmore, he attended the University of San Marcos in Lima, Peru, where he lived with a native family and learned to speak Spanish fluently. Inspired to public service by the career of John F. Kennedy, he became active in Brookline town meetings and, in 1962, was elected to the state legislature, where, over the rest of the decade, he rose to chairman of the public service committee, championed environmental protection and affordable housing, and engineered passage of the nation's first no-fault auto insurance law (1970). Defeated for lieutenant governor on the ticket with Mayor Kevin White of Boston in 1970, he organized the Dukakis Diggers, a state watchdog group of young volunteers patterned after Nader's Raiders. During 1971–1973 he was moderator of "The Advocates," a public television series on which the issues of the day were debated. In 1974 Dukakis ousted incumbent Republican Governor Francis Sargent on an unequivocal campaign pledge not to raise taxes. Faced with a larger deficit than anticipated, Governor Dukakis reneged on that pledge and was defeated for renomination in the 1978 primary by Edward King. He taught public policy at the Kennedy School of Government at Harvard University until regaining the governorship in 1982. He was reelected handily in 1986. Governor Dukakis fostered the growth of high-tech industry in the state to replace the dying textile mills, contributing to an economic transformation dubbed the "Massachusetts miracle," and set in place several innovative programs, including ET, the Employment and Training Choices program, which prodded tens of thousands of welfare recipients into useful, permanent employment; and REAP, the Revenue Enhancement and Protection program, which brought in tens of millions of dollars in unexpected revenue with a limited tax amnesty followed by a crackdown on tax cheats. In 1986 fellow governors of both parties elected him "the most effective governor" in the United States. The decision of Senator Edward Kennedy, the state's senior Democrat, not to run for president in 1988, made it possible for Dukakis to declare his candidacy. After Governor Mario Cuomo of New York declined to run and former Senator Gary Hart of Colorado withdrew from the race amid a sex scandal, Dukakis, well-financed and well-organized, broke out of the pack of remaining candidates about midway through the primary season. One by one his opponents withdrew: former Governor Bruce Babbitt of Arizona, Senator Paul Simon of Illinois, Representative Richard Gephardt of Missouri, and Senator Albert Gore, Jr., of Tennessee. By the time Democrats gathered in Atlanta in July 1988, Dukakis's nomination was assured. Only the Reverend Jesse Jackson remained in the race. Jackson, the most formidable black presidential candidate to date, challenged the Dukakis forces on the platform and subtly threatened to disrupt the convention unless offered a major role in the campaign, but in the end pledged his support for the ticket. Governor Bill Clinton of Arkansas, in a long-winded and poorly received address, placed Dukakis's name in nomination. Dukakis was nominated on the first ballot with 2,876 votes to 1,218 for Jackson. In a moving acceptance speech that far exceeded expectations, Dukakis began with an emotional tribute to his immigrant parents and went on to cast himself as the natural heir to the legacy of President John F. Kennedy. "If anyone tells you," he declared, "that the American dream belongs to the privileged few and not to all of us, you tell them that the Reagan era is over and a new era is about to begin. Because it's time to raise our sights to look beyond the cramped ideals and limited ambitions of the past eight years—to recapture the spirit of energy and of confidence and of idealism that John Kennedy and Lyndon Johnson inspired a generation ago." He went on to say, mistakenly as it turned out, that this election would turn on competence not ideology. The most memorable lines of the convention, however, were those that ridiculed George Bush. In the keynote speech, Texas state treasurer Ann Richards drew wild cheers for describing Bush as a creature of wealth and privilege who "was born with a silver foot in his mouth." Senator Kennedy recounted the failures of the Reagan administration and got the crowd to chant along as he repeatedly asked, "Where was George?" Other highlights of the convention were a stirring unity speech by Jesse Jackson and the brief television debut of John F. Kennedy, Jr. Dukakis chose Senator Lloyd Bentsen of Texas as his running mate, thus recreating the Boston-Austin axis that worked so well for the Democrats in 1960. The Democratic platform, a brief, broadly worded document barely a tenth of the size of the 1984 platform, papered over differences between the Dukakis and Jackson forces. After his defeat by Bush, Dukakis resumed his duties as governor just as the Massachusetts economy entered into a severe downturn. Faced with public opinion polls reflecting his extreme unpopularity in the state, Dukakis declined to seek reelection in 1990.

CAMPAIGN AND THE ISSUES, 1988: In one of the most negative presidential campaigns in recent memory, Bush and Dukakis seemed to spend more time attacking each other than offering voters positive reasons for their candidacies. An early Dukakis lead in the polls wilted under a barrage of Republican fire designed to define the little-known governor as a McGovern-style liberal far outside the mainstream of American politics. Bush implied that Governor Dukakis was unpatriotic for vetoing a Massachusetts bill that required all public school teachers in the state to lead their classes daily in the Pledge of Allegiance. For weeks, to the virtual exclusion of serious issues, Bush hammered away at the flag issue until television coverage of his visit to a New Jersey flag factory on the day Dukakis was offering a detailed and well-received health insurance plan trivialized the Republican strategy. While denouncing Dukakis as soft on crime for his longstanding opposition to the death penalty and a controversial Massachusetts prison furlough program, Bush called for the execution of major drug traffickers and drug-related murderers. Bush charged that Dukakis's opposition to certain land-based missile systems and the proposed space-based defense system known as Star Wars not only would threaten national security but also undermine U.S. negotiating leverage with the Soviet Union. For his part, Dukakis sought to sow public doubts about Bush's judgment. He condemned Bush for sitting silently at meetings in which the Reagan administration plotted to trade arms for hostages with Iran. He wondered how Bush, a former director of the Central Intelligence Agency and director of the Reagan administration's South Florida antidrug task force, could have been unaware of the drug smuggling activities of General Manuel Noriega of Panama. He reminded voters that Bush's first decision as a presidential nominee was to select young Dan Quayle as his running mate, passing over what many Republican leaders conceded were more qualified legislators. Neither candidate comprehensively addressed one of the most important issues of the day—the huge budget deficit. Dukakis vowed to step up tax collection efforts against chronic tax cheats and agreed to consider raising taxes but only as a last resort. Bush proposed a vague "flexible freeze" to hold down spending, but that seemed more than offset by the cost of his proposed new programs and the weapons systems he hoped to develop. Moreover, Bush vowed never to raise taxes under any circumstances. "Read my lips, no new taxes!" he cried at virtually every stop. Bush pledged to continue the Reagan economic program, which he boasted had improved the lives of most Americans. Dukakis countered that the Reagan Revolution had wrought "a Swiss-cheese economy," which brought prosperity to the coasts and other scattered areas but left isolated pockets of real hardship in the farm belt of the Midwest, the oil patch of the Southwest, and the rust belt of the Great Lakes region. Dukakis called for several new programs: employer-financed health insurance, federal tuition loans to be repaid by withholding a portion of future earnings for anyone willing and qualified to enter college, financial incentives for teachers, federal child-care facilities, and an antidrug czar. Bush proposed modest tax incentives to encourage personal savings and to offset the cost of private day-care facilities, a cut in the capital gains tax, more money for education, and an expansion of the Medicaid system to permit low-income workers without health insurance to buy into it. Bush supported voluntary prayer in public schools and a constitutional amendment to curb abortion; Dukakis opposed both. In the first presidential debate at Wake Forest University in Winston-Salem, North Carolina, on September 25, Dukakis appeared more poised and focused than Bush and succeeded in reinforcing the stereotype of Republicans as guardians of wealth and privilege by attacking Bush's proposed capital-gains tax cut as a gift to the richest 1 percent of Americans. But Bush scored points in denouncing Dukakis for his longstanding membership in the American Civil Liberties Union and sought to associate the governor with some of its more unpopular positions. In the vice presidential debate at Omaha on October 5, Lloyd Bentsen outperformed Dan Quayle. When Quayle sought to draw a parallel between his experience and that of Senator John F. Kennedy in 1960, Bentsen scored perhaps the most memorable sound bite of the campaign with the riposte, "Senator, you're no Jack Kennedy." Following the second presidential debate at Los Angeles on October 13, in which the candidates traded jabs, striking familiar themes, but broke no new ground, Bush surged to a double-digit lead in the polls. During the last week of the campaign, Dukakis began to climb back with a populist theme ("I'm on your side") aimed at Democrats who had voted for Reagan in 1984, but it proved too little, too late. Although Dukakis won over the late deciders 55–43 percent, according to a *New York Times/CBS News* exit poll, 86 percent of the electorate had already made up their minds more than a week before the election and the overwhelming majority of those supported Bush. A gender gap held down Bush's victory margin; he swept male voters 57–41 percent but the candidates split the women's vote. Although, as expected, Dukakis overwhelmingly carried the black vote, Bush managed to draw 12 percent of blacks, twice as much as President Reagan won in 1984. Similarly, Bush made slight inroads in the traditionally Democratic Jewish vote and even improved on Reagan's victory margin among white fundamentalist or evangelical Christians. Bush swept every southern state and carried every region of the country except the East, which the candidates split. For his part, Dukakis did better than either Jimmy Carter or Walter Mondale in the two previous elections. He was the first Democratic presidential candidate in 20 years to carry a West Coast state. He captured 64 counties in 17 northern tier states that had not gone Democratic since the Lyndon Johnson landslide of 1964. He won back half of the Democrats who had voted for Reagan in 1984. He outpaced Mondale among union households and those identifying themselves as liberals. Dukakis won the endorsement of the Friends of the Earth and other environmental groups. Bush scored a coup in Dukakis's backyard in winning the support of the Boston police association. In the battle for celebrity endorsements, Bush campaigned with Arnold Schwarzenegger, Charleston Heston, and Loretta Lynn; Dukakis stumped alongside Cher, Robert Redford, and Rob Lowe. Although foreign leaders rarely meddle in U.S. elections, this year China's Deng Xiao-ping voiced support for Bush. President Reagan campaigned extensively on behalf of his loyal vice president. Perhaps reflecting the anemic substance of the campaign, an unusually large number of newspapers declined to endorse either candidate and just 57 percent of the voting age population showed up at the polls, the lowest turnout since such figures were first compiled in 1964. In the most expensive presidential campaign in history, Bush outspent Dukakis, $115 million to $105 million, in private donations and public funds. Bush was the first president since Herbert Hoover to succeed a retiring president of his own party, the first president since William Howard Taft to win the White House while his party lost ground in both houses of Congress and the governorships, and the first sitting vice president since Martin Van Buren to be elected president.

ELECTION AS PRESIDENT, NOVEMBER 8, 1988:

Popular Vote. Bush (Republican), 47,946,422 (54%); Dukakis (Democrat), 41,016,429 (46%).

Electoral Vote. Bush, 426; Dukakis, 111. One elector from West Virginia voted for Lloyd Bentsen for president, Michael Dukakis for vice president.

States Carried. Bush won the electoral votes of 40 states—Alabama, Alaska, Arizona, Arkansas, California, Colorado, Connecticut, Delaware, Florida, Georgia, Idaho, Illinois, Indiana, Kansas, Kentucky, Louisiana, Maine, Maryland, Michigan, Mississippi, Missouri, Montana, Nebraska, Nevada, New Hampshire, New Jersey, New Mexico, North Carolina, North Dakota, Ohio, Oklahoma, Pennsylvania, South Carolina, South Dakota, Tennessee, Texas, Utah, Vermont, Virginia, and Wyoming. Dukakis won the electoral votes of the District of Columbia and 10 states—Hawaii, Iowa, Massachusetts, Minnesota, New York, Oregon, Rhode Island, Washington, West Virginia, and Wisconsin.

INAUGURAL ADDRESS: January 20, 1989. ". . . A new breeze is blowing. And a world refreshed by freedom seems reborn. For in man's heart, if not in fact, the day of the dictator is over. The totalitarian era is passing. Its old ideas blown away like the leaves from an ancient, lifeless tree. . . .

"This is a time when the future seems a door you can walk right through into a room called tomorrow. Great nations of the world are moving toward democracy through the door to freedom. Men and women of the world move toward free markets through the door to prosperity. The people of the world agitate for free expression and free thought through the door to the moral and intellectual satisfactions that only liberty allows. We know what works. Freedom works. We know what's right. Freedom is right. We know how to secure a more just and prosperous life for man on earth through free markets, free speech, free elections, and the exercise of free will unhampered by the state. . . .

"The president is neither prince nor pope; and I don't seek a window on men's souls. In fact, I yearn for a greater tolerance, an easygoingness about each other's attitudes and way of life. There are few clear areas in which we as a society must rise up united and express our intolerance. The most obvious now is drugs. And when that first cocaine was smuggled in on a ship it may as well have been a deadly bacteria, so much has it hurt the body, the soul, of our country. And there is much to be done and to be said. But take my word for it, this scourge will stop! . . ."

VICE PRESIDENT: (James) Dan(forth) Quayle (1947–   ), of Indiana, served 1989–1993. Born in Indianapolis, the grandson of Eugene Pulliam, publisher of the *Indianapolis Star* and other newspapers, Quayle was raised in Phoenix, Arizona and in Huntington, Indiana. A mediocre student, he graduated with a degree in political science from DePauw University in Greencastle, Indiana in 1969. Vulnerable to the draft during the Vietnam War, he won a place in the Indiana National Guard, having requested the aid of retired Major General Wendell Phillippi, an employee of the Pulliam chain and a former commander of the Guard. Quayle attended evening classes at Indiana University law school while working by turns in the consumer protection division of the Indiana attorney general's office, as an administrative assistant to the governor, and as director of the Indiana inheritance tax office. Receiving his law degree in 1974, he joined the family newspaper chain as associate publisher of the *Huntington Herald-Press*. In 1976 he surprised even members of his own family in upsetting two-term Democratic Representative J. Edward Roush of Indiana's 4th Congressional District, the Fort Wayne region. In the House, Quayle established a conservative voting record and was reelected in 1978. In 1980, he rode the coattails of Ronald Reagan in defeating Democratic Senator Birch Bayh, who was seeking an unprecedented fourth term, in a bitter campaign in which Quayle successfully portrayed Bayh as a captive of liberal special interests. Quayle was reelected in 1986 over Valparaiso councilwoman Jill Long with 61 percent of the vote, the largest majority of any popularly elected senator in Indiana history. In the Senate, Quayle established a solidly conservative voting record, supporting President Reagan nearly 90 percent of the time and earning consistently high marks from conservative rating groups, but he also developed a reputation as a lightweight with little patience for detail. His most significant achievement was passage of the Job Training Partnership Act of 1982, which he cosponsored with Democratic Senator Edward M. Kennedy of Massachusetts, promoting cooperation between local government and private employers in training unskilled youth to enter the job market. As a member of the Armed Services Committee, he surprised many of his colleagues by mastering the complexities of the defense budget and weapons systems. He was a leading advocate of Star Wars technology, Reagan's proposed space-based missile defense system. He consistently voted for tax cuts, aid for the contras fighting in Nicaragua, and the Reagan defense buildup. He was one of only 11 senators to oppose expanding Medicare to include certain catastrophic health benefits. However, he joined liberals in supporting economic sanctions against South Africa. His selection as vice president, for which he quietly campaigned, provoked a firestorm of controversy over his youth, poor academic record, draft avoidance during the Vietnam War, and lackluster congressional performance. Heckled at virtually every stop and the favorite butt of jokes for comics and cartoonists, he was scripted carefully by veteran Republican campaign staffers and restricted to low-visibility campaign swings. In the one chance he had to demonstrate a measure of substance, the vice presidential debate with Senator Lloyd Bentsen, he failed to rise above low expectations. Public opinion polls consistently ranked him as the most unpopular of the four national candidates with nearly half of those polled expressing an unfavorable view of him. As vice president, he never was able to erase doubts about his abilities. Such gaffes as misspelling the word potato only reinforced public misgivings. In 1992 he led the administration's appeal for "family values," most notably with a denunciation of the television show "Murphy Brown" for its title character's decision to bear a child out of wedlock and raise it as a single parent. "The elitists laughed at the reference to 'Murphy Brown,'" Quayle said defiantly before a Christian fundamentalist audience, "and sneered at my defense of basic values. But it wasn't just me they were laughing at, my friends. It was you and your families and your values." (*New York Times*, August 21, 1992). As chairman of the Council on Competitiveness, created by President Bush to consider ways to help U.S. companies compete in world markets, Quayle aggressively pressed to free business of government regulation, often running afoul of environmentalists who charged that his policies were contributing to pollution. He also served as chairman of the National Space Council. He was an outspoken advocate of term limits for Congress and a sharp critic of lawyers. He was dispatched abroad on various diplomatic missions, notably a two-week tour of Australia, Indonesia, Thailand, and Singapore in the spring of 1989 to reassure those governments that the United States intended to remain a major Pacific power despite uncertainty surrounding the renewal of leases for military bases in the Philippines.

CABINET:

Secretary of State. James A. Baker (1930–   ), of Texas, served 1989–1992. He served as Treasury secretary in the Reagan administration and was Bush's campaign manager. In March 1989, during weeks of personal negotiations with congressional leaders, he hammered out a bipartisan agreement on U.S. support for the contra rebels pending elections in Nicaragua. As the Soviet Union and the East bloc disintegrated, he fostered democratization and an orderly reunification of Germany. In the wake of the Persian Gulf War, during which he worked feverishly to keep the fragile anti-Iraq coalition intact, he advanced prospects for a comprehensive settlement of the Arab-Israeli conflict, winning Palestinian confidence by tying Israeli loan guarantees to a freeze on new Jewish settlements in the West Bank and Gaza Strip and arranging for Arab and Israeli leaders to engage in direct talks for the first time. He resigned in August 1992 to take over Bush's flagging reelection campaign. (2) Lawrence S. Eagleburger (1930–   ), of Wisconsin, served 1992–1993. A career diplomat, he had been Baker's deputy.

Secretary of the Treasury. Nicholas F. Brady (1930–   ), of New Jersey, served 1988–1993. A holdover from the Reagan administration, he cited as his overarching goal the reorientation of American business to end its preoccupation with current earnings and to begin to manage for the long term. He urged consideration of tax law changes as one way to curb the corporate buy-out frenzy of the 1980s, which he criticized as a misuse of talent and financial resources at a time when the United States is facing increasing competition abroad. He drafted the plans for bailing out the nation's troubled savings and loans and resolving the Third World debt crisis (see "Administration"). He solicited funds from other governments to help finance the Persian Gulf War. Amid widespread private criticism that he often appeared unprepared at meetings and is slow to grasp new information, he admitted in an interview with Alan Murray of the *Wall Street Journal* (April 19, 1989) that because of mild, though persistent dyslexia, he reads at a pace not much above that of a seventh-grade student.

Secretary of Defense. Richard Cheney (1941–   ), of Wyoming, served 1989–1993. Bush's first choice, former Senator John Tower of Texas, was rejected by the Senate amid charges of alcohol abuse, womanizing, and potential conflict of interest; this was the first Senate rejection of a cabinet appointment since 1959 (see "Dwight D. Eisenhower, 34th President," "Cabinet: Commerce"). Cheney was White House chief of staff during the Ford administration. At his first news conference as defense secretary he took an extraordinary step in demonstrating his authority by publicly rebuking Air Force Chief of Staff General Larry D. Welch for discussing the fate of certain nuclear weapons with members of Congress without authorization. He tightened procedures in the Pentagon's procurement system and overhauled the vast array of new weapons systems in various stages of development, scrapping some to strengthen others. He urged other NATO governments to increase defense spending to compensate for cutbacks in U.S. forces abroad. He oversaw the deployment of U.S. forces in the Persian Gulf War. In April 1991 he unveiled a controversial plan to close 31 of the 485 military installations around the country.

Attorney General. Richard Thornburgh (1932–   ), of Pennsylvania, served 1988–1991. A holdover from the Reagan administration, he encouraged the Supreme Court to restrict abortion rights and intervened in the trial of former National Security Council aide Lieutenant Colonel Oliver North to prevent disclosure of classified information. He won increased funding for law enforcement. He resigned to run, unsuccessfully, for the Senate. (2) William P. Barr (1950–   ), of New York, served 1991–1993. Barr shifted FBI attention from counter-intelligence, with which it had been preoccupied during the Cold War, to investigations of gang violence and health care fraud. He ran afoul of congressional Democrats for his resistance to appoint an independent special prosecutor in the case involving the Atlanta branch of an Italian bank, which had extended credit to Iraq.

Secretary of the Interior. Manuel Lujan (1928–   ), of New Mexico, served 1989–1993. The ranking Republican on the House Interior Committee, he twice was considered for this cabinet post by President Reagan. His nomination was opposed by the environmental group Friends of the Earth. He warned the oil industry that, although he generally supported controlled private drilling on public lands, including such ecologically sensitive areas as the Arctic National Wildlife Refuge, oil spills like the one off Alaska in 1989 (see "Administration") may poison popular support for oil development much like the accident at Three Mile Island (see "Jimmy Carter, 39th President," "Administration") halted further development of nuclear energy. He called for an easing of the Endangered Species Act to consider the economic impact of laws protecting wildlife.

Secretary of Agriculture. (1) Clayton Yeutter (1930–   ), of Nebraska, served 1989–1991. He was U.S. trade representative in the Reagan administration. He promoted U.S. farm products in foreign markets. He resigned to become chairman of the Republican National Committee. (2) Edward Madigan (1936–1994) of Illinois, 1991–1993. He was ranking Republican on the House Agriculture Committee.

Secretary of Commerce. Robert Mosbacher (1927–   ), of Texas, served 1989–1992. A friend of Bush's since their days together as Houston oilmen, he was financial director of the Bush presidential campaign. He fostered cooperation between government and industry to enable American companies to compete better abroad and won Japanese agreement for the operation of certain large retail stores in Japan. He resigned to direct Bush's reelection campaign. (2) Barbara H. Franklin (1940–   ) of Pennsylvania, served 1992–1993. One of the first women to receive an M.B.A. from Harvard, she was a management consultant at the time of her appointment. She eased controls on U.S. exports to former Communist countries.

Secretary of Labor. (1) Elizabeth H. Dole (1936–   ), of Kansas, served 1989–1990. She was transportation secretary in the Reagan administration. She led administration efforts in successfully limiting a rise in the minimum wage put forth by congressional Democrats, revitalized government efforts to provide jobs for disadvantaged youth, helped to settle the 1989 coal miners' strike in Appalachia, restored some of the cuts imposed by the Reagan administration on the Occupational Safety and Health Administration, and strengthened enforcement of the child labor laws. She resigned to become president of the American Red Cross. (2) Lynn Martin (1939–1993), of Illinois, served 1990–1993. A former schoolteacher and five-term veteran of the House, she had lost a bid to unseat Democratic Senator Paul Simon in 1990.

Secretary of Health and Human Services. Louis Sullivan (1933–   ), of

Georgia, served 1989–1993. A hematologist, he was president of the Morehouse School of Medicine at the time of his appointment. He was the only black in Bush's original cabinet. He mounted a highly visible campaign against the tobacco industry, speaking out against the introduction of new cigarettes aimed at women and blacks, calling for an end to tobacco company sponsorship of sporting events, and proposing a ban on cigarette vending machines.

Secretary of Housing and Urban Development. Jack Kemp (1935–   ), of New York, served 1989–1993. A former quarterback for the Buffalo Bills, nine-term congressman, and candidate for the 1988 Republican presidential nomination, he was an early advocate of supply-side economics and a principal architect of the Reagan-era tax cuts. He restored confidence in the department following the corruption of his predecessor's term. His calls for a renewed war on poverty, a national housing policy, and enterprise zones to encourage revitalization of the inner cities failed to attract administration support.

Secretary of Transportation. Samuel Skinner (1938–   ), of Illinois, served 1989–1991. Bush's Illinois campaign director, he was chairman of the Regional Transportation Authority of Northeastern Illinois at the time of his appointment. He persuaded President Bush not to intervene in the 1989 machinist strike against Eastern Airlines. He oversaw the military effort to assist Exxon in cleaning up the worst oil spill ever in U.S. waters (see "Administration") and facilitated the out-of-court settlement between Exxon and the state of Alaska. For his leadership role in the oil spill and such other calamities as Hurricane Hugo and an earthquake in San Francisco, he was dubbed the "Master of Disaster." He resigned to become White House chief of staff. (2) Andrew Card (1947–   ), of Massachusetts, served 1992–1993. An engineer who had directed Bush's opposition research team in 1988, which dug up the information that formed the basis for the Willie Horton prison furlough issue and other lines of attack against Democratic nominee Michael Dukakis, Card was deputy White House chief of staff at the time of his appointment. He supervised the federal government's relief effort in the wake of Hurricane Andrew in 1992.

Secretary of Energy. James Watkins (1927–   ), of California, served 1989–1993. A retired admiral and veteran of the nuclear submarine program, he was assigned the task of cleaning up and modernizing the nation's nuclear weapons production facilities. With the end of the Cold War, he helped draw up plans for the closing of certain nuclear weapons plants beginning in 1996. Citing safety reasons, he postponed the restarting of the government's Savannah River nuclear reactors in South Carolina, the only site where tritium gas for U.S. nuclear warheads is manufactured. Amid the shutdown of Middle East oil facilities during the Persian Gulf War, he oversaw the effort to conserve energy and increase domestic production. He encouraged opening up part of the Arctic National Wildlife Refuge in Alaska to oil drilling.

Secretary of Education. (1) Lauro F. Cavazos (1927–   ), of Texas, served 1988–1990. A holdover from the Reagan administration, he pressed for increased funding for education and set as a top priority a reduction in the nation's alarming high-school dropout rate. He resigned abruptly, reportedly because President Bush was dissatisfied with his performance. (2) Lamar Alexander (1940–   ) of Tennessee, served 1991–1993. A former governor of Tennessee, he was president of the University of Tennessee at the time of his appointment. A Senate inquiry into his financial investments held up his confirmation.

Secretary of Veterans Affairs. Edward Derwinski (1926–   ), of Illinois, served 1989–1992. The first secretary of this new department, he eased eligibility requirements for disability benefits for Vietnam veterans suffering from certain forms of cancer associated with the defoliant Agent Orange. He resigned under pressure from veterans groups who were upset over a controversial plan to open veterans hospitals to non-veterans. His deputy, Anthony J. Principi, was acting secretary for the remainder of Bush's term.

ADMINISTRATION: January 20, 1989–January 20, 1993.

The Economy. During the Bush administration, inflation eased to 3 percent annually, interest rates were driven down to their lowest levels in two decades, and swelling exports slashed the trade deficit. But by most other measures the economy worsened: Unemployment rose partly because under Bush fewer new jobs were created and more businesses failed than under any president since the Depression. Amid a lingering recession, the number of Americans qualifying for food stamps jumped to a record 10 percent of the population. The annual budget deficit doubled to about $350 billion, more than ten times what candidate Bush had promised in 1988 to deliver by the last year of his term.

No single action received more attention than Bush's reneging on his central campaign pledge not to raise taxes. In stark contrast to the fanfare attending his oft-repeated pledge, "Read my lips: No new taxes," throughout the presidential campaign, he announced his new position in a terse written statement released on June 26, 1990, a day in which the news was dominated by the Washington visit of Nelson Mandela. The turnaround outraged conservative Republicans, who torpedoed a budget compromise worked out by the White House and the Democratic leadership in Congress. Ironically, the White House looked to Senate Minority Leader Robert Dole to sell the package, even though it was Dole whom Bush had pummeled for his refusal to rule out a tax hike during the New Hampshire primary campaign in 1988. Following protracted negotiations, the White House and Congress agreed on a revised budget package for fiscal year 1991 that was expected to cut the deficit by hundreds of billions of dollars over the next several years. To achieve this, Bush agreed to a series of tax hikes aimed at the middle class (sharp increases in federal taxes on gasoline, cigarettes, and beer, and a boost in Medicare premiums) and the wealthy (luxury taxes on certain furs, jewels, cars, boats, and private aircraft, and an increase in the top income tax rate). In 1992 Bush publicly apologized for the tax increase, calling it a "mistake."

Savings and Loan Crisis. In 1989 President Bush signed into law a comprehensive plan to bail out the hundreds of insolvent savings and loans, which had been gutted by mismanagement or corruption or which simply failed to survive in the more competitive environment wrought by banking deregulation earlier in the decade. Having backed away from an early unpopular scheme to impose a fee on deposits, the administration approved a package that provided for more than $150 billion over the remainder of the century, with about 75 percent to be borne by the treasury and the rest from increased fees on healthy banks and thrifts. The bill anticipated a total cost, including interest and spread out over a 30-year period, of as much as $300 billion. It also imposed tough new restrictions on the accounting and lending practices of banks and thrifts and provided funds to prosecute cases of fraud. The Federal Home Loan Bank Board, which had supervised the thrift industry, and the Federal Savings and Loan Insurance Corporation, which had guaranteed deposits, were scrapped, their functions transferred, respectively, to the newly-created Office of Thrift Supervision within the Treasury Department and the Federal Deposit Insurance Corporation. A new agency, the Resolution Trust Corporation, was charged with closing and selling off the assets of failed institutions. Within months of the bill's enactment, the White House conceded what some analysts had been warning for some time, that the cost of the bailout might go even higher. Treasury Secretary Nicholas Brady predicted that the crisis might eventually wipe out as much as 40 percent of the thrift industry. In 1990 the General Accounting Office estimated the ultimate cost over 40 years will be $500 billion.

Third World Debt. In a reversal of Reagan administration policy, President Bush in March 1989 announced his support for a plan to induce international banks to forgive as much as 20 percent of the more than $300 billion in debts owed by 39 developing countries. Amid concerns that onerous debt service threatened to destabilize many Third World countries, including neighboring Mexico, Bush abandoned the Reagan administration's policy of encouraging new loans simply to help pay the interest on the old ones.

Nicaragua and the Fall of the Sandinistas. What the Reagan administration and the contras were unable to accomplish with bullets (see "Ronald Reagan, 40th President," "Administration: Nicaragua and the Contra Resistance"), the Bush administration and opposition presidential candidate Violeta Chamorro brought about with ballots. Soon after taking office, President Bush abandoned the Reagan administration's persistent efforts to rearm the contra rebels and topple the Marxist-led Sandinista regime in Managua. Admitting for the first time that the previous administration's Central American policy had failed, largely for lack of congressional support, the Bush administration struck a compromise with Democrats in Congress. Under the agreement, humanitarian aid for the contras, which was scheduled to run out at the end of March 1989, was extended through February 1990, the time of scheduled free elections in Nicaragua. The accord also offered for the first time assistance for expatriated contras wishing to resume peaceful residence in Nicaragua. The most controversial part of the $50 million package was a side letter in which President Bush pledged to cut off aid at the end of November 1989 unless he received letters of approval from four Democratic-controlled committees in Congress. Some legal observers expressed concern that the side letter appeared to give Congress a legislative veto over executive action, a power ruled unconstitutional by the Supreme Court, and might set a precedent for future congressional meddling in foreign policy. The plan was hailed by contra leaders and denounced by the Sandinistas as well as ultra-conservatives in Congress, including Republican Senator Jesse Helms of North Carolina. Separately, the administration slashed by 50 percent funding for the contras' political activities in exile in order to encourage rebel leaders to return home to take part in the 1990 elections.

Although most observers gave Mrs. Chamorro little chance against the entrenched Sandinista regime of Daniel Ortega, she proved to be a remarkably resourceful campaigner whose popularity never registered in public opinion polls. The widow of a crusading newspaper publisher whose assassination had sparked a revolt that brought down the dictatorship of Anastasio Somoza, she led the National Opposition Union, a fragile 14-party anti-Sandinista coalition, to victory on February 25, 1990 and was sworn in as president two months later. Delighted at her election, the Bush administration lifted the economic embargo against Nicaragua, promised more direct aid, and encouraged the contras to disband.

Invasion of Panama and the Capture of Noriega, 1989–1990. On December 20, 1989, U.S. forces invaded Panama to capture General Manuel Antonio Noriega, the de facto leader, who was wanted in Florida on drug trafficking charges and whose Panamanian Defense Forces had been harassing U.S. military personnel stationed in Panama. Operation Just Cause, as the campaign was called, ended on January 3, 1990, when Noriega surrendered to U.S. forces.

The United States had evidence as early as 1972 that Noriega was engaged in drug trafficking while serving as chief of intelligence under the then-ruler, General Omar Torrijos. According to John Ingersoll, then director of the U.S. Bureau of Narcotics and Dangerous Drugs, the Nixon administration considered but ultimately rejected a proposal to assassinate Noriega. At the same time, and for years thereafter, Noriega reportedly performed services, at times for pay, for the U.S. intelligence community. In 1988, after federal grand juries in Florida indicted Noriega on drug charges, the Reagan administration imposed sanctions against Panama, withdrawing trade preferences and suspending Panama Canal fees. By the time President Bush took office, the United States and Panama were on a collision course. In May 1989 Noriega nullified the apparent election of opposition presidential candidate Guillermo Endara and spoke defiantly of maintaining his iron grip on the country even as Bush increased the U.S. military presence there. When a group of Panamanian officers attempted to overthrow Noriega in October 1989, Bush refused to intervene to ensure their success, convincing many, perhaps including Noriega himself, that Bush lacked the will for war. In December of that year, Panamanian forces, which had for some time been harassing U.S. military personnel, shot one American officer and tortured another. "What changed my mind," Bush replied when asked why he ordered the invasion of Panama just two months after having refused to assist a coup, "was the death of the marine; the brutalizing, really obscene torture of the Navy lieutenant; and the threat of sexual abuse and the terror inflicted on that Navy lieutenant's wife; the declaration of war by Noriega; the fact that our people down there felt that they didn't know where this was going and they weren't sure what all that meant and whether that meant we could guarantee the safety of Americans there."[8]

The invasion was roundly criticized in most world capitals. The Organization of American States voted 20–1 (the United States was the lone dissenter) to condemn it. The United Nations General Assembly, in a vote of 75–20, with 40 abstentions, denounced it as a "flagrant violation" of international law. Among the major powers, the Soviet Union and China spoke out strongly against the invasion, while Britain, Canada, France, Italy, and Japan supported the United States. Those most affected by the invasion, the Panamanians themselves, overwhelmingly endorsed it. According to a public opinion poll conducted for CBS News, some 92 percent of Panamanians believed that the invasion was justified, including 80 percent of those whose property was destroyed in the process.

The fighting lasted about four days, while Noriega eluded capture. Resistance collapsed when it was learned that he had taken refuge inside the Vatican mission, which was quickly surrounded by U.S. forces. During the conflict, Captain Linda Bray, commander of the 988th Military Police Company, became the first woman ever to lead U.S. forces in combat, when she directed a 30-man unit in seizing control of a guard dog kennel from forces loyal to Noriega. On January 3, 1990, Noriega voluntarily walked out of the mission and was taken into U.S. custody. While awaiting trial on drug trafficking charges at a federal prison near Miami, Noriega declared himself a born-again Christian. On April 9, 1992, Noriega was found guilty on eight counts of cocaine trafficking, racketeering, and money laundering. He was sentenced to 40 years in prison.

Casualties: Of the 24,000 U.S. troops taking part in the conflict, 23 were killed, 322 were wounded. Among Panamanians, about 300 troops and 200 civilians were killed; about 100 troops and 2,000 civilians were wounded. Property damage exceeded $1 billion.

The Collapse of Communism. The hallmark of U.S. foreign policy since the end of World War II had been the containment of Communism. Presidents from Truman to Reagan were preoccupied with anticipating and countering the Soviet threat. The payoff came during Bush's term, as Communist governments seemed to fall of their own weight. With the Soviet Union, under Mikhail Gorbachev, no longer willing to impose Communism on other countries through force of arms, one by one the peoples of Eastern Europe rose up, dismantling their Marxist governments and, to varying degrees, embracing Western-style democracy:

• In Poland, the Solidarity labor movement, outlawed since 1982, was swept to power in elections in June 1989 and two months later formed the country's first non-Communist government since World War II. In December 1990 Lech Walesa, the shipyard electrician who had founded Solidarity, was elected president. In March 1991 Bush sought to advance Poland's transition to a free market economy by forgiving most of its debt to the United States.

• In East Germany, the Berlin Wall, erected in 1961 to stanch the exodus to the West, was opened to free travel on November 9, 1989. The two Germanys, divided since the end of World War II, were reunited on the terms of the Western powers at midnight on October 2–3, 1990.

• In Czechoslovakia, Vaclav Havel, a dissident playwright and leader of the Civic Forum reform movement, was elected president in December 1989.

• In Hungary, the Communist party officially disbanded in October 1989, paving the way for the election of a center-right government the following April. The first stock exchange in postwar Eastern Europe opened for trading in Budapest in 1990.

• In Yugoslavia, the Communist party renounced its constitutionally guaranteed leading role in society in January 1990, making possible the formation of opposition parties, but deep-seated ethnic divisions led to civil war.

• In Romania, President Nicolae Ceausescu and his wife were convicted by a military tribunal of genocide and plundering the treasury and, on Christmas Day, 1989, were executed. The subsequent government was criticized as authoritarian by the Bush administration.

• In Bulgaria, Todor Zhivkov, leader since 1954, resigned amid public protests in November 1989 and later was charged with corruption and abuse of power. A new party controlled by former Communists won a majority in the country's first free elections in June 1990.

• In Albania, the poorest and most hardline Marxist state in Eastern Europe, President Ramiz Alia took the first tentative steps to reform amid an exodus of tens of thousands of Albanians to Italy and Greece. Diplomatic relations between the United States and Albania, suspended since 1939, were resumed on March 15, 1991. The Communist party prevailed in the country's first free elections on March 31, 1991 but gave way to democratic forces in 1992.

• In the Soviet Union itself, dozens of Communist officials were rejected in March 1989, in the first free elections since the period of the Bolshevik Revolution, for seats in the newly-created legislature, the Congress of People's Deputies. A year later the Congress repealed the Communist Party's constitutionally-guaranteed monopoly in politics, paving the way for multi-party elections. In August 1991, as President Gorbachev prepared to grant more autonomy to the republics, hardliners staged a coup, placing Gorbachev under house arrest and crushing dissent. (Bush had warned Gorbachev personally as early as June about an impending coup, but Gorbachev told him not to worry about it.) Under the leadership of Russian President Boris Yeltsin, the forces of democracy restored Gorbachev to power. The failed coup only hastened the disintegration of the Soviet Union. Amid economic chaos there, Bush pledged $1.5 billion in food aid. In September 1991, the Baltic republics achieved their independence. Two months later Russia, Ukraine, and Byelorussia withdrew from the Soviet Union to form the Commonwealth of Independent States. Left to preside over an empty shell of a government, Gorbachev resigned as president on Christmas Day, 1991. Gorbachev formally rang down the "Iron Curtain" in a speech in May 1992 at Westminster College in Fulton, Missouri, where Winston Churchill had coined the phrase in 1946.

As President Bush left office, China, Cuba, and North Korea remained the last bastions of Communism.

Cold War Yields to the New World Order. At a summit meeting in Washington in the spring of 1990, Bush and Gorbachev agreed on the framework for a reduction in strategic arms and chemical stockpiles and to cooperate on atomic energy research. At a historic conference in Paris in November 1990, Bush, Gorbachev, and the leaders of 20 other nations that make up the North Atlantic Treaty Organization (NATO) and the Warsaw Pact, signed a mutual non-aggression pledge, thus proclaiming an end to the Cold War. The Warsaw Pact, created in 1955 to counter NATO, disbanded on March 31, 1991. The Paris conference also produced a comprehensive arms control treaty, in which the two sides agreed to sharply limit the numbers of tanks, artillery, and other non-nuclear weapons in Europe. The Soviet Union agreed to a disproportionately large share of the cuts to erase its superiority of armaments on the continent. Bush said the treaty signaled "the new world order." With the reunification of Germany and the democratization of much of the rest of Eastern Europe, the Soviet Union agreed to the phased withdrawal of all Soviet forces from its former satellites. In March 1991 the United States withdrew the last of the cruise nuclear missiles that the Reagan administration had installed on British soil amid intense local protest in 1983. On July 31, 1992, Bush and Gorbachev, using pens made of scrap metal from destroyed nuclear missiles, signed the Strategic Arms Reduction Treaty (START), which promised deep cuts in nuclear arsenals over seven years.

Persian Gulf War, 1990–1991. On August 2, 1990, Iraq invaded Kuwait. The Bush administration promptly mounted Operation Desert Shield, consisting of a comprehensive diplomatic campaign and economic embargo against Iraq and a defensive military operation, led by U.S. Army General H. Norman Schwarzkopf with headquarters in Saudi Arabia, to prevent Iraqi forces from pressing on to other Persian Gulf states. When economic sanctions failed to move Iraq by the January 15th deadline imposed by the UN Security Council, Allied forces, led by the United States, launched Operation Desert Storm, the offensive military campaign to liberate Kuwait, which began with the massive aerial bombardment of Baghdad on January 17, 1991. Despite five weeks of unremitting devastation, Iraqi President Saddam Hussein defied Bush's ultimatum to withdraw unconditionally by February 23rd. The next day Allied forces launched the ground offensive, which routed Iraq in 100 hours of combat.

Causes: The war was caused by Saddam's need for money in the wake of an eight-year war with Iran, his desire for greater access to the sea, and his miscalculation about Bush's reaction and resolve. The small but oil-rich emirate of Kuwait thought that its $10 billion contribution to Iraq's war with Iran had bought it immunity from Iraqi aggression. But Saddam, having failed to win concessions from Iran to expand its narrow access to the Persian Gulf, saw in the rich coast of Kuwait the answer to all its problems. Saddam, whose favorite motion picture was *The Godfather,* made the emir of Kuwait an offer that was hard to refuse: cede part of Kuwait to Iraq and remain friends or retain the present boundaries and risk the wrath of a powerful neighbor. The emir refused to yield ground.

Before the Iraqi invasion, the Bush administration had fostered closer ties with Saddam, aiding Iraq in its war with Iran, opposing congressional efforts to impose economic sanctions, and permitting the sale to Iraq of high technology equipment with potential military applications. On July 24, 1990, Margaret Tutwiler, the State Department spokeswoman, restated the U.S. commitment to its friends in the Gulf region but added that Washington had no specific security commitment to Kuwait. The next day Saddam summoned the U.S. ambassador, April Glaspie, for a lecture on Iraq's needs in the aftermath of its costly war with Iran. In a reference to Iraq's territorial dispute with Kuwait, Glaspie informed Saddam that the United States did not wish to meddle in inter-Arab affairs. "There was some reason to believe," Bush said in justifying his early overtures to Iraq, "that perhaps improved relations with the West would modify [Saddam's] behavior."[9] After the Iraqi invasion, the Bush administration gave various reasons for going to war, at times warning that Saddam was dangerously close to possessing nuclear weapons, at others arguing that American jobs were at stake. At length the administration set forth as its primary reason that Saddam, like Hitler, was a bloodthirsty aggressor who must be stopped sooner rather than later.

The war. After giving personal assurances to Egyptian President Hosni Mubarak and others that he would not invade Kuwait, Saddam did just that on August 2, 1990. Six days later he formally annexed the oil-rich emirate as a province of Iraq. Meanwhile, Bush, vowing to expel Iraq, mounted Operation Desert Shield. In a flurry of diplomacy, he marshalled the support of much of the rest of the world in isolating Iraq. The UN Security Council, in a series of resolutions adopted without dissent in August, condemned Iraq's aggression and demanded its immediate withdrawal, refused to recognize its annexation of Kuwait, and ordered a trade and financial embargo of Iraq. The Allied coalition nations that sent troops to the Gulf were, in the order of their troop strength, as of mid-February, 1991, the United States, Saudi Arabia, Great Britain, Egypt, France, Syria, Kuwait-in-exile, Pakistan, Morocco, Bangladesh, Canada, Italy, Senegal, Niger, and Argentina. Others that sent only naval vessels were Australia, Belgium, Denmark, Greece, Netherlands, Norway, Spain, and the Soviet

Union. Turkey participated with troops amassed on its own territory along the Iraqi border. Japan and Germany, constitutionally barred from military activity, contributed funds.

As Allied forces took up positions in Saudi Arabia, Iraqi troops dug into entrenched fortifications in Kuwait, terrorized Kuwaiti civilians, and looted the emirate of everything from computers and major appliances to light bulbs and school blackboards. They even stole videotapes of "Sesame Street" dubbed into Arabic from a Kuwaiti television station. In a crude attempt at psychological warfare, Iraq directed a "Voice of Peace" radio broadcast at U.S. troops. A female announcer, dubbed Baghdad Betty by GI's, sought to undermine U.S. morale with these improbable words: "While you're away, movie stars are taking your women. Robert Redford is dating your girlfriend. Tom Selleck is kissing your lady. Bart Simpson is making love to your wife."[10] Saddam ordered the roundup of some of the 3 million foreign civilians in Iraq and Kuwait, scattering them among strategic sites as human shields against an air war. They included more than a million Egyptians, the largest from any one nation, and thousands of Americans. Bush vowed that the presence of hostages would not deter him from war. By year's end, Iraq released them.

Under the aegis of the United Nations and with a clear, but not overwhelming mandate from the U.S. Congress, Bush launched the military offensive, Operation Desert Storm, on January 17, 1991. He left the conduct of the war to General Schwarzkopf, refusing, as President Lyndon Johnson had done during the Vietnam War, to micro-manage the conflict. In the first wave of air strikes in and around Baghdad, Stealth fighter jets knocked out Iraqi radar defenses, blinding the enemy and ensuring Allied control of the skies for the duration. For six weeks, more than 2,000 Allied warplanes dropped 88,500 tons of bombs over Iraq and parts of Kuwait, destroying nuclear and chemical weapons production facilities, power plants, roads and bridges, and conventional military targets. Laser-guided smart bombs zeroed in on government buildings in crowded downtown Baghdad. Iraq could do little but hunker down and hope to survive with enough strength to repel the long-awaited ground assault. In an attempt to goad Israel into the conflict and thereby destabilize the Allied coalition, Iraq launched Soviet-built Scud missiles at Israeli cities. Although some were destroyed in mid-flight by Patriot anti-missile missiles, many got through, injuring or killing small numbers of civilians. Under strong pressure from Washington, Israel reluctantly agreed to sit out the war. One Scud attack on Allied positions in Saudi Arabia survived its encounter with a Patriot missile and struck a barracks, killing 28 American reservists, including two women. When a last-minute peace plan offered by the Soviets failed to get Iraq to withdraw unconditionally, Bush imposed a February 23rd deadline, which Saddam let pass. The next day, General Schwarzkopf launched a bold ground offensive, the Hail Mary strategy, as he called it, in which a force of Marines feigned an amphibious assault, pinning down large numbers of Iraqis in defensive positions along the Kuwaiti coast, while the main force swept far west around a line of Iraqi defensive fortifications to strike the vaunted Republican Guard in the rear and effectively cut off demoralized front-line units. The action involved more than 800 U.S. tanks, the largest such engagement since the Battle of the Bulge. Meanwhile other coalition forces launched a frontal assault along the northern border of Saudi Arabia, easily penetrating what some had feared would be formidable defensive fortifications. The campaign proceeded much more quickly than planned, slowed down only by the masses of surrendering Iraqi soldiers. President Bush was called away from a paddleball game with Democratic Representative G. V. "Sonny" Montgomery of Mississippi to assess Iraq's desperate mid-battle offer to withdraw with their equipment intact. It was rejected as too little, too late. On February 27, marines liberated Kuwait City. In a mirror image of the humiliating evacuation of Saigon in 1975, a marine helicopter landed on the rooftop of the U.S. embassy, this time spilling out triumphant forces. With Iraqi troops in full rout, Bush ordered a suspension of hostilities on February 27. U.S. forces continued to occupy the southern fifth of Iraq pending a formal cease-fire. On April 3, 1991, the UN Security Council imposed strict terms as a basis for the cease-fire, demanding that Iraq pay war reparations, accept the pre-war boundary with Kuwait, and permit the elimination of its weapons of mass destruction. Near the end of his term, Bush resumed air strikes against selected targets in retaliation for Iraq's repeated violation of the cease-fire terms.

The cost: Of the 541,000 U.S. troops deployed to the Gulf, 148 were killed, 467 were wounded; about 15 percent of the casualties were from friendly fire. Another 141 foreign allied servicemen were killed in action. Pre-war planners had anticipated as many as 10,000 Allied casualties. Seventy-six U.S. aircraft crashed or were shot down or otherwise severely damaged. Iraq suffered an estimated 100,000 dead and 300,000 wounded and lost more than 50 percent of its armored personnel carriers and 85 percent of its tanks and artillery. Iraq flew much of its air force out of harm's way to Iran, where it was grounded for the duration. Foreign allied governments contributed $54 billion to help pay for the war; the United States furnished the remaining $7 billion. This marked the first time since the American Revolution that the United States accepted direct financial aid to fight a war.

The aftermath: After the euphoria of liberation faded, Kuwaitis set about the grim business of rebuilding their country. Withdrawing Iraqi forces had gone on a fresh looting spree and set fire to 732 oil wells, burning off six million barrels of oil daily, or enough to satisfy a third of U.S. consumption. The longterm health effects on Kuwaitis and GIs breathing the dense smoke from the blazes is unknown. Because some GI's returned home with a rare blood-borne parasite, the Pentagon refused blood donations from all Gulf War veterans. Calls for democracy in Kuwait, suppressed before the occupation, sprang anew. The emir of Kuwait, Jaber al-Sabah, was criticized for delaying his return to the homeland for 15 days after its liberation and for placing the luxuries of the royal family ahead of the basic necessities of ordinary citizens. While Kuwaitis awaited the first emergency shipment of food supplies, for example, laborers, some under the supervision of the U.S. Army Corps of Engineers, hastily refurbished the vandalized royal palace, replacing the crystal chandeliers and gold bathroom fixtures stolen by departing Iraqis. In Iraq, long-smoldering anti-Saddam sentiment by the Kurds in the north and Shiite Moslems in the south flared briefly into open rebellion, which brought death or hardship to the multitude of refugees from those areas. Fearful of being drawn into a protracted domestic struggle in Iraq, Bush only reluctantly intervened to provide humanitarian assistance to Kurdish refugees. Despite the humiliating defeat, Saddam Hussein managed to survive Bush in power, withstanding continued economic sanctions and diplomatic isolation. In the United States, the swift victory lifted Bush's public approval rating to a whopping 89 percent, the highest such rating ever recorded in a Gallup Poll, and spawned a renewed sense of patriotism and confidence in American technology and military prowess. Some senior military personnel, however, warned against blowing the victory out of proportion. "While we should be proud of what we have done," cautioned Marine Lieutenant General Walter Boomer, a division commander involved in the liberation of Kuwait City, "I don't think it's wise to get a big head about the war. I wouldn't want people to think that every war that you find yourself in would turn out to be quite as easy as this one."[11]

Oil Spill Off Alaska. Two weeks after the supertanker *Exxon Valdez* ran aground in Prince William Sound on March 24, 1989, spilling 10.8 million gallons of crude oil, the worst such disaster in North American history, President Bush dispatched federal troops to assist Exxon in its lagging cleanup effort. In a report issued in January 1990, the Alaska Oil Spill Commission blamed the disaster on the government's failure to regulate the oil tanker industry. In October 1991 Exxon agreed to pay $1 billion in damage claims and criminal penalties in an out-of-court settlement with the federal government and the state of Alaska. The company spent another $2.5 billion in clean-up costs. According to a wildlife damage assessment released by the federal government in April 1991, many hundreds of thousands of creatures were destroyed, including up to half of the area's sea otter population and possibly an entire generation of bald eagles.

Americans with Disabilities Act. In 1990 President Bush approved legislation requiring places of business, public transportation, and public accommodations to render their facilities accessible to those in wheelchairs. Taking effect in stages from 1992 to 1996, it was the most far-reaching anti-discrimination law since the Civil Rights Act of 1964.

Clean Air Act of 1990. In strengthening the anti-pollution standards imposed in 1977, this bill promised to sharply reduce acid rain, urban smog, and toxic chemical emissions from factories. It required stricter emission controls on cars and the use of cleaner-burning fuels. The cost of compliance, which was to be phased in over the remainder of the decade and in some instances even longer, was estimated to be $25 billion a year.

Aid to Somalia. In December 1992 President Bush dispatched U.S. troops to Somalia to help feed starving masses amid a civil war among competing warlords.

SUPREME COURT APPOINTMENTS: David H. Souter (1939–   ), of New Hampshire, served as associate justice 1990–   . He succeeded retiring Justice William J. Brennan. (2) Clarence Thomas (1948–   ), of Georgia, served as associate justice 1991–   . He survived sensational confirmation hearings, at which Anita Hill, a former employee, charged him with sexual harrassment. He was confirmed by a 52–48 margin. He succeeded retiring Justice Thurgood Marshall.

RETIREMENT: January 20, 1993–   . Having been defeated for reelection (see "Bill Clinton, 42d President,") for the election of 1992, Bush attended the inaugural of his successor and retired to Houston, Texas.

BUSH PRAISED: "George Bush is a man of action—a man accustomed to command. The vice presidency doesn't fit easily on such a man. But George Bush is a patriot. And so he made it fit, and he served with a distinction no one has ever matched."[12]—President Ronald Reagan, 1988

"I've always felt if there's one thing you could count on George Bush for, it's decency and fairness."[13]—Mayor Andrew Young of Atlanta, 1988

"Your principled, courageous and decisive position in the face of the Iraqi aggression on Kuwait is a true expression of the unabated faith and commitment of the American people to the humanitarian morals on which and for which the United States of America was founded."[14]—Sheik Jaber al-Ahmed al-Sabah, emir of Kuwait, 1990

"No president has followed Franklin Roosevelt's plan for a new world order more closely than George Bush in the gulf war. He has used the United Nations, deftly leading uneasy allies and outmaneuvering the not entirely friendly Soviets to extend American military power to defend vital interests and defend against aggression. . . . Like Roosevelt, he concentrates on diplomacy with heads of governments and high strategy and has left military micro-management to the top-notch military leaders he's chosen."[15]—Michael Barone, political analyst, 1991

"Some will ask why President Bush spent so much time on foreign policy during his first term, and here is my reply. The President saw a chance to take on the two central problems of our age—the struggle for freedom and the threat of nuclear war—and he seized it. No apologies for that."[16]—Secretary of State James Baker, 1992

BUSH CRITICIZED: "George is a damn good guy, but he doesn't come through well. It's a case of choking. It takes 11 hours to get George ready for an off-the-cuff remark."[17]—Robert Strauss, former chairman of the Democratic party, 1988

"Why wasn't he the education vice president? . . . Where has he been for eight years and why did he sit by with gauze in his mouth when they cut the programs if he cared so much? It just doesn't sell."[18]—Democratic Representative Pat Schroeder of Colorado, on Bush's pledge to become the "education president," 1988

"If ignorance ever goes to $40 a barrel, I want the drilling rights on George Bush's head."[19]—Jim Hightower, Agriculture Commissioner of Texas, 1988

"Yes, the president is doing what America says it wants in his latest poll. . . . But the reason the American people seem reluctant to embrace the changes in Eastern Europe; the reason they oppose increased investment in democracy in that region; the reason they aren't sure if the Cold War is over is because their president is not leading them. He is not explaining and interpreting these startling events for them. He is not helping them understand the new world we live in—its challenges, its opportunities, its dangers. . . . In short, the Bush foreign policy is a policy adrift, without vision, without imagination, without a guiding light save precious public opinion polls."[20]—Democratic Representative Richard Gephardt of Missouri, 1990

"For all the credit that President Bush deserves for his magnificent leadership after the Iraqi invasion, the truth is that his administration not only resisted imposing sanctions on Iraq before August 2, but, by giving Mr. Hussein the impression he could invade his defenseless neighbor with impunity, made the aggression more likely."[21]—Democratic Representative Stephen J. Solarz of New York, 1991

"All you hear [from Bush] is Lawrence Welk music, 'wonnerful, wonnerful, wonnerful,' and we're spending $400 billion of your children's money this year to try to get you to vote for us again."[22]—Ross Perot, 1992

BUSH QUOTES: "I'm a conservative, but I'm not a nut about it."[23]—1984

"I don't feel the compulsion to be the glamour, one shot, smart comment kind of guy. I think experience, steadiness, knowing how to interact with people is the way to get things done better."[24]—1987

"Terrorism attempts to erode the legitimacy of democratic institutions. Its real and lasting effects cannot be measured in body counts or property damage but rather by its long term psychological impact and the subsequent political results. The terrorists' cry is: Don't trust your government, your democratic institutions, your principles of law. None of these pillars of an open society can protect you. . . . Terrorism is a kind of violent graffiti, and simply by capturing headlines and television time the terrorist partially succeeds."[25]—1987

"If I have learned anything in a lifetime of politics and government, it is the truth of the famous phrase, 'History is biography,' that decisions are made by people, and they make them based on what they know of the world and how they understand it."[26]—1988

"The fact is prosperity has a purpose. It's to allow us to pursue 'the better angels,' to give us time to think and grow. Prosperity with a purpose means taking your idealism and making it concrete by certain acts of goodness."[27]—1988

"The surest way to win the war against poverty is to win the battle against ignorance. Even though we spend more on education than any other nation on Earth, we just don't measure up."[28]—1988

"I want to be remembered as the president who did more to help preserve and protect America's environment than any president since Teddy Roosevelt. . . ."[29]—1988

"We are a people whose energy and drive have fueled our rise to greatness. We're a forward looking nation, generous, yes, but ambitious as well, not for ourselves but for the world. Complacency is not in our character, not before, not now, not ever!"[30]—1989

"The day will come—and it is not far off—when the legacy of Lincoln will finally be fulfilled at 1600 Pennsylvania Avenue when a black man or woman will sit in the Oval Office. When that day comes, the most remarkable thing about it will be how naturally it occurs."[31]—1990

"We stand today at a unique and extraordinary moment. The crisis in the Persian Gulf, as grave as it is, also offers a rare opportunity to move toward an historic period of cooperation. Out of these troubled times . . . a new world order can emerge: a new era, freer from the threat of terror, stronger in the pursuit of justice, and more secure in the quest for peace. An era in which the nations of the world, east and west, north and south, can prosper and live in harmony. A hundred generations have searched for this elusive path to peace, while a thousand wars raged across the span of human endeavor. Today that new world is struggling to be born. A world quite different from the one we've known. A world where the rule of law supplants the rule of the jungle. A world in which nations recognize the shared responsibility for freedom and justice. A world where the strong respect the rights of the weak."[32]—1990

"Communism died this year. Even as president, with the most fascinating possible vantage point, there were times when I was so busy helping to manage progress and lead change that I didn't always show the joy that was in my heart. But the biggest thing that has happened in the world in my life, in our lives, is this: By the grace of God, America won the Cold War."[33]—1992

BOOKS BY BUSH: *All the Best, George Bush: My Life in Letters and Other Writings* (1999);
Looking Forward: An Autobiography (with Victor Gold, 1987);
Man of Integrity (with Doug Wead, 1988).

BOOKS ABOUT BUSH: Green, Fitshugh. *George Bush: An Intimate Portrait.* New York: Hippocrene Books, 1989.

Hyams, Joe. *Flight of the Avenger: George Bush at War.* New York: Harcourt, Brace Jovanovich, 1991.

Stinnett, Robert B. *George Bush: His World War II Years.* Washington: Brassey's, 1992.

NOTES:

1 *New York Newsday,* June 6, 1988, p. 53.

2 *Wall Street Journal,* August 15, 1988, p. 1.

3 *Congressional Quarterly Weekly Report,* January 14, 1989, p. 56.

4 George Bush, with Victor Gold, *Looking Forward: An Autobiography,* New York: Doubleday, 1987, p. 5.

5 Ibid., p. 101.

6 Ibid., p. 130.

7 *Newsweek,* February 8, 1988, p. 20.

8 *New York Times,* December 22, 1989, p. 8.

9 *New York Times,* September 19, 1990, p. A-8.

10 *New York Times,* January 14, 1991, p. A-14.

11 *Wall Street Journal,* March 11, 1991, p. A-16.

12 *Washington Post,* August 25, 1988, p. A-11.

13 *USA Today,* November 16, 1988, p. 4-A.

14 *New York Times,* September 29, 1990.

15 *U.S. News and World Report,* March 25, 1991, p. 32.

16 *New York Times,* August 14, 1992, p. A-10.

17 *Life,* May 1988, p. 139.

18 *Atlanta Journal,* July 20, 1988.

19 *Washington Post,* October 2, 1988, p. A-22.

20 *Washington Post,* March 7, 1990, p. A-18.

21 *New York Times,* March 18, 1991, p. A-11.

22 *New York Times,* April 24, 1992, p. A-10.

23 *Time,* November 19, 1984, p. 58.

24 *Christian Science Monitor,* December 28, 1987, p. 6.

25 *Department of State Bulletin,* April 1987, p. 4.

26 *Washington Post,* August 12, 1988, p. A-10.

27 *Facts on File,* August 19, 1988, p. 605.

28 *Christianity Today,* September 16, 1988, p. 40.

29 *Sports Afield,* October 1988, p. 13.

30 Speech to joint session of Congress, broadcast February 9, 1989.

31 *New York Times,* April 4, 1990, p. A-11.

32 *New York Times,* September 12, 1990, p. A-10.

33 *New York Times,* January 29, 1992, p. A-14.

BILL CLINTON

42D PRESIDENT

NAME: William Jefferson Clinton. He was born William Jefferson Blythe, 4th, having been named after his late father. At age 16, he legally changed his last name to that of his stepfather. As governor, he signed his name Bill Clinton. In issuing his first executive orders as president, he signed his name William J. Clinton.

PHYSICAL DESCRIPTION: Clinton stands 6 feet, 2½ inches tall and has intense blue-gray eyes and thick hair, which was mostly gray by the time of his election as president. His weight fluctuates between 205 and 230 pounds; at the time of his election, he weighed 215; on reelection, he reportedly was significantly trimmer. Like his predecessor, he is left-handed. He suffers from chronic laryngitis, caused by inhalant allergies and the leaking of stomach acid into his throat. During acute attacks, his vocal chords swell to the point where he loses his voice. To alleviate the problem, he drinks plenty of water, takes antacids and antihistamines, receives allergy shots regularly, and sleeps with his head slightly elevated. He is allergic, in varying degrees, to dust, mold, pollen, cats (including Chelsea's pet Socks), certain greenery (including Christmas trees), and dairy products. He is slightly hard of hearing. In 1984 he was diagnosed with bleeding hemorrhoids.

PERSONALITY: "Bill Clinton has a very true compass," observed Dick Morris, a former Clinton political adviser who also worked for Republicans. "I don't think that varies much with public opinion. But within the general proposition he wants to go north, he will take an endless variety of routes. He's constantly maneuvering, constantly picking the routes he wants to get there, maneuvering his opponents into positions where they can't get a clear shot at him. That is what leaves a legacy of 'Slick Willie.' " (*New York Times,* September 28, 1992). The nickname Slick Willie was coined by Paul Greenberg, a columnist for the *Arkansas Democrat-Gazette,* who was a frequent critic of the governor's tendency to compromise on state issues. Clinton's instinct for compromise is often

703

linked to an unwillingness to offend others. Like Franklin D. Roosevelt before him, he at times leaves people on opposite sides of an issue believing that he stands with them. Some have inferred that his aversion to making enemies is rooted in a childhood marred by the abuse of an alcoholic stepfather. Clinton concedes that he had to learn "not to overuse the peacemaking skills that I developed as a child." (*U.S. News and World Report,* July 20, 1992). But he insists that his early trials also provided him with a special empathy. "I can feel other people's pain a lot more than some people can. I think that is important for a politician. I think you literally have to be able to sit in the quiet of a room and accurately imagine what life must be like for people growing up on mean streets, people living their lives behind bars, people about to face death's door." (*New York Times Magazine,* March 8, 1992).

Clinton, personable and outgoing, seems to genuinely enjoy campaigning and talking to voters on a wide variety of topics. He is particularly persuasive in small groups, with whom he maintains strong eye contact. He is a tactile politician, who commonly strokes, pats, or hugs those with whom he is dealing. Out on the stump, Clinton can be a folksy speaker, with a ready store of down-home phrases laced with the rich Arkansas accent of his youth. His defense of a citizen's right to privacy, for example, can emerge as a call for the government "to give people a good lettin' alone." In more formal settings, however, his English straightens a bit and he has a tendency to become both long-winded and mired in statistical detail.

ANCESTORS: Clinton is of English, Irish, Scotch-Irish, German, and, according to his mother, Cherokee Indian heritage.

FATHER: William Jefferson Blythe, 3d (c. 1917–1946), traveling salesman. Born in Sherman, Texas, he was tall and handsome and said to be a natural salesman, charming, gregarious, and hard-working. Before World War II, he sold auto parts. After returning from overseas and being discharged from the service at the end of the war, he found work selling heavy construction equipment in the Midwest. Based in Chicago, he bought a house there in 1946 and was en route back to Arkansas to pick up his wife, who then was pregnant with the future president, when he was killed in a freak auto accident: While rounding a curve on Route 61 near Sikeston, Missouri, late in the night, one of his tires blew out. He skidded off the road and was thrown from his car. Knocked unconscious by a blow that left only a small mark on his forehead, he landed face down in a ditch, where he drowned in a few inches of rainwater. Throughout his life Clinton was haunted by the specter of a father he never knew. He believes that his father's untimely death made him impatient for success early in life. "Most kids never think about when they're going to have to run out of time, when they might die," he was quoted as saying by Charles F. Allen and Jonathan Portis in *The Comeback Kid* (1992). "I thought about it all the time, because my father died at twenty-nine, before I was born."

STEPFATHER: Roger Clinton (died 1967), car salesman. Having little luck selling Buicks in Hope, Arkansas, he moved the family to Hot Springs, where he went to work at his brother's dealership. An abusive alcoholic, he commonly flew into drunken rages, once firing a gun inside the house, at other times beating his wife. As a result, he had a strained relationship with his stepson. The two reconciled in the 1960s, while he was dying from cancer. Then a student at Georgetown University in Washington, Bill Clinton visited him on weekends at Duke University Hospital in Durham, North Carolina.

MOTHER: Virginia Cassidy Blythe Clinton Dwire Kelley (c. 1923–1994), retired nurse anesthetist. Born near Bodcaw, a small village in Nevada County, Arkansas, she was raised there and in Hope, where her father, who worked as a sawmill watchman and ice deliveryman, opened a grocery store. In 1943, while studying nursing at Tri-State Hospital in Shreveport, Louisiana, she met William Jefferson Blythe 3d, when he arrived at the hospital with a date who had been stricken with acute appendicitis. They married two months later just before he was to ship out overseas amid World War II. Following his death in an auto accident and the birth of Bill in 1946, she left her infant son with her parents for a year while she studied anesthesiology at Charity Hospital in New Orleans. In 1950 she married Roger Clinton, an automobile dealer, who moved the family to Hot Springs. His alcoholism led to their divorce in May 1962. At her divorce proceeding, she testified that he "continually tried to do bodily harm to myself and my son Billy." But three months later, over the vigorous objections of Bill, she remarried him out of a sense of pity. Following his death in 1967, she married Jeff Dwire, a hairdresser, who died from diabetes in 1974. Eight years later she married Richard Kelley, an executive with the Kelley Brokerage Company, a food distributor in Little Rock. Meanwhile, in 1981, she retired from nursing in the wake of inquiries involving the separate deaths of two patients under her care. One case ended with the out-of-court settlement of a lawsuit filed by the patient's survivors against her and a surgeon; in the other case, she was ruled blameless by the state medical examiner. An avid horseracing fan, Mrs. Kelley was a regular at the two-dollar window of the Oaklawn track in Hot Springs. She was such a devoted fan of Elvis Presley that Bill Clinton called her out of the operating room to break the news of the singer's sudden death in 1977. During the 1992 campaign, she expressed outrage at the news that the State Department had conducted a search of her passport file in an apparent attempt to unearth information damaging to her son. "She was, I thought, a good role model in three ways," Clinton said of his mother in *The Comeback Kid.* "She always worked; did a good job as a parent; and we had a lot of adversity in our life when I was growing up, and she handled it real well." Clinton's mother was buried on Elvis's birthday. Her best-selling autobiography, *Leading With My Heart*, was published posthumously in 1995.

SIBLINGS: Clinton has no full siblings. From his mother's second marriage, he has a half brother, Roger Clinton, a singer and television production assistant in Hollywood.

CHILD: Clinton has a daughter.

Chelsea Victoria Clinton (1980–   ). She was named after the 1969 song "Chelsea Morning," written by Joni Mitchell and popularized by Judy Collins. Clinton has taken special care to shield her from the pressures of his public life. Reporters have been denied interviews with her. A serious and bright student, she skipped a grade while attending public school in Little Rock while her father was governor. She spent parts of several summers studying German at the Waldsee foreign language camp in Moorhead, Minnesota. She also has taken ballet lessons. She played softball for the Molar Rollers, a team sponsored by a local dentist. In 1991 she was confirmed in her mother's Methodist church. At the time of Clinton's election as president, she was in the eighth grade at the Mann Magnet School, a predominantly black public junior high school in Little Rock. She transferred to the Sidwell Friends School, a private Quaker-run school in Washington. Her ambition is to become an astronautical engineer, building stations and colonies in space.

BIRTH: Clinton was born August 19, 1946 at Julia Chester Hospital in Hope, the seat of Hempstead County, in southwestern Arkansas. He weighed 6½ pounds at birth. The hospital subsequently was converted into an apartment building, which was destroyed by fire; the site now is a vacant lot. He was the first of the "baby boom" generation and the first native of Arkansas to become president.

CHILDHOOD: Clinton grew up in modest circumstances in Hope and, from age seven, in Hot Springs, Arkansas. When he was not quite two years old, he was taken in temporarily by his maternal grandparents, who ran a grocery store in a predominantly black section outside Hope, while his mother advanced her nurse's training in New Orleans. His grandparents taught him how to count and read by age three and impressed him at an early age with their example of racial tolerance amid the segregation then prevalent in Arkansas. From 1950 to 1953, he lived with his mother and stepfather in a small, single-story frame house at 321 East 13th Street in Hope. One of his earliest memories is that of being mauled by a sheep. As he recalled in an interview with the *Arkansas Democrat-Gazette* (April 15, 1990): "When I was seven or eight, a ram butted me and cut my head open. I was too young, fat and slow to run, even after he knocked me down the second time. He must have butted me 10 times. It was the awfullest beating I ever took and I had to go to the hospital for stitches." For a time the Clintons did not have indoor plumbing, presenting young Bill with a nighttime dilemma—whether to resist nature's call until sunrise or brave a dark outhouse that had become a favorite haven for snakes. Campaigning in San Francisco in 1992, Clinton was asked by a youngster how he handled the situation. "You just made real sure you wanted to go bad," Clinton replied, apparently oblivious to the C-SPAN camera recording the event.

Clinton benefited from a close extended family of aunts, uncles, and cousins. He was especially proud of his Uncle Oren Grisham, popularly known as Uncle Buddy, a firefighter with a seemingly endless store of colorful tales. His childhood, however, was seriously troubled by his stepfather's alcoholism. On March 27, 1959, Roger Clinton flew into a drunken rage at the news that his wife was going to visit a dying relative and fired a gun in her direction, sending a bullet into the wall of their home. Mrs. Clinton called the police, who locked him up for the night. When under the influence of alcohol, his stepfather often beat up Mrs. Clinton, leaving bruises, until the day that Bill, then fourteen years old, mustered the courage to confront him, warning him never to raise a hand again to his mother. "That was a dramatic thing," Clinton recalled. "It made me know I could do it if I had to. But it made me more conflict-averse. It's a really painful thing to threaten to beat up your stepfather." (*Time*, June 8, 1992). Few neighbors were aware of the conflict within the Clinton household, for Bill maintained a cheerful, positive attitude for the benefit of outsiders. Perhaps as part of that effort, he legally changed his name from Blythe to Clinton at age sixteen. His sunny disposition fooled even his mother. "If it was hard for him, I never knew it," she said in an interview for the PBS *Frontline* series ("Campaign '92," broadcast October 21, 1992). "But I look back now and see the tremendous responsibility he accepted for himself to protect me."

In all other respects, Clinton led a very typical babyboom childhood. He was a Boy Scout, sang in the church choir, played touch football, ran crossword puzzle races with a neighbor, sang along to Elvis Presley tunes on the jukebox at

Cook's ice cream parlor, attended band camp every summer, and won first place in a state saxophone competition. Along with two other boys, Joe Newman and Randy Goodrum, he formed a jazz combo of saxophone, piano, and drums. The trio, which performed in sunglasses, was known as The Three Blind Mice. Clinton also joined other boys in a popular neighborhood prank—calling up Maxine, a local prostitute, just to hear the string of expletives she yelled when she discovered the call was not from a paying customer. When the Clintons bought their first television set in 1956, Bill sat glued to the Democratic and Republican conventions that nominated Governor Adlai Stevenson of Illinois and President Dwight D. Eisenhower. "I was fascinated by it," he recalled in an interview for the *Arkansas Democrat-Gazette* (July 15, 1987). "I was the only person in my family who sat there and watched it all." But the most momentous year of his childhood was 1963: He was moved to tears by Martin Luther King's "I Have a Dream" speech. In July of that year he traveled to Washington as one of Arkansas' "senators" in the American Legion program Boys' Nation. At an outdoor reception for the group at the White House, he shook hands with President John F. Kennedy, an encounter that had a profound effect on him. Kennedy, using the occasion to criticize Republican foot-dragging on civil rights, commended the assembled youth for adopting a resolution calling racial discrimination a "cancerous disease" and added that they had shown "more initiative in some ways than the [Republican] Governors Conference in Miami" (*New York Times,* July 25, 1963), which had recently gone to great lengths to avoid taking a stand on the issue. Although Clinton had considered becoming a doctor or a musician, by the time he returned to Arkansas, he had decided on a career in politics. He later briefly considered becoming a journalist. After Kennedy, the most influential hero of his youth was Arkansas Senator J. William Fulbright, a Rhodes scholar who rose to national prominence as chairman of the Senate Foreign Relations Committee and was a leading critic of the Vietnam War.

EDUCATION: At age five, Clinton attended Miss Mary Purkins' School for Little Folks in Hope, Arkansas. When the Clintons moved to Hot Springs, he was enrolled in the second grade at St. John's Catholic school, because his mother felt that he was not yet ready for a large public school. He excelled during his two years there but once got a D in conduct for repeatedly shouting out answers without giving others in class a chance. He transferred to Ramble Elementary, a public school, in the fourth grade and went on to Central Junior High and Hot Springs High School. "Bill was the kind of person," recalled classmate Glenda Cooper for a profile in the *New York Times Magazine* (March 8, 1992), "who would come up to everyone new in high school and say: 'Hi. How are you? My name's Bill Clinton, and I'm running for something,' whatever it was. We always thought, well, someday Bill will be president." An outstanding student, he earned the school's Academically Talented Student Award, was a member of the National Honor Society, and made it to the semi-finals in the National Merit Scholarship contest. He was elected junior class president and served on the Student Council. He was defeated, however, for senior class secretary by Carolyn Staley, one of his best friends. He played saxophone in the school band and was band major. He graduated fourth of the 323 students of the class of 1964.

Clinton chose to attend Georgetown University because of its excellent foreign service program and because it was in the nation's capital. He shared a stone cottage off campus with four other students. The five boys had heated arguments about the Vietnam War, which Clinton opposed. Clinton was president of his freshman and sophomore classes. He ran for student body president in his senior year but was defeated by Terry Modglin, who had served under him as vice president of the freshman and sophomore classes. During his junior year, he worked part-time in the office of his home state's junior senator, J. William Fulbright, the chairman of the Senate Foreign Relations Committee, whose role as a leading critic of the Vietnam War greatly influenced Clinton. In the wake of the riots in reaction to the assassination of the Rev. Martin Luther King, Jr. in April 1968, Clinton worked with the Red Cross in delivering food to the burned-out section of Washington, relying on the Red Cross decals applied to his white Buick to protect him from the anti-white wrath of the neighborhood. Clinton graduated with a degree in international affairs in 1968.

That October Clinton sailed aboard the *USS United States* from New York to Southampton, England to begin study as a Rhodes scholar at Oxford University. During his first year he shared a cottage in Helen's Court with another American, a Palestinian, two white South Africans, and several Englishmen, and during his second year he roomed with two other Americans in a Victorian house at 46 Leckford Road. Fascinated by his new surroundings, he spent his first two weeks at Oxford on all-day walking tours. He studied politics, philosophy, and economics in his first year and focused more exclusively on politics, with emphasis on the Communist bloc, in his second year. One of his instructors, Zbigniew Pelczynski, recalled: "He was a very good student, receptive and intelligent. He was better in argument than on paper. His essay technique was not perhaps the best that I have seen, but he was obviously an avid reader." ([London] *Sunday Times,* October 25, 1992). While at Oxford he took part in public demonstrations against American involvement in the Vietnam War, attending a rally at Trafalgar Square in March 1969, helping to organize a teach-in at the University of London, and serving as a peace marshal at a protest outside the American embassy in London. He also traveled whenever a break in his studies allowed. An avid reader of Dylan Thomas, he made a pilgrimage to the birthplace of the Welsh poet. In December 1969 and January 1970, he traveled alone through Scandinavia, the Soviet Union, and Czechoslovakia. In Prague he stayed for six days with the Kopold family, the parents of one of his Oxford classmates, for a first-hand view of the city less than two years after the Soviet Union had invaded to crush the reform government of Alexander Dubcek.

Instead of completing his third year of the Rhodes scholarship, he returned to the United States in 1970 to accept a scholarship to the Yale University law school. To earn spending money, he taught at a community college, worked for a Hartford city councilman, and did investigative work for a lawyer in New Haven. He campaigned for the Rev. Joseph Duffy, an anti-war Democrat running for the Senate from Connecticut, in 1970. An early supporter of Senator George S. McGovern of South Dakota for the Democratic presidential nomination in 1972, Clinton managed, unsuccessfully, his general election campaign in Texas that year. He received his law degree in 1973.

RELIGION: Southern Baptist. "My faith tells me that all of us are sinners, and each of us has gone in our own way and fallen short of the glory of God," he declared in an interview on VISN, a religious cable network, as transcribed in the *New York Times* (October 8, 1992). "Religious faith has permitted me to believe in my continuing possibility of becoming a better person every day. If I didn't believe in God, if I weren't, in my view, a Christian, if I didn't believe ultimately in the perfection of life after death, my life would have been that much more difficult." Joining the Baptist church at age nine, Clinton grew up with more religious devotion than either his mother or his stepfather. From his student days at Georgetown in the late 1960s, however, until his defeat for reelection as governor in 1980, he attended Sunday services infrequently. Since then, he has resumed the more regular practice of his religion. He believes in an omniscient God who forgives sin and holds out the promise of redemption. He feels that one's faith is a private communication with God and should not be subject to public scrutiny. He is a member of the Immanuel Baptist Church in Little Rock, where he often has sung in the choir. He is occasionally joined at Sunday services by his wife and daughter, who belong to the First United Methodist Church in Little Rock. Among his favorite passages from the Bible is from St. Paul's letter to the Galatians, which he included in his inaugural address: "And let us not be weary in well-doing, for in due season we shall reap, if we faint not."

RECREATION: Clinton enjoys swimming, golf, and basketball, as well as playing cards, particularly hearts and pinochle, and Trivial Pursuit. He works crossword puzzles in ink at championship-rate speed. Together with Mrs. Clinton, he collects porcelain objects. He tries to keep his weight down by jogging and watching his diet. "He eats like a Tasmanian devil—Dunkin' Donuts, McDonald's, tin cans," said Mort Engleberg, a Hollywood producer and occasional Clinton adviser (*New York Times Magazine,* January 17, 1993). "You'll never find this guy asking for a splash more coffee. He's not a nervous eater. He enjoys it." His favorite foods include peanut-butter-and-banana sandwiches, tacos, chicken enchiladas, and mango ice cream. He drinks little besides an occasional beer. A voracious, eclectic reader, he rarely waits to finish one book before beginning one or more others. Visitors have marveled that he can read and carry on a conversation at the same time. He particularly enjoyed *One Hundred Years of Solitude* by Gabriel Garcia-Marquez, *The Meditations of Marcus Aurelius,* Tolstoy's *War and Peace,* and *Let Us Now Praise Famous Men* by James Agee. Other favorite authors are Tony Hillerman, P. D. James, Robert Ludlum, and Walter Mosley. He can and does read German language books and magazines. His favorite movies include such classics as *High Noon* and *Casablanca.* He plays jazz saxophone very well and does not mind showing off in public: He played a duet with Junior Walker at a Motown Review concert in Traverse City, Michigan in 1987, delivered a jazzy rendition of "Summertime" from *Porgy and Bess* on Johnny Carson's "Tonight Show" in 1988, and donned sunglasses to belt out "Heartbreak Hotel" on the Arsenio Hall show in 1992. He still appreciates the music of his youth, particularly the recordings of Elvis Presley, Judy Collins, the Supremes, the Four Tops, and Peter, Paul and Mary. He also likes jazz and classical music, particularly Bach.

MARRIAGE: Bill Clinton, 29, married Hillary Rodham, 27, on October 11, 1975 in a house he had recently purchased for them in Fayetteville, Arkansas. The First Lady was born October 26, 1947, in Chicago, the eldest child and only daughter of Hugh E. Rodham, the owner of a textile company, and Dorothy Howell Rodham. Raised in Park Ridge, Illinois, a northwestern suburb of Chicago, she was a high-achiever both inside and outside the classroom. She was elected class president at Maine Township High School in Park Ridge, where she earned numerous academic honors. She was active in Girl Scouts, worked summers in a public park, and organized neighborhood charity events for the benefit of migrant workers. Politically she was, like her parents, a conservative Repub-

lican, supporting Senator Barry Goldwater for president during the fall of her
senior year. As a student at Wellesley College, however, she turned against the
Vietnam War, so that by the next presidential primary campaign in 1968 she
was supporting the candidacy of Democratic Senator Eugene McCarthy of Minnesota. Graduating with high honors in 1969, she was class speaker at her
commencement, chosen by her classmates to provide an anti-establishment
counter-point to the address of Republican Senator Edward Brooke of Massachusetts. Excerpts of her speech were included in round-up articles on the nation's graduating classes that appeared in *Time* (June 13, 1969), entitled "Youth:
The Jeremiads of June," and *Life* (June 20, 1969), entitled "The Class of 1969:
With Eloquent Defiance, Top Students Protest Right Through Commencement."
In it she declared: "We are, all of us, exploring a world that none of us understands and attempting to create within that uncertainty. But there are some
things we feel—we feel that our prevailing, acquisitive and competitive corporate life, including, tragically, the universities, is not the way of life for us. We're
searching for more immediate, ecstatic and penetrating modes of living. And so
our questions, our questions about our institutions, about our colleges, about
our churches, about our government continue. Every protest, every dissent, is
unabashedly an attempt to forge an identity in this particular age. . . . For too
long, those who lead us have viewed politics as the art of the possible. The
challenge that faces them—and us—now is to practice politics as the art of
making possible what appears impossible."

Hillary Rodham attended Yale University Law School, where she met Bill
Clinton. While walking across the student lounge one day, she heard the tail
end of a sentence spoken in a distinctive Southern drawl: ". . . and not only
that, we have the biggest watermelons in the world." It was Clinton bragging to
a group of skeptical students about the allures of Arkansas. They met later at
the law library, when Hillary, annoyed at their furtive glances at one another,
stepped up to introduce herself, saying, "If you're going to keep looking at me,
and I'm going to keep looking back, we at least ought to know each other." They
began dating soon thereafter, but neither took the relationship seriously at first,
because she wanted no part of Clinton's plan to settle permanently in Arkansas.
At Yale she already had taken an interest in children's rights. On May 30, 1972,
she testified before a regional hearing of the Democratic National Convention
Platform Committee in Boston, urging the party to extend civil and political
rights to children. After receiving her law degree in 1973, she accepted a position with the Children's Defense Fund in Cambridge, Massachusetts. In an
article, "Children Under the Law," published in the Harvard Educational Review in 1973, she advocated expanding the rights of children—a position that
was picked up briefly as a campaign issue in 1992 by conservative Republicans,
most notably Pat Buchanan, who tried to recast its central thesis as an assault
on parental authority and the traditional family. In 1972 she joined Clinton in
Texas to campaign for Senator George McGovern for president. In 1974, she was
a staff lawyer of the House Judiciary Committee during its consideration of
impeachment charges against President Richard Nixon. Throughout this period, she maintained a long-distance relationship with Clinton, then a law professor at the University of Arkansas. During a visit to the Fayetteville campus,
she agreed to accept a teaching post at the law school there, which she held from
1974 to 1977. In 1975 Clinton purchased a house in Fayetteville that she had
admired and presented it to her along with a proposal of marriage. The cere-

mony, performed by a Methodist minister, was limited to the immediate family and close friends. Roger Clinton, the groom's half-brother, was best man. She retained her maiden name, despite much popular criticism during Clinton's first term as governor. Bowing to local convention in 1982, she began going by Mrs. Clinton largely to remove the matter as a campaign issue during her husband's comeback bid for governor. Meanwhile, in 1977, she gave up teaching to join the Rose Law Firm in Little Rock, one of the oldest and most prestigious in the state. In 1978 President Jimmy Carter appointed her as chair of the Legal Services Corporation Board, a federally-financed independent body that distributes legal aid funds. As First Lady of Arkansas, Mrs. Clinton headed the standards committee that recommended procedures for implementing the state's education reform program. At the same time, she earned a six-figure income as a top litigator with the Rose firm. In 1988 and again in 1991, she was named one of the "100 Most Influential Lawyers in America" by the National Law Journal. The major breadwinner of the family, she managed her husband's and her own investments. During the 1992 campaign, the Clintons were compelled to acknowledge that they had had marital problems but said that they had worked them out to their mutual satisfaction. In an extraordinary interview on "60 Minutes" (January 26, 1992) following charges that Bill Clinton had engaged in an affair with Gennifer Flowers (see "Extra-marital Affairs"), the Clintons asked the nation to respect the privacy of their marriage. With her husband looking on, she declared, in an acquired Arkansas accent: "I'm not sitting here because I'm some little woman standing by my man, like Tammy Wynette. I'm sitting here because I love him and I respect him and I honor what he's been through and what we've been through together, and you know, if that's not enough for people, then heck, don't vote for him." In what may have been the first time that the wife of a presidential candidate was attacked from the rostrum of a national convention, Pat Buchanan, in his address to GOP delegates in 1992, lashed out at Mrs. Clinton for her early writings on juvenile rights and, in mocking tones, referred several times to the Democratic ticket as "Clinton and Clinton." During the presidential transition, she took part in deliberations for the appointment of the Cabinet and other high-ranking officials. As First Lady, she broke precedent by occupying an office in the West Wing of the White House, where the president's senior staff members work. President Clinton appointed her as head of his Task Force on National Health Reform, charged with devising a comprehensive overhaul of the nation's health care system. Her work on the task force was considered unsuccessful and her involvement in several alleged scandals (see Administration entry below) resulted in a lower profile during the rest of Clinton's first term. Symbolic of this, Hillary Rodham Clinton (as she is usually known now) moved her office to the old Executive Office Building, away from the center of power. She is the author of *It Takes A Village* (1996), a study of the role of community in raising America's children. She is the first lawyer to become First Lady.

EXTRA-MARITAL AFFAIRS. For some time Clinton had been dogged by persistent, though unproven, rumors of affairs. In 1991 when he decided to run for president, he privately admitted to his most intimate supporters that he had had an affair but assured them that it was over, that the woman had vowed to remain silent, and that he would not endanger his candidacy by engaging in another affair during the campaign. "There aren't going to be any Donna Rices," he reportedly promised (*U.S. News and World Report,* March 30, 1992), referring to the woman whose much-publicized involvement with Gary Hart drove the Colorado senator from the 1988 presidential race. During the 1992 primary season, Gennifer Flowers, an Arkansas state employee and nightclub singer, sold an exclusive interview to the *Star,* in which she claimed that she had engaged in a 12-year affair with Governor Clinton. At a press conference on January 27, 1992, Flowers played recordings of telephone conversations with Clinton, taped by her without his knowledge, in which they appeared to discuss how to respond to eventual questions about their relationship. Clinton denied Flowers' charges.

MILITARY SERVICE: None. While a student at Oxford University, Clinton took steps to avoid the draft amid the Vietnam War. Writing in 1969, he called the conflict "a war I opposed and despised with a depth of feeling I had reserved solely for racism in America before Vietnam." He took part in peace demonstrations among Americans in England. After passing the Army induction physical in London in February 1969 and being classified 1-A, Clinton signed a letter of intent to join the Army Reserve Officers Training Corps program at the University of Arkansas and thus was removed from the draft pool. He began to have second thoughts, however, and notified Arkansas authorities that he would not be joining R.O.T.C. after all. In the national draft lottery, based on month and day of birth, held on December 1, 1969, Clinton drew number 311, safely above the 195 limit that satisfied the draft requirements that year. Two days later, he wrote Col. Eugene Holmes, director of the University of Arkansas R.O.T.C. program, thanking him "for saving me from the draft" and apologizing for misleading him about his attitude toward the war, according to the text of the letter reprinted in the *New York Times* (February 13, 1992). "I came to believe that the draft system itself is illegitimate," he continued. "No government really rooted in limited, parliamentary democracy should have the power to make its citizens fight and kill and die in a war they may oppose, a war which even possibly may be wrong, a war which, in any case, does not involve immediately the peace and freedom of the nation." He conceded that the draft was justified during World War II, because the very survival of the nation was at stake. The Korean War, he argued, was another conflict that did not warrant the use of a draft, though he supported the war itself. In the same letter, Clinton expressed admiration for conscientious draft resisters. The only reason that he had been willing to submit himself to the draft, he wrote, was "to maintain my political viability within the system. . . . to prepare myself for a political life characterized by both practical political ability and concern for rapid social progress."

CAREER BEFORE THE PRESIDENCY:

Law professor, University of Arkansas, 1973–1976. Upon graduation from law school in 1973, Clinton had intended to return to Hot Springs to practice law and await an opportunity to run for office. Instead, he accepted an offer to teach minor courses, among them admiralty law, at the University of Arkansas law school in Fayetteville. In 1974 he rejected a job offer from John Doar, special counsel to the House committee considering impeachment charges against President Nixon, in order to challenge the reelection of Representative John Paul Hammerschmidt of Arkansas' Third Congressional District, comprised of the predominantly Republican northwest quarter of the state. (Clinton recommended his girlfriend, Hillary Rodham, for the House job, and Doar hired her.) Having topped a four-man field in the Democratic primary with 44 percent of the vote, he went on to defeat State Senator Gene Rainwater, 69 percent to 31 percent, in the primary runoff. He then undertook a vigorous campaign against Hammerschmidt, a four-term veteran, criss-crossing the district in his 1970 Gremlin and later a Chevelle truck with an Astroturf bed-liner that served as his soapbox. Throughout the campaign Clinton kept Hammerschmidt on the defensive for his continued support of Nixon amid the Watergate scandal. Although Clinton was defeated, 52 percent to 48 percent, he was the toughest opponent Hammerschmidt ever faced.

Attorney General of Arkansas, 1977–1979. In 1976, in his first successful bid for public office, Clinton won the Democratic primary for state attorney general with 56 percent of the vote to 25 percent for former Arkansas secretary of state George Jernigan, Jr., and 19 percent for assistant state attorney general Clarence Cash, and ran unopposed in the general election. He also directed, successfully, the presidential campaign of Jimmy Carter in Arkansas that year. Attorney General Clinton developed a reputation as a consumer advocate, holding down utility rates and promoting environmental protection. But he opposed efforts to repeal the state's three percent sales tax on food and medicine because of its effect on the budget. In 1978 he was named one of the Ten Outstanding Young Men in the country by the United States Junior Chamber of Commerce.

Governor of Arkansas, 1979–81. In 1978 Clinton ran for governor, calling himself a "compromise progressive candidate," to succeed David Pryor. Although he played down his liberal origins, omitting from his campaign literature, for example, references to his work for Democratic presidential nominee George McGovern in 1972, he came under fire from conservative opponents in the primary for his support for gun control and the Equal Rights Amendment for women. On May 30, Clinton topped a five-man field with 59 percent of the vote, sweeping 71 of the state's 75 counties. Because Arkansas was overwhelmingly Democratic, the primary victory was tantamount to election. He went on to crush Lynne Lowe, the director of the state Republican party, 63 percent to 37 percent, in the general election. Looking back on the election, Clinton said, "I just think that people here voted their hopes. It sounds like apple pie and very simplistic, but they see me as another step in the struggle of the state to pull itself up from last place in so many areas." (*New York Times,* December 14, 1978). At age 32, Clinton was the youngest governor in the nation at that time and the youngest elected since Harold E. Stassen became governor of Minnesota at age 31 in 1938. Elected to statewide office along with him were Steve Clark, 31, the new state attorney general, and Paul Revere, 31, Arkansas secretary of state. The three young men, who had been friends since high school, were dubbed the Diaper Brigade. Clinton was the third successive governor, after Dale Bumpers and David Pryor, to take office in Little Rock as one of the so-called "new breed of Southern governors," who combined fiscal conservatism with progressive views on matters of race. Before he even took office as governor, Clinton already was being touted as a rising star in the Democratic party. As early as 1978, John White, the national party chairman, predicted, erroneously as it turned out, that Clinton would be on the presidential ticket by 1988.

But Clinton's surge to the top was short-circuited by an overly ambitious agenda. Surrounding himself with a team of brash, brilliant, though inexperienced, young men and women, he set out to enact a broad program of improvements in transportation and education. Bucking the national anti-tax fervor touched off by Proposition 13 in California, Clinton raised the state gasoline tax and automobile registration fee to pay for road improvements. Higher fuel costs particularly irked the state's influential poultry and trucking industries. He won passage of legislation that significantly raised spending on education, required prospective new teachers to pass the National Teacher Exam, and started a summer school program for gifted students, in which the governor and his wife participated directly as occasional teachers. Because of such programs, he was singled out as one of "Fifty Faces for America's Future" by *Time* magazine (August 6, 1979). Popular resentment against the young governor, already simmering from the tax increases, boiled over in June, 1980, when hundreds of Cuban refugees, which the administration of President Jimmy Carter had placed at Fort Chaffee, Arkansas, rioted and escaped into the countryside. Although the prisoners were rounded up with the help of the Arkansas National Guard, many blamed the governor for permitting the Cubans to be placed in Arkansas in the first place. Having supported President Carter's renomination over the challenge of Senator Edward M. Kennedy of Massachusetts in 1980, Clinton was given the opportunity to address the Democratic national convention that year. But even his emergence as a potential national figure began to work against him, as voters, who once took pride in a local boy winning recognition beyond the state's borders, came to feel that he was neglecting their problems to advance his own ambition. In 1980, Clinton was defeated for reelection, 52 percent to 48 percent, by Republican Frank White, a little-known savings and loan president, who had succeeded in casting the governor as arrogant and out of step with ordinary Arkansans. Clinton reportedly wept over the upset. "That defeat was really the seminal experience in his career," observed Dick Morris, a former Clinton political advisor (*New York Times,* September 28, 1992). He learned well, some say too well, the dangers of making political enemies and getting too far out in front of his constituents in pursuing an ambitious agenda. When he stepped down in 1981, he was at age 34 the youngest ex-governor in U.S. history.

Lawyer, 1981–1982. Clinton practiced commercial law with the Wright, Lindsey and Jennings firm in Little Rock. He spent much of his free time trying to figure out how and why he had lost the confidence of the people of Arkansas and planning his political comeback.

Governor of Arkansas, 1983–1992. Chastened by his loss, Clinton entered the 1982 campaign against Governor Frank White asking the people of Arkansas to give him another chance. "I made a young man's mistake," he admitted (*New York Times,* May 24, 1982). "I had an agenda a mile long that you couldn't achieve in a four-year term, let alone a two-year term. I was so busy doing what I wanted to do that I didn't leave enough time to correct mistakes." He apologized for raising the license fee, conceding it was a mistake, and vowed to listen better in a second term. In the May 25 primary, Clinton defeated four other Democratic candidates but, with just 42 percent of the vote, he was forced into a runoff with former Lieutenant Governor Joe Purcell. He went on to beat Purcell, 54 percent to 46 percent, in June. Squaring off against White, Clinton criticized the governor for a large utility rate hike approved by White's appointees to the Arkansas Public Utilities Commission and for failing to fulfill his campaign pledge to bring new industry into the state. For his part, White questioned Clinton's sincerity in admitting the mistakes of his first term. He appeared in television ads with a leopard, warning voters that Clinton, like the cat, could not change his spots. In the end, Arkansans welcomed Clinton back by a margin of 55 percent to 45 percent over White. He was the first former

Arkansas governor ever returned to office after having been defeated for reelection. In 1984 Clinton coasted to an easy (63 percent to 37 percent) win over Republican Elwood "Woody" Freeman, a contractor. The state legislature extended the gubernatorial term to four years, effective with the 1986 election. In a rematch with Frank White that year, Clinton rolled up an impressive (64 percent to 36 percent) victory. In 1990 he was returned for a fifth term over Sheffield Nelson by 57 percent to 42 percent. During that campaign he had vowed to serve out a full four-year term as governor. In 1991, however, he toured the state asking voters to release him from that pledge to allow him to run for president.

The centerpiece of Clinton's record as governor was education reform. In 1983 he won passage of a comprehensive package that included the first competency test for teachers in the nation. The Arkansas Education Association (AEA) bitterly opposed the test as demeaning and destructive of teacher morale, pointing out that other professionals, such as doctors and lawyers, are not required to prove their competence in mid-career. The organization enlisted the aid of other interest groups to lobby the governor to kill the measure. But Clinton insisted on the test, carefully coupling it with a significant increase in teacher pay for those who passed, as a way to upgrade the state's public school faculties. "The American people," he asserted, "are saying they are willing to take the shirts right off their backs if it will help improve education. But they demand accountability. They want us to get rid of the teachers who are really bad." (New York Times, January 17, 1984). In the end, fewer than four percent of the state's teachers were forced to leave education for repeatedly failing the test, which required the competence of an eighth-grader in reading, math, grammar, and basic knowledge. The teachers that remained saw their salaries rise at a faster rate than in any other state from 1983 to 1985. The new law also challenged students, imposing a high school entrance exam on eighth graders, the first such test in the nation, and increasing the age at which students can drop out to seventeen. What really got the students' attention was a provision revoking the driver's licenses of teenagers who leave high school without graduating. The program was financed by a one-cent increase in the sales tax and varying hikes in local property taxes around the state. One innovation designed to involve parents in their children's education was inspired by a program in Israel. The Home Instruction Program for Pre-school Youngsters, known locally by its acronym HIPPY, provided parents with elementary workbooks and help in planning brief daily lessons for their small children. Clinton also sought to decentralize education, giving teachers greater autonomy in the classroom. Although, under Clinton, Arkansas made measurable progress in such areas as the number of high school graduates who go on to college and improvements in curricula, particularly in the teaching of the sciences, it continued to rank near the bottom among the states in teacher salaries and per pupil expenditures, partly because other states also improved in those areas. But even many of Clinton's critics concede that he made a significant difference in the quality of the state's education. "We've fought him tooth and nail on things like teacher testing," said Sid Johnson, president of the AEA, as quoted in the New York Times (April 1, 1992). "But overall schools are a lot better now than they were before Bill Clinton arrived."

The Arkansas economy under Clinton was slow to recover from the national recession of the early 1980s. Required by state law to keep the budget in balance and unable to raise the state income tax without the approval of ¾ of the legislature, Clinton had few legislative levers with which to move the economy forward. He showcased Arkansas' low wage base and offered tax breaks to entice new businesses into the state, which translated into more than 200,000 new jobs during his administration in food processing and other areas of manufacturing. Job growth under Clinton outpaced the national average and in his last few years as governor was among the highest of any state. With the addition of new industry, however, came more environmental pollution. The biggest offender was the poultry industry, whose waste matter ended up in the state's waterways.

Arkansas consistently has ranked near the bottom of states in the quality of health. The Clinton administration made some modest gains in expanding health insurance coverage and improving health care for pregnant women and babies. Clinton appointed more blacks and women to high state office than any of his predecessors. Through the Arkansas Industrial Development Commission he fostered black-owned businesses. He created the Minority Business Advisory Council to monitor the state's progress in achieving its objective, adopted at Clinton's urging in 1991, to try to purchase 10 percent of its goods and services from black-owned enterprises.

Clinton's most difficult personal decision as governor involved his half-brother: In 1984 state police informed him that Roger Clinton had been snared in a cocaine sting operation. The police were prepared either to arrest him immediately on minor selling charges or to continue to send undercover agents to buy from him until the charges mounted to a point where he could more easily be turned against his supplier. At the suggestion of the police, Clinton agreed to the latter course. "I had to sit there on a secret for six weeks, while the undercover people kept setting him up over and over again," he recalled with fresh anguish in an interview with *U.S. News and World Report* (July 20, 1992). "It was a nightmare. But I think it was the right thing to do, and I think it probably saved his life." In January 1985 his brother pleaded guilty to five counts of distributing cocaine and one count of conspiring to distribute, and he was sentenced to two years in prison. He was paroled on April 25, 1986 and placed on three years' probation. The Clinton family, including the governor, his brother, and their mother, underwent group counseling to help him overcome his addiction.

Governor Clinton took an active role in national Democratic party affairs. In 1985 he was chosen to narrate the Democratic response to President Ronald Reagan's State of the Union Address. In it he acknowledged that "this is a party that knows it has to change." He was a prominent member of the Democratic Leadership Council (DLC), a group of moderate Democrats who set out to move the party toward the center and away from the liberal agenda of those responsible for the debacle of the 1984 campaign in which former Vice President Walter Mondale was buried in the reelection landslide of President Reagan. Clinton served as chairman of the DLC during 1990–1991. He also was chairman of the Southern Growth Policy Board during 1985–1986, chairman of the Education Commission of the States and the National Governors' Association during 1986–1987, and chairman of the National Governors' Association Task Force on Health Care during 1990–1991. In a poll of governors conducted by *Newsweek* in 1991, Clinton was named the most effective governor in the nation. In a similar poll in 1986, he ranked fifth among the 50 governors.

Meanwhile, in 1988, Clinton seriously considered running for president. He spent so much time traveling around the country assessing his chances that a Little Rock newspaper headlined an expected lull in such activity, "Governor to Stay in the State All Next Week." In July he surprised his closest supporters in announcing that he had decided not to run, primarily, he said, out of concern that his seven-year-old daughter was too young for such an ordeal. He denied suggestions that the real reason lay in the media's intensified interest in the personal lives of the candidates following the sex scandal that had driven Gary Hart from the race. But he did express concern about the new ground rules. "What are these people doing?" he wondered aloud about the press (*Washington Post*, June 8, 1987). "Are they going to print rumors? Are they going to print rumors that are 10 years old or 15 years old? Am I going to have to spend the whole campaign dealing with that and if they don't find anything it will still be debilitating?" At the 1988 Democratic convention, Clinton placed Governor Michael Dukakis' name in nomination in a 32-minute address that was poorly received by delegates, some of whom chanted "Get off, Get off" and cheered when Clinton said, "In conclusion. . . ." The speech was to have been Clinton's chance to shine in the national spotlight. Instead it was a source of acute embarrassment, which he shook off with a good-humored appearance with Johnny Carson on his late-night talk show. "Instead of running away from the problem, he faced it," Samuel Berger, a Clinton advisor, said of the incident (*New York Times*, July 16, 1992). "He took responsibility. He walked into the press room and took it. For me it foreshadowed the sort of resilience he showed in the dark days of the New Hampshire primary. I saw the same strength then—confronting a problem instead of running away from it." Clinton himself saw it as a learning experience. "I have to say even though it hurt in the beginning, I'm not so sure it's bad for politicians to get knocked on their rear every now and then . . . you can too easily forget the pain that basically comes on a regular basis to millions of Americans every day, people who feel like things are wrong with them or they're never doing things exactly right. I think that for years and years now, I'll be more sensitive than I otherwise would have been." (*Arkansas Democrat-Gazette*, July 30, 1988).

On October 3, 1991, Clinton announced his candidacy for the Democratic presidential nomination. On December 12, 1992, President-elect Clinton resigned as governor, failing by 31 days to tie the record of 12 years in office in Little Rock set by Governor Orval E. Faubus when he stepped down in 1967. Clinton was succeeded by Lieutenant Governor Jim Guy Tucker.

DEMOCRATIC PRESIDENTIAL NOMINATION, 1992: With President Bush's public approval rating soaring in the wake of the Persian Gulf War, many nationally-known Democrats, including Governor Mario Cuomo of New York, Senator Sam Nunn of Georgia, and Senator Bill Bradley of New Jersey, had chosen to sit out the race. Clinton's candidacy was nearly derailed by charges of marital infidelity and draft avoidance during the Vietnam War as well as the unexpected candidacy of Ross Perot, who emerged as the dominant agent of change in the months leading up to the Democratic convention. Clinton lost the symbolically important New Hampshire primary to former Senator Paul Tsongas of Massachusetts. But the Arkansas governor, dubbed "Robo-candidate" for his ability to absorb such blows, pressed on to roll up impressive primary victories in the South and elsewhere and locked up the nomination well before the convention. Driven from the field by convention time were Governor Douglas Wilder of Virginia, Senator Bob Kerrey of Nebraska, Senator Tom Harkin of Iowa, and Senator Tsongas. Only former Governor Jerry Brown of California refused to concede the nomination. After having his name placed in nomination by Governor Cuomo, Clinton was nominated on the first ballot with 3,372 delegate votes to 596 for Brown, and 209 for Tsongas. Defying the conventional wisdom of looking for regional balance in choosing a running mate, Clinton chose Al Gore, the junior senator from neighboring Tennessee, for vice president. The Clinton-Gore ticket is the youngest ever to be elected. In his acceptance speech, which was partially overshadowed by the sudden withdrawal earlier that day of independent candidate Ross Perot, Clinton called for a New Covenant, a phrase inspired by Carroll Quigley, Clinton's freshman history professor at Georgetown University. Clinton defined his New Covenant as "a solemn commitment between the people and their government, based not simply on what each of us can take, but on what all of us must give to make America work again." He challenged both parties to rethink their philosophies. "Republicans," he declared, "have campaigned against big government for a generation. But they've run big government for a generation, and they haven't changed a thing, except from bad to worse. They don't want to clean out the bureaucracy; they just want to run against it. But we Democrats have some changing to do, too. It is time for us to realize there is not a government program for every problem. And if we really want to use government to help people, we've got to make it work."

Other highlights of the convention: In a rousing keynote address, Governor Zell Miller of Georgia derided Bush as a president who "talks like Dirty Harry, but acts like Barney Fife" and criticized Ross Perot as a wheeler-dealer enriched by government contracts who "instead of shaking the system up, [has] been shaking it down." Jesse Jackson delivered a fiery speech remarkable for its lukewarm endorsement of Clinton. Jerry Brown spoke out angrily against the corrupting influence of money in politics without finding time to mention Clinton's name. The convention concluded with the traditional show of unity on stage, where the Clinton and Gore families swayed to the beat of Fleetwood Mac's 1977 single "Don't Stop (Thinking About Tomorrow)," the campaign's unofficial theme song. The Democratic party platform reflected the moderate philosophy of the candidate, emphasizing economic growth, welfare reform, and a strong defense consistent with the reduced demands of the post-Cold War era as well as abortion rights, universal access to health care, expanded child care, unpaid work leave for family emergencies, and new public works and environmental protection projects. It called for "a new social contract based neither on callous, do-nothing Republican neglect nor on an outdated faith in programs as the solution to every problem [but] a third way beyond the old approaches—to put government back on the side of citizens who play by the rules."

OPPONENTS: President George Bush (1924–) of Texas; Republican. After turning back a primary challenge from conservative columnist Patrick Buchanan, Bush entered the Republican convention in Houston in August 1992 assured of renomination but already behind Clinton in the polls. His name was placed in nomination by Secretary of Labor Lynn Martin. In his acceptance speech, Bush blamed much of the nation's ills on "the gridlock Democratic Congress," derided Clinton's plan as "Elvis economics," and claimed credit for the end of the Cold War. "My opponents say I spend too much time on foreign policy," he declared. "As if it didn't matter that schoolchildren once hid under their desks in drills to prepare for nuclear war. I saw the chance to rid our children's dreams of the nuclear nightmare, and I did." Other highlights of the convention included a slashing speech by Buchanan, who assailed both the Democratic nominee and his wife, referring to them repeatedly as "Clinton and Clinton," as though they were the ticket, and denounced Mrs. Clinton for embracing what he called "radical feminism." He called on the party to gird for a "religious war . . . for the soul of America." More subdued but no less conservative in tone was an address by Marilyn Quayle, the wife of the vice president, who in defending the value of full-time homemakers offended some by seeming to imply that working mothers were defying the essential nature of women. The Republican party platform underscored the prominence of hardline conservatives at the convention in calling, for example, for a constitutional ban on abortion without even the exceptions approved by President Bush. It also denounced the tax increase signed by Bush in 1990, though it stopped short of criticizing the president himself for doing so. The ultra-conservative tone of the convention disturbed many moderate Republicans, like Senator John Danforth of Missouri, who called it "a total disaster that in no way stood for what George Bush or this party believes in."

Ross Perot (1930–   ) of Texas; Independent. Defying all conventional wisdom, Ross Perot, a former IBM salesman who had parleyed a $1,000 investment in the creation of Electronic Data Systems in 1956 into a $2.5 billion enterprise by the time he sold it to General Motors in 1984, entered the presidential race almost as an afterthought during an interview with Larry King and tapped a reservoir of public discontent with his folksy, blunt speech and can-do spirit. In June 1992, before the conventions, he lead both Bush and Clinton in the polls, the first time an independent candidate ever scored better than the presumptive or actual nominees of either major party in the history of polling. Perot held no convention, made few public appearances, spurned political handlers, and otherwise gave the appearance of a most reluctant candidate who, like Macbeth, seemed to believe, "Chance may crown me without my stir." Then in July 1992 he suddenly withdrew from the race, explaining that his candidacy was no longer necessary now that the Democratic party had revived to seriously challenge Bush's reelection and that he did not want to act as a spoiler in denying the winner a majority of electoral votes and thus throw the race into the House of Representatives. Later he claimed that the real reason he had dropped out was because of reports that Republican party operatives had threatened to smear his daughter and disrupt her wedding. Whatever his motive, Perot reentered the race on October 1. He chose as his runningmate James Stockdale, a retired rear admiral and former prisoner of war in Vietnam.

CAMPAIGN AND THE ISSUES, 1992: This was at the same time one of the most unusual and most straightforward presidential campaigns of modern times. It was straightforward in that the campaign, for all the rhetoric and side-issues, boiled down to a simple referendum on President Bush and his handling of the economy. But this was no ordinary year:

• Never had the fortunes of an incumbent president fallen so far so fast in the absence of major scandal.

• Never before had an independent candidate ever led the two major party candidates in public opinion polls.

• Not since former President Theodore Roosevelt jumped into the 1912 race as the Bull Moose candidate had a third-party candidate won such a large percentage of the popular vote.

• The presidential candidates spurned the standard news interview programs, like "Meet the Press," in favor of informal talk shows hosted by the likes
of Phil Donahue, Arsenio Hall, and Larry King.

Soon after Ross Perot offered himself as a possible candidate, he soared ahead
of both President George Bush and Governor Bill Clinton in public opinion polls.
But in dropping out on July 16, just hours before the nation was to take a fresh
look at Clinton in his acceptance speech at the convention, Perot effectively
surrendered much of his following to the Democratic nominee. In the wake of
the convention Clinton surged from third to first place in the polls, solidifying
his lead in a successful bus trip across the American heartland with his running
mate and their wives. In a break with tradition, Clinton and Gore, the youngest
successful ticket in history, stumped frequently together, underscoring the
generational change they offered.

Bush was slow to react to the Democratic momentum. He delayed campaigning until after the Republican convention and was reluctant to pull Secretary of
State James Baker, his 1988 campaign manager, out of delicate negotiations in
the Middle East to salvage his campaign until late in the day. Reaching back to
the proven tactics of four years before, Bush resorted to hard negative campaigning, attacking Clinton, as he had Michael Dukakis, as an unpatriotic tax-
and-spend liberal. He lambasted Clinton for avoiding the draft during the Vietnam War and in particular for taking part in anti-war demonstrations while a
student in England. He implied that Clinton's youthful visit to Moscow was
born of some sinister motive, although he backed down from the charge amid
cries that it smacked of McCarthyism. Political appointees at the State Department poured over the passport files of Clinton and his mother in a futile attempt
to confirm rumors that Clinton had taken steps to renounce his citizenship in
order to avoid the draft. (After the election, the State Department's inspector
general concluded that the search was "politically motivated," was in violation
of department rules, and was condoned by senior White House officials, including James Baker.) Hitting his stride late in the campaign, Bush strung together
a series of Clinton inconsistencies—his varying explanations of how he had
avoided the draft, his ambivalence on the Persian Gulf War, his artfully crafted
position on the North American Free Trade Agreement that sought to support
free trade in principle without alienating organized labor—and offered it as
evidence of "a pattern of deception." He described a new disease, "Clintonesia,"
with the symptoms of "weak knees, sweaty palms and an incredible desire to
say anything on all sides of any issue, depending on who you're trying to
please." In short, he sought to portray Clinton as untried, untrustworthy, and at
heart un-American. Clinton, assisted by a computerized ready-response team,
set out to blunt each charge with a counter-charge, often within hours, so that
both sides were aired on that evening's news. When Bush began touting himself
as another Harry Truman who would prove the pundits wrong on election day,
Clinton, referring to the famous sign on Truman's desk, delivered this withering
contrast between the two presidents: Bush "has blamed his failures on everything from the Federal Reserve to Saddam Hussein, from Congress to consumers to the press. He says the recession is over; we just don't know it. And if it's
not really over, it is because we have an attitude problem. The buck doesn't stop
with George Bush; it doesn't even slow down there."

On issues of substance, the two major candidates reflected the traditional
philosophies of their parties: Bush wanted to limit the role of government in

solving the nation's problems. Clinton, though more restrained than the liberals of his party, saw more government intervention as the only way to stimulate growth and opportunity. Roiling the political waters was independent candidate Ross Perot, who focused attention on the corrosive effect of the budget deficit and the national debt, both of which had swelled under 12 years of Republican rule. Perot made deficit reduction a top priority, insisting on the need to raise taxes sharply on gasoline, cigarettes, and Social Security benefits. Bush, all but vowing again never to raise taxes, repeated his call for a cut in the capital gains tax as a proven stimulus to a sluggish economy. Clinton proposed a tax hike on the richest 2% of Americans and modest cuts for the middle class while relying largely on economic growth to gradually pay down the deficit. Both Clinton and Bush supported a line-item veto for the president. Clinton called for public works projects reminiscent of the New Deal to provide high speed rail service, a national computer network, and repair of the nation's infrastructure. Clinton proposed taking a step toward national health insurance by reforming the present system to eliminate bureaucratic duplication, rein in costs that have soared beyond inflation, and offer affordable coverage to all. Bush called for tax credits to offset the cost of health insurance. Clinton pledged to replace the current debt-ridden student loan program with a plan to offer college aid to all qualified applicants with the loans to be repaid either in cash at tax time or in community service. All three candidates envisioned cuts in the defense budget. Bush continued to support a constitutional amendment to ban abortion with exceptions for rape, incest, and threats to the mother's life. Clinton and Perot sought to reduce the incidence of abortion, but supported a woman's right to choose to end a pregnancy under the restrictions embodied in *Roe* v. *Wade*. Clinton called for welfare reform, providing recipients job training and other assistance but requiring them to go to work within two years or lose benefits. "Welfare," Clinton repeated often, "should be a second chance, not a way of life." Bush encouraged states to experiment with welfare reform. The three candidates agreed on the need to improve education by establishing national curriculum standards and tests and giving teachers more autonomy in the classroom. Clinton promised greater emphasis on preschool preparation and improvements in the health of women and children so that learning comes easier.

When Perot reentered the race on October 1, he scrambled an already unpredictable campaign, forcing the two major candidates to divine the course of his supporters. Outspending the other candidates, the billionaire businessman bought half-hour blocs of prime time television to talk about the nation's ills. His simple but effective presentations at times outdrew scheduled network shows on competing stations, including a baseball playoff game.

In the first debate in St. Louis on October 11, Bush failed to throw Clinton on the defensive or eat into his lead in the polls. When he again attacked Clinton for his youthful anti-war protests abroad, the governor pointedly reminded Bush that his own father had had the courage to stand up to Senator Joseph McCarthy in the 1950s, adding, "You were wrong to attack my patriotism." Perot got off the most memorable soundbites. Responding to charges that he lacked experience in government, Perot shot back, "Well, they've got a point. I don't have any experience in running up a $4 trillion debt." In the vice presidential debate in Atlanta on October 13, an animated Dan Quayle held his own against a reserved Al Gore. Perot's running mate, James Stockdale, appearing befuddled at times, candidly admitted that he was out of his depth. The format for the second presidential debate on October 15, insisted upon by Clinton, was an informal exchange among the candidates and an audience of undecided voters selected by an independent polling organization. Bush's strategy to continue to hammer away at Clinton's character was undermined by the audience's insistence that the candidates stick to the issues. His frustration seemed evident when he was unable to understand a clumsily-phrased question about how hard economic times had affected him personally. The camera caught bush peeking at his watch, a scene that was replayed on the news as emblematic of the president's impatience with the course of the campaign. In the final debate in East Lansing, Michigan on October 19, Bush performed better, effectively raising doubts about Clinton's preparedness for the presidency, but attention was diverted by Perot's pointed charges that Bush had coddled Saddam Hussein in advance of the Persian Gulf War and bungled the savings and loan crisis.

Not since 1964 had so many newspapers endorsed a Democratic presidential candidate. The *New York Daily News*, which last backed a Democrat in 1940, supported Clinton. The Canton (Ohio) *Repository* broke a 177-year tradition of supporting Republican candidates to endorse Clinton. While Bush won the backing of his adoptive hometown papers, the *Houston Post* and the *Houston Chronicle*, Clinton snared the *York County* (Maine) *Coast Star*, a weekly that serves Kennebunkport, and *The Philippians*, the student newspaper of Bush's old prep school. But Clinton failed to convince the Little Rock *Arkansas Democrat-Gazette*, the largest daily in his home state and a frequent critic of the governor, to break its tradition of remaining neutral in presidential contests. Among the newspapers to endorse Perot were the *Syracuse Herald-Journal*, the *Cedar Rapids* (Iowa) *Gazette*, and the *Bridgeport* (Connecticut) *Post*. Bush won the endorsement of the 240,000-member Fraternal Order of Police. But the National Rifle Association, which had supported Bush in 1988 and Ronald Reagan before him, withheld its endorsement this year in retaliation for Bush's ban on the importation of semi-automatic weapons. Clinton was endorsed by Governor Lowell Wicker of Connecticut and former Representative John Anderson of Illinois, both Republicans-turned-independent. John P. White, the architect of Perot's economic plan, opposed Perot's decision to reenter the race and endorsed Clinton. Sarah Brady, the wife of James Brady, the former Reagan administration spokesman who was severely wounded in the assassination attempt on Reagan, came out for Clinton because of his support for the Brady gun control bill. In the battle for celebrity endorsements, Clinton had the backing of Jack Nicholson, Roseanne Arnold, Glenn Close, and Robert DeNiro; Bush won support from Frank Sinatra, Charlton Heston, Arnold Schwarzenegger, and Sylvester Stallone; Perot was endorsed by Willie Nelson, Katharine Hepburn, and Kirstie Allie, though the latter two recanted.

In the campaign's closing days, Bush seemed reinvigorated by polls showing him narrowing the gap with Clinton. But it proved too little, too late. Clinton won a broad-based victory, piecing together much of the old New Deal coalition of the poor and middle class; blacks, Catholics, and Jews; labor and liberals; the young and the old. He carried every region of the country except the South, which he lost by the narrowest of margins to Bush. Perot did his best among self-described independents, carrying 30% of them, close behind Clinton (38%) and Bush (32%). Perot's best state was Maine, where he received 30% of the vote. Nationwide Perot siphoned votes equally from the two candidates. Although Perot carried no state, he drew a greater percentage of the popular vote than any independent candidate in 80 years. Clinton is the first

Democrat to win the White House without carrying Texas and the first president to have failed to win the New Hampshire primary as a candidate.

ELECTION AS PRESIDENT, FIRST TERM, NOVEMBER 3, 1992

Popular Vote. Clinton (Democrat), 44,908,233 (43%); Bush (Republican, 39,102,282 (37%); Perot (Independent), 19,741,048 (19%).

Electoral Vote. Clinton, 370; Bush, 168; Perot, 0.

States Carried. Clinton won the electoral votes of the District of Columbia and 32 states--Arkansas, California, Colorado, Connecticut, Delaware, Georgia, Hawaii, Illinois, Iowa, Kentucky, Louisiana, Maine, Maryland, Massachusetts, Michigan, Minnesota, Missouri, Montana, Nevada, New Hampshire, New Jersey, New Mexico, New York, Ohio, Oregon, Pennsylvania, Rhode Island Tennessee, Vermont, Washington, West Virginia, and Wisconsin. Bush won the electoral votes of 17 states--Alabama, Alaska, Arizona, Florida, Idaho, Indiana Kansas, Mississippi, Nebraska, North Caroline, North Dakota, Oklahoma South Carolina, South Dakota, Texas, Utah, Virginia, and Wyoming. Perot carried no state.

DEMOCRATIC NOMINATION FOR RE-ELECTION AS PRESIDENT 1996:

Clinton ran, for all intents and purposes, unopposed. His only consistent challenger was Lyndon LaRouche, a fringe politician who had vacillated between extreme left- and extreme right-wing positions over the years. LaRouche, a swindler, was convicted and jailed for mail fraud in December of 1988. He had been released from prison after five years and used the campaign as a platform for his incoherent ideas. He was never a serious challenger.

In many states there were local challengers, but Clinton won handily in every state that had a primary. Curiously, the public had now begun to separate Bill Clinton the person from Bill Clinton the politician. Polls showed that the public believed the president lacked character, they still thought he was doing a good job as president—an anomaly unprecedented in American history.

OPPONENTS: Robert "Bob" Dole, H. Ross Perot.

Bob Dole (1923-   ) of Kansas, Republican. Dole was the Senate Majority Leader. He was raised in Western Kansas in Russell, a small town on the Great Plains. During the Depression his family, like so many others, suffered economic hardship He credited this with making him appreciate the value of hard work. He was an athlete and a popular student in high school. In 1942 Dole joined the Army, became a second lieutenant, and fought in Italy in World War II. Dole was severely wounded and had to undergo nine operations before rehabilitation, but his wounds caused paralysis and left him unable to use his right arm. He was decorated with the Purple Heart twice and also with the Bronze Star.

Dole went to law school and earned a degree from Washburn University in Topeka, Kansas. In the early 1950s, the local hero in Russell was persuaded to enter politics and he won a seat in the state legislature and later served as county attorney. He was elected to the U.S. House of Representatives in 1961 and served until 1968. In 1968, Dole won a U.S. Senate seat and became Chairman of the Republican National Committee in 1971. He ran as the vice-presidential candidate with President Gerald Ford in an unsuccessful 1976 White House bid.

He married the former Elizabeth Hanford, a prominent Republican leader from North Carolina. Elizabeth Dole was the Secretary of Transportation for President Reagan and the Secretary of Labor for President Bush.

Dole was elected Senate Majority Leader in 1984, and became the longest serving Republican leader in the Senate until he resigned on June 11, 1996, to run for President of the United States. At seventy-three years of age, Dole was the oldest man in U.S. history to make a bid for the presidency.

Dole was the easy frontrunner for the Republicans as early as 1994. Former four-star general Colin Powell declined to run and the other candidates did not have Dole's name recognition or experience. His rivals for the nomination were Lamar Alexander, the former governor of Tennessee; Steve Forbes, publisher and financier; Phil Gramm, a senator from Texas; Bob Dornan, a congressman from California; Alan Keyes, a conservative talk-show host; Richard Lugar, a senator from Indiana; and Patrick Buchanan, a conservative writer.

Buchanan surprised everyone by winning the New Hampshire primary but it became evident that Dole would run away with the primaries. Dole won the key state of South Carolina on March 2, 1996, and in another month he essentially had enough delegates to secure the nomination. Buchanan ran a game second and Forbes third.

Dole was forced to pick up some of the rhetoric of his opponents in order to gain the support of their followers. After Forbes advocated a "flat tax," Dole proposed a 15 percent tax cut that would be a "fairer flatter tax." Dole tried to distance himself in the public's eyes from the radical Republicans such as Newt Gingrich, but he couldn't afford to alienate the right wing of his party either. Dole was a centrist politician who needed to appeal to conservative voters without alienating the middle.

Dole chose Jack Kemp, former NFL quarterback for the Buffalo Bills and a conservative congressman from New York, as his running mate. This choice may not have been the wisest. Middle America saw Kemp as conservative while Republicans viewed him as a neo-conservative in the mold of Reagan and Bush. In other words, Kemp was too conservative for average voters and not traditionalist enough for conservatives.

H. Ross Perot (1930-) of Texas; Reform Party. For more background information see "Opponents" in the 1992 campaign. Capitalizing on his popularity and a genuine grass-roots groundswell for a third party, Perot threw his hat into the ring for a second time while organizers formed the new Reform Party. He was challenged for the party nomination by former Colorado Governor Richard "Dick" Lamm who wasn't a serious threat to Perot's popularity.

Perot chose as his running mate, Pat Choate, an economist, a former public policy advisor for the TRW Corporation, and the author of several books. Choate, however, had almost no name recognition and added little to Perot's candidacy.

CAMPAIGN AND THE ISSUES 1996: Clinton, who had already distanced himself from his earlier liberal stances, tailored his campaign around centrist issues and even sounded like the Republicans on economic issues. He stole most of Dole's thunder by advocating a tax cut, a move he could now make with ease since he had raised taxes by a quarter of a trillion dollars in his earlier budget, and tax revenues were robust enough to make up for any difference.

The issues became less important as Clinton moved steadily to the middle, and Dole, who was firmly in the middle to begin with, could not move his platform any further to the right. What became evident was that the difference between the two major candidates was one of style rather than substance. Perot was virtually invisible since he was excluded from the debates by the two major parties. He sued to be allowed to participate in the nationally televised debates but lost. Also, one of his most important campaign issues, deficit reduction, which helped propel Perot into the national spotlight four years earlier, was a moot point because of Clinton's deficit reduction budget.

Clinton projected the image of a young forward-looking man of vigor. Dole's image was of an elderly man who longed to return to an idyllic past. In his nomination acceptance speech Dole said, "Age has its advantages. Let me be the bridge to an America that only the unknowing call myth. Let me be the bridge to a time of tranquillity, faith, and confidence in action. And to those who say it was never so, that America has not been better, I say, you're wrong, and I know, because I was there. And I have seen it. And I remember."

Clinton in his nomination acceptance speech said, "The real choice is whether we will build a bridge to the future or a bridge to the past, about whether we believe our best days are still out there or our best days are behind us, about whether we want a country of people all working together or one where you're on you're own. Let us commit ourselves this night to rise up and build the bridge we know we ought to build all the way to the twenty-first century. Let us have faith, American faith, that we are not leaving our greatness behind. We're going to carry it right on with us into that new century, a century of new challenge and unlimited promise."

Clinton, was now widely criticized by the opposition press as "Slick Willie." But he always played well to the television cameras and was an energetic speaker. Dole, on the other hand, was often called "Bob Dull." He held his own in his debates with Clinton, but since their platforms were not well differentiated to the public, Dole needed to win the debates with Clinton decisively, which he failed to do.

Dole accused Clinton of being too liberal but Clinton distanced himself from the liberals in his party and the conservatives elsewhere and put forth the image of a president who rejected extremist politics. He changed his emphasis from advocacy for the poor or special interest groups to a focus on issues for the middle class. By doing so, he helped the nascent Green Party under Ralph Nader, who took up the banner of environmentalism and traditional liberal causes.

Clinton firmly cemented his popularity with Middle America who were enjoying an economic boom by assuring them that he would protect the gains for which they had worked so hard.

In his nomination acceptance speech Clinton declared, "I want to build an America in the twenty-first century in which all Americans take personal responsibility for themselves, their families, their communities, and their country.... Well, for four years now, to realize our vision, we have pursued a simple but profound strategy: opportunity for all, responsibility from all, a strong, united American community.... Look at what's happened. We have the lowest combined rates of unemployment, inflation and home mortgages in twenty-eight years. Look at what happened: ten million new jobs, over half of them high-wage jobs. Ten million workers getting the raise they deserve with the minimum wage law.... On welfare, we worked with states to launch a quiet revolution. Today there are 1.8 million fewer people on welfare than there were the day I took the oath of office. We are moving people from welfare to work.... And the deficit has come down for four years in a row for the first time since before the Civil War, down 60 percent on the way to zero. We will do it. We are on the right track to the twenty-first century."

Dole, in his nomination acceptance speech said, "Now, which is more important? Wealth or honor? It is not, as was said by the victors four years ago, 'the economy, stupid.' It's the kind of nation we are. It's whether we still possess the wit and determination to deal with many questions, including economic questions, but certainly not limited to them. All things do not flow from wealth or poverty. I know this first hand, and so do you. All things flow from doing what is right. The triumph of this nation lies not in its material wealth but in courage, sacrifice and honor."

Clinton, on the one hand, was giving the American middle class facts and figures that they could visibly see in their daily lives, Dole, on the other hand, was talking vaguely about honor and sacrifice. Most people figured that they had sacrificed enough and were due some reward.

Dole's tax plan, which he outlined in his nomination acceptance speech, had broad appeal. He said, "It means you will have a president who will reduce taxes 15 percent across-the-board for every taxpayer in America. It will include a $500-per-child tax credit for lower- and middle-income families. Taxes for a family of four making $35,000 would be reduced by more than half — 56 percent to be exact. And that's a big, big reduction. It means you'll have a president who will help small businesses — the businesses that create most new jobs — by reducing the capital gains tax rate by 50 percent. Cut it in half."

Clinton countered with his own proposal, and said "Let me say again, every tax cut I call for tonight is targeted, it's responsible, and it is paid for within my balanced-budget plan. My tax cuts will not undermine our economy, they will speed economic growth. We should cut taxes for the family sending a child to college, for the worker returning to college, for the family saving to buy a home or for long-term health care, and a $500-per-child credit for middle-income families raising their children who need help with child care and what the children will do after school. That is the right way to cut taxes: pro-family, pro-education, pro-economic growth!

"Now, our opponents have put forward a very different plan, a risky, $50 billion tax scheme that will force them to ask for even bigger cuts in Medicare, Medicaid, education and the environment than they passed and I vetoed last year."

Clinton's appeal was strictly to the middle class while Dole offered both a middle and upper class tax cut. Not only did Dole's 50 percent cut in the capital gains tax smack of favoring the rich who owned stock, but Clinton further discredited the plan by intimating that the tax gains for the rich would come at the expense of the poor and middle class by cutting Medicare and other social programs that people had come to rely on.

On the defense issue, Dole came across as hawkish and Clinton as moderate. Dole said, "And on my first day in office, I will put America on a course that will end our vulnerability to missile attack and rebuild our armed forces. It is a course President Clinton has refused to take. On my first day in office, I will put terrorists on notice: If you harm one American, you harm all Americans. And America will pursue you to the ends of the earth. In short, don't mess with us if you're not prepared to suffer the consequences.... And furthermore, the lesson has always been clear. If we are prepared to defend

— if we are prepared to fight many wars, and greater wars, and any wars that come — we will have to fight fewer wars, and lesser wars, and perhaps no wars at all. It has always been so, and will ever be so."

Clinton responded with, "My fellow Americans, I want to build a bridge to the twenty-first century that makes sure we are still the nation with the world's strongest defense; that our foreign policy still advances the values of our American community in the community of nations. Our bridge to the future must include bridges to other nations. ... We cannot become the world's policeman, but where our values and our interests are at stake and where we can make a difference, we must act and we must lead. That is our job, and we are better, stronger and safer because we are doing it."

With his youthful good looks and polished TV persona in addition to his new middle class appeal, Clinton simply overwhelmed Dole, especially among women voters. Despite a growing scandal involving improper fundraising from foreign donors that was linked to his campaign, Clinton swept the "Soccer Moms" and enough of Middle America to win a plurality of votes. The "Comeback Kid" had done it once again. Clinton was the first Democrat to be re-elected president since Franklin Roosevelt and was elected twice without a popular majority of the vote either time.

ELECTION AS PRESIDENT, SECOND TERM, NOVEMBER 5, 1996:

Popular Vote: Bill Clinton (Democrat) 47,402,357 (49.2%); Bob Dole (Republican) 39,198,755(40.7%); Ross Perot (Reform Party) 8,085,402 (8.4%).

Electoral Vote: Bill Clinton 379; Bob Dole 159; Ross Perot 0.

States Carried: Bill Clinton won the electoral votes of the District of Columbia and thirty-one states: Arizona, Arkansas, California, Connecticut, Delaware, Florida, Hawaii, Illinois, Iowa, Kentucky, Louisiana, Maine, Maryland, Massachusetts, Michigan, Minnesota, Missouri, Nevada, New Hampshire, New Jersey, New Mexico, New York, Ohio, Oregon, Pennsylvania, Rhode Island, Tennessee, Vermont, Washington, West Virginia, and Wisconsin. Bob Dole won the electoral votes of nineteen states: Alabama, Alaska, Colorado, Georgia, Idaho, Indiana, Kansas, Mississippi, Montana, Nebraska, North Carolina, North Dakota, Oklahoma, South Carolina, South Dakota, Texas, Utah, Virginia, and Wyoming.

INAUGURAL ADDRESS (FIRST): January 20, 1993."...Our democracy must be not only the envy of the world but the engine or our own renewal. There is nothing wrong with America that cannot be cured by what is right with America. And so today we pledge an end to the era of deadlock and drift, and a new season of American renewal has begun.

"To renew America we must be bold. We must do what no generation has had to do before. We must invest more in our own people–in their jobs and in their future–and at the same time cut our massive debt. And we must do so in a world in which we must compete for every opportunity. It will not be easy. It will require sacrifice. But it can be done and done fairly. Not choosing sacrifice for its own sake, but for our own sake. We must provide for our nation the way a family provides for its children.

"Our founders saw themselves in the light of posterity, We can do no less. Anyone who has ever watched a child's eyes wander into sleep knows what posterity is. Posterity is the world to come; the world for whom we hold our ideals, from whom we have borrowed our planet, and to whom we bear sacred responsibility. We must do what America does best: offer more opportunity to all and demand more responsibility from all."

INAUGURAL ADDRESS (SECOND): "Now, for the third time, a new century is upon us, and another time to choose. We began the nineteenth century with a choice, to spread our nation from coast to coast. We began the twentieth century with a choice, to harness the Industrial Revolution to our values of free enterprise, conservation, and human decency. Those choices made all the difference. At the dawn of the twenty-first century a free people must now choose to shape the forces of the Information Age and the global society, to unleash the limitless potential of all our people, and, yes, to form a more perfect union....

"And once again, we have resolved for our time a great debate over the role of government. Today we can declare: Government is not the problem, and government is not the solution. We — the American people — we are the solution. Our founders understood that well and gave us a democracy strong enough to endure for centuries, flexible enough to face our common challenges and advance our common dreams in each new day.

"As times change, so government must change. We need a new government for a new century — humble enough not to try to solve all our problems for us, but strong enough to give us the tools to solve our problems for ourselves; a government that is smaller, lives within its means, and does more with less. Yet where it can stand up for our values and interests in the world, and where it can give Americans the power to make a real difference in their everyday lives, government should do more, not less. The preeminent mission of our new government is to give all Americans an opportunity — not a guarantee, but a real opportunity — to build better lives....

"As this new era approaches we can already see its broad outlines. Ten years ago, the Internet was the mystical province of physicists; today, it is a commonplace encyclopedia for millions of schoolchildren. Scientists now are decoding the blueprint of human life. Cures for our most feared illnesses seem close at hand. The world is no longer divided into two hostile camps. Instead, now we are building bonds with nations that once were our adversaries. Growing connections of commerce and culture give us a chance to lift the fortunes and spirits of people the world over. And for the very first time in all of history, more people on this planet live under democracy than dictatorship....

"Fellow citizens, let us build that America, a nation ever moving forward toward realizing the full potential of all its citizens. Prosperity and power — yes, they are important, and we must maintain them. But let us never forget: The greatest progress we have made, and the greatest progress we have yet to make, is in the human heart. In the end, all the world's wealth and a thousand armies are no match for the strength and decency of the human spirit....

"May those generations whose faces we cannot yet see, whose names we may never know, say of us here that we led our beloved land into a new century with the American Dream alive for all her children; with the American promise of a more perfect union a reality for all her people; with America's bright flame of freedom spreading throughout all the world."

VICE PRESIDENT: Albert Gore, Jr. (1948-), of Tennessee, served 1993-2000. A native of Washington, D.C., he grew up in a political family. His father Albert Gore, Sr., served in the House (1939-1944, 1945-1953) and Senate (1953-1971). As a child, Gore spent the school year in Washington, where he attended St. Alban's Episcopal School for Boys, a prestigious prep school, and lived in the Fairfax Hotel. Summers were spent on the family farm in Carthage, Tennessee. While a student at Harvard University in 1968, he campaigned for Senator Eugene McCarthy of Minnesota, who opposed the Vietnam policy of President Lyndon Johnson. His senior thesis was entitled, "The Impact of Television on the Conduct of the President, 1947-1969." Upon graduating cum laude with a degree in government in 1969, Gorge set aside his anti-war sentiment to enlist in the Army, at least in part to help his father, a leading critic of the war who faced an uphill reelection fight. The elder Gore was defeated anyway. After serving a tour in Vietnam as a reporter with an engineering unit, Gore attended the Vanderbilt School of Religion briefly and, from 1974 to 1976, Vanderbilt Law School. At the same time, from 1973 to 1976, he was a journalist for the *Nashville Tennessean*. When Representative Joe Evins retired from Tennessee's 4th Congressional District, the elder Gore's old seat, in 1976, Gore entered the race and won handily. As a member of the House Intelligence Committee he earned a reputation as an expert on arms control and generally and supported the Reagan administration's early defense buildup, though at reduced levels. In 1984 he was elected to the Senate, where he was recognized as an authority on the environment and maintained a liberal record on social issues, a more moderate record on foreign affairs. In 1988 he ran for the Democratic presidential nomination but dropped out when his strategy of focusing on the Southern primaries failed to give him sufficient momentum to take his message to other parts of the country. He declined to run in 1992 at least in part because his small son was still convalescing from an accident in which he was struck by a car and nearly killed. Gore was one of just 10 Democratic senators to vote to authorize the use of force to drive Iraq out of Kuwait. Gore is the author of *Earth in the Balance* (1991), a best-selling book that warns of "global ecological crisis." During the transition, Gore was a central figure in choosing senior appointments and helped to develop the administration's policies on the environment and technology. His wife, the former Mary Elizabeth "Tipper" Aitcheson, holds a master's degree in psychology and is the author of *Raising PG Kids in an X-Rated Society* (1987). (For more on Gore see "George W. Bush" : "Opponents.")

CABINET:

Secretary of State. (1) Warren M. Christopher (1925-   ) of California served 1993-1997. Christopher was a tireless worker and logged more miles (780,000) in representing the United States abroad than any Secretary of State in a comparable period. He took part in the Mid-East, Bosnian, and Haitian negotiations. (2) Madeleine Korbel Albright (1937-   ) of Washington, DC, served 1997-2001. Albright was the first female secretary of state and prior to her appointment served as the United States Permanent Representative to the United Nations. She spent much of her administration trying to broker a peace agreement in the Mid-East, but was unsuccessful at reaching an accord.

Secretary of the Treasury. 1) Lloyd M. Bentsen (1921-   ) of Texas served 1993-1994. Bentsen played a key role in reducing the federal deficit and promoted NAFTA and GATT. (2) Robert E. Rubin (1938-   ) of New York served 1995-1999. Rubin was an economic advisor to the president and director of the National Economic Council prior to taking over at the Treasury Department. He presided over the department during one of the country's greatest economic expansions. (3) Lawrence H. Summers (1954-   ) of Massachusetts served 1999-2001. Summers was deputy secretary under Robert Rubin and continued his policies, which brought about low inflation and steady economic growth. Summers was the first secretary to preside over a treasury with a surplus in thirty years.

Secretary of Defense. (1) Les Aspin, Jr. (1938-   ) of Wisconsin served 1993-1994. Aspin was faced with budgetary problems and the changing world order after the fall of communism. Increasingly the American military was dragged into regional wars as peacekeepers, trying to separate the warring factions. When a humanitarian mission to Somalia by American forces went awry and eighteen soldiers were killed, Aspin resigned over the debacle. (2) William J. Perry (1927-   ) of California served 1994-1997.

Perry was deputy secretary of defense under Aspin and inherited a department faced with budget shortfalls and base closings. Perry restructured defense acquisition policy and procedure, streamlined bureaucratic red tape, and eliminated arbitrary specifications. He promoted Partnership for Peace Programs that allowed the armies of the new Eastern European democracies to maneuver with NATO forces and paved the way for their entrance into NATO despite initial Russian opposition. He resigned because he could no longer take the strain of sending U.S. military personnel on life-threatening missions. (3) William S. "Bill" Cohen (1940-   ) of Maine served 1997-2001. Cohen was the only Republican on Clinton's cabinet. Cohen managed to get budget increases and to raise the pay of servicemen.

Attorney General. Janet Reno (1938-   ) of Florida served 1993-2001. Reno, the first female attorney general, was the subject of a great deal of controversy. Her departments were often accused of using excessive force, especially in the military-like assault on the Branch Davidian complex in Waco, Texas; the siege at Ruby Ridge, Idaho, in which a woman holding a child was shot and killed by an FBI sniper; and in the Elian Gonzalez custody fight in Miami, Florida. Under her administration the FBI solved the decades-old Unabomber killings and caught and convicted numerous terrorists, including the perpetrators of the bombings of the Oklahoma City federal building and the World Trade Center, as well as stopping bomb plots before any injury or loss of life.

Secretary of the Interior. Bruce Babbitt (1938-   ) of Arizona served 1993-2001. Babbitt was probably the most influential interior secretary in the history of the United States. By the end of his term in office he managed to convince Clinton to set aside more wilderness area than any other administration had since Theodore Roosevelt's. He pioneered the destruction of certain dams to restore the environmental integrity of river systems and used controlled burn-offs to prevent massive forest fires. Certain endangered species made a comeback during his tenure, including the gray wolf, bald eagle, and peregrine falcon. Babbitt, however, was not popular in Western states where his restrictions on commercial and private use of federal lands were seen as a threat to local economies.

Secretary of Agriculture. (1) Mike Espy (1953-   ) of Mississippi served 1993-1994. Espy, the first black agricultural secretary, was credited with reorganizing the agency and negotiating trade treaties to open foreign markets to American agricultural products. Espy resigned amid allegations of bribery and corruption but was never convicted of any charges. (2) Dan Glickman

(1944-) of Kansas served 1995-2001. Glickman inherited an unenviable position in which he had to guide American farmers through roller-coaster commodities and export markets. He helped institute mandatory price reporting in the livestock industry and encouraged farmers to diversify crops to sell to new markets. His administration established standards for labeling organic produce and for overseeing genetically altered food products.

Secretary of Commerce. (1) Ronald H. Brown (1941-1996) of New York served 1993-1996. Brown was the first black commerce secretary and a former DNC chairman. He negotiated trade deals with China and other Asian countries. He was killed in a plane crash while on trade mission to Bosnia. He was under investigation by an independent counsel at the time of his death and died under suspicious circumstances. (2) Mickey Kantor (1939-) of California served 1996-1997. Kantor never really wanted the Commerce position and just served out Brown's term after his death. He was a good negotiator and brokered a trade deal with Bosnia, but his abrasive personality was not suited to a high-profile job. He later became one of Clinton's personal lawyers. (3) William Daley (1948-) of Illinois served 1997-2001. Daley is a scion of Chicago's politically dominant Daley family and is the brother of Chicago Mayor Richard M. Daley. He helped to bring about the North American Free Trade Agreement prior to his appointment to the Commerce Department and got China permanent normal trade relations while secretary.

Secretary of Labor. (1) Robert B. Reich (1946-) of Massachusetts served 1993-1997. Reich helped to implement several key pieces of legislation: the School-to-Work Opportunities Act helped prepare young people for further education and careers in high-skill high-wage jobs; the Retirement Protection Act, which protects millions of Americans in under-funded pension plans; and the Family and Medical Leave Act, which gave workers up to twelve weeks of unpaid leave for medical reasons. (2) Alexis Herman (1947-) of Alabama served 1997-2001. Herman successfully brought about an end to the strike against United Parcel Service by the Teamsters Union by getting both sides to the negotiating table. The end to the strike was crucial to Internet and mail-order retailers who relied heavily on the delivery service, and to relieve the overburdened U.S. Postal Service.

Secretary of Health and Human Services. Donna E. Shalala (1941-) of Wisconsin served 1993-2001. Shalala was the longest serving Secretary of Health and Human Services in U.S. history. She guided the welfare reform process; made health insurance available to an estimated 2.5 million children through the Children's Health Insurance Programs (CHIP); raised child immunization rates to the highest levels in history; led the fight against young peoples' use of tobacco; created national initiatives to fight breast cancer, racial and ethnic health disparities, and violence against women; and crusaded for better access and better medications to treat AIDS.

Secretary of Housing and Urban Development. (1) Henry G. Cisneros (1947-) of Texas served 1993-1997. Cisneros lied to FBI agents in his vetting procedure about payments made to his mistress. He resigned and was later convicted of a misdemeanor in the incident and was given a presidential pardon by Clinton. After his resignation he became president of Univision, a Spanish-language television network. (2) Andrew M. Cuomo (1957-) of New York served 1997-2001. Cuomo, the son of New York Governor Mario Cuomo, shook up the Housing Department with his

Management Reform Plan, which created an Enforcement Center headed by an FBI agent to crack down on fraud and corruption the department. He also brokered a deal with Smith & Wesson, the largest maker of handguns in the U.S., to institute safer gun designs and to alter the distribution of firearms so that they would not fall into the hands of children.

Secretary of Transportation. (1) Federico F. Pena (1947-) of Colorado served 1993-1997. Pena reduced the size of the department and tightened safety standards for small airlines. Pena, however, came under heavy criticism after he defended the ValuJet airline after a crash in Florida in which 110 people were killed, and it was later found out that the company had poor maintenance and safety records. Pena resigned over the incident but was persuaded to take the position of Secretary of Energy by Clinton. (2) Rodney E. Slater (1955-) of Arkansas served 1997-2001. Slater worked at repairing America's infrastructure overseeing an ambitious road and bridge building effort. He brokered a deal to avoid an Amtrak strike and improved railroad safety. He also negotiated deals that allowed American-based airlines into fourteen new countries.

Secretary of Energy. (1) Hazel R. O'Leary (1937-) of Minnesota served 1993-1997. O'Leary presided over the declassification of documents concerning nuclear medical experiments carried out on American citizens. She promoted energy efficiency, nuclear non-proliferation, and waste management. (2) Federico F. Pena (1947-) of Colorado served 1997-1998. Pena's brief tenure at the Energy Department was not marred by any controversy. He was praised by environmentalists and business leaders alike for his endeavors in energy conservation. He was also very active in making sure that the nuclear components used in energy generation in foreign countries were safeguarded so that unauthorized persons could not get a hold of bomb-making components. (3) Bill Richardson (1947-) of New Mexico served 1998-2001.

Richardson helped to streamline the red tape in the department and increase efficiency. He negotiated deals with former Soviet countries for non-proliferation of nuclear materials and to give employment to nuclear scientists so that countries hostile to the United States would not employ them. He also tried to develop domestic oil and gas resources.

Secretary of Education. Richard W. Riley (1933-) of South Carolina served 1993-2001. Riley helped to create the Partnership for Family Involvement in Education, which included over 4,000 groups. Riley also helped to win a historic ruling by the F.C.C. to give schools and libraries deep discounts for Internet access and telecommunications services.

Secretary of Veterans Affairs. (1) Jesse Brown (1944-2002) of Illinois served 1993-1997. Under Brown's leadership, the VA expanded benefits for veterans who were prisoners of war, exposed to Agent Orange, radiation or mustard gas, and expanded treatment services to those suffering post-traumatic stress disorder. Brown also directed that VA undertake an aggressive research initiative to determine the causes of the illnesses of Persian Gulf War veterans. (2) Togo D. West, Jr., (1942-) of Washington, DC, served 1998-2001. West was secretary of the Army and served for four months as acting secretary of Veterans Affairs before the position was made permanent on May 5, 1998. West was at the center of a controversy in which he refuted allegations that large donors to the Democratic Party were given burial space in Arlington National Cemetery, a military resting-place.

ADMINISTRATION 1993-January 20, 2001: Clinton campaigned as a "New Democrat," progressive yet pragmatic. Nevertheless, his first two years in the White House brought back the same liberal agenda that echoed past Democratic presidencies. This was something that was not very popular with an American public that was conditioned to the moderate neo-conservatism of the Reagan-Bush years.

On the first day of his presidency Bill Clinton canceled the so-called "gag rule" in force for federally funded clinics that banned them from giving out information on abortions. He also reversed a ban on abortions in overseas military hospitals and on fetal-tissue research. His attempt to allow homosexuals into the military brought resistance and criticism, so he compromised by ordering recruiters not to ask about sexual preference and for recruits not to tell—a compromise that neither side liked.

These moves early in his administration angered conservatives. But the new president's goal wasn't to please conservatives. He further fanned their anger when he signed into law the Brady Bill. This was a gun-control law requiring both a background check and a waiting period before one could buy a handgun.

Then he signed the Family and Medical Leave Act, which provided protection to employees who took leaves of absence for pregnancy or illness. This law had more broad-based support but the duo still antagonized gun owners and some businessmen.

He put his wife, Hillary Rodham Clinton, in charge of a task force to develop a plan to reform the nation's health-insurance system. This had been a major campaign promise. The plan, when finally presented, was criticized by Democrats as well as Republicans and was quickly killed in Congress.

President Clinton did narrowly manage to get a budget through the Democratically controlled Congress with a deficit reduction package that had a beneficial effect on the economy although it did raise taxes by an unprecedented $240-$280 billion. However, two of his campaign promises remained unfulfilled: welfare reform and a tax cut for the middle class.

At this time, allegations of his involvement with fraudulent dealings in the failed Madison Savings and Loan and the Whitewater River real-estate scandal began to surface, as well as a scandal involving the firing of the White House travel staff (which was viewed as a purely vindictive move against staff members of the former Republican administration). The Clintons' failure to file proper tax returns resulted in them paying nearly $15,000 in back taxes.

Congress appointed a special prosecutor to investigate the Clintons involvement in the Whitewater scandal. Both Clintons were subpoenaed and forced to testify for the prosecutor. The Clintons' partners in the Whitewater deal, James and Susan McDougal, were later convicted of bank fraud and conspiracy.

On February 26, 1993, a bomb went off in New York City in the World Trade Center, one of the largest office buildings in the world. Six people were killed and more than one thousand injured, mostly from smoke inhalation. The bombing turned out to be the work of a group of Middle Eastern terrorists. Had the bombing gone off as planned, it would have killed thousands. Fortunately, the blast wasn't strong enough to topple one tower on top of the other.

The public uproar that followed generated widespread calls for tougher anti-terrorist laws. The terrorists were caught and each was sentenced to 240 years in prison without the possibility of parole. There were widespread calls for the death penalty in such cases.

On April 19, 1993, a combined FBI-BATF government siege at the Branch Davidian complex in Waco, Texas, went totally awry when the use of force was authorized and resulted in the death of seventy-six people. Many of these were children. Attorney General Janet Reno offered to resign over the disaster but Clinton turned down her offer.

On June 18, Clinton was given a $200 designer haircut on Air Force One, shutting down two runways at Los Angeles International Airport for one hour. This gave rise to a new storm of criticism. The incident was labeled by wags "Hairforce One."

On July 20, Vincent Foster, a top White House aide, died. His death was pronounced a suicide but strange circumstances surrounded the death. Foster, who was a good friend of Hillary Clinton, was linked to the Whitewater affair. Self-styled experts insisted that the evidence showed that Foster had died elsewhere and his body dumped in the park.

On September 30, Clinton signed a bill that gave the former Soviet Union $2.5 billion in aid. Despite widespread support for the bill on Capitol Hill, many peopled questioned giving gifts to former enemies.

In October 1993, a supposedly humanitarian mission to Somalia ended up with eighteen U.S. soldiers killed and seventy-eight wounded in an ambush attack. The Defense Department had ignored a request to send armored vehicles and Blackhawk helicopters for security backup in the area. The public was outraged by televised pictures of a dead American soldier being dragged by Somalians through the streets and began to question the stationing of U.S. troops overseas in precarious and ill-defined roles. In December 1993, Defense Secretary Les Aspin resigned over the debacle. Also in December, Clinton signed the North American Free Trade Act (NAFTA), eliminating trade barriers among the United States, Canada, and Mexico. Clinton and Gore had lobbied heavily for this legislation and alienated many Democratic supporters especially trade unionists.

In May 1994, Paula Jones, a former Arkansas government employee, filed a lawsuit against the president that charged him with sexual harassment. In August 1994, two Clinton staffers in the Treasury Department were forced to resign over improprieties in the use of their office regarding the ever-growing Whitewater scandal and Attorney General Reno requested an independent counsel to investigate Agriculture Secretary Mike Espy for accepting favors from firms regulated by his department.

Scandals were mushrooming and political advisors cautioned Democratic candidates to distance themselves from Clinton for the upcoming election. On September 20 1994, the Armed Forces sent 20,000 U.S. troops to Haiti to re-establish the popularly elected president, Jean-Bertrand Aristide. A previous attempt at this in October of 1993 failed when Haitians protested the landing of American troops. This time, Clinton sent a larger contingent of troops, and the Haitian military junta backed down and reinstated Aristide. However, the Somalian debacle had the public worried about what would happen to the troops in Haiti, and Clinton was criticized in the press for this action.

As if things couldn't get any worse, in late September 1994, the Justice Department announced an investigation of Housing and Urban Development Secretary Henry Cisneros. In October, Mike Espy resigned. As the 1994 elections approached, Clinton's popularity was understandably low and the Republicans capitalized on it by winning majorities in both houses of Congress for the first time in forty years. They gained fifty-two seats in the House and eight in the Senate. Not one Republican incumbent lost a Senate or House seat. By the 1996 presidential elections, more than two hundred elected Democratic office holders, including two Senators and six Congressmen, deserted the party and joined the Republicans.

Shortly after the elections, the White House asked the FBI for hundreds of files of Republican staffers still in government employ. A scandal later erupted over the misuse of these files.

Another Clinton appointee, Surgeon General Joycelyn Elders, was widely attacked over her advocacy of teaching children about masturbation in sex education classes. The president gave her no support and distanced himself from the controversy. She resigned.

On April 19, 1995, a huge bomb exploded in front of the federal building in Oklahoma City killing 169 people and injuring another 500. These included many children. Initially the bombing was believed to be the work of foreigners, but when the criminals were apprehended, they were found to be radical anti-government Americans who believed they were exacting revenge for the Branch Davidian massacre by government agents.

Clinton regained a measure of public respect for his handling of the terrorist attack and the swift passage of an anti-terrorist crime package, the Anti-terrorism and Effective Death Penalty Act. This enlarged the scope of federal jurisdiction to prosecute terrorist acts, deport foreign criminals, and abridge the appeals process. Clinton also managed to get a line-item veto bill passed but this was later declared unconstitutional by the United States Supreme Court.

Because of the public backlash exhibited in the triumph of the GOP in the 1994 polls, Clinton backed away from some of his liberal positions. However, when Republican radicals introduced drastic budget cuts and reductions in government, Clinton vetoed their proposals. This led to a budget impasse whereby Congress tried to force Clinton to accept their budget, which included a Balanced Budget Bill, and Clinton adamantly refused.

Since no budget bill had passed, many government offices were forced to shut down in late 1995 and early 1996 for lack of funds. In this impasse, the public sided with the president and Clinton regained much of his lost popularity. He cemented his gains in popularity by signing a major welfare reform bill, which altered the structure of welfare, essentially requiring recipients to find work within two years after entering the welfare rolls. This act was a departure from traditional liberal entitlement programs and Clinton began to refashion his image as a more moderate politician.

On August 21, 1996 he signed the Kennedy-Kassenbaum Act (the Health Insurance Portability and Accountability Act), which was a compromise between Clinton's original hope for universal health coverage and the Republican plan. One month later, in an effort to appeal to mainstream voters, he signed the Defense of Marriage Act that denied homosexual couples federal spousal status or benefits and permitted states to bar gay marriages.

Another mainstream issue, immigration reform, was passed and signed into law. It prohibited illegal immigrants from getting federal aid and Social Security benefits and changed the deportation laws to make deportation easier and swifter. Clinton prevented Republican right-wingers from adding more measures to the bill that would bar illegal immigrants from educational facilities and would deny other benefits to legal immigrants. GOP reactionaries had overplayed their hand by trying to cut funds for education and Medicare and Social Security benefits as part of their overall government reduction package. Clinton put this to good use in the coming election and was able to appear to be the voice of moderation against drastic reforms.

Despite the controversies and scandals that plagued his first administration, Clinton managed to accomplish the realization of a number of programs that he had promised during his election campaign. A National and Community Service Trust Act founded such programs as AmeriCorps, Learn and Serve America, and other national service programs. Students who volunteered for these programs could be forgiven all or part of the debt incurred by their student loans. Clinton resolved a dispute between environmentalists and local loggers over the endangered spotted owl through the Northwest Forest Plan, which reduced logging but provided other economic aid to local families, and by 1999 the Forestry Service declared the spotted owl was making a comeback. Just before the Democratic convention in August 1996, he signed a bill raising the minimum wage by ninety cents an hour.

Clinton also made some positive inroads in the foreign policy arena during his first administration. He got the leader of the Palestinian Liberation Organization, Yasser Arafat, and the Prime Minister of Israel, Yitzhak Rabin, to shake hands in front of cameras at the White House. The two had reached an accord in which the Israelis pledged limited autonomy for the Palestinians in return for a cease-fire from the PLO. In July 1994, he helped facilitate a pact between Israel and Jordan to end the state of war between the two countries that had existed since 1948. This agreement was also signed at the White House. The Haitian transfer of government to democracy went smoothly and most of the U.S. troops were quickly pulled out of the country.

In another Mid-East move in early September 1996, Clinton ordered missile attacks against Iraqi forces after they crossed the border of the internationally protected Kurdish zone of northern Iraq. Critics of Clinton said that this move was an election year ploy to divert attention away from his scandals, but continued Iraqi non-compliance with the cease-fire agreement after Operation Desert Storm would plague Clinton throughout his presidency. In September of 1995, the United States sent peacekeeping forces to Bosnia as part of a larger NATO peacekeeping contingent. By November 21, 1995, the Clinton administration had swiftly facilitated the negotiations that produced the Dayton Accords (named for Dayton, Ohio, where the deal was reached), an agreement between Croatia, Yugoslavia, and Bosnia-Herzegovina to bring peace to the region, which NATO troops would monitor.

On December 8, 1994 Clinton signed into law the General Agreement on Tariffs and Trade treaty (GATT) that established the World Trade Organization to arbitrate international trade controversies. Along with NAFTA, this enabled a freer flow of commerce between the United States and other countries.

A number of serendipitous economic factors helped propel Clinton as the

"Comeback Kid." Clinton was lucky that the advent of the Internet's exponential expansion coincided with his administration. The decision not to tax the Internet was a wise one and allowed an unprecedented boom in dot-com companies. The economy became robust because the Federal Reserve Board kept interest rates low, thus keeping inflation very low.

The budget deficit dropped precipitously because of spending cuts and rising tax revenues, both from the tax increase and from greatly enhanced normal revenues that were rising from increased economic activity. Unemployment decreased, falling to the lowest rates in years. America was experiencing the beginning of an unprecedented sustained economic boom and this was a major factor as Clinton sought re-election.

William Jefferson Clinton's moniker of "Slick Willie" surfaced constantly during his second administration. "Teflon Willie" would have been more appropriate since everything that was slung at him simply slid off. He survived numerous scandals, the resignation of half of his Cabinet, an impeachment trial in Congress, personal and family travails, and just about every nasty thing that ever could be said about anyone and it all bounced off of him.

Despite all this, Clinton departed the White House with one of the highest approval ratings of any president in history. This was due, in large measure, to the booming economy, for which he took credit.

History will judge his tenure in office. The country had come a long way since George Washington, one of whose legendary virtues was that he never told a lie. There are those who believe that William Jefferson Clinton never told the truth.

Before he took office for the second time, on January 14, 1997, Clinton facilitated a new accord between Israelis and Palestinians that paved the way for the withdrawal of Israeli forces from the West Bank city of Hebron. While the peace process in the Mid-East progressed slowly, it, nevertheless, was progressing. This, despite opposition from right-wing Israelis and radical Palestinians.

This good news became overshadowed by ever increasing charges of malfeasance in the fundraising activities of the Democratic National Committee (DNC) and Clinton's re-election committee. The DNC came under attack for accepting campaign contributions from foreign companies and individuals, including Greeks, South Koreans, Thais, Chinese, and Indonesians. Clinton had personal ties to many of the foreigners involved.

Vice president Gore was criticized for attending a fundraising event at a Buddhist temple, since religious institutions as non-profit organizations are not allowed to lobby or make campaign contributions. Then Clinton was charged with using the White House improperly when he allowed large donors to the Democratic Party to stay in the Lincoln bedroom overnight. On February 25, 1997, the administration somewhat reluctantly released to the press a list of people who were White House guests. It confirmed that many on the list were DNC donors.

In June 1997, Clinton introduced the President's Initiative on Race, which established a group of advisors to confer with the president on the status of race relations in America. This panel was widely seen as a boondoggle when, after a year it produced a two-hundred-plus-page report that offered virtually no solutions to the race problems of the nation.

While investigations into Clinton's conduct in the fundraising affair,

Whitewater, the misuse of FBI files, the Paula Jones suit, and the improper firing of the White House travel staff continued, there were nevertheless a couple of rays of sunshine over the White House.

For example, Congress and the president finally reached an accord on the U.S. budget and health care. On August 5, Clinton signed a bill that created a balanced budget. In return for agreeing to balance the budget, the Republicans got a tax cut of $91 billion (which was less than half of the tax raise of the previous budget passed by the Democratically controlled Congress), and an agreement to end the deficit by 2002 (which was longer than the Republicans wanted to wait). On the same day, Clinton signed the Children's Health Insurance Program, which gave $24 billion to poor families for health insurance for their children. This was far distant from the universal health coverage that Clinton wanted, but it was better than nothing.

In November, Clinton suffered a major defeat in Congress. He had asked that the office of the president be granted "fast track" authority to negotiate trade agreements with foreign countries. This would essentially eliminate congressional approval of treaties but neither the Democrats nor the Republicans were willing to surrender congressional authority to the president. The president tried to save face by asking the Congress to table the measure rather than openly defeating it..

On December 17, 1997 during the ongoing Paula Jones sexual harassment suit against Clinton, Monica Lewinsky, a White House intern, was subpoenaed to testify as to Clinton's pattern of conduct. On January 7, 1998, in an affidavit, Lewinsky denied having an affair with Clinton. Two weeks later, the Drudge Report, a muckraking Internet news site, published rumors of a sexual dalliance between the president and a White House intern.

Within two weeks the furor over the alleged affair forced Clinton to issue a public denial of the affair and any cover-up of the affair. He said "… I did not have sexual relations with that woman, Miss Lewinsky. I never told anybody to lie, not a single time—never. These allegations are false."

The president had previously made this denial under oath in the Paula Jones court case. To compound the problem, amid the ever-increasing Lewinsky scandal, on March 10, 1998, Kathleen Willey, a Democratic volunteer, testified before a grand jury that Bill Clinton groped her. On March 15, Willey went on national television and reiterated her story. The next day Clinton denied the allegation.

On April 1, 1998, a U.S. District Court judge dismissed Paula Jones's sexual harassment suit. Jones appealed the decision, but then her lawyers and Clinton agreed to a settlement. For a payment of $850,000, she withdrew her lawsuit and agreed not to pursue the matter. Clinton did not admit guilt or proffer an apology. Again, Bill Clinton had dodged a bullet. There were still other investigations pending.

Clinton got respite from the scandals when he facilitated the Good Friday Peace Accords in Northern Ireland. This agreement called for British withdrawal from Ireland and autonomy for Northern Ireland with warring Catholic and Protestant factions both sharing power and agreeing to end the violence.

In August, terrorists struck again; this time the targets were the American embassies in Nairobi, Kenya, and Dar es Salaam, Tanzania. Car bombs had been exploded and more than two hundred people were killed, including twelve Americans. Another five thousand people had been injured.

In the subsequent investigations, it was revealed that the Clinton administration had been warned about the vulnerability of the embassies but had done little to beef up security. The investigations also revealed that Osama bin Laden, a wealthy businessman who had been expelled from Saudi Arabia, was the mastermind behind the attacks. Several terrorists were apprehended and brought to trial, but bin Laden remained at large, allegedly hiding in Afghanistan. Later in the month, Clinton gave the order to fire missiles at locations in Sudan and Afghanistan to avenge the embassy bombings and deter future terrorist activity.

While the administration upheld the notion that the targets of the missiles were engaged in terrorist activities, the supposed chemical weapons factory in Sudan turned out to be a drug company.

On August 17, 1998, Clinton was forced to testify via videotape before a grand jury in the Lewinsky scandal. That night he said on national TV, "Indeed I did have a relationship with Ms. Lewinsky that was not appropriate. In fact it was wrong." To the amazement of political pundits. the public continued to give Clinton high ratings as president despite his perjury and adultery.

By the end of the year the budget deficit had been eliminated; this was four years ahead of schedule.

The Mid-East peace settlement ground to a halt, when the right-wing Israeli government refused to implement previously agreed upon measures. Talks had stalled for nearly two years and the intervention of Clinton administration officials, including Secretary of State Madeline Albright, did nothing to further the process. Finally Clinton personally intervened and invited Israeli Prime Minister Benjamin Netanyahu and Palestinian Authority leader Yasser Arafat together for negotiations at a retreat on the Wye River in Maryland in October 1998.

After nine days of negotiations, on October 23, Clinton managed to facilitate an agreement called the Wye River Memorandum, which spelled out the details of the 1995 agreement and a timetable for their implementation. In a historic move, the Palestine Liberation Organization formally renounced the clause in their charter that called for the destruction of Israel. In return, Israel agreed to give the Palestinian Authority jurisdiction over more territory in the West Bank and Gaza Strip if the Palestinian police would bring a halt to terrorist attacks on Israel.

Palestinian radicals rejected the agreement and initiated a series of bombings against Israelis. Netanyahu used this as an excuse to back out of the deal, but the Israeli public, sick of incessant warfare, toppled Prime Minister Netanyahu's government and elected Ehud Barak who favored the accord. Barak not only continued negotiations with the Palestinians but also carried on peace talks with the Syrians over the Golan Heights dispute. Clinton was a major factor in these flawed but continuing Mid-East negotiations.

In another Mid-East move, Clinton in conjunction with the British armed forces ordered missile bombardments on Iraqi military installations on December 16, 1998. This was called Operation Desert Fox and the attacks were initiated because of Iraqi non-compliance with U.N. weapons inspections, which was part of the cease-fire agreement between Iraq and the U.N. coalition after Operation Desert Storm. Iraq's continued refusal to allow inspections resulted in more missile reprisals over the following months.

On December 19, the House of Representatives voted to impeach Bill Clinton on two charges resulting from the Lewinsky scandal: obstruction of justice and perjury. He was the second president in American history to be impeached.

The Senate impeachment trial of Clinton began on January 14, 1999. Despite this, polls conducted after his State of the Union address on January 20 revealed that his popularity was higher than ever. Even before the Senate trial ended on February 12, it was evident that there were not enough votes in the Senate for the two-thirds majority needed to impeach. Bill Clinton had dodged yet another bullet although there were other investigations still continuing.

While the litigation in the numerous scandals consumed much of Clinton's time and energy, he continued to make inroads in his foreign policy. In March 1999, NATO and the U.S started a bombing campaign against Serbia. The bombings were to prevent the further ethnic cleansing of Albanians in the Kosovo region of the Serbian province of Yugoslavia. After two and a half months of bombing, Yugoslav President Slobodan Milosevic signed an accord with NATO to withdraw his forces from Kosovo.

During the bombing, U.S. warplanes accidentally bombed the Chinese embassy in Belgrade. Three people were killed and twenty were wounded. The incident sparked protests in China and put a severe strain on Chinese-American relations. In June 1999, 7,000 U.S. troops were committed to the Kosovo region along with other NATO ground forces to prevent further ethnic bloodshed. On July 11, 1999, Clinton sponsored a Mid-East peace summit at Camp David, Maryland. Clinton tried to facilitate an agreement between Ehud Barak and Yasser Arafat, but after two weeks the peace talks ended fruitlessly.

In October 1999, the Senate refused to ratify the Comprehensive Test Ban Treaty, which Clinton had lobbied heavily for. In November, however, the Clinton administration managed to open China to more U.S. products by signing an agreement that reduced tariffs. China, in turn, was allowed to join the World Trade Organization, paving the way for further trade deals with the world's most populous country. The deal, however, hinged on China receiving permanent normal trade relations, something which some members of Congress had expressed reluctance to grant, given China's poor record on human rights.

In December, the World Trade Organization met in Seattle but a storm of protestors nearly halted the conference. Clinton had hoped for a more productive meeting but was thwarted by the disruptions. On New Year's Eve, the United States formally ceded the Panama Canal to Panama, which had been promised in a treaty signed during the Carter administration.

After working behind the scenes for months, Clinton invited Israeli Prime Minister Ehud Barak and Syrian Foreign Minister Shara to Shepherdstown, West Virginia, on January 3, 2000. They discussed the withdrawal of Israel from the Golan Heights but reached an impasse. Clinton traveled to the meeting on January 7 in order to facilitate the negotiations, but came away from the table empty handed.

Clinton tried to be a negotiator in the mold of Jimmy Carter but the unstable Israeli political situation thwarted his efforts. Despite mixed results in his foreign policy, the economy of the United States kept booming and unemployment dropped to a thirty-year low at 4 percent by the end of January 2000. The end of 1999 saw a surplus in the U.S. budget for the first time in thirty years with over $100 billion in excess revenues. In February 2000 the economy set a record for the longest sustained expansion in history.

On January 4, 2000, the Clintons occupied a house in Chappaqua, New York, to establish residency for Hillary Clinton's bid for the U.S. Senate seat vacated by Daniel Moynihan. She was derided as a carpetbagger but polls indicated that she had a strong following despite never having lived in New York. On February 6, she announced her candidacy and became the only First Lady to run for office in U.S. history.

In March 2000, the scandal over the misuse of FBI files was put to rest when Robert Ray, the independent investigator, absolved the Clintons from any wrongdoing in the affair. Billy the Kid Clinton was now skilled at dodging bullets.

In April, the Clinton administration was severely criticized for the heavy-handed tactics used in the Elian Gonzalez case. Gonzalez, a young Cuban refugee, fled with his divorced mother and her lover to asylum in the United States. His mother and her lover were drowned during the stormy voyage but the boy was rescued after hours at sea and brought to Miami. There he was given shelter by his paternal great uncle.

Elian's father immediately applied for custody of the boy. The boy's relatives were unwilling to release him into the custody of his father who was still a resident of communist Cuba. The case became a cause celebre in Miami's Cuban exile community. After six months of legal wrangling, heavily armed federal agents took the boy from his relatives and returned him to his father. In doing so they were confirming the strong feelings of most Americans that the boy should indeed be united with his father.

In June 2000, as the Clinton presidency drew to a close, Clinton was mindful of the legacy he would leave. One of the constituencies that had supported him was the environmental movement. To reward them for their support, he set aside locations in Arizona, Colorado, Oregon, and Washington, and designated them as national monuments, which carried the same status as that of a national park. During his administration he also put a halt to commercial logging and the building of roads in nearly sixty million acres of national forest.

Environmentalists were pleased, but a large portion of the Western public and the state governments were not. They saw in Clinton's move an effort to frustrate economic development in the West, motivated by the fact that the Western States had voted Republican. Before his administration ended, Clinton had designated eleven areas as national monuments and had put restrictions on grazing and mining.

In July, Clinton tried yet once again to broker a peace deal between the Palestinians and the Israelis. Yasser Arafat and Ehud Barak met at Clinton's request at the Camp David retreat in Maryland. Negotiations lasted two weeks, but again Clinton came away empty handed. In November, bomb attacks on Israelis and air strike retaliations against Palestinian Authority targets in the Gaza Strip made the peace process seem all but impossible

Ehud Barak's coalition government collapsed in December and new elections were scheduled for February. Just before he left office, Clinton wrote letters to both the Israelis and Palestinians that were published in newspapers, telling them that they were closer than ever to peace and that they should continue to negotiate. The impasse was a major foreign policy defeat for Clinton despite his energetic efforts to broker the peace.

On September 20, 2000 after six years of investigation and an expenditure of more than $50 million, Robert Ray closed the Whitewater inquiry. The independent counsel couldn't find sufficient evidence that either of the Clintons committed fraud or any other crime. Oposition newspapers commented that "Slick Willie" had now become positively bulletproof.

October brought yet another victory to Clinton when Congress granted China permanent normal trade relations. This allowed the Chinese to enter the World Trade Organization and opened Chinese markets to American automobiles, films, and other products.

On October 12, 2000, terrorists struck again, this time igniting a bomb on the U.S.S. Cole, an American destroyer that was refueling in Yemen. The suspects who were apprehended were linked to Osama bin Laden, the mastermind of the World Trade Center bombing. Seventeen Americans were killed in the blast.

In the November Senate election in New York State, Hillary Clinton swept into office, soundly defeating Congressman Rick Lazio. Lazio, who entered the race when New York City Mayor Rudy Giuliani dropped out because of health problems and an infidelity scandal, had lacked the support that Giuliani had and could not overcome the name recognition of the First Lady.

On December 11, 2000, Independent Counsel Robert Ray postponed a lawsuit to bar Clinton from practicing law. The suit was related to his perjury in the Paula Jones case, which violated the ethical standards that attorneys must adhere to. Clinton spent his final two months as president in a flurry of last minute appointments, environmental measures, and the failed Mid-East peace talks.

On Clinton's last day in office, he announced a negotiated deal with Independent Counsel Robert Ray. He accepted a five-year suspension of his Arkansas law license and agreed to pay a $25,000 fine in return for a dismissal of the disbarment charges. "Slick Willie" was positively made of Teflon.

Then, when people believed he could do nothing to top his disgrace in the Monica Lewisky affair, he struck again just hours before saying farewell to the White House. He pardoned a number of people, including Susan McDougal, who had refused to testify against him in the Whitewater scandal.

The bombshell that shocked the nation was his pardon of Marc Rich, an arch criminal being sought by the government for trading with the enemy and evading nearly $50 million in taxes. Rich was on the FBI's most wanted list. His family had contributed more than $1 million to Clinton fundraisers since the early 1990s.

Denise Rich, Marc's former wife, vehemently denied that she'd asked Clinton to pardon her ex. The affair echoed Clinton's lying, "I have never had sex with that woman." Like Clinton, Denise Rich turned out to be a boldfaced liar. This was confirmed when it was revealed that she'd written a personal note asking the president for the pardon.

Clinton had topped himself in his lack of ethics and integrity.

Jack Newfield, a liberal columnist writing for the conservative *New York Post* commented: "Bill Clinton stained and diminished everything he touched. This pardon, which violated all the rules, and circumvented law enforcement, will stain Clinton's legacy much more than the semen-stained dress."

Time alone will tell.

SCANDALS AND IMPEACHMENT: To say that Bill Clinton made some poor choices while he was in the White House would be an understatement of the greatest magnitude. Mistakes from his past returned to haunt him in the Paula Jones sexual harassment suit and the Whitewater probe. These led to other investigations. He made several ill-advised appointments to government posts that ended in resignations and even indictments of those appointees. He had an adulterous affair with a young woman about which he lied, and it resulted in his impeachment. He improperly fired the White House travel staff, who were hired by the previous administrations, to put in their place cronies of his, including his cousin. He improperly asked for confidential FBI files on former Republican staffers who still held government posts. He accepted campaign funds from foreigners trying to influence foreign policy and inappropriately rewarded large contributors to his campaign with stays in the White House, as if it were a Hilton hotel. Throughout the investigations stemming from these scandals, the administration stonewalled investigators. Evidence disappeared and sometimes reappeared, and administration officials were caught trying to cover up evidence. The number of scandals was unprecedented. Not since Warren Harding had the office of the president been so disgraced.

Whitewater: The first scandal to surface and the most problematic was the Whitewater real estate deal, which was connected to the failure of the Madison Savings and Loan and the death of Vincent Foster. In 1978, just prior to assuming the governorship, Bill Clinton and his wife Hillary invested in a land scheme with partners and formed the Whitewater Development Corporation, which bought a tract of land along the Whitewater River in rural Arkansas to sell as individual plots. Their partners in the venture were James and Susan McDougal. Jim McDougal was an old friend of Bill Clinton's who worked with him on the staff of Senator William Fulbright (D-Ark.) during the 1960s. Clinton and McDougal placed a down payment of $20,000 on the land and received an unsecured loan for nearly $200,000 to mortgage the rest of the cost of the land.

In 1979, Clinton became governor of Arkansas and appointed Jim McDougal as an economic advisor. McDougal shortly afterward quit the administration and later bought Madison Guaranty Savings and Loan Corporation. The Whitewater accounts were then handled through Madison, including refinancing of the loan. The loan had to be refinanced numerous times since the interest on the loan was higher than profit derived from the slow-selling lots. Governor Clinton's banking advisor informed him that McDougal was employing very imprudent banking practices, but Clinton ignored the warning. McDougal apparently was using the Whitewater Corporation for questionable check transfers. Some of those checks were linked to payments directed to Clinton's 1984 gubernatorial re-election. By 1985, Madison was in financial straits. Arkansas State Securities Commissioner Beverly Bassett Schaffer, who was appointed by Clinton, approved a questionable stock issue by Madison to raise more money. Schaffer was a lawyer who had represented Madison prior to her appointment. Hillary Clinton also represented Madison. The McDougals apparently took out loans from Madison on property that already had other liens on it. Late in 1985, the Federal Savings and Loan Insurance Corporation informed McDougal that he would be audited shortly because of irregularities. McDougal raised capital to cover the shortfall at the bank by getting loan money from David Hale's Capital Management Services, Inc. to Susan McDougal's advertising firm, Master Marketing. Hale was a local Clinton-appointed judge who was allegedly asked by Clinton to make the loan to McDougal. The federally funded Capital Management, however, was only supposed to make loans to disadvantaged small businesses. Hale was later indicted for defrauding the Small Business Administration and for misusing federal money. Money that went to Master Marketing was allegedly disbursed in an elaborate check-kiting scheme involving the Whitewater Corporation. Records of the transactions at Madison were lost. In late 1986, federal-banking regulators relieved Jim McDougal of his office as head of Madison. In their report they cited faulty record keeping and diversion of funds. In 1987, McDougal said he sent all the Whitewater files to Hillary Clinton at her request. Capital Management in late 1988 sued Susan McDougal for default on the loan and in February 1989 a judgement was placed against her. By the end of the year Madison was bankrupt and depositors had to be bailed out by the Resolution Trust Corporation (RTC) at a cost to taxpayers of at least $47 million.

The Federal Deposit Insurance Corporation engaged the services of the Rose law firm to sue Madison's accounting firm to regain some of the lost money. The Rose firm had Webster Hubbell (later to become associate attorney general in Clinton's U.S. administration), Hillary Clinton, and Vincent Foster as part of its staff. Since Rose had represented Madison earlier, there was some question over conflict of interest. Rose settled with the accounting firm for a fraction of the monies of the original suit and charged 40 percent of the settlement as fees. The Clintons had turned over the legal aspects, including accounting, of the Whitewater Corporation to Vincent Foster. From 1990-1992, Whitewater failed to file tax returns.

In the spring of 1992, while Bill Clinton was on the campaign trail, the press broke the Whitewater story. After the story broke, Hillary Clinton was alleged to have shredded documents at the Rose law firm. In October 1992, the RTC recommended that the Justice Department investigate the McDougals and further stated that Whitewater Corporation benefited from their dubious practices. In December 1992, just before Bill Clinton was to take office as president, the Clintons sold their interest in the Whitewater Corporation to the McDougals for a token $1,000.

In late July 1993, a federal judge in Arkansas authorized a search warrant for the office of David Hale. Soon thereafter Vincent Foster's body was found in Fort Marcy, Virginia, on federal land belonging to the National Park Service. Foster, a White House counsel, was apparently warned that there was a probe of Hale's firm pending and feared the paper trail leading from Susan McDougal's loan to the Whitewater Corporation. After Foster's death became known, files relating to Whitewater were allegedly removed from his office by White House staffers.

On January 20, 1994, after a public outcry about the Clintons involvement in this affair, Attorney General Janet Reno appointed Robert Fiske as an Independent Counsel with the authority to investigate the circumstances of the case. He started a probe to find out whether money from Madison had gone to the Whitewater Corporation and whether Clinton used his political influence as governor to help Madison. As he investigated, the probe encompassed the death of Vincent Foster, the firing of the White House travel staff (see "Travelgate" below), and the misuse of FBI files by the Clinton administration (see "Filegate" below). Fiske indicted the McDougals and others who were involved with them. Subpoenaed documents in the Whitewater case were eventually turned over to investigators but not until after much foot dragging.

White House staff refused to turn over some documents in the Vincent Foster case. In March of 1994, White House counsel Bernard Nussbaum resigned over criticism that he interfered with the investigation. That same month U.S. Associate Attorney General Webster Hubbell resigned amid allegations of impropriety when he was with the Rose law firm. On March 22, David Hale reached a plea bargain with Fiske. In early August 1994, Fiske was replaced by Kenneth Starr who set up grand juries in Arkansas and the District of Columbia to further the probe. On August 17, 1994, Deputy Treasury Secretary Roger Altman resigned over allegations that he lied to Congress about the Whitewater affair. The next day, Treasury counsel Jean Hanson resigned amid charges that she apprised the White House about details of the RTC investigation into the Madison-Whitewater case. In December 1994, Webster Hubbell was convicted of mail fraud and tax evasion.

On August 17, 1995 Jim and Susan McDougal were indicted for mail fraud, misapplying funds, filing false bank reports, and conspiracy. Also indicted was Arkansas Governor Jim Guy Tucker, Clinton's successor. In January 1996, Hillary Clinton was subpoenaed and testified before the grand jury. In February, the White House handed over Whitewater records that had been subpoenaed two years before and were suddenly "found." In April, Bill Clinton testified in the Whitewater trial and denied he used his influence as governor to urge David Hale to lend money to Jim McDougal. The next month, Jim and Susan McDougal and Jim Guy Tucker were found guilty. The Starr investigation in Arkansas ended in 1998 but not enough evidence was found to indict either of the Clintons.

Paula Jones: On May 6, 1994 Paula Corbin Jones filed a civil lawsuit against Bill Clinton, seeking damages for sexual harassment stemming from an incident at the Excelsior Hotel in Little Rock on May 8, 1991, where it was alleged that she was sexually assaulted and harassed, and then later defamed by his denials of the incident. Jones, a former Arkansas State government secretary, said she rebuffed Clinton's advances but after the incident Clinton punished her by denying raises and promotion in her job. Clinton tried to get the suit dismissed citing presidential immunity but a U.S. District Court judge allowed depositions in the case to proceed but held that the trial itself could not take place until after Clinton fulfilled his presidential duties. In January of 1995, Jones appealed the decision to delay the case. It took an entire year for a decision to be made but the appeals judges ruled in Jones' favor. On May 15, 1996 Clinton appealed to the Supreme Court to delay the case until he left office. The Supreme Court agreed to hear the case, effectively delaying the case until after the election. A year after agreeing to review the case, the Supreme Court allowed the lawsuit to proceed. A trial date was set for May 1998.

On January 7, 1998, White House Intern Monica Lewinsky swore in an affidavit that she did not have an affair with Clinton. In a January 17 deposition, Clinton denied having an affair with Lewinsky. Independent Counsel Ken Starr was then allowed to expand the Whitewater investigation to find out whether Clinton suborned perjury in Lewinsky's testimony. In February, Clinton asked for dismissal of the suit. In March, Jones' lawyers presented evidence alleging that the Jones incident was part of a pattern of behavior of making sexual advances and that it had happened to several other women; they also contended that there were strenuous efforts being made to suppress evidence.

On April 1, 1998, the U.S. District Court judge dismissed the charges against Clinton as being without merit. Jones appealed the decision, and while waiting for the appeal, in November 1998 Clinton and her attorneys came to a settlement. Clinton paid Jones $850,000, in exchange, Jones dropped her suit and agreed not to ask for an apology or make Clinton admit guilt.

In April 1999, the U.S. District Court judge in the Jones case found Bill Clinton in contempt of court for lying in his deposition in January of 1998 and ordered him to pay legal costs.

Monica Lewinsky: In June of 1995, Monica Lewinsky joined the office of White House Chief of Staff Leon Paneta as an unpaid intern. By November she had met Clinton and begun an affair with him. She then worked in the mailroom in the Office of Legislative Affairs often delivering mail to the Oval Office. In April 1996, she was transferred to the Pentagon where she met Linda Tripp. Tripp and Lewinsky became friends and Lewinsky confided to Tripp about her affair with Clinton.

In August 1997, Tripp said she saw a distraught Kathleen Willey, a White House staff member, leave the Oval Office. Willey later claimed that Clinton had groped her. After the incident Tripp recorded her telephone talks with Lewinsky without Lewinsky's knowledge. In early December, Lewinsky left the Pentagon and was referred to Clinton's friend Vernon Jordan by Clinton's secretary for job referrals. On December 17, 1997, Lewinsky was subpoenaed in the Paula Jones case. On December 28, Lewinsky visited Clinton at the White House where he allegedly told her to evade the prosecutor's questions. On January 7, 1998, Lewinsky signed an affidavit denying a sexual affair with Clinton.

Linda Tripp then contacted Independent Counsel Ken Starr and told him about the tapes she made. The tapes allegedly contained details about the affair and Clinton suborning perjury by asking her to lie under oath. Starr asked the FBI for a body wire and arranged for Tripp to meet with Lewinsky to record their conversation on January 13.

Tripp was to testify in the Paula Jones case about Kathleen Willey, so the next day, Lewinsky brought her a "cheat sheet" in which it described how to make points in an affidavit. On January 16, 1998, Starr asked for authority to widen his investigation into charges of suborning perjury and obstruction of justice and was granted permission by a three-judge panel. That same day, when Lewinsky met with Tripp, she was intercepted and questioned by the FBI and offered immunity from prosecution for her testimony against Clinton. The next day, Clinton in a deposition in the Jones case flatly denied the Lewinsky affair. By January 19, the press had broken the story of the affair. On January 22, 1998, Clinton again denied the affair and also denied that he had asked her to lie. On January 25, Lewinsky's lawyer accepted the immunity-from-prosecution deal in exchange for her testimony. The next day Clinton said his famous line, "I did not have sexual relations with that woman, Miss Lewinsky," which began to sound a lot like Nixon's "I'm not a crook" quote.

In early February, Kenneth Starr withdrew the immunity deal because Lewinsky would not fully testify. Lewinsky's lawyers sued, saying they had a deal, but lost in court in April. In the next few months Clinton tried to avoid the case by invoking executive privilege but failed to do so. The Lewinsky family engaged in histrionics in the press over the case; and Clinton failed in a bid to keep Secret Service agents from testifying in the case. By the end of July the on-again off-again immunity deal with Lewinsky was resolved and she gave Starr a dress claiming it contained the president's semen, which DNA tests confirmed.

On August 6, 1998, Lewinsky began her grand-jury testimony. On August 17, Bill Clinton became the first president to testify before a grand jury while in office. That night he went on national TV and apologized for his behavior. On September 9, 1998, Starr submitted his report and an overwhelming amount of evidence to the House of Representatives. Two days later, the House Judiciary Committee started making the evidence public. On October 8, the House voted to hold an inquiry into the impeachment of the president and on December 11 approved impeachment articles, including two counts of perjury and one count of obstruction of justice. The next day they added another article of impeachment on the grounds of abuse of power.

The Democrats called for censure and not impeachment. The public perception was one of partisan politics where the Republicans were out to "get" the president, despite the obviously true nature of the charges. Much of the press tried to portray the case as a mere peccadillo, but the charges were not about the sexual affair, they were about trying to cover up the evidence of it. These were precisely the same charges brought against Nixon when he tried to cover up the bungled Watergate burglary and bugging, Nixon however, did not have Bill Clinton's Teflon shield.

Impeachment: On December 19, the House voted to impeach Bill Clinton and on January 7, 1999 the Senate opened the trial. The charges were one count of perjury and obstruction of justice, the other count of perjury and the misuse of power charge were dropped. From the outset the Senate was split along partisan lines but public opinion clearly was against the impeachment of the president. Nevertheless, the Senate proceeded because the president was not above the law. The Senate needed a two-thirds majority to convict and it became clear that they would not get the sixty-seven votes needed to convict.

On February 12, 1999, the Senate voted. The perjury article lost with forty-five votes for impeachment and fifty-five against with ten Republican senators voting against; the obstruction of justice article split fifty-fifty with five Republicans voting against. After the vote, Clinton appeared on national TV and apologized to the nation for his actions and asked for healing.

Travelgate: In May 1993, the seven-member White House travel staff was fired without notice. The staff was quickly replaced by Clinton staffers, including his cousin, Catherine Cornelius. Since there was no reason for the firings, protests were lodged and most of the fired government workers were transferred to other jobs within a week with their pay and benefits intact. However, Billy Dale, the travel director, was not only not reinstated, but the Clinton administration asked for his FBI files and charged him with financial malfeasance. Dale, who had been there since the Kennedy administration, was a respected long-term government worker and there was no basis for the charges. After a thirty-month investigation, Dale was brought to trial. On November 16, 1995, a jury acquitted Dale in less than an hour-and-a-half of deliberations,. The prosecution of Dale was widely seen as malicious. In September of 1996, the Senate voted to pay for Dale's legal fees.

In January 1996, the House Government Reform and Oversight Committee subpoenaed the Dale records from the White House. White House Counsel Jack Quinn invoked executive privilege for the president and refused to turn over three thousand documents relating to the travel office dismissals. When the House of Representatives threatened Quinn with contempt of Congress for his refusal, he sent one-third of the requested documents to the House. In the documents, there was evidence that the White House had asked the FBI for Dale's confidential file. When asked about the improper request for confidential information, a White House spokesman said it was a clerical error. The chairman of the Oversight Committee, Congressman William Clinger then asked for a list of all requests by the White House for confidential files from the FBI. This led to "Filegate" (see below). In September 1996, the Oversight Committee issued a report on Travelgate admonishing the White House and saying that the administration had "engaged in an unprecedented misuse of executive power and executive privilege."

Filegate: After Congressman Clinger asked for a list of the FBI files requested by the White House it was discovered that hundreds of confidential files had been transferred to the White House. The Clinton administration at first said that the General Accounting Office (GAO) requested the files but the GAO refuted the allegation. Then the White House admitted that it had requested over three hundred files but that the files were never read! They also claimed they were working off an outdated list generated by the Secret Service (a charge that the Secret Service denied). When people on the list found out that their personal and confidential FBI files had been given to the White House they were indignant and threatened legal action for violating the Privacy Act. By mid-June 1996, the FBI revealed that over four hundred files were obtained by the Clinton administration for no real official purpose. FBI director Louis Freeh stated, "Unfortunately, the FBI and I were victimized."

Then a White House spokesman admitted that the purpose of obtaining the files was to reconstruct the background information on employees held over from the Bush administration. Investigative journalists found out that Democratic Party activists Craig Livingstone, the White House personnel security director, and Anthony Marceca, a civilian army investigator, were the White House staffers who were handling the files. They both denied any wrongdoing connected with the affair. Clinton when questioned about the files dismissed it as "... a completely honest bureaucratic SNAFU." Livingstone, however, was blamed for the affair and placed on leave.

When the House Oversight Committee questioned Livingstone, he revealed that the files were kept in an unsecured room, meaning that virtually anyone in the White House had access to the files. There was a gap in the log kept in the White House for FBI file requests from March to September 1994.

Livingstone said that apparently entries weren't made in the log, but his assistant contradicted his statement by saying she did make the entries and that they were now missing. In the meantime, Clinton's Chief of Staff, Leon Panetta, blamed faulty procedures and instituted new guidelines for the personnel security office. Attorney General Janet Reno asked that Independent Counsel Kenneth Starr investigate the matter. By the end of June 1996, Craig Livingstone resigned, while Marceca refused to testify citing the Fifth Amendment.

By the time the investigation wrapped up, 900–1,000 files in all had been obtained from the FBI. Allegations were made that the White House had put together a database of political enemies using the files. In the fall of 1999, Independent Counsel Robert Ray took over the investigation when Ken Starr resigned.

On March 16, 2000, Ray's report was made public. Ray concluded that there had been "no substantial and credible evidence" to link any important White House official to the acquisition of confidential FBI files. The non-partisan Judicial Watch, a government watchdog organization, was outraged by the Filegate fiasco and brought a $90 million class-action civil lawsuit against Hillary Clinton and others in the administration for violating the Privacy Act and other privacy laws.

Chinagate: One of the most troubling of all the scandals surrounding Bill Clinton was the allegations of taking money from foreign individuals, companies, and governments. Federal fundraising laws prohibit accepting money from foreigners and from non-profit organizations, as well as using federal property to raise funds for partisan purposes, including using federal phones, faxes, or real estate for such purposes. Bill Clinton had a long history of involvement with Chinese and Asian businessmen from his days in the governor's mansion in Arkansas. Allegations of favoritism toward China and other Asian nations abounded when it was discovered that numerous foreigners had contributed to the Democratic National Committee and the Clinton campaign for re-election.

The DNC at first refused to file a list of donors with the Federal Elections Commission as required, and this prompted the Republican National Committee to threaten court action. The DNC later only submitted partial lists, claiming bureaucratic errors and faulty record keeping.

In Clinton's defense, it has been American foreign policy for hundreds of years (literally from the inception of the republic) to open China and other Asian nations to trade with America. Since the 1700s, America has exported goods to China, notably American ginseng, furs, and manufactured goods. In return, Americans have gotten tea, silk, spices, and other goods. In more modern times China has also exported cheap manufacturer goods, which have been eagerly absorbed in the American market.

The controversy did not arise over trade with China, something that even a hardened anticommunist such as Richard Nixon saw as good for American commerce. It revolved around cronyism with Asian businessmen who were friends of Clinton. It revolved around the fact that the Clinton administration changed certain policies, such as reversing the ban on not admitting siblings of immigrants into the country, and conferring diplomatic recognition, trade rights, or preferred nation status on various countries. It also revolved around the fact that Clinton was involved in a desperate race for the White

House in 1996. No matter what the polls said, he still had to defeat his opponents and that took money.

Both Clinton and Gore were accused of using White House telephone equipment for fundraising activities, and Clinton was accused of staging fundraising social gatherings in the White House and then rewarding large contributors with overnight stays in the White House's Lincoln bedroom. These were charges verified by White House records but never prosecuted.

Gore attended a fundraising event at a Buddhist temple, a non-profit organization, that netted $140,000 for the DNC, but much of the money was later returned. Various contributors to the DNC and the Clinton campaign, including the Riadys, ethnic Chinese Indonesians who control the Lippo Group banking interests; John Huang, a Lippo agent and fundraiser for the DNC; John H. K. Lee of Cheong Am America, a subsidiary of a South Korean company; Johnny Chung, an alleged hustler and friend to (communist) Chinese businessmen; and Charlie Trie, a Little Rock restaurateur and a longtime friend of President Clinton, had questionable contributions. This was only a partial list of questionable donors. Cheong gave $250,000 that was returned by the DNC after the press broke the story. The DNC returned $366,000 from Johnny Chung because they could not verify the source of the money, and later Chung admitted that the communist Chinese government had given him money for the DNC. Then the DNC returned $187,000 of Mr. Trie's personal contribution and planned to return another $458,000 that he had gotten from other people. The DNC acknowledged that the funds appeared to be from foreign sources. All in all, the DNC gave back millions of dollars after the press blew the whistle on them.

Since much of the money was returned, the DNC and the Clinton campaign could not be prosecuted, but the policy-for-contributions connection remained. During the 1996 campaign, Clinton called for campaign finance reform on a number of occasions.

SUPREME COURT APPOINTMENTS: In 1993, Clinton nominated Ruth Bader Ginsberg to replace retiring Justice Byron White. Ginsberg, a respected liberal justice, taught at Columbia Law School and later became one of the first attorneys to bring lawsuits for sexual discrimination. She had been a federal appeals judge prior to her appointment. In 1994, after the retirement of Justice Harry Blackmun, Clinton named moderate Chief Justice of the Circuit Court Stephen Breyer as his replacement.

CLINTON PRAISED: "Democrats have made a wise choice this year that can bring the needed change....This year he has endured—and survived—the false and misleading political attacks on his character. He is a man of honesty and intregrity." —former President Jimmy Carter) *New York Times* July 15, 1992, p.A-12)

"Bill Clinton knows the course from here, past peril, to a new era of growth and progress for this nation that will enable us to share our power and our abundance with the world community...He knows adversity: he has lived it, in the years before he entered public life, and in the many years of hard challenges since then. And with each new challenge he has grown wiser and stronger, as he demonstrated with his remarkable resiliency and unflappability in the recent bruising primaries." —Governor Mario Cuomo of New York (*New York Times* July 16, 1992, p, A-12)

"He has been through the hottest fire American politics has ever had to test somebody. And he's come out like fine-tempered Pennsylvania steel." —Senator

Harris Wofford of Pennsylvania (*New York Times* November 2, 1992, p.A-12)

CLINTON CRITICIZED: "He needs to get a hard slap of reality in the face every once in a while. He has an arrogant side." --Robert Savage, political scientist, University of Arkansas (*Congressional Quarterly Weekly Report*, January 11, 1992, p.61)

"At the [Democratic] convention, Clinton was like a used care salesman peddling his vehicle for change. The wax job was shiny, the hubcaps sparkled, the upholstery was spotless, the paint was new. But when you look under the hood you discover he is hawking a model from the Seventies, a Carter mobile with the axle broken and the frame bent to the left." --Senator Phil Gramm of Texas (*New York Times*, August 19, 1992, p.1)

"He would unite the Presidency and the Congress to achieve one end above all others--more government. A government that taxes more, spends more, regulates more, encourages more lawsuits and shuts off more products from the markets that Americans create."--President George Bush (*New York Times*, September 18, 1992, p.A-9)

"As the case of military service makes most clear, these different positions are, in fact, more than mere flip-flops. They reflect a fundamental element of Governor Clinton's character: the triumph of expediency over principle, of convenience over truth. Governor Clinton says he is the candidate of change, but he truly is the changing candidate." --Vice President Dan Quayle (*New York Times*, September 24, 1992, p.A-12)

CLINTON QUOTES: "Politics is about economics. People forget that the New Deal was an economic program. A lot of social good came out of it, but it was economic program." (*Atlanta Journal*, May 19, 1985)

"I think many of the lessons of the Eighties--the importance of competition, market economics, and individual responsibility--will remain with us in the Nineties. But I think there will be a reassertion of our more liberal impulse...to see common solutions to common problems, particularly in the areas of education and the environment." (*Change: The Magazine of Higher Learning*, March/April, 1990, p.73)

"I refuse to be part of a generation that celebrates the death of communism abroad with the loss of the American Dream at home." --declaration of candidacy for president, October 3, 1991

"The reason I'm still in public life is because I've kept my commitments. That's why I'm still here, that's why I'm still standing here. And I'm sick and tired of all these people who don't know me, know nothing about my life, know nothing about the battles that I've fought, know nothing about the life I've lived, making snotty-nose remarks about how I haven't done anything in my life and it's all driven by ambition. That's bull, and I'm tired of it." (*New York Times*, March 28, 1992, p.9)

BOOKS BY CLINTON: *My Life* New York: Knopf, 2004.
Putting People First (with Al Gore. 1992.)

BOOKS ABOUT CLINTON: Allen, Charles F. and Portis, Jonathan. *The Comeback Kid: The Life and Career of Bill Clinton*. New York: Birch Lane Press, 1992.

More, Jim and Inde, Rick. Clinton: *Young Man in a Hurry*. New York: Summit, 1992.

43D PRESIDENT

NAME: George Walker Bush. He was named for his father, George Herbert Walker Bush, the 41st President, and paternal great-grandfather, George Herbert Walker. He is often referred to as "George W" and "Dubya" (i.e., "W," "double-you," or as they say in Texas, "Dub-ya"). He is never called "George Jr." Like Ronald (Wilson) Reagan and his son, Ronald (Prescott) Reagan, George W. and his father have different middle names. He was known as "Bushtail" as a child in Midland, Texas, and "the Bombastic Bushkin" as a young adult. In prep school at Andover, he was called "Lip" and "Tweeds Bush." When he joined Yale University's Skull and Bones Society, he was called "Temporary" because he couldn't come up with a better secret name for himself.

PHYSICAL DESCRIPTION: Bush is often described as handsome and resembles his father, complete with the Bush family trademark uneven grin. He has his father's blue eyes and brown hair, which is graying, but he isn't quite as tall. George W. stands six-feet tall and weighs 192 pounds. He has an athletic build and runs several miles a day, five days a week. Bush's pace is about seven-and-a-half minutes per mile. This pace is so fast that his security detail need bicycles to keep up with him. He has been exercising regularly since 1972. Bush had an appendectomy at age 10, minor surgery to his chest wall at age 13, arthroscopic knee surgery in 1997, and two benign polyps removed from his colon in July 1998. Bush has excellent cardiovascular fitness and displays no signs of coronary artery disease.

Bush has mild hearing loss in the high-frequency range due to flying jets, but his hearing is excellent in the speech frequencies. He is farsighted, which was advantageous when he was a pilot. According to his doctor in a 1999 report, "He has totally abstained from alcohol during the past 13 years. He has no history of any alcohol, drug, mental, or psychiatric treatment or rehabilitation."

Bush dresses conservatively, but often sports a silver belt buckle and cowboy boots and hat. He never dresses down for public appearances, but he sometimes dresses casually to meet reporters, and, of course, wears a jogging suit when he runs. When he was younger, he did not always take as much care in his dress. His post-college dressing style has been described as "indifferent," "careless," "wretched," and "ratty." Perhaps his careless dress came as a result of a rebellion against having to follow jacket-and-tie dress codes in prep school and college. His sartorial epiphany came, apparently, when he first ran for public office.

Bush is a good public speaker, but, like his father, he occasionally mangles the English language. He has a history of malapropisms, bizarre grammar, and statements with a sort of backward logic. The following are a few notable quotes by George W. Bush during the 2000 campaign: "I understand small business growth. I was one." "They misunderestimated me." "Rarely is the question asked: Is our children learning?" "I think if you know what you believe, it makes it a lot easier to answer questions. I can't answer your question." "I do know I'm ready for the job. And, if not, that's just the way it goes."

Despite his verbal gaffes, Bush is considered a good communicator. He speaks with something of a Texas drawl and is his best when he reads from a TelePrompTer and is more likely to misspeak when he ad-libs or answers questions.

PERSONALITY: George W. Bush is lively and outgoing. He has a quick wit and tells frequent jokes, thus enabling strangers to feel at ease in his presence. When he was younger, George W. was considered the life of the party, going to great lengths to generate fun. Friends of Bush think that he took on this fun persona while trying to cheer up his mother after his sister's death from leukemia when he was seven years old. He is often described as a "late bloomer" since he had a devil-may-care attitude toward life until he was about 40 years old.

When he was a young man, President Bush generally lived the life of a playboy, dating a variety of women and partying hard. He was apt to make outrageous statements, once telling the Queen of England that he was the black sheep of the family and asking her who was the black sheep of her family. He could be obnoxious when he drank too much and once challenged his father to a fight, to which the elder Bush only expressed his disappointment in his son. After his marriage and the birth of his daughters, Bush began to mature. He admitted he had been drinking too much because of the reversals that his oil company was then undergoing.

His wife, Laura, warned that she would leave him if he didn't ease up on his drinking. After a particularly bad hangover following his 40th birthday party, Bush quit drinking and says he hasn't had a drink since. The year before, he had rekindled his interest in religion.

About this time, Bush also found direction in his life by participating in politics. First, he helped in his father's campaign and then he ran for office himself. George W. Bush is intensely loyal, especially to his father. He does not allow anyone in his presence to speak ill of his father.

Despite reversals in his life, such as those he suffered in the oil business, Bush's self-confidence has never flagged. He is a well-centered person, knowing who and what he is and what he is capable of accomplishing. Bush is punctual and expects others to be also. He likes to maintain schedules that he sets and his life falls into routine patterns, such as getting up and feeding the family animals in the morning and running at lunchtime. He allots only five minutes for each appointment and allows almost no interruptions of his meetings with others, giving them his full attention.

Bush is fiercely competitive, and if he cannot best an opponent in a sport, he may use psychological distractions, especially humorous ones, in order to win. When he was young, friends said that you had to keep playing until George won.

ANCESTORS: His maternal grandfather was Marvin Pierce, president of the firm that published *Redbook* and *McCall's* magazines, and a distant relative of the nation's 14th president, Franklin Pierce. For his paternal line see "George Bush, 41st President," "Ancestors."

FATHER: George Herbert Walker Bush, 41st President of the United States. George H. W. Bush and George W. Bush are the first father-son presidential combination since John Adams and John Quincy Adams. George W. succeeded his father just eight years after the latter left office. John Quincy Adams was elected 24 years after his father left office.

MOTHER: Barbara Pierce Bush. For background information, see "George Bush, 41st President," "Marriage." Barbara Bush worked on George W. Bush's presidential campaign with the same vigor she gave to her husband's campaigns. She had a great influence in shaping her son's educational policy, which stressed literacy. Mrs. Bush has long been a literacy volunteer and advocate. George W. has more of his mother's personality; he often says he has his father's looks and his "mother's mouth." In his 2000 presidential nomination speech, Bush said, "And mother, everyone loves you and so do I. Growing up, she gave me love and lots of advice. I gave her white hair."

SIBLINGS: For more background information see "George Bush, 41st President," "Children."

John Ellis "Jeb" Bush (1953-   ) was a highly successful real estate developer with the Codina Bush Group. He won the Republican nomination for governor of Florida handily, but was defeated in 1994 by incumbent Governor Lawton Chiles in a very close race. He returned to his real estate firm and published a book, *Profiles in Character*. He created the Foundation for Florida's Future, a conservative think tank.

In 1998, Jeb Bush again campaigned for governor of Florida on an education platform and defeated incumbent Buddy MacKay by ten percentage points. He campaigned for his brother for president as did his son, George P. Bush, who appealed especially to young people and Hispanic groups. In addition to George P., who became a lawyer, Jeb has a daughter, Noelle, who was arrested in 2002 for illegally attempting to buy a prescription drug and later was found with cocaine while in a rehab facility, and another son, Jeb Jr., who also got in trouble with the law when he was discovered having sex in a underage girl in a parking lot.

Jeb is a workhorse, often the first to arrive at his office and the last to leave. It is believed that he aspired to run for president of the United States and was dismayed when George W. told him of his decision to run. Jeb sublimated his disappointment and turned his energies toward helping his brother's campaign. Jeb won re-election as governor by a landslide against President Clinton's former attorney general, Janet Reno.

Neil Bush (1955-   ) is a Houston businessman and director of Interlink, an international consulting firm. While others went to prison, Neil wound up paying only $50,000 to the Federal Deposit Insurance Corporation to settle a lawsuit regarding his failed Silverado savings and loan bank that cost investors hundreds of millions of dollars. He also worked on his father's presidential campaigns. He was married to Sharon Smith and has three children, Lauren, Pierce, and Ashley.

Lauren achieved some success as a model. He left Sharon in 2002 to marry a woman who had served his mother as a secretary. That woman divorced her husband and collected a $5-million settlement.

This inspired Sharon Bush to seek $5 million from Neil, but her quest was fruitless since he claimed he was "broke," and she settled for considerably less. After their split, Neil described before a congressional investigative committee how, when he visited cities in Asia, there would be a knock on the door and a pretty lady would be waiting there to spend the night with him. With a straight face, he said he never knew who sent them or who paid them. Sharon tried to sell a book about her wrecked marriage and the failure of the senior Bush couple to give her any support, material or spiritual, but no publisher was interested. At a lunch with Kitty Kelley, the self-proclaimed "Queen of Sleaze," Sharon accused President Bush of selling drugs. When Kelley's book, *The Family: The Real Story of the Bush Dynasty*, was published in 2004, Sharon denied making that statement, but Kelley had witnesses to prove otherwise.

Marvin Bush (1956-   ) lives in Alexandria, Virginia, with his wife, Margaret, and their two children, Marshall and Walker. He is a venture capitalist and has been a fundraiser for both his father's and his brother's presidential campaigns.

Dorothy "Doro" Koch (1959-   ) resides in Bethesda, Maryland, where she does fundraising for charities. She is married to her second husband, Robert Koch. She has two children from her first marriage, William and LeBlond, and two from her second marriage, Ellie and Sam. She, too, worked on her brother's presidential campaign as a fundraiser.

COLLATERAL RELATIVES: His mother, Barbara Pierce Bush, is a cousin, four times removed, of President Franklin Pierce. For other relatives see "George Bush, 41st President," "Collateral Relatives."

CHILDREN: Jenna and Barbara Bush, fraternal twins, were born November 25, 1981. The girls were named for their maternal and paternal grandmothers respectively. Ironically, Jenna is said to be the one who inherited Grandma Barbara's personality.

George W. says that being their father is the most important job he has. Both girls went to public schools in Midland, an Episcopal school in Austin for a short while, and graduated from Stephen F. Austin High School, also in Austin. In high school, Jenna was senior class president, while Barbara was homecoming queen. Jenna attended the University of Texas, and Barbara attended Yale University, like her father. Both girls graduated college in 2004, in the midst of their father's re-election campaign. The girls appeared together at the 2004 Republican National Convention in New York City where they exchanged very carefully scripted witty remarks.

BIRTH: Bush was born in New Haven, Connecticut, on July 6, 1946.

CHILDHOOD: The family moved to Texas when George W. was two years old. Bush was raised mostly in Midland, a flat stretch of oil-rich desert in West Texas. Midland is so flat that a humorous local tee shirt has a straight horizontal line with a tiny bump in it that says, "Ski Midland." When he was four-and-a-half-years old, his father wrote to a friend, "Georgie has grown to be a near-man, talks dirty once in a while and occasionally swears. He lives in his cowboy clothes."

When he was seven, Bush's younger sister died of leukemia, an event that had a tremendous impact on him and his family. After his sister's death, George W. grew closer to his mother, partly to comfort her and partly to keep her company while his father was away on business. As the eldest child (he was older than his next sibling, Jeb, by six-and-a-half years), George W. spent most of his time with his friends rather than his brothers and sister. By all accounts, Bush had a remarkably ordinary childhood. Midland was small, relatively crime-free, and typical of 1950s and 1960s America. While his family was not poor, Bush did not spend his childhood in affluence either.

He attended public schools and led a rather mundane middle-class existence, despite the fact that by the time George W. was ten, his father had become a millionaire. He played all sorts of sports, including dodgeball and baseball. He loved to play baseball, often to the detriment of his schoolwork. He would play pickup games in the field behind his house at 2703 Sentinel Street in Midland, which was a buffalo wallow with a man-made baseball field. He also played catcher for the Cubs, a Little League team, and once made Midland's Little League All-Star team.

George engaged in the usual childhood high jinks, such as shooting frogs with his BB gun and blowing up a few with firecrackers. He was known as a class clown, once drawing sideburns and a beard on his face to get a laugh from his classmates. This was a prank that he paid for with a drubbing by the school principal.

Both his father and mother had a good sense of humor, and it rubbed off on George W. He was popular, not because his family was important but because he was likable and didn't act superior to anyone else. The virtually unanimous consensus from friends and relatives was that Bush was typical of children of his milieu.

EDUCATION: George W. attended public schools until eighth grade. He attended Sam Houston Elementary School and San Jacinto Junior High, both in Midland. He only attended San Jacinto Junior High for one year, during which he played quarterback on the football team and was elected seventh-grade class president. He spent the eighth and ninth grades at the elegant and private Kinkaid School in Houston, where his family moved in 1959.

High school was the elite Phillips Academy, which his father also attended, a New England prep school also known as "Andover" because of its location in Andover, Massachusetts. At the time, it was an all-boys school. Bush was the head cheerleader for Andover's football team and played varsity basketball and baseball. As the head cheerleader, he and his buddies once dressed in drag, complete with stuffed bras and short skirts. When school officials thought that his comic pranks had gone too far and were a distraction from the football team, his fellow students came to his rescue in a school newspaper article headlined "In Defense of George Bush's Antics."

He was a popular student but not a distinguished one. He placed second in a student poll as "Big Man on Campus." He was a decent athlete but not a distinguished one. Bush claims his education policy is a result of the years he spent at Andover, which was more like a college than a high school.

Following in the footsteps of his father and grandfather, George W. Bush attended Yale from 1964 until 1968. He graduated with a major in history. He played baseball during his freshman year and rugby during his junior and senior years. He joined Delta Kappa Epsilon, his father's fraternity, and was later elected president of the brotherhood. The DKE or "Deke" fraternity was known as a hard-partying group replete with beer bashes and bands playing soul music. One of the hazing rituals was to ask pledges to name the other pledges. The first few pledges who were asked could only name a few fellow pledges and were embarrassed (the whole point of the exercise). When Bush was asked, however, he could name every one. His friends remarked that when he went to a party he would talk with everyone at that party. He had a remarkable talent for connecting with people and remembering their names and the conversation he had with them.

By all accounts, George W. was a typical college student; he went to classes, drank beer, dated girls, and engaged in silly behavior. When Yale beat Princeton on the road in a football game, George W. helped tear down the Princeton goalposts. He was escorted out of town by the Princeton campus police for this caper.

He was arrested for disorderly conduct at Yale for stealing a Christmas wreath. The charges against him were dismissed since no real harm had been done. Like his father, he was also a member of the Skull and Bones Society, an elite "secret" society that singles out promising students and trains them for leadership roles later in life. His opponent in the 2004 general election, John F. Kerry, was also a Skull and Bones Society member.

After Bush graduated from Yale in 1968, he joined the Air National Guard. In 1973, he applied to the University of Texas Law School but was not accepted. He entered Harvard Business School that year instead and earned a master's of business administration (MBA) in 1975.

Throughout his school years, including college, it appears that Bush did enough work just to get by, but never excelled at anything except people skills. He has often been mocked by comedians for being dumb, but his marks in school gave him a "C" average—not that much lower than his rival in 2000, Al Gore. The fact that he attended public schools, unlike his father, gave George W. an insight into how ordinary Americans thought and how they lived. If Bush learned anything at school, it was how to understand people and get along with them.

RELIGION: Methodist. As a youngster, Bush attended Episcopal and Presbyterian churches, his father's and mother's preferences respectively. As he grew older, he generally attended Presbyterian services, but that depended on where he was living and which church was more convenient to attend. After he married, George W. attended the Methodist church, which is his wife's preference. When he was younger, George W. wasn't particularly religious, although he was raised in a religious household and served as an altar boy. When he matured, however, he developed a deep commitment to Christianity. Two incidents in his life transformed him: One was meeting evangelist Billy Graham, the other was his friend Don Evans gift of a 365-day version of the Bible and Evans's suggestion that Bush join his Bible study group.

Bush's parents arranged a meeting with Billy Graham at their Kennebunkport, Maine, home in the summer of 1985, and Bush was immediately taken with the charismatic Graham. They held long conversations about spiritual matters amid the natural splendors of the Maine coast. After that meeting, Bush read the Bible every day. The readings were made easier by Evans's gift, which was specially designed to read a selection from the Old Testament, New Testament, Psalms, and Proverbs daily. Bush still reads the Bible every day.

George W. Bush's religious revival coincided with his father's planning for a 1988 presidential bid. George W. worked as a liaison for his father's campaign with many members of the religious right. By doing so, he got to know and work with a group that became a part of his later constituency. Christian conservatives such as Ralph Reed and Pat Robertson became his allies. His knowledge of the Bible and his experience in the Bible classes allowed him to deal with the Christian right in a way that his father never could.

He once had a discussion with his mother about who gets into heaven. George W. maintained that non-Christians, according to the Bible, do not go to heaven. His mother disagreed and called up Billy Graham for some expert advice on the subject. Graham sided with the younger Bush, but added that one should not answer questions to which only God really knows the answers.

While the Christian evangelical right is a key component of his voting block, Bush claims not to be under its control. While governor of Texas, he infuriated some traditional Christians by denying their request to commute the death sentence of convicted murderess Karla Faye Tucker, who, while in jail, became a born-again Christian. They argued that she had repented and should be spared. Bush said that under Texas law, he couldn't commute the sentence, but it is doubtful that he would have even if he could since he is a firm believer in personal responsibility. Bush has shown himself insensitive to death-penalty cases, particularly where African-Americans are involved. For example, he refused to commute the death sentence of a young African-American boy who was shown to have the intelligence of an eight-year-old.

George W. Bush's religious beliefs can be characterized as devout but not fanatical. On the other hand, he is insensitive to the feelings of people who don't share his own superstitious beliefs. For example, as governor, he proclaimed "Jesus Day" in Texas for three straight years, ignoring separation-of-church-and-state doctrine and showing no concern for people who believed other than the way he did. His lack of understanding of or concern for the constitutional separation of church and state was made evident again and again by his actions as president.

Bush and his wife were members of the First United Methodist Church in Midland, where they were married and where their daughters were baptized. In 1989, Bush transferred the family membership to Highland Park United Methodist Church in Dallas. While in the governor's mansion, the family attended the Tarrytown United Methodist Church in Austin. After Bush led America into the invasion and occupation of Iraq, author and journalist Bob Woodward asked him in an interview if he ever consulted his father, the former president. He replied, "I consult a higher authority."

RECREATION: There is one thing that G. W. Bush is fanatical about: baseball. As a youngster and a young man, Bush played the game with enthusiasm. He was a catcher in Little League and a pitcher in college. He was never an outstanding player, but he compensated for his average skills by psyching out his opponents with a nonstop verbal assault.

Bush has been quoted as saying, "I never dreamed about being president. When I was growing up, I wanted to be Willie Mays." He started attending baseball games when he was a baby and his father played for Yale. His uncle, George Herbert Walker, was one of the owners of the New York Mets and took him to the games. As a youngster in Houston, he would watch the Astros at the Astrodome, especially if they played the Mets. He collected baseball cards and memorized the statistics. In Midland, he attended minor league games with Don Evans.

When he became part owner and managing partner of the Texas Rangers, a Major League baseball team, George W. was in his element. He shunned a private luxury box and would sit in the stands among the fans, handing out autographs and specially made baseball cards of himself. He may not have been Willie Mays, but this was the next best thing. He is still a Rangers fan, and he carries an electronic gadget that allows him to keep track of Rangers games when he can't watch them in person or on TV.

Bush also plays golf, and his handicap is "a legitimate fifteen" according to *Golf Magazine* reporter Harry Hurt. Overall, George W. is much too impatient to play golf and is not as avid a player as his father; instead, he plays video golf.

George W. often plays with his dog, Spot, an English springer spaniel, usually playing fetch with a rubber ball. He also has two cats, India and Ernie. Ernie has six toes and is named for Ernest Hemingway, who had a penchant for six-toed cats. George W. feeds the family pets every day as part of his morning routine.

Other sports George W. Bush engages in are hunting and fishing. He owns a few shotguns and hunts doves. He is a fan of country music and the Southern rock band ZZ Top. He reads few books and likes to play computer solitaire and surf the Internet.

MARRIAGE: Laura Welch Bush is an attractive woman with dark brown hair and striking blue eyes. She was born in Midland, Texas, to Harold and Jenna Welch. Her father was a house builder, and her mother kept the books for his firm. From a very early age, Laura aspired to become a teacher. Her father offered to send her to law school, but she opted to study education instead. She earned a bachelor's degree in education from Southern Methodist University and a master's degree in library science from the University of Texas at Austin. She was a librarian and taught in racially integrated public schools in Dallas, Houston, and Austin from 1968 to 1977.

Laura Welch met George W. Bush at a backyard barbeque held by their mutual friends Joe and Jan O'Neill in Midland in 1977. Curiously, Laura and George W. had crossed paths many times over the years, although neither of them remembered the other. Three months after meeting Laura in 1977, Bush married her in the First United Methodist Church in Midland.

Laura Bush's personality is almost the complete opposite of her husband's. Friends say that she is reserved compared to the highly outgoing George W. "I think I temper that personality," she said, referring to her husband's brashness, "but I also think that he makes life much more exciting for me."[1]

In 1981, Laura gave birth to fraternal twin girls. This was a blessed event for the Bushes since Laura experienced difficulty getting pregnant and was seriously considering adoption when she found out she was going to have children of her own. Her pregnancy was complicated by toxemia, a blood infection, and it was at first feared that she would lose one of the twins.

Laura, like her mother-in-law, Barbara Bush, is a literacy advocate. She has had a lifelong love of reading and literature. This is quite a contrast to her husband, who claims to read few books and boasts that he doesn't read newspapers. Mrs. Bush also takes an interest in women's health issues and is a breast cancer awareness advocate.

Prior to his marriage, George W. dated numerous women including Tricia Nixon, daughter of then-President Richard Nixon, and Christina Cassini, the beautiful daughter of fashion designer Oleg Cassini and actress Gene Tierney. In 1967, when he was a junior at Yale, George W. was engaged to Cathy Wolfman, a high-school cheerleader and student at Rice University in Houston. Shortly after graduation in 1968, the couple split up. Bush remained a bachelor until he was 31 years old.

Bush's marriage to Laura Welch was a turning point in his life. He gradually gave up his partying ways and settled down. Friends say that the Bushes' marriage has had its ups and downs, like any marriage, but that the two are a devoted couple. While Bush may have played the field when he was younger, friends say that he has been faithful to his wife.

MILITARY SERVICE: In May of 1968, just prior to his graduation from Yale, George W. Bush enlisted as an airman in the Texas Air National Guard with the 147th Fighter Group. Since there were no student deferments for graduate school, it is widely believed that Bush enlisted to avoid duty in the Vietnam War. After completing basic training at Lackland Air Force Base in Texas, Bush was briefly put on inactive duty while he worked for the Senate campaign of Edward Gurney in Florida. He applied to be a pilot, was commissioned as a second lieutenant, and took his flight training in Georgia. Bush has been criticized for his leap from airman to second lieutenant, but it is not uncommon in the armed forces for a pilot to become an officer.

In December 1969, George W. earned his National Guard pilot wings and was stationed at Ellington Air Force Base in Houston, Texas. In 1970, he graduated from Combat Crew Training School as a certified fighter pilot and for the next two years responded to alerts and drills frequently. In September 1972, Bush was allowed to transfer to the 187th Tactical Reconnaissance Group in Montgomery, Alabama, where he also worked on "Red" Blount's Senate race. In 1973, he was discharged from the service in order to enter Harvard Business School.

Some say Bush received preferential treatment in the Air National Guard, and to a certain extent, that may be true. Records have been conveniently lost. Then again, his preferred status may have had more to do with the fact that he was willing to undergo dangerous and time-consuming fighter-pilot training than the status of his father, who at that time was a U.S. congressman from Texas. George W. was given time off from his military duties to work on political campaigns, but the Air National Guard is not the Air Force, it is only a part-time job, and a leave of absence for a good reason is not uncommon. It is true that George W. was discharged from the service eight months early. His superiors, however, recognized that there was no real sense in keeping him for a few more months when the planes he flew, F-102s, were being phased out of service and retraining him on another type of plane would not be cost effective.

CAREER BEFORE THE PRESIDENCY: In 1968, Bush worked on the Senate campaign of Edward Gurney. In 1970, he worked on his father's unsuccessful campaign for Senate. In 1971, he held a position for nine months as a management trainee with Stratford of Texas, an agricultural company. In 1972, he was the political director for William "Red" Blount's losing Senate campaign in Alabama. In 1973, he was a counselor for nine months at the Professional United Leadership League (PULL), a mentoring program for Houston's inner-city children. Later that year, he entered Harvard Business School, from which he graduated in 1975.

After Harvard, George W. returned to Midland, which was experiencing an oil boom. He had money left over from his education trust fund and used it as seed money to break into the oil business. At first he worked as a landman, a broker who looks up land titles for oil companies and tries to buy or lease the land for them. In June 1977, Bush incorporated Arbusto Oil company (*arbusto* is Spanish for bush), although the company did not begin actual operations until the end of the following year. In the meantime, he decided that he would run for the congressional seat vacated by Texas Representative George Mahon.

While Bush considered himself a native Texan, he was characterized by his opponent, Democrat Kent Hance, as a Yankee from the Northeast due to his prep school and college education in New England. Bush lost that race, but learned some valuable lessons in public perception and the power of the Christian right, who criticized him for attending a rally where alcohol was served.

Bush resumed his business career and raised money for Arbusto. While his name and family connections helped in capitalizing the firm, Arbusto began to be called "El Busto" because of its poor performance. In 1982, Arbusto was renamed the Bush Exploration Company and recapitalized through a public offering of stock. The influx of capital was short lived as the oil boom subsided and Bush found it ever more difficult to acquire investors in the firm.

Two years later, Bush Exploration Company merged with Spectrum 7. George W. took over as chairman and CEO of the newly merged companies. In 1986, Spectrum 7 was sold to Harken Oil and Gas, one of whose investors was billionaire George Soros. (Soros would later consider Bush "the worst president our country has ever suffered" and spend more than $25 million of his own money to defeat Bush in 2004.) Bush became a Harken board member and consultant to the company. He has been criticized as a business failure, but Bush made money while others in the industry went broke. His talent lay not in discovering new oil and gas wells but in finding investors, many of whom used their losses as tax write-offs.

Before Bush decided to dispose of his stock, in June, 1990, the attorney for Harken warned him that he was acting on inside information. Bush, nevertheless, went ahead and sold his 212,140 shares for a net profit of $848,560. Shortly after, the stock fell from $4 to $1.25. A subsequent Securities and Exchange Commission (SEC) investigation concluded that it would not indict him for insider trading. Critics charge that this decision was made by members of the board, many of whom were close friends of the Bush family. As president, Bush refused to authorize the SEC to release its investigation report.[2] Bush's defense was his claim that he had filed his intention to sell on time and that the SEC had misplaced it.

Now George W. Bush's life took a new direction. He moved out of the oil business and into politics. He joined his family in Washington, D.C., and worked on his father's 1988 presidential campaign. It was during this time that he forged the alliances that were to help him in his later bids for political office, especially with Christian conservatives. After his father's victory, George W. led a transition team that apportioned jobs in the White House. With his work in Washington done, George W. returned to Texas intent on seeking a political office of his own. He was, however, advised against it by friends who pointed out to him that his accomplishments were few and that he would be perceived as riding on his father's coattails.

At the time, the Texas Rangers Major League Baseball team was for sale. He was approached to see if he was interested in putting together a group of investors to buy the team. For Bush, this was a deal made in heaven. It allowed him to combine his love of baseball with his talent for raising money. In 1989, he was introduced to investors who preferred to be silent partners while he served as the frontman, handling the day-to-day business of the team.

Bush bought the team from Eddie Chiles, a family friend, for $75 million. He invested $606,302 of his own money and became one of two managing general partners with Rusty Rose. Bush turned this job into a highly visible position by shunning the owner's box and mixing with the fans in the stands. The television exposure he received throughout Texas made him a household name.

The popularity of Bush and his baseball team soared to the point where, in 1991, he persuaded the residents of Arlington, Texas, to pass a referendum to raise $135 million through a sales tax to finance a new ball park for the Rangers. The new park greatly increased the value of the team and was opened at the beginning of the 1994 season. Bush's duties with the Rangers prevented him from taking part in his father's 1992 presidential re-election campaign.

In 1993, George W. threw his hat into the ring for the Texas gubernatorial election against popular incumbent Governor Ann Richards. Bush ran on four issues: welfare reform, raising the standards of public education, stricter penalties for juvenile crime, and reforming the tort (lawsuit) laws by reducing damages to reasonable amounts. He ran a simple but very effective campaign. His opponent made the mistake of ad hominem attacks, but he, in turn, did not attack her personally and stuck to the issues. He received endorsements from the largest newspapers in Texas and won 53 percent of the vote to Richards's 46 percent.

After the election, Bush gave up his managing general partner position with the Rangers and in 1998, sold his interest in the team for nearly $15 million. While George W. had not been poor before this, the sale of the Rangers gave him and his family financial security.

Bush's record as governor of Texas was mixed at best. He was successful in the area of juvenile crime. Young offenders were given a 16-hour-a-day routine to follow to instill discipline and to eliminate easy jail time. The age at which juveniles could be tried as adults was lowered, and those who illegally used a gun were given mandatory sentences. The "tough love" attitude toward juvenile crime resulted in lower crime rates for young offenders for the first time in a decade, especially for violent crime, which decreased by 38 percent. Adult crime decreased as well by 13 percent overall and by 20 percent for violent crime. This was partly due to the virtual abolishment of parole for violent and sex offenders, and partly due to the authorization of faith-based programs designed to reduce recidivism.

In the area of education, local control of schools was re-established, standards were raised, students who did not qualify for promotion to the next grade were held back, and reading comprehension was made a priority. There was a new emphasis on accountability, linking student performance to bonuses and promotions for the school district administrators. The result was that reading performance, especially among minority students, went up dramatically.

Bush wanted to cut taxes and got a billion-dollar tax cut for the rich, paid for by budget surpluses, passed. His initial plan to cut property taxes and raise sales taxes and taxes on businesses was opposed by many legislators, even Republicans, and failed to pass. While Bush slowed the growth of state spending to about 3.5 percent, he could not reverse the trend of ever-increasing government outlays.

Bush's tort reform, on the other hand, was criticized as benefiting the insurance companies, although that benefit was, in some small measure, passed on to consumers in the form of lower rates. His get-tough-on-crime measures, especially his advocacy of the death penalty, drew criticism as well.

While Bush was a conservative governor, he wasn't considered an extremist. When he ran for re-election as governor in November 1998, more than two out of three people voted for him over his opponent, Democratic land commissioner Garry Mauro. In 1997, early polls indicated that he was a front-runner for the GOP presidential nomination, and in 1999, he started a presidential exploratory committee. He put his excellent fund-raising abilities to work and amassed a war chest holding a record $36 million by July of 1999. By the end of the campaign, his funds had reached more than $175 million.

REPUBLICAN PRESIDENTIAL NOMINATION 2000: At the beginning of the campaign, the list of Republican presidential candidates was a long one: John McCain, a senator from Arizona; Elizabeth Dole, former secretary of labor; Alan Keyes, a conservative radio talk-show host; Lamar Alexander, a former Tennessee governor; Bob Smith, a senator from New Hampshire; Dan Quayle, former vice president; Steve Forbes, publisher and financier; Orrin Hatch, a senator from Utah; John Kasich, a congressman from Ohio; Donald Trump, wealthy real estate mogul and casino owner; Pat Buchanan, writer and former presidential hopeful; Gary Bauer, a conservative activist; and George W. Bush, governor of Texas. Buchanan and Trump dropped out of the crowded Republican race and vied for the Reform Party nomination, which Buchanan eventually won. Bob Smith dropped out of the Republican Party and ran as an Independent; he later gave up his Independent bid and rejoined the Republicans.

By the middle of July, John Kasich, who couldn't raise enough money, withdrew his bid and endorsed Bush. On August 14, 1999, Bush won the Iowa straw poll, a non-binding indicator of the Iowa caucuses to come. Two days later, Lamar Alexander also dropped out of the race citing poor performance in the Iowa poll and empty campaign coffers. Quayle and Dole followed, citing the inability to compete with Bush in raising funds. In November 1999, Bush was surprised by reporters who asked him the names of the leaders of some foreign countries; he didn't know the answer to their questions. At the end of the month, Bush called for $484 billion in tax cuts. By the end of December 1999, Bush had raised $67 million in campaign contributions.

In January 2000 Bush won the Iowa caucuses closely followed by Steve Forbes. Orrin Hatch dropped out of the primaries after garnering only 1 percent of the Iowa vote. February was a pivotal month for Bush. On February 1, 2000, John McCain won the New Hampshire primary with Bush in second place and Forbes a distant third. After New Hampshire, Gary Bauer pulled out of the race.

On February 8, 2000, Bush decisively won the Delaware primary with McCain a distant second. In the same primary, Steve Forbes garnered only 20 percent of the vote after extensive campaigning; he then dropped out of the race. At the end of the month, Bush won the South Carolina primary by 11 percentage points over McCain. Alan Keyes was a distant third with 5 percent of the vote and was never a real factor in any of the presidential primaries. On February 22, 2000, McCain won the Michigan primary by seven percentage points and his home state of Arizona by a whopping 24 percent over Bush.

On March 8, 2000, in the Super Tuesday primaries, Bush carried the populous states of California, New York, and Ohio, as well as Georgia, Maryland, Maine, Missouri, and Minnesota. The next day, McCain withdrew and left the field to Bush. On July 25, 2000, Bush selected Dick Cheney as his running mate and on August 3, 2000, he accepted the Republican presidential nomination in Philadelphia.

OPPONENTS: Al Gore (Albert Arnold Gore) (1948-   ). For background information, see "Bill Clinton, 42nd President," "Vice-President." Al Gore was probably one of the strongest vice presidents in American history. He was a presidential candidate in the 1988 campaign but dropped out after a poor showing in the primaries. Nevertheless, his popularity grew, and he was considered one of the

Democratic front-runners in the 1992 campaign but decided not to run, probably due to the unprecedented approval rating of George H. W. Bush. During the 1992 presidential campaign, the unexpected happened: a third-party candidate, Ross Perot, began to draw enormous numbers of votes away from the elder Bush. Since Gore was not in the race, the Democratic front-runner became Bill Clinton, a dark horse candidate from Arkansas. Clinton understood Gore's popularity and asked him to run on his ticket as vice president. Gore accepted the invitation, hoping to use the vice presidency as a springboard to the White House. Perot split the conservative vote and propelled Clinton into the White House with a plurality of votes.

In August 1993, while serving as vice president, Gore cast the tie-breaking vote in the Senate (as president of the Senate) to pass Bill Clinton's economic package. This was a major breakthrough for the Clinton administration, which had to deal with mainly Republican majorities in Congress.

In preparation for the 1996 presidential campaign, Gore was accused of inappropriately raising funds for the effort by using government offices and phones to carry on partisan activities and was implicated in accepting illegal campaign funds from a foreign country. An investigation was called for, but nothing happened until after he and Bill Clinton won re-election. In November 1998, Democratic Attorney General Janet Reno refused to appoint an independent counsel to investigate the affair. Throughout the Monica Lewinsky scandal and subsequent impeachment process, Al Gore supported Bill Clinton, even while trying to distance himself from the president.

In December 1998, Gore announced his candidacy for the Democratic presidential nomination. His only serious opposition was Bill Bradley, former National Basketball Association Knicks star player and senator from New Jersey. Gore tried to lose the image of a Washington Beltway insider by moving his campaign headquarters to Nashville, Tennessee (his home state), but his ploy of trying to appear as a regular guy really didn't wash with the reality of his privileged upbringing. Nevertheless, he was exceedingly popular among Democratic rank-and-file members, and when he won both the Iowa caucuses and the New Hampshire primary, it eliminated Bradley from the race, and the nomination was his. In early August, Gore selected Joseph Lieberman, a Jewish Democratic senator from Connecticut, as his running mate. On August 17, 2000, Gore accepted the Democratic presidential nomination in Los Angeles.

Gore's campaign suffered from numerous ill-advised image changes designed to counteract George W. Bush's growing popularity. He tried to project himself as more forceful and not just Clinton's second banana. He adopted a reformist image, which didn't quite work since he was trying to reform the very system that he had helped establish and of which he was a part. He attacked Bush's proposals as all wrong, but his alternatives were not much different.

When Bush's "compassionate conservatism" rhetoric began to affect the polls, Gore moved away from his more forceful image and toward an image of an intellectual with sensitivity to others. Despite all of his campaign posturing, Gore's popularity did not wane, but independent voters failed to see any real difference between him and George W. Bush on the issues.

Ralph Nader (1934-) was the Green Party candidate, and while he did not have any real chance to win the election, his candidacy held the swing votes in the states where the Gore-Bush race was close. It is ironic that a candidate whose platform rested originally on environmental issues would undermine the election of Al Gore, who had been an environmental champion. There was, however, considerable disillusionment among liberals with the Clinton administration, and a percentage of them voted for Nader as the more principled choice. Since the large mass of independent voters would have split fairly evenly between Bush and Gore, Nader's presidential run hurt Gore by drawing off liberal voters. Had Al Gore received the majority of Nader's 90,000 votes in Florida, the election would have been his.

Patrick Buchanan (1938-   ) was the Reform Party candidate, but not before an acrimonious split in the party and several lawsuits that tried to prevent his candidacy. The Reform Party that Ross Perot had built, mainly on the charisma of his personality, virtually disintegrated from internal squabbles. Buchanan didn't even come close to his previous popularity as a Republican hopeful.

Harry Browne (1933-   ) was the Libertarian Party candidate, and his claim to fame was a book he wrote called *How I Found Freedom in an Unfree World.* Much of the Libertarian platform had been co-opted by the Republican Party, and many Libertarians had deserted their party for the Republicans during the Reagan years. Browne, like Buchanan, was never a serious factor in the election.

CAMPAIGN AND THE ISSUES, 2000: As he did in his gubernatorial races, Bush focused on a few key issues: education, Social Security and Medicare, tax cuts, military overhaul and welfare reform. His speeches, time and again, focused on the slogan "prosperity with a purpose." In his acceptance speech for the Republican presidential nomination, he said, "This is a remarkable moment in the life of our nation. Never has the promise of prosperity been so vivid. . . . Prosperity can be a tool in our hands—used to build and better our country. Or it can be a drug in our system—dulling our sense of urgency, of empathy, of duty. . . . So tonight we vow to our nation . . . .We will use these good times for great goals."

"Prosperity with a purpose" dovetailed with another of Bush's campaign slogans: "compassionate conservatism." George W. Bush was probably the first Republican president since Lincoln who talked about compassion. In his acceptance speech for the Republican presidential nomination, he said, "When these [social] problems aren't confronted, it builds a wall within our nation. On one side are wealth and technology, education and ambition. On the other side of the wall are poverty and prison, addiction and despair. And, my fellow Americans, we must tear down that wall."

"Big government is not the answer. But the alternative to bureaucracy is not indifference. It is to put conservative values and conservative ideas into the thick of the fight for justice and opportunity. This is what I mean by compassionate conservatism."

Gore and Bush, the two major candidates, were not far apart on the issues, except for abortion, which Gore favored up to the second trimester and Bush only favored in cases of rape, incest, or when the mother's life was at stake. On the environment, Bush favored a more decentralized approach while Gore took a more proactive stance. Both of the major candidates were primarily political centrists, and the main contention on the other issues was more a matter of how to go about things rather than any real philosophical division.

ELECTION AS PRESIDENT, FIRST TERM, NOVEMBER 7, 2000: The 2000 presidential election was the most controversial and bitterly contested election since the 1876 presidential race between Rutherford B. Hayes and Samuel J. Tilden. On November 7, election night, confusion reigned as the media projected Al Gore the winner, only to retract the projection later that night. In the early hours of November 8, an executive at Fox News who happened to be George's first cousin declared George W. Bush the winner. Florida was the state with the pivotal electoral votes. Had Gore carried his own state of Tennessee, the election would have been over.

Gore called Bush to concede the election but retracted his concession when the media reported that Bush's lead was evaporating and some heavily Democratic districts in Florida were yet to be counted. By November 9, Bush was ahead by slightly less than 2,000 votes. Because of the slim margin, Florida law demanded that the votes be recounted in all counties by machine tabulation. At the end of the machine recount, Bush led by only 327 votes.

Democrats then demanded hand recounts in four heavily Democratic counties (Volusia, Broward, Palm Beach, and Miami-Dade). Hand or manual recounting is a process that is mandated in close elections under Florida law. While the Democrats pushed for hand recounts, the Republicans declined to exercise their privilege to ask for them. The law, however, was unclear as to the proper procedure to follow for hand recounts.

At this point, partisan politics played its corrupting role. Bush sued in federal district court to stop the hand recounts, despite the fact that the election had not yet been certified and the absentee ballots were still being counted. Democrats complained of irregularities in the counting of absentee ballots, while Republicans complained of irregularities in the hand counting. Numerous lawsuits were filed. Bush's suit to stop manual recounts was denied by the federal district court. November 14 was the deadline prescribed by Florida law to certify the election results with the exception of the absentee ballots. Gore sued to push back the date. A Florida state judge ruled the deadline was valid but allowed for further recounts at a later date. Florida's secretary of state, Katherine Harris, a Republican, refused to accept hand recounts. Democrats in the four counties sued to extend the deadline, and the Florida Supreme Court ruled that the hand recounts could continue, but did not rule on whether those recounts were required to be included in the certified total. A lower court allowed Ms. Harris to certify the vote on November 17, but was overruled by the Florida Supreme Court. By November 18, the absentee ballots were counted, and Bush led by 930 votes, although the vote still had not been certified.

On November 21, the Florida Supreme Court unanimously ruled that the hand recounts had to be included in the tally of votes. All of the Florida Supreme Court justices had been appointed by Democratic governors and were perceived to be partisan. The court set a deadline of 5 P.M. on November 26 for submission of the hand recounts. The Republicans appealed this decision to the U.S. Supreme Court, arguing that the Florida Supreme Court's decision amounted to an ex-post facto rewriting of the election law, especially regarding the deadline extension.

It was now Thanksgiving Day weekend, and Miami-Dade County officials decided not to recount, declaring there wasn't enough time for the procedure. Gore sued, demanding that they continue, but lost his suit in the Florida Supreme Court. Volusia, Broward, and Palm Beach counties continued the hand recounts amid controversy over the interpretation of what constituted a valid or invalid vote, since legal guidelines were lacking.

After 5 P.M. on November 26, Katherine Harris certified the vote with George W. Bush in the lead by 537 votes. Volusia and Broward counties had made the hand recount deadline, but Palm Beach was late and was not included in the tally. The next day, Gore sued to contest the election yet again and asked the Leon

County Circuit Court in the state capital to order that the disputed undervote ballots (i.e., ballots that did not register a vote for president on the machine count) in Miami-Dade and Palm Beach counties be submitted for a hand recount.

The judge denied his suit, and the case was appealed to the Florida Supreme Court. Meanwhile, on December 1, the U.S. Supreme Court heard Bush's appeal. Bush's lawyers reasoned that Article II of the U.S. Constitution gave the appointment of electors to the state legislature and not to the courts. The U.S. Supreme Court sidestepped the issue by sending it back to the Florida Supreme Court for explanation. On December 8, the seven Florida Supreme Court justices ruled in a 4-3 split decision that manual recounts of undervotes must continue and widened the field by declaring that all counties with such under-votes had to do a hand recount.

The court gave Gore 383 votes from previous hand recounts that had not been certified. Also on December 8, the partisanship of the Democratic Florida Supreme Court was matched by the partisanship of the Republican Florida state legislature. The lower house announced its prerogative in appointing the state's electors to the Electoral College if the election was still in dispute by the December 12 constitutional deadline. The next day, the U.S. Supreme Court agreed to hear a Bush appeal of the Florida Supreme Court decision and in a 5-4 decision (in which they oddly emphasized that their decision should not and would not serve as precedent for future election disputes) ordered a halt to manual recounts and upheld the certification of the vote. The next day, Al Gore conceded the race to Bush.

On December 12, the Republican-dominated lower house of the Florida legislature voted to appoint a slate of electors to the Electoral College to elect George W. Bush. Thus, after numerous lower court suits, Florida State Supreme Court suits, and two appeals to the U.S. Supreme Court, George W. Bush won the election with one electoral vote to spare.

ELECTION AS PRESIDENT, FIRST TERM, NOVEMBER 7, 2000

Popular Vote: George W. Bush (Republican) 50,456,167 (48%); Al Gore (Democrat) 50,996,064 (48.5%); Ralph Nader (Green Party) 2,864,810 (2.7%); Patrick Buchanan (Reform Party) 448,750 (0.4%); Harry Browne (Libertarian Party) 386,024 (0.4%).

Electoral Vote: Bush 271; Gore 266; Abstentions 1. One Gore elector from the District of Columbia, Barbara Lett-Simmons, submitted a blank ballot to protest the lack of representation of the district in Congress.

States Carried: Bush won the electoral votes of 30 states: Alabama, Alaska, Arizona, Arkansas, Colorado, Florida, Georgia, Idaho, Indiana, Kansas, Kentucky, Louisiana, Mississippi, Missouri, Montana, Nebraska, Nevada, New Hampshire, North Carolina, North Dakota, Ohio, Oklahoma, South Carolina, South Dakota, Tennessee, Texas, Utah, Virginia, West Virginia, Wyoming. It is noteworthy that Bush carried Gore's home state of Tennessee and Bill Clinton's home state of Arkansas. Gore won the electoral votes of the District of Columbia and twenty states: California, Connecticut, Delaware, Hawaii, Illinois, Iowa, Maine, Maryland, Massachusetts, Michigan, Minnesota, New Jersey, New Mexico, New York, Oregon, Pennsylvania, Rhode Island, Vermont, Washington, Wisconsin.

REPUBLICAN NOMINATION FOR RE-ELECTION AS PRESIDENT, 2004:
Bush ran unopposed.

OPPONENTS: John Forbes Kerry (1943-   ) of Massachusetts was the Democratic candidate. Kerry was the junior U.S. senator from Massachusetts. He was born on December 11, 1943, at Fitzsimons Military Hospital in Denver, Colorado, where his father, Richard, a test pilot in the Army Air Corps during World War II, was recovering from a bout with tuberculosis. His mother, Rosemary, was a life-long community activist, environmentalist, and devoted parent. Not long after Kerry's birth, his family settled in Massachusetts. Kerry was raised a Catholic and continued to be an active member of the Catholic Church.

His father was a Foreign Service officer in the Eisenhower administration, so Kerry traveled around the world a great deal when he was young. On these trips, he learned firsthand the value of building strong alliances with other nations. These experiences would later inform his foreign policy positions.

As he was graduating from Yale University, Kerry volunteered to serve in Vietnam, because, as he later said, "It was the right thing to do." He believed that "to whom much is given, much is required." Kerry served two tours of duty in Vietnam. On his second tour, he volunteered to serve on a Swift Boat in the river deltas, one of the most dangerous assignments of the war. He was awarded a Silver Star, a Bronze Star with Combat V, and three Purple Hearts.

By the time Kerry returned home from Vietnam, he questioned decisions he believed were being made to protect those in positions of authority in Washington at the expense of the soldiers carrying on the fighting in Vietnam. Kerry was a cofounder of the Vietnam Veterans of America and became a spokesman for the Vietnam Veterans Against the War. In April 1971, testifying before the Senate Foreign Relations Committee, Kerry asked the question of his fellow citizens, "How do you ask a man to be the last man to die for a mistake?" for which he would become widely known. Democratic Senator Claiborne Pell of Rhode Island thanked Kerry, then age 27, for testifying before the committee, expressing his hope that Kerry "might one day be a colleague of ours in this body."

Fourteen years later, Kerry had the opportunity to fulfill that hope—serving with Senator Pell as a member of the Senate Foreign Relations Committee. In the intervening years, Kerry graduated from Boston College Law School and found different ways to fight for those things in which he believed, such as holding the political system accountable.

In 1982, Kerry was elected lieutenant governor of Massachusetts. Two years later, he was elected to the U.S. Senate with a reputation for independence and strong conviction—and reinforced that reputation by making tough choices on difficult issues such as breaking with many in his own party to support the Gramm-Rudman Deficit Reduction bill, exposing the fraud and abuse at the heart of the Bank of Credit and Commerce International (BCCI) scandal, and investigating with Republican Senator John McCain reports and rumors surrounding Vietnam veterans declared POW/MIA.

Kerry was re-elected to the Senate in 1990, 1996 (this time defeating the popular Republican Governor William Weld in the most closely watched Senate race in the country), and 2002. In his fourth term, Kerry worked to reform public education, provide health insurance for millions of low-income children, protect the environment, and advance America's foreign policy interests around the globe. He has been praised as one of the leading environmentalists in the Senate and was instrumental in stopping the Bush-Cheney plan to drill in the Arctic National Wildlife Refuge.

Kerry married Teresa Heinz Kerry, the chairman of the Howard Heinz Endowment and the Heinz Family Philanthropies, in 1995. It was the second marriage for both. Teresa's first marriage was to Republican Senator John Heinz, who died in a plane crash in 1991. Kerry had two daughters, Alexandra and Vanessa, from a previous marriage. Teresa had three sons, John, André, and Christopher.

Kerry's rivals for the Democratic presidential nomination were Howard Dean, former Vermont governor and doctor; John Edwards, the freshman U.S. senator from North Carolina and a successful trial lawyer; Wesley Clark, a retired four-star army general and former supreme commander of NATO; Dennis Kucinich, a U.S. congressman from Ohio and former mayor of Cleveland; Reverend Al Sharpton, an ordained minister and civil rights activist; Richard Gephardt, former Democratic leader of the U.S. House of Representatives; Joe Lieberman, a U.S. senator from Connecticut and Al Gore's vice-presidential running mate in 2000; Carol Moseley Braun, the first African-American woman to serve in the U.S. Senate and former U.S. ambassador to New Zealand; and Bob Graham, a third-term U.S. senator from Florida and former Florida governor. Graham was the first candidate to drop out of the race.

Kerry fought an uphill battle to win his party's nomination. Dean was the first to enter the race, preceding the other candidates by six months, and was widely touted as the Democratic front-runner going into 2004. He attracted the attention of party activists with his strident denunciations of the Iraq war and grassroots use of the Internet to raise funds. Yet by the time he ended his campaign in mid-February 2004, he had not won a single primary or caucus. A few weeks later, on March 2 (Super Tuesday), his home state gave him his first and only primary victory. Dean's loss was attributed to voter sentiment that he was too radical to beat George W. Bush in the general election.

General Clark jumped into the race on September 17, 2003, and instantly soared to the top of most polls. The Arkansas native, who had never before sought elected office, was largely backed by those voters most concerned about national security and the Iraq war, but did not garner enough support to sustain his presidential run. After skipping the Iowa caucuses, he finished third in New Hampshire's primary and won Oklahoma, one of seven states in contention. Falling further and further behind Kerry, however, Clark ended his presidential run a day after placing a disappointing third in the Virginia and Tennessee primaries on February 10.

After suffering several campaign setbacks, and lagging behind Dean in voter polls, Kerry surprised the nation with a huge victory in Iowa's caucus on January 19, 2004. Edwards finished a strong second, Dean a disappointing third, and Gephardt came in fourth, ending his second presidential bid the following day. Kerry cemented his newfound front-runner status with a victory in New Hampshire on January 27. Senator Edwards became Kerry's chief competitor after winning the South Carolina primary on February 3, but withdrew from the race one month later, a day after failing to win even one race in the Super Tuesday primaries. Kerry won all but one of the 10 Super Tuesday primaries, and nearly every other primary or caucus that followed.

Senator Kerry underwent surgery for a cancerous prostate in February 2004, but returned to the campaign trail within weeks. After securing the Democratic Party nomination, he chose the charismatic Edwards as his running mate. Edwards had become known for his "Two Americas" stump speech, in which he argued that there were two Americas—an America of "haves" (composed of wealthy and privileged individuals like President Bush and Vice President Dick Cheney) and an America of "have-nots," comprising the working- and middle-classes. Edwards's lack of experience may have hurt Kerry's chance to win somewhat.

Ralph Nader (1934-   ) of Washington, D.C., was the Independent candidate. Nader was an attorney, author, and activist. For more background information, see "Opponents" in the 2000 campaign. Nader made his fourth presidential bid in 2004, despite not receiving the Green Party nomination. He ran, instead, as an Independent. Unlike in 2000, Nader's candidacy had no significant impact on the campaigns of the two major party candidates or the general election. Nader chose as his running mate, Peter Miguel Camejo, a financial investment advisor from California who had never before held public office.

Michael Badnarik (1954-   ) of Texas was the Libertarian candidate. A computer programmer and consultant, he ran as the Libertarian candidate for the Texas House of Representatives (Austin area) in 2000 and 2002. Badnarik traveled more than 25,000 miles across the U.S. in the 15 months leading up to the Libertarian Party National Convention in Atlanta and his nomination victory on May 30, 2004. Badnarik chose Richard Campagna, a businessman and university instructor from Texas, as his running mate.

David Cobb (1962-   ) of Texas was the Green Party candidate. He had a successful law practice until early 2002 when Ralph Nader asked him to manage the Green Party effort in Texas. He coordinated the ballot access drive in Texas that collected more than 76,000 signatures in 75 days. Cobb served as the general counsel for the Green Party of the United States until declaring his candidacy. Cobb selected Patricia LaMarche, a radio host and teacher from Maine, as his running mate.

Michael Anthony Peroutka (1952-   ) of Maryland, was the Constitution Party candidate. An attorney and activist, he was chairman of the Constitution Party of Maryland and a member of the executive committee of the Constitution Party National Committee. Peroutka chose Chuck Baldwin, a radio talk show host, activist, and Baptist minister from Florida, as his running mate.

CAMPAIGN AND THE ISSUES, 2004: The 2004 election was the most passionate and divisive battle since, well, the aftermath of the 2000 election. The 2004 campaign boiled down to a referendum on President Bush's handling of the economy and the war in Iraq, although other, so-called "moral issues," such as gay marriage, abortion, and stem-cell research played a role as well. In addition, the makeup of the Supreme Court hung in the balance as several justices would likely retire in the upcoming term, and the next president would nominate replacements.

President Bush and Senator Kerry espoused conflicting views on almost all of the key issues, including homeland security, the conduct of the war in Iraq, the economy and government spending, health care, taxes, job growth (or lack thereof—President Bush was the first president since Herbert Hoover to lose jobs and the only war-time president ever to do so), environmental protection, Social Security reform, and global alliances. Ralph Nader's voice was largely muted in 2004 as he lacked the backing of the Green Party and was excluded from the three televised presidential debates. Ultimately, Nader's name was left off the ballots in 16 states.

Senator Kerry attacked President Bush for his mishandling of the Iraq war. He criticized Bush for rushing into the war, snubbing U.S. allies and the United Nations, committing an insufficient number of troops, sending troops to battle without the necessary armor, lying about weapons of mass destruction (the Bush administration's primary explanation for going to war with Iraq was that Saddam Hussein had amassed weapons of mass destruction; no WMDs were ever found), lying about Hussein's alleged ties to the terrorist group al Qaeda, the gross negligence that made the Abu Ghraib prison torture abuses possible, and diverting precious resources from the war in Afghanistan to the war in Iraq. Specifically, Kerry criticized Bush for failing to capture Osama bin Laden, the real enemy, in the Tora Bora mountains of Afghanistan when the opportunity arose, and instead, "outsourcing" the job to Afghan warlords. Kerry promised to reach out to other nations to form an international coalition against terrorism.

President Bush refused to admit to a single mistake on his part. So what if the WMDs his administration claimed were in Iraq were never found—Saddam Hussein was a bad man and the world was safer without him in power. As for going to war without U.N. support, Bush declared that he would give no nation veto power over U.S. safety. Bush took a hawkish stance on fighting terrorists and criticized Kerry for his proposed "global test" and for being weak. The U.S. was sure to suffer another terrorist attack if Kerry were elected, his and Cheney's words implied.

On the domestic front, President Bush supported broad tax cuts as the best way to stimulate the economy and provide relief for American families, whereas Senator Kerry said he would raise taxes on individuals with incomes above $200,000, thereby lessening the burden on lower- and middle-income families.

Kerry promised universal health care coverage for all children and said he would work to give every American access to the same health plan that members of Congress receive. President Bush focused on keeping health care affordable by slowing the fast-growing medical liability insurance costs that doctors and hospitals often passed on to consumers and by limiting medical liability lawsuits. Unlike President Bush, Kerry endorsed the federal government's negotiating prescription drug prices on behalf of Americans, especially those on Medicare.

On "moral" issues such as gay marriage, abortion, and stem-cell research, President Bush stood firmly to the right, opposing essentially all three. He supported a constitutional amendment to protect marriage as an institution between a man and a woman (although he was not opposed necessarily to state-sanctioned civil unions for same-sex couples), declared that he would not spend taxpayers' money on abortion and promised to work toward reducing the number of abortions performed each year, and opposed federally funded stem-cell research beyond the stem-cell lines that were already in existence. Senator Kerry, despite his Catholic beliefs, fully supported *Roe v. Wade*. He stated his belief that marriage should be between a man and a woman, but supported civil unions and said he would leave that decision to the states. Kerry supported stem-cell research, a position that earned him the endorsement of quadriplegic actor Christopher Reeve and Reeve's wife, Dana.

In his nomination speech at the Democratic Convention in July 2004, Kerry was optimistic about America's future. "America can do better, and help is on the way," he declared repeatedly. "I defended this country as a young man, and I will defend it as president." In response to President Bush's religiosity, Kerry declared, "I don't want to claim that God is on our side. As Abraham Lincoln told us, I want to pray humbly that we are on God's side."

The convention theme, "Stronger at Home, Respected in the World," was stressed in speeches made by foreign policy experts, including former NATO Supreme Commander General Wesley Clark and former Secretary of State Madeleine Albright. Among the convention's highlights were energetic and inspirational speeches made by Bill Clinton, former presidential hopeful Al Sharpton, a group of Kerry's Vietnam "band of brothers," and perhaps most moving of all, Illinois state Senator Barack Obama (who won his U.S. Senate bid on November 2).

At the Republican National Convention in New York City, which started at the end of August, President Bush outlined the domestic agenda for his second term and pointed to the inroads he had made on the war on terrorism. "Since 2001, Americans have been given hills to climb and found the strength to climb them," he said in his nomination acceptance speech. "Now, because we have made the hard journey, we can see the valley below... and nothing will hold us back." Referring to his proposed domestic policy initiatives, Bush declared, "In all of these proposals, we seek to provide not just a government program, but a path— a path to greater opportunity, more freedom, and more control over your own life." A recurring theme of the convention was the September 11 terrorist attack, prompting many of Bush's critics to claim that he was capitalizing on the tragedy and to point out that Osama bin Laden remained at large. Bush's supporters, including former New York Mayor Rudolph Giuliani and California governor Arnold Schwarzenegger, touted Bush's courage in standing up to terrorists.

Kerry was judged as having won the first of the three presidential debates (interestingly, the debate that focused on U.S. foreign policy), but Bush held his own during the second and third debates. Overall, Kerry gained a slight edge coming out of the debates. The debate between Vice President Dick Cheney and Senator John Edwards, held in October, was largely deemed a draw.

Despite his firm resolve to hunt down and kill terrorists, and his appeals to the "everyman," Kerry largely failed to persuade undecided voters that he would be a tough commander-in-chief and may have been betrayed by his intellectualism and aristocratic background. His main challenge during the campaign was to appeal to conservative voters without losing his liberal constituency, while holding on to the middle. This proved tricky, and for his backpedaling and indecisiveness on several issues, Kerry earned the nickname "flip-flopper" from Bush and Bush's supporters. Indeed, Kerry's inability to take concise and forceful positions on many issues proved detrimental to his candidacy.

Bush, as his father, George H. W. Bush, did with Bill Clinton in 1992, resorted to hard negative campaigning. Unable to defend many of his policies and actions post-9/11, Bush focused instead on attacking Kerry's liberal record in the Senate and his vote on the Iraq war bill and criticized Kerry's antiwar actions after Vietnam. Bush accused Kerry of being unpatriotic and argued that Kerry would not be tough enough on terrorists. The Swift Boat Veterans for Truth ad, which featured men who claimed to have served with Kerry in Vietnam and criticized his service and post-combat testimony before Congress, was a source of great controversy among Democrats and Republicans and damaged Kerry's campaign. Presidential advisor Karl Rove was widely believed to have been behind the ad. Bush's questionable Texas National Guard service was also a point of contention.

Both candidates campaigned hard in the battleground states. Kerry courted the youth, Black, and "soccer mom" votes while Bush focused mainly on turning out his hard right, Evangelical Christian base, and "NASCAR dads." Both men raised unparalleled amounts of money: setting a record for a presidential challenger, Kerry raised $249.5 million; setting a presidential fund-raising record himself, Bush raised $274 million. Together, the candidates and their respective parties spent more than $1 billion.

Both candidates took advantage of the Internet to reach out to and mobilize their supporters. Voters could contribute money, raise money, sign up to volunteer, conduct phone banking, contact the media, and organize canvassing trips and other events through the candidates' Web sites.

Kerry received endorsements from a large number of newspapers, including the *New York Times, Washington Post, Boston Globe,* and *Minneapolis Star Tribune.* Kerry also was endorsed by the *Orlando Sentinel,* which had backed every Republican seeking the White House since Richard Nixon in 1968. Among Kerry's more surprising endorsements were those of *The New Yorker* magazine (which had never before endorsed a candidate), the *American Conservative* magazine, and *The Lone Star Iconoclast,* Bush's hometown newspaper in Crawford, Texas. Kerry was also endorsed by the AFL-CIO, the American Federation of Teachers, the International Association of Fire Fighters, and a slew of celebrities, including Howard Stern, Steven Spielberg, Morgan Freeman, Brad Pitt, Ben Affleck, and Tim Robbins. Kerry was also backed by a great number of music artists, including Bruce Springsteen, the Dixie Chicks, R.E.M., and Pearl Jam, who raised money for Kerry by organizing a Vote for Change tour across the country.

Overall, newspaper endorsements backed Kerry 3:1 over Bush, including 36 papers that endorsed Bush in 2000. The president did win the backing of publications such as the *Chicago Tribune, Rocky Mountain News, New York Post, Washington Times,* and *Boston Herald.* In addition, he won the support of the National Rifle Association and the Fraternal Order of Police.

More than 114 million total votes were cast in the November 2 election. With strong backing from his conservative base, in addition to increased support from Latino, Jewish, Catholic, and female voters, President Bush convincingly won both the popular vote and the electoral vote, although allegations of fraud and voting irregularities were made in Ohio. Perhaps not surprisingly, Ohio proved to be the key swing state in the 2004 election. Bush won Ohio by 119,000 votes.

Kerry conceded the election to Bush on November 3 at Fanueil Hall in Boston. In his concession speech, Kerry told his supporters, "We are required now to work together for the good of our country. In the days ahead, we must find common cause. We must join in common effort without remorse or recrimination, without anger or rancor. America is in need of unity and longing for a larger measure of compassion."

ELECTION AS PRESIDENT, SECOND TERM, NOVEMBER 2, 2004

Popular Vote: George W. Bush (Republican) 60,608,582 (51%); John Kerry (Democrat) 57,288,974 (48%); Ralph Nader (Independent) 406,924 (1%).

Electoral Vote: George W. Bush 286; John Kerry 252; Ralph Nader 0; Michael Badnarik 0; David Cobb 0; Michael Peroutka 0.

States Carried: George W. Bush won the electoral votes of 31 states: Alabama, Alaska, Arizona, Arkansas, Colorado, Georgia, Florida, Idaho, Indiana, Iowa, Kansas, Kentucky, Louisiana, Mississippi, Missouri, Montana, Nebraska, Nevada, New Mexico, North Carolina, North Dakota, Ohio, Oklahoma, South Carolina, South Dakota, Tennessee, Texas, Utah, Virginia, West Virginia, and Wyoming. John Kerry won the electoral votes of the District of Columbia and 18 states: California, Connecticut, Delaware, Hawaii, Illinois, Maine, Maryland, Massachusetts, Michigan, Minnesota, New Hampshire, New Jersey, New York, Oregon, Pennsylvania, Rhode Island, Vermont, and Washington.

INAUGURAL ADDRESS (FIRST): January 20, 2001. "The peaceful transfer of authority is rare in history, yet common in our country. With a simple oath, we affirm old traditions and make new beginnings. As I begin, I thank President Clinton for his service to our nation. And I thank Vice President Gore for a contest conducted with spirit and ended with grace. . . .

" . . . the American story, a story of flawed and fallible people, united across the generations by grand and enduring ideals. The grandest of these ideals is an unfolding American promise: that everyone belongs, that everyone deserves a chance, that no insignificant person was ever born. Americans are called to enact this promise in our lives and in our laws. . . .

"While many of our citizens prosper, others doubt the promise—even the justice—of our own country. The ambitions of some Americans are limited by failing schools and hidden prejudice and the circumstances of their birth. And sometimes our differences run so deep, it seems we share a continent, but not a country. We do not accept this, and we will not allow it. . . . And this is my solemn pledge: I will work to build a single nation of justice and opportunity. . . .

"Today we affirm a new commitment to live out our nation's promise through civility, courage, compassion, and character. America, at its best, matches a commitment to principle with a concern for civility. A civil society demands from each of us good will and respect, fair dealing and forgiveness. . . . Civility is not a tactic or a sentiment. It is the determined choice of trust over cynicism, of community over chaos. And this commitment, if we keep it, is a way to shared accomplishment."

INAUGURAL ADDRESS (SECOND): "For a half a century, America defended our own freedom by standing watch on distant borders. After the shipwreck of communism came years of relative quiet, years of repose, years of sabbatical. And then there came a day of fire. . . . For as long as whole regions of the world simmer in resentment and tyranny prone to ideologies that feed hatred and excuse murder, violence will gather and multiply in destructive power, and cross the most-defended borders, and raise a mortal threat. There is only one force of history that can break the reign of hatred and resentment . . . that is the force of human freedom. . . .

"The survival of liberty in our land increasingly depends on the success of liberty in other lands. The best hope for peace in our world is the expansion of freedom in all the world. . . .The rulers of outlaw regimes can know that we still believe as Abraham Lincoln did: Those who deny freedom to others deserve it not for themselves; and, under the rule of a just God, cannot long retain it. . . .

"[We will] give every American a stake in the promise and future of our country, we will bring the highest standards to our schools and build an ownership society. We will widen the ownership of homes and businesses, retirement savings and health insurance — preparing our people for the challenges of life in a free society."

VICE-PRESIDENT: Richard (Dick) Bruce Cheney (1941-   ) of Wyoming served 2001-   . According to his official biography from the Department of Defense, Cheney was born in Lincoln, Nebraska, and grew up in Casper, Wyoming. He attended Yale University, Casper College, and the University of Wyoming where he earned a B.A. (1965) and an M.A. (1966). He furthered his graduate study in political science at the University of Wisconsin and then went to Washington as a congressional fellow for the 1968-1969 year.

Cheney entered federal service in 1969 under the Nixon administration as a special assistant to the director of the Office of Economic Opportunity. In 1971 he became a White House staff assistant, and soon moved on to become assistant director of the Cost of Living Council, where he stayed until 1973. After a year in private business, he returned to the White House to become deputy assistant to President Gerald Ford (1974-1975) and then White House chief of staff (1975-1977).

In November 1978, Cheney was elected to the House of Representatives as Wyoming's sole congressman. He was re-elected five times, and he served several years on the House Intelligence Committee and the House Intelligence Budget Subcommittee. In December 1988 he became the Minority House Whip in the 101st Congress. On March 21, 1989, Cheney moved to the executive branch as George H. W. Bush's secretary of defense and served until 1993. He was a senior fellow at the American Enterprise Institute 1993-1995. In 1995 he took over as chairman and CEO of Halliburton Company, a large energy equipment and construction firm based in Dallas, that he left in 2000 to hit the campaign trail.

His steady rise from minor functionary in the Nixon administration to White House chief of staff under President Ford at only thirty-four years of age is a testament to his ability and acumen. In the House, Cheney had a strongly conservative voting record, but he built a reputation of willingness to listen to political opponents and of building friendships with them.

Cheney understood how Congress operated and used this knowledge and experience to avoid the kind of difficulties his predecessors had encountered on Capitol Hill. In general, Cheney got along well with the defense department's main oversight committees in Congress, although he suffered some disappointments and frustrations. After the collapse of the Soviet Union in 1991, Cheney worried about the dangers of nuclear proliferation from the Soviet nuclear arsenal to the Soviet republics and to possibly Iraq, Iran, and North Korea. He supported cutbacks in the production and deployment of nuclear weapons and new arms control agreements.

Several international crises arose during his tenure. In November 1989, Cheney approved the use of U.S. jets to deny rebel forces air cover during a coup against the government of President Corazon Aquino of the Philippines, and the coup collapsed. In December 1989, he directed the U.S. invasion of Panama in which U.S. forces arrested General Manuel Noriega, the dictator of the country, and brought him to trial and imprisonment on racketeering and drug-trafficking charges. After the Iraqi invasion of Kuwait in 1990, Cheney helped to put together Operation Desert Shield by securing Saudi Arabian cooperation to use their country as a base for a counter-invasion and directed the operation.

Bombing started on January 17, 1991. After five weeks of bombing Iraqi positions both in Kuwait and Iraq, the UN coalition launched the ground war and within four days, Iraqi forces had been routed from Kuwait, sustaining heavy losses. The UN coalition forces suffered relatively few casualties. Operation Desert Storm seemed an unprecedented military success. President George H. W. Bush awarded Cheney the Presidential Medal of Freedom, the highest civilian award, for his leadership in the Gulf War crisis. The reality was that this was a war about oil and had little to do with the interests of the average American citizen.

On several social issues involving the Department of Defense, Cheney's conservatism was evident. He favored the then-existing policies of a ban on homosexuals serving in the military and the exclusion of women from combat positions. He and his wife were embarrassed and defiant when, during the 2004 campaign, it was revealed in the national debates that his daughter was a lesbian, although she had been openly gay for years.

Cheney married his high-school sweetheart, Lynne Ann Vincent, in 1964. They have two adult daughters, Elizabeth and Mary. Lynne Cheney served as chair of the National Endowment for the Humanities from 1986 to 1993 during President Reagan's and the elder Bush's administrations and has been an outspoken leader in educational reform. Lynne Cheney has also been a senior fellow at the American Enterprise Institute and a co-host of CNN's *Crossfire Sunday*. She characterizes herself as more conservative than her husband. The Cheneys, like the Bushes, are Methodists.

There has been some concern over Dick Cheney's health. He had heart attacks in 1978, 1984, 1988, and 2000. He underwent quadruple-bypass surgery in 1988. The heart attack in 2000 occurred while he and George W. Bush were awaiting the results of the court decisions about the presidential election. His heart attacks have been characterized as mild, and he was up and about, putting together the transition team days after his last attack.

CABINET:

Secretary of State. (1) Colin Luther Powell (1937-   ) of Virginia served 2001-2005. Powell was born in Harlem and raised in the South Bronx, both areas in New York City. He was commissioned as a second lieutenant in 1958 and rose through the military to become a full general (four stars). He served two tours of duty in the Vietnam War, and commanded the 1st Battalion, 32nd Infantry in Korea in 1973 and the 2nd Brigade, 101st Airborne Division in 1976. He was a senior military assistant to the deputy secretary of defense 1977-1980 and 1983-1986. He was President Reagan's national security advisor 1987-1988, the commander-in-chief of the U.S. Forces Command 1989, and chairman of the Joint Chiefs of Staff 1989-1993 under George H. W. Bush. Powell turned down G. W. Bush's offer to run as his vice president. He is the first Black secretary of state. (2) Condoleezza Rice (1954-   ) of Alabama, nominated 2004. National security advisor to President Bush from 2001-2004, the first woman to serve in that capacity, she is considered one of the president's most trusted confidantes and had considerable influence over first-term foreign policy. Dr. Rice received a political science degree from the University of Denver in 1974, a master's from the University of Notre Dame in 1975, and a Ph.D. from the Graduate School of International Studies at the University of Denver in 1981. She was Stanford University provost for six years ending in 1999. A hard-liner, Dr. Rice was a fierce defender of the invasions of Afghanistan and Iraq. Some of her statements about the administration's response to pre-9/11 terrorists were called into question. Testifying before the 9/11 Commission, Dr. Rice tried to explain away why an August 6, 2001, memo titled "Bin Laden Determined to Attack within United States" didn't raise any red flags by saying it was "historical."

Secretary of the Treasury. (1) Paul Henry O'Neill (1935-   ) of Pennsylvania served 2001-2002. O'Neill was on the staff of the Office of Management and Budget 1967-1977. He was vice-president and later president of International Paper Company 1973-1985 and CEO of Alcoa Aluminum 1987-1999. O'Neill is a director of the conservative American Enterprise Institute in Washington and the Rand Corporation. After publicly criticizing Bush tax cuts, O'Neill was forced to resign. (2) John Snow (1939-   ) of Ohio served 2003-   . Snow became president of the rail company CSX in 1985 and later added CEO to his title. The company was large political contributor, the bulk of which went to Republicans. He was also chairman of the Business Roundtable, a group of 250 CEOs, and lobbied for the passage of the North American Free Trade Agreement. In addition, he worked at the Department of Transportation from 1972-1976 and was administrator of the National Highway Traffic Safety Administration from 1976-1977. Although Snow lobbied against government deficits in the 1980s, he defended President Bush's $455-billion deficit, saying, ". . .[the deficit] is manageable in the sense that it is not perceived as disruptive." He also pushed hard for tax cuts (which lowered his own taxes by more than $300,000). Snow was perceived as having little influence on bolstering the falling dollar.

Secretary of Defense. Donald Rumsfeld (1932-) of Illinois served 2001- . Rumsfeld is a former Illinois congressman, 1963-1969, and is a veteran of a number of Republican administrations. Rumsfeld held several posts in the Nixon administration 1969-1974, including ambassador to NATO 1973-1974. He also held various positions under Gerald Ford, including chief of staff and secretary of defense 1975-1977. He was the CEO of pharmaceutical giant G.D. Searle, 1977-1985, and has held various executive positions with different companies 1985-2000. Rumsfeld is an experienced defense secretary, and missile defense and antiterrorism are high on his list of priorities. Critics of his handling of the Iraq War demanded he be fired, but President Bush was disinclined to do so.

Attorney General. John Ashcroft (1942-) of Missouri served 2001-2004. Ashcroft began his political career as auditor for the state of Missouri 1973-1974. He was assistant attorney general 1975-1976 and attorney general of Missouri 1976-1985. He was elected governor of Missouri 1985-1993 and was the state's senator from 1994 to 2000. Ashcroft was very conservative, and his anti-abortion and pro-death penalty stances drew criticism from liberals. He has the unusual distinction of being defeated for re-election to the Senate by a dead man. His tenure was marked with controversy as critics charged he stomped on civil liberties with his enforcement of the Patriot Act, treating "dissent and criticism as if it was treason," as Georgetown University Law Professor David Cole put it.7 (2) Alberto Gonzales (1955-) of Texas, nominated 2004. He served as President Bush's White House counsel in the first term. He authored a highly controversial memo on the treatment of suspected terrorists, in which he maintained they did not fall under the Geneva Convention's definition of prisoners of war. Critics felt the memo "created a climate" that led to the abuses in Abu Ghraib prison (see Administration.) Governor Bush appointed him Texas Secretary of State in 1997, then a member of the Texas Supreme Court in 1999.

Secretary of the Interior. Gale Ann Norton (1954-) of Colorado served 2001- . Norton started her career as a clerk for the Colorado Court of Appeals, 1978-1979, and continued as a lawyer for the Mountain States Legal Foundation, 1979-1983. The foundation was founded by the former—and extremely controversial—Secretary of Interior James Watt. She was the assistant to the deputy secretary of the United States Department of Agriculture 1984-1985 and the associate solicitor of the United States Department of Interior 1985-1987. She went into a private law practice 1987-1990, served as attorney general of Colorado 1991-1999, and then returned to her private law practice 1999-2000. Environmental groups have criticized Norton for her advocacy of drilling for oil in the Arctic National Wildlife Refuge and the use of public lands for mineral and energy development.

Secretary of Agriculture. Ann M. Veneman (1949-) of California served 2001-2004. Veneman was the deputy undersecretary of the USDA 1989-1991 and the deputy secretary of the Department of Agriculture 1991-1993. She was the director of the California Department of Food and Agriculture 1995-1999. She was a partner in a private law firm 1999-2000. Veneman's parents were peach growers in the San Joaquin Valley of California, and her appointment was praised by various agricultural organizations, since she had a record of understanding what the industry needs and opening new markets for it. (2) Mike Johanns

(1950-   ) of Nebraska, nominated 2004. Raised on a dairy farm, Johanns was a two-term Nebraska governor when tapped by President Bush. According to the Associated Press, his choice to succeed Ann Veneman "may reflect the administration's desire to focus heavily on farm trade . . . " Governor Johanns was looked upon as pro-corporate, pro-subsidy, and pro-Bush.

Secretary of Commerce. Donald L. Evans (1946-   ) of Texas served 2001-2004. Evans was president and later CEO of Denver-based oil and gas company Tom Brown Inc. 1975-2000. He is a longtime fundraiser for George W. Bush and worked in his congressional campaign in 1978, his gubernatorial runs in 1994 and 1998, and his presidential bid in 2000. Evans became the Bush presidential campaign chairman. He was the chairman of the University of Texas System Board of Regents 1997-2000 and was appointed to the board by Bush when he was governor. Evans is a very close personal friend of Bush's, dating from the time he and Bush explored for oil in Texas in the mid-1970s. (2) Carlos Gutierrez (1953-   ) of Florida, nominated 2004. Gutierrez, whose family left Cuba in 1960, was chairman and CEO of the Kellogg Company at the time he was nominated. Gutierrez started with the company in 1975 selling cereal out of a van in Mexico. By leaving Kellogg, Gutierrez's salary would drop $7.4 million to $166,700. Highly regarded in the business community, his nomination was seen as an attempt to strengthen the administration's economic team as it tried to gather support for the restructuring of Social Security and rewriting the tax code.

Secretary of Labor. Elaine Lan Chao (1953-   ) of Kentucky served 2001-   . Elaine Chao was born in Taipei, Taiwan. She grew up in New York and is the wife of Republican Senator Mitch McConnell of Kentucky. She began her career as an investment banker at Citicorp bank 1973-1983 and worked for BankAmerica as a vice-president 1984-1986. She then had administrative posts in government, first as a deputy administrator in the Department of Transportation 1986-1988; chairwoman of the Federal Maritime Commission 1988-1989; then as deputy secretary in the Department of Transportation 1989-1991. She was director of the Peace Corps 1991-1992 and president of the United Way charities 1992-1996. She has been a fellow at the neo-conservative Heritage Foundation 1996-2000.

Secretary of Health and Human Services. (1) Tommy George Thompson (1941-   ) of Wisconsin served 2001-2005. Thompson practiced law 1966-1987 and was a member of the Wisconsin State Assembly, 1966-1986. He was also a real estate broker 1970-2000. He was an enormously popular politician and was elected governor of Wisconsin four times, 1987-2000. Planned Parenthood protested Thompson's appointment for his anti-abortion stand. Thompson worked hard for the passage of the Medicare bill, although he was against the ban on negotiating prices with drug companies. (2) Mike Leavitt (1951-   ) of Utah was nominated to succeed Thompson. See Administrator of Environmental Protection.

Secretary of Housing and Urban Development. (1) Melquiades "Mel" R. Martinez (1946-   ) of Florida served 2001-2004. Martinez was a lawyer for twenty-five years. He was president of the Orlando Utilities Commission 1994-1997 and also chairman of the Orlando Housing Authority. He was the chairman (ie., elected chief executive) of Orange County, Florida, which has the county seat at Orlando, 1998-2000. He is a Cuban immigrant who entered the United States as a refugee in 1962. (2) Alphonso Jackson served 2004-   . His 25 years of experience in both public and private sectors include serving as Director of Public Safety for the City of St. Louis; President and CEO of the Housing Authority of the City of Dallas; and Director of the Department of Public and

Assisted Housing in Washington D.C. Jackson first joined the Bush administration in June of 2001 as HUD's Deputy Secretary and Chief Operating Officer.

Secretary of Transportation. Norman Yoshio Mineta (1931-) of California served 2001- . Mineta sold insurance from 1956 to 1989. His political career started as a member of the San Jose City Council 1967-1971, then he became vice mayor of San Jose 1968-1971, and finally the city's mayor, 1971-1974. From local politics, he graduated to the national scene as member of the House of Representatives 1975-1995. He was a senior vice president for the Lockheed Martin Corporation 1995-2000. In July 2000, he entered the Clinton cabinet as secretary of commerce. He is the only Democrat in George W. Bush's cabinet.

Secretary of Energy. (1) Edmund Spencer Abraham (1952-) of Michigan served 2001-2004. Spencer Abraham taught at the Thomas M. Cooley School of Law 1981-1983. A longtime Republican Party official, he was the chairman of the Michigan Republican Party 1983-1989. In 1990 he was the deputy chief of staff to Vice President Dan Quayle and co-chairman of the National Republican Congressional Committee 1990-1992. He was a U.S. senator from Michigan, 1995-2000. Abraham was a conservative who long advocated the abolition of the Department of Energy, and his appointment was viewed as the first step toward dismantling the department although he has disavowed his earlier stand. Abraham pushed for using the Yucca Mountain in Nevada as a repository for nuclear waste and was praised by the International Atomic Energy Agency for his efforts in destroying Russian nuclear stockpiles. (2) Samuel W. Bodman (1938-) of Illinois, nominated 2004. Bodman worked in the private sector for 31 years, including a stint as president of Fidelity Investments, moving to Washington in 2001. He served first as deputy secretary in the Commerce Department, then held the same position at the Department of Treasury. It was expected that Bodman would be a strong advocate of oil drilling in Alaska's Arctic National Wildlife Refuge.

Secretary of Education. (1) Roderick Raynor Paige (1933-) of Texas served 2001-2004. Paige held numerous teaching posts and was head football coach of Utica (Mississippi) Junior College 1957-1967 and of Jackson State University 1962-1969. In 1971 he was hired by Texas Southern University and held a variety of positions, including head football coach, athletic director, assistant professor, and dean of the School of Education 1984-1990. He was elected to the Houston Independent School District Board of Education in 1989 and was its president in 1992. Paige was the superintendent of the Houston Independent School District 1994-2000, one of the country's top-ten largest. (2) Margaret Spellings (1958-) of Texas, nominated 2004. A longtime advisor to President Bush, she was one of the authors of the No Child Left Behind Act. Spellings worked on educational reform in Texas and was political director of George W. Bush's Texas gubernatorial campaign in 1994.

Secretary of Veterans Affairs. (1) Anthony Joseph Principi (1944-) of California served 2001-2005. Principi was a decorated naval line officer and served in the Vietnam War 1967-1972. He was an attorney in the Judge Advocate General Corps of the Navy 1975-1980 and a counselor for the Senate Armed Services Committee 1980-1983. He held various posts in the Veteran's Administration 1983-1993, including acting secretary 1992-1993. He has held various executive posts for a number of corporations 1995-1999 and was chairman of the Congressional Commission on Military Service Members and Veterans Transition Assistance 1996-1999. Principi brought a great deal of experience to the position, and the Paralyzed Veterans of America praised his appointment. (2) Jim Nicholson

(1938-) served 2005- . He graduated from the United States Military Academy at West Point, N.Y., in 1961 and then served eight years on active duty as a paratrooper and Army officer and 22 years in the Army Reserve. He holds a master's degree from Columbia and a law degree from the University of Denver. He served as chairman of the Republican National Convention from 1997-2000. Immediately prior to his nomination to the Bush administration, he served as U.S. Ambassador to the Holy See.

Administrator of Environmental Protection Agency. (1) Christine Todd Whitman (1947-) of New Jersey served 2001-2003. President Bush elevated the position of EPA administrator to cabinet level. Environmentalists had high hopes for Whitman when joined EPA because of her record as New Jersey governor. Those hopes evaporated when she had the unenviable task of announcing that the U.S. was backing out of the Kyoto Protocol. (See Administration, Kyoto Protocol). Although she denied it, it was believed she resigned EPA because of her unhappiness with administration environmental policies. (2) Mike Leavitt (1951-) of Utah served 2003-2005. Leavitt was governor of Utah 1992-2003. Under his watch, Utah played host to the 2002 Winter Olympics, which was praised for being environmentally sensitive. However, environmental groups protested his nomination—including many from Utah—saying he did little to enforce pollution regulations and made a deal with the Bush administration to open six million acres of Utah wild lands to oil and gas drilling, clear-cutting, mining, and bulldozing.

Secretary of Department of Homeland Security. (1) Tom Ridge (1945-) of Pennsylvania served 2001-2004. In response to the 9/11 terrorist attacks, President Bush created the Department of Homeland Security and placed its secretary on cabinet level. The department pulled 22 existing agencies under its umbrella, making it the second largest federal agency, only surpassed by the Pentagon. Ridge was a two-term governor (1995-2001) of Pennsylvania. A staff sergeant in Vietnam, he was awarded the Bronze Star for Valor. Before becoming governor, he served in the House of Representatives for fourteen years. He got mixed reviews as Homeland Security secretary, though some, like New York Senator Charles E. Schumer, said he was shackled by the administration not supplying him with necessary resources. Under his tenure, the color-coded security system was instituted. (See Administration, 9/11.) (2) Michael Chertoff (1953-) of New Jersey was nominated 2005. Chertoff was an assistant U.S. attorney in New York, 1983-1987, then in New Jersey, 1987-1990. He became U.S. attorney in the District of New Jersey, 1990-1994. He served as counsel to the Republican Whitewater committee that investigated the financial dealings of President Clinton. At the time of his nomination, Chertoff was a judge on the 3rd U.S. Circuit Court of Appeals.

ADMINISTRATION: January 20, 2001-

Tax cuts. President Bush wasted no time making good on the campaign promise he would continue as the "tax-cutting person" he had been as Texas governor. (Although an analysis by the *Dallas Morning News* brought into question whether Texans had actually saved any money under Governor Bush's leadership. "Many are still paying as much as [they] did in 1997, or more," the paper concluded. By lowering the property tax, Bush forced local districts to increase taxes to make up for school budget shortfalls.) President Bush's tax cut package, Economic Growth Tax Relief Reconciliation Act of 2001, was approved by Congress in May with the House voting 240-154 and the Senate 58-33. The

$1.35-trillion package, which had a 10-year life span, reduced the lowest tax rate from 15 percent to 10 percent, and the highest from 39.6 percent to 35 percent. In July 2001 the first of 95 million rebate checks hit the post office.

As physicists know, for every action, there is a reaction. The reaction to the Bush tax-cutting was the obliteration of the annual budget surplus of $230 billion inherited from Bill Clinton and the creation of a $413 billion deficit by 2004. Local governments complained they had to increase taxes and reduce services as they received less money from Washington while at the same time being saddled with unfunded or underfunded mandates. (See No Child Left Behind.) According to the nonpartisan Center of Budget and Policy Priorities, "federal policies are costing states and localities about $185 billion over the four-year course of the state fiscal crisis."

Also questioned was President Bush's assertion that "the vast majority of my tax cuts go to the bottom end of the spectrum." A study by the Tax Policy Center found that low- and middle-income Americans, the bottom 60 percent of the nation, received only 13.7 percent of the tax cuts. Two subsequent tax bills allowed businesses to write off half of their investments for two years, saving them billions of dollars, and reduced taxes on dividends and capital gains. In 2003, 10 Noble Laureates and 450 other U.S. economists warned that the tax cuts would not help the economy in the short run and the projected deficits would harm it over the long haul.

A goal of the tax cuts was to improve the economy. According to the Bureau of Labor Statistics (part of the Department of Labor), as of October 2004, there was a net job loss since President Bush took office of between 600,000 and 800,000 jobs based on its payroll survey. In the 2004 campaign, President Bush's camp cited the BLS household survey that showed a net job creation of 1.7 million. However, the BLS said the payroll survey measures job loss more accurately.

No Child Left Behind. Characterized as the most sweeping educational bill since 1965, the bill called for accountability in the nation's schools, improved performance results, and gave students the right to transfer out of unsafe or underperforming schools. President Bush called NCLB "the cornerstone of my administration." By the end of President Bush's first term, complaints about the act and the administration's failure to fund it were shelling the White House, not helped by Secretary of Education Rod Paige dismissing critics of NCLB as "guardians of mediocrity."

Environment.

• **Kyoto Protocol.** A binding addendum to a 1992 United Nation's treaty on climate control, the protocol set requirements for 38 industrialized nations to cut down on greenhouse gas emissions. The protocol was negotiated in 1996 by representatives from 160 nations, including the U.S. In March 2001, President Bush pulled out of the treaty. Christine Whitman, head of the Environmental Protection Agency, announced that the U.S. was "not interested" in it. The administration argued the treaty was flawed because it did not cover developing nations, that reining in emissions would hurt the American economy, and that there wasn't enough sound science showing global warming. Despite the U.S. withdrawal, the treaty was ratified in November 2004.

With the rejection of the protocol and the decision to withdraw from the Anti-Ballistic Missile Treaty, President Bush seemed to be leading the country on a road not traveled since after World War I, that of isolationism.

• **Domestic policies.** At home, President Bush came under fierce fire from environmentalists. The National Resources Defense Council said, "This administration, in catering to industries that put America's health and natural heritage at risk, threatens to do more damage to our environmental protections than any other in U.S. history." While the Bush administration can point to some pro-environmental accomplishments, they were outweighed by other legislation and changes in regulations that were seen as pandering to private industry. The Clear Skies initiative, it was charged, lowered the pollution standards for utilities. The Healthy Forests Initiative would increase logging in an attempt to reduce forest fires, something the Sierra Club rejected, saying the initiative "reveals the administration's true goal which is... to cut the public out of the public lands management decision making process and to give logging companies virtually free access to our National Forests."

Medicare and Social Security. With the endorsement of one of the country's strongest lobbying groups, the AARP, President Bush signed into law the Prescription Drug, Improvement and Modernization Act of 2003, later to be known as the Medicare Modernization Act. It created a tax-exempt Health Savings Account for people with high-deductible insurance plans. Prescription drug coverage became available under Medicare, but it also banned the federal government from negotiating lower prices from drug companies. Critics saw the act as the first step in a little-disguised plan to privatize Medicare and a boon for drug companies.

In his first term, President Bush talked about changing Social Security so that younger Americans could invest in private accounts. He accused the Democrats of wanting to make Social Security a federal program. However, Social Security has been a federal program since its inception under President Franklin D. Roosevelt in the 1930s.

Scientific Research. In his first term, President Bush earmarked $250 million for stem-cell research. Many scientists believe that such research will lead to cures for juvenile diabetes Alzheimer's, Parkinson's, and other diseases. The funds, however, could only be used for research with existing stem-cell lines. President Bush said there were 60 such lines; others have put that number as low as 12. For ethical reasons, the president said he would not allow federal money to be used on new lines, even from frozen embryos in fertility clinics. In response, the voters of California—with the endorsement of Republican Governor Arnold Schwarzenegger—passed an initiative allowing the state to fund stem-cell research using money raised from the sale of bonds.

The administration was also accused of discarding scientific studies with which it didn't agree, tossing people with opposing views from advisory committees, cutting back research budgets, backing reports from the industry being examined. In 2004, 4,000 scientists signed a statement decrying Bush's "misrepresenting and suppressing scientific knowledge for political purposes" and for undermining "the quality and independence of the scientific advisory system and the morale of the government's outstanding scientific personnel."

Religious Politics. Before 2003 federal money did not go directly to religious groups sponsoring social programs. To receive taxpayers' money, independent secular organizations had to be established. When President Bush couldn't get congressional backing, he circumvented this long-accepted principle by executive order, instituting the White House Faith-Based and Community Initiatives. In 2003, the White House reported that $1.17 billion grants went directly to religious groups. Besides being seen as breach in the separation of church and state, critics have pointed out that an accounting of which religious groups and the amount they have received was not readily available. It was argued that if taxpayers' money was going to one faith, Christianity, it would appear that President Bush was promoting a religion, thus violating the First Amendment.

President Bush's Born Alive Infants Protection Act changed the definition of "'person,' 'human being,' 'child,' and 'individual' to include 'every infant member of the species homo sapiens who is born alive at any stage of development.'" In lauding the act, he said, "Unborn children are members of the human family. They reflect our image, and they are created in God's own image." The act was seen as a victory for antiabortion groups. President Bush also reinstated a Reagan policy that stopped federal funds going to international organizations that advocated or paid for abortions.

9/11. At 8:45 A.M., Tuesday, September 11, 2001, American Airlines Flight 11 slammed into the North Tower of the World Trade Center in Lower Manhattan. Thus began the national nightmare of 9/11, which would result in the loss of more than 3,000 people and America's sense of security.

President Bush was listening to children read in a Sarasota, Florida, elementary school when he was informed of the second plane hitting the World Trade Center. He stayed for seven minutes before being whisked off to Air Force One. At that point, he was lost on the public's radar screen and did not reappear until later that day at a base near Omaha, Nebraska. He addressed the nation, saying, "Terrorist attacks can shake the foundations of our biggest buildings, but they cannot touch the foundation of America. These acts shattered steel, but they cannot dent the steel of American resolve."

In the ensuing days, President Bush declared war on terror and promised to hunt down those behind the attacks, specifically Osama bin Laden, a wealthy Saudi leader of the al Qaeda terrorist network. On October 8, the president announced the formation of the Office of Homeland Security, to be headed by former Pennsylvania Governor Tom Ridge. The office was charged with developing and coordinating a "comprehensive national strategy." In March 2002, Homeland Security unveiled its Homeland Security Advisory System. Depending on the seriousness of terrorist threats, the country would be on color-coded alert from the low-risk green through guarded blue, elevated yellow, high orange, and severe red.

The U.S. Patriot Act of 2001 (an acronym for Uniting and Strengthening America by Providing Appropriate Tools Required to Intercept and Obstruct Terrorism) was passed by Congress with a vote 357-66 in the House and followed by a 98-1 rout in the Senate. Only Democrat Russ Feingold of Wisconsin stood in opposition. Its purpose was "to deter and punish terrorist acts in the United States and around the world, to enhance law enforcement investigatory tools, and for other purposes."

The lengthy act (1,016 sections) gave the government increased domestic surveillance powers with reduced judicial oversight. One provision was nicknamed the "sneak and peek." Authorities could search a home or office without prior notification. Wiretaps for foreign intelligence and criminal activity within the U.S. could be obtained through a reduced standard of probable cause. The Justice Department could obtain records with "National Security Letters" that did not need judicial approval. The government could be granted a court order to search personal records, including what was checked out from the library.

To say that the strange bedfellows opposed the act would be a gross understatement. It angered the ACLU, librarians, libertarians, and some conservative Republicans who viewed it as an attack on civil liberties. Even legislators who voted for it worried that Congress was not receiving adequate reports on such things as how many national security letters had been issued. Certain provisions of the act were set to expire in 2005.

Invasion of Afghanistan. On October 7, 2001, President Bush, in keeping with his pledge to track down those responsible for the 9/11 attacks, launched Operation Enduring Freedom, the invasion of Afghanistan. Osama bin Laden was believed to be hiding out there, but the Taliban rulers refused to hand him over to the U.S. American and British planes and missiles bombarded the capital, Kabul, and elsewhere around the country, including al Qaeda training camps.

Taliban forces were no match against the United States, United Kingdom, Australia, and the Northern Alliance, a group of anti-Taliban factions. High-altitude bombers were out of range of Taliban antiaircraft fire. Carpet-bombing decimated their troops. On November 12, Taliban soldiers fled Kabul.

But Osama bin Laden was still at large. Intelligence put him in the caves of Tora Bora near the Pakistani border where the remnants of the Taliban army were regrouping. For whatever reason, the American military did not go after bin Laden, instead "outsourcing" the drive to local warlords. Bin Laden was not captured.

After the fall of the Taliban, a "roadmap" was announced to lead Afghanistan toward security and free elections. While the former may not have been achieved, elections were held in October 2004, propelling a Washington-friendly candidate into office. President Bush called the elections "a really great thing." At the time of the elections, there were still 17,000 American troops in Afghanistan. The cost through September 2004: $39.8 billion, according to the Pentagon.

Iraq War. In the 2002 State of the Union, President Bush stated that "we must prevent the terrorists and regimes who seek chemical, biological or nuclear weapons from threatening the United States and the world." The regimes mentioned in his "axis of evil" were North Korea, Iran, and Iraq. Iraq received the most attention in the address. President Bush accused the Iraqi government of plotting to develop weapons of mass destruction—anthrax, nerve gas, and nuclear—for more than a decade. The State of the Union was the opening salvo in what became known as the Bush Doctrine—that a cornerstone of American foreign policy would be "preemptive strikes" against any nation or group perceived to be a threat. Congress adopted a joint resolution authorizing the president to make preemptive, unilateral strikes against Iraq.

UN arms inspectors returned to Iraq November 27 and found no "smoking gun", as Hans Blix, chief UN inspector, put it. But President Bush wasn't buying it. In his 2003 State of the Union, he said Saddam Hussein "is not disarming. To the contrary, he is deceiving." Still attempting to obtain UN support for an invasion, in February 2003, Secretary of State Colin Powell went before the United Nations, stating he was sure that Hussein was working on developing nuclear weapons. Furthermore, Powell said, "[T]here can be no doubt that Saddam Hussein has biological weapons and the capability to rapidly produce more, many more." It was learned later that Powell had been skeptical of the "evidence," and an analysis of his speech by the State Department found numerous errors.

But despite Powell's appearance and lobbying by the United States and Great Britain, only Spain and Bulgaria climbed aboard the war bandwagon. Pulling together a coalition that included approximately 30 countries, although the U.S. and Britain supplied the bulk of the troops, armaments, and money, Operation Iraqi Freedom was launched on March 13 with air strikes. Ground troops moved in seven days later from Kuwait. Secretary of Defense Donald Rumsfeld promised that the war effort would be "of a force and a scope and a scale that has been beyond what we have seen before." As the catch phrase went, it would engender "shock and awe."

The administration had predicted coalition troops would be welcomed as liberators. To the contrary, fierce resistance was put up in towns on the way to Baghdad. Rumsfeld was assailed for waging the war on the cheap, not sending enough men or equipment. When questioned in 2004 about vehicles not being properly armored, his response was more were on the way, but "You go to war with the Army you have. They're not the Army you might want or wish to have at a later time."

The inevitable came quickly with Baghdad falling on April 9, 2003. Although the country was scoured, no weapons of mass destruction were found. On May 2, President Bush swooped down in Navy jet onto to the deck of the USS Lincoln wearing green flight suit and carrying a white helmet. Standing under a giant banner reading "Mission Accomplished," he informed the American people that "Major combat operations in Iraq have ended." Unfortunately for the troops in Iraq—and the Iraqi people—the conflict had only just begun as car-bombings and rocket attacks became daily occurrences. The United States did not seem to have a plan or adequately trained forces for restoration of services, security, and reconstruction.

This became painfully obvious in the Abu Ghraib scandal. Abu Ghraib was a Saddam Hussein prison, infamous for inhumane living conditions, torture, and executions. The Americans refurbished it and turned it into a military prison. The nation and international community were shocked when pictures and reports of abuse and torture were released. Arab American Institute President Dr. James Zogby laid the blame on the war "being fought by overworked, undertrained, unsupervised and overextended young Americans put in a situation they never should have been put in to begin with."

Violence increased in intensity as the scheduled January 2005 elections approached. Many had warned that there was not enough stability and protection for voters and candidates. While not claiming the elections would be "trouble free," President Bush said, "I'm confident that terrorists will fail, the elections will go forward and Iraq will be a democracy that reflects the values and traditions of its people."

Monetary cost through September 30: $102 billion, according to the Pentagon comptroller's office. Cost in terms of American lives: 1,355 U.S. service personnel died in Iraq as of January 13, 2005, 1,213 since May 1, 2003. Another 10,372 were wounded, according to the Pentagon's official Website.

BUSH PRAISED: "He doesn't panic. He knows how to play the hand he's dealt. He surveys his surroundings and, often at the last minute, finds a way to make the most of them. He's not imaginative, but he's patient and determined: a marathoner."—Howard Fineman[3]

"So I returned to my beloved Texas in 1995, Bush's first year as governor. I met him, and he impressed me. I thought then—and I think now—that he's a basically good man. He seems to have an abiding faith in God—and in himself—and an intense devotion to his family, his state, and our nation. And he's not a bigot... Bush truly doesn't know the meaning of the word 'intolerance.'"—Paul Begala[4]

"He's good on TV, great in a crowd and upon election began to build personal relationships with Democrats in the Statehouse—something [Gov. Ann] Richards never did. . . . So it could be that a country-club Republican who has learned the language of the Christian right is a better fit for a conservative state... than a progressive Democrat like Richards."—Louis Dubose[5]

BUSH CRITICIZED: "What former Texas Gov. Ann Richards, a Democrat, said about Bush's father is even more true about the son: 'He was born on third base and thinks he hit a triple.'"—Jack Newfield[6]

"I went to school with George. In fact, I knew him quite well, both through athletics, socializing, joint classes, and particularly as my immediate lab partner in a freshman science class. The fact that he is tantalizingly close to becoming the most powerful and important person in the world is both astonishing and terrifying. He was intellectually lazy, not particularly interested in anything serious, rather arrogant, contemptuous of studying, and purposeless. To think that someone so 'average' could be leading this nation is a scary proposition."—Dick Herman, former classmate at Andover[7]

" W... You were a poor student who somehow got into the finest schools. You were a National Guardsman who somehow disappeared from duty for a year. You were a failed businessman who somehow got rich. You were a minority investor who somehow was made managing partner of the Texas Rangers baseball team. And you were a defeated politician who somehow was made governor. Let's face it, Dub:... You're lighter than my grandma's biscuits. You know it. I know it.

"This book examines the real record of George Walker Bush: a man who presents the thinnest, weakest, least impressive record in public life of any major party nominee for the presidency this century. A man who at every critical juncture has been propelled upward by the forces of wealth, privilege, status, and special interests who would use his family's name for their private gain."—Paul Begala[8]

"Part of a governor's job is to review capital cases. The staggering pace of executions in Texas means that Bush has either (a) been doing little else but reviewing death sentences or (b) been signing death warrants as fast as they can be put in front of him."—Christopher Hitchens[9]

"George Bush dispenses with people who confront him with inconvenient facts. He truly believes he's on a mission from God. Absolute faith like that overwhelms a need for analysis. The whole thing about faith is to believe things for which there is no empirical evidence, but you can't run the world on faith." —Bruce Bartlett, domestic policy advisor to Ronald Reagan[10]

"A Bush presidency will result in radical-right activists on the Supreme Court and other judicial appointments, which would push public policy toward regressive directions on women's and gay rights, labor rights, criminal justice and other key issues. Also, Bush's blatant homophobia and his blood lust on the death penalty are chilling."—Torie Osborn, executive director, Liberty Hill Foundation[11]

"George W. Bush is the worst President the country has endured since Richard Nixon, and even mediocrity would be an improvement. Indeed, if one regards the Bush Administration's sins of governance—its distortion of intelligence in a time of crisis, its grotesque indulgence of the rich at the expense of the rest, its arrogant dissolution of American prestige and influence abroad, its heedless squandering of the world's resources—as worse than the third-rate burglary and second-rate coverup of thirty years ago, then President Bush is in a league only with the likes of Harding, Fillmore, Pierce and Buchanan."—David Remnick[12]

"Now that Bush wants a 15-minute election, it is much more sinister. The speed with which Bush wants to end the Florida presidential recount is the sign that the party animal is now a political gangster. He has gone from Eddie Haskell to Al Capone."—Derrick Z. Jackson[13]

BUSH QUOTES: "I'm not part of the problem. I'm a Republican."

"If this was a dictatorship, it would be a heck of a lot easier, just as long as I'm the dictator."

"We need an active exploration program in America. The only way to become less dependent on foreign sources of crude oil is to explore at home. And you bet I want to open up a small part of Alaska because when that field is on-line, it will produce a million barrels a day. Today we import a million barrels from Saddam Hussein. I would rather that a million come from our own hemisphere, our own country, as opposed from Saddam Hussein." (Presidential debate, Boston, Massachusetts, October 3, 2000)

"I will confront another form of bias—the soft bigotry of low expectations in education. Raise the bar of standards. Give schools the flexibility to meet them. Insist on results. Blow the whistle on failure. Provide parents with options to increase their influence." (Speech to the NAACP, "Renewing America's Purpose", July 10, 2000)

"I don't think you should support the death penalty to seek revenge. I don't think that's right. I think the reason to support the death penalty is because it saves other people's lives." (Presidential debate, St. Louis, Missouri, October 17, 2000)

"Now there's a role for our government, but it's not to tell the average folks how to live their lives." (Speech in Eau Claire, Wisconsin, October 18, 2000)

"I believe law-abiding citizens should be allowed to own guns to hunt and to protect themselves, and that our government should aggressively pursue people who illegally sell guns, illegally carry guns, or commit crimes with guns. I also believe that government should pass laws such as instant background checks to help keep guns out of the hands of felons and juveniles and others who should not have them." (*A Charge to Keep*, p. 35-36, 1999)

"These acts shattered steel, but they cannot dent the steel of American resolve... America was targeted for attack because we're the brightest beacons for freedom and opportunity in the world. And no one will keep that light from shining." (Presidential address, September 11, 2001)

"I am the master of low expectations."

BOOKS BY BUSH: *George W. Bush on God and Country: The President Speaks Out on Faith, Principle, and Patriotism* (with Thomas M. Freiling, Editor) Florida: Allegiance Press, 2004.

We Will Prevail: President George W. Bush on War, Terrorism, and Freedom (with Peggy Noonan and Jay Nordlinger) New York: National Review, 2003.

Compassionate Conservatism: What it Is, What it Does, and How It Can Transform America (with Marvin Olasky) New York: Free Press, 2000.

A Charge to Keep (with Karen Hughes) New York: William Morrow & Co., 1999.

BOOKS ABOUT BUSH: Begala, Paul. *Is Our Children Learning?: The Case Against George W. Bush.* New York: Simon & Schuster, 2000.

Cohen, Daniel. *George W. Bush: The Family Business.* Brookfield, Conn.:

Millbrook Press, 2000.

Hatfield, James. *Fortunate Son: George W. Bush and the Making of an American President.* New York: Soft Skull Press, 2000. [This book was originally published by St. Martin's Press but was withdrawn when allegations of drug use by Bush could not be substantiated and other "facts" could not be verified.]

Ivins, Molly and Dubose, Lou. *Shrub: The Short but Happy Political Life of George W. Bush.* New York: Random House, 2000.

Minutaglio, Bill. *First Son: George W. Bush and the Bush Family Dynasty.* New York: Times Books, 1999.

Mitchell, Elizabeth. *W.: Revenge of the Bush Dynasty.* New York: Hyperion, 2000.

Wade, Mary Dodson. *George W. Bush: Governor of Texas.* W S Benson & Co, 1999.

Woodward, Bob. *Bush at War.* New York: Simon & Schuster, 2002.

Woodward, Bob. *Plan of Attack.* New York: Simon & Schuster, 2004.

Wukovits, John F. *George W. Bush.* San Diego, Calif.: Lucent Books, 2000.

NOTES:

1 "For Laura Bush, a Direction That She Never Dreamed of" by Frank Bruni. *New York Times,* July 31, 2000, online version

2 *House of Bush, House of Saud* by Craig Unger. Scribner, March 2004.

3 "Postcard From the Primaries: The Marathon Man vs. Luke Skywalker" by Howard Fineman. *Newsweek,* March 1, 2000, online version

4 *Is Our Children Learning?,* Introduction, by Paul Begala. Simon & Schuster, September 2000.

5 "Running on Empty: The Truth About George W. Bush's 'Compassionate Conservatism'"; thenation.com, April 26, 1999

6 "Anti-Establishment Message Hits Home", *New York Post,* February 9, 2000 (The born-on-third-base quote has also been attributed to Texas Democratic Agricultural Commissioner Jim Hightower, and has been used repeatedly by various liberal critics.)

7 Justice for All Alerts, November 5, 2000, on www. jfanow.org, also distributed on other Web sites

8 *Is Our Children Learning?,* Introduction, by Paul Begala. Ibid.

9 "Gov. Death" on salon.com, August 7, 1999

10 reported by former *Wall Street Journal* national affairs reporter Ron Suskind in the *New York Times Magazine,* October 17, 2004

11 quoted in "The Great Divide" *LA Weekly,* September 3-9, 2000, online version

12 *The New Yorker.* August 9 & 15, 2004

13 "From Lazy Frat Boy to Political Gangster"; *Boston Globe* column, November 17, 2000, online version

POLITICAL COMPOSITION OF CONGRESS, 1789–2001

(Abbreviations: Fed—Federalist; Anti-Fed—Anti-Federalist; Dem-Rep—Democratic-Republican; proadmin—proadministration; antiadmin—antiadministration; Dem—Democrat; Nat Rep—National Republican; Rep—Republican)

President and Party	Congress	Years	Senate Composition	House Composition
Washington, Fed	1st	1789–1791	17 Fed, 9 Anti-Fed	38 Fed, 26 Anti-Fed
Washington, Fed	2d	1791–1793	16 Fed, 13 Dem-Rep	37 Fed, 33 Dem-Rep
Washington, Fed	3d	1793–1795	17 Fed, 13 Dem-Rep	57 Dem-Rep, 48 Fed
Washington, Fed	4th	1795–1797	19 Fed, 13 Dem-Rep	54 Fed, 52 Dem-Rep
J. Adams, Fed	5th	1797–1799	20 Fed, 12 Dem-Rep	58 Fed, 48 Dem-Rep
J. Adams, Fed	6th	1799–1801	19 Fed, 13 Dem-Rep	64 Fed, 42 Dem-Rep
Jefferson, Dem-Rep	7th	1801–1803	18 Dem-Rep, 14 Fed	69 Dem-Rep, 36 Fed
Jefferson, Dem-Rep	8th	1803–1805	25 Dem-Rep, 9 Fed	102 Dem-Rep, 39 Fed
Jefferson, Dem-Rep	9th	1805–1807	27 Dem-Rep, 7 Fed	116 Dem-Rep, 25 Fed
Jefferson, Dem-Rep	10th	1807–1809	28 Dem-Rep, 6 Fed	118 Dem-Rep, 24 Fed
Madison, Dem-Rep	11th	1809–1811	28 Dem-Rep, 6 Fed	94 Dem-Rep, 48 Fed
Madison, Dem-Rep	12th	1811–1813	30 Dem-Rep, 6 Fed	108 Dem-Rep, 36 Fed
Madison, Dem-Rep	13th	1813–1815	27 Dem-Rep, 9 Fed	112 Dem-Rep, 68 Fed
Madison, Dem-Rep	14th	1815–1817	25 Dem-Rep, 11 Fed	117 Dem-Rep, 65 Fed
Monroe, Dem-Rep	15th	1817–1819	34 Dem-Rep, 10 Fed	141 Dem-Rep, 42 Fed
Monroe, Dem-Rep	16th	1819–1821	35 Dem-Rep, 7 Fed	156 Dem-Rep, 27 Fed
Monroe, Dem-Rep	17th	1821–1823	44 Dem-Rep, 4 Fed	158 Dem-Rep, 25 Fed
Monroe, Dem-Rep	18th	1823–1825	44 Dem-Rep, 4 Fed	187 Dem-Rep, 26 Fed
J. Q. Adams	19th	1825–1827	26 proadmin, 20 antiadmin	105 proadmin, 97 antiadmin
J. Q. Adams	20th	1827–1829	28 antiadmin, 20 proadmin	119 antiadmin, 94 proadmin
Jackson, Dem	21st	1829–1831	26 Dem, 22 Nat Rep	139 Dem, 74 Nat Rep
Jackson, Dem	22d	1831–1833	25 Dem, 21 Nat Rep, 2 other	141 Dem, 58 Nat Rep, 14 other
Jackson, Dem	23d	1833–1835	20 Dem, 20 Nat Rep, 8 other	147 Dem, 53 Anti-Mason, 60 other

President and Party	Congress	Years	Senate Composition	House Composition
Jackson, Dem	24th	1835–1837	27 Dem, 25 Whig	145 Dem, 98 Whig
Van Buren, Dem	25th	1837–1839	30 Dem, 18 Whig, 4 other	108 Dem, 107 Whig, 24 other
Van Buren, Dem	26th	1839–1841	28 Dem, 22 Whig	124 Dem, 118 Whig
W. H. Harrison/Tyler, Whig	27th	1841–1843	28 Whig, 22 Dem, 2 other	133 Whig, 102 Dem, 6 other
Tyler, Whig	28th	1843–1845	28 Whig, 25 Dem, 1 other	142 Dem, 79 Whig, 1 other
Polk, Dem	29th	1845–1847	31 Dem, 25 Whig	143 Dem, 77 Whig, 6 other
Polk, Dem	30th	1847–1849	36 Dem, 21 Whig, 1 other	115 Whig, 108 Dem, 4 other
Taylor/Fillmore, Whig	31st	1849–1851	35 Dem, 25 Whig, 2 other	112 Dem, 109 Whig, 9 other
Fillmore, Whig	32d	1851–1853	35 Dem, 24 Whig, 3 other	140 Dem, 88 Whig, 5 other
Pierce, Dem	33d	1853–1855	38 Dem, 22 Whig, 2 other	159 Dem, 71 Whig, 4 other
Pierce, Dem	34th	1855–1857	42 Dem, 15 Rep, 5 other	108 Rep, 83 Dem, 43 other
Buchanan, Dem	35th	1857–1859	36 Dem, 20 Rep, 8 other	118 Dem, 92 Rep, 26 other
Buchanan, Dem	36th	1859–1861	36 Dem, 26 Rep, 4 other	114 Rep, 92 Dem, 31 other
Lincoln, Rep	37th	1861–1863	31 Rep, 10 Dem, 8 other	105 Rep, 43 Dem, 30 other
Lincoln, Rep	38th	1863–1865	36 Rep, 9 Dem, 5 other	102 Rep, 75 Dem, 9 other
Lincoln/Johnson, Union	39th	1865–1867	42 Union, 10 Dem	149 Union, 42 Dem
A. Johnson, Union	40th	1867–1869	42 Rep, 11 Dem	143 Rep, 49 Dem
Grant, Rep	41st	1869–1871	56 Rep, 11 Dem	149 Rep, 63 Dem
Grant, Rep	42d	1871–1873	52 Rep, 17 Dem 5 other	134 Rep, 104 Dem, 5 other
Grant, Rep	43d	1873–1875	49 Rep, 19 Dem, 5 other	194 Rep, 92 Dem, 14 other
Grant, Rep	44th	1875–1877	45 Rep, 29 Dem, 2 other	169 Dem, 109 Rep, 14 other
Hayes, Rep	45th	1877–1879	39 Rep, 36 Dem, 1 other	153 Dem, 140 Rep
Hayes, Rep	46th	1879–1881	42 Dem, 33 Rep, 1 other	149 Dem, 130 Rep, 14 other
Garfield/Arthur, Rep	47th	1881–1883	37 Rep, 37 Dem, 1 other	147 Rep, 135 Dem, 11 other
Arthur, Rep	48th	1883–1885	38 Rep, 36 Dem, 2 other	197 Dem, 118 Rep, 10 other
Cleveland, Dem	49th	1885–1887	43 Rep, 34 Dem	183 Dem, 140 Rep, 2 other
Cleveland, Dem	50th	1887–1889	39 Rep, 37 Dem	169 Dem, 152 Rep, 4 other
B. Harrison, Rep	51st	1889–1891	39 Rep, 37 Dem	166 Rep, 159 Dem
B. Harrison, Rep	52d	1891–1893	47 Rep, 39 Dem, 2 other	235 Dem, 88 Rep, 9 other

President and Party	Congress	Years	Senate Composition	House Composition
Cleveland, Dem	53d	1893–1895	44 Dem, 38 Rep, 3 other	218 Dem, 127 Rep, 11 other
Cleveland, Dem	54th	1895–1897	43 Rep, 39 Dem, 6 other	244 Rep, 105 Dem, 7 other
McKinley, Rep	55th	1897–1899	47 Rep, 34 Dem, 7 other	204 Rep, 113 Dem, 40 other
McKinley, Rep	56th	1899–1901	53 Rep, 26 Dem, 8 other	185 Rep, 163 Dem, 9 other
McKinley/T. Roosevelt, Rep	57th	1901–1903	56 Rep, 29 Dem, 3 other	197 Rep, 151 Dem, 9 other
T. Roosevelt, Rep	58th	1903–1905	57 Rep, 33 Dem	208 Rep, 178 Dem
T. Roosevelt, Rep	59th	1905–1907	57 Rep, 33 Dem	250 Rep, 136 Dem
T. Roosevelt, Rep	60th	1907–1909	61 Rep, 31 Dem	222 Rep, 164 Dem
Taft, Rep	61st	1909–1911	61 Rep, 32 Dem	219 Rep, 172 Dem
Taft, Rep	62d	1911–1913	51 Rep, 41 Dem	228 Dem, 161 Rep, 1 other
Wilson, Dem	63d	1913–1915	51 Dem, 44 Rep, 1 other	291 Dem, 127 Rep, 17 other
Wilson, Dem	64th	1915–1917	56 Dem, 40 Rep	230 Dem, 196 Rep, 9 other
Wilson, Dem	65th	1917–1919	53 Dem, 42 Rep	216 Dem, 210 Rep, 6 other
Wilson, Dem	66th	1919–1921	49 Rep, 47 Dem	240 Rep, 190 Dem, 3 other
Harding, Rep	67th	1921–1923	59 Rep, 37 Dem	300 Rep, 132 Dem, 1 other
Harding/Coolidge,	68th	1923–1925	51 Rep, 43 Dem, 2 other	225 Rep, 205 Dem, 5 other
Coolidge, Rep	69th	1925–1927	56 Rep, 39 Dem 1 other	247 Rep, 183 Dem, 4 other
Coolidge, Rep	70th	1927–1929	49 Rep, 46 Dem, 1 other	237 Rep, 195 Dem, 3 other
Hoover, Rep	71st	1929–1931	56 Rep, 39 Dem, 1 other	267 Rep, 163 Dem, 1 other
Hoover, Rep	72d	1931–1933	48 Rep, 47 Dem, 1 other	220 Dem, 214 Rep, 1 other
F. Roosevelt, Dem	73d	1933–1935	60 Dem, 35 Rep, 1 other	310 Dem, 117 Rep, 5 other
F. Roosevelt, Dem	74th	1935–1937	69 Dem, 25 Rep, 2 other	319 Dem, 103 Rep, 10 other
F. Roosevelt, Dem	75th	1937–1939	76 Dem, 16 Rep, 4 other	331 Dem, 89 Rep, 13 other
F. Roosevelt, Dem	76th	1939–1941	69 Dem, 23 Rep, 4 other	261 Dem, 164 Rep, 4 other
F. Roosevelt, Dem	77th	1941–1943	66 Dem, 28 Rep, 2 other	268 Dem, 162 Rep, 5 other
F. Roosevelt, Dem	78th	1943–1945	57 Dem, 38 Rep, 1 other	222 Dem, 209 Rep, 4 other
F. Roosevelt/Truman,	79th	1945–1947	56 Dem, 38 Rep, 1 other	242 Dem, 190 Rep, 2 other
Truman, Dem	80th	1947–1949	51 Rep, 45 Dem	245 Rep, 188 Dem, 1 other
Truman, Dem	81st	1949–1951	54 Dem, 42 Rep	263 Dem, 171 Rep, 1 other

President, Party	Congress	Years	Senate Composition	House Composition
Truman, Dem.	82d	1951-1953	49 Dem, 47 Rep.	234 Dem, 199 Rep, 1other
Eisenhower, Rep	83d	1951-1955	48 Rep, 47 Dem, 1 other	221 Rep, 211 Dem, 1 other
Eisenhower, Rep	84th	1955-1957	48 Dem, 47 Rep, 1 other	232 Dem, 203 Rep
Eisenhower, Rep	85th	1957-1959	49 Dem, 47 Rep	233 Dem, 200 Rep
Eisenhower, Rep	86th	1959-1961	64 Dem, 34 Rep	283 Dem, 153 Rep
Kennedy, Dem	87th	1961-1963	65 Dem, 35 Rep	263 Dem, 174 Rep
Kennedy/L. Johnson, Dem	88th	1963-1965	67 Dem, 33 Rep	258 Dem, 177 Rep
L. Johnson, Dem	89th	1965-1967	68 Dem, 32 Rep	295 Dem, 140 Rep
L. Johnson, Dem	90th	1967-1969	64 Dem, 36 Rep	248 Dem, 187 Rep
Nixon, Rep	91st	1969-1971	57 Dem, 43 Reo	244, Dem, 191 Rep
Nixon, Rep	92d	1971-1973	54 Dem, 44 Rep, 2 other	255 Dem, 180 Rep
Nixon/Ford, Rep	93d	1973-1975	56 Dem, 42 Rep 2 other	242 Dem, 192 Rep 1 other
Ford, Rep	94th	1975-1977	61 Dem, 37 Rep, 2 other	291 Dem, 144 Rep
Carter, Dem	95th	1977-1979	61 Dem, 38 Rep, 1 other	290 Dem, 145 Rep
Carter, Dem	96th	1979-1981	58 Dem, 41 Rep, 1 other	276 Dem, 159 Rep
Reagan, Rep	97th	1981-1983	53 Rep, 46 Dem, 1 other	244 Dem, 191 Rep
Reagan, Rep	98th	1983-1985	54 Rep, 46 Dem	269 Dem, 166 Rep
Reagan, Rep	99th	1985-1987	53 Rep, 47 Dem	253 Dem, 182 Rep
Reagan, Rep	100th	1987-1989	54 Dem, 46 Rep	258 Dem, 177 Rep
Bush, Rep	101st	1989-1991	55 Dem, 45 Rep	260 Dem, 175 Rep
Bush, Rep	102d	1991-1993	56 Dem, 44 Rep	267 Dem, 167 Rep 1 other
Clinton, Dem	103d	1993-1995	57 Dem, 43 Rep	258 Dem, 176 Rep, 1 other
Clinton, Dem	104th	1995-1997	52 Rep, 48 Dem	230 Rep, 204 Dem, 1 other
Clinton, Dem	105th	1997-1999	55 Rep, 45 Dem	228 Rep, 206 Dem, 1 other
Clinton, Dem	106th	1999-2001	54 Rep, 45 Dem 1 other	222 Rep, 211 Dem, 1 other, 1 vacancy
G.W. Bush, Rep	107th	2001-2003	50 Rep, 50 Dem	221 Rep, 211 Dem, 2 other, 1 vacancy
G.W. Bush, Rep	108th	2003-2005	51 Rep, 48 Dem 1 other	229 Rep, 205 Dem, 1 other, 0 vacancy

PRESIDENTIAL CURIOSITIES

The 20-Year Curse Cycle: Since 1840 every fifth quadrennial election has produced a president who either died in office or was shot. William Henry Harrison, elected in 1840, died a month after his inaugural. Abraham Lincoln, elected in 1860, was assassinated early in his second term. James A. Garfield, elected in 1880, also was shot to death in his first year in office. William McKinley, reelected in 1900, was mortally wounded the following year. Warren G. Harding, elected in 1920, succumbed to a stroke just as the Teapot Dome scandal was about to engulf his administration. Franklin D. Roosevelt, reelected to an unprecedented third term in 1940, was fatally stricken early in his fourth term. John F. Kennedy, elected in 1960, was murdered three years later. Ronald Reagan, elected in 1980 and the victim of an assassination attempt the next year, was the first president to survive the curse. Although his gunshot wound was at least as severe as Garfield's, he had the good fortune to be assaulted minutes away from a modern emergency medical facility.

The 50-Year Scandal Cycle: Every 50 years a major scandal has rocked the presidency. In the early 1870s, President Ulysses S. Grant was victimized by the "gold conspiracy" of James Fisk and Jay Gould, and members of his administration were implicated in the Crédit Mobilier and Whiskey Ring scandals. In the early 1920s, President Warren G. Harding died just as his administration was about to be engulfed in the Teapot Dome scandal and other improprieties. And, of course, in the early 1970s, Watergate destroyed the presidency of Richard Nixon. Brace yourself for the early 2020s.

Uncanny Similarities in the Lives of Abraham Lincoln and John F. Kennedy: Both were married in their thirties to women in their early twenties.

Lincoln was first elected to Congress in 1846, Kennedy in 1946.

Lincoln was an unsuccessful candidate for his party's vice presidential nomination in 1856, Kennedy in 1956.

In 1860 Lincoln was elected president with less than 50 percent of the vote over Stephen A. Douglas, born in 1813. In 1960 Kennedy was elected President with less than 50 percent of the vote over Richard Nixon, born in 1913.

Lincoln was younger than his vice president, Andrew Johnson, a southerner born in 1808. Kennedy was younger than his vice president, Lyndon Johnson, a southerner born in 1908.

Lincoln was shot in the back of the head in a theater on a Friday by an assassin who fled to a warehouse and was killed before he could be tried. Kennedy was shot in the back of the head from a warehouse on a Friday by an assassin who fled to a theater and was killed before trial.

APPENDIX C

THE RANKING OF PRESIDENTS 1982 v. 1962

In 1982 the *Chicago Tribune* asked 49 historians to rank the 38 presidents from Washington to Carter. The following is a comparison of that poll with the Arthur Schlesinger poll of 75 historians who ranked 31 presidents from Washington to Eisenhower, excluding W.H. Harrison and Garfield, in 1962:

Ranking

President	1982	1962
	Chicago Tribune	Schlesinger
Washington	3	2
J. Adams	14 (tie)	10
Jefferson	5	5
Madison	17	12
Monroe	16	18
J.Q. Adams	19	13
Jackson	6	6
Van Buren	18	17
W.H. Harrison	38	—
Tyler	29	25
Polk	11	8
Taylor	28	24
Fillmore	31	26
Pierce	35	28
Buchanan	36	29
Lincoln	1	1
A. Johnson	32	23
Grant	30	30
Hayes	22	14
Garfield	33	—
Arthur	24	21
Cleveland	13	11
B. Harrison	25	20
McKinley	10	15
T. Roosevelt	4	7
Taft	20	16
Wilson	7	4
Harding	37	31
Coolidge	27	27
Hoover	21	19
F.D. Roosevelt	2	3
Truman	8	9
Eisenhower	9	22
Kennedy	14 (tie)	—
L.B. Johnson	12	—
Nixon	34	—
Ford	23	—
Carter	26	—

INDEX

AAA (Agricultural Adjustment Act), 498
Abominations, Tariff of (1828), 99-100
Abraham, Edmund Spencer, 780
Abu Ghraib prison, 772, 778, 786
Acheson, Dean, 516
Adams, Abigail "Nabby", 20-21
Adams, Abigail Smith (Mrs, John Adams),
    23-24, 90
Adams, Brock, 626
Adams, Brooks, 91
Adams, Charles, 21
Adams, Charles Francis, 90
Adams, Charles Francis, Jr., 91
Adams, Charles Francis, III, 91, 471
Adams, Henry, 91, 341
Adams, John (father), 20
Adams, John (2nd President), 8, 14, 19-35,
    45, 52, 90
administration of, 29-30
birth of, 21
books about, 33
books by, 33
cabinet of, 28-29
campaign of, 27-28
career before presidency of:
    in Boston Massacre, 24-25
    Diplomat abroad, 26
    Continental Congress member, 26
    Massachusetts legislative member, 25-26
    Vice President, 26-27
childhood of, 21
criticized, 32-33
death of, 31-32
education of, 21-22
election of, 28
family of, 20-21, 32
inaugural address of, 28
marriage of, 23-24
midnight appointments of, 30
nomination of, 27
opponent of, 27
praise for, 32
quotes by, 33
rank in 1962 Historians' Poll of, 31

recreation of, 22-23
religion of, 22
retirement of, 31
romantic life of, 23
Supreme Court appointments by, 30-31
Vice President of, 28
Adams, John, II, 90
Adams, John Quincy (6th President), 21,
    80, 84, 89-103, 111, 118, 133, 146, 159,
    172, 194, 755
administration of, 99-100
birth of, 92
books about, 102
books by, 102
cabinet of, 98-99
campaign of, 97
career before presidency of:
    Chief Negotiator of Treaty of Ghent, 95
    Massachusetts State Senator, 95
    Minister to Great Britain, 96
    Minister to Netherlands, 94-95
    Minister to Prussia, 95
    Minister to Russia, 95
    Secretary of State, 96
    Senator, United States, 95
childhood of, 92
criticized, 101-102
death of, 100-101
education of, 92-93
election of, 97-98
family of, 90-92, 101
inaugural address of, 98
marriage of, 94
nomination of, 96
opponents of, 96-97
praise for, 101
quotes by, 102
rank in 1962 Historians' Poll of, 100
recreation of, 93
religion of, 93
retirement of, 100
romantic life of, 93-94
Supreme court appointment by, 100
Vice President of, 98

Iraq, 651, 664, 686, 693, 694, 695, 696, 697, 698,
771-72, 773, 776, 777, 778, 785-86
Iredell, James, 12
Iron Age Magazine, 388
Irving, Washington, 133
Israel, 519, 628, 395

Jackson, Alphonso, 779-80
Jackson, Andrew (father), 106
Jackson, Andrew (7th President), 96, 97, 99,
105-121, 127-28, 133, 146, 159, 168
administration of, 114-16
assassination attempt on, 116
birth of, 106-107
books about, 119
cabinet of, 113-114
campaigns of, 111, 112
career before presidency of:
in duel with Charles Dickinson (lawyer),
110
Justice of Tennessee Superior Court, 110
Representative, United States, 110
Senator, United States, 110, 111
childhood of, 107
criticized, 118
death of, 117-18
education of, 107
election of, 111-112
family of, 106, 118
inaugural address of, 112-13
marriage of, 108
military service of:
in American Revolution, 109
in Burr Conspiracy, 109
in First Seminole War, 110
In War of 1812, 109
nomination of, 111, 112
opponent of, 111, 112
praise for, 118
quotes by, 118-19
rank in 1962 Historians' Poll of, 117
recreation of, 107-108
religion of, 107
retirement of, 117
romantic life of, 108
Supreme Court appointments by, 116-17
Vice President of, 113
Jackson, Derrick Z., 788
Jackson, Elizabeth "Betty" Hutchinson, 106
Jackson, Howell E., 340
Jackson, Jesse, 645, 681-82, 718
Jackson, Mrs. Rachel Donelson (Robards),
108
Jackson, Robert H., 496, 503

James, Thomas L., 301, 302, 312
Japan, 193
Jardine, William M., 457
Jay, John, 12
Jay's Treaty (1795), 10-11
Jefferson, Jane Randolph, 38
Jefferson, Martha (née Wayles Skelton), 42
Jefferson, Martha "Patsy", 38-39
Jefferson, Mary "Polly", 39
Jefferson, Peter, 38
Jefferson, Thomas (3rd President), 8, 15, 27,
28, 32, 37-53, 61-62, 68, 84, 118
administration of, 49-50
birth of, 39
book by, 53
books about, 53
cabinet of, 48-49
campaigns of, 45-47
career before presidency of:
Continental Congress member, 44
Declaration of Independence and, 43-44
Governor of Virginia, 44
House of Burgesses member, 43
Minister to France, 45
Secretary of State, 45
Vice President, 45
Virginia House of Delegates member, 44
childhood of, 39
criticized, 52
death of, 51-52
education of, 39-40
elections of, 46, 47
family of, 38-39, 51
inaugural address of, 47
marriage of, 42
nomination of, 45, 46
opponent of, 45, 46
praise for, 52
quotes by, 52-53
rank in 1962 Historians' Poll of, 51
recreation of, 40-41
religion of, 40
retirement of, 51
romantic life of, 41-43
Supreme Court appointments by, 50-51
Vice President of, 47-48
Jenner, William, 523
Jernigan, George, 713
Jewell, Marshall, 270
Job Corps, 574
Job Training Partnership Act (1982), 685
Johanns, Mike, 778-79
John Birch Society, 673
Johnson, Andrew (17th President), 172, 235,
237, 247-57, 274